LITURGICAL
HYMNS OLD & NEW

Compiled by
  Robert Kelly
  Sister Sheila McGovern SSL
  Kevin Mayhew
  Father Andrew Moore
  Sister Louisa Poole SSL

Acknowledgements

The publishers wish to express their gratitude to the copyright holders who have granted permission to include their material in this book.

Every effort has been made to trace the copyright holders of all the songs in this collection and we hope that no copyright has been infringed. Apology is made and pardon sought if the contrary be the case, and a correction will be made in any reprint of this book.

Important Copyright Information

We would like to remind users of this hymnal that the reproduction of any song texts or music without the permission of the copyright holder is illegal. Details of all copyright holders are clearly indicated under each song.

Many of the song *texts* may be covered either by a Christian Copyright Licensing (CCL) licence or a Calamus licence. If you possess a CCL or Calamus licence, it is essential that you check your instruction manual to ensure that the song you wish to use is covered.

If you are *not* a member of CCL or Calamus, or the song you wish to reproduce is not covered by your licence, you must contact the copyright holder direct for their permission.

Christian Copyright Licensing (Europe) Ltd, have also now introduced a *Music Reproduction Licence*. Again, if you hold such a licence it is essential that you check your instruction manual to ensure that the song you wish to reproduce is covered. The reproduction of any music not covered by your licence is both illegal and immoral.

If you are interested in joining CCL or Calamus they can be contacted at the following addresses:

Christian Copyright Licensing (Europe) Ltd, P.O. Box 1339, Eastbourne, East Sussex, BN21 4YF
Tel: 01323 417711, Fax: 01323 417722.

Calamus, 30 North Terrace, Mildenhall, Suffolk, IP28 7AB
Tel: 01638 716579, Fax: 01638 510390.

First published in Great Britain in 1999 by
KEVIN MAYHEW LIMITED
Buxhall, Stowmarket
Suffolk IP14 3DJ

Compilation © Kevin Mayhew Ltd 1999

The right of Robert Kelly, Sister Sheila McGovern, Kevin Mayhew, Father Andrew Moore and Sister Louisa Poole to be identified as the compilers and editors of this work has been asserted by them in accordance with the Copyright, Designs and Patents Act 1988.

All rights reserved. No part of this publication may be reproduced, stored in a retrieval system, or transmitted, in any form or by any means, electronic, mechanical, photocopying, recording or otherwise, without the prior written permission of the publisher.

The following editions are available

People's copy (standard)	Catalogue No. 1413081	
	ISBN No. 1 84003 303 7	ISMN No. M 57004 570 9
People's copy (plastic)	Catalogue No. 1413082	
	ISBN No. 1 84003 318 5	ISMN No. M 57004 560 0
Melody/guitar	Catalogue No. 1413083	
	ISBN No. 1 84003 304 5	ISMN No. M 57004 501 3
Organ/choir	Catalogue No. 1413084	
	ISBN No. 1 84003 305 3	ISMN No. M 57004 502 0

Front cover design by Jonathan Stroulger
Printed and bound in Great Britain by William Clowes Ltd, Beccles, Suffolk

Contents

Mass Music	1 - 93
Hymns and Songs	94 - 759
Children's Hymns and Songs	760 - 858
Chants	859 - 899
Responsorial Psalms	900 - 1078
Eucharistic Adoration with Benediction	1079 - 1085
Indexes	Following 1085

    Composers and Sources of Music
    Alphabetical Index of Tunes
    Metrical Index of Tunes
    Authors and Sources of Text
    Scriptural Index
    Index of Uses
    Index of Sunday and Feastday Themes
    Responsorial Psalm Index
    Index of First Lines

Liturgical
HYMNS OLD & NEW

Production Team

ROB DANTER
DONALD THOMSON
Music Setters

RICHARD WEAVER
LOUISE SELFE
MATTHEW LOCKWOOD
Text Setters

HUBERT J. RICHARDS
JANET SIMPSON
ANNE GILBERT
Indexes

GEOFF PEACHEY
ELISABETH BATES
HELEN ELLIOT
KATE GALLAHER
HELEN GOODALL
RACHEL JUDD
GEOFFREY MOORE
Proof Readers

JONATHAN STROULGER
Cover Design

JANE RAYSON
Copyright Manager

JANET SIMPSON
Project Manager

Foreword

The first edition of *Hymns Old and New* appeared in 1977. The principle underlying its production was simple: to offer in one, single, conveniently sized book, a selection of the hymns most used by Catholic communities in Britain and Ireland. The contents ranged from the stalwart songs of the traditional pre-Vatican II hymnals to the best of the new as discovered and tested by the series of *20th Century Folk Hymnals*.

By 1984 it was clear that a major revision of this basically sound idea was needed. Very little adjustment to the 'old' traditional material was needed, but by now the repertoire of 'new' material had broadened. This was largely due to the work of people like the late Brother Damian Lundy in encouraging young people to be brave enough to express their faith in song, and which had made the influential *Songs of the Spirit* series possible. There was also the papal visit of 1982, where the various public celebrations had opened the eyes of many parishes to the role that music could and should play in their liturgy. Not only did parishes and other communities seem to have developed an immense appetite for music for their celebrations, but they were demanding a wider repertoire of material, and expecting higher standards from the words. As a response to these pastoral demands, *Hymns Old and New with Supplement* was published. It was the first popular hymnal to offer a scriptural index, and to equip parishes to be able to sing the Responsorial Psalm for every Sunday and major feast. This edition soon became, and for many years has remained, Britain's best-selling hymnal.

A decade later seemed an opportune moment to offer a new edition. There was, of course, the need to include the good new material that had been emerging in the rest of Europe and the United States. The result, *Hymns Old and New, New Century Edition*, was also a far more elegant product, thanks to the improvements in computer-based music-setting which did not exist ten years earlier. The somewhat summary scriptural index of its predecessor was now far more generous, matching the growing realisation that scripture should be the primary source for what we proclaim in song in our liturgies. This edition's main innovation, though, was to try and serve those parishes whose musical repertoire was almost exclusively traditional material by offering 'hymns for the Lectionary': a comprehensive range of new texts, explicitly constructed on the scripture readings for the Sundays and feasts – but all singable to traditional hymn-tunes.

The need so clearly felt to renew the material for our celebrations is a healthy one, because it is a sign of the Church's vitality. Quite naturally, parishes and communities are now looking for the pastoral tool that will take them and their celebrations forward into the third millennium. This latest edition of the series is designed to serve that purpose. It has consciously taken the best insights and initiatives of its predecessors, and added another very important one. The basic title *Hymns Old and New* has gained the significant adjective *'Liturgical'*. Parishes are now more discerning in the material they choose for their celebrations: they are demanding songs that have clear and coherent connections with the scripture texts that are proclaimed; the people are reclaiming the parts of the Mass and the celebration of the sacraments that belong to them by wanting – as they should – to sing them; it is, happily, becoming standard practice for the Responsorial Psalm to be sung. These are all profoundly 'liturgical' aspirations, and this book is designed to satisfy them.

Robert Kelly
Sister Sheila McGovern SSL
Kevin Mayhew
Father Andrew Moore
Sister Louisa Poole SSL

LITURGICAL
HYMNS OLD & NEW

Mass Music

1 A New People's Mass (Gregory Murray)

Penitential Rite

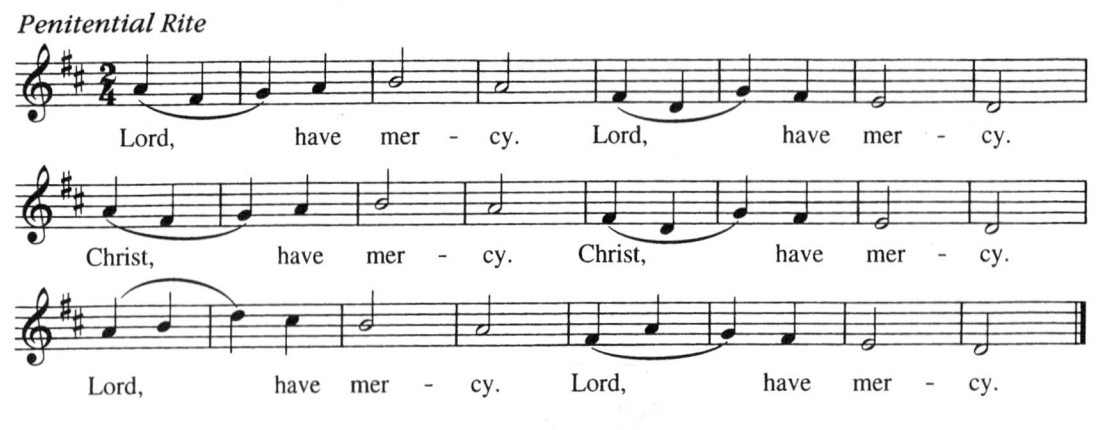

Lord, have mer-cy. Lord, have mer-cy.

Christ, have mer-cy. Christ, have mer-cy.

Lord, have mer-cy. Lord, have mer-cy.

Gloria

Glo-ry to God in the high-est, and peace to his peo-ple on earth. Lord God, hea-ven-ly King, al-migh-ty God and Fa-ther, we wor-ship you, we give you thanks, we praise you for your glo-ry. Lord Je-sus Christ, on-ly Son of the Fa-ther, Lord God, Lamb of God, you take a-way the sins of the world, have mer-cy on us; you are seat-ed at the right hand of the Fa-ther, re-ceive our prayer. For you a-lone are the Ho-ly One, you a-lone are the

© Copyright McCrimmon Publishing Co. Ltd., 10-12 High Street, Great Wakering, Southend-on-Sea, Essex SS3 0EQ, UK. Used by permission.

Text: from the Roman Missal
Music: Gregory Murray (1905-1992)

2 A Simple Mass (Andrew Moore)

Penitential Rite

Lord, have mer-cy. Lord, have mer-cy. Christ, have mer-cy.
Christ, have mer-cy. Lord, have mer-cy. Lord, have mer-cy.

Gloria

Glo-ry to God in the high - est, and peace to his peo-ple on earth. Lord God, heav'n-ly King, al - migh-ty God and Fa-ther, we wor-ship you, we give you thanks, we praise you for your glo - ry, we praise you for your glo - ry. Lord Je-sus Christ, on-ly Son of the Fa-ther, Lord God, Lamb of God, you take a-way the sins of the world: have mer - cy on us; you are seat-ed at the right hand of the Fa - ther: re - ceive our prayer. For you a - lone are the Ho - ly One, you a - lone are the Lord, you a - lone are the Most High, Je - sus Christ, with the Ho - ly Spi - rit, in the glo - ry of God the Fa - ther. A - men. A - men.

© Copyright 1999 Kevin Mayhew Ltd.

Text: from the Roman Missal
Music: Andrew Moore (b.1954)

F Gm11 Fmaj7 Gm11 F Gm11 Fmaj7
you a - lone are the Lord, you a - lone are the Most High,
Bbm7 Eb Abmaj7 Dbmaj7 Gm7 C Fm
f
Je - sus Christ, with the Ho - ly Spi - rit, in the
Bbm7 Eb Abmaj7 Dbmaj7 G7sus4 G7 Csus4 C
glo - ry, the glo - ry, the glo - ry of God the Fa - ther.
Optional Descant
F Gm11 Fmaj7 Gm11 F Gm11 Fmaj7 Gm11
mf
A - men, a - men, a - men,
mf
A - men, a - men, a - men,
Largo
F Dm Fmaj7 Bbmaj7 Gm7 F
f cresc. e rit.
ff cresc.
a - men, a - men, a - men.
f cresc.
ff cresc.
a - men, a - men, a - men.
Sanctus
Moderato (♩. = c. 56)
rall.
F Gm11 Fmaj7 Gm11 Fmaj7 Gm11 Fmaj7 Gm11
mf
dim.
F Gm11 Fmaj7 Gm11 F Gm11 Fmaj7 Gm11
a tempo
mp
Ho - ly, ho - ly, ho - ly Lord, God of pow'r and God of might,

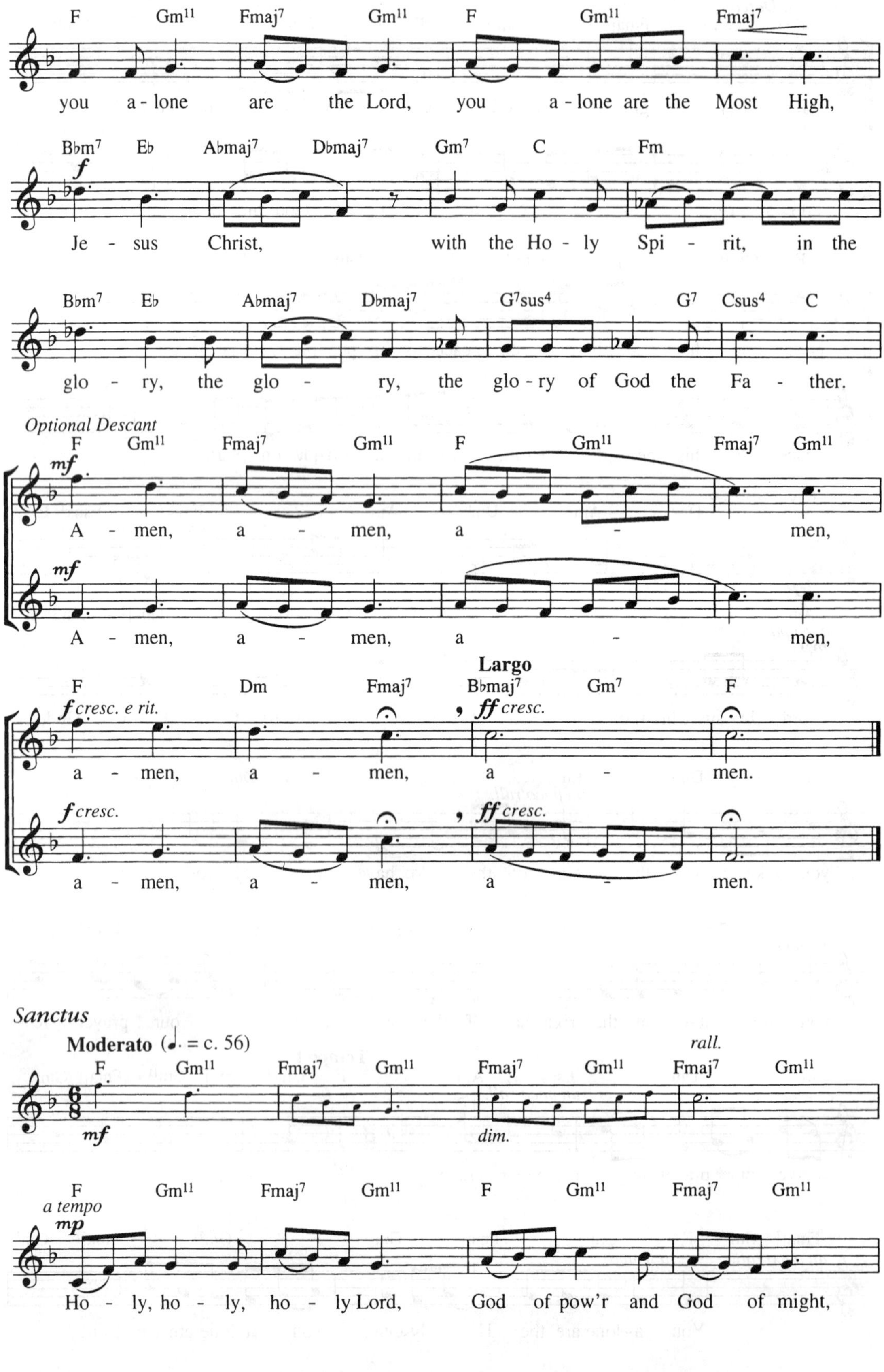

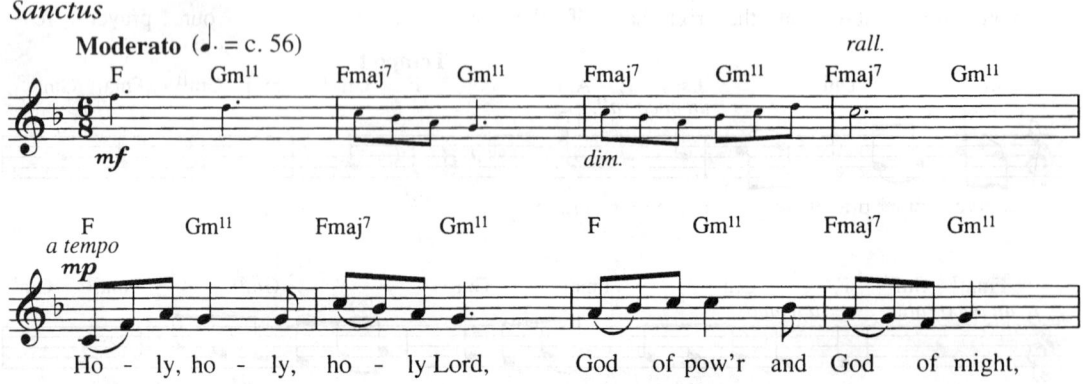

Text: from the Roman Missal
Music: Margaret Rizza (b. 1929)

5 Missa de Angelis (Plainsong)

6 Mass XVIII (Plainsong)

Penitential Rite

Ky - ri - e, e - le - i - son. Chris-te, e - le - i - son.

Ky - ri - e, e - le - i - son. Ky - ri - e, e - le - i - son.

Sanctus

San-ctus, san-ctus, san-ctus Do-mi-nus De-us sa-ba-oth.

Ple-ni sunt cæ-li et ter-ra glo-ri-a tu-a. Ho-san-na in ex-cel-sis.

Be-ne-di-ctus qui ve-nit in no-mi-ne Do-mi-ni. Ho-san-na in ex-cel-sis.

Agnus Dei

A-gnus De - i, qui tol-lis pec-ca-ta mun-di: mi-se-re-re no - bis.

A-gnus De - i, qui tol-lis pec-ca-ta mun-di: do-na no-bis pa - cem.

Text: from the Roman Missal
Music: Plainsong

7 The 'American' Eucharist

Penitential Rite

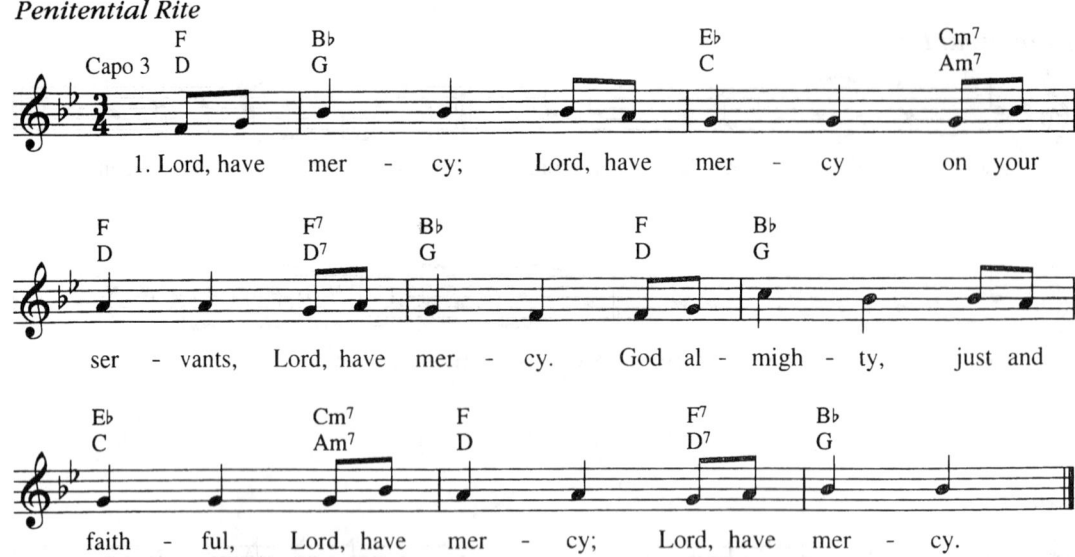

1. Lord, have mercy; Lord, have mercy on your servants, Lord, have mercy. God almighty, just and faithful, Lord, have mercy; Lord, have mercy.

2. Christ, have mercy; Christ, have mercy;
gift from heaven, Christ, have mercy.
Light of truth and light of justice,
Christ, have mercy; Christ, have mercy.

3. Lord, have mercy; Lord, have mercy;
on your servants, Lord, have mercy.
God almighty, just and faithful,
Lord, have mercy; Lord, have mercy.

Gospel acclamation

Alleluia, alleluia,
let us praise Christ, our Lord Jesus.
Alleluia, let us praise him,
now among us in his Gospel.

Memorial acclamation

When we eat this bread you give us,
and we drink this cup you left us,
we proclaim your death, Lord Jesus,
till you come again in glory.

Sanctus

1. Holy, holy, holy, holy,
Lord of hosts. You fill with glory
all the earth and all the heavens.
Sing hosanna, sing hosanna.

2. Blest and holy, blest and holy,
he who comes now in the Lord's name.
In the highest sing hosanna,
in the highest sing hosanna.

Agnus Dei

1. Jesus, Lamb of God, have mercy,
bearer of our sins, have mercy.
Jesus, Lamb of God, have mercy,
bearer of our sins, have mercy.

2. Saviour of the world, Lord Jesus,
may your peace be with us always.
Saviour of the world, Lord Jesus,
may your peace be always with us.

Kyrie, Sanctus, Agnus Dei © Copyright McCrimmon Publishing Co. Ltd., 10-12 High Street,
Great Wakering, Southend-on-Sea, Essex SS3 0EQ. Used by arrangement.
Gospel & Memorial acclamations © Copyright 1983, 1999 Kevin Mayhew Ltd.
Text: Kyrie, Sanctus, Agnus Dei adapted from the Liturgy by Sandra Joan Billington (b.1946)
Gospel Acclamation and Memorial Acclamation adapted from the Liturgy by Robert B. Kelly (b.1948)
Music: traditional American Melody

8 The 'Hopwood' Mass

Penitential Rite

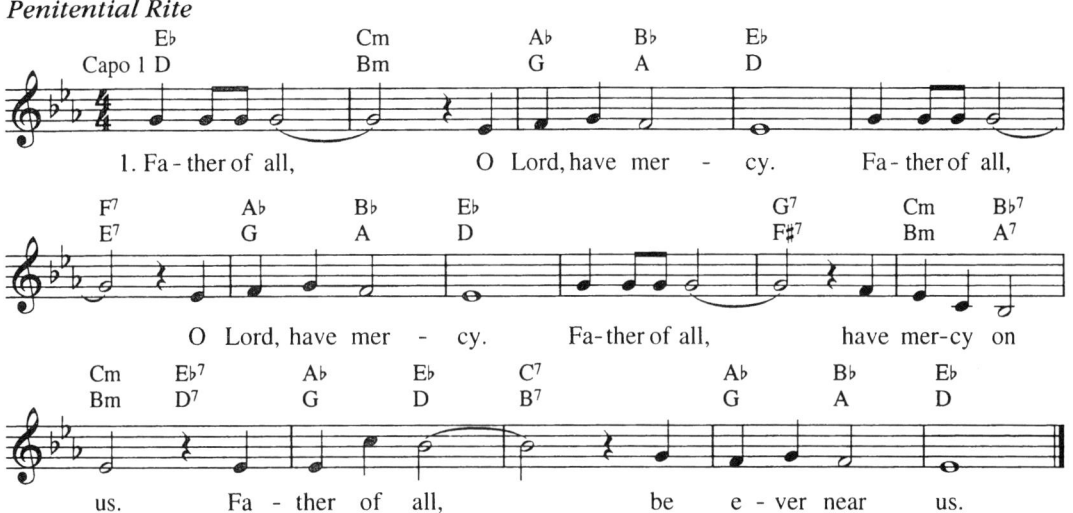

1. Father of all, O Lord, have mercy. Father of all, O Lord, have mercy. Father of all, have mercy on us. Father of all, be ever near us.

2. Saviour of all, O Christ, have mercy.
   Saviour of all, O Christ, have mercy.
   Saviour of all, have mercy on us.
   Saviour of all, be ever near us.

3. Spirit of all, O Lord, have mercy.
   Spirit of all, O Lord, have mercy.
   Spirit of all, have mercy on us.
   Spirit of all, be ever near us.

Sanctus

1. Holy are you, Lord of creation!
   Holy are you, Lord God of angels!
   Holy are you, God of all people!
   Heaven and earth proclaim your glory.

2. Glory to you! Your name is holy.
   Blessèd is he who comes in your name!
   Glory to him! We sing his praises.
   Heaven and earth proclaim your glory.

Agnus Dei

O Lamb of God, you bore our sinning.
O Lamb of God, you bore our dying.
O Lamb of God, have mercy on us.
O Lamb of God, your peace be with us.

Text: adapted from the Liturgy by Terence Collins (b. 1938)
Music: Welsh melody adapted by Terence Collins (b.1938) and David Bentley
© Copyright 1978 Kevin Mayhew Ltd.

9 The 'Israeli' Mass

Penitential Rite

1. Lord, have mer-cy. Lord, have mer-cy. Lord, have mer-cy on us all.
Lord, have mer-cy. Lord, have mer-cy. Lord, have mer-cy on us all.

2. Christ, have mercy. Christ, have mercy.
   Christ, have mercy on us all.
   Christ, have mercy. Christ, have mercy.
   Christ, have mercy on us all.

3. Lord, have mercy. Lord, have mercy.
   Lord, have mercy on us all.
   Lord, have mercy. Lord, have mercy.
   Lord, have mercy on us all.

Sanctus

1. Holy, holy, holy, holy,
   Lord of pow'r, Lord of might.
   Heav'n and earth are filled with glory.
   Sing hosanna evermore.

2. Blest and holy, blest and holy,
   he who comes from God on high.
   Raise your voices, sing his glory,
   praise his name for evermore.

Agnus Dei

1. Lamb of God, you take away the sin,
   the sin of all the world:
   give us mercy, give us mercy,
   give us mercy, Lamb of God.

2. Lamb of God, you take away the sin,
   the sin of all the world:
   give us mercy, give us mercy,
   give us mercy, Lamb of God.

3. Lamb of God, you take away the sin,
   the sin of all the world:
   grant us peace, Lord; grant us peace, Lord;
   grant us peace, Lamb of God.

Text: adapted from the Liturgy by Anthony Hamson
Music: traditional Iraeli melody collected by Anthony Hamson

© McCrimmon Publishing Co. Ltd., 10-12 High Street, Great Wakering,
Southend-on-Sea, Essex SS3 0EQ. Used by arrangement.

10 Lord, have mercy (Missa de Angelis)

Text: from the Roman Missal
Music: Alan Rees (b.1941) adapted from Plainsong
© Copyright 1999 Kevin Mayhew Ltd.

11 Lord, have mercy (Orbis Factor)

Text: from the Roman Missal
Music: Alan Rees (b.1941) adapted from Plainsong
© Copyright 1999 Kevin Mayhew Ltd.

12 Lord, have mercy (Alme Pater)

Text: from the Roman Missal
Music: Alan Rees (b.1941) based on Plainsong
© Copyright 1999 Kevin Mayhew Ltd.

13 Kyrie eleison (Haugen)

© Copyright 1984 GIA Publications Inc, 7404 S. Mason Avenue, Chicago, Illinois 60638, USA.
All rights reserved. Used by permission.

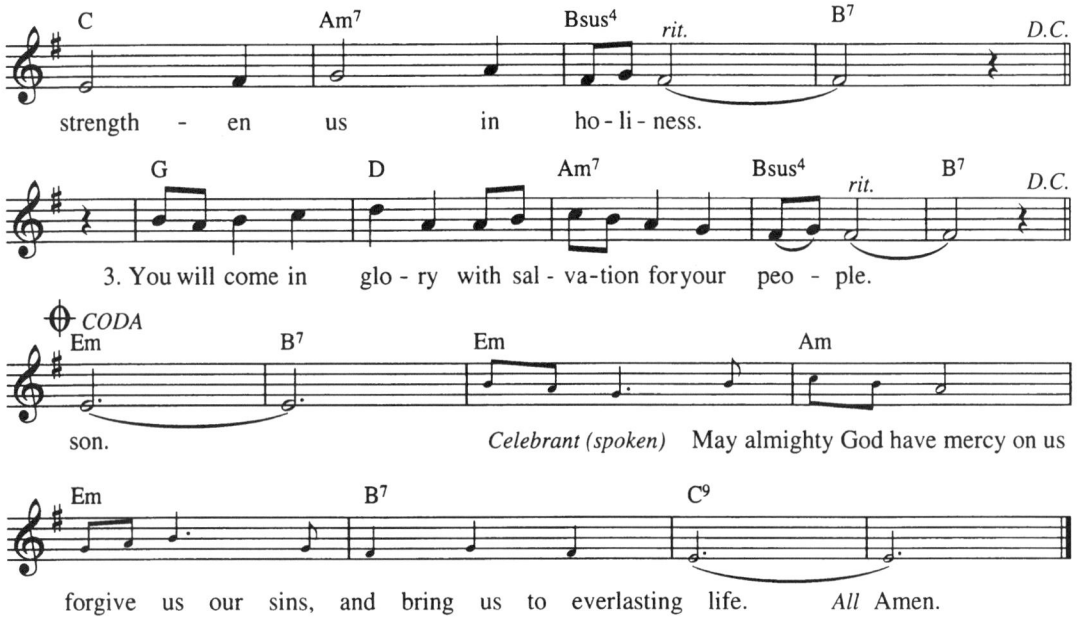

Text: adapted from the Liturgy by Marty Haugen (b.1950)
Music: Marty Haugen (b.1950)

14 Lord, have mercy (Archer)

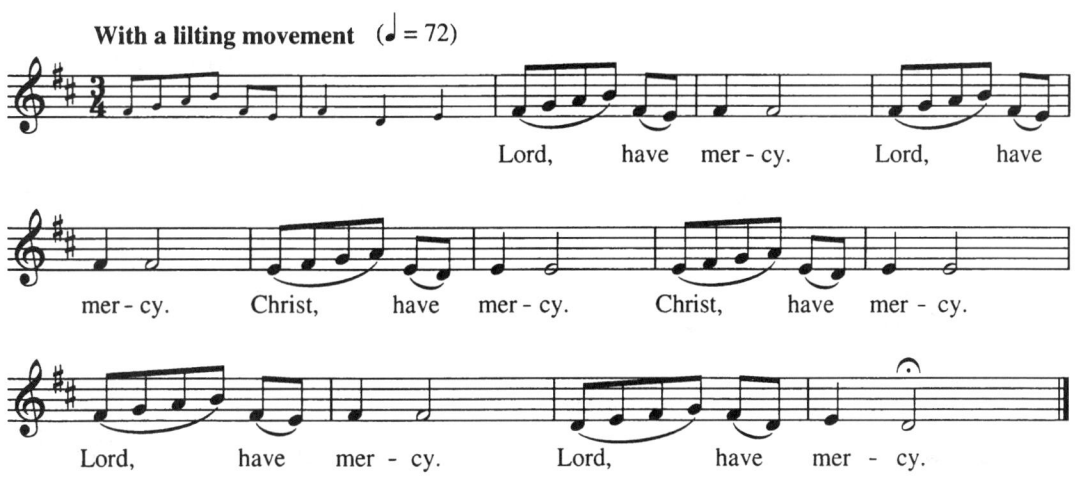

Text: from the Roman Missal
Music: Malcolm Archer (b.1952) from 'The Halesworth Setting'
© Copyright 1995 Kevin Mayhew Ltd.

15 Lord, have mercy (Rock)

2. Christ, have mercy on us all.
Christ, have mercy on us all.
Christ, have mercy,
Christ, have mercy,
Christ, have mercy on us all.

3. Lord, have mercy . . .

Text: from the Roman Missal
Music: Gordon Rock from 'The Pilgrim's Mass'
© Copyright Gordon Rock. Used by permission.

16 Kyrie eleison (Rizza)

Text: from the Roman Missal
Music: Margaret Rizza (b. 1929)
© Copyright 1997 Kevin Mayhew Ltd.

17 Kyrie (Mawby)

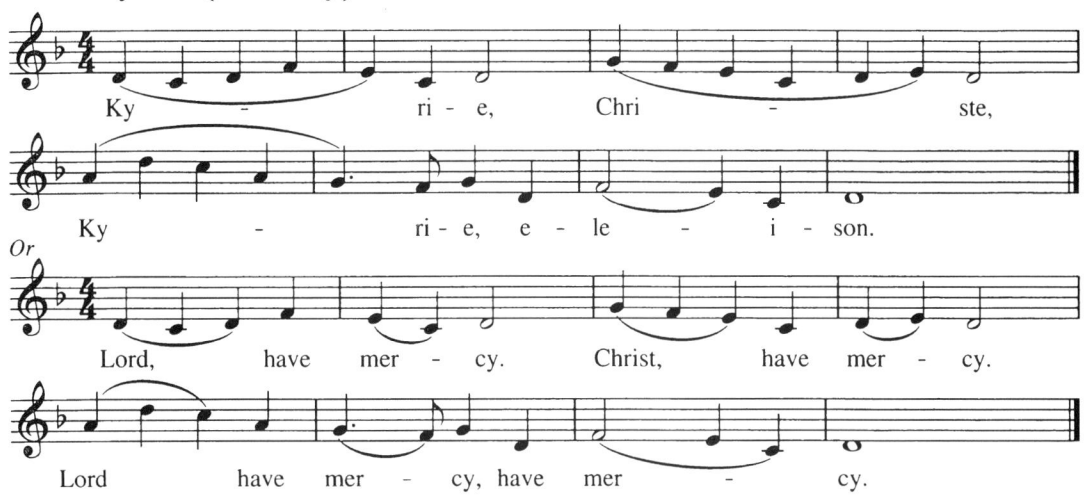

Kyrie, Christe, Kyrie, eleison.

Or

Lord, have mercy. Christ, have mercy. Lord have mercy, have mercy.

Text: from the Roman Missal
Music: Colin Mawby (b.1936)
© Copyright 1991 Kevin Mayhew Ltd.

18 Kyrie 7

Kyrie, Kyrie, eleison.
Kyrie, Kyrie, eleison. *(hum under the invocations)*

* ad lib, 2nd time only

Text: from the Roman Missal
Music: Jacques Berthier (1923-1994)
© Copyright Ateliers et Presses de Taizé, Taizé Communauté, F-71250, France. Used by permission.

19 Lord, have mercy (Filitz)

CASWALL 65 65

1. Lord, have mercy on us, hear us as we pray;
   Lord, have mercy on us, take our sin away.

2. Christ, have mercy on us,
   hear us as we pray;
   Christ, have mercy on us,
   take our sin away.

3. Lord, have mercy on us,
   hear us as we pray;
   Lord, have mercy on us,
   take our sin away.

Text: Michael Forster (b.1946)
Music: Friedrich Filitz (1804-1876)
Text © Copyright 1997 Kevin Mayhew Ltd.

20 Coventry Gloria

© Copyright 1981, 1982 Peter Jones. Published by OCP Publications, 5536 NE Hassalo, Portland, OR 97213, USA. All rights reserved. Used by permission.

Text: from the Roman Missal
Music: Peter Jones

21 Gloria (Rees)

Text: from the Roman Missal
Music: Alan Rees (b.1941)
© Copyright 1992 Kevin Mayhew Ltd.

22 Glory to God (Archer)

With vigour ($\quarter = 126$)

Glory to God in the highest, and peace to his people on earth. Lord God, heav'nly King, almighty God and Father, we worship you, we give you thanks, we praise you for your glory. Lord Jesus Christ, only Son of the Father, Lord God, Lamb of God, you take away the sins of the world: have mercy on us; you are seated at the right hand of the Father; receive our prayer. For you alone are the Holy One, you alone are the Lord, you alone are the Most High, Jesus Christ, with the Holy Spirit, in the glory of

rall.

God the Father. Amen.

Text: from the Roman Missal
Music: Malcolm Archer (b.1952) from 'The People's Setting'
© Copyright 1995 Kevin Mayhew Ltd.

23 Gloria 3

This setting may be sung as a canon with entries as indicated.

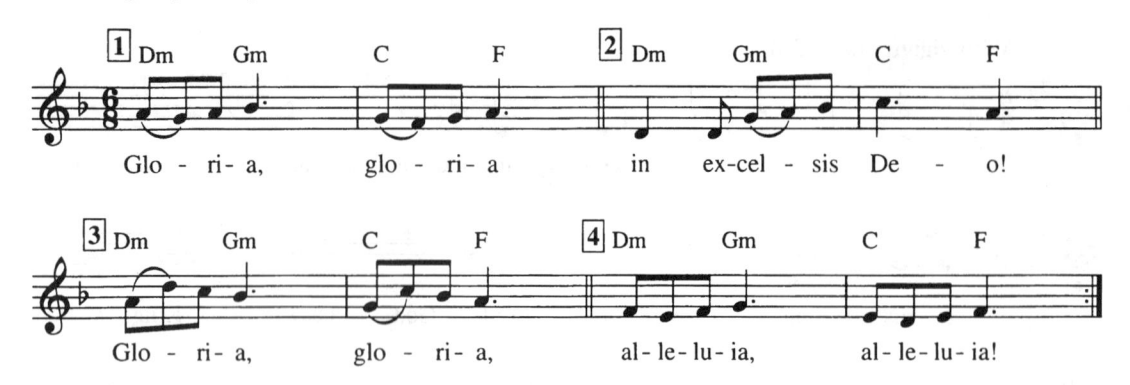

Glo - ri - a, glo - ri - a in ex-cel - sis De - o!

Glo - ri - a, glo - ri - a, al - le - lu - ia, al - le - lu - ia!

Text: Taizé Community, from the Roman Missal
Music: Jacques Berthier (1923-1994)
© Copyright Ateliers et Presses de Taizé, Taizé Communauté, F-71250, France. Used by permission.

24 Glory, glory in the highest

Bright. joyful feel

Glo-ry, glo-ry in the high-est; glo-ry to the Al-migh-ty; glo-ry to the Lamb of God, and glo-ry to the liv-ing Word; glo-ry to the Lamb!

I give glo-ry, glo-ry, glo-ry, glo-ry, glo-ry, glo-ry to the Lamb!

I give I give glo-ry to the Lamb!

Text and Music: Danny Daniels
© Copyright 1987 Mercy/Vineyard Publishing/Music Services. Administered by CopyCare,
P.O. Box 77, Hailsham, East Sussex BN27 3EF, UK. Used by permission.

25 Gloria (Anderson)

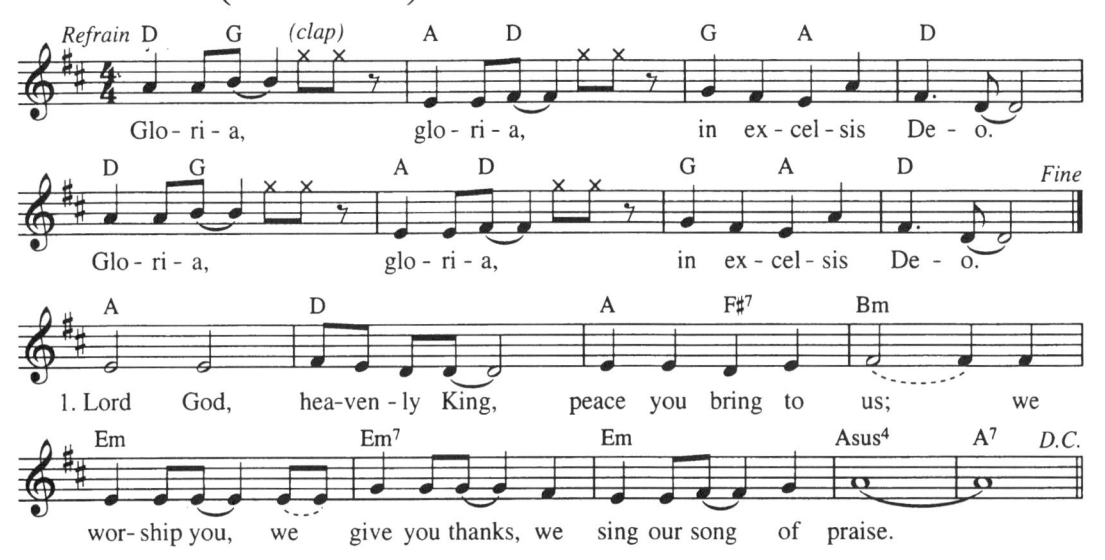

Refrain: Gloria, gloria, in excelsis Deo.
Gloria, gloria, in excelsis Deo.

1. Lord God, heavenly King, peace you bring to us; we worship you, we give you thanks, we sing our song of praise.

2. Jesus, Saviour of all,
   Lord God, Lamb of God,
   you take away our sins,
   O Lord, have mercy on us all.

3. At the Father's right hand,
   Lord receive our prayer,
   for you alone are the Holy One,
   and you alone are Lord.

4. Glory, Father and Son,
   glory, Holy Spirit,
   to you we raise our hands up high,
   we glorify your name.

Text: Mike Anderson (b.1956) adapted from the Liturgy
Music: Mike Anderson (b.1956)
© Copyright 1999 Kevin Mayhew Ltd.

26 Gloria (Salazar)

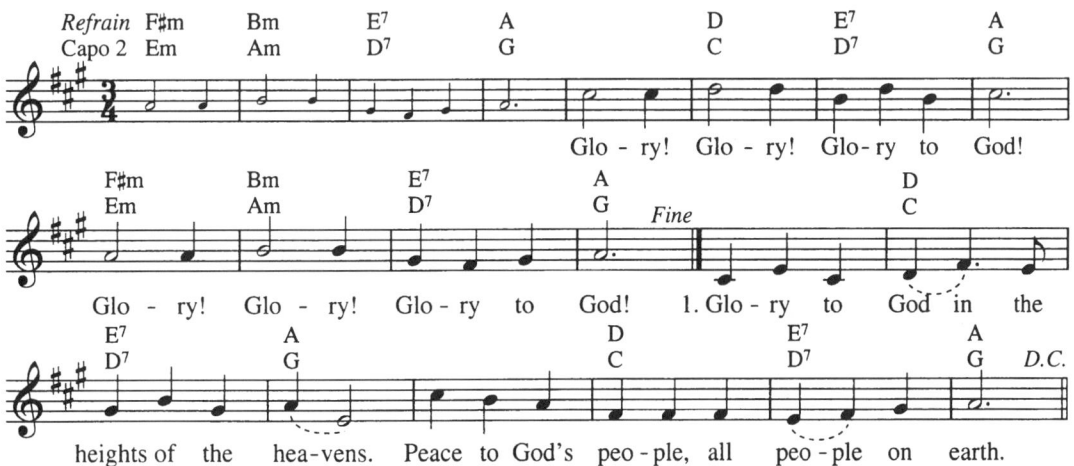

Refrain (Capo 2)

Glory! Glory! Glory to God!
Glory! Glory! Glory to God!

1. Glory to God in the heights of the heavens. Peace to God's people, all people on earth.

2. Son of the Father, all glory and worship;
   praise and thanksgiving to you, Lamb of God.

3. You take away the sin of the world;
   have mercy on us, receive our prayer.

4. Seated in pow'r at the right of the Father,
   Jesus alone is the Lord, the Most High.

5. And with the Spirit of love everlasting,
   reigning in glory for ever. Amen.

Text: George Salazar trans. Paul Inwood
Music: George Salazar arr. Paul Inwood
Original text and music © Copyright 1984 George Salazar.
English translation © Copyright 1984, 1993, Paul Inwood. Published by
OCP Publications, 5536 NE Hassalo, Portland OR 97213, USA. All rights reserved. Used by permission.

27 Gloria (Duffy)

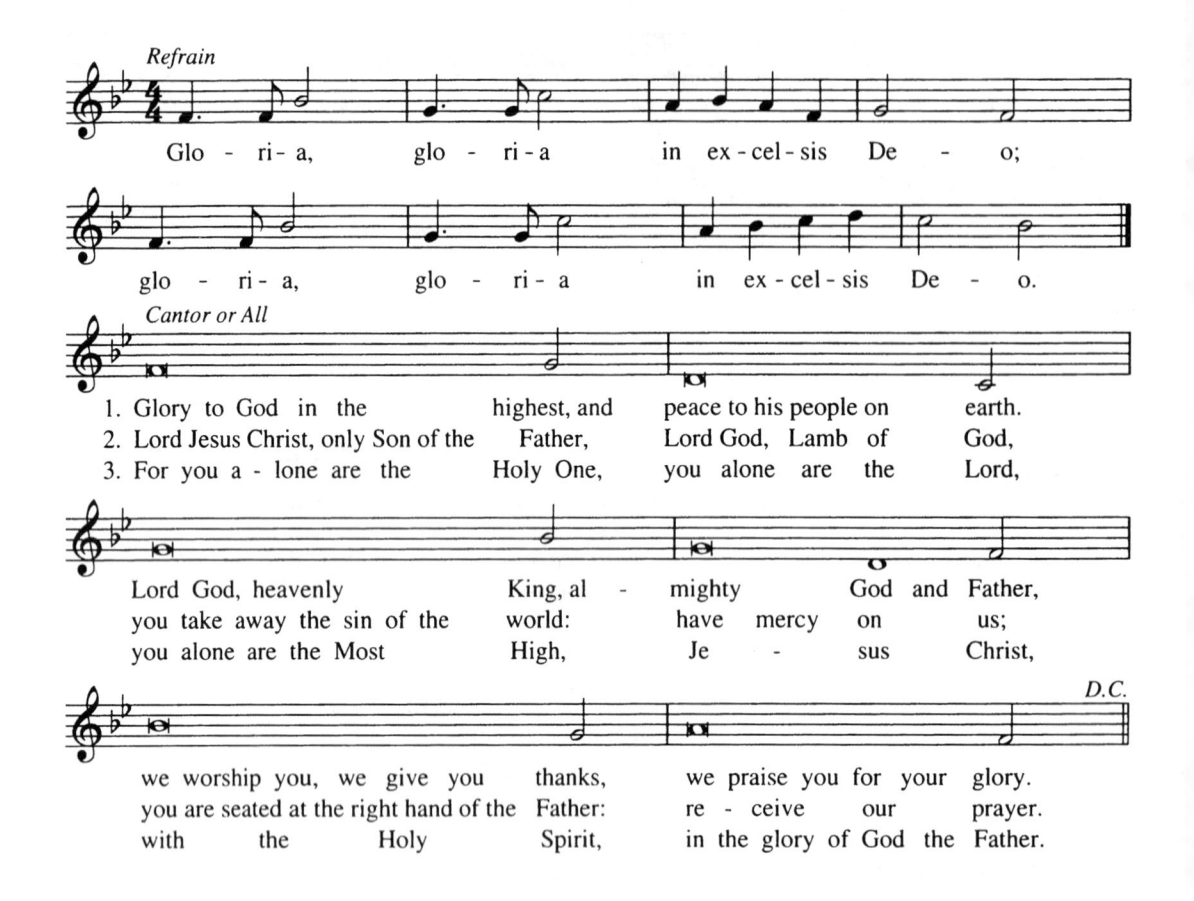

Refrain

Gloria, gloria in excelsis Deo;
gloria, gloria in excelsis Deo.

Cantor or All

1. Glory to God in the highest, and peace to his people on earth.
2. Lord Jesus Christ, only Son of the Father, Lord God, Lamb of God,
3. For you alone are the Holy One, you alone are the Lord,

Lord God, heavenly King, almighty God and Father,
you take away the sin of the world: have mercy on us;
you alone are the Most High, Jesus Christ,

D.C.

we worship you, we give you thanks, we praise you for your glory.
you are seated at the right hand of the Father: receive our prayer.
with the Holy Spirit, in the glory of God the Father.

Text: from the Roman Missal
Music: Francis Duffy
© Copyright 1999 Kevin Mayhew Ltd.

28 Lourdes Gloria

Refrain

Gloria, gloria in excelsis Deo.

Fine

Gloria, gloria in excelsis Deo.

© Copyright 1988 Kevin Mayhew Ltd.

1. Glory to God in the highest, and peace to his people on earth.
2. Lord Jesus Christ, only Son of the Father. Lord God, Lamb of God.
3. For you alone are the Holy One, you alone are the Lord.

Lord God, heavenly King, almighty God and Father,
you take away the sin of the world: have mercy on us;
you alone are the Most High, Jesus Christ,

we worship you, we give you thanks, we praise you for your glory.
you are seated at the right hand of the Father: receive our prayer.
with the Holy Spirit, in the glory of God the Father. A - men.

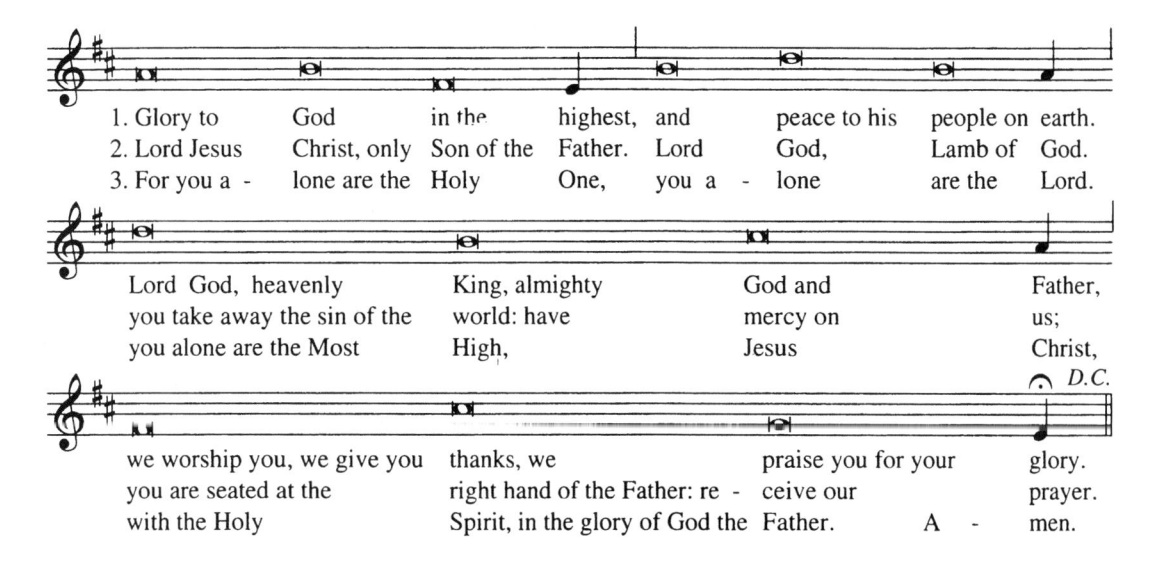

D.C.

Text: from the Roman Missal
Music: Jean-Paul Lécot (b.1947)

29 Sing to God a song of glory

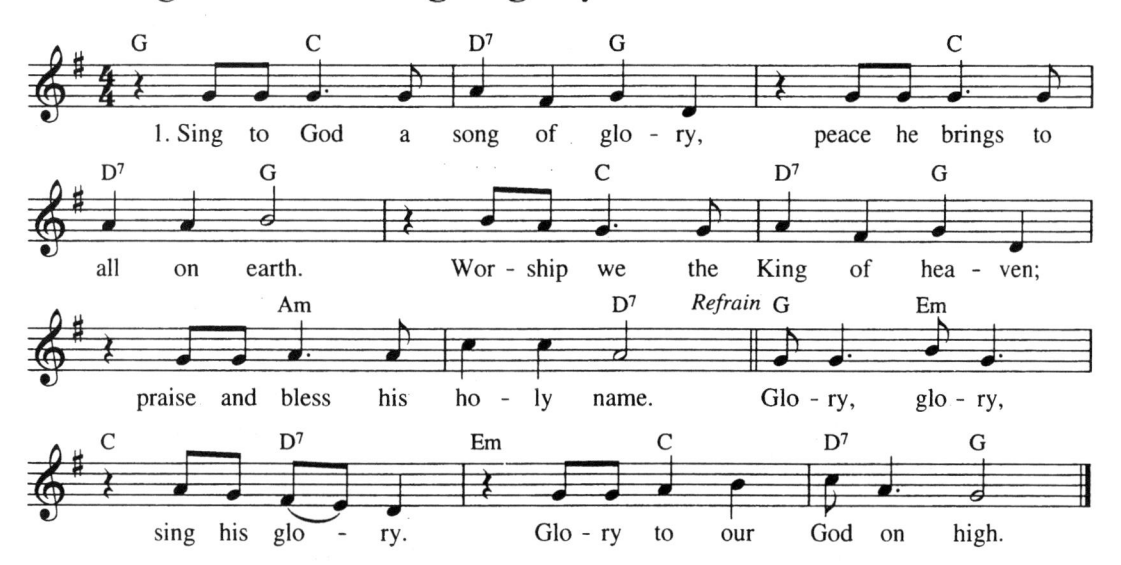

1. Sing to God a song of glory, peace he brings to all on earth. Worship we the King of heaven; praise and bless his holy name. *Refrain* Glory, glory, sing his glory. Glory to our God on high.

2. Sing to Christ, the Father's loved one,
   Jesus, Lord and Lamb of God:
   hear our prayer, O Lord, have mercy,
   you who bear the sins of all.

3. Sing to Christ, the Lord and Saviour,
   seated there at God's right hand:
   hear our prayer, O Lord, have mercy,
   you alone the Holy One.

4. Glory sing to God the Father,
   glory to his only Son,
   glory to the Holy Spirit,
   glory to the Three in One.

Text: Francesca Leftley (b.1955) based on the 'Gloria'
Music: Francesca Leftley (b.1955) arr. Christopher Tambling
© Copyright 1978 Kevin Mayhew Ltd.

30 Peruvian Gloria

Cantor
1. Glory to God, glory to God, glory to the Father.

All
Glory to God, glory to God, glory to the Father.

Refrain
Cantor To him be glory for ever. *All* **To him be glory for ever.**

Cantor Alleluia, amen, *All* **alleluia, amen, alleluia, amen, alleluia, amen.**

2. Glory to God, glory to God,
   Son of the Father.
   **Glory to God, glory to God,
   Son of the Father.**
   To him be glory for ever.
   To him be glory for ever.
   Alleluia, amen.
   **Alleluia, amen,
   alleluia, amen,
   alleluia, amen.**

3. Glory to God, glory to God,
   glory to the Spirit.
   **Glory to God, glory to God,
   Son of the Spirit.**
   To him be glory for ever.
   To him be glory for ever.
   Alleluia, amen.
   **Alleluia, amen,
   alleluia, amen,
   alleluia, amen.**

This is best sung accompanied only by bongos or a similar percussion instrument. The optional harmony notes give added effect, but those singing the tune should remain on the lower notes.

Text and Music: traditional Peruvian, collected and arr. John Ballantine (b.1945)
© Copyright 1976 Kevin Mayhew Ltd.

31 Glory to God, to God in the height
Country Gardens Gloria

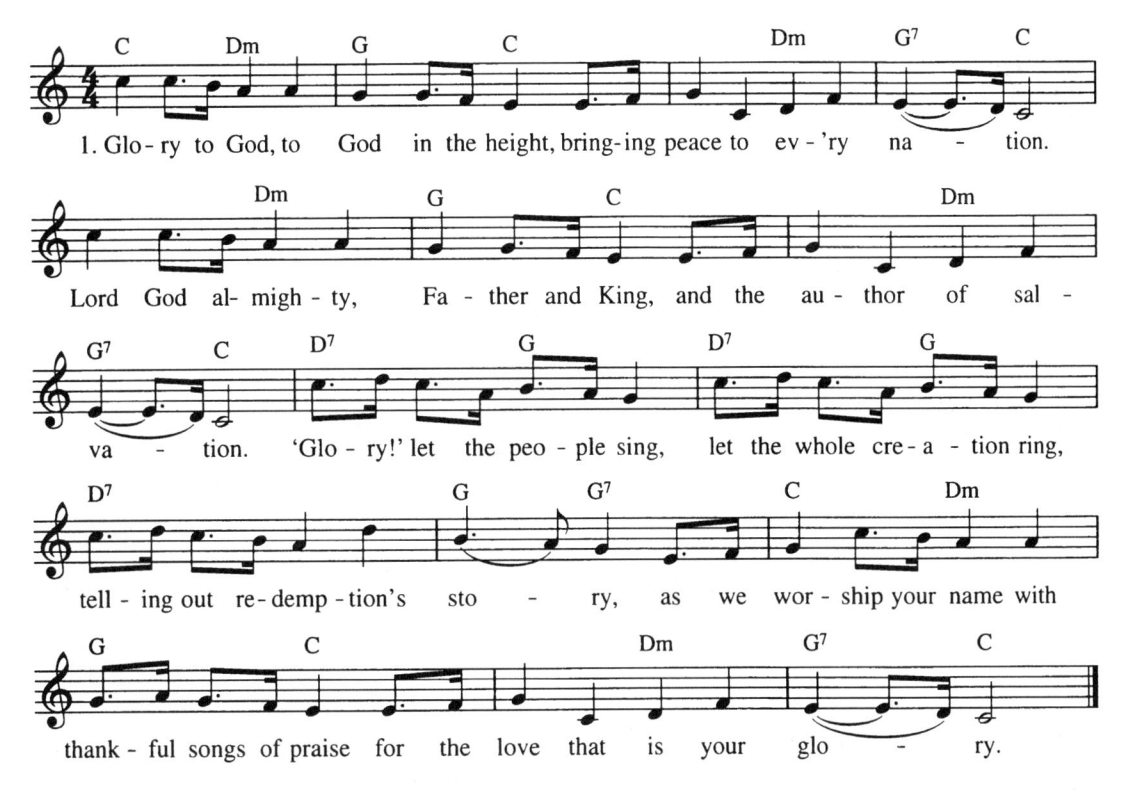

1. Glory to God, to God in the height, bringing peace to ev-'ry nation.
Lord God almighty, Father and King, and the author of salvation.
'Glory!' let the people sing, let the whole creation ring,
telling out redemption's story, as we worship your name with
thankful songs of praise for the love that is your glory.

2. Jesus, the Father's one holy Son,
all creation bows before you.
You are the God, the God we acclaim,
and we worship and adore you.
Lamb of God, to you we pray,
you who take our sin away,
mercy, grace and truth revealing.
At the right hand of God,
receive our humble prayer
for forgiveness, hope and healing.

3. You, Jesus Christ, alone are the Lord,
by your own eternal merit;
sharing by right the glory of God
in the presence of the Spirit.
You alone are Lord Most High,
you alone we glorify,
reigning over all creation.
To the Father, the Son and
Spirit, Three in One,
be eternal acclamation!

Text: Michael Forster (b.1946) based on the Gloria
Music: traditional English melody
Text © Copyright 1995, 1999 Kevin Mayhew Ltd.

32 Sing glory to God
Ash Grove Gloria

1. Sing glory to God in the height of the heavens, salvation and peace to his people on earth; our King and our Saviour, our God and our Father, we worship and praise you and sing of your worth. *Refrain* Creation unites in the power of the Spirit, in praise of the Father, through Jesus, the Son. So complex, so simple, so clear, so mysterious, our God ever three, yet eternally one.

2. Lord Jesus, the Christ, only Son of the Father,
   the Lamb who has carried our burden of shame,
   now seated on high in the glory of heaven,
   have mercy upon us who call on your name.

3. For you, only you, we acknowledge as holy,
   we name you alone as our Saviour and Lord;
   you only, O Christ, with the Spirit exalted,
   at one with the Father, for ever adored.

Text: Michael Forster (b.1946) based on the 'Gloria'
Music: traditional Welsh melody
Text © Copyright 1995, 1999 Kevin Mayhew Ltd.

33 Advent Alleluia

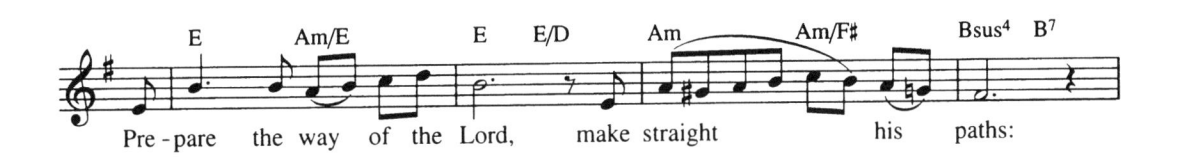

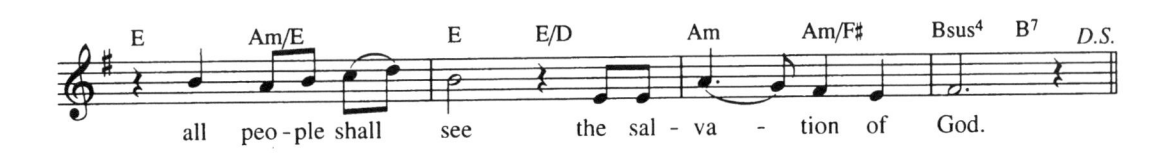

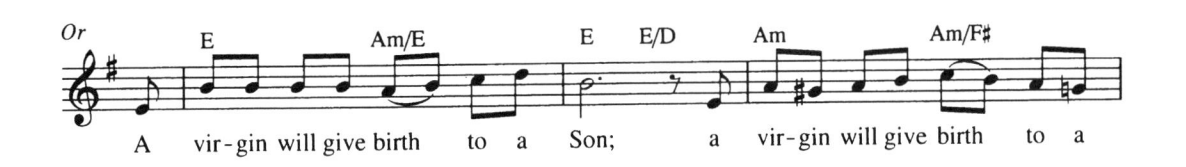

Alleluia, alleluia, alleluia, alleluia!

Prepare the way of the Lord, make straight his paths: all people shall see the salvation of God.

Or

A virgin will give birth to a Son; a virgin will give birth to a Son; his name will be Emmanuel: God is with us.

Text: from the Lectionary
Music: Michael Joncas (b.1951)

Text © Copyright ICEL, 1522 K. Street NW, Suite 1000, Washington DC 20005-1202, USA.
Music © Copyright 1981, 1983 New Dawn Music, 5536 NE Hassalo, Portland, OR 97213, USA.
All rights reserved. Used by permission.

34 Alleluia (Lloyd)

Al-le-lu-ia, al-le-lu-ia, al-le-lu-ia, al-le-lu-ia! *Fine*

Either: (1 Samuel 3: 9; John 6: 68) *D.C.*

Speak, Lord, your servant is listening: you have the message of eternal life.

Or: (John 1: 14,12)

The Word was made flesh and lived among us; to all who did accept him he gave power to become children of God. *D.C.*

Text: from the Lectionary
Music: Richard Lloyd (b.1933)
© Copyright 1995 Kevin Mayhew Ltd.

35 Scottish Alleluia

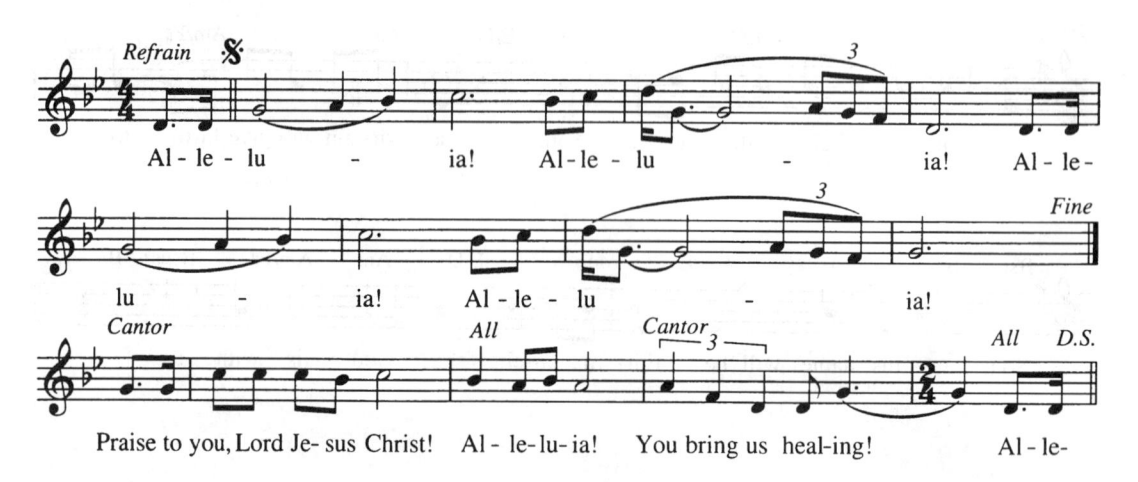

Refrain

Al-le-lu-ia! Al-le-lu-ia! Al-le-lu-ia! Al-le-lu-ia! *Fine*

Cantor: Praise to you, Lord Jesus Christ! *All:* Al-le-lu-ia! *Cantor:* You bring us healing! *All:* Al-le- *D.S.*

Other texts may be substituted for 'You bring us healing' to reflect the Gospel reading:

Light for our darkness! . . . Way to the Father! . . . Shepherd eternal! . . .

Strength in our weakness! . . . Word here among us!

Text and Music: Frances M. Kelly
© Copyright 1998, 1999 Kevin Mayhew Ltd.

36 Irish Alleluia

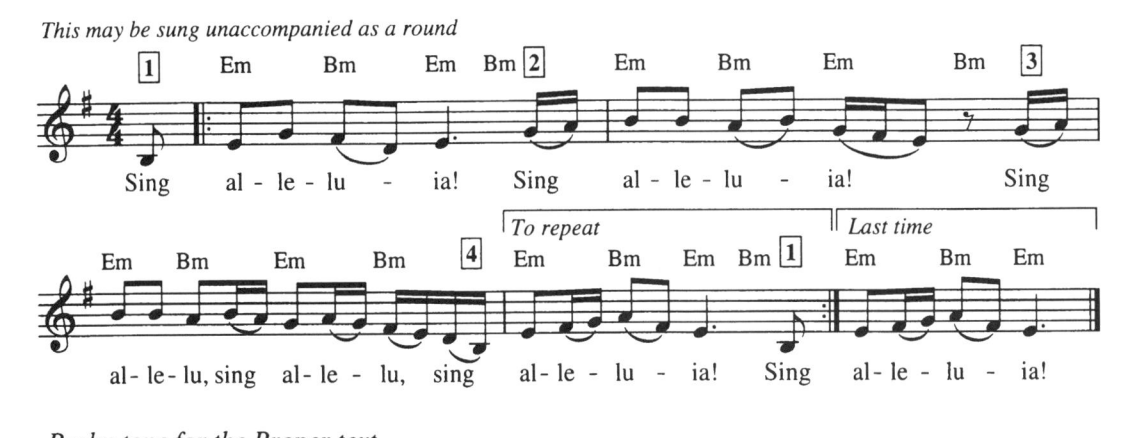

This may be sung unaccompanied as a round

Sing alleluia! Sing alleluia! Sing alleluia, sing alleluia, sing alleluia! Sing alleluia!

Psalm tone for the Proper text

Music: Response – traditional Irish
Psalm tone – Gregory Murray (1905-1992)
Psalm tone © Copyright Downside Abbey. Used by permission.

37 Celtic Alleluia

Alleluia, alleluia, alleluia, alleluia.

Psalm tone for the Proper text

Music: Response – Fintan O'Carroll
Psalm tone – Gregory Murray (1905-1992)
Response © Copyright 1985 Fintan O'Carroll and Christopher Walker. Published by OCP Publications, 5536 NE Hassalo, Portland OR 97213, USA. All rights reserved. Used by permission.
Psalm tone © Copyright Downside Abbey. Used by permission.

38 Eightfold Alleluia

1. Al-le-lu-ia, al-le-lu-ia, al-le-lu-ia, al-le-lu-ia, al-le-lu-ia, al-le-lu-ia, al-le-lu-ia, al-le-lu-ia.

Psalm tone for the Proper text

Music: Response – unknown
Psalm tone – Gregory Murray (1905-1992)
Psalm tone © Copyright Downside Abbey. Used by permission.

39 Easter Alleluia

Al-le-lu-ia, al-le-lu-ia, al-le-lu-ia.

Psalm tone for the Proper text

Music: Response – Plainsong
Psalm tone – Gregory Murray (1905-1992)
Psalm tone © Copyright Downside Abbey. Used by permission.

40 Alleluia 7

Al-le-lu-ia, al-le-lu-ia, al-le-lu-ia. Al-le-lu-ia! (Al-le-lu-ia!)

Music: Jaques Berthier (1923-1994)
© Copyright Ateliers et Presses de Taizé, Taizé-Communauté, F-71250, France.

41 Alleluia (Archer)

Al - le - lu - ia, al - le - lu - ia, al - le - lu - ia, al - le - lu - ia,
al - le - lu - ia, al - le - lu - ia, al - le - lu - ia, al - le - lu - ia.

Psalm tone for the Proper text

Music: Response - Malcolm Archer (b.1956)
Psalm tone - Gregory Murray (1905-1992)
Response © Copyright 1998 Kevin Mayhew Ltd.
Psalm Tone © Copyright Downside Abbey. Used by permission.

42 Alleluia (Plainsong)

Al - le - lu - ia, al - le - lu - ia, al - le - lu - ia.

Psalm tone for the Proper text

Music: Response - Plainsong
Psalm tone - Gregory Murray (1905-1992)
Psalm Tone © Copyright Downside Abbey. Used by permission.

43 Alleluia (Moore No. 1)

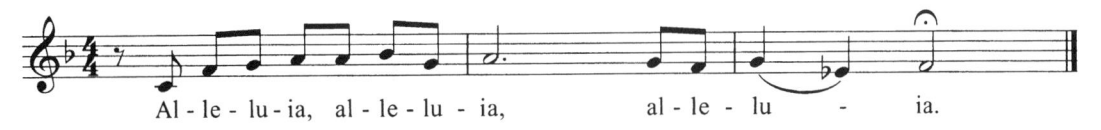

Al - le - lu - ia, al - le - lu - ia, al - le - lu - ia.

Psalm tone for the Proper text

Music: Response - Andrew Moore (b.1954)
Psalm tone - Gregory Murray (1905-1992)
Psalm Tone © Copyright Downside Abbey. Used by permission.

44 Alleluia (Moore No. 2)

Optional Introduction

Al - le - lu - ia, al - le - lu - ia, al - le - lu - ia.

Psalm tone for the Proper text

Music: Response - Andrew Moore (b.1954)
Psalm tone - Gregory Murray (1905-1992)
Response © Copyright 1998 Kevin Mayhew Ltd.
Psalm Tone © Copyright Downside Abbey. Used by permission.

45 Alleluia (White)

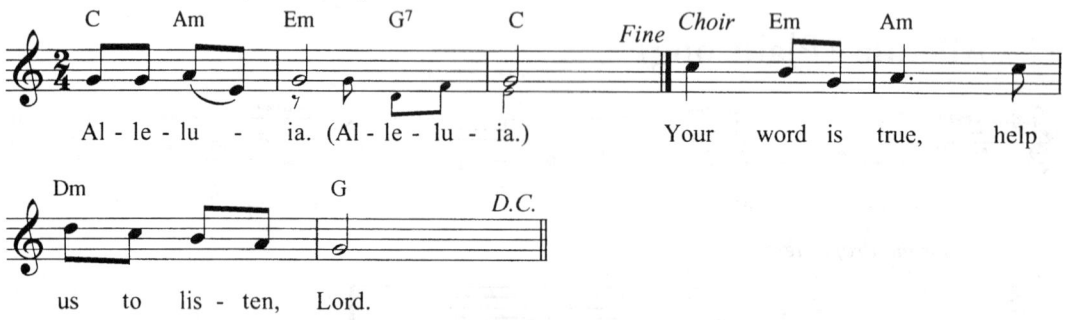

Al - le - lu - ia. (Al - le - lu - ia.) Your word is true, help us to lis - ten, Lord.

Text and Music: Estelle White (b.1925)
© Copyright 1976 Kevin Mayhew Ltd.

46 Alleluia (Moore No. 3)

Al - le - lu - ia, al - le - lu - ia, al - le - lu - ia, al - le - lu - ia, al - le - lu - ia, al - le - lu - ia.

Psalm tone for the Proper text

Music: Response - Andrew Moore (b.1954)
Psalm tone - Gregory Murray (1905-1992)
Psalm Tone © Copyright Downside Abbey. Used by permission.

47 Alleluia (Bevenot)

Al - le-lu - ia, al - le-lu - ia, al - le - lu - ia.

Psalm tone for the Proper text

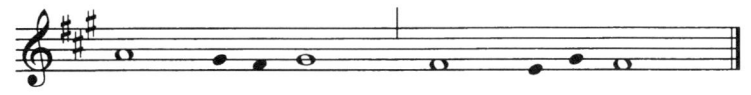

Music: Response and Psalm tone – Laurence Bevenot
Response © Copyright 1998 Kevin Mayhew Ltd.
Psalm tone © Copyright Downside Abbey. Used by permission.

48 Alleluia (Lundy)

Al - le - lu - ia, al - le - lu - ia, al - le - lu - ia.

Easter

1. Lord Jesus, you are risen from the dead: you are our companion on the road of life, and we know you in the breaking of the bread.

Advent and Christmas

2. Lord Jesus, Word of God made man for us,
you reveal your glory to our broken world,
and we worship you. Come again in glory!

Pentecost

3. Lord Jesus, you are at the Father's side:
you have sent your Spirit to renew our joy,
and we praise you. Come again in glory!

Text: Damian Lundy (b.1944-1997))
Music: adapted from Plainsong arr. John Ballantine
© Copyright 1979 Kevin Mayhew Ltd.

49 Alleluia! Magnificat!

A good way to sing this is as follows: The 'Alleluia' is sung by a cantor then echoed by the congregation; the congregation continue to sing the 'Alleluia' while the cantor sings the verse; all then sing the 'Alleluia'.

Al - le - lu - ia, al - le - lu - ia! Al - le - lu -
My soul now glo - ri - fies the Lord!

ia, al - le - lu - ia! Al - le - lu - ia, al - le - lu -
And how my spi - rit re - joi - ces in my

To repeat — *Last time*
ia! Al - le - lu - ia! Al - le - ia!
sav - ing God!

Original Text and Music © Copyright ARTEMAS – CCN, 10 Rue Henri IV,
69287 Lyon Cedex 02, France. Used by permission.
English translation © Copyright 1999 Kevin Mayhew Ltd.

50 Alleluia: We will hear your Word

Refrain
Al - le - lu - ia, al - le - lu - ia, al - le -
lu - ia, al - le - lu - ia, al - le - lu - ia. We will hear your Word, one in
love; we will live your Word, one in love; we will spread your Word, one in love.

Text and Music: Joe Wise (b.1939)
© Copyright GIA Publications Inc., 7404 S. Mason Avenue, Chicago, Illinois 60638, USA.
All rights reserved. Used by permission.

51 Halle, halle, halle

Halle, halle, hallelujah! Halle, halle, hallelujah! Halle, halle, hallelujah! Hallelujah, hallelujah!

Text: traditional
Music: unknown

52 Sing praises to the Lord

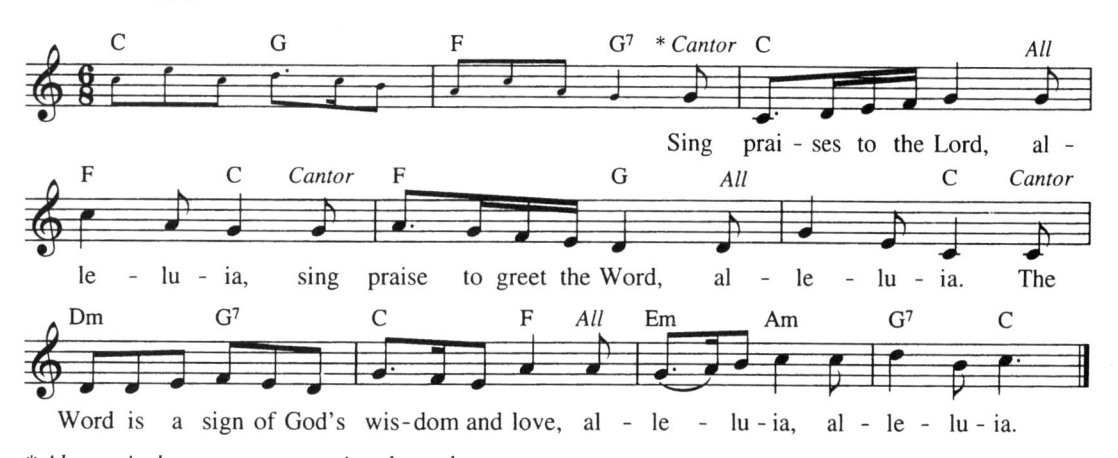

Cantor: Sing praises to the Lord, alleluia, *All:* sing praise to greet the Word, alleluia. *Cantor:* The Word is a sign of God's wisdom and love, *All:* alleluia, alleluia.

*Alternatively, everyone may sing throughout

2. God's truth can set us free, alleluia,
Christ Jesus is the key, alleluia.
Our ears hear the Word,
but it lives in our hearts,
alleluia, alleluia.

3. We listen to your voice, alleluia,
we praise you and rejoice, alleluia.
Your Spirit is with us,
she breathes in your Word:
alleluia, alleluia.

4. Sing praises to the Lord, alleluia,
sing praise to greet the Word, alleluia.
Creator and Son
with the Spirit adored:
alleluia, alleluia.

Text and Music: Christopher Walker (b.1947)

© Copyright 1985 Christopher Walker. Published by OCP Publications, 5536 NE Hassalo, Portland, OR 97213, USA. All rights reserved. Used by permission.

53 Lent and Holy Week Gospel Acclamation (Lundy)

All   *Fine*

Praise to you, Lord, praise to you, Lord, praise to you, Lord.

Passiontide

Lord Jesus, obedient to the Father's will, you became a

D.C.

slave, enduring death for us. Now you reign as Lord. Come again in glory!

Text: Damian Lundy (1944-1997)
Music: adapted from Plainsong arr. John Ballantine
© Copyright 1979 Kevin Mayhew Ltd.

54 Lent and Holy Week Gospel Acclamation (Walsh)

Glory and praise to you, O Christ!

Glory and praise to you, O Christ!

Psalm tone for the Proper text

Music: James Walsh
© Copyright Rev. James Walsh. Used by permission.

55 Lent and Holy Week Gospel Acclamation (Moore)

Andante — *Response*

Praise to you, O Christ, King of eternal glory!

Praise to you, O Christ, King of eternal glory! *Fine*

Lent

From the bright cloud, the Father's voice was heard: 'This is my Son, the Beloved. Listen to him!' *rit. a tempo D.S.*

Holy Week
Slower

Christ was humbler yet, even to accepting death, death on a cross. But God raised him high and gave him the name which is above all names. *rit. a tempo D.S.*

© Copyright 1995 Kevin Mayhew Ltd.

Text: Matthew 17:5; Philippians 2:8-9
Music: Andrew Moore (b.1954)

56 Credo 3

Credo in unum Deum, Patrem omnipotentem, factorem cæli et terræ, visibilium omnium, et invisibilium. Et in unum Dominum Jesum Christum, Filium Dei unigenitum, et ex patre natum ante omnia sæcula. Deum de Deo, lumen de lumine, Deum verum de Deo vero, genitum non factum, consubstantialem Patri: per quem omnia facta sunt. Qui propter nos homines, et propter nostram salutem descendit de cælis.

This arrangement © Copyright 1994 Kevin Mayhew Ltd.

Et in-car-na-tus est de Spi-ri-tu San-cto ex Ma-ri-a Vir-gi-ne:
et ho-mo fa-ctus est. Cru-ci-fi-xus et-i-am pro no-bis
sub Pon-ti-o Pi-la-to, pas-sus et se-pul-tus est.
Et re-sur-re-xit ter-ti-a di-e, se-cun-dum Scri-ptu-ras,
et as-cen-dit in cæ-lum: se-det ad dex-te-ram Pa-tris.
Et i-te-rum ven-tu-rus est cum glo-ri-a, ju-di-ca-re vi-vos et mor-tu-os:
cu-jus reg-ni non e-rit fi-nis. Et in Spi-ri-tum San-ctum, Do-mi-num,
et vi-vi-fi-can-tem: qui ex Pa-tre Fi-li-o-que pro-ce-dit.
Qui cum Pa-tre et Fi-li-o si-mul a-do-ra-tur,
et con-glo-ri-fi-ca-tur: qui lo-cu-tus est per Pro-phe-tas.

Et u-nam, san-ctam cath-o-li-cam et a-po-sto-li-cam Ec-cle-si-am.

Con-fi-te-or un-um ba-pti-sma in re-mis-si-o-nem pec-ca-to-rum.

Et ex-spe-cto re-sur-re-cti-o-nem mor-tu-o-rum.

Et vi-tam ven-tu-ri sæ-cu-li.

A - - - men.

Text: from the Roman Missal
Music: Plainsong

57 Lourdes Credo

Fine

Cre-do, cre-do, cre-do, A-men!

Unaccompanied

I believe in God the Fa-ther, Cre-ator of heaven and earth

I believe in Jesus his Son, who was made man, who died and rose a-gain.

D.C.

I believe in the Ho-ly Spirit, who gives life to the Church.

Text and Music: Jean-Paul Lécot (b.1947)
© Copyright Jean-Paul Lécot, 'Espélugues', 1 Ave. Mgr. Théas, 65100 Lourdes, France. Used by permission.

58 We believe (Fitzpatrick)

Celebrant

1. Do you believe in God, the Father almighty, creator of heav'n and earth?

All

We be-lieve, we do be-lieve.

Celebrant

2. Do you believe in Jesus Christ, his only Son, our Lord, who was born of the Virgin Mary, was crucified, died and was buried? We be-lieve, we do be-lieve.

Celebrant

3. Do you believe in Jesus Christ, who rose from the dead, and is now seated at the right hand of the Father? We be-lieve, we do be-lieve.

Celebrant

4. Do you believe in the Holy Spirit, the holy Catholic Church, the com - mun - ion of saints?

All

We be-lieve, we do be-lieve.

Celebrant

5. Do you believe in the forgiveness of sins, the resurrection of the body and the life e - ver-lasting?

All

We be-lieve, we do be-lieve.

Text: from the Roman Missal
Music: Gerry Fitzpatrick (b.1940)
© Copyright 1986 Kevin Mayhew Ltd.

59 Holy, holy, holy (MacMillan)

Moderato

Ho - ly, ho - ly, ho - ly Lord, God of pow'r and might. Heav'n and earth are full of your glo - ry. Ho - san - na in the high - est. Bles - sed is he, O bles - sed is he who comes in the name of the Lord. Ho - san - na in the high - est. Ho - san - na in the high - est.

Text: from the Roman Missal
Music: James MacMillan from 'St. Anne's Mass'
© Copyright 1997 Boosey & Hawkes Music Publishers Ltd., 295 Regent Street, London W1R 8JH. Used by permission.

60 Holy, holy, holy (Celtic Liturgy)

1. Ho - ly, ho - ly, ho - ly Lord, God of pow - er and might, hea - ven and earth are full of your glo - ry. Ho - san - na, ho - san - na in the high - est. 2. Bles - sed is he who comes in the name of the Lord. Ho - san - na in the high - est, ho - san - na in the high - est.

Text: from the Roman Missal
Music: Christopher Walker (b.1947) from 'A Celtic Liturgy'
© Copyright 1982 Christopher Walker. Published by OCP Publications, 5536 NE Hassalo, Portland, OR 97213, USA. All rights reserved. Used by permission.

61 Sanctus (Donnelly)

To be sung unaccompanied. A Cantor may sing each phrase first.

Ho - ly, ho - ly, ho - ly Lord, God of pow'r and might, hea - ven and earth are full of your glo - ry. Ho - san - na in the high - est. Bles - sed is he who comes in the name of the Lord. Ho - san - na in the high - est.

Text: from the Roman Missal
Music: Noel Donnelly (b.1932)
© Copyright 1986 Kevin Mayhew Ltd.

62 Holy, holy, holy (Deutsche Messe)

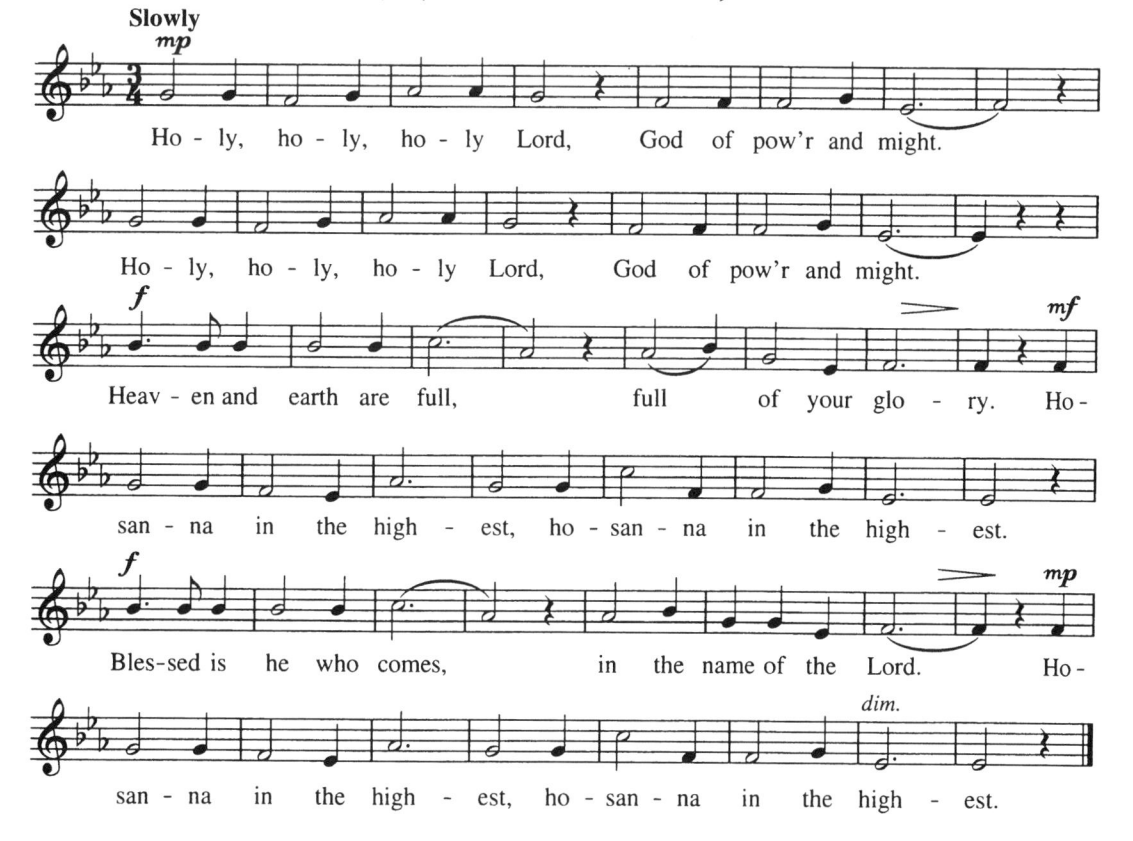

Slowly
mp

Ho - ly, ho - ly, ho - ly Lord, God of pow'r and might.

Ho - ly, ho - ly, ho - ly Lord, God of pow'r and might.

f — *mf*

Heav - en and earth are full, full of your glo - ry. Ho - san - na in the high - est, ho - san - na in the high - est.

f — *mp*

Bles - sed is he who comes, in the name of the Lord. Ho-

dim.

san - na in the high - est, ho - san - na in the high - est.

Text: from the Roman Missal
Music: Franz Schubert (1797-1828) adapted by Richard Proulx
© Copyright 1984 GIA Publications Inc., 7404 S. Mason Avenue, Chicago, Illinois 60638, USA.
All rights reserved. Used by permission.

63 Sanctus (Taizé)

Lento ($\newline$ = 60)

Sanctus, sanctus, sanctus Dominus
Deus Sabaoth, Deus, Sabaoth.

Holy, holy, holy Lord, God of pow'r and might.
Heaven and earth are full of your glory. Hosanna in the highest.
Blest is he who comes in the name of the Lord. Hosanna in the highest.

*Choose either part.

Text: from the Roman Missal
Music: Jacques Berthier (1923-1994)
© Copyright Ateliers et Presses de Taizé, Taizé-Communauté, F-71250, France. Used by permission.

64 Lourdes Sanctus

Refrain

Holy, holy, holy Lord, God of pow'r and might!

1. Full of your glory are heav'n and earth, God of pow'r and might.

© Copyright 1988 Kevin Mayhew Ltd.

2. Bles - sed is he who comes a - mong us in the name of the Lord.

3. Ho - san - na in the high - est!

Text: adapted by W.R. Lawrence (1925-1997)
Music: Jean-Paul Lécot (b.1947)

65 Holy, holy, holy is the Lord

1. Ho - ly, ho - ly, ho - ly is the Lord, ho - ly is the Lord God al - migh - ty! Ho - ly, ho - ly, ho - ly is the Lord, ho - ly is the Lord God al - migh - ty! Who was and is, and is to come; ho - ly, ho - ly, ho - ly is the Lord.

2. Blessèd, blessèd, blest is he who comes,
blest is he who comes in the Lord's name.
Blessèd, blessèd, blest is he who comes,
blest is he who comes in the Lord's name.
Hosanna in the heights of heav'n.
Blessèd, blessèd, blessèd is the Lord.

Text: John Ballantine (b.1945)
Music: Unknown
© Copyright 1984, 1988 Kevin Mayhew Ltd.

66 Holy, most holy, all holy the Lord
Slane Sanctus

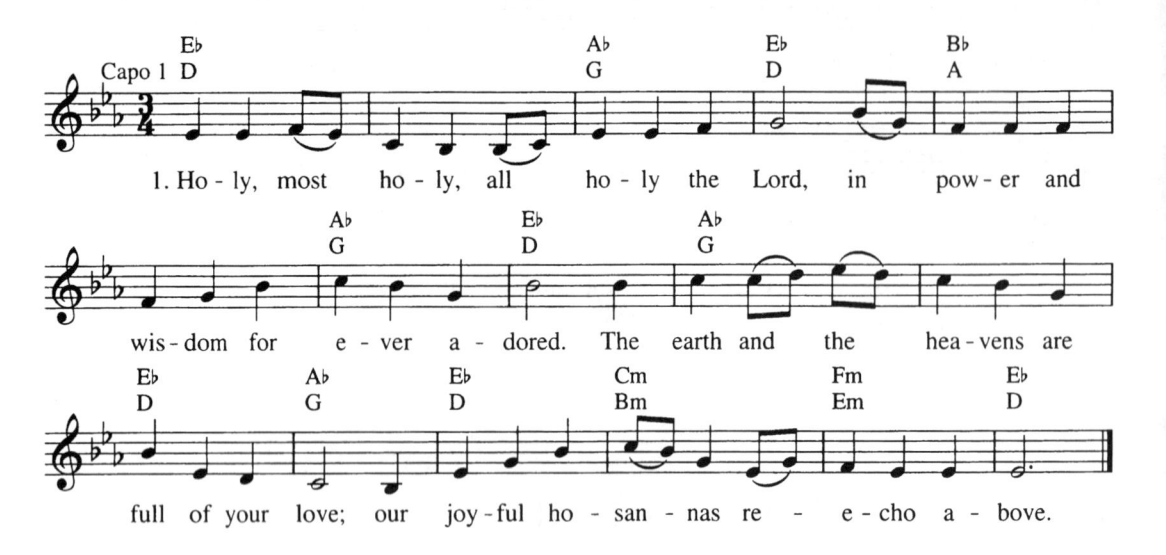

1. Holy, most holy, all holy the Lord, in power and wisdom for ever adored. The earth and the heavens are full of your love; our joyful hosannas re-echo above.

2. Blessèd, most blessèd, all blessèd is he
whose life makes us whole, and whose death sets us free:
who comes in the name of the Father of light,
let endless hosannas resound in the height.

Text: Michael Forster (b.1946) based on the Sanctus
Music: traditional Irish melody
Text © Copyright 1995, 1999 Kevin Mayhew Ltd.

67 O holy, most holy
Ash Grove Sanctus

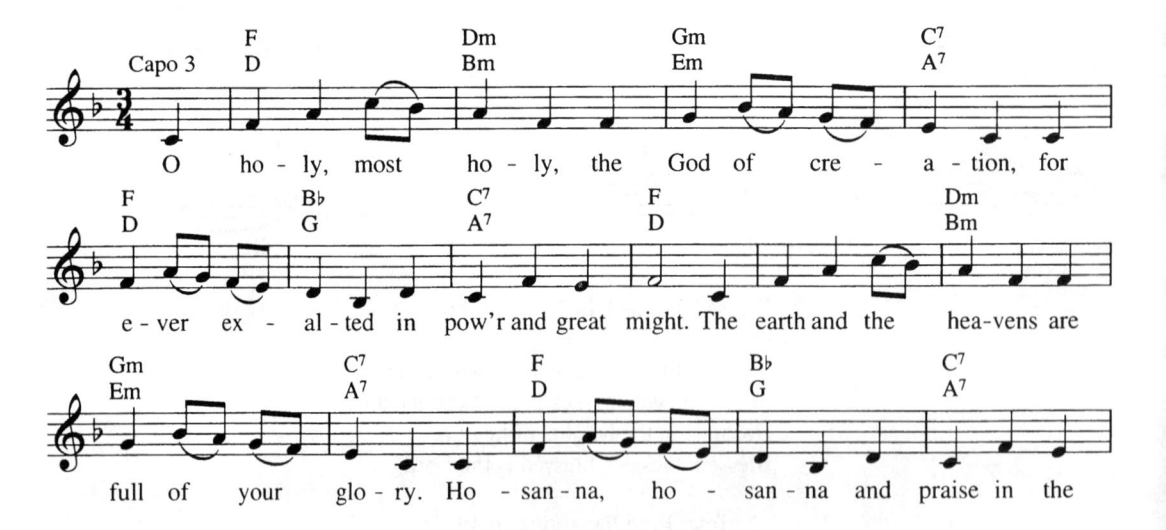

O holy, most holy, the God of creation, for ever exalted in pow'r and great might. The earth and the heavens are full of your glory. Hosanna, hosanna and praise in the

Text © Copyright 1995, 1999 Kevin Mayhew Ltd.

height! How bles-sèd is he who is sent to re-deem us, who
puts ev-'ry fear and in-jus-tice to flight; who comes in the name of the
Lord as our Sa-viour. Ho-san-na, ho-san-na and praise in the height!

Text: Michael Forster (b.1946) based on the 'Sanctus'
Music: traditional Welsh melody

68 Christ has died (Celtic Liturgy)

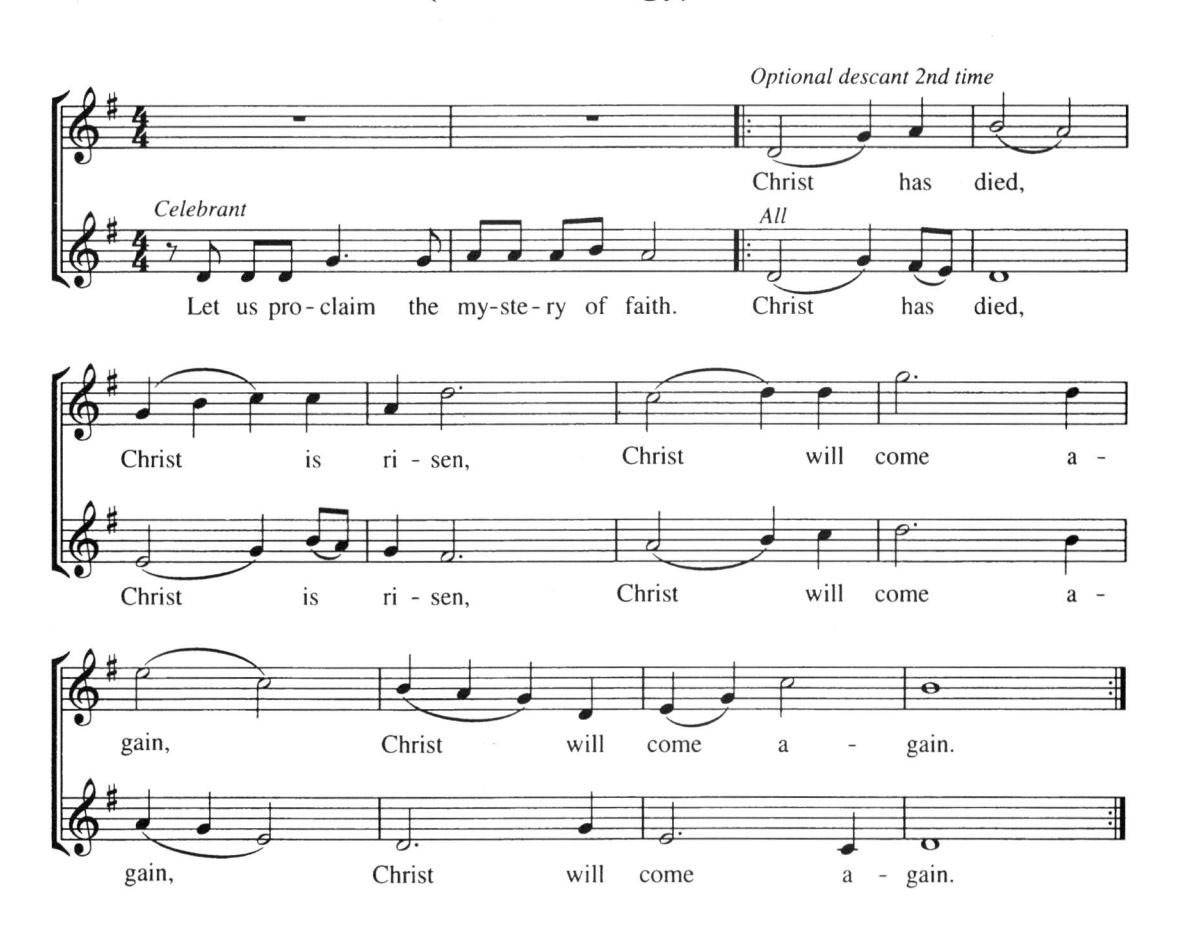

Optional descant 2nd time

Christ has died,

Celebrant Let us pro-claim the my-ste-ry of faith. *All* Christ has died,

Christ is ri-sen, Christ will come a-

Christ is ri-sen, Christ will come a-

gain, Christ will come a-gain.

gain, Christ will come a-gain.

Text: from the Roman Missal
Music: Christopher Walker (b.1947) from 'A Celtic Liturgy'
© Copyright 1982 Christopher Walker. Published by OCP Publications, 5536 NE Hassalo,
Portland, OR 97213, USA. All rights reserved. Used by permission.

69 Christ has died (Duffy)

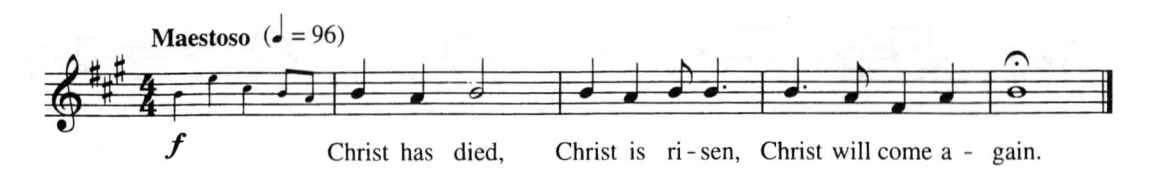

Maestoso ($\quarternote = 96$)

f Christ has died, Christ is ri-sen, Christ will come a-gain.

Text: from the Roman Missal
Music: Philip Duffy
© Copyright 1979 Philip Duffy. Used by permission.

70 Christ has died (Donnelly)

Celebrant — Let us pro-claim the mys-t'ry of faith. *All* — Christ has died, al-le-lu-ia. Christ is ri-sen, al-le-lu-ia. Christ will come a-gain.

Text: from the Roman Missal
Music: Noel Donnelly (b.1932)
© Copyright 1986 Kevin Mayhew Ltd.

71 Christ has died (Hill)

f Christ has died, Christ is ri-sen, Christ will come a-gain.

Optional descant — Christ has died, Christ is ri-sen, Christ will come a-gain.

Melody — Christ has died, Christ is ri-sen, Christ will come a-gain.

Text: from the Roman Missal
Music: David Hill
© Copyright 1999 Kevin Mayhew Ltd.

72 Christ has died (Wise)

Christ has died, al-le-lu-ia. Christ is ri-sen, al-le-lu-ia. Christ will come a-gain, al-le-lu-ia, al-le-lu-ia.

Text: from the Roman Missal
Music: Joe Wise (b.1939)
© Copyright 1970 GIA Publications Inc., 7404 S. Mason Avenue, Chicago, Illinois 60638, USA.
All rights reserved. Used by permission.

73 Dying you destroyed our death (Duffy)

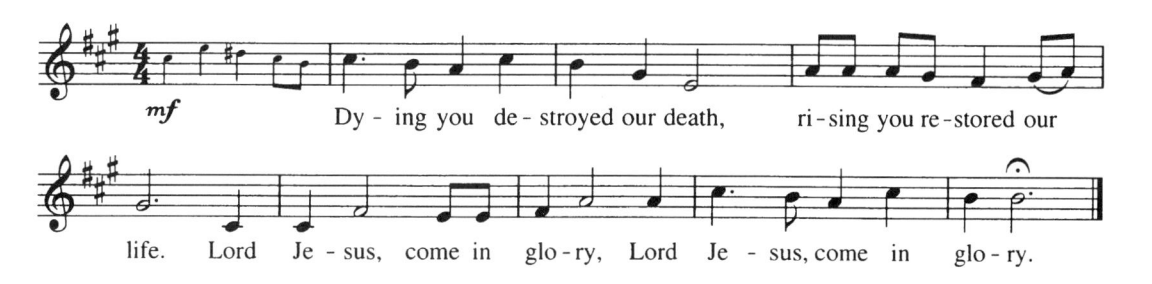

Dy-ing you de-stroyed our death, ri-sing you re-stored our life. Lord Je-sus, come in glo-ry, Lord Je-sus, come in glo-ry.

Text: from the Roman Missal
Music: Philip Duffy
© Copyright 1999 Kevin Mayhew Ltd.

74 When we eat this bread (Irish melody)

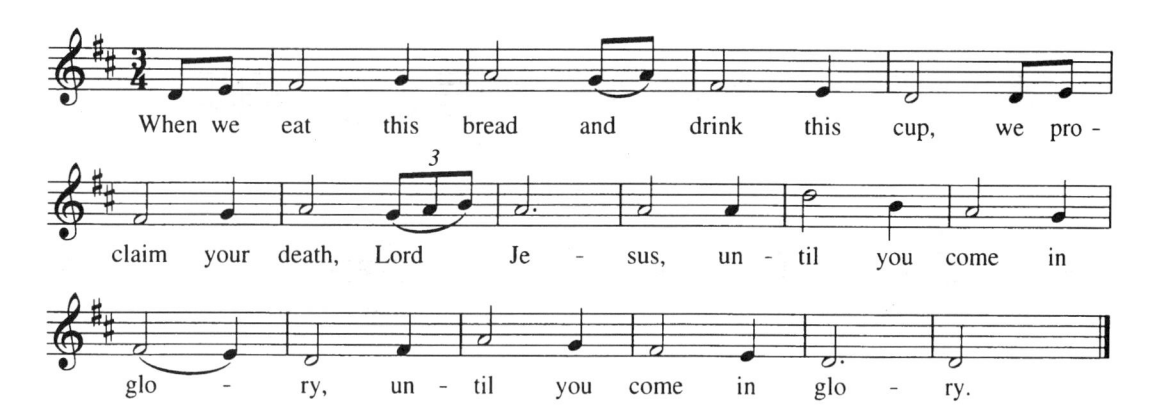

When we eat this bread and drink this cup, we pro-claim your death, Lord Je-sus, un-til you come in glo-ry, un-til you come in glo-ry.

Text: from the Roman Missal
Music: Irish melody (Petrie Collection)

75 When we eat this bread (MacMillan)

Moderato

When we eat this bread and drink this cup we proclaim your death, Lord Jesus, until you come in glory, until you come in glory.

Text: from the Roman Missal
Music: James MacMillan from 'St. Anne's Mass'
© Copyright 1997 Boosey & Hawkes Music Publishers Ltd., 295 Regent Street, London W1R 8JH, UK.
Used by permission.

76 When we eat this bread (Proulx)

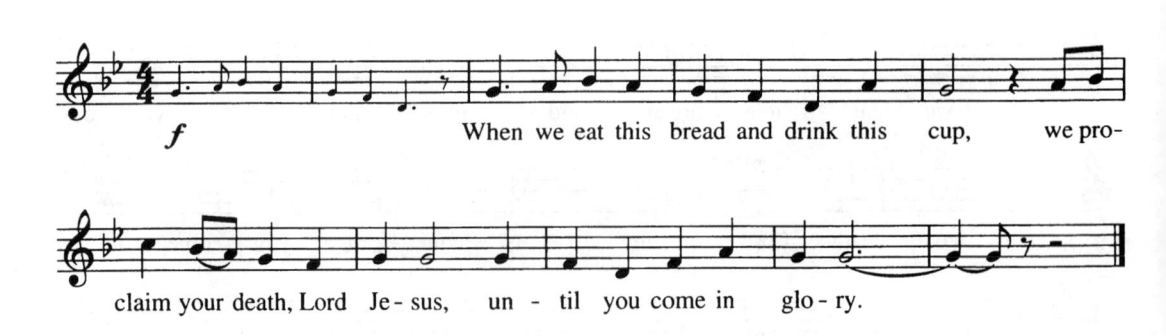

When we eat this bread and drink this cup, we proclaim your death, Lord Jesus, until you come in glory.

Text: from the Roman Missal
Music: Richard Proulx (b.1937) from 'A Festival Eucharist'
© Copyright GIA Publications Inc., 7404 S. Mason Avenue, Chicago, Illinois 60638, USA.
All rights reserved. Used by permission.

77 Great Amen (Mayhew)

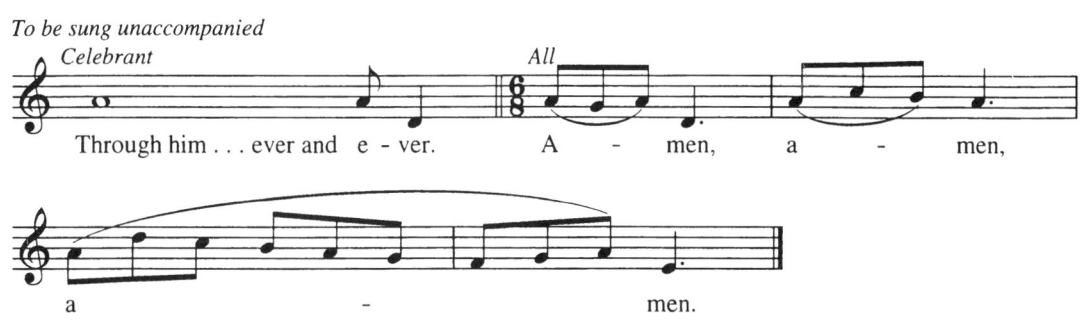

To be sung unaccompanied

Through him ... ever and e - ver. A - men, a - men, a - men.

Music: Kevin Mayhew (b.1942)
© Copyright 1986 Kevin Mayhew Ltd.

78 Great Amen (Lourdes)

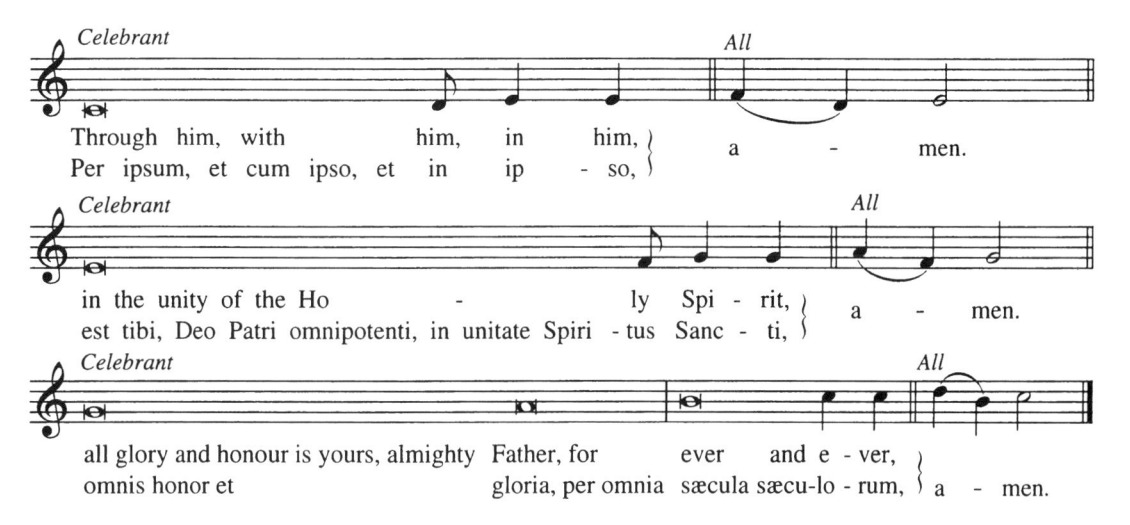

Through him, with him, in him, a - men.
Per ipsum, et cum ipso, et in ip - so,

in the unity of the Ho - ly Spi - rit, a - men.
est tibi, Deo Patri omnipotenti, in unitate Spiri - tus Sanc - ti,

all glory and honour is yours, almighty Father, for ever and e - ver,
omnis honor et gloria, per omnia sæcula sæcu-lo - rum, a - men.

Text: from the Roman Missal
Music: Jean-Paul Lécot (b.1947)
© Copyright 1988 Kevin Mayhew Ltd.

79 Great Amen (Plainsong)

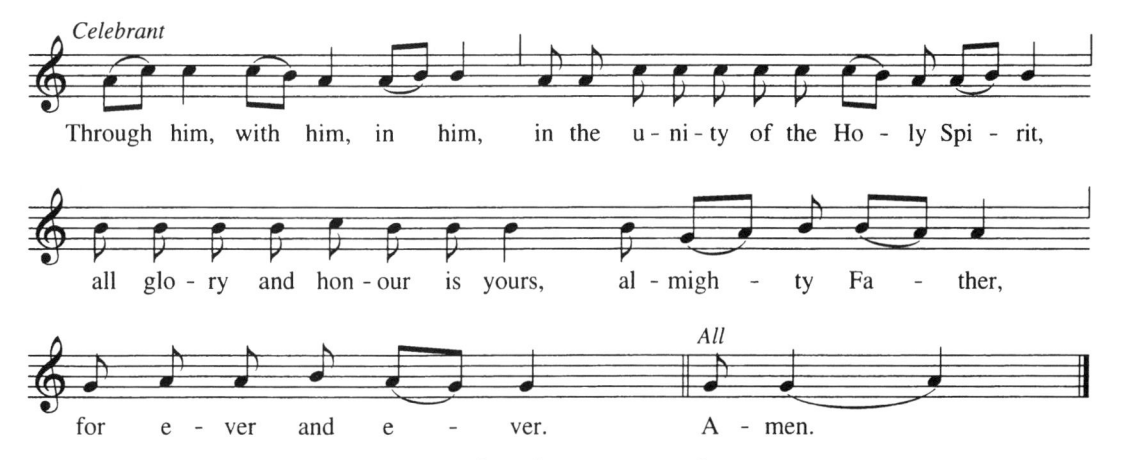

Through him, with him, in him, in the u - ni - ty of the Ho - ly Spi - rit,

all glo - ry and hon - our is yours, al - migh - ty Fa - ther,

for e - ver and e - ver. A - men.

Text: from the Roman Missal
Music: adapted from Plainsong

80 Great Amen (Hill)

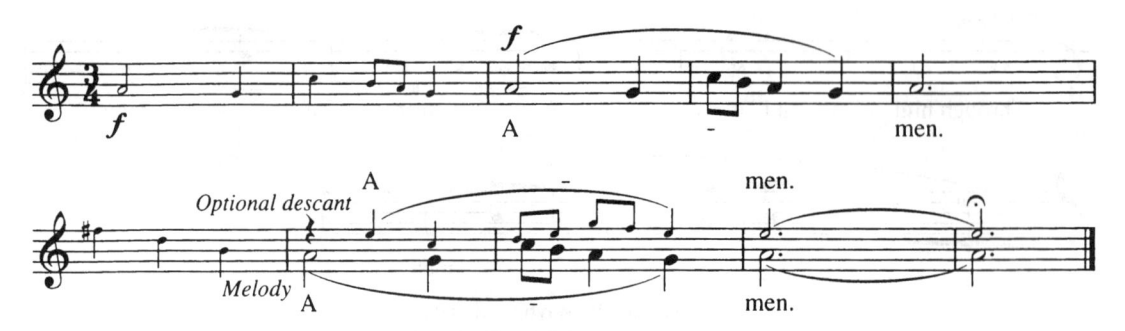

Text: from the Roman Missal
Music: David Hill
© Copyright 1999 Kevin Mayhew Ltd.

81 Great Amen (Proulx)

Text: from the Roman Missal
Music: Richard Proulx (b.1937) from 'A Festival Eucharist'
© Copyright GIA Publications Inc., 7404 S. Mason Avenue, Chicago, Illinois 60638, USA.
All rights reserved. Used by permission.

82 Great Amen (South African)

Text: Robert B. Kelly (b.1948)
Music: traditional South African melody
© Copyright 1999 Kevin Mayhew Ltd.

83 Our Father (White)

Our Father, who art in heaven, hallowed be thy name; thy kingdom come; thy will be done on earth as it is in heaven. Give us this day our daily bread; and forgive us our trespasses as we forgive those who trespass against us; and lead us not into temptation, but deliver us from evil.

Doxology
For the kingdom, the pow'r and the glory are yours, now and for ever.

Text: Matthew 6:9-13 and Luke 11:2-4
Music: Estelle White (b.1925)
© Copyright 1974, 1976 Kevin Mayhew Ltd.

84 Our Father (Wiener)

Our Fa - ther, who art in hea - ven, hal-lowed be thy name; thy king-dom come; thy will be done on earth as it is in hea - ven. Give us this day our dai-ly bread; and for-give us our tres-pas - ses as we for-give those who tres-pass a-gainst us; and lead us not in-to temp-ta-tion, but de-li-ver us from all that is e - vil.

Doxology
For the king - dom the pow'r and the glo - ry are yours, now and for e-ver. A - men.

Text: Matthew 6:9-13 and Luke 11:2-4
Music: Julian Wiener
© Copyright 1984, 1999 Kevin Mayhew Ltd.

85 Our Father (Rimsky-Korsakov)

Our Fa-ther, who art in hea-ven, hal-lowed be thy name;

thy king-dom come; thy will be done on earth as it is in hea-ven.

Give us this day our dai-ly bread; and for-give us our tres-pas-es

as we for-give those who tres-pass a-gainst us;

and lead us not in-to temp-ta-tion, but de-li-ver us from e-vil.

Doxology

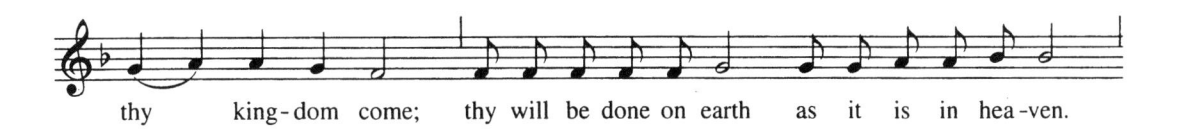

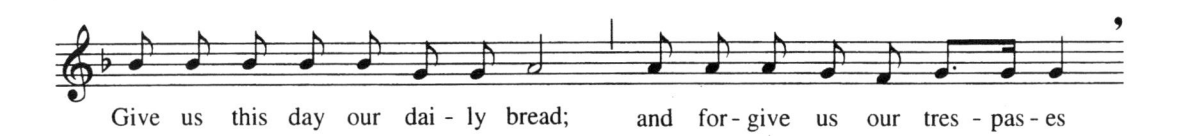

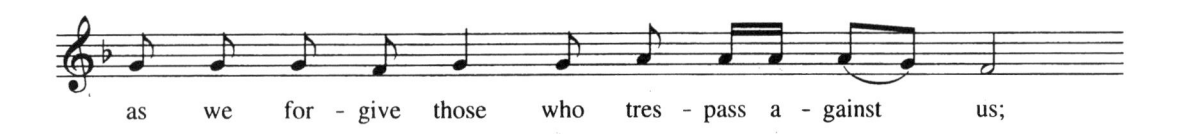

For the king-dom, the pow'r, and the glo-ry are yours, now and for e-ver. A-men.

Text: traditional based on Matthew 6:9-13 ; Luke 11:2-4
Music: Nicholai Rimsky-Korsakov (1844-1908) based on traditional Russian Orthodox sources,
adapted by Joseph Gelineau and Robert B. Kelly (b.1948)
© Copyright 1984 Kevin Mayhew Ltd.

86 'Echo' Our Father

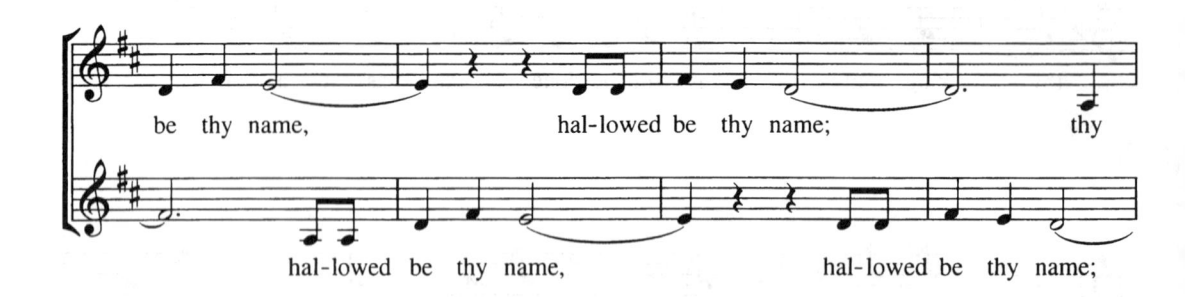

© Copyright 1978 Kevin Mayhew Ltd.

Words: Matthew 6:9-13 and Luke 11:2-4
Music: Jacqueline Emery

87 Our Father (Caribbean)

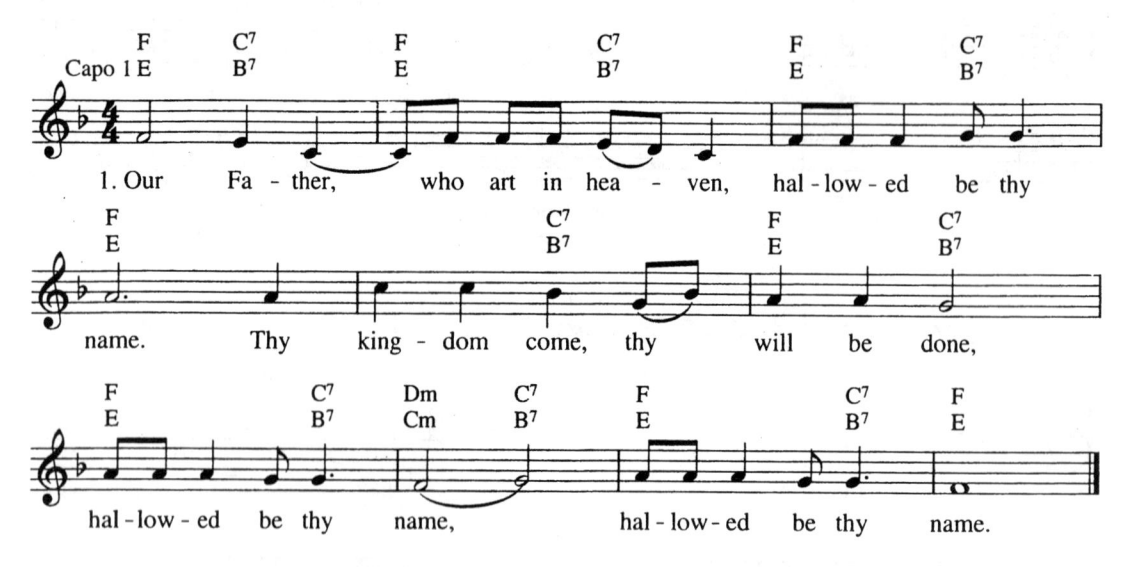

1. Our Father, who art in heaven, hallowed be thy name. Thy kingdom come, thy will be done, hallowed be thy name, hallowed be thy name.

2. On earth as it is in heaven,
   hallowed be thy name.
   Give us this day our daily bread,
   hallowed be thy name,
   hallowed be thy name.

3. Forgive us our trespasses,
   as we forgive those who
   trespass against us.

4. Lead us not into temptation,
   but deliver us from all that is evil.

5. For thine is the kingdom,
   the power, and the glory,
   for ever, and for ever and ever.

6. Amen, amen, it shall be so.
   Amen, amen, it shall be so.

Text: traditional Caribbean based on Matthew 6:9-13 and Luke 11:2-4
Music: traditional Caribbean

88 Lamb of God (Fitzpatrick)

Lamb of God, you take away the sins of the world; have mercy on us, have mercy on us. Lamb of God, you take away the sins of the world: grant us peace, grant us peace.

Text: from the Roman Missal
Music: Gerry Fitzpatrick (b.1940)
© Copyright 1986 Kevin Mayhew Ltd.

89 Lamb of God (Archer)

($\quarternote = 66$)

Lamb of God, you take a-way the sins of the world: have mer-cy, have mer-cy on us. Lamb of God, you take a-way the sins of the world: grant us, grant us peace.

Text: from the Roman Missal
Music: Malcolm Archer (b.1952) from 'The Halesworth Setting'
© Copyright 1995 Kevin Mayhew Ltd.

90 Lamb of God (Rees)

Lamb of God, you take a-way the sins of the world: have mer-cy on us. Lamb of God, you take a-way the sins of the world: grant us peace.

Text: from the Roman Missal
Music: Alan Rees (b.1941)
© Copyright 1992 Kevin Mayhew Ltd.

91 Jesus, Lamb of God (Inwood)

1. Jesus, Lamb of God, have mercy on us. Jesus, Lamb of God, have mercy on us. Jesus, Word made flesh, bearer of our sins: Jesus, Lamb of God, have mercy on us.

2. Jesus, Bread of Life, have mercy on us. Jesus, Bread of Life, have mercy on us. Jesus, Morning Star; Jesus, Prince of Peace: Jesus, Bread of Life, have mercy on us.

3. Jesus, Lamb of God, have mercy on us. Jesus, Lamb of God, have mercy on us. Jesus, King of kings; Jesus, Lord of all: Jesus, Lamb of God, give us your peace.

Text: adapted from the Liturgy by Paul Inwood (b.1947)
Music: Paul Inwood (b.1947)

© Copyright 1982, 1989 Paul Inwood. Published by OCP Publications, 5536 NE Hassalo, Portland, OR 97213, USA. All rights reserved. Used by permission.

92 Jesus, Lamb of God (Duffy)

Calmly and peacefully

Jesus, Lamb of God, have mercy on us.
Jesus, Lamb of God, have mercy on us. God's beloved Son, Saviour of us all. Jesus, Lamb of God, have mercy on us.

Bearer of our sins, have mercy on us: Bearer of our sins, have mercy on us. Healer of our wounds, comfort of our ills: Bearer of our sins, have mercy on us.

Jesus, Lamb of God, have mercy on us. Jesus, Lamb of God, have mercy on us. Christ, eternal priest, Shepherd of the flock: Jesus, Lamb of God, have mercy on us.

Hope of those who fail, rest for those who toil;

© Copyright 1999 Kevin Mayhew Ltd.

Bearer of our sins, have mercy on us. Solace of the sick, comfort in distress: Bearer of our sins, have mercy on us.

Jesus, Lamb of God, give us your peace: Jesus, Lamb of God, give us your peace. God's beloved Son, promise now fulfilled, Jesus, Lamb of God, give us your peace.

Text and Music: Philip Duffy

93 O Lamb of God

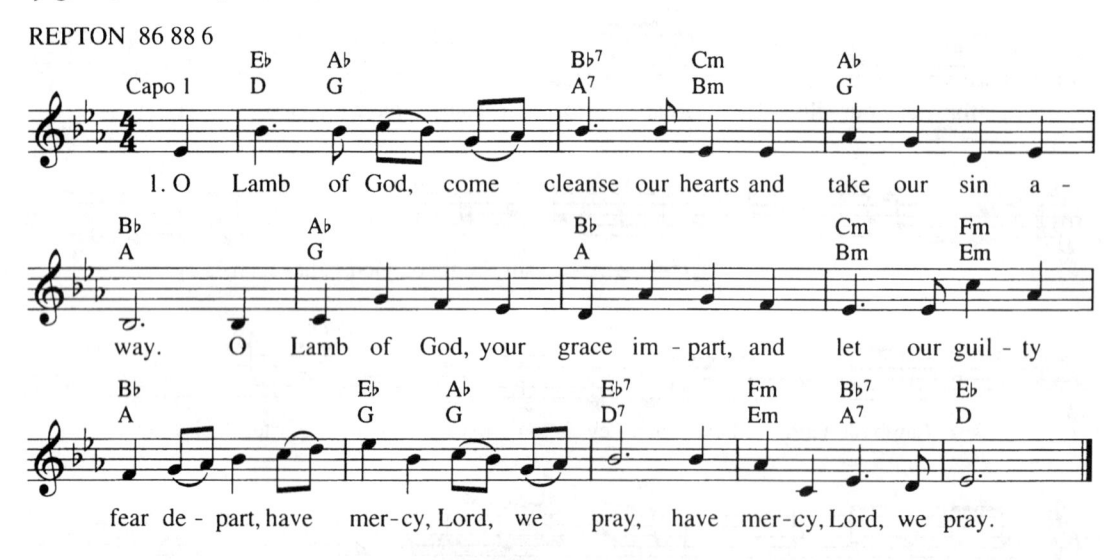

REPTON 86 88 6

1. O Lamb of God, come cleanse our hearts and take our sin away. O Lamb of God, your grace impart, and let our guilty fear depart, have mercy, Lord, we pray, have mercy, Lord, we pray.

2. O Lamb of God, our lives restore,
   our guilty souls release.
   Into our lives your Spirit pour
   and let us live for evermore
   in perfect heav'nly peace,
   in perfect heav'nly peace.

Text: Michael Forster (b.1946) based on the 'Agnus Dei'
Music: Hubert Parry (1848-1918)
Text © Copyright 1997, 1999 Kevin Mayhew Ltd.

Hymns and Songs

Hymns and Songs

94 Abba, Abba, Father

Ab - ba, Ab - ba, Fa - ther, you are the pot - ter, we are the clay, the work of your hands.

1. Mould us, mould us and fa - shion us in - to the im - age of Je - sus, your Son, of Je - sus, your Son.

2. Father, may we be one in you,
   as he is in you and you are in him,
   and you are in him.

3. Glory, glory and praise to you,
   glory and praise to you for ever, amen,
   for ever, amen.

Text and Music: Carey Landry

© Copyright 1977, Carey Landry and North American Liturgy Resources (NALR), 5536 NE Hassalo, Portland, OR 97213, USA. All rights reserved. Used by permission.

95 Abba, Father, from your hands

1. Abba Father, from your hands the living waters flow.
In your love you give me joy, joy so I may grow.
Abba Father, from your hands the living waters flow.

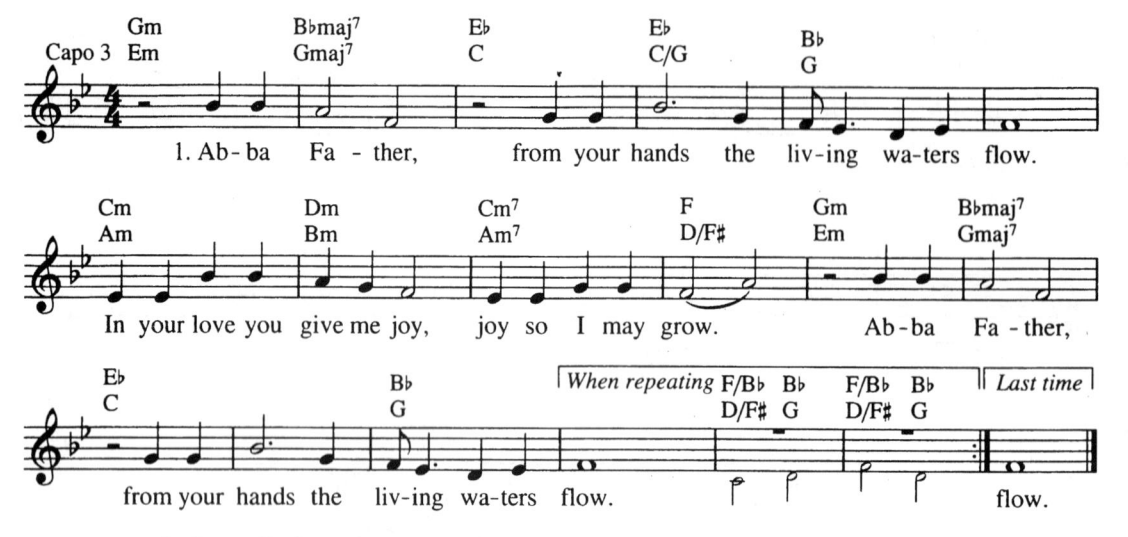

2. Jesus, Saviour, from your wounds
the living waters flow.
In your love you give me peace,
peace so I may grow.
Jesus, Saviour, from your wounds
the living waters flow.

3. Holy Spirit, from your pow'r
the living waters flow.
In your love you give me pow'r,
pow'r so I may grow.
Holy Spirit, from your pow'r
the living waters flow.

4. Alleluia! From your life
the living waters flow.
In your love you give me joy,
joy so I may grow.
Alleluia! From your life
the living waters flow.

Text: Damian Lundy (1944-1997)
Music: Gerard Markland (b.1953)
© Copyright 1982 Kevin Mayhew Ltd.

96 Abba, Father, send your Spirit

1. Abba, Father, send your Spirit. Glory, Jesus Christ.
Abba, Father, send your Spirit. Glory, Jesus Christ.

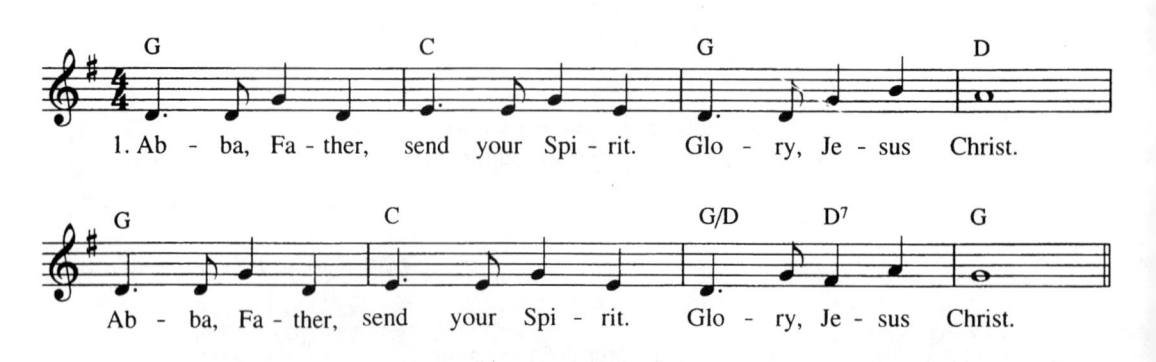

© Copyright 1974, 1998 Sisters of St. Mary of Namur, 909 West Shaw, Ft. Worth, Texas 76110, USA.
All rights reserved. Used by permission.

Refrain

Glo - ry, hal - le - lu - jah, glo - ry, Je - sus Christ!

Glo - ry, hal - le - lu - jah, glo - ry, Je - sus Christ! Christ!

Text and Music: Virginia Vissing

97 Abide with me

EVENTIDE 10 10 10 10

1. A - bide with me, fast falls the e - ven - tide; the dark-ness deep-ens; Lord, with me a - bide: when o - ther help - ers fail, and com-forts flee, help of the help - less, O a - bide with me.

2. Swift to its close ebbs out life's little day;
   earth's joys grow dim, its glories pass away;
   change and decay in all around I see;
   O thou who changest not, abide with me.

3. I need thy presence ev'ry passing hour;
   what but thy grace can foil the tempter's pow'r?
   Who like thyself my guide and stay can be?
   Through cloud and sunshine, Lord, abide with me.

4. I fear no foe with thee at hand to bless;
   ills have no weight, and tears no bitterness.
   Where is death's sting? Where, grave, thy victory?
   I triumph still, if thou abide with me.

5. Hold thou thy cross before my closing eyes;
   shine through the gloom, and point me to the skies;
   heav'n's morning breaks, and earth's vain shadows flee;
   in life, in death, O Lord, abide with me.

Text: Henry Francis Lyte (1793-1847)
Music: William Henry Monk (1823-1889)

98 A child is born in Bethlehem

1. A child is born in Beth-le-hem, al-le-lu-ia, there-fore re-joice, Je-ru-sa-lem,
2. The babe who lies up-on the straw, al-le-lu-ia, will rule the world for e-ver-more
3. Up-on this joy-ful ho-ly night, al-le-lu-ia, we bless your name, O Lord of light,
4. We praise you, Ho-ly Tri-ni-ty, al-le-lu-ia, a-dor-ing you e-ter-nal-ly,

al-le-lu-ia, al-le-lu-ia. Our joy-ful hearts we raise,

Christ is born, O come a-dore him in new-found songs of praise.

Text: 14th century Latin, trans. Ruth Fox Hume
Music: Plainsong
© Copyright 1964, 1986 GIA Publications Inc., 7404 S. Mason Avenue, Chicago, Illinois 60638, USA.
All rights reserved. Used by permission.

99 Across the years there echoes still

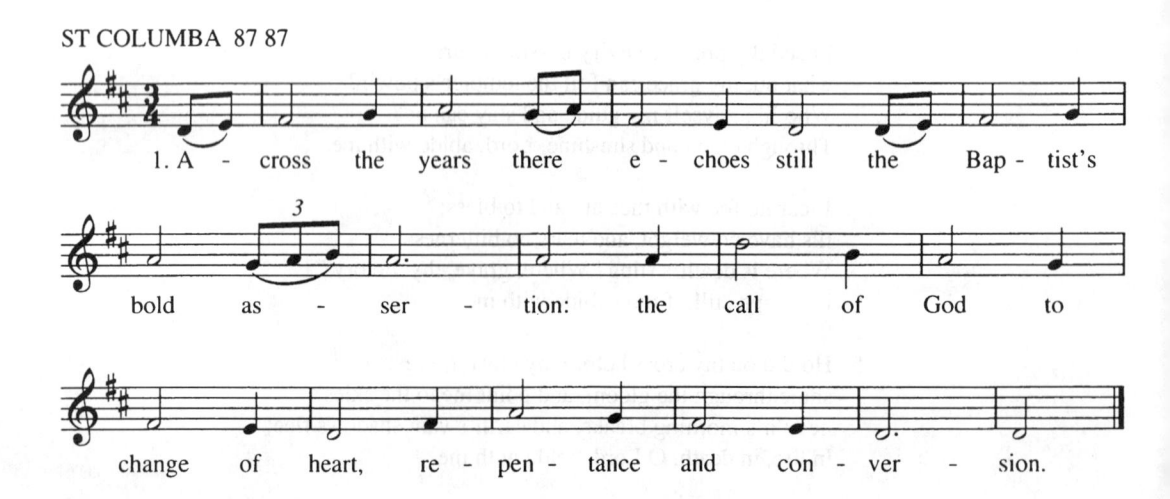

ST COLUMBA 87 87

1. A-cross the years there e-choes still the Bap-tist's bold as-ser-tion: the call of God to change of heart, re-pen-tance and con-ver-sion.

Words © Copyright The Archdiocese of Durban, 408 Innes Road, Durban 4001, South Africa. Used by permission.

2. The word that John more boldly spoke
   in dying, than in living,
   now Christ takes up, as he proclaims
   a Father all-forgiving.

3. The erring son he welcomes home
   when all is spent and squandered.
   He lovingly pursues the sheep
   that from the flock has wandered.

4. Forgive us, Lord, all we have done
   to you and one another.
   So often we have gone our way,
   forgetful of each other.

5. Forgetful of the cross they bear
   of hunger, want, oppression –
   grant, Lord, that we may make amends,
   who humbly make confession.

Text: Denis E. Hurley
Music: Irish melody (Petrie Collection)

100 Adeste fideles

ADESTE FIDELES Irregular and Refrain

1. Adeste fideles, laeti triumphantes;
   venite, venite in Bethlehem;
   natum videte regem angelorum:

   Refrain
   venite adoremus, venite adoremus,
   venite adoremus Dominum.

A higher setting will be found at No. 501

2. Deum de Deo, lumen de lumine,
   gestant puellæ viscera:
   Deum verum, genitum, non factum:

3. Cantet nunc Io! Chorus angelorum:
   cantet nunc aula cælestium;
   Gloria in excelsis Deo!

4. Ergo qui natus die hodierna,
   Jesu tibi sit gloria:
   Patris æterni Verbum caro factum!

Text and Music: John Francis Wade (1711-1786)

101 A hymn of glory let us sing!

LASST UNS ERFREUEN 88 44 88 and Alleluias

1. A hymn of glo-ry let us sing! New hymns through-out the world shall ring. Alleluia! Alleluia! Christ, by a road be-fore un-trod, as-cends un-to the throne of God. *Refrain* Al-le-lu-ia! Al-le-lu-ia! Al-le-lu-ia! Al-le-lu-ia! Al-le-lu-ia!

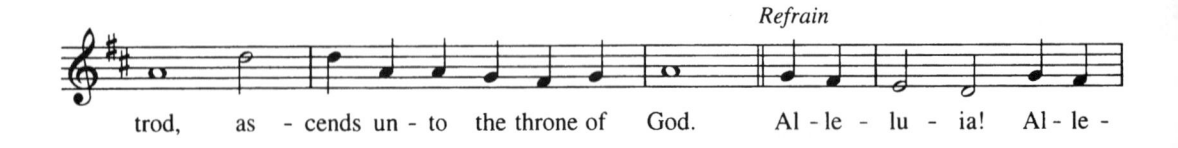

A lower setting will be found at No. 184

2. The holy apostolic band
upon the Mount of Olives stand.
Alleluia! Alleluia!
And with his faithful foll'wers see
their Lord ascend in majesty.
Alleluia! Alleluia!
Alleluia! Alleluia! Alleluia!

3. To whom the shining angels cry,
'Why stand and gaze upon the sky?'
Alleluia! Alleluia!
'This is the Saviour!' Thus they say,
'This is his glorious triumph day!'
Alleluia! Alleluia!
Alleluia! Alleluia! Alleluia!

4. O risen Christ, ascended Lord,
all praise to you let earth accord:
Alleluia! Alleluia!
You are, while endless ages run,
with Father and with Spirit one.
Alleluia! Alleluia!
Alleluia! Alleluia! Alleluia!

Text: 'Hymnum canamus gloria' by Venerable Bede (673-735) trans. 'Lutheran Book of Worship' (1978)
Music: melody from 'Geistliche Kirchengesang', Cologne (1623)

102 All creation, bless the Lord

BENEDICITE 77 75 D

1. All creation, bless the Lord.
   Earth and heaven, bless the Lord.
   Spirits, powers, bless the Lord.
   Praise him for ever.
   Sun and moon, bless the Lord.
   Stars and planets, bless the Lord.
   Dews and showers, bless the Lord.
   Praise him for ever.

2. Winds and breezes, bless the Lord.
   Spring and autumn, bless the Lord.
   Winter, summer, bless the Lord.
   Praise him for ever.
   Fire and heat, bless the Lord.
   Frost and cold, bless the Lord.
   Ice and snow, bless the Lord.
   Praise him for ever.

3. Night and daytime, bless the Lord.
   Light and darkness, bless the Lord.
   Clouds and lightning, bless the Lord.
   Praise him for ever.
   All the earth, bless the Lord.
   Hills and mountains, bless the Lord.
   Trees and flowers, bless the Lord.
   Praise him for ever.

4. Springs and rivers, bless the Lord.
   Seas and oceans, bless the Lord.
   Whales and fishes, bless the Lord.
   Praise him for ever.
   Birds and insects, bless the Lord.
   Beasts and cattle, bless the Lord.
   Let all creatures bless the Lord.
   Praise him for ever.

5. Let God's people bless the Lord.
   Men and women, bless the Lord.
   All creation, bless the Lord.
   Praise him for ever.
   Let God's people bless the Lord.
   Men and women, bless the Lord.
   All creation, bless the Lord.
   Praise him for ever.

Text: based on the 'Canticle of Daniel', Hayward Osborne
Music: Hayward Osborne

© Copyright 1975 Josef Weinberger Ltd., 12-14 Mortimer Street, London W1N 7RD.
All rights reserved. Used by permission.

103 All creatures of our God and King

LASST UNS ERFREUEN 88 44 88 and Alleluias

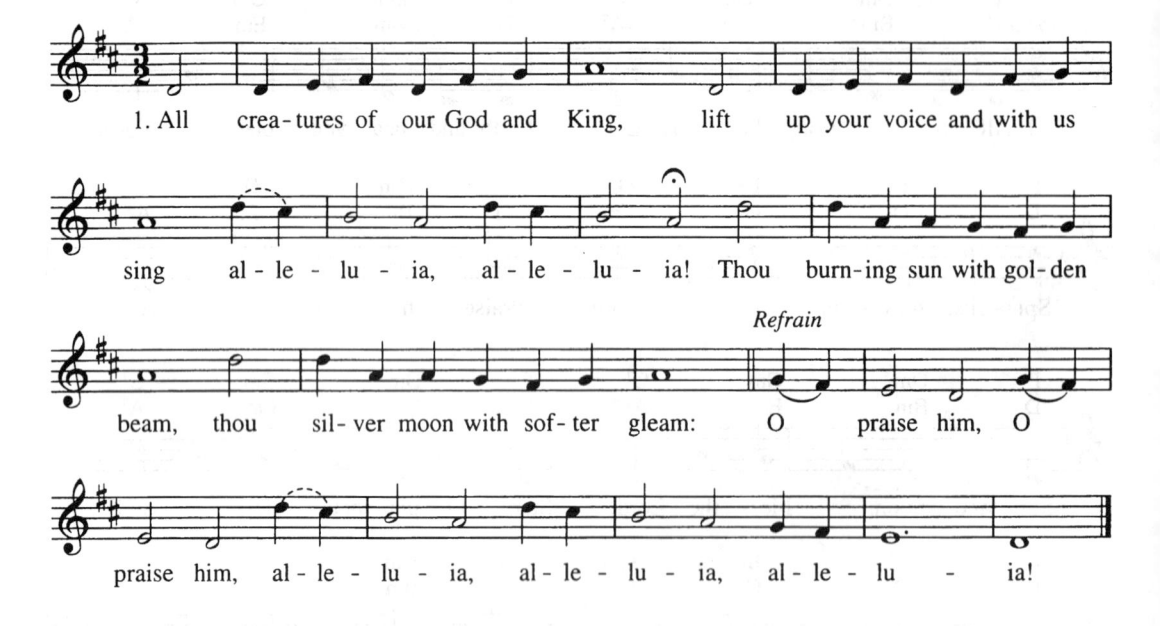

1. All crea-tures of our God and King, lift up your voice and with us sing al-le-lu-ia, al-le-lu-ia! Thou burn-ing sun with gol-den beam, thou sil-ver moon with sof-ter gleam:

Refrain

O praise him, O praise him, al-le-lu-ia, al-le-lu-ia, al-le-lu-ia!

2. Thou rushing wind that art so strong,
ye clouds that sail in heav'n along,
O praise him, alleluia!
Thou rising morn, in praise rejoice,
ye lights of evening, find a voice:

3. Thou flowing water, pure and clear,
make music for thy Lord to hear,
alleluia, alleluia!
Thou fire so masterful and bright,
that givest us both warmth and light:

4. Dear mother earth, who day by day
unfoldest blessings on our way,
O praise him, alleluia!
The flow'rs and fruits that in thee grow,
let them his glory also show.

5. All you with mercy in your heart,
forgiving others, take your part,
O sing ye, alleluia!
Ye who long pain and sorrow bear,
praise God and on him cast your care:

6. And thou, most kind and gentle death,
waiting to hush our latest breath,
O praise him, alleluia!
Thou leadest home the child of God,
and Christ our Lord the way hath trod:

7. Let all things their Creator bless,
and worship him in humbleness,
O praise him, alleluia!
Praise, praise the Father, praise the Son,
and praise the Spirit, Three in One.

A lower setting will be found at No. 184

Text: William Henry Draper (1855-1933) alt.
based on the 'Cantico di Frate Sole' of St. Francis of Assisi (1182-1226)
Music: melody from 'Geistliche Kirchengesang', Cologne (1623)
Text © Copyright J. Curwen & Sons Ltd, 8/9 Frith Street, London W1V 5TZ. Used by permission.

104 Alleluia: All the earth

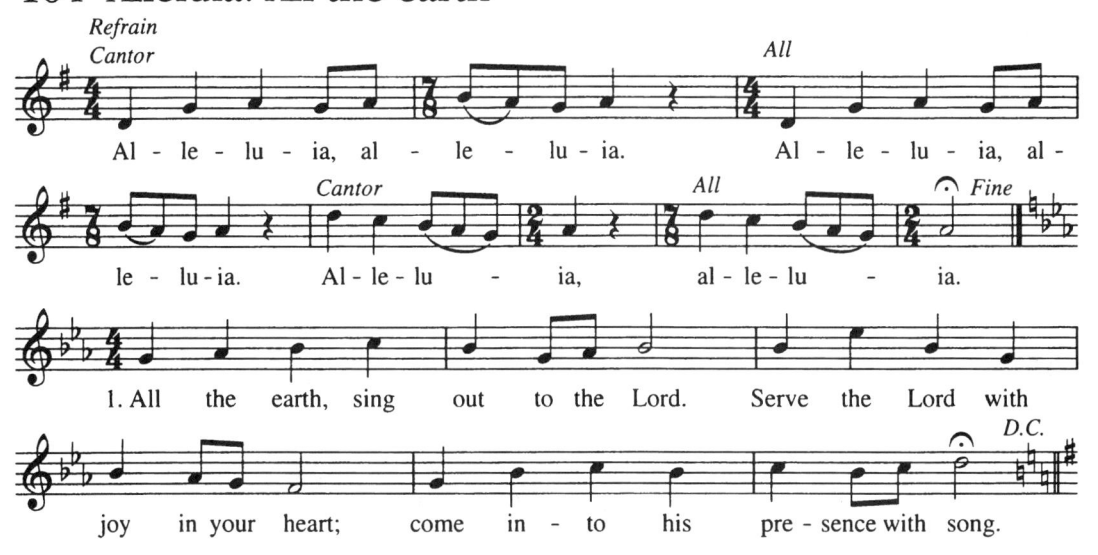

Al-le-lu-ia, al-le-lu-ia. Al-le-lu-ia, al-le-lu-ia. Al-le-lu-ia, al-le-lu-ia.

1. All the earth, sing out to the Lord.
   Serve the Lord with joy in your heart;
   come into his presence with song.

2. Come and bring your gifts to the Lord.
   Come before him, singing his praise;
   he is Lord, and he is our God.

3. God is good, his love never ends;
   he is always true to his word,
   he is faithful, age upon age.

Text: Hubert J. Richards (b.1921) based on Psalm 99
Music: Andrew Moore (b.1954)
© Copyright 1996 Kevin Mayhew Ltd.

105 Alleluia, alleluia, give thanks to the risen Lord

Alleluia, alleluia, give thanks to the risen Lord, alleluia, alleluia, give praise to his name. 1. Jesus is Lord of all the earth. He is the King of creation.

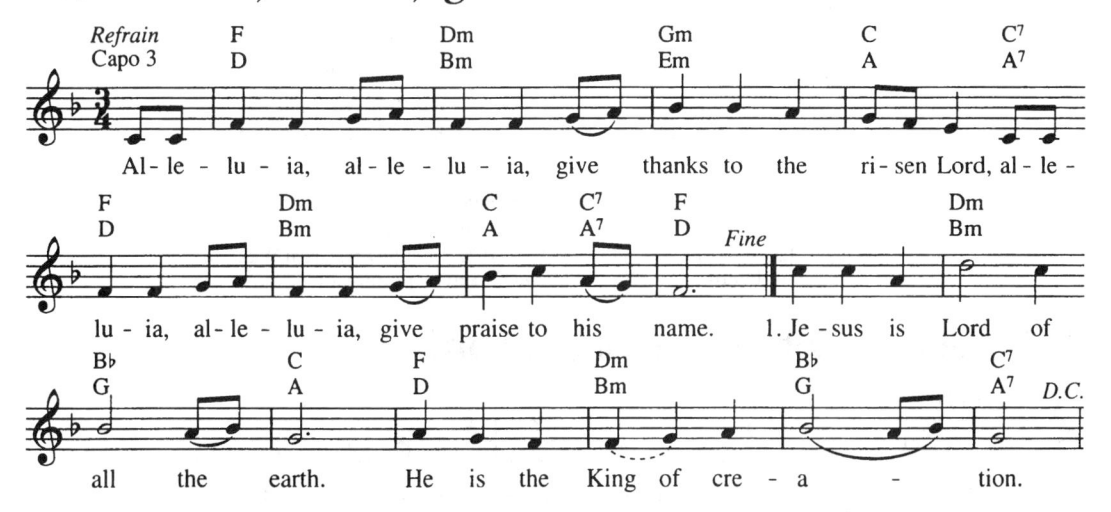

2. Spread the good news o'er all the earth.
   Jesus has died and is risen.

3. We have been crucified with Christ.
   Now we shall live for ever.

4. God has proclaimed the just reward:
   'Life for us all, alleluia!'

5. Come, let us praise the living God,
   joyfully sing to our Saviour.

Text: Donald Fishel (b.1950) alt.
Music: Donald Fishel (b.1950)
© Copyright 1973 Word of God Music. Administered by CopyCare,
P.O. Box 77, Hailsham, East Sussex BN27 3EF, UK. Used by permission.

106 Alleluia, alleluia! I will praise the Father

CONFIDO 12 4 11 5

Refrain

Al-le-lu - ia, al-le-lu - ia! I will praise the Fa-ther for all of my life. I will sing to my God as long as I live. Al-le-lu - ia, al-le-lu - ia, al-le-lu - ia! *(Last time only — Fine)* al - le-lu - ia!

To verses

1. Do not place all your trust in a wo-man or man: they can-not save. Their schemes will all per-ish when they yield up their breath at the end of their days.

2. But so happy are those
    who will trust in their God:
   they will find help.
   For God is the maker
    of the heavens and earth
   and of all that these hold.

3. All the searchers for justice,
    for freedom, for love,
   God will fulfil.
   The widow, the orphan,
    and the blind and the lame
   in his love are restored.

Text: Michael Cockett (b.1938) based on Psalm 145
Music: Gregory Murray (1905-1992)
© Copyright McCrimmon Publishing Co. Ltd, 10-12 High Street, Great Wakering,
Southend-on-Sea, Essex SS3 0EQ. Used by permission.

107 Alleluia: Let us sing of the Lord

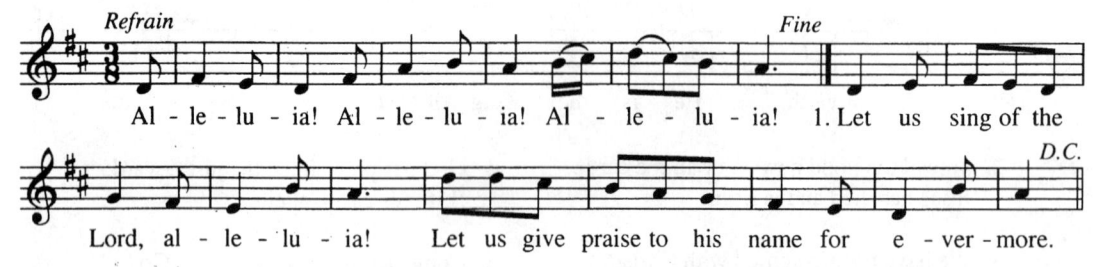

Refrain ... *Fine*

Al - le - lu - ia! Al - le - lu - ia! Al - le - lu - ia! 1. Let us sing of the Lord, al - le - lu - ia! Let us give praise to his name for e - ver - more. *D.C.*

2. We give thanks to the Lord, for he is good;
   his loving kindness endures eternally.

3. All the works of the Lord proclaim his love;
   he is the source of contentment for his friends.

Text: Jean-Paul Lécot (b.1947) based on Psalms 110, 111, 117, 118 trans. W.R. Lawrence (1925-1997)
Music: Paul Décha
© Copyright 1988 Kevin Mayhew Ltd.

108 Alleluia: Praise God

Alleluia, alleluia, alleluia.

1. Praise God, who forgives all our sins
   and heals us of ev'rything evil;
   he rescues our life from the grave
   and clothes us in mercy and love.

2. Our God is all kindness and love,
   so patient and rich in compassion;
   not treating us as we deserve:
   not paying us back for our sins.

3. As heaven is high over earth,
   so strong is his love for his people.
   As far as the east from the west,
   so far he removes all our sins.

4. As fathers take pity on sons,
   we know God will show us compassion;
   for he knows of what we are made:
   no more than the dust of the earth.

Text: Hubert J. Richards (b.1921) based on Psalms 102 and 104
Music: Richard Lloyd (b.1933)
© Copyright 1995 Kevin Mayhew Ltd.

109 Alleluia: Sing, my soul

Alleluia! Alleluia! Alleluia!

1. Sing with gladness, my soul, and praise the Lord,
   let my spirit rejoice in God my Saviour.

2. He has honoured me in my lowliness,
   and all people to come shall call me blessèd.

3. The Almighty has shown his pow'r in me,
   and his mercy is known by all his people.

4. He has brought down the mighty and the proud,
   and exalted on high the poor and humble.

5. He has satisfied all the hungry ones,
   but has sent back the wealthy empty-handed.

6. He protected his servant, Israel,
   as he promised to Abraham, our father.

7. Praise the Father, the Spirit and the Son,
   God who was, who is now and ever shall be.

Text: Christina Wilde based on Luke 1:46-55
Music: Paul Décha
© Copyright 1988, 1999 Kevin Mayhew Ltd.

110 Alleluia, sing to Jesus

HYFRYDOL 87 87 D

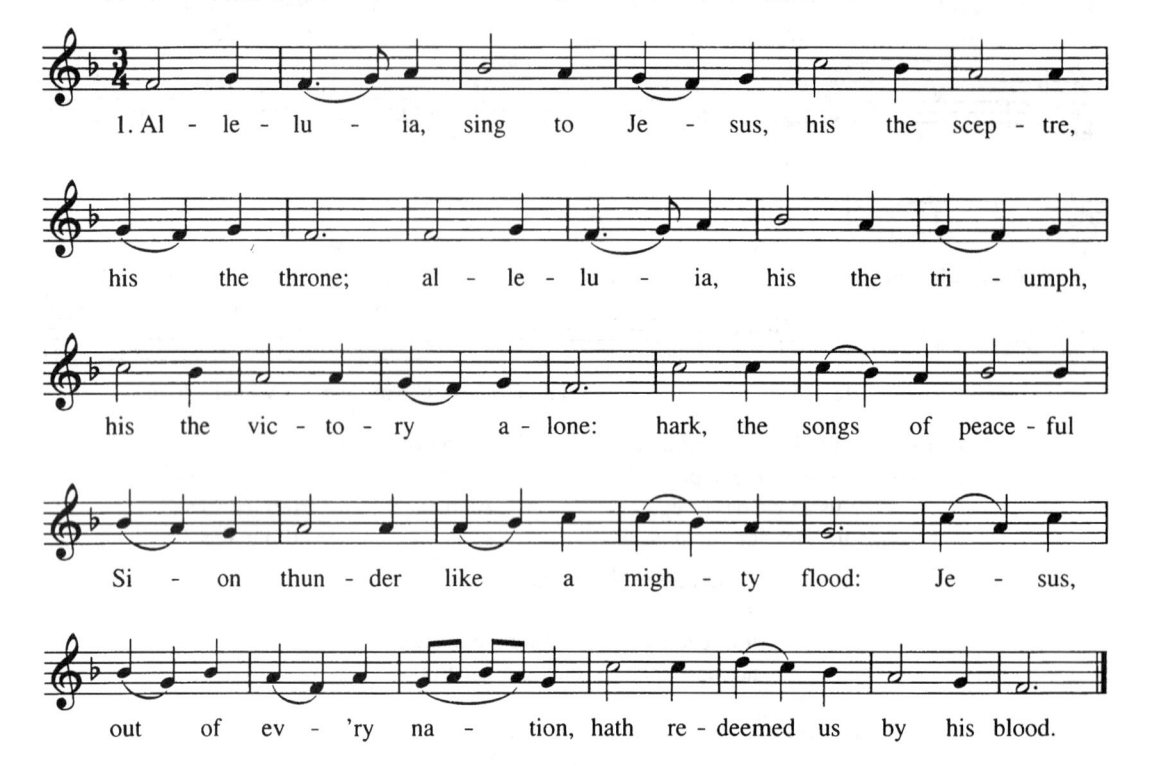

1. Alleluia, sing to Jesus, his the sceptre, his the throne;
alleluia, his the triumph, his the victory alone:
hark, the songs of peaceful Sion thunder like a mighty flood:
Jesus, out of ev'ry nation, hath redeemed us by his blood.

2. Alleluia, not as orphans
are we left in sorrow now;
alleluia, he is near us,
faith believes, nor questions how;
though the cloud from sight received him
when the forty days were o'er,
shall our hearts forget his promise,
'I am with you evermore'?

3. Alleluia, bread of angels,
here on earth our food, our stay;
alleluia, here the sinful
come to you from day to day.
Intercessor, friend of sinners,
earth's redeemer, plead for me,
where the songs of all the sinless
sweep across the crystal sea.

4. Alleluia, King eternal,
he the Lord of lords we own;
alleluia, born of Mary,
earth his footstool, heav'n his throne;
he within the veil has entered
robed in flesh, our great High Priest;
he on earth both priest and victim
in the Eucharistic Feast.

Text: William Chatterton Dix (1837-1898) alt. the editors.
Music: Rowland Huw Pritchard (1811-1887)
This version of text © Copyright 1999 Kevin Mayhew Ltd.

111 Alleluia, thank you for fathers

Al - le - lu - ia, al - le - lu - ia, al - le - lu - ia, al - le - lu - ia.

1. Thank you for fa-thers, the men on this earth! Thank you for mo-thers, who gave us our birth! Thank you for chil-dren, their smiles and their tears! Thank-you for help-ing us con-quer our fears!

2. Praise for the mountains, the hills and ravines;
   praise for the rivers, the brooks and the streams;
   praise for the oceans, the sand and the sea;
   praise for the natural beauties we see!

3. Sing of the blossoms that flow'r on the trees;
   sing of the wind, and the calm and the breeze;
   sing of the autumn, and winter and spring;
   sing of the sunshine the summer will bring!

4. Thank you for giving the life that we know!
   Praise for the honesty we all must show.
   Sing against tyrants and despots and greed.
   Love be our message and peace be our creed!

Text and Music: Mike Anderson (b.1956)
© Copyright 1980 Kevin Mayhew Ltd.

112 All for Jesus

ALL FOR JESUS 87 87

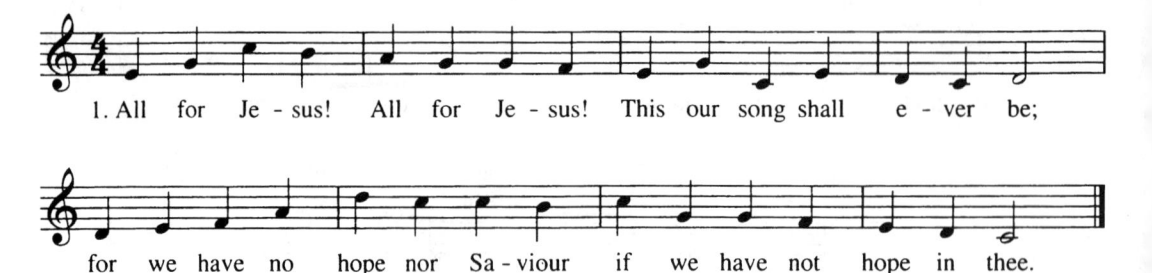

1. All for Jesus! All for Jesus! This our song shall ever be; for we have no hope nor Saviour if we have not hope in thee.

2. All for Jesus! thou wilt give us
   strength to serve thee hour by hour;
   none can move us from thy presence
   while we trust thy love and pow'r.

3. All for Jesus! at thine altar
   thou dost give us sweet content;
   there, dear Saviour, we receive thee
   in thy holy sacrament.

4. All for Jesus! thou hast loved us,
   all for Jesus! thou hast died,
   all for Jesus! thou art with us,
   all for Jesus, glorified!

5. All for Jesus! All for Jesus!
   This the Church's song shall be,
   till at last the flock is gathered
   one in love, and one in thee.

Text: William John Sparrow-Simpson (1859-1952) alt.
Music: John Stainer (1840-1901)
Text © Copyright Novello & Co. Ltd. 8/9 Frith Street, London W1V 5TZ. Used by permission.

113 All glory, laud and honour

ST THEODULPH 76 76 and Refrain

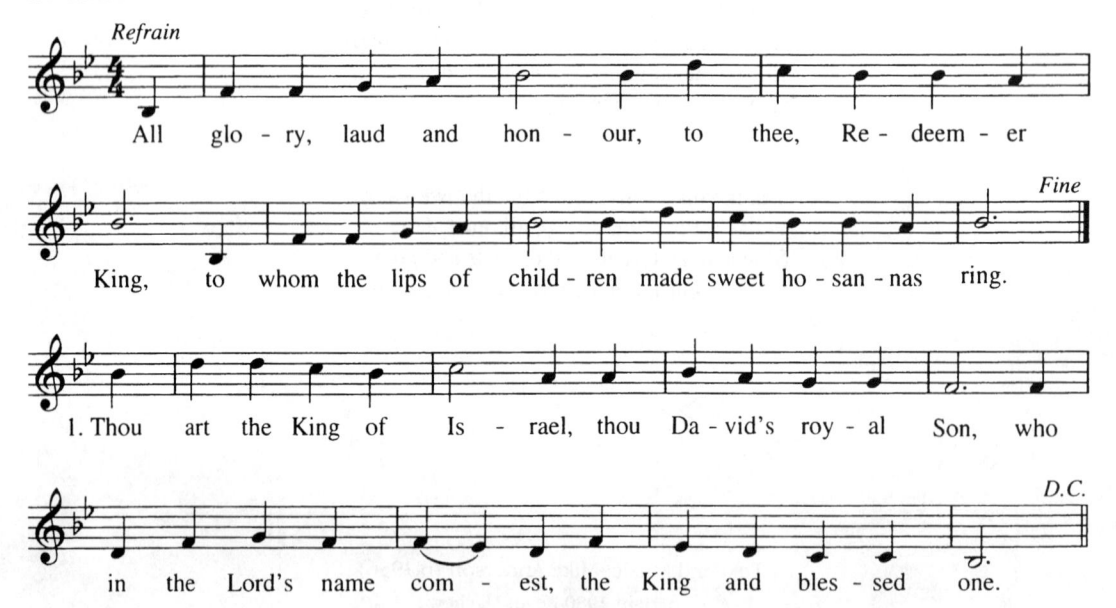

Refrain
All glory, laud and honour, to thee, Redeemer King, to whom the lips of children made sweet hosannas ring. *Fine*

1. Thou art the King of Israel, thou David's royal Son, who in the Lord's name comest, the King and blessed one. *D.C.*

2. The company of angels
   are praising thee on high,
   and mortals, joined with all things
   created, make reply.

3. The people of the Hebrews
   with palms before thee went:
   our praise and prayer and anthems
   before thee we present.

4. To thee before thy passion
   they sang their hymns of praise:
   to thee now high exalted
   our melody we raise.

5. Thou didst accept their praises,
   accept the prayers we bring,
   who in all good delightest,
   thou good and gracious king.

Text: 'Gloria, laus et honor' by St Theodulph of Orleans (d.821)
trans. John Mason Neale (1818-1866)
Music: Melchior Teschner (1584-1635)

114 All glory to you, Redeemer and Lord

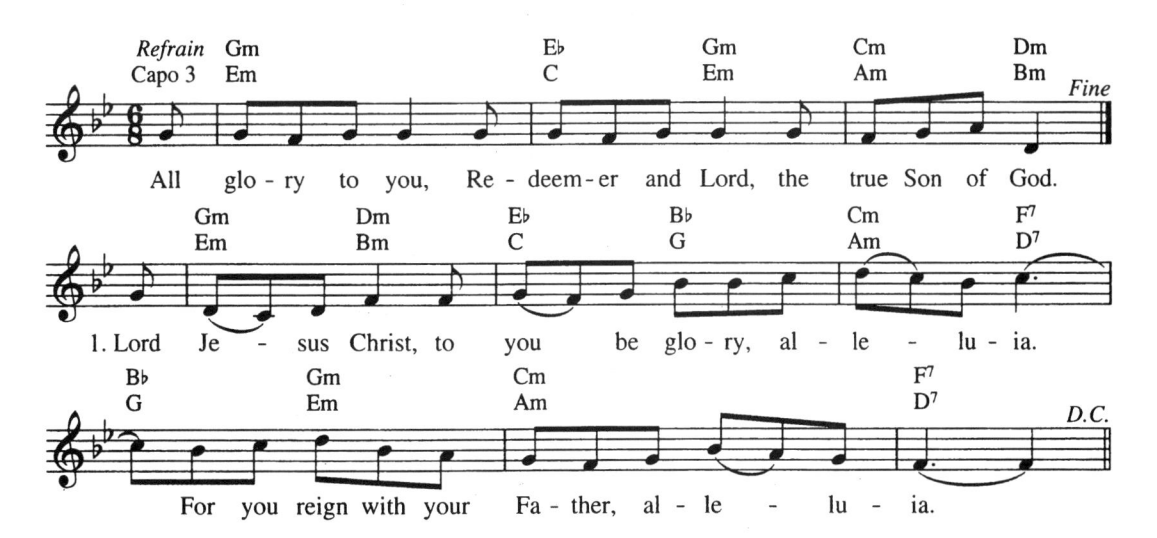

Refrain: All glory to you, Redeemer and Lord, the true Son of God.

1. Lord Jesus Christ, to you be glory, alleluia.
   For you reign with your Father, alleluia.

2. Lord Jesus Christ, to you be glory, alleluia.
   You were born of the virgin, alleluia.

3. Lord Jesus Christ, to you be glory, alleluia.
   You fought evil and conquered, alleluia.

4. Lord Jesus Christ, to you be glory, alleluia.
   Risen Lord, we acclaim you, alleluia.

5. Lord Jesus Christ, to you be glory, alleluia.
   You have ransomed God's people, alleluia.

6. Lord Jesus Christ, to you be glory, alleluia.
   You have made us God's children, alleluia.

7. Lord Jesus Christ, to you be glory, alleluia.
   Lead us all to your kingdom, alleluia.

Text: Damian Lundy (1944-1997)
Music: R. Jef
Text © Copyright 1979 Kevin Mayhew Ltd.
Music © Copyright Edition du Chalet/SEFIM, 13 Avenue Savornin, 94249 L'Hay-les-Roses, France. All rights reserved.

115 All God's people, here together

AR HYD Y NOS 84 84 88 84

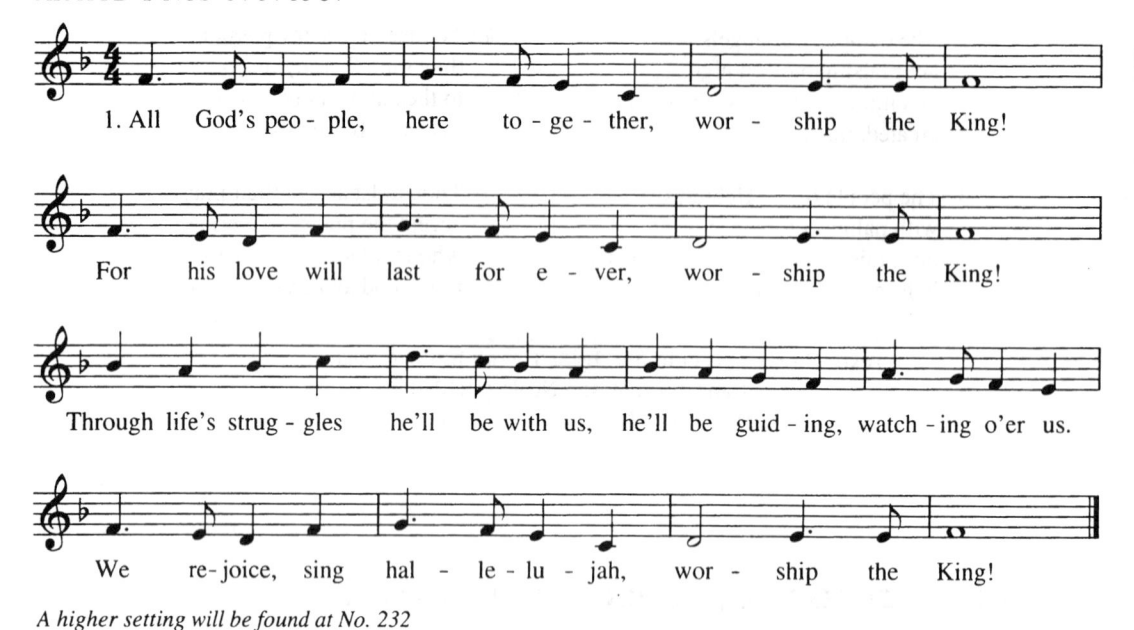

1. All God's peo-ple, here to-ge-ther, wor-ship the King!
For his love will last for e-ver, wor-ship the King!
Through life's strug-gles he'll be with us, he'll be guid-ing, watch-ing o'er us.
We re-joice, sing hal-le-lu-jah, wor-ship the King!

A higher setting will be found at No. 232

2. All God's people, pray together,
peace to the world,
loving brother, loving sister,
peace to the world!
God is love and God is kindness,
he will guide us through the darkness.
We rejoice, sing hallelujah,
peace to the world!

3. All God's people, love each other,
glory to God!
Though we die we live for ever,
glory to God!
We will enter life eternal,
chosen, blessed, for ever praising.
We rejoice, sing hallelujah,
glory to God!

Text: Peter Watcyn-Jones (b.1944)
Music: traditional Welsh melody
Text © Copyright 1978, 1999 Kevin Mayhew Ltd.

116 All hail the power of Jesus' name

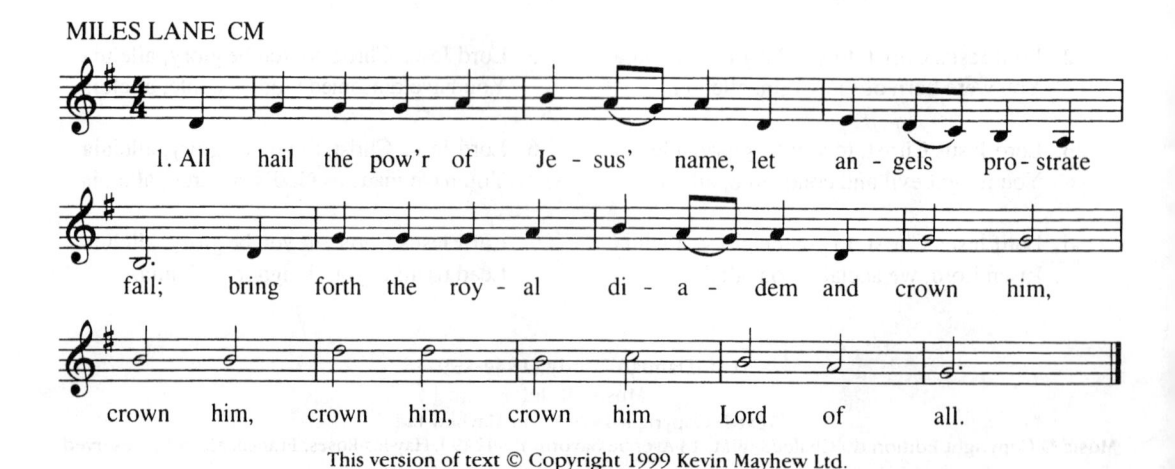

MILES LANE CM

1. All hail the pow'r of Je-sus' name, let an-gels pro-strate fall;
bring forth the roy-al di-a-dem and crown him,
crown him, crown him, crown him Lord of all.

This version of text © Copyright 1999 Kevin Mayhew Ltd.

2. Crown him, all martyrs of your God,
who from his altar call;
praise him whose way of pain you trod,
and crown him Lord of all.

3. O prophets faithful to his word,
in matters great and small,
who made his voice of justice heard,
now crown him Lord of all.

4. All sinners, now redeemed by grace,
who heard your Saviour's call,
now robed in light before his face,
O crown him Lord of all.

5. Let every tribe and every race
who heard the freedom call,
in liberation, see Christ's face
and crown him Lord of all.

6. Let every people, every tongue
to him their heart enthral:
lift high the universal song
and crown him Lord of all.

Text: Edward Perronet (1726-1792) adapted by Michael Forster (b.1946)
Music: William Shrubsole (1760-1806)

117 All heaven declares

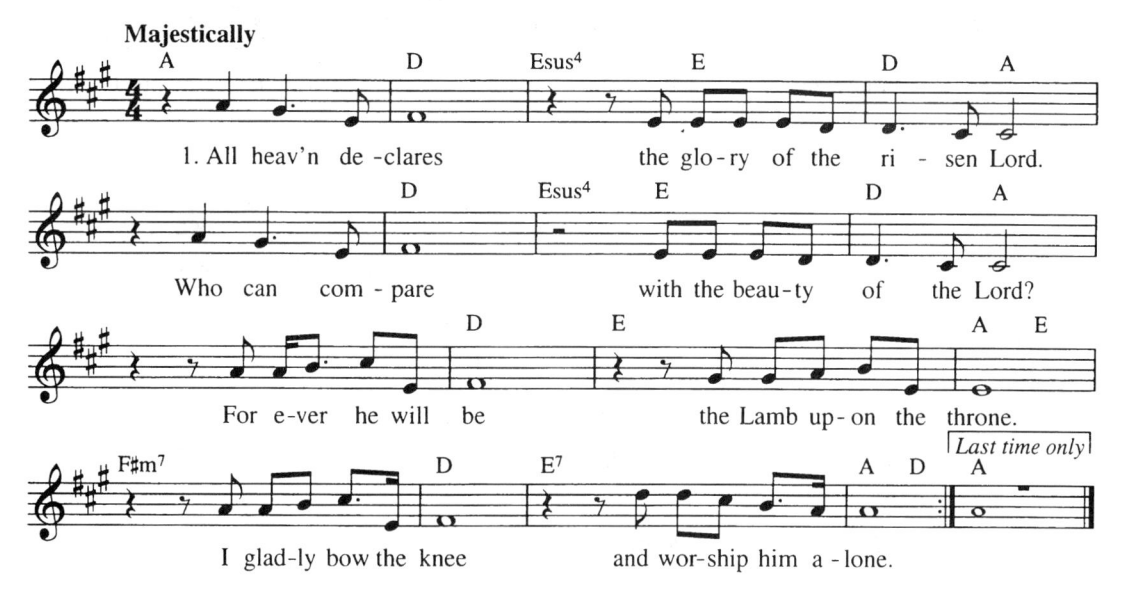

Majestically

1. All heav'n declares
the glory of the risen Lord.
Who can compare
with the beauty of the Lord?
For ever he will be
the Lamb upon the throne.
I gladly bow the knee
and worship him alone.

2. I will proclaim
the glory of the risen Lord.
Who once was slain
to reconcile us all to God.
For ever you will be
the Lamb upon the throne.
I gladly bow the knee
and worship you alone.

Text: Tricia Richards
Music: Noel Richards
© Copyright 1987 Kingsway's Thankyou Music, P.O. Box 75, Eastbourne, East Sussex BN23 6NW, UK.
Used by permission.

118 All I once held dear
Knowing you

1. All I once held dear, built my life upon, all this world reveres, and wars to own, all I once thought gain I have counted loss; spent and worthless now, compared to this. Knowing you, Jesus, knowing you, there is no greater thing. You're my all, you're the best, you're my joy, my righteousness, and I love you, Lord.

2. Now my heart's desire
is to know you more,
to be found in you
and known as yours.
To possess by faith
what I could not earn,
all-surpassing gift
of righteousness.

3. Oh, to know the pow'r
of your risen life,
and to know you in
your sufferings.
To become like you
in your death, my Lord,
so with you to live
and never die.

Text: Graham Kendrick (b.1950) based on Philippians 3:8-12
Music: Graham Kendrick (b.1950)
© Copyright 1993 Make Way Music, P.O. Box 263, Croydon, Surrey CR9 5AP, UK.
International copyright secured. All rights reserved. Used by permission.

119 All my hope on God is founded
MICHAEL 87 87 33 7

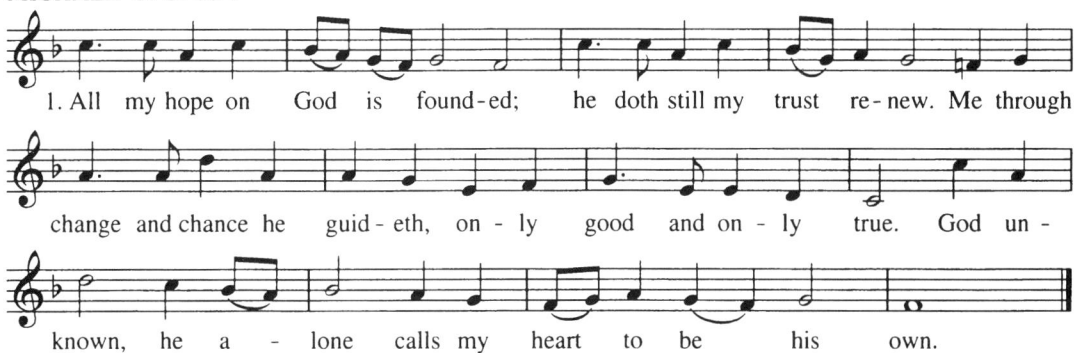

1. All my hope on God is found-ed; he doth still my trust re-new. Me through change and chance he guid-eth, on-ly good and on-ly true. God un-known, he a-lone calls my heart to be his own.

2. Human pride and earthly glory,
sword and crown betray his trust;
what with care and toil he buildeth,
tow'r and temple, fall to dust.
But God's pow'r, hour by hour,
is my temple and my tow'r.

3. God's great goodness aye endureth,
deep his wisdom, passing thought:
splendour, light and life attend him,
beauty springeth out of naught.
Evermore, from his store,
new-born worlds rise and adore.

4. Still from earth to God eternal
sacrifice of praise be done,
high above all praises praising
for the gift of Christ his Son.
Christ doth call one and all:
ye who follow shall not fall.

Text: paraphrased by Robert Bridges (1844-1930) alt.
based on 'Meine Hoffnung stehet feste' by Joachim Neander (1650-1680)
Music: Herbert Howells (1892-1983)
Text © Copyright Oxford University Press, Great Clarendon Street, Oxford OX2 6DP.
Used by permission from 'The Yattendon Hymnal'.
Music © Copyright Novello & Co Ltd, 8/9 Frith Street, London W1V 5TZ. Used by permission.

120 All over the world

1. All o-ver the world the Spi-rit is mov-ing, all o-ver the world, as the proph-ets said it would be. All o-ver the world there's a migh-ty re-ve-la-tion of the glo-ry of the Lord, as the wa-ters co-ver the sea.

2. All over this land the Spirit is moving . . .
3. All over the Church the Spirit is moving . . .
4. All over us all the Spirit is moving . . .
5. Deep down in my heart the Spirit is moving . . .

Text and Music: Roy Turner (b.1940)
© Copyright 1984 Kingsway's Thankyou Music, P.O. Box 75, Eastbourne, East Sussex BN23 6NW, UK.
Used by permission.

121 All people that on earth do dwell

OLD HUNDREDTH LM

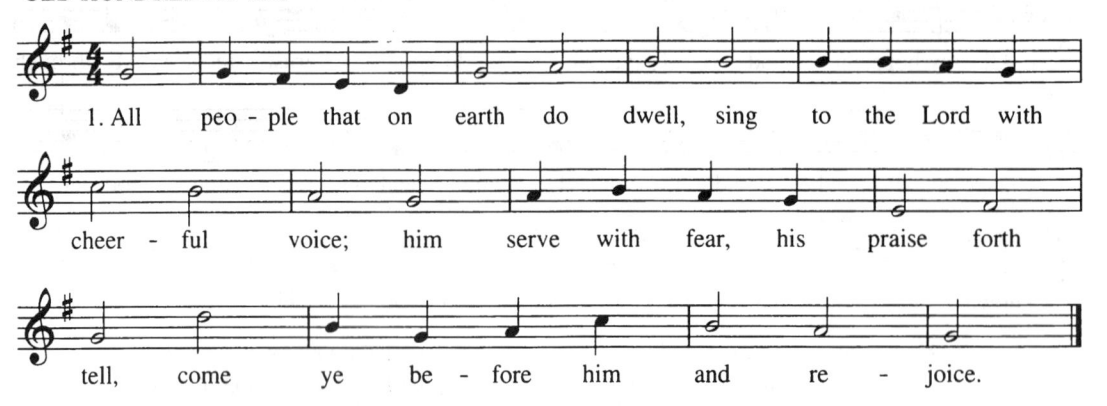

1. All people that on earth do dwell, sing to the Lord with cheerful voice; him serve with fear, his praise forth tell, come ye before him and rejoice.

2. The Lord, ye know, is God indeed,
without our aid he did us make;
we are his folk, he doth us feed
and for his sheep he doth us take.

3. O enter then his gates with praise,
approach with joy his courts unto;
praise, laud and bless his name always,
for it is seemly so to do.

4. For why? the Lord our God is good:
his mercy is for ever sure;
his truth at all times firmly stood,
and shall from age to age endure.

5. To Father, Son and Holy Ghost,
the God whom heav'n and earth adore,
from us and from the angel-host
be praise and glory evermore.

Text: William Kethe (d.1594) from 'Day's Psalter' (1560) alt.
Music: from the 'Genevan Psalter' (1551), attributed to Louis Bourgeois (c.1510-c.1561)

122 All that I am

1. All that I am, all that I do, all that I'll ever have, I offer now to you. Take and sanctify these gifts for your honour, Lord. Knowing that I love and serve you

* Omit chords if using Organ accompaniment (2nd version)

© Copyright 1967 OCP Publications, 5536 NE Hassalo, Portland OR 97213, USA.
All rights reserved. Used by permission.

is e-nough re-ward. All that I am, all that I
do, all that I'll e-ver have I of-fer now to you.

    2. All that I dream, all that I pray,
       all that I'll ever make I give to you today.
       Take and sanctify these gifts for your honour, Lord.
       Knowing that I love and serve you is enough reward.
       All that I am, all that I do,
       all that I'll ever have I offer now to you.

Text and Music: Sebastian Temple (1928-1997)

123 All the earth proclaim the Lord

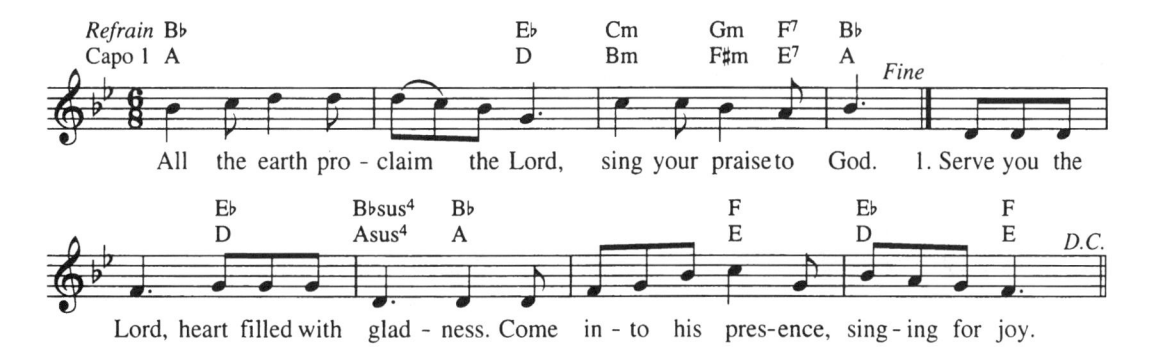

All the earth pro-claim the Lord, sing your praise to God. 1. Serve you the
Lord, heart filled with glad-ness. Come in-to his pres-ence, sing-ing for joy.

  2. Know that the Lord is our creator.
     Yes, he is our Father, we are his own.

  3. We are the sheep of his green pasture,
     for we are his people; he is our God.

  4. Enter his gates bringing thanksgiving,
     O enter his courts while singing his praise.

  5. Our Lord is good, his love enduring,
     his Word is abiding now with us all.

  6. Honour and praise be to the Father,
     the Son, and the Spirit, world without end.

Text: Lucien Deiss (b.1921) based on Psalm 99
Music: Lucien Deiss (b.1921)
© Copyright 1965 World Library Publications, a division of J.S. Paluch Co. Inc., 3825 N.Willow Road,
Schiller Park, Illinois 60176, USA. All rights reserved. Used by permission.

124 All the ends of the earth

Refrain
All the ends of the earth have seen the salvation of our God.

1. Let us sing a new song to the Lord
for the wonderful things he has done;
by his holy and powerful arm,
his salvation is brought to us all.

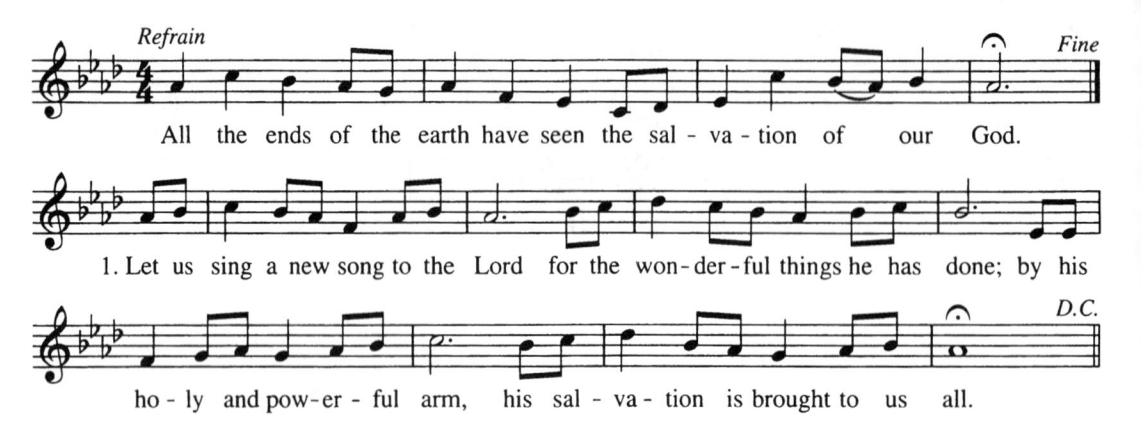

2. His salvation is known on the earth,
all the nations can see he is just;
he will never neglect to be true
to the people he knows as his own.

3. Ev'ry part of creation has seen
the salvation our God has bestowed.
Let the earth shout aloud to our God,
and the universe ring with delight.

4. O sing songs to our God with the harp,
and with music sing praise to the Lord;
let the horn and the trumpet give voice,
we acknowledge the Lord who is King.

Text: Susan Sayers (b.1946) based on Psalm 97
Music: Andrew Moore (b.1954)
© Copyright 1995 Kevin Mayhew Ltd.

125 All things bright and beautiful

TUNE 1: ALL THINGS BRIGHT AND BEAUTIFUL 76 76 and Refrain

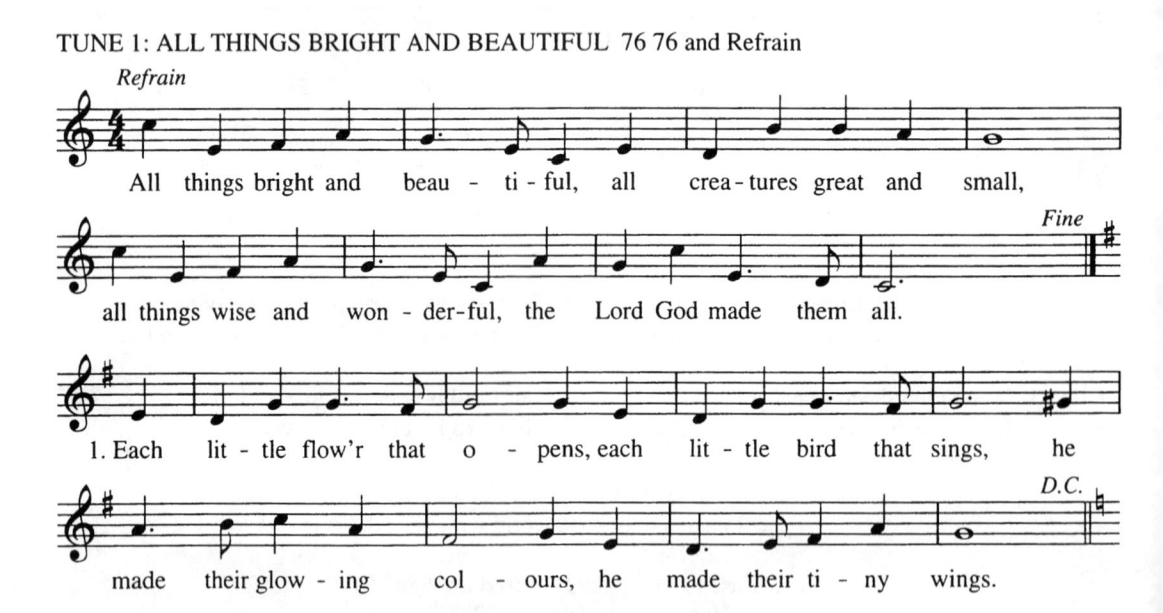

Refrain
All things bright and beautiful, all creatures great and small,
all things wise and wonderful, the Lord God made them all.

1. Each little flow'r that opens, each little bird that sings,
he made their glowing colours, he made their tiny wings.

2. The purple-headed mountain,
   the river running by,
   the sunset and the morning
   that brightens up the sky.

3. The cold wind in the winter,
   the pleasant summer sun,
   the ripe fruits in the garden,
   he made them every one.

4. The tall trees in the greenwood,
   the meadows for our play,
   the rushes by the water,
   to gather ev'ry day.

5. He gave us eyes to see them,
   and lips that we might tell
   how great is God Almighty,
   who has made all things well.

TUNE 2: ROYAL OAK 76 76 and Refrain

Refrain

All things bright and beautiful, all creatures great and small, all things wise and wonderful, the Lord God made them all. *Fine*

1. Each little flow'r that opens, each little bird that sings, he made their glowing colours, he made their tiny wings. *D.C.*

Text: Cecil Frances Alexander (1818 - 1895)
Music: Tune 1 – William Henry Monk (1823-1889)
Tune 2 – traditional English melody

126 All you nations, sing out your joy

All you na-tions, sing out your joy to the Lord; al-le-lu-ia, al-le-lu-ia. 1. Joy-ful-ly shout, all you on earth, give praise to the glo-ry of God; and with a hymn sing out his glo-ri-ous praise; al-le - lu - ia!

2. Lift up your hearts; sing to your God:
   tremendous his deeds on the earth!
   Vanquished your foes, struck down by
   power and might; alleluia!

3. Let all the earth kneel in his sight,
   extolling his marvellous fame;
   honour his name, in highest
   heaven give praise; alleluia!

4. Come forth and see all the great works
   that God has brought forth by his might;
   fall on your knees before his
   glorious throne; alleluia!

5. Parting the seas with might and power,
   he rescued his people from shame;
   let us give thanks for all his
   merciful deeds; alleluia!

6. His eyes keep watch on all the earth,
   his strength is forever renewed;
   and let no one rebel
   against his commands; alleluia!

7. Tested are we by God the Lord,
   as silver is tested by fire;
   burdened with pain, we fall
   ensnared in our sins; alleluia!

8. Over our heads wicked ones rode,
   we passed through the fire and the flood;
   then, Lord, you brought your people
   into your peace; alleluia!

9. Glory and thanks be to the Father;
   honour and praise to the Son;
   and to the Spirit, source of life
   and of love; alleluia!

Text: Lucien Deiss (b.1921) based on Psalm 65
Music: Lucien Deiss (b.1921)

© Copyright 1965 World Library Publications Inc., a division of J.S. Paluch Co. Inc., 3825 N. Willow Road, Schiller Park, Illinois 60176, USA. All rights reserved. Used by permission.

127 All you who seek a comfort sure
ST BERNARD CM

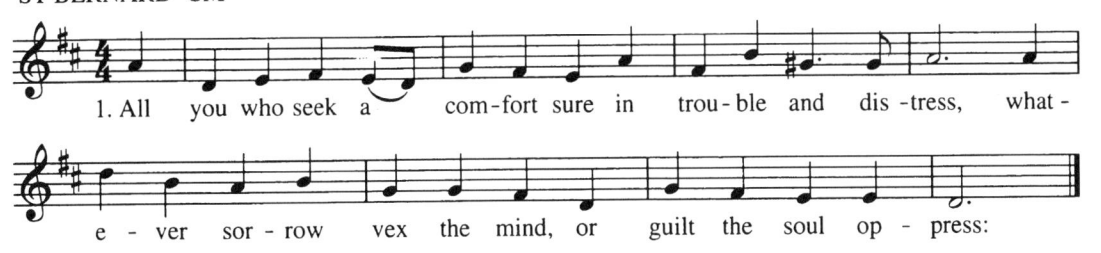

1. All you who seek a comfort sure in trouble and distress, whatever sorrow vex the mind, or guilt the soul oppress:

2. Jesus, who gave himself for you
upon the cross to die,
opens to you his sacred heart;
O, to that heart draw nigh.

3. You hear how kindly he invites;
you hear his words so blest:
'All you that labour, come to me,
and I will give you rest.'

4. What meeker than the Saviour's heart?
As on the cross he lay,
it did his murderers forgive,
and for their pardon pray.

5. Jesus, the joy of saints on high,
the hope of sinners here,
attracted by those loving words
to you I lift my prayer.

6. Wash then my wounds in that dear blood
which forth from you does flow;
by grace a better hope inspire,
and risen life bestow.

Text: 'Quincunque centum quæritis' (18th century) trans. Edward Caswall (1814-1878) alt. the editors
Music: adapted from a melody in 'Tochter Sion' (1741)
This version of text © Copyright 1999 Kevin Mayhew Ltd.

128 Alma redemptoris mater

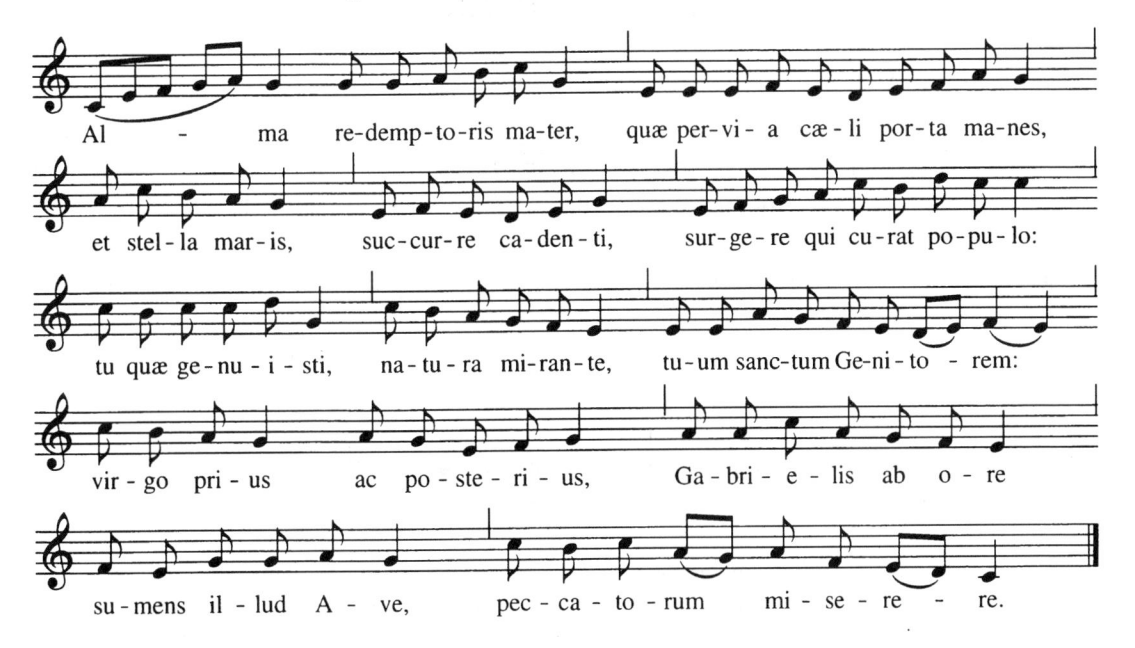

Alma redemptoris mater, quæ pervia cæli porta manes,
et stella maris, succurre cadenti, surgere qui curat populo:
tu quæ genuisti, natura mirante, tuum sanctum Genitorem:
virgo prius ac posterius, Gabrielis ab ore
sumens illud Ave, peccatorum miserere.

Text: Hermann the Lame (d.1054)
Music: Plainsong

129 Almighty Father, Lord most high

TALLIS'S CANON LM

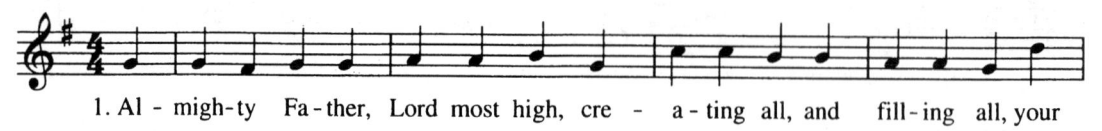

1. Almighty Father, Lord most high, creating all, and filling all, your name we praise and magnify, for all our needs on you we call.

A lower setting will be found at No. 282

2. We offer to you of your own,
   ourselves and all that we can bring,
   in bread and cup before you shown,
   our universal offering.

3. Were we to offer all we own,
   our wealth combined could not suffice.
   Yet all has value through your love
   and Christ's atoning sacrifice.

4. By this command in bread and cup,
   his body and his blood we plead;
   what on the cross he offered up
   is here our sacrifice indeed.

5. For all your gifts of life and grace,
   here we your servants humbly pray
   that you would look upon the face
   of your anointed Son today.

Text: Vincent Stuckey Stratton Coles (1845-1929) alt. Michael Forster (b.1946)
Music: Thomas Tallis (c.1550-1585)
This version of text © Copyright 1999 Kevin Mayhew Ltd.

130 Almighty Father, take this bread

TUNE1: ST BERNARD CM

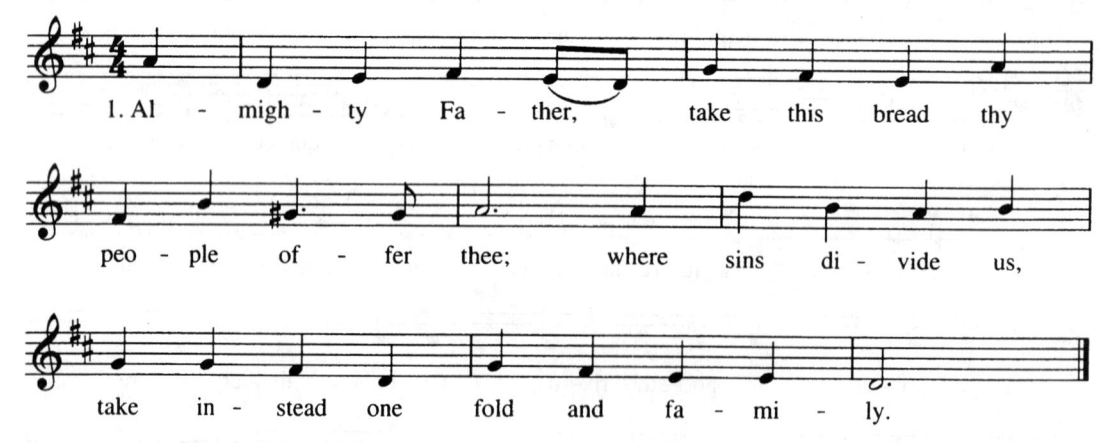

1. Almighty Father, take this bread thy people offer thee; where sins divide us, take instead one fold and family.

2. The wine we offer soon will be
   Christ's blood, redemption's price;
   receive it, Holy Trinity,
   this holy sacrifice.

3. O God, by angels' choirs adored,
   thy name be praised on earth;
   on all may be that peace outpoured
   once promised at his birth.

TUNE 2: FARRANT CM

1. Al-mighty Father, take this bread thy
people offer thee; where sins divide us,
take instead one fold and family.

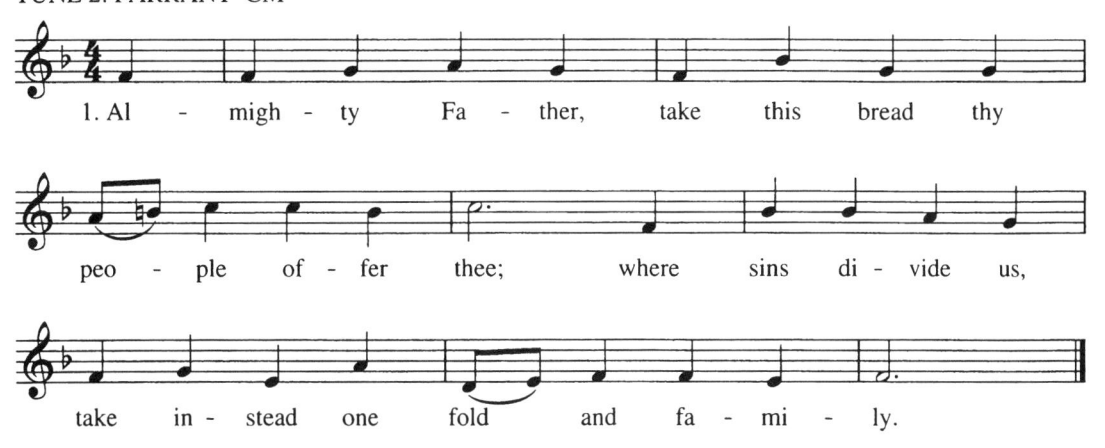

Text: unknown, alt.
Music: Tune 1 – adapted from a melody in 'Tochter Sion' (1741)
Tune 2 – Richard Farrant (c.1530-1585)

131 Amazing grace

AMAZING GRACE CM

1. A-mazing grace! How sweet the sound that saved a wretch like me. I once was lost, but now I'm found; was blind, but now I see.

2. 'Twas grace that taught my heart to fear,
and grace my fears relieved.
How precious did that grace appear
the hour I first believed.

3. Through many dangers, toils and snares
I have already come.
'Tis grace that brought me safe thus far,
and grace will lead me home.

4. The Lord has promised good to me,
his word my hope secures;
he will my shield and portion be
as long as life endures.

5. When we've been there a thousand years,
bright shining as the sun,
we've no less days to sing God's praise
than when we first begun.

Text: vs. 1-4: John Newton (1725-1807) alt; v.5: John Rees (1828-1900)
Music: American folk melody

132 And did those feet in ancient time
Jerusalem

JERUSALEM DLM

1. And did those feet in ancient time walk upon England's mountains green? And was the holy Lamb of God on England's pleasant pastures seen? And did the countenance divine shine forth upon our clouded hills? And was Jerusalem builded here among those dark satanic mills?

2. Bring me my bow of burning gold! Bring me my arrows of desire! Bring me my spear! O clouds, unfold! Bring me my chariot of fire! I will not cease from mental fight, nor shall my sword sleep in my hand, till we have built Jerusalem in England's green and pleasant land.

Text: William Blake (1757-1827)
Music: Hubert Parry (1848-1918)

133 A new commandment

Refrain

A new commandment I give unto you: that you love one another as I have loved you, that you love one another as I have loved you. *Fine* 1. By this shall all know that you are my disciples if you have love one for another. By this shall all know that you are my disciples if you have love one for another. *D.C.*

* *Omit chords if accompanied by Organ (2nd version)*

2. You are my friends if you do what I command you.
   Without my help you can do nothing. *(Repeat)*

3. I am the true vine, my Father is the gard'ner.
   Abide in me: I will be with you. *(Repeat)*

4. True love is patient, not arrogant nor boastful;
   love bears all things, love is eternal. *(Repeat)*

Text: v.1 unknown based on John 13:34-35; vs. 2-4 Aniceto Nazareth based on John 15 and 1 Corinthians 13
Music: unknown arr. Andrew Moore
© Copyright 1984, 1999 Kevin Mayhew Ltd.

134 Angels we have heard in heaven

IRIS 87 87 and Refrain

1. Angels we have heard in heaven sweetly singing o'er our plains;
and the mountain tops in answer echoing their joyous strains.

Refrain
Glo - - - ria in excelsis Deo.
Glo - - - ria in excelsis Deo.

2. Shepherds, why this exultation?
Why your rapt'rous strain prolong?
Tell us of the gladsome tidings
which inspire your joyous song.

3. Come to Bethlehem, and see him
o'er whose birth the angels sing:
come, adore, devoutly kneeling,
Christ the Lord, the new-born King.

4. See him in a manger lying
whom the choir of angels praise!
Mary, Joseph, come to aid us
while our hearts in love we raise.

Text: James Chadwick (1813-1882)
Music: traditional French melody

135 Angels we have heard on high

IRIS 77 77 and Refrain

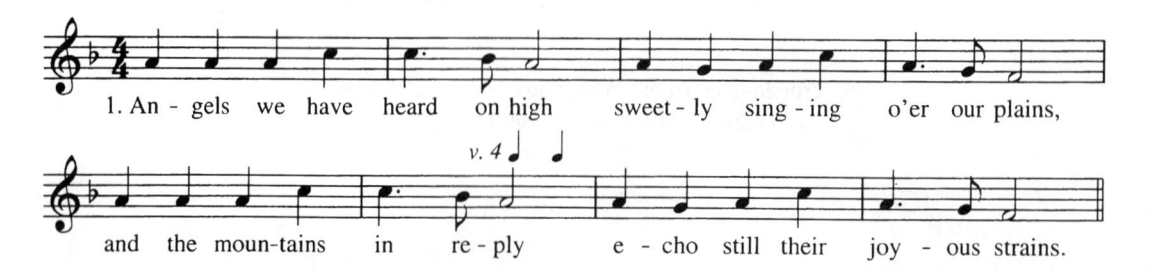

1. Angels we have heard on high sweetly singing o'er our plains,
and the mountains in reply echo still their joyous strains.

This arrangement © Copyright control. Refrain © Copyright 1999 Kevin Mayhew Ltd.

Refrain

Gloria in excelsis Deo.

Gloria in excelsis Deo.

2. Shepherds, why this jubilee?
   Why your rapt'rous strain prolong?
   Say, what may your tidings be,
   which inspire your heav'nly song.

3. Come to Bethlehem and see
   him whose birth the angels sing:
   come, adore on bended knee
   th'infant Christ, the new-born King.

4. See within a manger laid,
   Jesus, Lord of heav'n and earth!
   Mary, Joseph, lend your aid
   to celebrate our Saviour's birth.

Text: James Chadwick (1813-1882)
Music: traditional French melody

136 A noble flower of Judah

ES IST EIN' ROS' ENTSPRUNGEN 76 76 676

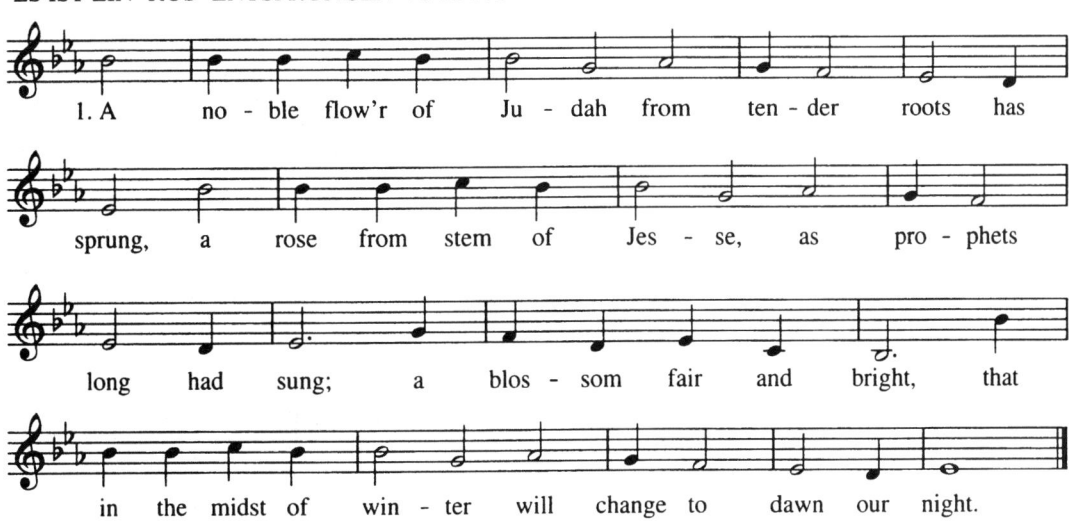

1. A noble flow'r of Judah from tender roots has sprung, a rose from stem of Jesse, as prophets long had sung; a blossom fair and bright, that in the midst of winter will change to dawn our night.

2. The rose of grace and beauty
   of which Isaiah sings
   is Mary, virgin mother,
   and Christ the flow'r she brings.
   By God's divine decree
   she bore our loving Saviour
   who died to set us free.

3. To Mary, dearest mother,
   with fervent hearts we pray:
   grant that your tender infant
   will cast our sins away,
   and guide us with his love
   that we shall ever serve him
   and live with him above.

Text: Vorreformatorisch (Cologne, 1599), cento paraphrased by Anthony G. Petti
Music: German carol melody

137 Arise, come to your God

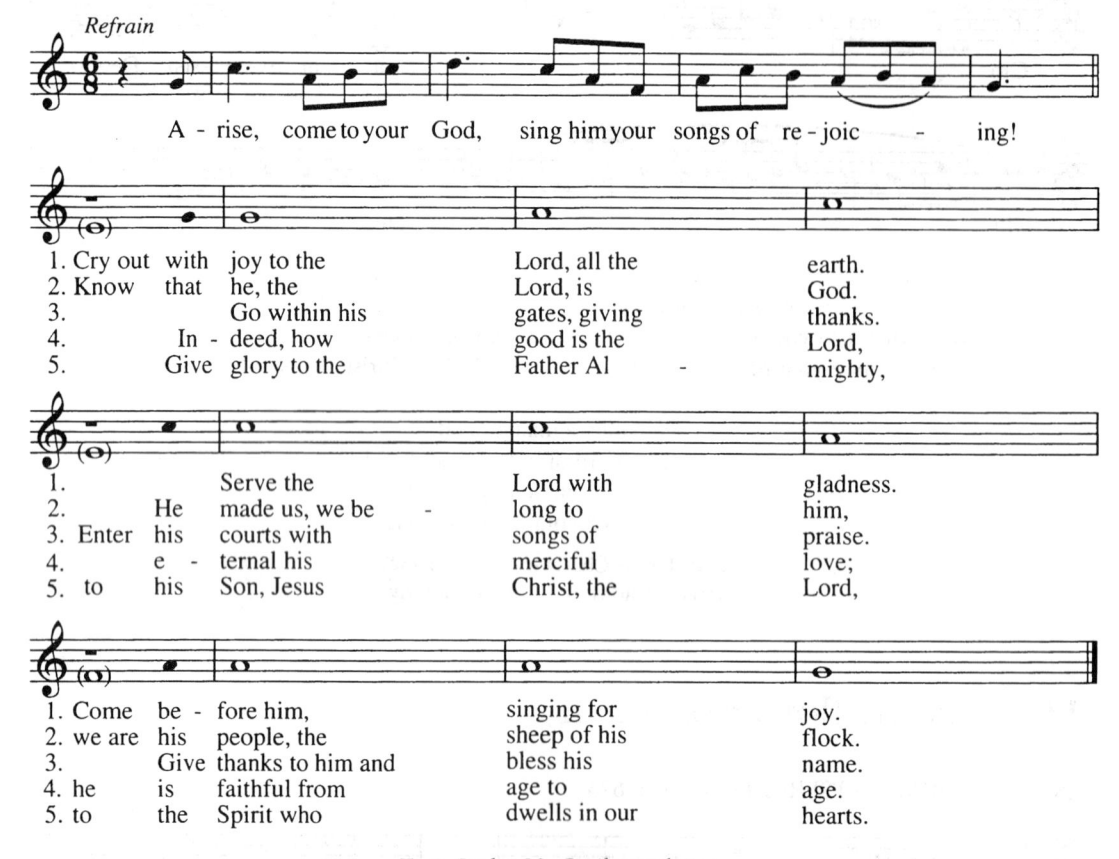

Refrain

A-rise, come to your God, sing him your songs of re-joic - ing!

1. Cry out with joy to the Lord, all the earth.
2. Know that he, the Lord, is God.
3. Go within his gates, giving thanks.
4. In-deed, how good is the Lord,
5. Give glory to the Father Al - mighty,

1. Serve the Lord with gladness.
2. He made us, we be - long to him,
3. Enter his courts with songs of praise.
4. e - ternal his merciful love;
5. to his Son, Jesus Christ, the Lord,

1. Come be - fore him, singing for joy.
2. we are his people, the sheep of his flock.
3. Give thanks to him and bless his name.
4. he is faithful from age to age.
5. to the Spirit who dwells in our hearts.

Text: Psalm 99, Grail translation
Music: Joseph Gelineau (b.1920)

© Copyright 1963, 1986, 1993 The Grail, England. Used by permission of A.P. Watt Ltd., 20 John Street, London WC1N 2DR. Taken from 'The Psalms: A New Inclusive Language Version', published by HarperCollins Religious.

138 Arise to greet the Lord of light

REPTON 86 88 6

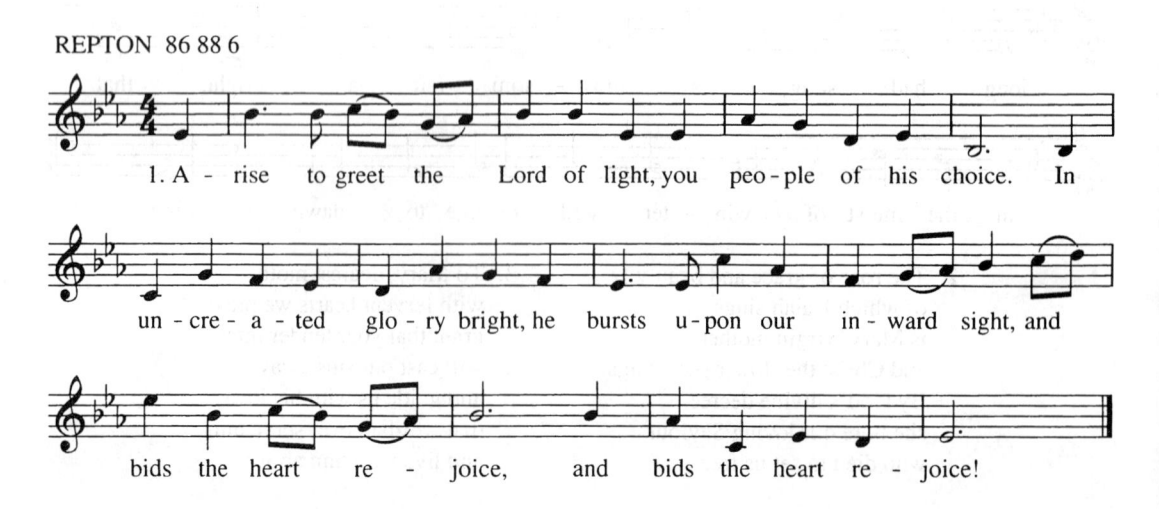

1. A - rise to greet the Lord of light, you peo-ple of his choice. In un - cre - a - ted glo - ry bright, he bursts u-pon our in - ward sight, and bids the heart re - joice, and bids the heart re - joice!

Text © Copyright 1993 Kevin Mayhew Ltd.

2. Towards his light shall kings be drawn
   this majesty to see;
   and in the brightness of the dawn
   shall see the world in hope reborn,
   in justice full and free,
   in justice full and free.

3. The holy light in Judah's skies
   calls sages from afar.
   The hope of kings they recognise
   which, in the virgin mother's eyes,
   outshines the guiding star,
   outshines the guiding star.

4. This majesty for long concealed
   from longing human sight,
   in Jesus Christ is now revealed,
   and God's eternal promise sealed
   in love's unending light,
   in love's unending light.

Text: Michael Forster (b.1946) based on Isaiah 60:1-6
Music: Hubert Parry (1848-1918)

139 As bread my Lord comes to me

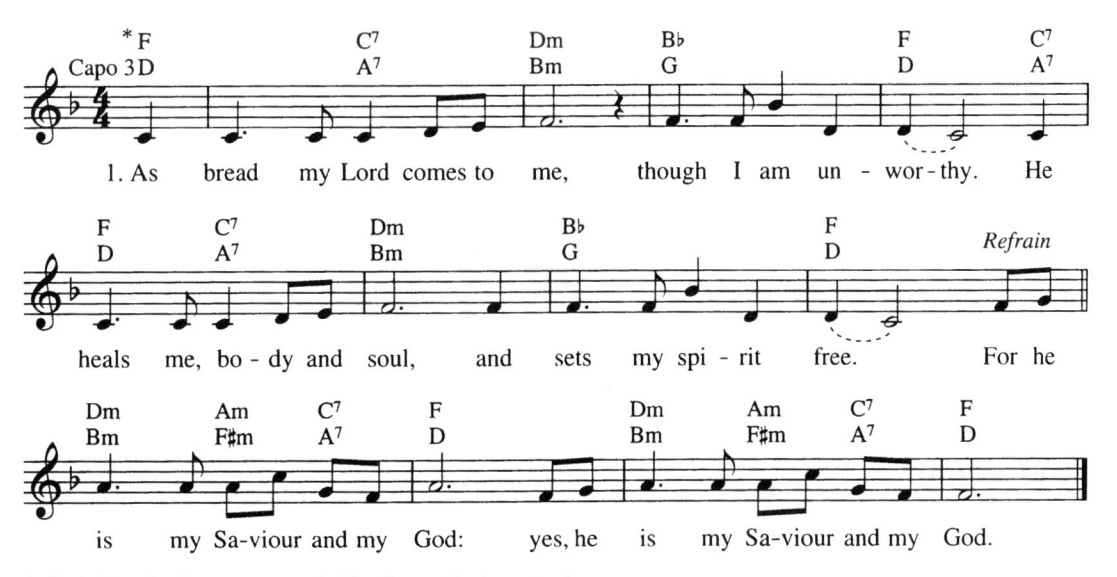

1. As bread my Lord comes to me, though I am un-wor-thy. He heals me, bo-dy and soul, and sets my spi-rit free. For he is my Sa-viour and my God: yes, he is my Sa-viour and my God.

* *Omit chords when accompanied by Organ (2nd version)*

2. I am far nearer to him
   than the air I breathe.
   With joy I welcome him home;
   he satisfies my heart's need.

3. The still, small voice that I hear,
   always is reminding
   my soul of love and of peace,
   that passes understanding.

Text and Music: Estelle White (b.1925)
© Copyright 1976, 1999 Kevin Mayhew Ltd.

140 As earth that is dry

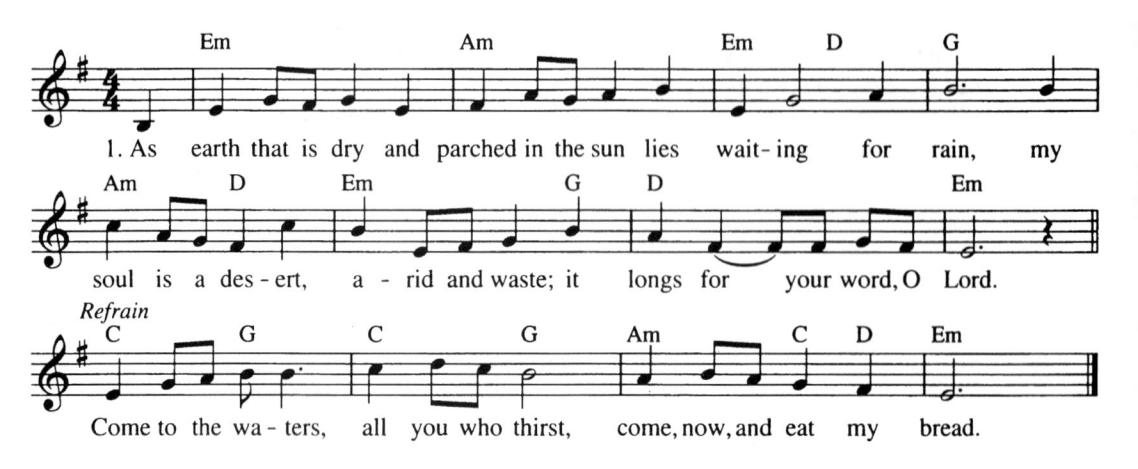

1. As earth that is dry and parched in the sun lies waiting for rain, my soul is a desert, arid and waste; it longs for your word, O Lord.

Refrain
Come to the waters, all you who thirst, come, now, and eat my bread.

2. Though you have no money,
come, buy my corn
and drink my red wine.
Why spend precious gold
on what will not last?
Hear me, and your soul will live.

3. As one on a journey
strays from the road
and falls in the dark,
my mind is a wand'rer,
choosing wrong paths
and longing to find a star.

4. The Lord is your light,
the Lord is your strength,
turn back to him now,
for his ways are not
the ways you would choose,
and his thoughts are always new.

5. As rain from the mountains
falls on the land
and brings forth the seed,
the word of the Lord
sinks deep in our hearts,
creating the flow'r of truth.

Text: Anne Conway (b.1940) based on Isaiah 55
Music: Anne Conway (b.1940)
© Copyright 1984 Kevin Mayhew Ltd.

141 As I kneel before you

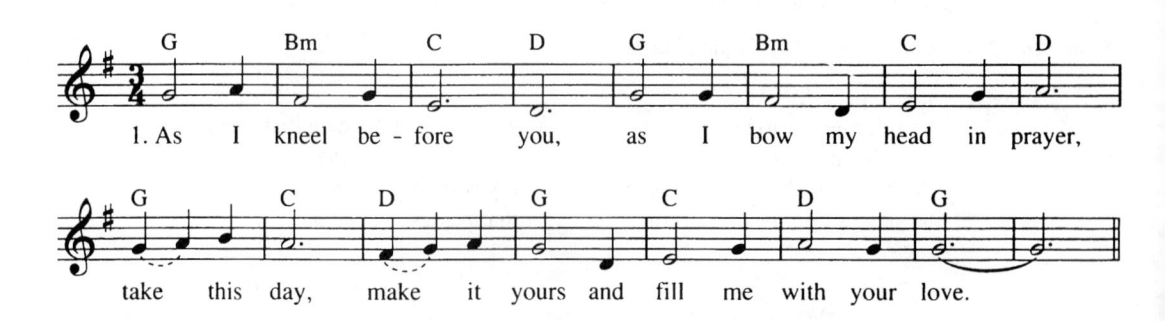

1. As I kneel before you, as I bow my head in prayer, take this day, make it yours and fill me with your love.

© Copyright 1978 Kevin Mayhew Ltd.

Refrain

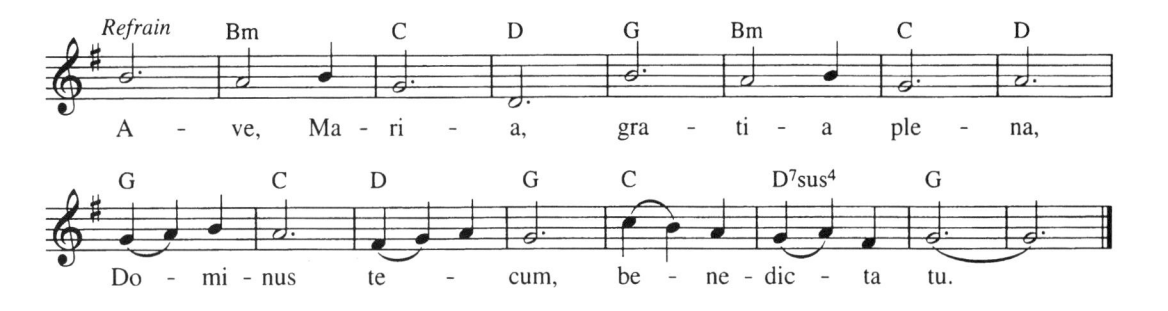

A - ve, Ma - ri - a, gra - ti - a ple - na,
Do - mi - nus te - cum, be - ne - dic - ta tu.

2. All I have I give you,
   ev'ry dream and wish are yours;
   mother of Christ, mother of mine,
   present them to my Lord.

3. As I kneel before you,
   and I see your smiling face,
   ev'ry thought, ev'ry word
   is lost in your embrace.

Text and Music: Maria Parkinson (b.1956)

142 As the deer pants for the water

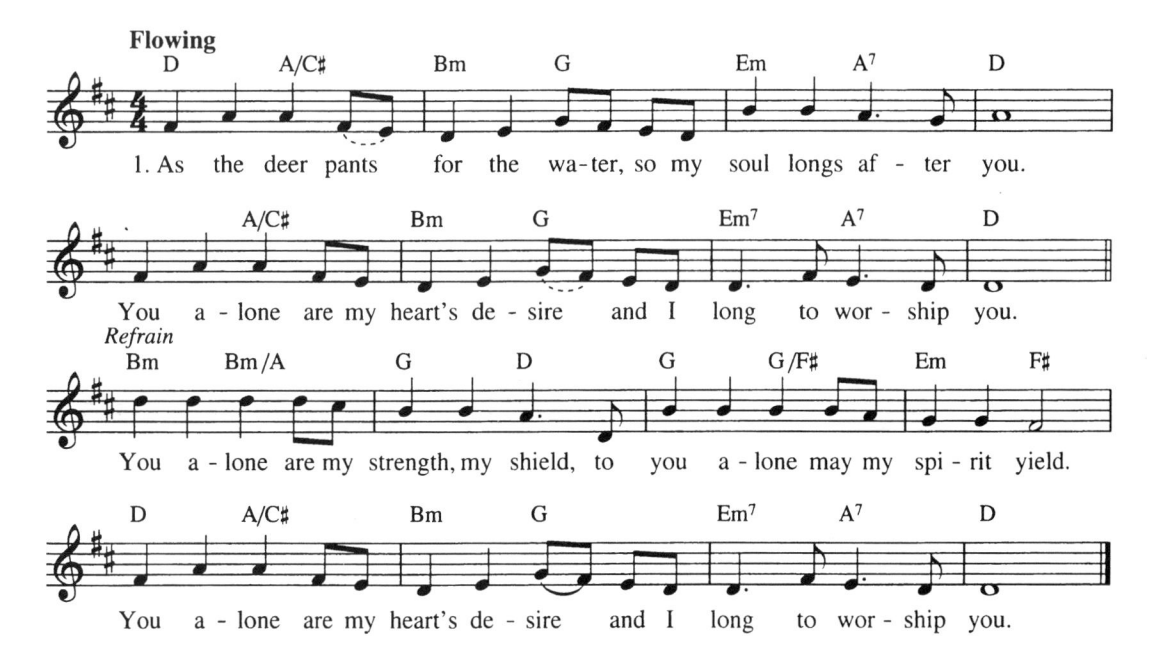

Flowing

1. As the deer pants for the wa - ter, so my soul longs af - ter you.
   You a - lone are my heart's de - sire and I long to wor - ship you.

Refrain
You a - lone are my strength, my shield, to you a - lone may my spi - rit yield.
You a - lone are my heart's de - sire and I long to wor - ship you.

2. I want you more than gold or silver,
   only you can satisfy.
   You alone are the real joy-giver
   and the apple of my eye.

3. You're my friend and you are my brother,
   even though you are a king.
   I love you more than any other,
   so much more than anything.

Text and Music: Martin Nystrom, based on Psalm 41:1-2
© Copyright 1983 Restoration Music Ltd, administered by Sovereign Music UK,
P.O. Box 356, Leighton Buzzard, Beds. LU7 8WP, UK for Europe. Used by permission.

143 As we are gathered

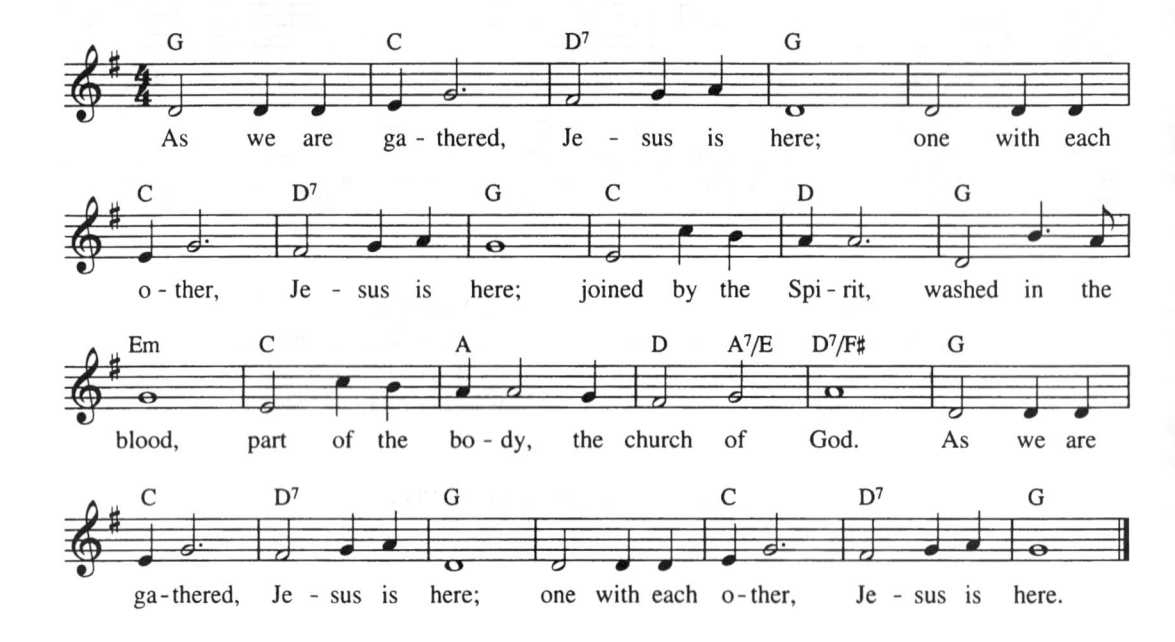

As we are gathered, Jesus is here;
one with each other, Jesus is here;
joined by the Spirit, washed in the blood,
part of the body, the church of God.
As we are gathered, Jesus is here;
one with each other, Jesus is here.

Text and Music: John Daniels
© Copyright 1979 Word's Spirit of Praise Music. Administered by CopyCare,
P.O. Box 77, Hailsham, East Sussex BN27 3EF, UK. Used by permission.

144 As with gladness men of old

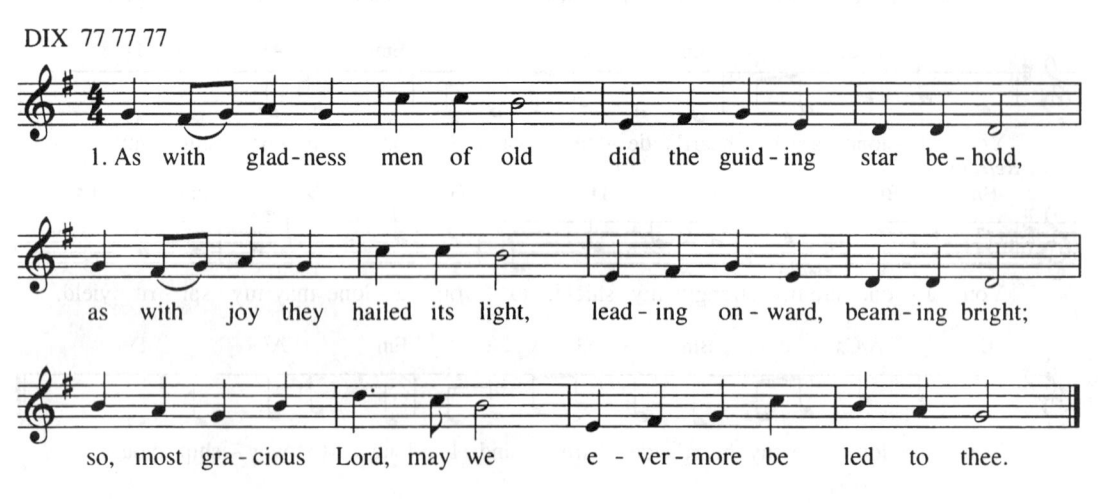

DIX 77 77 77

1. As with gladness men of old
did the guiding star behold,
as with joy they hailed its light,
leading onward, beaming bright;
so, most gracious Lord, may we
evermore be led to thee.

2. As with joyful steps they sped,
to that lowly manger-bed,
there to bend the knee before
him whom heav'n and earth adore,
so may we with willing feet
ever seek thy mercy-seat.

3. As their precious gifts they laid,
at thy manger roughly made,
so may we with holy joy,
pure, and free from sin's alloy,
all our costliest treasures bring,
Christ, to thee our heav'nly King.

4. Holy Jesu, ev'ry day
   keep us in the narrow way;
   and, when earthly things are past,
   bring our ransomed souls at last
   where they need no star to guide,
   where no clouds thy glory hide.

5. In the heav'nly country bright
   need they no created light,
   thou its light, its joy, its crown,
   thou its sun which goes not down;
   there for ever may we sing
   alleluias to our King.

Text: William Chatterton Dix (1837-1898) alt.
Music: adapted from Conrad Kocher (1786-1872) by William Henry Monk (1823-1889)

145 At the cross her station keeping

STABAT MATER 887

1. At the cross her station keeping,
   stood the mournful mother weeping,
   close to Jesus to the last.

2. Through her heart, his sorrow sharing,
   all his bitter anguish bearing,
   now at length the sword has passed.

3. O, how sad and sore distressed
   was that mother highly blest,
   of the sole-begotten One.

4. Christ above in torment hangs;
   she beneath beholds the pangs
   of her dying glorious Son.

5. Is there one who would not weep,
   whelmed in miseries so deep,
   Christ's dear mother to behold?

6. Can the human heart refrain
   from partaking in her pain,
   in that mother's pain untold?

7. Bruised, derided, cursed, defiled,
   she beheld her tender child,
   all with bloody scourges rent.

8. For the sins of his own nation,
   saw him hang in desolation,
   till his spirit forth he sent.

9. O thou mother! Fount of love!
   Touch my spirit from above,
   make my heart with thine accord.

10. Make me feel as thou hast felt;
    make my soul to glow and melt
    with the love of Christ my Lord.

11. Holy Mother, pierce me through,
    in my heart each wound renew
    of my Saviour crucified.

12. Let me share with thee his pain
    who for all my sins was slain,
    who for me in torments died.

13. Let me mingle tears with thee,
    mourning him who mourned for me,
    all the days that I may live.

14. By the cross with thee to stay,
    there with thee to weep and pray,
    this I ask of thee to give.

Another hymn for the Stations of the Cross will be found at No. 402

Text: 'Stabat mater', ascribed to Jacopone da Todi (d.1306) trans. Edward Caswall (1814-1878)
Music: from 'Mainz Gesangbuch' (1661)

146 At the Lamb's high feast we sing

SALZBURG 77 77 D

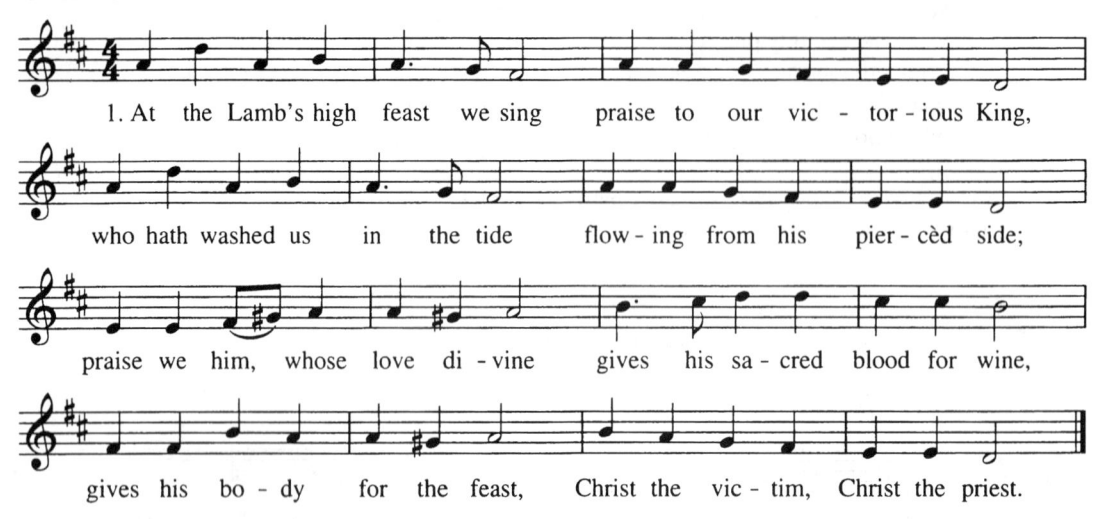

1. At the Lamb's high feast we sing
praise to our victorious King,
who hath washed us in the tide
flowing from his piercèd side;
praise we him, whose love divine
gives his sacred blood for wine,
gives his body for the feast,
Christ the victim, Christ the priest.

2. Where the paschal blood is poured,
death's dark angel sheathes his sword;
faithful hosts triumphant go
through the wave that drowns the foe.
Praise we Christ, whose blood was shed,
paschal victim, paschal bread;
with sincerity and love
eat we manna from above.

3. Mighty victim from above,
conqu'ring by the pow'r of love;
thou hast triumphed in the fight,
thou hast brought us life and light.
Now no more can death appal,
now no more the grave enthral:
thou hast opened paradise,
and in thee thy saints shall rise.

4. Easter triumph, Easter joy,
nothing now can this destroy;
from sin's pow'r do thou set free
souls new-born, O Lord, in thee.
Hymns of glory and of praise,
risen Lord, to thee we raise;
holy Father, praise to thee,
with the Spirit, ever be.

Text: 'Ad regias Agni dapes' (7th century) trans. Robert Campbell (1814-1868)
Music: Jacob Hintze (1622-1702)

147 At the name of Jesus

TUNE 1: EVELYNS 65 65 D

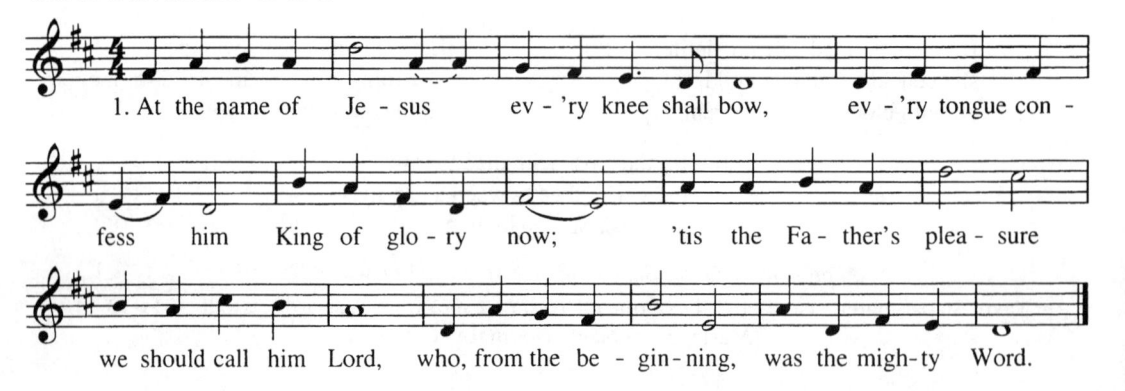

1. At the name of Jesus ev'ry knee shall bow,
ev'ry tongue confess him King of glory now;
'tis the Father's pleasure we should call him Lord,
who, from the beginning, was the mighty Word.

2. At his voice creation
   sprang at once to sight,
   all the angels' faces,
   all the hosts of light,
   thrones and dominations,
   stars upon their way,
   all the heav'nly orders
   in their great array.

3. Humbled for a season,
   to receive a name
   from the lips of sinners
   unto whom he came,
   faithfully he bore it,
   spotless to the last,
   brought it back victorious
   when from death he passed.

4. Bore it up triumphant,
   with its human light,
   through all ranks of creatures
   to the central height,
   to the throne of Godhead,
   to the Father's breast,
   filled it with the glory
   of that perfect rest.

5. In your hearts enthrone him;
   there let him subdue
   all that is not holy,
   all that is not true;
   crown him as your captain
   in temptation's hour;
   let his will enfold you
   in its light and pow'r.

6. Truly, this Lord Jesus
   shall return again,
   with his Father's glory,
   with his angel train;
   for all wreaths of empire
   meet upon his brow,
   and our hearts confess him
   King of glory now.

TUNE 2: CAMBERWELL 65 65 D

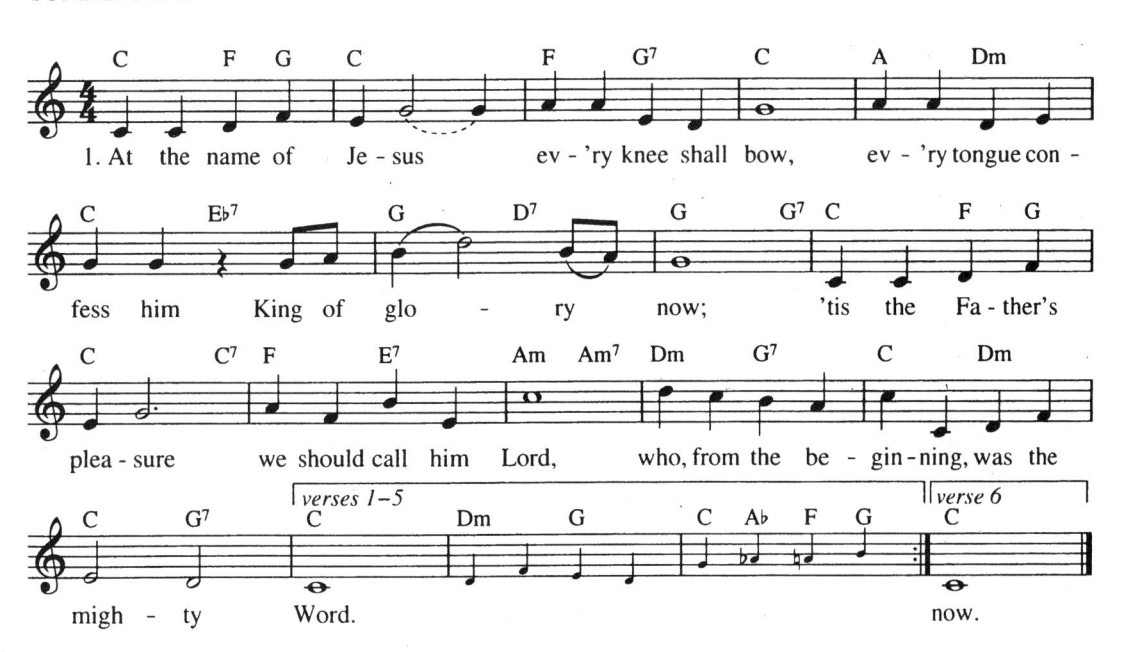

1. At the name of Jesus ev-'ry knee shall bow, ev-'ry tongue con-fess him King of glo-ry now; 'tis the Fa-ther's plea-sure we should call him Lord, who, from the be-gin-ning, was the migh-ty Word. now.

Text: Caroline Maria Noel (1817-1877) alt.
Music: Tune 1 - William Henry Monk (1823-1889) Tune 2 - Michael Brierley (b.1932)
Tune 2: Music © Copyright 1960 Josef Weinberger Ltd, 12-14 Mortimer Street, London W1N 7RD.
Used by permission.

148 At your feet

SACRUM CONVIVIUM 87 87 87

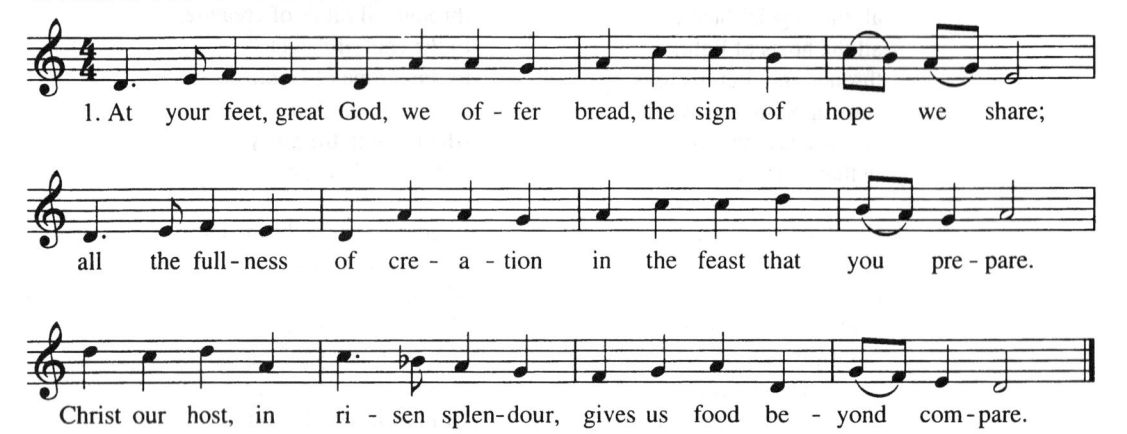

1. At your feet, great God, we offer bread, the sign of hope we share;
all the fullness of creation in the feast that you prepare.
Christ our host, in risen splendour, gives us food beyond compare.

2. Now, in humble adoration,
drawn by grace, we offer here
wine that speaks of love's oblation,
life from death and hope from fear.
Sharing in his cup of sorrow,
our Redeemer we revere.

3. Here, most holy God, we offer,
with the saints in full accord,
hearts and gifts for your acceptance,
broken dreams to be restored.
All creation cries for healing;
you alone such grace afford!

Text: Michael Forster (b.1946)
Music: Alan Rees (b.1941)
© Copyright 1992 Kevin Mayhew Ltd.

149 Ave Maria, O maiden, O mother

AVE MARIA 11 10 11 10 and Refrain

1. Ave Maria, O maiden, O mother, fondly thy children are calling on thee; thine are the graces unclaimed by another, sinless and beautiful star of the sea.

Music © Copyright Burns & Oates Ltd, Wellwood, North Farm Road,
Tunbridge Wells, Kent TN2 3QR, UK. Used by permission.

Refrain

Mater amabilis, ora pro nobis, pray for thy children who call upon thee, ave sanctissima, ave purissima, sinless and beautiful star of the sea.

2. Ave Maria, the night shades are falling,
softly, our voices arise unto thee;
earth's lonely exiles for succour are calling,
sinless and beautiful star of the sea.

3. Ave Maria, thy children are kneeling,
words of endearment are murmured to thee;
softly thy spirit upon us is stealing,
sinless and beautiful star of the sea.

Text: 'Sister M.'
Music: Richard Runciman Terry (1865-1938)

150 Ave, Regina cælorum

Ave, Regina cælorum! Ave, Domina angelorum!
Salve radix, salve porta, ex qua mundo lux est orta.
Gaude Virgo gloriosa, super omnes speciosa:
vale, o valde decora, et pro nobis Christum exora.

An English version of this antiphon, 'O Queen of heaven', will be found at No. 550

Text: unknown, 12th Century
Music: Plainsong

151 Ave verum corpus

A - ve ve-rum cor-pus, na-tum ex Ma-ri-a vir - gi-ne;

ve - re pas-sum, im-mo-la-tum in cru-ce pro ho - mi-ne.

Cu-jus la-tus per-fo-ra - tum un-da flux-it et san - gui-ne;

es-to no-bis præ-gu-sta - tum mor-tis in ex - a - mi-ne.

O Je-su dul - cis! O Je-su pi - e!

O Je - su fi - li Ma-ri - æ.

Text: Traditional
Music: Plainsong

152 Awake, awake and greet the new morn

REJOICE, REJOICE 98 98 87 89

1. A-wake, a-wake and greet the new morn, for an-gels he-rald its dawn-ing, sing out your joy, for now he is born, be-hold, the child of our long - ing. Come as a ba-by weak and poor, to bring all hearts to - ge - ther, he o-pens wide the heav'n-ly door and lives now in-side us for e - ver.

© Copyright 1983 GIA Publications Inc, 7404 S. Mason Avenue, Chicago, Illinois 60638, USA.
All rights reserved. Used by permission.

2. To us, to all in sorrow and fear,
   Emmanuel comes a-singing,
   his humble song is quiet and near,
   yet fills the earth with its ringing;
   music to heal the broken soul
   and hymns of loving kindness,
   the thunder of his anthems roll
   to shatter all hatred and blindness.

3. In darkest night his coming shall be,
   when all the world is despairing,
   as morning light so quiet and free,
   so warm and gentle and caring.
   Then shall the mute break forth in song,
   the lame shall leap in wonder,
   the weak be raised above the strong,
   and weapons be broken asunder.

4. Rejoice, rejoice, take heart in the night,
   though dark the winter and cheerless,
   the rising sun shall crown you with light,
   be strong and loving and fearless;
   love be our song and love our prayer,
   and love our endless story,
   may God fill ev'ry day we share,
   and bring us at last into glory.

Text and Music: Marty Haugen (b.1950)

153 Awake, awake: fling off the night

DEUS TUORUM MILITUM LM

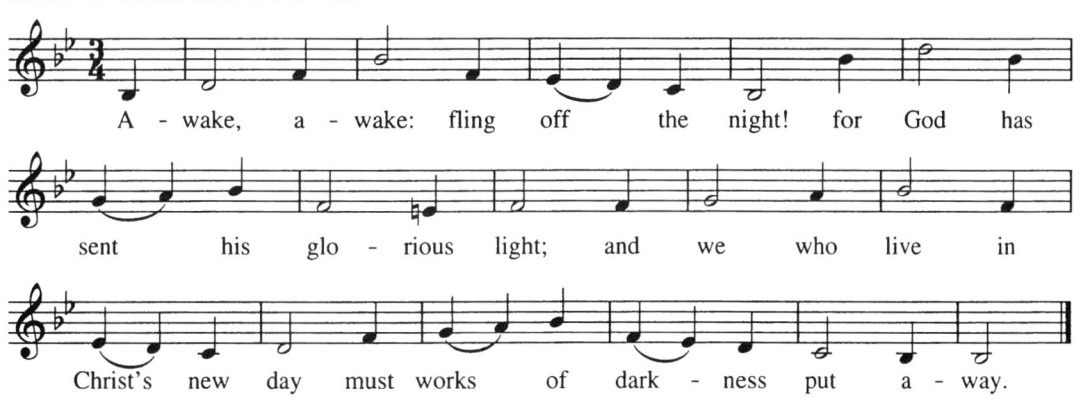

A-wake, a-wake: fling off the night! for God has sent his glorious light; and we who live in Christ's new day must works of darkness put away.

2. Awake and rise, in Christ renewed,
   and with the Spirit's pow'r endued.
   The light of life in us must glow,
   and fruits of truth and goodness show.

3. Let in the light; all sin expose
   to Christ, whose life no darkness knows.
   Before his cross for guidance kneel;
   his light will judge and, judging, heal.

4. Awake, and rise up from the dead,
   and Christ his light on you will shed.
   Its pow'r will wrong desires destroy,
   and your whole nature fill with joy.

5. Then sing for joy, and use each day;
   give thanks for everything alway.
   Lift up your hearts; with one accord
   praise God through Jesus Christ our lord.

Text: John Raphael Peacey (1896-1971) based on Ephesians 5:6-20 alt.
Music: melody from 'Grenoble Antiphoner' (1753)
Text © Copyright the Revd. M. J. Hancock. Used by kind permission.

154 Awake from your slumber
City of God

1. A-wake from your slum-ber! A-rise from your sleep!
   A new day is dawn-ing for all those who weep.
   The peo-ple in dark-ness have seen a great light.
   The Lord of our long-ing has con-quered the night.

2. We are sons of the morn-ing, we are daugh-ters of day.
   The one who has loved us has bright-ened our way.
   The Lord of all kind-ness has called us to be.
   a light for his peo-ple to set their hearts free.

Refrain
Let us build the ci-ty of God, may our tears be turned in-to dan-cing! For the Lord, our light and our love, has turned the night in-to day.

© Copyright 1981 Daniel L. Schutte and New Dawn Music, 5536 NE Hassalo, Portland, OR 97213, USA.
All rights reserved. Used by permission.

3. God is light; in him there is no darkness. Let us walk in his light, his children, one and all. O comfort my people, make gentle your words. Proclaim to my city the day of her birth.

Refrain
Let us build the city of God, may our tears be turned into dancing! For the Lord, our light and our love, has turned the night into day.

4. O city of gladness, now lift up your voice! Proclaim the good tidings that all may rejoice!

Text and Music: Dan Schutte

155 Away in a manger

CRADLE SONG 11 11 11 11

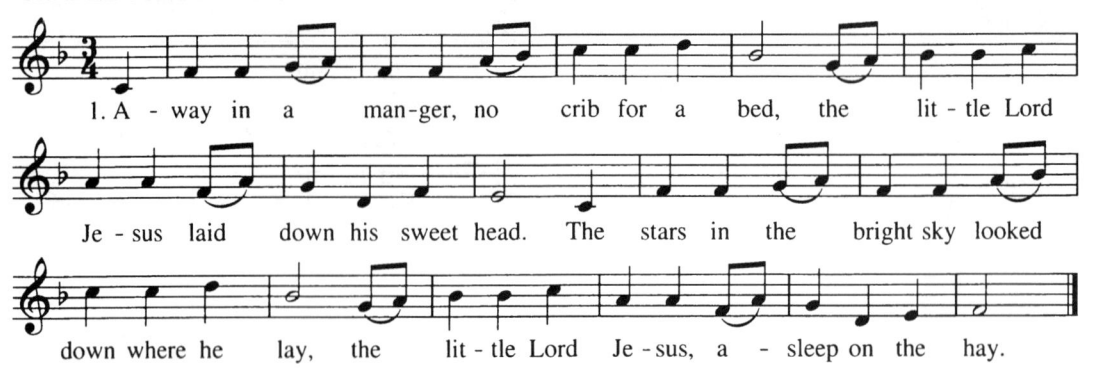

1. A-way in a man-ger, no crib for a bed, the lit-tle Lord Je-sus laid down his sweet head. The stars in the bright sky looked down where he lay, the lit-tle Lord Je-sus, a-sleep on the hay.

An alternative version of verses 2 and 3

2. The cattle are lowing, the baby awakes,
   but little Lord Jesus no crying he makes.
   I love thee, Lord Jesus! Look down from the sky,
   and stay by my side until morning is nigh.

3. Be near me Lord Jesus; I ask thee to stay
   close by me for ever, and love me, I pray.
   Bless all the dear children in thy tender care,
   and fit us for heaven, to live with thee there.

2. The cattle are lowing, they also adore
   the little Lord Jesus who lies on the straw.
   I love you, Lord Jesus, I know you are near
   to love and protect me till morning is here.

3. Be near me, Lord Jesus; I ask you to stay
   close by me for ever, and love me, I pray.
   Bless all the dear children in your tender care,
   prepare us for heaven, to live with you there.

Original text: William James Kirkpatrick (1838-1921)
Alternative text, verses 2 and 3: Michael Forster (b.1946)
Music: William James Kirkpatrick (1838-1921)
Alternative verses © Copyright 1996 Kevin Mayhew Ltd.

156 Battle is o'er, hell's armies flee

SURREXIT 888 and Alleluias.

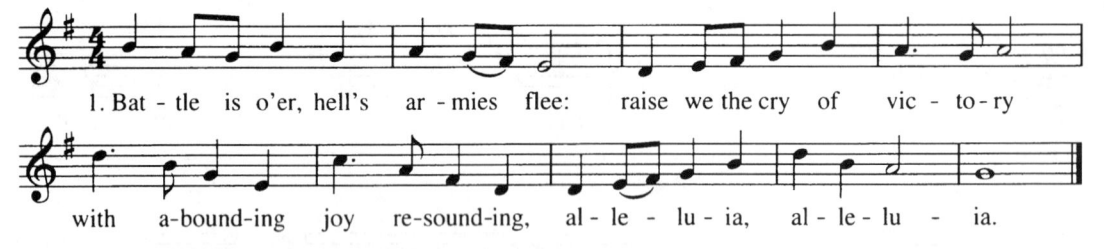

1. Bat-tle is o'er, hell's ar-mies flee: raise we the cry of vic-to-ry with a-bound-ing joy re-sound-ing, al-le-lu-ia, al-le-lu-ia.

2. Christ who endured the shameful tree,
   o'er death triumphant welcome we,
   our adoring praise outpouring,
   alleluia, alleluia.

3. On the third morn from death rose he,
   clothed with what light in heav'n shall be,
   our unswerving faith deserving,
   alleluia, alleluia.

4. Hell's gloomy gates yield up their key,
   paradise door thrown wide we see;
   never-tiring be our choiring,
   alleluia, alleluia.

5. Lord, by the stripes men laid on thee,
   grant us to live from death set free,
   this our greeting still repeating,
   alleluia, alleluia.

Text: 'Finita iam sunt proelia' from 'Simphonia Sirenum' (1695), trans. Ronald Arbuthnott Knox (1888-1957)
Music: Gregory Murray (1905-1992)

Text © Copyright Burns and Oates Ltd, Wellwood, North Farm Road, Tunbridge Wells, Kent, TN2 3DR. Used by permission.
Music © Copyright the Estate of Gregory Murray. Used by permission of the Trustees of Downside Abbey,
Stratton-on-the-Fosse, Bath BA3 4RH, UK. Used by permission.

157 Beauty for brokenness
God of the poor

1. Beauty for brokenness, hope for despair,
   Lord, in the suff'ring, this is our prayer:
   bread for the children, justice, joy, peace,
   sunrise to sunset your kingdom increase.
   God of the poor, friend of the weak,
   give us compassion we pray;
   melt our cold hearts, let tears fall like rain,
   come, change our love from a spark to a flame.

2. Shelter for fragile lives,
   cures for their ills,
   work for the craftsmen,
   trade for their skills.
   Land for the dispossessed,
   rights for the weak,
   voices to plead the cause
   of those who can't speak.

3. Refuge from cruel wars,
   havens from fear,
   cities for sanctu'ry,
   freedoms to share.
   Peace to the killing fields,
   scorched earth to green,
   Christ for the bitterness,
   his cross for pain.

4. Rest for the ravaged earth,
   oceans and streams,
   plundered and poisoned,
   our future, our dreams.
   Lord, end our madness,
   carelessness, greed;
   make us content with
   the things that we need.

5. Lighten our darkness,
   breathe on this flame,
   until your justice
   burns brightly again;
   until the nations
   learn of your ways,
   seek your salvation
   and bring you their praise.

Text and Music: Graham Kendrick (b.1950)

© Copyright 1993 Make Way Music, P.O. Box 263, Croydon, Surrey CR9 5AP, UK.
International copyright secured. All rights reserved. Used by permission.

LITURGICAL
HYMNS OLD & NEW

158 Be blessed, pure of heart

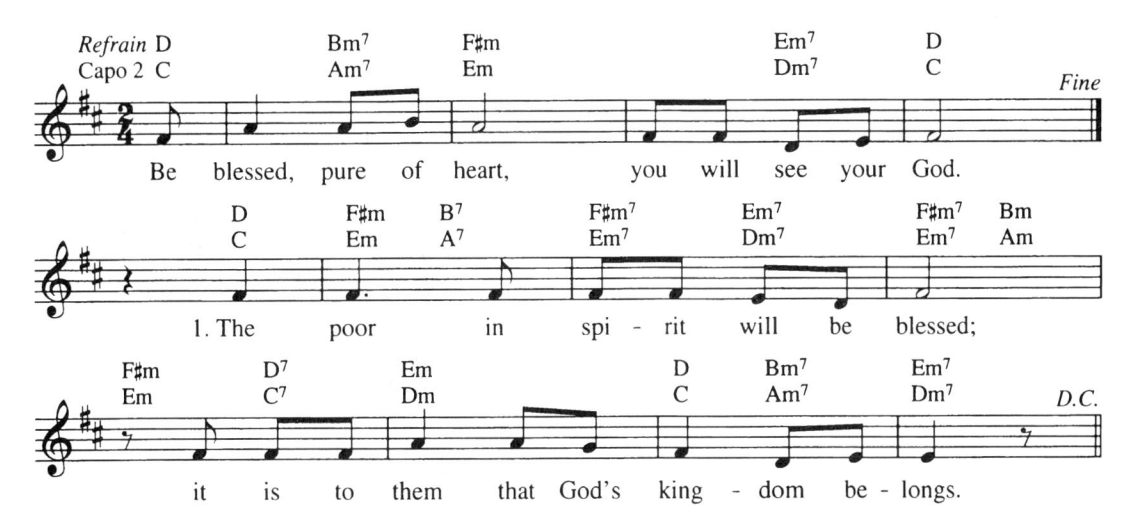

Be blessed, pure of heart, you will see your God.

1. The poor in spirit will be blessed;
   it is to them that God's kingdom belongs.

2. The meek and patient will be blessed;
   they will succeed and inherit the earth.

3. All those who suffer will be blessed;
   they will be comforted in their distress.

4. All those who thirst for what is right
   will be blessed and be given their fill.

5. The merciful will all be blessed;
   they will have mercy and love shown to them.

6. The clean of heart will all be blessed;
   they will be given the vision of God.

7. Those making peace will all be blessed;
   they will be known as the children of God.

8. Those suff'ring in the cause of right
   will all be blessed in the kingdom of heav'n.

Text: W.R. Lawrence (1925-1997), from Matthew 5:3-12
Music: Alexandre Lesbordes
© Copyright 1988 Kevin Mayhew Ltd.

159 Before the light of evening fades

1. Before the light of evening fades we pray, O Lord of all,
   that by your love we may be saved from ev-'ry grievous fall.

2. Repel the terrors of the night
   and Satan's pow'r of guile,
   impose a calm and restful sleep
   that nothing may defile.

3. Most holy Father, grant our prayer
   through Christ your only Son,
   that in your Spirit we may live
   and praise you ever one.

Text: 'Te Lucis ante terminum' (7th century) trans. Ralph Wright (b.1938)
Music: Laurence Bevenot
Text © Copyright Dom Ralph Wright OSB, St.Louis Abbey, 500 S. Mason Road,
St. Louis, Missouri 63141, USA. Used by permission.
Music © Copyright Ampleforth Abbey Trustees, Ampleforth Abbey, York YO6 4EY. Used by permission.

160 Behold, the Lamb of God

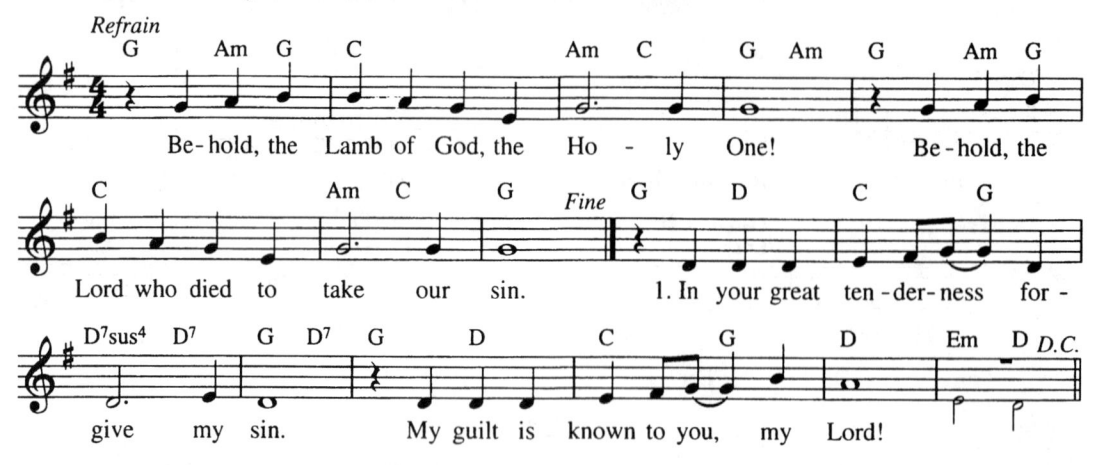

Be-hold, the Lamb of God, the Ho-ly One! Be-hold, the Lord who died to take our sin. *Fine*

1. In your great ten-der-ness for-give my sin. My guilt is known to you, my Lord! *D.C.*

2. My sin is constantly before my eyes,
   so wash me whiter than the snow.

3. Give me your joy and take away my shame,
   and fill my body with new life.

4. Create in me, O Lord, a heart renewed,
   and keep me always pure and clean.

5. Do not deprive me of your spirit, Lord,
   open my lips to sing your praise!

6. I come to offer you a sacrifice:
   the broken heart you have made new.

Text: Damian Lundy (b.1944-1997) based on Psalm 50
Music: Gerard Markland (b.1953)
© Copyright 1997 Kevin Mayhew Ltd.

161 Behold, the Saviour of the nations

ST CLEMENT 98 98

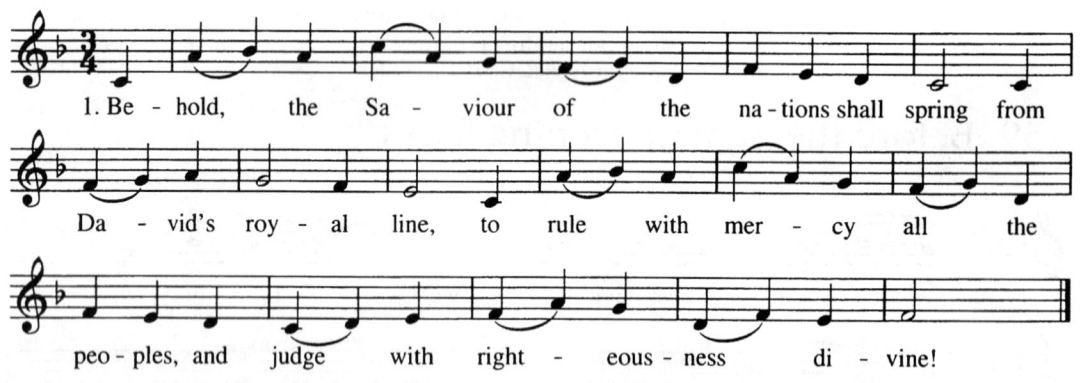

1. Be-hold, the Sa-viour of the na-tions shall spring from Da-vid's roy-al line, to rule with mer-cy all the peo-ples, and judge with right-eous-ness di-vine!

A higher setting will be found at No. 563

2. He shall delight in truth and wisdom,
   with justice for the meek and poor,
   and reconcile his whole creation,
   where beasts of prey shall hunt no more.

3. Here may his word, with hope abounding,
   unite us all in peace and love,
   to live as one with all creation,
   redeemed by mercy from above.

4. Prepare the way with awe and wonder;
   salvation comes on judgement's wing,
   for God will purify his people,
   and 'Glory!' all the earth shall sing.

Text: Michael Forster (b.1946) based on Isaiah 11:1-10
Music: Clement Cotterill Scholefield (1839-1904)
Text © Copyright 1993 Kevin Mayhew Ltd.

162 Beloved, let us love

SONG 46 11 10

1. Beloved, let us love: for love is of God; in God alone love has its true abode.

2. Beloved, let us love:
for those who love,
they only, are his children from above.

3. Beloved, let us love:
for love is rest,
and those who do not love cannot be blessed.

4. Beloved, let us love:
for love is light,
and those who do not love still live in night.

5. Beloved, let us love:
for only thus
shall we see God, the Lord who first loved us.

Text: Horatius Bonar (1808-1889) based on 1 John 4:7
Music: Orlando Gibbons (1583-1625)

163 Be still and know I am with you

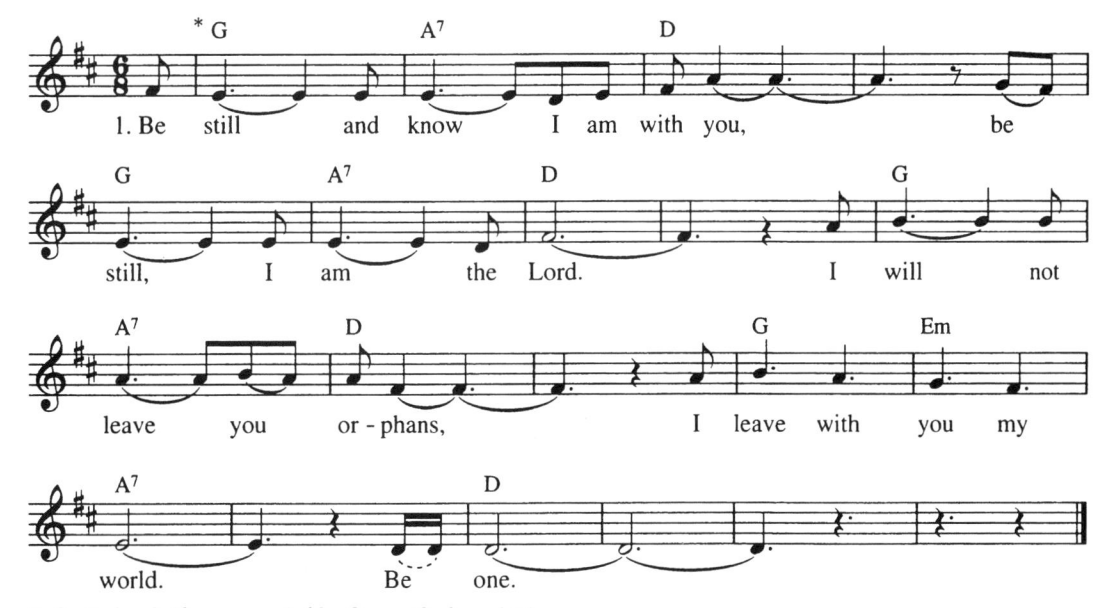

1. Be still and know I am with you, be still, I am the Lord. I will not leave you orphans, I leave with you my world. Be one.

* *Omit chords if accompanied by Organ (2nd version)*

2. You fear the light may be fading,
you fear to lose your way.
Be still, and know I am near you.
I'll lead you to the day and the sun.

3. Be glad the day you have sorrow,
be glad, for then you live.
The stars shine only in darkness,
and in your need I give my peace.

Text and Music: Anne Conway (b.1940)
© Copyright Anne Scott. Used by permission.

164 Be still and know that I am God

BE STILL AND KNOW 888

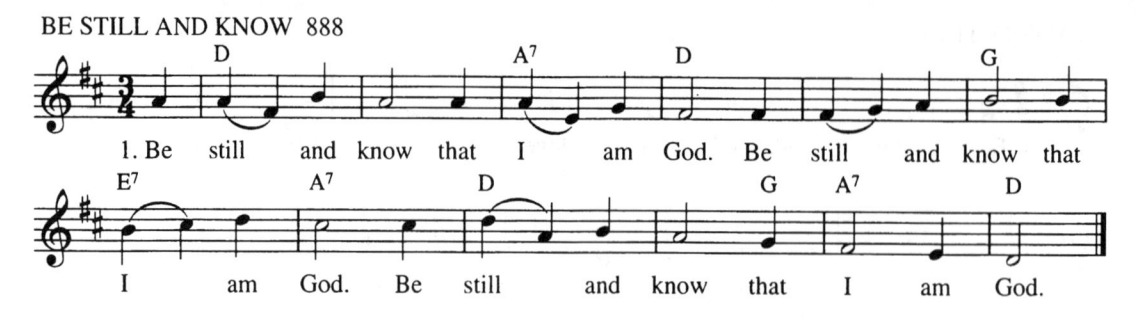

1. Be still and know that I am God.
Be still and know that I am God.
Be still and know that I am God.

2. I am the Lord that healeth thee.
I am the Lord that healeth thee.
I am the Lord that healeth thee.

3. In thee, O Lord, I put my trust.
In thee, O Lord, I put my trust.
In thee, O Lord, I put my trust.

Text: unknown based on Psalm 45
Music: unknown

165 Be still, for the presence of the Lord

1. Be still, for the presence of the Lord, the Holy One, is here.
Come, bow before him now, with reverence and fear.
In him no sin is found, we stand on holy ground.
Be still, for the presence of the Lord, the Holy One, is here.

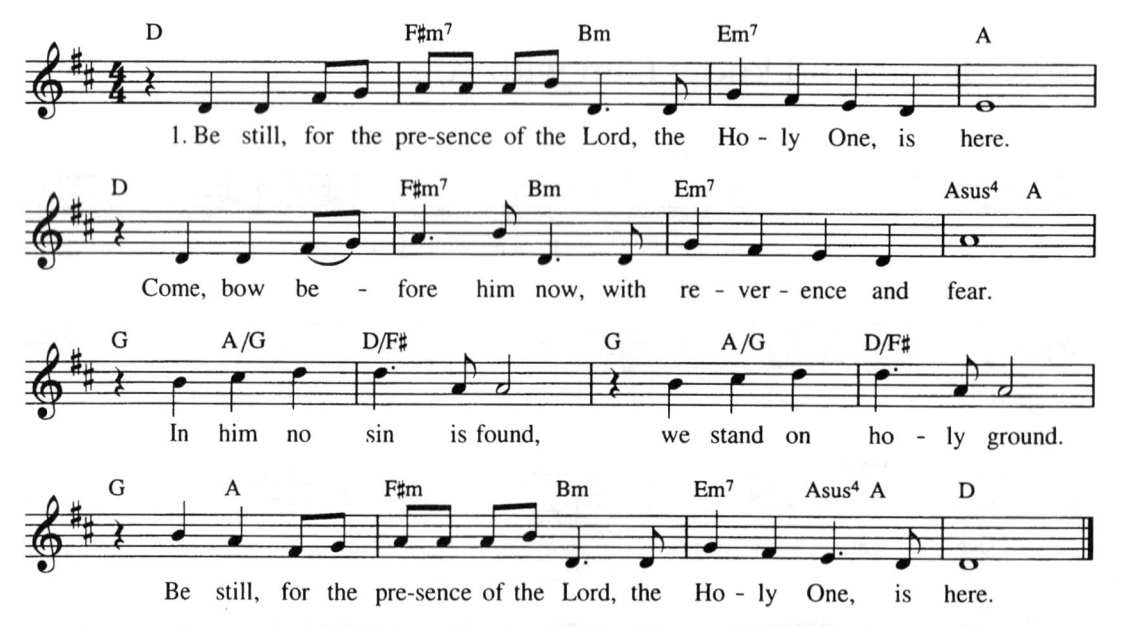

2. Be still, for the glory of the Lord is shining all around;
he burns with holy fire, with splendour he is crowned.
How awesome is the sight, our radiant King of light!
Be still, for the glory of the Lord is shining all around.

3. Be still, for the power of the Lord is moving in this place;
he comes to cleanse and heal, to minister his grace.
No work too hard for him, in faith receive from him.
Be still, for the power of the Lord is moving in this place.

Text and Music: David J. Evans (b.1957)
© Copyright 1986 Kingsway's Thankyou Music, P.O. Box 75, Eastbourne,
East Sussex BN23 6NW, UK. Used by permission.

166 Be still, my soul

FINLANDIA 10 10 10 10 10 10

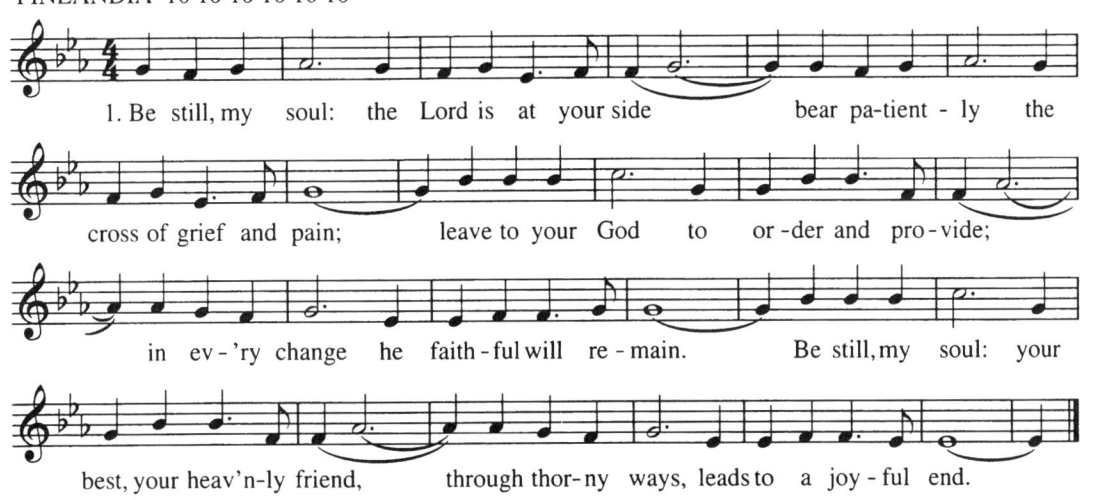

1. Be still, my soul: the Lord is at your side
bear patiently the cross of grief and pain;
leave to your God to order and provide;
in ev'ry change he faithful will remain.
Be still, my soul: your best, your heav'nly friend,
through thorny ways, leads to a joyful end.

2. Be still, my soul: your God will undertake
to guide the future as he has the past.
Your hope, your confidence let nothing shake,
all now mysterious shall be clear at last.
Be still, my soul: the tempests still obey
his voice, who ruled them once on Galilee.

3. Be still, my soul: the hour is hastening on
when we shall be for ever with the Lord,
when disappointment, grief and fear are gone,
sorrow forgotten, love's pure joy restored.
Be still, my soul: when change and tears are past,
all safe and blessèd we shall meet at last.

Text: Katherina von Schlegel (b.1697) trans. Jane L. Borthwick alt.
Music: Jean Sibelius (1865-1957)
Music © Copyright Breitkopf and Härtel, Walkmühlstrasse 52, D-65195 Wiesbaden, Germany.
Used by permission.

167 Bethlehem, of noblest cities

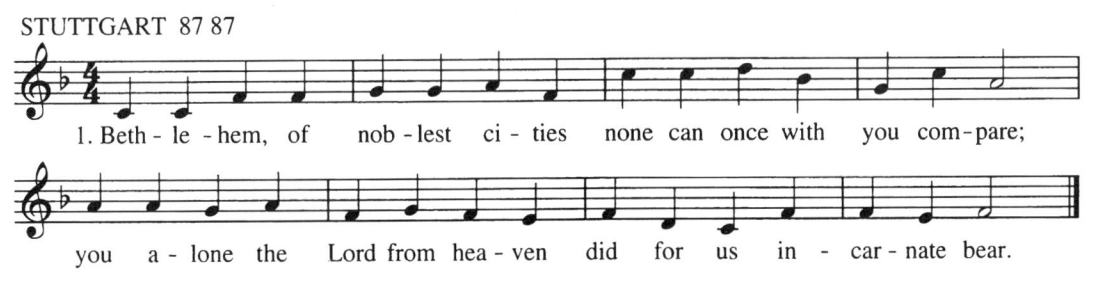

STUTTGART 87 87

1. Bethlehem, of noblest cities
none can once with you compare;
you alone the Lord from heaven
did for us incarnate bear.

2. Fairer than the sun at morning
was the star that told his birth,
to the lands their God announcing,
veiled in human form on earth.

3. Guided by its shining glory
did the eastern kings appear;
see them bend, their gifts to offer,
for a greater King is here.

4. Solemn things of mystic meaning!
incense shows God's presence here,
gold proclaims his sovereign kingship,
myrrh foreshadows death and tears.

5. Holy Jesus, in your brightness
to the gentile world displayed,
with the Father and the Spirit
endless praise to you be paid.

Text: 'O sola magnarum urbium' by Clemens Prudentius (348-413)
trans. Edward Caswall (1814-1878) alt. Michael Forster (b.1946)
Music: German melody
This version of text © Copyright 1999 Kevin Mayhew Ltd.

168 Be thou my vision

SLANE 10 10 10 10

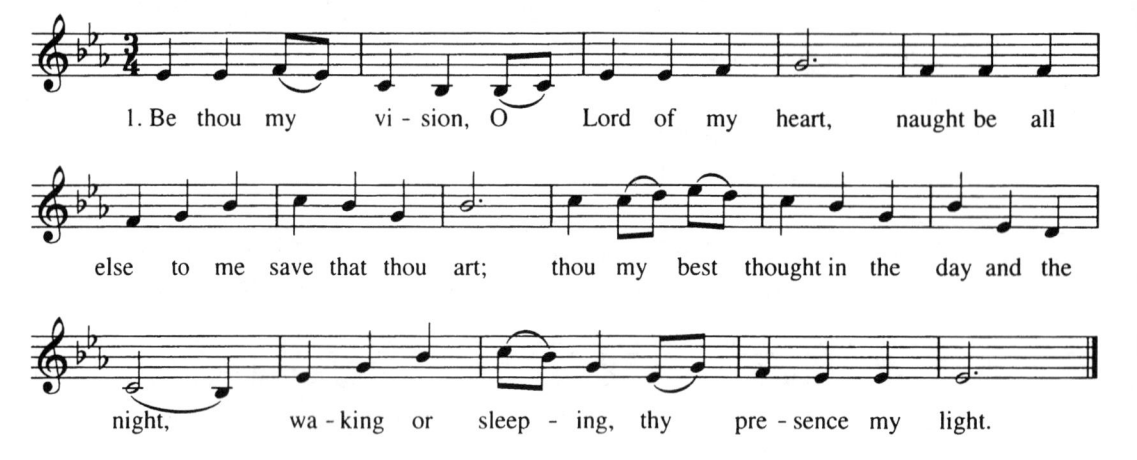

1. Be thou my vi-sion, O Lord of my heart,
naught be all else to me save that thou art;
thou my best thought in the day and the night,
wa-king or sleep-ing, thy pre-sence my light.

2. Be thou my wisdom, be thou my true word,
I ever with thee and thou with me, Lord;
thou my great Father, and I thy true heir;
thou in me dwelling, and I in thy care.

3. Be thou my breastplate, my sword for the fight,
be thou my armour, and be thou my might,
thou my soul's shelter, and thou my high tow'r,
raise thou me heav'nward, O Pow'r of my pow'r.

4. Riches I need not, nor all the world's praise,
thou mine inheritance through all my days;
thou, and thou only, the first in my heart,
high King of heaven, my treasure thou art!

5. High King of heaven, when battle is done,
grant heaven's joy to me, O bright heav'n's sun;
Christ of my own heart, whatever befall,
still be my vision, O Ruler of all.

Text: Irish (c.8th century) trans. Mary Byrne (1880-1931) and Eleanor Hull (1860-1935)
Music: traditional Irish melody
Text © Copyright control

169 Bind us together, Lord

Refrain

Bind us to-geth-er, Lord, bind us to-geth-er with cords that can-not be bro-ken. Bind us to-geth-er, Lord, bind us to-geth-er, Lord, bind us to-geth-er in love.

© Copyright 1977 Kingsway's Thankyou Music, P.O. Box 75, Eastbourne, East Sussex BN23 6NW, UK.
Used by permission.

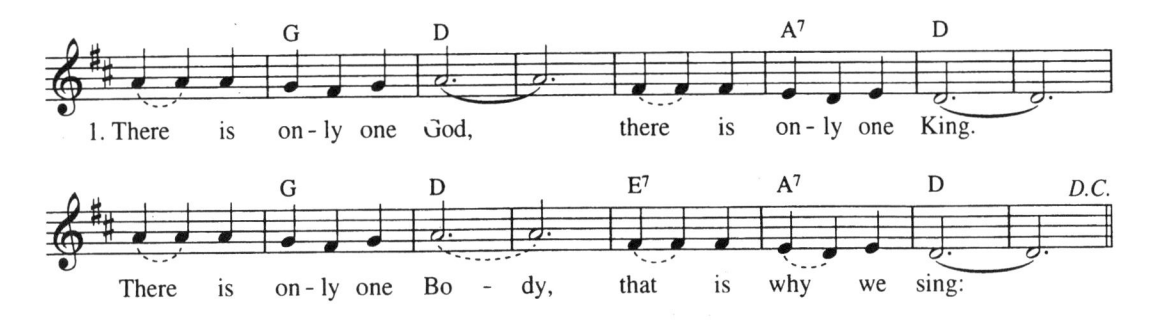

1. There is only one God,
there is only one King.
There is only one Body,
that is why we sing:

2. Fit for the glory of God,
   purchased by his precious Blood,
   born with the right to be free:
   Jesus the vict'ry has won.

3. We are the fam'ly of God,
   we are his promise divine,
   we are his chosen desire,
   we are the glorious new wine.

Text and Music: Bob Gillman

170 Blessed assurance

BLESSED ASSURANCE Irregular
Capo 5

1. Blessed assurance, Jesus is mine: O what a foretaste of glory divine! Heir of salvation, purchase of God; born of his Spirit, washed in his blood.

Refrain
This is my story, this is my song, praising my Saviour all the day long. This is my story, this is my song, praising my Saviour all the day long.

2. Perfect submission, perfect delight,
   visions of rapture burst on my sight;
   angels descending, bring from above
   echoes of mercy, whispers of love.

3. Perfect submission, all is at rest,
   I in my Saviour am happy and blest;
   watching and waiting, looking above,
   filled with his goodness, lost in his love.

Text: Frances Jane van Alstyne (Fanny J. Crosby) (1820-1915)
Music: Phoebe Palmer Knapp (1839-1908)

171 Blessed be God

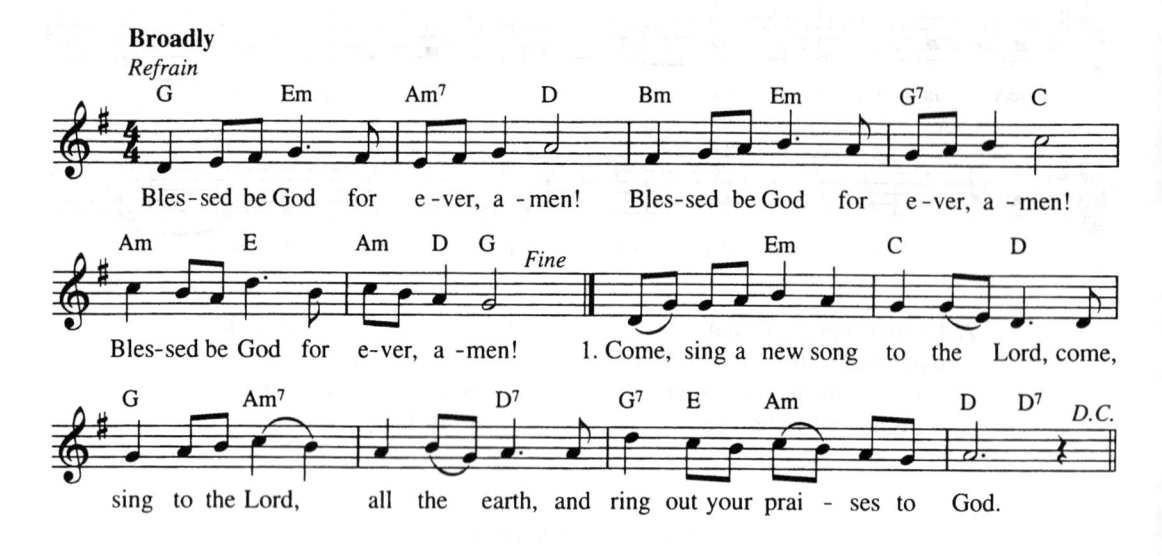

Broadly

Refrain

Bles-sed be God for e-ver, a-men! Bles-sed be God for e-ver, a-men! Bles-sed be God for e-ver, a-men! 1. Come, sing a new song to the Lord, come, sing to the Lord, all the earth, and ring out your prai-ses to God.

2. Come, tell of all his wondrous deeds,
   come, thank him for all he has done,
   and offer your gifts to the Lord.

3. Let all creation shout for joy;
   come worship the Lord in his house,
   the Lord who made heaven and earth.

Text: Hubert J. Richards (b.1921) based on Psalm 95
Music: Richard Lloyd (b.1933)
© Copyright 1996 Kevin Mayhew Ltd.

172 Blessed be the God of Jesus Christ

OLD HUNDREDTH LM

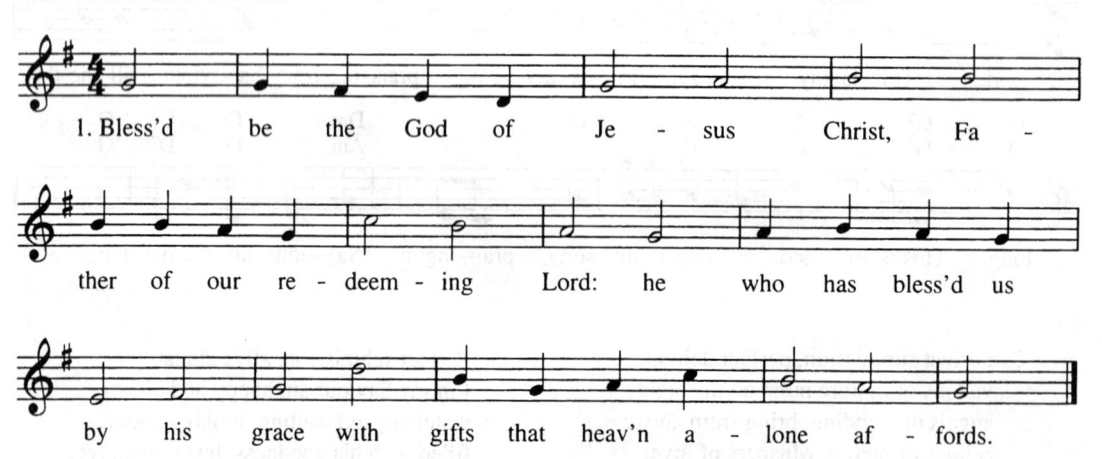

1. Bless'd be the God of Je-sus Christ, Fa-ther of our re-deem-ing Lord: he who has bless'd us by his grace with gifts that heav'n a-lone af-fords.

Text © Copyright 1996 Kevin Mayhew Ltd.

2. Chosen in Christ, by God's good will,
before the earth was set in place,
called to be children of his love,
and holy stand before his face:

3. We have redemption through his blood,
pardon by his abundant grace,
blessing eternal from above,
by Christ made known in time and space.

4. Wisdom and insight of our God
make known the myst'ry of his ways;
to him all things of heav'n and earth
shall gather on the final day.

5. In him the gospel truth is known,
his word of wholeness is revealed.
All who believe and trust in him
are with the Holy Spirit sealed.

6. This is the pledge that we receive,
sign of redemption as his own;
then shall the heav'ns and earth unite
to make his praise and glory known.

Text: Michael Forster (b.1946) based on Ephesians 1:3-14
Music: from the 'Genevan Psalter' (1551)

173 Bless the Lord, my soul

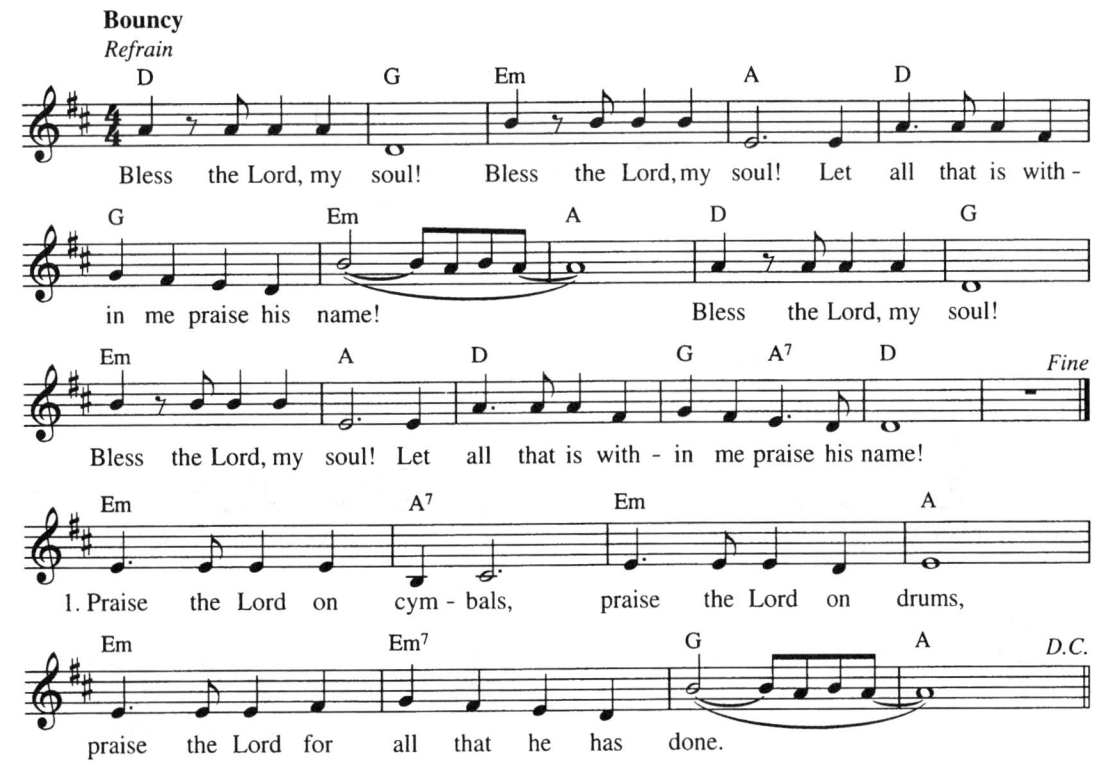

Bouncy

Refrain

Bless the Lord, my soul! Bless the Lord, my soul! Let all that is within me praise his name! Bless the Lord, my soul! Bless the Lord, my soul! Let all that is within me praise his name!

1. Praise the Lord on cymbals,
praise the Lord on drums,
praise the Lord for all that he has done.

2. Praise the Lord on trumpet,
praise the Lord in song,
praise him all who stand before his throne.

3. Praise him for his mercy,
praise him for his pow'r,
praise him for his love which conquers all.

Text and Music: Mike Anderson (b.1956)
© Copyright 1999 Kevin Mayhew Ltd.

174 Blest are the pure in heart

FRANCONIA SM

1. Blest are the pure in heart, for they shall see our God; the secret of the Lord is theirs, their soul is Christ's abode.

2. The Lord who left the heav'ns
our life and peace to bring,
to dwell in lowliness with us,
our pattern and our King.

3. Still to the lowly soul
he doth himself impart,
and for his dwelling and his throne
chooseth the pure in heart.

4. Lord, we thy presence seek;
may ours this blessing be:
give us a pure and lowly heart,
a temple meet for thee.

Text: vs. 1, 3: John Keble (1792-1866)
vs. 2, 4: William John Hall's 'Psalms and Hymns' (1836) alt.
Music: from 'Harmonischer Liederschatz' (1738)
adapted by William Henry Havergal (1793-1870)

175 Blest are you, Lord
Blessed be God

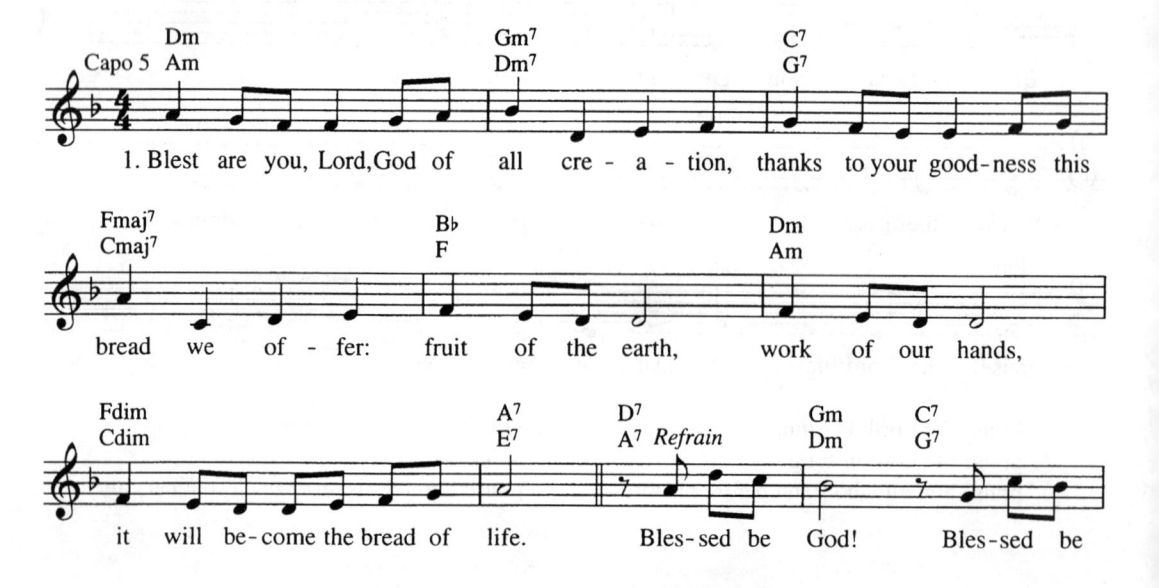

1. Blest are you, Lord, God of all creation, thanks to your goodness this bread we offer: fruit of the earth, work of our hands, it will become the bread of life. Blessed be God! Blessed be

© Copyright 1984 Kevin Mayhew Ltd.

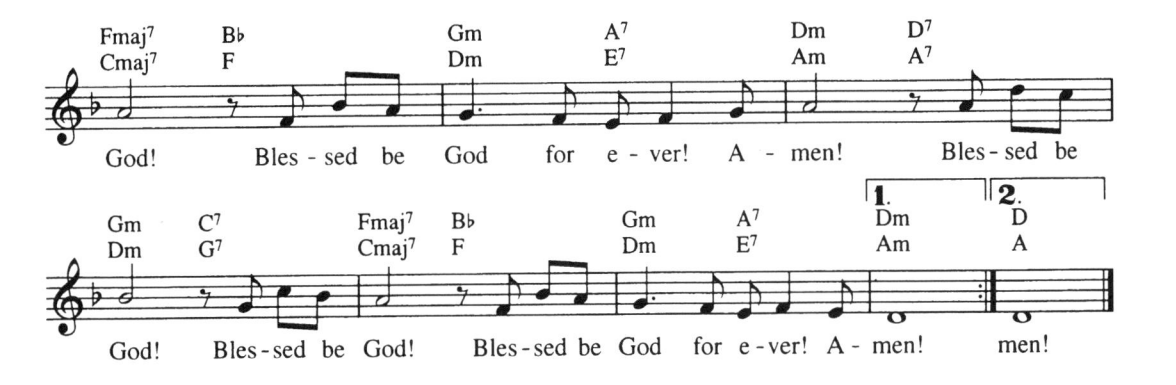

God! Bles - sed be God for e - ver! A - men! Bles - sed be
God! Bles - sed be God! Bles - sed be God for e - ver! A - men! men!

2. Blest are you, Lord, God of all creation,
   thanks to your goodness this wine we offer:
   fruit of the earth, work of our hands,
   it will become the cup of life.

Text: Aniceto Nazareth, based on the Roman Missal
Music: Aniceto Nazareth

176 Blest are you, Lord of creation

1. Blest are you, Lord of cre - a - tion, you pro-vide the bread we of - fer,
   fruit of your earth and work of our hands. Blest be the Lord for
   e - ver, A - men. Blest be the Lord for e - ver, A - men.

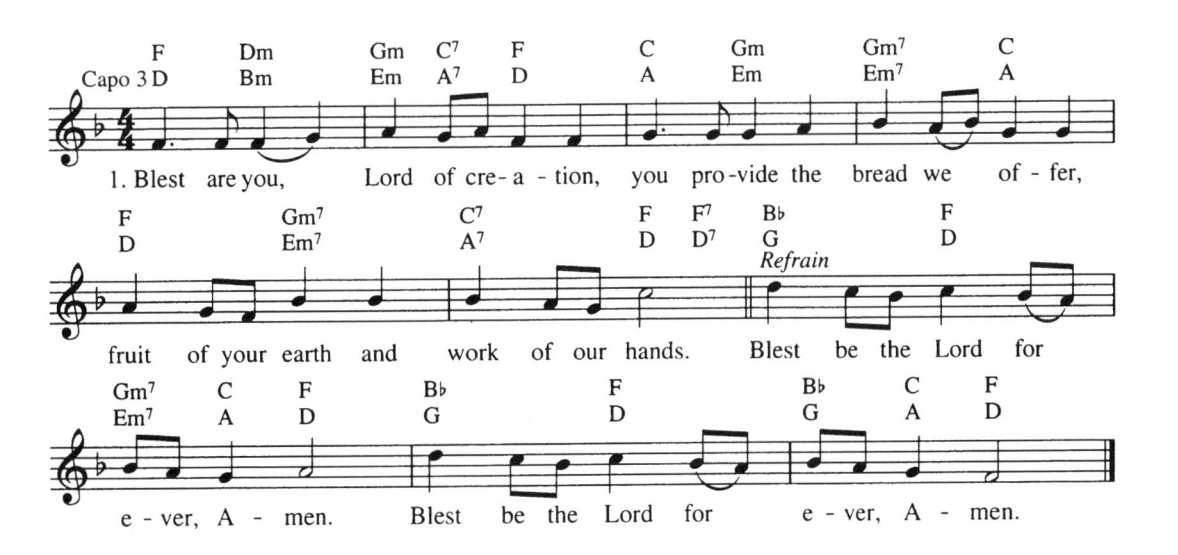

2. Blest are you, Lord of creation,
   you provide the wine we offer,
   fruit of your earth and work of our hands.

3. Blest are you, Lord of creation,
   look with favour on our off'rings,
   pour out your Spirit over these gifts.

Text: Hubert J. Richards (b.1921) based on the prayers at the preparation of the gifts (Roman Missal)
Music: Richard Shephard (b.1949)
© Copyright 1996 Kevin Mayhew Ltd.

177 Blest are you, O God

ODE TO JOY 87 87 D

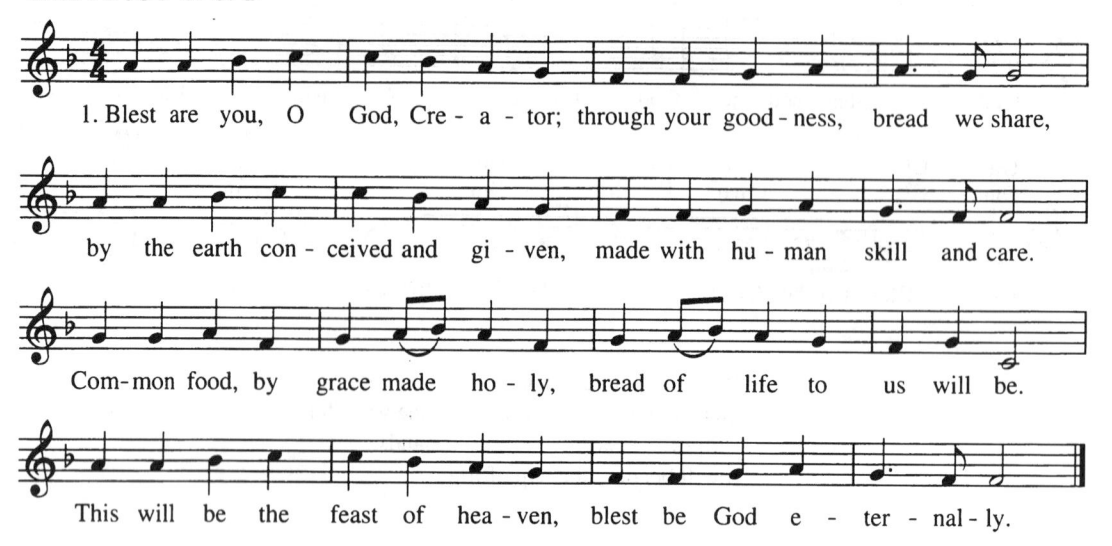

1. Blest are you, O God, Cre - a - tor; through your good - ness, bread we share,
by the earth con - ceived and gi - ven, made with hu - man skill and care.
Com - mon food, by grace made ho - ly, bread of life to us will be.
This will be the feast of hea - ven, blest be God e - ter - nal - ly.

2. Blest are you, O God, Creator;
by your grace we bring you wine,
work of human hands combining
with the goodness of the vine;
cup of blessing yet of sorrow,
cup of life and love to be;
sign of covenant eternal;
blest be God eternally.

3. Blest are you, O God, Creator;
Light of lights and Pow'r of pow'rs,
yet in humble love accepting
gifts from hands as poor as ours.
In our gifts our lives are given,
by your grace Christ's life to be.
In the giving and receiving,
blest be God eternally.

Text: Michael Forster (b.1946)
Music: Ludwig van Beethoven (1770-1827)
Text © Copyright 1993, 1999 Kevin Mayhew Ltd.

178 Blest be the Lord

Refrain

Blest be the Lord; blest be the Lord, the God of mer - cy, the God who saves. I shall not fear the dark of night, nor the ar - row that flies by day.

© Copyright 1976 Daniel L. Schutte and New Dawn Music, 5536 NE Hassalo, Portland, OR 97213, USA.
All rights reserved. Used by permission.

1. He will release me from the nets of all my foes. He will protect me from their wicked hands. Beneath the shadow of his wings I will rejoice to find a dwelling place secure.

2. I need not shrink before the terrors of the night,
   nor stand alone before the light of day.
   No harm shall come to me, no arrow strike me down,
   no evil settle in my soul.

3. Although a thousand strong have fallen at my side,
   I'll not be shaken with the Lord at hand.
   His faithful love is all the armour that I need
   to wage my battle with the foe.

Text: Dan Schutte based on Psalm 90
Music: Dan Schutte

179 Born in the night, Mary's child

MARY'S CHILD 76 76

1. Born in the night, Mary's child, a long way from your home;
   coming in need, Mary's child, born in a borrowed room.

2. Clear shining light,
   Mary's child,
   your face lights up our way;
   light of the world,
   Mary's child,
   dawn on our darkened day.

3. Truth of our life,
   Mary's child,
   you tell us God is good;
   prove it is true,
   Mary's child,
   go to your cross of wood.

4. Hope of the world,
   Mary's child,
   you're coming soon to reign;
   King of the earth,
   Mary's child,
   walk in our streets again.

Text and Music: Geoffrey Ainger (b.1925)
© Copyright 1964 Stainer & Bell Ltd, P.O. Box 110, Victoria House, 23 Gruneisen Road, Finchley, London N3 1DZ.
Used by permission.

180 Bread from the earth

AMOR DEI 13 13 13

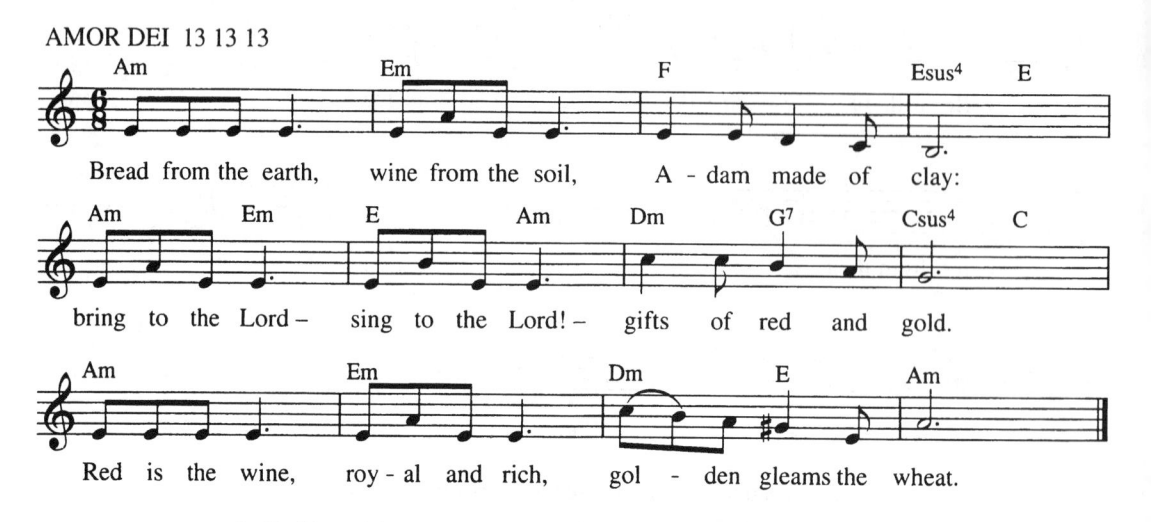

Bread from the earth, wine from the soil, Adam made of clay:
bring to the Lord – sing to the Lord! – gifts of red and gold.
Red is the wine, royal and rich, golden gleams the wheat.

2. Fashioned from dust, what can you give, Adam, weak and poor?
   Bring to the Lord – sing to the Lord! – what he gave to you:
   spirit of flame, mastering mind, body fine and proud.

3. Cry on his name, worship your God, all who dwell on earth.
   Bring to the Lord – sing to the Lord! – heart and voice and will.
   Father and Son, Spirit most high, worship Three in One.

Text: Luke Connaughton (1917-1979)
Music: Kevin Mayhew (b.1942)

© Copyright McCrimmon Publishing Co. Ltd., 10-12 High Street, Great Wakering, Southend-on-Sea, Essex SS3 0EQ. Used by arrangement.

181 Bread is blessed and broken

GRACE IN ESSENCE 65 63

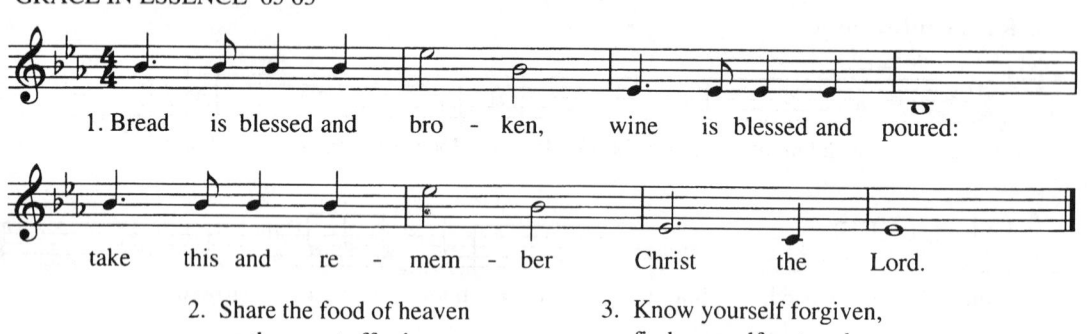

1. Bread is blessed and broken, wine is blessed and poured:
   take this and remember Christ the Lord.

2. Share the food of heaven
   earth cannot afford.
   Here is grace in essence –
   Christ the Lord

3. Know yourself forgiven,
   find yourself restored,
   meet a friend for ever –
   Christ the Lord.

4. God has kept his promise
   sealed by sign and word:
   here, for those who want him –
   Christ the Lord.

Text and Music: John L. Bell (b.1949) and Graham Maule (b.1958)
© Copyright 1989 WGRG, Iona Community, 840 Govan Road, Glasgow G51 3UU, Scotland, from the 'Love From Below' collection (Wild Goose Publications 1989). Used by permission.

182 Breathe on me, breath of God

CARLISLE SM

1. Breathe on me, breath of God, fill me with life anew, that as you love, so I may love, and do what you would do.

2. Breathe on me, breath of God,
   until my heart is pure:
   until my will is one with yours
   to do and to endure.

3. Breathe on me, breath of God,
   fulfil my heart's desire,
   until this earthly part of me
   glows with your heav'nly fire.

4. Breathe on me, breath of God,
   so shall I never die,
   but live with you the perfect life
   of your eternity.

Text: Edwin Hatch (1835-1889) alt. the editors
Music: Charles Lockhart (1745-1815)
This version of text © Copyright 1999 Kevin Mayhew Ltd.

183 Breath of God, O Holy Spirit

1. Breath of God, O Holy Spirit, breath of God, O Holy Spirit, breath of God, O Holy Spirit, breathe on us now.

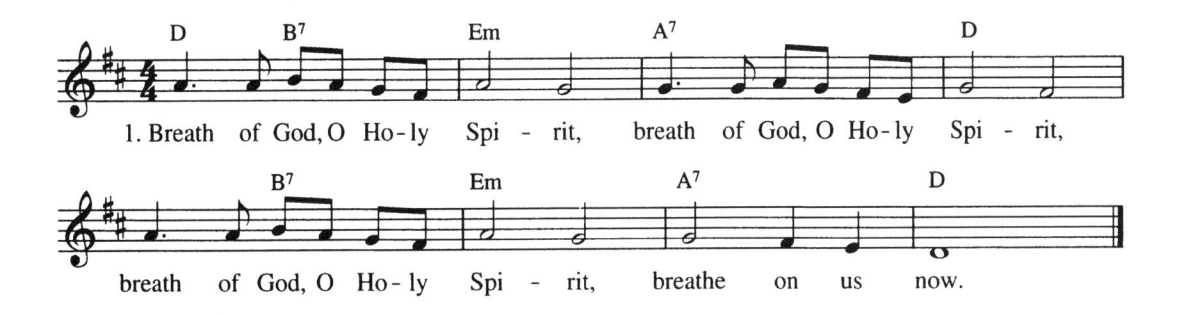

2. Comforter in time of sorrow,
   comforter in time of sorrow,
   comforter in time of sorrow,
   give us your peace.

3. Fount of joy and of all beauty,
   fount of joy and of all beauty,
   fount of joy and of all beauty,
   come, fill our minds.

4. Light divine and flame eternal,
   light divine and flame eternal,
   light divine and flame eternal,
   burn in us now.

5. Promise of our Saviour, Jesus,
   promise of our Saviour, Jesus,
   promise of our Saviour, Jesus,
   speak through us now.

Text and Music: Estelle White (b.1925)
© Copyright 1982 Kevin Mayhew Ltd.

184 Bring, all ye dear-bought nations

LASST UNS ERFREUEN 88 44 88 and Alleluias

1. Bring, all ye dear-bought na-tions, bring, your rich-est prai-ses to your King, al-le-lu-ia, al-le-lu-ia, that spot-less Lamb, who more than due, paid for his sheep, and those sheep you, *Refrain* al-le-lu-ia, al-le-lu-ia, al-le-lu-ia, al-le-lu-ia, al-le-lu-ia!

A higher setting will be found at No. 101

2. That guiltless Son, who bought your peace,
and made his Father's anger cease,
alleluia, alleluia,
then, life and death together fought,
each to a strange extreme were brought.

3. Life died, but soon revived again,
and even death by it was slain,
alleluia, alleluia.
Say, happy Magdalen, O, say,
what didst thou see there by the way?

4. 'I saw the tomb of my dear Lord,
I saw himself, and him adored,
alleluia, alleluia,
I saw the napkin and the sheet,
that bound his head and wrapped his feet.'

5. 'I heard the angels witness bear,
Jesus is ris'n; he is not here,
alleluia, alleluia;
go, tell his foll'wers they shall see
thine and their hope in Galilee.'

6. We, Lord, with faithful hearts and voice,
on this thy rising day rejoice,
alleluia, alleluia.
O thou, whose pow'r o'ercame the grave,
by grace and love us sinners save.

Text: 'Victimae Paschali Laudes' attributed to Wipo of Burgundy (11th century),
trans. Walter Kirkham Blount (d.1717)
Music: melody from 'Geistliche Kirchengesang', Cologne (1623)

185 Bring flowers of the rarest

1. Bring flow'rs of the rarest, bring blos-soms the fairest, from garden and woodland and hillside and dale; our full hearts are swelling, our glad voices telling the praise of the loveliest flow'r of the vale.

Refrain
O Mary, we crown thee with blossoms today, Queen of the angels and Queen of the May. O Mary we crown thee with blossoms today, Queen of the angels and Queen of the May.

2. Their lady they name thee,
   their mistress proclaim thee.
   O, grant that thy children on earth be as true,
   as long as the bowers
   are radiant with flowers
   as long as the azure shall keep its bright hue.

3. Sing gaily in chorus,
   the bright angels o'er us
   re-echo the strains we begin upon earth;
   their harps are repeating
   the notes of our greeting,
   for Mary herself is the cause of our mirth.

Text and Music: A Sister of Notre Dame

186 Brother, sister, let me serve you
The servant song

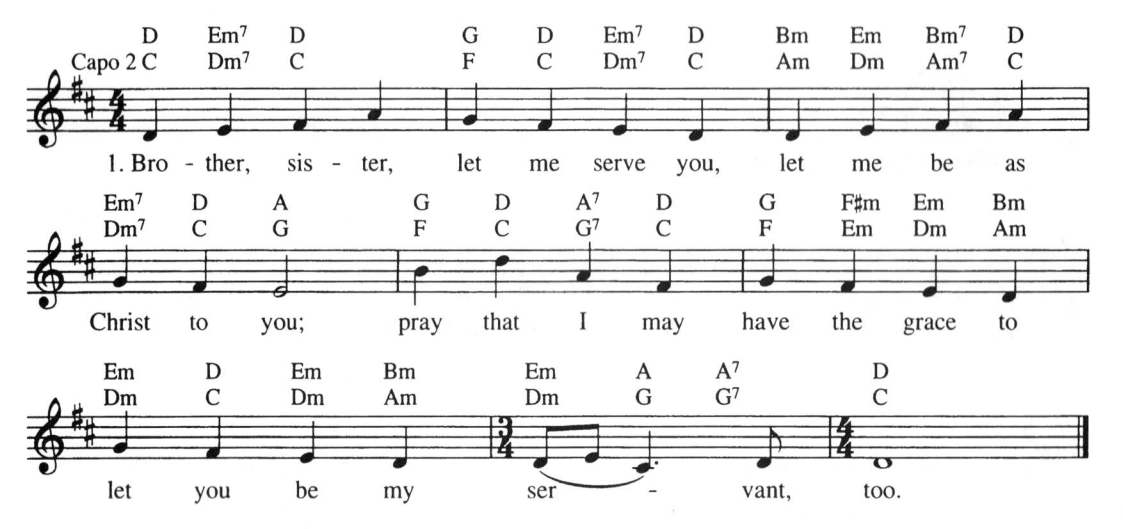

1. Brother, sister, let me serve you,
let me be as Christ to you;
pray that I may have the grace to
let you be my servant, too.

2. We are pilgrims on a journey,
fellow trav'llers on the road;
we are here to help each other
walk the mile and bear the load.

3. I will hold the Christlight for you
in the night-time of your fear;
I will hold my hand out to you,
speak the peace you long to hear.

4. I will weep when you are weeping;
when you laugh, I'll laugh with you.
I will share your joy and sorrow
till we've seen this journey through.

5. When we sing to God in heaven,
we shall find such harmony,
born of all we've known together
of Christ's love and agony.

6. Brother, sister, let me serve you,
let me be as Christ to you;
pray that I may have the grace to
let you be my servant, too.

Text and Music: Richard Gillard
© Copyright 1977 Scripture in Song, a division of Integrity Music. Administered by Kingsway's Thankyou Music, P.O. Box 75, Eastbourne, East Sussex BN23 6NW, UK. For the territory of the UK only. Used by permission.

187 By his grace

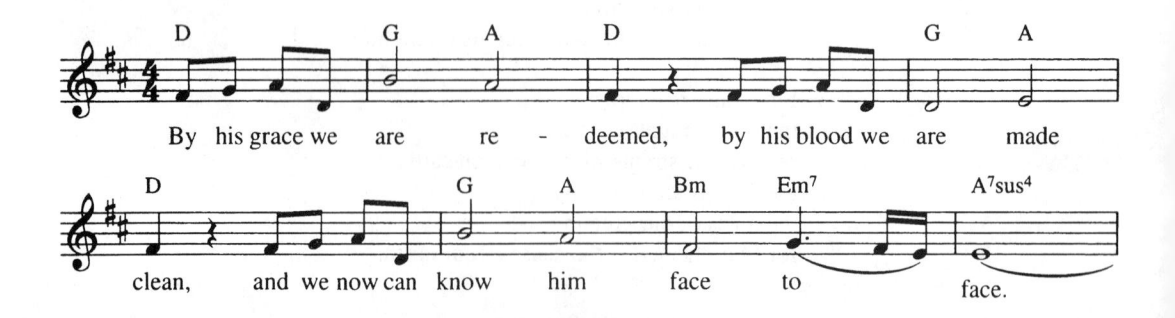

By his grace we are redeemed, by his blood we are made clean, and we now can know him face to face.

© Copyright 1994 Deep Fryed Music/Word Music/Maranatha! Music. Administered by CopyCare, P.O. Box 77, Hailsham, East Sussex BN27 3EF, UK. Used by permission.

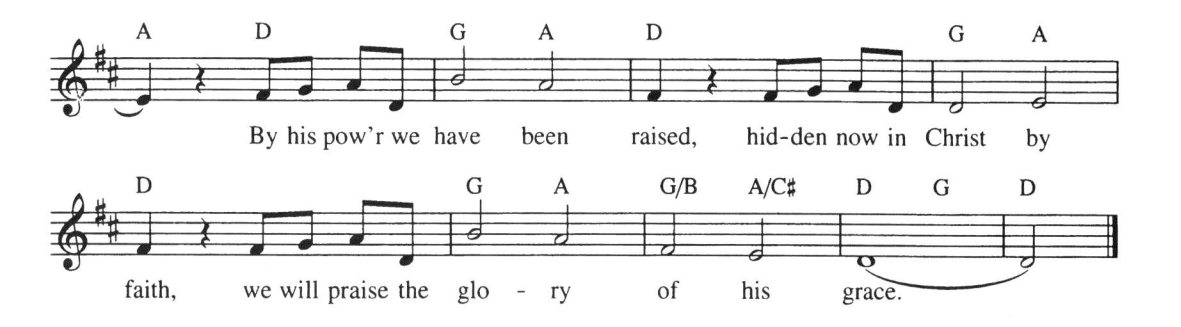

By his pow'r we have been raised, hidden now in Christ by faith, we will praise the glory of his grace.

Text and Music: Steven Fry
© Copyright 1994 Deep Fryed Music/Word Music/Maranatha! Music. Administered by CopyCare, P.O. Box 77, Hailsham, East Sussex BN27 3EF, UK. Used by permission.

188 By the blood that flowed from thee

WESTMINSTER OLD 77 77 and Refrain

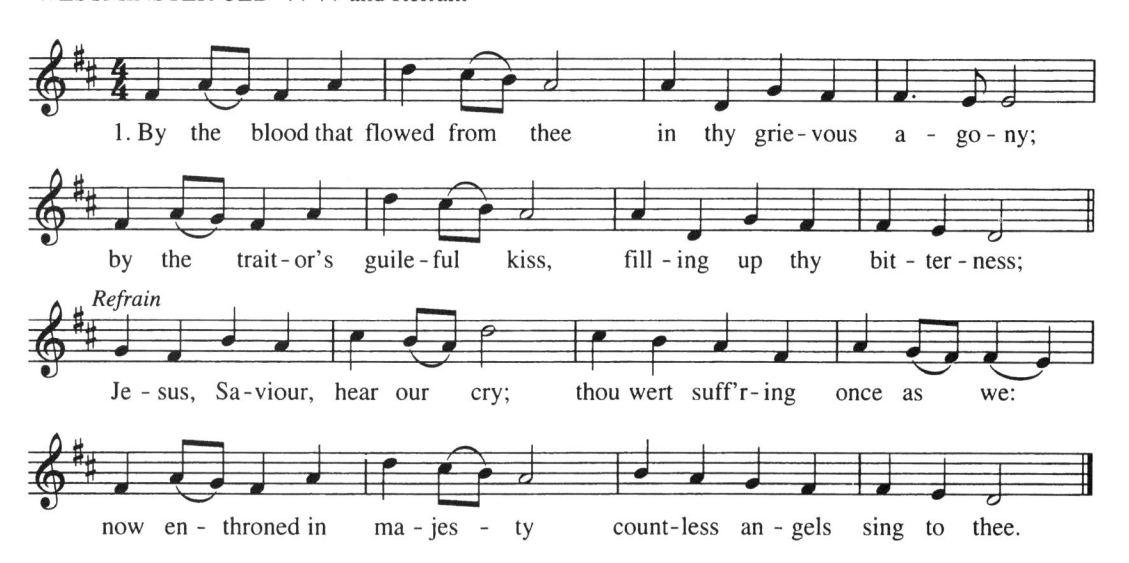

1. By the blood that flowed from thee in thy grievous agony; by the traitor's guileful kiss, filling up thy bitterness;

Refrain
Jesus, Saviour, hear our cry; thou wert suff'ring once as we: now enthroned in majesty countless angels sing to thee.

2. By the cords that, round thee cast, bound thee to the pillar fast, by the scourge so meekly borne, by the purple robe of scorn.

3. By the thorns that crowned thy head; by the sceptre of a reed; by thy foes on bended knee, mocking at thy royalty.

4. By the people's cruel jeers; by the holy women's tears; by thy footsteps, faint and slow, weighed beneath thy cross of woe.

5. By thy weeping mother's woe; by the sword that pierced her through, when in anguish standing by, on the cross she saw thee die.

Text: Frederick William Faber (1814-1863)
Music: John Richardson (1816-1879)

189 By the cross

Refrain (Capo 3)

By the cross we are marked for life! We are cho-sen as God's peo-ple!
To this Tree of life we are branched by Christ, and its fruit will last for e-ver. *Fine*

1. Made in the i-mage and the like-ness of the one true God, we are the daugh-ters and the sons of God, our Fa-ther. But, for a tree and its fruit, we turned a-gainst him, we chose to clothe our-selves in self-ish-ness and shame. *D.C.*

2. Made in our image and the likeness of humanity,
   Christ came from God and taught us how to call him 'Father'!
   Then, by the Tree, did he lead us to the Garden,
   where God awaits in welcome if we're clothed in Christ.

Text and Music: Robert B. Kelly (b.1948)
© Copyright 1999 Kevin Mayhew Ltd.

190 By the waters of Babylon

This may be sung as a round, with entries at A, B *and* C

1. By the waters, the waters of Babylon,
we sat down and wept, and wept for thee, Zion;
we remember thee, remember thee, remember thee, Zion.

2. On the willows, the willows of Babylon,
we hung up our harps, our harps, for thee, Zion;
how can we sing, can we sing, sing of thee, Zion?

3. There our captors, our captors from Babylon,
tried to make us sing, to sing of thee, Zion;
but we could not sing, we could not sing, we could not sing, Zion.

Text: based on Psalm 137
Music: Don McClean and Lee Hays
© Copyright control.

191 Called to be servants

Refrain

Called to be servants, called to be sons, called to be daughters, we're called to be one. Called into service, called to be free; you are called to be you, and I'm called to be me.

1. Children, come with wide open eyes.
   Look at the water; you have been baptised.
   You're free from the slav-'ry that bound you to sin,
   so live now as children in the kingdom of heav'n.

2. We are saints! Forgiveness is sure,
   not of ourselves, but the cross Christ endured.
   We're free from the law that said 'You must provide!'
   We're free to be servants; we're called, we're baptised.

3. Jesus closed the dark pit of death.
   He has breathed on us with his holy breath.
   He gives us the faith to respond to his News.
   We're free to show mercy, to love, to be bruised.

Text and Music: James G. Johnson

© Copyright James G. Johnson, Eighth Day Creations Music, Box 375, Red Lodge, Montana 59068, USA. Used by permission.

192 Change my heart, O God

Change my heart, O God, make it ever true;
change my heart, O God, may I be like you.

You are the potter, I am the clay;
mould me and make me: this is what I pray.

Text: Eddie Espinosa based on Isaiah 64:8
Music: Eddie Espinosa
© Copyright 1982 Mercy/Vineyard Publishing/Music Services. Administered by CopyCare,
P.O. Box 77, Hailsham, East Sussex BN27 3EF. Used by permission.

193 Child in the manger

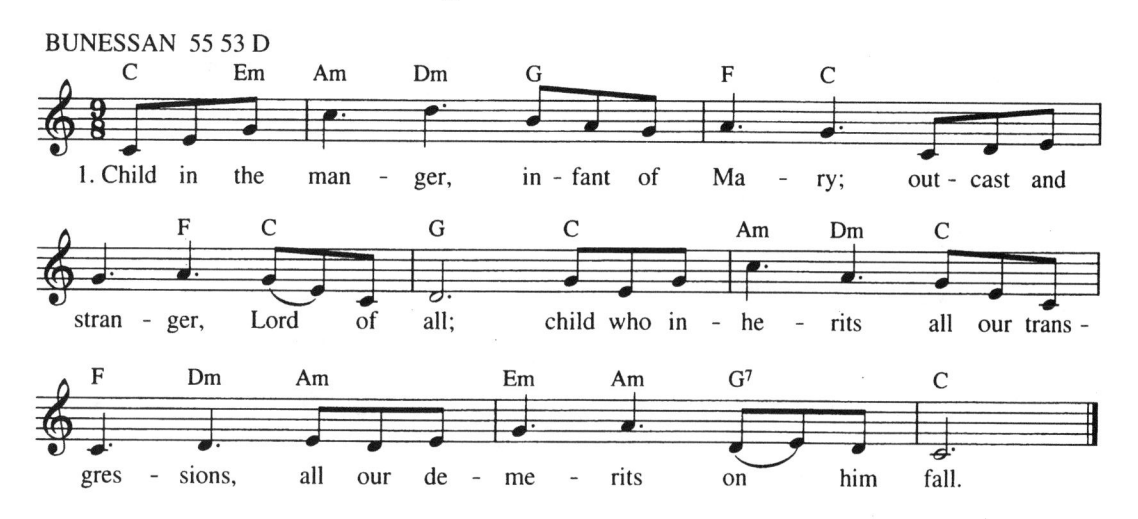

BUNESSAN 55 53 D

1. Child in the manger, infant of Mary;
   outcast and stranger, Lord of all;
   child who inherits all our transgressions,
   all our demerits on him fall.

2. Once the most holy child of salvation
   gently and lowly lived below;
   now as our glorious mighty Redeemer,
   see him victorious o'er each foe.

3. Prophets foretold him, infant of wonder;
   angels behold him on his throne;
   worthy our Saviour of all their praises;
   happy for ever are his own.

Text: Mary MacDonald (1817-1890) trans. Lachlan MacBean (1853-1931)
Music: traditional Gaelic melody
Text © Copyright control.

194 Christ be beside me

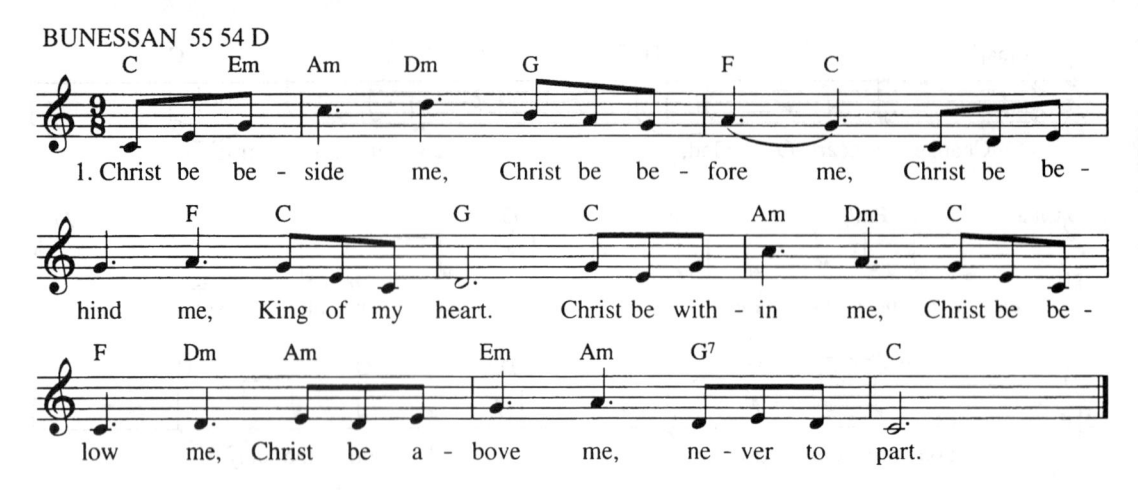

BUNESSAN 55 54 D

1. Christ be beside me, Christ be before me, Christ be behind me, King of my heart. Christ be within me, Christ be below me, Christ be above me, never to part.

2. Christ on my right hand, Christ on my left hand,
Christ all around me, shield in the strife.
Christ in my sleeping, Christ in my sitting,
Christ in my rising, light of my life.

3. Christ be in all hearts thinking about me.
Christ be in all tongues telling of me.
Christ be the vision in eyes that see me,
in ears that hear me, Christ ever be.

Text: adapted from 'St Patrick's Breastplate' by James Quinn (b.1919)
Music: traditional Gaelic melody
Text © Copyright 1969 Geoffrey Chapman, an imprint of Cassell plc, 125 Strand, London WC2R 0BB, UK.
Used by permission.

195 Christians, lift up your hearts

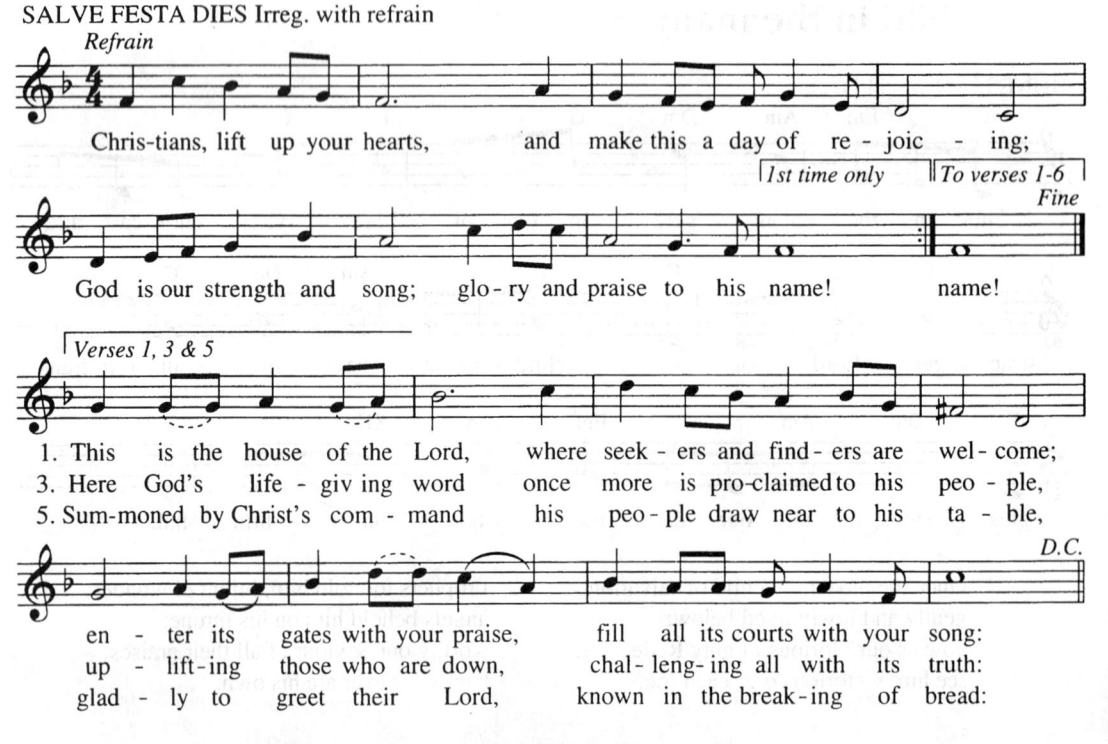

SALVE FESTA DIES Irreg. with refrain

Refrain
Christians, lift up your hearts, and make this a day of rejoicing; God is our strength and song; glory and praise to his name!

Verses 1, 3 & 5
1. This is the house of the Lord, where seekers and finders are welcome;
3. Here God's life-giving word once more is proclaimed to his people,
5. Summoned by Christ's command his people draw near to his table,

enter its gates with your praise, fill all its courts with your song:
uplifting those who are down, challenging all with its truth:
gladly to greet their Lord, known in the breaking of bread:

Text: © Copyright John E. Bowers. Used by permission.
Music: © Copyright Oxford University Press, Great Clarendon Street, Oxford OX2 6DP.
Used by permission from the 'English Hymnal'.

Verses 2, 4 & 6

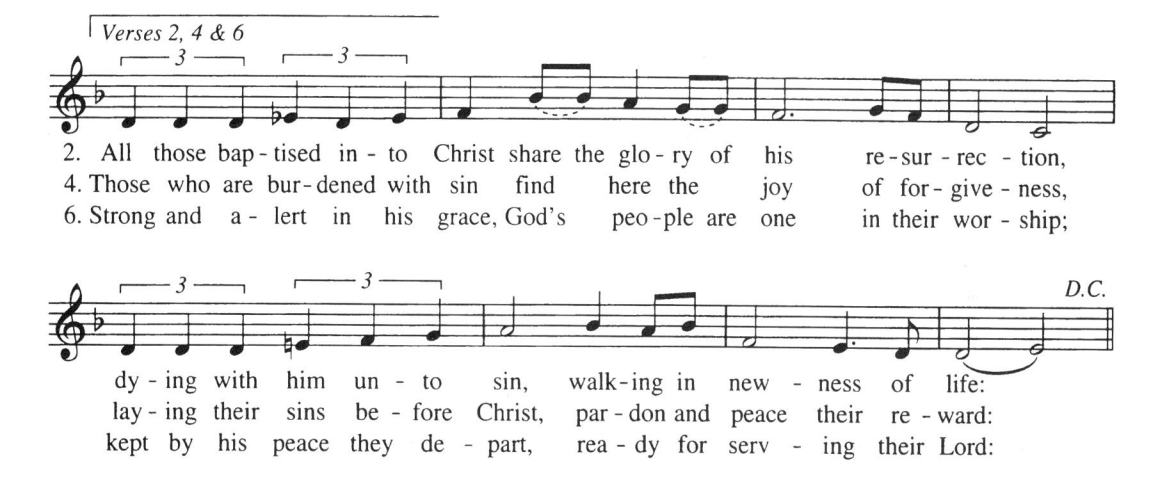

2. All those baptised into Christ share the glory of his resurrection,
   dying with him unto sin, walking in newness of life:
4. Those who are burdened with sin find here the joy of forgiveness,
   laying their sins before Christ, pardon and peace their reward:
6. Strong and alert in his grace, God's people are one in their worship;
   kept by his peace they depart, ready for serving their Lord:

Text: John E. Bowers
Music: Ralph Vaughan Williams (1872-1958)

196 Christ is King of earth and heaven

LAUS DEO (REDHEAD NO. 46) 87 87

1. Christ is King of earth and heaven! Let his subjects all proclaim,
   in the splendour of his temple, honour to his holy name.

A lower setting will be found at No. 340

2. Christ is King! No soul created
   can refuse to bend the knee
   to the God made man who reigneth,
   as 'twas promised, from the tree.

3. Christ is King! Let humble sorrow
   for our past neglect atone,
   for the lack of faithful service
   to the Master whom we own.

4. Christ is King! Let joy and gladness
   greet him; let his courts resound
   with the praise of faithful subjects
   to his love in honour bound.

5. Christ is King! In health and sickness,
   till we breathe our latest breath,
   till we greet in highest heaven,
   Christ the victor over death.

Text: Ivor J.E. Daniel (1883-1967)
Music: German melody adapted and arranged by Richard Redhead (1820-1901)
Text © Copyright Burns & Oates Ltd, Wellwood, North Farm Road,
Tunbridge Wells, Kent TN2 3QR. Used by permission.

197 Christ is made the sure foundation

TUNE 1: WESTMINSTER ABBEY 87 87 87

1. Christ is made the sure foundation, Christ the head and cornerstone,
chosen of the Lord, and precious, binding all the Church in one,
holy Zion's help for ever, and her confidence alone.

2. To this temple, where we call you,
come, O Lord of hosts, today;
you have promised loving kindness,
hear your servants as we pray,
bless your people now before you,
turn our darkness into day.

3. Hear the cry of all your people,
what they ask and hope to gain;
what they gain from you, for ever
with your chosen to retain,
and hereafter in your glory
evermore with you to reign.

4. Praise and honour to the Father,
praise and honour to the Son,
praise and honour to the Spirit,
ever Three and ever One,
One in might and One in glory,
while unending ages run.

TUNE 2: REGENT SQUARE 87 87 87

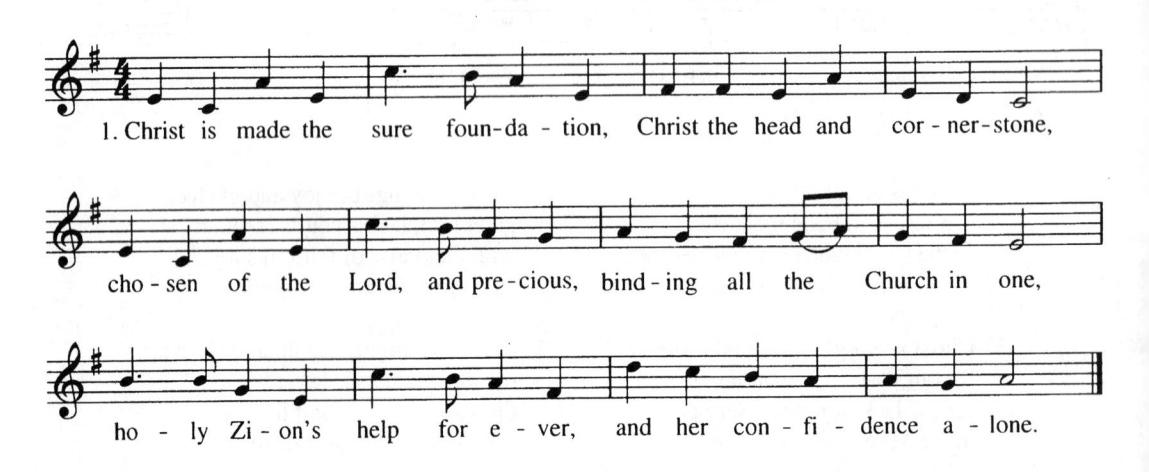

1. Christ is made the sure foundation, Christ the head and cornerstone,
chosen of the Lord, and precious, binding all the Church in one,
holy Zion's help for ever, and her confidence alone.

Text: 'Urbs beata Jerusalem' (c.7th century) trans. John Mason Neale (1818-1866) alt.
Music: Tune 1 – Henry Purcell (1659-1695)
Tune 2 – Henry Smart (1813-1879)

198 Christ's is the world
A touching place

DREAM ANGUS Irregular

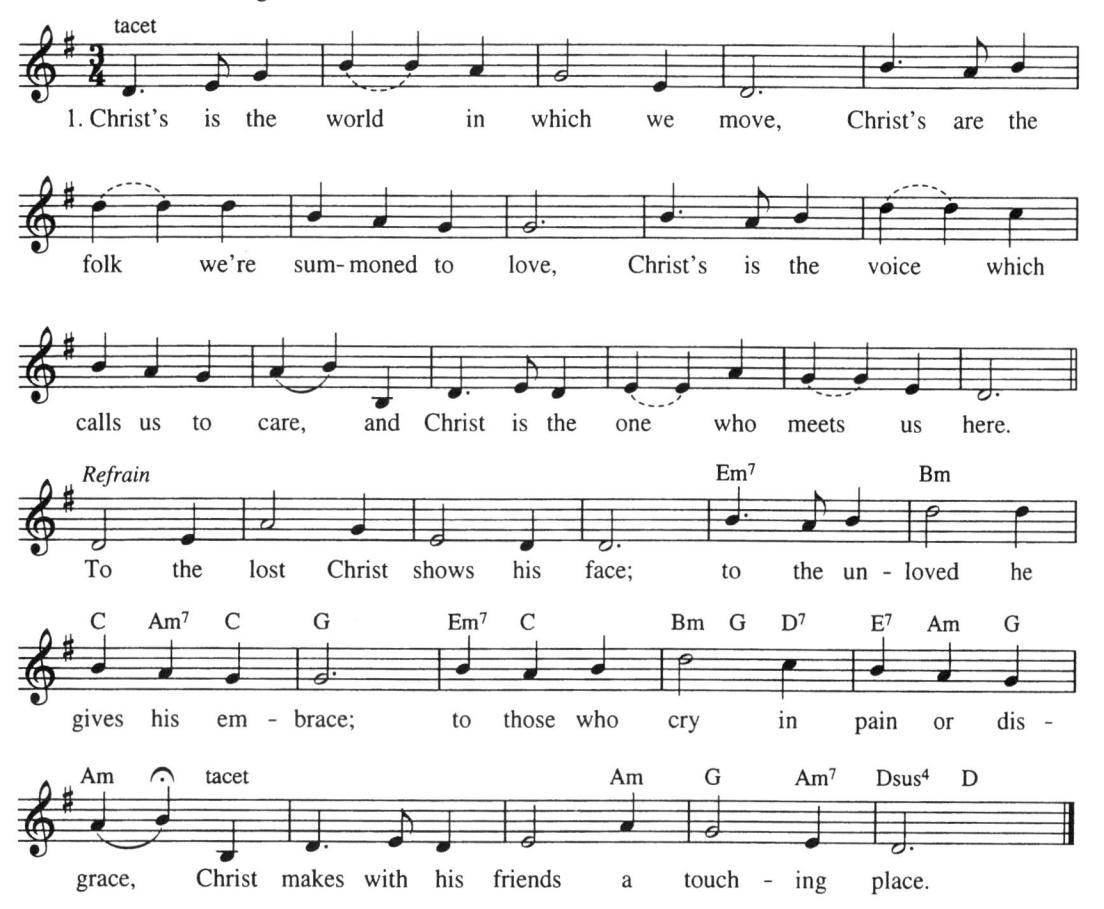

1. Christ's is the world in which we move,
Christ's are the folk we're summoned to love,
Christ's is the voice which calls us to care,
and Christ is the one who meets us here.

Refrain
To the lost Christ shows his face;
to the unloved he gives his embrace;
to those who cry in pain or disgrace,
Christ makes with his friends a touching place.

2. Feel for the people we most avoid,
strange or bereaved or never employed;
feel for the women, and feel for the men
who fear that their living is all in vain.

3. Feel for the parents who've lost their child,
feel for the women whom men have defiled,
feel for the baby for whom there's no breast,
and feel for the weary who find no rest.

4. Feel for the lives by life confused,
riddled with doubt, in loving abused;
feel for the lonely heart, conscious of sin,
which longs to be pure but fears to begin.

Text: John L. Bell (b.1949) and Graham Maule (b.1958)
Music: traditional Scottish
Text © 1989 WGRG, Iona Community, 840 Govan Road, Glasgow G51 3UU, Scotland.
Used by permission from the 'Love from Below' collection.

199 Christ the Lord is risen today

EASTER HYMN 77 77 D

1. Christ the Lord is ris'n to-day! Christians, haste your vows to pay,
of-fer ye your praises meet at the pas-chal victim's feet;
for the sheep the Lamb hath bled, sinless in the sinner's stead.
Christ the Lord is ris'n on high; now he lives, no more to die.

A higher setting will be found at No. 389

2. Christ, the victim undefiled,
God and sinners reconciled
when in strange and awful strife
met together death and life;
Christians, on this happy day,
haste with joy your vows to pay.
Christ the Lord is ris'n on high;
now he lives, no more to die.

3. Say, O wond'ring Mary, say,
what thou sawest on thy way.
'I beheld, where Christ had lain,
empty tomb and angels twain,
I beheld the glory bright
of the rising Lord of light;
Christ my hope is ris'n again;
now he lives, and lives to reign.'

4. Christ, who once for sinners bled,
now the first-born from the dead,
throned in endless might and power,
lives and reigns for evermore.
Hail, eternal hope on high!
Hail, thou King of victory!
Hail, thou Prince of life adored!
Help and save us, gracious Lord.

Text: 'Victimae Paschali Laudes' attributed to Wipo of Burgundy (11th century)
trans. Jane Elizabeth Leeson (1809-1881) alt.
Music: from 'Lyra Davidica' (1708)

200 Christ triumphant

GUITING POWER 85 85 and Refrain

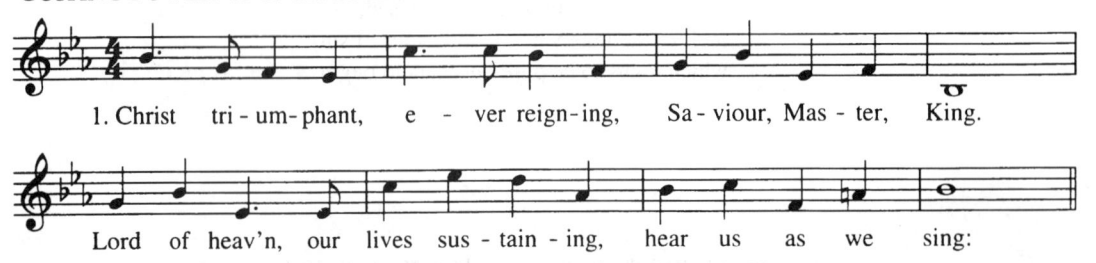

1. Christ triumphant, ever reigning, Saviour, Master, King.
Lord of heav'n, our lives sustaining, hear us as we sing:

Text © Copyright Michael Saward/Jubilate Hymns
Music © Copyright John Barnard/Jubilate Hymns, 4 Thorne Park Road, Chelston, Torquay, Devon TQ2 6RX, UK.
Used by permission.

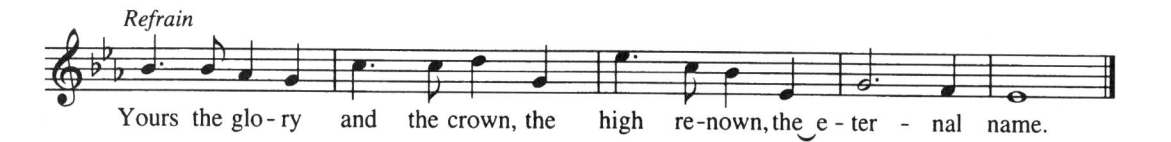

Yours the glo-ry and the crown, the high re-nown, the e-ter-nal name.

2. Word incarnate, truth revealing,
   Son of Man on earth!
   Pow'r and majesty concealing
   by your humble birth:

3. Suff'ring servant, scorned, ill-treated,
   victim crucified!
   Death is through the cross defeated,
   sinners justified:

4. Priestly King, enthroned for ever
   high in heav'n above!
   Sin and death and hell shall never
   stifle hymns of love:

5. So, our hearts and voices raising
   through the ages long,
   ceaselessly upon you gazing,
   this shall be our song:

Text: Michael Saward (b.1932)
Music: John Barnard (b.1948)

201 Christus vincit

Chri-stus vin-cit, Chri-stus re-gnat, Chri-stus im-pe-rat.

Psalm Tone for the verses

1. God has delivered us from the dominion of darkness
   and transferred us to the kingdom of his beloved Son:
   in Christ we gain our freedom,
   in him, the forgiveness of our sins.

2. Christ is the image of the unseen God,
   he is the first-born of all creation:
   in Christ, all things were created, in heaven and on earth,
   all things, visible and invisible.

3. In Christ, all things were created,
   through him and for him.
   Christ is, and was before all things,
   all things are held in unity by Christ.

4. The Church is the Body of Christ,
   he is its head:
   he is the beginning,
   the first-born from the dead.

5. In Christ all the fullness of God was pleased to dwell,
   and through Christ to reconcile all things to himself;
   to reconcile everything in heaven or on earth,
   making peace by the blood of the cross.

Text: Colossians 1:13-20 adapted by Robert B. Kelly (b.1948)
Music: Refrain – Plainsong
Psalm Tone – Gregory Murray (1905-1992)
© Copyright 1999 Kevin Mayhew Ltd.

202 Colours of day
Light up the fire

1. Col-ours of day dawn in-to the mind, the sun has come up, the night is be-hind. Go down in the ci-ty, in-to the street, and let's give the mes-sage to the peo-ple we meet.

Refrain
So light up the fire and let the flame burn, o-pen the door, let Je-sus re-turn, take seeds of his Spi-rit, let the fruit grow, tell the peo-ple of Je-sus, let his love show.

2. Go through the park, on into the town;
the sun still shines on; it never goes down.
The light of the world is risen again;
the people of darkness are needing our friend.

3. Open your eyes, look into the sky,
the darkness has come, the sun came to die.
The evening draws on, the sun disappears,
but Jesus is living, and his Spirit is near.

Text and Music: Sue McClellan (b.1951), John Paculabo (b.1946) and Keith Ryecroft (b.1949)
© Copyright 1974 Kingsway's Thankyou Music, P.O. Box 75, Eastbourne, East Sussex BN23 6NW.
Used by permission.

203 Come and be filled

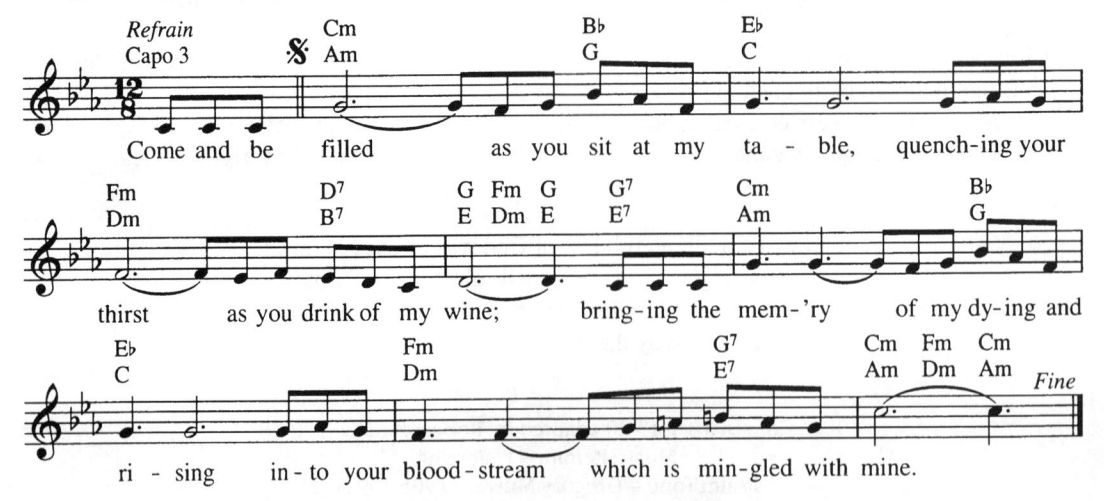

Refrain
Capo 3

Come and be filled as you sit at my ta-ble, quench-ing your thirst as you drink of my wine; bring-ing the mem-'ry of my dy-ing and ri-sing in-to your blood-stream which is min-gled with mine.

Fine

© Copyright 1984 Kevin Mayhew Ltd.

1. This is the bread that has come down from heaven. This is my blood for the life of the world. Come and be

2. He leads us out of the power of darkness
and brings us safe to his kingdom of life.

3. No longer I, but now Christ lives within me.
I live by faith in the Son of God.

4. For those in Christ there is no condemnation.
He sets them free through the Spirit he sends.

5. Thus shall the world know you are my disciples,
if you can love, and if you can forgive.

Text: Aniceto Nazareth based on Scripture
Music: Aniceto Nazareth

204 Come and be light for our eyes

Come and be light for our eyes; be the air we breathe, be the voice we speak! Come, be the song we sing, be the path we seek!

1. Your life was given; food for all people, body and blood new life in our midst! Death is no longer, life is our future, Jesus, Messiah; name of all names!

2. We hold your presence;
risen for ever!
Your Name now names us people of God!
Filled with your vision, people of mission,
healing, forgiving;
light for the world!

3. Lead us to justice,
light in the darkness;
singing, proclaiming Jesus is Lord!
Teach us to speak, and help us to listen
for when your truth
and our dreams embrace!

Text and Music: David Haas (b.1957)
© Copyright 1985 GIA Publications Inc., 7404 S. Mason Avenue, Chicago, Illinois 60638, USA.
All rights reserved. Used by permission.

205 Come and go with me

1. Come and go with me to my Father's house, to my Father's house, to my Father's house. Come and go with me to my Father's house where there's joy, joy, joy.

2. It's not very far to my Father's house,
   to my Father's house, to my Father's house.
   It's not very far to my Father's house
   where there's joy, joy, joy.

3. There is room for all in my Father's house,
   in my Father's house, in my Father's house.
   There is room for all in my Father's house
   where there's joy, joy, joy.

4. Ev'rything is free in my Father's house,
   in my Father's house, in my Father's house.
   Ev'rything is free in my Father's house
   where there's joy, joy, joy.

5. Jesus is the way to my Father's house,
   to my Father's house, to my Father's house.
   Jesus is the way to my Father's house
   where there's joy, joy, joy.

6. Jesus is the light in my Father's house,
   in my Father's house, in my Father's house.
   Jesus is the light in my Father's house
   where there's joy, joy, joy.

Other verses may be added spontaneously, such as:

We will clap our hands...
There is liberty...
We will praise the Lord...

Text: v.1 unknown; vs. 2 - 6 and additional verses, Damian Lundy (1944-1997)
Music: unknown
Additional words © Copyright 1994 Kevin Mayhew Ltd.

206 Come and praise him

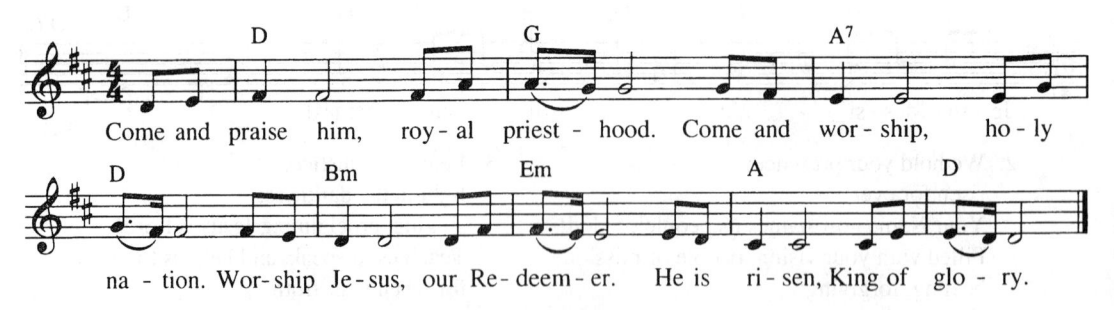

Come and praise him, royal priesthood. Come and worship, holy nation. Worship Jesus, our Redeemer. He is risen, King of glory.

Text and Music: Andy Carter (b.1951)
© Copyright 1977 Kingsway's Thankyou Music, P.O. Box 75, Eastbourne, East Sussex BN23 6NW, UK.
Used by permission.

207 Come back to me

1. Come back to me with all your heart, don't let fear keep us a-part. Trees do bend, though straight and tall; so must we to o-thers' call.

(2.) wild-er-ness will lead you to your heart where I will speak. In-te-gri-ty and jus-tice with ten-der-ness you shall know

Refrain
Long have I wait-ed for your com-ing home to me and liv-ing deep-ly our new life.

2. The life.

3. You shall sleep se-cure with peace; faith-ful-ness will be your joy.

Final Refrain
Long have I wait-ed for your com-ing home to me and liv-ing deep-ly our new life. *Fine*

Text: Gregory Norbert based on Hosea
Music: Gregory Norbert

© Copyright 1972 The Benedictine Foundation of the State of Vermont, Inc., Weston Priory, Weston, Vermont 05161, USA. Used by permission from the recording 'Listen'.

208 Come, come, come to the manger

COME TO THE MANGER Irregular

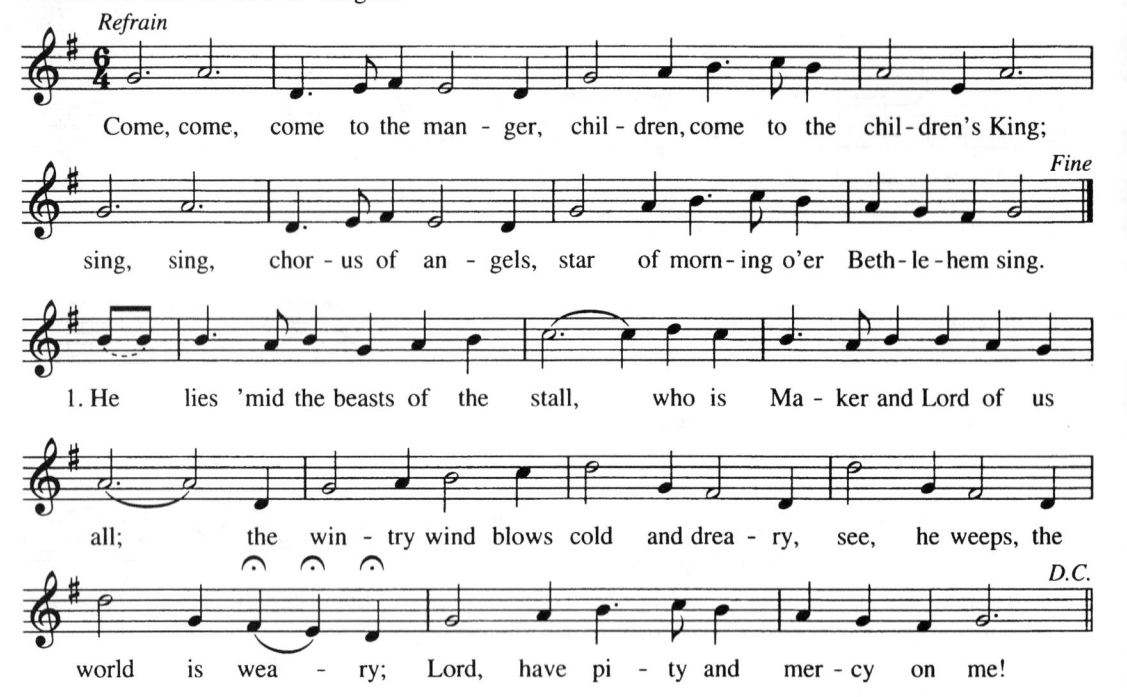

Refrain

Come, come, come to the manger, children, come to the children's King;
sing, sing, chorus of angels, star of morning o'er Bethlehem sing. *Fine*

1. He lies 'mid the beasts of the stall, who is Maker and Lord of us all; the wintry wind blows cold and dreary, see, he weeps, the world is weary; Lord, have pity and mercy on me! *D.C.*

2. He leaves all his glory behind,
to be Saviour of all humankind,
with grateful beasts his cradle chooses,
thankless world his love refuses;
Lord, have pity and mercy on me!

3. To the manger of Bethlehem come,
to the Saviour Emmanuel's home;
the heav'nly hosts above are singing,
set the Christmas bells a-ringing;
Lord, have pity and mercy on me!

Text: unknown, alt.
Music: traditional melody adapted by S. P. Waddington

209 Come down, O Love divine

DOWN AMPNEY 66 11 D

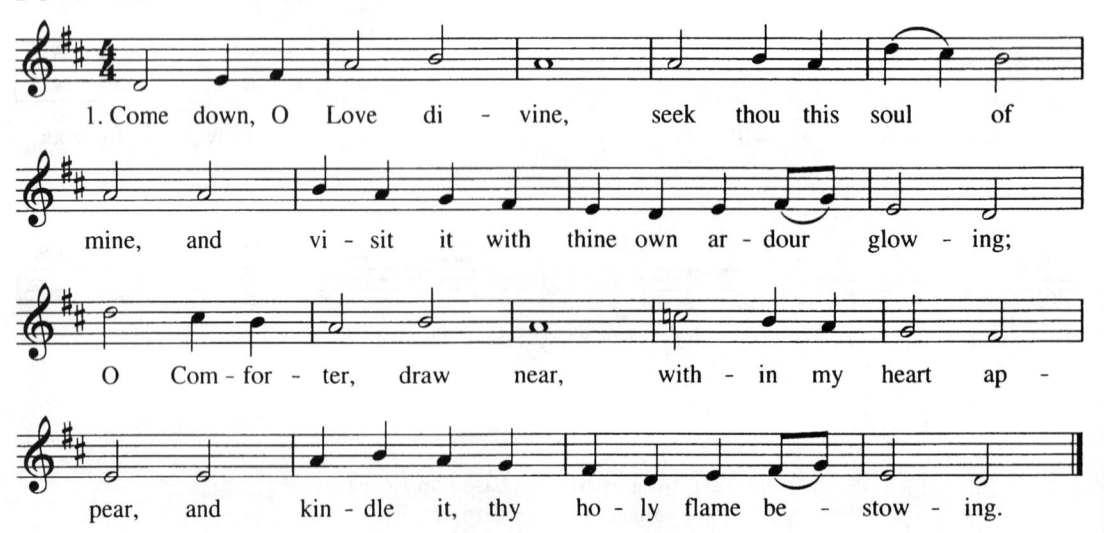

1. Come down, O Love divine, seek thou this soul of mine, and visit it with thine own ardour glowing; O Comforter, draw near, within my heart appear, and kindle it, thy holy flame bestowing.

Music © Copyright Oxford University Press, Great Clarendon Street, Oxford OX2 6DP.
Used by permission from the 'English Hymnal.'

2. O let it freely burn,
   till earthly passions turn
   to dust and ashes in its heat consuming;
   and let thy glorious light
   shine ever on my sight,
   and clothe me round,
   the while my path illuming.

3. Let holy charity
   mine outward vesture be,
   and lowliness become mine inner clothing;
   true lowliness of heart,
   which takes the humbler part,
   and o'er its own shortcomings
   weeps with loathing.

4. And so the yearning strong,
   with which the soul will long,
   shall far outpass the pow'r of human telling;
   nor can we guess its grace,
   till we become the place
   wherein the Holy Spirit makes his dwelling.

Text: 'Discendi, amor santo' by Bianco da Siena (d.1434) trans. Richard F. Littledale (1833-1890) alt.
Music: Ralph Vaughan Williams (1872-1958)

210 Come, Holy Ghost, Creator, come

TALLIS'S ORDINAL CM

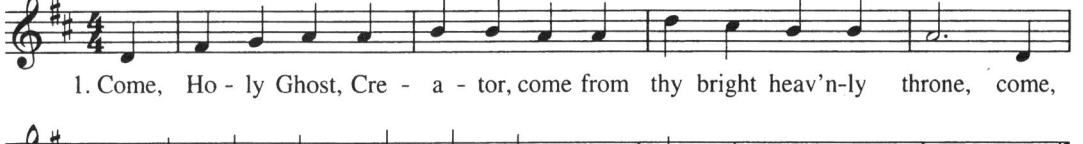

1. Come, Holy Ghost, Creator, come from thy bright heav'nly throne, come, take possession of our souls, and make them all thine own.

2. Thou who art called the Paraclete,
   best gift of God above,
   the living spring, the living fire,
   sweet unction and true love.

3. Thou who art sev'nfold in thy grace,
   finger of God's right hand;
   his promise, teaching little ones
   to speak and understand.

4. O guide our minds with thy blest light,
   with love our hearts inflame;
   and with thy strength, which ne'er decays,
   confirm our mortal frame.

5. Far from us drive our deadly foe;
   true peace unto us bring;
   and through all perils lead us safe
   beneath thy sacred wing.

6. Through thee may we the Father know,
   through thee th'eternal Son,
   and thee the Spirit of them both,
   thrice-blessèd Three in One.

7. All glory to the Father be,
   with his co-equal Son:
   the same to thee, great Paraclete,
   while endless ages run.

Text: 'Veni, Creator Spiritus', ascribed to Rabanus Maurus (776-856) trans. unknown
Music: Thomas Tallis (c.1505-1585)

211 Come, Holy Spirit, come

DONNYBROOK DSM

1. Come, Holy Spirit, come! Inflame our souls with love, transforming ev'ry heart and home with wisdom from above. O let us not despise the humble path Christ trod, but choose, to shame the worldly-wise, the foolishness of God.

2. All-knowing Spirit, prove
the poverty of pride,
by knowledge of the Father's love
in Jesus crucified.
And grant us faith to know
the glory of that sign,
and in our very lives to show
the marks of love divine.

3. Come with the gift to heal
the wounds of guilt and fear,
and to oppression's face reveal
the kingdom drawing near.
Where chaos longs to reign,
descend, O holy Dove,
and free us all to work again
the miracles of love.

4. Spirit of truth, arise;
inspire the prophet's voice:
expose to scorn the tyrant's lies,
and bid the poor rejoice.
O Spirit, clear our sight,
all prejudice remove,
and help us to discern the right,
and covet only love.

5. Give us the tongues to speak,
in ev'ry time and place,
to rich and poor, to strong and weak,
the word of love and grace.
Enable us to hear
the words that others bring,
interpreting with open ear
the special song they sing.

6. Come, Holy Spirit, dance
within our hearts today,
our earthbound spirits to entrance,
our mortal fears allay.
And teach us to desire,
all other things above,
that self-consuming holy fire,
the perfect gift of love!

Text: Michael Forster (b.1946)
Music: Colin Mawby (b.1936)
© Copyright 1992 Kevin Mayhew Ltd.

212 Come, let us raise a joyful song

Refrain

Come, let us raise a joyful song to the Lord, a shout of triumph!
Come, let us raise a joyful song to the Lord, and give him thanks!

1. The furthest places on the earth are in his hands.
   He made them, and we sing his praise.

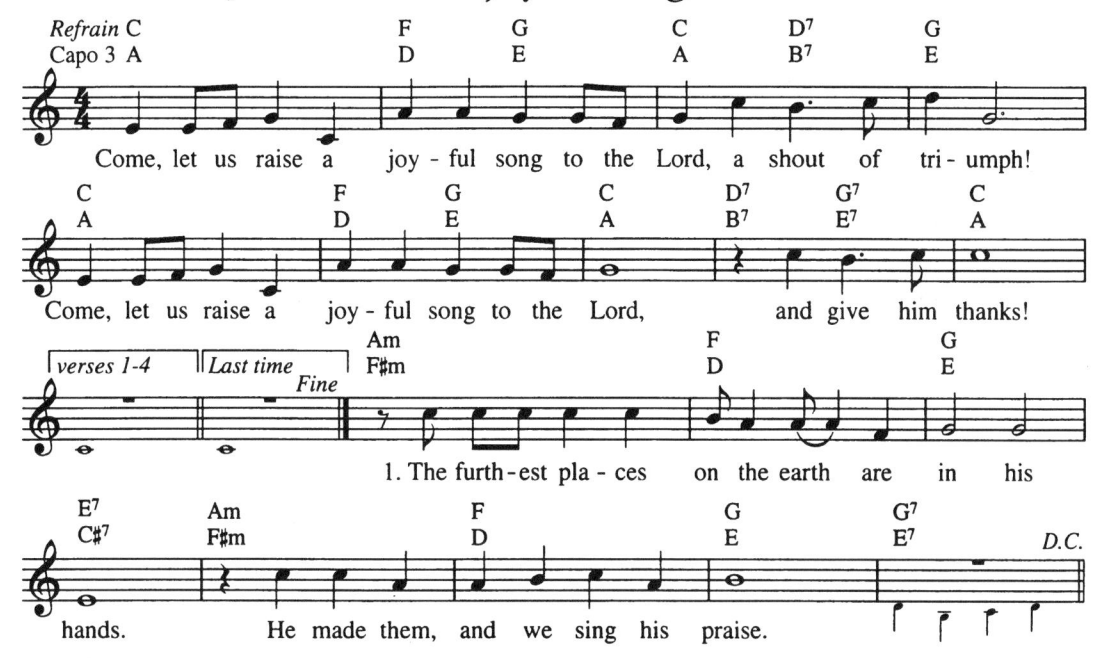

2. The seas and waters on the earth
   are in his hands.
   He made them, and we sing his praise.

3. The hills and valleys on the earth
   are in his hands.
   He made them, and we sing his praise.

4. All living creatures on the earth
   are in his hands.
   He made them, and we sing his praise.

5. And we his people on the earth
   are in his hands.
   He saved us, and we sing his praise.

Text and Music: Mike Anderson (b.1956) based on Psalm 95
Music: Mike Anderson (b.1956)
© Copyright 1982 Kevin Mayhew Ltd.

213 Come, Lord Jesus
Advent song

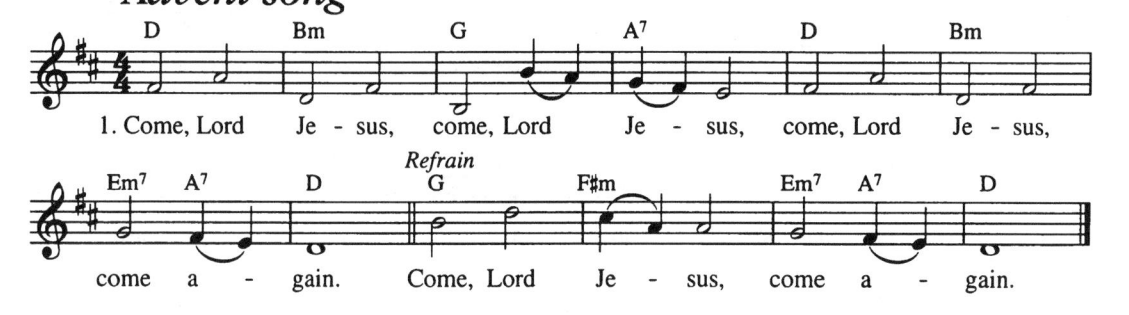

1. Come, Lord Jesus, come, Lord Jesus, come, Lord Jesus, come again.

Refrain
Come, Lord Jesus, come again.

2. Born of Mary, *(x3)*
   come again.

3. Slain to save us, *(x3)*
   come again.

4. Raised to new life, *(x3)*
   come again.

5. At God's right hand, *(x3)*
   come again.

6. Send your Spirit, *(x3)*
   come again.

7. Come in glory, *(x3)*
   come again.

Text and Music: Damian Lundy (1944-1997)
© Copyright 1986 Kevin Mayhew Ltd.

214 Come, Lord Jesus, come

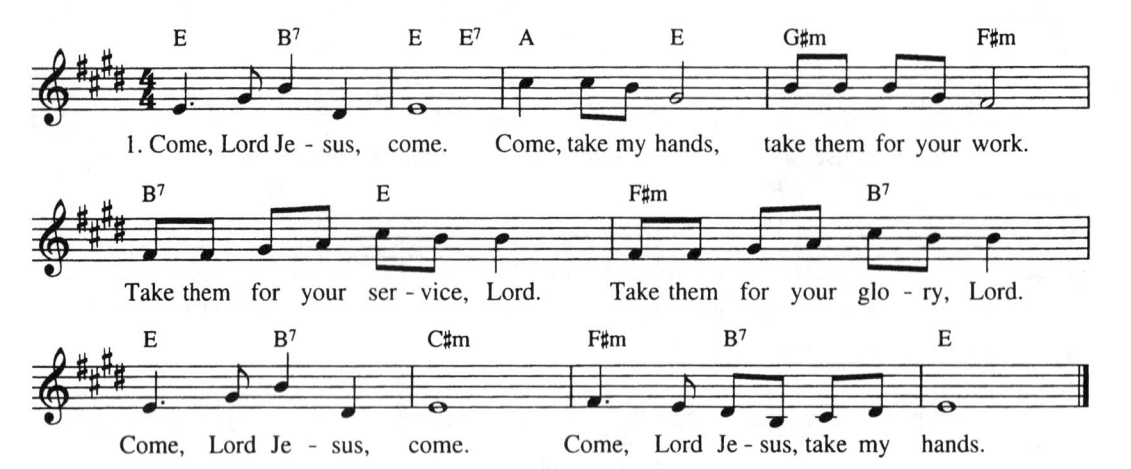

1. Come, Lord Jesus, come. Come, take my hands, take them for your work.
Take them for your ser-vice, Lord. Take them for your glo-ry, Lord.
Come, Lord Je-sus, come. Come, Lord Je-sus, take my hands.

2. Come, Lord Jesus, come.
Come, take my eyes,
may they shine with joy.
Take them for your service, Lord.
Take them for your glory, Lord.
Come, Lord Jesus, come.
Come, Lord Jesus, take my eyes.

3. Come, Lord Jesus, come.
Come, take my lips,
may they speak your truth.
Take them for your service, Lord.
Take them for your glory, Lord.
Come, Lord Jesus, come.
Come, Lord Jesus, take my lips.

4. Come, Lord Jesus, come.
Come, take my feet,
may they walk your path.
Take them for your service, Lord.
Take them for your glory, Lord.
Come, Lord Jesus, come.
Come, Lord Jesus, take my feet.

5. Come, Lord Jesus, come.
Come, take my heart,
fill it with your love.
Take it for your service, Lord.
Take it for your glory, Lord.
Come, Lord Jesus, come.
Come, Lord Jesus, take my heart.

6. Come, Lord Jesus, come.
Come, take my life,
take it for your own.
Take it for your service, Lord.
Take it for your glory, Lord.
Come, Lord Jesus, come.
Come, Lord Jesus, take my life.

A lower setting

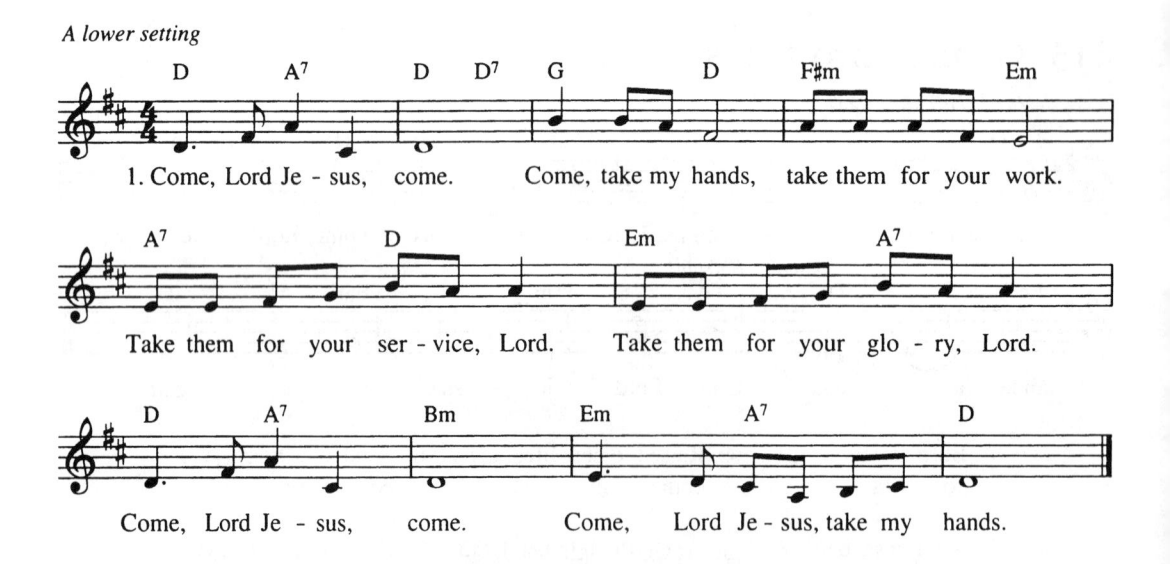

1. Come, Lord Je-sus, come. Come, take my hands, take them for your work.
Take them for your ser-vice, Lord. Take them for your glo-ry, Lord.
Come, Lord Je-sus, come. Come, Lord Je-sus, take my hands.

Text and Music: Kevin Mayhew (b.1942)
© Copyright 1974, 1976 Kevin Mayhew Ltd.

215 Come, my Way, my Truth, my Life

THE CALL 77 77

1. Come, my Way, my Truth, my Life: such a way as gives us breath; such a truth as ends all strife; such a life as killeth death.

2. Come, my Light, my Feast, my Strength:
such a light as shows a feast;
such a feast as mends in length;
such a strength as makes his guest.

3. Come, my Joy, my Love, my Heart:
such a joy as none can move;
such a love as none can part;
such a heart as joys in love.

Text: George Herbert (1593-1633)
Music: Ralph Vaughan Williams (1872-1958), adapted by E.H. Green
Music: © Copyright 1911 Stainer & Bell Ltd, P.O. Box 110, Victoria House, 23 Gruneisen Road, Finchley, London N3 1DZ. Used by permission.

216 Come, O divine Messiah!

VENEZ, DIVIN MESSIE 78 76 and Refrain

1. Come, O divine Messiah! The world in silence waits the day when hope shall sing its triumph, and sadness flee away. *Refrain* Sweet Saviour, haste: come, come to earth: dispel the night, and show thy face, and bid us hail the dawn of grace. Come, O divine Messiah! The world in silence waits the day when hope shall sing its triumph, and sadness flee away.

2. O thou, whom nations sighed for,
whom priests and prophets long foretold,
wilt break the captive fetters,
redeem the long-lost fold.

3. Shalt come in peace and meekness,
and lowly will thy cradle be:
all clothed in human weakness
shall we thy Godhead see.

Text: Sister Mary of St. Philip
Music: French traditional carol

217 Come, O God of all the earth
Sing out, earth and skies

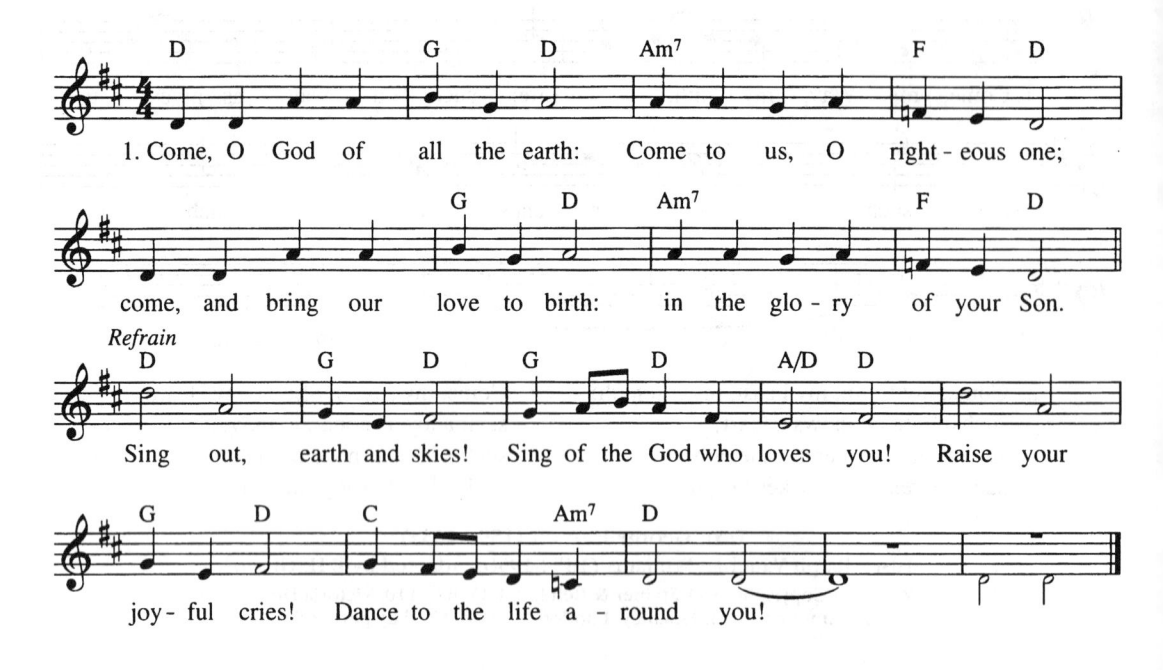

1. Come, O God of all the earth: Come to us, O righteous one;
come, and bring our love to birth: in the glory of your Son.

Refrain
Sing out, earth and skies! Sing of the God who loves you! Raise your joyful cries! Dance to the life around you!

2. Come, O God of wind and flame:
fill the earth with righteousness;
teach us all to sing your name:
may our lives your love confess.

3. Come, O God of flashing light:
twinkling star and burning sun;
God of day and God of night:
in your light we all are one.

4. Come, O God of snow and rain:
shower down upon the earth;
come, O God of joy and pain:
God of sorrow, God of mirth.

5. Come, O justice, come, O peace:
come and shape our hearts anew;
come and make oppression cease:
bring us all to life to you.

Text and Music: Marty Haugen (b.1950)
Copyright © 1985 GIA Publications, Inc., 7404 S. Mason Avenue, Chicago, Illinois 60638, USA. Used by permission. All rights reserved.

218 Come, O long-expected Jesus

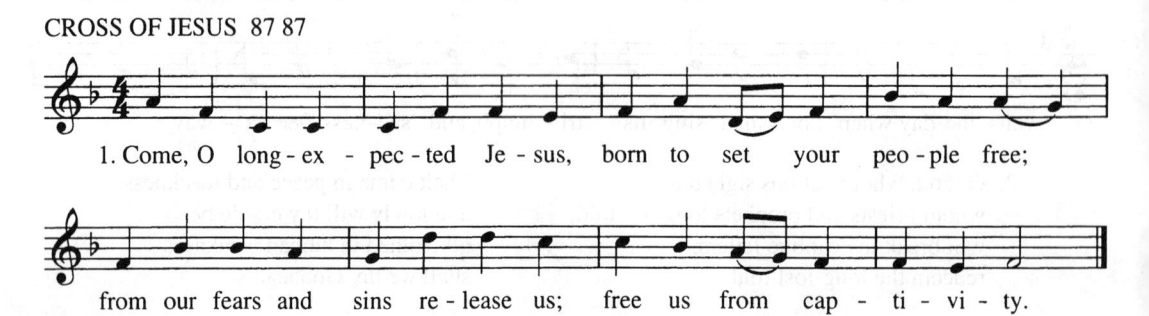

CROSS OF JESUS 87 87

1. Come, O long-expected Jesus, born to set your people free;
from our fears and sins release us; free us from captivity.

2. Israel's strength and consolation,
   you the hope of all the earth,
   dear desire of ev'ry nation,
   come, and save us by your birth!

3. Born your people to deliver;
   born a child and yet a King!
   Born to reign in us for ever,
   now your gracious kingdom bring.

4. By your own eternal Spirit
   rule in all our hearts alone;
   by your all-sufficient merit
   raise us to your glorious throne.

Text: Charles Wesley (1701-1788) based on Haggai 2:7, alt. the editors.
Music: John Stainer (1840-1901)

219 Come on and celebrate

Very lively

Come on and celebrate his gift of love, we will celebrate
the Son of God who loved us and gave us life.
We'll shout your praise, O King, you give us joy nothing else can bring;
we'll give to you our offering in celebration praise. Come on and
celebrate, celebrate, celebrate and sing, celebrate and

To repeat: sing to the King!
Last time: Come on and sing to the King!

Words and Music: Patricia Morgan and Dave Bankhead
© Copyright 1984 Kingsway's Thankyou Music, P.O. Box 75, Eastbourne,
East Sussex, BN23 6NW, UK. Used by permission.

220 Come, praise the Lord

LOBE DEN HERREN 14 14 4 7 8

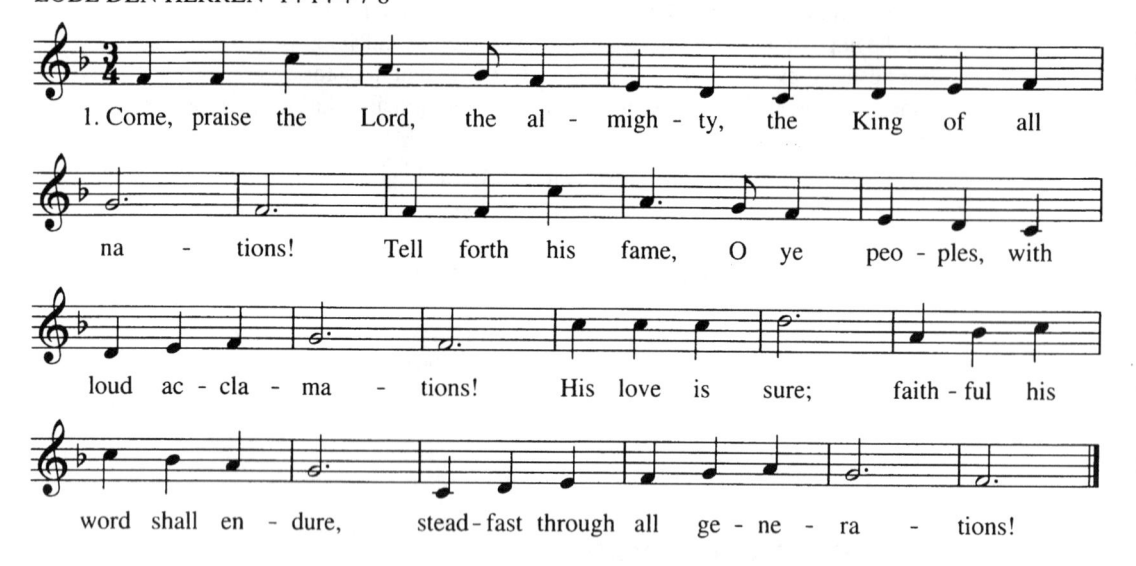

1. Come, praise the Lord, the almighty, the King of all nations! Tell forth his fame, O ye peoples, with loud acclamations! His love is sure; faithful his word shall endure, steadfast through all generations!

2. Praise to the Father most gracious,
the Lord of creation!
Praise to his Son, the Redeemer,
who wrought our salvation!
O heav'nly Dove,
praise to thee, fruit of their love,
giver of all consolation!

Text: Psalm 116 versified by James Quinn (b.1919)
Music: melody from 'Praxis Pietatis Melica' (1668)
Text © Copyright 1969 Geoffrey Chapman, an imprint of Cassell plc, Wellington House, 125 Strand, London WC2R 0BB. Used by permission.

221 Come, prepare the way
Song of the Advent Prophets

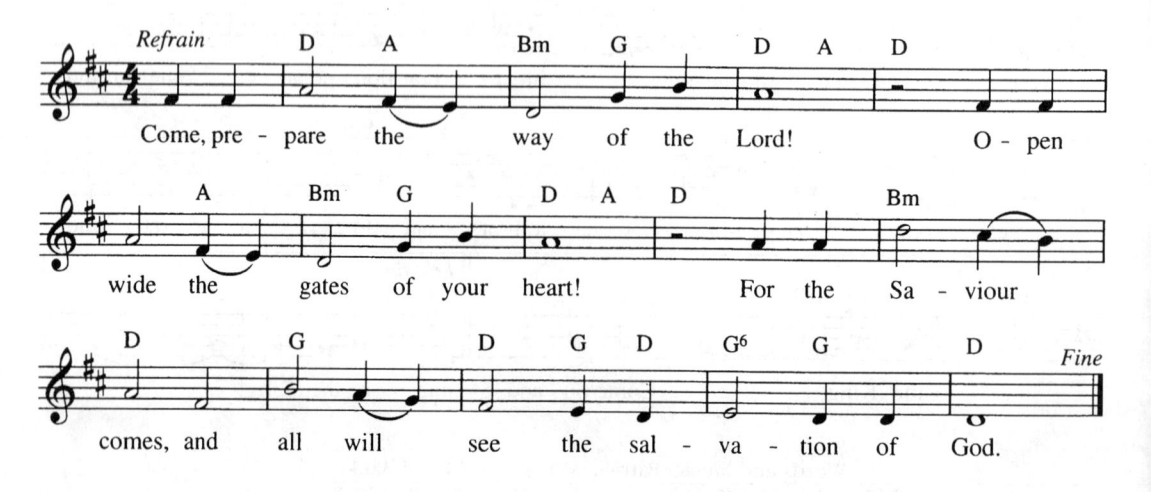

Refrain
Come, prepare the way of the Lord! Open wide the gates of your heart! For the Saviour comes, and all will see the salvation of God.

© Copyright 1999 Kevin Mayhew Ltd.

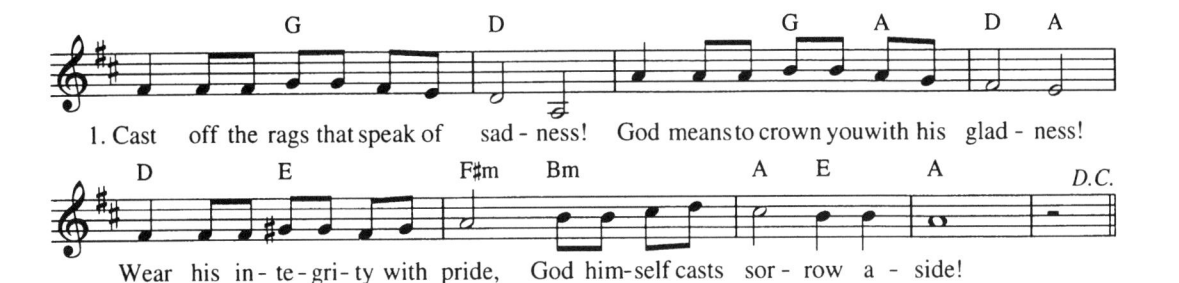

1. Cast off the rags that speak of sadness!
God means to crown you with his gladness!
Wear his integrity with pride,
God himself casts sorrow aside!

2. Tell the faint-hearted, tell the fearful,
no need to worry, God will save you!
God comes, salvation in his hand,
leads you to the new Promised Land!

3. See them laid low, the hills and mountains.
Valleys are filled, becoming great plains.
We are no longer left to roam,
God himself will shepherd us home.

4. Those who were blind now see God's glory,
those who were deaf now hear God's story.
Those who were hungry eat their fill,
those once lame now cannot keep still!

5. Fresh water irrigates the dry land,
flowers now grow in what was dead sand.
Earth now lies ready for the grain,
earth is ripe for planting the vine!

Text: Joseph Gelineau (b.1920) and Robert B. Kelly (b.1948) based on Isaiah 35 and 40 and Baruch 5
Music: Joseph Gelineau (b.1920)

222 Come to me

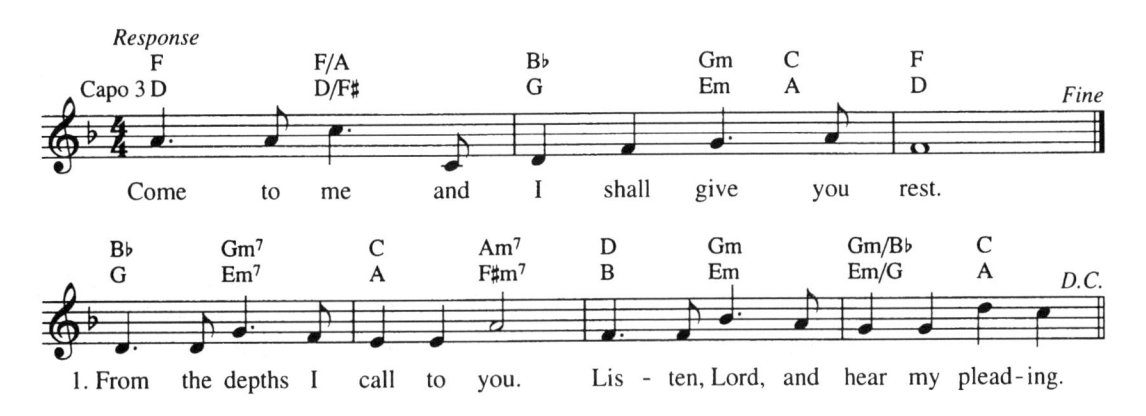

Response

Come to me and I shall give you rest.

1. From the depths I call to you.
Listen, Lord, and hear my pleading.

2. Love and mercy flow from you,
Lord of life and kind Redeemer.

3. In the dark I hope for you,
you are light of new day dawning.

4. Weak and frail we come to you,
God of love and new beginning.

Text: Noel Donnelly (b.1932) based on Psalm 129
Music: Noel Donnelly (b.1932)
© Copyright Noel S. Donnelly. Used by permission.

223 Come to me, all who labour

Come to me, all who labour and are heavy burdened, and I shall give you rest. Take up my yoke and learn from me, for I am meek and humble of heart. And you'll find rest for your souls. Yes, my yoke is easy and my burden is light. The Lord is my shepherd, I shall never be in need. Fresh and green are the meadows where he gives me rest. Come to

Text: Gregory Norbert based on Psalm 22 and Matthew 11:8-30
Music: Gregory Norbert

© Copyright 1971 The Benedictine Foundation of the State of Vermont, Inc., Weston Priory, Weston, Vermont 05161, USA.
Used by permission from the recording 'Locusts and Wild Honey'.

224 Come to me, come, my people
Be humble of heart

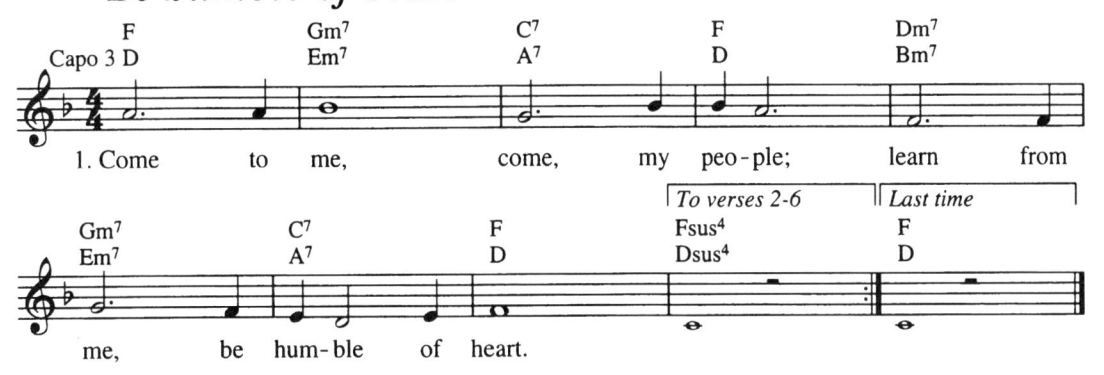

1. Come to me, come, my people; learn from me, be humble of heart.

2. I your Lord, I your master;
   learn from me, be humble of heart.

3. Follow me to my Father;
   learn from me, be humble of heart.

4. In my death, in my rising;
   learn from me, be humble of heart.

5. Be transformed by my Spirit;
   learn from me, be humble of heart.

6. Glory be to my Father;
   learn from me, be humble of heart.

Text and Music: Gerard Markland (b.1953)
© Copyright 1998 Kevin Mayhew Ltd.

225 Come to the table of the Lord

Refrain
Come to the table of the Lord, sinners by faith and grace restored; taste here what earth cannot afford, alleluia!

1. How I rejoiced when Jesus said,
   'Come to my table, share my bread, where souls and bodies both are fed.'

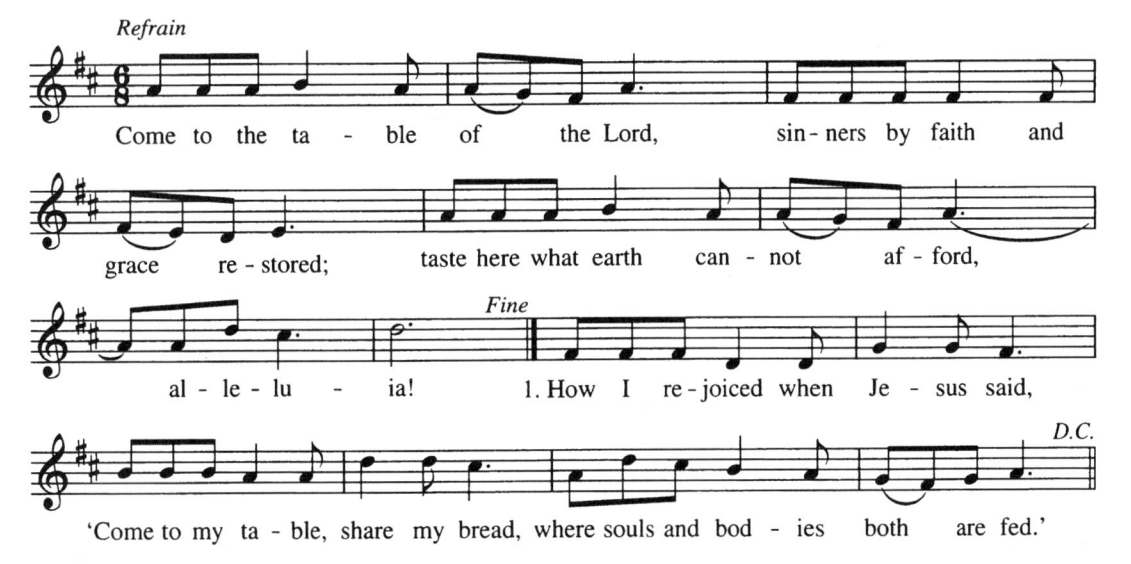

2. 'This is my body, giv'n to be
   broken for you eternally:
   do this when you remember me.'

3. This is my lifeblood, flowing free,
   shed for the world eternally:
   do this when you remember me.'

Text: Michael Forster (b.1946)
Music: Refrain – G.P. da Palestrina (c.1525-1594)
Verses – Jean Paul Lécot (b.1947)
Text © Copyright 1999 Kevin Mayhew Ltd.
Music (verse) © Copyright Jean-Paul Lécot, 'Espélugues', 1 Ave Mgr. Théas, 65100 Lourdes, France. Used by permission.

226 Come, ye thankful people, come

SAINT GEORGE'S WINDSOR 77 77 D

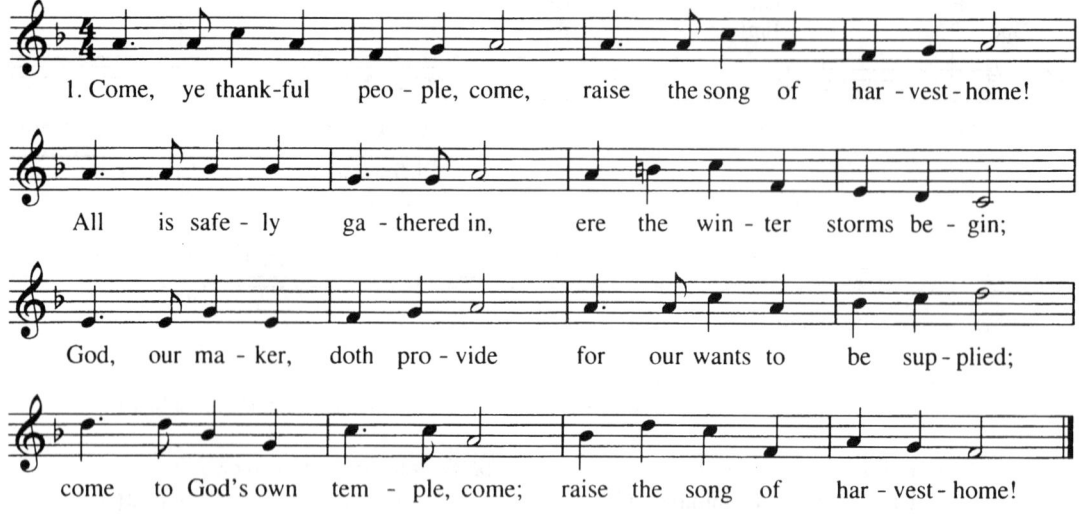

1. Come, ye thankful people, come, raise the song of harvest-home!
All is safely gathered in, ere the winter storms begin;
God, our maker, doth provide for our wants to be supplied;
come to God's own temple, come; raise the song of harvest-home!

2. We ourselves are God's own field,
fruit unto his praise to yield;
wheat and tares together sown,
unto joy or sorrow grown;
first the blade and then the ear,
then the full corn shall appear:
grant, O harvest Lord, that we
wholesome grain and pure may be.

3. For the Lord our God shall come,
and shall take his harvest home,
from his field shall purge away
all that doth offend, that day;
give his angels charge at last
in the fire the tares to cast,
but the fruitful ears to store
in his garner evermore.

4. Then, thou Church triumphant, come,
raise the song of harvest-home;
all be safely gathered in,
free from sorrow, free from sin,
there for ever purified
in God's garner to abide:
come, ten thousand angels, come,
raise the glorious harvest-home!

Text: Henry Alford (1810-1871) alt.
Music: George Job Elvey (1816-1893)

227 Comfort, comfort my people

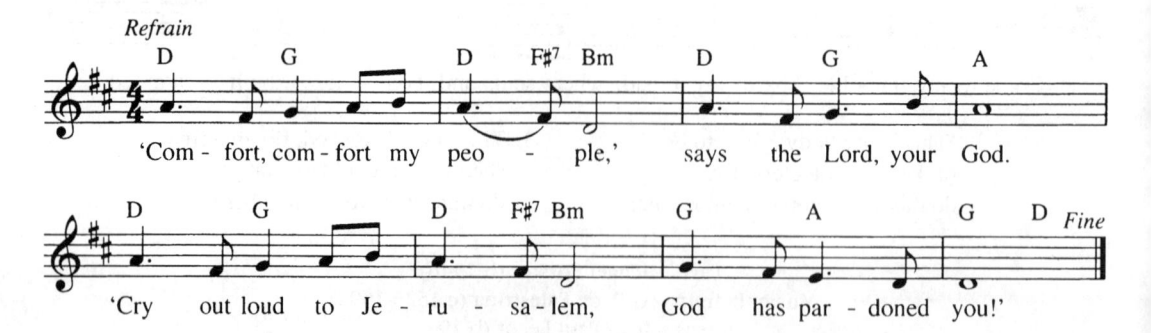

Refrain

'Comfort, comfort my people,' says the Lord, your God.
'Cry out loud to Jerusalem, God has pardoned you!' *Fine*

© Copyright 1984 Kevin Mayhew Ltd.

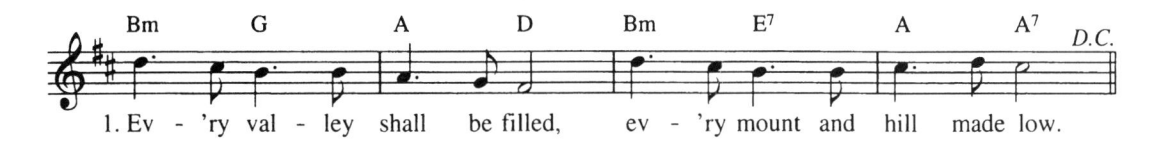

1. Ev-'ry val-ley shall be filled, ev-'ry mount and hill made low.

2. In the desert make a path
   for the Lord Emmanuel.

3. For the glory of the Lord
   soon shall be revealed to me.

Text: Anthony D'Souza (b.1950) based on Isaiah 40
Music: Anthony D'Souza (b.1950)

228 Creator of the day

GLORIA CHRISTI 88 88 and Refrain

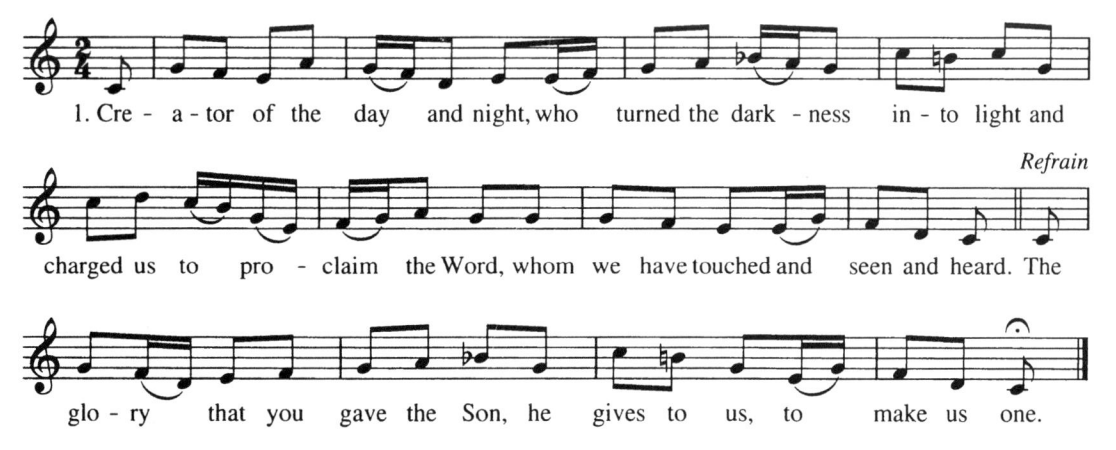

1. Cre-a-tor of the day and night, who turned the darkness in-to light and charged us to pro-claim the Word, whom we have touched and seen and heard. The glo-ry that you gave the Son, he gives to us, to make us one.

2. Your kingdom in a mystery,
   began with twelve in Galilee,
   through whom the Son would teach and cure;
   whose fruit would ripen and endure.

3. At Pentecost, with wind and flame,
   you sent the Spirit in his name,
   to make the Church a present Christ;
   anointed Prophet, King and Priest.

4. And when your purpose is complete,
   the Son of Man will take his seat;
   and Christ will be identified
   with these, the least, for whom he died.

Text: Michael Hodgetts (b.1936)
Music: Seóirse Bodley
Text © Copyright Michael Hodgetts. Used by permission.
Music © Copyright Seóirse Bodley. Used by permission.

LITURGICAL
HYMNS OLD & NEW

229 Crown him with many crowns

TUNE 1: CORONA DSM

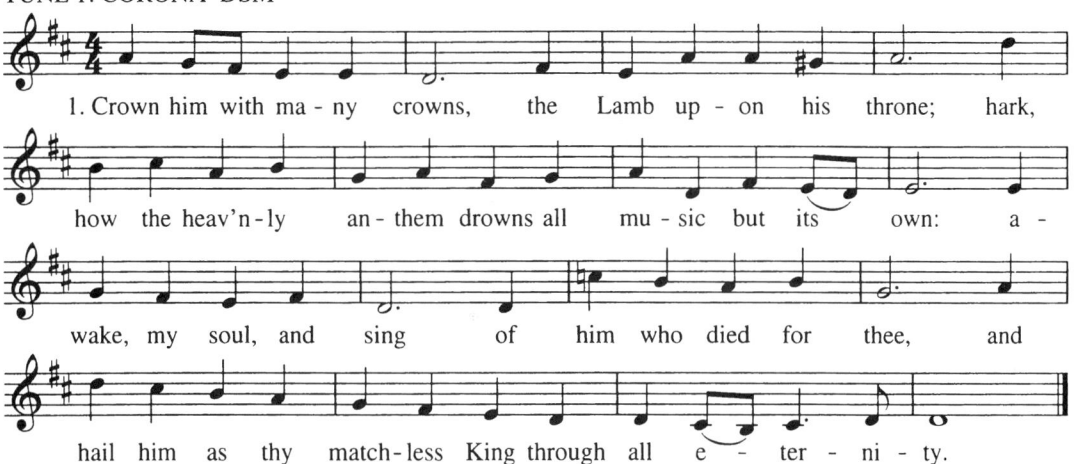

1. Crown him with many crowns, the Lamb upon his throne; hark, how the heav'nly anthem drowns all music but its own: awake, my soul, and sing of him who died for thee, and hail him as thy matchless King through all eternity.

2. Crown him the Virgin's Son,
the God incarnate born,
whose arm those crimson trophies won
which now his brow adorn;
fruit of the mystic Rose,
as of that Rose the Stem,
the Root, whence mercy ever flows,
the Babe of Bethlehem.

3. Crown him the Lord of love;
behold his hands and side,
rich wounds, yet visible above,
in beauty glorified:
no angel in the sky
can fully bear that sight,
but downward bends each burning eye
at mysteries so bright.

4. Crown him the Lord of peace,
whose pow'r a sceptre sways
from pole to pole, that wars may cease,
absorbed in prayer and praise:
his reign shall know no end,
and round his piercèd feet
fair flow'rs of paradise extend
their fragrance ever sweet.

5. Crown him the Lord of years,
the Potentate of time,
Creator of the rolling spheres,
ineffably sublime.
All hail, Redeemer, hail!
for thou hast died for me;
thy praise shall never, never fail
throughout eternity.

TUNE 2: DIADEMATA DSM

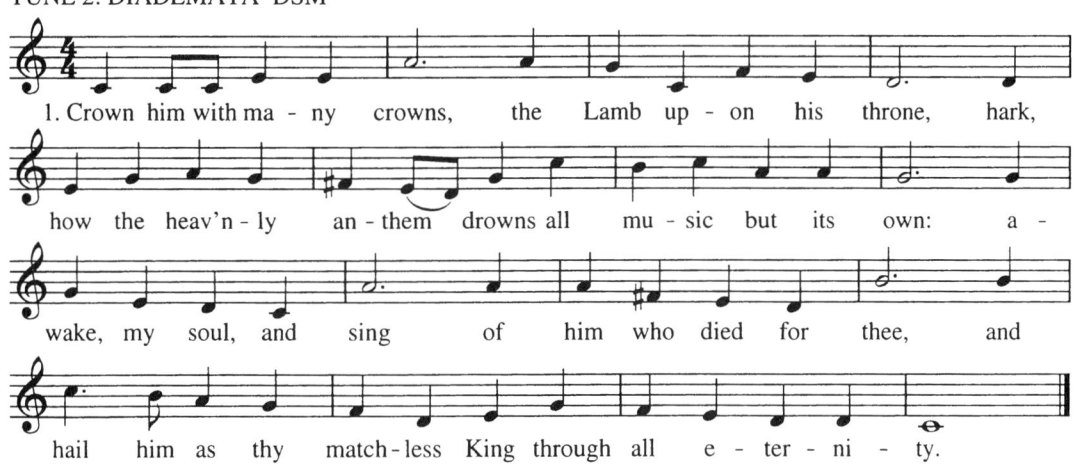

1. Crown him with many crowns, the Lamb upon his throne, hark, how the heav'nly anthem drowns all music but its own: awake, my soul, and sing of him who died for thee, and hail him as thy matchless King through all eternity.

A higher setting will be found at No. 292

Text: Matthew Bridges (1800-1894)
Music: Tune 1 – Richard Runciman Terry (1865-1938)
Tune 2 – George Job Elvey (1816-1893)
Tune 1 © Copyright control

230 Daily, daily, sing to Mary

TUNE 1: DAILY, DAILY 87 87 D

1. Daily, daily, sing to Mary,
sing, my soul, her praises due;
all her feasts, her actions worship,
with her heart's devotion true.
Lost in wond'ring contemplation
be her majesty confessed:
call her mother, call her virgin,
happy mother, virgin blest.

2. She is mighty to deliver;
call her, trust her lovingly.
When the tempest rages round thee,
she will calm the troubled sea.
Gifts of heaven she has given,
noble lady, to our race:
she, the queen, who decks her subjects,
with the light of God's own grace.

3. Sing, my tongue, the virgin's trophies,
who for us her Maker bore;
for the curse of old inflicted,
peace and blessings to restore.
Sing in songs of praise unending,
sing the world's majestic queen;
weary not, nor faint in telling
all the gifts she gives to men.

4. All my senses, heart, affections,
strive to sound her glory forth;
spread abroad, the sweet memorials,
of the virgin's priceless worth.
Where the voice of music thrilling,
where the tongues of eloquence,
that can utter hymns beseeming
all her matchless excellence?

5. All our joys do flow from Mary,
all then join her praise to sing;
trembling, sing the virgin mother,
mother of our Lord and King,
while we sing her awful glory,
far above our fancy's reach,
let our hearts be quick to offer
love the heart alone can teach.

TUNE 2: LAUDES MARIAE 87 87 D

1. Daily, daily, sing to Mary,
sing, my soul, her praises due;
all her feasts, her actions worship,
with her heart's devotion true.
Lost in wond'ring contemplation
be her majesty confessed:
call her mother, call her virgin,
happy mother, virgin blest.

2. She is mighty to deliver;
call her, trust her lovingly.
When the tempest rages round thee,
she will calm the troubled sea.
Gifts of heaven she has given,
noble lady, to our race:
she, the queen, who decks her subjects,
with the light of God's own grace.

3. Sing, my tongue, the virgin's trophies,
who for us her Maker bore;
for the curse of old inflicted,
peace and blessings to restore.
Sing in songs of praise unending,
sing the world's majestic queen;
weary not, nor faint in telling
all the gifts she gives to men.

4. All my senses, heart, affections,
strive to sound her glory forth;
spread abroad, the sweet memorials,
of the virgin's priceless worth.
Where the voice of music thrilling,
where the tongues of eloquence,
that can utter hymns beseeming
all her matchless excellence?

5. All our joys do flow from Mary,
all then join her praise to sing;
trembling, sing the virgin mother,
mother of our Lord and King,
while we sing her awful glory,
far above our fancy's reach,
let our hearts be quick to offer
love the heart alone can teach.

TUNE 3: OMNI DIE DIC MARIAE 87 87 D

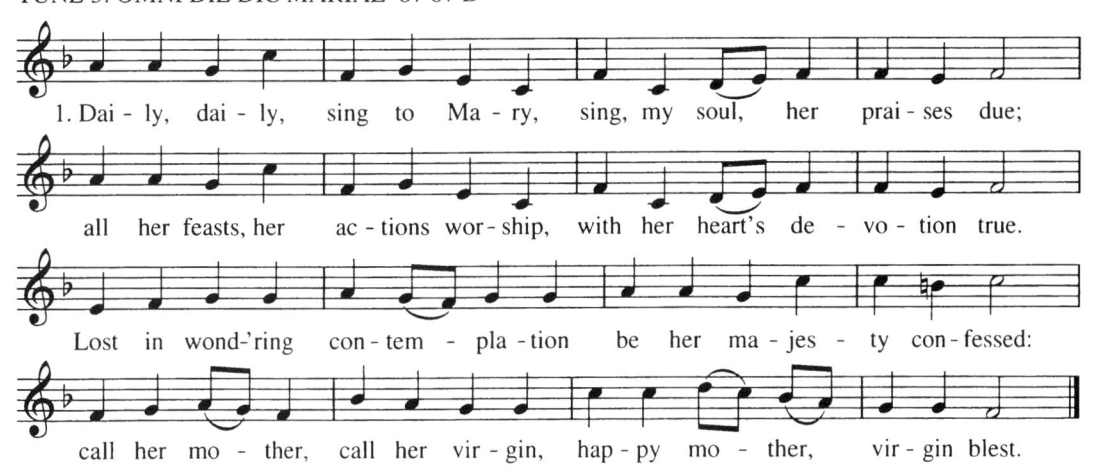

1. Daily, daily, sing to Mary,
sing, my soul, her praises due;
all her feasts, her actions worship,
with her heart's devotion true.
Lost in wond'ring contemplation
be her majesty confessed:
call her mother, call her virgin,
happy mother, virgin blest.

Text: 'Omni die dic Mariae', ascribed to St. Bernard of Cluny (12th century)
trans. Henry Bittleston (1818 - 1886)
Music: Tune 1 – from the 'Paderborn Gesangbuch' (1765)
Tune 2 – Henri Friedrich Hémy (1818-1888)
Tune 3 – German melody

LITURGICAL
HYMNS OLD & NEW

231 Dance in your Spirit

Refrain

Dance in your Spirit, we dance in your Spirit, we dance in your Spirit of joy! Dance in your Spirit, we dance in your Spirit, we dance in your Spirit of joy!

1. Jesus, you showed us the way to live,
and your Spirit sets us free,
free now to sing, free to dance and shout,
'Glory, glory' to your name.

2. Jesus, you opened your arms for us,
but we nailed them to a cross;
but you are risen and now we live,
free from, free from ev'ry fear.

3. Your Spirit brings peace and gentleness,
kindness, self-control and love,
patience and goodness and faith and joy,
Spirit, Spirit fill us now.

Text and Music: Mike Anderson (b.1956)
© Copyright 1999 Kevin Mayhew Ltd.

232 Day is done, but love unfailing

AR HYD Y NOS 84 84 88 84

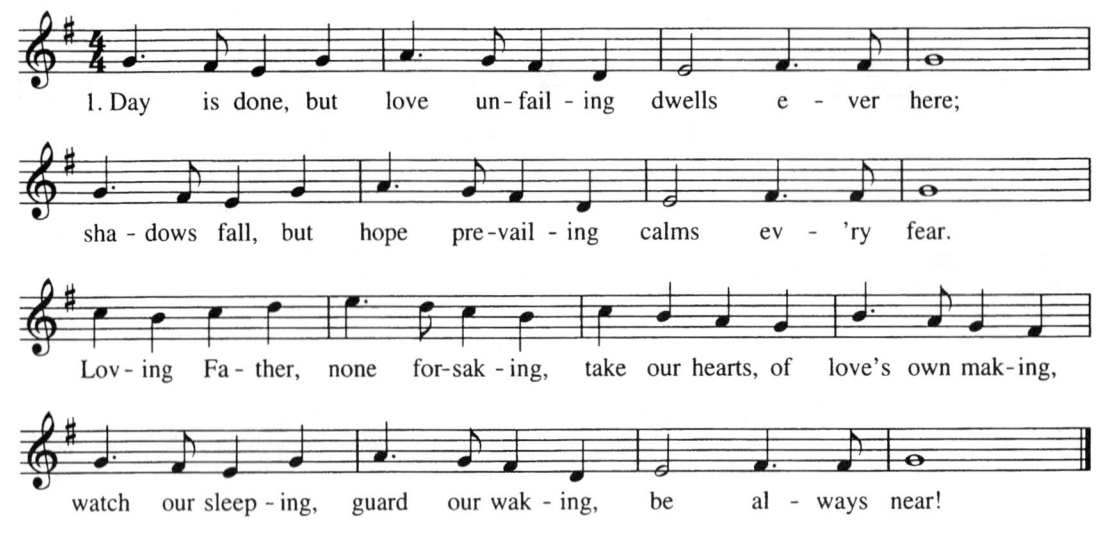

1. Day is done, but love un-fail-ing dwells e-ver here;
sha-dows fall, but hope pre-vail-ing calms ev-'ry fear.
Lov-ing Fa-ther, none for-sak-ing, take our hearts, of love's own mak-ing,
watch our sleep-ing, guard our wak-ing, be al-ways near!

A lower setting will be found at No. 233

2. Dark descends, but light unending
shines through our night;
you are with us, ever lending
new strength to sight;
one in love, your truth confessing,
one in hope of heaven's blessing,
may we see, in love's possessing,
love's endless light!

3. Eyes will close, but you, unsleeping,
watch by our side;
death may come; in love's safe keeping
still we abide.
God of love, all evil quelling,
sin forgiving, fear dispelling,
stay with us, our hearts indwelling,
this eventide!

Text: James Quinn (b.1919)
Music: traditional Welsh melody
Text © Copyright Geoffrey Chapman, an imprint of Cassell plc, Wellington House,
125 Strand, London WC2R 0BB, UK. Used by permission.

233 Day of wrath and day of wonder

AR HYD Y NOS 84 84 88 84   *A higher setting will be found at No. 232*

1. Day of wrath and day of won-der, whence hope has fled!
See the bo-dy torn a-sun-der, blood free-ly shed.
Stripped of ma-jes-ty we saw him, hu-man sight re-coiled be-fore him,
yet it was our sor-rows tore him; for us he bled.

Text © Copyright 1993 Kevin Mayhew Ltd.

2. Day of hope and day of glory,
though unperceived!
See redemption's dreadful story,
long, long conceived.
Evil pow'rs, in downfall lying,
knowing death itself is dying,
hear the voice triumphant crying,
'All is achieved!'

3. Day of majesty and splendour,
here ends the race!
Christ, our Priest, our soul's defender,
us will embrace.
He who walked this earth before us,
tried and tempted, yet victorious,
calls us to the kingdom glorious,
O perfect grace!

Text: Michael Forster (b.1946)
Music: traditional Welsh melody

234 Dear Lord and Father of mankind

REPTON 86 88 6

1. Dear Lord and Father of mankind, forgive our foolish ways! Re-clothe us in our rightful mind, in purer lives thy service find, in deeper rev-'rence praise, in deeper rev-'rence praise.

2. In simple trust like theirs who heard,
beside the Syrian sea,
the gracious calling of the Lord,
let us, like them, without a word,
rise up and follow thee,
rise up and follow thee.

3. O Sabbath rest by Galilee!
O calm of hills above,
where Jesus knelt to share with thee
the silence of eternity,
interpreted by love!
Interpreted by love!

4. Drop thy still dews of quietness,
till all our strivings cease;
take from our souls the strain and stress,
and let our ordered lives confess
the beauty of thy peace,
the beauty of thy peace.

5. Breathe through the heats of our desire
thy coolness and thy balm;
let sense be dumb, let flesh retire;
speak through the earthquake, wind and fire,
O still small voice of calm!
O still small voice of calm!

Text: John Greenleaf Whittier (1807-1892)
Music: Charles Hubert Hastings Parry (1848-1918)

235 Deep calls to deep

DEEP CALLS TO DEEP 4 10 4 10 and Refrain

1. Deep calls to deep, and my soul finds no rest-ing place but him.
He is my God, the yearn-ings of my heart his touch can still. And each rare mo-ment that I've felt his pres-ence, I shall re-mem-ber and for-ev-er cher-ish. cher-ish.

2. Deep calls to deep,
   and at his feast I am a welcome guest.
   He gives me food,
   the hunger of my soul is laid to rest.

3. Deep calls to deep,
   for he created me to be his own.
   He understands,
   the joy and pain of life he too has known.

Text and Music: Estelle White (b.1925)
© Copyright 1978 Kevin Mayhew Ltd.

236 Deep peace of the running wave to you

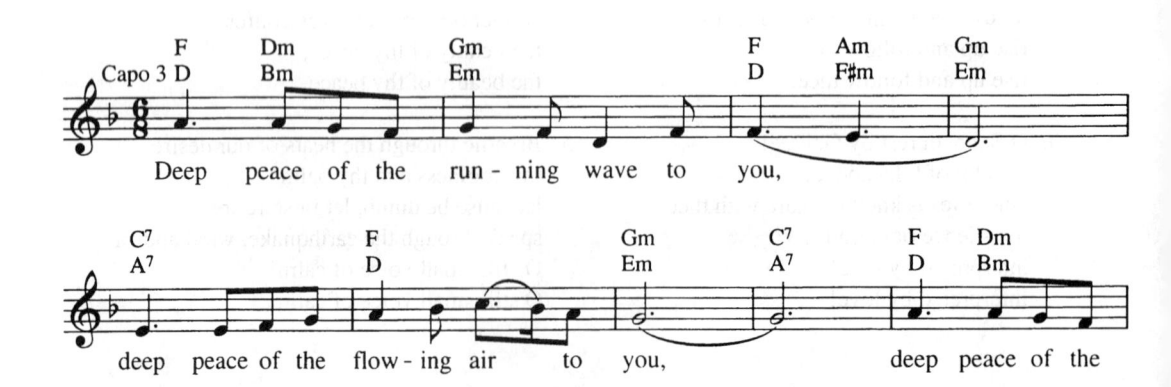

Deep peace of the run-ning wave to you, deep peace of the flow-ing air to you, deep peace of the

Music © Copyright 1976, 1999 Kevin Mayhew Ltd.

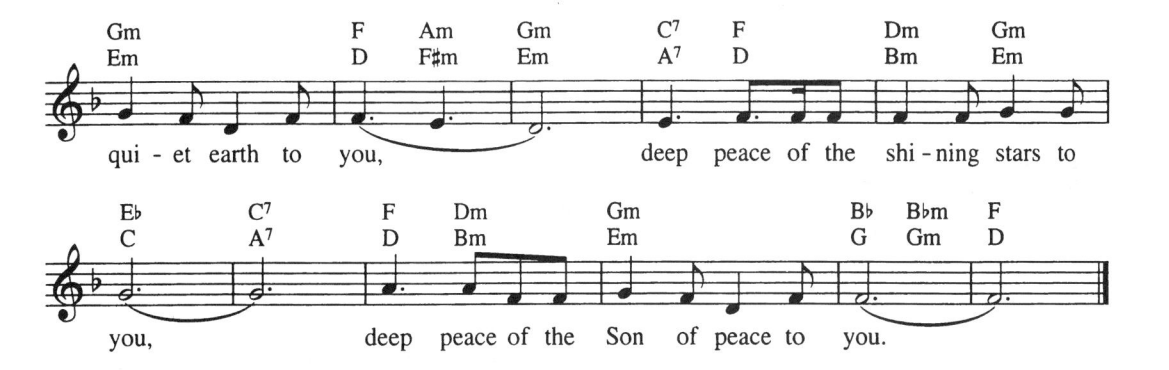

qui - et earth to you, deep peace of the shi - ning stars to you, deep peace of the Son of peace to you.

Text: Fiona MacLeod (1855-1905)
Music: Robert B. Kelly (b.1948)ß

237 Deep within my heart

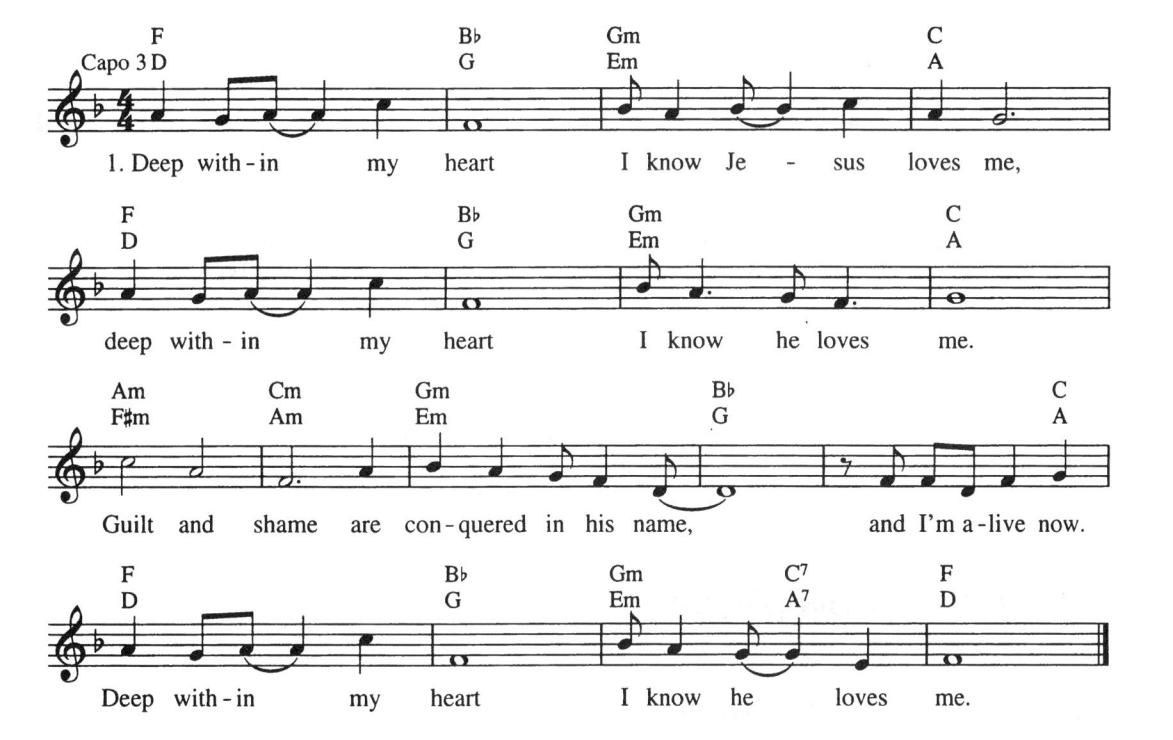

1. Deep with-in my heart I know Je - sus loves me,
deep with-in my heart I know he loves me.
Guilt and shame are con-quered in his name, and I'm a-live now.
Deep with-in my heart I know he loves me.

2. Deep within my heart I know I'm forgiven,
deep within my heart I know that I'm free.
Free from sin, a new life to begin, and I'm alive now.
Deep within my heart I know that I'm free.

3. Deep within my heart Jesus' love is healing,
deep within my heart he is healing me.
Tears like rain are flooding out the pain, and I'm alive now.
Deep within my heart he is healing me.

Text and Music: Mike Anderson (b.1956)
© Copyright 1999 Kevin Mayhew Ltd.

238 Ding dong, merrily on high

BRANSLE DE L'OFFICIAL 77 77 and Refrain

1. Ding dong, mer-ri-ly on high! In heav'n the bells are ring-ing;
ding dong, ve-ri-ly the sky is riv'n with an-gels sing-ing.

Refrain
Glo - - - - ri - a, ho-san-na in ex-cel-sis.

D.C.

2. E'en so here below, below,
   let steeple bells be swungen,
   and io, io, io,
   by priest and people sungen.

3. Pray you, dutifully prime
   your matin chime, ye ringers;
   may you beautifully rhyme
   your evetime song, ye singers.

Text: George Ratcliffe Woodward (1848-1934)
Music: traditional French melody
Text © Copyright SPCK, Holy Trinity Church, Marylebone Road, London NW1 4DU. Used by permission.

239 Dona nobis pacem

This may be sung as a round, the voices entering as indicated

[1] F   C   F   C   B♭
Capo 3 D   A   D   A   G

Do - na no - bis, no - bis pa - cem, do - na

F   C7   F   C   F
D   A7   D   [2] A   D

no - bis pa - cem. Do - na no - bis

This arrangement © Copyright 1999 Kevin Mayhew Ltd.

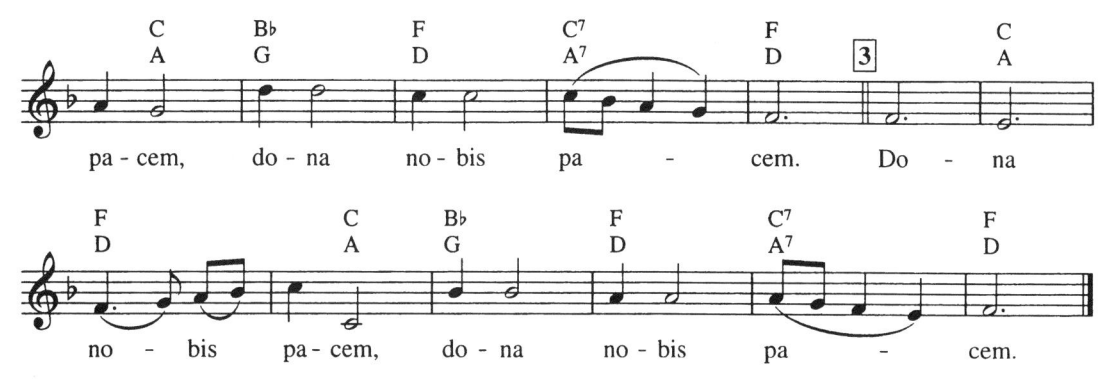

pa - cem, do - na no - bis pa - cem. Do - na no - bis pa - cem, do - na no - bis pa - cem.

Translation: Give us peace

Text: Traditional
Music: Unknown

240 Do not be afraid

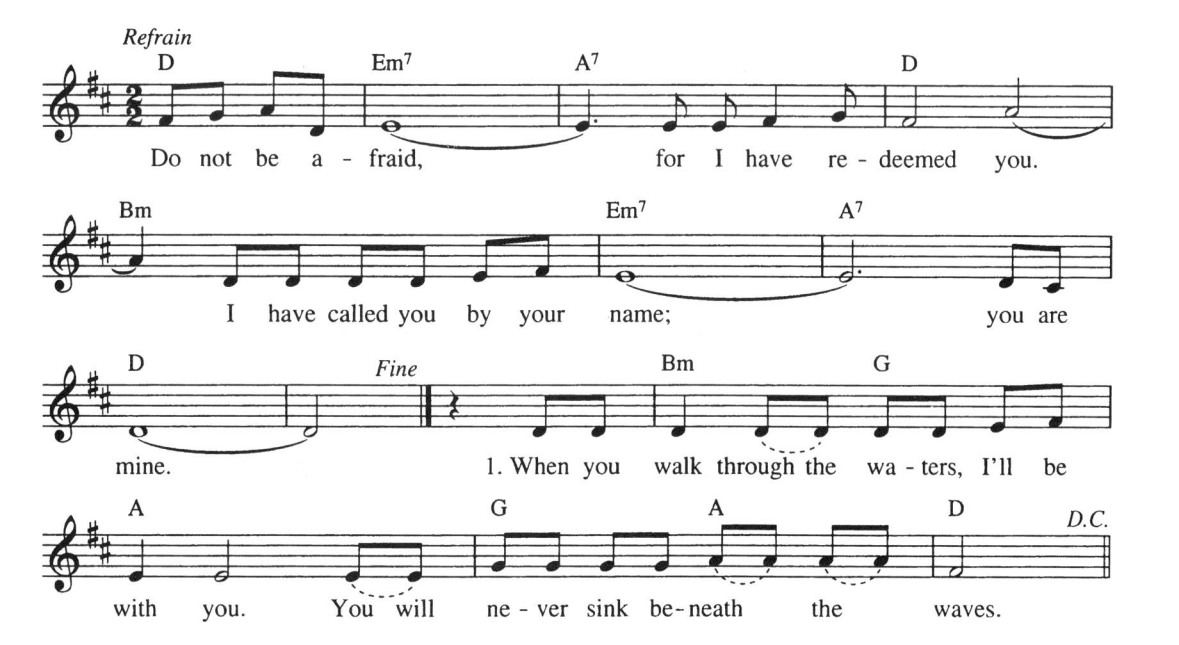

Refrain

Do not be a - fraid, for I have re - deemed you. I have called you by your name; you are mine. 1. When you walk through the wa - ters, I'll be with you. You will ne - ver sink be - neath the waves.

2. When the fire is burning all around you,
   you will never be consumed by the flames.

3. When the fear of loneliness is looming,
   then remember I am at your side.

4. When you dwell in the exile of the stranger,
   remember you are precious in my eyes.

5. You are mine, O my child, I am your Father,
   and I love you with a perfect love.

Text: Gerard Markland (b.1953) based on Isaiah 43:1-4
Music: Gerard Markland
© Copyright 1978 Kevin Mayhew Ltd.

241 Dying you destroyed our death
Song of farewell

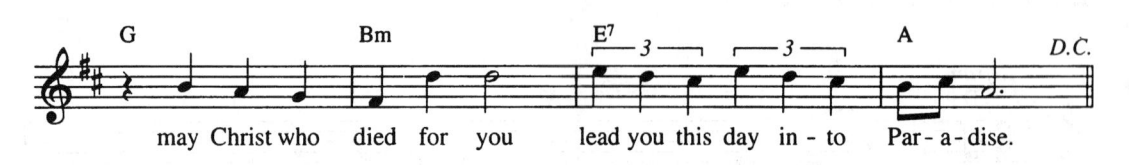

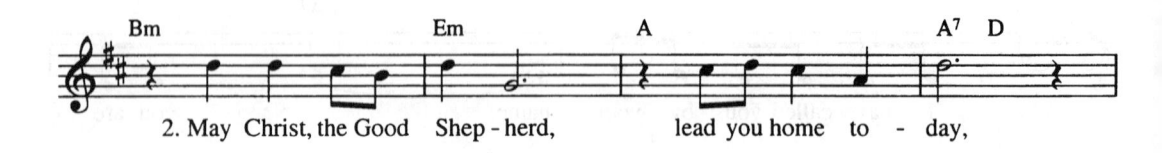

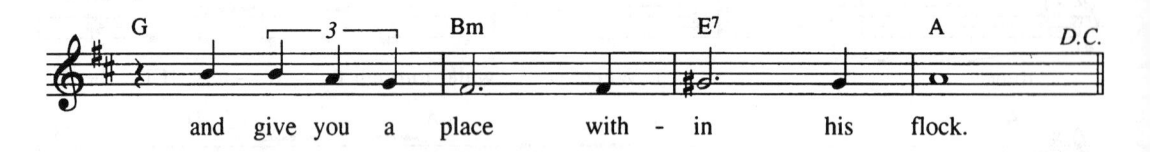

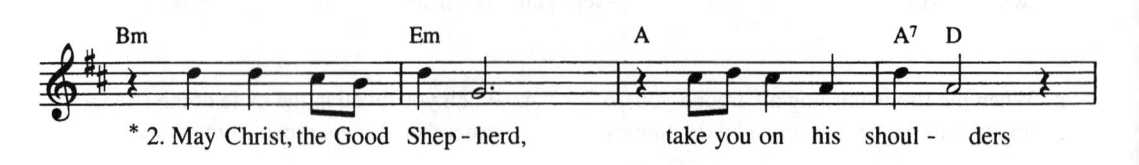

Refrain

Dying you destroyed our death; rising you restored our life.
Lord Jesus, Lord Jesus, come in glory!

1. May Christ who died for you lead you into his kingdom;
may Christ who died for you lead you this day into Paradise.

2. May Christ, the Good Shepherd, lead you home today,
and give you a place within his flock.

* 2. May Christ, the Good Shepherd, take you on his shoulders

* *Alternative children's verses*

Text © Copyright 1973 ICEL 1522 K Street NW, Suite 1000, Washington DC 20005-1202, USA.
Music © Copyright 1988 GIA Publications Inc., 7404 S. Mason Avenue, Chicago, Illinois 60638, USA.
Used by permission.

and bring you home, bring you home to-day.

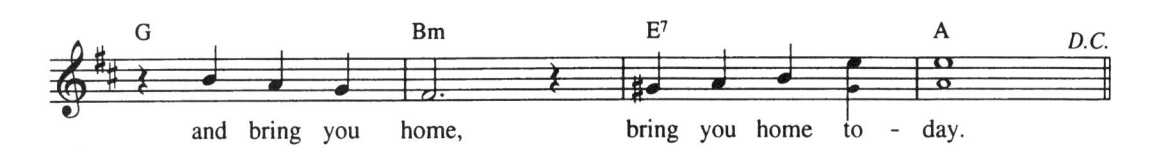

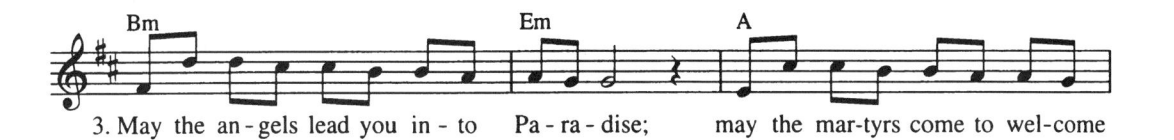

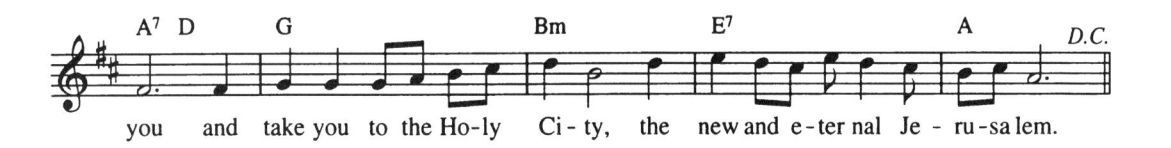

3. May the an-gels lead you in-to Pa-ra-dise; may the mar-tyrs come to wel-come you and take you to the Ho-ly Ci-ty, the new and e-ter-nal Je-ru-sa-lem.

4. May the choirs of an-gels come to meet you, may the choirs of an-gels come to meet you where Laz-a-rus is poor no long-er, may you have e-ter-nal life in Christ.

*4. May the choirs of an-gels come to meet you, may the choirs of an-gels come to meet you; and with all God's chil-dren may you have e-ter-nal life in Christ.

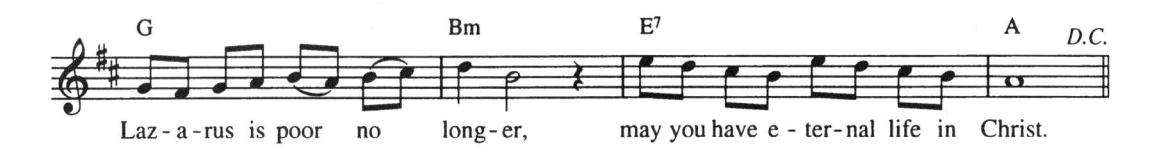

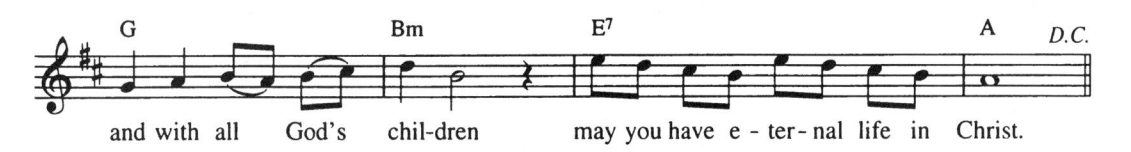

*Alternative children's verses

Text: Michael Marchal
Music: Michael Joncas (b.1951)

242 Enter in the wilderness

En-ter in the wil-der-ness, the Lord is com-ing, in the des-ert make the high-way straight. Ev-'ry val-ley shall be lif-ted up be-fore him, ev-'ry moun-tain lev-elled at his feet. 1. God comes, run out to meet him; God comes, hur-ry to greet him; God comes, try to be rea-dy, for the King is on his way. So,

2. Christ comes, now we will heed him;
Christ comes, all of us need him;
Christ comes, hope of the nations,
Son of justice, Prince of Peace. So,

3. Look up, bonds cut asunder;
look up, waiting in wonder;
look up, soon you will see him,
Christ the Lord is on his way. So,

Text: Willard F. Jabusch (b.1930)
Music: Hasidic melody
Text © Copyright 1998 Willard F. Jabusch, 5735 University Avenue, Chicago, Illinois 60637, USA. Used by permission.

243 Eternal Father, strong to save

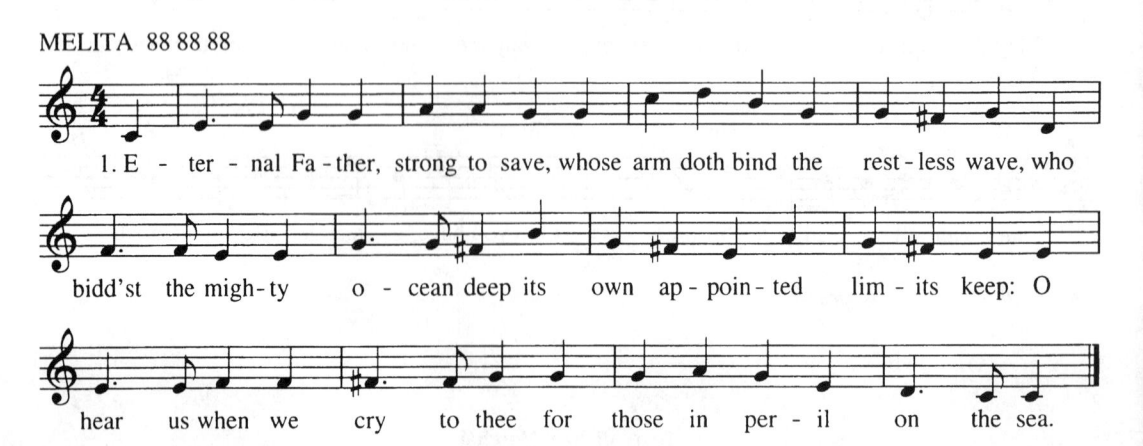

MELITA 88 88 88

1. E-ter-nal Fa-ther, strong to save, whose arm doth bind the rest-less wave, who bidd'st the migh-ty o-cean deep its own ap-poin-ted lim-its keep: O hear us when we cry to thee for those in per-il on the sea.

2. O Saviour, whose almighty word
the winds and waves submissive heard,
who walkedst on the foaming deep,
and calm, amid its rage, didst sleep:
O hear us when we cry to thee
for those in peril on the sea.

3. O sacred Spirit, who didst brood
upon the waters dark and rude,
and bid their angry tumult cease,
and give, for wild confusion, peace:
O hear us when we cry to thee
for those in peril on the sea.

4. O Trinity of love and pow'r,
our brethren shield in danger's hour.
From rock and tempest, fire and foe,
protect them whereso'er they go,
and ever let there rise to thee
glad hymns of praise from land and sea.

Text: William Whiting (1825-1878) alt.
Music: John Bacchus Dykes (1823-1876)

244 Faithful Cross

BLAENWERN 87 87 D

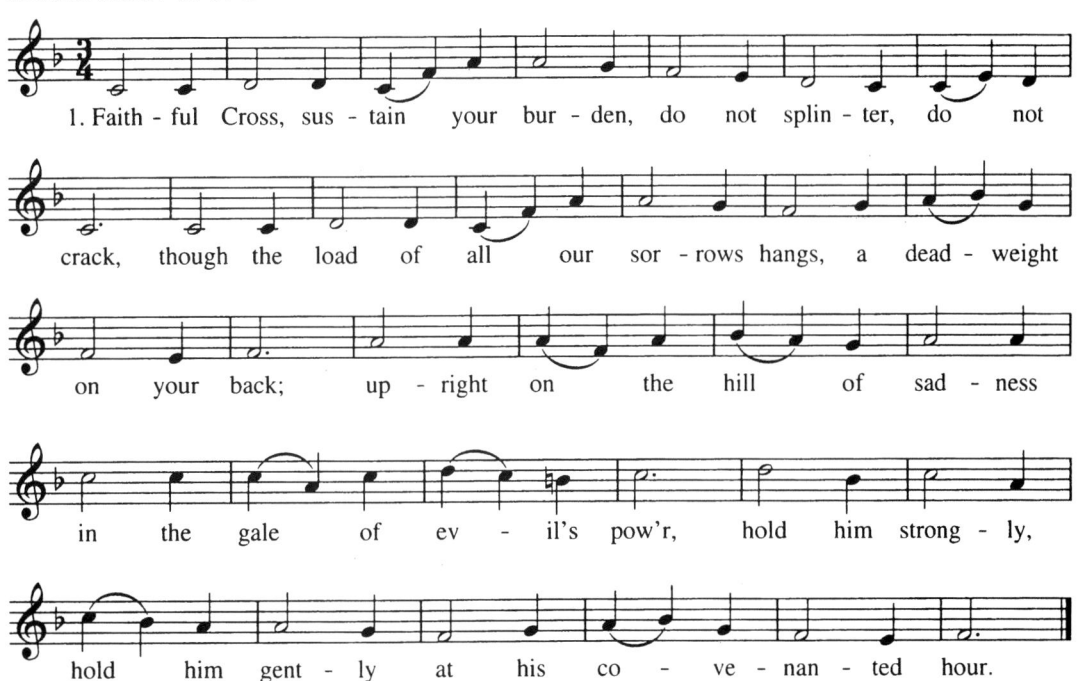

1. Faith-ful Cross, sus-tain your bur-den, do not splin-ter, do not crack, though the load of all our sor-rows hangs, a dead-weight on your back; up-right on the hill of sad-ness in the gale of ev-il's pow'r, hold him strong-ly, hold him gent-ly at his co-ve-nan-ted hour.

2. Nameless in the forest mounting,
shoot and sapling, branch and tree,
felled, dismembered, planed and jointed
for this day's dark mystery.
Gibbet, infamous, ennobled
by this death and by this birth,
hold your cross-grained branches open
harbour for a shipwrecked earth.

3. When, the noontide darkness ending,
he whom you have borne is dead,
in his mother's arms laid gently
you are left untenanted:
sharp against the soul's horizon
still uphold us, shining tree,
emblem of the Saviour's passion
standard of his victory.

Text: Kevin Nichols (b.1929) based on 'Crux fidelis'
Music: William Penfro Rowlands (1860-1937)
Text © Copyright Kevin Nichols. Used by permission. Music © Copyright control.

245 Faith in God

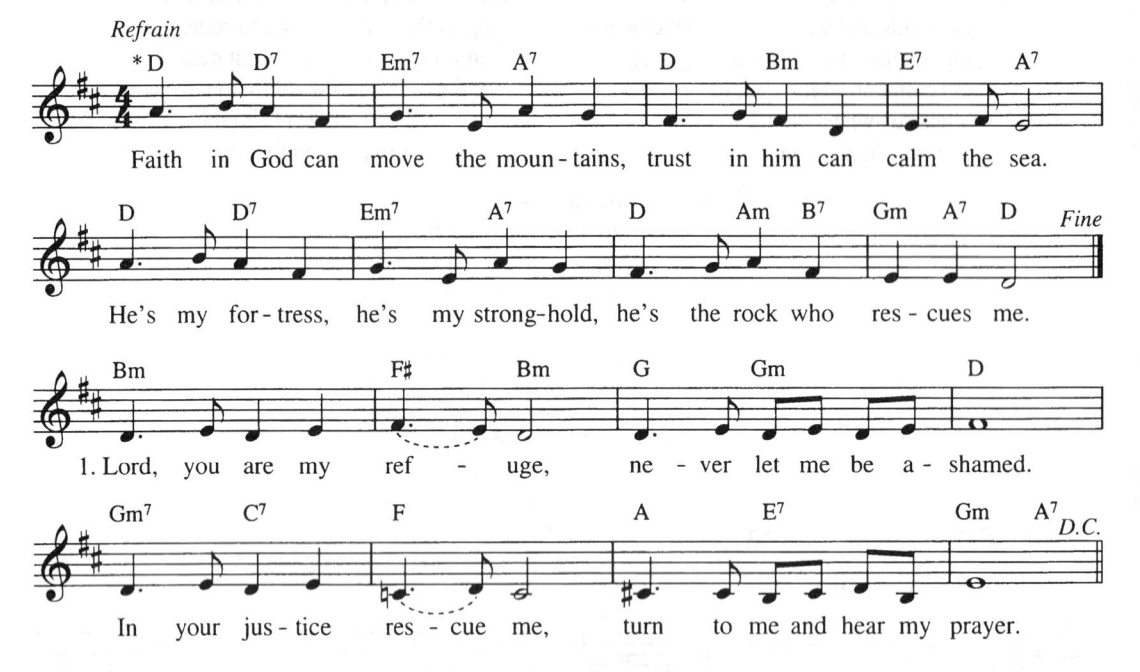

Faith in God can move the mountains, trust in him can calm the sea.
He's my fortress, he's my stronghold, he's the rock who rescues me.

1. Lord, you are my refuge, never let me be ashamed.
   In your justice rescue me, turn to me and hear my prayer.

* The guitar and keyboard parts should not be played together

2. You are my salvation,
   from oppression set me free.
   Ever since my childhood,
   you have been my only hope.

3. Bitter troubles burden me,
   but you fill me with new life.
   From the grave you raise me up,
   so my tongue will sing your praise.

Text: Aniceto Nazareth, based on Psalm 61
Music: Aniceto Nazareth
© Copyright 1984 Kevin Mayhew Ltd.

246 Faith of our fathers

SAWSTON LM and Refrain

1. Faith of our fathers, living still in spite of dungeon, fire and sword; O, how our hearts beat high with joy when-e'er we hear that glorious word! Faith of our fathers! Holy Faith! We will be true to thee till death, we will be true to thee till death.

2. Our fathers, chained in prisons dark,
    were still in heart and conscience free;
    how sweet would be their children's fate,
    if they, like them, could die for thee!

3. Faith of our fathers, Mary's prayers
    shall win our country back to thee;
    and through the truth that comes from God
    this land shall then indeed be free.

4. Faith of our fathers, we will love
    both friend and foe in all our strife,
    and preach thee too, as love knows how,
    by kindly words and virtuous life.

Text: Frederick William Faber (1814-1863)
Music: traditional melody from 'Crown of Jesus' hymnal (1864)

247 Father and life-giver

PRINCETHORPE 65 65 D

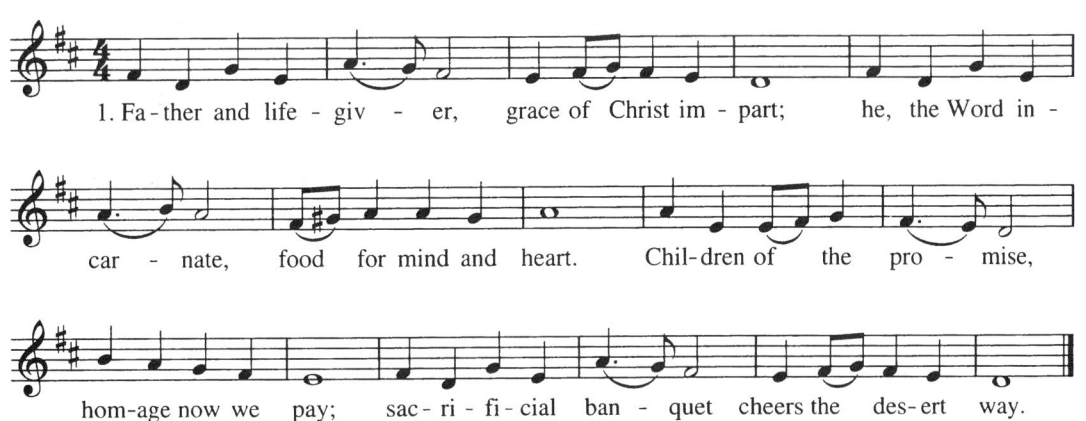

1. Father and life-giver, grace of Christ impart;
   he, the Word incarnate, food for mind and heart.
   Children of the promise, homage now we pay;
   sacrificial banquet cheers the desert way.

A higher setting will be found at No. 392

2. Wine and bread the symbols, love and life convey,
    offered by your people, work and joy portray.
    All we own consigning, nothing is retained;
    tokens of our service, gifts and song contain.

3. Transformation wondrous, water into wine;
    mingled in the Godhead we are made divine.
    Birth into his body brought us life anew,
    total consecration, fruit from grafting true.

4. Christ, the head, and members living now as one,
    offered to the Father by his holy Son;
    and our adoration purified we find,
    through the Holy Spirit breathing in mankind.

Text: A.J. Newman
Music: William Pitts (1829-1903)

248 Father God, gentle Father God

Gently

Father God, gentle Father God, my Lord of consolation, I lift up my heart to you. 1. O Lord, you search me, you know me, my ev-'ry move. My thoughts you read from afar, all my ways lie there before you.

2. My heart, my innermost being
   was made by you.
   My body, secretly formed in the womb,
   was always with you.

3. What place, what heavens could
   hide me away from you?
   Were I to fly to the ends of the sea,
   your hand would guide me.

4. Your works, your knowledge, your love
   are beyond my mind.
   My Lord, I thank you for these
   and the wonder of my being.

5. O Lord, come search me, come find
   what is in my heart;
   that I may never stray far
   from your path of life eternal.

Text: Gerard Markland (b.1953) based on Psalm 138
Music: Gerard Markland (b.1953)
© Copyright 1998 Kevin Mayhew Ltd.

249 Father God, I wonder
I will sing your praises

Lively

Father God, I wonder how I managed to exist without the knowledge of your parenthood and your loving care. But now I am your child, I am adopted in your family and I can never be alone 'cause, Father God, you're there beside me.

I will sing your praises, I will sing your praises, I will sing your praises, for evermore. for evermore.

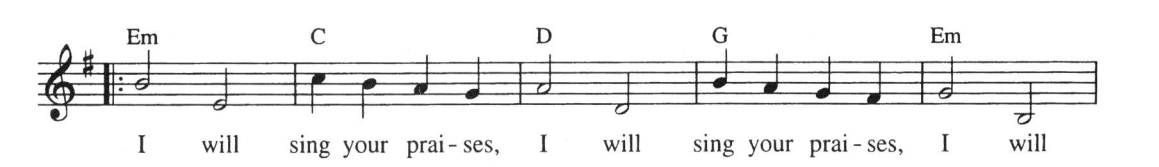

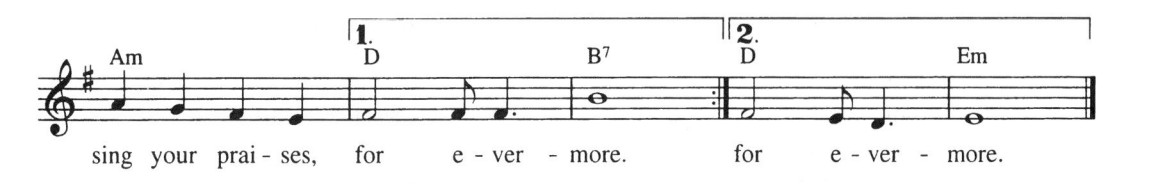

Text and Music: Ian Smale

© Copyright 1984 Kingsway's Thankyou Music, P.O. Box 75, Eastbourne, East Sussex BN23 6NW, UK. Used by permission.

250 Father, in my life I see
Trinity Song

Effective when men's voices sing one line, and women's the other

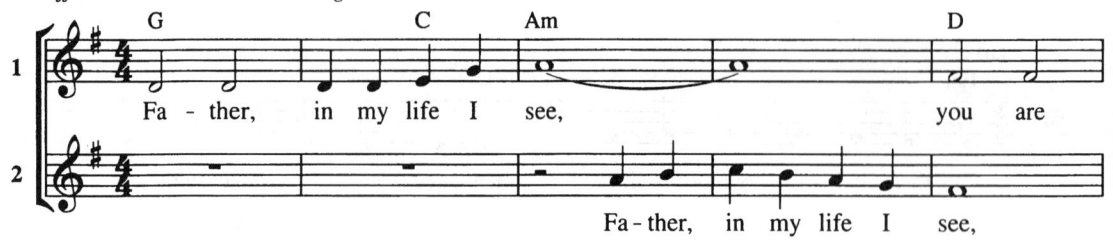

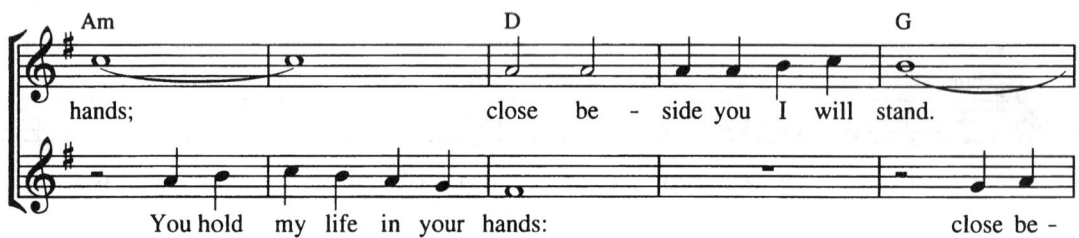

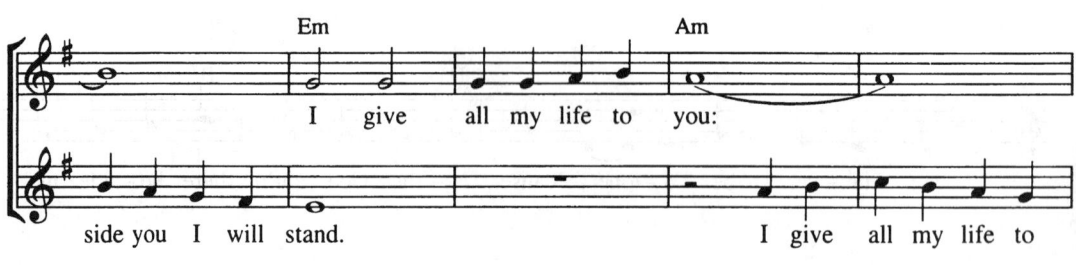

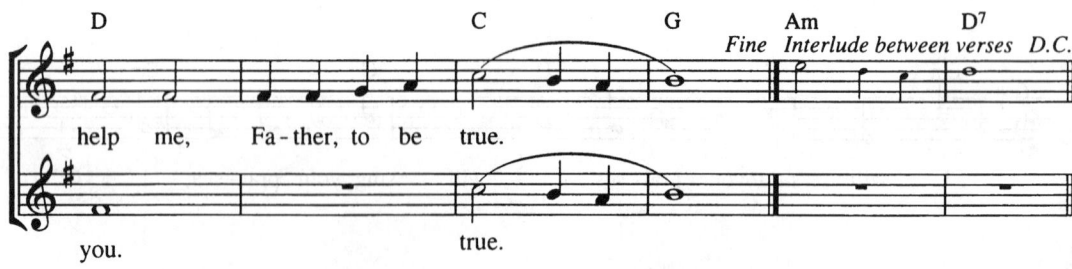

1. Father, in my life I see,
   you are God who walks with me.
   You hold my life in your hands;
   close beside you I will stand.
   I give all my life to you:
   help me, Father, to be true.

2. Jesus, in my life I see
   you are God who walks with me.
   You hold my life in your hands;
   close beside you I will stand.
   I give all my life to you:
   help me, Jesus, to be true.

3. Spirit, in my life I see
   you are God who walks with me.
   You hold my life in your hands;
   close beside you I will stand.
   I give all my life to you:
   help me, Spirit, to be true.

Text and Music: Frank Andersen

© Copyright Word of Life International, P.O. Box 2322, Burleigh MDC, Queensland 4220, Australia.
Used by permission.

251 Father, I place into your hands

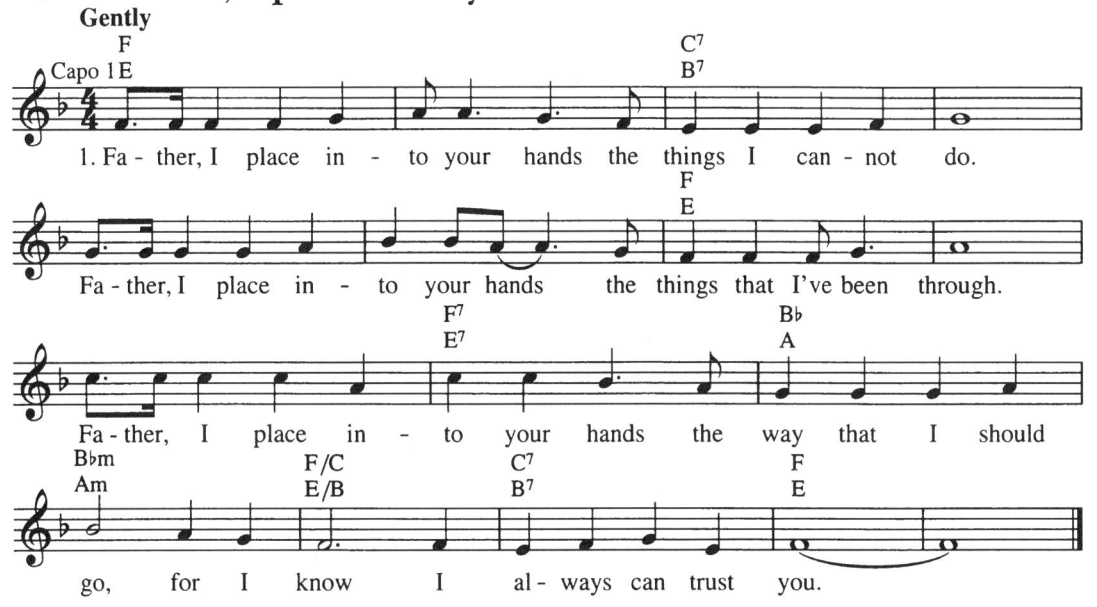

Gently

1. Father, I place into your hands the things I cannot do.
Father, I place into your hands the things that I've been through.
Father, I place into your hands the way that I should go,
for I know I always can trust you.

2. Father, I place into your hands
my friends and family.
Father, I place into your hands
the things that trouble me.
Father, I place into your hands
the person I would be,
for I know I always can trust you.

3. Father, we love to see your face,
we love to hear your voice.
Father, we love to sing your praise
and in your name rejoice.
Father, we love to walk with you
and in your presence rest,
for we know we always can trust you.

4. Father, I want to be with you
and do the things you do.
Father, I want to speak the words
that you are speaking too.
Father, I want to love the ones
that you will draw to you,
for I know that I am one with you.

Text and Music: Jenny Hewer (b.1945)

© Copyright 1975 Kingsway's Thankyou Music, P.O. Box 75, Eastbourne,
East Sussex BN23 6NW, UK. Used by permission.

252 Father, we adore you

This may be sung in unison as a round, with entries at A, B and C

1. Father, we adore you, lay our lives before you. How we love you!

2. Jesus, we adore you, lay our lives before you.
How we love you!

3. Spirit, we adore you, lay our lives before you.
How we love you!

Text and Music: Terrye Coelho (b.1952)

© Copyright 1972 Maranatha! Music. Administered by CopyCare, P.O. Box 77, Hailsham,
East Sussex BN27 3EF, UK. Used by permission.

253 Father, we come to you

Strong, steady rhythm

Cantor: Father, we come to you, God of all pow'r and might. Show us your glory: give us your life.

All: Father, we come to you, God of all pow'r and might. Show us your glory: give us your life.

Cantor: You have united us, bound us in love and peace: God in the midst of us, holy, unseen.

All: Blessed is he who comes, piercing our night of sin. Open your hearts to him. Great is his name.

Cantor: Bread of life shared with us, *(poco rall.)* body of Christ the Lord, broken and died for us: life for the world.

a tempo *All:* Father, we come to you, God of all pow'r and might. Show us your glory: give us your life. Blessed is he who comes, piercing our night of sin. Open our hearts to you: great is your name. *(rall.)* Open our hearts to you: great is your name!

Text and Music: James Walsh

© Copyright 1997 James Walsh, OSB. Published by OCP Publications, 5536 NE Hassalo, Portland, OR 97213, USA. All rights reserved. Used by permission.

254 Father, we love you
Glorify your name

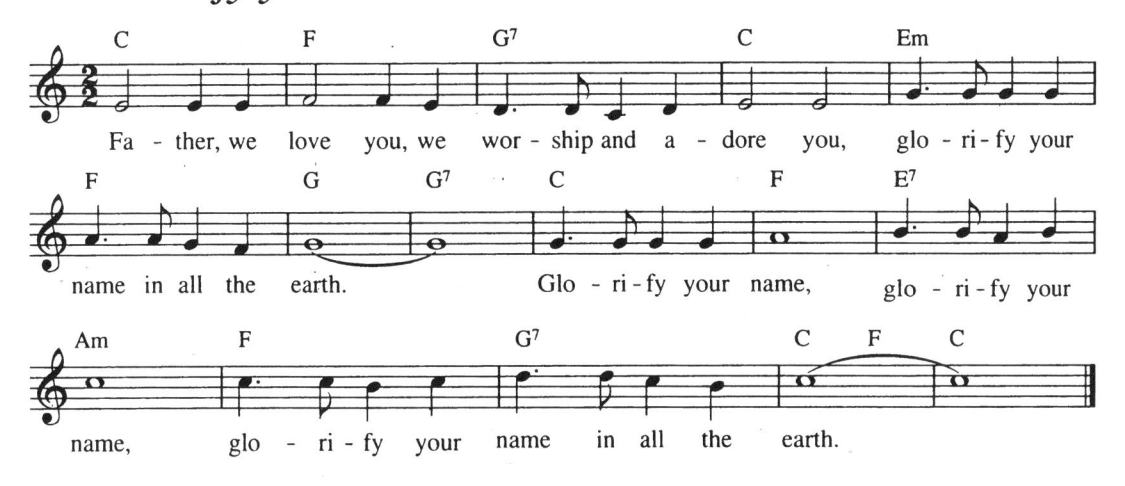

Father, we love you, we worship and adore you, glorify your name in all the earth. Glorify your name, glorify your name, glorify your name in all the earth.

2. Jesus, we love you . . .

3. Spirit, we love you . . .

Text and Music: Donna Adkins (b.1940)
© Copyright 1976 Maranatha! Music. Administered by CopyCare,
P.O. Box 77, Hailsham, East Sussex BN27 3EF, UK. Used by permission.

255 Fight the good fight

DUKE STREET LM

1. Fight the good fight with all thy might; Christ is thy strength, and Christ thy right; lay hold on life, and it shall be thy joy and crown eternally.

2. Run the straight race through God's good grace,
   lift up thine eyes and seek his face;
   life with its way before us lies;
   Christ is the path, and Christ the prize.

3. Cast care aside, lean on thy guide;
   his boundless mercy will provide;
   trust, and thy trusting soul shall prove
   Christ is its life, and Christ its love.

4. Faint not nor fear, his arms are near;
   he changeth not, and thou art dear;
   only believe, and thou shalt see
   that Christ is all in all to thee.

Text: John Samuel Bewley Monsell (1811-1875) alt.
Music: melody attributed to John Hatton (d.1793)

256 Fill my house

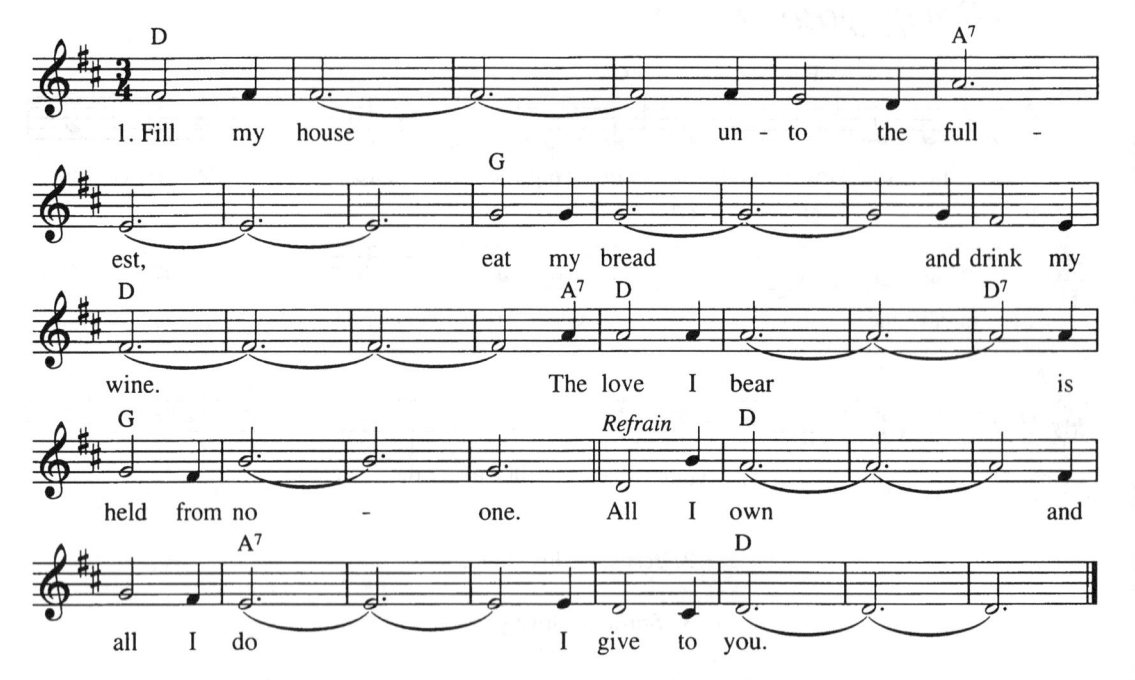

1. Fill my house unto the fullest,
eat my bread and drink my wine.
The love I bear is held from no-one.

Refrain
All I own and all I do
I give to you.

2. Take my time unto the fullest,
find in me the trust you seek,
and take my hands to you outreaching.

3. Christ our Lord with love enormous
from the cross his lesson taught:
'Show love to all, as I have loved you.'

4. Join with me as one in Christ-love,
may our hearts all beat as one,
and may we give ourselves completely.

Text and Music: Peter Kearney
© Copyright 1966 J. Albert & Son Pty Ltd. /B. Feldman & Co. Ltd. /EMI Music Publishing Ltd.,
London WC2H 0EA, UK. Reproduced by permission of IMP Ltd.

257 Fill your hearts with joy and gladness

ODE TO JOY 87 87 D

1. Fill your hearts with joy and gladness,
sing and praise your God and mine!
Great the Lord in love and wisdom,
might and majesty divine.
He who framed the starry heavens
knows and names them as they shine.
Fill your hearts with joy and gladness,
sing and praise your God and mine!

Text © Copyright Timothy Dudley-Smith, 9 Ashlands, Ford, Salisbury, Wiltshire SP4 6DY. Used by permission.

2. Praise the Lord, his people, praise him!
   Wounded souls his comfort know.
   Those who fear him find his mercies,
   peace for pain and joy for woe;
   humble hearts are high exalted,
   human pride and pow'r laid low.
   Praise the Lord, his people, praise him!
   Wounded souls his comfort know.

3. Praise the Lord for times and seasons,
   cloud and sunshine, wind and rain;
   spring to melt the snows of winter
   till the waters flow again;
   grass upon the mountain pastures,
   golden valleys thick with grain.
   Praise the Lord for times and seasons,
   cloud and sunshine, wind and rain.

4. Fill your hearts with joy and gladness,
   peace and plenty crown your days!
   Love his laws, declare his judgements,
   walk in all his words and ways;
   he the Lord and we his children,
   praise the Lord, all people, praise!
   Fill your hearts with joy and gladness,
   peace and plenty crown your days!

Text: Timothy Dudley-Smith (b.1926)
Music: Ludwig van Beethoven (1770-1827)

258 Firmly I believe

OMNI DIE 87 87

1. Firm-ly I be-lieve and tru-ly God is three, and God is one, and I next ac-know-ledge du-ly man-hood ta-ken by the Son.

2. And I trust and hope most fully
   in the Saviour crucified;
   and each thought and deed unruly
   do to death, as he has died.

3. Simply to his grace and wholly
   light and life and strength belong;
   and I love supremely, solely,
   him the holy, him the strong.

4. And I hold in veneration,
   for the love of him alone,
   Holy Church, as his creation,
   and her teachings, as his own.

5. Adoration aye be given,
   with and through th'angelic host,
   to the God of earth and heaven,
   Father, Son and Holy Ghost.

Text: John Henry Newman (1801-1890) alt.
Music: from 'Corners Gesangbuch' (1631) arr. W.S. Rockstro (1823-1895)

259 Follow me

Refrain

Fol-low me, fol-low me, leave your home and fa-mi-ly, leave your fish-ing nets and boats u-pon the shore. Leave the seed you have sown, leave the crops that you've grown, leave the peo-ple you have known and fol-low me.

1. The fox-es have their holes and the swal-lows have their nests, but the Son of Man has no place to lie down, I do not of-fer com-fort, I do not of-fer wealth, but in me will all hap-pi-ness be found. Fol-low

2. If you would follow me,
   you must leave old ways behind.
   You must take my cross and
   follow on my path.
   You may be far from loved ones,
   you may be far from home,
   but my Father will welcome you at last.

3. Although I go away
   you will never be alone,
   for the Spirit will be
   there to comfort you.
   Though all of you may scatter,
   each follow his own path,
   still the Spirit of love will lead you home.

Text: Michael Cockett (b.1938)
Music: Sister Madeleine
© Copyright 1978 Kevin Mayhew Ltd.

260 For all the saints

SINE NOMINE 10 10 10 4

1. For all the saints who from their la-bours rest, who
thee by faith be-fore the world con-fessed, thy
name, O Je-sus, be for e-ver blest. Al-
le-lu-ia, al-le-lu-ia!
(cue notes v.3)

2. Thou wast their rock, their fortress and their might;
thou, Lord, their captain in the well-fought fight;
thou in the darkness drear their one true light.
Alleluia, alleluia.

3. O may thy soldiers, faithful, true and bold,
fight as the saints who nobly fought of old,
and win, with them, the victor's crown of gold.
Alleluia, alleluia.

4. O blest communion! fellowship divine!
we feebly struggle, they in glory shine:
yet all are one in thee, for all are thine.
Alleluia, alleluia.

5. And when the strife is fierce, the warfare long,
steals on the ear the distant triumph song,
and hearts are brave again, and arms are strong.
Alleluia, alleluia.

6. The golden evening brightens in the west;
soon, soon to faithful warriors cometh rest;
sweet is the calm of paradise the blest.
Alleluia, alleluia.

7. But lo! there breaks a yet more glorious day;
the saints triumphant rise in bright array:
the King of glory passes on his way.
Alleluia, alleluia.

8. From earth's wide bounds, from ocean's farthest coast,
through gates of pearl stream in the countless host,
singing to Father, Son and Holy Ghost.
Alleluia, alleluia.

Text: William Walsham How (1823-1897)
Music: Ralph Vaughan Williams (1872-1958)
Music © Copyright Oxford University Press, Great Clarendon Street, Oxford OX2 6DP.
Used by permission from 'The English Hymnal'.

261 For the fruits of his creation

EAST ACKLAM 84 84 888 4

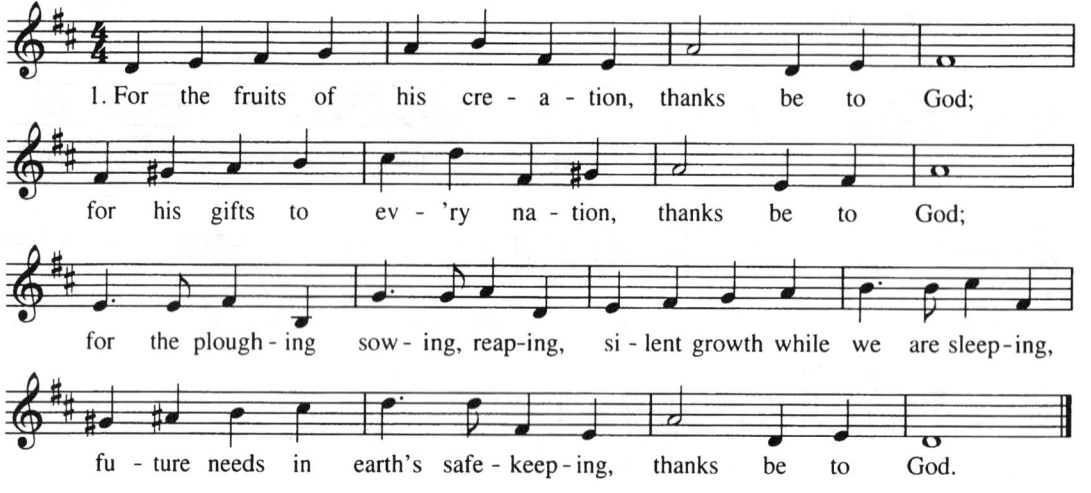

1. For the fruits of his creation, thanks be to God;
for his gifts to ev-'ry nation, thanks be to God;
for the plough-ing sow-ing, reap-ing, si-lent growth while we are sleep-ing,
fu-ture needs in earth's safe-keep-ing, thanks be to God.

2. In the just reward of labour,
God's will is done;
in the help we give our neighbour,
God's will is done;
in our world-wide task of caring
for the hungry and despairing,
in the harvests we are sharing,
God's will is done.

3. For the harvests of his Spirit,
thanks be to God;
for the good we all inherit,
thanks be to God;
for the wonders that astound us,
for the truths that still confound us,
most of all, that love has found us,
thanks be to God.

Text: Fred Pratt Green (b.1903)
Music: Francis Jackson (b.1917)
Text © Copyright 1970 Stainer & Bell Ltd, P.O. Box 110, Victoria House, 23 Gruneisen Road, Finchley, London N3 1DZ. Used by permission.
Music © Copyright Dr. Francis Jackson. Used by permission of the composer.

262 For the healing of the nations

PICARDY 87 87 87

1. For the heal-ing of the na-tions, Lord, we pray with one ac-cord; for a just and e-qual shar-ing of the things that earth af-fords. To a life of love in act-ion help us rise and pledge our word.

Text © Copyright 1968 Stainer & Bell Ltd., P.O. Box 110, Victoria House, 23 Gruneisen Road, Finchley, London N3 1DZ. Used by permission.

2. Lead us, Father, into freedom,
   from despair your world release;
   that, redeemed from war and hatred,
   all may come and go in peace.
   Show us how through care and goodness
   fear will die and hope increase.

3. All that kills abundant living,
   let it from the earth be banned;
   pride of status, race or schooling
   dogmas that obscure your plan.
   In our common quest for justice
   may we hallow life's brief span.

4. You, creator-God, have written
   your great name on humankind;
   for our growing in your likeness
   bring the life of Christ to mind;
   that by our response and service
   earth its destiny may find.

Text: Fred Kaan (b. 1929)
Music: traditional French melody

263 Forth in the peace of Christ we go

SONG 34 (ANGELS' SONG) LM

1. Forth in the peace of Christ we go; Christ to the world with joy we bring; Christ in our minds, Christ on our lips, Christ in our hearts, the world's true King.

2. King of our hearts, Christ makes us kings;
   kingship with him his servants gain;
   with Christ, the Servant-Lord of all,
   Christ's world we serve to share Christ's reign.

3. Priests of the world, Christ sends us forth
   this world of time to consecrate,
   our world of sin by grace to heal,
   Christ's world in Christ to re-create.

4. Prophets of Christ, we hear his word:
   he claims our minds, to search his ways,
   he claims our lips, to speak his truth,
   he claims our hearts, to sing his praise.

5. We are his Church, he makes us one:
   here is one hearth for all to find,
   here is one flock, one Shepherd-King,
   here is one faith, one heart, one mind.

Text: James Quinn (b.1919)
Music: Orlando Gibbons (1583-1625)
Text © Copyright 1969 Geoffrey Chapman, an imprint of Cassell plc,
Wellington House, 125 Strand, London WC2R 0BB. Used by permission.

264 Forty days and forty nights
AUS DER TIEFE (HEINLEIN) 77 77

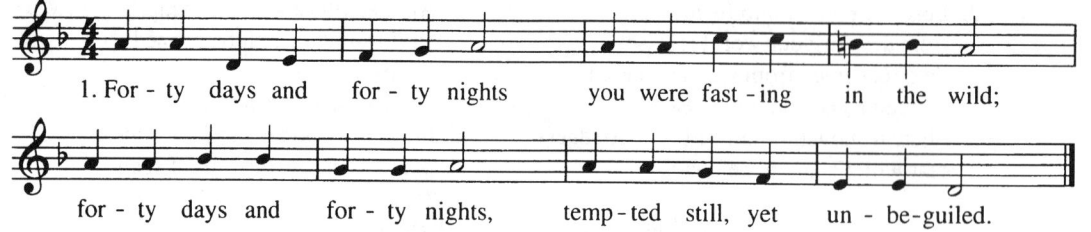

1. For-ty days and for-ty nights you were fast-ing in the wild;
for-ty days and for-ty nights, temp-ted still, yet un-be-guiled.

2. Sunbeams scorching all the day,
chilly dew-drops nightly shed,
prowling beasts about your way,
stones your pillow, earth your bed.

3. Let us your endurance share,
and from earthly greed abstain,
with you vigilant in prayer,
with you strong to suffer pain.

4. Then if evil on us press,
flesh or spirit to assail,
Victor in the wilderness,
help us not to swerve or fail.

5. So shall peace divine be ours;
holy gladness, pure and true:
come to us, angelic powers,
such as ministered to you.

6. Keep, O keep us, Saviour dear,
ever constant by your side,
that with you we may appear
at th' eternal Eastertide.

Text: George Hunt Smyttan (1822-1870) adapted by Michael Forster (b.1946)
Music: melody from 'Nürnbergisches Gesangbuch' (1676)
This version of text © Copyright 1999 Kevin Mayhew Ltd.

265 For you my soul is thirsting

Refrain
For you my soul is thirst-ing, O Lord, for you my soul is thirst-ing O Lord, for you my soul is thirst-ing.

1. You are my God, it is you that I seek. I am thirst-ing for you; just as a land that is wea-ry and parched, longs my bo-dy for you.

2. Day after day I will watch in your house.
You are glory and pow'r;
better than life is your love for your child,
I shall sing to your praise.

3. All my life long I will bless you, my God,
lift my hands in your name;
richly my soul will be feasted with love,
I shall praise you with joy.

4. I will remember you, Lord, when I sleep.
I will watch through the night;
you are my help and with you I am safe
in the shade of your wing.

Text: Susan Sayers (b.1946) based on Psalm 62
Music: Andrew Moore (b.1954)
© Copyright 1995 Kevin Mayhew Ltd.

266 Freedom for my people

Refrain:
Freedom for my people! Freedom for my people! Call them to liberty! Alleluia! Healing! Liberation for a new creation! Set all my people free!

1. Moses was the man I called to liberty;
   sent him back to Pharaoh's court to set my people free.
   He led all my people out to liberty,
   calling them to leave that land of their slavery.

2. Through the desert they were led to liberty;
   with the manna they were fed so they could be free.
   And I gave my law to them for liberty,
   so that they might live in peace and in unity.

3. Oh, when will my people know how to be free?
   All my prophets tried to show: the people would not see.
   So I gave my only Son, precious to me;
   on the cross he hung in pain for your liberty.

4. Jesus rose on Easter Day to liberty.
   He will never go away - he will set you free!
   Never will he die again! He is with me,
   and we have begun our reign with his victory!

   (after vs.4 and 5) Gloria! Alleluia!
   Gloria! Alleluia!
   Sing of his victory! Alleluia!
   Gloria! Alleluia!
   Gloria! Alleluia!
   Set all my people free!

5. I'm your God and you are mine: now you are free!
   Eat my bread and drink my wine! Come and follow me!
   You will know my Spirit's love and you will see
   power coming from above to set all people free!

Text: Damian Lundy (1944-1997)
Music: Traditional South American melody
Text © Copyright 1982, 1999 Kevin Mayhew Ltd.

267 From heaven you came
The Servant King

Worshipfully

1. From heav'n you came, helpless babe, entered our world, your glory veiled; not to be served but to serve, and give your life that we might live.

Refrain
This is our God, the Servant King, he calls us now to follow him, to bring our lives as a daily offering of worship to the Servant King.

2. There in the garden of tears,
   my heavy load he chose to bear;
   his heart with sorrow was torn.
   'Yet not my will but yours,' he said.

3. Come see his hands and his feet,
   the scars that speak of sacrifice,
   hands that flung stars into space,
   to cruel nails surrendered.

4. So let us learn how to serve,
   and in our lives enthrone him;
   each other's needs to prefer,
   for it is Christ we're serving.

Text and Music: Graham Kendrick (b.1950)
© Copyright 1983 Kingsway's Thankyou Music, P.O. Box 75, Eastbourne,
East Sussex BN23 6NW, UK. Used by permission.

268 From many grains

SONG 1   10 10 10 10 10 10

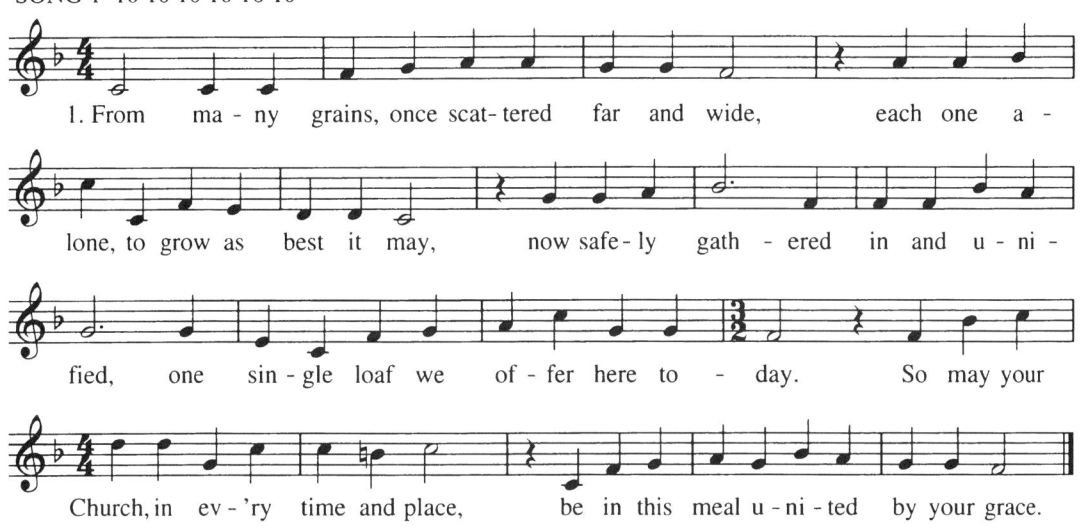

1. From many grains, once scattered far and wide,
each one alone, to grow as best it may,
now safely gathered in and unified,
one single loaf we offer here today.
So may your Church, in ev'ry time and place,
be in this meal united by your grace.

2. From many grapes, once living on the vine,
now crushed and broken under human feet,
we offer here this single cup of wine:
the sign of love, unbroken and complete.
So may we stand among the crucified,
and live the risen life of him who died.

3. From many places gathered, we are here,
each with a gift that we alone can bring.
O Spirit of the living God, draw near,
make whole by grace our broken offering.
O crush the pride that bids us stand alone;
let flow the love that makes our spirits one.

Text: Michael Forster (b.1946) based on the Didaché
Music: Orlando Gibbons (1583-1625)
Text © Copyright 1992 Kevin Mayhew Ltd.

269 From the depths we cry to thee

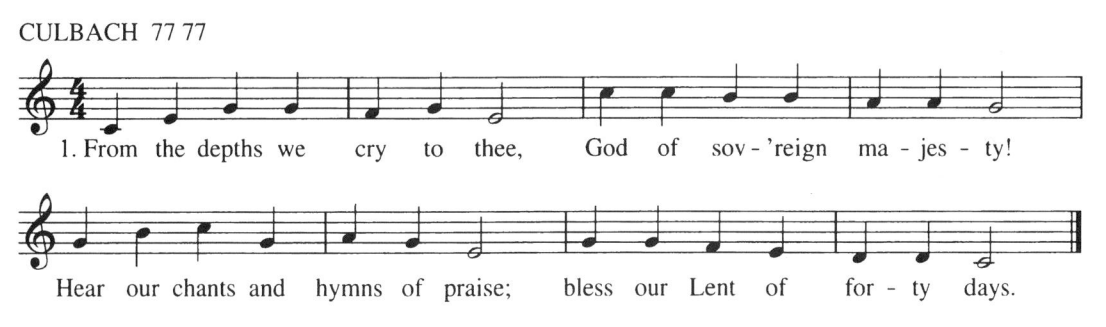

CULBACH   77 77

1. From the depths we cry to thee,
God of sov-'reign majesty!
Hear our chants and hymns of praise;
bless our Lent of forty days.

2. Though our consciences proclaim
our transgressions and our shame,
cleanse us, Lord, we humbly plead,
from our sins of thought and deed.

3. Lord, accept our Lenten fast
and forgive our sinful past,
that we may partake with thee
in the Easter mystery.

This may also be sung to the tune of 'Forty days and forty nights' at No. 264

Text: Sister M. Teresine based on Psalm 129
Music: Johann Scheffler 'Heilige Seelenlust' (1657)

LITURGICAL
HYMNS OLD & NEW

270 From the sun's rising

1. From the sun's rising unto the sun's setting,
Jesus, our Lord, shall be great in the earth;
and all earth's kingdoms shall be his dominion,
all of creation shall sing of his worth.

Refrain
Let ev'ry heart, ev'ry voice, ev'ry tongue join with spirits ablaze;
one in his love, we will circle the world with the song of his praise.
O let all his people rejoice,
and let all the earth hear his voice.

2. To evr'y tongue, tribe and nation he sends us,
to make disciples, to teach and baptise.
For all authority to him is given;
now, as his witnesses, we shall arise.

3. Come, let us join with the Church from all nations,
cross ev'ry border, throw wide ev'ry door;
workers with him as he gathers his harvest,
till earth's far corners our Saviour adore.

Text and Music: Graham Kendrick (b.1950)

© Copyright 1988 Make Way Music, P.O. Box 263, Croydon, Surrey CR9 5AP, UK.
International copyright secured. All rights reserved. Used by permission.

271 From the very depths of darkness

TUNE 1: CAMERON'S 15 15 15 7 and Refrain

1. From the very depths of darkness springs a bright and living light; out of falsehood and deceit a greater truth is brought to sight; in the halls of death, defiant, life is dancing with delight! The Lord is risen indeed!

Refrain
Christ is risen! Hallelujah!
Christ is risen! Hallelujah!
The Lord is risen indeed!

2. Jesus meets us at the dawning
of the resurrection day;
speaks our name with love, and gently
says that here we may not stay:
'Do not cling to me, but go to all
the fearful ones and say,
"The Lord is risen indeed!"'

3. So proclaim it in the high-rise,
in the hostel let it ring;
make it known in Cardboard City,
let the homeless rise and sing:
'He is Lord of life abundant,
and he changes everything;
the Lord is risen indeed!'

4. In the heartlands of oppression,
sound the cry of liberty;
where the poor are crucified,
behold the Lord of Calvary;
from the fear of death and dying,
Christ has set his people free;
the Lord is risen indeed!

5. To the tyrant, tell the gospel
of a love he's never known
in his guarded palace tomb,
condemned to live and die alone:
'Take the risk of love and freedom;
Christ has rolled away the stone!
The Lord is risen indeed!'

6. When our spirits are entombed
in mortal prejudice and pride;
when the gates of hell itself
are firmly bolted from inside;
at the bidding of his Spirit,
we may fling them open wide;
The Lord is risen indeed!

Text: Michael Forster (b.1946)
Music: Christopher Tambling (b.1964)
© Copyright 1992 Kevin Mayhew Ltd.

TUNE 2: BATTLE HYMN 77 87 87 6 and Refrain

1. From the very depths of darkness springs a bright and living light; out of falsehood and deceit a greater truth is brought to sight; in the halls of death, defiant, life is dancing with delight! The Lord is risen indeed!

Refrain
Christ is risen! Hallelujah! Christ is risen! Hallelujah! Christ is risen! Hallelujah! The Lord is risen indeed!

2. Jesus meets us at the dawning
of the resurrection day;
speaks our name with love, and gently
says that here we may not stay:
'Do not cling to me, but go to all
the fearful ones and say,
"The Lord is risen indeed!"'

3. So proclaim it in the high-rise,
in the hostel let it ring;
make it known in Cardboard City,
let the homeless rise and sing:
'He is Lord of life abundant,
and he changes everything;
the Lord is risen indeed!'

4. In the heartlands of oppression,
sound the cry of liberty;
where the poor are crucified,
behold the Lord of Calvary;
from the fear of death and dying,
Christ has set his people free;
the Lord is risen indeed!

5. To the tyrant, tell the gospel
of a love he's never known
in his guarded palace tomb,
condemned to live and die alone:
'Take the risk of love and freedom;
Christ has rolled away the stone!
The Lord is risen indeed!'

6. When our spirits are entombed
in mortal prejudice and pride;
when the gates of hell itself
are firmly bolted from inside;
at the bidding of his Spirit,
we may fling them open wide;
The Lord is risen indeed!

Text: Michael Forster (b.1946)
Music: traditional American
Text © Copyright 1992, 1994 Kevin Mayhew Ltd.

LITURGICAL
HYMNS OLD & NEW

272 Gather around, for the table is spread

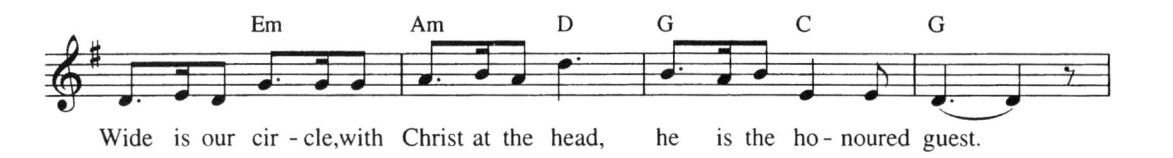

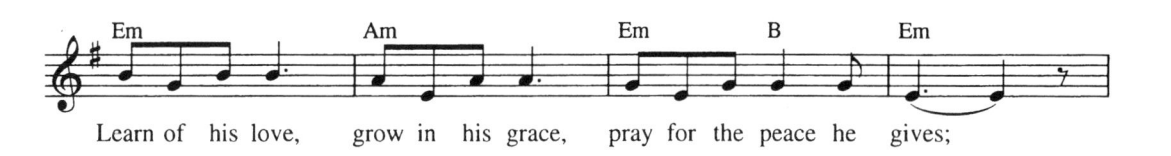

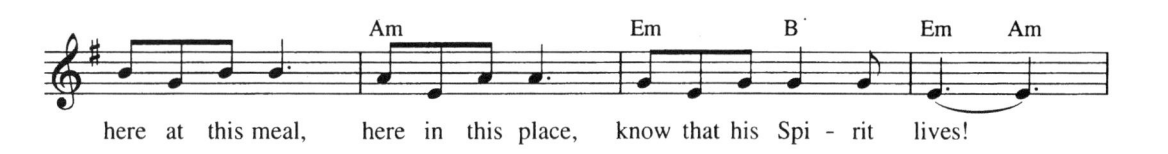

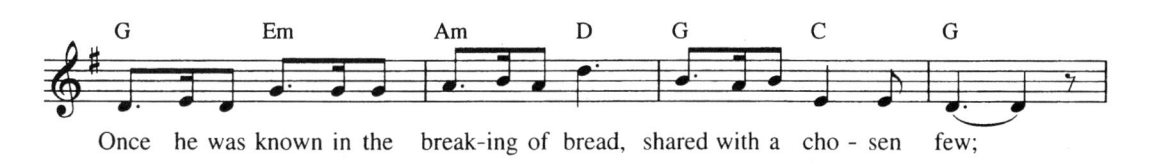

1. Gather around, for the table is spread, welcome the food and rest!
Wide is our circle, with Christ at the head, he is the honoured guest.
Learn of his love, grow in his grace, pray for the peace he gives;
here at this meal, here in this place, know that his Spirit lives!
Once he was known in the breaking of bread, shared with a chosen few;
multitudes gathered and by him were fed, so will he feed us too.

Text: Jean Holloway (b.1939)
Music: traditional Scottish melody
Text © Copyright 1994, 1999 Kevin Mayhew Ltd.

273 Gifts of bread and wine

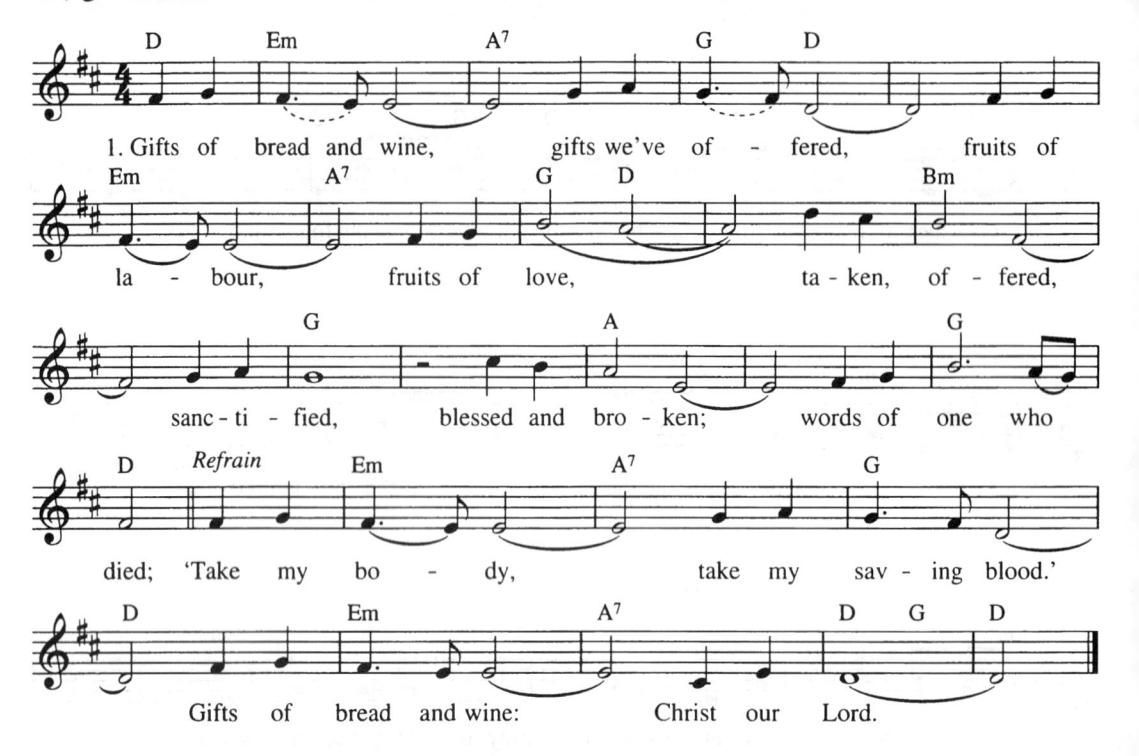

1. Gifts of bread and wine, gifts we've of-fered, fruits of la-bour, fruits of love, ta-ken, of-fered, sanc-ti-fied, blessed and bro-ken; words of one who died; *Refrain* 'Take my bo-dy, take my sav-ing blood.' Gifts of bread and wine: Christ our Lord.

2. Christ our Saviour, living presence here,
   as he promised while on earth:
   'I am with you for all time,
   I am with you in this bread and wine.'

3. To the Father, with the Spirit,
   one in union with the Son,
   for God's people, joined in prayer,
   faith is strengthened by the food we share.

Text and Music: Christine McCann (b.1951)
© Copyright 1978 Kevin Mayhew Ltd.

274 Give me joy in my heart
Sing hosanna

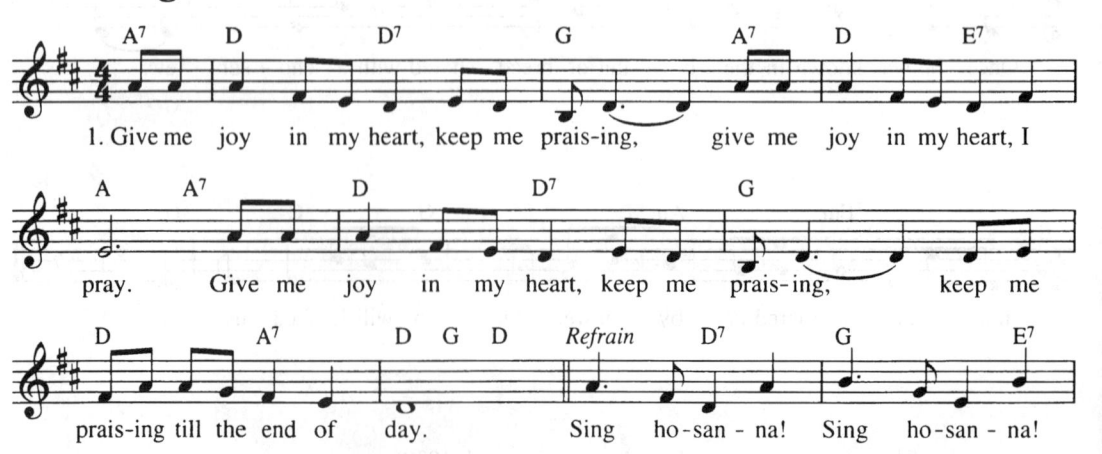

1. Give me joy in my heart, keep me prais-ing, give me joy in my heart, I pray. Give me joy in my heart, keep me prais-ing, keep me prais-ing till the end of day. *Refrain* Sing ho-san-na! Sing ho-san-na!

Sing ho-san-na to the King of kings! Sing ho-san-na!
Sing ho-san-na! Sing ho-san-na to the King!

2. Give me peace in my heart, keep me resting,
   give me peace in my heart, I pray.
   Give me peace in my heart, keep me resting,
   keep me resting till the end of day.

3. Give me love in my heart, keep me serving,
   give me love in my heart, I pray.
   Give me love in my heart, keep me serving,
   keep me serving till the end of day.

4. Give me oil in my lamp, keep me burning,
   give me oil in my lamp, I pray.
   Give me oil in my lamp, keep me burning,
   keep me burning till the end of day.

Text and Music: traditional

275 Give thanks to God

1. Give thanks to God, for he is good, his love will ne-ver end. To our e-ter-nal Sa-viour let songs of praise as-cend. Let all his peo-ple say with joy, 'His love will ne-ver end.' Sing al-le-lu-ia! Praise the Lord! Al-le-lu-ia! Sing al-le-lu-ia! Praise the Lord!

2. The Lord has triumphed gloriously,
   his hand has raised me high.
   Now I shall tell his wonders,
   and never shall I die.
   Let all his people sing with joy,
   'His hand has raised me high.'

3. The stone the builders cast aside
   is now the cornerstone,
   a work by which God's glory
   and faithfulness are shown.
   Let all his people sing with joy,
   'He is our cornerstone.'

Text: Michael Forster (b.1946) based on Psalm 117
Music: Christopher Tambling (b.1964)
© Copyright 1997 Kevin Mayhew Ltd.

276 Give thanks with a grateful heart

Give thanks with a grateful heart, give thanks to the Holy One, give thanks because he's given Jesus Christ, his Son. And now let the weak say, 'I am strong', let the poor say, 'I am rich', because of what the Lord has done for us. And now let the weak say, 'I am strong', let the poor say, 'I am rich', because of what the Lord has done for us, us, for us.

Text and Music: Henry Smith
© Copyright 1978 Integrity's Hosanna! Music. Administered by Kingsway's Thankyou Music, P.O. Box 75, Eastbourne, East Sussex BN23 6NW, UK. Used by permission.

277 Glorify the Lord

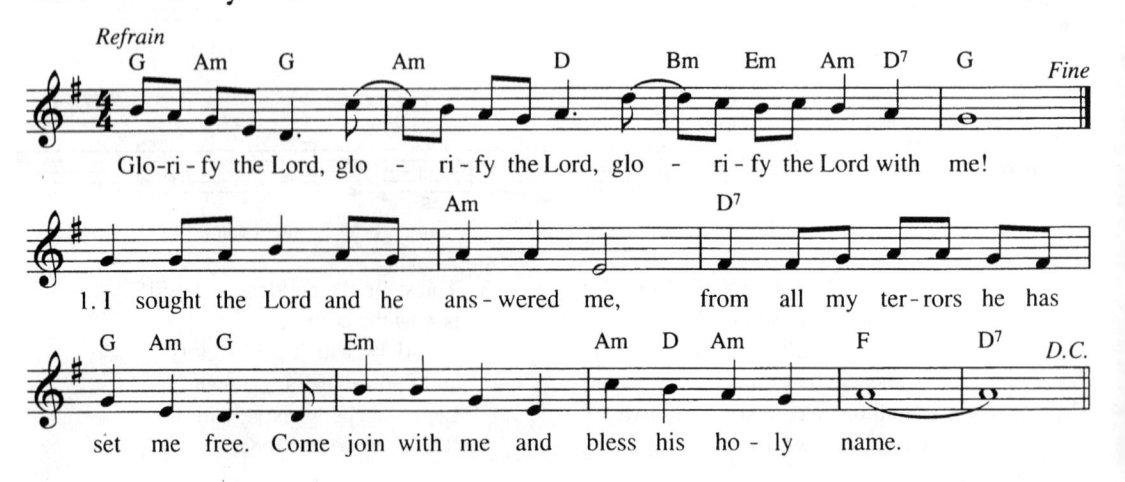

Refrain
Glorify the Lord, glorify the Lord, glorify the Lord with me!

1. I sought the Lord and he answered me, from all my terrors he has set me free. Come join with me and bless his holy name.

© Copyright 1984 Kevin Mayhew Ltd.

2. Look at the Lord, do not be ashamed,
   he will deliver those who call his name.
   The poor have called, the Lord has heard their plea.

3. O taste and see that the Lord is good.
   Happy are those who put their trust in him.
   So fear the Lord and you will know no want.

Text: Peter Gonsalves based on Psalm 33
Music: Peter Gonsalves

278 Glorious God, King of creation

1. Glo-ri-ous God, King of cre-a-tion, we praise you, we bless you, we wor-ship you in song. Glo-ri-ous God in ad-o-ra-tion, at your feet we be-long. *Fine*

Refrain
Lord of life, Fa-ther al-migh-ty, Lord of hearts, Christ the King. Lord of love, Ho-ly Spi-rit, to whom we hom-age bring. *D.C.*

2. Glorious God, magnificent, holy,
   we love you, adore you,
   and come to you in pray'r.
   Glorious God, mighty, eternal,
   we sing your praise ev'rywhere.

Text and Music: Sebastian Temple (1928-1997)
© Copyright 1967 OCP Publications, 5536 NE Hassalo, Portland, OR 97213, USA.
All rights reserved. Used by permission.

279 Glory and praise to our God

Refrain

Glo-ry and praise to our God, who a-lone gives light to our days. Ma-ny are the bless-ings he bears to those who trust in his ways.

1. We, the daugh-ters and sons of him who built the val-leys and plains, praise the won-ders our God has done in ev-'ry heart that sings.

2. In his wisdom he strengthens us,
like gold that's tested in fire.
Though the power of sin prevails,
our God is there to save.

3. Ev'ry moment of ev'ry day
our God is waiting to save,
always ready to seek the lost,
to answer those who pray.

4. God has wa-tered our bar-ren land and sent his mer-ci-ful rain. Now the riv-ers of life run full for a-ny-one to drink.

Text: Dan Schutte based on Psalm 64, 65
Music: Dan Schutte
© Copyright 1976 Daniel L. Schutte and New Dawn Music, 5536 NE Hassalo, Portland, OR 97213, USA.
All rights reserved. Used by permission.

280 Glory be to Jesus
CASWALL 65 65

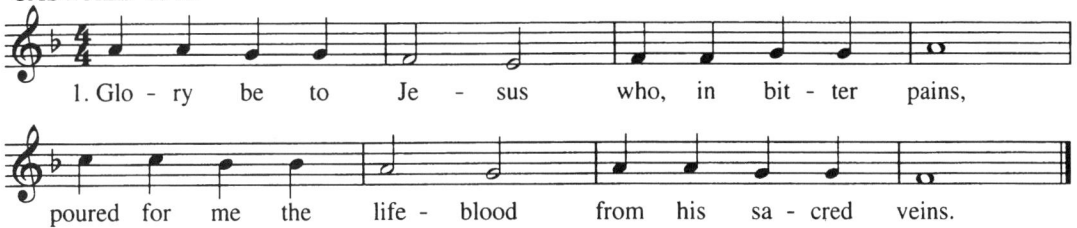

1. Glory be to Jesus
who, in bitter pains,
poured for me the lifeblood
from his sacred veins.

2. Grace and life eternal
in that blood I find:
blest be his compassion,
infinitely kind.

3. Blest, through endless ages,
be the precious stream
which, from endless torment,
did the world redeem.

4. There the fainting spirit
drinks of life her fill;
there, as in a fountain,
laves herself at will.

5. Abel's blood for vengeance
pleaded to the skies,
but the blood of Jesus
for our pardon cries.

6. Oft as it is sprinkled
on our guilty hearts
Satan in confusion
terror-struck departs.

7. Oft as earth exulting
wafts its praise on high
angel hosts rejoicing,
make their glad reply.

8. Lift, then, all your voices,
swell the mighty flood;
louder still and louder,
praise the precious blood.

Text: 'Viva, viva, Gesù' (18th century) trans. Edward Caswall (1814-1878) alt.
Music: Friedrich Filitz (1804-1876)

281 Glory to thee, Lord God
CORONA DSM

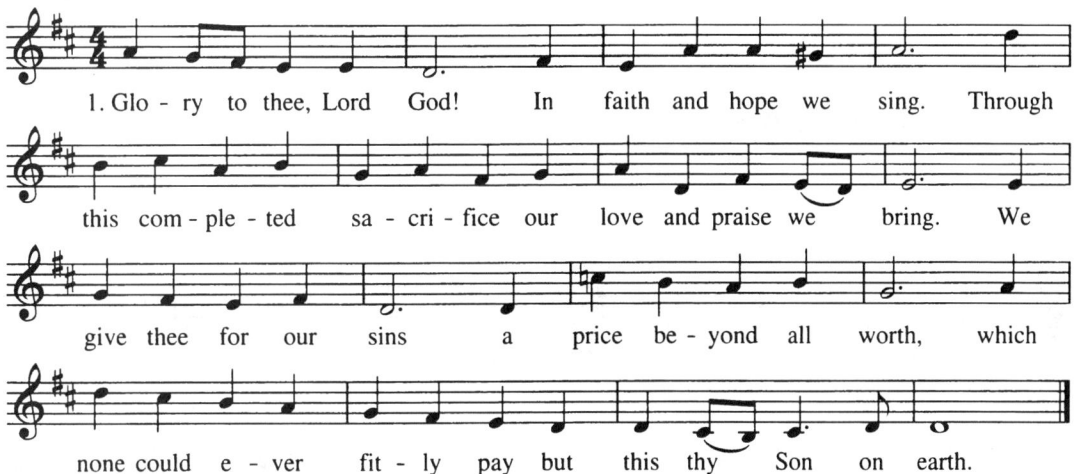

1. Glory to thee, Lord God! In faith and hope we sing. Through this completed sacrifice our love and praise we bring. We give thee for our sins a price beyond all worth, which none could ever fitly pay but this thy Son on earth.

2. Here is the Lord of all,
to thee in glory slain;
of worthless givers, worthy gift,
a victim without stain.
Through him we give thee thanks,
with him we bend the knee,
in him be all our life, who is
our one true way to thee.

3. So may this sacrifice
we offer here this day,
be joined with our poor lives in all
we think and do and say.
By living true to grace,
for thee and thee alone,
our sorrows, labours, and our joys
will be his very own.

Text: John Greally
Music: Richard Runciman Terry (1865-1938)
Text © Copyright The Trustees for Roman Catholic Purposes Registered,
114 Mount Street, London W1Y 6AH. Used by permission. Music © Copyright control.

282 Glory to thee, my God, this night

TALLIS'S CANON LM

1. Glo-ry to thee, my God, this night for all the bless-ings of the light; keep me, O keep me, King of kings, be-neath thine own al-migh-ty wings.

A higher setting will be found at No. 129

2. Forgive me, Lord, for thy dear Son,
the ill that I this day have done,
that with the world, myself and thee,
I, ere I sleep, at peace may be.

3. Teach me to live, that I may dread
the grave as little as my bed;
teach me to die, that so I may
rise glorious at the awful day.

4. O may my soul on thee repose,
and with sweet sleep mine eyelids close;
sleep that may me more vig'rous make
to serve my God when I awake.

5. Praise God, from whom all blessings flow;
praise him, all creatures here below;
praise him above, ye heav'nly host;
praise Father, Son and Holy Ghost.

Text: Thomas Ken (1637-1710)
Music: Thomas Tallis (c.1505-1585)

283 God be in my head

GOD BE IN MY HEAD Irregular

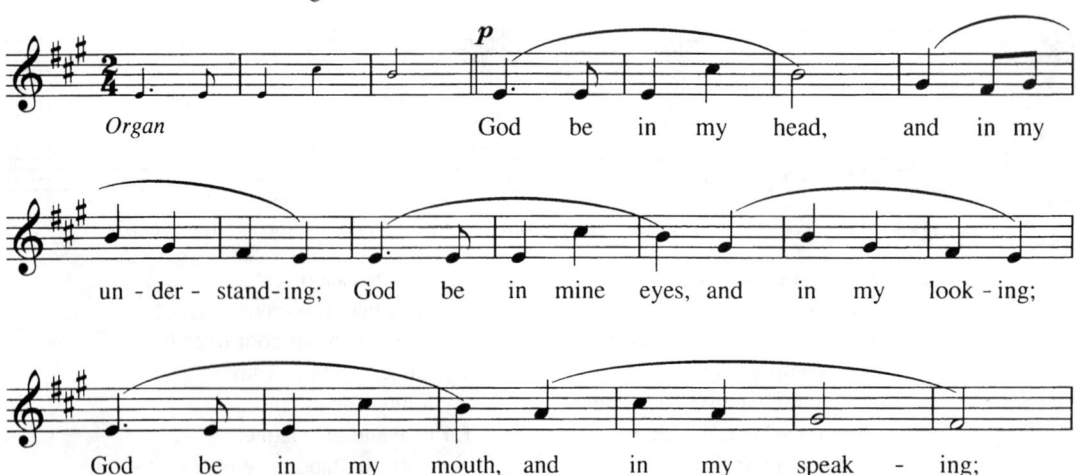

Organ God be in my head, and in my un-der-stand-ing; God be in mine eyes, and in my look-ing; God be in my mouth, and in my speak-ing;

Music © Copyright The Trustees of Sir Walford Davies. Used by permission of Oxford University Press, Great Clarendon Street, Oxford OX2 6DP.

God be in my heart, and in my think-ing;

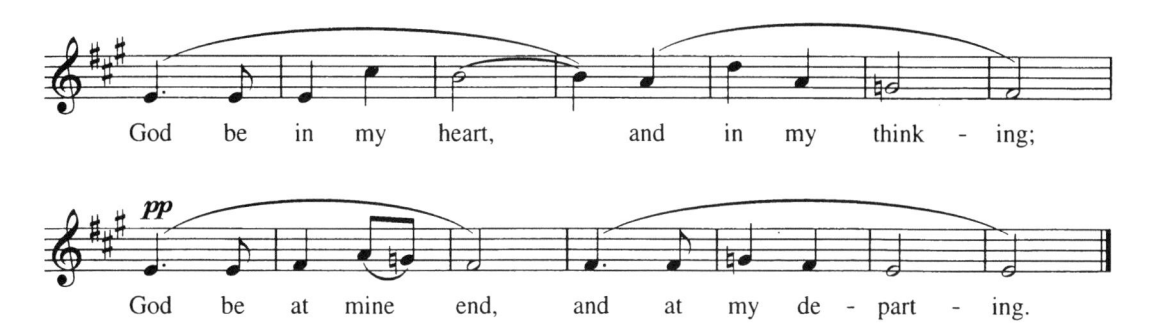

God be at mine end, and at my de-part-ing.

Text: 'Book of Hours' (1514)
Music: Henry Walford Davies (1869-1941)

284 God everlasting, wonderful and holy

CHRISTE SANCTORUM 11 11 11 5

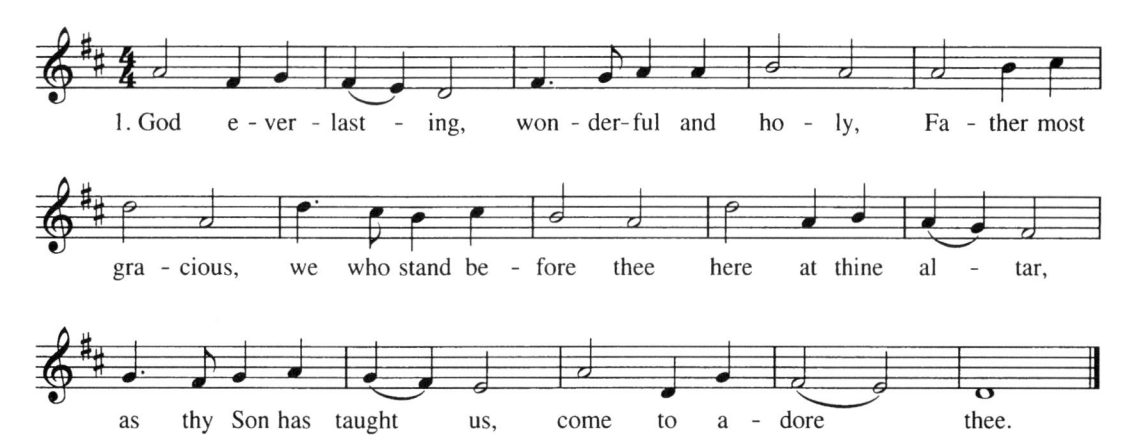

1. God e-ver-last-ing, won-der-ful and ho-ly, Fa-ther most gra-cious, we who stand be-fore thee here at thine al-tar, as thy Son has taught us, come to a-dore thee.

A lower setting will be found at No. 615

2. Countless the mercies thou has lavished on us,
source of all blessing to all creatures living;
to thee we render, for thy love o'erflowing,
humble thanksgiving.

3. Now in remembrance of our great Redeemer,
dying on Calv'ry, rising and ascending,
through him we offer what he ever offers,
sinners befriending.

4. Strength to the living, rest to the departed,
grant, Holy Father, through this pure oblation:
may the life-giving bread for ever bring us
health and salvation.

Text: Harold Riley
Music: from the 'Paris Antiphoner' (1681)

285 God fills me with joy

God fills me with joy, alleluia. His holy presence is my robe, alleluia.

1. My soul, now glorify the Lord who is my Saviour. Rejoice, for who am I, that God has shown me favour.

2. The world shall call me blest
and ponder on my story.
In me is manifest
God's greatness and his glory.

3. For those who are his friends,
and keep his laws as holy,
his mercy never ends,
and he exalts the lowly.

4. But by his pow'r the great,
the proud, the self-conceited,
the kings who sit in state,
are humbled and defeated.

5. He feeds the starving poor,
he guards his holy nation,
fulfilling what he swore
long since in revelation.

6. Then glorify with me
the Lord who is my Saviour:
one holy Trinity
for ever and for ever.

Text: Jean-Paul Lécot (b.1947) based on Luke 1:46-55 trans. Michael Hodgetts (b.1936)
Music: Paul Décha
Text © 1974 Michael Hodgetts. Used by permission.
Music © Copyright 1988 Kevin Mayhew Ltd.

286 God forgave my sin
Freely, freely

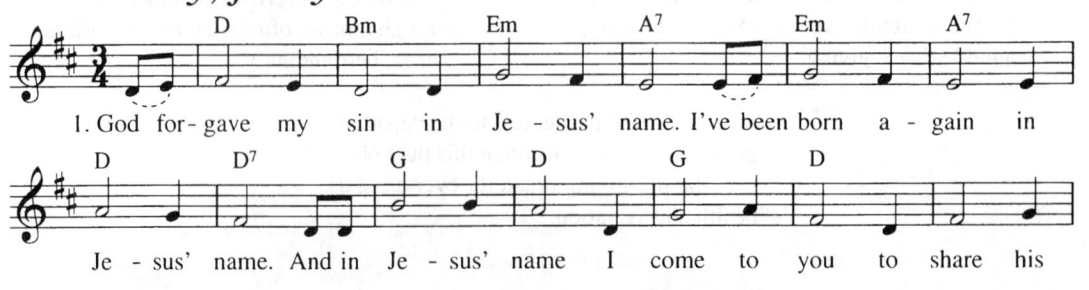

1. God forgave my sin in Jesus' name. I've been born again in Jesus' name. And in Jesus' name I come to you to share his

© Copyright 1972 Bud John Songs /EMI Christian Music Publishing. Administered by CopyCare Ltd, P.O. Box 77, Hailsham, East Sussex BN27 3EF, UK. Used by permission.

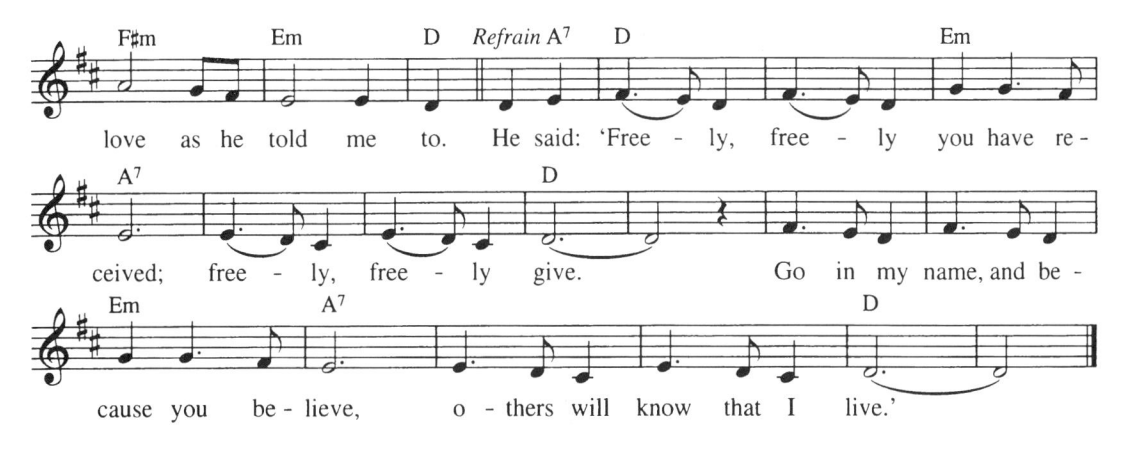

love as he told me to. He said: 'Free-ly, free-ly you have re-ceived; free-ly, free-ly give. Go in my name, and be-cause you be-lieve, o-thers will know that I live.'

2. All pow'r is giv'n in Jesus' name,
in earth and heav'n in Jesus' name.
And in Jesus' name I come to you
to share his pow'r as he told me to.

3. God gives us life in Jesus' name,
he lives in us in Jesus' name.
And in Jesus' name I come to you
to share his peace as he told me to.

Text and Music: Carol Owens

287 Godhead here in hiding

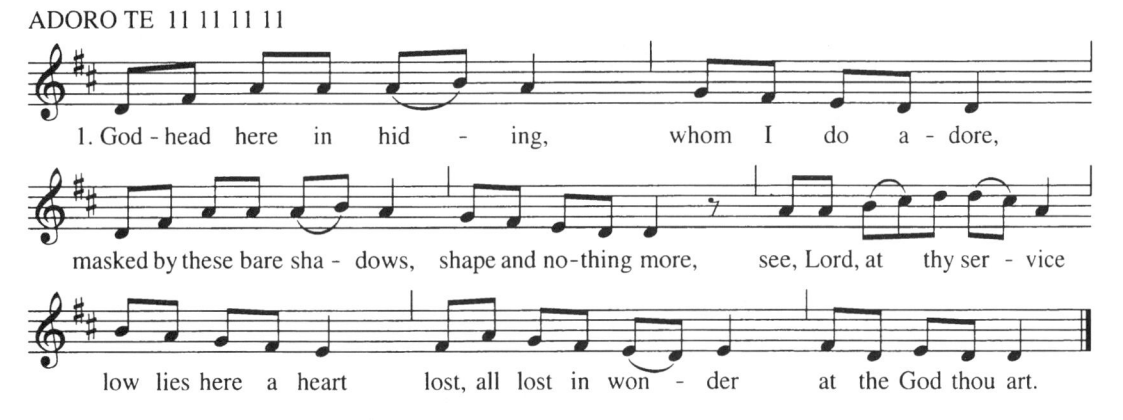

ADORO TE 11 11 11 11

1. God-head here in hid-ing, whom I do a-dore,
masked by these bare sha-dows, shape and no-thing more,
see, Lord, at thy ser-vice low lies here a heart
lost, all lost in won-der at the God thou art.

Another translation of this hymn will be found at No. 396

2. Seeing, touching, tasting are in thee deceived;
how, says trusty hearing, that shall be believed?
What God's Son hath told me, take for truth I do;
truth himself speaks truly, or there's nothing true.

3. On the cross thy Godhead made no sign to men;
here thy very manhood steals from human ken;
both are my confession, both are my belief;
and I pray the prayer of the dying thief.

4. I am not like Thomas, wounds I cannot see,
but can plainly call thee Lord and God as he;
this faith each day deeper be my holding of,
daily make me harder hope and dearer love.

5. O thou our reminder of Christ crucified,
living Bread, the life of us for whom he died,
lend this life to me then; feed and feast my mind,
there be thou the sweetness man was meant to find.

6. Jesu, whom I look at shrouded here below,
I beseech thee send me what I long for so,
some day to gaze on thee face to face in light
and be blest for ever with thy glory's sight.

Text: ascribed to St. Thomas Aquinas (1227-1274)
trans. Gerard Manley Hopkins (1844-1889) alt.
Music: Plainsong

288 God in the planning
Bridegroom and bride

SLANE 10 10 10 10

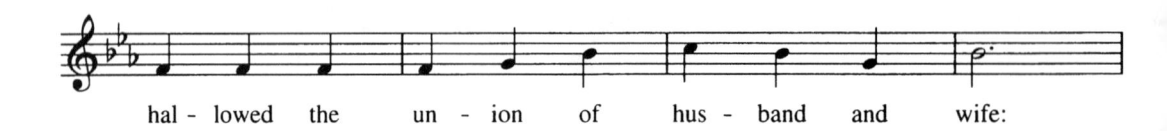

1. God, in the plan-ning and pur-pose of life,
hal-lowed the un-ion of hus-band and wife:
this we em-bo-dy where love is dis-played,
rings are pre-sen-ted and pro-mi-ses made.

2. Jesus was found, at a similar feast,
taking the roles of both water and priest,
turning the worldly towards the divine,
tears into the laughter and water to wine.

3. Therefore we pray that his Spirit preside
over the wedding of bridegroom and bride,
fulfilling all that they've hoped will come true,
lighting with love all they dream of and do.

4. Praise then the Maker, the Spirit, the Son,
source of the love through which two are made one.
God's is the glory, the goodness and grace
seen in this marriage and known in this place.

Text: John L. Bell (b.1949) and Graham Maule (b. 1958)
Music: traditional Irish melody
Text © Copyright 1989 WGRG, Iona Community, 840 Govan Road, Glasgow G51 3UU, Scotland.
Used by permission from 'Love from Below' (Wild Goose Publications, 1989)

289 God is love

1. God is love, and the one who lives in love lives in God, and God lives in him. God is love, and the one who lives in love lives in God, and God lives in her. And we have come to know and have believed the love which God has for us. God is love, and all those who live in love live in God, and God lives in them.

2. God is hope, and the one who lives in hope lives in God, and God lives in him.
God is hope, and the one who lives in hope lives in God, and God lives in her.
And we have come to know and have believed the love which God has for us.
God is hope, and all those who live in hope live in God, and God lives in them.

3. God is peace, and the one who lives in peace lives in God, and God lives in him.
God is peace, and the one who lives in peace lives in God, and God lives in her.
And we have come to know and have believed the love which God has for us.
God is peace, and all those who live in peace live in God, and God lives in them.

4. God is joy, and the one who lives in joy lives in God, and God lives in him.
God is joy, and the one who lives in joy lives in God, and God lives in her.
And we have come to know and have believed the love which God has for us.
God is joy, and all those who live in joy live in God, and God lives in them.

Text and Music: traditional

290 God is love: his the care

VERSION 1: PERSONENT HODIE (THEODORIC) 666 66 and Refrain

1. God is love: his the care, tend-ing each, ev-'ry-where. God is love, all is there! Je-sus came to show him, that we all might know him!

Refrain
Sing a-loud, loud, loud! Sing a-loud, loud, loud! God is good! God is truth! God is beau-ty! Praise him!

2. None can see God above;
   we can share life and love;
   thus may we Godward move,
   seek him in creation,
   holding ev'ry nation.

3. Jesus lived on the earth,
   hope and life brought to birth
   and affirmed human worth,
   for he came to save us
   by the truth he gave us.

4. To our Lord praise we sing,
   light and life, friend and King,
   coming down, love to bring,
   pattern for our duty,
   showing God in beauty.

VERSION 2: PERSONENT HODIE (THEODORIC) 666 66 and Refrain

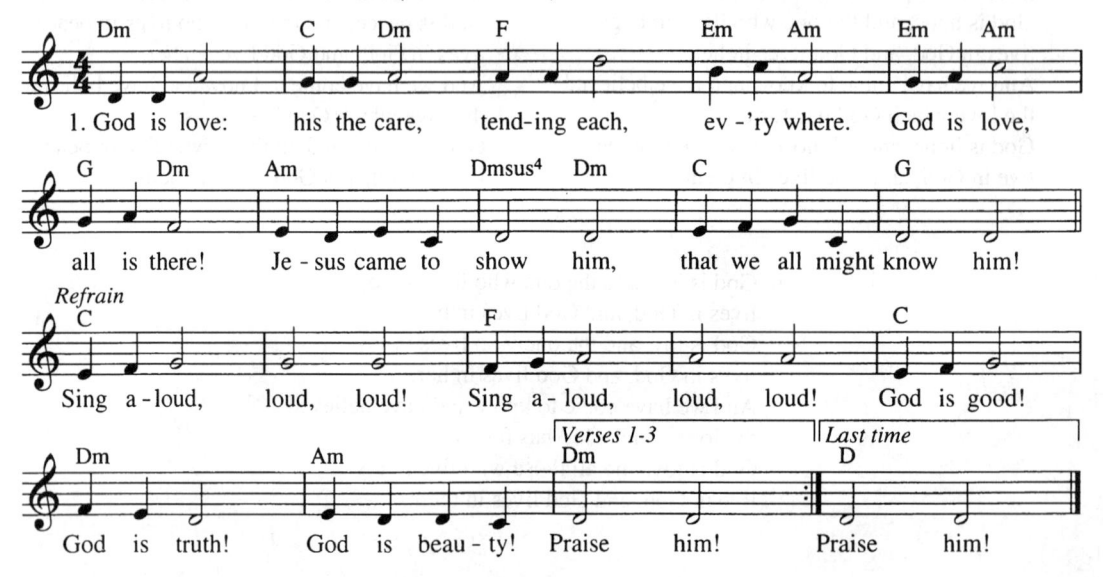

1. God is love: his the care, tend-ing each, ev-'ry where. God is love, all is there! Je-sus came to show him, that we all might know him!

Refrain
Sing a-loud, loud, loud! Sing a-loud, loud, loud! God is good! God is truth! God is beau-ty! Praise him! Praise him!

Verses 1-3 / Last time

Text: Percy Dearmer (1867-1936) alt.
Music: from 'Piae Cantones' (1582)
Text © Copyright Oxford University Press, Great Clarendon Street, Oxford OX2 6DP. Used by permission.

291 God is my great desire
LEONI 66 84 D

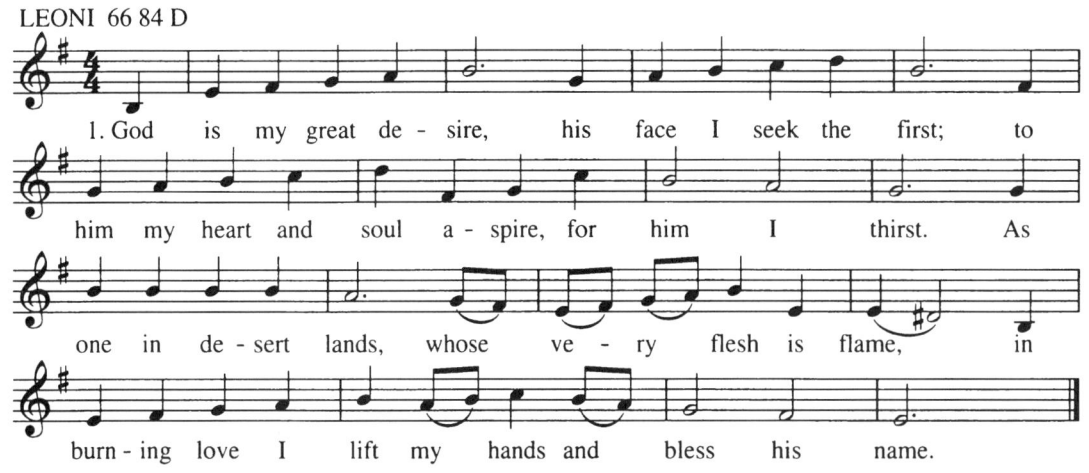

1. God is my great desire, his face I seek the first;
to him my heart and soul aspire, for him I thirst.
As one in desert lands, whose very flesh is flame,
in burning love I lift my hands and bless his name.

2. God is my true delight,
my richest feast his praise,
through silent watches of the night,
through all my days.
To him my spirit clings,
on him my soul is cast;
beneath the shadow of his wings
he holds me fast.

3. God is my strong defence
in ev'ry evil hour;
in him I face with confidence
the tempter's pow'r.
I trust his mercy sure,
with truth and triumph crowned:
my hope and joy for evermore
in him are found.

Text: Timothy Dudley-Smith (b.1926) based on Psalm 62
Music: transcribed from the 'Yigdal' by Meyer Lyon (c.1751-1797)
Text © Copyright Timothy Dudley-Smith, 9 Ashlands, Ford, Salisbury, Wiltshire SP4 6DY. Used by permission.

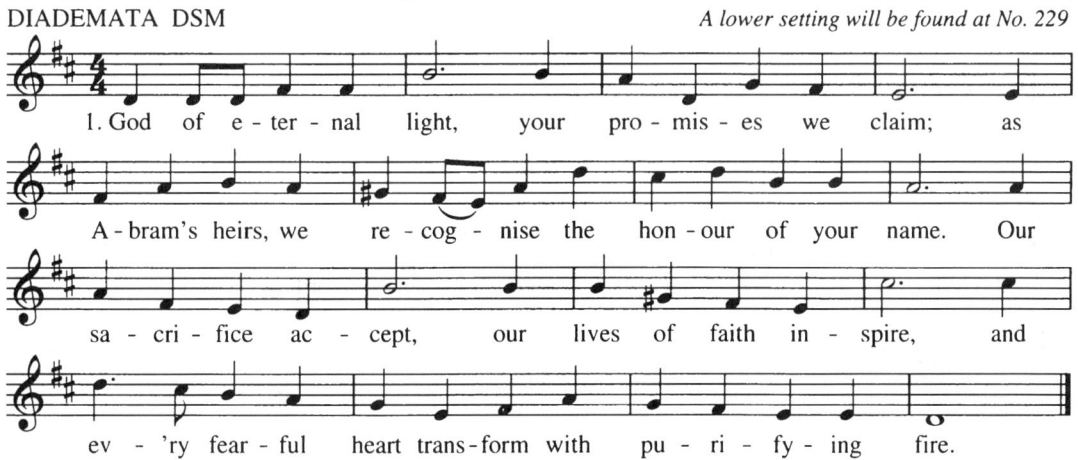

292 God of eternal light
DIADEMATA DSM   *A lower setting will be found at No. 229*

1. God of eternal light, your promises we claim;
as Abram's heirs, we recognise the honour of your name.
Our sacrifice accept, our lives of faith inspire,
and ev'ry fearful heart transform with purifying fire.

2. High on the mountain side
your glory was revealed,
and yet, that great mysterious light
a deeper truth concealed!
What fearful shadows still
those sights and sounds portray:
a dreadful kind of majesty
that words cannot convey!

3. Christ, from the heav'ns descend,
eternal life make known,
and all our mortal bodies change
to copies of your own.
Your great and glorious light
creation then shall see,
when truth and peace are all around,
and justice flowing free!

Text: Michael Forster (b.1946)
Music: George Job Elvey (1816-1893)
Text © Copyright 1993 Kevin Mayhew Ltd.

293 God of mercy and compassion

AU SANG QU'UN DIEU 87 87 D

1. God of mercy and compassion, look with pity upon me;
Father, let me call thee Father, 'tis thy child returns to thee.

Refrain
Jesus, Lord, I ask for mercy, knowing it is not in vain:
all my sins I now detest them, help me not to sin again.

2. Only by thy grace and mercy
may I hope for heav'n above,
where the Saints rejoice for ever
in a sea of boundless love.

3. See our Saviour, bleeding, dying
on the cross of Calvary;
to that cross my sins have nailed him,
yet he bleeds and dies for me.

Text: Edmund Vaughan (1827-1908) alt.
Music: French melody adapted by Giovanni Battista Pergolesi (1710-1736)

294 God of the covenant

LOBE DEN HERREN 14 14 4 7 8

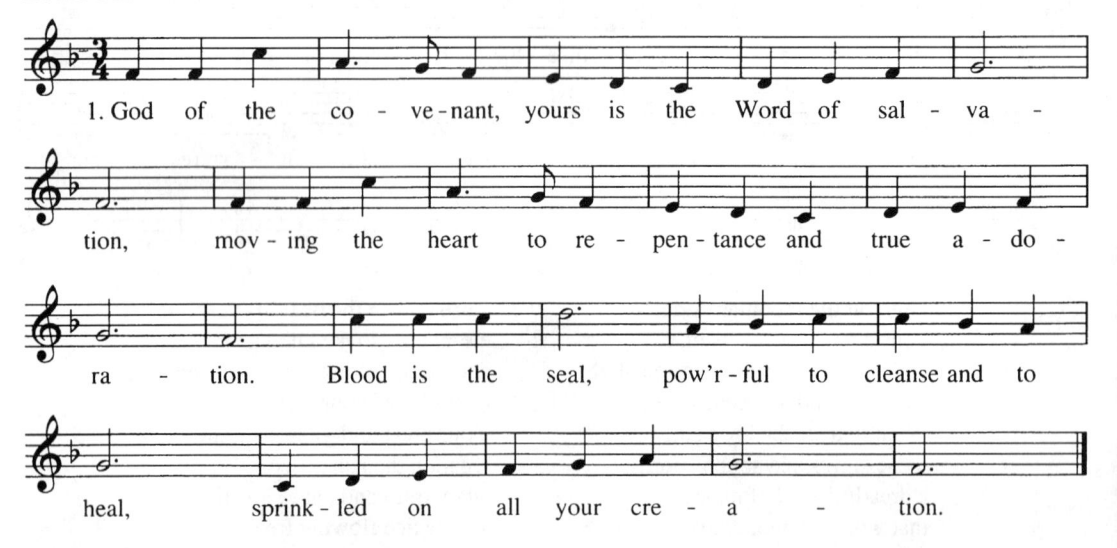

1. God of the covenant, yours is the Word of salvation,
moving the heart to repentance and true adoration.
Blood is the seal, pow'r-ful to cleanse and to heal,
sprinkled on all your creation.

Text © Copyright 1993 Kevin Mayhew Ltd.

2. God of the covenant, known in the breaking and pouring,
   body and blood of the Saviour, creation restoring:
   here we prepare,
   Christ, in your passion to share,
   humbly your presence adoring.

3. God of the covenant, yours is the Word of salvation
   bearing the terrible cost of the world's liberation.
   Freedom at last!
   Christ through the curtain has passed.
   God is at one with creation!

   Text: Michael Forster (b.1946)
   Music: melody from 'Praxis Pietatis Melica' (1668)

295 God of the Passover

LOBE DEN HERREN 14 14 4 7 8

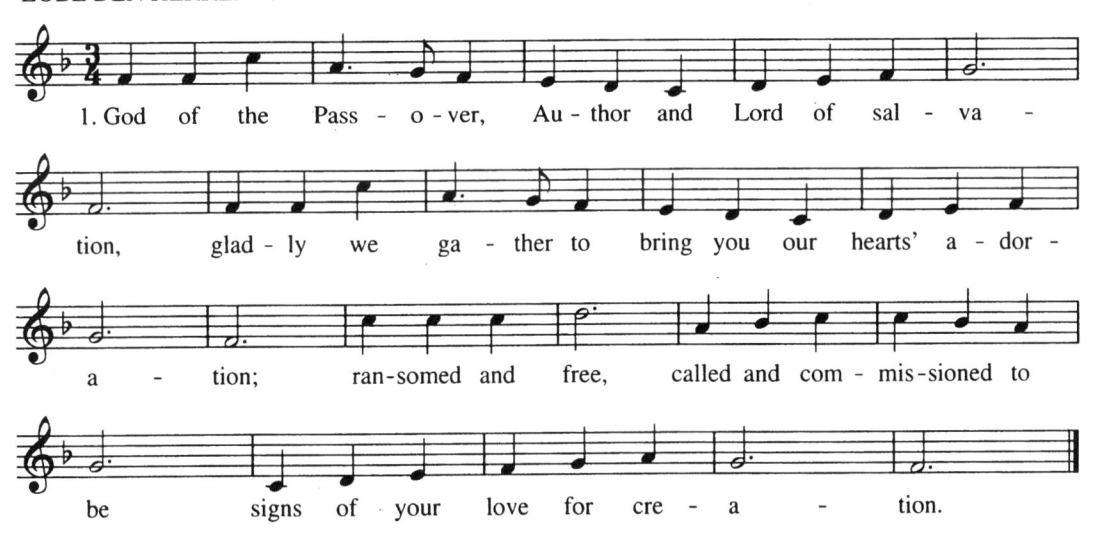

1. God of the Passover, Author and Lord of salvation,
   gladly we gather to bring you our hearts' adoration;
   ransomed and free,
   called and commissioned to be
   signs of your love for creation.

2. Here we remember that evening of wonder enthralling,
   myst'ry of passion divine, and betrayal appalling.
   Breaking the bread,
   'This is my body,' he said,
   'do this, my passion recalling.'

3. God of the Eucharist, humbly we gather before you
   and, at your table, for pardon and grace we implore you.
   Under the cross,
   counting as profit our loss,
   safe in its shade, we adore you.

   Text: Michael Forster (b.1946)
   Music: melody from 'Praxis Pietatis Melica' (1668)
   Text © Copyright 1993 Kevin Mayhew Ltd.

296 God rest you merry, gentlemen

GOD REST YOU MERRY 86 86 86 and Refrain

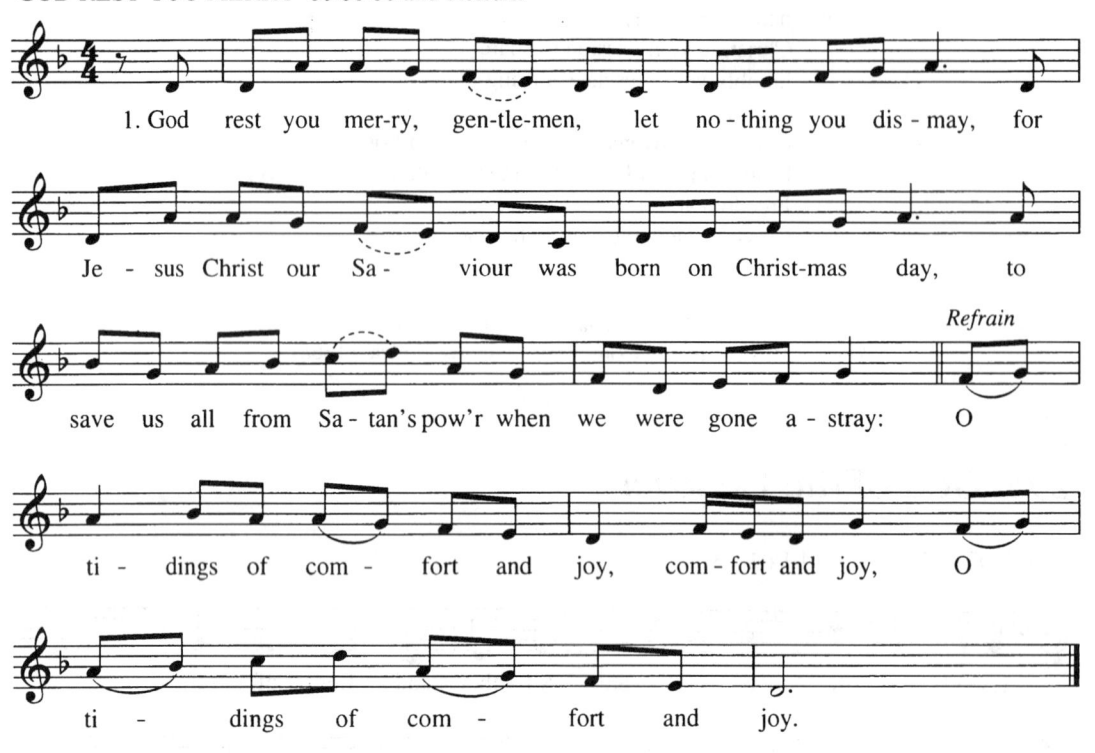

1. God rest you merry, gentlemen, let nothing you dismay,
for Jesus Christ our Saviour was born on Christmas day,
to save us all from Satan's pow'r when we were gone astray:

Refrain
O tidings of comfort and joy, comfort and joy,
O tidings of comfort and joy.

2. In Bethlehem, in Jewry,
this blessèd babe was born,
and laid within a manger,
upon this blessèd morn;
the which his mother Mary
did nothing take in scorn.

3. From God, our heav'nly Father,
a blessèd angel came,
and unto certain shepherds
brought tidings of the same,
how that in Bethlehem was born
the Son of God by name.

4. 'Fear not,' then said the angel,
'let nothing you affright,
this day is born a Saviour,
of virtue, pow'r and might;
by him the world is overcome
and Satan put to flight.'

5. The shepherds at those tidings
rejoicèd much in mind,
and left their flocks a-feeding,
in tempest, storm and wind,
and went to Bethlehem straightway
this blessèd babe to find.

6. But when to Bethlehem they came,
whereat this infant lay,
they found him in a manger,
where oxen feed on hay;
his mother Mary kneeling,
unto the Lord did pray.

7. Now to the Lord sing praises,
all you within this place,
and with true love and fellowship
each other now embrace;
this holy tide of Christmas
all others doth deface.

Text: traditional English alt.
Music: traditional English melody

297 God's Spirit is in my heart
Go, tell everyone

Tempo rubato

1. God's Spi-rit is in my heart. He has called me and set me a-part. This is what I have to do, what I have to do.

Refrain

He sent me to give the Good News to the poor, tell pris-'ners that they are pris-'ners no more, tell blind peo-ple that they can see, and set the down-trod-den free, and go tell ev-'ry-one the news that the king-dom of God has come, and go tell ev-'ry-one the news that God's king-dom has come. 3/4. Don't

2. Just as the Father sent me,
   so I'm sending you out to be
   my witnesses throughout the world,
   the whole of the world.

3. Don't carry a load in your pack,
   you don't need two shirts on your back.
   A workman can earn his own keep,
   can earn his own keep.

4. Don't worry what you have to say,
   don't worry because on that day
   God's Spirit will speak in your heart,
   will speak in your heart.

Text: Alan Dale and Hubert J. Richards (b.1921)
Music: Hubert J. Richards (b.1921)
© Copyright 1982 Kevin Mayhew Ltd.

298 Going home

1. Go - ing home, mov - ing on, through God's o - pen door; hush, my soul, have no fear, Christ has gone be - fore. Part - ing hurts, love pro - tests, pain is not de - nied; yet, in Christ, life and hope span the great di - vide. Go - ing home, mov - ing on, through God's o - pen door; hush, my soul, have no fear, Christ has gone be - fore, Christ has gone be - fore.

2. No more guilt, no more fear,
   all the past is healed:
   broken dreams now restored,
   perfect grace revealed.
   Christ has died, Christ is ris'n,
   Christ will come again:
   death destroyed, life restored,
   love alone shall reign.
   Going home, moving on,
   through God's open door;
   hush, my soul, have no fear,
   Christ has gone before,
   Christ has gone before.

Text: Michael Forster (b.1946)
Music: adapted from Dvořák's 'New World Symphony'
Text © Copyright 1999 Kevin Mayhew Ltd.

299 Go in peace

Refrain

Go in peace to be Christ's body. Go in peace, proclaim his Word.
You have shared his dying and his rising. Go in peace, Christ lives in you.

1. But our treasure is in earthen vessels, proving we are weak and need God's strength.
Bearing in our flesh the death of Jesus, we must show his life at work in us.

2. Though our outer nature may seem wasted,
daily is the inner self renewed.
For the love of Jesus Christ controls us,
since we know that one man died for all.

Text and Music: Aniceto Nazareth
© Copyright 1984 Kevin Mayhew Ltd.

300 Good Christians all, rejoice

IN DULCI JUBILO Irregular

1. Good Christians all, rejoice with heart and soul and voice!
Give ye heed to what we say: News! News! Jesus Christ is born today; ox and ass before him bow, and he is in the manger now: Christ is born today, Christ is born today!

2. Good Christians all, rejoice
with heart and soul and voice!
Now ye hear of endless bliss:
Joy! Joy! Jesus Christ was born for this.
He hath opened heaven's door,
and we are blest for evermore:
Christ was born for this,
Christ was born for this.

3. Good Christians all, rejoice
with heart and soul and voice!
Now ye need not fear the grave:
Peace! Peace! Jesus Christ was born to save;
calls you one, and calls you all,
to gain his everlasting hall:
Christ was born to save,
Christ was born to save.

Text: John Mason Neale (1818-1866) alt.
Music: 14th century German carol melody

301 Good King Wenceslas

TEMPUS ADEST FLORIDUM 76 76 D

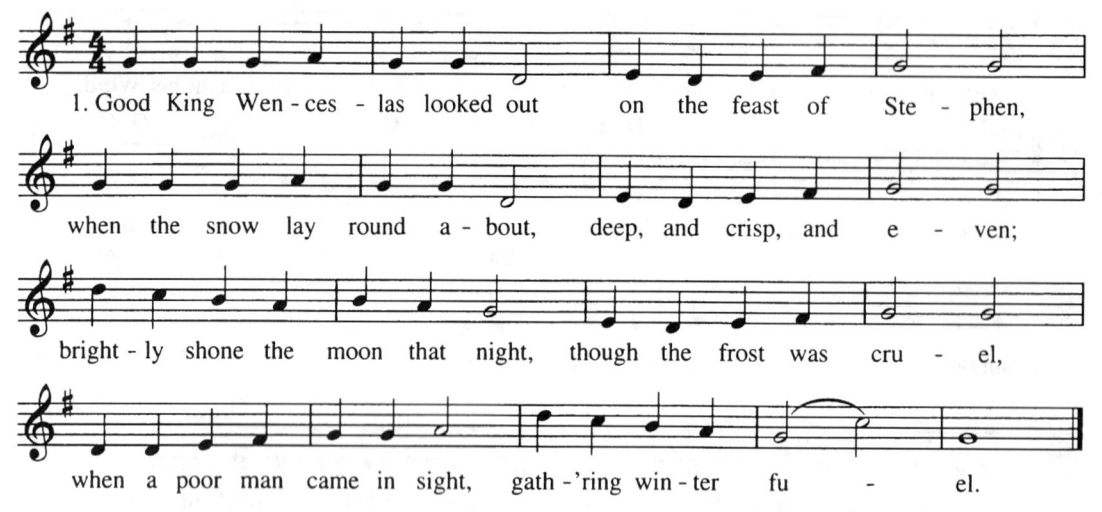

1. Good King Wenceslas looked out
on the feast of Stephen,
when the snow lay round about,
deep, and crisp, and even;
brightly shone the moon that night,
though the frost was cruel,
when a poor man came in sight,
gath'ring winter fuel.

2. 'Hither, page, and stand by me,
if thou know'st it, telling,
yonder peasant, who is he,
where and what his dwelling?'
'Sire, he lives a good league hence,
underneath the mountain,
right against the forest fence,
by Saint Agnes' fountain.'

3. 'Bring me flesh, and bring me wine,
bring me pine logs hither:
thou and I will see him dine,
when we bring them thither.'
Page and monarch, forth they went,
forth they went together;
through the rude wind's wild lament,
and the bitter weather.

4. 'Sire, the night is darker now,
and the wind blows stronger;
fails my heart, I know not how;
I can go no longer.'
'Mark my footsteps good, my page;
tread thou in them boldly:
thou shalt find the winter's rage
freeze thy blood less coldly.'

5. In his master's steps he trod,
where the snow lay dinted;
heat was in the very sod
which the Saint had printed.
Therefore, Christians all, be sure,
wealth or rank possessing,
ye who now will bless the poor,
shall yourselves find blessing.

Text: John Mason Neale (1818-1866) alt.
Music: from 'Piae Cantiones' (1582)

302 Go, tell it on the mountain

Refrain

Go, tell it on the mountain, over the hills and ev'rywhere,
go, tell it on the mountain that Jesus Christ is born.

Fine

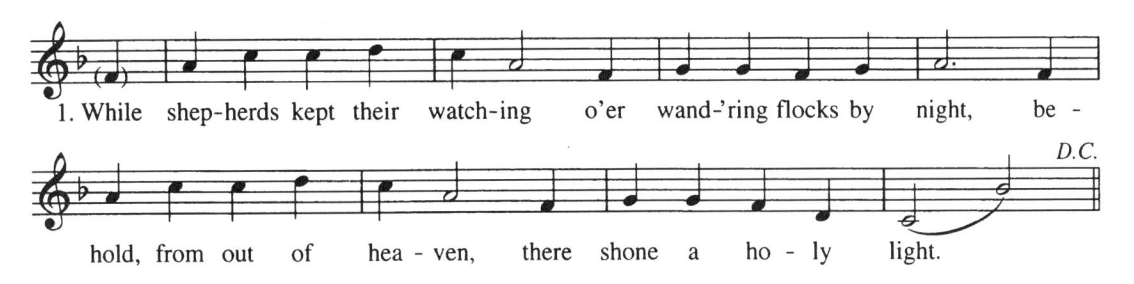

1. While shepherds kept their watching o'er wand'ring flocks by night, behold, from out of heaven, there shone a holy light.

2. And lo, when they had seen it,
   they all bowed down and prayed;
   they travelled on together
   to where the babe was laid.

3. When I was a seeker,
   I sought both night and day:
   I asked my Lord to help me
   and he showed me the way.

4. He made me a watchman
   upon the city wall,
   and, if I am a Christian,
   I am the least of all.

Text and Music: traditional

303 Go, the Mass is ended

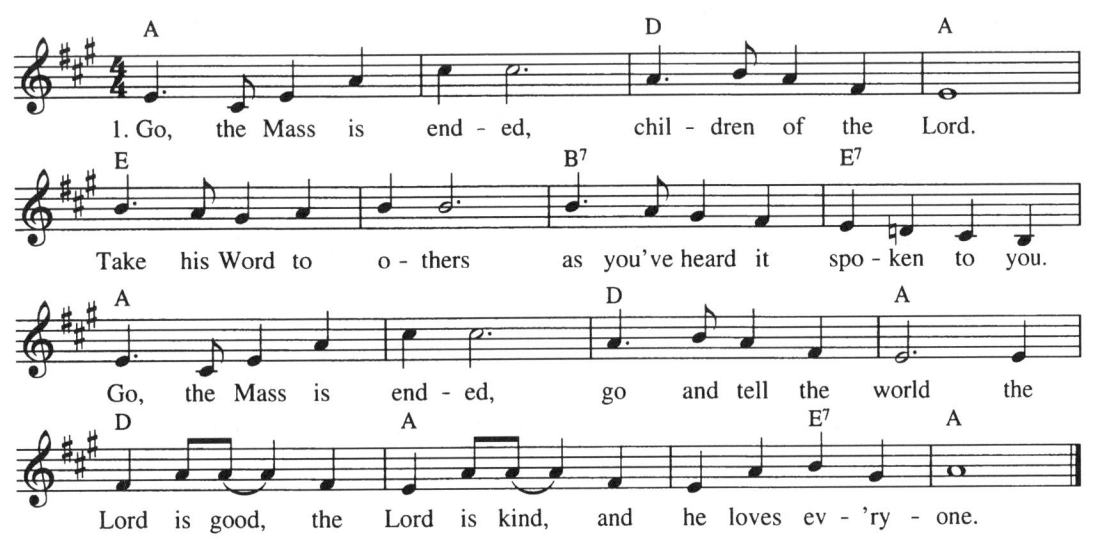

1. Go, the Mass is ended, children of the Lord.
Take his Word to others as you've heard it spoken to you.
Go, the Mass is ended, go and tell the world the
Lord is good, the Lord is kind, and he loves ev'ryone.

2. Go, the Mass is ended,
   take his love to all.
   Gladden all who meet you,
   fill their hearts with hope and courage.
   Go, the Mass is ended,
   fill the world with love,
   and give to all what you've received
   – the peace and joy of Christ.

3. Go, the Mass is ended,
   strengthened in the Lord,
   lighten ev'ry burden,
   spread the joy of Christ around you.
   Go, the Mass is ended,
   take his peace to all.
   This day is yours to change the world
   – to make God known and loved.

Text and Music: Marie Lydia Pereira (b.1920)
© Copyright 1976 Kevin Mayhew Ltd.

304 Grant to us, O Lord

Refrain

Grant to us, O Lord, a heart re-newed;
re-cre-ate in us your own Spi-rit, Lord! *Fine*

1. Be-hold, the days are com-ing, says the Lord our God, when I will make a new co-ve-nant with the house of Is-ra-el. *D.C.*

2. Deep with-in their be-ing I will im-plant my law; I will write it in their hearts. *D.C.*

3. I will be their God, and they shall be my peo-ple. *D.C.*

4. And for all their faults I will grant for-give-ness; ne-ver-more will I re-mem-ber their sins. *D.C.*

Text: Lucien Deiss (b.1921) adapted from Ezekiel 36:26 and Jeremiah 31: 31-34
Music: Lucien Deiss (b.1921)
© Copyright 1965, 1966, 1968, 1973 World Library Publications Inc., a division of J.S. Paluch Co. Inc., 3825 N. Willow Road, Schiller Park, IL 60176, USA. All rights reserved. Used by permission.

305 Grant us your peace

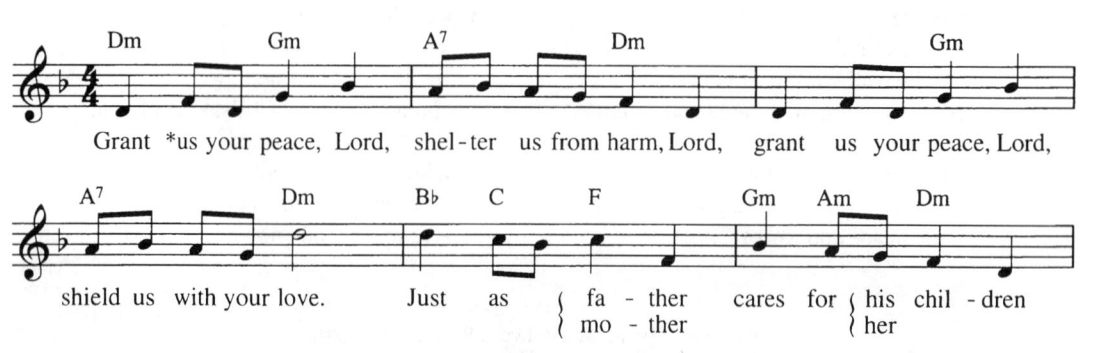

Grant *us your peace, Lord, shel-ter us from harm, Lord, grant us your peace, Lord, shield us with your love. Just as { fa-ther cares for { his chil-dren
{ mo-ther { her

Text © Copyright 1976, 1999 Kevin Mayhew Ltd.

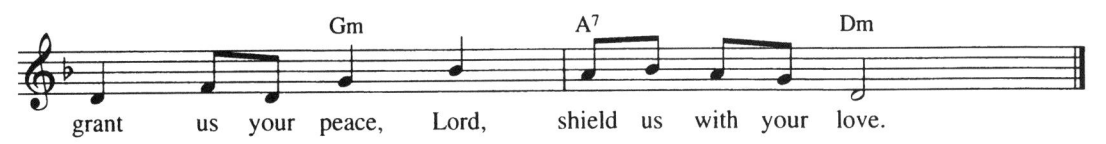

grant us your peace, Lord, shield us with your love.

* or 'them'; 'her'; 'him' as appropriate

2. Grant us your strength, Lord,
shelter us from harm, Lord,
grant us your strength, Lord,
shield us with your love.
From dusk till daybreak,
each waking moment,
grant us your strength, Lord,
shield us with your love.

Text: Francesca Leftley (b.1955)
Music: traditional Israeli melody

306 Great indeed are your works, O Lord

Great in-deed are your works, O Lord, now and e-ver-more!

Great in-deed are your works, O Lord, now and e-ver-more! more!

1. The u-ni-verse, night and day, tells of all your won-ders.

You are our life and our light: we shall praise you al-ways.

2. You are the path which we tread,
you will lead us onward.
From ev'ry corner of earth
all the nations gather.

3. You lead them all by the hand
to the heav'nly kingdom.
Then, at the end of all times,
you will come in glory.

Text: Aniceto Nazareth based on the Psalms
Music: Aniceto Nazareth
© Copyright 1984 Kevin Mayhew Ltd.

307 Guide me, O thou great Redeemer

CWM RHONDDA 87 87 47

1. Guide me, O thou great Redeemer, pilgrim through this barren land; I am weak, but thou art mighty, hold me with thy pow'r-ful hand: Bread of Heaven, Bread of Heaven, feed me till I want no more, (want no more) feed me till I want no more.

A lower setting will be found at No. 338

2. Open now the crystal fountain,
whence the healing stream doth flow;
let the fire and cloudy pillar
lead me all my journey through;
strong deliv'rer, strong deliv'rer,
be thou still my strength and shield,
be thou still my strength and shield.

3. When I tread the verge of Jordan,
bid my anxious fears subside;
death of death, and hell's destruction,
land me safe on Canaan's side;
songs of praises, songs of praises,
I will ever give to thee,
I will ever give to thee.

Text: William Williams (1717-1791) trans. Peter Williams (1727-1796) and others
Music: John Hughes (1873-1932)
Music © Copyright control

308 Hail, glorious Saint Patrick

SAINT PATRICK 11 11 11 11 and Refrain

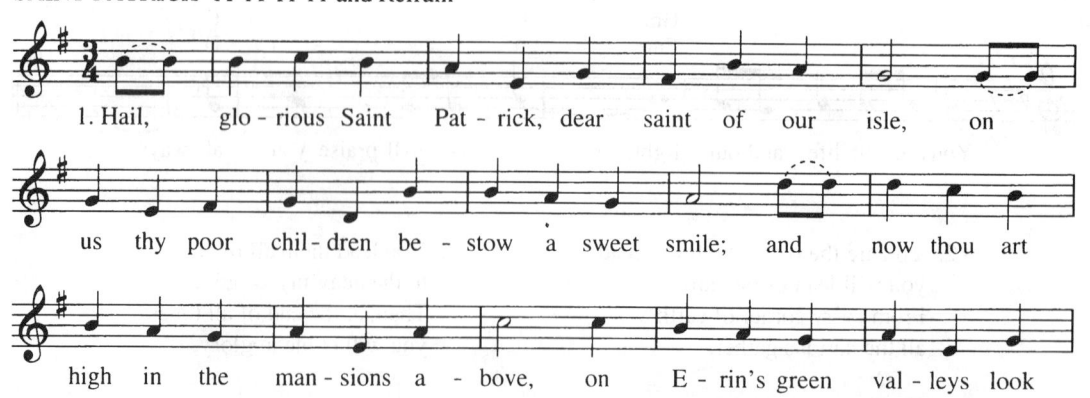

1. Hail, glorious Saint Patrick, dear saint of our isle, on us thy poor children bestow a sweet smile; and now thou art high in the mansions above, on Erin's green valleys look

Refrain

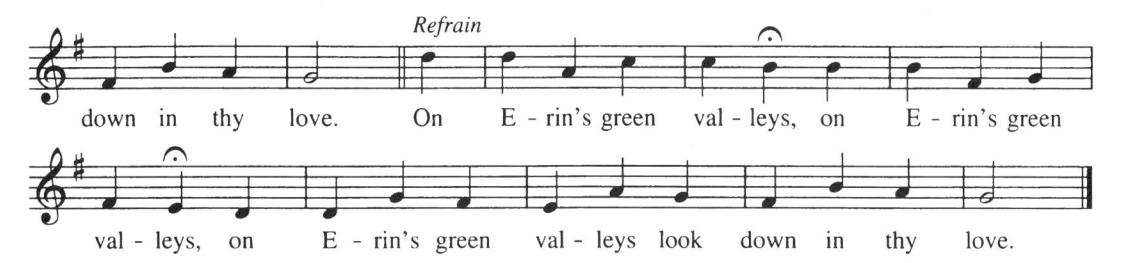

down in thy love. On E-rin's green val-leys, on E-rin's green val-leys, on E-rin's green val-leys look down in thy love.

2. Hail, glorious Saint Patrick, thy words were once strong
against Satan's wiles and an infidel throng;
not less is thy might where in heaven thou art;
O, come to our aid, in our battle take part.

3. In the war against sin, in the fight for the faith,
dear saint, may thy children resist unto death;
may their strength be in meekness, in penance, in prayer,
their banner the Cross which they glory to bear.

4. Thy people, now exiles on many a shore,
shall love and revere thee till time be no more;
and the fire thou hast kindled shall ever burn bright,
its warmth undiminished, undying its light.

5. Ever bless and defend the sweet land of our birth,
where the shamrock still blooms as when thou wert on earth,
and our hearts shall yet burn, wheresoever we roam,
for God and Saint Patrick, and our native home.

Text: Sister Agnes
Music: traditional melody

309 Hail, Queen of heaven

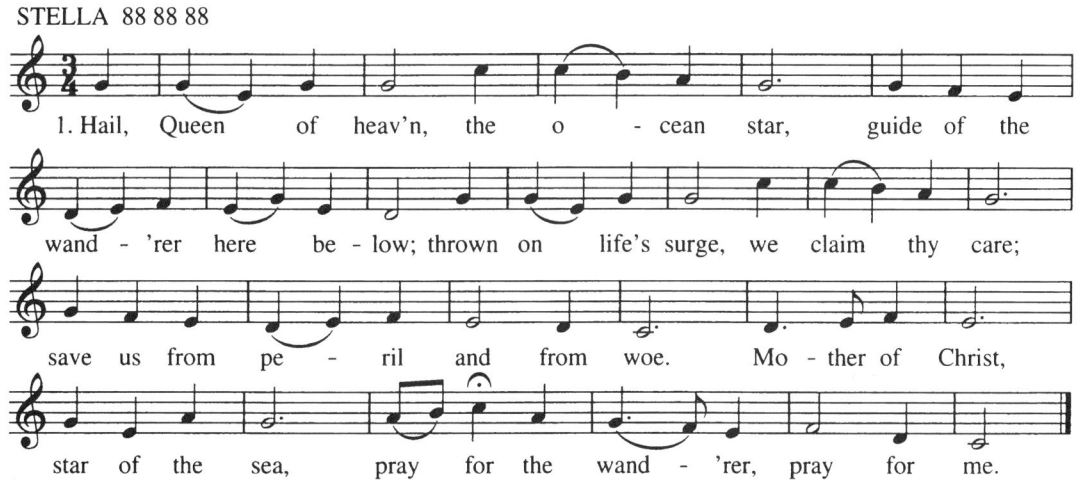

STELLA 88 88 88

1. Hail, Queen of heav'n, the o-cean star, guide of the wand-'rer here be-low; thrown on life's surge, we claim thy care; save us from pe-ril and from woe. Mo-ther of Christ, star of the sea, pray for the wand-'rer, pray for me.

2. O gentle, chaste and spotless maid,
we sinners make our prayers through thee;
remind thy Son that he has paid
the price of our iniquity.
Virgin most pure, star of the sea,
pray for the sinner, pray for me.

3. Sojourners in this vale of tears,
to thee, blest advocate, we cry;
pity our sorrows, calm our fears,
and soothe with hope our misery.
Refuge in grief, star of the sea,
pray for the mourner, pray for me.

4. And while to him who reigns above,
in Godhead One, in persons Three,
the source of life, of grace, of love,
homage we pay on bended knee,
do thou, bright Queen, star of the sea,
pray for thy children, pray for me.

Text: John Lingard (1771-1851)
Music: traditional melody

310 Hail, Redeemer, King divine

KING DIVINE 77 77 and Refrain

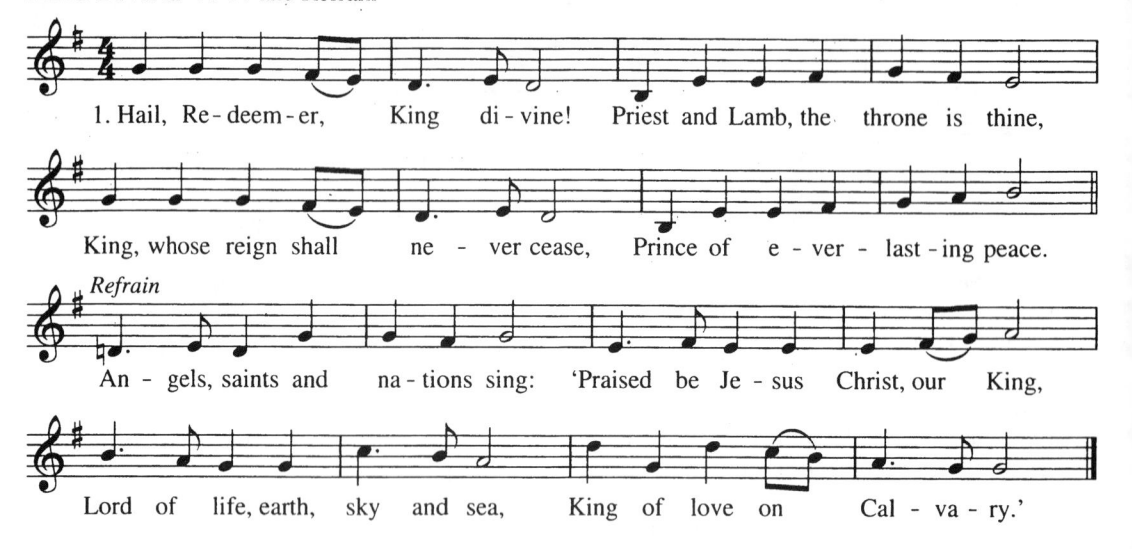

1. Hail, Redeemer, King divine!
Priest and Lamb, the throne is thine,
King, whose reign shall never cease,
Prince of everlasting peace.

Refrain
Angels, saints and nations sing:
'Praised be Jesus Christ, our King,
Lord of life, earth, sky and sea,
King of love on Calvary.'

2. King whose name creation thrills,
rule our minds, our hearts, our wills,
till in peace each nation rings
with thy praises, King of kings.

3. King most holy, King of truth,
guide the lowly, guide the youth;
Christ thou King of glory bright,
be to us eternal light.

4. Shepherd-King, o'er mountains steep,
homeward bring the wand'ring sheep,
shelter in one royal fold
states and kingdoms, new and old.

Text: Patrick Brennan (1877-1952)
Music: Charles Rigby (1901-1962)
© Copyright Burns & Oates Ltd, Wellwood, North Farm Road,
Tunbridge Wells, Kent TN2 3QR. Used by permission.

311 Hail the day that sees him rise

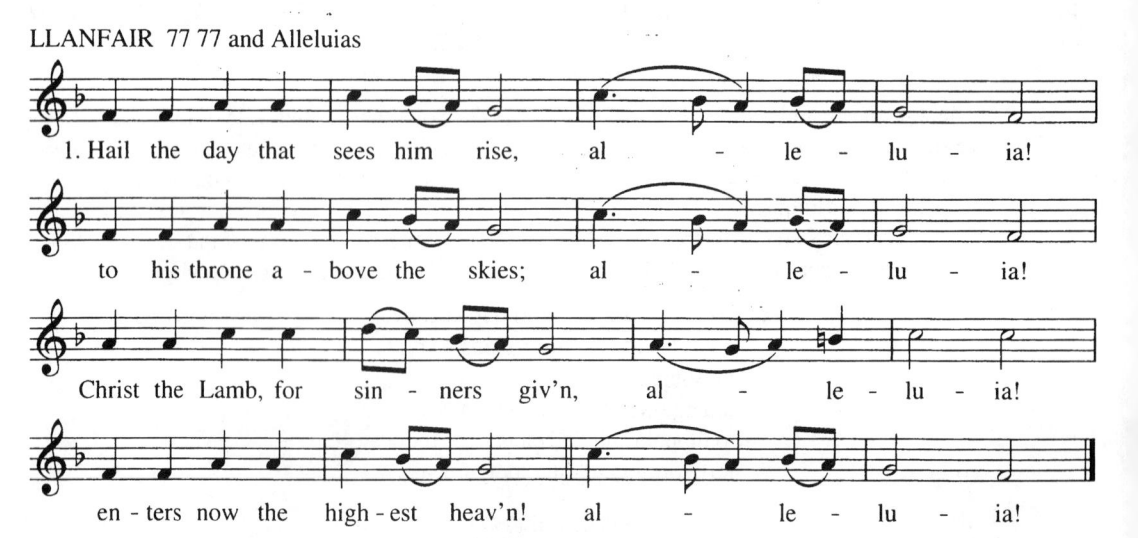

LLANFAIR 77 77 and Alleluias

1. Hail the day that sees him rise, alleluia!
to his throne above the skies; alleluia!
Christ the Lamb, for sinners giv'n, alleluia!
enters now the highest heav'n! alleluia!

2. There for him high triumph waits;
   lift your heads, eternal gates!
   He hath conquered death and sin;
   take the King of Glory in!

3. Circled round with angel-pow'rs,
   their triumphant Lord and ours;
   wide unfold the radiant scene,
   take the King of Glory in!

4. Lo, the heav'n its Lord receives,
   yet he loves the earth he leaves;
   though returning to his throne,
   calls the human race his own.

5. See, he lifts his hands above;
   see, he shows the prints of love;
   hark, his gracious lips bestow
   blessings on his Church below.

6. Still for us he intercedes,
   his prevailing death he pleads;
   near himself prepares our place,
   he the first-fruits of our race.

7. Lord, though parted from our sight,
   far above the starry height,
   grant our hearts may thither rise,
   seeking thee above the skies.

8. Ever upward let us move,
   wafted on the wings of love;
   looking when our Lord shall come,
   longing, sighing after home.

Text: Charles Wesley (1707-1788), Thomas Cotterill (1779-1823) and others, alt.
Music: Robert Williams (1781-1821)

312 Hail the risen Lord, ascending

PRAISE MY SOUL 87 87 87

1. Hail the risen Lord, ascending to his holy Father's side,
   angels lost in awe and wonder now acclaim the Lord who died.
   Alleluia, alleluia, Christ triumphant, glorified!

2. He who once, from royal splendour,
   came to share our state of blame,
   now ascends in clouds of glory
   to the heights from which he came.
   Alleluia, alleluia,
   Christ for evermore the same!

3. He will grant his praying servants,
   from the riches of his power,
   grace to live as risen people
   in this present watching hour.
   Alleluia, alleluia,
   God on us his blessings shower.

4. Now he bids us tell his story,
   where the lost and fearful roam:
   he will come again triumphant,
   and will lead his people home.
   Alleluia, alleluia,
   Maranatha! Come, Lord, come!

Text: Michael Forster (b.1946)
Music: John Goss (1800-1880)
Text © Copyright 1993 Kevin Mayhew Ltd.

313 Hail, thou star of ocean

LAUDES 65 65 D

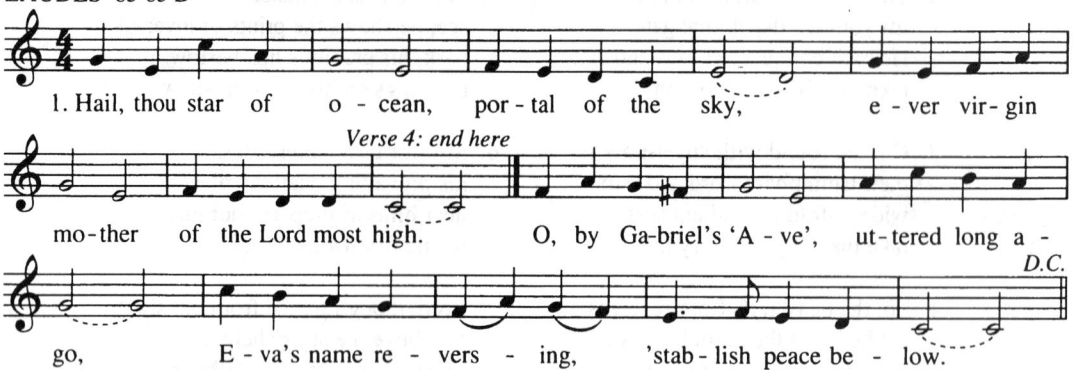

1. Hail, thou star of ocean, portal of the sky,
ever virgin mother of the Lord most high.
O, by Gabriel's 'Ave', uttered long ago,
Eva's name reversing, 'stablish peace below.

2. Break the captive's fetters, light on blindness pour,
all our ills expelling, ev'ry bliss implore.
Show thyself a mother; offer him our sighs,
who for us incarnate did not thee despise.

3. Virgin of all virgins, to thy shelter take us;
gentlest of the gentle, chaste and gentle make us.
Still, as on we journey, help our weak endeavour;
till with thee and Jesus we rejoice for ever.

4. Through the highest heaven, to th'almighty Three,
Father, Son and Spirit, One same glory be.

Text: 'Ave, maris stella' (9th century) trans. Edward Caswall (1814-1878)
Music: John Richardson (1816-1879)

314 Hail to the Lord's anointed

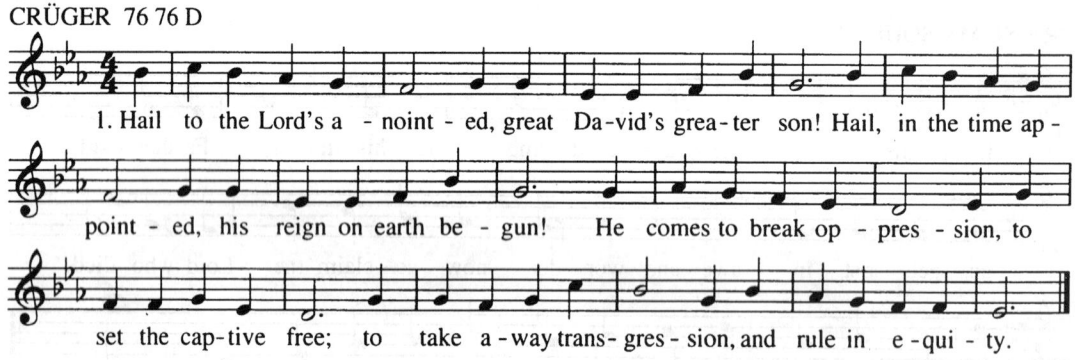

CRÜGER 76 76 D

1. Hail to the Lord's anointed, great David's greater son!
Hail, in the time appointed, his reign on earth begun!
He comes to break oppression, to set the captive free;
to take away transgression, and rule in equity.

2. He comes with succour speedy
to those who suffer wrong;
to help the poor and needy,
and bid the weak be strong;
to give them songs for sighing,
their darkness turn to light,
whose souls, condemned and dying,
were precious in his sight.

3. He shall come down like showers
upon the fruitful earth,
and love, joy, hope, like flowers,
spring in his path to birth:
before him on the mountains
shall peace the herald go;
and righteousness in fountains
from hill to valley flow.

4. Kings shall fall down before him,
and gold and incense bring;
all nations shall adore him,
his praise all people sing;
to him shall prayer unceasing
and daily vows ascend;
his kingdom still increasing,
a kingdom without end.

5. O'er ev'ry foe victorious,
he on his throne shall rest,
from age to age more glorious,
all-blessing and all-blest;
the tide of time shall never
his covenant remove;
his name shall stand for ever;
that name to us is love.

Text: paraphrase of Psalm 71 by James Montgomery (1771-1854)
Music: from a melody in Johann Crüger's 'Gesangbuch' adapted by William Henry Monk (1823-1889)

315 Hail, true Body

TUNE 1: PLAINSONG Irregular

1. Hail, true Body, born of Mary, by a wondrous virgin birth.
You who on the cross were offered to redeem us all on earth.

2. You whose side became a fountain pouring forth your precious blood,
give us now, and at our dying, your own self to be our food.

O kindest Jesu, O gracious Jesu,
O Jesu, blessed Mary's Son.

TUNE 2: STANDISH Irregular

1. Hail, true Body, born of Mary, by a wondrous virgin birth. You who on the Cross were offered to redeem us all on earth;
2. You whose side became a fountain pouring forth your precious blood, give us now, and at our dying, your own self to be our food.

After verse 2

O kindest Jesu, O gracious Jesu, O Jesu, blessed Mary's Son.

The original Latin text of this hymn, Ave Verum, will be found at No. 151

Text: Latin 14th century trans. H.N. Oxenham (1852-1941) alt.
Music: Tune 1 – Plainsong
Tune 2 – J. Dykes Bower (1905-1981)
Text © Copyright control.
Tune 2: Music © Copyright Hymns Ancient & Modern,
St Mary's Works, St Mary's Plain, Norwich NR3 3BH. Used by permission.

316 Hark! a herald voice is calling

MERTON 87 87

1. Hark! a herald voice is calling: 'Christ is nigh!' it seems to say;
'Cast away the dreams of darkness, O ye children of the day!'

2. Startled at the solemn warning,
let the earth-bound soul arise;
Christ, her sun, all sloth dispelling,
shines upon the morning skies.

3. Lo, the Lamb, so long expected,
comes with pardon down from heav'n;
let us haste, with tears of sorrow,
one and all to be forgiv'n.

4. So when next he comes with glory,
wrapping all the earth in fear,
may he then, as our defender,
on the clouds of heav'n appear.

5. Honour, glory, virtue, merit,
to the Father and the Son,
with the co-eternal Spirit,
while unending ages run.

Text: 'Vox clara ecce intonat' (6th century) trans. Edward Caswall (1814-1878)
Music: William Henry Monk (1823-1889)

317 Hark, the herald-angels sing

MENDELSSOHN 77 77 D and Refrain

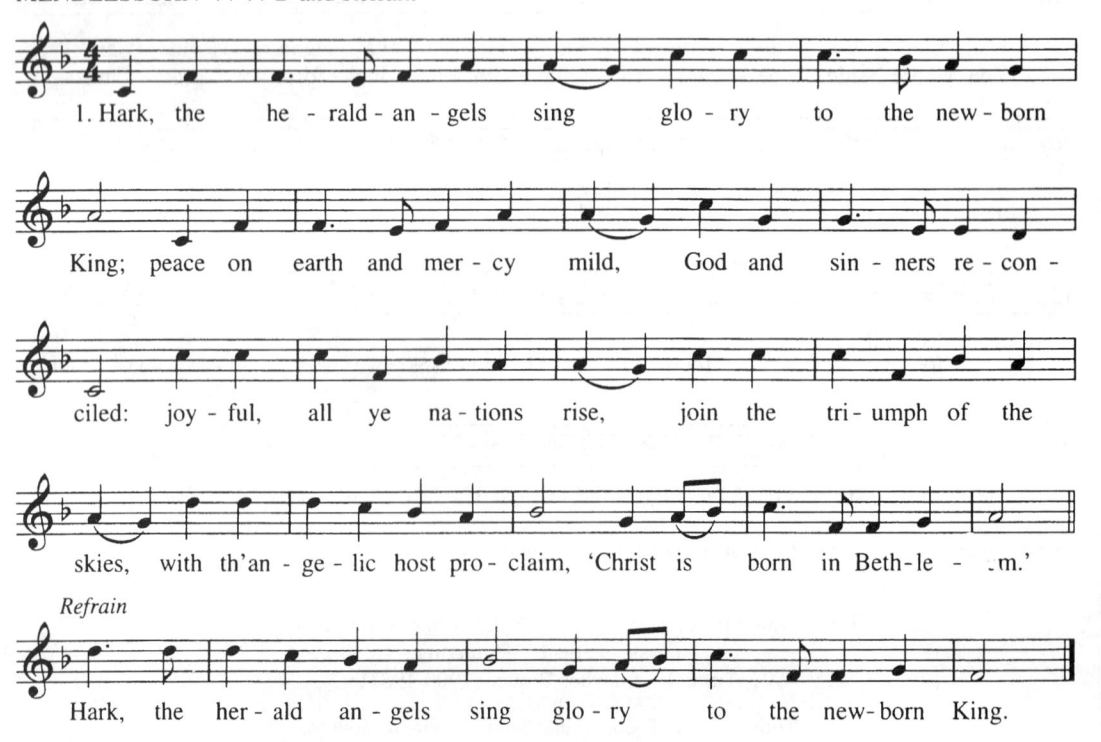

1. Hark, the herald-angels sing glory to the new-born King; peace on earth and mercy mild, God and sinners reconciled: joyful, all ye nations rise, join the triumph of the skies, with th'angelic host proclaim, 'Christ is born in Bethlehem.'

Refrain
Hark, the herald angels sing glory to the new-born King.

2. Christ, by highest heav'n adored,
   Christ, the everlasting Lord,
   late in time behold him come,
   offspring of a virgin's womb!
   Veiled in flesh the Godhead see,
   hail, th'incarnate Deity!
   Pleased as man with us to dwell,
   Jesus, our Emmanuel.

3. Hail, the heav'n-born Prince of Peace!
   Hail, the Sun of Righteousness!
   Light and life to all he brings,
   ris'n with healing in his wings;
   mild he lays his glory by,
   born that we no more may die,
   born to raise us from the earth,
   born to give us second birth.

Text: Charles Wesley (1707-1788), George Whitefield (1714-1770),
Martin Madan (1726-1790) and others, alt.
Music: adapted from Felix Mendelssohn (1809-1847)
by William Hayman Cummings (1831-1915)

318 Have mercy on us, O Lord

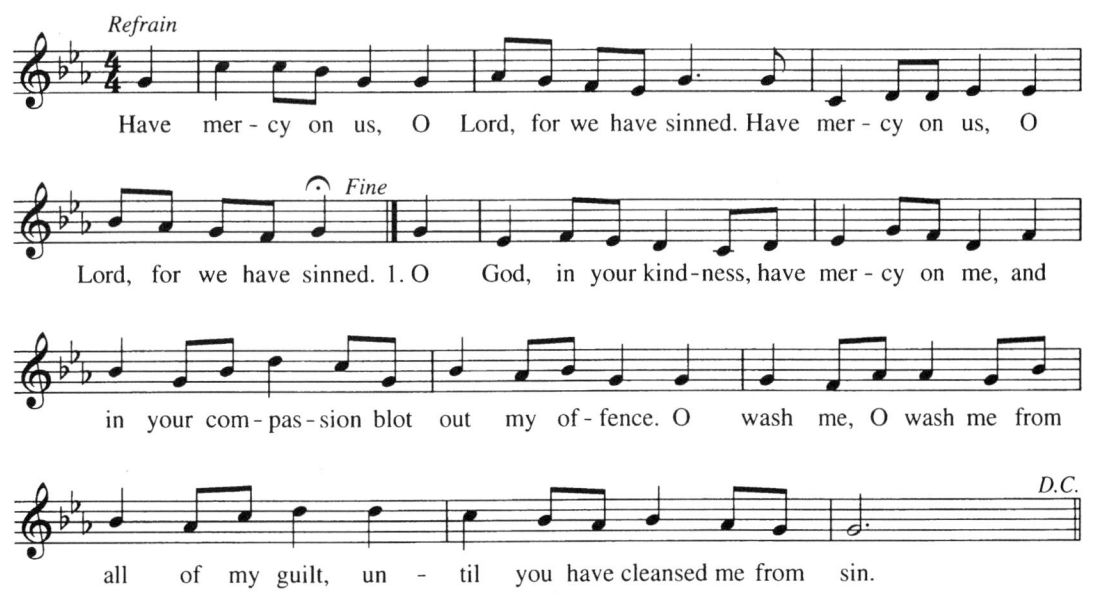

Refrain

Have mercy on us, O Lord, for we have sinned. Have mercy on us, O Lord, for we have sinned.

1. O God, in your kindness, have mercy on me, and in your compassion blot out my offence. O wash me, O wash me from all of my guilt, until you have cleansed me from sin.

2. For all my offences I know very well.
   I cannot escape from the sight of my sin.
   Against you, O Lord, only you, have I sinned,
   and done what is wrong in your eyes.

3. A pure heart create in your servant, O Lord;
   a steadfast and trustworthy spirit in me.
   O cast me not out from your presence, I pray,
   and take not your spirit from me.

4. Restore to me, Lord, all the joy of your help;
   sustain me with fervour, sustain me with zeal.
   Then open my lips, and my mouth shall declare
   the praise of my Lord and my God.

Text: Susan Sayers (b.1946) based on Psalm 50
Music: Alan Ridout (1934-1996)
© Copyright 1989 Kevin Mayhew Ltd.

319 Healer of our every ill

Healer of our ev-'ry ill, light of each tomorrow,
give us peace beyond our fear, and hope beyond our sorrow.

1. You who know our fears and sadness,
grace us with your peace and gladness.
Spirit of all comfort: fill our hearts.

2. In the pain and joy beholding,
how your grace is still unfolding.
Give us all your vision: God of love.

3. Give us strength to love each other,
ev'ry sister, ev'ry brother.
Spirit of all kindness: be our guide.

4. You who know each thought and feeling,
teach us all your way of healing.
Spirit of compassion: fill each heart.

Text and Music: Marty Haugen (b.1950)
© Copyright 1987 GIA Publications Inc., 7404 S. Mason Avenue, Chicago, Illinois 60638, USA.
All rights reserved. Used by permission.

320 Healer of the sick

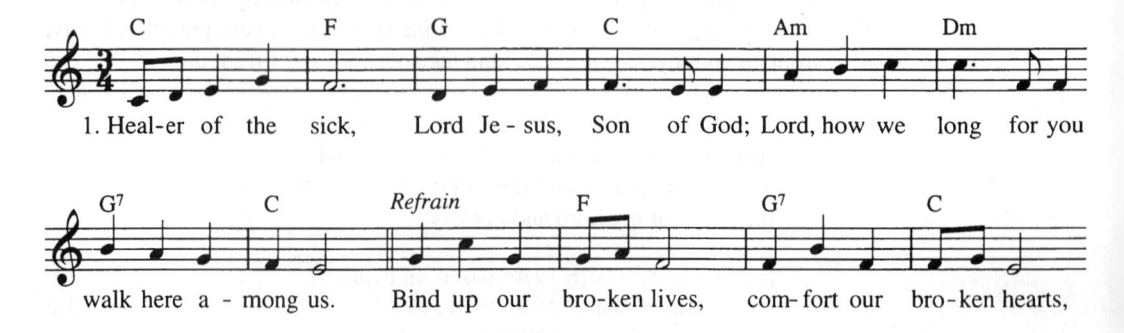

1. Healer of the sick, Lord Jesus, Son of God;
Lord, how we long for you walk here among us.
Bind up our broken lives, comfort our broken hearts,

© Copyright 1999 Kevin Mayhew Ltd.

banish our hidden fears. Lord, come with power, bring new light to the blind, bring peace to troubled minds, hold us now in your arms, set us free now.

2. Bearer of our pain,
Lord Jesus, Lamb of God;
Lord, how we cry to you:
walk here among us.

3. Calmer of our fears,
Lord Jesus, Prince of Peace;
Lord, how we yearn for you:
walk here among us.

4. Saviour of the world,
Lord Jesus, mighty God;
Lord, how we sing to you:
walk here among us.

Text and Music: Francesca Leftley (b.1955)

321 Hear my cry

Hear my cry, O Lord, my God, listen to my prayer; from earth's end I call to you when my heart is faint.

1. Set me high on a rock; you are my refuge, O Lord.

2. Let me stay in your tent;
safe in the shade of your wings.

3. I will echo your praise;
pay my vows day after day.

Text: Anthony D'Souza (b.1950) based on Psalm 60
Music: Anthony D'Souza (b.1950)
© Copyright 1984 Kevin Mayhew Ltd.

322 Hear our cry

(Cantor) Hear our cry, O hear our cry: 'Jesus, come!' *(All)* Hear our cry, O hear our cry: 'Jesus, come!'

Verse
(All)
1. The tide of prayer is rising —
   a deeper passion burning —
2. We lift our eyes with longing
   to see your kingdom coming —

(Cantor) Hear our cry, O hear our cry: 'Jesus, come!' *(All)* Hear our cry, O hear our cry: 'Jesus, come!'

Refrain
(Cantor) Whoever is thirsty, come now and drink the waters
(All) Whoever is thirsty, come now and drink the waters
(Cantor) of life;
(All) of life. 'Jesus, come!' 'Jesus, come!'

(Cantor) Hear our cry, O hear our cry: Hear our cry, O hear our cry: Come!'

3. The streets of teeming cities
   cry out for healing rivers —

4. Refresh them with your presence,
   give grace for deep repentance —

5. Tear back the shroud of shadows
   that covers all the peoples —

6. Revealing your salvation
   in ev'ry tribe and nation —

Text and Music: Graham Kendrick (b.1950)

© Copyright 1996 Make Way Music, P.O. Box 263, Croydon, Surrey CR9 5AP, UK.
International copyright secured. All rights reserved. Used by permission.

323 Heaven is open wide

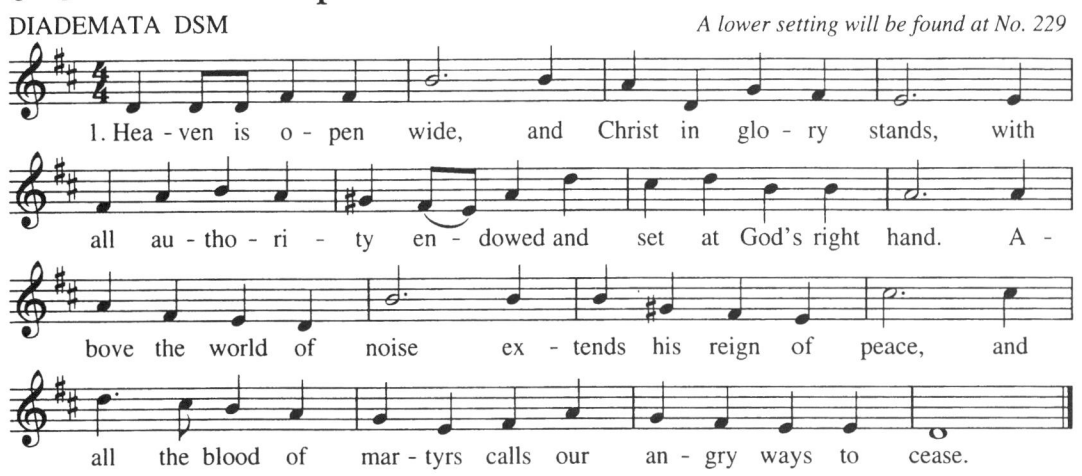

DIADEMATA DSM *A lower setting will be found at No. 229*

1. Heaven is open wide, and Christ in glory stands,
with all authority endowed and set at God's right hand.
Above the world of noise extends his reign of peace,
and all the blood of martyrs calls our angry ways to cease.

2. Heaven is open wide,
and perfect love we see
in God's eternal self revealed:
the blessèd Trinity.
Christ for the Church has prayed,
that we may all be one,
and share the triune grace whereby
creation was begun.

3. Heaven is open wide,
and Christ in glory stands:
the Source and End, the First and Last,
with justice in his hands.
Let all the thirsty come
where life is flowing free,
and Christ, in splendour yet unknown,
our morning star will be.

Text: Michael Forster (b.1946)
Music: George Job Elvey (1816-1893)
Text © Copyright 1993 Kevin Mayhew Ltd.

324 He brings us into his banqueting table
His banner over me is love

1. He brings us into his banqueting table, his banner over me is love;
he brings us into his banqueting table, his banner over me is love;
he brings us into his banqueting table, his banner over me is love,
his banner over me is love.

2. The one way to peace is the power of the cross,
his banner over me is love;

3. He builds his Church on a firm foundation,
his banner over me is love;

4. In him we find a new creation,
his banner over me is love;

5. He lifts us up to heavenly places,
his banner over me is love;

Text: traditional
Music: unknown

325 He is Lord

1. He is Lord, he is Lord.
   He is risen from the dead and he is Lord.
   Ev'ry knee shall bow, ev'ry tongue confess
   that Jesus Christ is Lord.

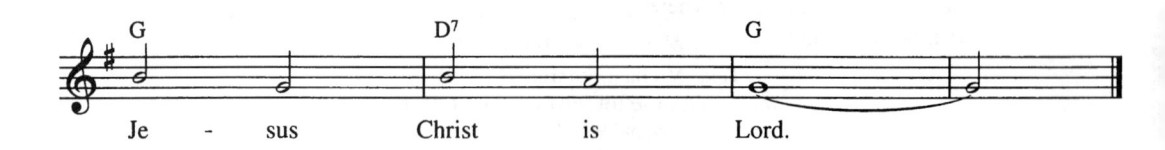

2. He is King, he is King.
   He is risen from the dead and he is King.
   Ev'ry knee shall bow, ev'ry tongue confess
   that Jesus Christ is King.

3. He is love, he is love.
   He is risen from the dead and he is love.
   Ev'ry knee shall bow, ev'ry tongue confess
   that Jesus Christ is love.

Text and Music: unknown
This arrangement © Copyright 1994 Kevin Mayhew Ltd.

326 He is risen, tell the story

WZLOBIE LEZY 87 87 88 7

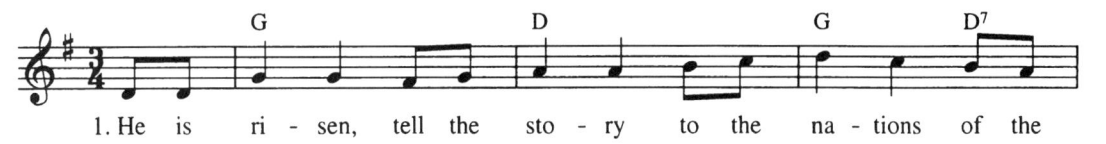

1. He is risen, tell the story
to the nations of the night;
from their sin and from their blindness,
let them walk in Easter light.
Now begins a new creation,
now has come our true salvation,
Jesus Christ, the Son of God!

2. Mary goes to tell the others
of the wonders she has seen;
John and Peter come a-running
– what can all this truly mean?
O Rabboni, Master holy,
to appear to one so lowly!
Jesus Christ, the Son of God!

3. He has cut down death and evil,
he has conquered all despair;
he has lifted from our shoulders
all the weight of anxious care.
Risen Brother, now before you,
we will worship and adore you,
Jesus Christ, the Son of God!

4. Now get busy, bring the message,
so that all may come to know
there is hope for saint and sinner,
for our God has loved us so.
Ev'ry church bell is a-ringing,
ev'ry Christian now is singing,
Jesus Christ, the Son of God!

Text: Willard F. Jabusch (b.1930)
Music: traditional Polish melody
Text © Copyright 1998 Willard F. Jabusch, 5735 University Avenue, Chicago, Illinois 60637, USA.
Used by permission.

LITURGICAL
HYMNS OLD & NEW

327 Here in this place
Gather us in

1. Here in this place, new light is streaming,
now is the darkness vanished away;
see in this space, our fears and our dreamings,
brought here to you in the light of this day.
Gather us in, the lost and forsaken,
gather us in, the blind and the lame;
call to us now, and we shall awaken,
we shall arise at the sound of your name.

2. We are the young, our lives are a myst'ry,
we are the old who yearn for your face;
we have been sung throughout all of hist'ry,
called to be light to the whole human race.
Gather us in, the rich and the haughty,
gather us in, the proud and the strong;
give us a heart so meek and so lowly,
give us the courage to enter the song.

3. Here we will take the wine and the water,
here we will take the bread of new birth;
here you shall call your sons and your daughters,
call us anew to be salt for the earth.
Give us to drink the wine of compassion,
give us to eat the bread that is you;
nourish us well, and teach us to fashion
lives that are holy and hearts that are true.

4. Not in the dark of buildings confining,
not in some heaven, light years away,
but here in this place the new light is shining,
now is the kingdom, now is the day.
Gather us in and hold us for ever,
gather us in and make us your own;
gather us in, all peoples together,
fire of love in our flesh and our bone.

Text and Music: Marty Haugen (b.1950)

© Copyright 1982 GIA Publications Inc., 7404 S. Mason Avenue, Chicago, Illinois 60638, USA.
All rights reserved. Used by permission.

328 Here is bread

1. Here is bread, here is wine, Christ is with us, he is with us.
Break the bread, taste the wine, Christ is with us here.

Refrain
In this bread there is healing, in this cup is life for ever.
In this moment, by the Spirit, Christ is with us here.

2. Here is grace, here is peace,
Christ is with us, he is with us;
know his grace, find his peace,
feast on Jesus here.

3. Here we are, joined in one,
Christ is with us, he is with us;
we'll proclaim, till he comes,
Jesus crucified.

Text and Music: Graham Kendrick (b.1950)
© Copyright 1991 Make Way Music, P.O. Box 263, Croydon, Surrey CR9 5AP, UK.
International copyright secured. All rights reserved. Used by permission.

329 Here's a child for you, O Lord

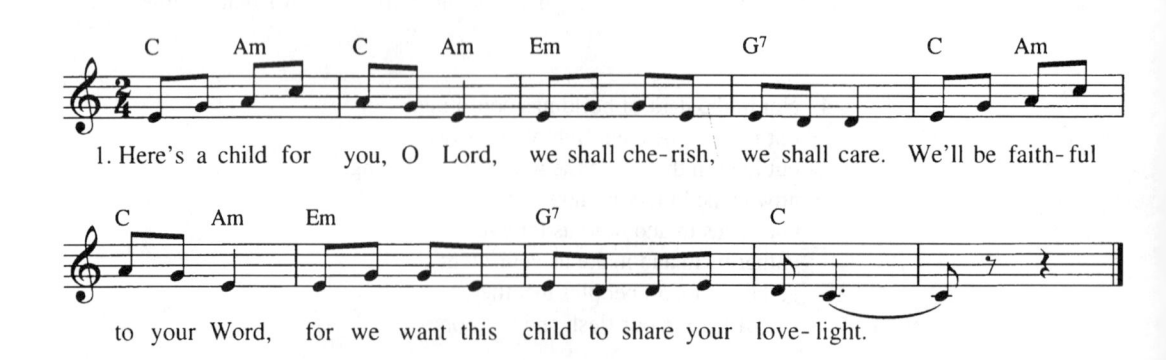

1. Here's a child for you, O Lord, we shall cherish, we shall care. We'll be faithful to your Word, for we want this child to share your love-light.

© Copyright 1976 Kevin Mayhew Ltd.

2. May he *(she)* hold his *(her)* head up high,
graceful, joyful, strong of limb.
May his *(her)* eyes be clear and bright,
seeing beauty in all things
that you've made.

3. We were young ourselves, O Lord,
we were eager, we were fresh
like the op'ning buds of spring,
and we wanted happiness
in your way.

4. Then, at times, we went astray,
we were foolish, we were weak,
and the innocence we had
vanished like the trace of feet
when snow melts.

5. But we come, O Lord and King,
at your bidding, and we pray
that the precious gift we bring
will grow stronger ev'ry day
in your love.

6. By the water poured out here
and your promise, we believe,
he *(she)* will master ev'ry fear,
and at last will come to see
your Godhead.

Text and Music: Estelle White (b.1925)

330 He's got the whole world in his hand

1. He's got the whole world in his hand. He's got the whole world in his hand. He's got the whole world in his hand. He's got the whole world in his hand.

2. He's got you and me, brother, in his hand. *(x3)*
He's got the whole world in his hand.

3. He's got you and me, sister, in his hand. *(x3)*
He's got the whole world in his hand.

4. He's got the little tiny baby in his hand. *(x3)*
He's got the whole world in his hand.

5. He's got ev'rybody here in his hand. *(x3)*
He's got the whole world in his hand.

Text and Music: traditional
This arrangement © Copyright 1994 Kevin Mayhew Ltd.

331 He who would valiant be

MONKS GATE 65 65 66 65

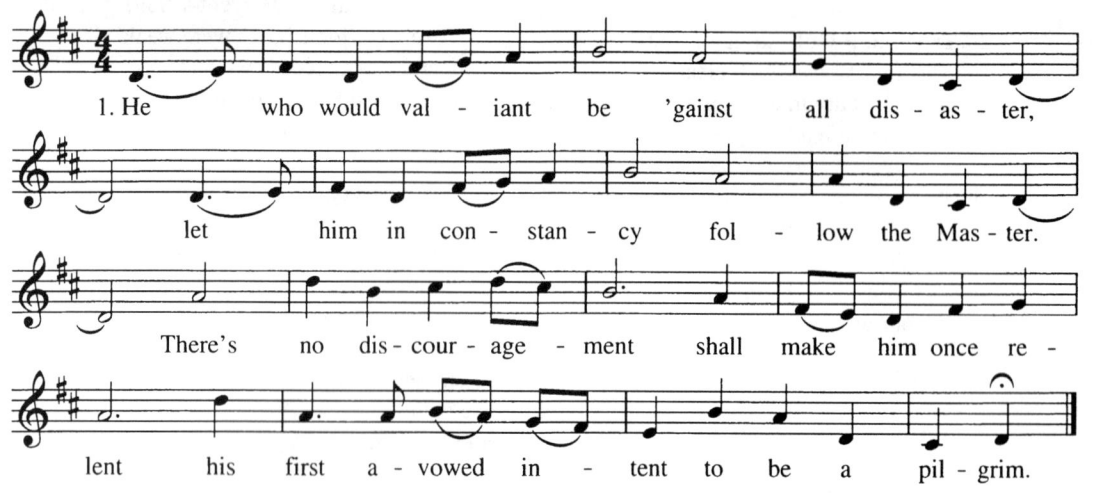

1. He who would valiant be 'gainst all disaster,
let him in constancy follow the Master.
There's no discouragement shall make him once relent
his first avowed intent to be a pilgrim.

2. Who so beset him round
with dismal stories,
do but themselves confound –
his strength the more is.
No foes shall stay his might,
though he with giants fight:
he will make good his right
to be a pilgrim.

3. Since, Lord, thou dost defend
us with thy Spirit,
we know we at the end
shall life inherit.
Then fancies flee away!
I'll fear not what men say,
I'll labour night and day
to be a pilgrim.

Text: Percy Dearmer (1867-1936) after John Bunyan (1628-1688)
Music: traditional English melody collected and arranged by
Ralph Vaughan Williams (1872-1958)
Text © Copyright Oxford University Press.
Music © Copyright Oxford University Press, Great Clarendon Street, Oxford OX2 6DP.
Used by permission from the 'English Hymnal'.

332 Holy God, of righteous glory

BLAENWERN 87 87 D

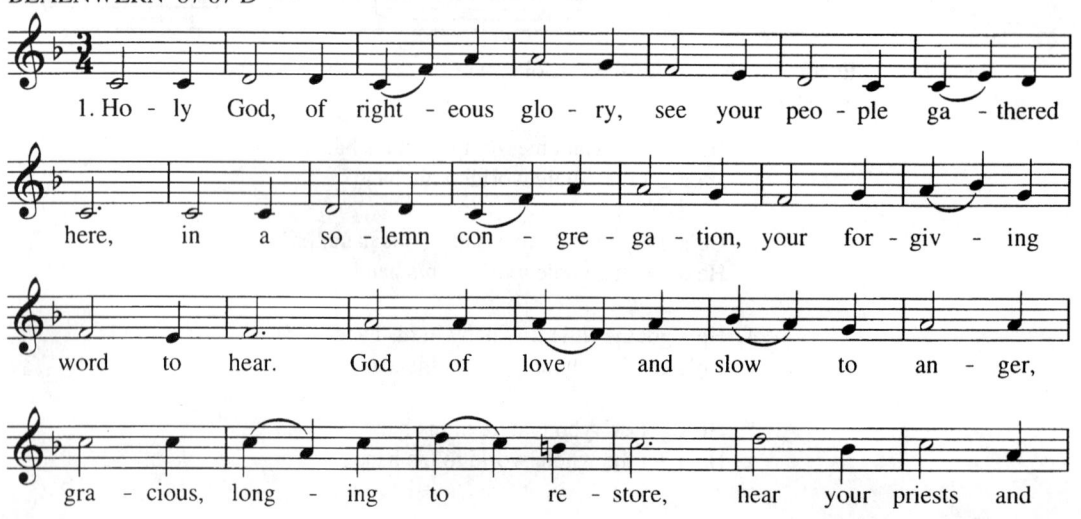

1. Holy God, of righteous glory, see your people gathered here,
in a solemn congregation, your forgiving word to hear.
God of love and slow to anger, gracious, longing to restore,
hear your priests and

Text © Copyright 1993 Kevin Mayhew Ltd.
Music © Copyright control

peo - ple call - ing, give us grace to sin no more.

2. We confess the pride we suffer,
needs which none can satisfy;
how we love the praise of mortals,
swift to flow'r and quick to die.
Let us find rewards eternal
as we quietly seek your face,
and our open, public living
witness only to your grace.

3. Free us from our self-bound living,
better witnesses to be,
to the world by grace appealing,
telling forth the mystery:
how creation's pure Redeemer
walked among us undefiled,
by his deathless love proclaiming,
God with us is reconciled.

Text: Michael Forster (b.1946)
Music: William Penfro Rowlands (1860-1937)

333 Holy God, we praise thy name

GROSSER GOTT 78 78 77

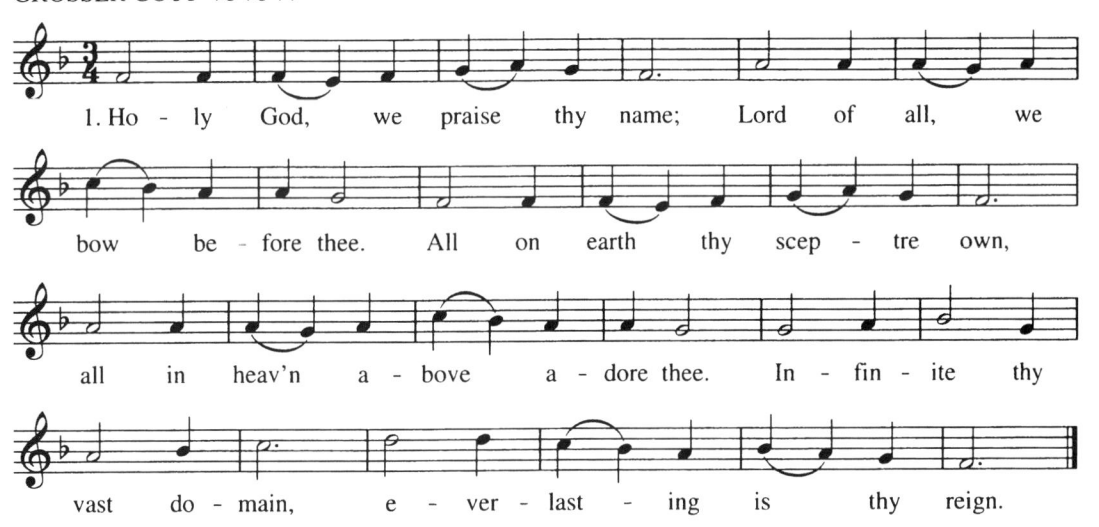

1. Ho - ly God, we praise thy name; Lord of all, we bow be - fore thee. All on earth thy scep - tre own, all in heav'n a - bove a - dore thee. In - fin - ite thy vast do - main, e - ver - last - ing is thy reign.

2. Hark, the loud celestial hymn,
angel choirs above are raising;
cherubim and seraphim,
in unceasing chorus praising,
fill the heav'ns with sweet accord,
holy, holy, holy Lord.

3. Holy Father, Holy Son,
Holy Spirit, three we name thee,
while in essence only one
undivided God we claim thee;
and adoring bend the knee,
while we own the mystery.

4. Spare thy people, Lord, we pray,
by a thousand snares surrounded;
keep us without sin today;
never let us be confounded.
Lo, I put my trust in thee,
never, Lord, abandon me.

Text: adaptation of a hymn by Ambrose (d.397) ascribed to Ignaz Franz (1719-1790)
trans. Clarence Walworth (1820-1900)
Music: from 'Katholisches Gesangbuch' (c.1774)

334 Holy God, your pilgrim people

AR HYD Y NOS 84 84 88 84

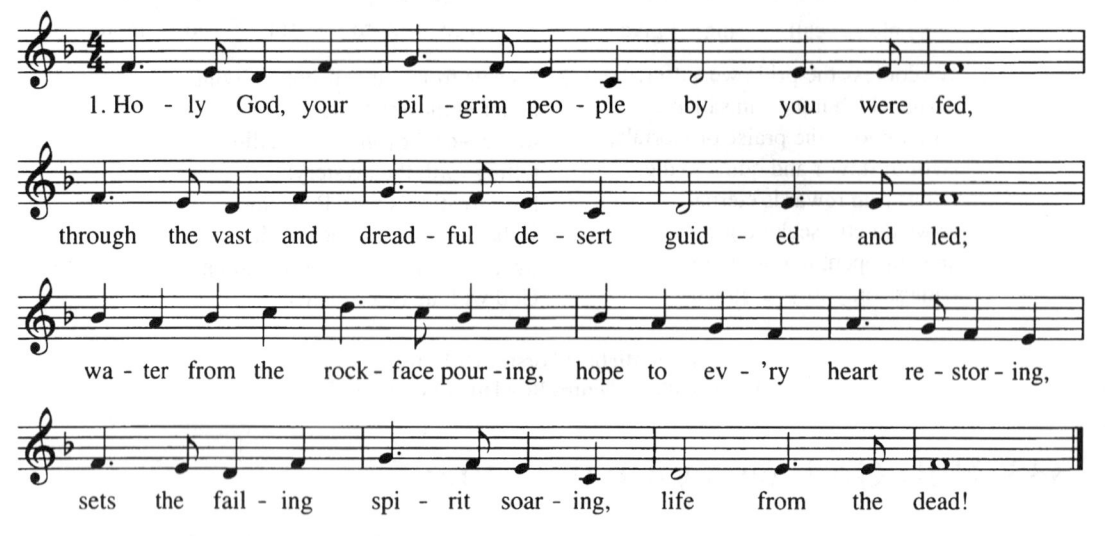

1. Holy God, your pilgrim people by you were fed,
through the vast and dreadful desert guided and led;
water from the rock-face pouring, hope to ev'ry heart restoring,
sets the failing spirit soaring, life from the dead!

A higher setting will be found at No. 232

2. Living bread for mortals broken,
gift from above,
live in us the life eternal,
perfect in love.
Come, the word of wholeness bringing,
where our fearful souls are clinging;
and of life abundant singing,
all fear remove.

3. One the bread and one the chalice,
one work of grace;
one the Church of Christ, united
in his embrace.
One the gospel of salvation,
for the wholeness of creation;
Christ is poured in ev'ry nation,
and ev'ry race.

Text: Michael Forster (b.1946)
Music: traditional Welsh melody
Text © Copyright 1996, 1999 Kevin Mayhew Ltd.

335 Holy, holy, holy

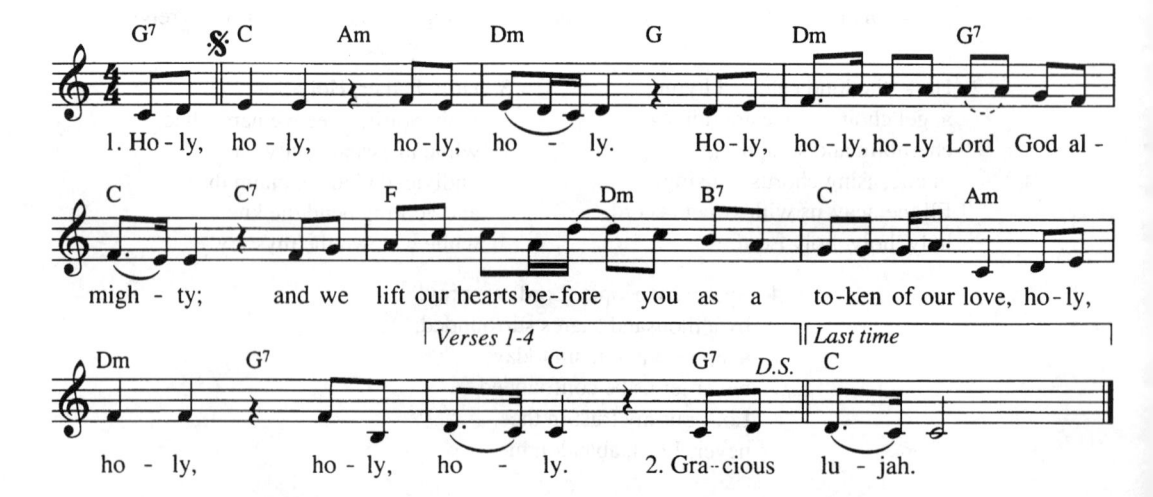

1. Holy, holy, holy, holy. Holy, holy, holy Lord God almighty;
and we lift our hearts before you as a token of our love, holy,
holy, holy, holy. 2. Gracious lujah.

© Copyright 1972 Bud John Songs/EMI Christian Music Publishing. Administered by CopyCare,
P.O. Box 77, Hailsham, East Sussex BN27 3EF, UK. Used by permission.

2. Gracious Father, gracious Father,
    we are glad to be your children, gracious Father;
    and we lift our heads before you
    as a token of our love,
    gracious Father, gracious Father.

3. Risen Jesus, risen Jesus,
    we are glad you have redeemed us, risen Jesus;
    and we lift our hands before you
    as a token of our love,
    risen Jesus, risen Jesus.

4. Holy Spirit, Holy Spirit,
    come and fill our hearts anew, Holy Spirit;
    and we lift our voice before you
    as a token of our love,
    Holy Spirit, Holy Spirit.

5. Hallelujah, hallelujah,
    hallelujah, hallelujah, hallelujah;
    and we lift our hearts before you
    as a token of our love,
    hallelujah, hallelujah.

Text and Music: Jimmy Owens

336 Holy, holy, holy is the Lord

1. Holy, holy, holy is the Lord, holy is the Lord God almighty. Holy, holy, holy is the Lord, holy is the Lord God almighty: who was, and is, and is to come; holy, holy, holy is the Lord.

2. Jesus, Jesus, Jesus is the Lord,
    Jesus is the Lord God almighty.
    Jesus, Jesus, Jesus is the Lord,
    Jesus is the Lord God almighty:
    who was, and is, and is to come;
    Jesus, Jesus, Jesus is the Lord.

3. Worthy, worthy, worthy is the Lord,
    worthy is the Lord God almighty.
    Worthy, worthy, worthy is the Lord,
    worthy is the Lord God almighty:
    who was, and is, and is to come;
    worthy, worthy, worthy is the Lord.

4. Glory, glory, glory to the Lord,
    glory to the Lord God almighty.
    Glory, glory, glory to the Lord,
    glory to the Lord God almighty:
    who was, and is, and is to come;
    glory, glory, glory to the Lord.

For liturgical version (Sanctus) see hymn No. 65

Text and Music: unknown

337 Holy, holy, holy! Lord God almighty

NICAEA 11 12 12 10

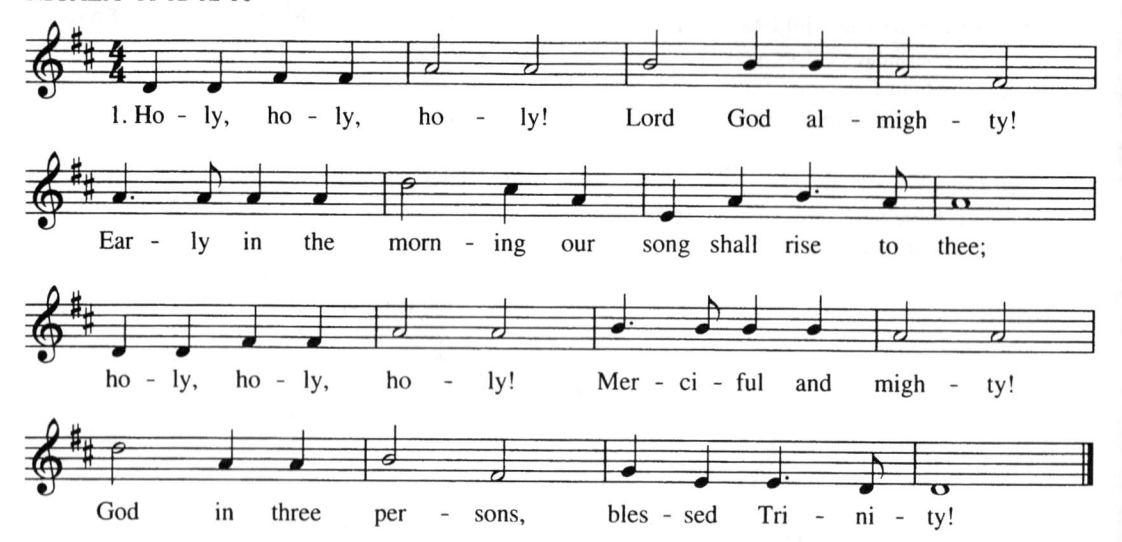

1. Holy, holy, holy! Lord God almighty!
Early in the morning our song shall rise to thee;
holy, holy, holy! Merciful and mighty!
God in three persons, blessèd Trinity!

* 2. Holy, holy, holy! All the saints adore thee,
casting down their golden crowns around the glassy sea;
cherubim and seraphim falling down before thee,
which wert, and art, and evermore shall be.

3. Holy, holy, holy! Though the darkness hide thee,
though the eye made blind by sin thy glory may not see,
only thou art holy, there is none beside thee,
perfect in pow'r, in love, and purity.

4. Holy, holy, holy! Lord God almighty!
All thy works shall praise thy name, in earth, and sky and sea;
holy, holy, holy! Merciful and mighty!
God in three persons, blessèd Trinity!

May be omitted

Text: Reginald Heber (1783-1826)
Music: John Bacchus Dykes (1823-1876)

338 Holy Jesus, in our likeness born

CWM RHONDDA 87 87 47

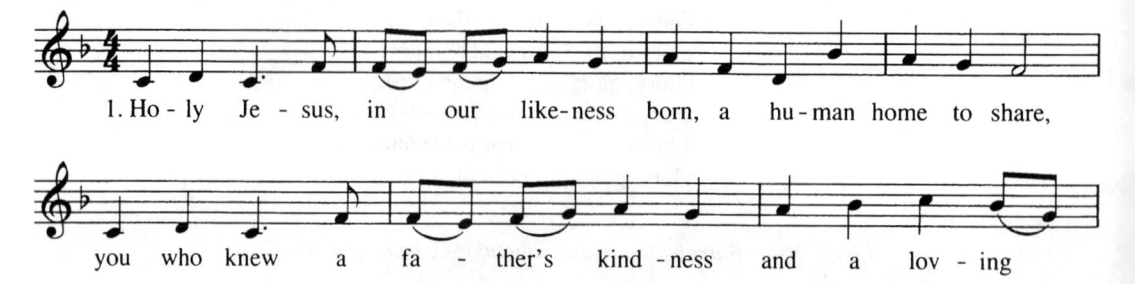

1. Holy Jesus, in our likeness born, a human home to share,
you who knew a father's kindness and a loving

Text © Copyright 1993 Kevin Mayhew Ltd.
Music © Copyright control

mo - ther's care, by your e - ver - pre - sent mer - cy,
may we catch this vi - sion fair, (vi-sion fair) may we catch this vi - sion fair!

A higher setting will be found at No. 307

2. Look with kindness and compassion
   on each mortal family.
   Give us joy in one another,
   touching here eternity!
   Saviour, hold your many people
   in the sweetest harmony,
   in the sweetest harmony.

3. May we live for one another,
   growing through life's ev'ry stage,
   with protection for the youngest
   and respect for greater age;
   all a common value sharing,
   what a holy heritage,
   what a holy heritage!

Text: Michael Forster (b.1946)
Music: John Hughes (1873-1932)
Text © Copyright 1993 Kevin Mayhew Ltd.
Music © Copyright control

339 Holy Mary, you were chosen

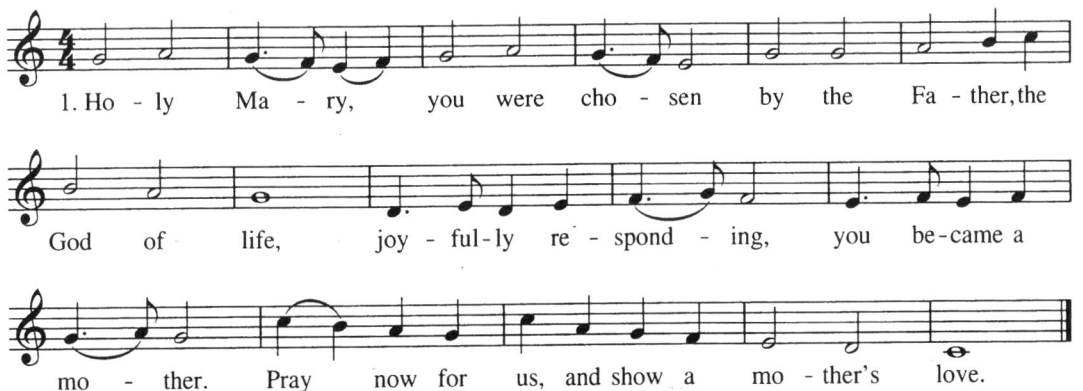

O SANCTISSIMA Irregular

1. Ho - ly Ma - ry, you were cho - sen by the Fa - ther, the God of life, joy - ful - ly re - spond - ing, you be - came a mo - ther. Pray now for us, and show a mo - ther's love.

2. Holy Mary, you were chosen,
   called to carry the Son of God.
   Gratefully responding,
   you became his mother.
   Pray now for us, and show a mother's love.

3. Holy Mary, you were chosen,
   so the Spirit could work in you.
   Faithfully responding,
   you became God's mother.
   Pray now for us, and show a mother's love.

4. Holy Mary, you were chosen
   all God's children are blessed in you.
   Joyfully responding,
   you became our mother.
   Pray now for us, and show a mother's love.

Text: Damian Lundy (1944-1997)
Music: traditional Sicilian melody
Text © Copyright 1987, 1999 Kevin Mayhew Ltd.

340 Holy Spirit, come, confirm us

LAUS DEO (REDHEAD NO. 46) 87 87

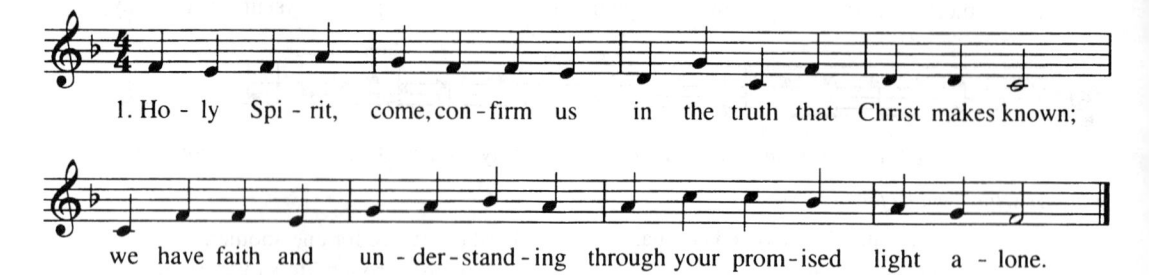

1. Holy Spirit, come, confirm us in the truth that Christ makes known;
we have faith and understanding through your promised light alone.

A higher setting will be found at No. 196

2. Holy Spirit, come, console us,
come as Advocate to plead;
loving Spirit from the Father,
grant in Christ the help we need.

3. Holy Spirit, come renew us,
come yourself to make us live;
holy through your loving presence,
holy through the gifts you give.

4. Holy Spirit, come, possess us,
you the love of Three in One,
Holy Spirit of the Father,
Holy Spirit of the Son.

Text: Brian Foley (b.1919)
Music: German melody adapted by Richard Redhead (1820-1901)
Text Copyright © 1971 Faber Music Ltd, 3 Queen Square, London WC1N 3AU.
Reproduced from 'New Catholic Hymnal' by permission of the publishers.

341 Holy Spirit, Lord of light

VENI SANCTE SPIRITUS 777 D

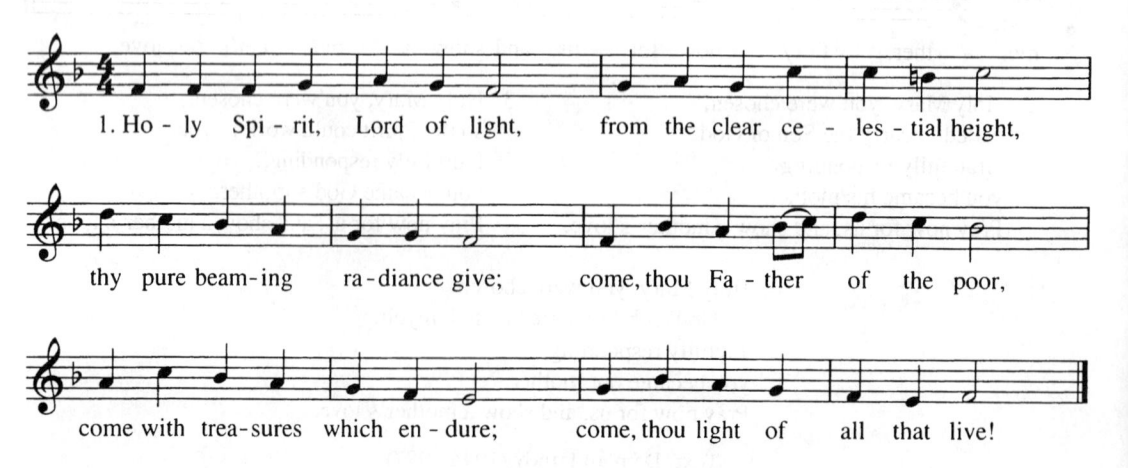

1. Holy Spirit, Lord of light, from the clear celestial height,
thy pure beaming radiance give; come, thou Father of the poor,
come with treasures which endure; come, thou light of all that live!

2. Thou, of all consolers best,
    thou, the soul's delightsome guest,
    dost refreshing peace bestow:
    thou in toil art comfort sweet;
    pleasant coolness in the heat;
    solace in the midst of woe.

3. Light immortal, light divine,
    visit thou these hearts of thine,
    and our inmost being fill:
    if thou take thy grace away,
    nothing pure in us will stay;
    all his good is turned to ill.

4. Heal our wounds, our strength renew;
    on our dryness pour thy dew;
    wash the stains of guilt away;
    bend the stubborn heart and will;
    melt the frozen, warm the chill;
    guide the steps that go astray.

5. Thou, on those who evermore
    thee confess and thee adore,
    in thy sev'nfold gifts descend:
    give them comfort when they die;
    give them life with thee on high;
    give them joys that never end.

Text: ascribed to Stephen Langton (d.1228) trans. Edward Caswall (1814-1878) alt.
Music: Samuel Webbe (1740-1816)

342 Holy Spirit of fire

Holy Spirit of fire, flame e-ver-last-ing, so bright and clear, speak this day in our hearts. Light-en our dark-ness and purge us of fear, Ho-ly Spi-rit of fire. *Refrain* The wind can blow or be still, or wa-ter be parched by the sun. A fire can die in-to dust: but here the e-ter-nal Spi-rit of God tells us a new world's be-gun.

2. Holy Spirit of love,
    strong are the faithful who trust your pow'r.
    Love who conquers our will,
    teach us the words of the gospel of peace,
    Holy Spirit of love.

3. Holy Spirit of God,
    flame everlasting so bright and clear,
    speak this day in our hearts.
    Lighten our darkness and purge us of fear,
    Holy Spirit of God.

Text and Music: John Glynn (b.1948)
© Copyright 1976 Kevin Mayhew Ltd.

343 Holy virgin, by God's decree
New Lourdes Hymn

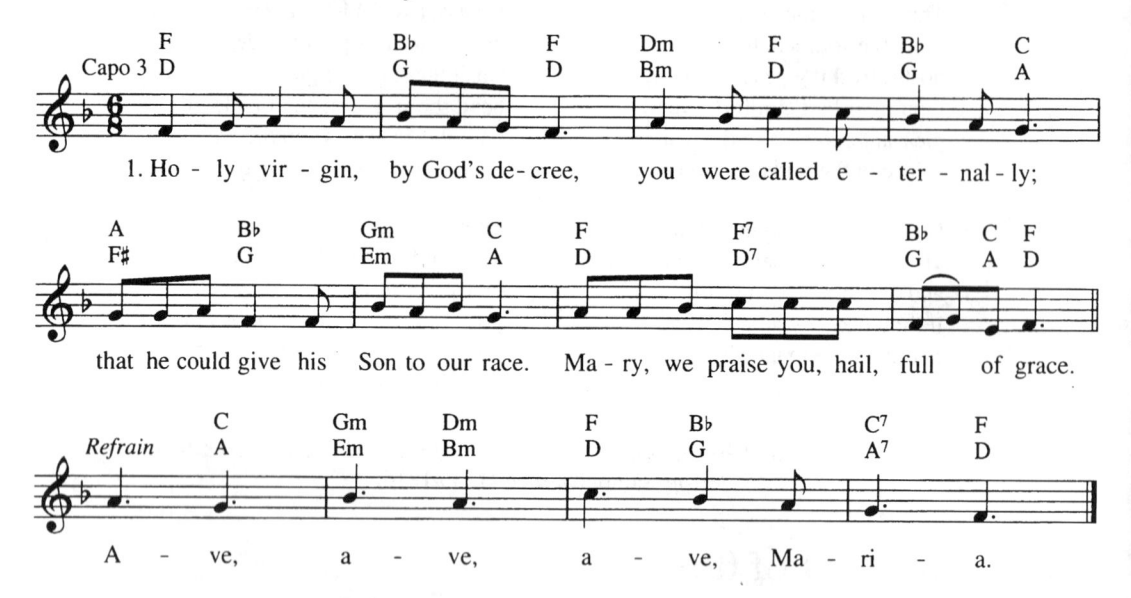

1. Holy virgin, by God's decree, you were called eternally; that he could give his Son to our race. Mary, we praise you, hail, full of grace.

Refrain
Ave, ave, ave, Maria.

2. By your faith and loving accord,
as the handmaid of the Lord,
you undertook God's plan to embrace.
Mary, we thank you, hail, full of grace.

3. Joy to God you gave and expressed,
of all women none more blessed,
when in our flesh your Son took his place.
Mary, we love you, hail, full of grace.

4. Refuge for your children so weak,
sure protection all can seek.
Problems of life you help us to face.
Mary, we trust you, hail, full of grace.

5. To our needy world of today
love and beauty you portray,
showing the path to Christ we must trace.
Mary, our mother, hail, full of grace.

Text: Jean-Paul Lécot (b. 1947) trans. W.R. Lawrence (1925-1997), alt.
Music: Paul Dècha
© Copyright 1988 Kevin Mayhew Ltd.

344 Hosanna, hosanna

1. Hosanna, hosanna, hosanna in the highest! Hosanna, hosanna, hosanna in the highest!

© Copyright 1985 Mercy/Vineyard Publishing/Music Services. Administered by CopyCare,
P.O. Box 77, Hailsham, East Sussex BN27 3EF, UK. Used by permission.

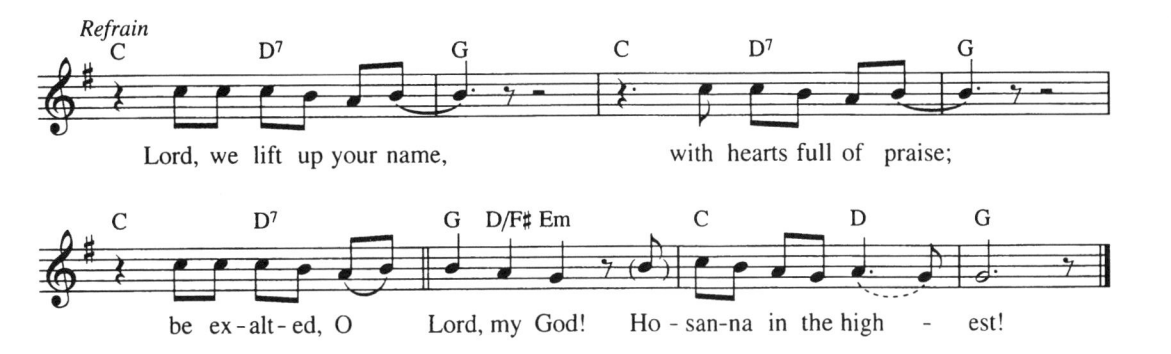

Lord, we lift up your name, with hearts full of praise;
be exalted, O Lord, my God! Hosanna in the highest!

2. Glory, glory, glory to the King of kings!
   Glory, glory, glory to the King of kings!

Text and Music: Carl Tuttle

345 How great is our God

How great is our God, how great is his name!
How great is our God, for ever the same! same!

1. He rolled back the waters of the mighty Red Sea,
   and he said: 'I'll never leave you. Put your trust in me.'

2. He sent his Son, Jesus,
   to set us all free,
   and he said: 'I'll never leave you.
   Put your trust in me.'

3. He gave us his Spirit,
   and now we can see.
   And he said: 'I'll never leave you.
   Put your trust in me.'

Text and Music: unknown

346 How lovely on the mountains
Our God reigns

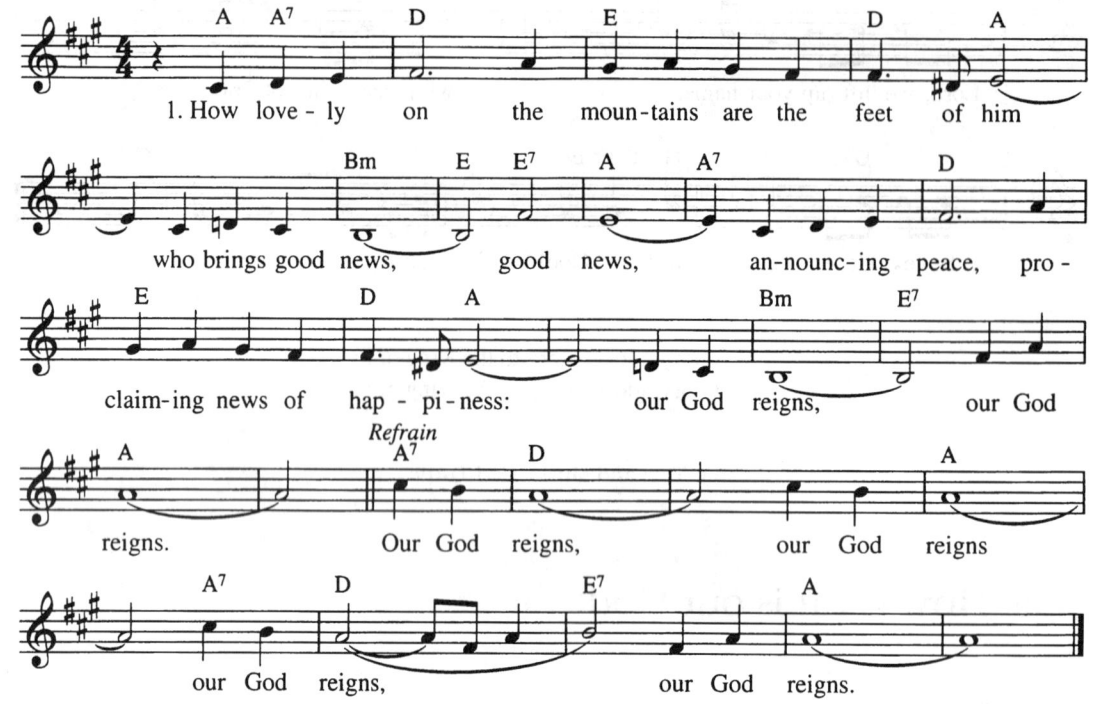

1. How lovely on the mountains are the feet of him who brings good news, good news, announcing peace, proclaiming news of happiness: our God reigns, our God reigns.

Refrain
Our God reigns, our God reigns, our God reigns, our God reigns.

2. You watchmen, lift your voices joyfully as one,
shout for your King, your King!
See eye to eye the Lord restoring Zion:
our God reigns, our God reigns.

3. Wasteplaces of Jerusalem, break forth with joy!
We are redeemed, redeemed.
The Lord has saved and comforted his people:
our God reigns, our God reigns.

4. Ends of the earth, see the salvation of our God!
Jesus is Lord, is Lord!
Before the nations he has bared his holy arm:
our God reigns, our God reigns.

Text: v.1 Leonard E. Smith Jnr. (b.1942) based on Isaiah 52,53; vs. 2-4 unknown
Music: Leonard E. Smith Jnr. (b.1942)
© Copyright 1974 Kingsway's Thankyou Music, P.O. Box 75, Eastbourne, East Sussex BN23 6NW, UK.
Europe only. Used by permission.

347 How shall they hear the word of God

VERBUM DEI 86 86 88

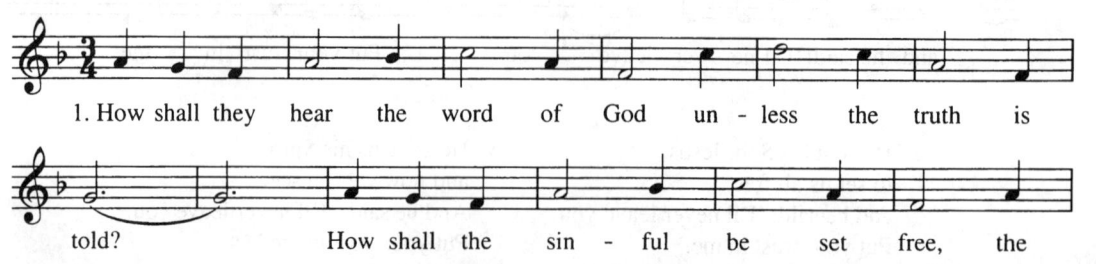

1. How shall they hear the word of God unless the truth is told? How shall the sinful be set free, the

Text © Copyright 1980 Mrs B. Perry/Jubilate Hymns, 4 Thorne Park Road, Chelston, Torquay TQ2 6RX.
Used by permission. Music © Copyright 1999 Kevin Mayhew Ltd.

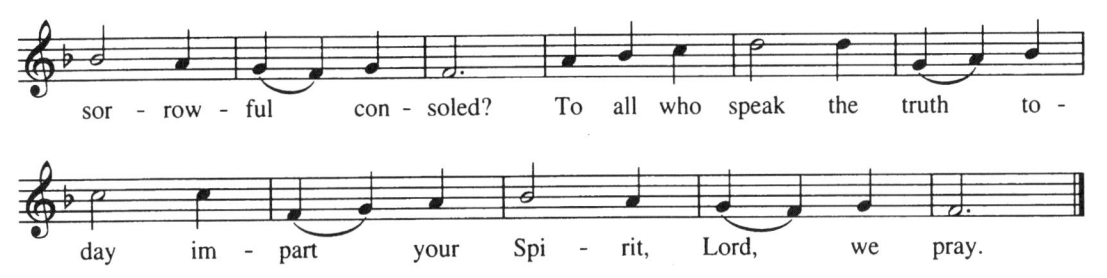

sor - row - ful con - soled? To all who speak the truth to -
day im - part your Spi - rit, Lord, we pray.

2. How shall they call to God for help
unless they have believed?
How shall the poor be given hope,
the prisoner reprieved?
To those who help the blind to see
give light and love and clarity.

3. How shall the gospel be proclaimed
that sinners may repent?
How shall the world find peace at last
if heralds are not sent?
So send us, Lord, for we rejoice
to speak of Christ with life and voice.

Text: Michael Perry (b.1942)
Music: Andrew Moore (b.1954)

348 I am the bread of life (Konstant)

I am the bread of life. You who come to me will ne - ver be hun - gry.
I will raise you up, I will raise you up, I will
raise you up to e - ter - nal life. I am the bread of life.

2. I am the spring of life.
You who hope in me will never be thirsty.
I will raise you up, I will raise you up,
I will raise you up to eternal life.
I am the spring of life.

3. I am the way of life.
You who follow me will never be lonely.
I will raise you up, I will raise you up,
I will raise you up to eternal life.
I am the way of life.

4. I am the truth of life.
You who look for me will never seek blindly.
I will raise you up, I will raise you up,
I will raise you up to eternal life.
I am the truth of life.

5. I am the life of life.
You who die with me will never die vainly.
I will raise you up, I will raise you up,
I will raise you up to eternal life.
I am the life of life.

Text: David Konstant (b.1930)
Music: Kevin Mayhew (b.1942)
© Copyright 1976 Kevin Mayhew Ltd.

349 I am the bread of life (Toolan)

1. I am the bread of life. You who come to me shall not hunger; and who believe in me shall not thirst. No one can come to me unless the Father beckons.

Refrain
And I will raise you up, and I will raise you up, and I will raise you up on the last day.

2. The bread that I will give is my flesh for the life of the world, and if you eat of this bread, you shall live for ever, you shall live for ever.

© Copyright 1966 GIA Publications Inc., 7404 S. Mason Avenue, Chicago, Illinois 60638, USA. All rights reserved. Used by permission.

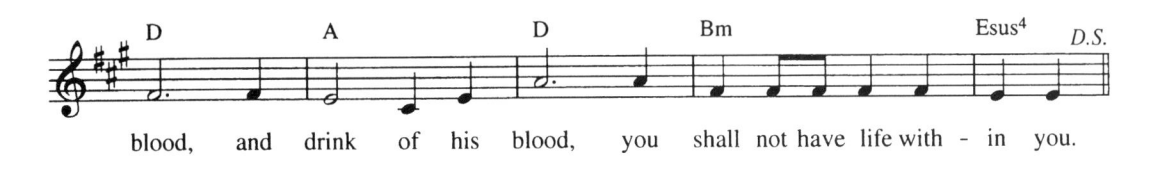

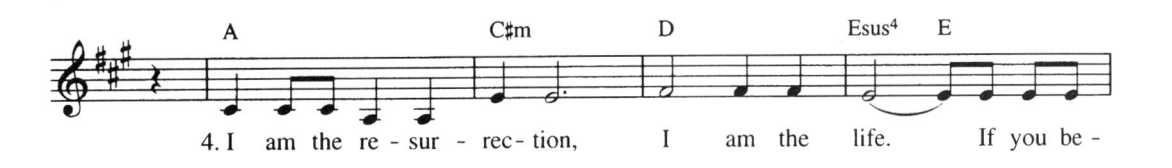

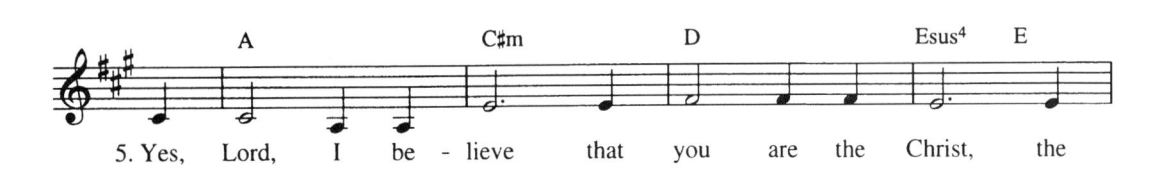

3. Unless you eat of the flesh of the Son of Man, and drink of his blood, and drink of his blood, you shall not have life within you.

4. I am the resurrection, I am the life. If you believe in me, even though you die, you shall live forever.

5. Yes, Lord, I believe that you are the Christ, the Son of God, who has come into the world.

Text and Music: Suzanne Toolan (b.1927)

350 I am the Light
Come, follow me

1. I am the Light, bringing you out of darkness, so come, take my light to the world. I am the Bread you must feed to the hungry, the Wine that must fill ev'ry heart. Foxes have holes, birds have their nests, but the Son of Man has no place to rest.

Refrain
Come, follow me; be the light of the nations. Leave your nets and come, follow me.

2. I am the Life
   that must change ev'ry life
   and the Way that must alter your ways.
   I am the Truth and my word is the cross
   you must take if you want to be free.
   Foxes have holes, birds have their nests,
   but the Son of Man has no place to rest.

3. I am the Sower,
   come, work in my vineyard, my field.
   Tend my vines, sow the grain.
   And should it fall to the ground,
   it can only spring up
   with new life, hundredfold.
   Foxes have holes, birds have their nests,
   but the Son of Man has no place to rest.

4. I am the Shepherd,
   come into the sheepfold
   to help feed my lambs, feed my sheep.
   Bring back the straying,
   and bind up their wounds, and rejoice
   when you've found what was lost.
   Foxes have holes, birds have their nests,
   but the Son of Man has no place to rest.

Text: Aniceto Nazareth based on the Gospel of John
Music: Aniceto Nazareth
© Copyright 1984 Kevin Mayhew Ltd.

351 I cannot tell

LONDONDERRY AIR 11 10 11 10 11 10 11 12

1. I cannot tell how he whom angels worship
should stoop to love the peoples of the earth,
or why as shepherd he should seek the wand'rer
with his mysterious promise of new birth.
But this I know, that he was born of Mary,
when Beth-l'em's manger was his only home,
and that he lived at Nazareth and laboured,
and so the Saviour, Saviour of the world, is come.

2. I cannot tell how silently he suffered,
   as with his peace he graced this place of tears,
   or how his heart upon the cross was broken,
   the crown of pain to three and thirty years.
   But this I know, he heals the broken-hearted,
   and stays our sin, and calms our lurking fear,
   and lifts the burden from the heavy laden,
   for yet the Saviour, Saviour of the world, is here.

3. I cannot tell how he will win the nations,
   how he will claim his earthly heritage,
   how satisfy the needs and aspirations
   of east and west, of sinner and of sage.
   But this I know, all flesh shall see his glory,
   and he shall reap the harvest he has sown,
   and some glad day his sun shall shine in splendour
   when he the Saviour, Saviour of the world, is known.

4. I cannot tell how all the lands shall worship,
   when, at his bidding, ev'ry storm is stilled,
   or who can say how great the jubilation
   when ev'ry heart with perfect love is filled.
   But this I know, the skies will thrill with rapture,
   and myriad, myriad human voices sing,
   and earth to heav'n and heav'n to earth, will answer:
   'At last the Saviour, Saviour of the world, is King!'

Text: William Young Fullerton (1857-1932) alt.
Music: traditional Irish melody
Text © Copyright control

352 I come like a beggar

I come like a beggar with a gift in my hand, I come like a beggar with a gift in my hand.

Refrain
By the hungry I will feed you, by the poor I make you rich, by the broken I will mend you, tell me, which one is which?

2. I come like a prisoner to set you free,
   I come like a prisoner to set you free.

3. The need of another is the gift that I bring,
   the need of another is the gift that I bring.

4. I come like a beggar, what you do for my sake
   is the wine that I offer you, the bread that I break.

Text and Music: Sydney Carter (b.1915)
© Copyright 1974 Stainer & Bell Ltd., P.O. Box 110, Victoria House, 23 Gruneisen Road, Finchley, London N3 1DZ. Used by permission.

353 I danced in the morning
Lord of the dance

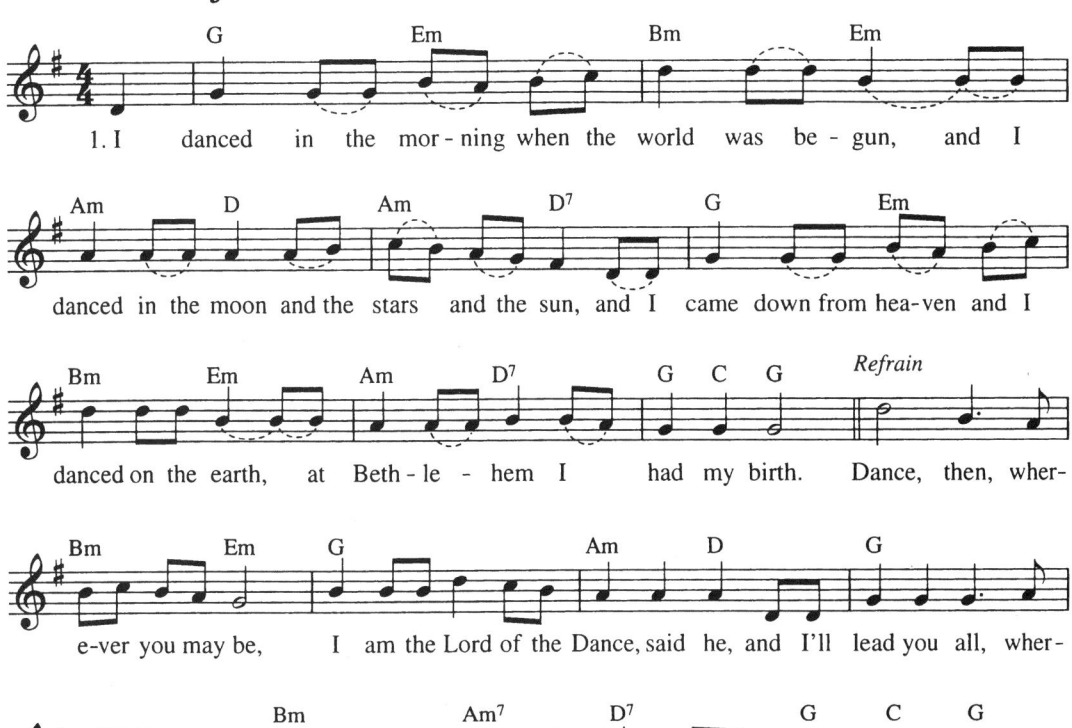

1. I danced in the morning when the world was begun, and I
danced in the moon and the stars and the sun, and I came down from heaven and I
danced on the earth, at Bethlehem I had my birth.
Dance, then, wherever you may be, I am the Lord of the Dance, said he, and I'll lead you all, wherever you may be, and I'll lead you all in the dance, said he.

2. I danced for the scribe and the Pharisee,
but they would not dance and they wouldn't follow me.
I danced for the fishermen, for James and John –
they came with me and the dance went on.

3. I danced on the Sabbath and I cured the lame;
the holy people, they said it was a shame.
They whipped and they stripped and they hung me on high,
and they left me there on a cross to die.

4. I danced on a Friday when the sky turned black –
it's hard to dance with the devil on your back.
They buried my body, and they thought I'd gone,
but I am the dance, and I still go on.

5. They cut me down and I leapt up high;
I am the life that'll never, never die;
I'll live in you if you'll live in me –
I am the Lord of the Dance, said he.

Text: Sydney Carter (b.1915)
Music: traditional American melody adapted by Sydney Carter (b.1915)
© Copyright 1963 Stainer & Bell Ltd, P.O. Box 110, Victoria House, 23 Gruneisen Road, Finchley, London N3 1DZ, UK.
Used by permission.

354 If God is for us

Refrain

If God is for us, who can be a-gainst, if the Spi-rit of God has set us free? If God is for us, who can be a-gainst, if the Spi-rit of God has set us free? *Fine* 1. I know that no-thing in this world can e-ver take us from his love. If

2. Nothing can take us from his love,
   poured out in Jesus, the Lord.

3. And nothing present or to come
   can ever take us from his love.

4. I know that neither death nor life
   can ever take us from his love.

Text: John Foley based on Romans 8:31-39
Music: John Foley

© Copyright 1975 John B. Foley, S.J. and New Dawn Music, 5536 NE Hassalo, Portland, Oregon 97213, USA.
All rights reserved. Used by permission.

355 If I am lacking love

Refrain (Capo 3)

If I am lacking love, then I am nothing, Lord. On love I set my heart; my joy and my reward. *Fine*

1. Without love my words ring hollow, my intentions are disgraced, all my sacrifices empty, ev'ry hope and pray'r misplaced. *D.C.*

2. Love is patient, love is kindly,
   never jealous, never proud;
   not conceited, nor ill-mannered,
   never selfish, never rude.

3. Love is gracious and forgiving,
   taking no delight in sin;
   love rejoices in the truth,
   will not lose heart, will not give in.

4. I know love is everlasting;
   other gifts will pass away.
   Only faith and hope and love
   will never die, will ever stay.

5. God is bountiful in giving;
   all his gifts are my desire,
   but I set my heart on love.
   May his love set my heart on fire!

Text: Damian Lundy (1944-1997) based on 1 Corinthians 13
Music: South American melody
Text © Copyright 1982, 1998 Kevin Mayhew Ltd.

LITURGICAL
HYMNS OLD & NEW

356 I give you love
Reproaches

FINLANDIA 10 10 10 10 10 10

1. I give you love, and how do you re-pay? When you were slaves I strove to set you free; I led you out from un-der Pha-raoh's yoke, but you led out your Christ to Cal-va-ry.

Refrain
My peo-ple, tell me, what is my of-fence,
What have I done to harm you? Ans-wer me!

2. For forty years I was your constant guide,
   I fed you with my manna from on high.
   I led you out to live in hope and peace,
   but you led out my only Son to die.

3. With cloud and fire I marked the desert way,
   I heard your cries of rage and calmed your fear.
   I opened up the sea and led you through,
   but you have opened Christ with nail and spear.

4. When in distress you cried to me for food,
   I sent you quails in answer to your call,
   and saving water from the desert rock,
   but to my Son you offered bitter gall.

5. I gave you joy when you were in despair,
   with songs of hope, I set your hearts on fire;
   crowned you with grace, the people of my choice,
   but you have crowned my Christ with thorny briar.

6. When you were weak, exploited and oppressed,
   I heard your cry and listened to your plea.
   I raised you up to honour and renown,
   but you have raised me on a shameful tree.

Text: Michael Forster (b.1946) based on the Good Friday Reproaches
Music: Jean Sibelius (1865-1957)
Text © Copyright 1996 Kevin Mayhew Ltd.
Music © Copyright Breitkopf and Härtel, Walkmühlstrasse 52, D-65195 Wiesbaden, Germany.
Used by permission.

357 I have loved you with an everlasting love

I have loved you with an e-ver last-ing love, I have called you, and you are mine. I have loved you with an e-ver-last-ing love, I have called you, and you are mine. 1. Seek the face of the Lord and long for him: he will bring you his light and his peace. I have

2. Seek the face of the Lord and long for him:
he will bring you his joy and his hope.

3. Seek the face of the Lord and long for him:
he will bring you his care and his love.

Text and Music: Michael Joncas (b.1951)

© Copyright 1979 New Dawn Music, 5536 NE Hassalo, Portland, OR 97213, USA. All rights reserved. Used by permission.

358 I'll sing a hymn to Mary

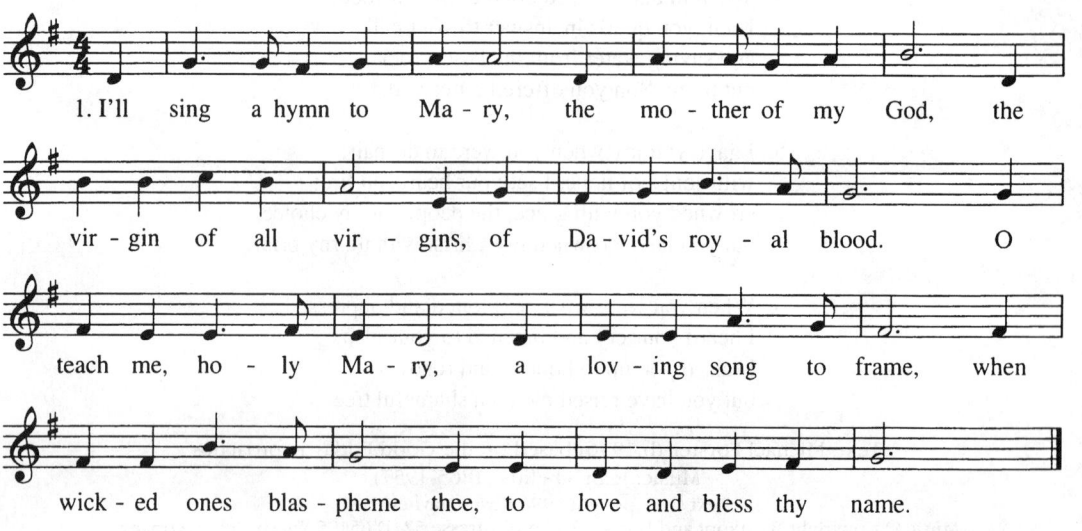

TURRIS DAVIDICA 76 76 D

1. I'll sing a hymn to Ma-ry, the mo-ther of my God, the vir-gin of all vir-gins, of Da-vid's roy-al blood. O teach me, ho-ly Ma-ry, a lov-ing song to frame, when wick-ed ones blas-pheme thee, to love and bless thy name.

2. O noble Tower of David,
   of gold and ivory,
   the Ark of God's own promise,
   the gate of heav'n to me,
   to live and not to love thee,
   would fill my soul with shame;
   when wicked ones blaspheme thee,
   I'll love and bless thy name.

3. The saints are high in glory,
   with golden crowns so bright;
   but brighter far is Mary,
   upon her throne of light.
   O that which God did give thee,
   let mortal ne'er disclaim;
   when wicked ones blaspheme thee,
   I'll love and bless thy name.

4. But in the crown of Mary,
   there lies a wondrous gem,
   as queen of all the angels,
   which Mary shares with them:
   no sin hath e'er defiled thee,
   so doth our faith proclaim;
   when wicked ones blaspheme thee,
   I'll love and bless thy name.

Text: John Wyse (1825-1898) alt.
Music: Henri Friedrich Hémy (1818-1888)

359 I'll turn my steps to the altar of God

I'll turn my steps to the al-tar of God, I'll turn my steps to the glad-ness of my life. 1. Show your jus-tice in plead-ing my cause, let me walk in the way of your laws. I'll turn my

2. Lead me on with your power and strength,
   then my courage will never be spent.

3. Fill my heart with your truth and your light
   as I enter with joy in your sight.

4. Holy praises of God will I sing;
   I will trust and will hope in my King.

5. Glory be to the Father, the Son
   and the Spirit, while endless years run.

Text: Aniceto Nazareth based on Psalm 42
Music: Aniceto Nazareth
© Copyright 1984 Kevin Mayhew Ltd.

360 Immaculate Mary
Lourdes Hymn

LOURDES 65 65 and Refrain

1. Immaculate Mary! Our hearts are on fire; that title so wondrous fills all our desire. A-ve, a-ve, a-ve Maria! A-ve, a-ve, a-ve Maria!

2. We pray for God's glory,
may his kingdom come!
We pray for his vicar,
our father, and Rome.

4. For poor, sick, afflicted
thy mercy we crave;
and comfort the dying,
thou light of the grave.

5. In grief and temptation,
in joy or in pain,
we'll ask thee, our mother,
nor seek thee in vain.

3. We pray for our mother
the Church upon earth,
and bless, sweetest lady,
the land of our birth.

6. In death's solemn moment,
our mother, be nigh;
as children of Mary,
O teach us to die.

7. And crown thy sweet mercy
with this special grace,
and worship in heaven
God's ravishing face.

8. To God be all glory
and worship for aye;
to God's virgin mother
an endless Ave.

Text: unknown
Music: traditional French melody
This arrangement © Copyright 1978 Kevin Mayhew Ltd.

361 Immortal, invisible, God only wise

SAINT DENIO 11 11 11 11

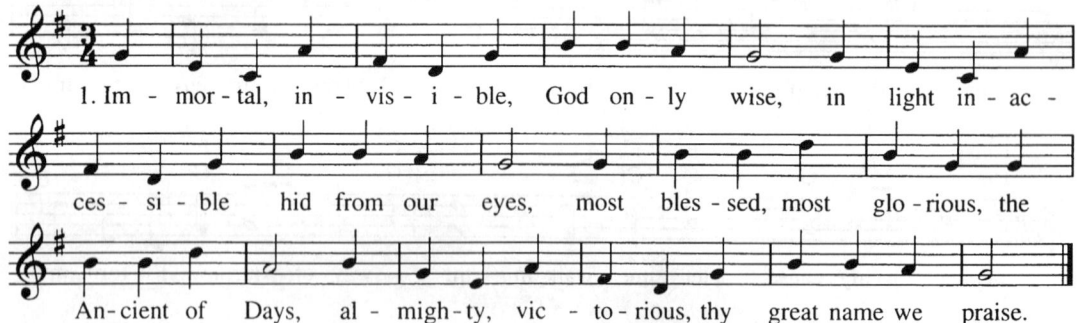

1. Immortal, invisible, God only wise, in light inaccessible hid from our eyes, most blessed, most glorious, the Ancient of Days, almighty, victorious, thy great name we praise.

2. Unresting, unhasting, and silent as light,
nor wanting, nor wasting, thou rulest in might;
thy justice like mountains high soaring above
thy clouds which are fountains of goodness and love.

3. To all life thou givest, to both great and small;
in all life thou livest, the true life of all;
we blossom and flourish as leaves on the tree,
and wither and perish; but naught changeth thee.

4. Great Father of glory, pure Father of light,
thine angels adore thee, all veiling their sight;
all laud we would render, O help us to see
'tis only the splendour of light hideth thee.

Text: Walter Chalmers Smith (1824-1908) based on 1 Timothy 1:17
Music: adapted from a traditional Welsh hymn melody in John Roberts' 'Caniadu y Cyssegr' (1839)

362 In bread we bring you, Lord

1. In bread we bring you, Lord, our bodies' labour.
   In wine we offer you our spirits' grief.
   We do not ask you, Lord, who is my neighbour,
   but stand united now, one in belief.
   O we have gladly heard your Word, your holy Word,
   and now in answer, Lord, our gifts we bring.
   Our selfish hearts make true, our failing faith renew,
   our lives belong to you, our Lord and King.

2. The bread we offer you is blessed and broken,
   and it becomes for us our spirits' food.
   Over the cup we bring your Word is spoken;
   make it your gift to us, your healing blood.
   Take all that daily toil plants in our hearts' poor soil,
   take all we start and spoil, each hopeful dream,
   the chances we have missed, the graces we resist,
   Lord, in thy Eucharist, take and redeem.

Text and Music: Kevin Nichols (b.1929)
© Copyright 1976 Kevin Mayhew Ltd.

363 In company with Christians past

TALLIS' CANON LM

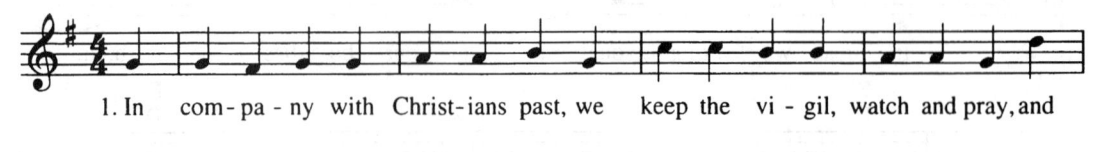

1. In company with Christ-ians past, we keep the vi-gil, watch and pray, and with the temp-ted Christ, re-ject the su-per-fi-cial, ea-sy way.

A lower setting will be found at No. 282

2. We will not turn our stones to bread,
or from the temple's heights be hurled;
nor look for cheap success within
the ways and values of the world.

3. Forgive us, Lord, the times we fail
to keep that promise day by day,
and give us grace to follow you
on faith's more costly, rocky way.

4. Then lead us on to find once more
the glory veiled but never lost:
the image of our God in us,
restored by grace at such a cost!

5. O perfectly related God,
eternal Father, Spirit, Son,
renew us in the Covenant
that makes your many people one.

6. Then move us on from fast to feast.
where life and wholeness are restored,
and you, in triune majesty
are honoured, worshipped and adored.

Text: Michael Forster (b.1946) based on St Gregory the Great (540-604)
Music: Thomas Tallis (c.1505-1585)
Text © Copyright 1999 Kevin Mayhew Ltd.

364 Infant holy, infant lowly

WZLOBIE LEZY 87 87 88 77

1. In-fant ho-ly, in-fant low-ly, for his bed a cat-tle stall; ox-en low-ing, lit-tle know-ing Christ the babe is Lord of all. Swift are wing-ing an-gels sing-ing, no-wells ring-ing, ti-dings

Text © Copyright control

bring-ing, Christ the babe is Lord of all, Christ the babe is Lord of all.

    2. Flocks were sleeping, shepherds keeping
       vigil till the morning new;
       saw the glory, heard the story,
       tidings of a gospel true.
       Thus rejoicing, free from sorrow,
       praises voicing, greet the morrow,
       Christ the babe was born for you,
       Christ the babe was born for you.

Text: trans. from the Polish by Edith Margaret Gellibrand Reed (1885-1933)
Music: traditional Polish melody

365 In the bleak mid-winter

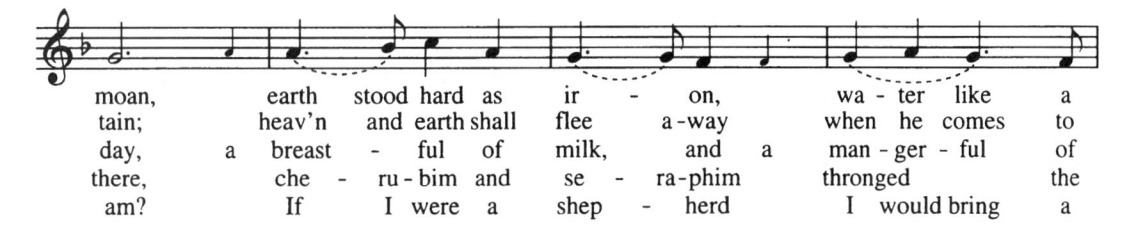

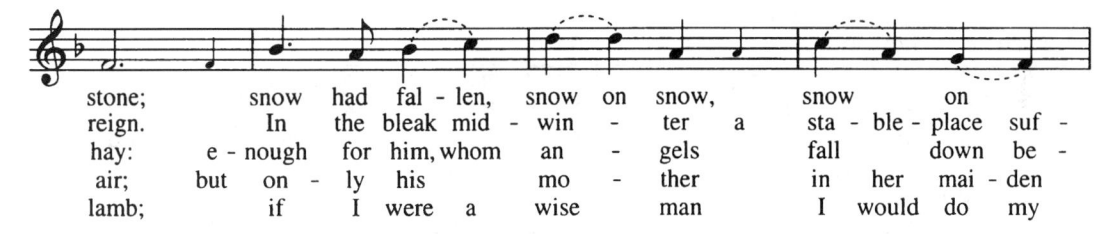

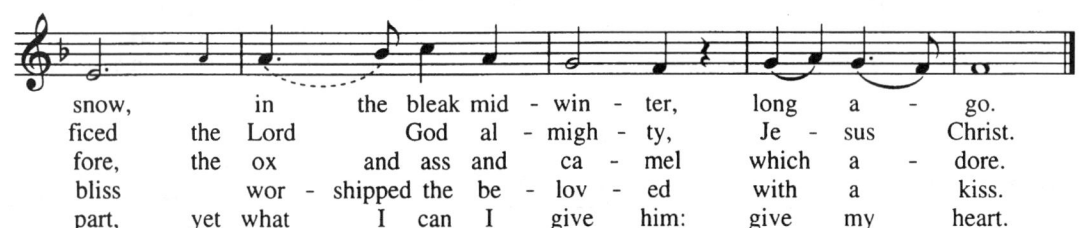

CRANHAM Irregular

1. In the bleak mid-winter frosty wind made moan, earth stood hard as iron, water like a stone; snow had fallen, snow on snow, snow on snow, in the bleak mid-winter, long ago.
2. Our God, heav'n cannot hold him nor earth sustain; heav'n and earth shall flee away when he comes to reign. In the bleak mid-winter a stable-place sufficed the Lord God almighty, Jesus Christ.
3. Enough for him, whom cherubim worship night and day, a breastful of milk, and a mangerful of hay: enough for him, whom angels fall down before, the ox and ass and camel which adore.
4. Angels and archangels may have gathered there, cherubim and seraphim thronged the air; but only his mother in her maiden bliss worshipped the beloved with a kiss.
5. What can I give him, poor as I am? If I were a shepherd I would bring a lamb; if I were a wise man I would do my part, yet what I can I give him: give my heart.

Text: Christina Georgina Rossetti (1830-1894)
Music: Gustav Holst (1874-1934)
Music © Copyright Oxford University Press, Great Clarendon Street, Oxford OX2 6DP.
Used by permission from 'The English Hymnal'.

366 In the love of God and neighbour

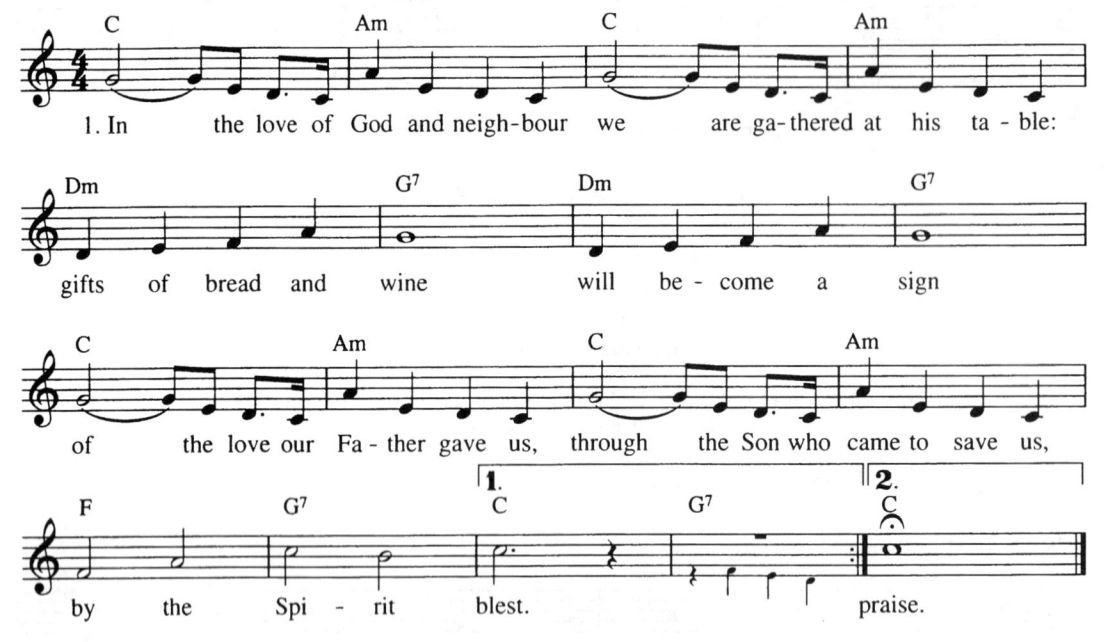

1. In the love of God and neighbour
we are gathered at his table:
gifts of bread and wine
will become a sign
of the love our Father gave us,
through the Son who came to save us,
by the Spirit blest.
praise.

2. So we offer our tomorrows,
all our present joys and sorrows,
ev'ry heart and will, talent, gift and skill.
For the riches we've been given
to the Trinity of heaven
we give thanks and praise.

Text and Music: Estelle White (b.1925)
© Copyright 1978 Kevin Mayhew Ltd.

367 In the tomb so cold
Christ is risen!

1. In the tomb so cold they laid him, death its victim claimed.
Pow'rs of hell, they could not hold him; back to life he came!

Refrain
(Men) Christ is risen! (Women) Christ is risen! (Men) Death has been conquered.

© Copyright 1986 Kingsway's Thankyou Music, P.O. Box 75,
Eastbourne, East Sussex BN23 6NW, UK. Used by permission.

(Women) Death has been con-quered. (Men) Christ is ri - sen! (Women) Christ is ri - sen!

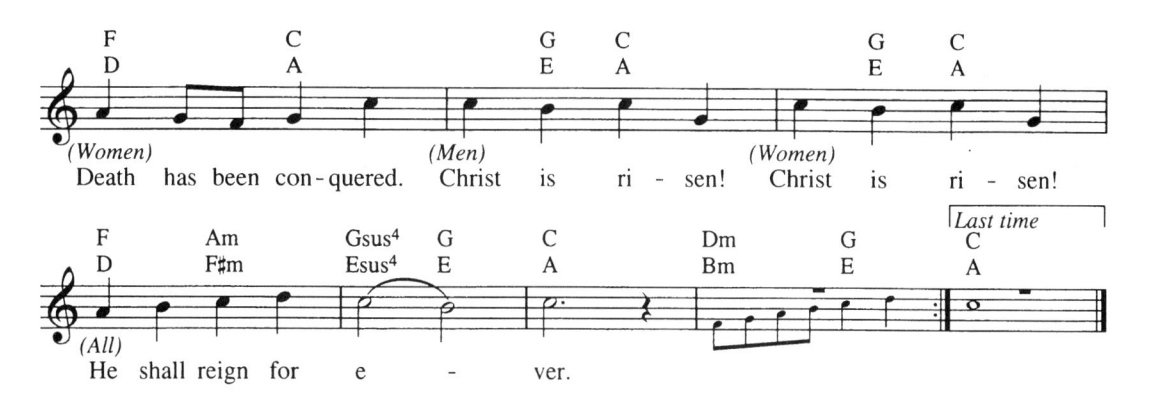

(All) He shall reign for e - ver.

2. Hell had spent its fury on him,
   left him crucified.
   Yet, by blood, he boldly conquered,
   sin and death defied.

3. Now the fear of death is broken,
   love has won the crown.
   Pris'ners of the darkness listen,
   walls are tumbling down.

4. Raised from death to heav'n ascending,
   love's exalted King.
   Let his song of joy, unending,
   through the nations ring!

Text and Music: Graham Kendrick (b.1950)

368 Into one we all are gathered

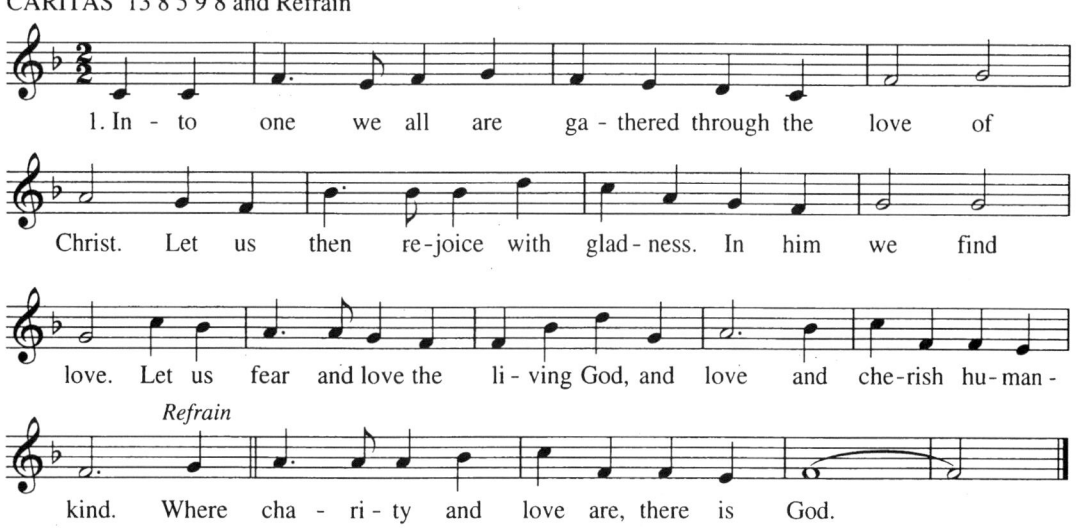

CARITAS 13 8 5 9 8 and Refrain

1. In - to one we all are ga - thered through the love of Christ. Let us then re-joice with glad-ness. In him we find love. Let us fear and love the li - ving God, and love and che-rish hu-man-kind.

Refrain
Where cha - ri - ty and love are, there is God.

2. Therefore, when we are together
   in the love of Christ,
   let our minds know no division,
   strife or bitterness;
   may the Christ our God be in our midst.
   Through Christ our Lord all love is found.

3. May we see your face in glory,
   Christ our loving God.
   With the blessèd saints of heaven
   give us lasting joy.
   We will then possess true happiness,
   and love for all eternity.

Text: Michael Cockett (b.1938) adapted from 'Ubi Caritas'
Music: Eric Welch

© Copyright McCrimmon Publishing Co. Ltd, 10-12 High Street, Great Wakering,
Southend-on-Sea, Essex SS3 0EQ. Used by arrangement.

369 In you, my God

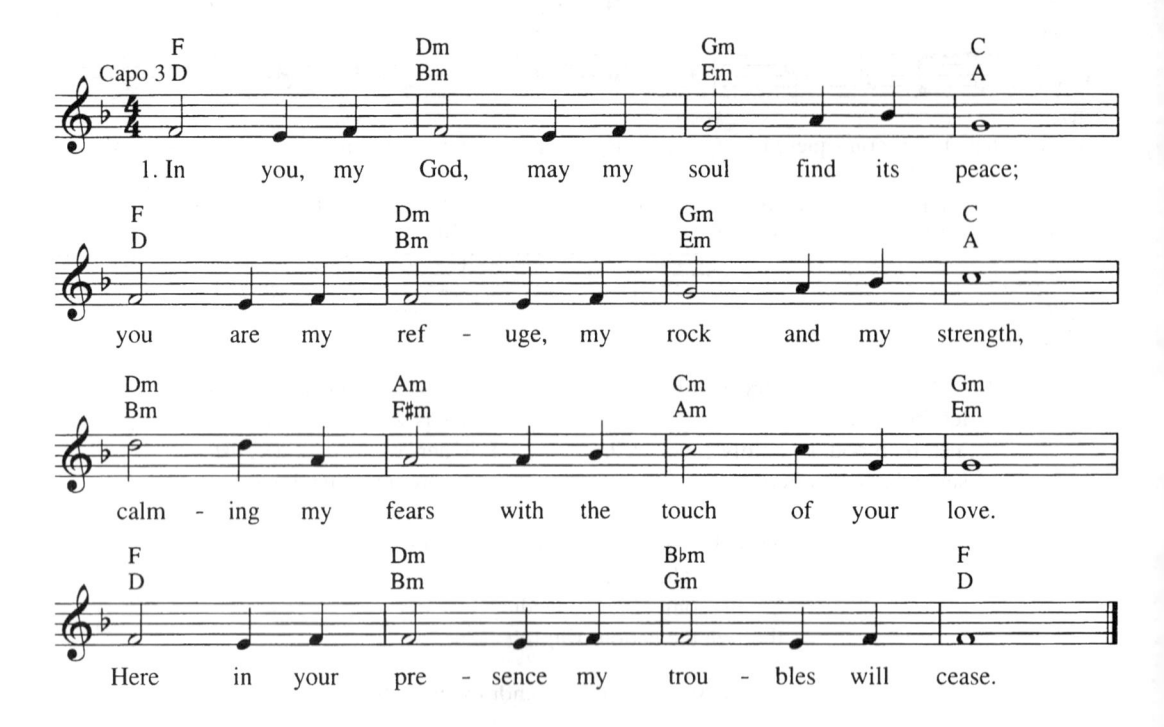

1. In you, my God, may my soul find its peace;
you are my refuge, my rock and my strength,
calming my fears with the touch of your love.
Here in your presence my troubles will cease.

2. In you, my God, may my soul find its joy;
you are the radiance, the song of my heart,
drying my tears with the warmth of your love.
Here in your presence my troubles will cease.

3. In you, my God, may my soul find its rest;
you are the meaning, the purpose of life,
drawing me near to the fire of your love,
safe in your presence my yearning will cease.

Text and Music: Francesca Leftley (b.1955)
© Copyright 1978 Kevin Mayhew Ltd.

370 In your coming and going

HILLSDOWN 11 11 8 9 and Refrain

Refrain
In your coming and going God is with you, He will keep you in safety night and day.

1. You raise your eyes and you look at the

© Copyright 1978, 1999 Kevin Mayhew Ltd.

...moun-tains; you cry a-loud to the hills, 'Come and help me!' Now, see our God is on his way; he will stay be-side you night and day.

2. His arm outstretched to protect you in danger,
he never sleeps all the time he is watching.
He is the maker of the skies,
but he knows your name, he hears your cries.

3. His loving care shelters you like a shadow,
to keep you safe from the evil around you.
He shields you from the burning sun,
and the moon at night will do no harm.

Text: Damian Lundy (1944-1997) based on Psalm 120
Music: Andrew Moore (b.1954)

371 I received the living God

Refrain
I re-ceived the liv-ing God, and my heart is full of joy. I re-ceived the liv-ing God, and my heart is full of joy.

1. He has said: I am the Bread, knead-ed long to give you life; you who will par-take of me need not e-ver fear to die.

2. He has said: I am the Way,
and my Father longs for you;
so I come to bring you home
to be one with him anew.

3. He has said: I am the Truth;
if you follow close to me
you will know me in your heart,
and my word shall make you free.

4. He has said: I am the Life
far from whom no thing can grow,
but receive this living bread,
and my Spirit you shall know.

Text: from the Gospel of John
Music: Unknown

372 I saw streams of water flowing

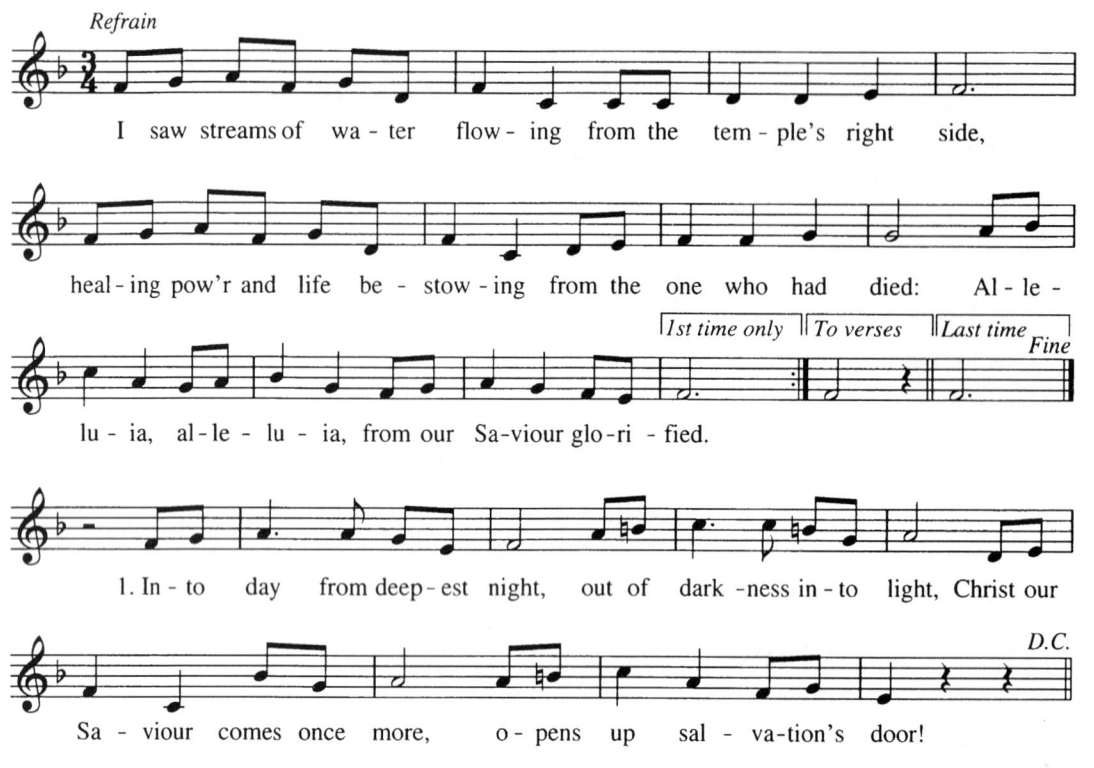

Refrain

I saw streams of water flowing from the temple's right side,
healing pow'r and life bestowing from the one who had died: Alleluia, alleluia, from our Saviour glorified.

1. Into day from deepest night, out of darkness into light, Christ our Saviour comes once more, opens up salvation's door!

2. He has healed us with his blood,
led us safe through Jordan's flood,
on the further bank we stand,
gazing on the promised land!

3. He has raised us from the grave,
from the Red Sea's mighty wave;
dead to sin we rise with Christ,
paschal Lamb now sacrificed.

Text and Music: Stephen Dean
© Copyright 1993 Stephen Dean. Published by OCP Publications, 5536 NE Hassalo, Portland, OR 97213, USA. All rights reserved. Used by permission.

373 I saw the holy city

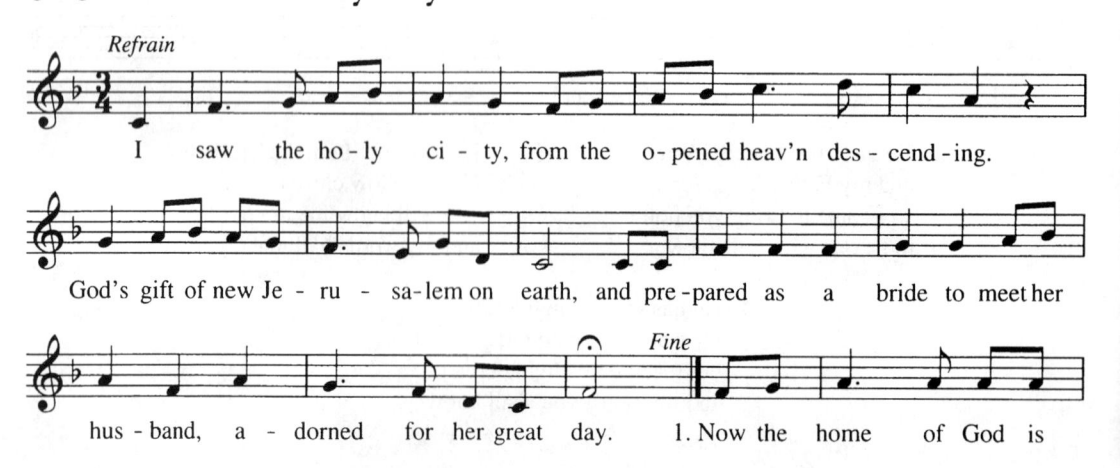

Refrain

I saw the holy city, from the opened heav'n descending,
God's gift of new Jerusalem on earth, and prepared as a bride to meet her husband, adorned for her great day. 1. Now the home of God is

© Copyright 1988, 1999 Kevin Mayhew Ltd.

made up-on the earth, he will dwell a-mong his peo - ple and be with them.

2. He will wipe away the tears from ev'ry eye,
   and no more will death be known, that is his promise.

3. No more mourning, no more pain, and no more tears,
   for the former things have passed away for ever.

4. Praise the Father, Son and Spirit, Three in One,
   God who was, and who is now, and ever shall be.

Text: Michael Forster (b.1946) based on Revelation 21
Music: Alexandre Lesbordes

374 I sing a song to you, Lord

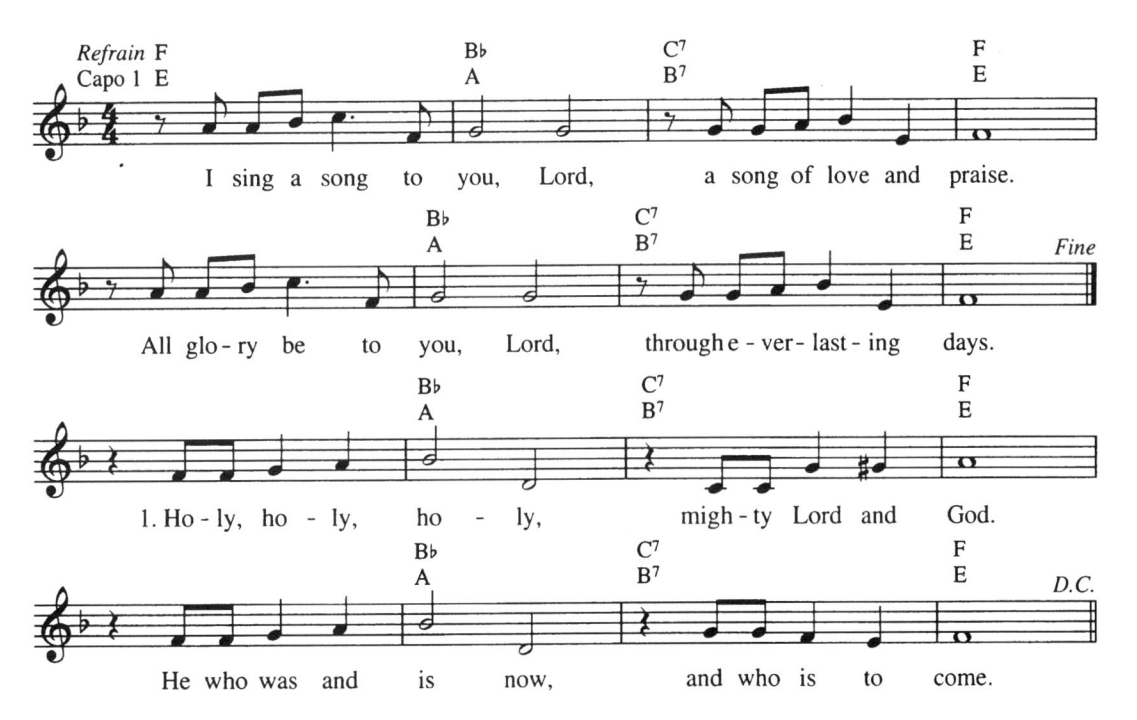

I sing a song to you, Lord, a song of love and praise.
All glo-ry be to you, Lord, through e-ver-last-ing days.
1. Ho-ly, ho-ly, ho - ly, migh-ty Lord and God.
He who was and is now, and who is to come.

2. Worthy is the slain Lamb,
   honour him and praise.
   We rejoice with gladness,
   sing our love today.

3. He has used his power,
   has begun his reign.
   So rejoice, you heavens,
   and proclaim his name.

4. Shine your light on us, Lord,
   let us know your way.
   Be our guide for ever,
   make us yours today.

Text and Music: Richard Beaumont (b.1974)
© Copyright 1974, 1998 Sisters of St Mary of Namur, 909 West Shaw, Ft. Worth, Texas 76110, USA.
All rights reserved. Used by permission.

375 It came upon the midnight clear

NOEL DCM

1. It came upon the midnight clear, that glorious song of old,
from angels bending near the earth to touch their harps of gold:
'Peace on the earth, good-will to all, from heav'ns all-gracious King!'
The world in solemn stillness lay to hear the angels sing.

2. Still through the cloven skies they come,
with peaceful wings unfurled;
and still their heav'nly music floats
o'er all the weary world:
above its sad and lowly plains
they bend on hov'ring wing;
and ever o'er its Babel-sounds
the blessèd angels sing.

3. Yet with the woes of sin and strife
the world has suffered long;
beneath the angel-strain have rolled
two thousand years of wrong;
and warring humankind hears not
the love-song which they bring:
O hush the noise of mortal strife,
and hear the angels sing!

4. And ye, beneath life's crushing load,
whose forms are bending low,
who toil along the climbing way
with painful steps and slow:
look now! for glad and golden hours
come swiftly on the wing;
O rest beside the weary road,
and hear the angels sing.

5. For lo, the days are hast'ning on,
by prophets seen of old,
when with the ever-circling years
comes round the age of gold;
when peace shall over all the earth
its ancient splendours fling,
and all the world give back the song
which now the angels sing.

Text: Edmund Hamilton Sears (1810-1876) alt.
Music: traditional English melody

376 I, the Lord of sea and sky
Here I am, Lord

HERE I AM 77 74 D and Refrain

1. I, the Lord of sea and sky, I have heard my people cry. All who dwell in dark and sin my hand will save. I who made the stars of night, I will make their darkness bright. Who will bear my light to them? Whom shall I send?

Refrain
Here I am, Lord. Is it I, Lord? I have heard you calling in the night. I will go, Lord, if you lead me. I will hold your people in my heart.

2. I, the Lord of snow and rain,
I have borne my people's pain.
I have wept for love of them.
They turn away.
I will break their hearts of stone,
give them hearts for love alone.
I will speak my word to them.
Whom shall I send?

3. I, the Lord of wind and flame,
I will tend the poor and lame.
I will set a feast for them.
My hand will save.
Finest bread I will provide
till their hearts be satisfied.
I will give my life to them.
Whom shall I send?

Text and Music: Dan Schutte

© Copyright 1981 Daniel L. Schutte and New Dawn Music, 5536 NE Hassalo, Portland, Oregon 97213, USA.
All rights reserved. Used by permission.

377 I, the Servant-Lord

Response

I, the Servant-Lord, serve you; serve one another.
Love and service are the signs you are my disciples.

1. Jesus rose from table, put a tow'l around him,
poured some water in a dish, knelt before his friends.

2. In the manner of a slave
Jesus washed their feet.
One by one he came to them,
all who were at supper.

3. With the tow'l he wiped their feet –
Judas too – and Peter.
'Do you understand,' he said,
'this is my example.'

4. 'Happiness will come to you
if you serve each other.
I, the Lord, have washed your feet;
be each other's servant.'

5. 'Trust in God and trust in me;
let no heart be troubled.
I'll prepare a place for you,
I will come back for you.'

6. Thomas said, 'What do you mean?
Which way are you going?'
'Through the darkness follow me;
I go to the Father.'

7. 'Way and truth and life am I.
Learn my way as servant.
Love each other as I do;
serve me in each other.'

8. 'Let us see the Father, Lord.'
Philip asked of Jesus.
'He is in me,' Jesus said,
'I am in the Father.'

9. 'I in you and you in me,
we are one together.
Father, may we all be one,
serving one another.'

10. 'If you love me, keep my word.
Thus my Father loves you.
We shall make our home in you.
You shall live for ever.'

11. 'I have said these things to you
while I still am with you.
In my name the Spirit comes,
sent soon from my Father.'

12. 'My own peace I give to you,
not of this world's giving.
Fear must not constrain your heart.
My own peace I leave you.'

Text: Noel Donnelly (b.1932) based on John 13 and 14
Music: Noel Donnelly (b.1932)
© Copyright 1986 Kevin Mayhew Ltd.

378 I watch the sunrise
Close to you

1. I watch the sunrise lighting the sky,
casting its shadows near.
And on this morning, bright though it be,
I feel those shadows near me.

Refrain
But you are always close to me,
following all my ways.
May I be always close to you,
following all your ways, Lord.

2. I watch the sunlight shine through the clouds,
warming the earth below.
And at the mid-day, life seems to say:
'I feel your brightness near me.'
For you are always . . .

3. I watch the sunset fading away,
lighting the clouds with sleep.
And as the evening closes its eyes,
I feel your presence near me.
For you are always . . .

4. I watch the moonlight guarding the night,
waiting till morning comes.
The air is silent, earth is at rest
– only your peace is near me.
Yes you are always . . .

Text: John Glynn (b.1948)
Music: Colin Murphy
© Copyright 1976 Kevin Mayhew Ltd.

379 I will be with you

Refrain

I will be with you wher-e-ver you go.
Go now through-out the world!
I will be with you in all that you say.
Go now and spread my word!

1. Come, walk with me on stor-my wa-ters.
Why fear? Reach out, and I'll be there.

2. And you, my friend, will you now leave me,
or do you know me as your Lord?

3. Your life will be transformed with power
by living truly in my name.

4. And if you say: 'Yes, Lord, I love you,'
then feed my lambs and feed my sheep.

Text and Music: Gerard Markland (b.1953)
© Copyright 1978 Kevin Mayhew Ltd.

380 I will bless the Lord

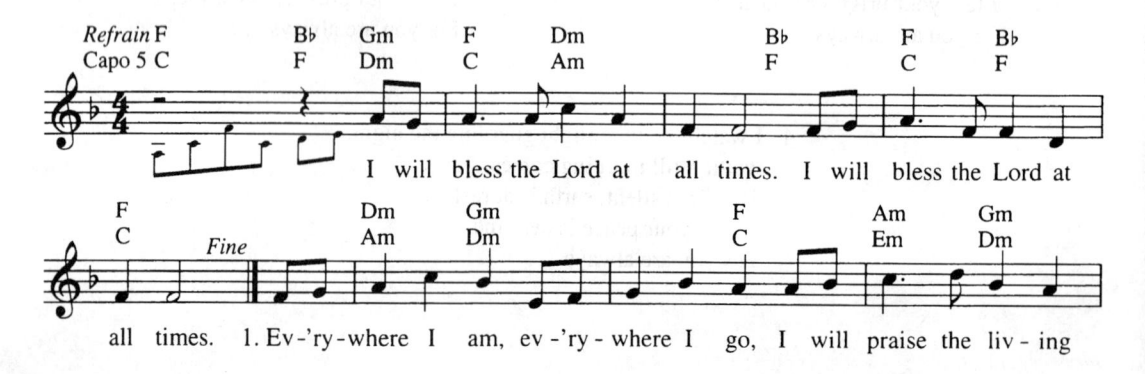

Refrain Capo 5

I will bless the Lord at all times. I will bless the Lord at all times. 1. Ev-'ry-where I am, ev-'ry-where I go, I will praise the liv-ing

© Copyright 1996 Kevin Mayhew Ltd.

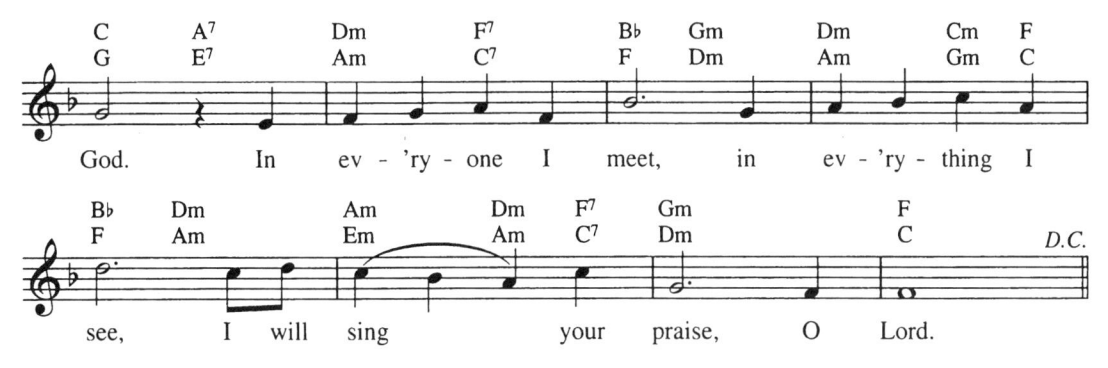

God. In ev-'ry-one I meet, in ev-'ry-thing I
see, I will sing your praise, O Lord.

2. When I was in pain,
when I lived in fear,
I was calling out to him.
He rescued me from death,
he wiped my tears away,
I will sing your praise, O Lord.

3. Trust him with your life,
trust him with today,
come and praise the Lord with me;
O come and know his love,
O taste and understand,
let us sing your praise, O Lord.

Text: Susan Sayers (b.1946) based on Psalm 33
Music: Andrew Moore (b.1954)

381 I will enter his gates
He has made me glad

I will en-ter his gates with thanks-giv-ing in my heart, I will
en-ter his courts with praise, I will say this is the day that the
Lord has made, I will re-joice for he has made me glad.
He has made me glad, he has made me glad, I
will re-joice for he has made me glad. He has made me glad,
he has made me glad, I will re-joice for he has made me glad.

Words and Music: Leona von Brethorst
© Copyright 1976 Maranatha! Music. Administered by CopyCare,
P.O. Box 77, Hailsham, East Sussex BN27 3EF, UK. Used by permission.

382 I will never forget you

1. I will never forget you, my people; I have carved you on the palm of my hand. I will never forget you; I will not leave you orphaned. I will never forget my own.

2. Does a mother forget her baby? Or a woman the child within her womb? Yet even if these forget, yes, even if these forget, I will never forget my own.

Text: Carey Landry based on Isaiah 49:15-16
Music: Carey Landry
© Copyright 1983 North American Liturgy Resources (NALR), 5536 NE Hassalo, Portland, OR 97213, USA. All rights reserved. Used by permission.

383 I will seek your face, O Lord

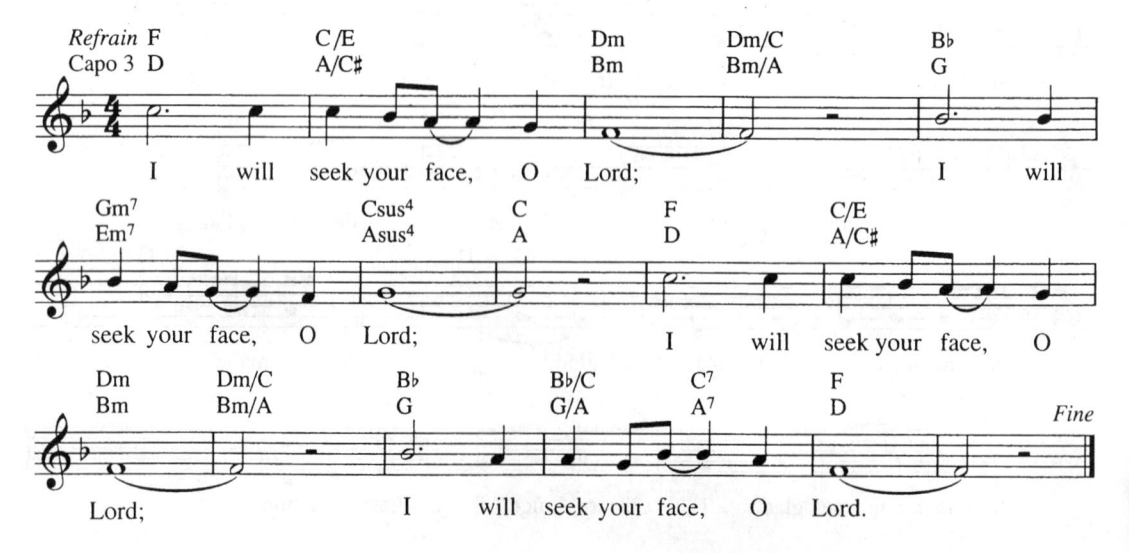

Refrain

I will seek your face, O Lord; I will seek your face, O Lord; I will seek your face, O Lord; I will seek your face, O Lord.

© Copyright 1990 Kingsway's Thankyou Music, P.O. Box 75, Eastbourne, East Sussex BN23 6NW, UK. Used by permission.

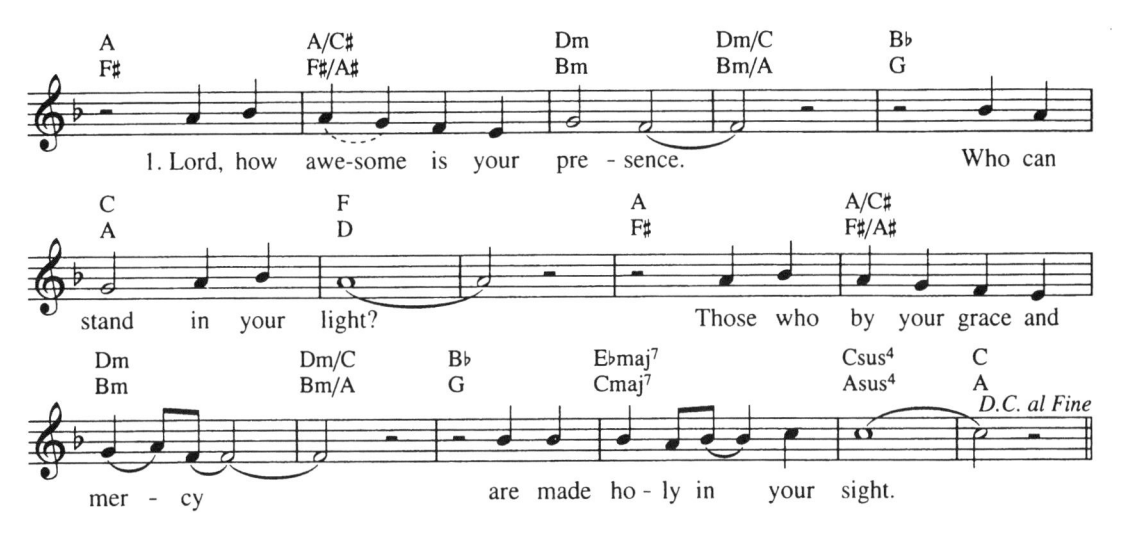

1. Lord, how awe-some is your pre - sence. Who can stand in your light? Those who by your grace and mer - cy are made ho - ly in your sight.

2. I will dwell in your presence
all the days of my life;
there to gaze upon your glory,
and to worship only you.

Text and Music: Noel and Tricia Richards

384 I will sing a song

I will sing a song, a song to please our God, a song from all his peo - ple. 1. For he builds us a ci - ty of peace, and he calls us to - ge - ther as one.

2. We were scattered, but he called us home;
broken-hearted but now we are whole.

3. We are healed – he has bound up our wounds,
he who calls all the stars by their names.

4. He is God of the world that he made,
he is God of the poor that he helps.

5. How he covers the heavens with clouds!
How he clothes mountain valleys with green!

6. He sends food to young ravens in need.
he will come if you wait for his love.

7. To the Father and Son sing a song,
to the Spirit who fills us with life.

Text: Damian Lundy (1944-1997) based on Psalm 146
Music: Joseph Gelineau (b.1920)
Text © Copyright 1978 Kevin Mayhew Ltd.
Music © Copyright Editions Musique et Liturgie, administered by SEFIM, 13 Ave Savornin,
94240 L'Hay-les-Roses, France. All rights reserved.

385 I will sing, I will sing

1. I will sing, I will sing a song unto the Lord. I will sing, I will sing a song unto the Lord. I will sing, I will sing a song unto the Lord. Alleluia, glory to the Lord.

Refrain: Alle-lu, alleluia, glory to the Lord. Alle-lu, alleluia, glory to the Lord. Alleluia, glory to the Lord.

2. We will come, we will come as one before the Lord. *(x3)*
   Alleluia, glory to the Lord.

3. If the Son, if the Son shall make you free, *(x3)*
   you shall be free indeed.

4. They that sow in tears shall reap in joy. *(x3)*
   Alleluia, glory to the Lord.

5. Ev'ry knee shall bow and ev'ry tongue confess *(x3)*
   that Jesus Christ is Lord.

6. In his name, in his name we have the victory. *(x3)*
   Alleluia, glory to the Lord.

Text and Music: Max Dyer (b.1951)

© Copyright 1974 Celebration. Administered by Kingsway's Thankyou Music, P.O. Box 75, Eastbourne, East Sussex BN23 6NW, UK. Europe and British Commonwealth (excl. Canada, Australasia & Africa) Used by permission.

386 I will walk in the presence of God

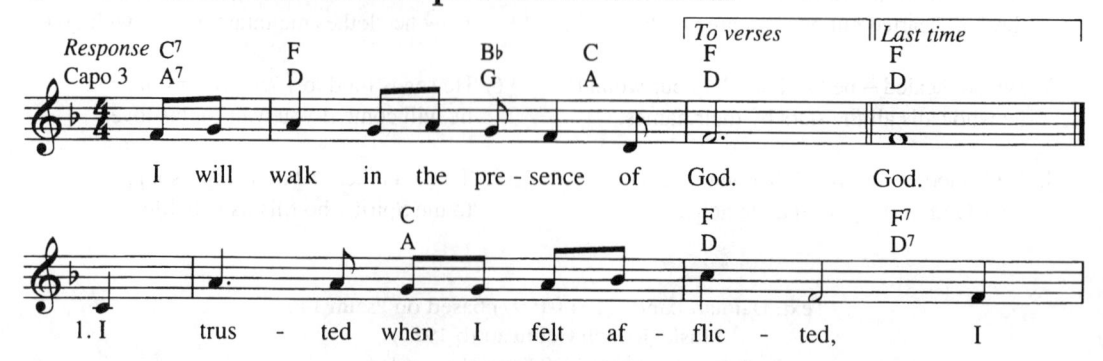

I will walk in the presence of God. God.

1. I trusted when I felt afflicted, I

© Copyright Noel Donnelly. Used by permission.

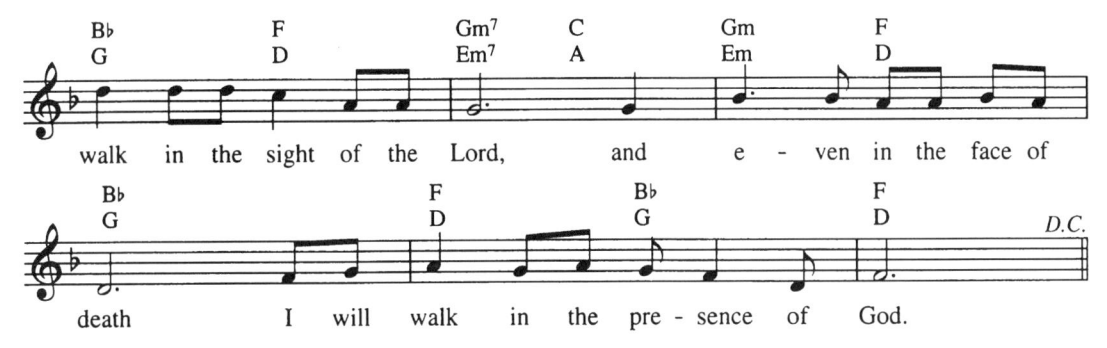

walk in the sight of the Lord, and even in the face of
death I will walk in the presence of God.

2. Your servant, Lord, is ever trusting.
My bonds you have loosened with care.
I offer thanks and sacrifice,
I will walk in the presence of God.

3. My vows to God I keep with gladness,
I dwell in the house of my Lord.
My promises I will fulfil.
I will walk in the presence of God.

Text: Noel Donnelly (b.1931) based on Psalm 115
Music: Noel Donnelly (b.1931)

387 Jerusalem the golden

EWING 76 76 D

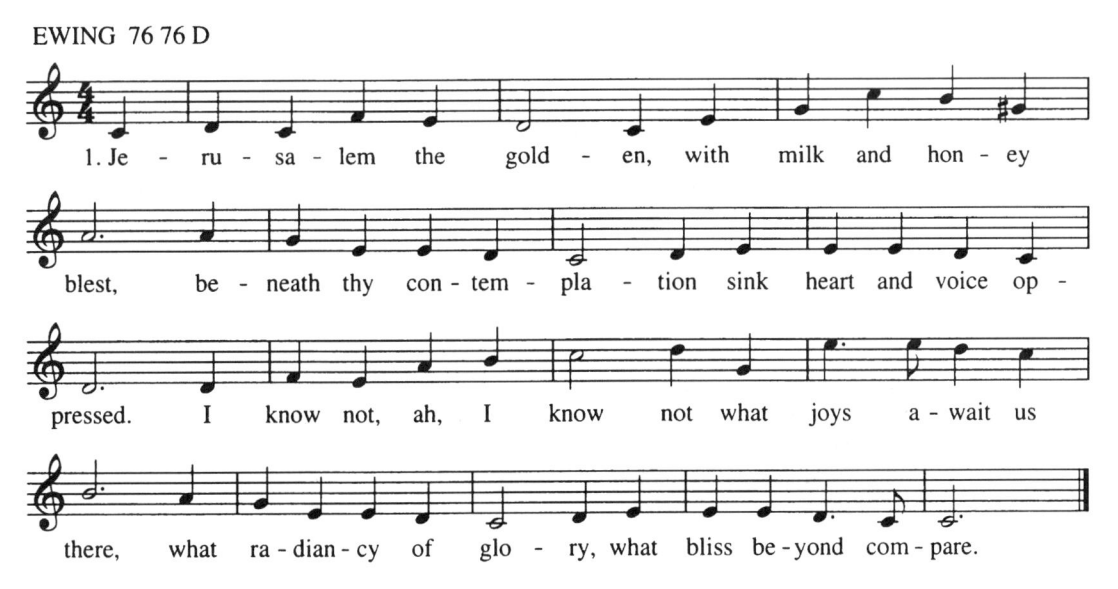

1. Jerusalem the golden, with milk and honey blest, beneath thy contemplation sink heart and voice oppressed. I know not, ah, I know not what joys await us there, what radiancy of glory, what bliss beyond compare.

2. They stand, those halls of Zion,
all jubilant with song,
and bright with many angels,
and all the martyr throng;
the prince is ever with them,
the daylight is serene;
the pastures of the blessèd
are decked in glorious sheen.

3. There is the throne of David;
and there, from care released,
the shout of them that triumph,
the song of them that feast;
and they, who with their leader
have fully run the race,
are robed in white for ever
before their Saviour's face.

4. O sweet and blessèd country,
the home of God's elect!
O sweet and blessèd country
that eager hearts expect!
Jesus, in mercy, bring us
to that dear land of rest;
who art, with God the Father
and Spirit, ever blest.

Text: from 'De Contemptu Mundi' by St Bernard of Cluny (12th century)
trans. John Mason Neale (1818-1866) alt.
Music: Alexander Ewing (1830-1895)

388 Jesus calls us

Jesus calls us here to meet him as, through word and song and prayer, we affirm God's promised presence where his people live and care. Praise the God who keeps his promise; praise the Son who calls us friends; praise the Spirit who, among us, to our hopes and fears attends.

2. Jesus call us to confess him
 Word of life and Lord of All,
 sharer of our flesh and frailness
 saving all who fail or fall.
 Tell his holy human story;
 tell his tales that all may hear;
 tell the world that Christ in glory
 came to earth to meet us here.

3. Jesus calls us to each other:
 found in him are no divides.
 Race and class and sex and language –
 such are barriers he derides.
 Join the hand of friend and stranger;
 join the hands of age and youth;
 join the faithful and the doubter
 in their common search for truth.

4. Jesus calls us to his table,
 rooted firm in time and space,
 where the Church in earth and heaven
 finds a common meeting place.
 Share the bread and wine, his body;
 share the love of which we sing;
 share the feast for saints and sinners
 hosted by our Lord and King.

Text: John L. Bell (b.1949) and Graham Maule (b.1958)
Music: Gaelic air, adapted John L. Bell (b.1949) and Graham Maule (b.1958)
© Copyright 1989 WGRG, Iona Community, 840 Govan Road, Glasgow G51 3UU, Scotland. Used by permission.

389 Jesus Christ is risen today

EASTER HYMN 77 77 and Alleluias

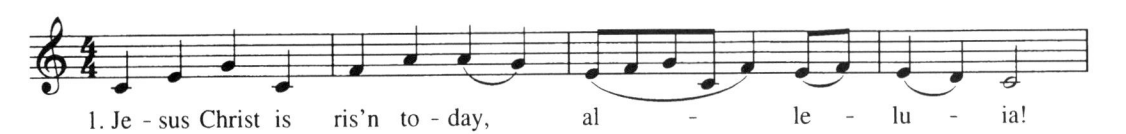

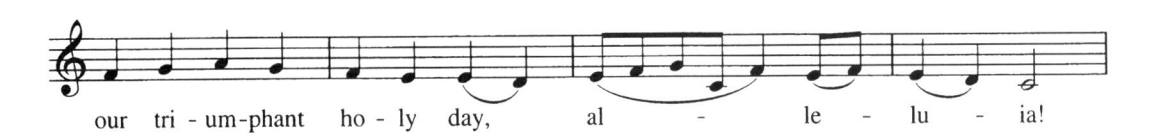

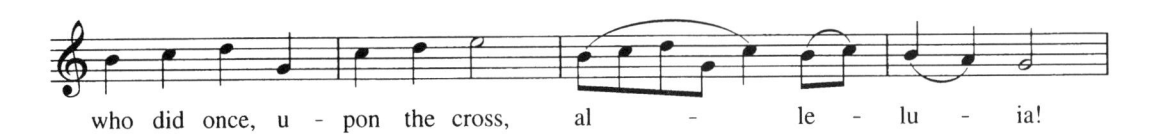

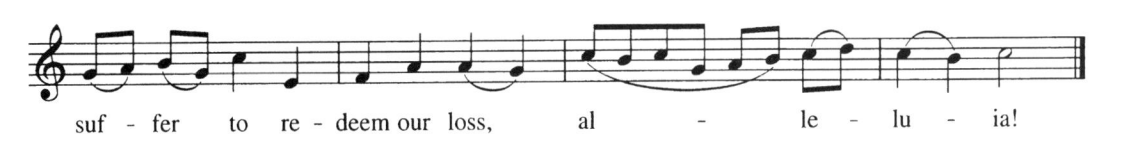

1. Je-sus Christ is ris'n to-day, alleluia!
our tri-um-phant ho-ly day, alleluia!
who did once, u-pon the cross, alleluia!
suf-fer to re-deem our loss, alleluia!

A lower setting will be found at No. 199

2. Hymns of praise then let us sing, alleluia!
unto Christ, our heav'nly King, alleluia!
who endured the cross and grave, alleluia!
sinners to redeem and save, alleluia!

3. But the pains that he endured, alleluia!
our salvation have procured; alleluia!
now above the sky he's King, alleluia!
where the angels ever sing, alleluia!

Text: v.1 'Surrexit hodie' (14th century), anonymous translation, as in 'Lyra Davidica' (1708);
vs. 2-3 from J. Arnold's 'Compleat Psalmodist' (1749)
Music: melody from 'Lyra Davidica' (1708), harmony by William Henry Monk (1823-1889)

390 Jesus Christ is waiting

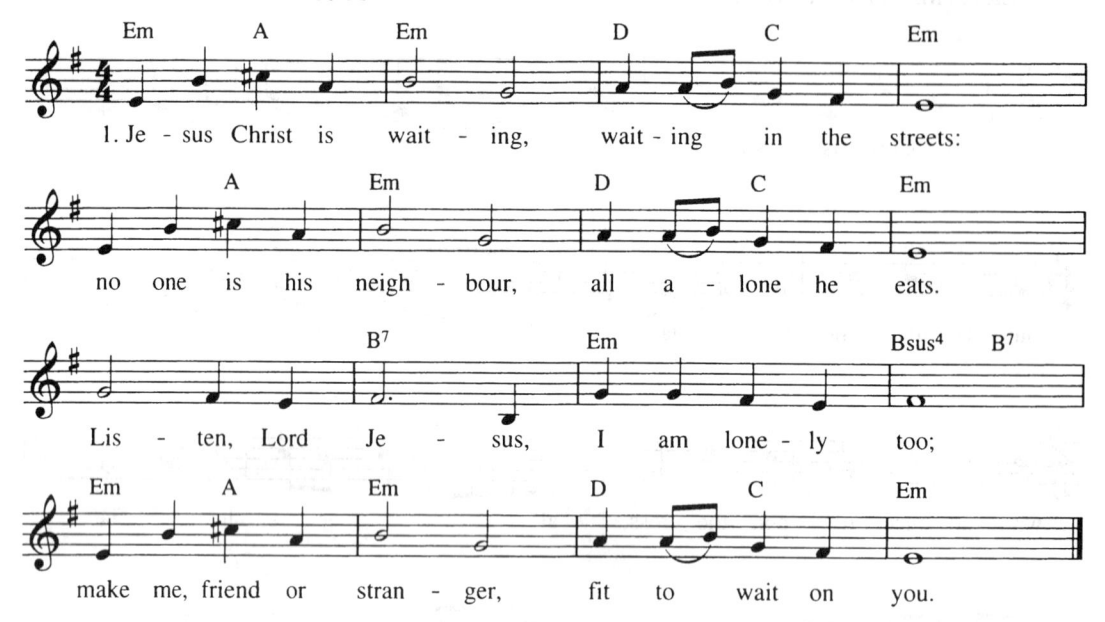

NOEL NOUVELET 11 11 10 11

1. Je-sus Christ is wait-ing, wait-ing in the streets:
no one is his neigh-bour, all a-lone he eats.
Lis-ten, Lord Je-sus, I am lone-ly too;
make me, friend or stran-ger, fit to wait on you.

2. Jesus Christ is raging,
raging in the streets
where injustice spirals
and all hope retreats.
Listen, Lord Jesus,
I am angry too;
in the kingdom's causes
let me rage with you.

3. Jesus Christ is healing,
healing in the streets
curing those who suffer,
touching those he greets.
Listen, Lord Jesus,
I have pity too;
let my care be active,
healing just like you.

4. Jesus Christ is dancing,
dancing in the streets,
where each sign of hatred
his strong love defeats.
Listen, Lord Jesus,
I feel triumph too;
on suspicion's graveyard,
let me dance with you.

5. Jesus Christ is calling,
calling in the streets,
'Come and walk faith's tightrope,
I will guide your feet.'
Listen, Lord Jesus,
let my fears be few;
walk one step before me,
I will follow you.

Text: John L. Bell (b.1949) and Graham Maule (b.1958)
Music: traditional French melody
Text © Copyright 1988 WGRG, Iona Community, 840 Govan Road, Glasgow G51 3UU, Scotland.
Used by permission from 'Enemy of Apathy' (Wild Goose Publications, 1988).

391 Jesus, ever-flowing fountain
Come to me

COME TO ME 87 87 and Refrain

Refrain
Jesus, ever-flowing fountain, give us water from your well.
In the gracious gift you offer there is joy no tongue can tell.

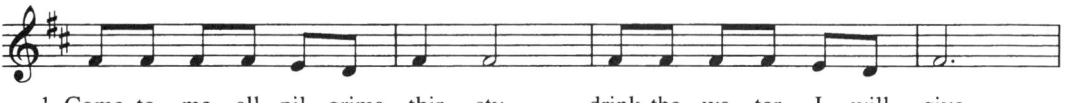

1. Come to me, all pilgrims thirsty,
   drink the water I will give.
   If you knew what gift I offer,
   you would come to me and live.

2. Come to me, all trav'lers weary,
   come that I may give you rest.
   Drink the cup of life I offer;
   at this table be my guest.

3. Come to me, believers burdened,
   find refreshment in this place.
   If you knew the gift I offer,
   you would turn and seek my face.

4. Come to me, repentant sinners;
   leave behind your guilt and shame.
   If you knew divine compassion,
   you would turn and call my name.

5. Come to me distressed and needy;
   I would be your trusted friend.
   If you seek the gift I offer,
   come, your open hands extend.

6. Come to me abandoned, orphaned;
   lonely ways no longer roam.
   If you knew the gift I offer,
   you would make in me your home.

Text: Delores Dufner
Music: Rosalie Bonighton (b.1946)
Text © Copyright 1992, 1996 Sisters of the Order of St Benedict, 104 Chapel Lane,
St Joseph, MN 56374-0220, USA. Used by permission. Music © Copyright 1997 Kevin Mayhew Ltd.

392 Jesus, gentlest Saviour

PRINCETHORPE 65 65 D

1. Jesus, gentlest Saviour, God of might and power,
thou thyself art dwelling in us at this hour.
Nature cannot hold thee, heav'n is all too strait
for thine endless glory, and thy royal state.

A lower setting will be found at No. 247

2. Yet the hearts of children,
hold what worlds cannot,
and the God of wonders
loves the lowly spot.
Jesus, gentlest Saviour,
thou art in us now,
fill us full of goodness,
till our hearts o'erflow.

3. Pray the prayer within us
that to heav'n shall rise;
sing the song that angels
sing above the skies;
multiply our graces,
chiefly love and fear;
and, dear Lord, the chiefest,
grace to persevere.

Text: Frederick William Faber (1814-1863)
Music: William Pitts (1829-1903)

393 Jesus is God

ELLACOMBE 76 76 D

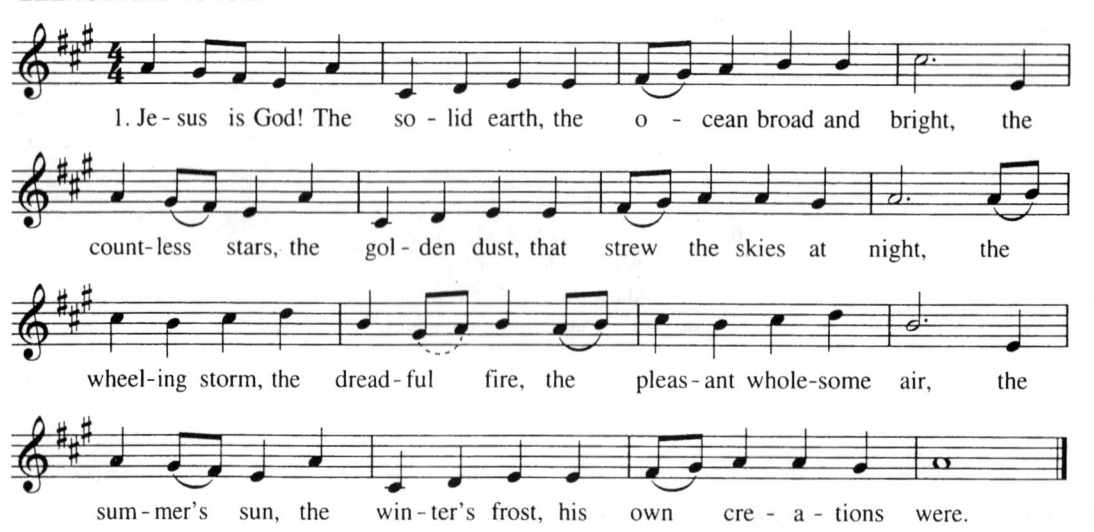

1. Jesus is God! The solid earth, the ocean broad and bright,
the countless stars, the golden dust, that strew the skies at night,
the wheeling storm, the dreadful fire, the pleasant wholesome air,
the summer's sun, the winter's frost, his own creations were.

2. Jesus is God! The glorious bands
   of golden angels sing
   songs of adoring praise to him,
   their Maker and their King.
   He was true God in Bethlehem's crib,
   on Calv'ry's cross, true God,
   he who in heav'n eternal reigned,
   in time on earth abode.

3. Jesus is God! Let sorrow come,
   and pain and ev'ry ill;
   all are worthwhile, for all are meant
   his glory to fulfil;
   worthwhile a thousand years of life
   to speak one little word,
   if by our Credo we might own
   the Godhead of our Lord.

Text: Frederick William Faber (1814-1863)
Music: from the 'Württemberg Gesangbuch' (1784)

394 Jesus is Lord! Creation's voice proclaims it

JESUS IS LORD 11 12 11 12 and Refrain

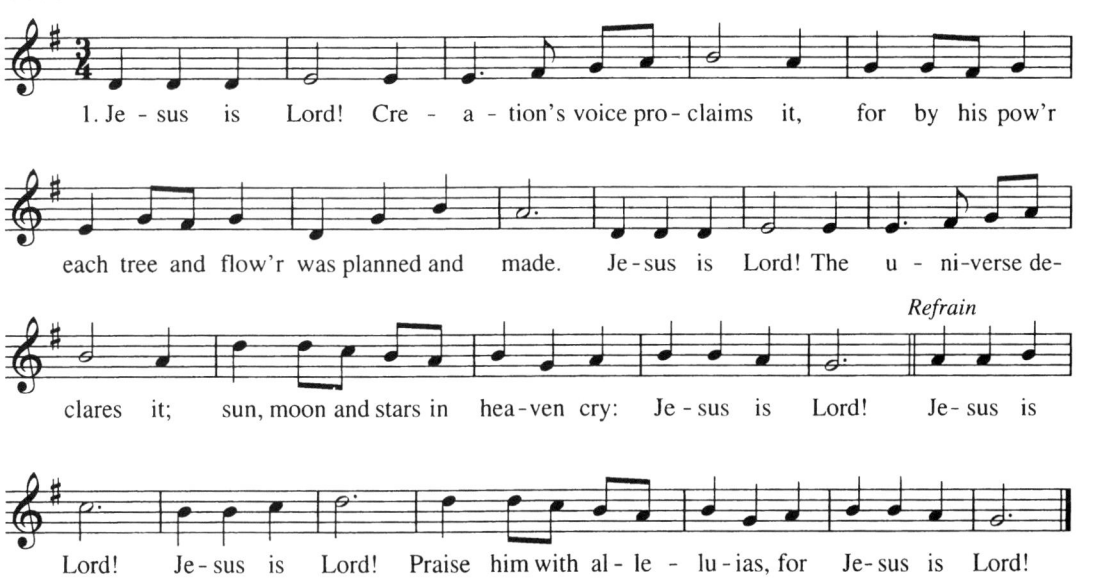

1. Jesus is Lord! Creation's voice proclaims it, for by his pow'r each tree and flow'r was planned and made. Jesus is Lord! The universe declares it; sun, moon and stars in heaven cry: Jesus is Lord!

Refrain
Jesus is Lord! Jesus is Lord! Praise him with alleluias, for Jesus is Lord!

2. Jesus is Lord! Yet from his throne eternal
   in flesh he came to die in pain on Calv'ry's tree.
   Jesus is Lord! From him all life proceeding,
   yet gave his life as ransom thus setting us free.

3. Jesus is Lord! O'er sin the mighty conqu'ror,
   from death he rose and all his foes shall own his name.
   Jesus is Lord! God sends his Holy Spirit
   to show by works of power that Jesus is Lord.

Text and Music: David J. Mansell
© Copyright 1982 Word's Spirit of Praise Music. Administered by CopyCare, P.O. Box 77,
Hailsham, East Sussex BN27 3EF, UK. Used by permission.

395 Jesus is Lord! In love he came

MALVERN 88 88 8

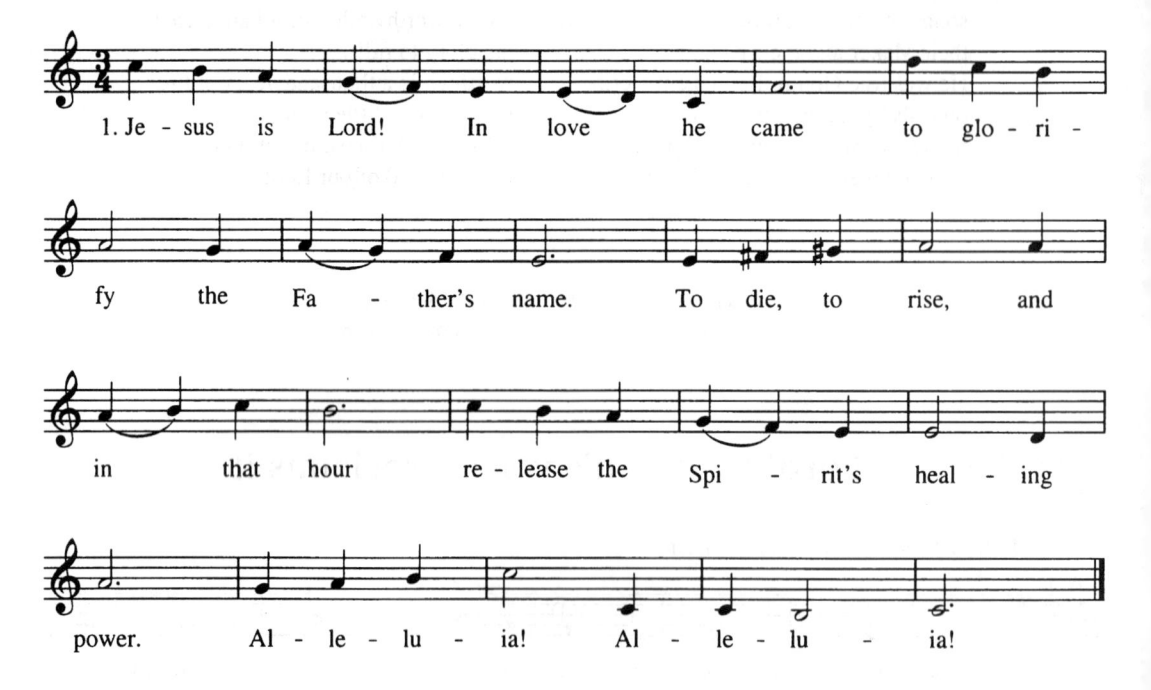

1. Je-sus is Lord! In love he came to glo-ri-fy the Fa-ther's name. To die, to rise, and in that hour re-lease the Spi-rit's heal-ing power. Al-le-lu-ia! Al-le-lu-ia!

2. Jesus is Lord! He'll come again,
   in empty hearts take up his reign;
   where living springs of water flow
   in desert land, new orchards grow.

3. Jesus is Lord! Be still for he
   will come with healing, quietly.
   Deep in your heart, you'll hear his voice,
   and in that stillness you'll rejoice.

4. Jesus is Lord! Be glad and know
   he is the way by which we go
   into our Father's home to share
   the joyful welcome waiting there.

5. Jesus is Lord! His victory
   the deaf will hear, the blind will see,
   and from their graves the dead will rise,
   with saints and angels crowd the skies.

Text: Damian Lundy (1944-1997)
Music: Edward Elgar (1857-1934) adapted by Alan Ridout (1934-1996)
Text and this arrangement © Copyright 1982, 1992 Kevin Mayhew Ltd.

396 Jesus, Lord of glory

ADORO TE 11 11 11 11

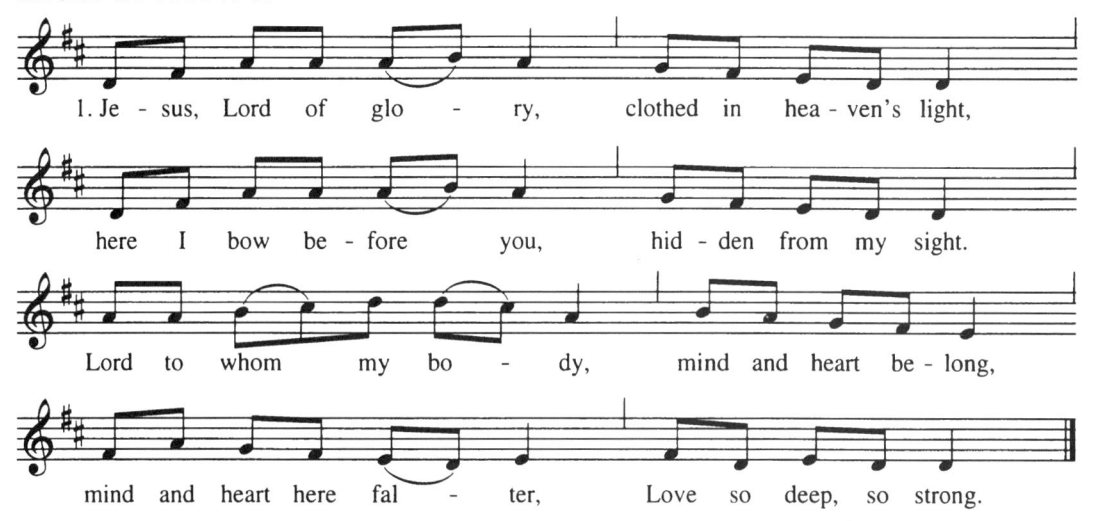

1. Je-sus, Lord of glo-ry, clothed in hea-ven's light,
here I bow be-fore you, hid-den from my sight.
Lord to whom my bo-dy, mind and heart be-long,
mind and heart here fal-ter, Love so deep, so strong.

Another translation of this hymn will be found at No. 287

2. Here distrust, my spirit, eye and tongue and hand,
   trust faith's ear and listen, hear and understand.
   Hear the voice of Wisdom, speaking now to you;
   when God's Word has spoken, what can be more true?

3. Once you hid your glory, Jesus crucified,
   now you hide your body, Jesus glorified.
   When you come in judgement, plain for all to see,
   God and man in splendour, Lord, remember me.

4. Once you showed to Thomas wounded hands and side.
   Here I kneel adoring, faith alone my guide.
   Help me grow in faith, Lord, grow in hope and love,
   living by your Spirit, gift of God above.

5. Here I see your dying, Jesus, victim-priest,
   here I know your rising, host and guest and feast.
   Let me taste your goodness, manna from the skies,
   feed me, heal me, save me, food of Paradise.

6. Heart of Jesus, broken, pierced and open wide,
   wash me in the water flowing from your side.
   Jesus' blood so precious that one drop could free
   all the world from evil, come and ransom me.

7. How I long to see you, Jesus, face to face,
   how the heart is thirsting, living spring of grace.
   Show me soon your glory, be my great reward,
   be my joy for ever, Jesus, gracious Lord.

Text: 'Adoro te devote' ascribed to St Thomas Aquinas (1227-1274) trans. James Quinn (b.1919)
Music: Plainsong
Text © Copyright Geoffrey Chapman, an imprint of Cassell plc, Wellington House,
125 Strand, London WC2R 0BB, UK. Used by permission.

397 Jesus, my Lord, my God, my all

CORPUS CHRISTI LM and Refrain

1. Jesus, my Lord, my God, my all, how can I love thee as I ought? And how revere this wondrous gift so far surpassing hope or thought? *Refrain* Sweet Sacrament, we thee adore; O make us love thee more and more.

2. Had I but Mary's sinless heart
to love thee with, my dearest King,
O, with what bursts of fervent praise
thy goodness, Jesus, would I sing!

3. Ah, see, within a creature's hand
the vast Creator deigns to be,
reposing, infant-like, as though
on Joseph's arm, or Mary's knee.

4. Thy body, soul and Godhead, all;
O mystery of love divine!
I cannot compass all I have,
for all thou hast and art are mine.

5. Sound, sound, his praises higher still,
and come, ye angels, to our aid;
'tis God, 'tis God, the very God
whose pow'r both us and angels made.

Text: Frederick William Faber (1814-1863)
Music: from 'Crown of Jesus' hymn book (1894)

398 Jesus, Name above all names

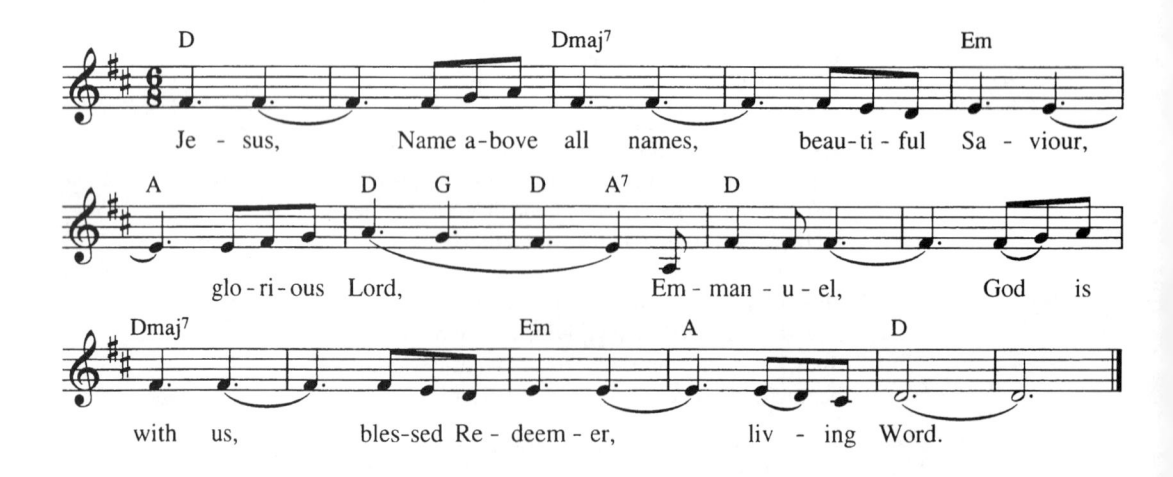

Jesus, Name above all names, beautiful Saviour, glorious Lord, Emmanuel, God is with us, blessed Redeemer, living Word.

Text and Music: Naida Hearn (b.1944)

© Copyright 1974 Scripture in Song, a division of Integrity Music. Administered by Kingsway's Thankyou Music, P.O. Box 75, Eastbourne, East Sussex BN23 6NW, UK. For the territory of the UK only. Used by permission.

399 Jesus rose on Easter Day

RESONET IN LAUDIBUS 777 11

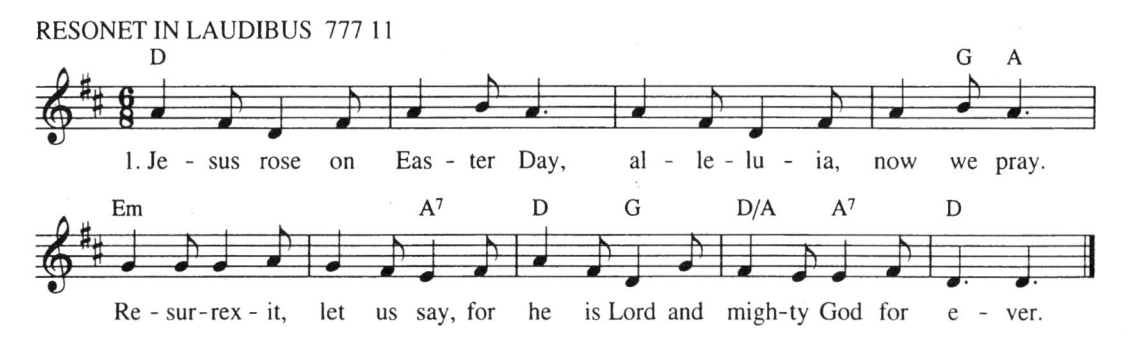

1. Jesus rose on Easter Day,
   alleluia, now we pray.
   Resurrexit, let us say,
   for he is Lord and mighty God for ever.

2. He has conquered death and sin.
   All God's people now begin
   singing praises unto him,
   for he is Lord and mighty God for ever.

3. 'Alleluia' is our cry,
   for he lives, no more to die.
   Glory be to God on high,
   for he is Lord and mighty God for ever.

4. Alleluia! May we know
   all the joy which long ago
   set the Easter sky aglow,
   for he is Lord and mighty God for ever.

5. Alleluia! Let us be
   filled with love, our hearts set free
   as we praise his victory,
   for he is Lord and mighty God for ever.

Text: Damian Lundy (1944-1997)
Music: German carol melody (16th century)
Text © Copyright 1988, 1999 Kevin Mayhew Ltd.

400 Jesu, the very thought of thee

TOZER CM

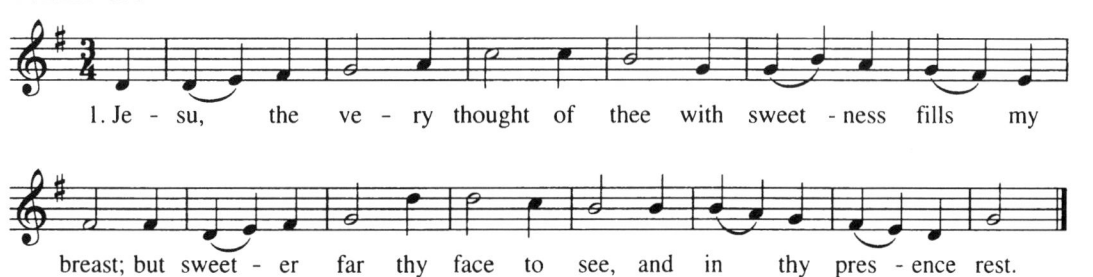

1. Jesu, the very thought of thee
   with sweetness fills my breast;
   but sweeter far thy face to see,
   and in thy presence rest.

2. No voice can sing, no heart can frame,
   nor can the mind recall,
   a sweeter sound than thy blest name,
   O Saviour of us all.

3. O hope of ev'ry contrite heart,
   O joy of all the meek,
   to those who fall, how kind thou art,
   how good to those who seek!

4. But what to those who find? Ah, this
   no tongue nor pen can show;
   the love of Jesus, what it is
   none but his lovers know.

5. Jesu, our only joy be thou,
   as thou our prize wilt be,
   Jesu, be thou our glory now,
   and through eternity.

Text: 11th century trans. Edward Caswall (1814-1878) alt.
Music: A. Edmunds Tozer (1857-1910)
This version of text © Copyright 1999 Kevin Mayhew Ltd.

401 Jesus, the Word, has lived among us

WHENCE IS THAT GOODLY FRAGRANCE? 98 98 98

1. Jesus, the Word, has lived among us, sharing his fullness, truth and grace, God's only Son, the Father's loved one reveals him to the human race. Jesus, the Word, has lived among us sharing his fullness, truth and grace.

2. He was with God from the beginning
and through him all things came to be.
He lightens darkness, conquers evil,
gives life for living, glad and free.
He was with God from the beginning
and through him all things came to be.

3. Sing praise to God who sent Christ Jesus
to be his sign of endless love;
sent him to live his life among us,
lifting our hearts to things above.
Sing praise to God who sent Christ Jesus
to be his sign of endless love!

Text: Keith D. Pearson based on John 1 and 3
Music: French carol melody
Text © 1996 Keith D. Pearson. Used by permission.

402 Jesus, who condemns you?
The Stations of the Cross

HOLY CROSS 65 65

1. Jesus, who condemns you?
   Who cries 'Crucify'?
   Priest or politician?
   Jesus, is it I?

2. Heavy, oh too heavy,
   weighs a world of hate;
   Christ, be our Redeemer,
   Jesus, bear the weight.

3. Perfect in obedience
   to your Father's call,
   Christ, creation's glory,
   shares creation's fall.

4. Where the humble suffer,
   and the proud deride,
   Mary, blessed Mother,
   calls us to your side.

5. Christ, our only Saviour,
   you must bear the loss;
   yet give us compassion,
   let us bear the cross.

6. Christ, where now you suffer,
   in each painful place,
   let each act of kindness
   still reveal your face.

7. Mortal flesh exhausted,
   tortured sinews fail,
   yet the spirit triumphs,
   and the will prevails.

8. Still the faithful women
   stand beside the way,
   weeping for the victims
   of the present day.

9. Bowed beneath the burden
   of creation's pain,
   Saviour, be beside us
   when we fall again.

10. Church of God, resplendent
    in the robes of pow'r,
    be the Saviour's body,
    share his triumph hour!

11. All the pow'rs of evil
    join to strike the nail;
    patience and compassion
    silently prevail.

12. Lonely and forsaken,
    in this dying breath,
    love alone can bear him
    through the veil of death.

13. Arms that cradled Jesus,
    both at death and birth,
    cradle all who suffer
    in the pains of earth.

14. Christ, who came with nothing
    from your Mother's womb,
    rest in destitution,
    in a borrowed tomb.

15. Broken but triumphant,
    birthing gain from loss,
    let us share your glory,
    let us share your cross.

Text: Michael Forster (b.1946)
Music: Andrew Moore (b.1954)
© Copyright 1997 Kevin Mayhew Ltd.

LITURGICAL
HYMNS OLD & NEW

403 Join in the dance

Refrain:
Join in the dance of the earth's jubilation! This is the feast of the love of God. Shout from the heights to the ends of creation: Jesus the Saviour is risen from the grave!

1. Wake, O people, sleep no longer;
   greet the breaking day!
   Christ, Redeemer, Lamb and Lion,
   turns the night away!

2. All creation, like a mother,
   labours to give birth.
   Soon the pain will be forgotten,
   joy for all the earth!

3. Now our shame becomes our glory
   on this holy tree.
   Now the reign of death is ended;
   now we are set free!

4. None on earth, no prince or power,
   neither death nor life,
   nothing now can ever part us
   from the love of Christ.

5. Love's triumphant day of vict'ry
   heaven opens wide.
   On the tree of hope and glory
   death itself has died!

6. Christ for ever, Lord of ages,
   love beyond our dreams:
   Christ our hope of heaven's glory,
   all that yet will be!

Text and Music: Dan Schutte

© Copyright 1992, Daniel L. Schutte. Published by OCP Publications, 5536 NE Hassalo, Portland OR 97213, USA.
All rights reserved. Used by permission.

404 Joy to the world

ANTIOCH CM

1. Joy to the world! The Lord is come; let earth receive her King; let ev-'ry heart prepare him room, and heav'n and nature sing, and heav'n and nature sing, and heav'n, and heav'n and nature sing.

2. Joy to the earth! The Saviour reigns;
let us our songs employ;
while fields and floods, rocks, hills and plains
repeat the sounding joy,
repeat the sounding joy,
repeat, repeat the sounding joy.

3. He rules the world with truth and grace,
and makes the nations prove
the glories of his righteousness,
and wonders of his love,
and wonders of his love,
and wonders, and wonders of his love.

Text: Isaac Watts (1674-1748) based on Psalm 97 alt.
Music: George Frideric Handel (1685-1759)

405 Jubilate Deo

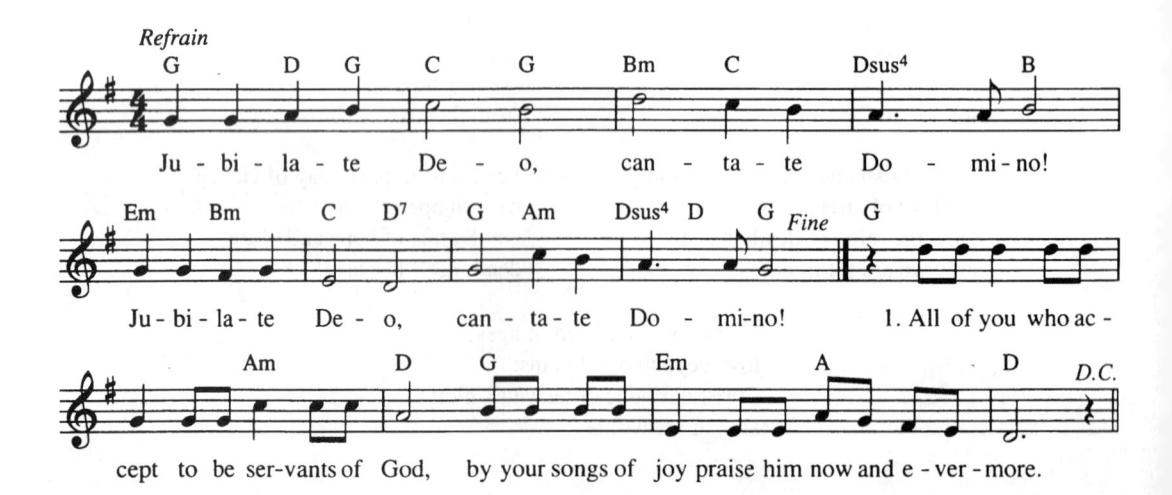

Refrain

Ju-bi-la-te De-o, can-ta-te Do-mi-no!
Ju-bi-la-te De-o, can-ta-te Do-mi-no! 1. All of you who accept to be servants of God, by your songs of joy praise him now and e-ver-more.

© Copyright 1988 Kevin Mayhew Ltd.

2. To the Lord offer thanks and give praise to his name;
   sing aloud new songs to proclaim his mighty power.

3. For the Word of the Lord is both faithful and sure;
   all the things he does show his justice, truth and love.

4. All creation is filled with the love of the Lord;
   everything that is was created through the Word.

5. May the People of God in all ages be bless'd;
   day by day his grace is outpoured upon us all.

6. May our hearts never waver, but trust in the Lord;
   he, the living God, is both merciful and good.

7. May your love, Lord, be with us in all that we do;
   all our hope and longing we humbly place in you.

Text: Jean-Paul Lécot (b.1947) based on Psalm 32 trans. W. R. Lawrence alt.
Music: Jean-Paul Lécot (b.1947)

406 Jubilate, everybody

JUBILATE DEO 88 87 88 86

Ju-bi-la-te, ev-'ry bo-dy, serve the Lord in all your ways and
come be-fore his pre-sence sing-ing; en-ter now his courts with praise.
For the Lord our God is gra-cious, and his mer-cy e-ver-last-ing.
Ju-bi-la-te, ju-bi-la-te, ju-bi-la-te De - o!

Text and Music: Fred Dunn (1907-1979)
© Copyright 1977 Kingsway's Thankyou Music, P.O. Box 75, Eastbourne, East Sussex BN23 6NW, UK.
Used by permission.

407 Keep in mind

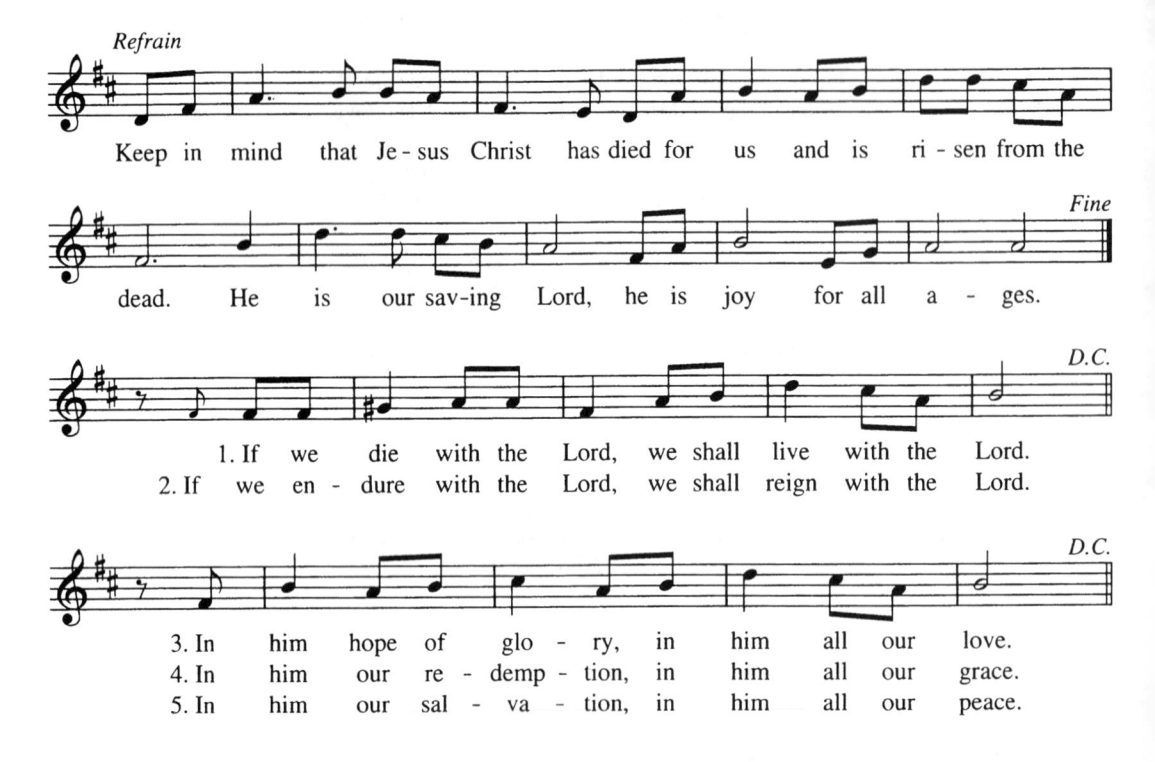

Refrain

Keep in mind that Jesus Christ has died for us and is risen from the dead. He is our saving Lord, he is joy for all ages.

1. If we die with the Lord, we shall live with the Lord.
2. If we endure with the Lord, we shall reign with the Lord.

3. In him hope of glory, in him all our love.
4. In him our redemption, in him all our grace.
5. In him our salvation, in him all our peace.

Text: Lucien Deiss (b.1921) based on 2 Timothy 2:8-11
Music: Lucien Deiss (b.1921)
© Copyright 1965 World Library Publications, a division of J.S. Paluch Co. Inc., 3825 N. Willow Road, Schiller Park, Illinois 60176, USA. All rights reserved. Used by permission.

408 King of glory, King of peace

GWALCHMAI 74 74 D

1. King of glory, King of peace, I will love thee;
and, that love may never cease, I will move thee.
Thou hast granted my appeal, thou hast heard me;
thou didst note my ardent zeal, thou hast spared me.

2. Wherefore with my utmost art,
   I will sing thee,
   and the cream of all my heart
   I will bring thee.
   Though my sins against me cried,
   thou didst clear me,
   and alone, when they replied,
   thou didst hear me.

3. Sev'n whole days, not one in sev'n,
   I will praise thee;
   in my heart, though not in heav'n,
   I can raise thee.
   Small it is, in this poor sort
   to enrol thee:
   e'en eternity's too short
   to extol thee.

Text: George Herbert (1593-1633)
Music: John David Jones (1827-1870)

409 King of kings and Lord of lords

May be sung as a 2-part round, the second voices beginning when the first voices reach [B]

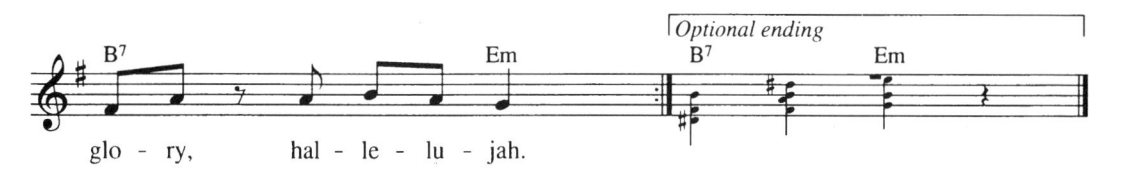

King of kings and Lord of lords, glo-ry, hal-le-lu-jah.

King of kings and Lord of lords, glo-ry, hal-le-lu-jah.

Je-sus, Prince of Peace, glo-ry, hal-le-lu-jah. Je-sus, Prince of Peace,

Optional ending

glo-ry, hal-le-lu-jah.

Text and Music: Naomi Batya and Sophie Conty
© Copyright 1980 Maranatha! Music. Administered by CopyCare,
P.O. Box 77, Hailsham, East Sussex BN27 3EF, UK. Used by permission.

410 Lamb of God, Holy One

Lamb of God, Holy One, Jesus Christ, Son of God,
lifted up willingly to die;
that I the guilty one may know the blood once shed
still freely flowing, still cleansing, still healing.
I exalt you, Jesus my sacrifice,
I exalt you, my Redeemer and my Lord.
I exalt you, worthy Lamb of God,
and in honour I bow down before your throne.

Text and Music: Chris Bowater
© Copyright 1988 Sovereign Lifestyle Music Ltd., P.O. Box 356,
Leighton Buzzard, Bedfordshire LU7 8WP, UK. Used by permission.

411 Lauda, Jerusalem

Response

Lau-da, Je-ru-sa-lem, Do-mi-num. Lau-da De-um tu-um Zi - on.
Ho - san - na! Ho - san - na! Ho - san - na fi - li - o Da - vid! *Fine*

1. O praise the Lord, Jerusalem! O Zion, sing praise to your God!
2. He has strengthened the bars of your gates, he has blessed the children within you.
3. He has established peace on your borders, he feeds you with finest wheat.
4. He sends out his word to the earth and swiftly runs his command.
5. He showers down snow white as wool, he scatters hoar frost like ashes.
6. He hurls down hailstones like crumbs. The waters are frozen at his touch.
7. He sends forth his word and it melts them: at the breath of his mouth the waters flow.
8. He makes his word known to Jacob, to Israel his laws and decrees.
9. He has not dealt thus with other nations; he has not taught them his decrees.

Text: Psalm 147, Grail translation
Music: Response – Th. Deckers; Verses – Alexandre Lesbordes
Text © Copyright 1963, 1986, 1993 The Grail, England. Used by permission of
A.P. Watt Ltd., 20 John Street, London WC1N 2DR, UK.
Music © Copyright 1988 Kevin Mayhew Ltd.

412 Laudato sii, O mi Signore

(Sheet music with lyrics:)

Lau-da-to sii, O mi Sig-no-re. Lau-da-to sii, O mi Sig-no-re. Lau-da-to sii, O mi Sig-no-re. Lau-da-to sii, O mi Sig-no-re. Lau-da-to sii, O mi Sig-no-re. Lau-da-to sii!

1. Yes, be praised in all your crea-tures, bro-ther sun and sis-ter moon; in the stars and in the wind, air and fire and flow-ing wa-ter.

2. For our sister, mother earth,
   she who feeds us and sustains us;
   for her fruits, her grass, her flowers,
   for the mountains and the oceans.

3. Praise for those who spread forgiveness,
   those who share your peace with others,
   bearing trials and sickness bravely!
   Even sister death won't harm them.

4. For our life is but a song,
   and the reason for our singing
   is to praise you for the music;
   join the dance of your creation.

5. Praise to you, Father most holy,
   praise and thanks to you, Lord Jesus,
   praise to you, most Holy Spirit,
   life and joy of all creation!

The Italian phrase 'Laudate sii, O mi Signore'
translates as 'Praise be to you, O my Lord'.

Text: Damian Lundy (1944-1997) from St Francis of Assisi (1182-1226)
Music: unknown Italian origin
Text © Copyright 1981, 1994 Kevin Mayhew Ltd.

413 Lay your hands gently upon us

Refrain
Capo 3

Lay your hands gent-ly u-pon us, let their touch ren-der your peace, let them bring your for-give-ness and heal-ing, lay your hands, gent-ly lay your hands.

1. You were sent to free the bro-ken-heart-ed. You were sent to give sight to the blind. You de-sire to heal all our ill-ness. Lay your hands, gent-ly lay your hands.

2. Lord, we come to you through one another,
   Lord, we come to you in all our need.
   Lord, we come to you seeking wholeness.
   Lay your hands, gently lay your hands.

Text and Music: Carey Landry
© Copyright 1977 North American Liturgy Resources (NALR), 5536 NE Hassalo, Portland, OR 97213, USA.
All rights reserved. Used by permission.

414 Leader, now on earth no longer

SWAVESEY 87 87 and Refrain

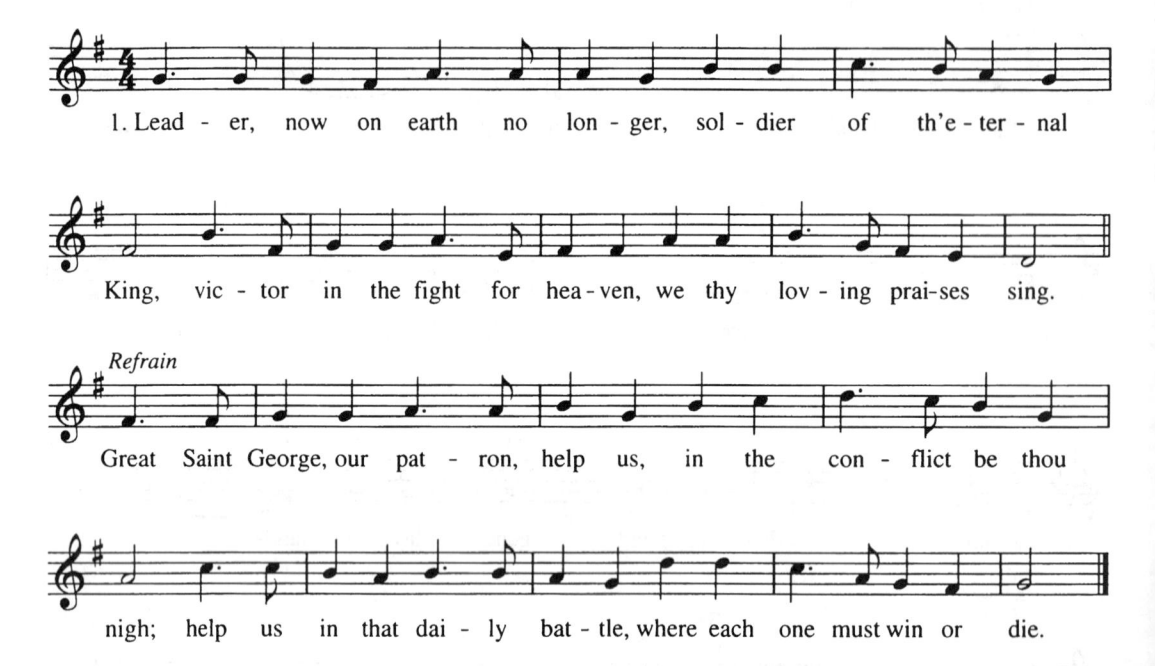

1. Leader, now on earth no longer, soldier of th'eternal King, victor in the fight for heaven, we thy loving praises sing.

Refrain
Great Saint George, our patron, help us, in the conflict be thou nigh; help us in that daily battle, where each one must win or die.

2. Praise him who in deadly battle
   never shrank from foeman's sword,
   proof against all earthly weapon,
   gave his life for Christ the Lord.

3. Who, when earthly war was over,
   fought, but not for earth's renown;
   fought, and won a nobler glory,
   won the martyr's purple crown.

4. Help us when temptation presses,
   we have still our crown to win;
   help us when our soul is weary
   fighting with the pow'rs of sin.

5. Clothe us in thy shining armour,
   place thy good sword in our hand;
   teach us how to wield it, fighting
   onward t'wards the heav'nly land.

6. Onward till, our striving over,
   on life's battlefield we fall,
   resting then, but ever ready,
   waiting for the angel's call.

Text: Joseph W. Reeks (1849-1900)
Music: J. Crookall (1821-1887)

415 Lead, kindly light

TUNE 1: SANDON 10 4 10 4 10 10

1. Lead, kind-ly light, amid th'en-cir-cling gloom, lead thou me on; the night is dark, and I am far from home; lead thou me on. Keep thou my feet; I do not ask to see the dis-tant scene; one step e-nough for me.

2. I was not ever thus, nor prayed that thou
   shouldst lead me on;
   I loved to choose and see my path; but now
   lead thou me on.
   I loved the garish day, and, spite of fears,
   pride ruled my will: remember not past years.

3. So long thy pow'r hath blest me, sure it still
   will lead me on,
   o'er moor and fen, o'er crag and torrent, till
   the night is gone;
   and with the morn those angel faces smile,
   which I have loved long since, and lost awhile.

TUNE 2: LUX BENIGNA 10 4 10 4 10 10

1. Lead, kind-ly light, a-mid th'en-cir-cling gloom, lead thou me on; the night is dark, and I am far from home; lead thou me on. Keep thou my feet; I do not ask to see the dis-tant scene; one step e-nough for me.

Text: John Henry Newman (1801-1890)
Music: Tune 1 – Charles Henry Purday (1799-1885)
Tune 2 – John Bacchus Dykes (1823-1876)

416 Lead us, heavenly Father, lead us

MANNHEIM 87 87 87

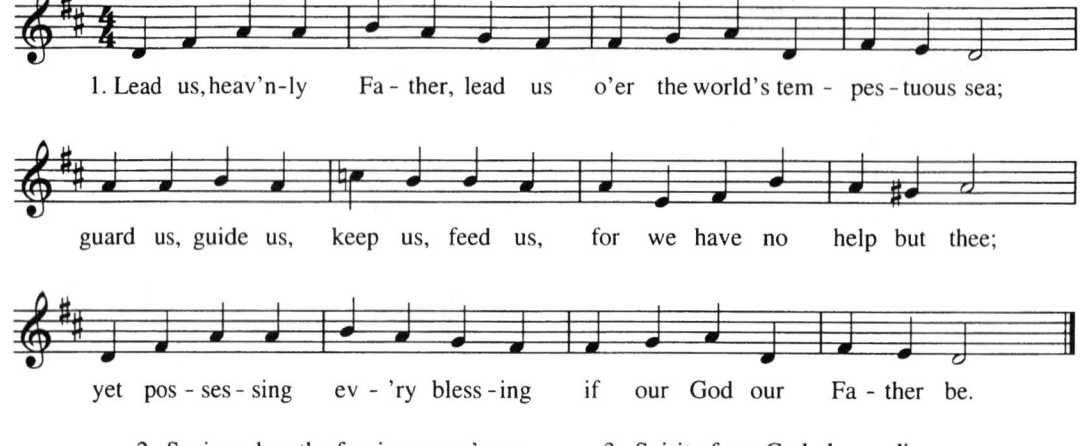

1. Lead us, heav'nly Father, lead us
o'er the world's tempestuous sea;
guard us, guide us, keep us, feed us,
for we have no help but thee;
yet possessing ev-'ry blessing
if our God our Father be.

2. Saviour, breathe forgiveness o'er us,
all our weakness thou dost know,
thou didst tread this earth before us,
thou didst feel its keenest woe;
lone and dreary, faint and weary,
through the desert thou didst go.

3. Spirit of our God, descending,
fill our hearts with heav'nly joy,
love with ev'ry passion blending,
pleasure that can never cloy;
thus provided, pardoned, guided,
nothing can our peace destroy.

Text: James Edmeston (1791-1867)
Music: Friedrich Filitz (1804-1876)

417 Leave your country and your people

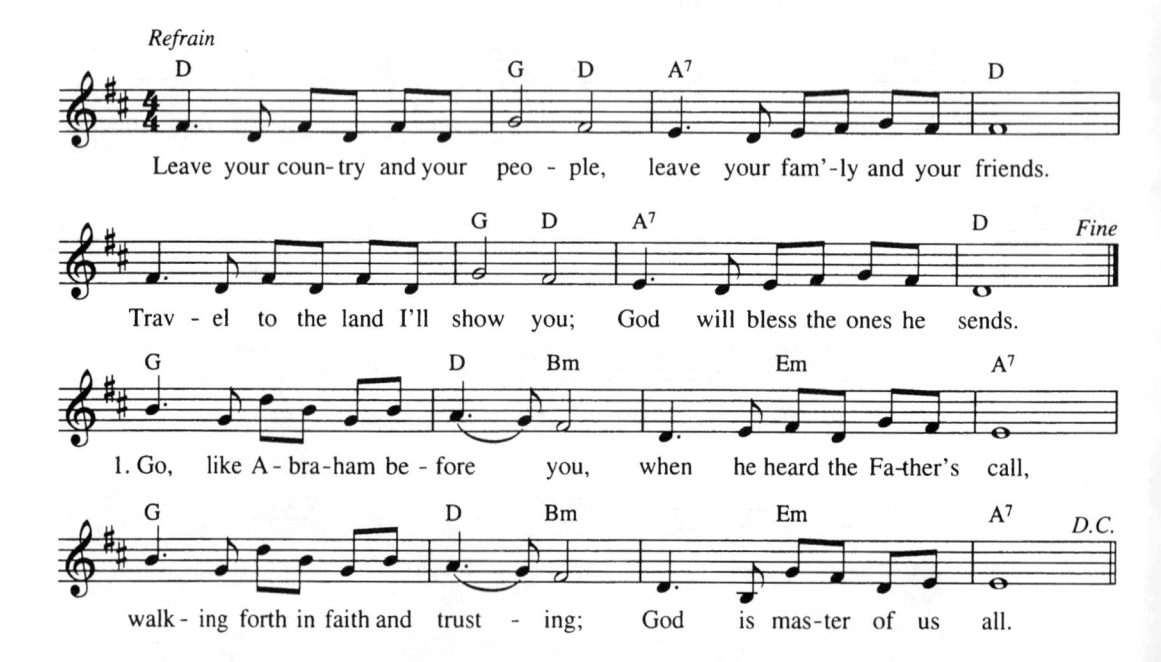

Refrain
Leave your country and your people,
leave your fam'-ly and your friends.
Travel to the land I'll show you;
God will bless the ones he sends.

1. Go, like Abraham before you,
when he heard the Father's call,
walking forth in faith and trusting;
God is master of us all.

© Copyright 1998 Willard F. Jabusch /OCP Publications, 5536 NE Hassalo, Portland, OR 97213, USA.
All rights reserved. Used by permission.

2. Sometimes God's word is demanding,
   leave security you know,
   breaking ties and bonds that hold you,
   when the voice of God says, 'Go'.

3. Take the path into the desert;
   barren seems the rock and sand.
   God will lead you through the desert
   when you follow his command.

4. Go with courage up the mountain,
   climb the narrow, rocky ledge,
   leave behind all things that hinder,
   go with only God as pledge.

Text and Music: Willard Jabusch (b.1930)

418 Let all mortal flesh keep silence

PICARDY 87 87 87

1. Let all mortal flesh keep silence and with fear and trembling stand; ponder nothing earthly-minded, for with blessing in his hand Christ our God on earth descendeth, our full homage to demand.

2. King of kings, yet born of Mary,
   as of old on earth he stood,
   Lord of lords, in human vesture,
   in the body and the blood.
   He will give to all the faithful
   his own self for heav'nly food.

3. Rank on rank the host of heaven
   spreads its vanguard on the way,
   as the Light of light descendeth
   from the realms of endless day,
   that the pow'rs of hell may vanish
   as the darkness clears away.

4. At his feet the six-winged seraph;
   cherubim, with sleepless eye,
   veil their faces to the Presence,
   as with ceaseless voice they cry,
   alleluia, alleluia,
   alleluia, Lord most high.

Text: Liturgy of St James trans. G. Moultrie (1829-1885)
Music: traditional French melody

419 Let all that is within me

*1. Let all that is within me cry: holy.
Let all that is within me cry: holy.
Holy, holy, holy is the Lamb that was slain.*

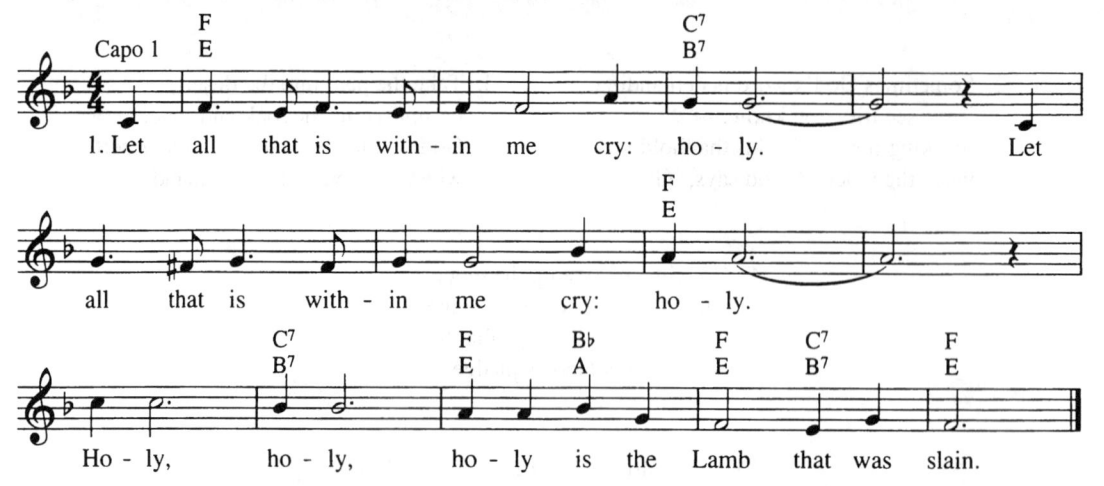

2. Let all that is within me cry: mighty. *(x2)*
Mighty, mighty, mighty is the
Lamb that was slain.

3. Let all that is within me cry: worthy. *(x2)*
Worthy, worthy, worthy is the
Lamb that was slain.

4. Let all that is within me cry: blessèd. *(x2)*
Blessèd, blessèd, blessèd is the
Lamb that was slain.

5. Let all that is within me cry: Jesus. *(x2)*
Jesus, Jesus, Jesus is the
Lamb that was slain.

Text and Music: unknown

420 Let all the world in every corner sing

LUCKINGTON 10 4 66 66 10 4

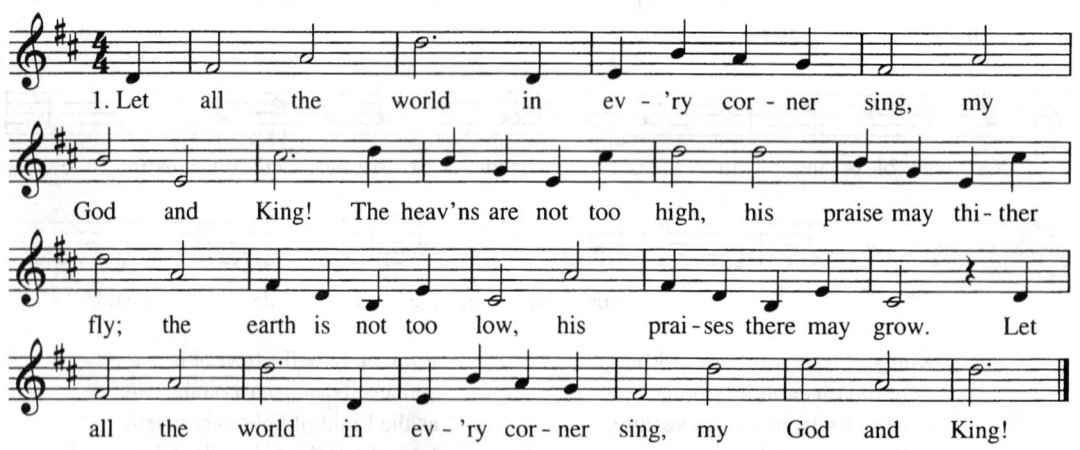

1. Let all the world in ev-'ry cor-ner sing, my God and King! The heav'ns are not too high, his praise may thi-ther fly; the earth is not too low, his prai-ses there may grow. Let all the world in ev-'ry cor-ner sing, my God and King!

2. Let all the world in ev'ry corner sing,
my God and King!
The Church with psalms must shout,
no door can keep them out;
but, above all, the heart
must bear the longest part.
Let all the world in ev'ry corner sing,
my God and King!

Text: George Herbert (1593-1633)
Music: Basil Harwood (1859-1949)

Music © Copyright The Estate of Dr. Basil Harwood. Reproduced by permission of the Trustees of the late Dr. Basil Harwood Settlement Trust, Public Trust Office, 24 Kingsway, London WC2B 6XJ.

421 Let love be real

1. Let love be real, in giving and receiving,
   without the need to manage and to own;
   a haven free from posing and pretending,
   where ev'ry weakness may be safely known.
   Give me your hand, along the desert pathway,
   give me your love wherever we may go.

   Refrain
   As God loves us, so let us love each other:
   with no demands, just open hands and space to grow.

2. Let love be real, not grasping or confining,
   that strange embrace that holds yet sets us free;
   that helps us face the risk of truly living,
   and makes us brave to be what we might be.
   Give me your strength when all my words are weakness;
   give me your love in spite of all you know.

3. Let love be real, with no manipulation,
   no secret wish to harness or control;
   let us accept each other's incompleteness,
   and share the joy of learning to be whole.
   Give me your hope through dreams and disappointments;
   give me your trust when all my failings show.

Text: Michael Forster (b.1946)
Music: Christopher Tambling (b.1964)
© Copyright 1995 Kevin Mayhew Ltd.

422 Let our praise to you be as incense

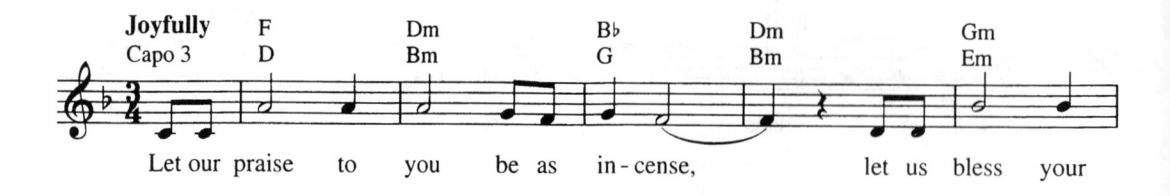

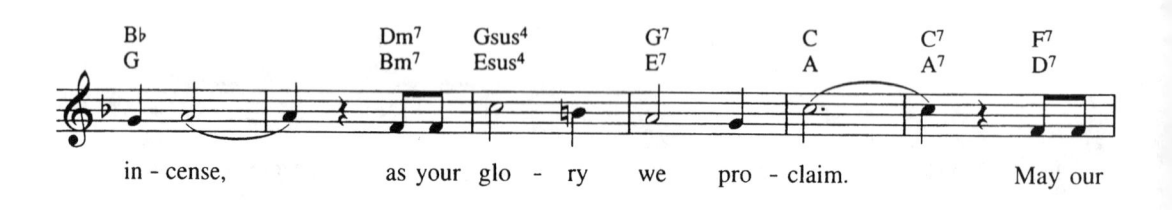

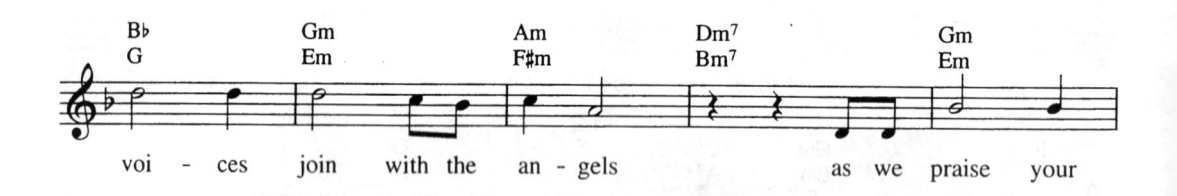

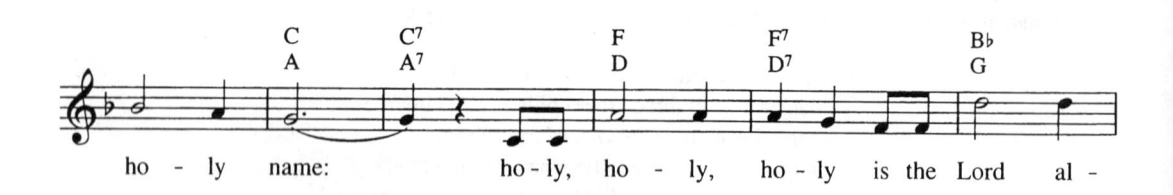

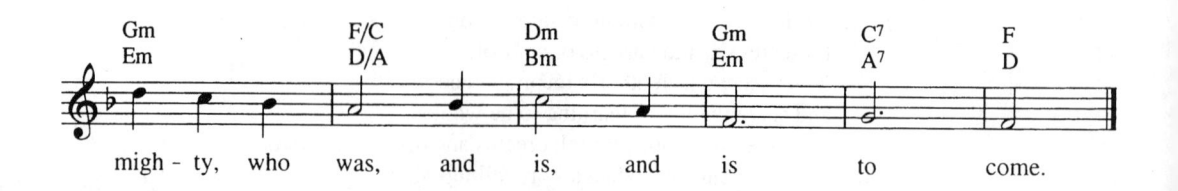

Joyfully
Capo 3

Let our praise to you be as in-cense, let us bless your ho-ly name; let our praise to you be as in-cense, as your glo-ry we pro-claim. May our voi-ces join with the an-gels as we praise your ho-ly name: ho-ly, ho-ly, ho-ly is the Lord al-migh-ty, who was, and is, and is to come.

Text: Bryan Spinks based on Psalm 140
Music: Malcolm Archer (b.1952)
© Copyright 1996 Kevin Mayhew Ltd.

423 Let the heavens declare

Lively
Refrain

Let the heavens declare, let the mountains sing,
let the oceans roar that Jesus lives and is our King.
Lift your hands in praise, let your spirits soar,
let the heavens declare, let the mountains sing, let the oceans roar. *Fine*

1. All the sins we've ever sinned died upon the cross with him,
but we know he lives again: the vict'ry is won, the vict'ry is won, the vict'ry is won, the vict'ry is won. *D.C.*

2. Hanging on the cross for me
Jesus died in agony.
Blood and tears he shed for me,
that I might have life. *(x4)*

3. In the kingdom he revealed
broken hearts can all be healed,
through the covenant he sealed
with his holy blood. *(x4)*

Text and Music: Mike Anderson (b.1956)
© Copyright 1999 Kevin Mayhew Ltd.

424 Let the hungry come to me

ADORO TE Plainsong

1. Let the hun-gry come to me, let the poor be fed. Let the thir-sty come and drink, share my wine and bread. Though you have no mon-ey, come to me and eat. Drink the cup I of-fer, feed on fin-est wheat!

2. I myself am living bread;
   feed on me and live.
   In this cup, my blood for you;
   drink the wine I give.
   All who eat my body,
   all who drink my blood
   shall have joy for ever,
   share the life of God.

3. Here among you shall I dwell,
   making all things new.
   You shall be my very own,
   I, your God with you.
   Blest are you invited
   to my wedding feast.
   You shall live for ever,
   all your joys increased.

4. Nourished by the Word of God,
   now we eat the bread.
   With the gift of God's own life,
   hungry hearts are fed.
   Manna in the desert,
   in our darkest night!
   Food for pilgrim people,
   pledge of glory bright!

5. Many grains become one loaf,
   many grapes, the wine.
   So shall we one body be,
   who together dine.
   As the bread is broken,
   as the wine is shared:
   so must we be given,
   caring as Christ cared.

6. Risen Saviour, walk with us,
   lead us by the hand.
   Heal our blinded eyes and hearts,
   help us understand.
   Lord, make known your presence
   at this table blest.
   Stay with us for ever,
   God, our host and guest!

Text: Delores Dufner
Music: Plainsong

Text: © Copyright 1985, 1989 Sisters of St Benedict. Published by World Library Publications, a division of J.S. Paluch Co. Inc, 3825 N. Willow Road, Schiller Park, IL 60176, USA. All rights reserved. Used by permission.

425 Let there be love

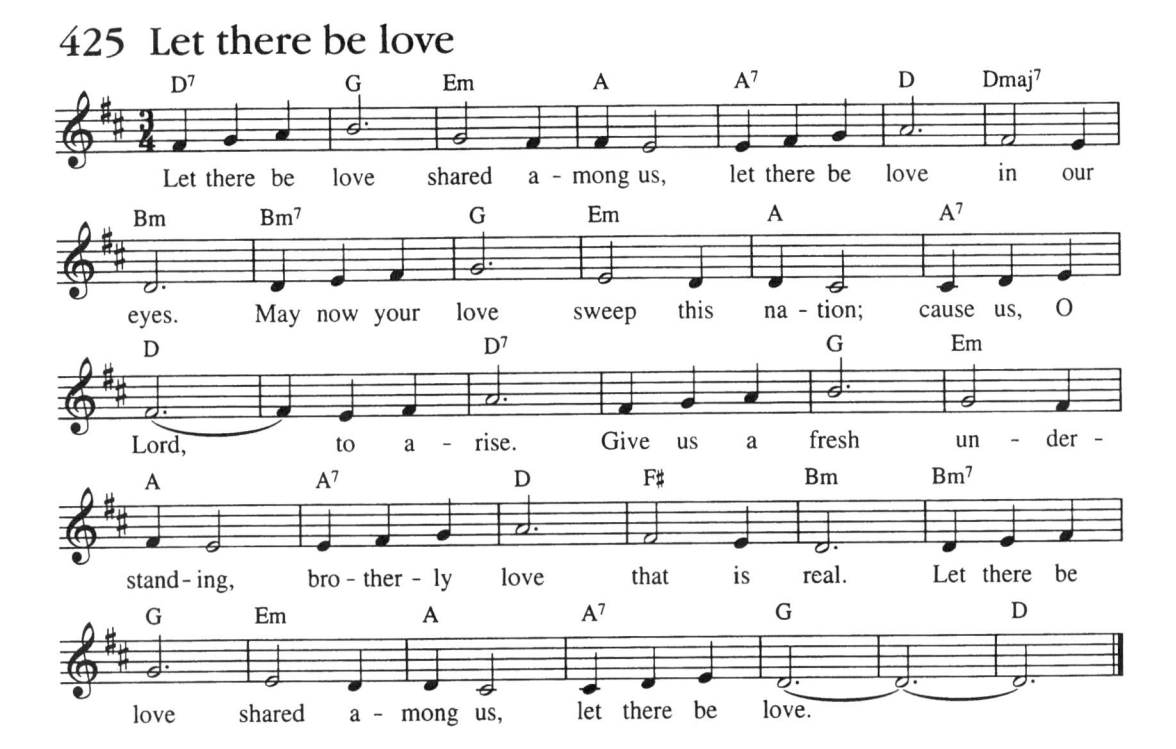

Let there be love shared a-mong us, let there be love in our eyes. May now your love sweep this na-tion; cause us, O Lord, to a-rise. Give us a fresh un-der-stand-ing, bro-ther-ly love that is real. Let there be love shared a-mong us, let there be love.

Text and Music: Dave Bilbrough
© Copyright 1979 Kingsway's Thankyou Music, P.O. Box 75, Eastbourne,
East Sussex BN23 6NW, UK. Used by permission.

426 Let the world in concert sing

This song should be unaccompanied

1. Let the world in con-cert sing prai-ses to our glo-rious King.*
Let the world in con-cert sing prai-ses to our glo-rious King.

Refrain
Al-le-lu-ia, al-le-lu-ia to our King!
Al-le-lu-ia, al-le-lu-ia to our King!

2. Of his pow'r and glory tell;
all his work he does right well:

3. Come, behold what he has done,
deeds of wonder, ev'ry one:

4. O you fearful ones, draw near;
praise our God who holds you dear:

5. Let us now in concert sing
praises to our glorious King: *

* For Eastertide 'risen King' may be substituted

Text: traditional Zulu trans. Helen Taylor, adapted by Tom Colvin
Music: 'Charu chose ngoni' traditional Zulu dance tune

© Copyright Hope Publishing. Administered by CopyCare, P.O. Box 77, Hailsham, East Sussex BN27 3EF, UK.
Used by permission.

427 Let us sing your glory

Steadily

1. Let us sing your glory, Lord, alleluia,
   let us praise your name adored, alleluia.
   Joy and beauty come from you, alleluia,
   and each hour your love shines through, alleluia.

   Refrain
   Alleluia, alleluia, allelu, alleluia.

2. Leaf that quivers on the tree, alleluia,
   flow'rs that we delight to see, alleluia.
   Planets as they reel in space, alleluia,
   tell us of your pow'r and grace, alleluia.

3. All creation sings your praise, alleluia,
   young and old their voices raise, alleluia.
   Children as they laugh and sing, alleluia,
   to your goodness homage bring, alleluia.

Text and Music: Marie Lydia Pereira
© Copyright 1999 Kevin Mayhew Ltd.

428 Let us, with a gladsome mind

MONKLAND 77 77

1. Let us, with a gladsome mind, praise the Lord, for he is kind;

   Refrain
   for his mercies ay endure, ever faithful, ever sure.

2. Let us blaze his name abroad,
   for of gods he is the God;

3. He, with all-commanding might,
   filled the new-made world with light;

4. He the golden-tressèd sun
   caused all day his course to run;

5. And the moon to shine at night,
   'mid her starry sisters bright;

6. All things living he doth feed,
   his full hand supplies their need;

7. Let us, with a gladsome mind,
   praise the Lord, for he is kind;

Text: John Milton (1608-1674) based on Psalm 135
Music: from 'Hymn Tunes of the United Brethren' (1824)
adapt. by John Bernard Wilkes (1785-1869)

429 Lift high the Cross

CRUCIFER 10 10 and Refrain

Refrain
Lift high the Cross, the love of Christ proclaim till all the world adore his sacred name!

1. Come, Christians, follow where our Saviour trod, o'er death victorious, Christ the Son of God.

2. Led on their way by this triumphant sign,
   the hosts of God in joyful praise combine:

3. Each new disciple of the Crucified
   is called to bear the seal of him who died:

4. Saved by the Cross whereon their Lord was slain,
   now Adam's children their lost home regain:

5. From north and south, from east and west they raise
   in growing harmony their song of praise:

6. O Lord, once lifted on the glorious tree,
   as thou hast promised, draw us unto thee:

7. Let ev'ry race and ev'ry language tell
   of him who saves from fear of death and hell:

8. From farthest regions, let them homage bring,
   and on his Cross adore their Saviour King:

9. Set up thy throne, that earth's despair may cease
   beneath the shadow of its healing peace:

10. For thy blest Cross which doth for all atone,
    creation's praises rise before thy throne:

11. So let the world proclaim with one accord
    the praises of our ever-living Lord.

Text: George William Kitchin (1827-1912) and Michael Robert Newbolt (1874-1956) alt.
Music: Sydney Hugo Nicholson (1875-1947)
© Copyright Hymns Ancient & Modern Ltd, St Mary's Works, St Mary's Plain, Norwich NR3 3BH.
Used by permission.

430 Lift up your hearts

Refrain
Lift up your hearts to the Lord in praise of his mer-cy!
Sing out your joy to the Lord: his love is en-dur-ing. *Fine*

1. Shout with joy to the Lord, all the earth!
Praise the glo-ry of his name!
Say to God 'How won-drous your works,
how glo-rious your name!' *D.C.*

2. Let the earth worship, singing your praise.
Praise the glory of your name!
Come and see the deeds of the Lord;
come, worship his name!

3. At his touch the dry land did appear;
paths were opened in the sea.
Let the earth rejoice in his might,
the might of his love.

4. Listen now, all you servants of God,
as I tell of his great works.
Blessed be the Lord of my life!
His love shall endure!

Text: Roc O'Connor based on Psalm 66
© Copyright 1981, 1993, Robert F. O'Connor, S.J. and New Dawn Music,
5536 NE Hassalo, Portland, OR 97213, USA. All rights reserved. Used by permission.

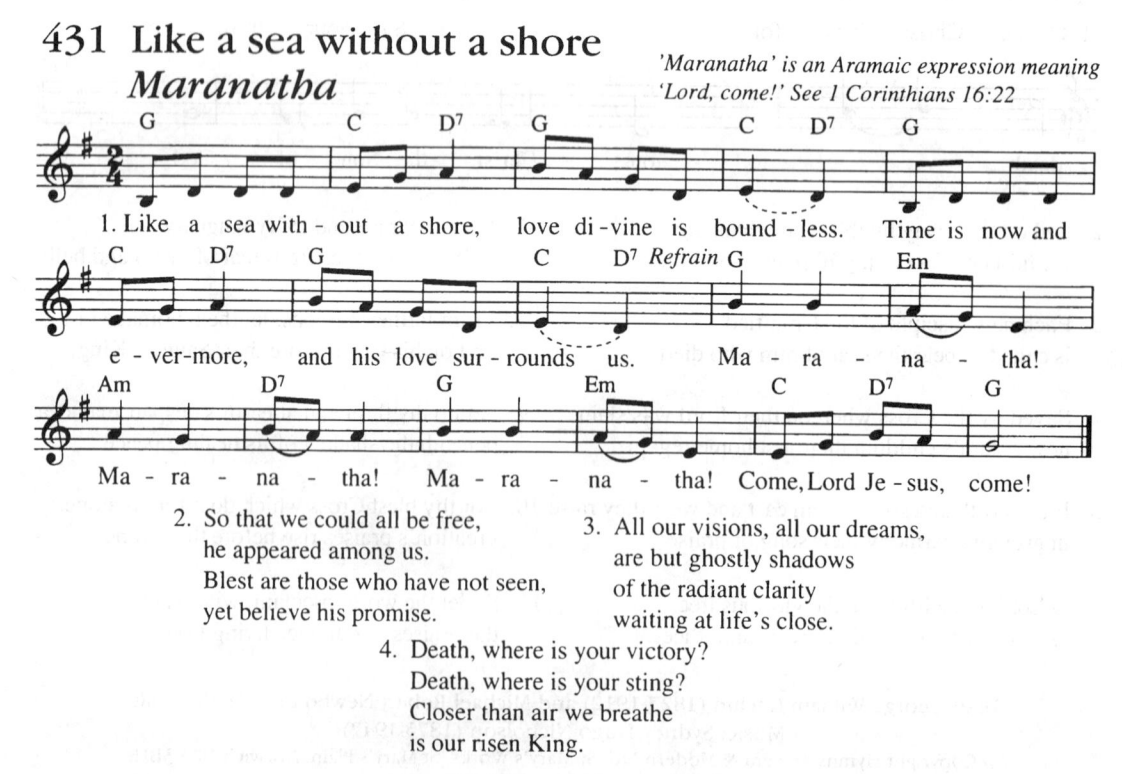

431 Like a sea without a shore
Maranatha

'Maranatha' is an Aramaic expression meaning 'Lord, come!' See 1 Corinthians 16:22

1. Like a sea with-out a shore, love di-vine is bound-less. Time is now and e-ver-more, and his love sur-rounds us. *Refrain* Ma-ra-na-tha! Ma-ra-na-tha! Ma-ra-na-tha! Come, Lord Je-sus, come!

2. So that we could all be free,
he appeared among us.
Blest are those who have not seen,
yet believe his promise.

3. All our visions, all our dreams,
are but ghostly shadows
of the radiant clarity
waiting at life's close.

4. Death, where is your victory?
Death, where is your sting?
Closer than air we breathe
is our risen King.

Text and Music: Estelle White (b.1925)
© Copyright 1976 Kevin Mayhew Ltd.

432 Like as the deer

Slow and reflective

Response

Like as the deer that yearns for flow-ing wa-ters, so longs my soul for God, the liv-ing God. *Fine*

1. My soul is thirst-ing for God, the God of my life; when can I en-ter and see the face of God? *D.C.*

2. These things will I re-mem-ber as I pour out my soul: how I would lead the re-joic-ing crowd in-to the house of God. *D.C.*

3. Send forth your light and your truth, let these be my guide; let them bring me to your ho-ly moun-tain, to the place where you dwell. *D.C.*

4. And I will come to the al-tar of God, the God of my joy! My Re-deem-er, I will thank you on the harp, O God, my God! *D.C.*

Text: Psalm 41, Grail translation
Music: Abbaye de Notre Dame de Tamié

Text: © Copyright 1963, 1986, 1993 The Grail, England. Used by permission of A.P. Watt Ltd,
20 John Street, London WC1N 2DR.
Music © Copyright Abbaye de Notre Dame de Tamié.

433 Like the deer that yearns

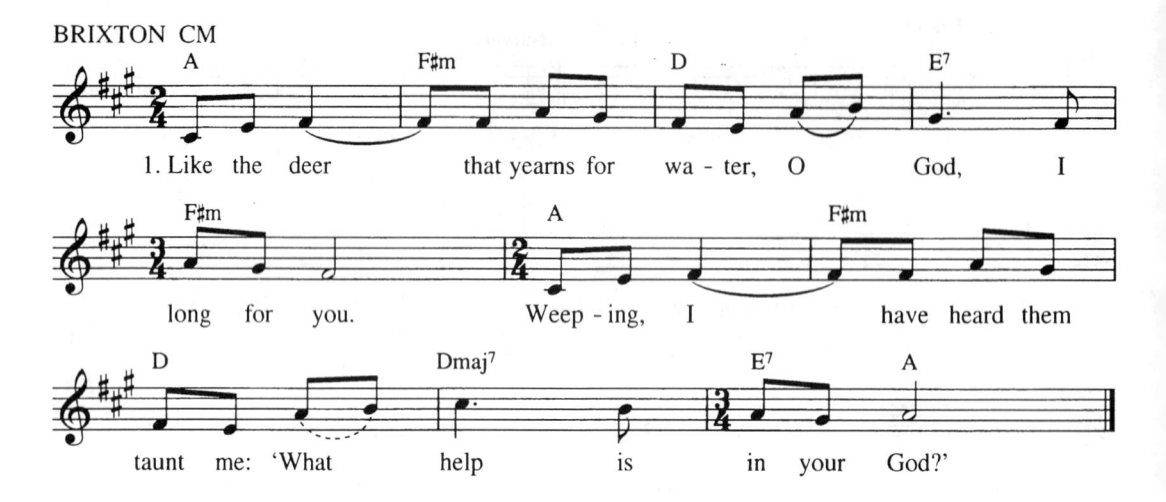

BRIXTON CM

1. Like the deer that yearns for water, O God, I long for you. Weeping, I have heard them taunt me: 'What help is in your God?'

2. Gladly I would lead your people,
rejoicing to your house.
Trust in God, my soul, and praise him,
and he will dry your tears.

3. Grief and pain, like roaring torrents,
had swept my soul away.
But his mercy is my rescue,
I will praise him all my days.

4. Weeping, I have heard them taunt me:
'What help is in your God?'
Rock of strength, do not forget me,
in you alone I trust.

5. To the Father praise and honour,
all glory to the Son,
honour to the Holy Spirit:
let God be glorified.

Text: Luke Connaughton (1917-1979) and Kevin Mayhew (b.1942) based on Psalm 41
Music: Kevin Mayhew (b.1942)
© Copyright 1976 Kevin Mayhew Ltd.

434 Like the murmur of the dove's song

BRIDEGROOM 87 87 6

1. Like the murmur of the dove's song, like the challenge of her flight, like the vigour of the wind's rush, like the new flame's eager might: come, Holy Spirit, come.

© Copyright 1989 Hope Publishing. Administered by CopyCare, P.O. Box 77, Hailsham,
East Sussex BN27 3EF, UK. Used by permission.

2. To the members of Christ's body,
   to the branches of the Vine,
   to the Church in faith assembled,
   to her midst as gift and sign:
   come, Holy Spirit, come.

3. With the healing of division,
   with the ceaseless voice of prayer,
   with the pow'r to love and witness,
   with the peace beyond compare:
   come, Holy Spirit, come.

Text: Carl P. Daw Jr.
Music: Peter Cutts

435 Listen, let your heart keep seeking

Refrain

Listen, let your heart keep seeking; listen to his constant speaking;
listen to the Spirit calling you.
Listen to his inspiration; listen to his invitation;
listen to the Spirit calling you.

1. He's in the sound of the thunder, in the whisper of the breeze.
   He's in the might of the whirlwind, in the roaring of the seas.

2. He's in the laughter of children,
   in the patter of the rain.
   Hear him in cries of the suff'ring,
   in their moaning and their pain.

3. He's in the noise of the city,
   in the singing of the birds.
   And in the night-time the stillness
   helps you listen to his word.

Text and Music: Aniceto Nazareth
© Copyright 1984 Kevin Mayhew Ltd.

436 Listen to me, Yahweh

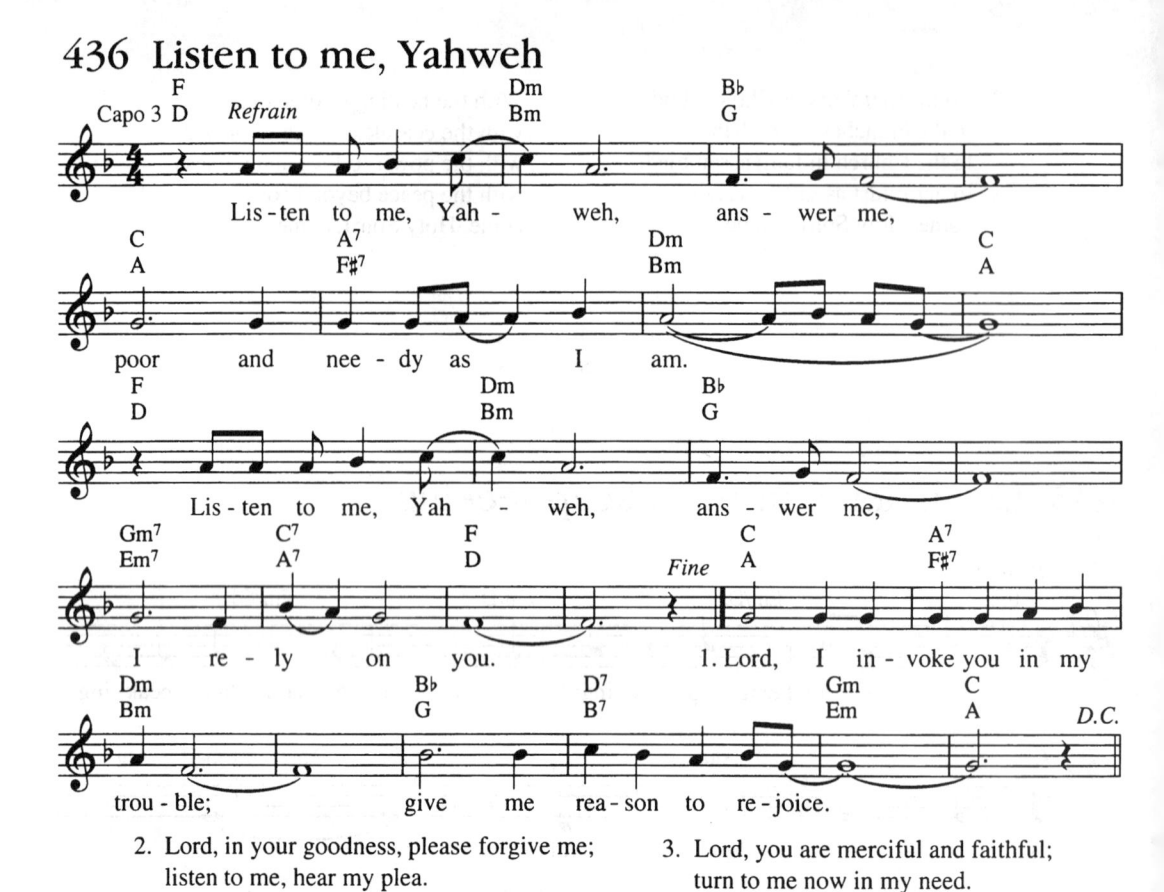

Capo 3 D   *Refrain*

Lis-ten to me, Yah-weh, ans-wer me,
poor and nee-dy as I am.
Lis-ten to me, Yah-weh, ans-wer me,
I re-ly on you. *Fine*

1. Lord, I in-voke you in my trou-ble;
   give me rea-son to re-joice. *D.C.*

2. Lord, in your goodness, please forgive me;
   listen to me, hear my plea.

3. Lord, you are merciful and faithful;
   turn to me now in my need.

4. Lord, give me strength, I am your servant;
   show me that you really care.

Text: Mike Anderson (b.1956) based on Psalm 85
Music: Mike Anderson (b.1956)
© Copyright 1999 Kevin Mayhew Ltd.

437 Listen to my voice
A healing song

1. Lis-ten to my voice, and then turn back to me:
   I will heal your heart, and I will set you free.
   Oh, my dear-est child, how much you mean to me:
   let me fill your life and love you ten-der-ly.

© Copyright 1999 Kevin Mayhew Ltd.

2. Rest within my arms and let your fears depart,
   feel my peace and joy bind up your broken heart.
   I will wipe your tears and make you whole again:
   come to me, my child, and turn away from sin.

3. Take my hand, and now we will begin once more,
   I will walk beside you as I did before.
   I have never left you, though your eyes were dim:
   walk with me in light, and turn away from sin.

Text and Music: Francesca Leftley (b.1955)

438 Lo, he comes with clouds descending

HELMSLEY 87 87 47

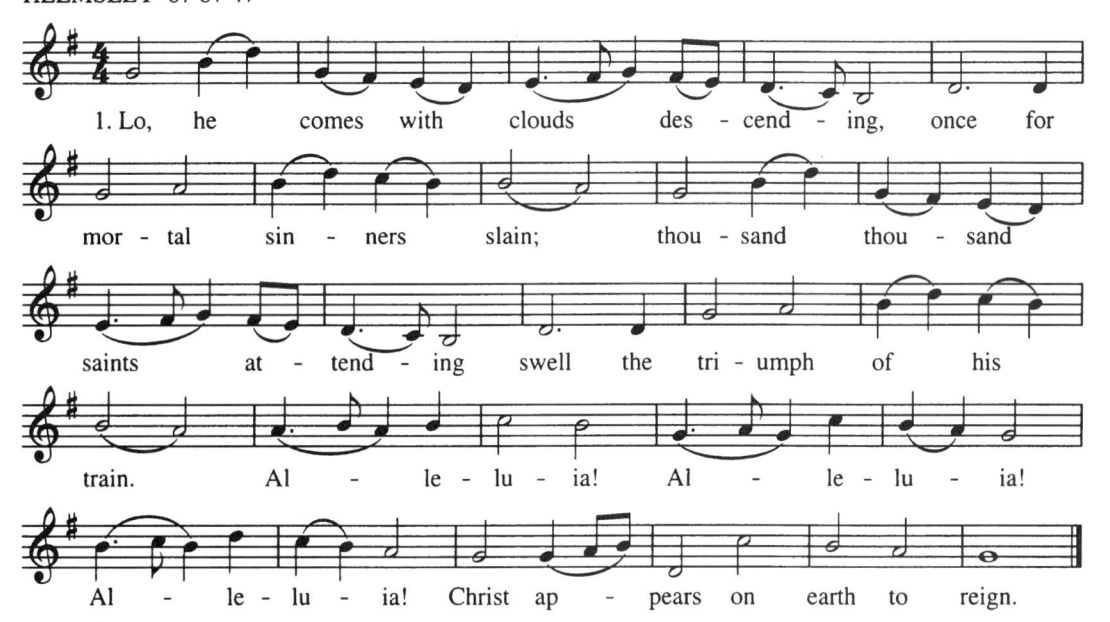

1. Lo, he comes with clouds descending, once for mortal sinners slain; thousand thousand saints attending swell the triumph of his train. Alleluia! Alleluia! Alleluia! Christ appears on earth to reign.

2. Ev'ry eye shall now behold him
   robed in dreadful majesty;
   we who set at naught and sold him,
   pierced and nailed him to the tree,
   deeply grieving, deeply grieving,
     deeply grieving,
   shall the true Messiah see.

3. Those dear tokens of his passion
   still his dazzling body bears,
   cause of endless exultation
   to his ransomed worshippers:
   with what rapture, with what rapture,
     with what rapture
   gaze we on those glorious scars!

4. Yea, amen, let all adore thee,
   high on thine eternal throne;
   Saviour, take the pow'r and glory,
   claim the kingdom for thine own.
   Alleluia! Alleluia! Alleluia!
   Thou shalt reign, and thou alone.

Text: Charles Wesley (1707-1788), John Cennick (1718-1755)
and Martin Madan (1726-1790) alt.
Music: from John Wesley's 'Select Hymns with Tunes Annext' (1765)

439 Longing for light
Christ be our light

1. Longing for light, we wait in darkness.
Longing for truth, we turn to you.
Make us your own, your holy people,
light for the world to see.

Refrain
Christ, be our light! Shine in our hearts.
Shine through the darkness.
Christ, be our light!
Shine in your Church gathered today.

2. Longing for peace, our world is troubled.
Longing for hope, many despair.
Your word alone has power to save us.
Make us your living voice.

3. Longing for food, many are hungry.
Longing for water, still many thirst.
Make us your bread, broken for others,
shared until all are fed.

4. Longing for shelter, many are homeless.
Longing for warmth, many are cold.
Make us your building, sheltering others,
walls made of living stone.

5. Many the gifts, many the people,
many the hearts that yearn to belong.
Let us be servants to one another,
making your kingdom come.

Text and Music: Bernadette Farrell
© Copyright 1993 Bernadette Farrell. Published by OCP Publications, 5536 NE Hassalo, Portland, OR 97213, USA.
All rights reserved. Used by permission.

440 Look around you
Kyrie eleison

1. Look around you, can you see?
Times are troubled, people grieve.
See the violence, feel the hardness;

© Copyright 1976 Celebration. Administered by Kingsway's Thankyou Music, P.O. Box 75, Eastbourne, East Sussex BN23 6NW, UK.Europe and British Commonwealth, (excl. Canada, Australasia & Africa). Used by permission.

all my peo - ple, weep with me. Ky - ri - e, e - lei - son. Chris - te, e - lei - son. Ky - ri - e, e - le - i - son.

2. Walk among them, I'll go with you.
   Reach out to them with my hands.
   Suffer with me, and together
   we will serve them, help them stand.

3. Forgive us, Father; hear our prayer.
   We'll walk with you anywhere,
   through your suff'ring, with forgiveness,
   take your life into the world.

Text and Music: Jodi Page Clark (b.1941)

441 Look at the sky

1. Look at the sky! The stars pro-claim my glo - ry. I am the Lord, the auth - or of your sto - ry. Sing and make mu - sic, share my ce - le - bra - tion! Spread the good news! Bring joy to ev-'ry na - tion. *Refrain* I am your God, your Fa - ther and your joy. You are my own, my chil - dren and my joy!

2. See I am near you, in my own creation!
   May ev'ry moment bring you my salvation!
   The moon is your sister and the sun your brother!
   Living and fruitful is the earth, your mother.

3. Listen to all my Word is still revealing!
   Filled with my Spirit, you will know my healing,
   for I am near you – in your heart I'm living.
   You'll recognise me, loving and forgiving.

4. Know I am with you, I am all around you.
   All my attention and my love surround you.
   You are my children: Jesus is your brother.
   Find me in him, and him in one another.

Text: Damian Lundy (1944-1997)
Music: Traditional Italian melody
Text © Copyright 1982, 1999 Kevin Mayhew Ltd.

442 Look down, O mother Mary

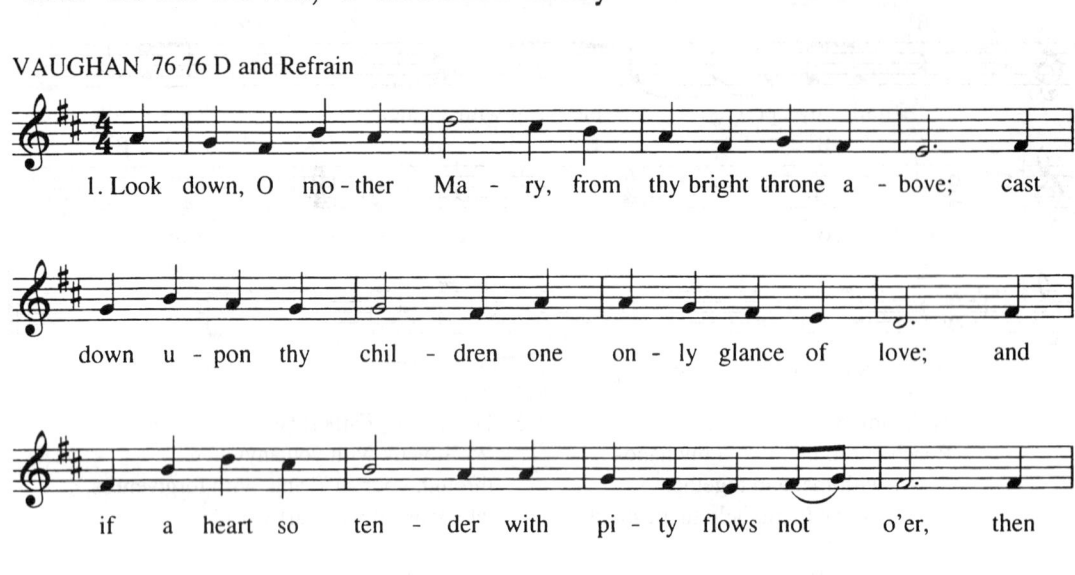

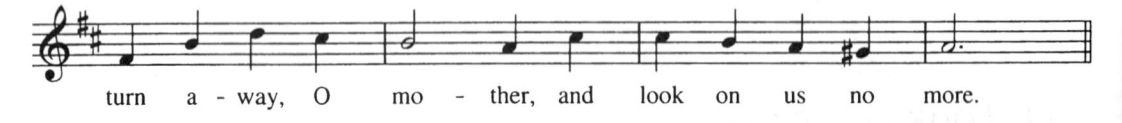

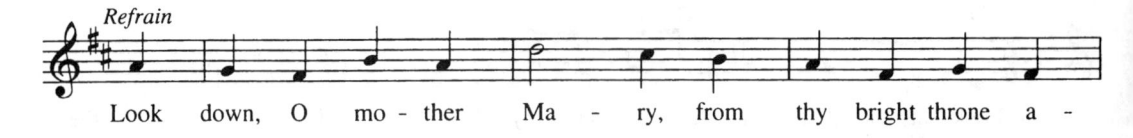

VAUGHAN 76 76 D and Refrain

1. Look down, O mother Mary, from thy bright throne above;
cast down upon thy children one only glance of love;
and if a heart so tender with pity flows not o'er,
then turn away, O mother, and look on us no more.

Refrain
Look down, O mother Mary, from thy bright throne above,
cast down upon thy children one only glance of love.

2. See how, ungrateful sinners,
we stand before thy Son;
his loving heart upbraids us
the evil we have done,
but if thou wilt appease him,
speak for us but one word;
for thus thou canst obtain us,
the pardon of our Lord.

3. O Mary, dearest mother,
if thou wouldst have us live,
say that we are thy children,
and Jesus will forgive.
Our sins make us unworthy
that title still to bear,
but thou art still our mother;
then show a mother's care.

4. Unfold to us thy mantle,
there stay we without fear;
what evil can befall us
if, mother, thou art near?
O kindest, dearest mother,
thy sinful children save;
look down on us with pity,
who thy protection crave.

Text: 'Dal tuo celeste' by St Alphonsus (1696-1787) trans. Edmund Vaughan (1827-1908)
Music: John Richardson (1816-1879)

443 Lord, accept the gifts we offer

ST THOMAS 87 87 87

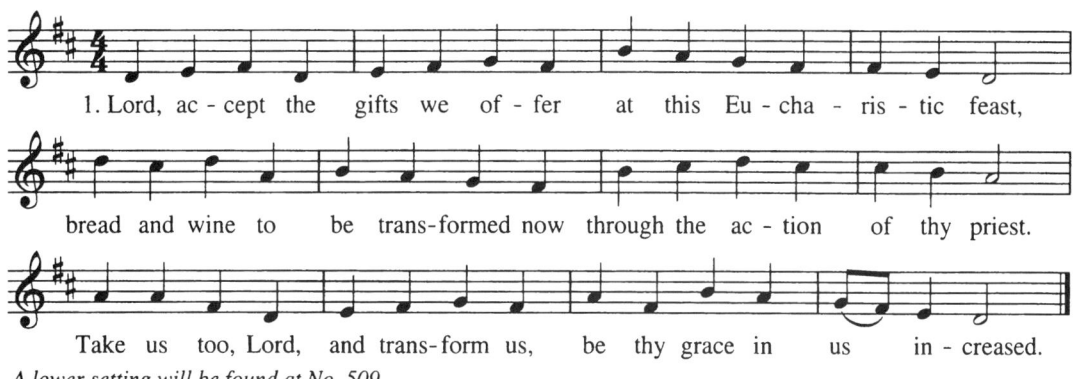

1. Lord, accept the gifts we offer at this Eucharistic feast,
bread and wine to be transformed now through the action of thy priest.
Take us too, Lord, and transform us, be thy grace in us increased.

A lower setting will be found at No. 509

2. May our souls be pure and spotless
as the host of wheat so fine;
may all stain of sin be crushed out,
like the grape that forms the wine,
as we, too, become partakers,
in the sacrifice divine.

3. Take our gifts, almighty Father,
living God, eternal, true,
which we give through Christ our Saviour,
pleading here for us anew.
Grant salvation to all present,
and our faith and love renew.

Text: Sister M. Teresine
Music: Samuel Webbe (1740-1816)

444 Lord, enthroned in heavenly splendour

REGENT SQUARE 87 87 87

1. Lord, enthroned in heav'nly splendour, glorious firstborn from the dead,
you alone our strong defender lifting up your people's head:
alleluia, alleluia, Jesus, true and living bread!

2. Prince of life, for us now living,
by your body souls are healed;
Prince of peace, your pardon giving,
by your blood our peace is sealed:
Alleluia, alleluia,
Word of God in flesh revealed.

3. Paschal Lamb! your off'ring finished,
once for all, when you were slain;
in its fulness undiminished
shall for evermore remain:
Alleluia, alleluia,
cleansing souls from ev'ry stain.

4. Great High Priest of our profession,
through the veil you entered in,
by your mighty intercession
grace and mercy there to win:
Alleluia, alleluia,
only sacrifice for sin.

5. Life-imparting heav'nly Manna,
stricken rock, with streaming side;
heav'n and earth, with loud hosanna,
worship you, the Lamb who died:
Alleluia, alleluia,
ris'n, ascended, glorified!

Text: George Hugh Bourne (1840-1925)
Music: Henry Smart (1813-1879)

445 Lord, for tomorrow and its needs
LORD FOR TOMORROW (PROVIDENCE) 84 84

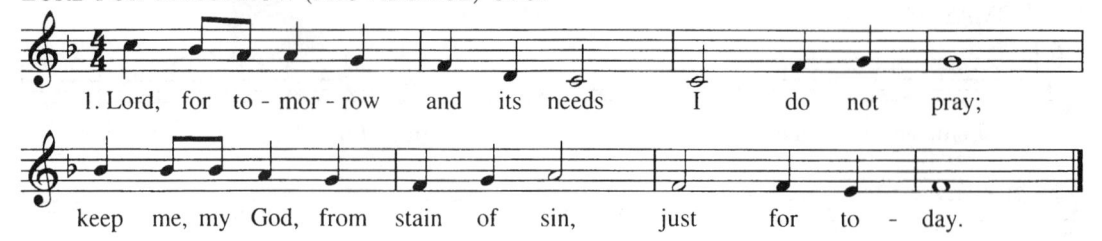

1. Lord, for to-mor-row and its needs I do not pray;
keep me, my God, from stain of sin, just for to-day.

2. Let me both diligently work
and duly pray;
let me be kind in word and deed,
just for today.

3. Let me no wrong or idle word
unthinking say;
set thou a seal upon my lips,
just for today.

4. And if today my tide of life
should ebb away,
give me thy sacraments divine,
sweet Lord, today.

5. So, for tomorrow and its needs
I do not pray;
but keep me, guide me, love me, Lord,
just for today.

Text: Sister M. Xavier
Music: Richard Runciman Terry (1865-1938)
Music © Copyright Burns & Oates Ltd, Wellwood, North Farm Road, Tunbridge Wells, Kent TN2 3QR. Used by permission.

446 Lord, have mercy
EZECHIEL 88 88 98 11 7

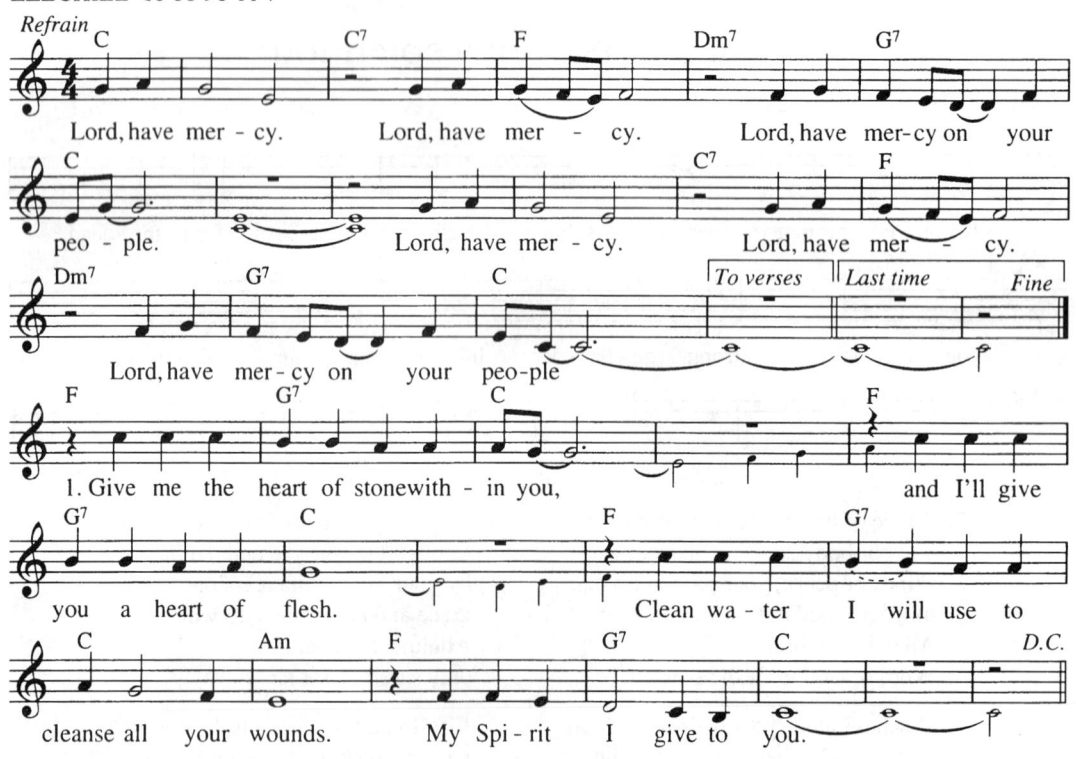

Refrain
Lord, have mer-cy. Lord, have mer-cy. Lord, have mer-cy on your peo-ple. Lord, have mer-cy. Lord, have mer-cy. Lord, have mer-cy on your peo-ple

1. Give me the heart of stone with-in you, and I'll give you a heart of flesh. Clean wa-ter I will use to cleanse all your wounds. My Spi-rit I give to you.

2. You'll find me near the broken-hearted:
those crushed in spirit I will save.
So turn to me, for my pardon is great;
my word will heal all your wounds.

Text: Gerard Markland based on Ezekiel
Music: Gerard Markland
© Copyright 1978 Kevin Mayhew Ltd.

447 Lord Jesus Christ
Living Lord

LIVING LORD 9 8 88 83

1. Lord Jesus Christ, you have come to us, you are one with us, Mary's Son. Cleansing our souls from all their sin, pouring your love and goodness in, Jesus, our love for you we sing, living Lord.

2. Lord Jesus Christ,
   now and ev'ry day
   teach us how to pray,
   Son of God.
   You have commanded us to do
   this in remembrance, Lord, of you.
   Into our lives your pow'r breaks through,
   living Lord.

3. Lord Jesus Christ,
   you have come to us,
   born as one of us,
   Mary's Son.
   Led out to die on Calvary,
   risen from death to set us free,
   living Lord Jesus, help us see
   you are Lord.

4. Lord Jesus Christ,
   I would come to you,
   live my life for you,
   Son of God.
   All your commands I know are true,
   your many gifts will make me new,
   into my life your pow'r breaks through,
   living Lord.

Text and Music: Patrick Appleford (b.1925)

© Copyright 1960 Josef Weinberger Ltd., 12-14 Mortimer Street, London W1N 7RD.
All rights reserved. Used by permission.

448 Lord Jesus, think on me

SOUTHWELL (DAMON) SM

1. Lord Jesus, think on me, and purge away my sin; from earth-born passions set me free, and make me pure within.

2. Lord Jesus, think on me,
   with care and woe opprest;
   let me thy loving servant be,
   and taste thy promised rest.

3. Lord Jesus, think on me
   amid the battle's strife;
   in all my pain and misery
   be thou my health and life.

4. Lord Jesus, think on me,
   nor let me go astray;
   through darkness and perplexity
   point thou the heav'nly way.

5. Lord Jesus, think on me,
   when flows the tempest high:
   when on doth rush the enemy,
   O Saviour, be thou nigh.

6. Lord Jesus, think on me,
   that, when the flood is past,
   I may th'eternal brightness see,
   and share thy joy at last.

Text: 'Mnōeo Christe' by Bishop Synesius (375-430) trans. Allen William Chatfield (1808-1896)
Music: from 'The Psalms in English Metre' (1570) adapted by William Damon (1540-1591)

449 Lord, make me a means of your peace

1. Lord, make me a means of your peace. Where there's hatred grown, let me sow your love. Where there's in-j'ry, Lord, let forgiveness be my sword. Lord, make me a means of your peace.

© Copyright 1976 John B. Foley SJ and New Dawn Music, 5536 NE Hassalo, Portland, OR 97213, USA.
All rights reserved. Used by permission.

2. Lord, make me a means of your peace.
   Where there's doubt and fear,
   let me sow your faith.
   In this world's despair,
   give me hope in you to share.
   Lord, make me a means of your peace.

3. Lord, make me a means of your peace.
   When there's sadness here,
   let me sow your joy.
   When the darkness nears,
   may your light dispel our fears.
   Lord, make me a means of your peace.

4. Lord, grant me to seek and to share:
   less to be consoled
   than to help console,
   less be understood
   than to understand your good.
   Lord, make me a means of your peace.

5. Lord, grant me to seek and to share:
   to receive love less
   than to give love free,
   just to give in thee,
   just receiving from your tree.
   Lord, make me a means of your peace.

6. Lord, grant me to seek and to share:
   to forgive in thee,
   you've forgiven me;
   for to die in thee
   is eternal life to me.
   Lord, make me a means of your peace.

Text: John B. Foley based on the Prayer of St Francis
Music: John B. Foley

450 Lord of all hopefulness

SLANE 10 11 11 12

1. Lord of all hopefulness, Lord of all joy, whose trust, ever childlike, no cares could destroy, be there at our waking, and give us, we pray, your bliss in our hearts, Lord, at the break of the day.

2. Lord of all eagerness,
   Lord of all faith,
   whose strong hands were skilled
   at the plane and the lathe,
   be there at our labours,
   and give us, we pray,
   your strength in our hearts, Lord,
   at the noon of the day.

3. Lord of all kindliness,
   Lord of all grace,
   your hands swift to welcome,
   your arms to embrace,
   be there at our homing,
   and give us, we pray,
   your love in our hearts, Lord,
   at the eve of the day.

4. Lord of all gentleness,
   Lord of all calm,
   whose voice is contentment,
   whose presence is balm,
   be there at our sleeping,
   and give us, we pray,
   your peace in our hearts, Lord,
   at the end of the day.

Text: Jan Struther (1901-1953)
Music: traditional Irish melody
Text © Copyright Oxford University Press, Great Clarendon Street, Oxford OX2 6DP.
Used by permission from 'Enlarged Songs of Praise.'

451 Lord of life

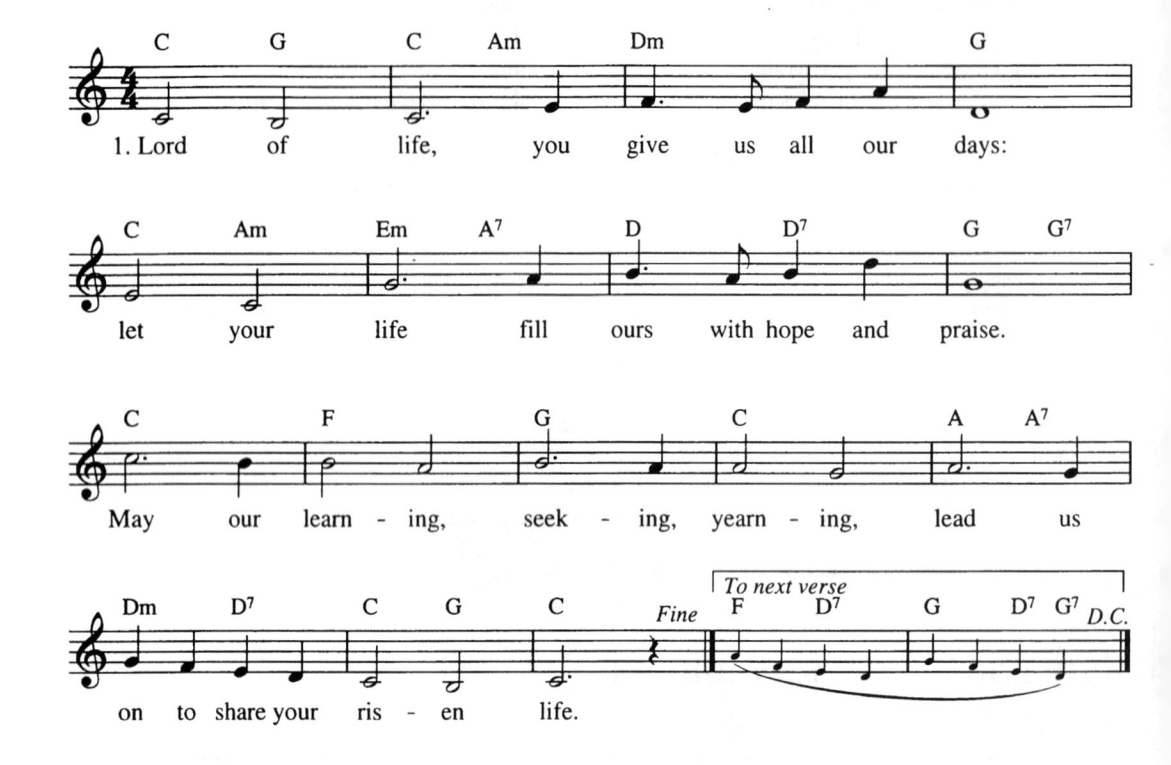

1. Lord of life, you give us all our days:
let your life fill ours with hope and praise.
May our learning, seeking, yearning,
lead us on to share your risen life.

2. 'Come to me, and I will give you rest.'
   Help us see your Way is richly blest;
   guide our questing, working, resting,
   till we hear you calling 'follow me'.

3. Lord, we come, encouraged by your grace,
   Lord, we come, and things fall into place;
   pilgrims ever, we endeavour,
   Lord, to follow as you bring us home.

4. Lord, may we bring all our strength and skill:
   help us be prepared to do your will.
   Turn our living into giving
   love and service as you set us free.

5. Glory be to God for all his love;
   here may we with saints below, above,
   go rejoicing, ever voicing
   praise for such a welcome 'Come to me'.

Text and Music: Patrick Appleford (b.1925)
© Copyright 1984 Kevin Mayhew Ltd.

452 Lord our God

LAMBOURN 87 87

1. Lord our God, O Lord our Father, Lord of love and Lord of fear, now we gather round your altar and we know your Word is near.

2. All our lives lie open to you,
   Lord of age, and Lord of youth,
   as we bring our sins and falsehoods
   to the judgement of your truth.

3. Lord of times and Lord of seasons,
   Lord of calmness, Lord of stress,
   heart that sees our secret terrors,
   Lord of strength and gentleness.

4. Lord of storms and Lord of sunsets,
   Lord of darkness, Lord of light,
   cast the shadow of your blessing
   on us gathered in your sight.

5. Lord of foes and Lord of friendships,
   Lord of laughter, Lord of tears,
   Lord of toil and Lord of Sabbath,
   Master of the hurrying years.

6. Lord of hope and Lord of hunger,
   Lord of atoms, Lord of space,
   take this world we bring before you
   to the haven of your grace.

Text: Kevin Nichols (b.1929)
Music: Andrew Moore (b.1954)
© Copyright 1976, 1999 Kevin Mayhew Ltd.

LITURGICAL
HYMNS OLD & NEW

453 Lord, the light of your love
Shine, Jesus, shine

SHINE, JESUS, SHINE 9 9 10 10 6

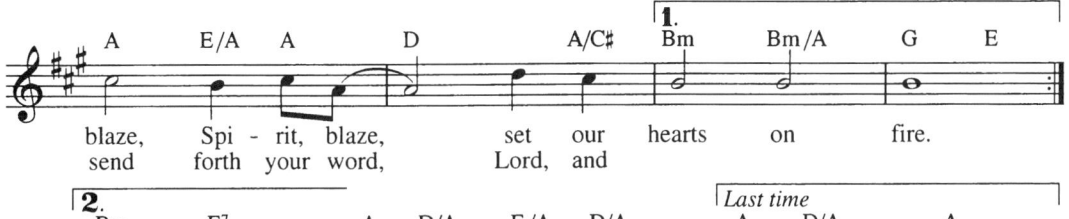

1. Lord, the light of your love is shining, in the midst of the darkness, shining; Jesus, Light of the World, shine upon us, set us free by the truth you now bring us. Shine on me, shine on me.

Refrain
Shine, Jesus, shine, fill this land with the Father's glory;
Blaze, Spirit, blaze, set our hearts on fire.
Flow, river, flow, flood the nations with grace and mercy;
Send forth your word, Lord, and let there be light.

2. Lord, I come to your awesome presence,
from the shadows into your radiance;
by the blood I may enter your brightness,
search me, try me, consume all my darkness.
Shine on me, shine on me.

3. As we gaze on your kingly brightness,
so our faces display your likeness,
ever changing from glory to glory;
mirrored here may our lives tell your story.
Shine on me, shine on me.
(Refrain twice to end)

Text and Music: Graham Kendrick (b.1950)

© Copyright 1987 Make Way Music, P.O. Box 263, Croydon, Surrey CR9 5AP, UK.
International copyright secured. All rights reserved. Used by permission.

454 Lord, thy word abideth

RAVENSHAW 66 66

1. Lord, thy word abideth,
and our footsteps guideth;
who its truth believeth
light and joy receiveth.

2. When our foes are near us,
then thy word doth cheer us,
word of consolation,
message of salvation.

3. When the storms are o'er us,
and dark clouds before us,
then its light directeth,
and our way protecteth.

4. Who can tell the pleasure,
who recount the treasure,
by thy word imparted
to the simple-hearted?

5. Word of mercy, giving
succour to the living;
word of life, supplying
comfort to the dying.

6. O that we, discerning
its most holy learning,
Lord, may love and fear thee,
evermore be near thee.

Text: Henry Williams Baker (1821-1877)
Music: melody from M. Weisse's 'Neu Gesangbüchlein' (1531)
adapted by William Henry Monk (1823-1889)

455 Lord, unite all nations

Lord, unite all nations in your love. Bless us with your bounty from above. And may all in heaven one day sing at the banquet of their Lord and King. 1. Draw us in love, grant us your

© Copyright 1999 Kevin Mayhew Ltd.

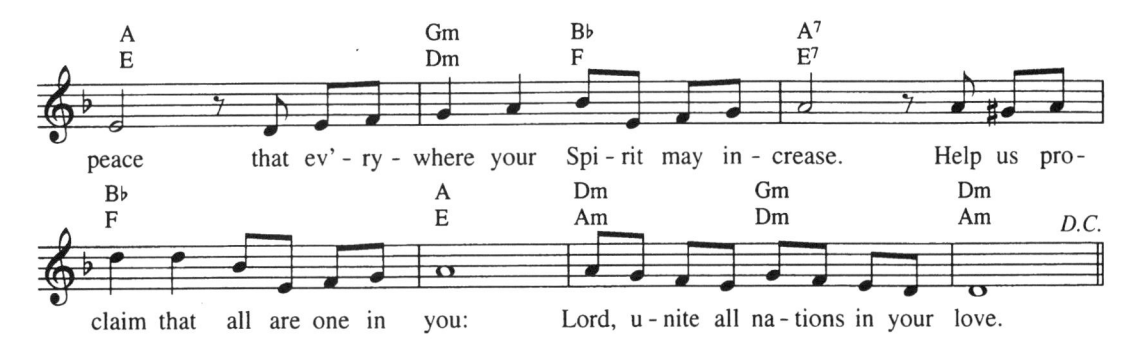

peace that ev'-ry-where your Spi-rit may in-crease. Help us pro-claim that all are one in you: Lord, u-nite all na-tions in your love.

2. Fill us with love, give us your peace,
   let grace abound and charity increase.
   From East to West may all be one in love:
   Lord, unite all nations in your love.

3. Teach us your love, teach us your peace,
   that joy may grow and happiness increase.
   Help us to work to make all nations one;
   Lord, unite all nations in your love.

Text and Music: Marie Lydia Pereira (b.1920)

456 Lord, we come to ask your healing

AR HYD Y NOS 84 84 88 84

A higher setting will be found at No. 232

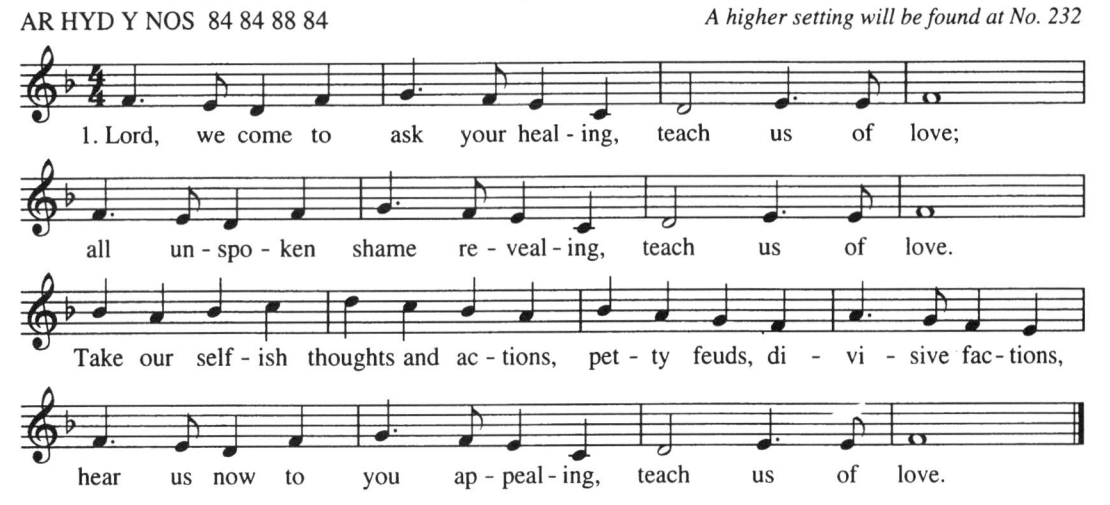

1. Lord, we come to ask your heal-ing, teach us of love;
   all un-spo-ken shame re-veal-ing, teach us of love.
   Take our self-ish thoughts and ac-tions, pet-ty feuds, di-vi-sive fac-tions,
   hear us now to you ap-peal-ing, teach us of love.

2. Soothe away our pain and sorrow,
   hold us in love;
   grace we cannot buy or borrow,
   hold us in love.
   Though we see but dark and danger,
   though we spurn both friend and stranger,
   though we often dread tomorrow,
   hold us in love.

3. When the bread is raised and broken,
   fill us with love;
   words of consecration spoken,
   fill us with love.
   As our grateful prayers continue,
   make the faith that we have in you
   more than just an empty token,
   fill us with love.

4. Help us live for one another,
   bind us in love;
   stranger, neighbour, father, mother –
   bind us in love.
   All are equal at your table,
   through your Spirit make us able
   to embrace as sister, brother,
   bind us in love.

Text: Jean Holloway (b.1939)
Music: traditional Welsh melody
Text © Copyright 1995 Kevin Mayhew Ltd.

457 Lord, when I wake I turn to you

MELCOMBE LM

1. Lord, when I wake I turn to you,
your-self my day's first thought and prayer,
your strength to help, your peace to bless,
your will to guide me ev-'ry-where!

2. I live with many in our world
   – their worldly eyes too blind to see –
   who never think what is your will,
   or why you brought our world to be!

3. Your thought for me, your loving care,
   those favours I could never earn,
   call for my thanks in praise and prayer,
   call me to love you in return!

4. There is no blessing, Lord, from you
   for those who make their will their way,
   no praise for those who do not praise,
   no peace for those who do not pray!

5. Make then my life a life of love,
   keep me from sin in all I do,
   your way to be my only way,
   your will my will for love of you!

Text: Brian Foley (b.1919) based on Psalm 5
Music: Samuel Webbe (1740-1816)
Text © Copyright 1971 Faber Music Ltd, 3 Queen Square, London WC1N 3AU.
Used by permission from 'New Catholic Hymnal'

458 Lord, who throughout these forty days

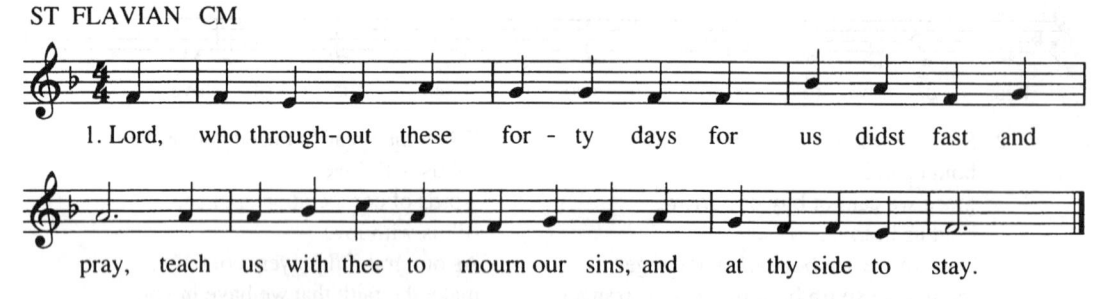

ST FLAVIAN CM

1. Lord, who through-out these for-ty days
for us didst fast and pray,
teach us with thee to mourn our sins,
and at thy side to stay.

2. As thou with Satan didst contend
   and didst the vict'ry win,
   O give us strength in thee to fight,
   in thee to conquer sin.

3. As thirst and hunger thou didst bear,
   so teach us, gracious Lord,
   to die to self, and daily live
   by thy most holy word.

4. And through these days of penitence,
   and through thy Passiontide,
   yea, evermore, in life and death,
   Lord Christ, with us abide.

Text: Claudia Frances Hernaman (1838-1898)
Music: from 'Day's Psalter' (1563)

459 Lord, you give the great commission

ABBOT'S LEIGH 87 87 D

1. Lord, you give the great commission:
'Heal the sick and preach the word.'
Lest the Church neglect its mission,
and the Gospel go unheard,
help us witness to your purpose
with renewed integrity;
with the Spirit's gifts empow'r us
for the work of ministry.

2. Lord, you call us to your service:
'In my name baptise and teach,'
that the world may trust your promise,
life abundant meant for each,
give us all new fervour,
draw us closer in community;
with the Spirit's gifts empow'r us
for the work of ministry.

3. Lord, you make the common holy:
'This my body, this my blood.'
Let us all, for earth's true glory,
daily lift life heavenward,
asking that the world around us
share your children's liberty;
with the Spirit's gifts empow'r us
for the work of ministry.

4. Lord, you show us love's true measure;
'Father what they do, forgive.'
Yet we hoard as private treasure
all that you so freely give.
May your care and mercy lead us
to a just society;
with the Spirit's gifts empow'r us
for the work of ministry.

5. Lord, you bless with words assuring:
'I am with you to the end.'
Faith and hope and love restoring,
may we serve as you intend,
and, amid the cares that claim us,
hold in mind eternity;
with the Spirit's gifts empow'r us
for the work of ministry.

Text: Jeffrey Rowthorn (b.1934)
Music: Cyril Vincent Taylor (1907-1991)

Text © Copyright 1978 Hope Publishing. Administered by CopyCare,
P.O. Box 77, Hailsham, East Sussex BN27 3EF, UK. Used by permission.
Music © Copyright Oxford University Press, Great Clarendon Street, Oxford OX2 6DP. Used by permission.

460 Love came down at Christmas

LOVE CAME DOWN 67 67

1. Love came down at Christmas, Love all lovely, Love divine;
Love was born at Christmas, star and angels gave the sign.

2. Worship we the Godhead,
Love incarnate, Love divine;
worship we our Jesus:
but wherewith for sacred sign?

3. Love shall be our token,
love be yours and love be mine,
love to God and all men,
love for plea and gift and sign.

Text: Christina Georgina Rossetti (1830-1894)
Music: Malcolm Archer (b.1952)
Music © Copyright 1991 Kevin Mayhew Ltd.

461 Love divine, all loves excelling

TUNE 1: LOVE DIVINE 87 87

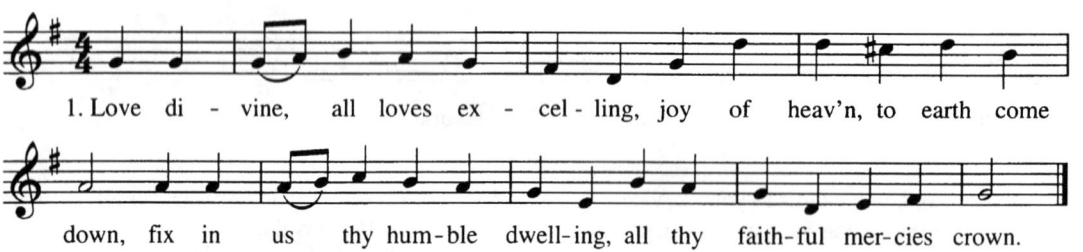

1. Love divine, all loves excelling, joy of heav'n, to earth come down, fix in us thy humble dwelling, all thy faithful mercies crown.

2. Jesu, thou art all compassion,
pure unbounded love thou art;
visit us with thy salvation,
enter ev'ry trembling heart.

3. Breathe, O breathe thy loving Spirit
into ev'ry troubled breast;
let us all in thee inherit,
let us find thy promised rest.

4. Take away the love of sinning,
Alpha and Omega be;
end of faith, as its beginning,
set our hearts at liberty.

5. Come, almighty to deliver,
let us all thy grace receive;
suddenly return, and never,
nevermore thy temples leave.

6. Thee we would be always blessing,
serve thee as thy hosts above;
pray, and praise thee without ceasing,
glory in thy perfect love.

7. Finish then thy new creation,
pure and spotless let us be;
let us see thy great salvation
perfectly restored in thee.

8. Changed from glory into glory,
till in heav'n we take our place,
till we cast our crowns before thee,
lost in wonder, love, and praise.

Tune 2 © Copyright control

TUNE 2: BLAENWERN 87 87 D

1. Love divine, all loves excelling, joy of heav'n, to
earth come down, fix in us thy humble dwelling, all thy
faithful mercies crown. Jesu, thou art all compassion,
pure unbounded love thou art; visit us with
thy salvation, enter ev'ry trembling heart.

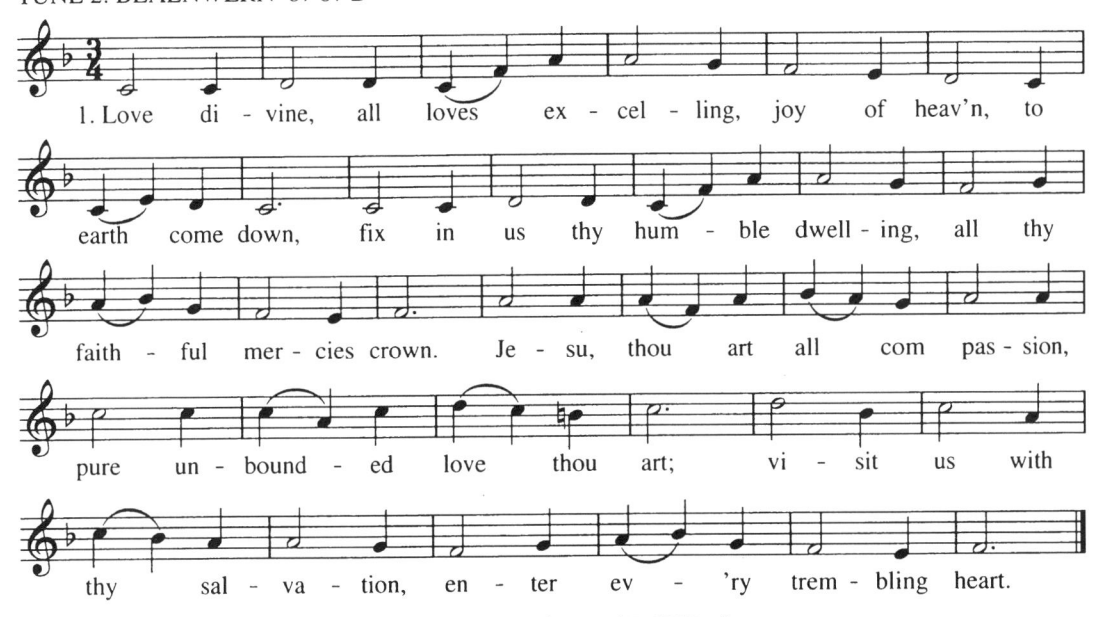

Text: Charles Wesley (1707-1788) alt.
Music: Tune 1: – John Stainer (1840-1901)
Tune 2: – William Penfro Rowlands (1860-1937)

462 Love is his word

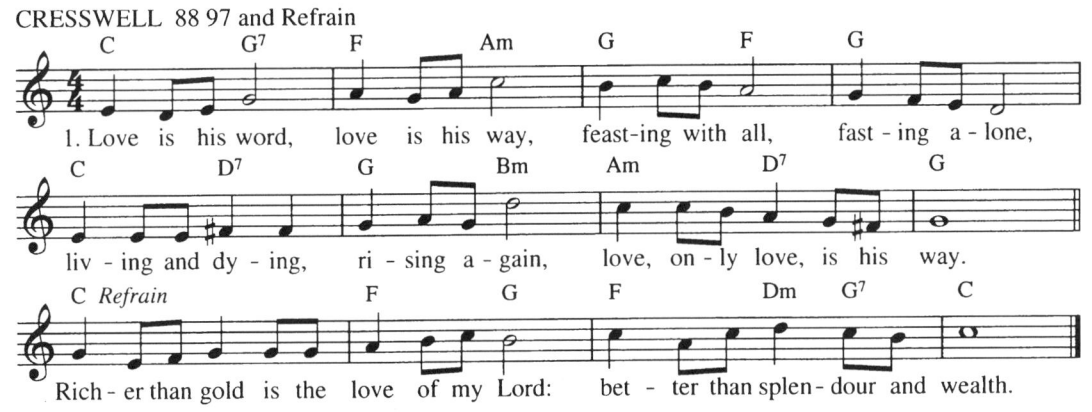

CRESSWELL 88 97 and Refrain

1. Love is his word, love is his way,
feasting with all, fasting alone,
living and dying, rising again,
love, only love, is his way.

Refrain
Richer than gold is the love of my Lord:
better than splendour and wealth.

2. Love is his way, love is his mark,
sharing his last Passover feast,
Christ at the table, host to the twelve,
love, only love, is his mark.

3. Love is his mark, love is his sign,
bread for our strength, wine for our joy,
'This is my body, this is my blood.'
Love, only love, is his sign.

4. Love is his sign, love is his news,
'Do this,' he said, 'lest you forget
all my deep sorrow, all my dear blood.'
Love, only love, is his name.

5. Love is his news, love is his name,
we are his own, chosen and called,
family, brethren, cousins and kin.
Love, only love, is his name.

6. Love is his name, love is his law,
hear his command, all who are his,
'Love one another, I have loved you.'
Love, only love, is his law.

7. Love is his law, love is his word:
love of the Lord, Father and Word,
love of the Spirit, God ever one,
love, only love, is his word.

Text: Luke Connaughton (1917-1979) alt.
Music: Anthony Milner (b.1925)

© Copyright McCrimmon Publishing Co. Ltd., 10-12 High Street, Great Wakering, Southend-on-Sea,
Essex SS3 0EQ. All rights reserved. Used by arrangement.

463 Love is patient

Refrain

Love is patient, love is always kind, love can take the roughest path and never seem to mind. Love is never boastful or jealous of the rest, love is strong and faces ev'ry test.

1. If I speak with eloquence and make the angels stare, I'm a tinkling cymbal, if love is never there. If I am a prophet and know all things to come, if I have not love, I might as well be dumb!

2. If my faith is strong,
   then I might make the mountains move,
   feed the hungry people,
   but what does all that prove?
   I can give up all things –
   possessions come and go –
   but unless there's love
   it doesn't count, I know.

3. Love goes on for evermore
   but prophecies will pass;
   tongues will cease their wagging,
   and knowledge will not last;
   for we know so little,
   the future's very dim,
   but with faith and hope,
   our love leads us to him.

Text: Sister Patrick Ignatius, based on 1 Corinthians 13
Music: Adapted from a Spiritual by Sister Patrick Ignatius
© Copyright 1978 Kevin Mayhew Ltd.

464 Love is the only law

1. Love is the only law for God and humankind,
love your God with all your heart, your strength and soul and mind.
Love your neighbour as yourself, of ev'ry creed and race,
turn the water of endless laws into the wine of grace.

Refrain
Love is God's only law, love is God's only law;
love is God's wisdom, love is God's strength, love of such height, such depth, such length, love is God's only law.

2. Give to the poor a voice
and help the blind to see,
feed the hungry, heal the sick
and set the captive free.
All that God requires of you
will then fall into place,
turn the water of endless laws
into the wine of grace.

3. Let love like fountains flow
and justice like a stream,
faith become reality
and hope your constant theme.
Then shall freedom, joy and peace
with righteousness embrace,
turn the water of endless laws
into the wine of grace.

Text: Michael Forster (b.1946)
Music: Andrew Moore (b.1954)
© Copyright 1997 Kevin Mayhew Ltd.

465 Lovely in your littleness
Jesus is our joy

Semplice, con gioia (♩ = 80)

1. Love - ly in your lit - tle - ness, long - ing for our low - li - ness,
long - ing for our low - li - ness, search - ing for our meek - ness:
Je - sus is our joy, Je - sus is our joy.

Last time
Je - sus is our joy, Je - sus is our joy.

2. Peace within our powerlessness,
hope within our helplessness,
hope within our helplessness,
love within our loneliness:
Jesus is our joy, Jesus is our joy.

3. Held in Mary's tenderness,
tiny hands are raised to bless,
tiny hands are raised to bless,
touching us with God's caress:
Jesus is our joy, Jesus is our joy.

4. Joy, then, in God's graciousness,
peace comes with gentleness,
peace comes with gentleness,
filling hearts with gladness:
Jesus is our joy, Jesus is our joy.

Text: Pamela Hayes
Music: Margaret Rizza (b.1929)
© Copyright 1998 Kevin Mayhew Ltd.

466 Loving shepherd of thy sheep

LÜBECK 77 77

1. Lov - ing shep - herd of thy sheep, keep me, Lord, in safe - ty keep;
noth - ing can thy pow'r with - stand, none can pluck me from thy hand.

2. Loving shepherd, thou didst give
thine own life that I might live;
may I love thee day by day,
gladly thy sweet will obey.

3. Loving shepherd, ever near,
teach me still thy voice to hear;
suffer not my steps to stray
from the straight and narrow way.

4. Where thou leadest may I go,
walking in thy steps below;
then, before thy Father's throne,
Jesu, claim me for thine own.

Text: Jane Elizabeth Leeson (1809-1881)
Music: from Freylinghausen's 'Gesangbuch' (1704)

467 Lumen Christi

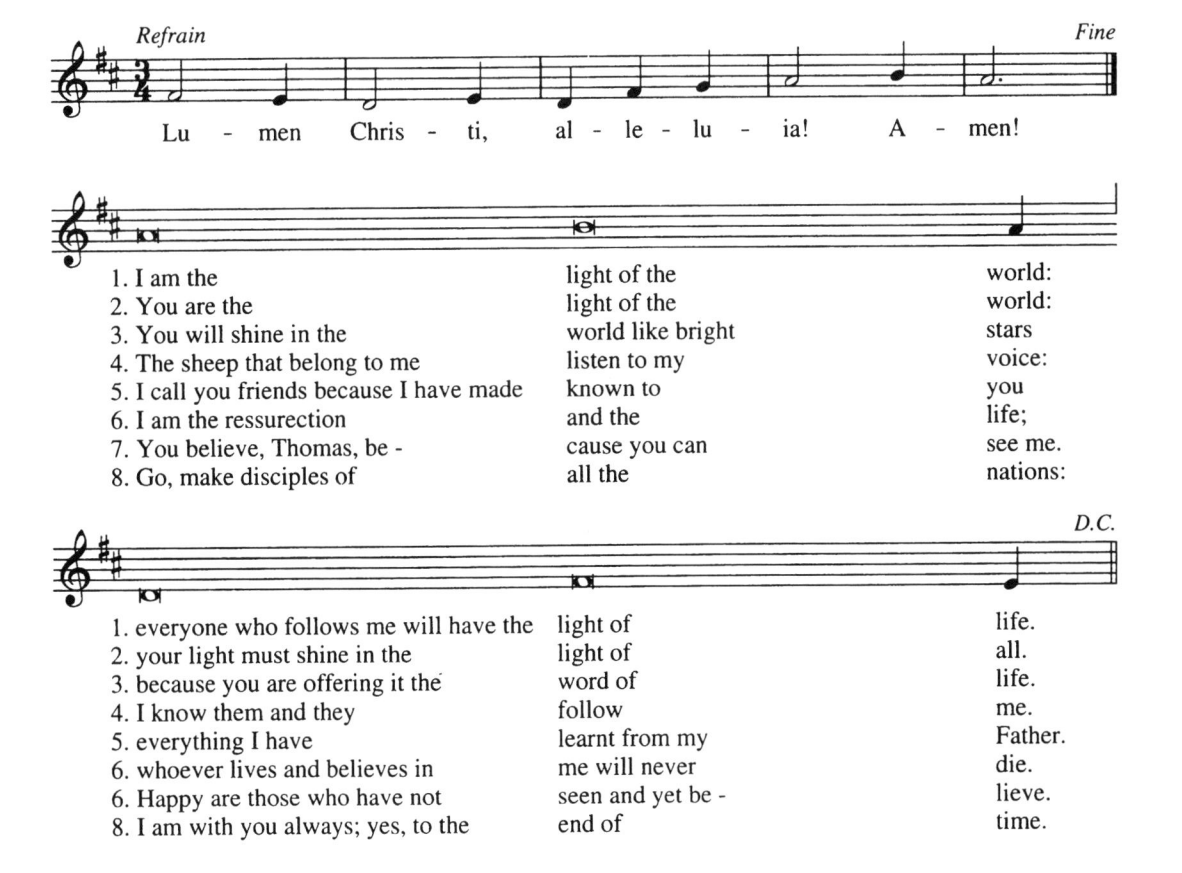

Refrain

Lu - men Chris - ti, al - le - lu - ia! A - men!

1. I am the / light of the / world:
2. You are the / light of the / world:
3. You will shine in the / world like bright / stars
4. The sheep that belong to me / listen to my / voice:
5. I call you friends because I have made / known to / you
6. I am the ressurection / and the / life;
7. You believe, Thomas, be - / cause you can / see me.
8. Go, make disciples of / all the / nations:

1. everyone who follows me will have the / light of / life.
2. your light must shine in the / light of / all.
3. because you are offering it the / word of / life.
4. I know them and they / follow / me.
5. everything I have / learnt from my / Father.
6. whoever lives and believes in / me will never / die.
6. Happy are those who have not / seen and yet be - / lieve.
8. I am with you always; yes, to the / end of / time.

Text: from the Gospel of John
Music: Jean-Paul Lécot (b.1947)
© Copyright 1988 Kevin Mayhew Ltd.

468 Maiden, yet a mother

NOEL NOUVELET 11 11 11 11

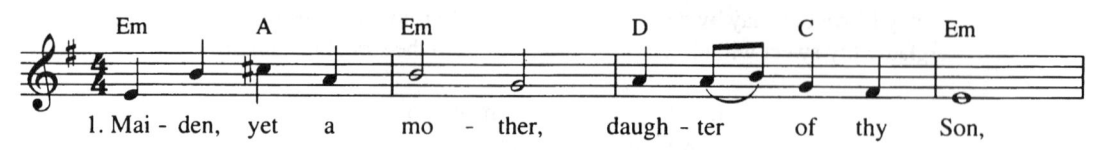

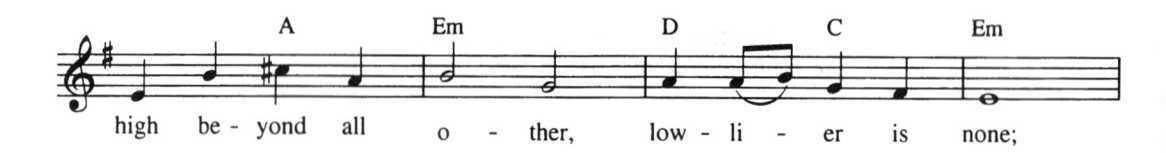

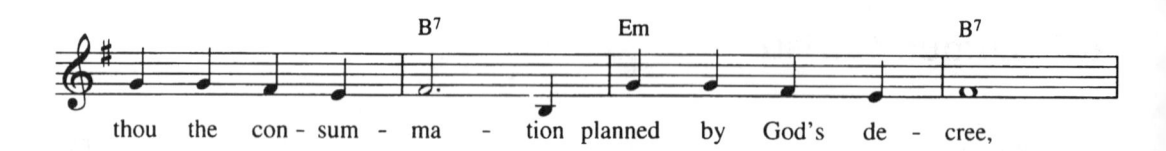

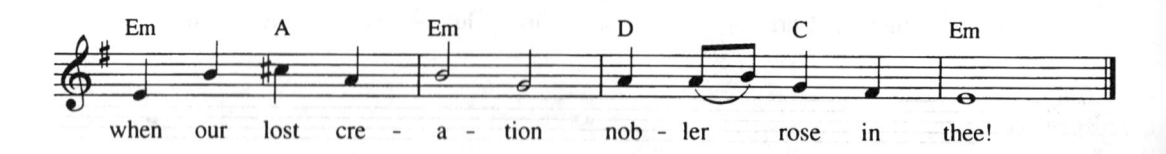

1. Mai-den, yet a mo-ther, daugh-ter of thy Son,
high be-yond all o-ther, low-li-er is none;
thou the con-sum-ma-tion planned by God's de-cree,
when our lost cre-a-tion nob-ler rose in thee!

2. Thus his place preparèd,
he who all things made
'mid his creatures tarried,
in thy bosom laid;
there his love he nourished,
warmth that gave increase
to the root whence flourished
our eternal peace.

3. Lady, lest our vision,
striving heav'nward, fail,
still let thy petition
with thy Son prevail,
unto whom all merit,
pow'r and majesty
with the Holy Spirit
and the Father be.

Text: Dante Alighieri (1265-1321) trans. Ronald Arbuthnott Knox (1888-1957)
Music: traditional French melody
Text © Copyright Burns & Oates Ltd, Wellwood, North Farm Road, Tunbridge Wells, Kent TN2 3QR.
Used by permission.

469 Majesty, worship his majesty

Majesty, worship his majesty; unto Jesus be glory, honour and praise.

Majesty, kingdom authority flow from his throne unto his own: his anthem raise. So exalt, lift up on high the name of Jesus; magnify, come glorify Christ Jesus the King.

Majesty, worship his majesty, Jesus who died, now glorified, King of all kings.

Text and Music: Jack W. Hayford (b.1934)

© Rocksmith Music Inc. Administered by Leosong Copyright Service Ltd., Independent House, 54 Larkshall Road, Chingford, London E4 6PD. Used by permission.

LITURGICAL
HYMNS OLD & NEW

470 Make me a channel of your peace

1. Make me a chan-nel of your peace. Where there is ha-tred, let me bring your love. Where there is in-ju-ry, your par-don, Lord; and where there's doubt, true faith in you.

2. Make me a chan-nel of your peace. Where there's des-pair in life, let me bring hope. Where there is dark-ness, on-ly light, and where there's sad-ness, e-ver joy.

3. O, Mas-ter, grant that I may ne-ver seek so much to be con-soled as to con-sole, to be un-der-stood as to un-der-stand, to be loved as to love with all my soul.

4. Make me a chan-nel of your peace. It is in par-don-ing that we are par-doned, in giv-ing to all that we re-ceive, and in dy-ing that we're born to e-ter-nal life.

Text: Sebastian Temple (1928-1997) based on the Prayer of St Francis
Music: Sebastian Temple (1928-1997)

© Copyright 1967 OCP Publications, 5536 NE Hassalo, Portland, OR 97213, USA.
All rights reserved. Used by permission. (Dedicated to Mrs. Frances Tracy).

471 Make way, make way

1. Make way, make way, for Christ the King in splendour arrives; fling wide the gates and welcome him into your lives.

Refrain
Make way, make way, make way, *make way*, for the King of kings; *for the King of kings;* make way, *make way*, make way, *make way*, and let his kingdom in!

2. He comes the broken hearts to heal,
   the pris'ners to free;
   the deaf shall hear, the lame shall dance,
   the blind shall see.

3. And those who mourn with heavy hearts,
   who weep and sigh,
   with laughter, joy and royal crown
   he'll beautify.

4. We call you now to worship him
   as Lord of all,
   to have no gods before him,
   their thrones must fall.

Text and Music: Graham Kendrick (b.1950)
© Copyright 1986 Kingsway's Thankyou Music, P.O. Box 75, Eastbourne,
East Sussex BN23 6NW, UK. Used by permission.

472 Mary had a baby

Mary had a baby, yes, Lord, Mary had a baby, yes, my Lord, Mary had a baby, yes, Lord, the people came to Bethlehem to see her son.

Text © Copyright 1999 Kevin Mayhew Ltd.

2. What did she name him, yes, Lord? *(x3)*
   The people came to Bethlehem to see her son.

3. Mary named him Jesus, yes, Lord. *(x3)*
   The people came to Bethlehem to see her son.

4. Where was he born, yes, Lord? *(x3)*
   The people came to Bethlehem to see her son.

5. Born in a stable, yes, Lord. *(x3)*
   The people came to Bethlehem to see her son.

6. Where did she lay him, yes, Lord? *(x3)*
   The people came to Bethlehem to see her son.

7. Laid him in a manger, yes, Lord. *(x3)*
   The people came to Bethlehem to see her son.

Text: West Indian Spiritual alt.
Music: West Indian Spiritual

473 Mary immaculate

LIEBSTER IMMANUEL 11 10 11 10

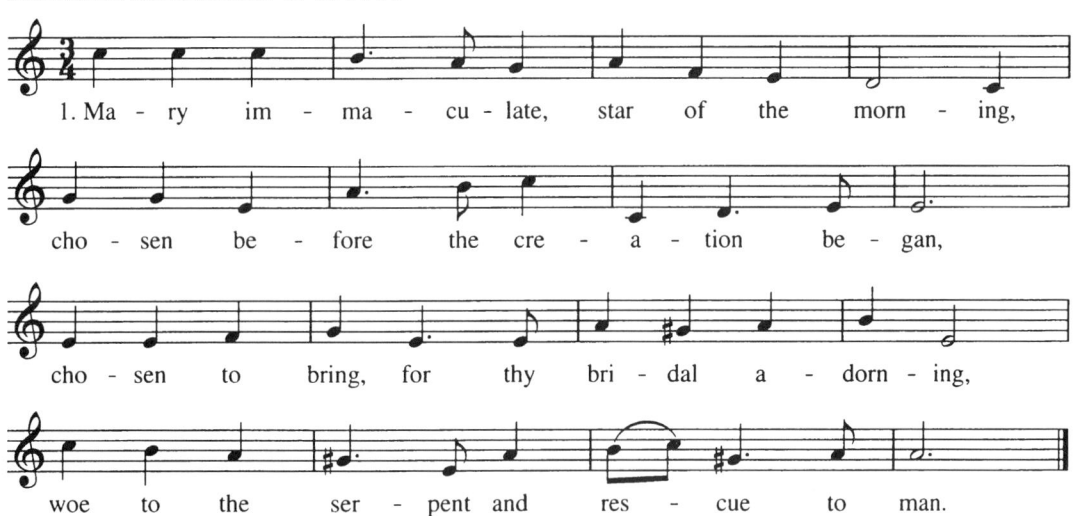

1. Mary immaculate, star of the morning,
   chosen before the creation began,
   chosen to bring, for thy bridal adorning,
   woe to the serpent and rescue to man.

2. Here, in an orbit of shadow and sadness
   veiling thy splendour, thy course thou hast run;
   now thou art throned in all glory and gladness,
   crowned by the hand of thy Saviour and Son.

3. Sinners, we worship thy sinless perfection,
   fallen and weak, for thy pity we plead;
   grant us the shield of thy sov'reign protection,
   measure thine aid by the depth of our need.

4. Frail is our nature and strict our probation,
   watchful the foe that would lure us to wrong,
   succour our souls in the hour of temptation,
   Mary immaculate, tender and strong.

5. See how the wiles of the serpent assail us,
   see how we waver and flinch in the fight;
   let thine immaculate merit avail us,
   make of our weakness a proof of thy might.

6. Bend from thy throne at the voice of our crying;
   bend to this earth which thy footsteps have trod;
   stretch out thine arms to us living and dying,
   Mary immaculate, mother of God.

Text: F. W. Weatherell
Music: melody adapted from 'Himmels-Lust', Jena (1679)

474 May you see the face of God

LUX PERPETUA 12 12 and Refrain

1. May you see the face of God, your loving Father.
May you live in joy with him whose hands once made you.
Refrain
May the light of God now shine on you for ever.

2. May you rest in Christ the Shepherd-King who feeds you.
May his peace be yours where sorrow may not enter.

3. May the flame of love, the Holy Spirit, warm you.
May he welcome you to perfect love in heaven.

Text and Music: Gregory Murray (1905-1992)
© Copyright 1999 Kevin Mayhew Ltd.

475 Meekness and majesty
This is your God

THIS IS YOUR GOD 66 65 D and Refrain

Capo 3 A

1. Meek-ness and ma-jes-ty, man-hood and de-i-ty, in per-fect har-mo-ny the Man who is God. Lord of e-ter-ni-ty dwells in hu-ma-ni-ty, kneels in hu-mi-li-ty and wash-es our feet. O what a my-ste-ry meek-ness and ma-jes-ty. Bow down and wor-ship for this is your God,

© Copyright 1986 Kingsway's Thankyou Music, P.O. Box 75, Eastbourne,
East Sussex BN23 6NW, UK. Used by permission.

this is your God.

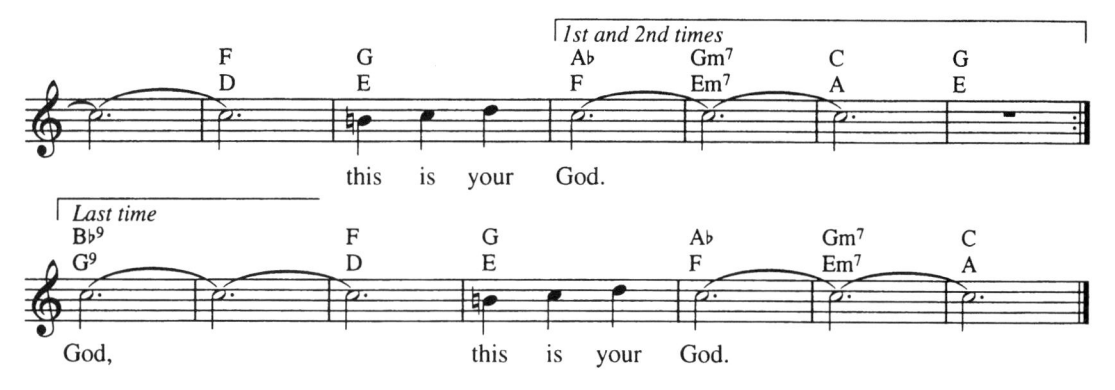

God, this is your God.

2. Father's pure radiance,
perfect in innocence,
yet learns obedience
to death on a cross.
Suff'ring to give us life,
conqu'ring through sacrifice,
and as they crucify
prays: 'Father forgive.'

3. Wisdom unsearchable,
God the invisible,
love indestructible
in frailty appears.
Lord of infinity,
stooping so tenderly,
lifts our humanity
to the heights of his throne.

Text and Music: Graham Kendrick (b.1950)

476 Morning has broken

BUNESSAN 55 54 D

1. Morning has broken like the first morning, blackbird has spoken like the first bird. Praise for the singing! Praise for the morning! Praise for them, springing fresh from the Word!

2. Sweet the rain's new fall,
sunlit from heaven,
like the first dew-fall
on the first grass.
Praise for the sweetness
of the wet garden,
sprung in completeness
where his feet pass.

3. Mine is the sunlight!
Mine is the morning
born of the one light
Eden saw play!
Praise with elation,
praise ev'ry morning,
God's re-creation
of the new day!

Text: Eleanor Farjeon (1881-1965)
Music: traditional Gaelic melody

Text © Copyright David Higham Associates, 5-8 Lower John Street, Golden Square, London W1R 4HA.
Used by permission from 'The Children's Bells', published by Oxford University Press.

477 Moses, I know you're the man

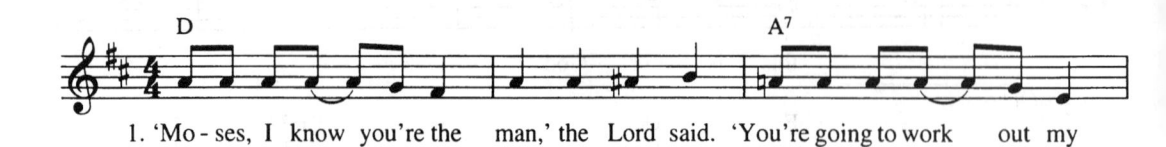

1. 'Moses, I know you're the man,' the Lord said. 'You're going to work out my plan,' the Lord said. 'Lead all the Israelites out of slavery, and I shall make them a wandering race called the people of God.'

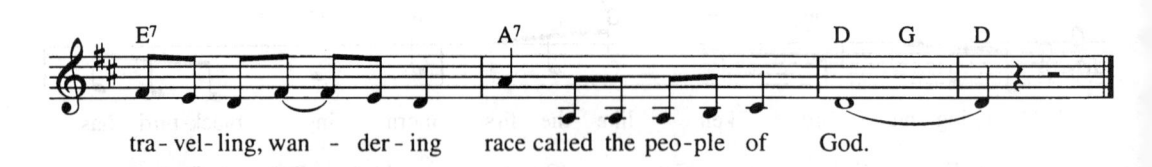

Refrain
So ev'ry day we're on our way, for we're a travelling, wandering race called the people of God.

2. 'Don't get too set in your ways,'
the Lord said.
'Each step is only a phase,'
the Lord said.
'I'll go before you and I shall be a sign
to guide my travelling, wandering race.
You're the people of God.'

3. 'No matter what you may do,'
the Lord said,
'I shall be faithful and true,'
the Lord said.
'My love will strengthen you as you go along,
for you're my travelling, wandering race.
You're the people of God.'

4. 'Look at the birds in the air,'
the Lord said.
'They fly unhampered by care,'
the Lord said.
'You will move easier if you're trav'lling light,
for you're a wandering, vagabond race.
You're the people of God.'

5. 'Foxes have places to go,'
the Lord said,
'but I've no home here below,'
the Lord said.
'So if you want to be with me all your days,
keep up the moving and travelling on.
You're the people of God.'

Text and Music: Estelle White (b.1925)

© Copyright McCrimmon Publishing Co. Ltd., 10-12 High Street, Great Wakering, Southend-on-Sea, Essex SS3 0EQ and Stainer & Bell Ltd. Used by arrangement.

478 Mother of God's living Word
ORIENTIS PARTIBUS 77 77

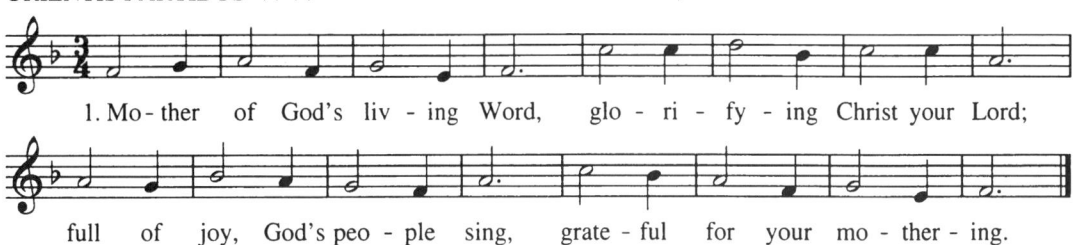

1. Mother of God's living Word,
   glorifying Christ your Lord;
   full of joy, God's people sing,
   grateful for your mothering.

2. Virgin soil, untouched by sin,
   for God's seed to flourish in;
   watered by the Spirit's dew,
   in your womb the Saviour grew.

3. Sharing his humility,
   Bethlehem and Calvary,
   with him in his bitter pain,
   now as queen with him you reign.

4. We are God's new chosen race,
   new-born children of his grace,
   citizens of heaven who
   imitate and honour you.

5. We, God's people on our way,
   travelling by night and day,
   moving to our promised land,
   walk beside you hand in hand.

6. Christ, your Son, is always near,
   so we journey without fear,
   singing as we walk along:
   Christ our joy, and Christ our song!

7. Sing aloud to Christ with joy,
   who was once a little boy.
   Sing aloud to Mary, sing,
   grateful for her mothering.

Text: Damian Lundy (1944-1997)
Music: 'L'Office de la Circoncision' attributed to Pierre de Corbeil (d.1222)
Text © Copyright 1978 Kevin Mayhew Ltd.

479 My God, accept my heart this day
BELMONT CM

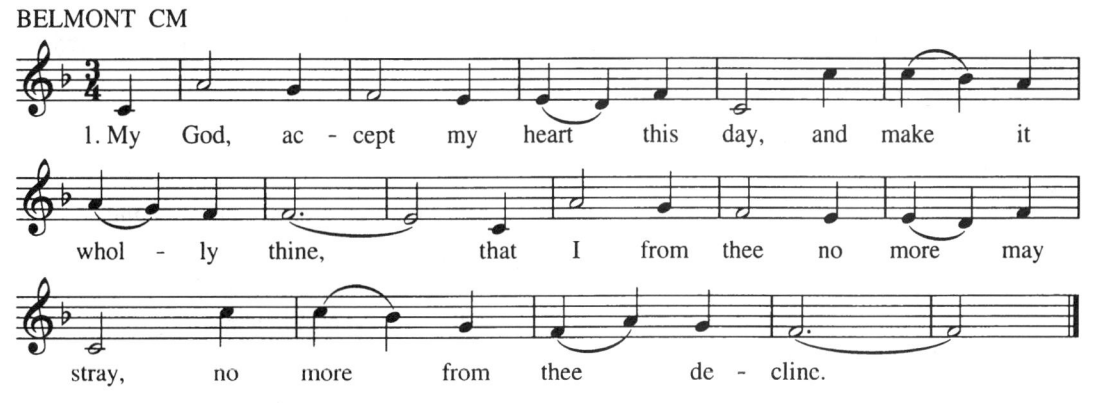

1. My God, accept my heart this day,
   and make it wholly thine,
   that I from thee no more may stray,
   no more from thee decline.

2. Before the cross of him who died,
   behold, I prostrate fall;
   let ev'ry sin be crucified,
   and Christ be all in all.

3. Anoint me with thy heav'nly grace,
   and seal me for thine own,
   that I may see thy glorious face,
   and worship at thy throne.

4. Let ev'ry thought and work and word
   to thee be ever giv'n,
   then life shall be thy service, Lord,
   and death the gate of heav'n.

5. All glory to the Father be,
   all glory to the Son,
   all glory, Holy Ghost, to thee,
   while endless ages run.

Text: Matthew Bridges (1800-1894)
Music: adapted from William Gardiner's 'Sacred Melodies' (1812)

480 My God, and is thy table spread
ROCKINGHAM LM *A higher setting will be found at No. 731*

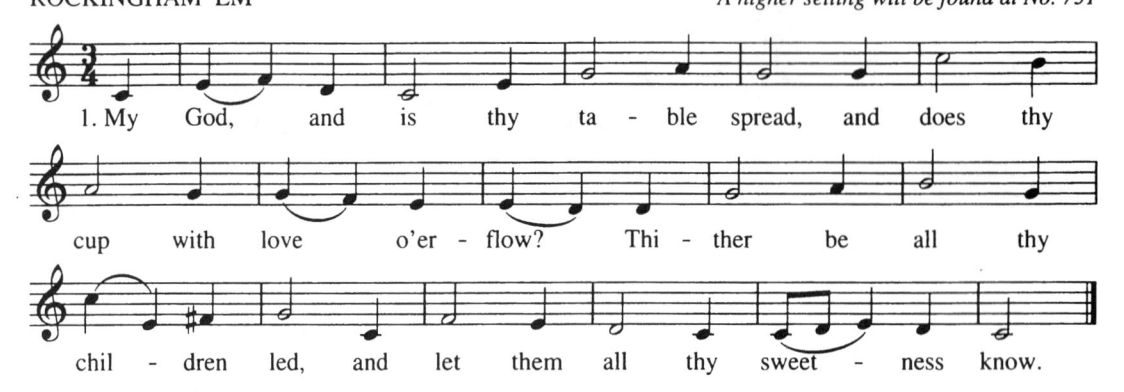

1. My God, and is thy table spread, and does thy cup with love o'er-flow? Thither be all thy children led, and let them all thy sweetness know.

2. Hail, sacred feast, which Jesus makes!
   Rich banquet of his flesh and blood!
   Thrice happy all, who here partake
   that sacred stream, that heav'nly food.

3. What wondrous love! What perfect grace,
   for Jesus, our exalted host,
   invites us to this special place
   who offer least and need the most.

4. O let thy table honoured be,
   and furnished well with joyful guests:
   and may each soul salvation see,
   that here its sacred pledges tastes.

Text: Philip Doddridge (1702-1751) alt., v. 3: Michael Forster (b.1946)
Music: from A. Williams' 'Second supplement to Psalmody in Miniature' (c.1780)
adapted by Edward Miller (1735-1807)
This version of text © Copyright 1996 Kevin Mayhew Ltd.

481 My God, how wonderful you are
WESTMINSTER CM

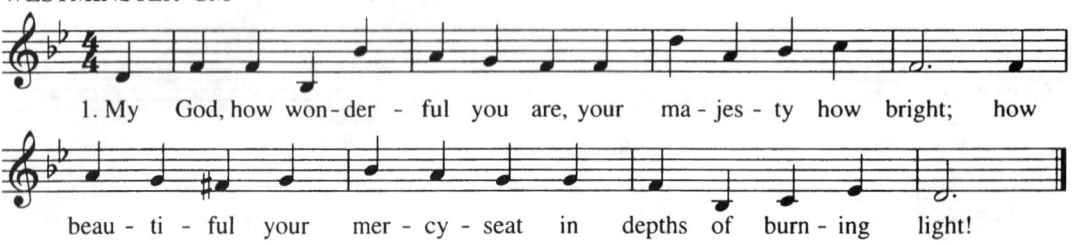

1. My God, how wonderful you are, your majesty how bright; how beautiful your mercy-seat in depths of burning light!

2. Creator from eternal years
   and everlasting Lord,
   by holy angels day and night
   unceasingly adored!

3. How wonderful, how beautiful
   the sight of you must be –
   your endless wisdom, boundless pow'r,
   and awesome purity!

4. O how I fear you, living God,
   with deepest, tenderest fears,
   and worship you with trembling hope
   and penitential tears!

5. But I may love you too, O Lord,
   though you are all-divine,
   for you have stooped to ask of me
   this feeble love of mine.

6. Father of Jesus, love's reward,
   great King upon your throne,
   what joy to see you as you are
   and know as I am known!

Text: Frederick William Faber (1814-1863) alt.
Music: James Turle (1802-1882)
This version of text © Copyright Jubilate Hymns, 4 Thorne Park Road,
Chelston, Torquay TQ2 6RX. Used by permission.

482 My God, my God, why have you forsaken me?

My God, my God, why have you for-sa-ken me?

1. Peo-ple who see me are scorn-ful, sneer-ing at me, and tos-sing their heads, 'His trust was in God, let God save him, come to the aid of his own spe-cial friend!'

2. Dogs have surrounded me, howling;
criminal gangs approach and attack.
My hands and my feet they are tearing,
all of my bones can be easily seen.

3. They have divided my clothing,
gambling with straws or dice for my robe.
Please, God, do not leave me forsaken,
hasten to help me, O God of my strength.

4. I will proclaim to my people;
your name, O Lord, they worship and praise.
All children of Jacob, give glory,
children of Israel, come worship your God.

Text: Susan Sayers (b.1946) based on Psalm 21
Music: Andrew Moore (b.1954)
© Copyright 1995 Kevin Mayhew Ltd.

483 My God said to me, 'Follow!'

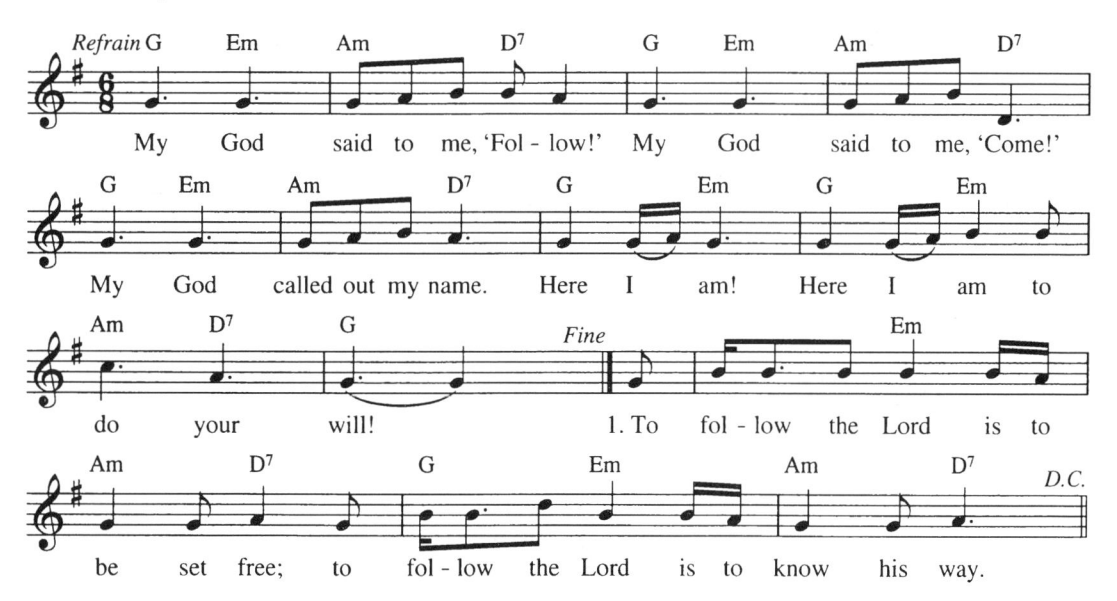

My God said to me, 'Fol-low!' My God said to me, 'Come!' My God called out my name. Here I am! Here I am to do your will! 1. To fol-low the Lord is to be set free; to fol-low the Lord is to know his way.

2. To live with the Lord is to live in love;
to live with the Lord is to live in peace.

Text and Music: Louis Welker
© Copyright 1982 Kevin Mayhew Ltd.

484 My heart will sing to you
Great love

1. My heart will sing to you be-cause of your great love,
a love so rich, so pure, a love be-yond com-pare;
the wil-der-ness, the bar-ren place,
be-come a bles-sing in the warmth of your em-brace.

Refrain
May my heart sing your praise for e-ver,
may my voice lift your name, my God;
may my soul know no o-ther trea-sure than your love,
than your love.

2. When earthly wisdom dims the light of knowing you,
or if my search for understanding clouds your way,
to you I fly, my hiding-place,
where revelation is beholding face to face.

Text and Music: Robin Mark
© Copyright 1996 Daybreak Music Ltd, Silverdale Road,
Eastbourne, East Sussex BN20 7AB, UK. Used by permission.

485 My people, what have I done to you?

Refrain

My people, what have I done to you? How have I hurt you? Answer me.

1. I led you out of Egypt, I set you free, I set you free. I led you through the desert, and yet you turn away from me.

2. I fed you in the desert,
   I led you through the raging sea.
   I gave you saving water,
   and yet you found a cross for me.

3. I gave you a royal sceptre;
   you offered me a crown of thorns.
   I raised you as a nation;
   you mocked and treated me with scorn.

Text: Francesca Leftley (b.1955) based on the Good Friday Reproaches
Music: Francesca Leftley (b.1955)
© 1984 Kevin Mayhew Ltd.

486 My shepherd is the Lord

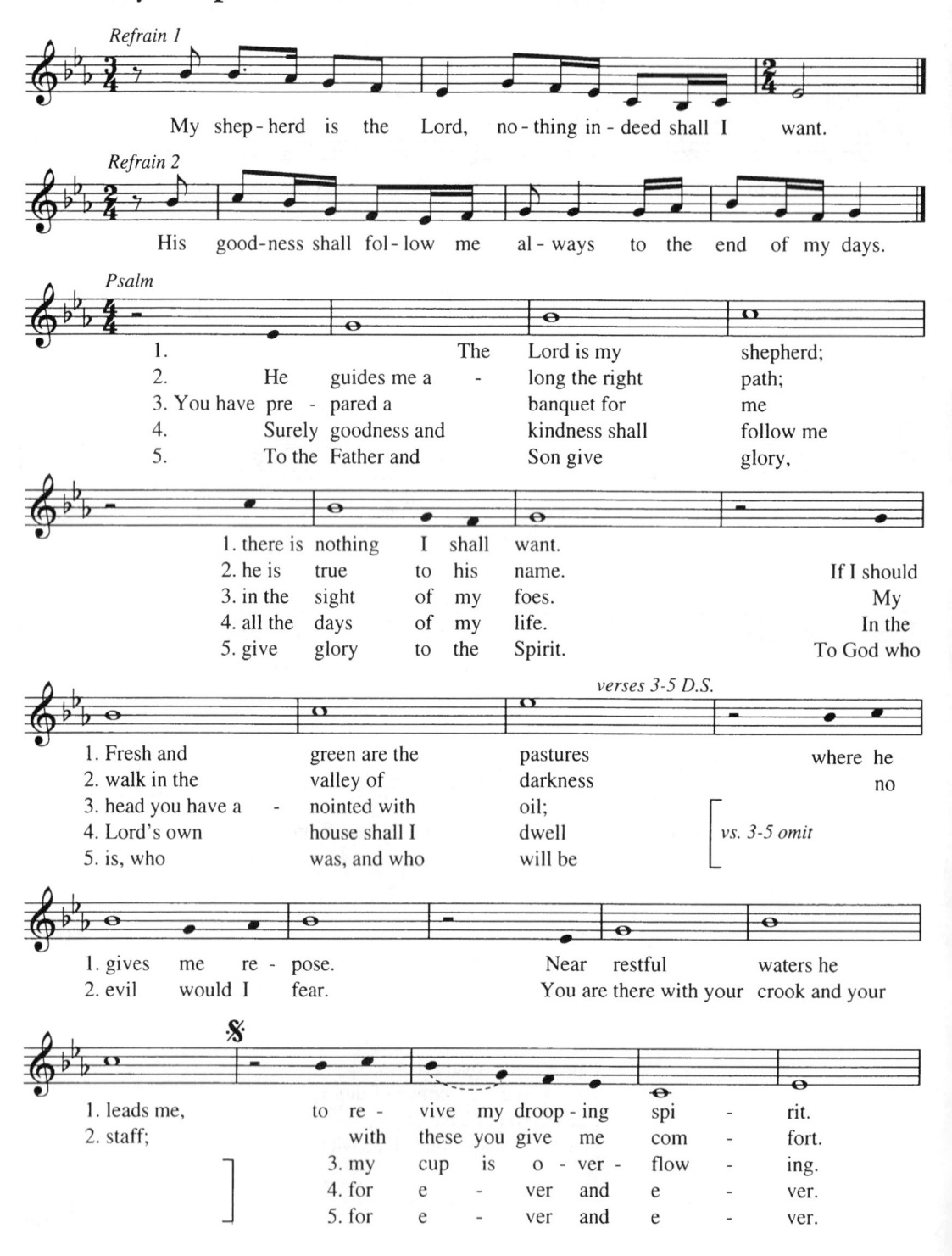

Refrain 1
My shep-herd is the Lord, no-thing in-deed shall I want.

Refrain 2
His good-ness shall fol-low me al-ways to the end of my days.

Psalm

1. The Lord is my shepherd;
2. He guides me a-long the right path;
3. You have pre-pared a banquet for me
4. Surely goodness and kindness shall follow me
5. To the Father and Son give glory,

1. there is nothing I shall want.
2. he is true to his name. If I should
3. in the sight of my foes. My
4. all the days of my life. In the
5. give glory to the Spirit. To God who

verses 3-5 D.S.

1. Fresh and green are the pastures where he
2. walk in the valley of darkness no
3. head you have a-nointed with oil;
4. Lord's own house shall I dwell   [vs. 3-5 omit
5. is, who was, and who will be

1. gives me re-pose.   Near restful waters he
2. evil would I fear.   You are there with your crook and your

1. leads me, to re-vive my droop-ing spi - rit.
2. staff;   with these you give me com - fort.
3. my cup is o - ver - flow - ing.
4. for e - ver and e - ver.
5. for e - ver and e - ver.

Text: Psalm 22, Grail translation
Music: Psalm and Response 1 – Joseph Gelineau (b.1920)
Response 2 – Gregory Murray (1905-1992)

Text and response 1 © Copyright 1963, 1986, 1993 The Grail, England.
Used by permission of A.P. Watt Ltd, 20 John Street, London WC1N 2DR, UK.
Response 2 © 1984 Kevin Mayhew Ltd.

487 My song is love unknown

LOVE UNKNOWN 66 66 44 44

1. My song is love unknown, my Saviour's love to me, love to the loveless shown, that they might lovely be. O who am I, that for my sake, my Lord should take frail flesh and die?

2. He came from his blest throne,
   salvation to bestow;
   but sin made blind, and none
   the longed-for Christ would know.
   But O, my friend, my friend indeed,
   who at my need his life did spend!

3. Sometimes they strew his way,
   and his sweet praises sing;
   resounding all the day
   hosannas to their King;
   then 'Crucify'! is all their breath,
   and for his death they thirst and cry.

4. Why, what hath my Lord done?
   What makes this rage and spite?
   He made the lame to run,
   he gave the blind their sight.
   Sweet injuries! Yet they at these
   themselves displease, and 'gainst him rise.

5. They rise, and needs will have
   my dear Lord made away;
   a murderer they save,
   the Prince of Life they slay.
   Yet cheerful he to suff'ring goes,
   that he his foes from thence might free.

6. Here might I stay and sing,
   no story so divine;
   never was love, dear King,
   never was grief like thine.
   This is my friend in whose sweet praise
   I all my days could gladly spend.

Text: Samuel Crossman (c.1624-1684) alt.
Music: John Ireland (1879-1962)

Music © Copyright The John Ireland Trust, 35 St Mary's Mansions, St Mary's Terrace, London W2 1SQ, UK.
Used by permission.

488 My soul doth magnify the Lord

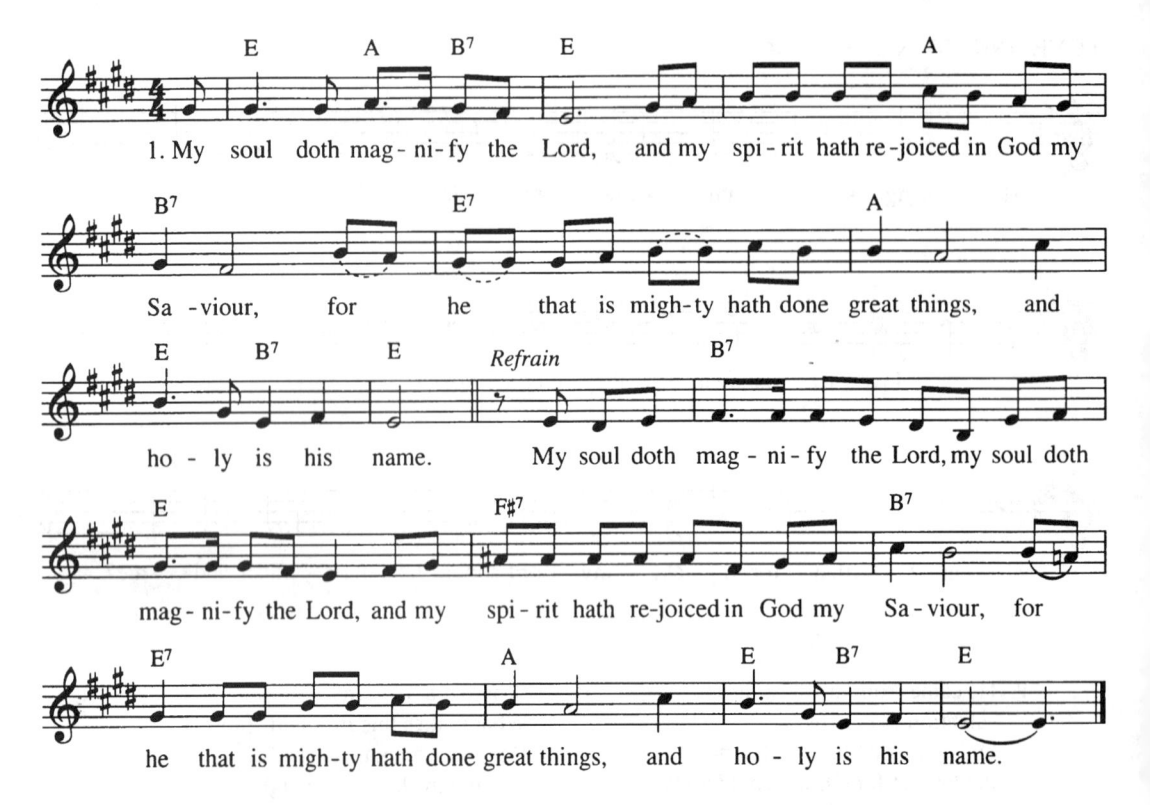

1. My soul doth magnify the Lord, and my spirit hath rejoiced in God my Saviour, for he that is mighty hath done great things, and holy is his name.

Refrain
My soul doth magnify the Lord, my soul doth magnify the Lord, and my spirit hath rejoiced in God my Saviour, for he that is mighty hath done great things, and holy is his name.

2. From age to age he shows his love,
and his mercy is for ever to his servants,
for he stretches out his arm,
casts down the mighty,
and raises up the meek.

3. He fills the hungry with good food.
When the rich demand their share,
their hands are empty.
He has kept all his promises to Israel:
his mercy is made known.

4. To God the Father we sing praise,
and to Jesus, whom he sent to be our Saviour!
To the Spirit of God be all glory,
for holy is his name!

Text: v.1 unknown based on Luke 1:46-55; vs.2-4 Damian Lundy (1944-1997)
Music: unknown
Text © Copyright 1987, 1999 Kevin Mayhew Ltd.

489 My soul is filled with joy

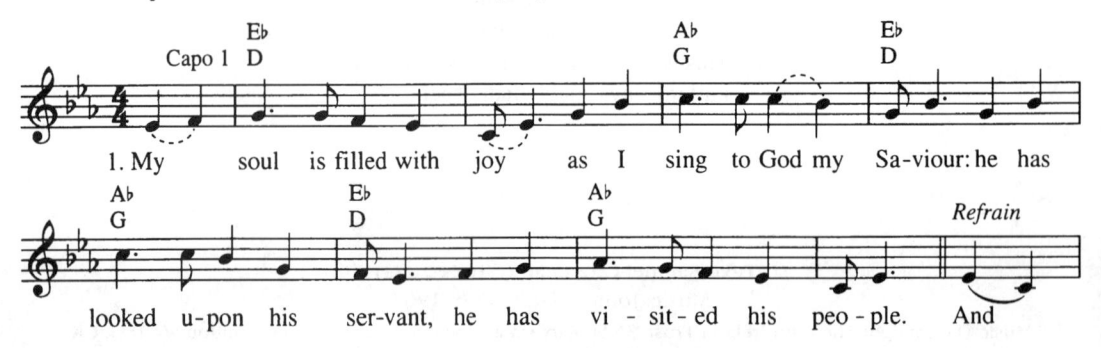

1. My soul is filled with joy as I sing to God my Saviour: he has looked upon his servant, he has visited his people. And

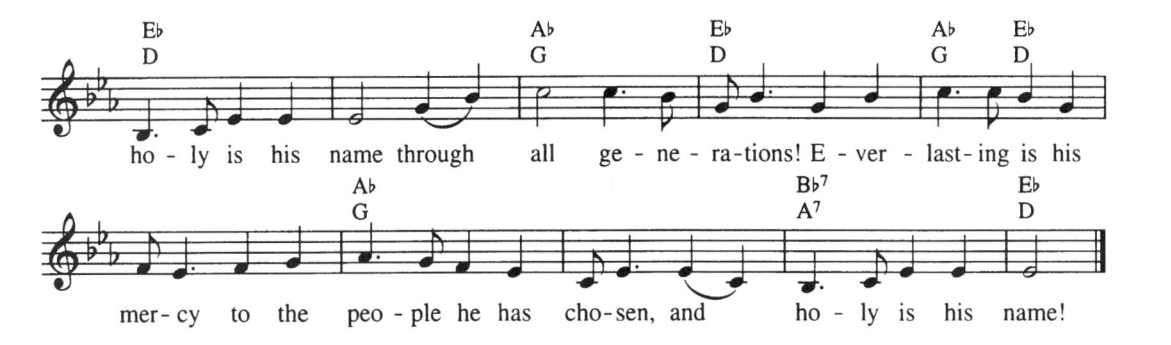

holy is his name through all generations! Everlasting is his
mercy to the people he has chosen, and holy is his name!

2. I am lowly as a child,
but I know from this day forward
that my name will be remembered
and the world will call me blessèd.

3. I proclaim the pow'r of God!
He does marvels for his servants;
though he scatters the proud-hearted
and destroys the might of princes.

4. To the hungry he gives food,
sends the rich away empty.
In his mercy he is mindful
of the people he has chosen.

5. In his love he now fulfills
what he promised to our fathers.
I will praise the Lord, my Saviour.
Everlasting is his mercy.

Text: unknown based on Luke 1:46-55
Music: Scottish Folk melody

490 My soul is longing for your peace

My soul is longing for your peace, near to you, my God.

1. Lord, you know that my heart is not proud and my eyes are not lifted from the earth.

2. Lofty thoughts have never filled my mind,
far beyond my sight all ambitious deeds.

3. In your peace I have maintained my soul,
I have kept my heart in your quiet peace.

4. As a child rests on a mother's knee,
so I place my soul in your loving care.

5. Israel, put all your hope in God,
place your trust in him, now and evermore.

Text: Lucien Deiss (b.1921) based on Psalm 130
Music: Lucien Deiss (b.1921)
© Copyright 1965 World Library Publications, a division of J.S. Paluch Co. Inc.,
3825 N. Willow Road, Schiller Park, Illinois 60176-9936, USA.
All rights reserved. Used by permission.

491 My soul proclaims you, mighty God

AMAZING GRACE CM

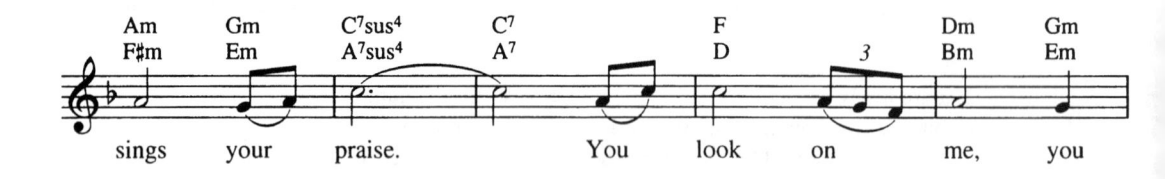

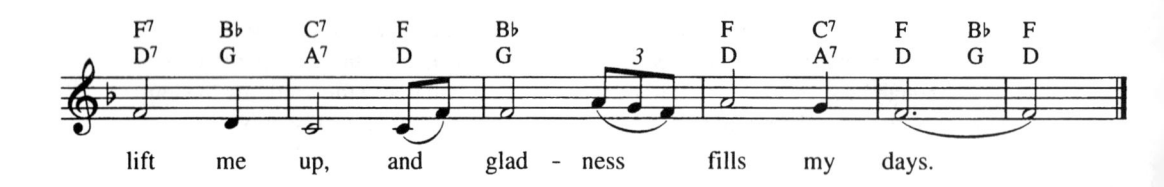

1. My soul proclaims you, mighty God.
My spirit sings your praise.
You look on me, you lift me up,
and gladness fills my days.

2. All nations now will share my joy;
your gifts you have outpoured.
Your little one you have made great;
I magnify my God.

3. For those who love your holy name,
your mercy will not die.
Your strong right arm puts down the proud
and lifts the lowly high.

4. You fill the hungry with good things,
the rich you send away.
The promise made to Abraham
is filled to endless day.

5. Magnificat, magnificat,
magnificat, praise God!
Praise God, praise God, praise God, praise God,
magnificat, praise God!

Text: Anne Carter (1944-1993) based on Luke 1:46-55
Music: American folk melody
Text © Copyright 1988 Society of the Sacred Heart, 4389 West Pine Blvd., St. Louis, Missouri 63198, USA.
Used by permission.

492 New daytime dawning

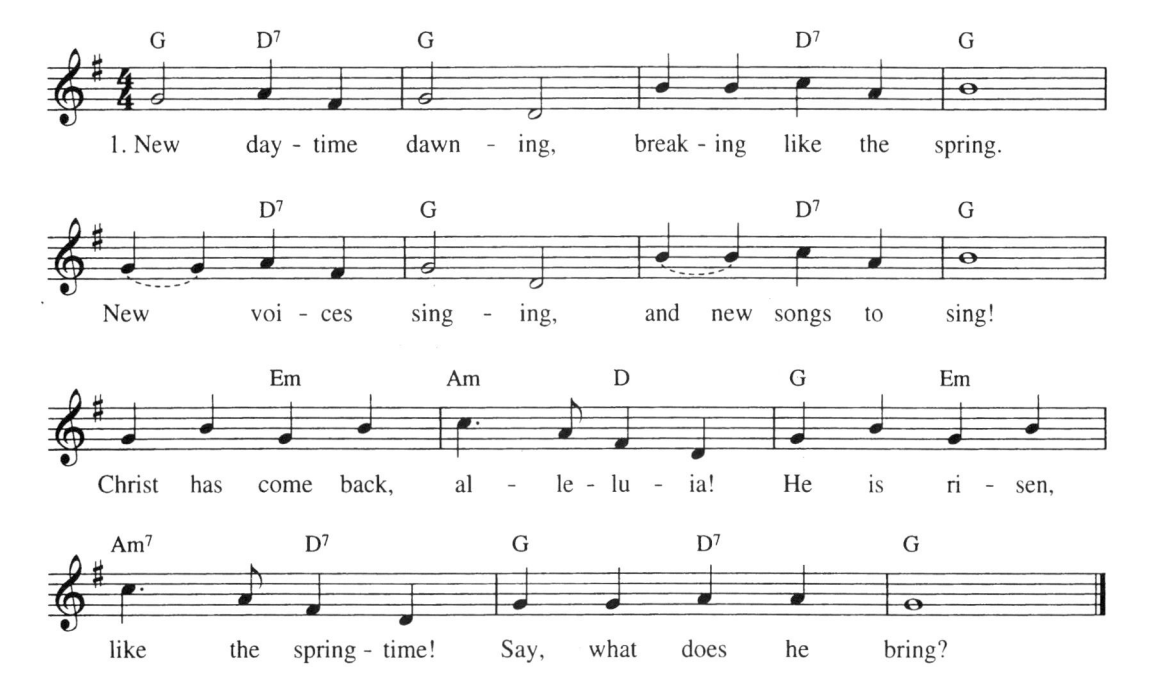

1. New daytime dawning, breaking like the spring.
   New voices singing, and new songs to sing!
   Christ has come back, alleluia! He is risen,
   like the springtime! Say, what does he bring?

2. Death in the tree tops!
   Jesus cried with pain,
   hanging in the branches. Now he lives again!
   For the tree of death has flowered,
   life has filled the furthest branches!
   Sunlight follows rain.

3. The man of sorrows,
   sleeping in his tomb,
   the man of sorrows, he is coming home.
   He is coming like the springtime.
   Suddenly you'll hear him talking,
   you will see him come.

4. Say, are you hungry?
   Come and eat today!
   Come to the table, nothing to pay!
   Take your place, the meal is waiting.
   Come and share the birthday party,
   and the holiday.

5. Look where the garden
   door is open wide!
   Come to the garden, there's no need to hide.
   God has broken down the fences
   and he stands with arms wide open.
   Come along inside!

Text: Damian Lundy (1944-1997) based on a French poem
Music: traditional Polish melody
Text © Copyright 1978, 1994 Kevin Mayhew Ltd.

493 New praises be given

ST DENIO 11 11 11 11

1. New praises be given to Christ newly crowned, who
back to his heaven a new way hath found;
God's blessedness sharing before us he goes,
what mansions preparing, what endless repose!

2. His glory still praising on thrice holy ground,
th'apostles stood gazing, his mother around;
with hearts that beat faster, with eyes full of love,
they watched while their master ascended above.

3. 'No star can disclose him,' the bright angels said;
'eternity knows him, your conquering head;
those high habitations, he leaves not again,
till, judging all nations, on earth he shall reign.'

4. Thus spoke they and straightway, where legions defend
heav'n's glittering gateway, their Lord they attend,
and cry, looking thither, 'Your portals let down
for him who rides hither in peace and renown.'

5. They asked, who keep sentry in that blessèd town,
'Who thus claimeth entry, a king of renown?'
'The Lord of all valiance,' that herald replied,
'who Satan's battalions laid low in their pride.'

6. Grant, Lord, that our longing may follow thee there,
on earth who are thronging thy temples with prayer;
and unto thee gather, Redeemer, thine own,
where thou with thy Father dost sit on the throne.

Text: 'Hymnum canamus gloria' by the Venerable Bede (673-735)
trans. Ronald Arbuthnott Knox (1888-1957)
Music: Welsh melody from John Roberts' 'Caniadau y Cyssegr' (1839)
Text © Copyright Burns and Oates Ltd, Wellwood, North Farm Road,
Tunbridge Wells, Kent TN2 3QR. Used by permission.

494 Nothing shall separate us

Refrain

No - thing shall se - pa - rate us from the love of God.

No - thing shall se - pa - rate us from the love of God. God.

1. God did not spare his on - ly Son, gave him to save us all.
Sin's price was met by Je - sus' death and hea - ven's mer - cy falls.

2. Up from the grave Jesus was raised
to sit at God's right hand;
pleading our cause in heaven's courts,
forgiven we can stand.

3. Now by God's grace we have embraced
a life set free from sin;
we shall deny all that destroys
our union with him.

Text and Music: Noel and Tricia Richards
© Copyright 1989 Kingsway's Thankyou Music, P.O. Box 75, Eastbourne,
East Sussex BN23 6NW, UK. Used by permission.

495 Now as the evening shadows fall

TUNE 1: TE LUCIS LM

1. Now as the evening shadows fall, God our Creator, hear our call:
help us to trust your constant grace, though darkness seems to hide your face.

2. Help us to find, in sleep's release,
bodily rest and inner peace;
so may the darkness of the night
refresh our eyes for morning light.

3. Father almighty, holy Son,
Spirit eternal, Three in One,
grant us the faith that sets us free
to praise you for eternity.

TUNE 2: BLACKHEATH LM

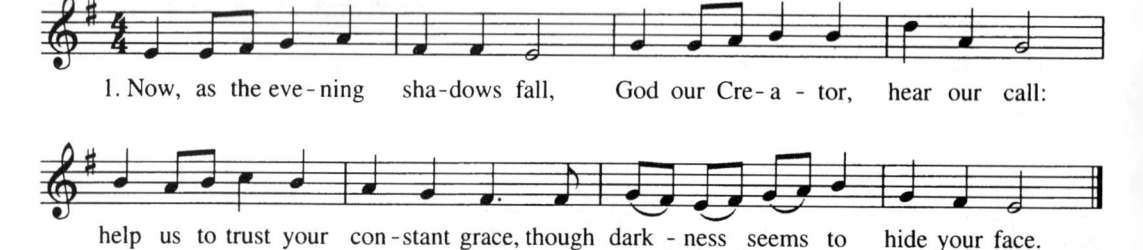

1. Now, as the evening shadows fall, God our Creator, hear our call:
help us to trust your constant grace, though darkness seems to hide your face.

Text: Michael Forster (b.1946) based on 'Te lucis ante terminum'
Music: Tune 1 – Plainsong
Tune 2 – Anthony Milner (b.1928)
Text © Copyright 1999 Kevin Mayhew Ltd.
Tune 2 © Copyright 1958, 1979 Anthony Milner. Used by permission.

496 Now I know what love is

Refrain Bb / Capo 3 G

Now I know what love is, now I know your Spirit is here,
living deep within me, now I know love is real.

© Copyright 1999 Kevin Mayhew Ltd.

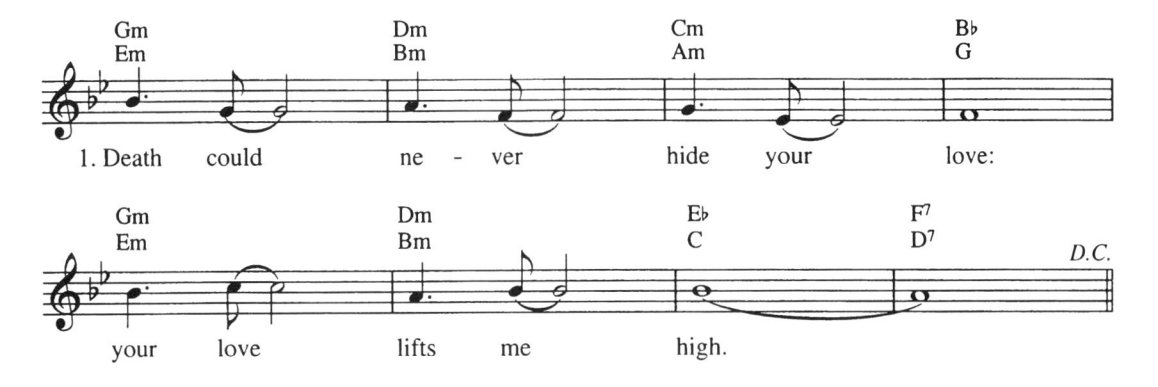

1. Death could never hide your love:
your love lifts me high.

2. Darkness will not hide your love,
shining like a star.

3. What could ever quench your love,
love that changes hearts.

Text and Music: Mike Anderson (b.1956)

497 Now thank we all our God

NUN DANKET 67 67 66 66

1. Now thank we all our God, with hearts and hands and voices, who wondrous things hath done, in whom his world rejoices; who from our mother's arms hath blessed us on our way with countless gifts of love, and still is ours today.

A lower setting will be found at No. 586

2. O may this bounteous God
through all our life be near us,
with ever joyful hearts
and blessèd peace to cheer us;
and keep us in his grace,
and guide us when perplexed,
and free us from all ills
in this world and the next.

3. All praise and thanks to God
the Father now be given,
the Son and him who reigns
with them in highest heaven,
the one eternal God,
whom earth and heav'n adore;
for thus it was, is now,
and shall be evermore.

Text: 'Nun danket alle Gott' by Martin Rinkart (1586-1649) trans. Catherine Winkworth (1827-1878)
Music: melody by Johann Crüger (1598-1662); harmony by William Henry Monk (1823-1889)

498 Now the green blade riseth

NOEL NOUVELET 11 11 10 11

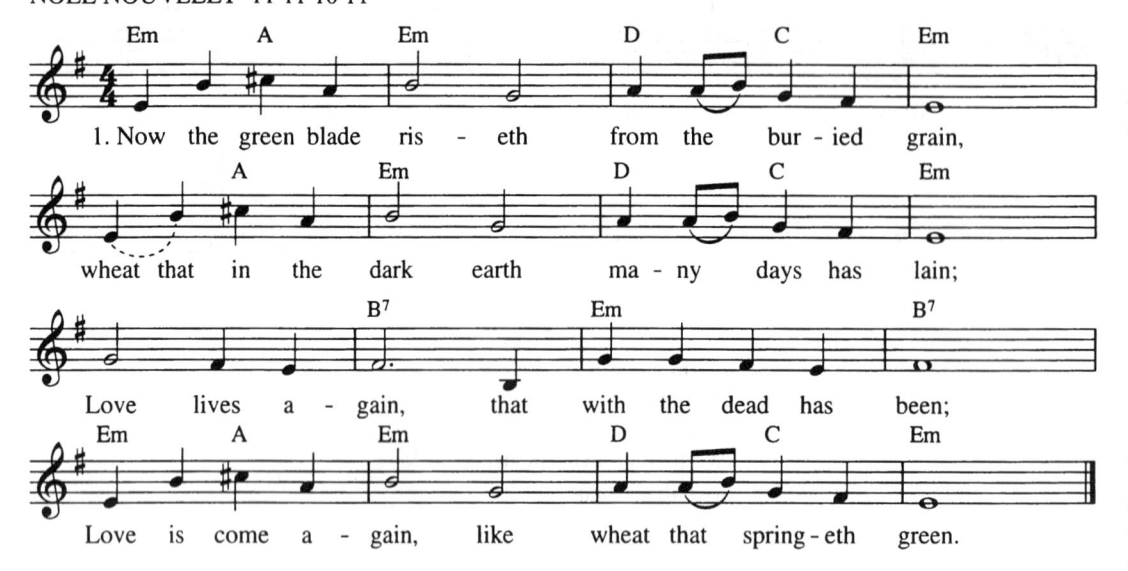

1. Now the green blade riseth from the buried grain,
wheat that in the dark earth many days has lain;
Love lives again, that with the dead has been;
Love is come again, like wheat that springeth green.

2. In the grave they laid him, Love by hatred slain,
thinking that never he would wake again,
laid in the earth like grain that sleeps unseen:
Love is come again, like wheat that springeth green.

3. Forth he came at Easter, like the risen grain,
he that for three days in the grave had lain;
quick from the dead, my risen Lord is seen:
Love is come again, like wheat that springeth green.

4. When our hearts are wintry, grieving or in pain,
thy touch can call us back to life again;
fields of our hearts, that dead and bare have been:
Love is come again, like wheat that springeth green.

Text: John Macleod Campbell Crum (1872-1958) alt.
Music: traditional French melody
Text © Copyright 1928 Oxford University Press, Great Clarendon Street, Oxford OX2 6DP.
Used by permission from 'The Oxford Book of Carols.'

499 Now with the fast-departing light

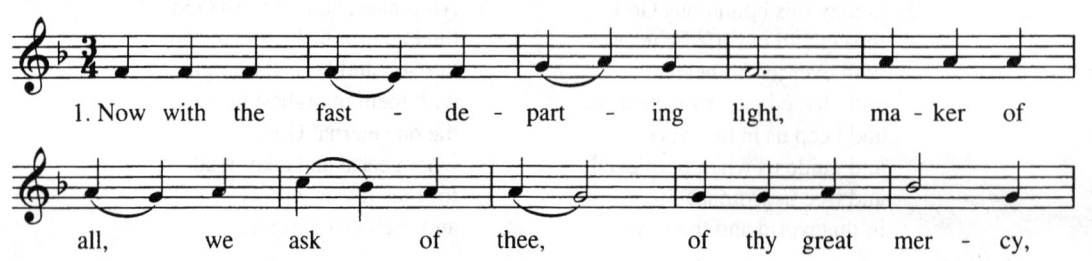

GROSSER GOTT LM

1. Now with the fast-departing light, maker of
all, we ask of thee, of thy great mercy,

through the night our guardian and defence to be.

2. Far off let idle visions fly,
no phantom of the night molest;
curb thou our raging enemy,
that we in chaste repose may rest.

3. Father of mercies, hear our cry,
hear us, O sole-begotten Son
who, with the Holy Ghost most high,
reignest while endless ages run.

Text: 'Te lucis ante terminum' trans. Edward Caswall (1814-1878)
Music: from 'Katholisches Gesangbuch' (c.1774)

500 O bread of heaven

ST CATHERINE (TYNEMOUTH) 88 88 88

1. O bread of heav'n beneath this veil thou dost my very God conceal; my Jesus, dearest treasure, hail; I love thee and adoring kneel; each loving soul by thee is fed with thine own self in form of bread.

2. O food of life, thou who dost give
the pledge of immortality;
I live; no, 'tis not I that live;
God gives me life, God lives in me:
he feeds my soul, he guides my ways,
and ev'ry grief with joy repays.

3. O bond of love, that dost unite
the servant to his living Lord;
could I dare live, and not requite
such love – then death were meet reward:
I cannot live unless to prove
some love for such unmeasured love.

4. Beloved Lord in heav'n above,
there, Jesus, thou awaitest me;
to gaze on thee with changeless love,
yes, thus I hope, thus shall it be:
for how can he deny me heav'n
who here on earth himself hath giv'n?

Text: St Alphonsus (1696-1787) trans. Edmund Vaughan (1827-1908)
Music: Henri Friedrich Hémy (1818-1888)

501 O come, all ye faithful

ADESTE FIDELES Irregular and Refrain

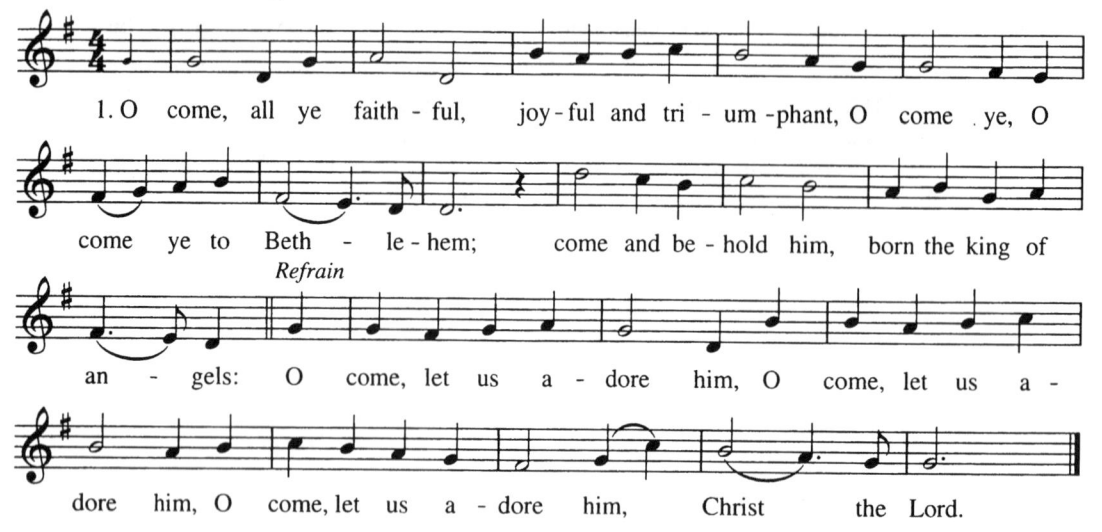

1. O come, all ye faithful, joyful and triumphant, O come ye, O come ye to Bethlehem; come and behold him, born the king of angels: O come, let us adore him, O come, let us adore him, O come, let us adore him, Christ the Lord.

A lower setting will be found at No. 100

2. God of God,
Light of Light,
lo, he abhors not the Virgin's womb;
very God, begotten not created:

3. Sing, choirs of angels,
sing in exultation,
sing, all ye citizens of heav'n above;
glory to God in the highest:

4. Yea, Lord, we greet thee,
born this happy morning,
Jesu, to thee be glory giv'n;
Word of the Father, now in flesh appearing:

Text: original Latin attributed to John Francis Wade (1711-1786)
trans. Frederick Oakeley (1802-1880)
Music: attributed to John Francis Wade (1711-1786)

502 O come and mourn with me awhile

OLD HALL GREEN 888 and Refrain

1. O come and mourn with me awhile; see, Mary calls us to her side; O come and let us mourn with her; Jesus our love, Jesus our love, is crucified.

This version of text © Copyright 1999 Kevin Mayhew Ltd.

2. Have we no tears to shed for him
while soldiers scoff and people sneer?
Ah, look how patiently he hangs!

3. How fast his feet and hands are nailed,
his blessèd tongue with thirst is tied;
his failing eyes are blind with blood;

4. Sev'n times he spoke, sev'n words of love,
and all three hours his silence cried
for mercy on poor human souls.

5. O break, O break, hard heart of mine:
thy weak self-love and guilty pride
his Pilate and his Judas were:

6. A broken heart, a fount of tears,
ask, and they will not be denied;
a broken heart, love's cradle is;

7. O love of God! O mortal sin!
In this dread act your strength is tried;
and victory remains with love;

Text: Frederick William Faber (1814-1863) alt. the Editors
Music: J. Crookall (1821-1887)

503 O come, O come, Emmanuel

VENI EMMANUEL LM and Refrain

1. O come, O come, Emmanuel, and ransom captive Israel, that mourns in lonely exile here, until the Son of God appear. Rejoice, rejoice! Emmanuel shall come to thee, O Israel.

2. O come, thou rod of Jesse, free
thine own from Satan's tyranny;
from depths of hell thy people save,
and give them vic'try o'er the grave.

3. O come, thou dayspring, come and cheer
our spirits by thine advent here;
disperse the gloomy clouds of night,
and death's dark shadows put to flight.

4. O come, thou key of David, come
and open wide our heav'nly home;
make safe the way that leads on high,
and close the path to misery.

5. O come, O come, thou Lord of might,
who to thy tribes on Sinai's height
in ancient times didst give the Law,
in cloud and majesty and awe.

Text: from the 'Great O Antiphons' (12th-13th century) trans. John Mason Neale (1818-1866)
Music: adapted by Thomas Helmore (1811-1890) from a French Missal

504 O, come to the water

FELSHAM 86 96 and Refrain

O, come to the water, all you who are thirsty, and drink, drink deeply. Though you don't have a penny and your clothes are in rags, you'll be welcome to drink all you can.

1. Come, take your choice of wine and milk: ev-'ry-thing here is free! Why spend your money on worthless food: ev-'ry-thing here is free!

2. Now, listen well and you will find
   food that will feed your soul.
   Just come to me to receive your share,
   food that will feed your soul.

3. I promise you good things to come;
   you are my chosen ones.
   I name you witnesses to my world;
   you are my chosen ones.

Text: Kevin Mayhew (b.1942) based on Isaiah 55:1-4
Music: Kevin Mayhew (b.1942)
© Copyright 1984 Kevin Mayhew Ltd.

505 O comfort my people
COMFORT 11 11 11 11

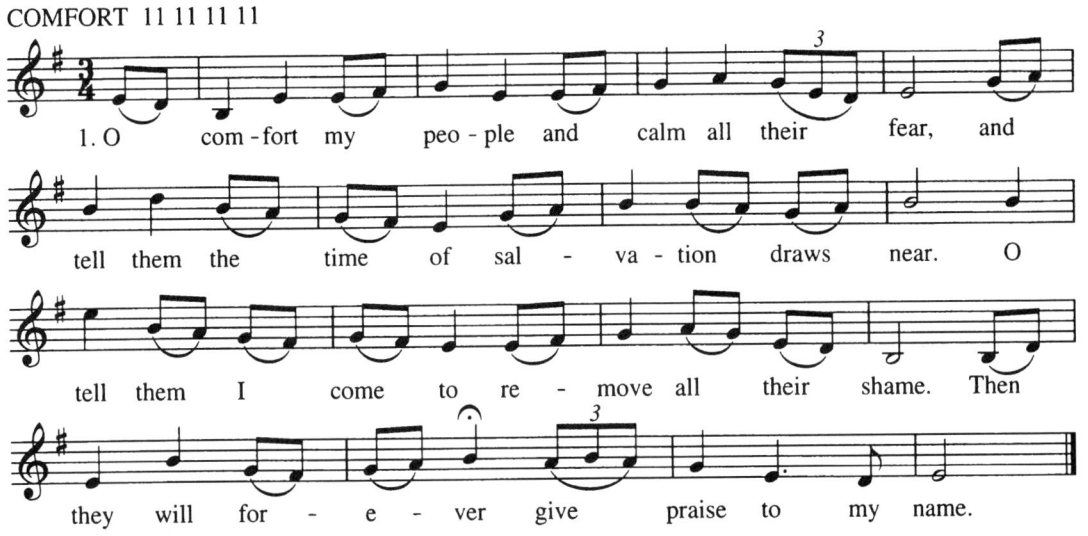

1. O comfort my people and calm all their fear,
and tell them the time of salvation draws near.
O tell them I come to remove all their shame.
Then they will for ever give praise to my name.

2. Proclaim to the cities
of Judah my word;
that 'gentle yet strong is
the hand of the Lord.
I rescue the captives,
my people defend,
and bring them to justice
and joy without end.'

3. 'All mountains and hills
shall become as a plain,
for vanished are mourning
and hunger and pain.
And never again shall
these war against you.
Behold, I come quickly
to make all things new.'

Text: Chrysogonus Waddell based on Isaiah 40
Music: Irish traditional melody
Text © Copyright Chysogonus Waddell

506 O food of travellers
EISENACH LM

1. O food of trav-'llers, angels' bread,
manna wherewith the blest are fed,
come nigh, and with thy sweetness fill
the hungry hearts that seek thee still.

2. O fount of love, O well unpriced,
outpouring from the heart of Christ,
give us to drink of very thee,
and all we pray shall answered be.

3. O Jesus Christ, we pray to thee
that this thy presence which we see,
though now in form of bread concealed,
to us may be in heav'n revealed.

Text: 'O esca viatorum' from 'Maintzisch Gesangbuch' (1661) trans. Walter H. Shewring and others
Music: melody by Johann Hermann Schein (1586-1630)
harmonised by Johann Sebastian Bach (1685-1750)

507 O fountain of life

Guitar tacet

O fountain of life and infinite grace, unaltered by time, unhindered by space. Immortal wellspring of holiness and peace; eternal, infinite love without cease.

1. Preserve and keep me all my days,
   in good intent and faithful ways.
   And lead me to such holiness
   as mortal pray'rs cannot express.

2. Lord, lead me out and guide me in.
   Protect me both from fear and sin.
   Enfold me in your constant love,
   with grace abundant from above.

3. Be there to guide me when I speak.
   To strengthen when my love is weak:
   be there to calm my final breath,
   and light the way to life through death.

Text: Michael Forster (b.1946)
Music: Margaret Rizza (b.1929)
© Copyright 1997 Kevin Mayhew Ltd.

508 Of the Father's love begotten

CORDE NATUS (DIVINUM MYSTERIUM) 87 87 87 7

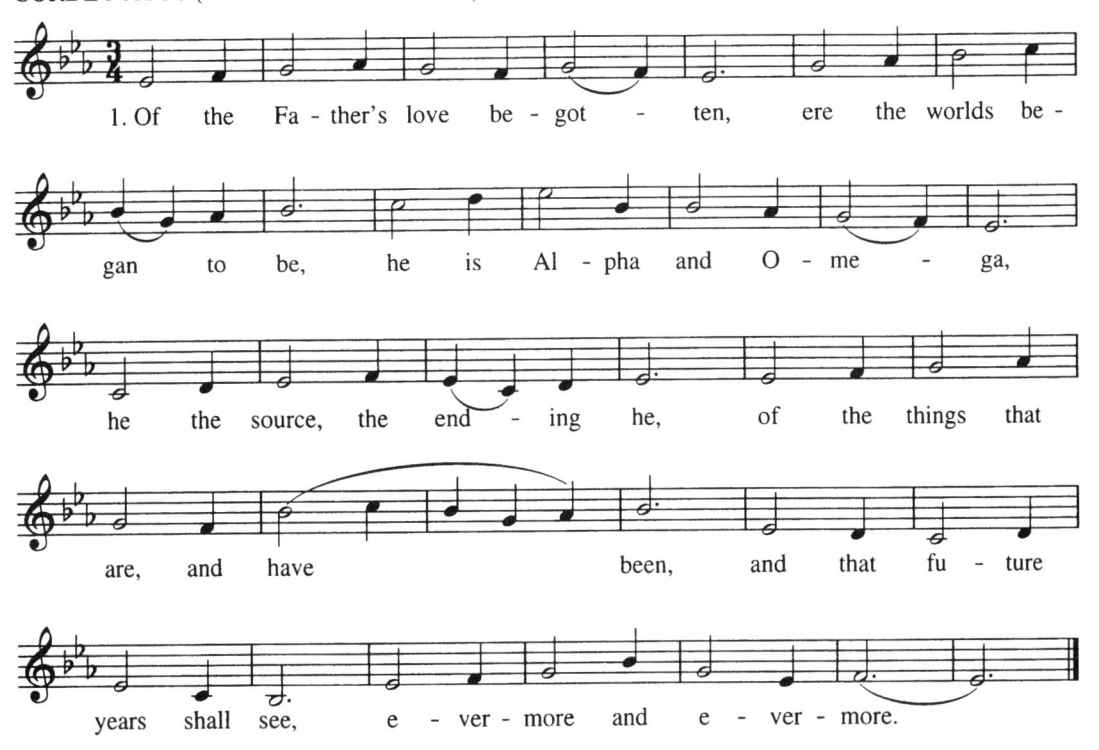

1. Of the Father's love begotten, ere the worlds began to be, he is Alpha and Omega, he the source, the ending he, of the things that are, and have been, and that future years shall see, evermore and evermore.

2. At his word they were created;
he commanded; it was done:
heav'n and earth and depths of ocean
in their threefold order one;
all that grows beneath the shining
of the light of moon and sun,
evermore and evermore.

3. O that birth for ever blessèd,
when the Virgin, full of grace,
by the Holy Ghost conceiving,
bore the Saviour of our race,
and the babe, the world's Redeemer,
first revealed his sacred face,
evermore and evermore.

4. O ye heights of heav'n, adore him;
angel hosts, his praises sing;
pow'rs, dominions, bow before him,
and extol our God and King:
let no tongue on earth be silent,
ev'ry voice in concert ring,
evermore and evermore.

5. This is he whom seers and sages
sang of old with one accord;
whom the writings of the prophets
promised in their faithful word;
now he shines, the long-expected:
let our songs declare his worth,
evermore and evermore.

6. Christ, to thee, with God the Father,
and, O Holy Ghost, to thee,
hymn and chant and high thanksgiving,
and unwearied praises be;
honour, glory, and dominion,
and eternal victory,
evermore and evermore.

Text: 'Corde natus ex parentis' by Aurelius Clemens Prudentius (348-413)
trans. John Mason Neale (1818-1866) alt.
Music: Plainsong melody (13th century) adapted by Theodoricus Petrus in 'Piae Cantiones' (1582)

509 Of the glorious body telling

ST THOMAS 87 87 87

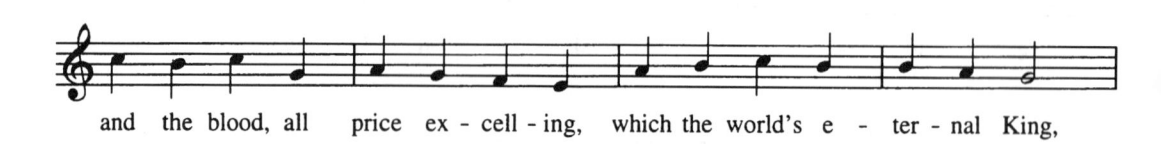

1. Of the glorious body telling,
O my tongue, its myst-'ries sing,
and the blood, all price excelling,
which the world's eternal King,
in a noble womb once dwelling,
shed for this world's ransoming.

A higher setting will be found at No. 443

2. Giv'n for us, for us descending,
of a virgin to proceed,
he with us in converse blending,
scattered he the gospel seed,
till his sojourn drew to ending,
which he closed in wondrous deed.

3. At the last great supper lying,
circled by his brethren's band,
meekly with the law complying,
first he finished its command.
Then, immortal food supplying,
gave himself with his own hand.

4. Word made flesh, by word is making
very bread his flesh to be;
we, in wine, Christ's blood partaking,
and if senses fail to see,
faith alone the true heart waking,
to behold the mystery.

5. Therefore, we before him bending,
this great sacrament revere;
types and shadows have their ending,
for the newer rite is here;
faith, our outward sense befriending,
makes the inward vision clear.

6. Glory let us give, and blessing,
to the Father and the Son,
honour, might and praise addressing,
while eternal ages run;
ever too his love confessing,
who from both, with both is one.

Text: St Thomas Aquinas (1227-1274) trans. John Mason Neale (1818-1866) alt.
Music: Samuel Webbe (1740-1816)

510 O God beyond all praising

THAXTED 13 13 13 13 13 13

1. O God beyond all praising, we worship you today, and
sing the love amazing that songs cannot repay; for
we can only wonder at ev'ry gift you send, at
blessings without number and mercies without end: we
lift our hearts before you and wait upon your word, we
honour and adore you, our great and mighty Lord.

2. Then hear, O gracious Saviour,
accept the love we bring,
that we who know your favour
may serve you as our King;
and whether our tomorrows
be filled with good or ill,
we'll triumph through our sorrows
and rise to bless you still:
to marvel at your beauty
and glory in your ways,
and make a joyful duty
our sacrifice of praise.

Text: Michael Perry (1942-1996)
Music: Gustav Holst (1874-1934)

Text © Copyright Mrs. B. Perry Jubilate Hymns, 4 Thorne Park Road, Chelston, Torquay TQ2 6RX. Used by permission.
Music © Copyright control.

511 O Godhead hid

AQUINAS 11 11 11 11

1. O Godhead hid, devoutly I adore thee, who truly
art within the forms before me; to thee my heart I
bow with bended knee, as failing quite in contemplating thee.

2. Sight, touch and taste in thee are each deceived,
the ear alone most safely is believed:
I believe all the Son of God has spoken;
than Truth's own word there is no truer token.

3. God only on the cross lay hid from view;
but here lies hid at once the manhood too;
and I, in both professing my belief,
make the same prayer as the repentant thief.

4. Thy wounds, as Thomas saw, I do not see;
yet thee confess my Lord and God to be;
make me believe thee ever more and more,
in thee my hope, in thee my love to store.

5. O thou memorial of our Lord's own dying!
O bread that living art and vivifying!
Make ever thou my soul on thee to live;
ever a taste of heav'nly sweetness give.

6. O loving Pelican! O Jesus, Lord!
Unclean I am, but cleanse me in thy blood,
of which a single drop, for sinners spilt,
is ransom for a world's entire guilt.

7. Jesus, whom for the present veiled I see,
what I so thirst for, O, vouchsafe to me:
that I may see thy countenance unfolding,
and may be blest thy glory in beholding.

Text: 'Adoro te devote,' ascribed to St Thomas Aquinas (1227-1274) trans. Edward Caswall (1814-1878)
Music: Richard Runciman Terry (1865-1938)
Music © Copyright control.

512 O God of earth and altar

TUNE 1: KING'S LYNN 76 76 D

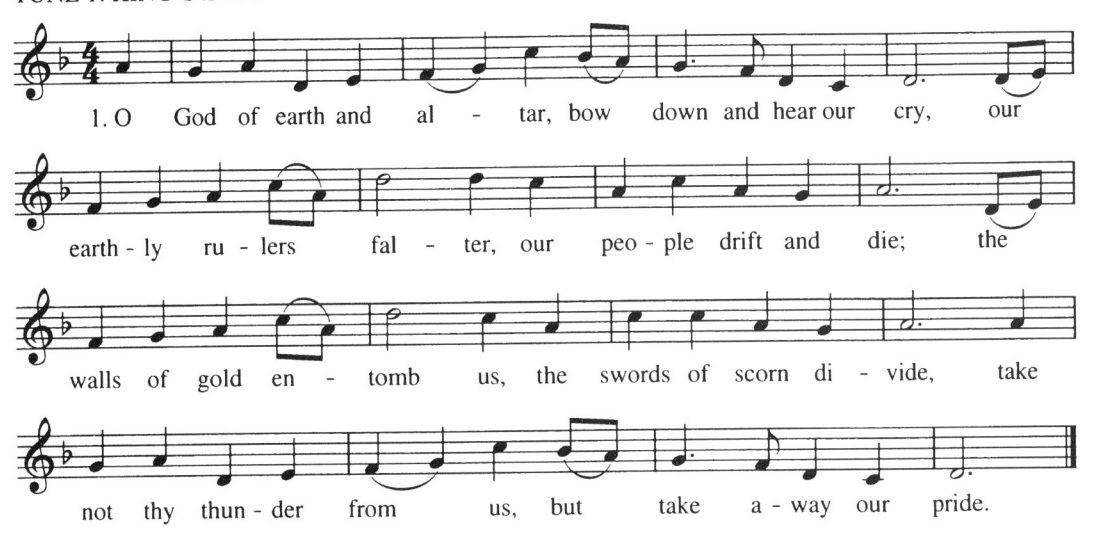

1. O God of earth and altar, bow down and hear our cry, our earthly rulers falter, our people drift and die; the walls of gold entomb us, the swords of scorn divide, take not thy thunder from us, but take away our pride.

2. From all that terror teaches,
from lies of tongue and pen,
from all the easy speeches
that comfort cruel men,
from sale and profanation
of honour and the sword,
from sleep and from damnation,
deliver us, good Lord!

3. Tie in a living tether
the prince and priest and thrall,
bind all our lives together,
smite us and save us all;
in ire and exultation
aflame with faith and free,
lift up a living nation,
a single sword to thee.

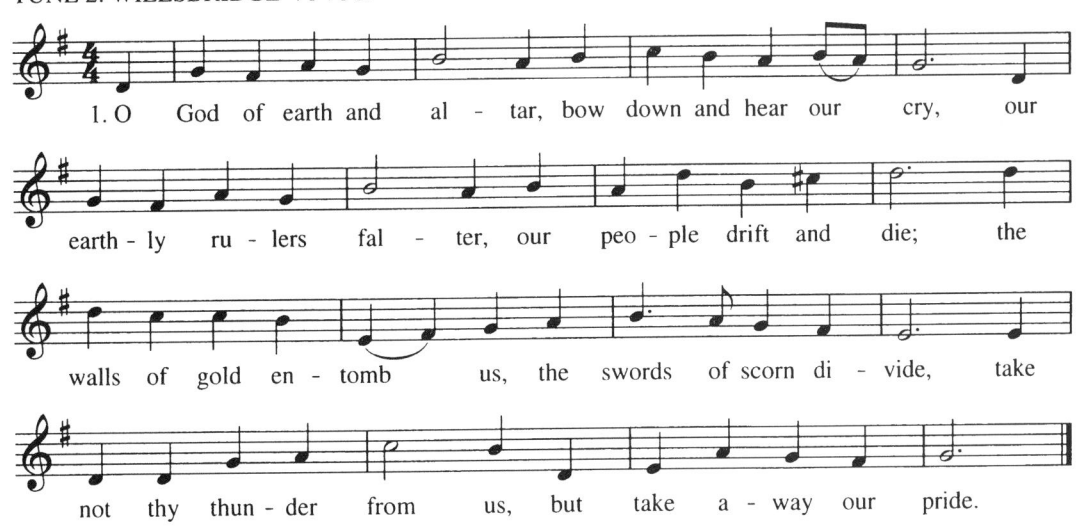

TUNE 2: WILLSBRIDGE 76 76 D

1. O God of earth and altar, bow down and hear our cry, our earthly rulers falter, our people drift and die; the walls of gold entomb us, the swords of scorn divide, take not thy thunder from us, but take away our pride.

Text: Gilbert Keith Chesterton (1874-1936)
Music: Tune 1– traditional English melody collected Ralph Vaughan Williams (1872-1958)
Tune 2– Robert Lucas de Pearsall (1795-1856)
Text © Copyright control.
Tune 1 © Copyright Oxford University Press, Great Clarendon Street, Oxford OX2 6DP.
Used by permission from the 'English Hymnal.'

LITURGICAL
HYMNS OLD & NEW

513 O God of grace, we thank you

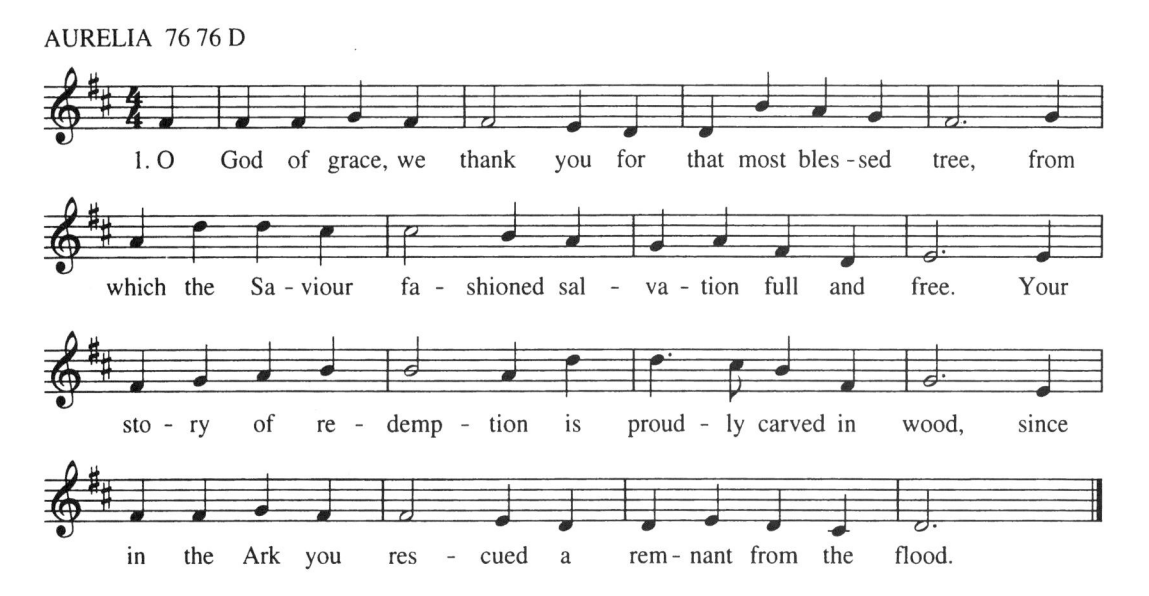

AURELIA 76 76 D

1. O God of grace, we thank you for that most blessed tree, from which the Saviour fashioned salvation full and free. Your story of redemption is proudly carved in wood, since in the Ark you rescued a remnant from the flood.

A lower setting will be found at No. 521

2. The bush that lit the desert –
   'though burned, yet not consumed –
   became the seed of promise
   from which salvation bloomed.
   The light of life eternal
   still shines with hope and joy,
   from him whom hell's inferno
   could burn but not destroy.

3. The staff which Moses carried,
   as shepherd of your choice,
   is lifted high to rally
   the sheep who know your voice.
   From farthest bounds, you call us,
   as people of the cross,
   to find eternal value
   in your most bitter loss.

4. Christ is the vine eternal,
   producing wholesome fruit;
   the rod that brings salvation,
   the branch from Jesse's root.
   In crib and crucifixion,
   in boats upon the sea,
   the Saviour's earthly journey
   is shadowed by the tree.

5. This tree of life gives knowledge
   of love that conquers all,
   the fruits of goodness ripen,
   and evil's strongholds fall.
   It sprang from this creation
   of which we all are made,
   and where, by sign and symbol,
   your purpose is displayed.

6. The log which, in the desert,
   made bitter water sweet,
   transforms the foulest hatred,
   and renders hope complete;
   for in its awesome presence
   all earthly glory pales:
   the Carpenter is reigning,
   enthroned on wood and nails.

Text: Michael Forster (b.1946)
Music: Samuel Sebastian Wesley (1810-1876)
Text © Copyright 1996 Kevin Mayhew Ltd.

514 O God, our help in ages past

ST ANNE CM

1. O God, our help in ages past, our hope for years to come, our shelter from the stormy blast, and our eternal home.

2. Beneath the shadow of thy throne,
   thy saints have dwelt secure;
   sufficient is thine arm alone,
   and our defence is sure.

3. Before the hills in order stood,
   or earth received her frame,
   from everlasting thou art God,
   to endless years the same.

4. A thousand ages in thy sight
   are like an evening gone;
   short as the watch that ends the night
   before the rising sun.

5. Time, like an ever-rolling stream,
   will bear us all away;
   we fade and vanish, as a dream
   dies at the op'ning day.

6. O God, our help in ages past,
   our hope for years to come,
   be thou our guard while troubles last,
   and our eternal home.

Text: Isaac Watts (1674-1748) alt.
Music: William Croft (1678-1727)

515 O God, please listen
In the shadow of your wings

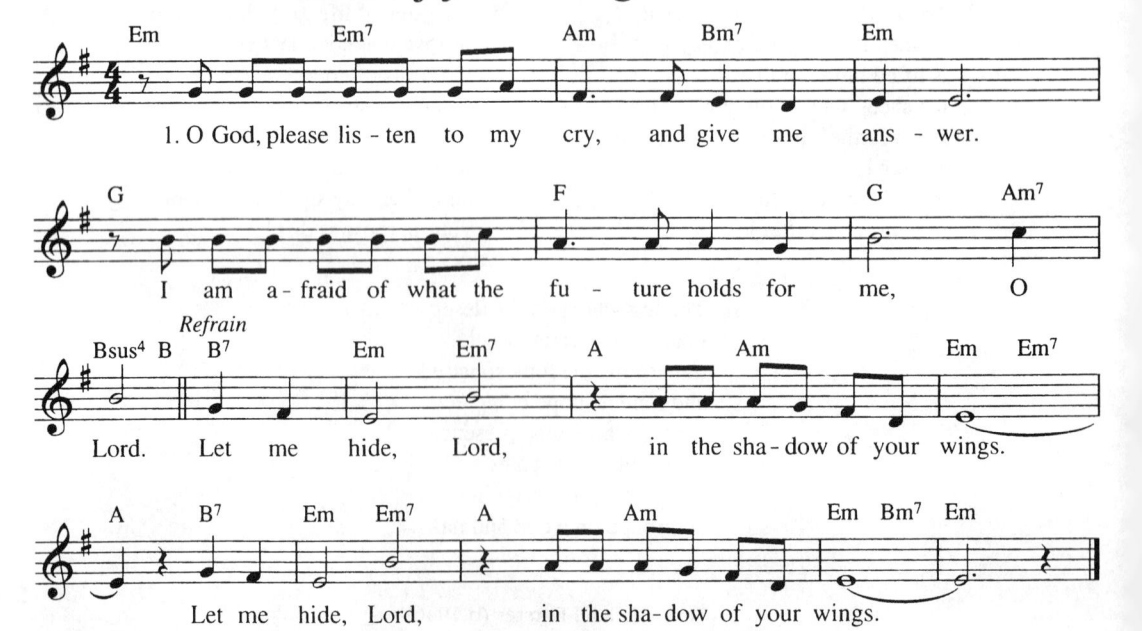

1. O God, please listen to my cry, and give me answer.
I am afraid of what the future holds for me, O Lord.

Refrain
Let me hide, Lord, in the shadow of your wings.
Let me hide, Lord, in the shadow of your wings.

© Copyright 1999 Kevin Mayhew Ltd.

2. If only I had wings to fly I would escape, Lord:
I'd fly as far as I could go to find some peace of mind.

3. I feel defeated by life's trials and disappointments.
My days and nights are spent in fear, with no one I can trust.

4. But all of this I can survive if you are with me:
my life is here, my life is now, and I must carry on.

5. Within the shadow of your wings I find my refuge.
You are the only one I have; I count on you, O Lord.

Text: Frances M. Kelly based on Psalm 54
Music: Frances M. Kelly

516 O God, we give ourselves today

IRISH CM

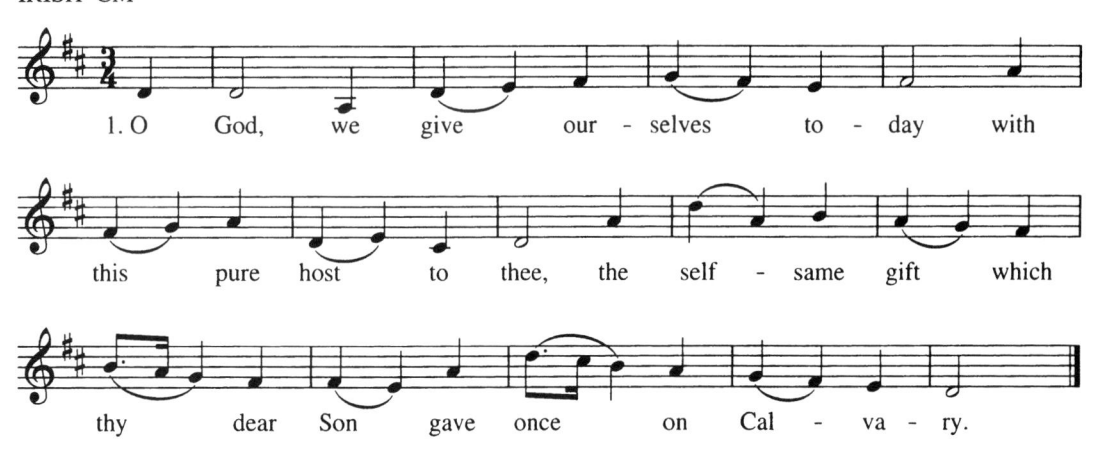

1. O God, we give ourselves today with this pure host to thee, the self-same gift which thy dear Son gave once on Calvary.

2. Entire and whole, our life and love
with heart and soul and mind,
for all our errors, faults and needs,
thy Church and humankind.

3. With humble and with contrite heart
this bread and wine we give
because thy Son once gave himself
and died that we might live.

4. Though lowly now, soon by thy word
these offered gifts will be
the very body of our Lord,
his soul and deity.

5. His very body, offered up,
a gift beyond all price,
he gives to us, that we may give,
in loving sacrifice.

6. O Lord, who took our human life,
as water mixed with wine,
grant through this sacrifice that we
may share thy life divine.

Text: Anthony Nye (b.1932) alt.
Music: Melody from 'Hymns and Sacred Poems', Dublin (1749)
Text © Copyright The Trustees for Roman Catholic Purposes Registered,
114 Mount Street, London W1Y 6AH. Used by permission.

517 O God, your people gather

TUNE 1: THORNBURY 76 76 D

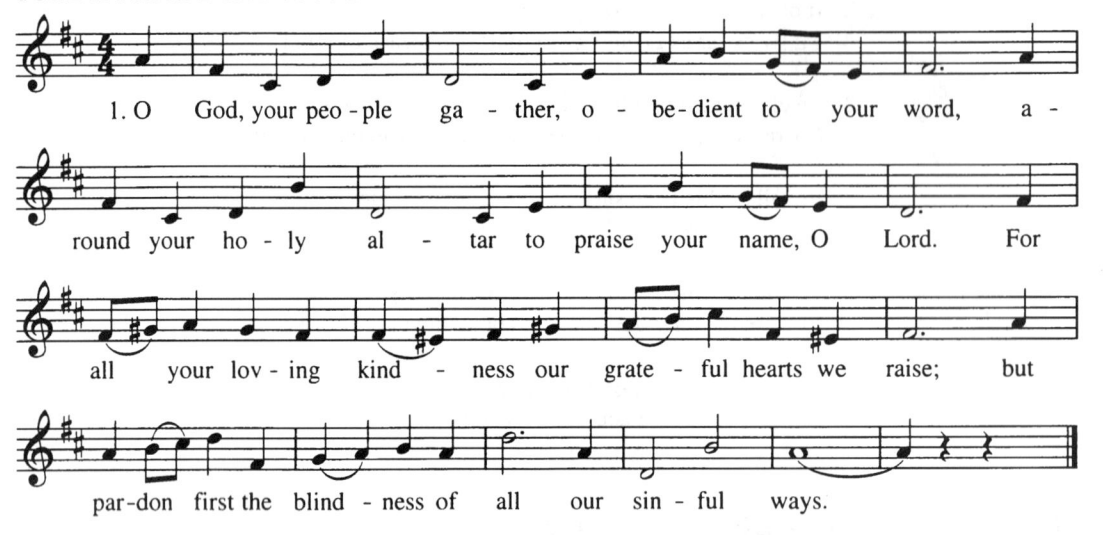

1. O God, your people gather, obedient to your word,
around your holy altar to praise your name, O Lord.
For all your loving kindness our grateful hearts we raise;
but pardon first the blindness of all our sinful ways.

2. You are our loving Father,
you are our holiest Lord,
but we have sinned against you,
by thought and deed and word.
Before the court of heaven
we stand and humbly pray
our sins may be forgiven,
our faults be washed away.

3. Though sinful, we implore you
to turn and make us live,
that so we may adore you,
and our due off'ring give,
and may the prayers and voices
of your glad people rise,
as your whole Church rejoices
in this great sacrifice.

TUNE 2: PINNER 76 76 D

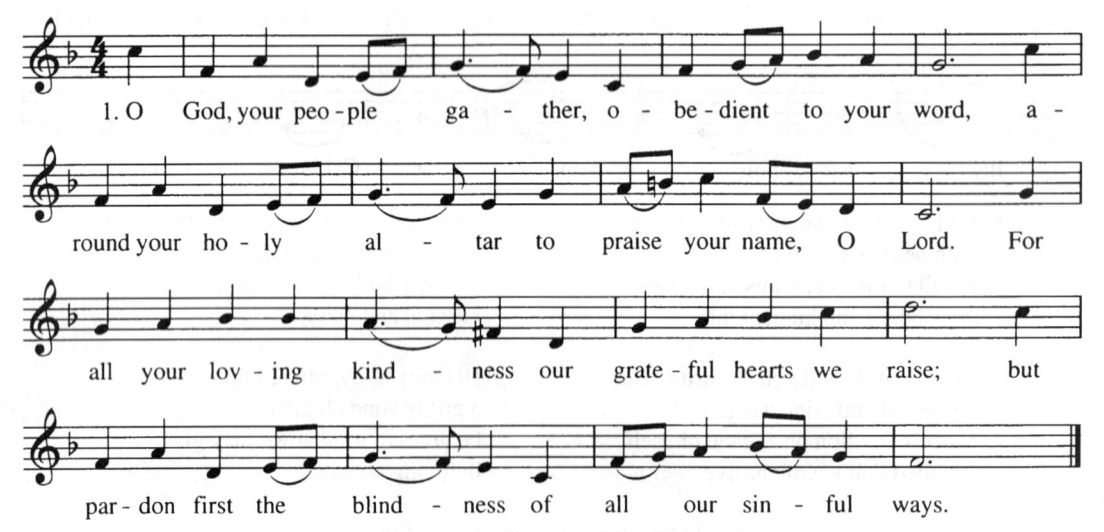

Text: Anthony Nye (b.1932)
Music: Tune 1 – Basil Harwood (1859-1949)
Tune 2 – Wilfrid Trotman

Text © Copyright the Trustees for Roman Catholic Purposes Registered,
114 Mount Street, London W1Y 6AH. Used by permission.
Music: Tune 1 – © Copyright the Executors of the late Dr. Basil Harwood.
Reproduced by permission of the Trustees of the late Dr. Basil Harwood Settlement Trust,
Stewart House, 24 Kingsway, London WC2B 6JX.
Tune 2 – © Copyright control.

518 O healing river

(echo) O healing river, send down your waters,
send down your waters, send down your waters upon this land.
O healing river, O healing river, send down your waters,
and wash the blood from off the sand.

2. This land is parching, this land is burning,
no seed is growing in the barren ground.
O healing river, send down your waters,
O healing river, send your waters down.

3. Let the seed of freedom awake and flourish,
let the deep roots nourish, let the tall stalks rise.
O healing river, send down your waters,
O healing river, from out of the skies.

Text and Music: traditional Baptist hymn

519 O holy Lord, by all adored

MIT FREUDEN ZART 87 87 887

1. O holy Lord, by all adored, our trespasses confessing, to thee this day thy children pray, our holy faith professing! Accept, O King, the gifts we bring, our songs of praise, the prayers we raise, and grant us, Lord, thy blessing.

2. To God on high be thanks and praise,
who deigns our bond to sever;
his care shall guide us all our days,
and harm shall reach us never;
on him we rest with faith assured
of all that live he is the Lord,
for ever and for ever.

Text: Maurice F. Bell (1862-1947) alt.
Music: The Bohemian Brethren's 'Kirchengesang' (1566)
Text © Copyright Oxford University Press, Great Clarendon Street, Oxford OX2 6DP.
Used by permission from the 'English Hymnal'

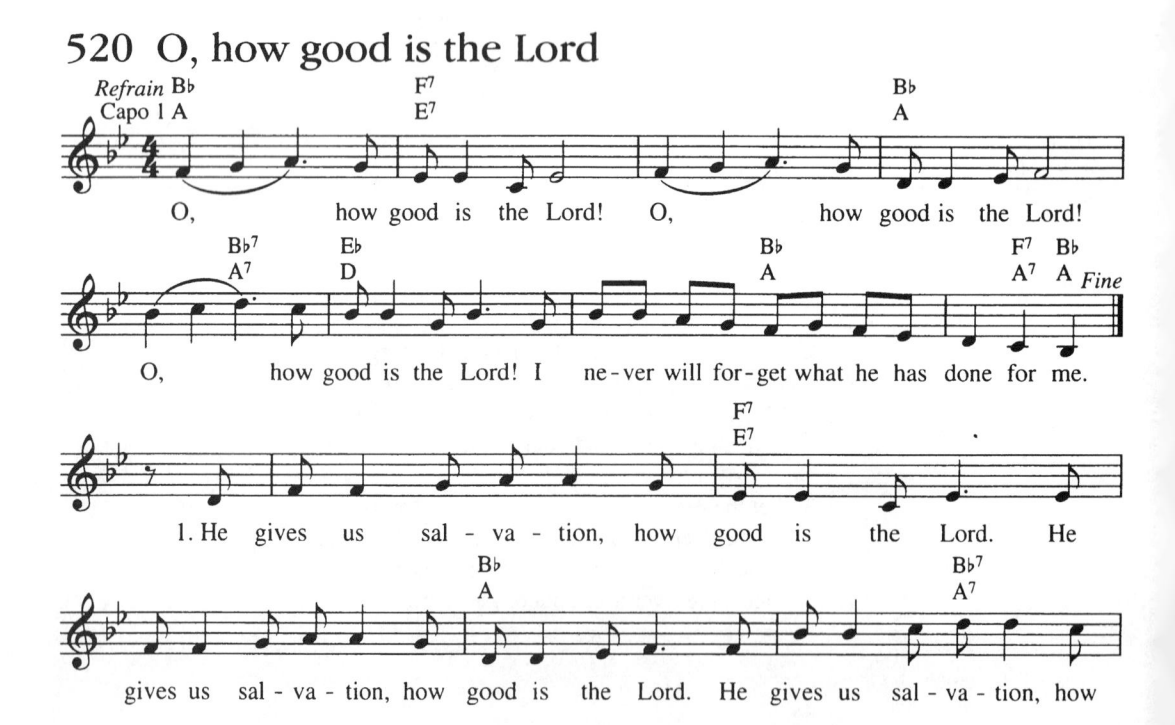

520 O, how good is the Lord

Refrain

O, how good is the Lord! O, how good is the Lord! O, how good is the Lord! I never will forget what he has done for me.

1. He gives us salvation, how good is the Lord. He gives us salvation, how good is the Lord. He gives us salvation, how

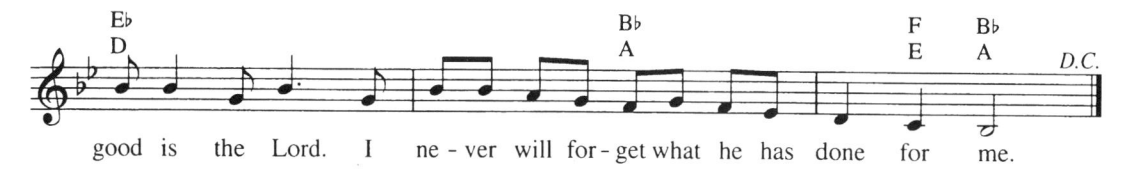

good is the Lord. I ne-ver will for-get what he has done for me.

2. He gives us his Spirit, how good is the Lord. *(x3)*
   I never will forget what he has done for me.

3. He gives us his healing, how good is the Lord. *(x3)*
   I never will forget what he has done for me.

4. He gives us his body, how good is the Lord. *(x3)*
   I never will forget what he has done for me.

5. He gives us his freedom, how good is the Lord. *(x3)*
   I never will forget what he has done for me.

6. He gives us each other, how good is the Lord. *(x3)*
   I never will forget what he has done for me.

7. He gives us his glory, how good is the Lord. *(x3)*
   I never will forget what he has done for me.

Text and Music: traditional

521 O Jesus Christ, remember
AURELIA 76 76 D

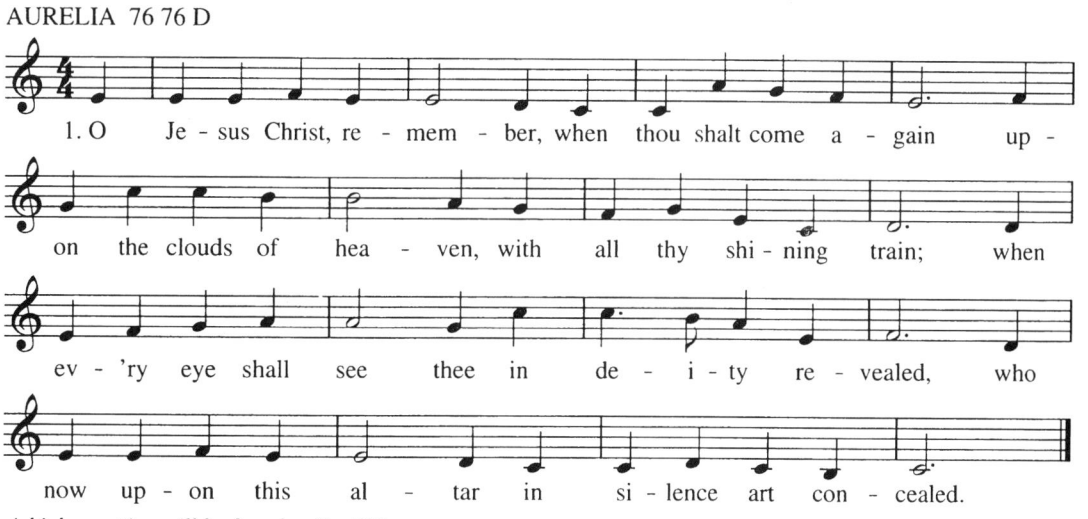

1. O Jesus Christ, remember, when thou shalt come again upon the clouds of heaven, with all thy shining train; when ev-'ry eye shall see thee in deity revealed, who now upon this altar in silence art concealed.

A higher setting will be found at No. 513

2. Remember then, O Saviour,
   I supplicate of thee,
   that here I bowed before thee
   upon my bended knee;
   that here I owned thy presence,
   and did not thee deny,
   and glorified thy greatness
   though hid from human eye.

3. Accept, divine Redeemer,
   the homage of my praise;
   be thou the light and honour
   and glory of my days.
   Be thou my consolation
   when death is drawing nigh;
   be thou my only treasure
   through all eternity.

This hymn may be sung to the tune 'Kings Lynn' at No. 512

Text: Edward Caswall (1814-1878)
Music: Samuel Sebastian Wesley (1810-1876)

522 O Jesus, I have promised

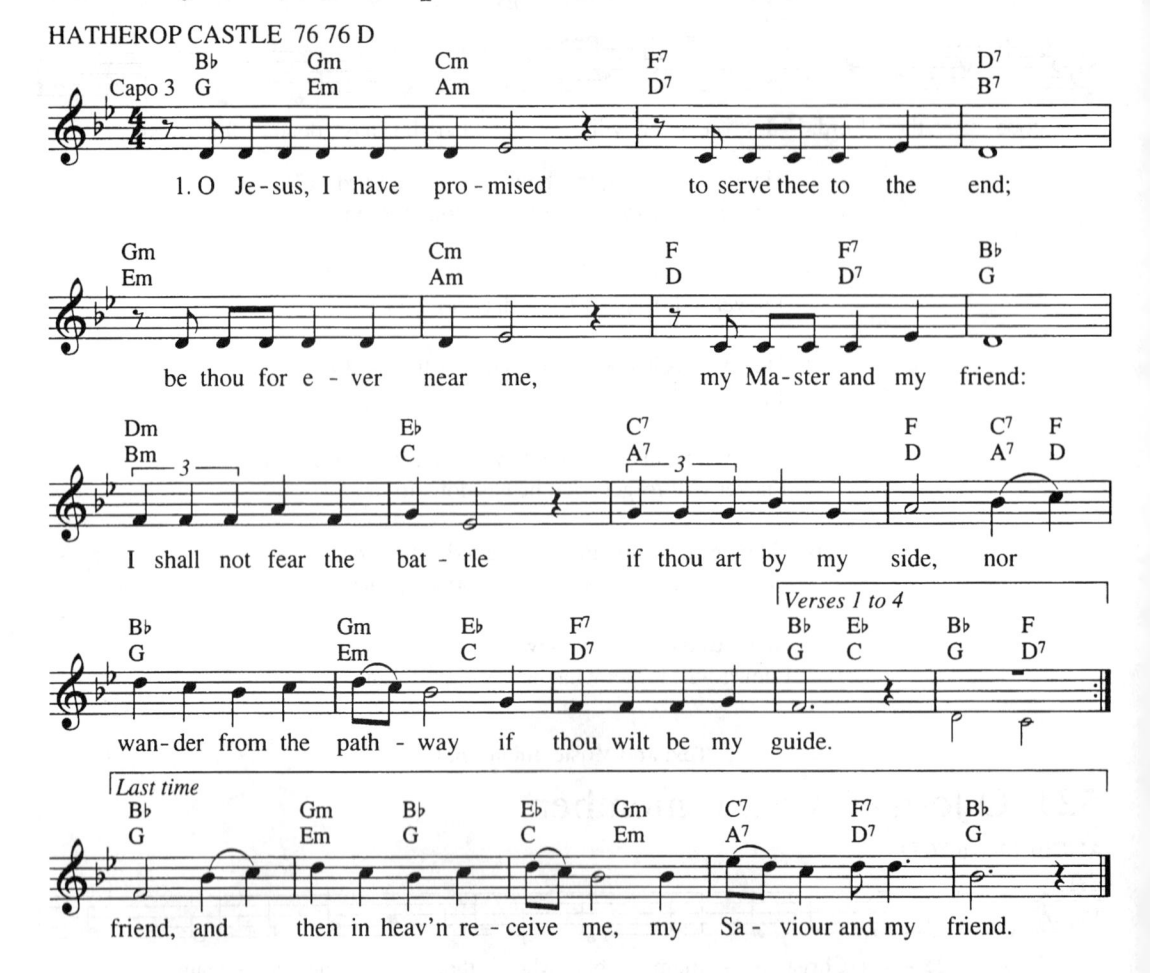

HATHEROP CASTLE 76 76 D

1. O Jesus, I have promised
to serve thee to the end;
be thou for ever near me,
my Master and my friend:
I shall not fear the battle
if thou art by my side,
nor wander from the pathway
if thou wilt be my guide.
[Last time] friend, and then in heav'n receive me, my Saviour and my friend.

2. O let me feel thee near me:
the world is ever near;
I see the sights that dazzle,
the tempting sounds I hear;
my foes are ever near me,
around me and within;
but, Jesus, draw thou nearer,
and shield my soul from sin.

3. O let me hear thee speaking
in accents clear and still,
above the storms of passion,
the murmurs of self-will;
O speak to reassure me,
to hasten or control;
O speak and make me listen,
thou guardian of my soul.

4. O Jesus, thou hast promised,
to all who follow thee,
that where thou art in glory
there shall thy servant be;
and, Jesus, I have promised
to serve thee to the end:
O give me grace to follow,
my Master and my friend.

5. O let me see thy foot-marks,
and in them plant mine own;
my hope to follow duly
is in thy strength alone:
O guide me, call me, draw me,
uphold me to the end;
and then in heav'n receive me,
my Saviour and my friend.

Text: John E. Bode (1816-1874)
Music: Geoffrey Beaumont (1903-1970)
Music © Copyright 1960 Josef Weinberger Ltd, 12-14 Mortimer Street, London W1N 7RD.
Used by permission.

523 O King of might and splendour

O KING OF MIGHT 76 76 D

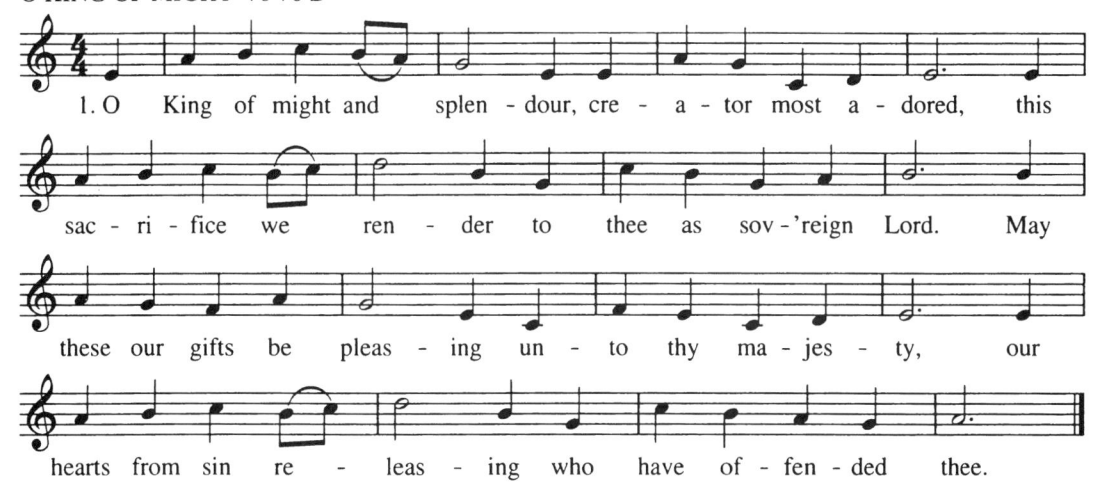

1. O King of might and splendour, creator most adored,
this sacrifice we render to thee as sov-'reign Lord.
May these our gifts be pleasing unto thy majesty,
our hearts from sin releasing who have offended thee.

2. Thy body thou hast given, thy blood thou hast outpoured,
that sin might be forgiven, O Jesus, loving Lord.
As now with love most tender, thy death we celebrate,
our lives in self-surrender to thee we consecrate.

Text and Music: Gregory Murray (1905-1992)
© Copyright the Estate of Gregory Murray. Reproduced by permission of the Trustees of Downside Abbey, Stratton-on-the-Fosse, Bath BA3 4RH.

524 O lady, full of God's own grace

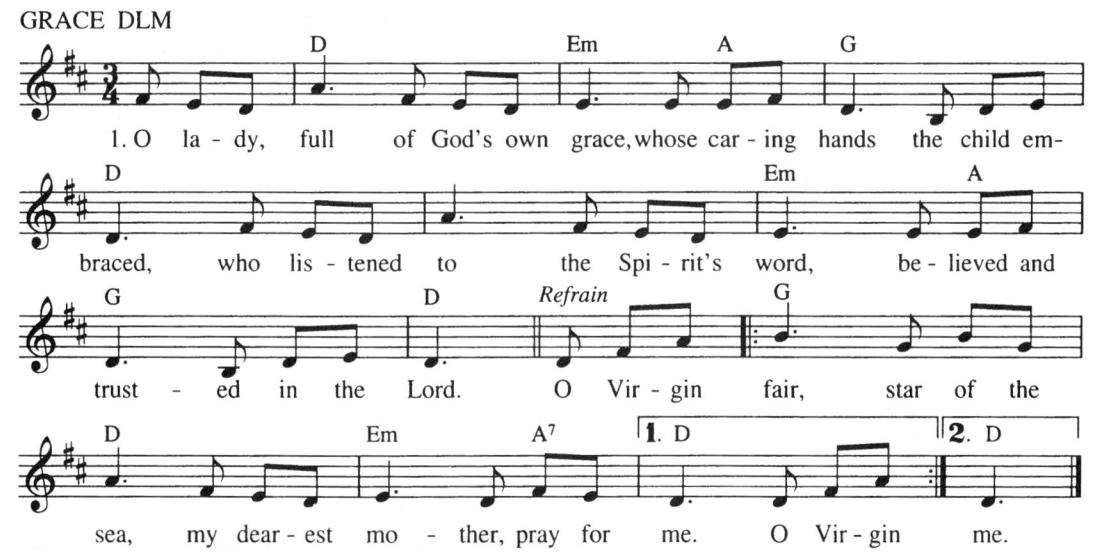

GRACE DLM

1. O lady, full of God's own grace, whose caring hands the child embraced,
who listened to the Spirit's word, believed and trusted in the Lord.
Refrain: O Virgin fair, star of the sea, my dearest mother, pray for me.
O Virgin me.

2. O lady, who felt daily joy
in caring for the holy boy,
whose home was plain and shorn of wealth,
yet was enriched by God's own breath.

3. O lady, who bore living's pain
but still believed that love would reign,
who on a hill watched Jesus die,
as on the cross they raised him high.

4. O lady, who, on Easter day,
had all your sorrow wiped away
as God the Father's will was done
when from death's hold he freed your Son.

Text and Music: Estelle White (b.1925)
© Copyright 1976 Kevin Mayhew Ltd.

525 O let all who thirst
Come to the water

1. O let all who thirst, let them come to the water. And let all who have nothing, let them come to the Lord: without money, without price. Why should you pay the price, except for the Lord?

2. And let all who seek,
   let them come to the water.
   And let all who have nothing,
   let them come to the Lord:
   without money, without strife.
   Why should you spend your life,
   except for the Lord?

3. And let all who toil,
   let them come to the water.
   And let all who are weary,
   let them come to the Lord:
   all who labour, without rest.
   How can your soul find rest,
   except for the Lord?

4. And let all the poor,
   let them come to the water.
   Bring the ones who are laden,
   bring them all to the Lord:
   bring the children without might.
   Easy the load and light:
   oh come to the Lord.

Text: John Foley based on Isaiah 55:1,2 and Matthew 11:28-30
Music: John Foley
© Copyright 1978 John B. Foley, SJ and New Dawn Music, 5536 NE Hassalo, Portland, OR 97213, USA.
All rights reserved. Used by permission.

526 O little town of Bethlehem

FOREST GREEN DCM

1. O little town of Bethlehem, how still we see thee lie! Above thy deep and dreamless sleep the silent stars go

Music © Copyright Oxford University Press, Great Clarendon Street, Oxford OX2 6DP.
Used by permission from the 'English Hymnal'.

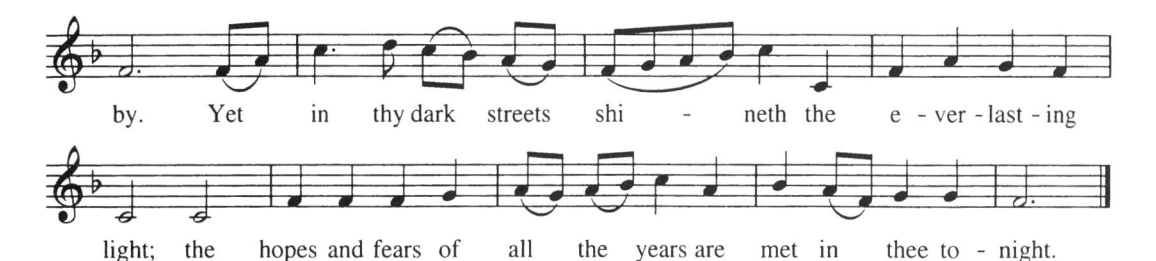

by. Yet in thy dark streets shineth the everlasting light; the hopes and fears of all the years are met in thee to-night.

2. O morning stars, together
proclaim the holy birth,
and praises sing to God the King,
and peace to all the earth;
For Christ is born of Mary;
and, gathered all above,
while mortals sleep, the angels keep
their watch of wond'ring love.

3. How silently, how silently,
the wondrous gift is giv'n!
So God imparts to human hearts
the blessings of his heav'n.
No ear may hear his coming;
but in this world of sin,
where meek souls will receive him, still
the dear Christ enters in.

4. O holy child of Bethlehem,
descend to us, we pray;
cast out our sin, and enter in,
be born in us today.
We hear the Christmas angels
the great glad tidings tell:
O come to us, abide with us,
our Lord Emmanuel.

Text: Phillips Brooks (1835-1893) alt.
Music: traditional English melody collected and arr. Ralph Vaughan Williams (1872-1958)

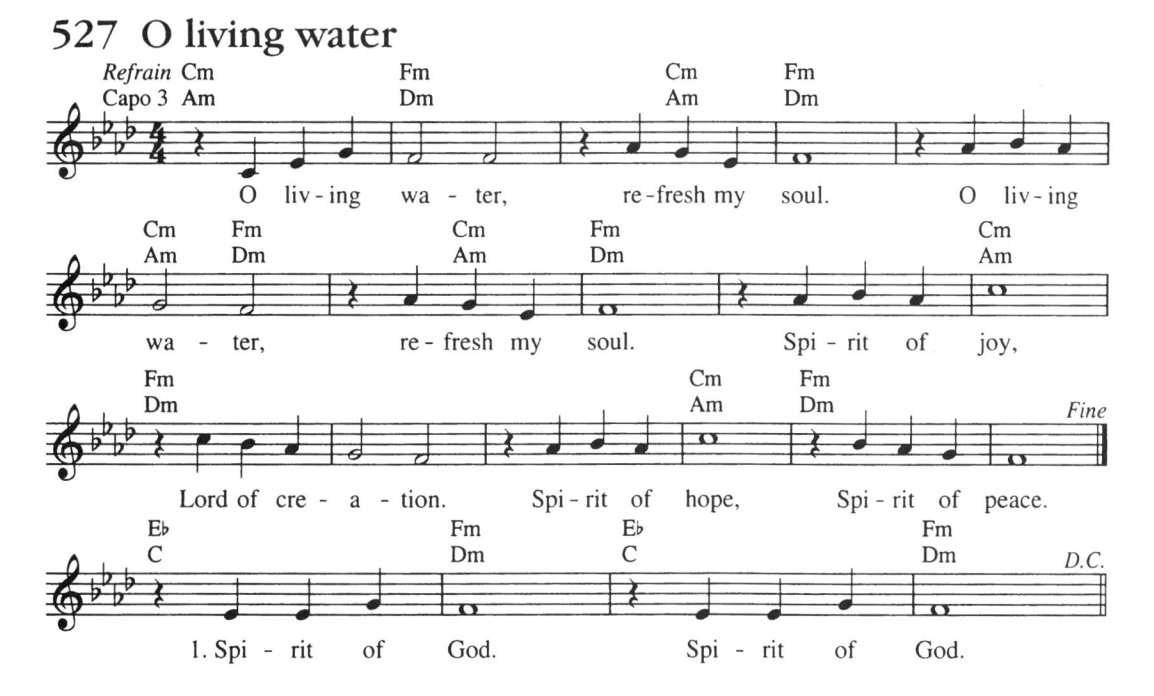

527 O living water

O living water, refresh my soul. O living water, refresh my soul. Spirit of joy, Lord of creation. Spirit of hope, Spirit of peace.

1. Spirit of God. Spirit of God.
2. O set us free. O set us free.
3. Come, pray in us. Come, pray in us.

Text and Music: Virginia Vissing
© Copyright 1974, 1998 Sisters of St Mary of Namur, 909 West Shaw, Ft. Worth, Texas 76110, USA.
All rights reserved. Used by permission.

528 O Lord, be not mindful

Refrain

O Lord, be not mind-ful of our guilt and our sins;

O Lord, do not judge us for our faults and of-fences. May your mer-ci-ful love be up-on us. *Fine*

1. Help your peo-ple, Lord, O God our Sa-viour, de-liv-er us for the glo-ry of your name! *D.C.*

2. Par-don us, O Lord, all our sins, de-liv-er us for the glo-ry of your name! *D.C.*

3. Praise to you, O Lord, through all a-ges with-out end, de-li-ver us for the glo-ry of your name! *D.C.*

Text: Lucien Deiss (b.1921) based on Psalm 102:17-18 (Refrain) and Psalm 78:9 (verses)
Music: Lucien Deiss (b.1921)
© Copyright 1965 World Library Publications, a division of J.S. Paluch Co. Inc.,
3825 N. Willow Road, Schiller Park, Illinois 60176-9936, USA.
All rights reserved. Used by permission.

529 O Lord, my God
How great thou art

HOW GREAT THOU ART 11 10 11 10 and Refrain

1. O Lord, my God, when I in awe-some won-der con-si-der
all the works thy hand has made, I see the stars, I hear the roll-ing
thun-der, thy pow'r through-out the u-ni-verse dis-played.

Refrain
Then sings my soul, my Sa-viour God, to thee: how great thou
art, how great thou art. Then sings my soul, my Sa-viour God, to
thee; how great thou art, how great thou art.

2. When through the woods and forest glades I wander
and hear the birds sing sweetly in the trees;
when I look down from lofty mountain grandeur,
and hear the brook, and feel the gentle breeze.

3. And when I think that God, his Son not sparing,
sent him to die, I scarce can take it in
that on the cross, my burden gladly bearing,
he bled and died to take away my sin.

4. When Christ shall come with shout of acclamation
and take me home, what joy shall fill my heart;
when I shall bow in humble adoration,
and there proclaim: my God, how great thou art.

Text: 'O Støre Gud' by Karl Boberg (1859-1940) trans. Stuart K. Hine (1899-1989)
Music: Swedish folk melody

© Copyright 1953 Stuart K. Hine. Administered by Kingsway's Thankyou Music,
P.O. Box 75, Eastbourne, East Sussex BN23 6NW, UK. Worldwide (excl. USA and Canada). Used by permission.

530 O Lord, your tenderness

With feeling

O Lord, your ten-der-ness, melt-ing all my bit-ter-ness, O Lord, I re-ceive your love. O Lord, your love-li-ness, chang-ing all my ug-li-ness, O Lord, I re-ceive your love. O Lord, I re-ceive your love, O Lord, I re-ceive your love.

Text and Music: Graham Kendrick (b.1950)
© Copyright 1986 Kingsway's Thankyou Music, P.O. Box 75, Eastbourne, East Sussex BN23 6NW, UK. Used by permission.

531 O Mary, when our God chose you

1. O Ma-ry, when our God chose you to bring his on-ly Son to birth, a new cre-a-tion made in you gave joy to all the earth.

Text © Copyright 1978 Kevin Mayhew Ltd.

2. When he was born on Christmas night
and music made the rafters ring,
the stars were dancing with delight;
now all God's children sing.

3. One winter's night, a heap of straw
becomes a place where ages meet,
when kings come knocking at the door
and kneeling at your feet.

4. In you, our God confounds the strong
and makes the crippled dance with joy;
and to our barren world belong
his mother and her boy.

5. In empty streets and broken hearts
you call to mind what he has done;
where all his loving kindness starts
in sending you a Son.

6. And, Mary, while we stand with you,
may once again his Spirit come,
and all his people follow you
to reach our Father's home.

Text: Damian Lundy (1944-1997)
Music: Swiss folk melody

532 O Mother blest

ST URSULA 86 86 and Refrain

1. O Mother blest, whom God bestows on sinners and on just, what joy, what hope thou givest those who in thy mercy trust.

Refrain
Thou art clement, thou art chaste, Mary, thou art fair; of all mothers sweetest, best, none with thee compare.

2. O heav'nly mother, maiden sweet!
It never yet was told
that suppliant sinner left thy feet
unpitied, unconsoled.

3. O mother pitiful and mild,
cease not to pray for me;
for I do love thee as a child
and sigh for love of thee.

4. O mother blest, for me obtain,
ungrateful though I be,
to love that God who first could deign
to show such love for me.

Text: 'Sei pura, sei pia' by St Alphonsus (1696-1787) trans. Edmund Vaughan (1827-1908)
Music: F. Westlake (1840-1898)

533 O my Lord, within my heart

1. O my Lord, within my heart pride will have no home, ev-'ry talent that I have comes from you a-lone. And like a child at rest close to its mo-ther's breast, safe in your arms my soul is calmed.

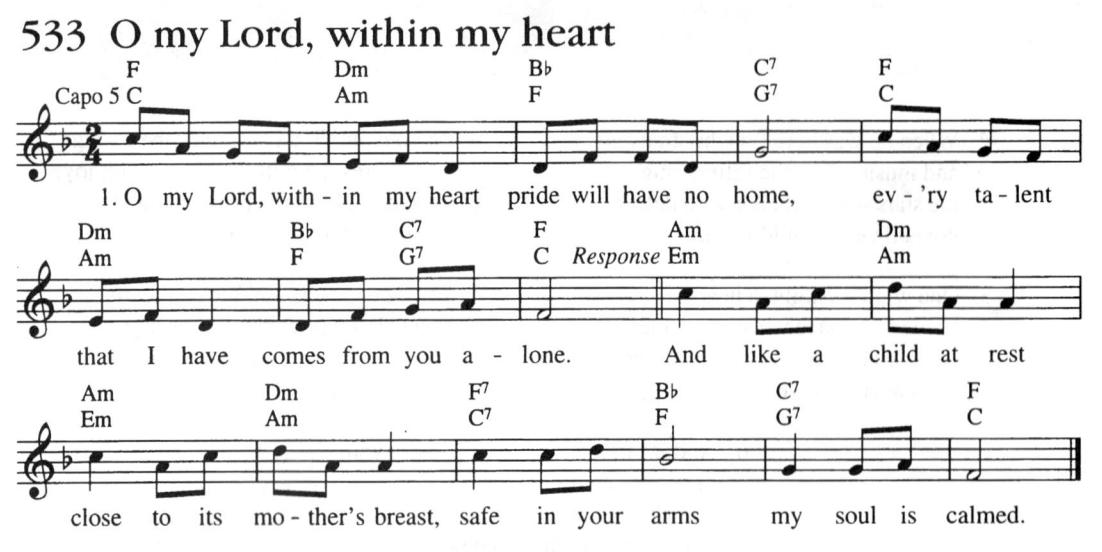

2. Lord, my eyes do not look high
 nor my thoughts take wings,
 I can find such treasures in
 ordinary things.

3. Great affairs are not for me,
 deeds beyond my scope.
 In the simple things I do
 I find joy and hope.

Text: Estelle White (b.1925) based on Psalm 130
Music: Estelle White (b.1925)
© Copyright 1976, 1997 Kevin Mayhew Ltd.

534 O my people, what have I done to you?

REPROACHES 7 8 9 8 and Refrain

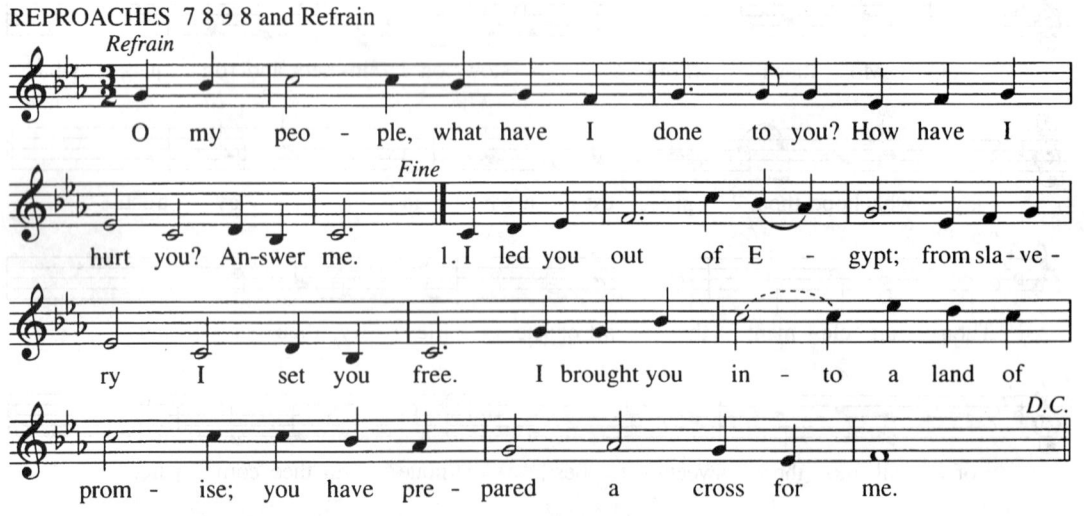

Refrain
O my peo-ple, what have I done to you? How have I hurt you? An-swer me.

1. I led you out of E-gypt; from sla-ve-ry I set you free. I brought you in-to a land of prom-ise; you have pre-pared a cross for me.

2. I led you as a shepherd,
 I brought you safely through the sea,
 fed you with manna in the desert;
 you have prepared a cross for me.

3. I fought for you in battles,
 I won you strength and victory,
 gave you a royal crown and sceptre:
 you have prepared a cross for me.

4. I planted you, my vineyard,
 and cared for you most tenderly,
 looked for abundant fruit, and found none
 – only the cross you made for me.

5. Then listen to my pleading,
 and do not turn away from me.
 You are my people: will you reject me?
 For you I suffer bitterly.

Text: Damian Lundy (1944-1997) based on the Good Friday 'Reproaches'
Music: Damian Lundy (1944-1997)
© Copyright 1978 Kevin Mayhew Ltd.

535 On a hill far away
The old rugged cross

THE OLD RUGGED CROSS 66 8 D and Refrain

1. On a hill far away stood an old rugged cross, the emblem of suff'ring and shame; and I loved that old cross where the dearest and best for a world of lost sinners was slain. So I'll cherish the old rugged cross, till my trophies at last I lay down; I will cling to the old rugged cross and exchange it some day for a crown.

    2. O that old rugged cross,
       so despised by the world,
       has a wondrous attraction for me:
       for the dear Lamb of God
       left his glory above
       to bear it to dark Calvary.

    3. In the old rugged cross,
       stained with blood so divine,
       a wondrous beauty I see.
       For 'twas on that old cross
       Jesus suffered and died
       to pardon and sanctify me.

    4. To the old rugged cross
       I will ever be true,
       its shame and reproach gladly bear.
       Then he'll call me some day
       to my home far away;
       there his glory for ever I'll share.

Text and Music: George Bennard (1873-1958)

© Copyright The Rodeheaver Co./Word Music. Administered by CopyCare, P.O. Box 77, Hailsham, East Sussex BN27 3EF, UK. Used by permission.

536 Once in royal David's city
IRBY 87 87 77

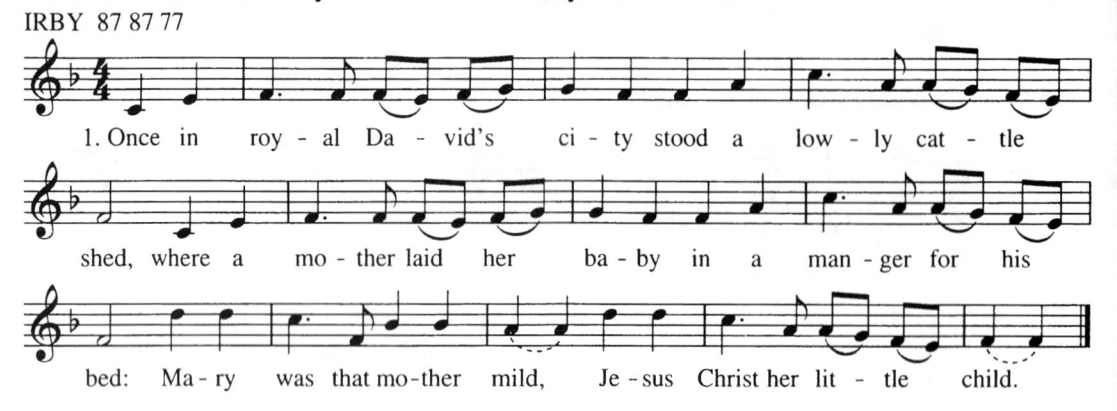

1. Once in royal David's city stood a lowly cattle shed, where a mother laid her baby in a manger for his bed: Mary was that mother mild, Jesus Christ her little child.

2. He came down to earth from heaven,
who is God and Lord of all,
and his shelter was a stable,
and his cradle was a stall;
with the needy, poor and lowly,
lived on earth our Saviour holy.

3. For he is our childhood's pattern,
day by day like us he grew;
he was little, weak and helpless,
tears and smiles like us he knew;
and he feeleth for our sadness,
and he shareth in our gladness.

4. And our eyes at last shall see him
through his own redeeming love,
for that child so dear and gentle
is our Lord in heav'n above;
and he leads his children on
to the place where he is gone.

Text: Cecil Frances Alexander (1818-1895) alt.
Music: Henry John Gauntlett (1805-1876)
This version of text © Copyright 1996 Kevin Mayhew Ltd.

537 On Christmas night all Christians sing
SUSSEX CAROL 88 88 88

1. On Christmas night all Christians sing, to hear the news the angels bring, on Christmas night all Christians sing, to hear the news the angels bring, news of great joy, news of great mirth, news of our merciful King's birth.

Music © Copyright Stainer and Bell Ltd., P.O. Box 110, Victoria House, 23 Gruneisen Road, Finchley, London N3 1DZ. Used by permission.

2. Then why should we on earth be so sad,
   since our Redeemer made us glad,
   then why should we on earth be so sad,
   since our Redeemer made us glad,
   when from our sin he set us free,
   all for to gain our liberty?

3. When sin departs before his grace,
   then life and health come in its place,
   when sin departs before his grace,
   then life and health come in its place,
   angels and earth with joy may sing,
   all for to see the new-born King.

4. All out of darkness we have light,
   which made the angels sing this night:
   all out of darkness we have light,
   which made the angels sing this night:
   'Glory to God and peace to men,
   now and for evermore. Amen.'

Text: traditional English carol alt.
Music: traditional English melody collected Ralph Vaughan Williams (1872-1958)

538 One bread, one body

One bread, one body, one Lord of all,
one cup of blessing which we bless:
and we, though many,
throughout the earth,
we are one body in this one Lord.

1. Gentile or Jew, servant or free,
   woman or man, no more. One

2. Many the gifts,
   many the works,
   one in the Lord of all.

3. Grain for the fields,
   scattered and grown,
   gathered to one, for all.

Text: John Foley based on 1 Cor. 10:16, 17; 12:4, Gal. 3:28; Didaché 9
Music: John Foley
© Copyright 1978 John B. Foley, SJ and New Dawn Music, 5536 NE Hassalo, Portland, Oregon 97213, USA.
All rights reserved. Used by permission.

539 One cold night in spring

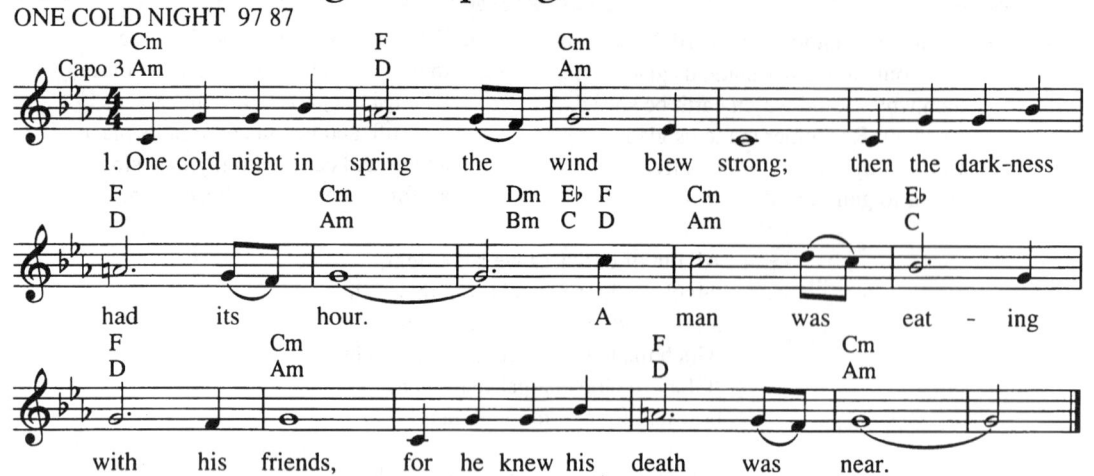

ONE COLD NIGHT 97 87

1. One cold night in spring the wind blew strong; then the darkness had its hour. A man was eating with his friends, for he knew his death was near.

2. And he broke a wheaten loaf to share,
for his friends a last goodbye.
'My body is the bread I break.
O, my heart will break and die.'

3. Then he poured good wine into a cup,
blessed it gently, passed it round.
'This cup is brimming with my blood.
Soon the drops will stain the ground.'

4. See a dying man with arms outstretched
at the setting of the sun.
He stretches healing hands to you.
Will you take them for your own?

5. Soon a man will come with arms outstretched
at the rising of the sun.
His wounded hands will set you free
if you take them for your own.

Text and Music: Damian Lundy (1944-1997)
© Copyright 1978 Kevin Mayhew Ltd.

540 One Father
One God

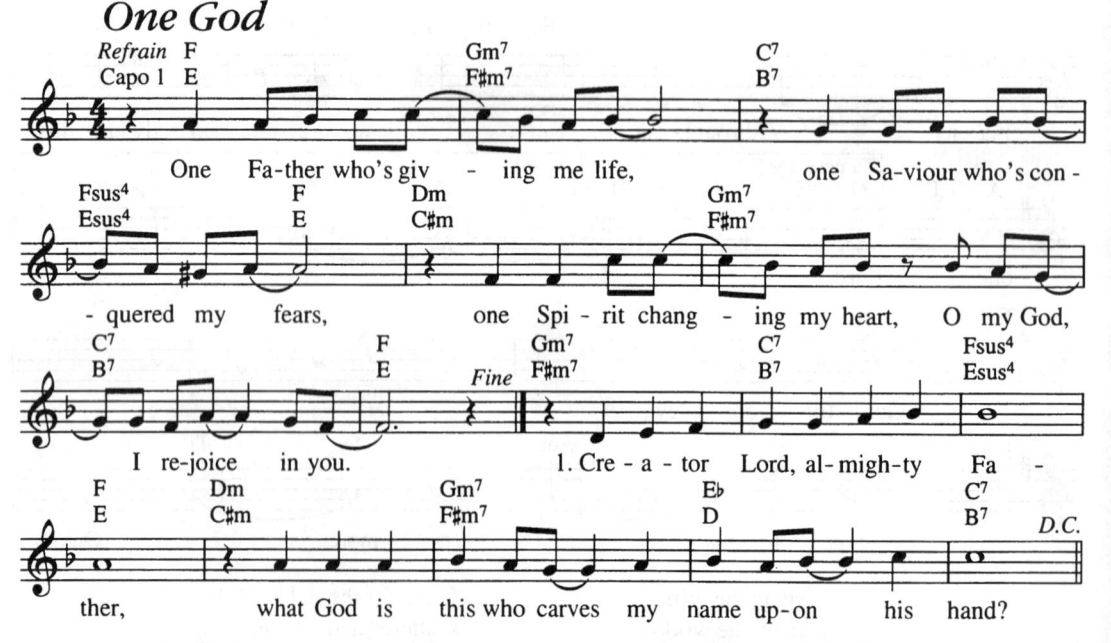

Refrain
One Father who's giving me life, one Saviour who's conquered my fears, one Spirit changing my heart, O my God, I rejoice in you.

Fine

1. Creator Lord, almighty Father, what God is this who carves my name upon his hand?

D.C.

2. Lord Jesus, now enthroned in glory,
what God is this who gives his life
to set me free?

3. O loving breath of God almighty,
what God is this who through my weakness
sings his praise?

Text and Music: Gerard Markland (b.1953)
© Copyright 1998 Kevin Mayhew Ltd.

541 On Jordan's bank the Baptist's cry
WINCHESTER NEW LM

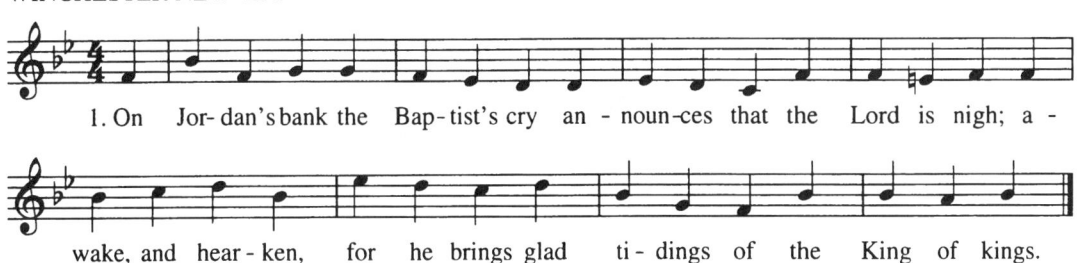

1. On Jordan's bank the Baptist's cry announces that the Lord is nigh; awake, and hearken, for he brings glad tidings of the King of kings.

A lower setting will be found at No. 593

2. Then cleansed be ev'ry breast from sin;
make straight the way for God within;
prepare we in our hearts a home,
where such a mighty guest may come.

3. For thou art our salvation, Lord,
our refuge and our great reward;
without thy grace we waste away,
like flow'rs that wither and decay.

4. To heal the sick stretch out thine hand,
and bid the fallen sinner stand;
shine forth and let thy light restore
earth's own true loveliness once more.

5. All praise, eternal Son, to thee
whose advent doth thy people free,
whom with the Father we adore
and Holy Ghost for evermore.

Text: Charles Coffin (1676-1749) trans. John Chandler (1806-1876) alt.
Music: from 'Musikalisches Handbuch' (1690)

542 On this day of joy

Refrain
On this day of joy, on this day of hope, we come to you in love, O Lord, on this day of joy, on this day of hope, we come to you in love.

1. With this bread and wine we come to this eucharistic feast. On this day of joy, on this day of hope, we come to you in love.

2. Bread to be your body, Lord,
wine to be your saving blood;
on this day of joy, on this day of hope,
we come to you in love.

Text and Music: Marie Lydia Pereira (b.1920)
© Copyright 1999 Kevin Mayhew Ltd.

543 On this house your blessing, Lord

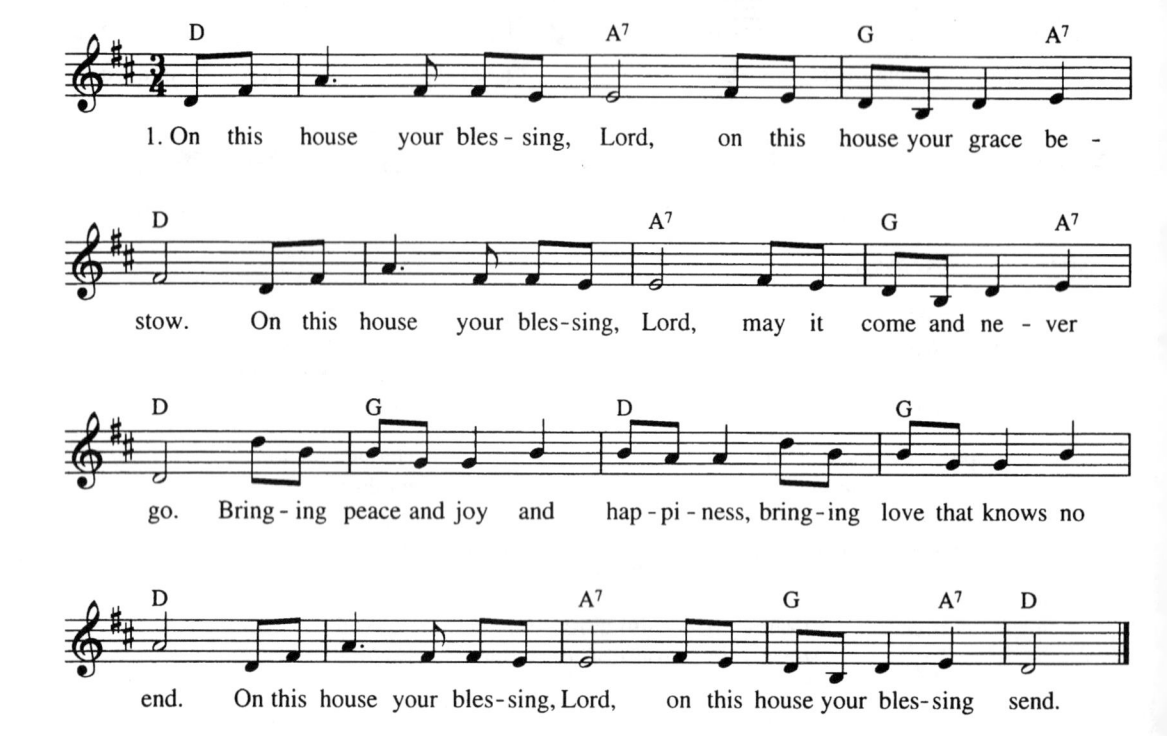

1. On this house your blessing, Lord,
   on this house your grace bestow.
   On this house your blessing, Lord,
   may it come and never go.
   Bringing peace and joy and happiness,
   bringing love that knows no end.
   On this house your blessing, Lord,
   on this house your blessing send.

2. On this house your loving, Lord,
   may it overflow each day.
   On this house your loving, Lord,
   may it come and with us stay.
   Drawing us in love and unity
   by the love received from you.
   On this house your loving, Lord,
   may it come each day anew.

3. On this house your giving, Lord,
   may it turn and ever flow.
   On this house your giving, Lord,
   on this house your wealth bestow.
   Filling all our hopes and wishes, Lord,
   in the way you know is best.
   On this house your giving, Lord,
   may it come and with us rest.

4. On this house your calling, Lord,
   may it come to us each day.
   On this house your calling, Lord,
   may it come to lead the way.
   Filling us with nobler yearnings, Lord,
   calling us to live in you.
   On this house your calling, Lord,
   may it come each day anew.

The word 'house' may be replaced throughout by 'school', 'church', etc.

Text and Music: Marie Lydia Pereira (b.1920)
© Copyright 1976 Kevin Mayhew Ltd.

544 Onward, Christian pilgrims

ST GERTRUDE 65 65 D and Refrain

1. Onward, Christian pilgrims,
   Christ will be our light;
   see, the heav'nly vision
   breaks upon our sight!
   Out of death's enslavement
   Christ has set us free,
   on then to salvation,
   hope and liberty.

   Refrain
   Onward, Christian pilgrims,
   Christ will be our light;
   see, the heav'nly vision
   breaks upon our sight!

2. Onward, Christian pilgrims,
   up the rocky way,
   where the dying Saviour
   bids us watch and pray.
   Through the darkened valley
   walk with those who mourn,
   share the pain and anger,
   share the promised dawn!

3. Onward, Christian pilgrims,
   in the early dawn;
   death's great seal is broken,
   life and hope reborn!
   Faith in resurrection
   strengthens pilgrim's hearts,
   ev'ry load is lightened,
   ev'ry fear departs.

4. Onward, Christian pilgrims,
   hearts and voices raise,
   till the whole creation
   echoes perfect praise:
   swords are turned to ploughshares,
   pride and envy cease,
   truth embraces justice,
   hope resolves in peace.

Text: Michael Forster (b.1946)
Music: Arthur Seymour Sullivan (1842-1900)
Text © Copyright 1996 Kevin Mayhew Ltd.

545 Open our eyes, Lord

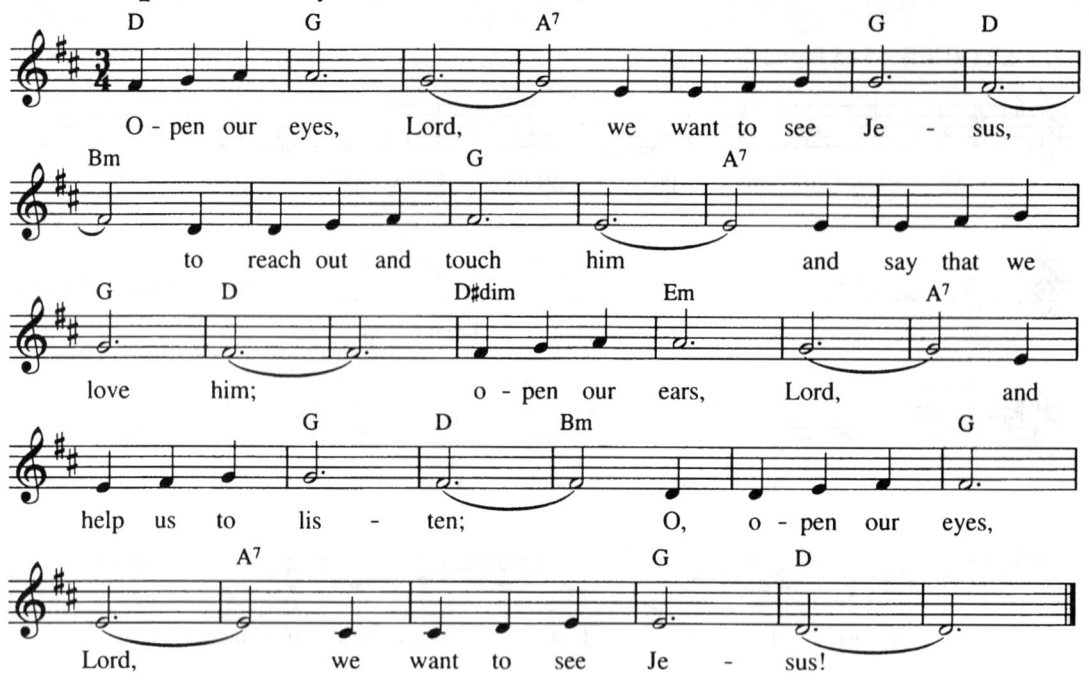

O-pen our eyes, Lord, we want to see Je-sus,
to reach out and touch him and say that we love him;
o-pen our ears, Lord, and help us to lis-ten;
O, o-pen our eyes, Lord, we want to see Je-sus!

Text and Music: Robert Cull (b.1949)
© Copyright 1976 Maranatha! Music. Administered by CopyCare, P.O. Box 77,
Hailsham, East Sussex BN27 3EF, UK. Used by permission.

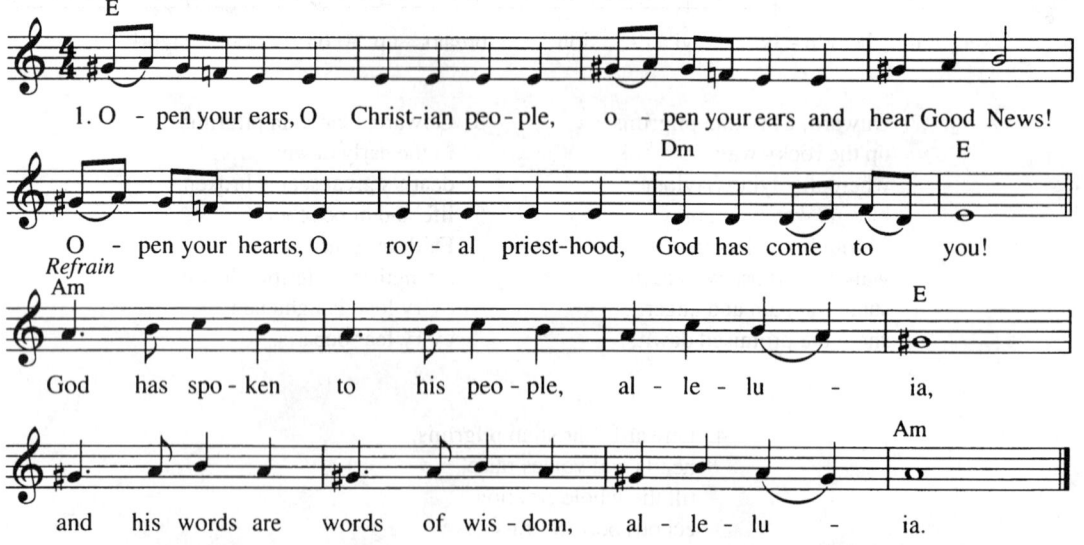

546 Open your ears, O Christian people

1. O-pen your ears, O Christ-ian peo-ple, o-pen your ears and hear Good News!
O-pen your hearts, O roy-al priest-hood, God has come to you!

Refrain
God has spo-ken to his peo-ple, al-le-lu-ia,
and his words are words of wis-dom, al-le-lu-ia.

2. Israel comes to greet the Saviour,
   Judah is glad to see his day.
   From east and west the peoples travel,
   he will show the way.

3. All who have ears to hear his message,
   all who have ears then let them hear.
   All who would learn the way of wisdom,
   let them hear God's words.

Text: Willard F. Jabusch (b.1930)
Music: Israeli melody
Text © Copyright 1998 Willard F. Jabusch, 5735 University Avenue,
Chicago, Illinois 60637, USA. Used by permission.

547 O perfect love

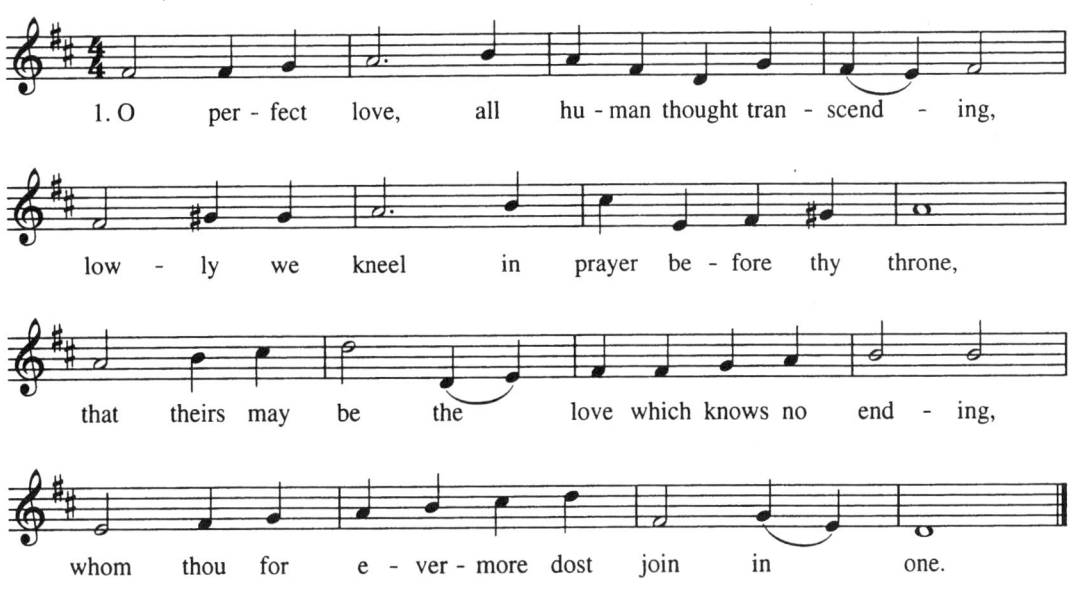

TUNE 1: STRENGTH AND STAY 11 10 11 10

1. O perfect love, all human thought transcending,
lowly we kneel in prayer before thy throne,
that theirs may be the love which knows no ending,
whom thou for evermore dost join in one.

2. O perfect life,
be thou their full assurance
of tender charity
and steadfast faith,
of patient hope
and quiet, brave endurance,
with childlike trust
that fears not pain nor death.

3. Grant them the joy
which brightens earthly sorrow,
grant them the peace
which calms all earthly strife;
and to life's day
the glorious unknown morrow
that dawns upon
eternal love and life.

TUNE 2: HIGHWOOD 11 10 11 10

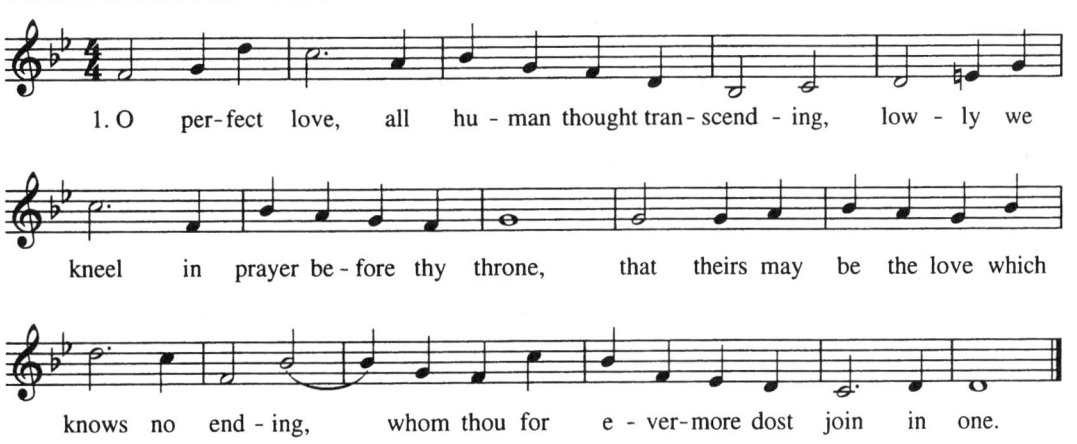

1. O perfect love, all human thought transcending, lowly we kneel in prayer before thy throne, that theirs may be the love which knows no ending, whom thou for evermore dost join in one.

Text: Dorothy F. Gurney (1858-1932)
Music: Tune 1 – John Bacchus Dykes (1823-1876)
Tune 2 – Richard Runciman Terry (1865-1938)
Text © Copyright control.
Tune 2 © Copyright Oxford University Press, Great Clarendon Street, Oxford OX2 6DP, UK. Used by permission.

548 O praise ye the Lord!

LAUDATE DOMINUM (PARRY) 10 10 11 11

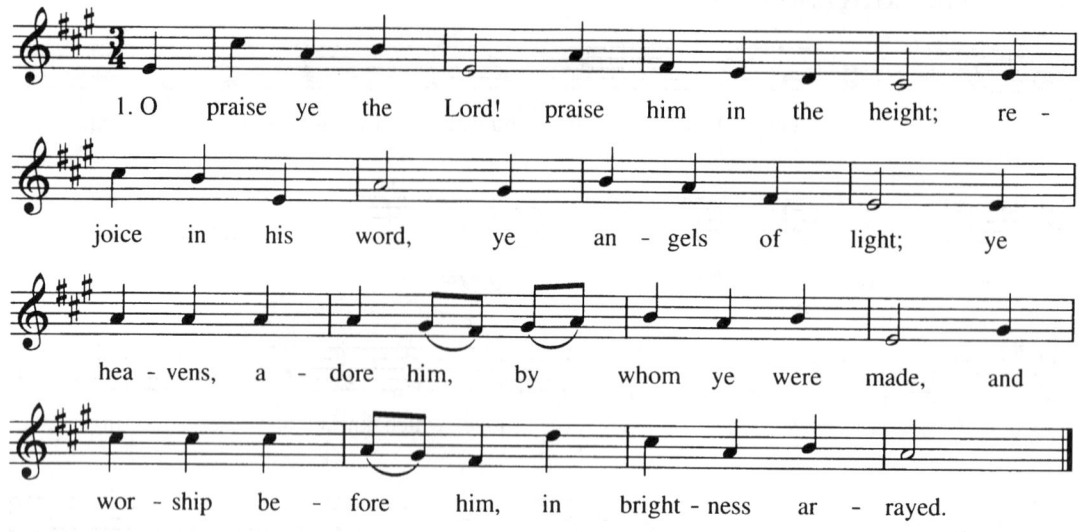

1. O praise ye the Lord! praise him in the height;
rejoice in his word, ye angels of light;
ye heavens, adore him, by whom ye were made,
and worship before him, in brightness arrayed.

A higher setting will be found at No. 669

2. O praise ye the Lord! praise him upon earth,
in tuneful accord, all you of new birth;
praise him who hath brought you his grace from above,
praise him who hath taught you to sing of his love.

3. O praise ye the Lord! all things that give sound;
each jubilant chord re-echo around;
loud organs his glory forth tell in deep tone,
and, sweet harp, the story of what he hath done.

4. O praise ye the Lord! thanksgiving and song
to him be outpoured all ages along:
for love in creation, for heaven restored,
for grace of salvation, O praise ye the Lord!

Text: Henry Williams Baker (1821-1877) based on Psalms 148 and 150 alt.
Music: Charles Hubert Hastings Parry (1848-1918)

549 O purest of creatures

MARIA ZU LIEBEN 11 11 11 11

1. O purest of creatures! Sweet mother, sweet maid:
the one spotless womb wherein Jesus was laid.
Dark night hath come down on us, mother, and we
look out for thy shining, sweet star of the sea.

2. Earth gave him one lodging;
   'twas deep in thy breast,
   and God found a home where
   the sinner finds rest;
   his home and his hiding-place,
   both were in thee;
   he was won by thy shining,
   sweet star of the sea.

3. O, blissful and calm
   was the wonderful rest
   that thou gavest thy God
   in thy virginal breast;
   for the heaven he left
   he found heaven in thee,
   and he shone in thy shining,
   sweet star of the sea.

Text: Frederick William Faber (1814-1863)
Music: from 'Paderborn Gesangbuch' (1765)

550 O Queen of heaven

1. O Queen of heav'n, to you the angels sing, the Maiden-Mother of their Lord and King. O Woman raised above the stars, receive the homage of your children, sinless Eve.

2. O full of grace, in grace your womb did bear
   Emmanuel, King David's promised heir.
   O Eastern Gate, whom God had made his own,
   by you, God's glory came to Zion's throne.

3. O Burning Bush, you gave the world its light,
   when Christ, your Son, was born on Christmas night.
   O Mary Queen, who bore God's holy one,
   for us your children, pray to God your Son.

Text: James Quinn (b.1919)
Music: Gregory Murray (1905-1992)
Text © Copyright Geoffrey Chapman, an imprint of Cassell plc,
Wellington House, 125 Strand, London WC2R 0BB. Used by permission.
Music © Copyright 1999 Kevin Mayhew Ltd.

551 O sacred head ill-used

PASSION CHORALE 76 76 D

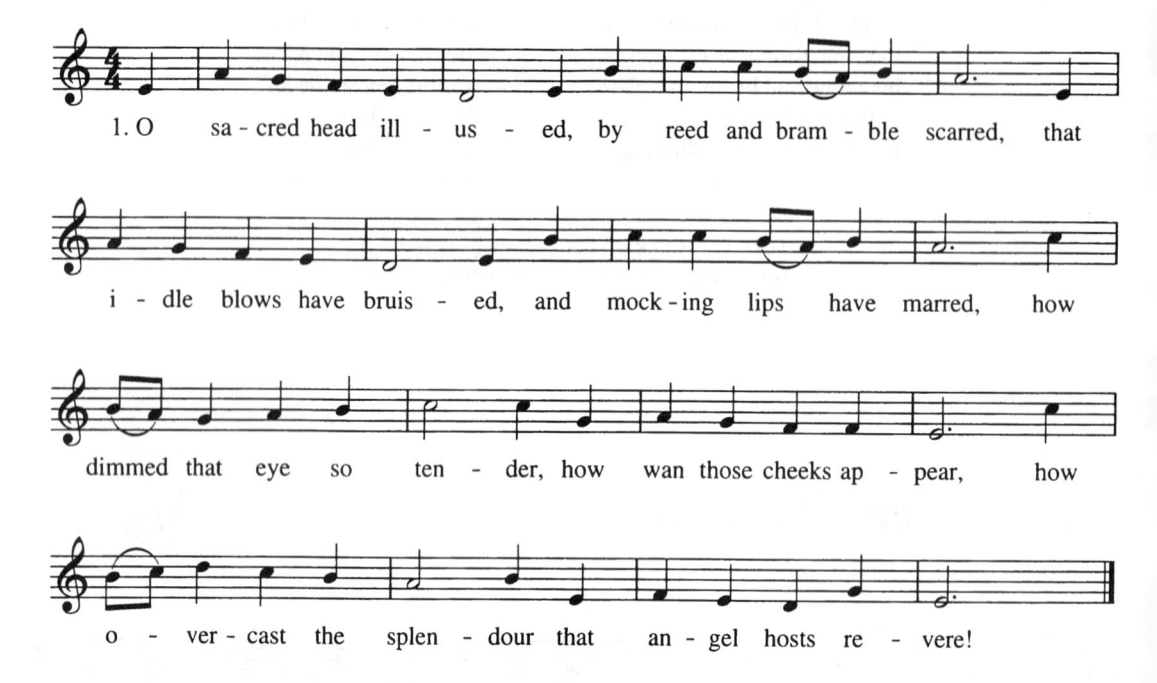

1. O sacred head ill-used, by reed and bramble scarred, that idle blows have bruised, and mocking lips have marred, how dimmed that eye so tender, how wan those cheeks appear, how overcast the splendour that angel hosts revere!

2. What marvel if thou languish,
vigour and virtue fled,
wasted and spent with anguish,
and pale as are the dead?
O by thy foes' derision,
that death endured for me,
grant that thy open vision
a sinner's eyes may see.

3. Good Shepherd, spent with loving,
look on me, who have strayed,
oft by those lips unmoving
with milk and honey stayed;
spurn not a sinner's crying
nor from thy love outcast,
but rest thy head in dying
on these frail arms at last.

4. In this thy sacred passion
O that some share had I!
O may thy Cross's fashion
o'erlook me when I die!
For these dear pains that rack thee
a sinner's thanks receive;
O, lest in death I lack thee,
a sinner's care relieve.

5. Since death must be my ending,
in that dread hour of need,
my friendless cause befriending,
Lord, to my rescue speed;
thyself, dear Jesus, trace me
that passage to the grave,
and from thy cross embrace me
with arms outstretched to save.

Text: Paul Gerhardt (1607-1676) based on 'Salve caput cruentatum'
trans. Ronald Arbuthnott Knox (1888-1957)
Music: Hans Leo Hassler (1564-1612) harmonised by Johann Sebastian Bach (1685-1750)
Text © Copyright Burns and Oates Ltd, Wellwood, North Farm Road,
Tunbridge Wells, Kent TN2 3QR. Used by permission.

552 O sacred head sore wounded

PASSION CHORALE 76 76 D

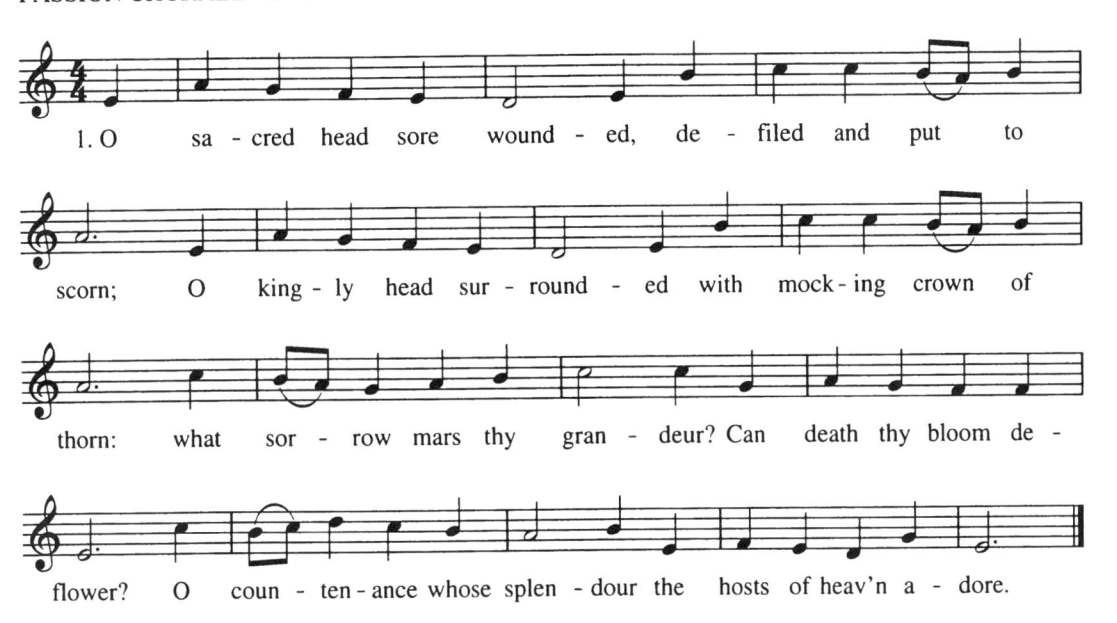

1. O sacred head sore wounded, defiled and put to scorn;
O kingly head surrounded with mocking crown of thorn:
what sorrow mars thy grandeur? Can death thy bloom deflower?
O countenance whose splendour the hosts of heav'n adore.

2. Thy beauty, long-desirèd,
hath vanished from our sight;
thy pow'r is all expirèd,
and quenched the light of light.
Ah me, for whom thou diest,
hide not so far thy grace:
show me, O love most highest,
the brightness of thy face.

3. I pray thee, Jesus, own me,
me, shepherd good, for thine;
who to thy fold hast won me,
and fed with truth divine.
Me guilty, me refuse not,
incline thy face to me,
this comfort that I lose not,
on earth to comfort thee.

4. In thy most bitter passion
my heart to share doth cry,
with thee for my salvation
upon the cross to die.
Ah, keep my heart thus movèd,
to stand thy cross beneath,
to mourn thee, well-belovèd,
yet thank thee for thy death.

5. My days are few, O fail not,
with thine immortal power,
to hold me that I quail not
in death's most fearful hour:
that I may fight befriended,
and see in my last strife
to me thine arms extended
upon the cross of life.

Text: Paul Gerhardt (1607-1676) based on 'Salve caput cruentatum' trans. Robert Bridges (1844-1930)
Music: Hans Leo Hassler (1564-1612) harmonised by Johann Sebastian Bach (1685-1750)
Text © Copyright Oxford University Press, Great Clarendon Street, Oxford OX2 6DP.
Used by permission from the 'Yaltendon Hymnal'.

553 O Sacred Heart

LAURENCE 4 6 88 4

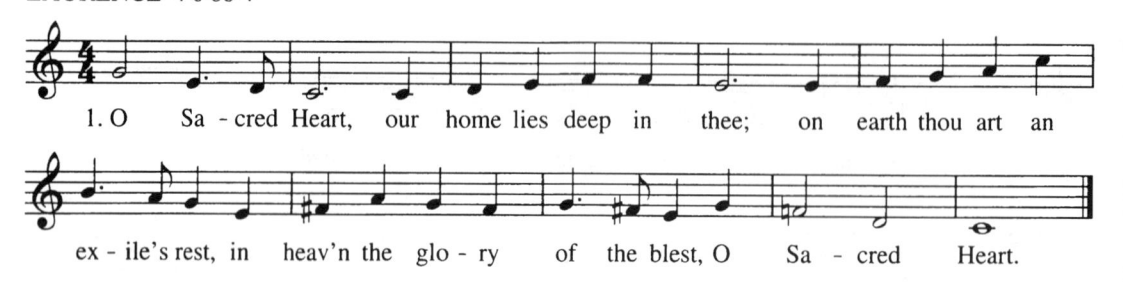

1. O Sacred Heart, our home lies deep in thee; on earth thou art an exile's rest, in heav'n the glory of the blest, O Sacred Heart.

2. O Sacred Heart,
thou fount of contrite tears;
where'er those living waters flow,
new life to sinners they bestow,
O Sacred Heart.

3. O Sacred Heart,
our trust is all in thee,
for though earth's night be dark and drear,
thou breathest rest where thou art near,
O Sacred Heart.

4. O Sacred Heart,
lead exiled children home,
where we may ever rest near thee,
in peace and joy eternally,
O Sacred Heart.

Text: Francis Stanfield (1835-1914)
Music: Richard Runciman Terry (1865-1938)
Music © Copyright control

554 O sing a new song

Refrain
O sing a new song giving praise to the Lord, alleluia, alleluia, alleluia!

Advent:
1. People of God, be glad and rejoice, your Saviour comes: harken his voice!
2. He who will save the world from its stain comes from the clouds, gentle as rain.

© Copyright 1988 Kevin Mayhew Ltd.

Christmas:
3. This is the day the Saviour was born;
   God's love and peace shine in this dawn.

Our Lady:
4. Mother of God, we honour your worth;
   you gave us Christ to ransom earth.

Epiphany:
5. This Child you see is Saviour and Lord,
   God's Son made Man, by kings adored.

Presentation:
6. Glory to Christ who brought us his light;
   coming from God, he gives us sight.

Ascension:
7. As we have died with Christ unto sin,
   so we now share new life with him.

Pentecost:
8. God's Spirit fills the earth with his love,
   makes all things new, draws them above.

9. Spirit of God, come dwell in our hearts;
   kindle the fire your love imparts.

Doxology:
10. To Father, Son and Spirit be giv'n
    eternal praise, here and in heav'n.

Verses 1, 6, 7, 8, 9 & 10 can also be for General use

Text: Jean-Paul Lécot (b.1947) based on Matthew 2:11; Romans 6:8; Wisdom 8:1 trans. W.R. Lawrence
Music: Alexandre Lesbordes

555 O suffering Jesus

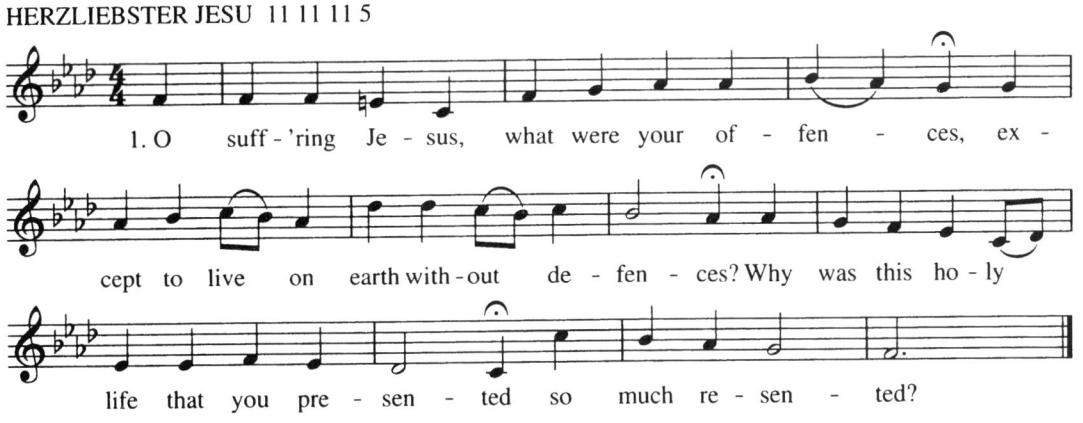

HERZLIEBSTER JESU 11 11 11 5

1. O suff-'ring Jesus, what were your offences, except to live on earth without defences? Why was this holy life that you presented so much resented?

2. The challenge of perfection made us tremble
   – a love we knew we never could resemble –
   and so you bore the sins of all creation
   for our salvation.

3. Those sins were ours – how grudgingly we own them!
   We treat them lightly, pardon and condone them.
   Yet, through the pain, your love shines out, revealing
   judgement and healing.

4. O suff'ring Christ, still found in ev'ry nation,
   you bear the pain and hope of all creation.
   Love reigns triumphant, sin and death defeated:
   all is completed.

Text: Michael Forster (b.1946)
Music: Johann Crüger (1598-1662)
Text © Copyright 1999 Kevin Mayhew Ltd.

556 O that today you would listen to his voice

Response

O that to-day you would lis-ten to his voice, 'Hard-en not your hearts.' *Fine*

1. Come let us joy-ful-ly sing to the Lord, sa-lut-ing the rock who pre-serves us.

Let us ap-proach him to of-fer him thanks, with songs let us wel-come our God. *D.C.*

2. Let us come in, let us kneel and adore
in rev'rence for God who has made us.
We are his people, the sheep of his flock,
we graze in the pastures of God.

3. Out in the desert they hardened their hearts,
at Massah they tested their Saviour,
O that today you would listen to him,
and open your hearts to his love.

Text: Susan Sayers (b.1946) based on Psalm 94
Music: Andrew Moore (b.1954)
© Copyright 1995 Kevin Mayhew Ltd.

557 O, the love of my Lord
As gentle as silence

AS GENTLE AS SILENCE 10 9 12 10

1. O, the love of my Lord is the es-sence of all that I love here on earth. All the beau-ty I see he has gi-ven to me, and his giv-ing is gen-tle as si-lence. 2. Ev-'ry
3. There've been

© Copyright McCrimmon Publishing Co. Ltd., 10-12 High Street, Great Wakering,
Southend-on-Sea, Essex SS3 0EQ. Used by arrangement.

2. Ev'ry day, ev'ry hour, ev'ry moment
   have been blessed by the strength of his love.
   At the turn of each tide he is there at my side,
   and his touch is as gentle as silence.

3. There've been times when I've turned from his presence,
   and I've walked other paths, other ways;
   but I've called on his name in the dark of my shame,
   and his mercy was gentle as silence.

Text and Music: Estelle White (b.1925)

558 O the word of my Lord

Refrain

O the word of my Lord, deep with-in my be-ing,
O the word of my Lord, you have filled my mind. mind.

1. Before I formed you in the womb,
   I knew you through and through,
   I chose you to be mine.
   Before you left your mother's side,
   I called to you, my child, to be my sign.

2. I know that you are very young,
   but I will make you strong,
   I'll fill you with my word;
   and you will travel through the land,
   fulfilling my command which you have heard.

3. And ev'rywhere you are to go
   my hand will follow you;
   you will not be alone.
   In all the danger that you fear
   you'll find me very near, your words my own.

4. With all my strength you will be filled:
   you will destroy and build,
   for that is my design.
   You will create and overthrow,
   reap harvests I will sow, your word is mine.

Text: Damian Lundy (1944-1997) based on Jeremiah 1
Music: Damian Lundy (1944-1997)
© Copyright 1978 Kevin Mayhew Ltd.

559 O thou, who at thy Eucharist didst pray

SONG 1 10 10 10 10 10 10

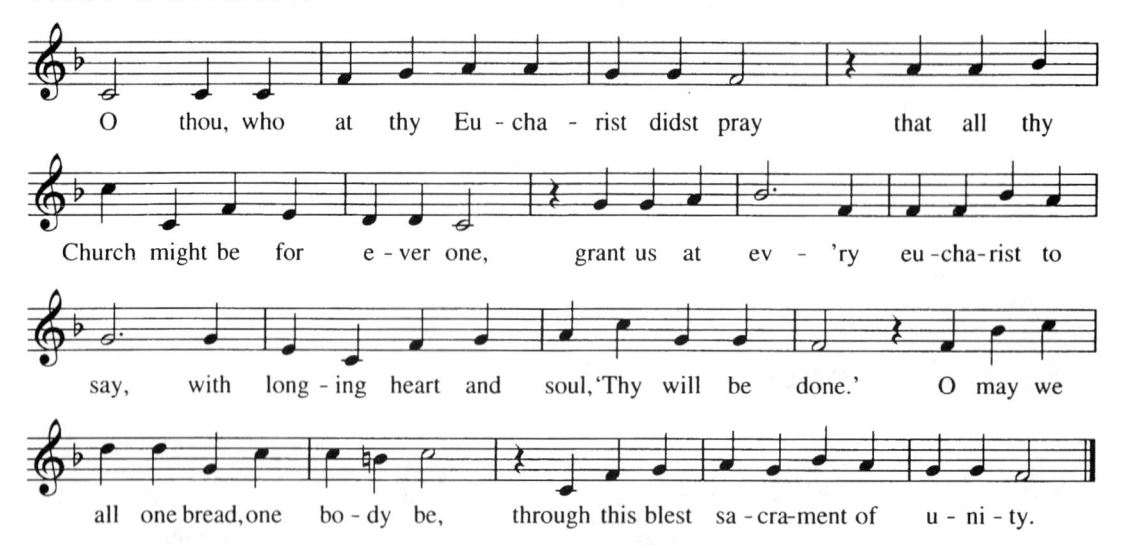

O thou, who at thy Eu-cha-rist didst pray that all thy Church might be for e-ver one, grant us at ev-'ry eu-cha-rist to say, with long-ing heart and soul, 'Thy will be done.' O may we all one bread, one bo-dy be, through this blest sa-cra-ment of u-ni-ty.

2. For all thy Church, O Lord, we intercede;
   make thou our sad divisions soon to cease;
   draw us the nearer each to each, we plead,
   by drawing all to thee, O Prince of Peace:
   thus may we all one bread, one body be,
   through this blest sacrament of unity.

3. We pray thee too for wand'rers from thy fold;
   O bring them back, good Shepherd of the sheep,
   back to the faith which saints believed of old,
   back to the Church which still that faith doth keep:
   soon may we all one bread, one body be,
   through this blest sacrament of unity.

4. So, Lord, at length when sacraments shall cease,
   may we be one with all thy Church above,
   one with thy saints in one unbroken peace,
   one with thy saints in one unbounded love:
   more blessèd still, in peace and love to be
   one with the Trinity in unity.

Text: William Harry Turton (1856-1938) based on John 17
Music: Orlando Gibbons (1583-1625)
Text © Copyright control

560 Our God loves us

PLAISIR D'AMOUR 4 6 6 5

1. Our God loves us, his love will ne-ver end. He rests with-in our hearts for our God loves us.

Text © Copyright 1976 Kevin Mayhew Ltd.

2. His gentle hand
   he stretches over us.
   Though storm-clouds threaten the day,
   he will set us free.

3. He comes to us
   in sharing bread and wine.
   He brings us life that will reach
   past the end of time.

4. Our God loves us,
   his faithful love endures,
   and we will live like his child
   held in love secure.

5. The joys of love
   as off'rings now we bring.
   The pains of love will be lost
   in the praise we sing.

Text: v.1 unknown; vs. 2-5 Sandra Joan Billington (b.1946)
Music: traditional

561 Our God sent his Son long ago

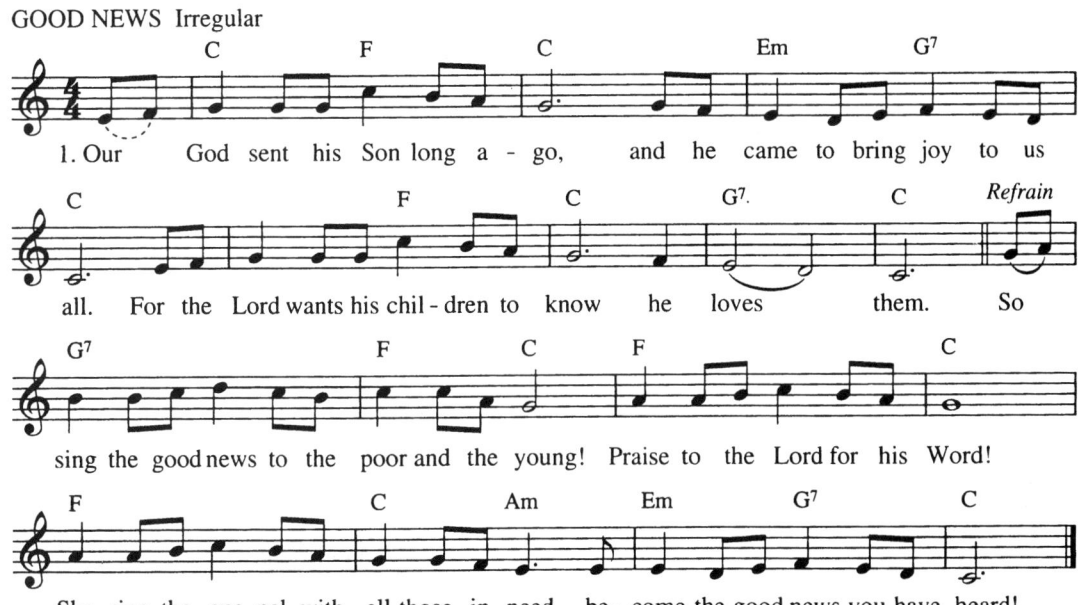

GOOD NEWS Irregular

1. Our God sent his Son long a-go, and he came to bring joy to us all. For the Lord wants his chil-dren to know he loves them. So sing the good news to the poor and the young! Praise to the Lord for his Word! Sha-ring the gos-pel with all those in need, be-come the good news you have heard!

2. But how will the good news be heard?
   When we answer the call of our Lord,
   when we live so our faith can be shared with others.

3. From the Spirit of God comes our call,
   bringing pow'r to be joyful and free,
   to be brothers and sisters to all: to love them.

4. Praise and glory to God for his Word,
   always living in those who believe,
   still made flesh in our lives to be shared with others.

Text and Music: Damian Lundy (1944-1997)
© Copyright 1982 Kevin Mayhew Ltd.

562 Our hearts were made for you

Our hearts were made for you, Lord, our hearts were made for you; they'll ne-ver find, ne-ver find, ne-ver find rest un-til they find their rest in you.

1. When you call me I will an-swer, when you seek me you will find. I will lead you back from ex-ile, and re-veal to you my mind.

2. I will take you from the nations, and will bring you to your land. From your idols I will cleanse you and you'll cherish my command.

3. I will put my law within you, I will write it on your heart; I will be your God and Saviour, you, my people set apart.

Text: Aniceto Nazareth based on Scripture
Music: Aniceto Nazareth
© Copyright 1984 Kevin Mayhew Ltd.

563 Our Saviour, Christ

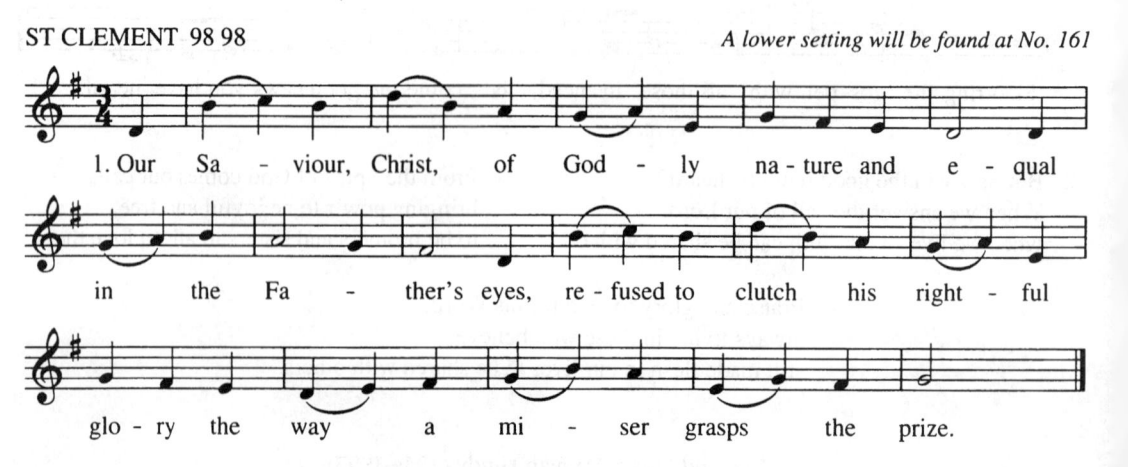

ST CLEMENT 98 98 *A lower setting will be found at No. 161*

1. Our Sa-viour, Christ, of God-ly na-ture and e-qual in the Fa-ther's eyes, re-fused to clutch his right-ful glo-ry the way a mi-ser grasps the prize.

Text © Copyright 1997 Kevin Mayhew Ltd.

2. Of all his heav'nly glory emptied,
his very self he freely gave,
to clothe himself in human nature
and wear the mantle of a slave.

3. Immortal God for us made mortal,
the God-breathed Word drew human breath,
then gave up even that to save us,
obedient to the very death.

4. From death to life did God exalt him,
to heaven's joy and earth's acclaim;
on him, and him alone, bestowing
the Name above all other names:

5. That at the glorious Name of Jesus
all nations shall acclaim his worth,
and every knee shall bow before him
above, below and on the earth.

6. Let ev'ry tongue in earth and heaven
proclaim that Jesus Christ is Lord,
who shows the glory of the Father,
our God for evermore adored.

Text: Michael Forster (b.1946) based on Philippians 2:6-11
Music: Clement Cotterill Scholefield (1839-1904)

564 Ours were the sufferings he bore

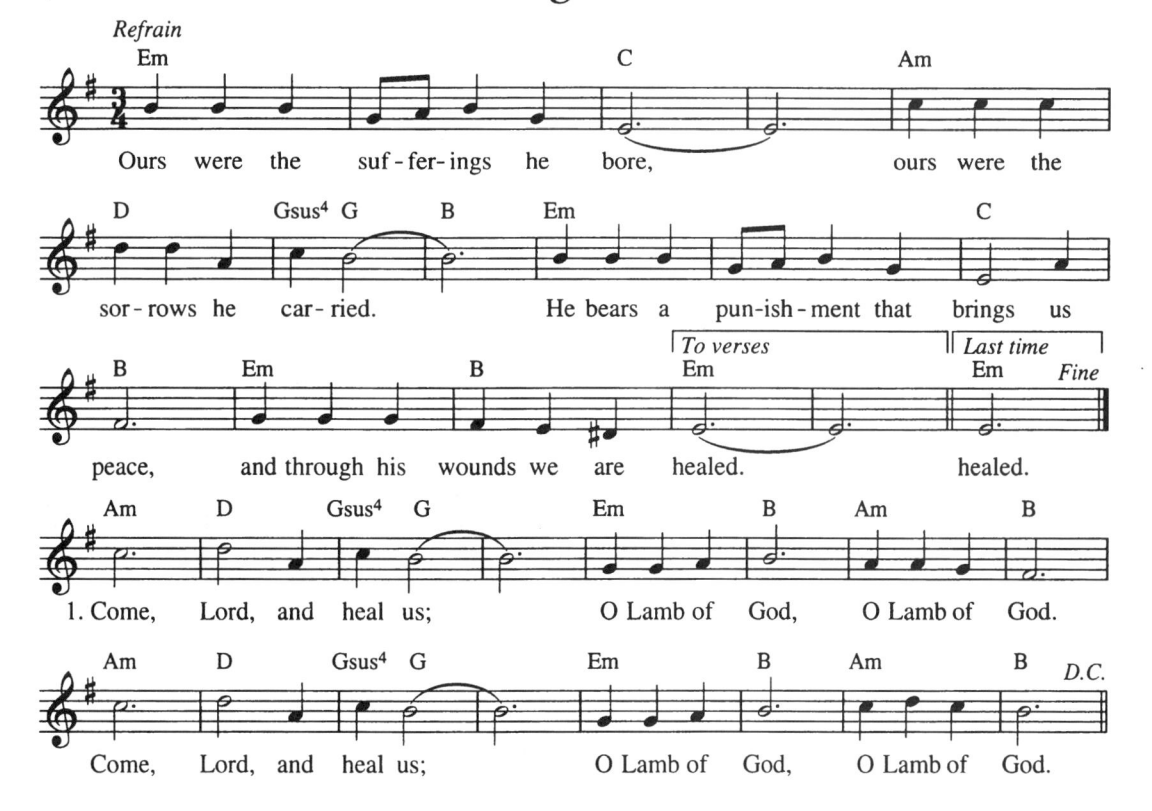

Refrain

Ours were the sufferings he bore, ours were the sorrows he carried. He bears a punishment that brings us peace, and through his wounds we are healed. healed.

1. Come, Lord, and heal us; O Lamb of God, O Lamb of God.
   Come, Lord, and heal us; O Lamb of God, O Lamb of God.

2. Come, Lord, and heal us;
   you died for us, you died for us.
   Come, Lord, and heal us;
   you died for us, you died for us.

3. Come, Lord, and heal us;
   grant us your peace, grant us your peace.
   Come, Lord, and heal us;
   grant us your peace, grant us your peace.

Text and Music: Francesca Leftley (b.1955)
© Copyright 1985, 1994 Francesca Leftley. Used by permission.
(Originally published by Clifton Music, Clifton Cathedral House, Clifton Park, Bristol BS8 3BX.)

565 Out of darkness

Refrain

Out of dark-ness God has called us, claimed by Christ as God's own peo-ple. Ho-ly na-tion, roy-al priest-hood, walk-ing in God's marv'-lous light. marv'-lous light. marv'-lous light. A-men.

1. Let us take the words you give,
   strong and faith-ful words to live,
   words that in our hearts are sown,
   words that bind us as your own.

2. Let us take the Christ you give,
   Broken Body Christ we live,
   Christ, the risen from the tomb,
   Christ, who calls us as your own.

3. Let us take the love you give,
   that the way of love we live,
   love to bring your people home,
   love to make us all your own.

Text and Music: Christopher Walker (b.1947)
© Copyright 1989 Christopher Walker. Published by OCP Publications, 5536 NE Hassalo, Portland, OR 97213, USA.
All rights reserved. Used by permission.

566 O Wisdom, source of harmony

O WALY WALY LM

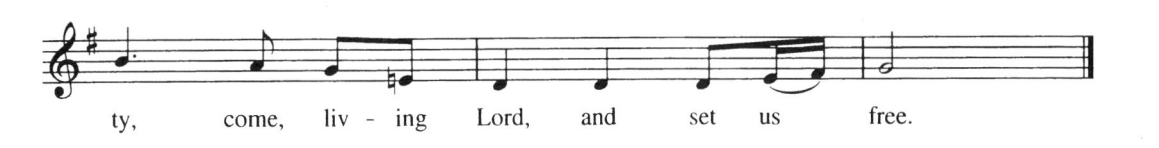

1. O Wisdom, source of harmony, the Word of God who made the world, sustaining life and liberty, come, living Lord, and set us free.

2. O sov'reign Lord who long ago
led Israel to liberty,
come once again! On earth below
your pow'r and loving-kindness show.

3. O Root of Jesse, hope for all
who long to see a new life grow,
come, raise your people when we fall,
come, flow'r among us when we call.

4. Oh shine on us, dear Morning Star!
Your radiant light be over all,
for death is banished where you are.
Come, shine in darkness from afar!

5. O David's key, your people wait
to know your faithfulness and care.
Come, save us from our gloomy state!
Oh come and open heaven's gate!

6. O King of ev'ry nation, come
and bring the joy for which we wait.
Lord, to the earth you made us from
come once again and be at home.

7. Emmanuel, God with us, Lord,
the ancient Word dispelling gloom,
in human flesh the living Word,
fulfil the promise we have heard.

8. Lord Jesus, come again, we pray,
come, live with us! Lord, with us stay!
Take all our shame and fear away.
Come, Lord! Be born again today.

Text: Damian Lundy (1944-1997) based on the 'O' Antiphons
Music: Somerset folk song collected by Cecil Sharp (1859-1924)
Text © Copyright 1987, 1996 Kevin Mayhew Ltd.

567 O Word, in uncreated light

CREATOR ALME SIDERUM LM

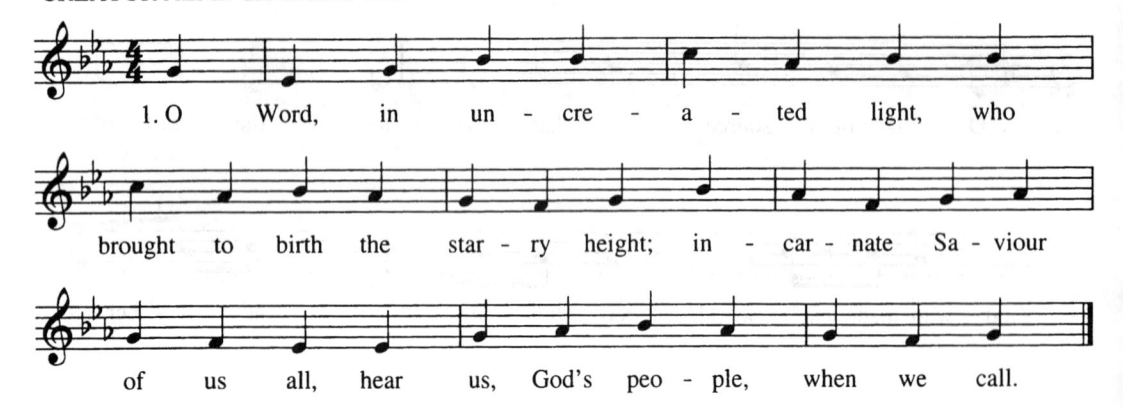

1. O Word, in uncreated light, who brought to birth the starry height; incarnate Saviour of us all, hear us, God's people, when we call.

2. Attentive to our helpless cry
as mortals, so afraid to die,
you took our flesh in truth and grace
to save the fallen human race.

3. When earth was in its crisis' hour,
you came in love's redeeming pow'r,
with life and grace to burst the tomb,
unsealing first the Virgin's womb.

4. Now to the glory of your Name
let praise be sung and due acclaim;
let all on earth and all above
declare you Lord of life and love.

5. Prepare us, Lord and Judge, we pray
to face you on the final day;
and keep us in this present hour
from yielding to temptation's pow'r.

6. To God the Father, God the Son,
and God the Spirit, Three in One,
all glory, praise and honour be,
from age to age eternally.

Alternative plainsong setting

CREATOR ALME SIDERUM

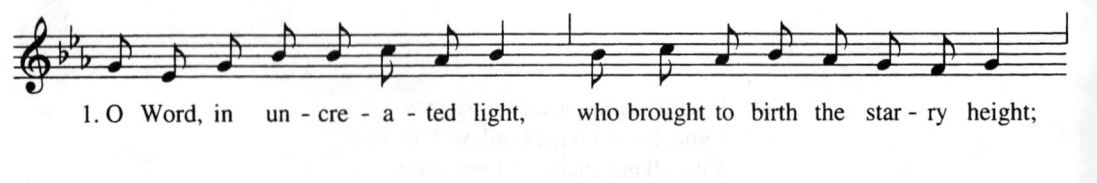

1. O Word, in uncreated light, who brought to birth the starry height; incarnate Saviour of us all, hear us, God's people, when we call.

Text: Michael Forster (b.1946) based on 'Creator alme siderum' (7th century)
Music: Plainsong
Text © Copyright 199 Kevin Mayhew Ltd.

568 O worship the King

HANOVER 10 10 11 11

1. O worship the King all glorious above;
O gratefully sing his pow'r and his love:
our shield and defender, the Ancient of Days,
pavilioned in splendour, and girded with praise.

2. O tell of his might, O sing of his grace,
whose robe is the light, whose canopy space;
his chariots of wrath the deep thunder-clouds form,
and dark is his path on the wings of the storm.

3. This earth, with its store of wonders untold,
almighty, thy pow'r hath founded of old:
hath stablished it fast by a changeless decree,
and round it hath cast, like a mantle, the sea.

4. Thy bountiful care what tongue can recite?
It breathes in the air, it shines in the light;
it streams from the hills, it descends to the plain,
and sweetly distils in the dew and the rain.

5. Frail children of dust, and feeble as frail,
in thee do we trust, nor find thee to fail;
thy mercies how tender, how firm to the end!
Our maker, defender, redeemer, and friend.

6. O measureless might, ineffable love,
while angels delight to hymn thee above,
thy humbler creation, though feeble their lays,
with true adoration shall sing to thy praise.

Text: Robert Grant (1779-1838) based on Psalm 103
Music: melody and bass by William Croft (1678-1727)
in 'A Supplement to the New Version' (1708)

569 O worship the Lord in the beauty of holiness

WAS LEBET 13 10 13 10

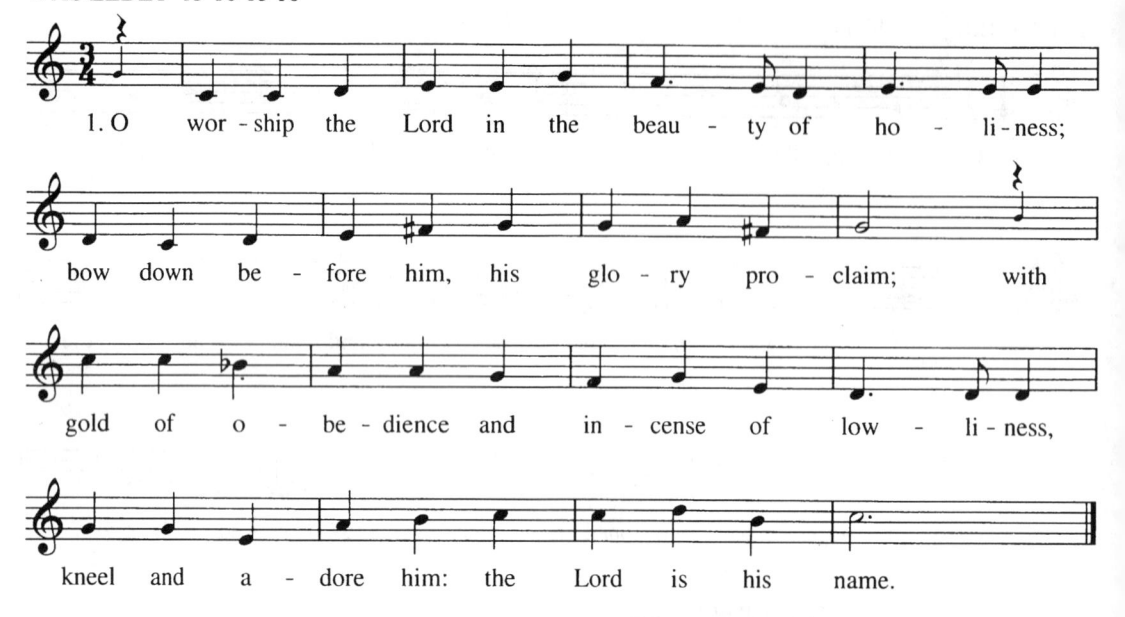

1. O worship the Lord in the beauty of holiness;
bow down before him, his glory proclaim;
with gold of obedience and incense of lowliness,
kneel and adore him: the Lord is his name.

2. Low at his feet lay thy burden of carefulness:
high on his heart he will bear it for thee,
comfort thy sorrows, and answer thy prayerfulness,
guiding thy steps as may best for thee be.

3. Fear not to enter his courts in the slenderness
of the poor wealth thou wouldst reckon as thine:
truth in its beauty, and love in its tenderness,
these are the off'rings to lay on his shrine.

4. These, though we bring them in trembling and fearfulness,
he will accept for the name that is dear;
mornings of joy give for evenings of tearfulness,
trust for our trembling and hope for our fear.

Text: John Samuel Bewley Monsell (1811-1875)
Music: melody from the 'Rheinhardt MS', Üttingen (1754)

570 Pange lingua gloriosi

PANGE LINGUA 87 87 87

Pange lingua gloriosi, Corporis Mysterium,
Sanguinisque pretiosi quem in mundi pretium,
fructus ventris generosi Rex effudit gentium.

Last time

A - men.

2. Nobis datus, nobis natus
ex intacta Virgine;
et in mundo conversatus,
sparso verbi semine,
sui moras incolatus
miro clausit ordine.

3. In supremæ nocte coenæ
recumbens cum fratribus,
observata lege plene
cibis in legalibus:
cibum turbæ duodenæ
se dat suis manibus.

4. Verbum caro, panem verum,
verbo carnem efficit:
fitque sanguis Christi merum;
et si sensus deficit,
ad firmandum cor sincerum
sola fides sufficit.

5. Tantum ergo Sacramentum
veneremur cernui:
et antiquum documentum
novo cedat ritui;
præstet fides supplementum
sensuum defectui.

6. Genitori, genitoque
laus, et jubilatio,
salus, honor, virtus quoque
sit et benedictio;
procedenti ab utroque
compar sit laudatio. Amen.

Text: St Thomas Aquinas (1227-1274)
Music: Plainsong

571 Peace I leave with you

Peace I leave with you, peace I give to you;
not as the world gives peace, do I give.
Take and pass it on, on to ev-'ry one;
thus the world will know, you are my friends.

Text and Music: Peter Madden
© Copyright 1976 Kevin Mayhew Ltd.

572 Peace is flowing like a river

VERSION 1

1\. Peace is flowing like a river, flowing out through you and me,
spreading out into the desert, setting all the captives free.

2. Love is flowing like a river,
   flowing out through you and me,
   spreading out into the desert,
   setting all the captives free.

3. Joy is flowing like a river,
   flowing out through you and me,
   spreading out into the desert,
   setting all the captives free.

4. Hope is flowing like a river,
   flowing out through you and me,
   spreading out into the desert,
   setting all the captives free.

5. Christ brings peace to all creation,
   flowing out through you and me,
   love, joy, hope and true salvation,
   setting all the captives free.

VERSION 2: with Refrain

1\. Peace is flowing like a river, flowing out through you and me, spreading out into the desert, setting all the captives free. *Refrain* Let it flow through me, let it flow through me, let the mighty peace of God flow

Verse 5 © Copyright 1999 Kevin Mayhew Ltd.

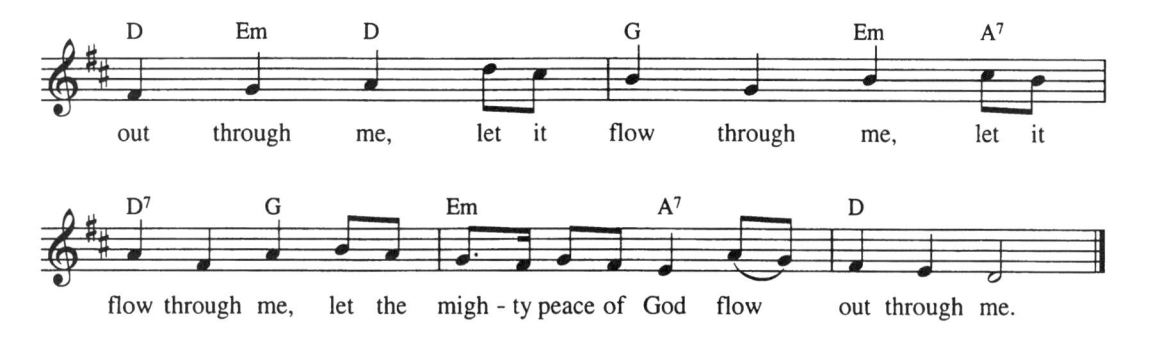

out through me, let it flow through me, let it flow through me, let the migh-ty peace of God flow out through me.

Text: vs.1-4 unknown; v.5 the Editors
Music: unknown

573 Peace is the gift

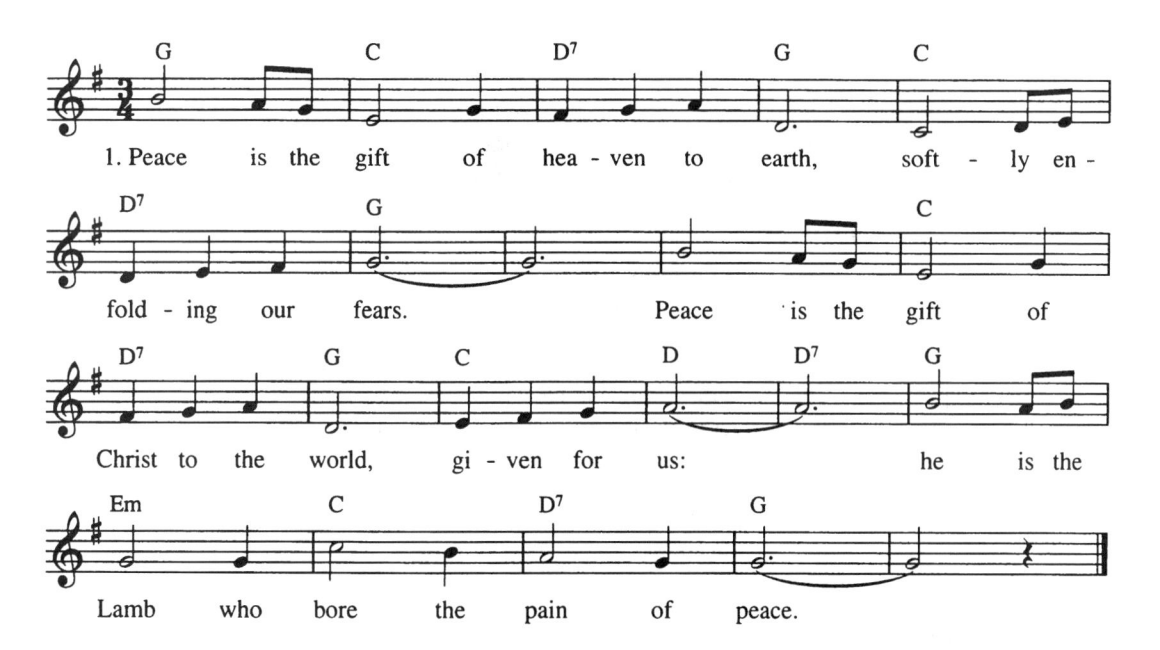

1. Peace is the gift of hea-ven to earth, soft-ly en-fold-ing our fears. Peace is the gift of Christ to the world, gi-ven for us: he is the Lamb who bore the pain of peace.

2. Peace is the gift of Christ to his Church,
   wound of the lance of his love.
   Love is the pain he suffered for all,
     offered to us:
   O, to accept the wound that brings us peace!

3. Joy is the gift the Spirit imparts,
   born of the heavens and earth.
   We are his children, children of joy,
     people of God:
   he is our Lord, our peace, our love, our joy!

Text and Music: John Glynn (b.1948)
© Copyright 1976 Kevin Mayhew Ltd.

574 Peace, perfect peace

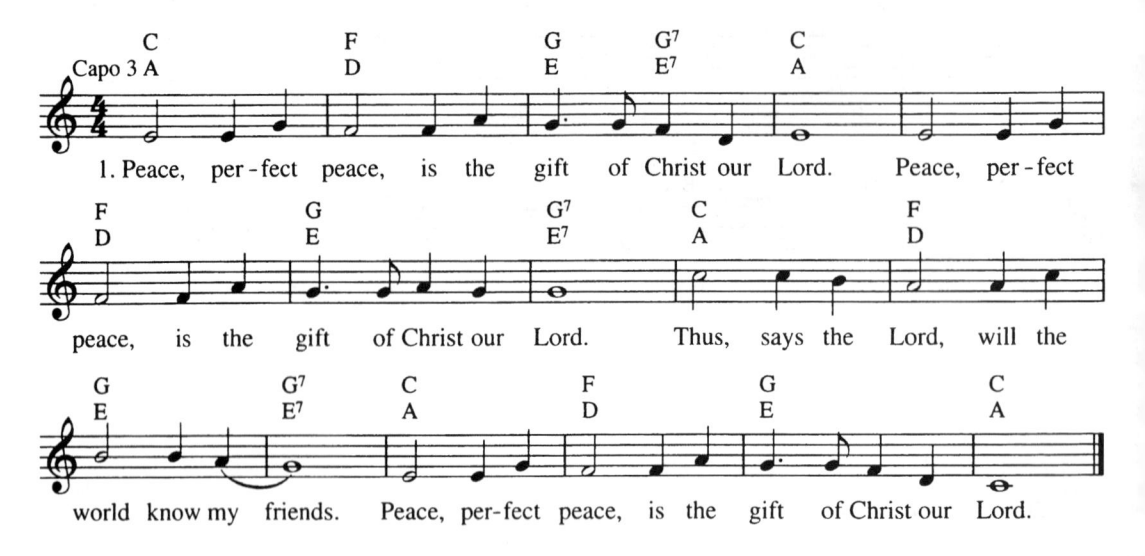

1. Peace, perfect peace, is the gift of Christ our Lord. Peace, perfect peace, is the gift of Christ our Lord. Thus, says the Lord, will the world know my friends. Peace, perfect peace, is the gift of Christ our Lord.

2. Love, perfect love, is the gift of Christ our Lord. *(x2)*
   Thus, says the Lord, will the world know my friends.
   Love, perfect love, is the gift of Christ our Lord.

3. Faith, perfect faith, is the gift of Christ our Lord. *(x2)*
   Thus, says the Lord, will the world know my friends.
   Faith, perfect faith, is the gift of Christ our Lord.

4. Hope, perfect hope, is the gift of Christ our Lord. *(x2)*
   Thus, says the Lord, will the world know my friends.
   Hope perfect hope, is the gift of Christ our Lord.

5. Joy, perfect joy, is the gift of Christ our Lord. *(x2)*
   Thus, says the Lord, will the world know my friends.
   Joy, perfect joy, is the gift of Christ our Lord.

Text and Music: Kevin Mayhew (b.1942)
© Copyright 1976 Kevin Mayhew Ltd.

575 Praise him

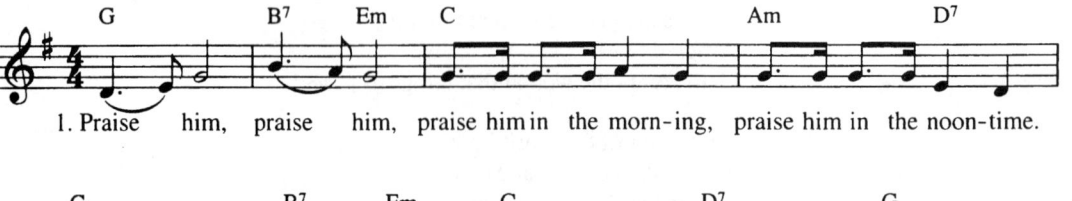

1. Praise him, praise him, praise him in the morning, praise him in the noon-time. Praise him, praise him, praise him when the sun goes down.

2. Love him, love him,
   love him in the morning,
   love him in the noontime.
   Love him, love him,
   love him when the sun goes down.

3. Trust him, trust him,
   trust him in the morning,
   trust him in the noontime.
   Trust him, trust him,
   trust him when the sun goes down.

4. Serve him, serve him,
   serve him in the morning,
   serve him in the noontime.
   Serve him, serve him,
   serve him when the sun goes down.

5. Jesus, Jesus,
   Jesus in the morning,
   Jesus in the noontime.
   Jesus, Jesus,
   Jesus when the sun goes down.

Text and Music: unknown

576 Praise, my soul, the King of heaven

PRAISE, MY SOUL 87 87 87

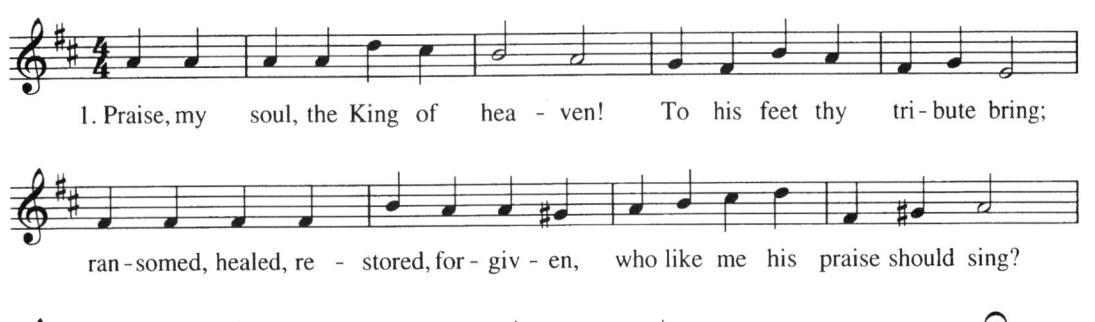

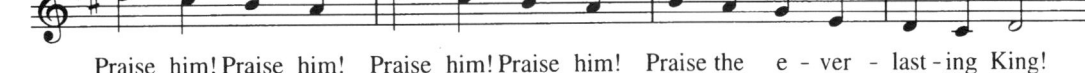

1. Praise, my soul, the King of heaven!
   To his feet thy tribute bring;
   ransomed, healed, restored, forgiven,
   who like me his praise should sing?
   Praise him! Praise him! Praise him! Praise him!
   Praise the everlasting King!

2. Praise him for his grace and favour
   to our fathers in distress;
   praise him still the same for ever,
   slow to chide and swift to bless.
   Praise him! Praise him!
   Praise him! Praise him!
   Glorious in his faithfulness!

3. Father-like, he tends and spares us;
   well our feeble frame he knows;
   in his hands he gently bears us,
   rescues us from all our foes.
   Praise him! Praise him!
   Praise him! Praise him!
   Widely as his mercy flows!

4. Angels, help us to adore him;
   ye behold him face to face;
   sun and moon, bow down before him,
   dwellers all in time and space.
   Praise him! Praise him!
   Praise him! Praise him!
   Praise with us the God of grace!

Text: Henry Frances Lyte (1793-1847) alt. based on Psalm 103
Music: John Goss (1800-1880)

577 Praise the Lord

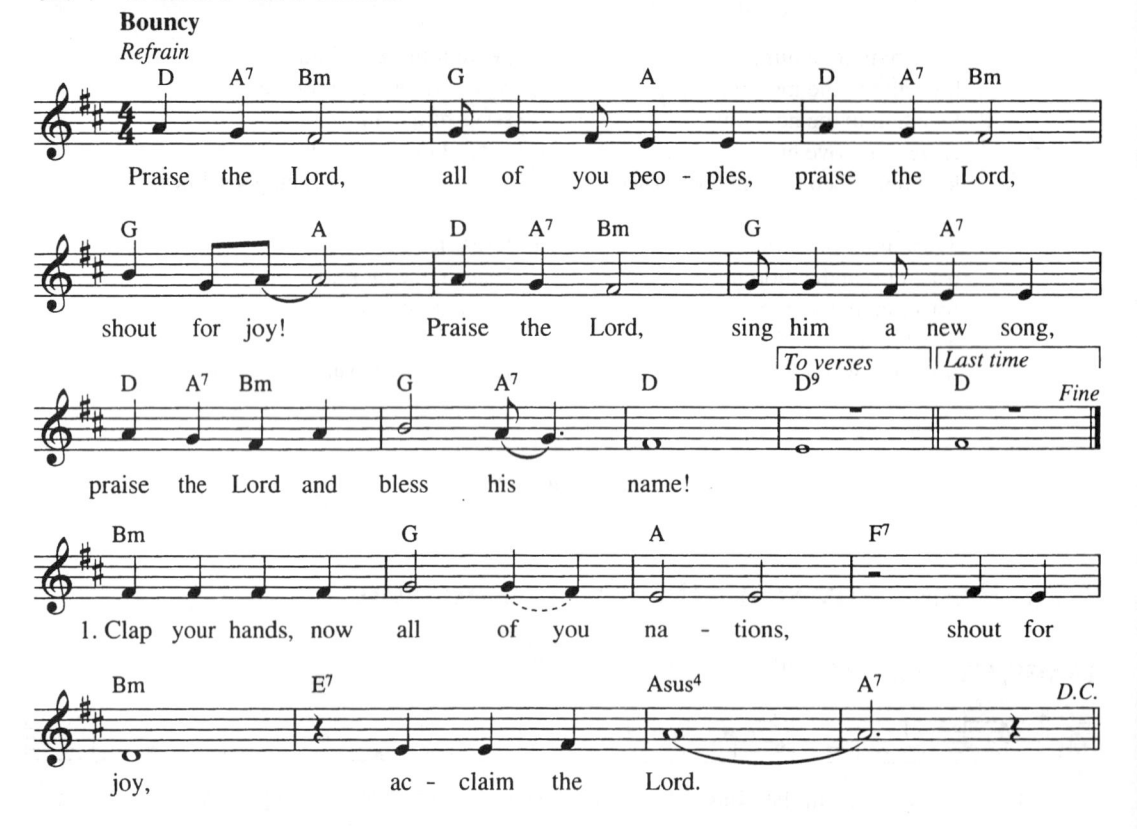

Bouncy

Refrain

Praise the Lord, all of you peo-ples, praise the Lord, shout for joy! Praise the Lord, sing him a new song, praise the Lord and bless his name!

1. Clap your hands, now all of you na-tions, shout for joy, ac-claim the Lord.

2. He goes up to shouts which acclaim him;
   he goes up to trumpet blast.

3. Let the music sound for the Lord, now;
   let your chords resound in praise.

4. He is King of all the nations;
   honour him by singing psalms.

Text: Mike Anderson (b.1956) based on Psalm 46
Music: Mike Anderson (b.1956)
© Copyright 1999 Kevin Mayhew Ltd.

578 Praise the Lord in his holy house

Refrain

Praise the Lord in his ho-ly house, in the fir-ma-ment of his ma-jes-ty. Praise the Lord! Praise the Lord! (Praise the Lord! Praise the Lord!)

1. Praise the Lord in his ho-ly house, in the fir-ma-

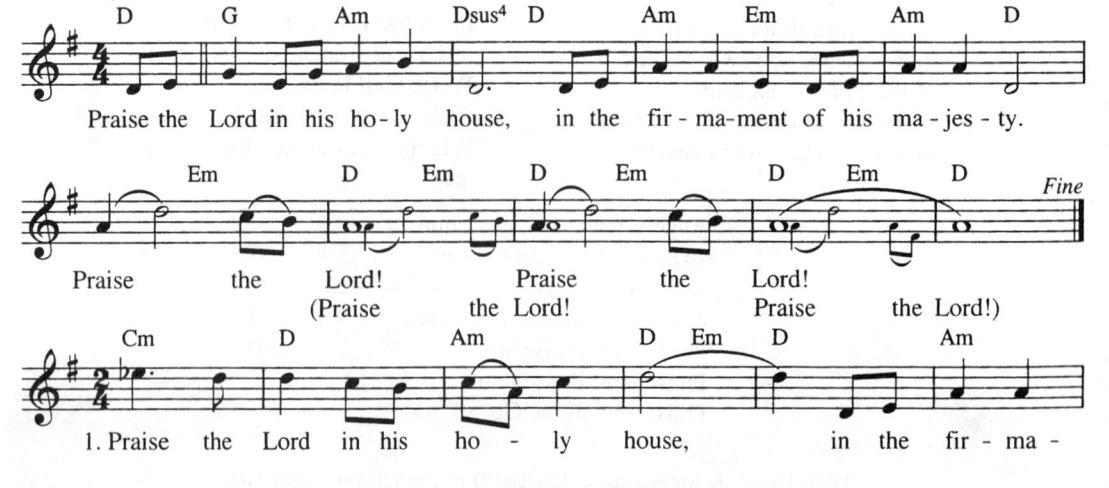

© Copyright 1984 Kevin Mayhew Ltd.

ment of his majesty. Praise him for all his pow'r-ful works.

Praise him, he is truly great.

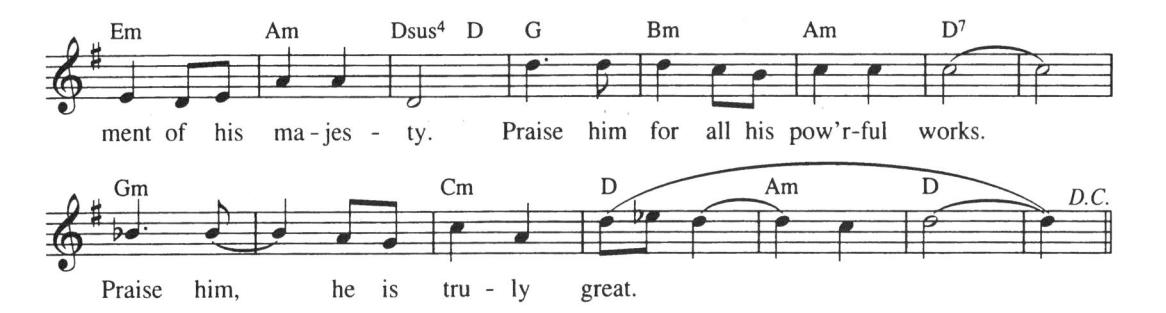

2. Praise him with your resounding horns,
   praise him with your lutes,
   your guitars and harps.
   Praise with dancing and tambourines,
   tune your strings and play your flute!

3. Praise with cymbals and pounding drums,
   praise him, brass and woodwind,
   let choirs rejoice.
   Alleluia, alleluia!
   All living, sing praise to God!

Text: Frances M. Kelly based on Psalm 150
Music: Frances M. Kelly

579 Praise the Lord, ye heavens, adore him

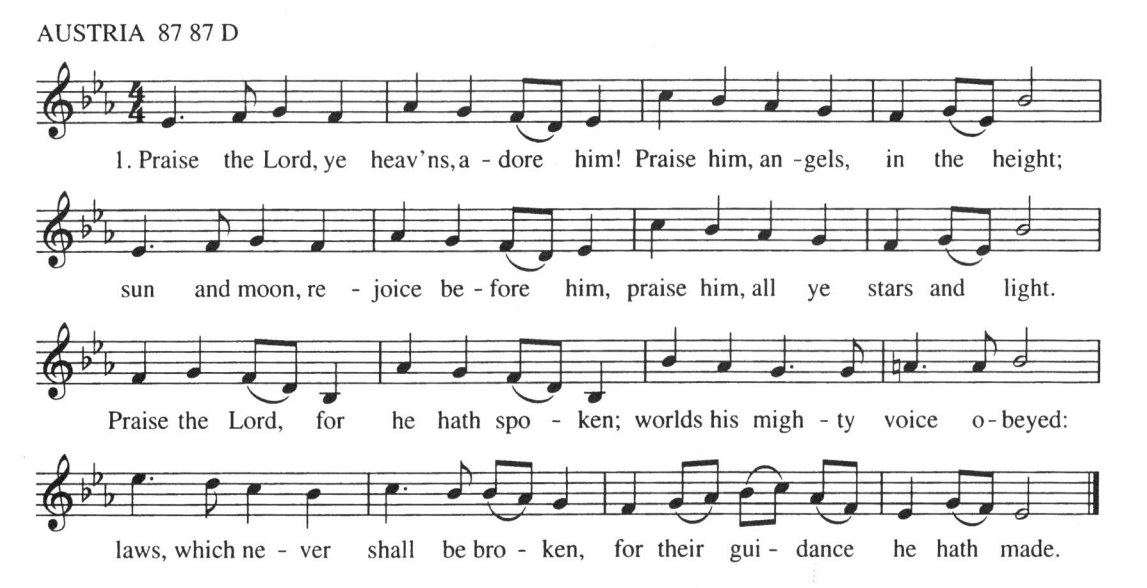

AUSTRIA 87 87 D

1. Praise the Lord, ye heav'ns, adore him! Praise him, angels, in the height;
sun and moon, rejoice before him, praise him, all ye stars and light.
Praise the Lord, for he hath spoken; worlds his mighty voice obeyed:
laws, which never shall be broken, for their guidance he hath made.

2. Praise the Lord, for he is glorious:
   never shall his promise fail.
   God hath made his saints victorious;
   sin and death shall not prevail.
   Praise the God of our salvation,
   hosts on high, his pow'r proclaim;
   heav'n and earth and all creation,
   laud and magnify his name!

3. Worship, honour, glory, blessing,
   Lord, we offer to thy name;
   young and old, thy praise expressing,
   join their Saviour to proclaim.
   As the saints in heav'n adore thee,
   we would bow before thy throne;
   as thine angels serve before thee,
   so on earth thy will be done.

Text: vs. 1 & 2: from 'Foundling Hospital Collection' (1796)
v. 3: Edward Osler (1798-1863)
Music: Croatian folk melody adapted by Franz Joseph Haydn (1732-1809)

580 Praise to God for saints and martyrs

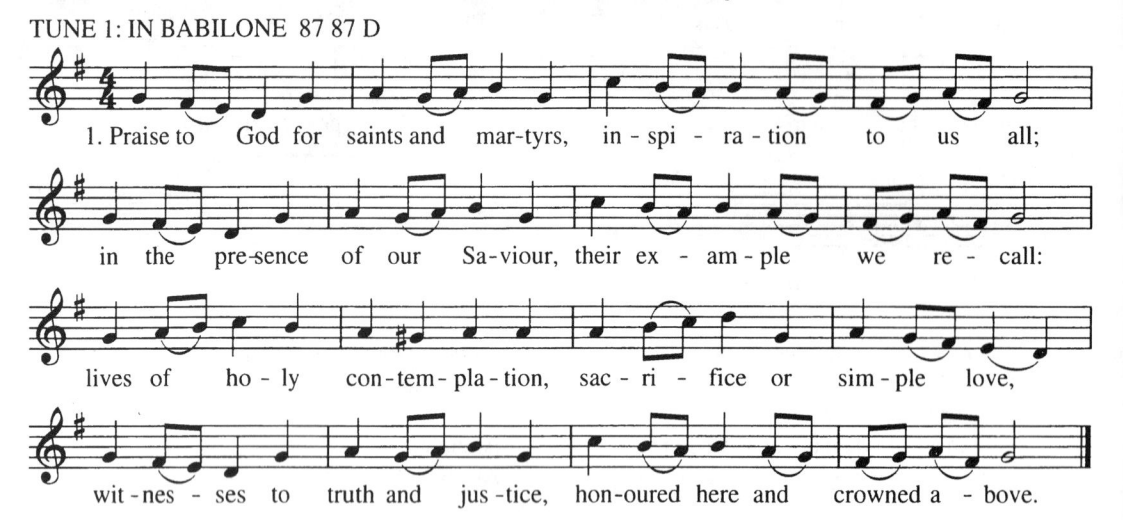

TUNE 1: IN BABILONE 87 87 D

1. Praise to God for saints and martyrs, inspiration to us all;
in the presence of our Saviour, their example we recall:
lives of holy contemplation, sacrifice or simple love,
witnesses to truth and justice, honoured here and crowned above.

2. How we long to share their story, faithful in response to grace,
signs of God's eternal presence in the realm of time and space.
Now, their pilgrimage completed, cross of Christ their only boast,
they unite their own rejoicing with the great angelic host.

3. Saints and martyrs, now in glory, robed before your Saviour's face,
let us join your intercession for God's holy human race.
Let us join with you in singing Mary's liberation song,
till a just and free creation sings, with the angelic throng:

4. Praise and honour to the Father, adoration to the Son,
with the all-embracing Spirit wholly Three and wholly One.
All the universe, united in complete diversity,
sings as one your endless praises, ever-blessèd Trinity!

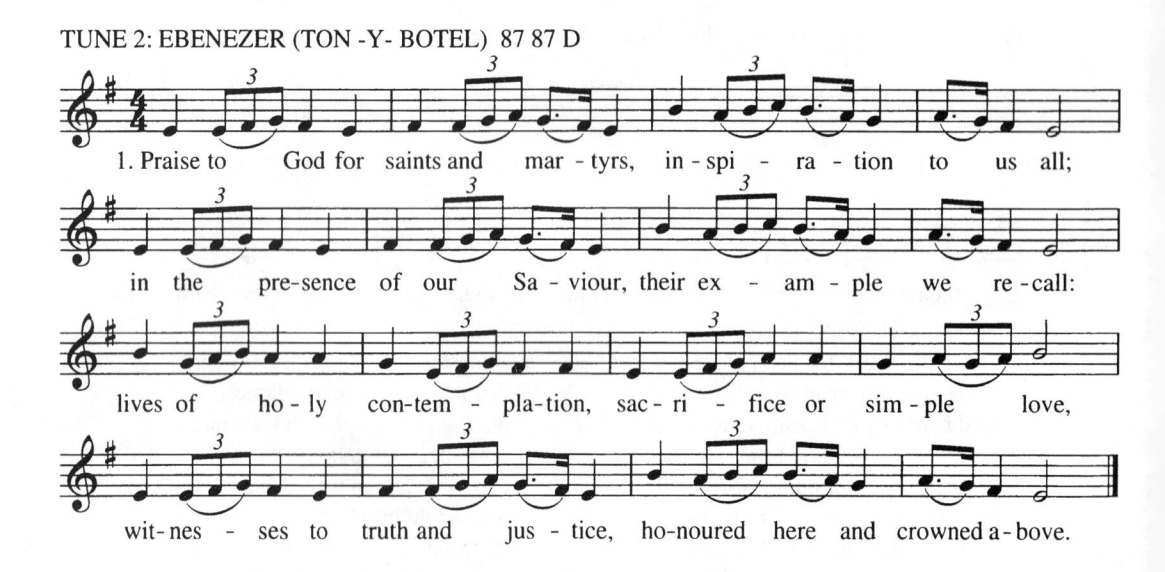

TUNE 2: EBENEZER (TON -Y- BOTEL) 87 87 D

1. Praise to God for saints and martyrs, inspiration to us all;
in the presence of our Saviour, their example we recall:
lives of holy contemplation, sacrifice or simple love,
witnesses to truth and justice, honoured here and crowned above.

Text : Michael Forster (b.1946)
Music: Tune 1 – traditional Dutch melody arr. Julius Röntgen
Tune 2 – from an anthem by Thomas Williams (1869 - 1944))
Text © Copyright 1999 Kevin Mayhew Ltd.
Tune 2 © Copyright control.

581 Praise to God in the highest

Cantor
1. Praise to God in the highest!
All
Bless us, O Father! Praise to you!

2. Guide and prosper the nations,
   rulers and peoples.

3. May the truth in its beauty
   flourish triumphant.

4. May the mills bring us bread
   for food and for giving.

5. May the good be obeyed
   and evils be conquered.

6. Give us laughter and set
   all your people rejoicing.

7. Peace on earth and goodwill
   be ever among us.

Text and Music: unknown

582 Praise to the Holiest

BILLING CM *A higher setting will be found at No. 704*

1. Praise to the Holiest in the height, and in the depth be praise; in all his words most wonderful, most sure in all his ways.

2. O loving wisdom of our God!
   when all was sin and shame,
   a second Adam to the fight,
   and to the rescue came.

3. O wisest love! that flesh and blood,
   which did in Adam fail,
   should strive afresh against the foe,
   should strive and should prevail.

4. And that a higher gift than grace
   should flesh and blood refine,
   God's presence and his very self,
   and essence all-divine.

5. And in the garden secretly,
   and on the cross on high,
   should teach his brethren, and inspire
   to suffer and to die.

6. Praise to the Holiest in the height,
   and in the depth be praise;
   in all his words most wonderful,
   most sure in all his ways.

Text: John Henry Newman (1801-1890)
Music: Richard Runciman Terry (1865-1938)
Music © Copyright Burns & Oates Ltd, Wellwood, North Farm Road,
Tunbridge Wells, Kent TN2 3QR. Used by permission.

583 Praise to the Lord, the Almighty (Version A)

LOBE DEN HERREN 14 14 4 7 8

1. Praise to the Lord, the Almighty, the King of creation!
O my soul, praise him, for he is your health and salvation.
All you who hear, now to his altar draw near;
join in profound adoration.

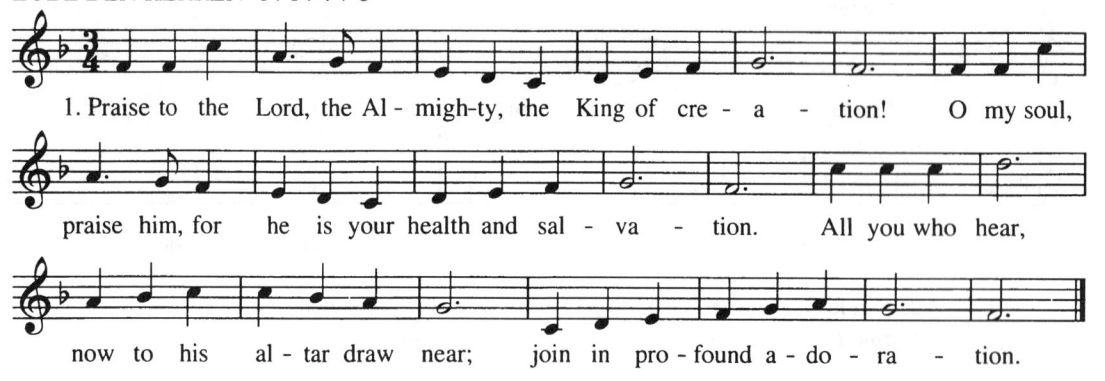

2. Praise to the Lord, let us
    offer our gifts at his altar;
    let not our sins and transgressions
    now cause us to falter.
    Christ, the High Priest,
    bids us all join in his feast;
    victims with him on the altar.

3. Praise to the Lord, O let all that
    is in us adore him!
    All that has life and breath,
    come now with praises before him.
    Let the 'Amen'
    sound from his people again,
    now as we worship before him.

Text: Joachim Neander (1650-1680) trans. Catherine Winkworth (1827-1878) alt.
Music: from 'Praxis Pietatis Melica' (1668)

584 Praise to the Lord, the Almighty (Version B)

LOBE DEN HERREN 14 14 4 7 8

For use on Ecumenical occasions

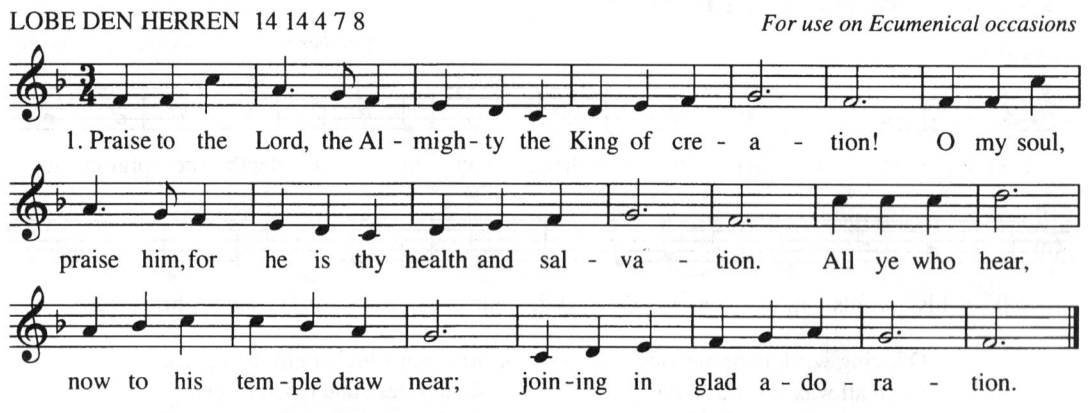

1. Praise to the Lord, the Almighty the King of creation!
O my soul, praise him, for he is thy health and salvation.
All ye who hear, now to his temple draw near;
joining in glad adoration.

2. Praise to the Lord, who o'er all
    things so wondrously reigneth,
    shieldeth thee gently from harm,
    or when fainting sustaineth:
    hast thou not seen
    how thy heart's wishes have been
    granted in what he ordaineth?

3. Praise to the Lord, who doth prosper
    thy work and defend thee,
    surely his goodness and mercy
    shall daily attend thee:
    ponder anew what the Almighty can do,
    if to the end he befriend thee.

4. Praise to the Lord, O let all
    that is in us adore him!
    All that hath life and breath,
    come now with praises before him.
    Let the 'Amen' sound from his people again,
    gladly for ay we adore him.

Text: Joachim Neander (1650-1680) trans. Catherine Winkworth (1827-1878)
Music: from 'Praxis Pietatis Melica' (1668)

585 Praise to you, O Christ, our Saviour

Refrain

Praise to you, O Christ, our Saviour, Word of the Father, calling us to life; Son of God who leads us to freedom: glory to you, Lord Jesus Christ! Christ!

1. You are the Word who calls us out of darkness; you are the Word who leads us into light; you are the Word who brings us through the desert: glory to you, Lord Jesus Christ!

2. You are the one whom prophets hoped and longed for;
   you are the one who speaks to us today;
   you are the one who leads us to our future:
   glory to you, Lord Jesus Christ!

3. You are the Word who calls us to be servants;
   you are the Word whose only law is love;
   you are the Word-made-flesh who lives among us:
   glory to you, Lord Jesus Christ!

4. You are the Word who binds us and unites us;
   you are the Word who calls us to be one;
   you are the Word who teaches us forgiveness:
   glory to you, Lord Jesus Christ!

Text and Music: Bernadette Farrell

© Copyright 1986 Bernadette Farrell. Published by OCP Publications, 5536 NE Hassalo, Portland, OR 97213, USA.
All rights reserved. Used by permission.

586 Praise we our God with joy

NUN DANKET 67 67 66 66 *A higher setting will be found at No. 497*

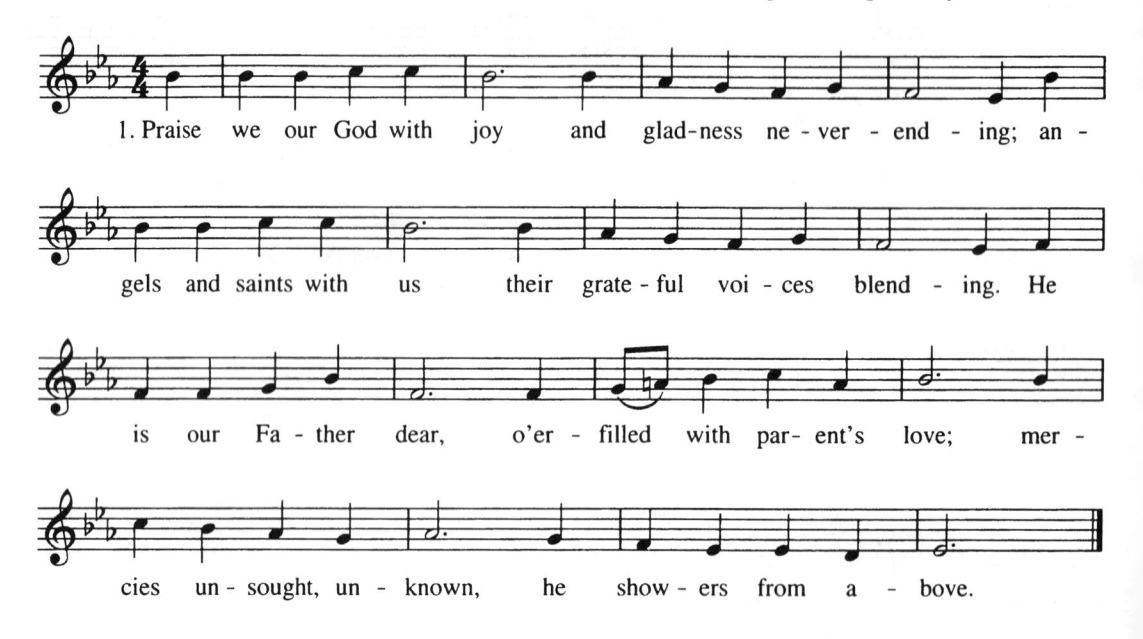

1. Praise we our God with joy and gladness never-ending; angels and saints with us their grateful voices blending. He is our Father dear, o'er-filled with parent's love; mercies unsought, unknown, he showers from above.

2. He is our shepherd true;
   with watchful care unsleeping,
   on us, his erring sheep,
   an eye of pity keeping;
   he with a mighty arm
   the bonds of sin doth break,
   and to our burdened hearts
   in words of peace doth speak.

3. Graces in copious stream
   from that pure fount are welling,
   where, in our heart of hearts,
   our God hath set his dwelling.
   His word our lantern is;
   his peace our comfort still;
   his sweetness all our rest;
   our law, our life, his will.

Text: Frederick Oakeley (1802-1880) and others
Music: Johann Crüger (1598-1662)

587 Reap me the earth

JUCUNDA LAUDATIO 10 7 10 7 and Refrain

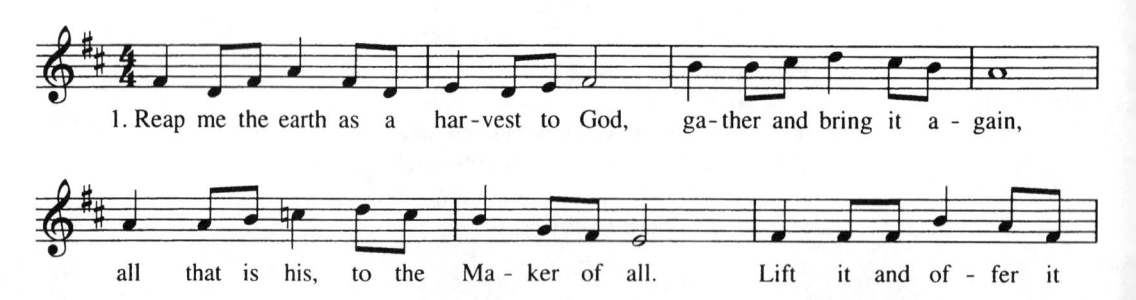

1. Reap me the earth as a harvest to God, gather and bring it again, all that is his, to the Maker of all. Lift it and offer it

© Copyright McCrimmon Publishing Co. Ltd, 10-12 High Street, Great Wakering, Southend-on-Sea, Essex SS3 0EQ.
Used by permission.

Refrain

high. Bring bread, bring wine, give glory to the Lord; whose is the earth but God's, whose is the praise but his?

2. Go with your song and your music with joy,
   go to the altar of God.
   Carry your offerings, fruits of the earth,
   work of your labouring hands.

3. Gladness and pity and passion and pain,
   all that is mortal in man,
   lay all before him, return him his gift,
   God, to whom all shall go home.

Text: Luke Connaughton (1917-1979)
Music: Gregory Murray (1905-1992)

588 Regina cæli

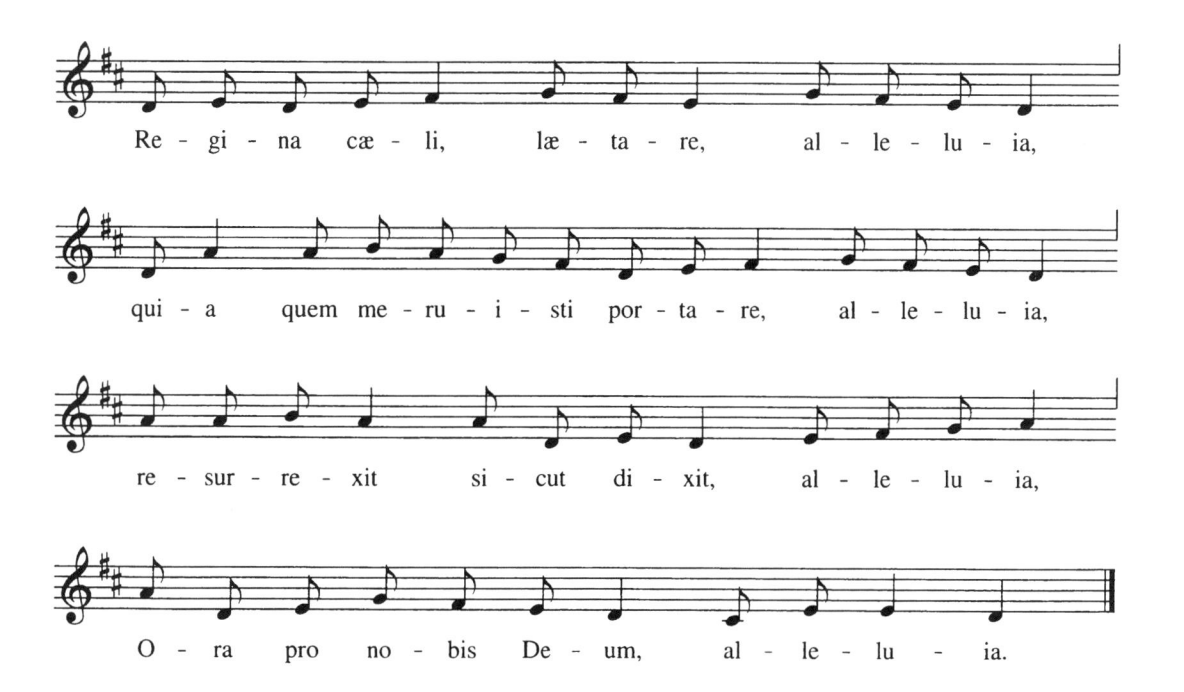

Re - gi - na cæ - li, læ - ta - re, al - le - lu - ia,

qui - a quem me - ru - i - sti por - ta - re, al - le - lu - ia,

re - sur - re - xit si - cut di - xit, al - le - lu - ia,

O - ra pro no - bis De - um, al - le - lu - ia.

Text: unknown, 12th century
Music: Plainsong

589 Rejoice, all heavenly powers

DARWALL'S 148TH 66 66 44 44

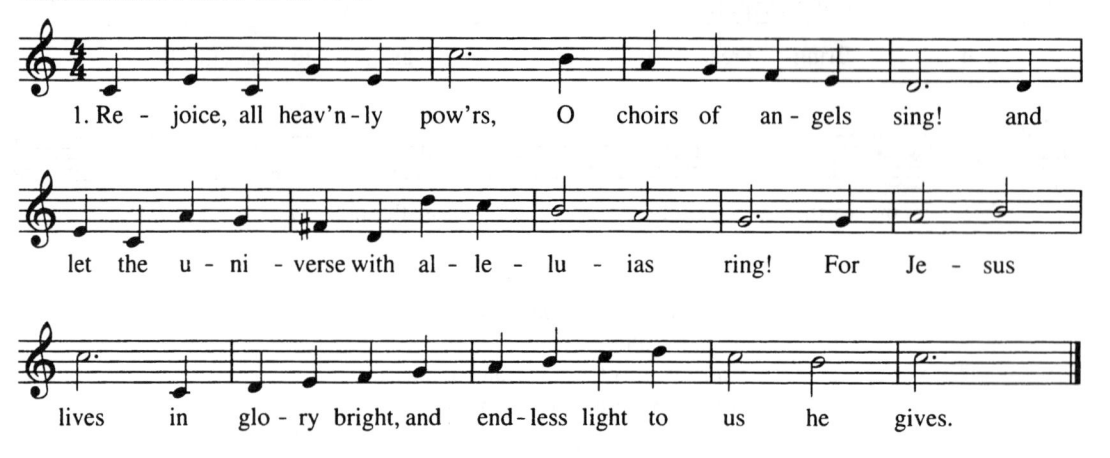

1. Rejoice, all heav'nly pow'rs, O choirs of angels sing! and let the universe with alleluias ring! For Jesus lives in glory bright, and endless light to us he gives.

2. Rejoice, O shining earth,
in glorious hope reborn,
and praise the Light who wrought
the first creation's dawn.
Redeemed and free,
in Christ we rise,
and darkness dies
eternally.

3. Rejoice, O Mother church;
on you the Saviour shines:
then let the vaults resound
with joy and peace divine!
His truth proclaim,
and loud and long,
in glorious song,
exalt his name.

4. The people who have walked
in terror through the night,
from shades of death released,
have seen a glorious light.
God's word is sure,
and he will bless
with righteousness
the humble poor.

5. O God of hope and love,
who lit the desert way,
and led from slav'ry's night
to liberation's day:
still go before,
till we rejoice,
with heart and voice,
on Canaan's shore.

6. We light these gentle flames
to be our pledge and sign:
we share the risen life
of Christ, the light divine.
Throughout the earth,
oppression's night
shall flee the light
of human worth.

7. Arise, O Morning Star,
O Sun who never sets,
and bring these humble flames
to greater glory yet.
Let all adore,
in glorious strains,
the Christ who reigns
for evermore.

Text: Michael Forster (b.1946) based on the 'Exsultet' from the Easter Vigil Liturgy
Music: John Darwall (1731-1789)
Text © Copyright 1997 Kevin Mayhew Ltd.

590 Rejoice in the Lord always

This may be sung as a round, the second voice entering at the double bar.

Rejoice in the Lord always and again I say rejoice. Rejoice in the Lord always and again I say re-

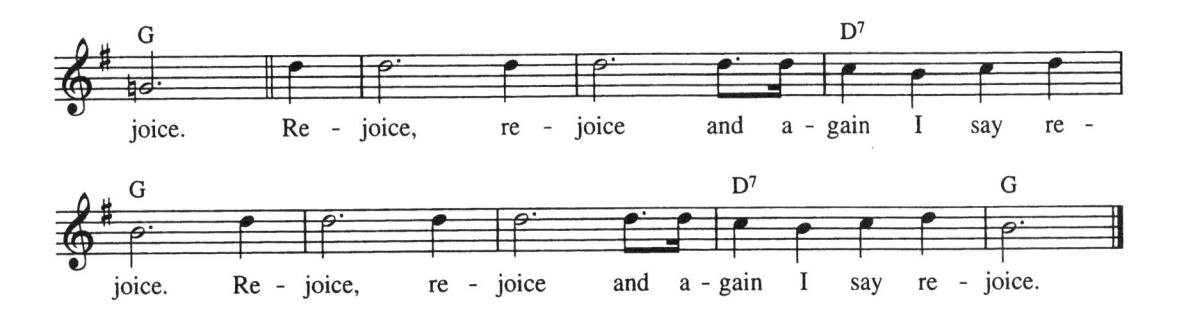

joice. Re - joice, re - joice and a - gain I say re -
joice. Re - joice, re - joice and a - gain I say re - joice.

Text: based on Philippians 4:4
Music: unknown

591 Rejoice, the Lord is King

GOPSAL 66 66 and Refrain

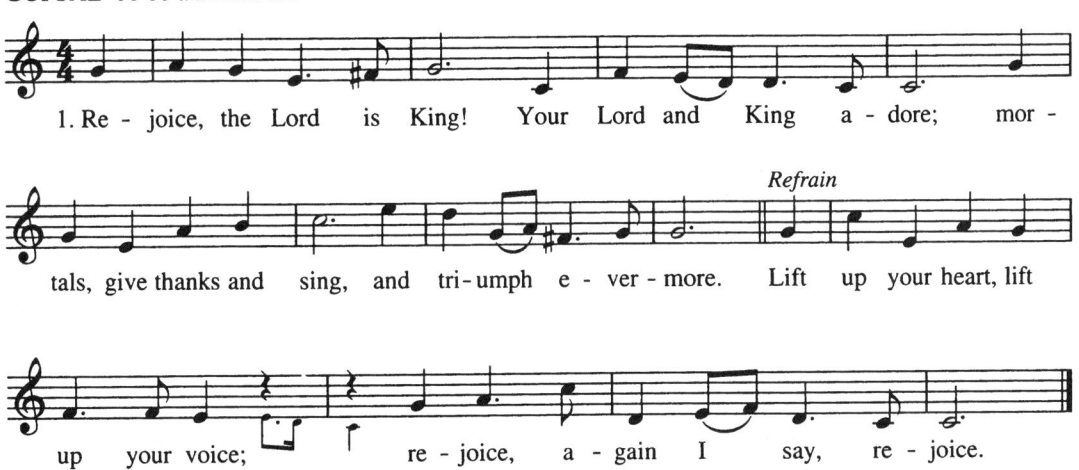

1. Re - joice, the Lord is King! Your Lord and King a - dore; mor - tals, give thanks and sing, and tri - umph e - ver - more. *Refrain* Lift up your heart, lift up your voice; re - joice, a - gain I say, re - joice.

2. Jesus the Saviour reigns,
   the God of truth and love;
   when he had purged our stains,
   he took his seat above.

3. His kingdom cannot fail;
   he rules o'er earth and heav'n;
   the keys of death and hell
   are to our Jesus giv'n.

4. He sits at God's right hand
   till all his foes submit,
   and bow to his command,
   and fall beneath his feet.

Text: Charles Wesley (1707-1788)
Music: George Frideric Handel (1685-1759)

592 Remember your mercy, Lord

Cantor
Re-member, re-member your mer-cy, Lord. Re-member, re-member your mer-cy, Lord. Hear your peo-ple's prayer as they call to you: re-member, re-member your mer-cy, Lord.

All
Re-member, re-member your mer-cy, Lord. Re-member, re-member your mer-cy, Lord. Hear your peo-ple's prayer as they call to you: re-member, re-member your mer-cy, Lord.

To verses
1.
2. Re-
3. The

Last time
mer-cy, Lord. *Fine*

Text © Copyright 1963, 1986, 1993 The Grail, England.
Used by permission of A.P. Watt, 20 John Street, London WC1N 2DR.
Music and refrain text © Copyright 1981, Paul Inwood. Published by OCP Publications,
5536 NE Hassalo, Portland, OR 97213, USA. All rights reserved. Used by permission.

1. Lord, make me know your ways. Lord, teach me your paths. Make me walk in your truth, and teach me: for you are God my Saviour.

2. member your mercy, Lord, and the love you have shown from of old. Do not remember the sins of my youth. In your love remember me, in your love remember me, because of your goodness, O Lord.

3. Lord is good and upright. He shows the path to all who stray, he guides the humble in the right path; he teaches his way to the poor.

Text: Psalm 24, Grail Translation
Music: Paul Inwood

593 Ride on, ride on in majesty

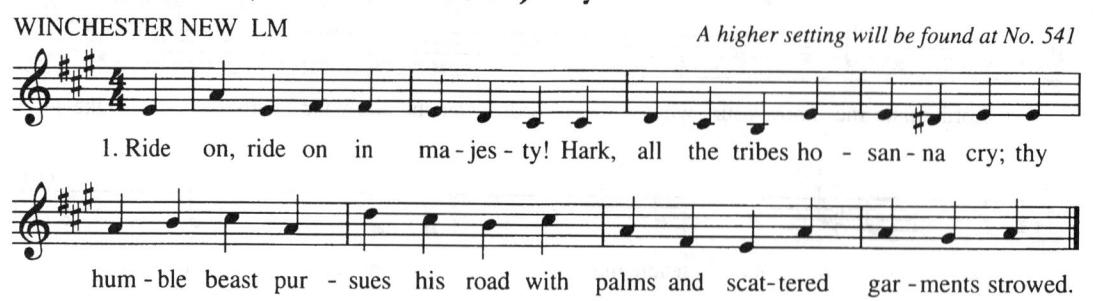

WINCHESTER NEW LM

A higher setting will be found at No. 541

1. Ride on, ride on in majesty! Hark, all the tribes hosanna cry; thy humble beast pursues his road with palms and scattered garments strowed.

2. Ride on, ride on in majesty!
In lowly pomp ride on to die;
O Christ, thy triumphs now begin
o'er captive death and conquered sin.

3. Ride on, ride on in majesty!
The wingèd squadrons of the sky
look down with sad and wond'ring eyes
to see th'approaching sacrifice.

4. Ride on, ride on in majesty!
Thy last and fiercest strife is nigh;
the Father, on his sapphire throne,
awaits his own appointed Son.

5. Ride on, ride on in majesty!
In lowly pomp ride on to die;
bow thy meek head to mortal pain,
then take, O God, thy pow'r, and reign.

Text: Henry Hart Milman (1791-1868) alt.
Music: from 'Musikalisches Handbuch' (1690)

594 Ring out your joy

Ring out your joy, give glory to God. Lift up your hearts and sing. Let all creation tell of his name. Praise him for evermore!

1. Blessed are you, God of creation; glory and praise for evermore!
Blest be your holy, glorious, great name; glory and praise for evermore!

© Copyright 1984 Kevin Mayhew Ltd.

2. Blest in the temple of your glory;
   glory and praise for evermore!
   Blessèd, enthroned over your kingdom;
   glory and praise for evermore!

3. Blest, you who know the deeps and highest;
   glory and praise for evermore!
   Blest in the firmament of heaven;
   glory and praise for evermore!

4. All things the Lord has made, now bless him;
   glory and praise for evermore!
   Angels and saints, now bless and praise him;
   glory and praise for evermore!

Text: Aniceto Nazareth based on the Canticle of Daniel
Music: Aniceto Nazareth

595 Said Judas to Mary
Judas and Mary

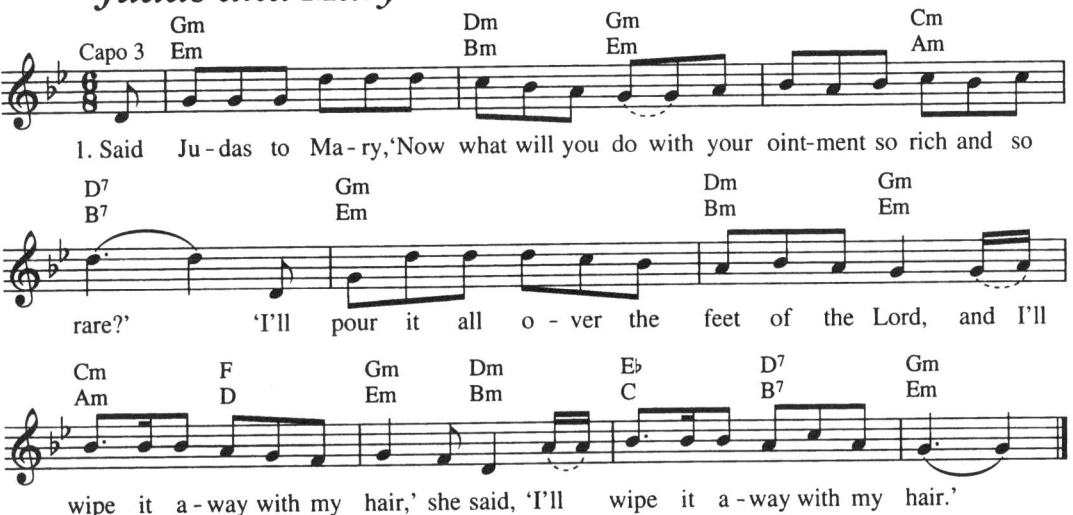

1. Said Judas to Mary, 'Now what will you do with your ointment so rich and so rare?' 'I'll pour it all over the feet of the Lord, and I'll wipe it away with my hair,' she said, 'I'll wipe it away with my hair.'

2. 'Oh Mary, oh Mary, oh think of the poor,
   this ointment, it could have been sold,
   and think of the blankets and think of the bread
   you could buy with the silver and gold,' he said,
   'you could buy with the silver and gold.'

3. 'Tomorrow, tomorrow, I'll think of the poor,
   tomorrow,' she said, 'not today;
   for dearer than all of the poor in the world
   is my love who is going away,' she said,
   'my love who is going away.'

4. Said Jesus to Mary, 'Your love is so deep,
   today you may do as you will.
   Tomorrow you say I am going away,
   but my body I leave with you still,' he said,
   'my body I leave with you still.'

5. 'The poor of the world are my body,' he said,
   'to the end of the world they shall be.
   The bread and the blankets you give to the poor
   you'll find you have given to me,' he said,
   'you'll find you have given to me.'

6. 'My body will hang on the cross of the world,
   tomorrow,' he said, 'and today,
   and Martha and Mary will find me again
   and wash all my sorrow away,' he said,
   'and wash all my sorrow away.'

Text and Music: Sydney Carter (b.1915)

© Copyright 1964 Stainer and Bell Ltd, P.O. Box 110, Victoria House, 23 Gruneisen Road, Finchley, London N3 1DZ. Used by permission.

596 Salvation is God's

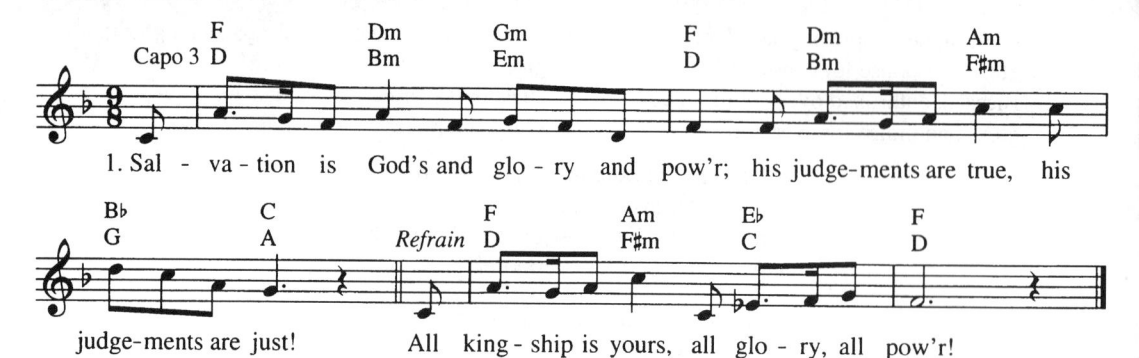

1. Salvation is God's and glory and pow'r; his judgements are true, his judgements are just! *Refrain* All kingship is yours, all glory, all pow'r!

2. Give praise to our God,
you servants of God,
both little and great,
revering his name!

3. The Lord is now King,
the Ruler of all;
give glory to him,
in him take your joy!

4. The wedding day dawns
for Lamb and for Bride;
in beauty adorned,
she waits for the Lamb.

5. The grace of the Lamb
has robed her in white;
in glory she shines,
fit Bride for the Lamb.

6. How happy are those
invited to share
the Supper prepared
for Bridegroom and Bride!

Text: James Quinn (b.1919) based on Revelation 19:1, 2, 5-9
Music: Noel Donnelly (b.1932)
Text © Geoffrey Chapman, an imprint of Cassell plc, Wellington House, 125 Strand, London WC2R 0BB.
Used by permission.
Music © 1986 Kevin Mayhew Ltd.

597 Salve, Regina

Salve, Regina, mater misericordiæ; vita, dulcedo, et spes nostra, salve. Ad te clamamus, exules filii hevæ. Ad te suspiramus, gementes et flentes in hac lacrimarum valle.

E - ia er - go, ad - vo - ca - ta no - stra,
il - los tu - os mi - se - ri - cor - des o - cu - los ad nos con - ver - te.
Et Je - sum, be - ne - di - ctum fru - ctum ven - tris tu - i,
no - bis post hoc ex - i - li - um o - sten - de.
O cle - mens, O pi - a,
O dul - cis Vir - go Ma - ri - a.

Text: Hermann the Lame (d.1054)
Music: Plainsong

598 Save us, O Lord

Save us, O Lord, while we are a-wake, and guard us while we sleep,
that a-wake we may watch with Christ, and a-sleep we may rest in peace,
in Je - sus' name, in Je - sus' name.

Text: The Office of Night Prayer
Music: Kevin Mayhew (b.1942)
Music © Copyright 1996 Kevin Mayhew Ltd.

599 Save us, O Lord
Song of Simeon

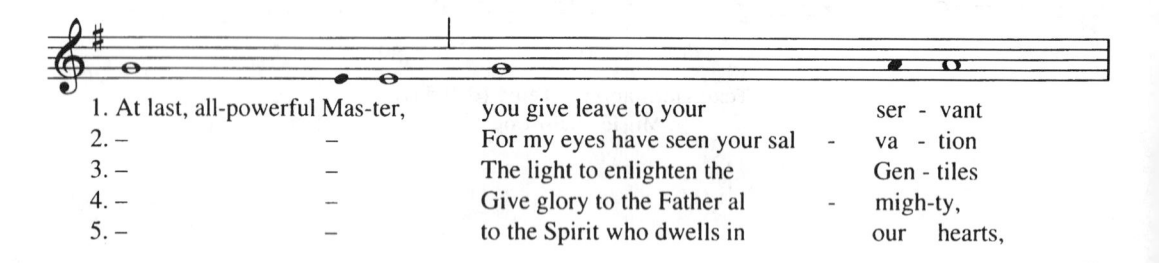

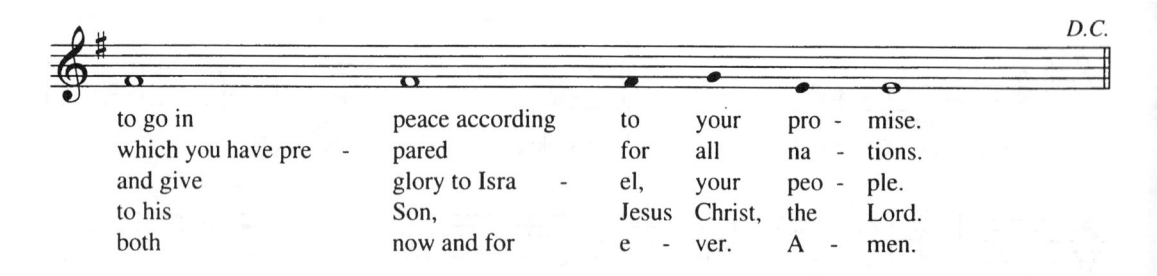

Refrain

Save us, O Lord, while we're a-wake. Guard us, O Lord, when we're a-sleep that we may watch with Christ and rest in peace, that we may watch with Christ and rest in peace. *Fine*

1. At last, all-powerful Master, you give leave to your ser-vant to go in peace according to your pro-mise.
2. — — For my eyes have seen your sal-va-tion which you have pre-pared for all na-tions.
3. — — The light to enlighten the Gen-tiles and give glory to Isra-el, your peo-ple.
4. — — Give glory to the Father al-migh-ty, to his Son, Jesus Christ, the Lord.
5. — — to the Spirit who dwells in our hearts, both now and for e-ver. A-men.

D.C.

Text: Luke 2:29-32 trans. The Grail
Music: Aniceto Nazareth

Text © Copyright 1963, 1986, 1993 The Grail, England. Used by permission of A. P. Watt Ltd,
20 John Street, London WC1N 2DR.
Music © Copyright 1984 Kevin Mayhew Ltd.

600 Save us, O Lord

Refrain: Save us, O Lord. Carry us back. Rouse your power and come. Rescue your people, show us your face. Bring us back.

1. O Shepherd of Israel, hear us; return and we shall be saved. Arise, O Lord; hear our cries, O Lord. Bring us back!

2. How long will you hide from your people. We long to see your face. Give ear to us, draw near to us, Lord God of hosts!

3. Turn again, care for your vine, protect what your right hand has planted. Your vineyards are trampled, uprooted and burned. Come to us, Father of might!

Text and Music: Bob Dufford

© Copyright 1981 Robert J. Dufford, SJ & New Dawn Music, 5536 NE Hassalo, Portland, OR 97213, USA.
All rights reserved. Used by permission

601 See, amid the winter's snow

TUNE 1: HUMILITY (OXFORD) 77 77 and Refrain

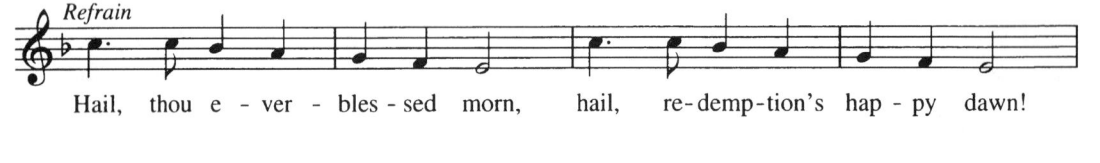

1. See, amid the winter's snow,
born for us on earth below,
see, the tender Lamb appears,
promised from eternal years.

Refrain
Hail, thou ever-blessed morn,
hail, redemption's happy dawn!
Sing through all Jerusalem,
Christ is born in Bethlehem.

2. Lo, within a manger lies
he who built the starry skies;
he who, throned in heights sublime,
sits amid the cherubim.

3. Say, you holy shepherds, say,
what your joyful news today?
Wherefore have you left your sheep
on the lonely mountain steep?

4. 'As we watched at dead of night,
there appeared a wondrous light;
angels, singing peace on earth,
told us of the Saviour's birth.'

5. Sacred infant, all divine,
what a tender love was thine,
thus to come from highest bliss,
down to such a world as this!

6. Virgin mother, Mary, blest,
by the joys that fill thy breast,
pray for us, that we may prove
worthy of the Saviour's love.

TUNE 2: CHRISTMAS MORN 77 77 and Refrain

1. See, amid the winter's snow,
born for us on earth below,
see, the tender Lamb appears,
promised from eternal years.

Refrain

Hail, thou ever-blessed morn, hail, redemption's happy dawn!
Sing through all Jerusalem Christ is born in Bethlehem.

Text: Edward Caswall (1814-1878)
Music: Tune 1 – John Goss (1800-1880)
Tune 2 – traditional melody

602 See, Christ was wounded

EISENACH LM

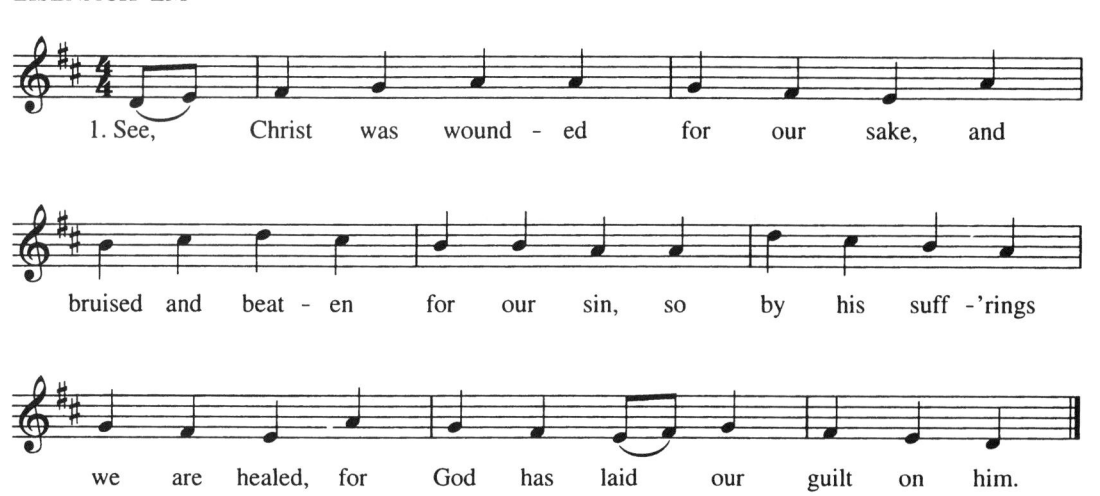

1. See, Christ was wounded for our sake, and
bruised and beaten for our sin, so by his suff'rings
we are healed, for God has laid our guilt on him.

2. Look on his face, come close to him
   – see, you will find no beauty there;
   despised, rejected, who can tell
   the grief and sorrow he must bear?

3. Like sheep that stray we leave God's path,
   to choose our own and not his will;
   like lamb to slaughter he has gone,
   obedient to his Father's will.

4. Cast out to die by those he loved,
   reviled by those he died to save,
   see how sin's pride has sought his death,
   see how sin's hate has made his grave.

5. For on his shoulders God has laid
   the weight of sin that we should bear;
   so by his passion we have peace,
   through his obedience and his prayer.

Text: Brian Foley (b.1919)
Music: melody by Johann Hermann Schein (1586-1630) harmonised by Johann Sebastian Bach (1685-1750)
Text © Copyright 1971 Faber Music Ltd, 3 Queen Square, London WC1N 3AU.
Used by permission from 'New Catholic Hymnal.'

603 See him lying on a bed of straw

CALYPSO CAROL Irregular and Refrain

1. See him lying on a bed of straw: a draughty stable with an open door. Mary cradling the babe she bore: the Prince of Glory is his name.

Refrain
O now carry me to Bethlehem to see the Lord of love again: just as poor as was the stable then, the Prince of Glory when he came!

2. Star of silver, sweep across the skies,
show where Jesus in the manger lies;
shepherds, swiftly from your stupor rise
to see the Saviour of the world!

3. Angels, sing again the song you sang,
sing the glory of God's gracious plan;
sing that Bethl'em's little baby can
be salvation to the soul.

4. Mine are riches, from your poverty;
from your innocence, eternity;
mine, forgiveness by your death for me,
child of sorrow for my joy.

Text and Music: Michael Perry (1942-1996)

© Copyright 1965 Mrs. B. Perry/Jubilate Hymns, 4 Thorne Park Road, Chelston, Torquay TQ2 6RX.
Used by permission.

604 Seek ye frst

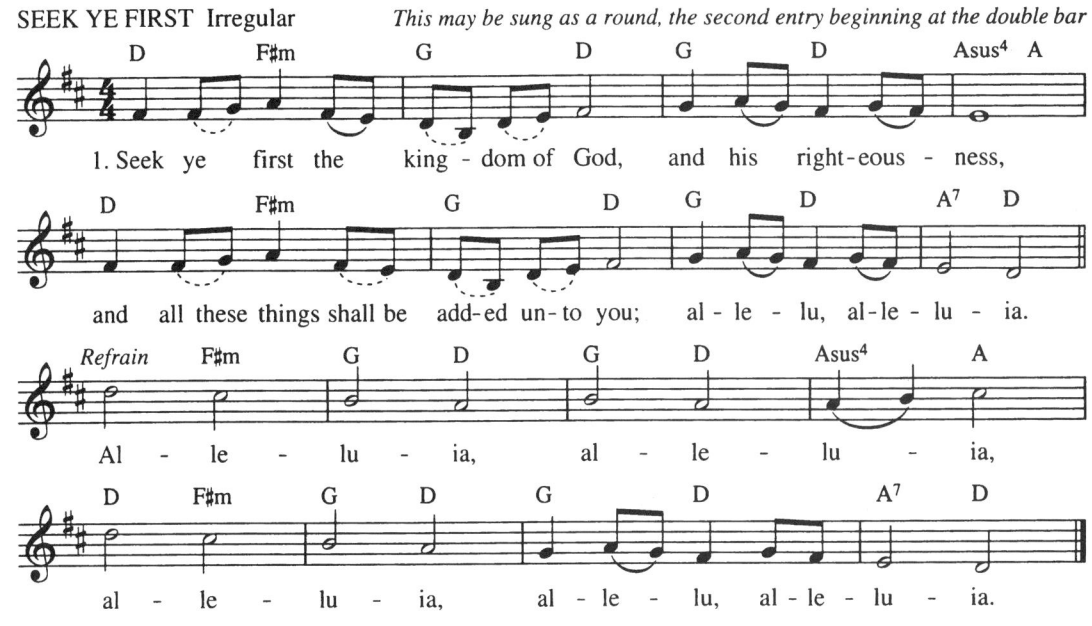

SEEK YE FIRST Irregular *This may be sung as a round, the second entry beginning at the double bar*

1. Seek ye first the kingdom of God, and his righteousness,
and all these things shall be added unto you; al-le-lu, al-le-lu-ia.

Refrain
Alleluia, alleluia,
alleluia, al-le-lu, al-le-lu-ia.

2. You shall not live by bread alone,
but by ev'ry word
that proceeds from the mouth of God;
allelu, alleluia.

3. Ask and it shall be given unto you,
seek and ye shall find;
knock, and it shall be opened unto you;
allellu, alleluia.

Text: v.1 Karen Lafferty (b.1948); vs. 2 & 3 unknown, based on Matthew 6:33, 7:7
Music: Karen Lafferty (b.1948)
© Copyright 1972 Maranatha! Music. Administered by CopyCare Ltd., P.O. Box 77, Hailsham, East Sussex BN27 3EF. Used by permission.

605 See the holy table, spread for our healing

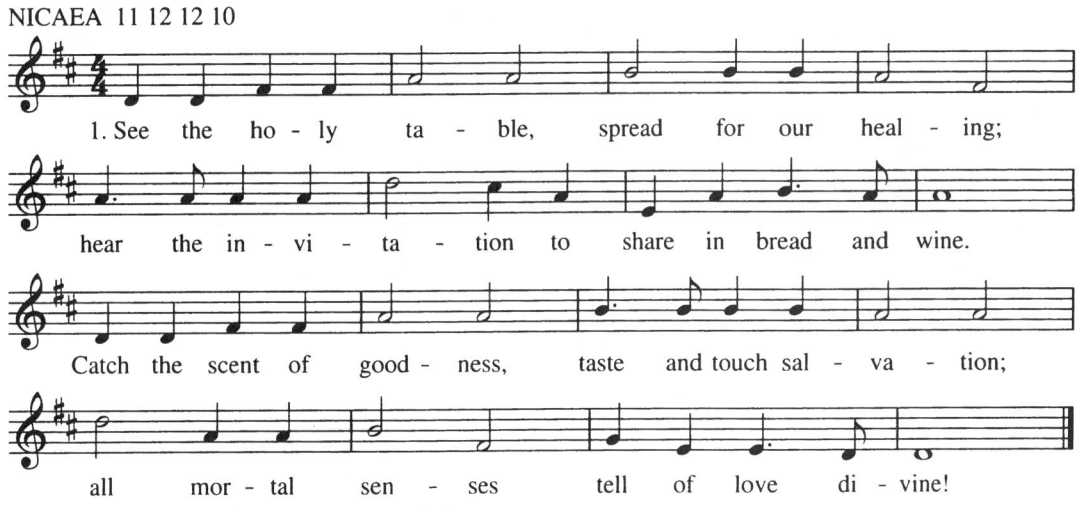

NICAEA 11 12 12 10

1. See the holy table, spread for our healing;
hear the invitation to share in bread and wine.
Catch the scent of goodness, taste and touch salvation;
all mortal senses tell of love divine!

2. As the bread is broken, Christ is remembered;
as the wine is flowing, his passion we recall;
as redemption's story opens up before us,
hope is triumphant, Christ is all in all.

3. Tell again the story, wonder of wonders:
Christ, by grace eternal, transforms the simplest food!
Sign of hope and glory, life in all its fullness,
God's whole creation ransomed and renewed!

Text: Michael Forster (b.1946)
Music: John Bacchus Dykes (1823-1876)
Text © Copyright 1993 Kevin Mayhew Ltd.

606 See us, Lord, about your altar

LAUS DEO (Redhead No. 46) 87 87

A lower setting will be found at No. 340

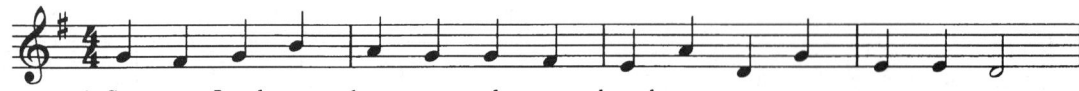

1. See us, Lord, about your altar; though so many, we are one;
many souls by love united in the heart of Christ your Son.

2. Hear our prayers, O loving Father,
hear in them your Son, our Lord;
hear him speak our love and worship,
as we sing with one accord.

3. Once were seen the blood and water;
now he seems but bread and wine;
then in human form he suffered,
now his form is but a sign.

4. Wheat and grape contain the meaning;
food and drink he is to all;
one in him, we kneel adoring,
gathered by his loving call.

5. Hear us yet; so much is needful
in our frail, disordered life;
stay with us and tend our weakness
till that day of no more strife.

6. Members of his mystic body,
now we know our prayer is heard,
heard by you, because your children
have received th'eternal Word.

Text: John Greally
Music: German melody adapted by Richard Redhead (1820-1901)
Text © Copyright Trustees for Roman Catholic Purposes Registered, 114 Mount Street, London W1Y 6AH.
Used by permission.

607 See, your Saviour comes

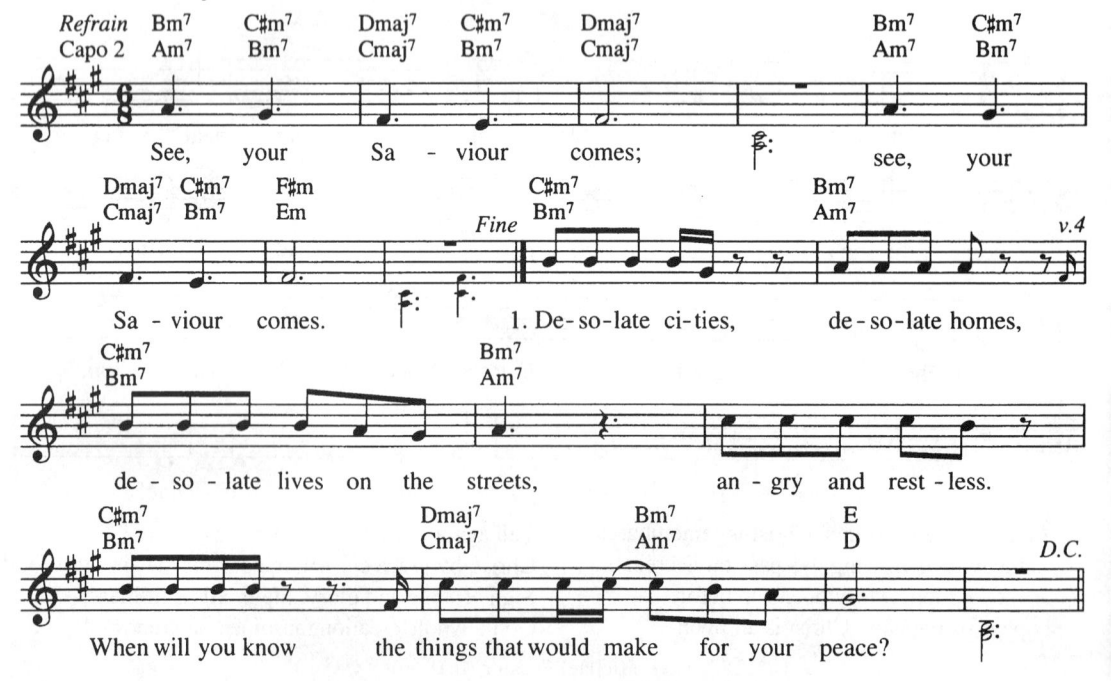

See, your Saviour comes; see, your Saviour comes.

1. Desolate cities, desolate homes,
desolate lives on the streets,
angry and restless.
When will you know the things that would make for your peace?

© Copyright 1996 Make Way Music. P.O. Box 263, Croydon, Surrey CR9 5AP, UK.
International copyright secured. All rights reserved. Used by permission.

2. Father of mercy, hear as we cry
   for all who live in this place;
   show here your glory, come satisfy
   your longing that all should be saved.

3. Where lives are broken, let there be hope,
   where there's division bring peace;
   where there's oppression, judge and reprove,
   and rescue the crushed and the weak.

4. Lord, let your glory dwell in this land,
   in mercy restore us again:
   pour out salvation, grant us your peace,
   and strengthen the things that remain.

Text and Music: Graham Kendrick (b.1950)

608 Send forth your Spirit

Refrain

Send forth, send forth your Spi-rit, O Lord, to re-new, re-new the face of the earth, send your Spi-rit to re-new the earth.

Fine

1. Send the Spi-rit of wis-dom and un-der-stand-ing, the Spi-rit of right judge-ment and cou-rage, send the Spi-rit of know-ledge and re-ve-rence, send your Spi-rit to re-new us all. *D.C.*

2. Send your Spi-rit up-on us as help-er and guide, may he fill us with won-der and awe. Seal us, O Lord, with your ho-ly gift, send your Spi-rit to re-new our lives. *D.C.*

Text: from the Rite of Confirmation
Music: Alan Rees (b.1941)
Music © Copyright 1998 Kevin Mayhew Ltd.

609 Send forth your Spirit

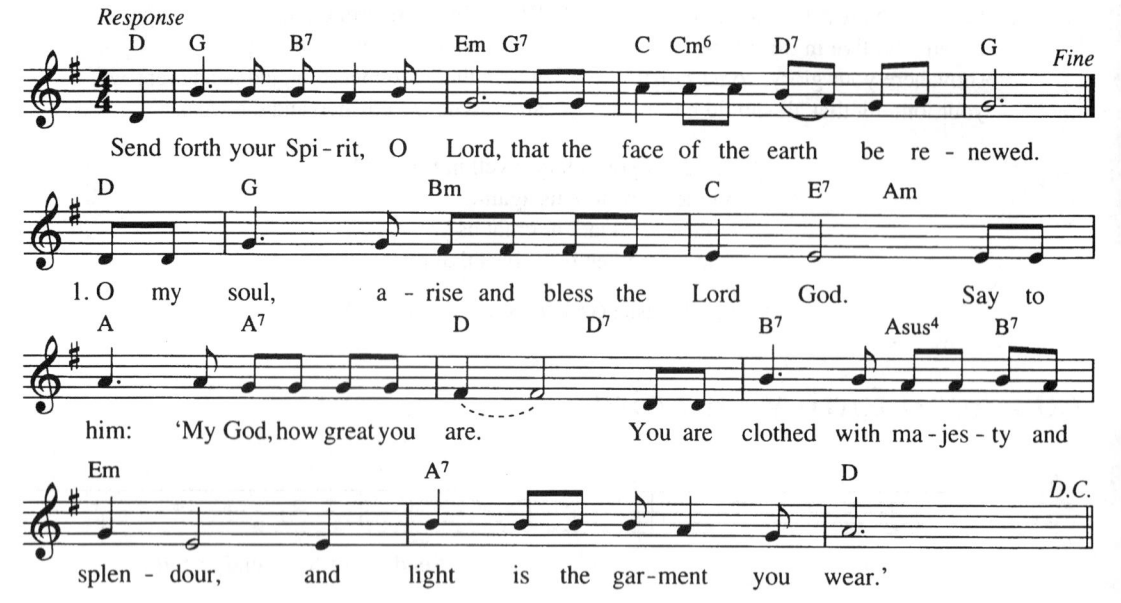

Response

Send forth your Spi-rit, O Lord, that the face of the earth be re-newed.

1. O my soul, a-rise and bless the Lord God. Say to him: 'My God, how great you are. You are clothed with ma-jes-ty and splen-dour, and light is the gar-ment you wear.'

2. 'You have built your palace on the waters.
   Like the winds, the angels do your word.
   you have set the earth on its foundations,
   so firm, to be shaken no more.'

3. 'All your creatures look to you for comfort;
   from your open hand they have their fill,
   you send forth your Spirit and revive them,
   the face of the earth you renew.'

4. While I live, I sing the Lord God's praises;
   I will thank the author of these marvels.
   Praise to God, the Father, Son and Spirit
   both now and for ever. Amen.

Text: Aniceto Nazareth based on Psalm 104
Music: Aniceto Nazareth
© Copyright 1984 Kevin Mayhew Ltd.

610 Send forth your Spirit, Lord

Allegretto

Refrain

Send forth your Spi-rit, Lord, re-new the face of the earth.
Send forth your Spi-rit, Lord, re-new the face of the earth.

Last time

earth, re-new the face of the earth. 1. Bless the Lord, O my

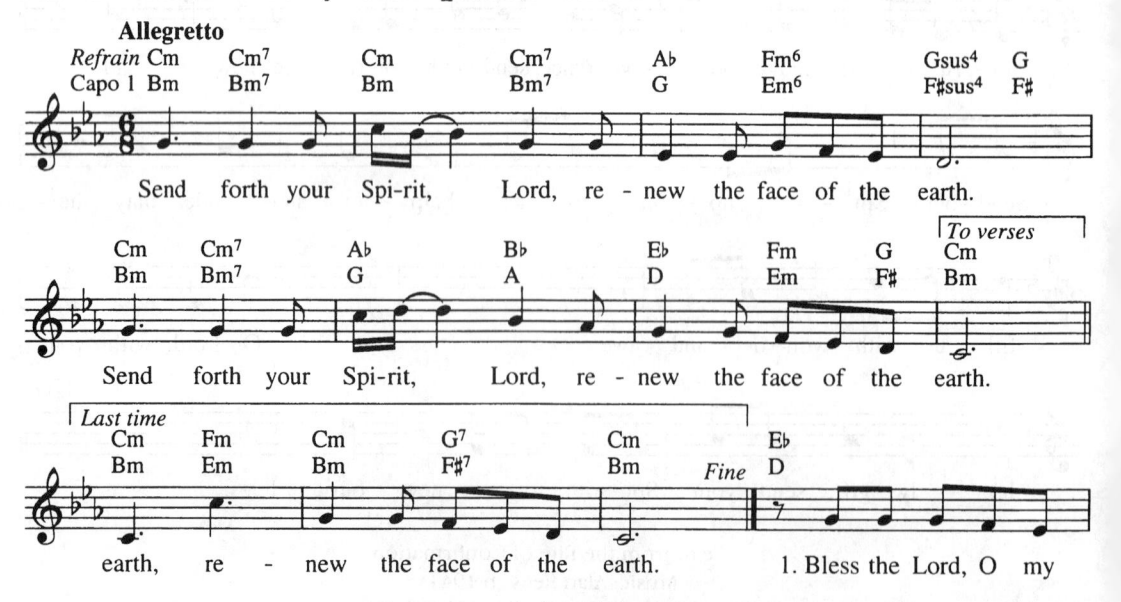

© Copyright 1997 Kevin Mayhew Ltd.

soul, O Lord God, how great you are; you are clothed in hon-our and

glo - ry, you set the world on its foun - da - tions.

2. Lord, how great are your works,
in wisdom you made them all;
all the earth is full of your creatures,
your hand always open to feed them.

3. May your wisdom endure,
rejoice in your works, O Lord.
I will sing for ever and ever,
in praise of my God and my King.

Text: Michael Forster (b.1946) based on Psalm 104
Music: Margaret Rizza (b.1929)
© Copyright 1997 Kevin Mayhew Ltd.

611 Send me, Lord
Thuma mina

1. Send me, Lord.
Thu - ma mi - na.

1. Send me, Je - sus. Send me, Je - sus. Send me, Je - sus. Send me, Lord.
Thu - ma mi - na, thu - ma mi - na, thu - ma mi - na, So - man - dla.

2. Lead me, Lord.
Thu - ma mi - na.

Send me, Lord.
Thu - ma dla.

2. Lead me, Lord. *(x3)*
Lead me, Jesus.
Lead me, Lord.

3. Fill me, Lord. *(x3)*
Fill me, Jesus.
Fill me, Lord.

Text and Music: traditional South African, collected and translated by Anders Nyberg
© Copyright 1990 WGRG, Iona Community, 840 Govan Road, Glasgow G51 3UU, Scotland.
Used by permission from 'Freedom is coming' (Wild Goose Publications, 1990).

612 Shalom, my friend

Sha-lom, my friend, sha-lom, my friend, sha-lom, sha-lom. The peace of Christ I give you to-day, sha-lom, sha-lom.

This may be sung as a round, the second part entering at B
* Omit chords if using Alternative Harmonisation

Text: Sandra Joan Billington (b.1946)
Music: traditional Hebrew melody
Text © Copyright 1976, 1999 Kevin Mayhew Ltd.

613 She sits like a bird
Enemy of apathy

THAINAKE 11 11 11 11

1. She sits like a bird, brood-ing on the wa-ters, hov-'ring on the cha-os of the world's first day; she sighs and she sings, mo-ther-ing cre-a-tion, wait-ing to give birth to all the Word will say. dove.

Text and Music © Copyright 1988 WGRG, Iona Community, 840 Govan Road, Glasgow G51 3UU, Scotland.
Used by permission from 'Enemy of Apathy' (Wild Goose Publications, 1988)

2. She wings over earth, resting where she wishes,
   lighting close at hand or soaring through the skies;
   she nests in the womb, welcoming each wonder,
   nourishing potential hidden to our eyes.

3. She dances in fire, startling her spectators,
   waking tongues of ecstasy where dumbness reigned;
   she weans and inspires all whose hearts are open,
   nor can she be captured, silenced or restrained.

4. For she is the Spirit, one with God in essence,
   gifted by the Saviour in eternal love;
   she is the key opening the scriptures,
   enemy of apathy and heav'nly dove.

Text and Music: John L. Bell (b.1949) and Graham Maule (b.1958)

614 Silent night

STILLE NACHT Irregular

1. Si-lent night, ho-ly night. All is calm, all is bright,
round yon vir-gin mo-ther and child; ho-ly in-fant, so ten-der and mild,
sleep in hea-ven-ly peace, sleep in hea-ven-ly peace.

2. Silent night, holy night.
   Shepherds quake at the sight,
   glories stream from heaven afar,
   heav'nly hosts sing alleluia:
   Christ, the Saviour is born,
   Christ, the Saviour is born.

3. Silent night, holy night.
   Son of God, love's pure light,
   radiant beams from thy holy face,
   with the dawn of redeeming grace:
   Jesus, Lord, at thy birth,
   Jesus, Lord, at thy birth.

Text: Joseph Mohr (1792-1848) trans. John Freeman Young (1820-1885)
Music: Franz Grüber (1787-1863)

615 Sing, all creation

CHRISTE SANCTORUM 11 11 11 5

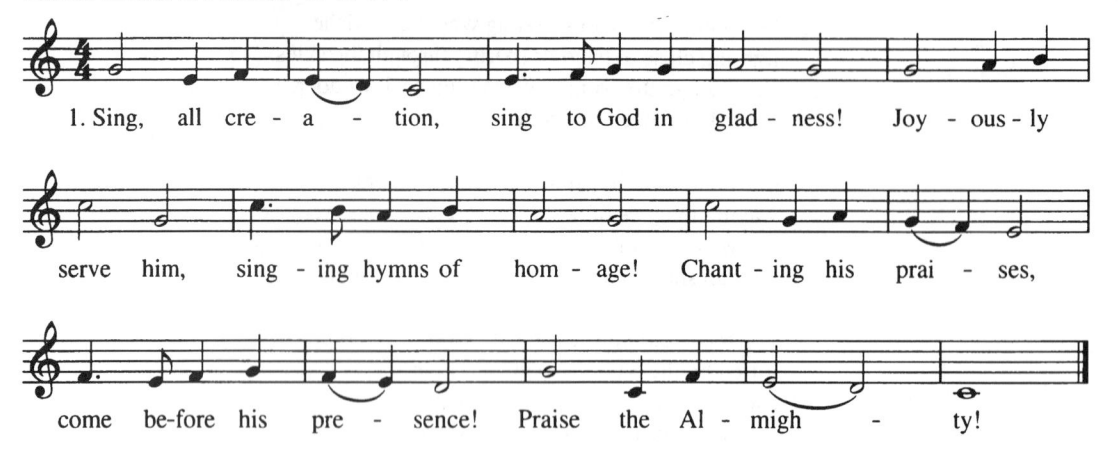

1. Sing, all creation, sing to God in gladness!
Joyously serve him, singing hymns of homage!
Chanting his praises, come before his presence!
Praise the Almighty!

A higher setting will be found at No. 284

2. Know that our God is Lord of all the ages!
He is our maker; we are all his creatures,
people he fashioned, sheep he leads to pasture!
Praise the Almighty!

3. Enter his Temple, ringing out his praises!
Sing in thanksgiving as you come before him!
Blessing his bounty, glorify his greatness!
Praise the Almighty!

4. Great in his goodness is the Lord we worship;
steadfast his kindness, love that knows no ending!
Faithful his word is, changeless, everlasting!
Praise the Almighty!

Text: James Quinn (b. 1919) based on Psalm 99
Music: from the 'Paris Antiphoner' (1681)
Text © Copyright 1969 Geoffrey Chapman, an imprint of Cassell plc, Wellington House, 125 Strand, London WC2R 0BB. Used by permission.

616 Sing a new song

Refrain

Sing a new song unto the Lord, let your song be sung from mountains high. Sing a new song unto the Lord, singing alleluia.

1. All God's people dance for

© Copyright 1972, 1974 Daniel L. Schutte. Administered by New Dawn Music, 5536 NE Hassalo, Portland, OR 97213, USA. All rights reserved. Used by permission.

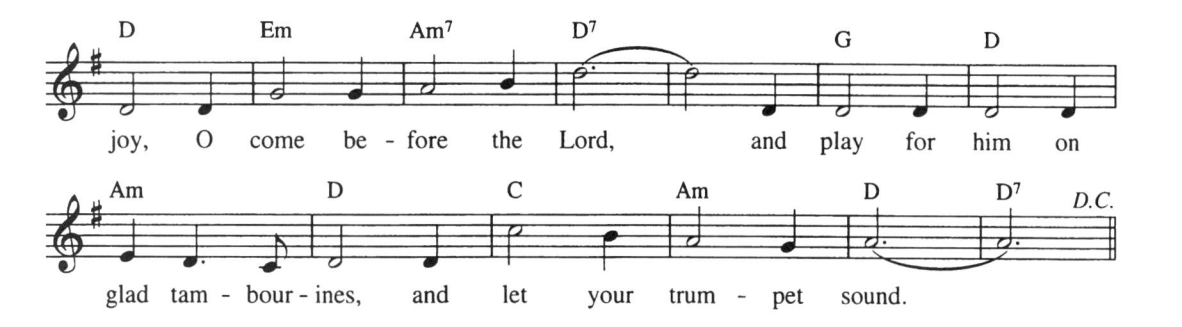

joy, O come be-fore the Lord, and play for him on
glad tam-bour-ines, and let your trum-pet sound.

2. Rise, O children, from your sleep,
   your Saviour now has come,
   and he has turned your sorrow to joy,
   and filled your soul with song.

3. Glad my soul, for I have seen
   the glory of the Lord.
   The trumpet sounds, the dead shall be raised.
   I know my Saviour lives.

Text: Dan Schutte based on Psalm 97
Music: Dan Schutte

617 Sing hallelujah to the Lord

Sing hal-le-lu-jah to the Lord.
Sing hal-le-lu-jah to the
Sing hal-le-lu-jah to the Lord. Sing hal-le-lu-jah,
Lord. Sing hal-le-lu-jah, hal-le-
sing hal-le-lu-jah, sing hal-le-lu-jah to the Lord.
lu-jah, sing hal-le-lu-jah to the Lord.

Text and Music: Linda Stassen
© Copyright 1974 Linda Stassen, New Song Creations, R.R.I., Box 454, Erin, TN 37061, USA.
All rights reserved. International copyright secured. Used by permission.

618 Sing, holy mother

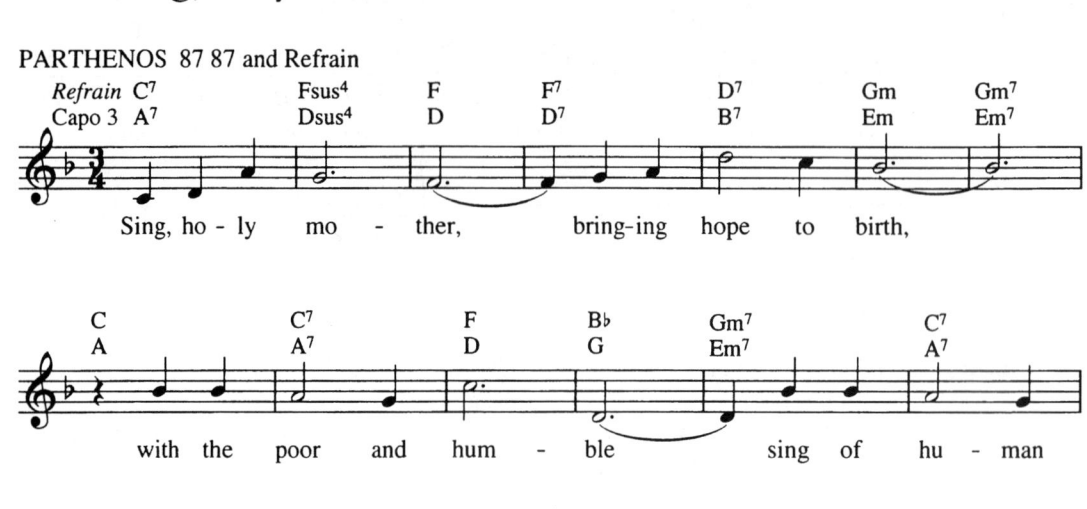

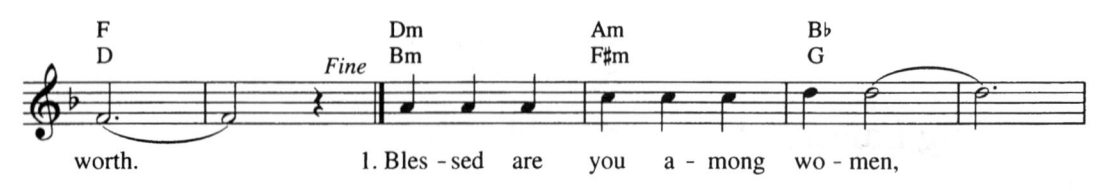

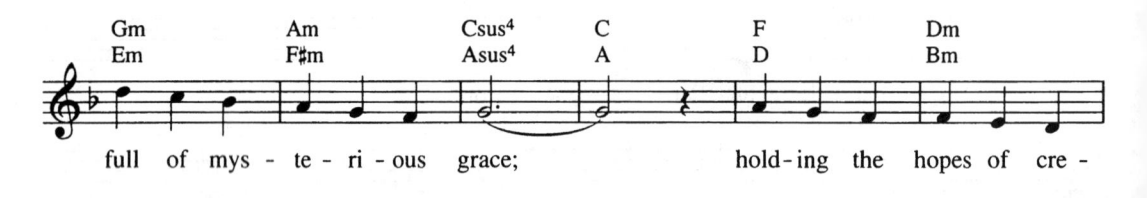

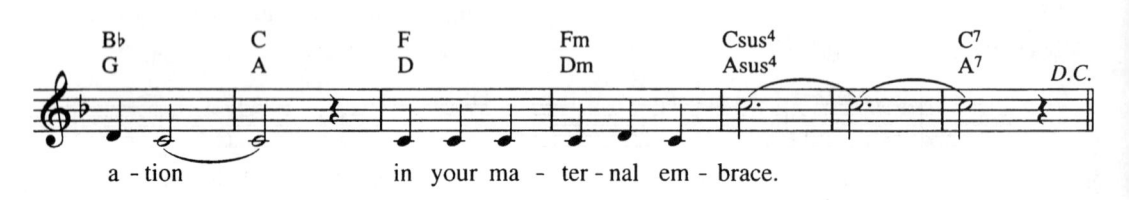

PARTHENOS 87 87 and Refrain

Sing, holy mother, bringing hope to birth, with the poor and humble sing of human worth.

1. Blessed are you among women, full of mysterious grace; holding the hopes of creation in your maternal embrace.

2. Stand with the lost and the lonely,
   those whom the vain world denies,
   join with the weak and the foolish,
   humbling the strong and the wise!

3. Sing of the values of heaven,
   shame our respectable pride!
   Sing to the spurned and the faithful,
   tell them no longer to hide!

Text: Michael Forster (b.1946)
Music: Kevin Mayhew (b.1942)
© Copyright 1997 Kevin Mayhew Ltd.

619 Sing it in the valleys

Refrain

Sing it in the valleys, shout it from the mountain tops,
Jesus came to save us, and his saving never stops.
He is King of kings, and new life he brings,
sing it in the valleys, shout it from the mountain tops,
Oh, shout it from the mountain tops.

1. Jesus, you are by my side, you take all my fears.
   If I only come to you, you will heal the pain of years.

2. You have not deserted me,
   though I go astray.
   Jesus, take me in your arms,
   help me walk with you today.

3. Jesus, you are living now,
   Jesus, I believe;
   Jesus, take me, heart and soul,
   yours alone I want to be.

Text and Music: Mike Anderson (b.1956)
© Copyright 1999 Kevin Mayhew Ltd.

620 Sing, my soul

Sing, my soul. Sing, my soul. Sing, my soul of his mer-cy. Sing, my soul. Sing, my soul. Sing, my soul of his mer-cy.

To verses / Last time Fine

1. The Lord is good to me.
   His light will shine on me.
   When ci-ty lights would blind my eyes.
   He hears my si-lent call.
   His hands help when I fall.
   His gen-tle voice stills my sighs.

2. The Lord is good to me.
   His word will set me free
   when men would tie me to the ground.
   He mocks my foolish ways
   with love that never fails.
   When I'm most lost then I'm found.

3. The Lord is good to me.
   I hear him speak to me.
   His voice is in the rain that falls.
   He whispers in the air
   of his unending care.
   If I will hear, then he calls.

Text: Michael Cockett (b.1938)
Music: Estelle White (b.1925)
© Copyright 1976 Kevin Mayhew Ltd.

621 Sing, my tongue, the song of triumph

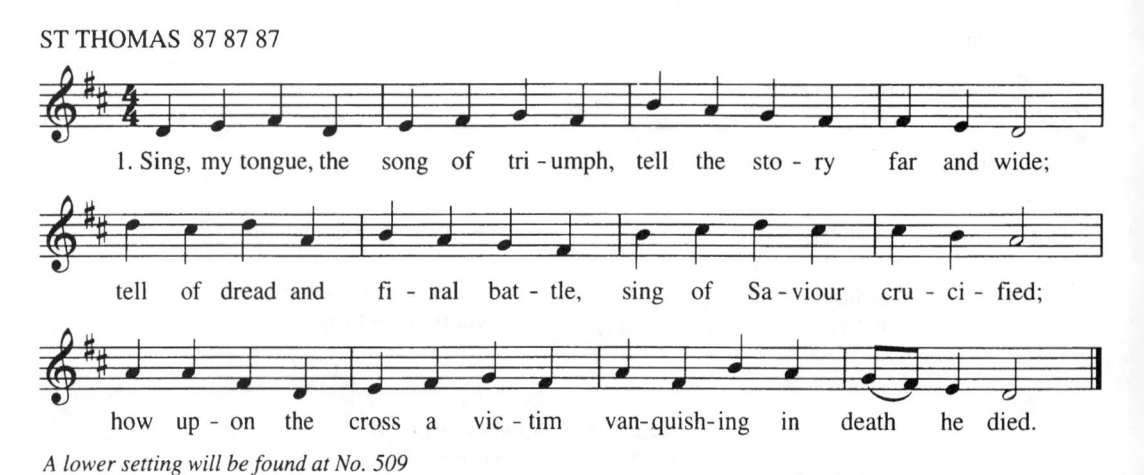

ST THOMAS 87 87 87

1. Sing, my tongue, the song of tri-umph, tell the sto-ry far and wide;
   tell of dread and fi-nal bat-tle, sing of Sa-viour cru-ci-fied;
   how up-on the cross a vic-tim van-quish-ing in death he died.

A lower setting will be found at No. 509

2. He endured the nails, the spitting,
vinegar and spear and reed;
from that holy body broken
blood and water forth proceed;
earth and stars and sky and ocean
by that flood from stain are freed.

3. Faithful Cross, above all other,
one and only noble tree,
none in foliage, none in blossom,
none in fruit your peer may be;
sweet the wood and sweet the iron
and your load, most sweet is he.

4. Bend your boughs, O Tree of glory!
all your rigid branches, bend!
For a while the ancient temper
that your birth bestowed, suspend;
and the King of earth and heaven
gently on your bosom tend.

This may also be sung to the tune 'Westminster Abbey' at No. 197

Text: translation of 'Pange, lingua, gloriosi proelium certaminis'
by Venantius Fortunatus (c.530-609) from 'The Three Days' (1981)
Music: Samuel Webbe (1740-1816)

622 Sing of Mary, pure and lowly

PLEADING SAVIOUR 87 87 D

1. Sing of Mary, pure and lowly,
virgin mother undefiled.
Sing of God's own Son most holy,
who became her little child.
Fairest child of fairest mother,
God, the Lord, who came to earth,
Word made flesh, our very brother,
takes our nature by his birth.

2. Sing of Jesus, son of Mary,
in the home at Nazereth.
Toil and labour cannot weary
love enduring unto death.
Constant was the love he gave her,
though he went forth from her side,
forth to preach and heal and suffer,
till on Calvary he died.

3. Glory be to God the Father,
glory be to God the Son,
glory be to God the Spirit,
glory to the Three in One.
From the heart of blessèd Mary,
from all saints the song ascends,
and the Church the strain re-echoes
unto earth's remotest ends.

Text: anonymous (c.1914)
Music: from 'The Christian Lyre' (1831)

623 Sing praises to the living God

1. Sing prai-ses to the liv-ing God, glo-ry, al-le-lu-ia.
Come, a-dore the liv-ing God, glo-ry, al-le-lu-ia.
Though sun and moon may pass a-way his words will e-ver stay. His pow-er is for e-ver-more, glo-ry, al-le-lu-ia.

Refrain
Glo-ry to the Tri-ni-ty. The un-di-vi-ded U-ni-ty, the Fa-ther, Son and Spi-rit one, from whom all life and great-ness come.

2. And to the living God we sing,
glory, alleluia.
Let our love and praises ring,
glory, alleluia.
To all of us he always gives
his mercy and his love.
So praise him now for evermore,
glory, alleluia.

3. And to the God who cannot die,
glory, alleluia.
To the living God we cry,
glory, alleluia.
He promised to be with us and
he lives in ev'ryone.
We love him now for evermore,
glory, alleluia.

Text and Music: Sebastian Temple (1928-1997)
© Copyright 1971 OCP Publications, 5536 NE Hassalo, Portland, OR 97213, USA.
All rights reserved. Used by permission.

624 Sing the gospel of salvation
AUSTRIA 87 87 D

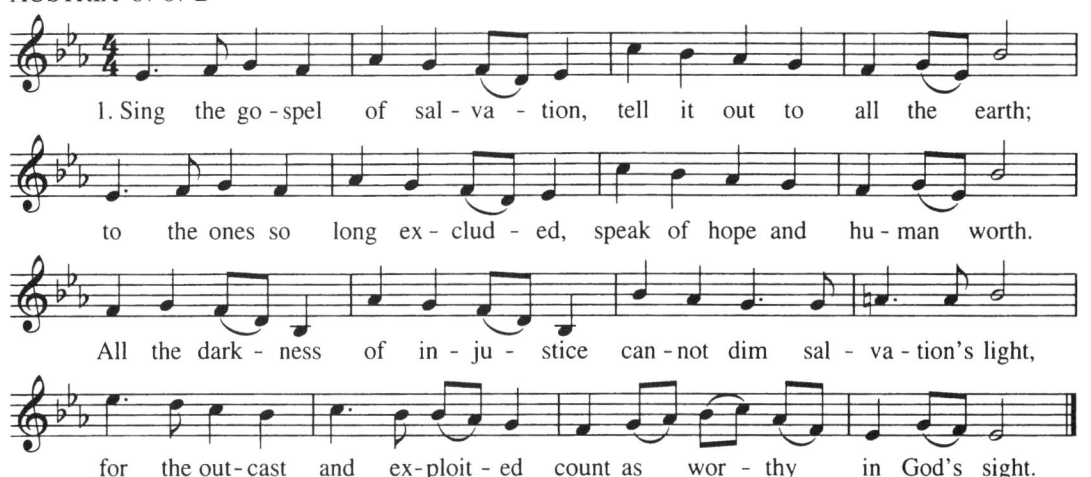

1. Sing the gospel of salvation, tell it out to all the earth;
to the ones so long excluded, speak of hope and human worth.
All the darkness of injustice cannot dim salvation's light,
for the outcast and exploited count as worthy in God's sight.

2. Christ, the one eternal Shepherd,
   calls creation to rejoice,
   and the victims of oppression
   thrill to hear salvation's voice.
   All who recognise the Saviour
   take their place within the fold,
   there, in perfect truth and freedom,
   life's eternal joys to hold.

3. See, the host that none can number
   gathers in from ev'ry side,
   once the victims of injustice,
   now redeemed and glorified.
   Fear and weeping here are ended,
   hunger and oppression cease.
   Now the Lamb becomes the Shepherd!
   Now begins the reign of peace!

Text: Michael Forster (b.1946)
Music: Croatian folk melody adapted by Franz Joseph Haydn (1732-1809)
Text © Copyright 1993 Kevin Mayhew Ltd.

625 Sing to the Lord, alleluia

Refrain
Sing to the Lord, alleluia, sing to the Lord.

1. Bless his name, announce his salvation, day after day, alleluia.

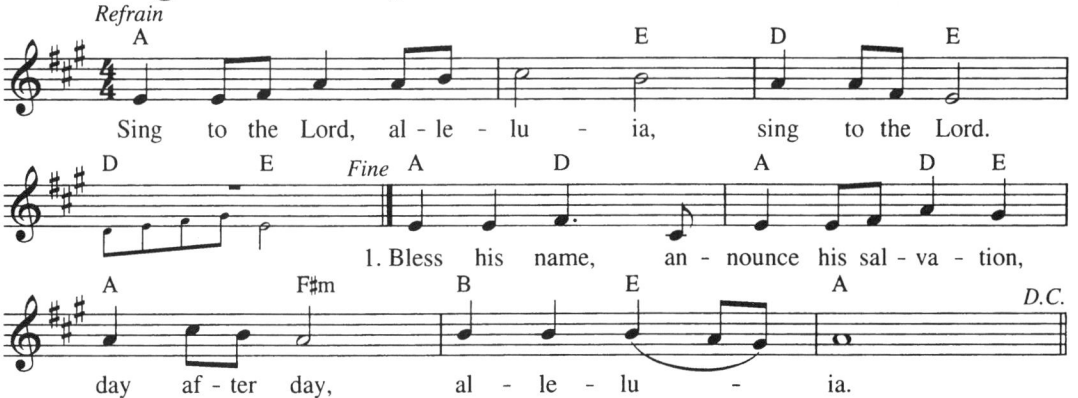

2. Give to him, you fam'lies of peoples,
   glory and praise, alleluia.

3. Great is he and worthy of praises,
   day after day, alleluia.

4. He it is who gave us the heavens,
   glory to God, alleluia.

5. Tell his glories, tell all the nations,
   day after day, alleluia.

6. Bring your gifts and enter his temple,
   worship the Lord, alleluia.

Text: John Foley based on Psalm 95
Music: John Foley
© Copyright 1970, 1974 John B. Foley, SJ and New Dawn Music, 5536 NE Hassalo, Portland, OR 97213, USA.
All rights reserved. Used by permission.

626 Sing to the mountains

Refrain

Sing to the moun-tains, sing to the sea, raise your voi-ces, lift your hearts. This is the day the Lord has made, let all the earth re-joice. *Fine*

1. I will give thanks to you, my Lord, you have an-swered my plea; you have saved my soul from death, you are my strength and my song. *D.C.*

2. Ho-ly, ho-ly, ho-ly Lord, hea-ven and earth are full of your glo-ry. *D.C.*

3. This is the day that the Lord has made, let us be glad and re-joice. He has turned all death to life, sing of the glo-ry of God. *D.C.*

Text: Bob Dufford based on Psalm 117
Music: Bob Dufford

© Copyright 1975 Robert J. Dufford and New Dawn Music, 5536 NE Hassalo, Portland, Oregon 97213, USA. All rights reserved. Used by permission.

627 Sleep, holy babe

EDGBASTON 46 886

1. Sleep, holy babe, upon thy mother's breast; great Lord of earth and sea and sky, how sweet it is to see thee lie in such a place of rest.

2. Sleep, holy babe, thine angels watch around,
   all bending low, with folded wings,
   before th'incarnate King of kings,
   in reverent awe profound.

3. Sleep, holy babe, while I with Mary gaze
   in joy upon thy face awhile,
   upon the loving infant smile,
   which there divinely plays.

4. Sleep, holy babe, ah, take thy brief repose;
   too quickly will thy slumbers break,
   and thou to lengthened pains awake,
   that death alone shall close.

5. O lady blest, sweet virgin, hear my cry;
   forgive the wrong that I have done
   to thee, in causing thy dear Son
   upon the cross to die.

Text: Edward Caswall (1814-1878)
Music: traditional English melody

628 Soul of my Saviour

ANIMA CHRISTI 10 10 10 10

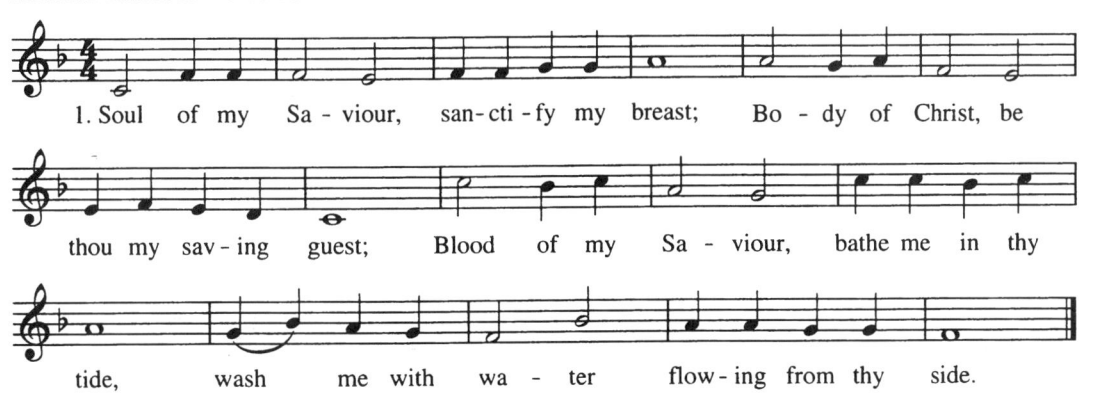

1. Soul of my Saviour, sanctify my breast; Body of Christ, be thou my saving guest; Blood of my Saviour, bathe me in thy tide, wash me with water flowing from thy side.

2. Strength and protection may thy passion be;
   O blessèd Jesus, hear and answer me;
   deep in thy wounds, Lord, hide and shelter me;
   so shall I never, never part from thee.

3. Guard and defend me from the foe malign;
   in death's dread moments make me only thine;
   call me, and bid me come to thee on high,
   where I may praise thee with thy saints for aye.

Text: 'Anima Christi' ascribed to John XXII (1249-1334) trans. unknown
Music: W.J. Maher (1823-1877)

629 Spirit hovering o'er the waters
Veni, veni, Sancte Spiritus

2. Spirit speaking through the prophets
when they cried for justice and peace,
living Spirit, come renew us,
fill the earth with peace and love.

3. Spirit hov'ring o'er the virgin,
Word and flesh are mothered in her.
living Spirit, breath of Yahweh,
bring the Word to life in us.

4. Spirit breathed on John and Mary
as they stood here under the cross,
living Spirit, strengthen, comfort,
guide, unite your church today.

5. Spirit hov'ring o'er apostles,
wind and fire of Pentecost Day,
living Spirit, now confirm us,
come inspire us, come, we pray.

Text and Music: Noel Donnelly (b.1932)
© Copyright Noel Donnelly. Used by permission.

630 Spirit of the living God

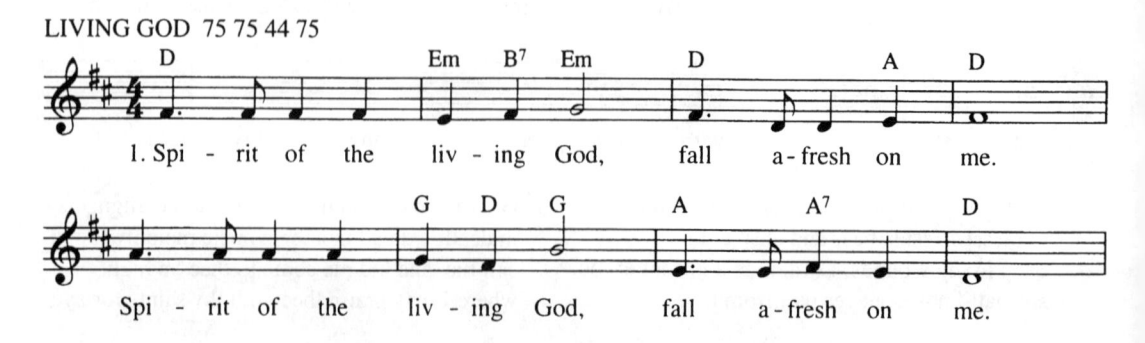

LIVING GOD 75 75 44 75

1. Spirit of the living God, fall afresh on me.
Spirit of the living God, fall afresh on me.

© Copyright 1963 Birdwing Music/EMI Christian Music Publishing. Administered by CopyCare, P.O. Box 77, Hailsham, East Sussex BN27 3EF, UK. Used by permission.

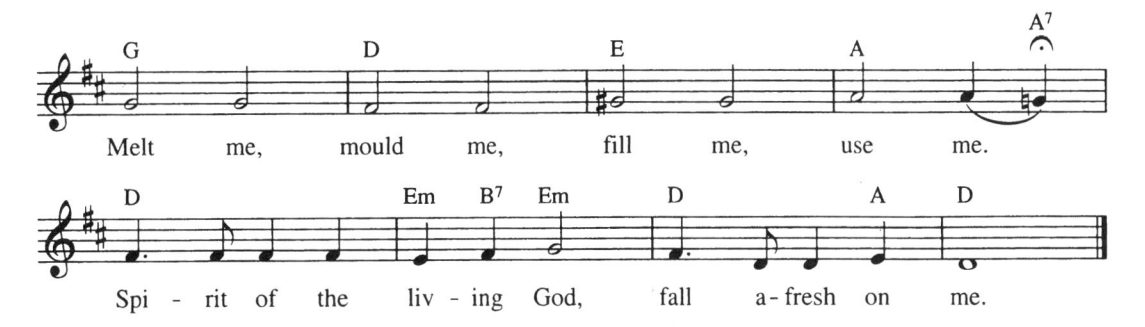

Melt me, mould me, fill me, use me.
Spirit of the living God, fall afresh on me.

2. Spirit of the living God, fall afresh on us.
   Spirit of the living God, fall afresh on us.
   Melt us, mould us, fill us, use us.
   Spirit of the living God, fall afresh on us.

When appropriate, a third verse may be added, singing 'on them',
for example, before Confirmation, or at a service for the sick.

Text and Music: Daniel Iverson (1890-1972)

631 Springs of water, bless the Lord

Springs of water, bless the Lord! Praise be God for evermore!

1. With this gift of water, Lord, you have given us a sign, our baptismal sacrament.

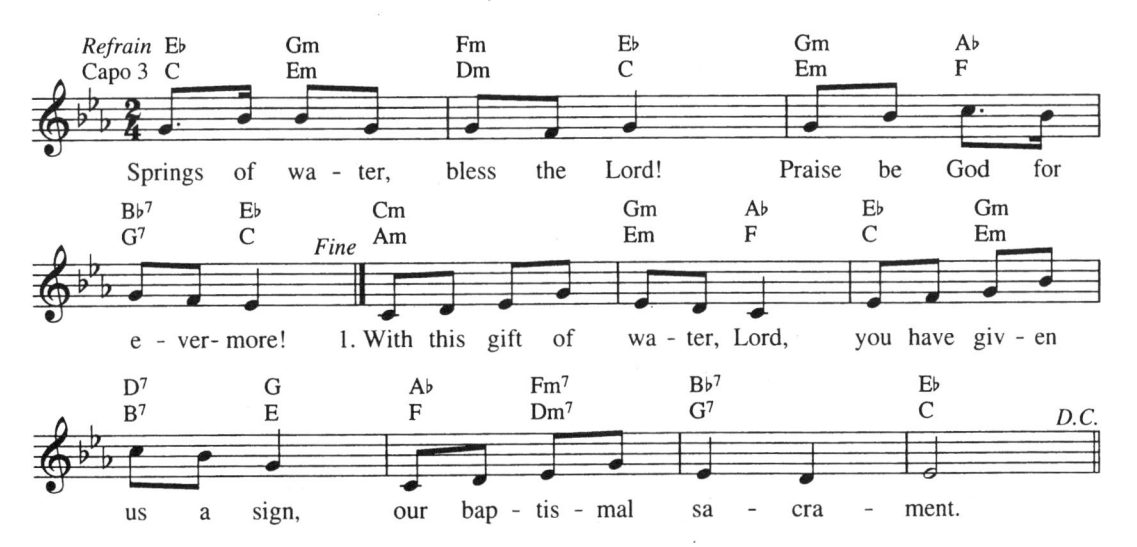

2. At the wat'ry dawn of all,
   order out of chaos came,
   when your Spirit hovered there.

3. With the waters of the flood
   you renewed baptismal sign.
   Sin gave way to spring of life.

4. Through the waters of the sea
   you led Israel, set her free,
   image of your baptised Church.

5. In the Jordan waters, John
   saw your Son baptised and sealed
   with your Spirit resting there.

6. Blood and water from his side,
   symbols of his life outpoured,
   as he hung upon the cross.

7. Then the risen Lord proclaimed:
   'Go and teach, baptising all.
   I will always be with you!'

Text: Noel Donnelly (b.1932) based on the Blessing of baptismal waters (Roman Missal)
Music: Noel Donnelly (b.1932)
© Copyright 1986 Kevin Mayhew Ltd.

632 Star of sea and ocean

AVE MARIS STELLA 66 66

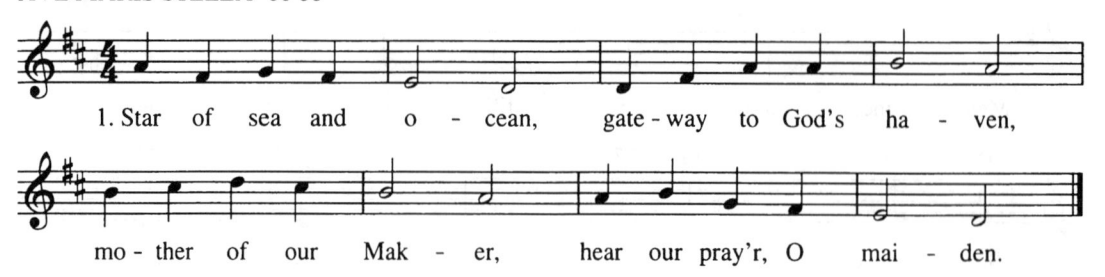

1. Star of sea and o-cean, gate-way to God's ha-ven,
mo-ther of our Mak-er, hear our pray'r, O mai-den.

2. Welcoming the Ave
of God's simple greeting,
you have borne a Saviour,
far beyond all dreaming.

3. Loose the bonds that hold us
bound in sin's own blindness
that with eyes now opened
God's own light may guide us.

4. Show yourself our mother;
he will hear your pleading
whom your womb has sheltered
and whose hand brings healing.

5. Gentlest of all virgins,
that our love be faithful
keep us from all evil
gentle, strong and grateful.

6. Guard us through life's dangers,
never turn and leave us.
May our hope find harbour
in the calm of Jesus.

7. Sing to God our Father
through the Son who saves us,
joyful in the Spirit,
everlasting praises.

Text: 'Ave Maris Stella' (9th century) trans. Ralph Wright (b.1938)
Music: Casper Ett (1788-1847)
Text © Copyright Ralph Wright OSB, St Louis Abbey,
500 S. Mason Road, St. Louis, Missouri 63141, USA. Used by permission.

633 Steal away

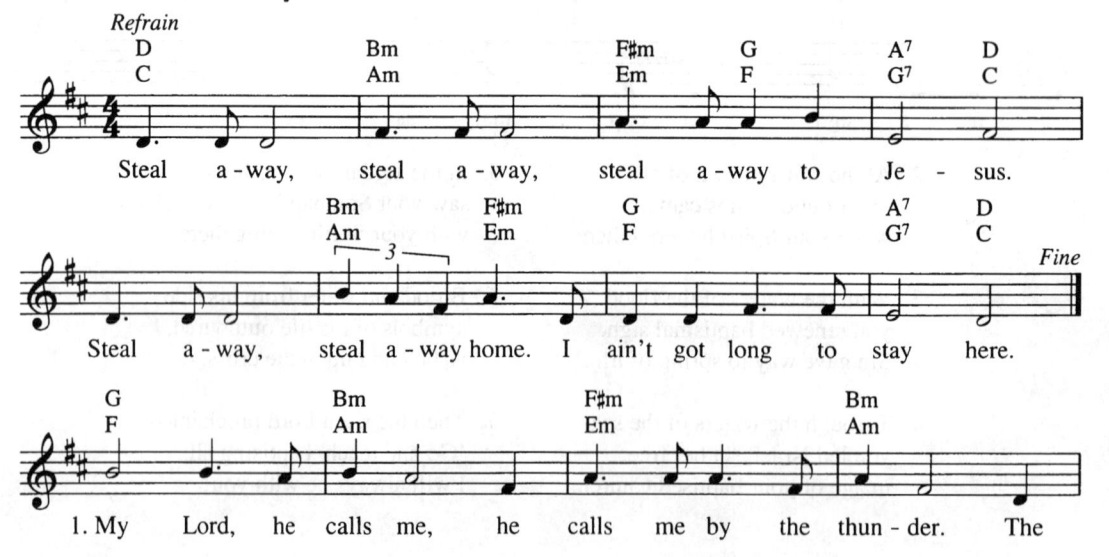

Refrain

Steal a-way, steal a-way, steal a-way to Je-sus.
Steal a-way, steal a-way home. I ain't got long to stay here.

1. My Lord, he calls me, he calls me by the thun-der. The

trum-pet sounds with-in my soul; I ain't got long to stay here.

2. Green trees are bending,
the sinner stands a-trembling.
The trumpet sounds within my soul;
I ain't got long to stay here.

3. My Lord, he calls me,
he calls me by the lightning.
The trumpet sounds within my soul;
I ain't got long to stay here.

Text and Music: Spiritual

634 Sweet heart of Jesus

FONS AMORIS 11 10 11 10 88 and Refrain

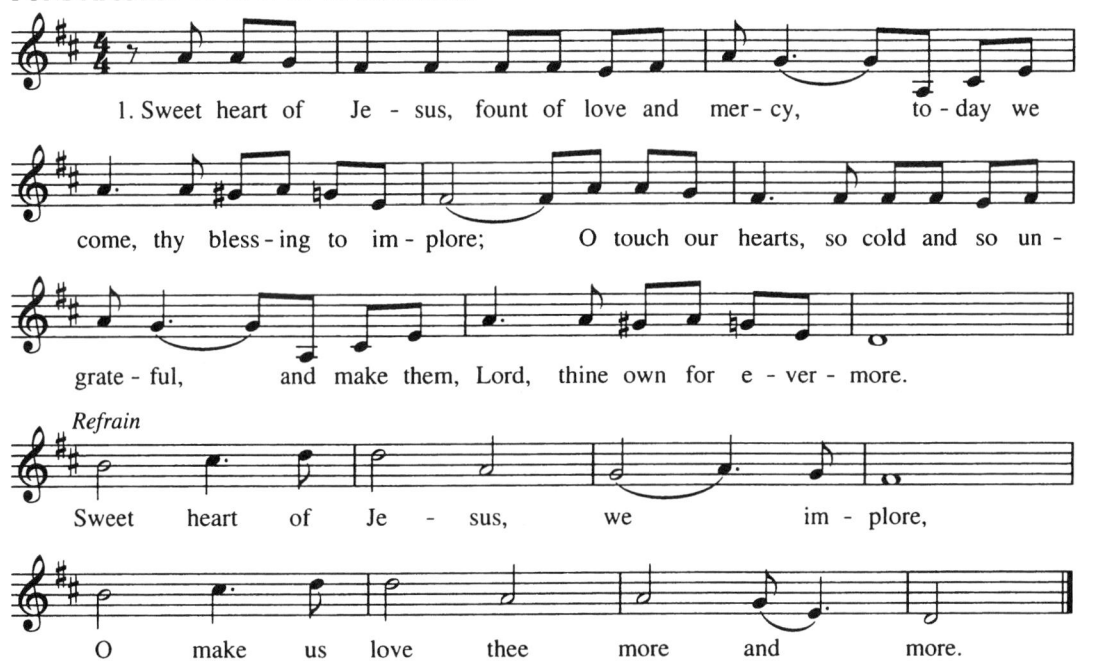

1. Sweet heart of Jesus, fount of love and mercy, today we come, thy blessing to implore; O touch our hearts, so cold and so ungrateful, and make them, Lord, thine own for evermore.

Refrain
Sweet heart of Jesus, we implore,
O make us love thee more and more.

2. Sweet heart of Jesus, make us know and love thee,
unfold to us the treasures of thy grace;
that so our hearts, from things of earth uplifted,
may long alone to gaze upon thy face.

3. Sweet heart of Jesus, make us pure and gentle,
and teach us how to do thy blessèd will;
to follow close the print of thy dear footsteps,
and when we fall – sweet heart, O love us still.

4. Sweet heart of Jesus, bless all hearts that love thee,
and may thine own heart ever blessèd be;
bless us, dear Lord, and bless the friends we cherish,
and keep us true to Mary and to thee.

Text: Sister Marie Josephine
Music: traditional melody

635 Sweet sacrament divine

TUNE 1: DIVINE MYSTERIES 66 66 88 6

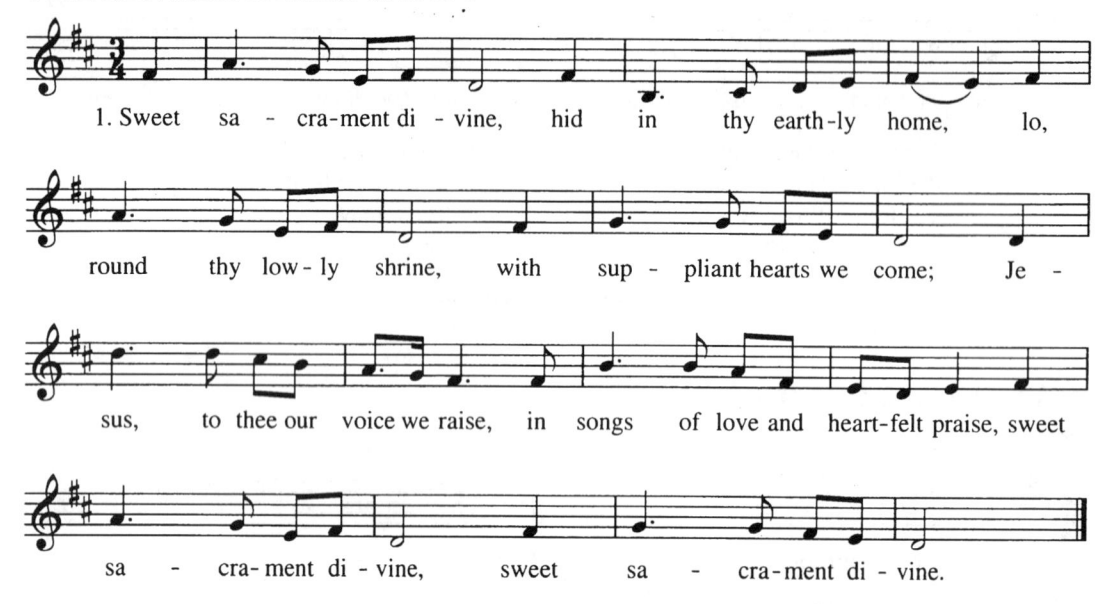

1. Sweet sacrament divine, hid in thy earthly home, lo, round thy lowly shrine, with suppliant hearts we come; Jesus, to thee our voice we raise, in songs of love and heart-felt praise, sweet sacrament divine, sweet sacrament divine.

2. Sweet sacrament of peace,
   dear home of ev'ry heart,
   where restless yearnings cease,
   and sorrows all depart,
   there in thine ear all trustfully
   we tell our tale of misery,
   sweet sacrament of peace.

3. Sweet sacrament of rest,
   Ark from the ocean's roar,
   within thy shelter blest
   soon may we reach the shore;
   save us, for still the tempest raves;
   save, lest we sink beneath the waves,
   sweet sacrament of rest.

4. Sweet sacrament divine,
   earth's light and jubilee,
   in thy far depths doth shine
   thy Godhead's majesty;
   sweet light, so shine on us, we pray,
   that earthly joys may fade away,
   sweet sacrament divine.

TUNE 2: SANCTISSIMUM 66 66 88 6

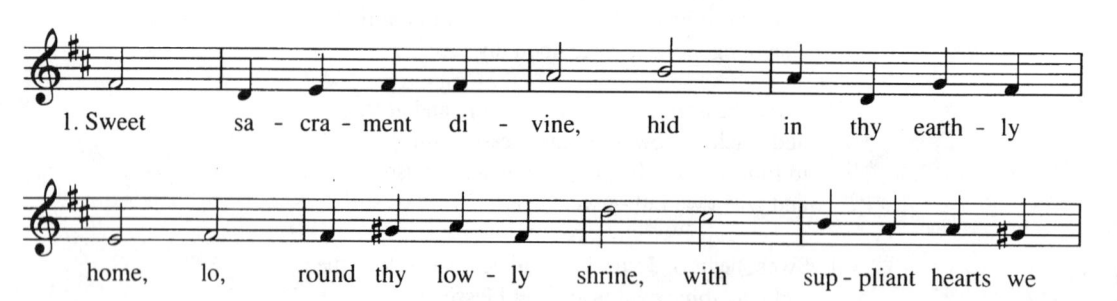

1. Sweet sacrament divine, hid in thy earthly home, lo, round thy lowly shrine, with suppliant hearts we

Tune 2: © Copyright The Estate of Gregory Murray. Used by permission of the Trustees of Downside Abbey, Stratton-on-the-Fosse, Bath BA3 4RH.

come; Je - sus, to thee our voice we raise, in
songs of love and heart-felt praise, sweet sa - cra - ment di - vine.

Text: Francis Stanfield (1835-1914)
Music: Tune 1 – Francis Stanfield (1835-1914)
Tune 2 – Gregory Murray (1905-1992)

636 Sweet Saviour, bless us

SUNSET 88 88 88

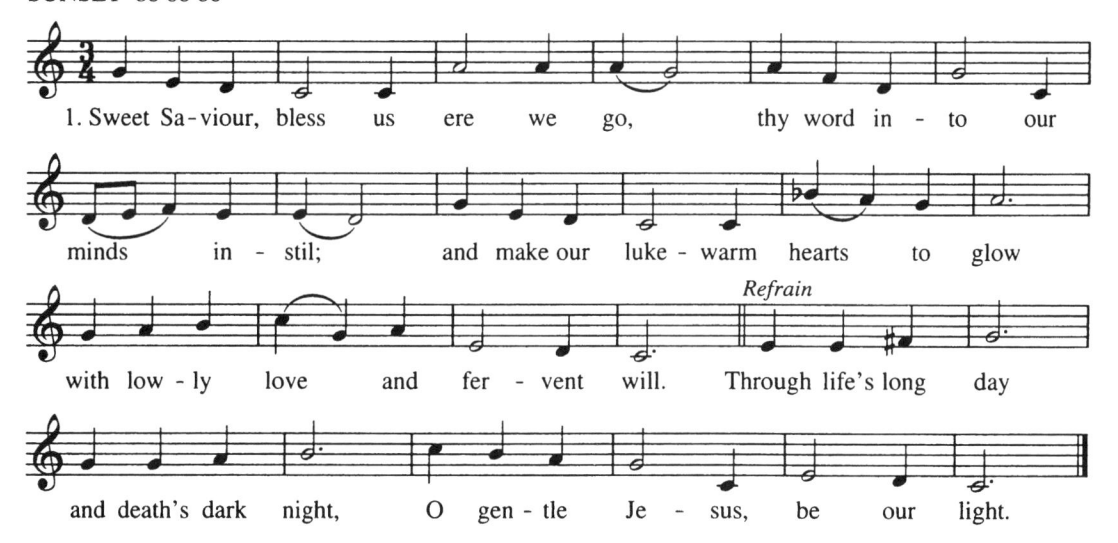

1. Sweet Sa-viour, bless us ere we go, thy word in - to our minds in - stil; and make our luke - warm hearts to glow with low - ly love and fer - vent will. *Refrain* Through life's long day and death's dark night, O gen - tle Je - sus, be our light.

2. The day is done; its hours have run,
and thou hast taken count of all
the scanty triumphs grace has won,
the broken vow, the frequent fall.

3. Grant us, dear Lord, from evil ways,
true absolution and release;
and bless us more than in past days
with purity and inward peace.

4. Do more than pardon; give us joy,
sweet fear and sober liberty,
and loving hearts without alloy,
that only long to be like thee.

5. Labour is sweet, for thou hast toiled,
and care is light, for thou hast cared;
let not our works with self be soiled,
nor in unsimple ways ensnared.

6. For all we love – the poor, the sad,
the sinful – unto thee we call;
O let thy mercy make us glad,
thou art our Jesus and our all.

Text: Frederick William Faber (1814-1863)
Music: George Herbert (1817-1906)

LITURGICAL
HYMNS OLD & NEW

637 Take and bless our gifts

Refrain / Capo 5

Take and bless our gifts, take and bless our gifts, take and bless our gifts, take and bless them, Lord. Take and bless our gifts, take and bless our gifts, take and bless our gifts, take and bless them, Lord.

1. Bles-sed are you, Lord, God of all cre-a-tion. Through your good-ness we of-fer you this bread, which earth has giv'n and hu-man hands have made. It will be-come for us the bread of life.

2. Blessed are you, Lord, God of all creation.
Through your goodness we offer you this wine,
fruit of the vine and work of human hands.
It will become for us the wine of life.

3. Blessed are you, Lord, God of all creation.
Through your goodness we offer you our lives.
Accept, make holy all we try to do,
offered in praise and glory of your name.

Text and Music: Christine McCann (b.1951)
© Copyright 1999 Kevin Mayhew Ltd.

638 Take me, Lord

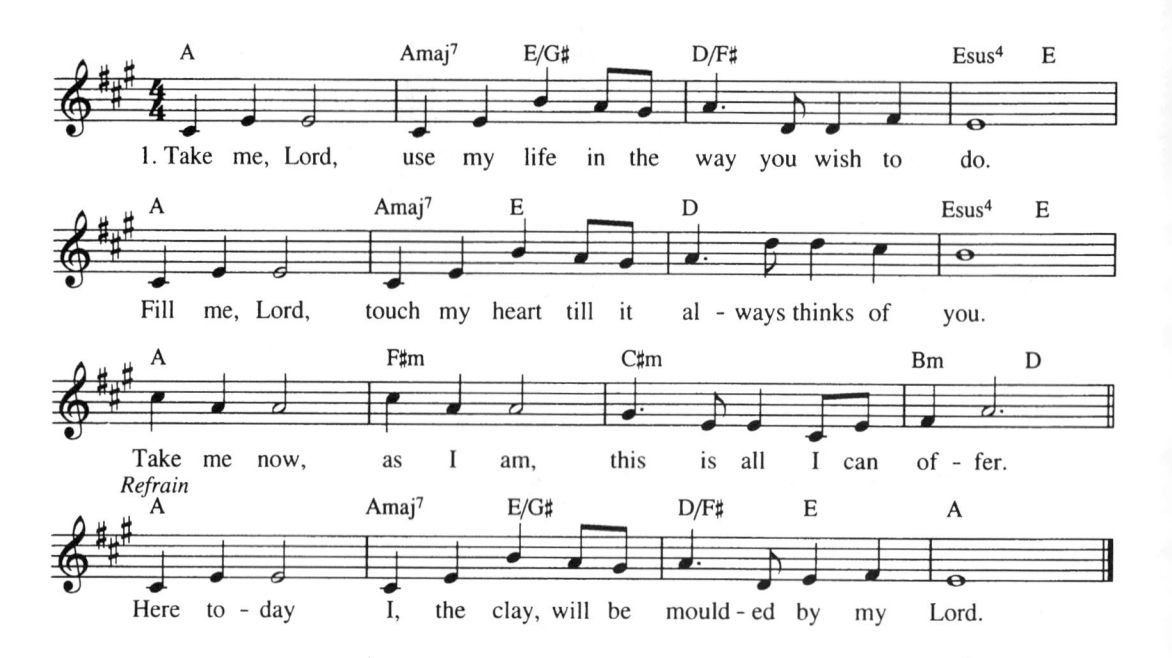

1. Take me, Lord, use my life in the way you wish to do.
Fill me, Lord, touch my heart till it al-ways thinks of you.
Take me now, as I am, this is all I can of-fer.

Refrain
Here to-day I, the clay, will be mould-ed by my Lord.

2. Lord, I pray that each day I will listen to your will.
Many times I have failed but I know you love me still.
Teach me now, guide me, Lord, keep me close to you always.

3. I am weak, fill me now with your strength and set me free.
Make me whole, fashion me so that you will live in me.
Hold me now in your hands, form me now with your Spirit.

Text and Music: Francesca Leftley (b.1955)
© Copyright 1984 Kevin Mayhew Ltd.

639 Take my hands

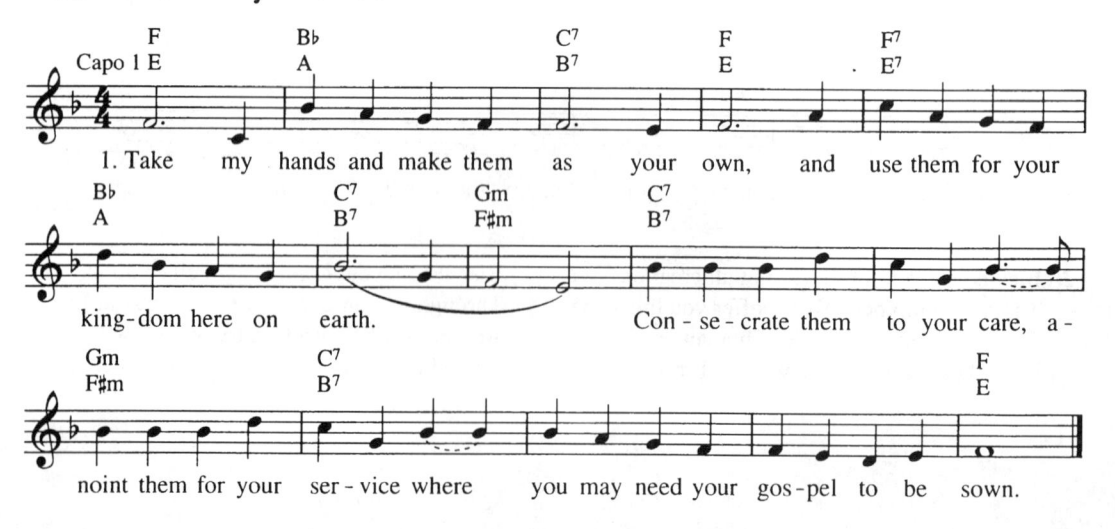

1. Take my hands and make them as your own, and use them for your kingdom here on earth. Con-se-crate them to your care, a-noint them for your ser-vice where you may need your gos-pel to be sown.

© Copyright 1967 OCP Publications, 5536 NE Hassalo,
Portland, OR 97213, USA. All rights reserved. Used by permission.

2. Take my hands, they speak now for my heart,
and by their actions they will show their love.
Guard them on their daily course,
be their strength and guiding force
to ever serve the Trinity above.

3. Take my hands, I give them to you, Lord.
Prepare them for the service of your name.
Open them to human need
and by their love they'll sow your seed
so all may know the love and hope you give.

Text and Music: Sebastian Temple (1928-1997)

640 Take my hands, Lord
Take my life

1. Take my hands, Lord, to share in your la-bours, take my eyes, Lord, to see your needs, let me hear the voice of lone-ly peo-ple, let my love, Lord, bring ri-ches to the poor.

yours, take my life, Lord, and make it tru-ly yours.

2. Give me someone to feed when I'm hungry,
when I'm thirsty give water for their thirst.
When I stand in need of tenderness,
give me someone to hold who longs for love.

3. Keep my heart ever open to others,
may my time, Lord, be spent with those in need;
may I tend to those who need your care.
Take my life, Lord, and make it truly yours.

Text: vs. 1 & 3 Margaret Rizza (b.1929); v.2 unknown
Music: Margaret Rizza (b.1929)
© Copyright 1998 Kevin Mayhew Ltd.

641 Take our bread

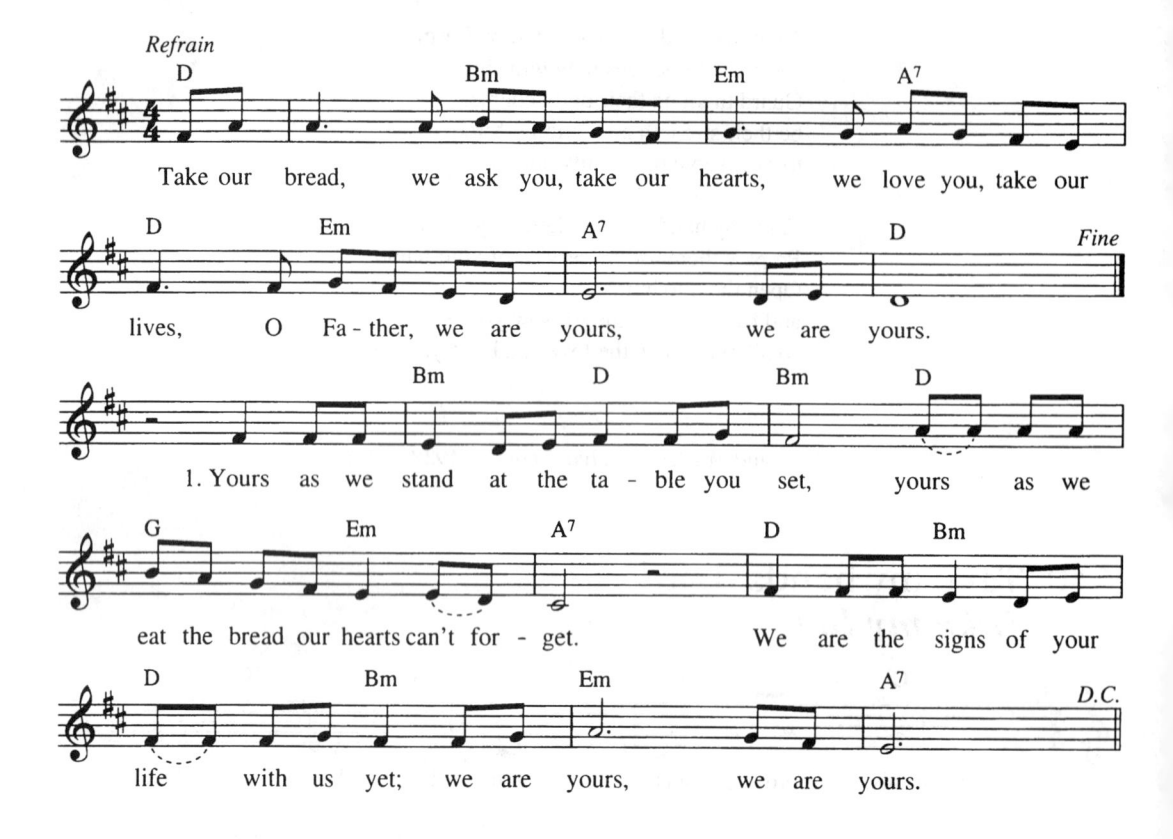

Refrain

Take our bread, we ask you, take our hearts, we love you, take our lives, O Father, we are yours, we are yours.

1. Yours as we stand at the table you set, yours as we eat the bread our hearts can't forget. We are the signs of your life with us yet; we are yours, we are yours.

2. Your holy people stand washed in your blood,
   Spirit-filled, yet hungry, we await your food.
   Poor though we are, we have brought ourselves to you:
   we are yours, we are yours.

Text and Music: Joe Wise (b.1939)
© Copyright 1966 GIA Publications Inc, 7404 S. Mason Avenue, Chicago, Illinois 60638, USA.
All rights reserved. Used by permission.

642 Take this and eat

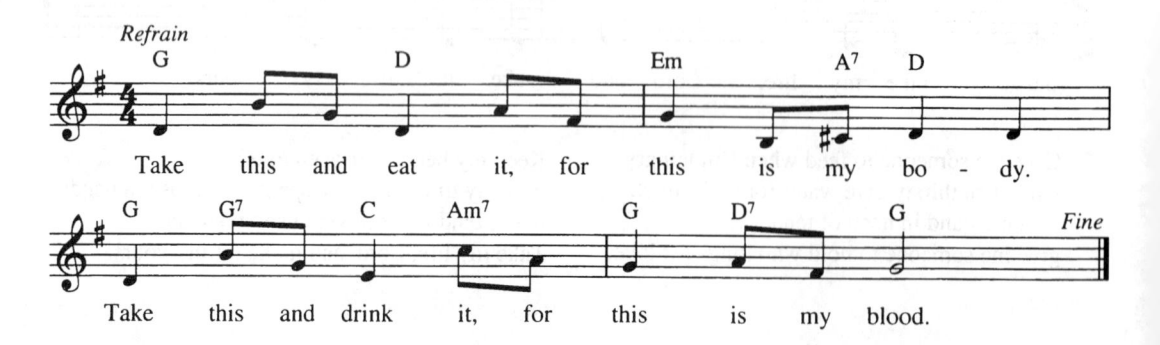

Refrain

Take this and eat it, for this is my body.
Take this and drink it, for this is my blood.

© 1984 Kevin Mayhew Ltd.

1. Taste and see that the Lord is all goodness.
   Happy those who take refuge in him.

2. 'Come to me, you who are heavy laden;
   take my yoke, for my burden is light.'

3. When you eat and you drink at this table,
   Jesus' death you proclaim, till he comes.

4. Eat, you poor, and be filled, you afflicted.
   Those who seek him, give praise to the Lord.

5. Come, be filled as you sit at my table;
   quench your thirst as you drink of my wine.

6. You who eat, break your bread with the hungry;
   you who drink of his Spirit, give praise.

7. Beautiful is the place of your dwelling;
   how my soul longs for you, O my God.

8. See how good and delightful that brethren
   share this meal to bring true unity.

9. You commanded the heavens to open,
   raining manna upon Israel.

10. This, indeed, is the bread come from heaven;
    those who eat it will never know death.

Text: Aniceto Nazareth based on Scripture
Music: Aniceto Nazareth
© 1984 Kevin Mayhew Ltd.

643 Taste and see the goodness of the Lord

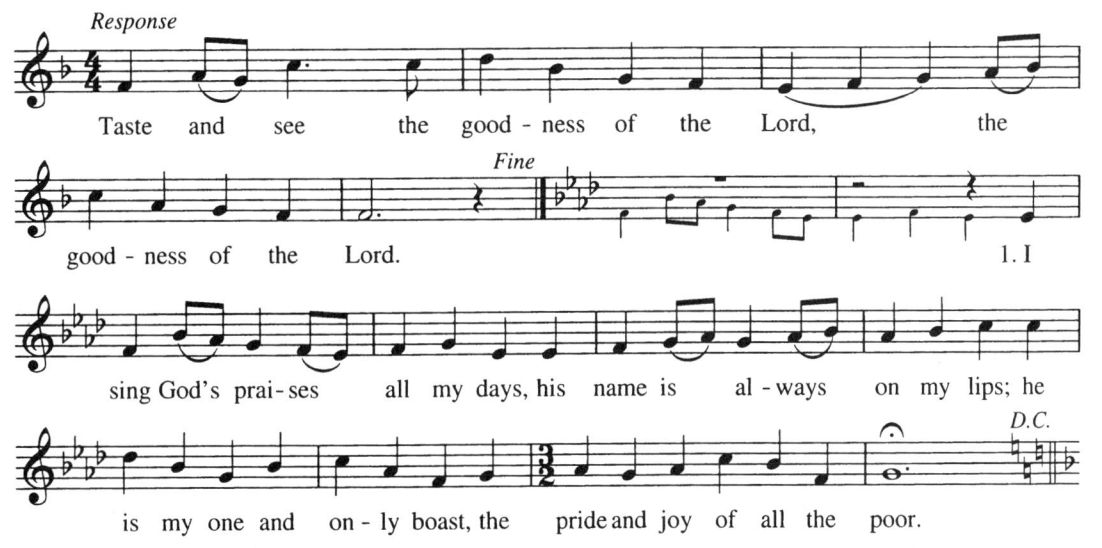

Taste and see the goodness of the Lord, the goodness of the Lord.

I sing God's praises all my days, his name is always on my lips; he is my one and only boast, the pride and joy of all the poor.

2. So come with me to sing his praise,
   together let us praise his name.
   I seek the Lord, he answers me,
   and rescues me from all my fears.

3. The Lord is quick to heed the poor
   and liberate them from their chains.
   The Lord is close to broken hearts,
   he rescues slaves and sets them free.

Text: Hubert J. Richards (b.1921) based on Psalm 33
Music: Andrew Moore (b.1954)
© Copyright 1996 Kevin Mayhew Ltd.

644 Tell out, my soul

WOODLANDS 10 10 10 10

1. Tell out, my soul, the greatness of the Lord: unnumbered blessings, give my spirit voice; tender to me the promise of his word; in God my Saviour shall my heart rejoice.

2. Tell out, my soul, the greatness of his name:
make known his might, the deeds his arm has done;
his mercy sure, from age to age the same;
his holy name, the Lord, the mighty one.

3. Tell out, my soul, the greatness of his might:
pow'rs and dominions lay their glory by;
proud hearts and stubborn wills are put to flight,
the hungry fed, the humble lifted high.

4. Tell out, my soul, the glories of his word:
firm is his promise, and his mercy sure.
Tell out, my soul, the greatness of the Lord
to children's children and for evermore.

Text: Timothy Dudley Smith (b.1926) based on Luke 1:46-55
Music: Walter Greatorex (1877-1949)
Text © Copyright 1961 Timothy Dudley-Smith, 9 Ashlands, Ford, Salisbury, Wiltshire SP4 6DY, UK.
Music © Copyright Oxford University Press, Great Clarendon Street, Oxford OX2 6DP.
Used by permission from 'Enlarged Songs of Praise.'

645 Thanks for the fellowship

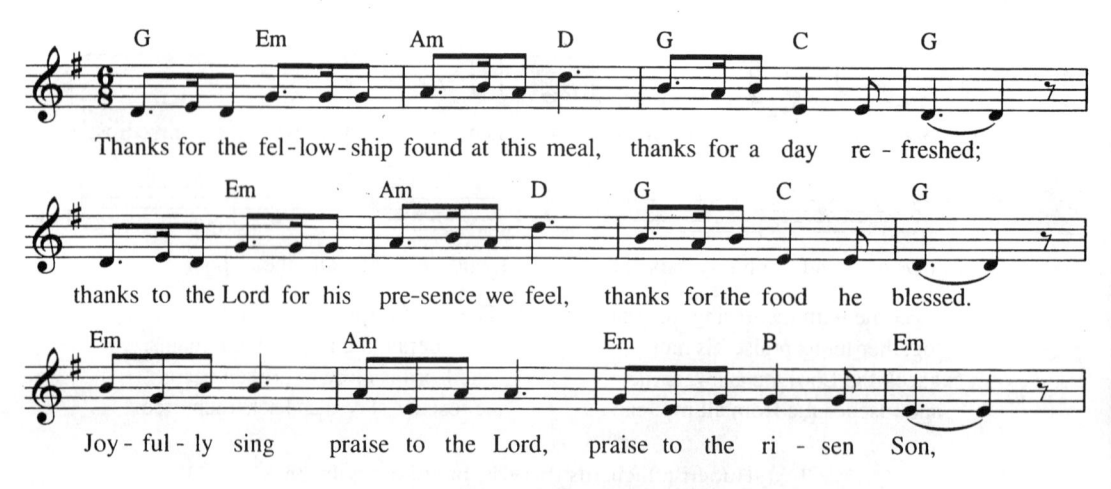

Thanks for the fellowship found at this meal, thanks for a day refreshed;
thanks to the Lord for his presence we feel, thanks for the food he blessed.
Joyfully sing praise to the Lord, praise to the risen Son,

Text © Copyright 1994 Kevin Mayhew Ltd.

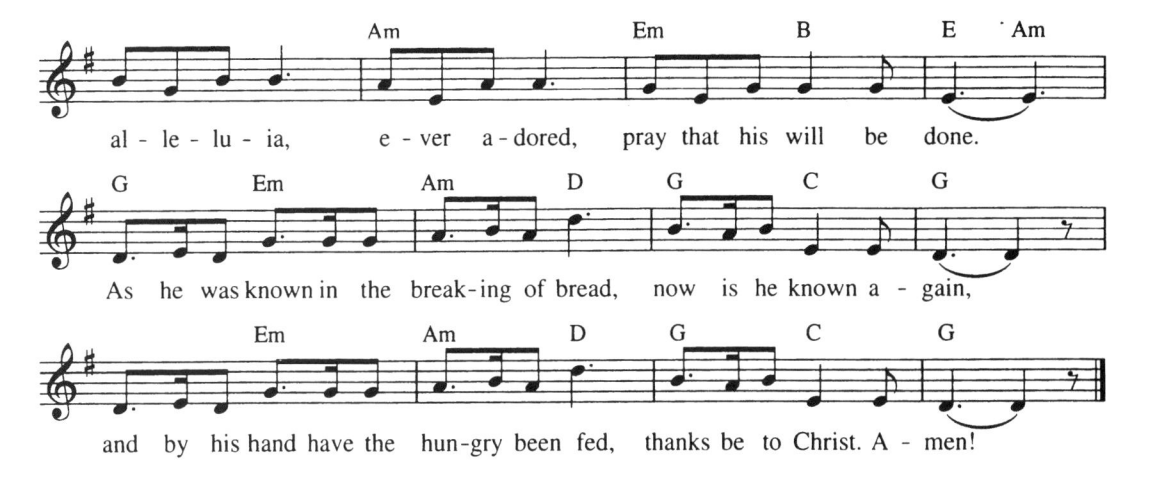

alleluia, ever adored, pray that his will be done.
As he was known in the breaking of bread, now is he known again,
and by his hand have the hungry been fed, thanks be to Christ. Amen!

Text: Jean Holloway (b.1939)
Music: traditional Scottish melody

646 The angel Gabriel from heaven came

BIRJINA GAZTETTOBAT ZEGOEN 10 10 12 10

1. The angel Gabriel from heaven came, his wings as drifted snow, his eyes as flame. 'All hail,' said he, 'thou lowly maiden, Mary, most highly favoured lady.' Gloria!

2. 'For known a blessèd Mother thou shalt be.
All generations laud and honour thee.
Thy Son shall be Emmanuel, by seers foretold,
most highly favoured lady.' Gloria!

3. Then gentle Mary meekly bowed her head.
'To me be as it pleaseth God,' she said.
'My soul shall laud and magnify his holy name.'
Most highly favoured lady! Gloria!

4. Of her, Emmanuel, the Christ, was born
in Bethlehem, all on a Christmas morn;
and Christian folk throughout the world will ever say:
'Most highly favoured lady.' Gloria!

Text: Sabine Baring-Gould (1843-1924) based on 'Birjina gaztettobat zegoen'
Music: traditional Basque melody

647 The Church's one foundation

AURELIA 76 76 D

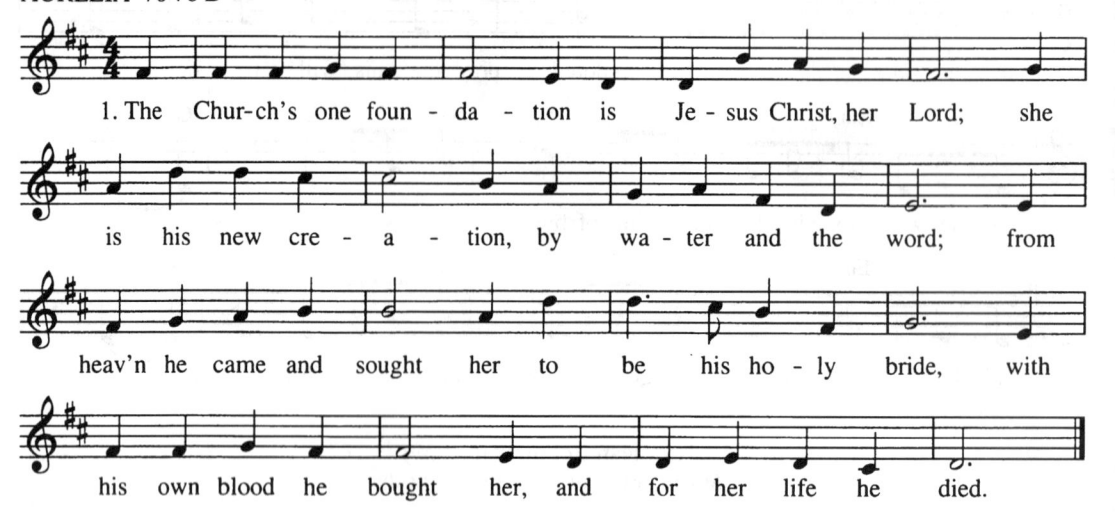

1. The Church's one foundation is Jesus Christ, her Lord;
she is his new creation, by water and the word;
from heav'n he came and sought her to be his holy bride,
with his own blood he bought her, and for her life he died.

A lower setting will be found at No. 521

2. Elect from ev'ry nation, yet one o'er all the earth,
her charter of salvation, one Lord, one faith, one birth;
one holy name she blesses, partakes one holy food,
and to one hope she presses, with ev'ry grace endued.

3. 'Mid toil and tribulation, and tumult of her war,
she waits the consummation of peace for evermore;
till with the vision glorious her longing eyes are blest,
and the great Church victorious shall be the Church at rest.

4. Yet she on earth hath union with God the Three in One,
and mystic sweet communion with those whose rest is won:
O happy ones and holy! Lord, give us grace that we
like them, the meek and lowly, on high may dwell with thee.

Text: Samuel John Stone (1839-1900)
Music: Samuel Sebastian Wesley (1810-1876)

648 The coming of our God

TUNE 1: FRANCONIA SM

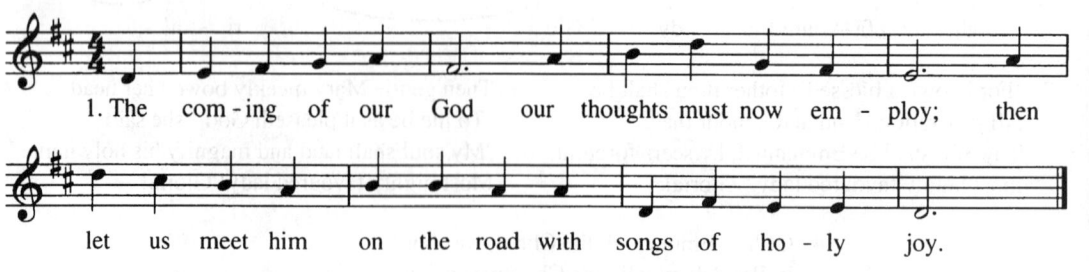

1. The coming of our God our thoughts must now employ;
then let us meet him on the road with songs of holy joy.

2. The co-eternal Son,
a maiden's offspring see;
a servant's form Christ putteth on,
to set his people free.

3. Daughter of Sion, rise
to greet thine infant king,
nor let thy stubborn heart despise
the pardon he doth bring.

4. In glory from his throne
   again will Christ descend,
   and summon all that are his own
   to joys that never end.

5. Let deeds of darkness fly
   before th'approaching morn,
   for unto sin 'tis ours to die,
   and serve the virgin-born.

6. Our joyful praises sing
   to Christ, that set us free;
   like tribute to the Father bring
   and, Holy Ghost, to thee.

TUNE 2: BELLWOODS SM

1. The coming of our God our thoughts must now employ;
   then let us meet him on the road with songs of holy joy.

Text: 'Instantis adventum Dei' by Charles Coffin (1676-1749) trans. Robert Campbell (1814-1868) and others
Music: Tune 1 – traditional melody
Tune 2 – James Hopkirk (b.1908)
Tune 2 © Copyright control

649 The day of resurrection

ELLACOMBE 76 76 D

1. The day of resurrection! Earth, tell it out abroad;
   the passover of gladness, the passover of God!
   From death to life eternal, from earth unto the sky,
   our Christ hath brought us over with hymns of victory.

2. Our hearts be pure from evil, that we may see aright
   the Lord in rays eternal of resurrection-light;
   and list'ning to his accents, may hear so calm and plain
   his own 'All hail' and, hearing, may raise the victor strain.

3. Now let the heav'ns be joyful, and earth her song begin,
   the round world keep high triumph, and all that is therein;
   let all things, seen and unseen, their notes of gladness blend,
   for Christ the Lord hath risen, our joy that hath no end.

Text: St. John of Damascus (c.750) trans. John Mason Neale (1818-1866)
Music: 'Württemberg Gesangbuch' (1784)

650 The day thou gavest, Lord, is ended

ST CLEMENT 98 98

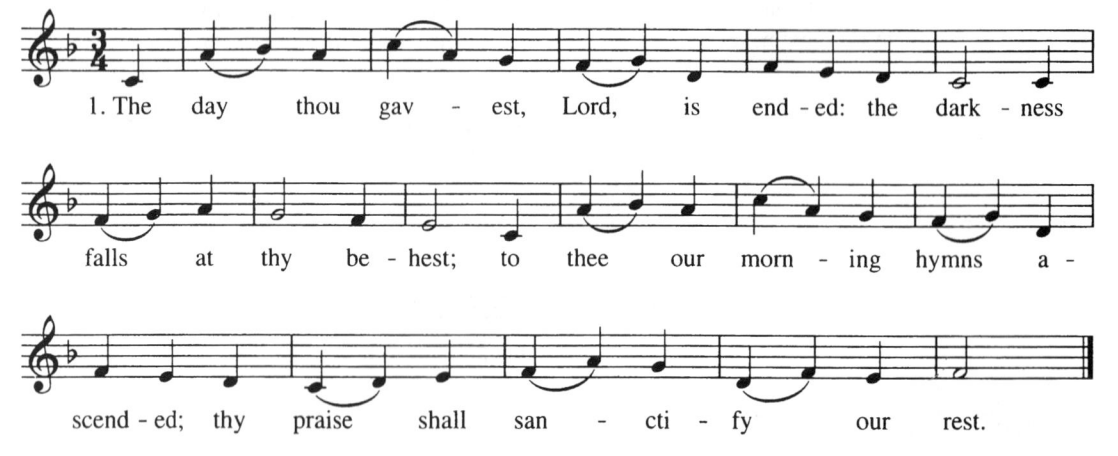

1. The day thou gavest, Lord, is ended: the darkness
falls at thy behest; to thee our morning hymns ascended;
thy praise shall sanctify our rest.

A higher setting will be found at No. 563

2. We thank thee that thy Church unsleeping,
while earth rolls onward into light,
through all the world her watch is keeping,
and rests not now by day or night.

3. As o'er each continent and island
the dawn leads on another day,
the voice of prayer is never silent,
nor dies the strain of praise away.

4. The sun that bids us rest is waking
our brethren 'neath the western sky,
and hour by hour fresh lips are making
thy wondrous doings heard on high.

5. So be it, Lord; thy throne shall never,
like earth's proud empires, pass away;
thy kingdom stands, and grows for ever,
till all thy creatures own thy sway.

Text: John Ellerton (1826-1893)
Music: Clement Cotterill Scholefield (1839-1904)

651 The first Nowell

THE FIRST NOWELL   Irregular

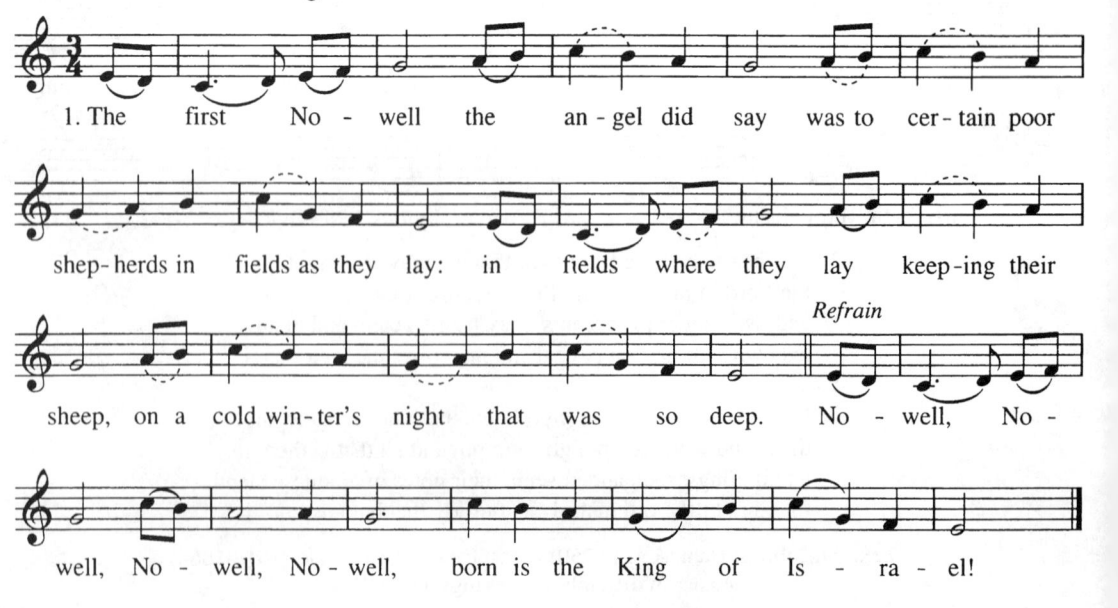

1. The first Nowell the angel did say
was to certain poor shepherds in fields as they lay:
in fields where they lay keeping their sheep,
on a cold winter's night that was so deep.

Refrain
Nowell, Nowell, Nowell, Nowell,
born is the King of Israel!

2. They lookèd up and saw a star,
   shining in the east, beyond them far,
   and to the earth it gave great light,
   and so it continued both day and night.

3. And by the light of that same star,
   three wise men came from country far;
   to seek for a king was their intent,
   and to follow the star wherever it went.

4. This star drew nigh to the north-west,
   o'er Bethlehem it took its rest,
   and there it did both stop and stay
   right over the place where Jesus lay.

5. Then entered in those wise men three,
   full rev'rently upon their knee,
   and offered there in his presence,
   their gold and myrrh and frankincense.

6. Then let us all with one accord
   sing praises to our heav'nly Lord,
   who with the Father we adore
   and Spirit blest for evermore.

Text: from William Sandys' 'Christmas Carols, Ancient and Modern' (1833) alt.
Music: traditional English melody

652 The head that once was crowned with thorns

ST MAGNUS CM

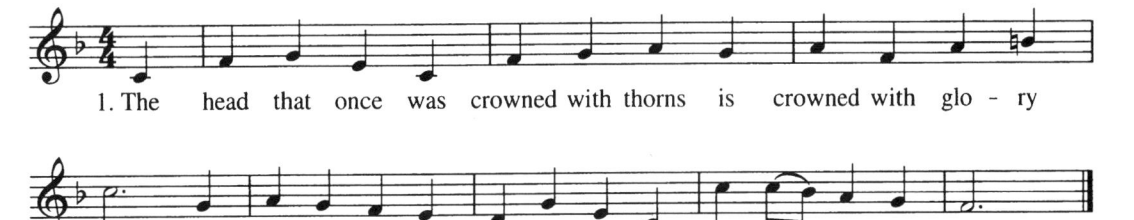

1. The head that once was crowned with thorns is crowned with glory now: a royal diadem adorns the mighty victor's brow.

2. The highest place that heav'n affords
   is his, is his by right.
   The King of kings and Lord of lords,
   and heav'n's eternal light.

3. The joy of all who dwell above,
   the joy of all below,
   to whom he manifests his love,
   and grants his name to know.

4. To them the cross, with all its shame,
   with all its grace is giv'n;
   their name an everlasting name,
   their joy the joy of heav'n.

5. They suffer with their Lord below,
   they reign with him above,
   their profit and their joy to know
   the myst'ry of his love.

6. The cross he bore is life and health,
   though shame and death to him;
   his people's hope, his people's wealth,
   their everlasting theme.

Text: Thomas Kelly (1769-1855)
Music: Jeremiah Clarke (1670-1707)

653 The holly and the ivy

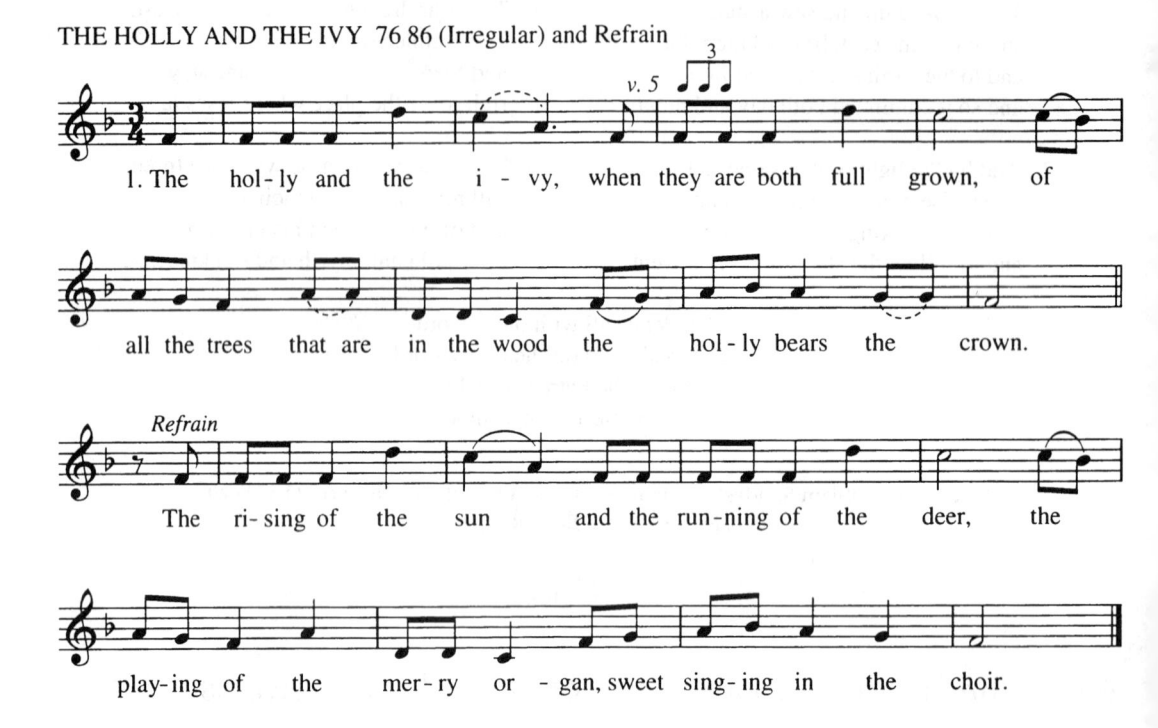

THE HOLLY AND THE IVY 76 86 (Irregular) and Refrain

1. The holly and the ivy, when they are both full grown, of all the trees that are in the wood the holly bears the crown.

Refrain
The rising of the sun and the running of the deer, the playing of the merry organ, sweet singing in the choir.

2. The holly bears a blossom,
   white as the lily flower,
   and Mary bore sweet Jesus Christ
   to be our sweet Saviour.

3. The holly bears a berry,
   as red as any blood,
   and Mary bore sweet Jesus Christ
   to do poor sinners good.

4. The holly bears a prickle,
   as sharp as any thorn,
   and Mary bore sweet Jesus Christ
   on Christmas day in the morn.

5. The holly bears a bark,
   as bitter as any gall,
   and Mary bore sweet Jesus Christ
   for to redeem us all.

6. The holly and the ivy,
   when they are both full grown,
   of all the trees that are in the wood
   the holly bears the crown.

Text: traditional
Music: English folk carol

654 The kingdom of heaven
The Beatitudes

The kingdom of heaven, the kingdom of heaven is yours. A new world in Jesus, a new world in Jesus is yours.

1. Blessed are you in sorrow and grief, for you shall all be consoled; blessed are you, the gentle of heart, you shall inherit the earth. The

2. Blessed are you who hunger for right,
   for you shall be satisfied;
   blessed are you the merciful ones,
   for you shall be pardoned too.

3. Blessed are you whose hearts are pure,
   your eyes shall gaze on the Lord;
   blessed are you who strive after peace,
   the Lord will call you his own.

4. Blessed are you who suffer for right,
   the heav'nly kingdom is yours;
   blessed are you who suffer for me,
   for you shall reap your reward.

Text: Mike Anderson (b.1956) based on Matthew 5:3-10
Music: Mike Anderson (b.1956)
© Copyright 1999 Kevin Mayhew Ltd.

655 The King of glory comes

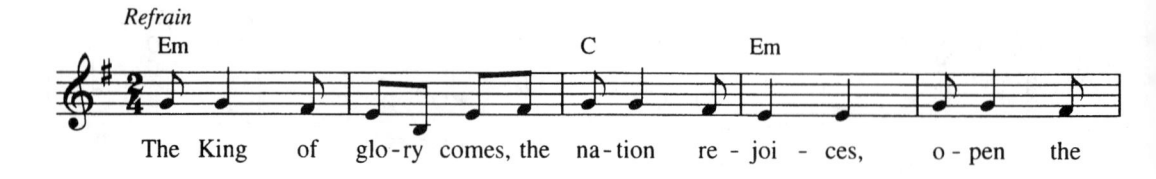

Refrain

The King of glo-ry comes, the na-tion re-joi-ces, o-pen the gates be-fore him, lift up your voi-ces. *Fine* 1. Who is the King of glo-ry, how shall we call him? He is Em-ma-nu-el, the pro-mised of a-ges. *D.C.*

2. In all of Galilee,
   in city and village,
   he goes among his people,
   curing their illness.

3. Sing then of David's Son,
   our Saviour and brother;
   in all of Galilee
   was never another.

4. He gave his life for us,
   the pledge of salvation.
   He took upon himself
   the sins of the nation.

5. He conquered sin and death;
   he truly has risen;
   and he will share with us
   his heavenly vision.

Text: Willard F. Jabusch (b.1930)
Music: Israeli melody

Text © Copyright 1998 Willard F. Jabusch, 5735 University Avenue, Chicago, Illinois 60637, USA. Used by permission.

656 The King of love my shepherd is

TUNE 1: DOMINUS REGIT ME 87 87

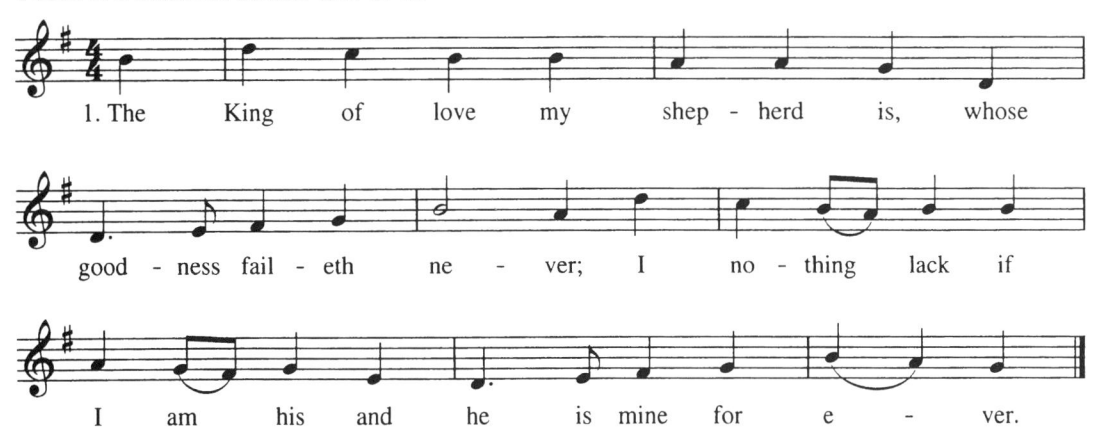

1. The King of love my shepherd is, whose goodness faileth never; I nothing lack if I am his and he is mine for ever.

A lower setting will be found at No. 671

2. Where streams of living water flow
my ransomed soul he leadeth,
and where the verdant pastures grow
with food celestial feedeth.

3. Perverse and foolish oft I strayed,
but yet in love he sought me,
and on his shoulder gently laid,
and home, rejoicing, brought me.

4. In death's dark vale I fear no ill
with thee, dear Lord, beside me;
thy rod and staff my comfort still,
thy cross before to guide me.

5. Thou spread'st a table in my sight,
thy unction grace bestoweth:
and O what transport of delight
from thy pure chalice floweth!

6. And so through all the length of days
thy goodness faileth never;
good Shepherd, may I sing thy praise
within thy house for ever.

TUNE 2: ST COLUMBA 87 87

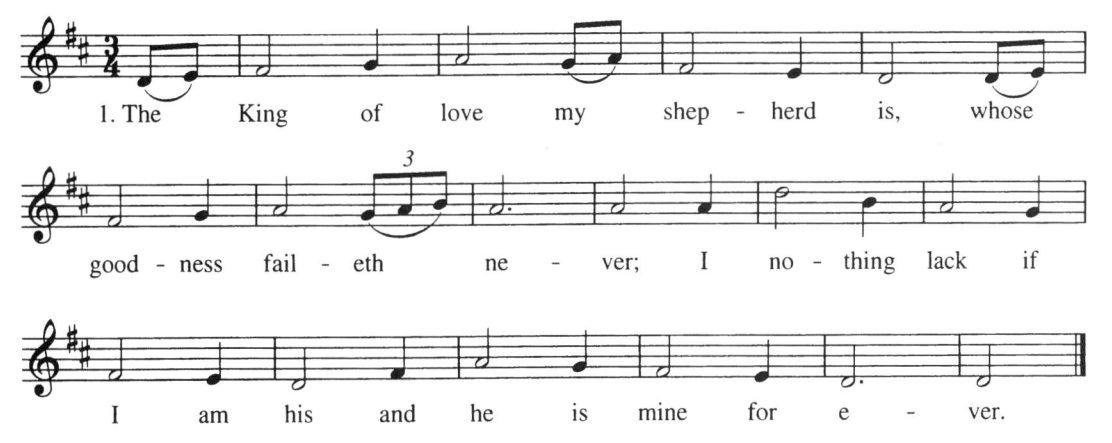

1. The King of love my shepherd is, whose goodness faileth never; I nothing lack if I am his and he is mine for ever.

Text: Henry Williams Baker (1821-1877) based on Psalm 22
Music: Tune 1 – John Bacchus Dykes (1823-1876)
Tune 2 – Irish melody (Petrie Collection)

657 The light of Christ

Capo 3 *Optional*

The light of Christ has come in-to the world.

Refrain
The light of Christ has come in-to the world. The
light of Christ has come in-to the world. (3. The) world.

The light of Christ has come.

1. We must all be born a-gain to see the king-dom of God. The
2. God gave up his on-ly Son out of love for the world, so that
3. light of God has come to us so that we might have sal - va-tion; from the

wa - ter and the Spi - rit bring new life in God's love. The
all who be - lieve in him will live for e - ver. The
dark-ness of our sins we walk in-to glo - ry with Christ Je - sus. The

Text and Music: Donald Fishel (b.1950)

© Copyright 1973 The Word of God Music. Administered by CopyCare, P.O. Box 77, Hailsham, East Sussex, BN27 3EF, UK. Used by permission.

658 The Lord hears the cry of the poor

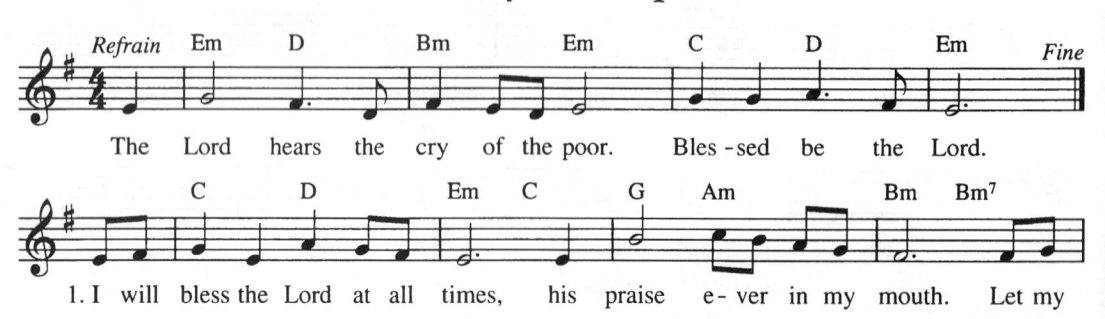

Refrain
The Lord hears the cry of the poor. Bles-sed be the Lord.

1. I will bless the Lord at all times, his praise e-ver in my mouth. Let my

© Copyright 1978, 1991 John B. Foley, SJ and New Dawn Music, 5536 NE Hassalo, Portland, OR 97213, USA. All rights reserved. Used by permission.

soul glo-ry in the Lord, for he hears the cry of the poor.

    2. Let the lowly hear and be glad:
       the Lord listens to their pleas;
       and to hearts broken he is near,
       for he hears the cry of the poor.

    3. Ev'ry spirit crushed he will save;
       will be ransom for their lives;
       will be safe shelter for their fears,
       for he hears the cry of the poor.

    4. We proclaim the greatness of God,
       his praise ever in our mouth;
       ev'ry face brightened in his light,
       for he hears the cry of the poor.

Text: John Foley based on Psalm 33
Music: John Foley

659 The Lord is alive

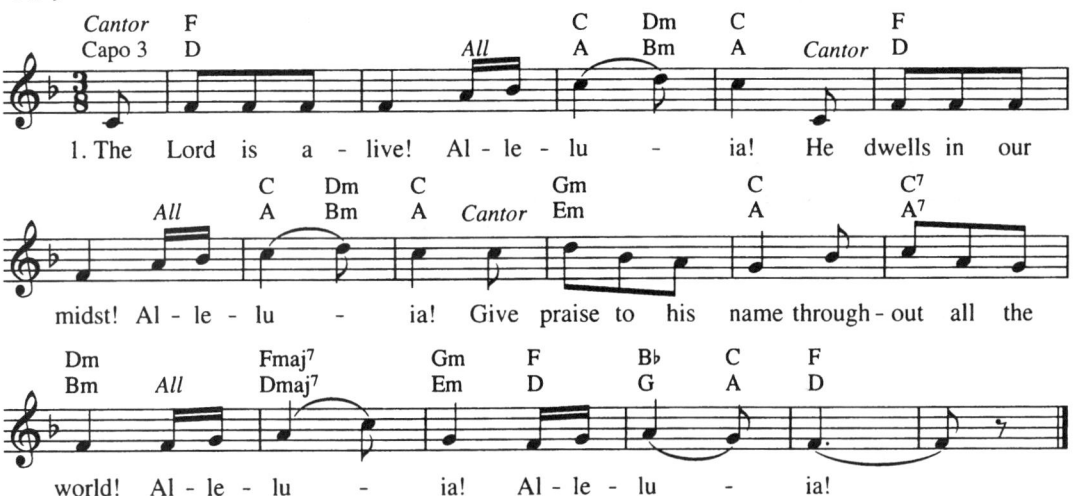

1. The Lord is a-live! Al-le-lu - ia! He dwells in our midst! Al-le-lu - ia! Give praise to his name through-out all the world! Al-le-lu - ia! Al-le-lu - ia!

The division between Cantor and Congregation is suggested for responsorial use.
Verse 5 may be used as a Memorial Acclamation after the Consecration.

    2. He brings us great joy! Alleluia!
       He fills us with hope! Alleluia!
       He comes as our food,
       he gives us our life!
       Alleluia! Alleluia!

    3. So let us rejoice! Alleluia!
       Give praise to the Lord! Alleluia!
       He showed us his love,
       by him we are saved!
       Alleluia! Alleluia!

    4. The Lord is alive! Alleluia!
       So let us proclaim, alleluia,
       the Good News of Christ
       throughout all the world!
       Alleluia! Alleluia!

    5. Christ Jesus has died! Alleluia!
       Christ Jesus is ris'n! Alleluia!
       Christ Jesus will come
       again as the Lord!
       Alleluia! Alleluia!

    6. Sing praises to God, alleluia,
       who reigns without end! Alleluia!
       The Father, the Son,
       and Spirit – all One!
       Alleluia! Alleluia!

Text: Jean-Paul Lécot (b.1947) trans. W.R. Lawrence (1925-1997)
Music: J. Herrera
© Copyright 1988 Kevin Mayhew Ltd.

660 The Lord is my life

Refrain

The Lord is my life, the Lord is my strength, the Lord is my light and my salvation. The Lord is my hope, the Lord is my song, the Lord is my light and my salvation.

1. The Lord is my light and my salvation; whom shall I fear? The Lord is the refuge of my life; of whom should I be afraid? *The*

2. One thing I ask of the Lord, only one thing I seek: to live in the presence of the Lord, to dwell in the house of my God. *The*

3. I believe I shall see the Lord's goodness in the land where the living dwell. Wait for the Lord and be brave; yes, wait for the living God! *The*

Text: Michael Joncas (b.1951) based on Psalm 27
Music: Michael Joncas (b.1951)
© Copyright GIA Publications Inc., 7404 South Mason Avenue, Chicago, Illinois 60638, USA.
All rights reserved. Used by permission.

661 The Lord's my shepherd

TUNE 1: CRIMOND CM

1. The Lord's my shepherd, I'll not want.
   He makes me down to lie
   in pastures green. He leadeth me
   the quiet waters by.

2. My soul he doth restore again,
   and me to walk doth make
   within the paths of righteousness,
   e'en for his own name's sake.

3. Yea, though I walk in death's dark vale,
   yet will I fear no ill.
   For thou art with me, and thy rod
   and staff me comfort still.

4. My table thou has furnishèd
   in presence of my foes,
   my head thou dost with oil anoint,
   and my cup overflows.

5. Goodness and mercy all my life
   shall surely follow me.
   And in God's house for evermore
   my dwelling-place shall be.

TUNE 2: BROTHER JAMES'S AIR CM

1. The Lord's my shepherd, I'll not want. He makes me down to lie in pastures green. He leadeth me the quiet waters by. In pastures green, he leadeth me the quiet waters by.

Text: Psalm 22 from 'The Scottish Psalter' (1650)
Music: Tune 1 – melody by Jessie Seymour Irvine (1836-1887)
Tune 2 – Brother James Leith Macbeth Bain (d.1925)

LITURGICAL
HYMNS OLD & NEW

662 The love I have for you
Only a shadow

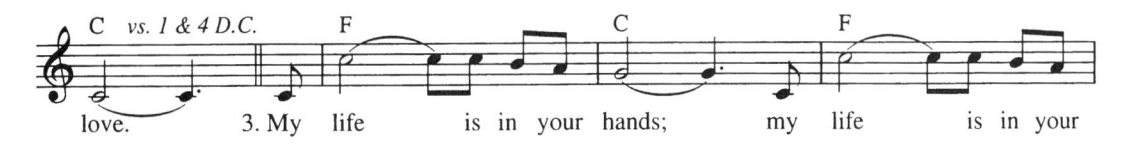

1. The love I have for you, my Lord, is only a shadow of your love for me; only a shadow of your love for me; your deep abiding love.

2. My own belief in you, my Lord,
   is only a shadow of your faith in me;
   only a shadow of your faith in me;
   your deep and lasting faith.

3. My life is in your hands; my life is in your hands. My love for you will grow, my God. Your light in me will shine.

4. The dream I have today, my Lord,
   is only a shadow of your dreams for me;
   only a shadow of all that will be;
   if I but follow you.

5. The joy I feel today, my Lord,
   is only a shadow of your joys for me;
   only a shadow of your joys for me;
   when we meet face to face.

6. *Repeat verse 3.*

Text and Music: Carey Landry

© Copyright 1971 Carey Landry and North American Liturgy Resources (NALR),
5536 NE Hassalo, Portland, OR 97213, USA. All rights reserved. Used by permission.

663 The Mass is ended

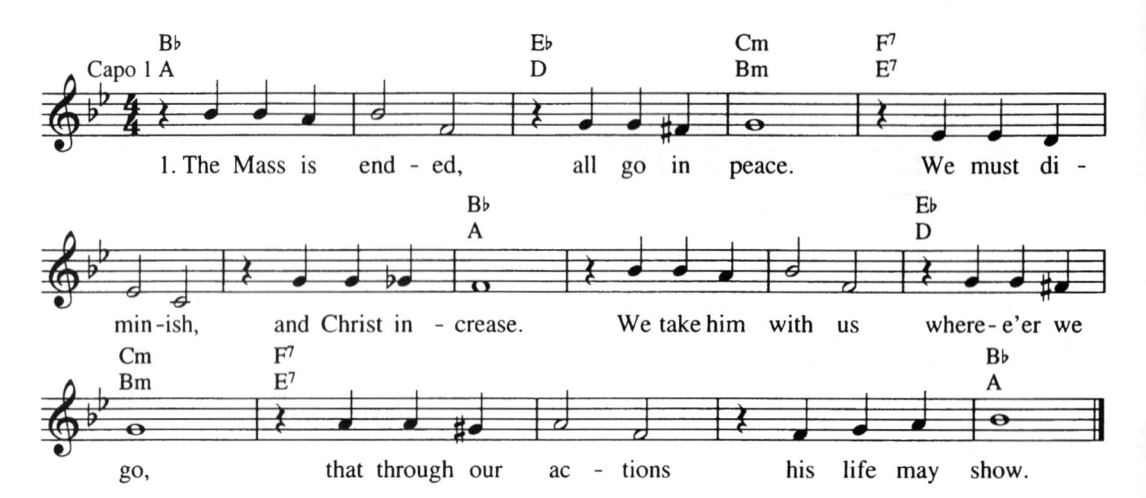

1. The Mass is end-ed, all go in peace. We must di-minish, and Christ in-crease. We take him with us where-e'er we go, that through our ac-tions his life may show.

2. We witness his love to ev'ryone
by our communion with Christ the Son.
We take the Mass to where people are
that Christ may shine forth, their Morning Star.

3. Thanks to the Father who shows the way.
His life within us throughout each day.
Let all our living and loving be
to praise and honour the Trinity.

4. *Repeat verse 1.*

Text: Sebastian Temple (1928-1997) alt.
Music: Sebastian Temple (1928-1997)
© Copyright 1967 OCP Publications, 5536 NE Hassalo, Portland, OR 97213, USA.
All rights reserved. Used by permission.

664 The night was dark
Come and see

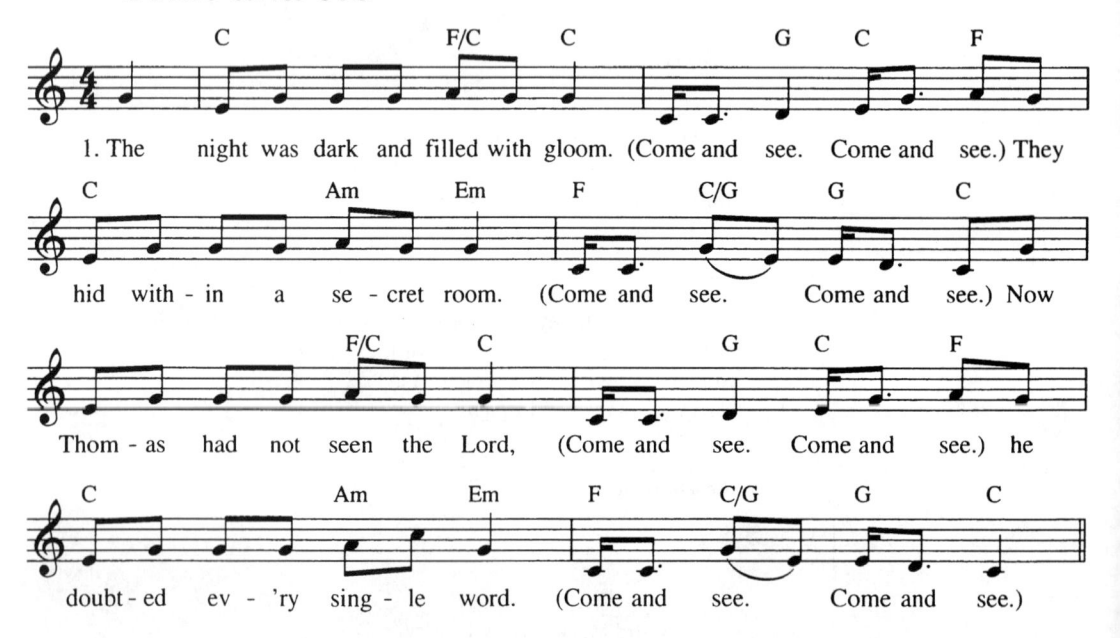

1. The night was dark and filled with gloom. (Come and see. Come and see.) They hid with-in a se-cret room. (Come and see. Come and see.) Now Thom-as had not seen the Lord, (Come and see. Come and see.) he doubt-ed ev-'ry sin-gle word. (Come and see. Come and see.)

Text © Copyright 1991 John C. Ylvisaker, Box 321, Waverly, IA 50677-0321, USA. Used by permission.

Refrain

I be-lieve this is Je-sus. (Come and see. Come and see.) Oh,
I be-lieve this is Je-sus. (Come and see. Come and see.)

2. Then suddenly the Lord appeared
   (Come and see. Come and see.)
   to see his friends and calm their fears.
   (Come and see. Come and see.)
   'Now Thomas,' he said, 'see my hand,'
   (Come and see. Come and see.)
   'it happened just as God had planned.'

3. 'Well,' Thomas said, 'my God, my Lord.
   (Come and see. Come and see.)
   'Now I believe the living Word.'
   (Come and see. Come and see.)
   Go tell the people far and wide,
   (Come and see. Come and see.)
   'twas for their sins that Jesus died.

Text: John Ylvisaker
Music: Traditional American

665 The race that long in darkness pined

TUNE 1: ST FULBERT CM

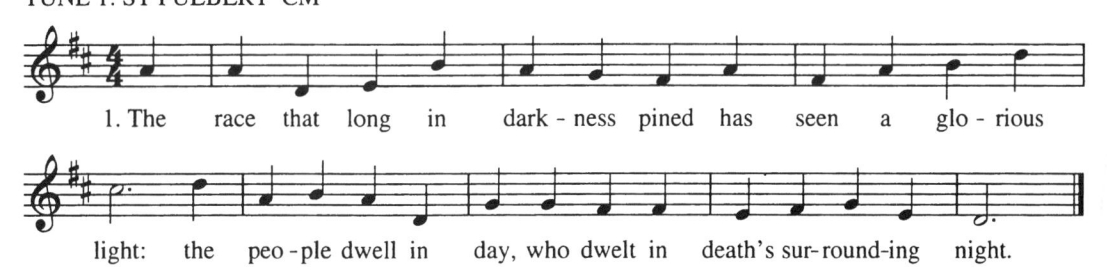

1. The race that long in dark-ness pined has seen a glo-rious light: the peo-ple dwell in day, who dwelt in death's sur-round-ing night.

2. To hail thy rise, thou better sun,
   the gath'ring nations come,
   joyous as when the reapers bear
   the harvest treasures home.

3. To us a child of hope is born,
   to us a Son is giv'n;
   him shall the tribes of earth obey,
   him all the hosts of heav'n.

4. His name shall be the Prince of Peace
   for evermore adored,
   the Wonderful, the Counsellor,
   the great and mighty Lord.

5. His pow'r increasing still shall spread,
   his reign no end shall know;
   justice shall guard his throne above,
   and peace abound below.

TUNE 2: DUNDEE CM

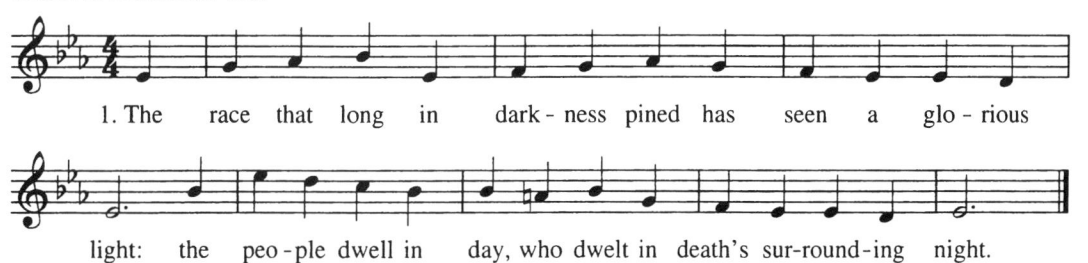

1. The race that long in dark-ness pined has seen a glo-rious light: the peo-ple dwell in day, who dwelt in death's sur-round-ing night.

Text: John Morrison (1750-1798) based on Isaiah 9:2-7
Music: Tune 1 – Henry John Gauntlett (1805-1876)
Tune 2 – melody from 'Psalms', Edinburgh (1615)

666 There is a green hill far away

HORSLEY CM

1. There is a green hill far a-way, outside a ci-ty wall, where the dear Lord was cru-ci-fied who died to save us all.

2. We may not know, we cannot tell
   what pains he had to bear,
   but we believe it was for us
   he hung and suffered there.

3. He died that we might be forgiv'n,
   he died to make us good;
   that we might go at last to heav'n,
   saved by his precious blood.

4. There was no other good enough
   to pay the price of sin;
   he only could unlock the gate
   of heav'n, and let us in.

5. O, dearly, dearly has he loved,
   and we must love him too,
   and trust in his redeeming blood,
   and try his works to do.

Text: Cecil Frances Alexander (1818-1895) alt.
Music: William Horsley (1774-1858)

667 There is a river

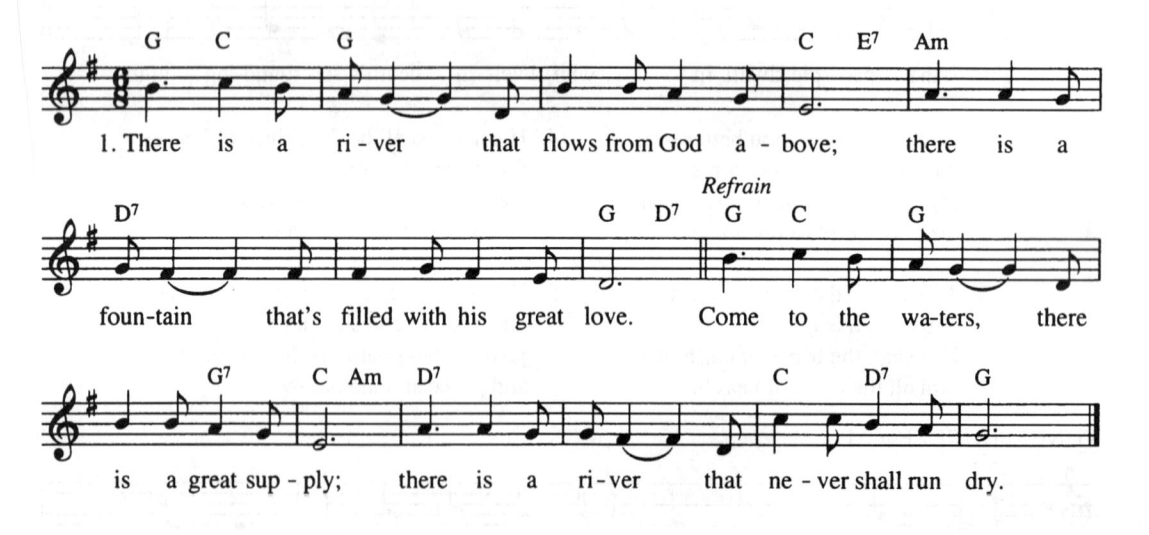

1. There is a ri-ver that flows from God a-bove; there is a foun-tain that's filled with his great love.

Refrain
Come to the wa-ters, there is a great sup-ply; there is a ri-ver that ne-ver shall run dry.

2. Wash me with water, and then I shall be clean;
   white as the new snow, if you remove my sin.

3. Plunged in the water, the tomb of our rebirth,
   so may we rise up to share in Christ's new life.

Text © Copyright 1999 Kevin Mayhew Ltd.

4. All who are thirsty, now hear God as he calls;
   come to the Lord's side, his life pours out for all.

5. Safe in the new Ark, the Church of Christ our Lord,
   praise God for water, his sign to save the world.

Text: v.1 Unknown; vs. 2-5 Robert B. Kelly (b.1948) from Scripture
Music: Traditional melody

668 The royal banners forward go

TUNE 1: TRURO LM

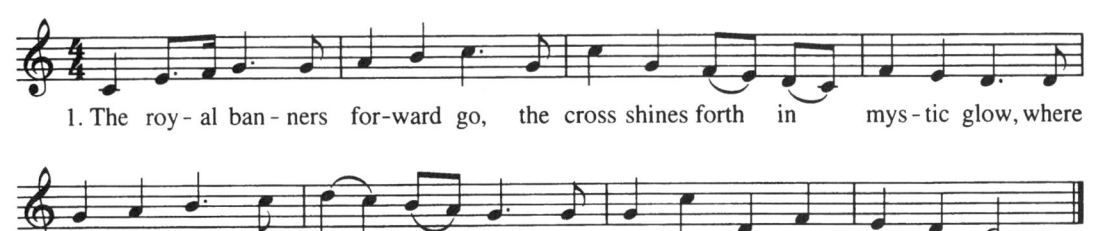

1. The royal banners forward go, the cross shines forth in mystic glow, where he in flesh, our flesh who made, our sentence bore, our ransom paid.

2. There whilst he hung, his sacred side
   by soldier's spear was opened wide,
   to cleanse us in the precious flood
   of water mingled with his blood.

3. Fulfilled is now what David told
   in true prophetic song of old,
   how God the heathen's king should be;
   for God is reigning from the tree.

4. O tree of glory, tree most fair,
   ordained those holy limbs to bear,
   how bright in purple robe it stood,
   the purple of a Saviour's blood!

5. Upon its arms, like balance true,
   he weighed the price for sinners due,
   the price which none but he could pay:
   and spoiled the spoiler of his prey.

6. To thee, eternal Three in One,
   let homage meet by all be done,
   as by the cross thou dost restore,
   so rule and guide us evermore.

TUNE 2: WINCHESTER NEW LM

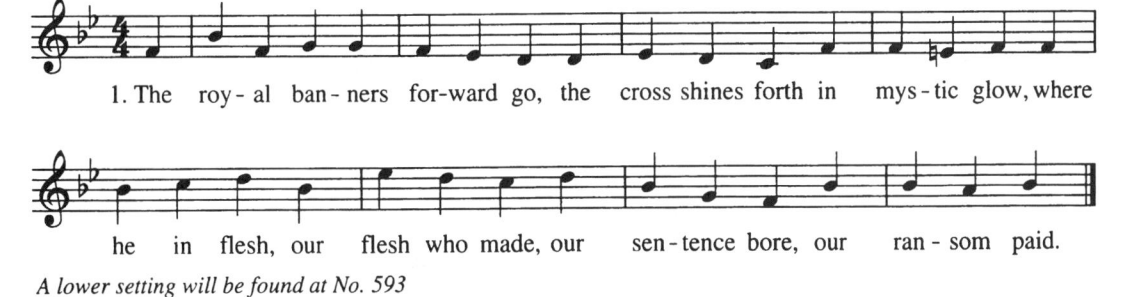

1. The royal banners forward go, the cross shines forth in mystic glow, where he in flesh, our flesh who made, our sentence bore, our ransom paid.

A lower setting will be found at No. 593

Text: 'Vexilla regis prodeunt' by Venantius Fortunatus (530-609)
trans. John Mason Neale (1818-1866) and others
Music: Tune 1 – from 'Psalmodia Evangelica' (1789)
Tune 2 – from 'Musikalisches Handbuch' (1690)

669 The Saviour will come, resplendent in joy

LAUDATE DOMINUM 10 10 11 11

1. The Saviour will come, resplendent in joy;
the lame and the sick new strength will enjoy.
The desert, rejoicing, shall burst into flow'r,
the deaf and the speechless will sing in that hour!

A lower setting will be found at No. 548

2. The Saviour will come, like rain on the earth,
to harvest at last his crop of great worth.
In patience await him, with firmness of mind;
both mercy and judgement his people will find.

3. The Saviour will come, his truth we shall see:
where lepers are cleansed and captives set free.
No finely clad princeling in palace of gold,
but Christ with his people, O wonder untold!

Text: Michael Forster (b.1946) based on Isaiah 35
Music: Hubert Parry (1848-1918)
Text © Copyright 1993 Kevin Mayhew Ltd.

670 The seed is Christ's

AG CRÍOST AN SÍOL Irregular

The seed is Christ's, the harvest his: may we be stored within God's barn. The sea is Christ's, the fish are his: may we be caught within God's net. From birth to age, from

Text © Copyright Geoffrey Chapman, an imprint of Cassell plc, Wellington House,
125 Strand, London WC2R 0BB. Used by permission.

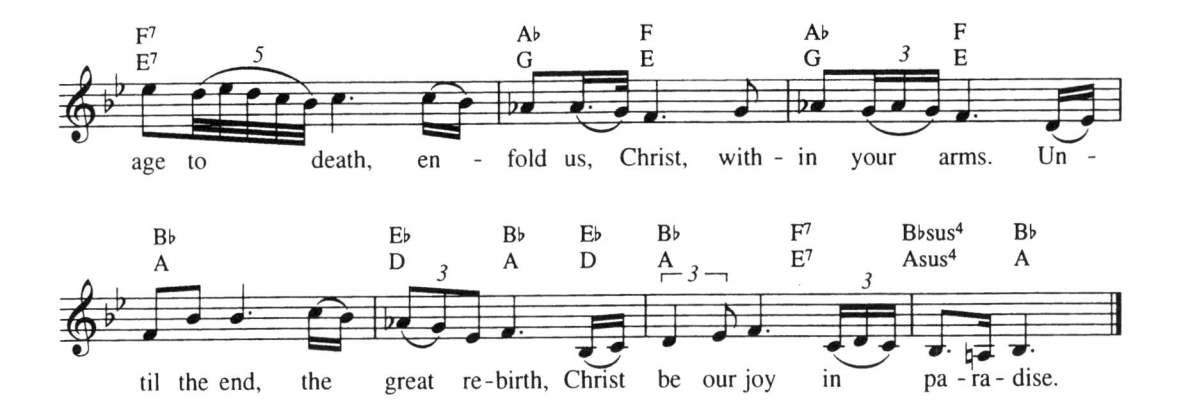

age to death, en - fold us, Christ, with - in your arms. Un -
til the end, the great re-birth, Christ be our joy in pa - ra - dise.

Text: James Quinn (b.1919)
Music: Seán Ó Riada

671 The sign of hope, creation's joy

DOMINUS REGIT ME 87 87

1. The sign of hope, cre - a - tion's joy, is born of pur - est beau - ty: the vir - gin's womb, now glo - ri - fied, where grace u-nites with du - ty.

A higher setting will be found at No. 656

2. Emmanuel shall be his name,
   a title pure and holy,
   for God with us will truly be
   among the poor and lowly.

3. Where love divine concurs with trust
   to share redemption's story,
   Emmanuel in hope is born,
   and earth exults in glory.

4. Now we, by grace and duty called,
   proclaim to ev'ry nation
   the Sign of hope which Mary bore,
   and promise of salvation.

Text: Michael Forster (b.1946)
Music: John Bacchus Dykes (1823-1876)
Text © Copyright 1993 Kevin Mayhew Ltd.

672 The Spirit lives to set us free
Walk in the light

1. The Spirit lives to set us free, walk, walk in the light.
He binds us all in unity, walk, walk in the light.

Refrain
Walk in the light, walk in the light, walk in the light, walk in the light of the Lord.

2. Jesus promised life to all,
   walk, walk in the light.
   The dead were wakened by his call,
   walk, walk in the light.

3. He died in pain on Calvary,
   walk, walk in the light,
   to save the lost like you and me,
   walk, walk in the light.

4. We know his death was not the end,
   walk, walk in the light.
   He gave his Spirit to be our friend,
   walk, walk in the light.

5. By Jesus' love our wounds are healed,
   walk, walk in the light.
   The Father's kindness is revealed,
   walk, walk in the light.

6. The Spirit lives in you and me,
   walk, walk in the light.
   His light will shine for all to see,
   walk, walk in the light.

Text: Damian Lundy (1944-1997)
Music: unknown
Text © Copyright 1978, 1993 Kevin Mayhew Ltd.

673 The Spirit of the Lord

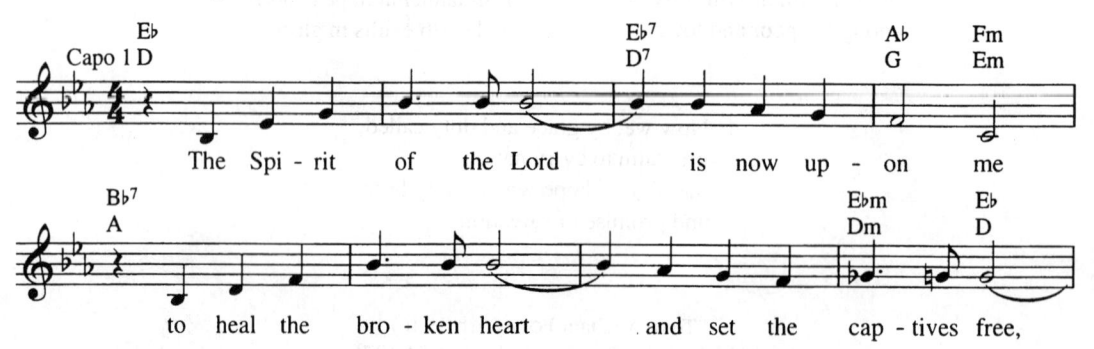

The Spirit of the Lord is now upon me to heal the broken heart and set the captives free,

to open prison doors and make the blind to see.
The Spirit of the Lord is now on me.

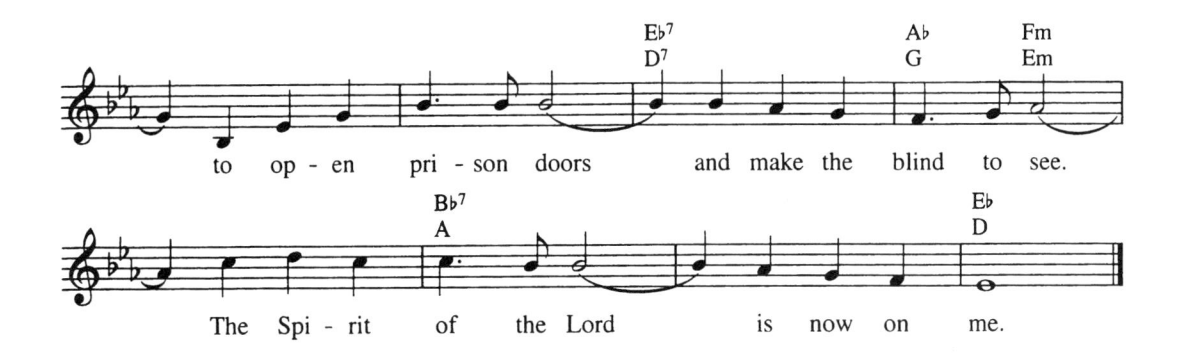

Text: Luke 4:18 and Isaiah 61:1-2
Music: unknown

674 The table's set, Lord

1. The table's set, Lord, your people gathered; around this table each finds their place. Sign of the kingdom, the greatest gath'ring, around Christ Jesus each has their place.

2. At this same table in other places,
so many people here in Christ's name.
Those gone before us, who will succeed us,
one single table throughout all time.

3. One Lord inviting, one Church responding;
one single bread and one cup of wine.
May what we do here change and transform us,
one single presence, Christ through all time.

Text and Music: Robert B. Kelly (b.1948)
© Copyright 1999 Kevin Mayhew Ltd.

675 The temple of the living God

ELLACOMBE DCM

1. The temple of the living God is built of living stones,
a holy people, called to live by light of Christ alone.
With special joy we celebrate the word the psalmist said:
'The stone the builders cast aside is now the corner's head!'

2. The temple of the living God
is set secure above,
where Christ invites the world to share
his perfect reign of love.
And we who seek the Father's face
are summoned to obey,
and follow where he goes before,
the Life, the Truth, the Way.

3. The temple of the living God
upon the earth must grow,
and those of ev'ry race and class
his true compassion know.
The widow and the fatherless
receive a special care,
till all creation, just and free,
his perfect peace will share.

Text: Michael Forster (b.1946)
Music: 'Württemberg Gesangbuch' (1784)
Text © Copyright 1993 Kevin Mayhew Ltd.

676 The Virgin Mary had a baby boy

1. The Virgin Mary had a baby boy, the Virgin Mary had a baby boy, the Virgin Mary had a baby boy, and they said that his name was Jesus.

Refrain
He came from the glory, he came from the glorious kingdom.
He came from the glory, he came from the glorious kingdom.
O yes, believer. O yes, believer.
He came from the glory, he came from the glorious kingdom.

2. The glorious kingdom.

2. The angels sang when the baby was born, *(x3)*
   and proclaimed him the Saviour Jesus.

3. The wise men saw where the baby was born, *(x3)*
   and they saw that his name was Jesus.

Text and Music: traditional West Indian

677 The wandering flock of Israel

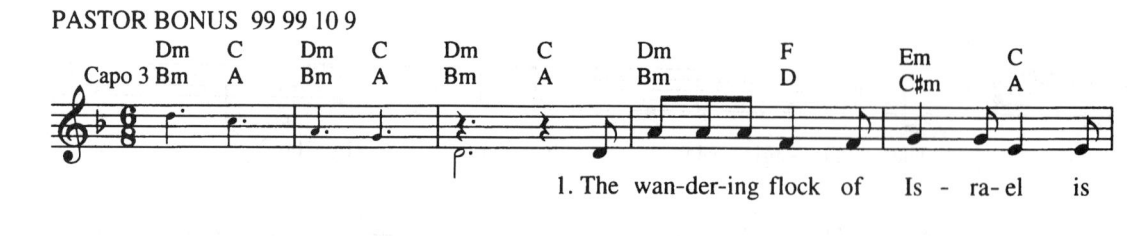

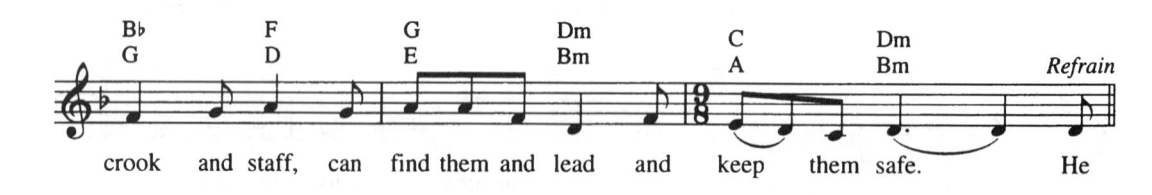

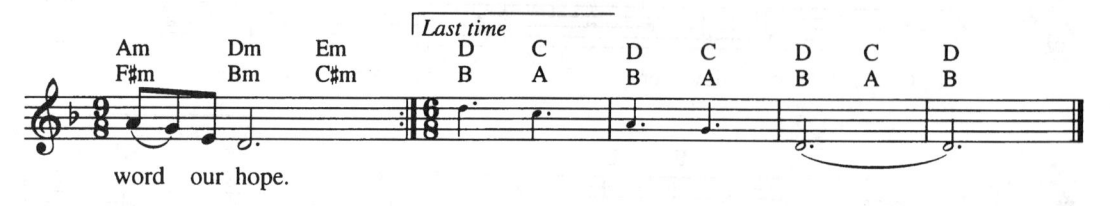

PASTOR BONUS 99 99 10 9

1. The wan-der-ing flock of Is-ra-el is
scat-tered and far from home and hope;
the shep-herd a-lone with
crook and staff, can find them and lead
and keep them safe. *Refrain* He
made and up-held us, grant-ed grace;
his smile is our peace, his
word our hope.

2. I walk on the heights, I climb and cling,
the terrors beneath, the ice aloft.
I look for his tracks, await his hand
to help and to hold, to guide and save.

3. I thirst for his word as grass in drought,
dry, brittle and barren, parched and brown;
no shower can fall, no sap rise green
no hope, if the Lord should send no rain.

4. Creator of all, your craftsman's care
with fashioning hand caressed our clay;
this vine is the work your hands have wrought,
your love is the sun, our soil of growth.

Text: Luke Connaughton (1917-1979)
Music: Gregory Murray (1905-1992)

© Copyright McCrimmon Publishing Co. Ltd, 10-12 High Street,
Great Wakering, Southend-on-Sea, Essex SS3 0EQ. Used by permission.

678 Thine be the glory

MACCABAEUS 10 11 11 11 and Refrain

1. Thine be the glory, risen, conqu'ring Son,
endless is the vic-t'ry thou o'er death hast won;
angels in bright raiment rolled the stone away,
kept the folded grave-clothes where thy body lay.

Refrain
Thine be the glory, risen, conqu'ring Son,
endless is the vic-t'ry thou o'er death hast won.

2. Lo! Jesus meets us, risen from the tomb;
lovingly he greets us, scatters fear and gloom.
Let the Church with gladness hymns of triumph sing,
for her Lord now liveth; death hath lost its sting.

3. No more we doubt thee, glorious Prince of Life!
Life is naught without thee: aid us in our strife.
Make us more than conqu'rors through thy deathless love.
Bring us safe through Jordan to thy home above.

Text: 'À toi la gloire' by Edmond Louis Budry (1854-1932) trans. Richard Birch Hoyle (1875-1939)
Music: George Frideric Handel (1685-1759)
Text © Copyright control

679 This Child

Calypso

1. This Child, secretly comes in the night, O this Child, hiding a heavenly light, O this Child, coming to us like a stranger, this heavenly Child.

Refrain
This Child, heaven come down now to be with us here, heavenly love and mercy appear, softly in awe and wonder come near to this heavenly Child.

2. This Child, rising on us like the sun,
   O this Child, given to light everyone,
   O this Child, guiding our feet on the pathway
   to peace on earth.

3. This Child, raising the humble and poor,
   O this Child, making the proud ones to fall;
   O this Child, filling the hungry with good things,
   this heavenly Child.

Text and Music: Graham Kendrick (b.1950)

© Copyright 1988 Make Way Music, P.O. Box 263, Croydon, Surrey CR9 5AP, UK.
International copyright secured. All rights reserved. Used by permission.

680 This day God gives me

BUNESSAN 55 54 D

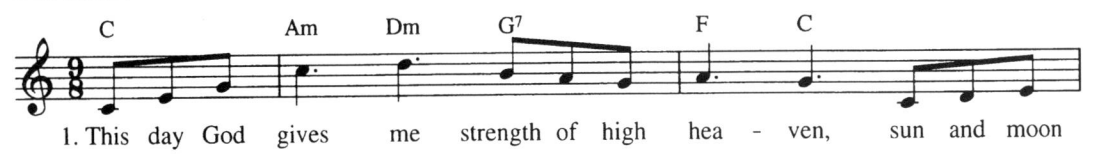

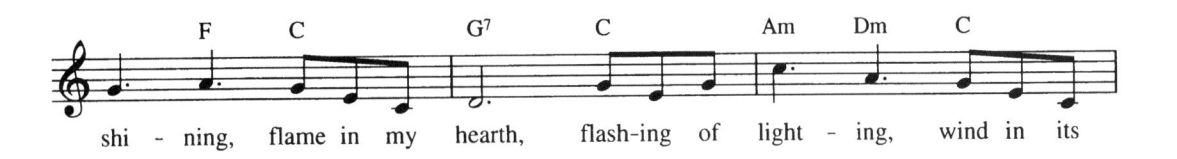

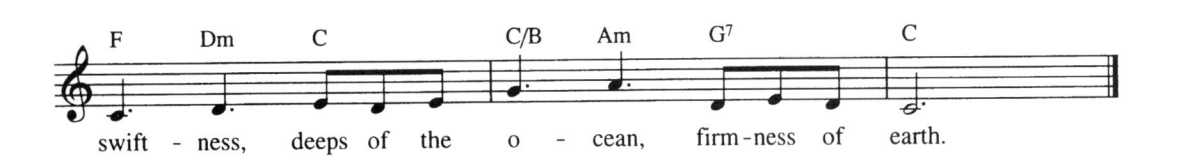

1. This day God gives me
strength of high heaven,
sun and moon shining,
flame in my hearth,
flashing of lightning,
wind in its swiftness,
deeps of the ocean,
firmness of earth.

2. This day God sends me
strength to sustain me,
might to uphold me,
wisdom as guide.
Your eyes are watchful,
your ears are list'ning,
your lips are speaking,
friend at my side.

3. God's way is my way,
God's shield is round me,
God's host defends me,
saving from ill.
Angel of heaven,
drive from me always
all that would harm me,
stand by me still.

4. Rising, I thank you,
mighty and strong One,
King of creation,
giver of rest,
firmly confessing
Threeness of persons,
Oneness of Godhead,
Trinity blest.

Text: ascribed to St. Patrick (372-466) adapted by James Quinn (b.1919)
Music: traditional Gaelic melody

Text © 1969 Geoffrey Chapman, an imprint of Cassell plc, Wellington House, 125 Strand, London WC2R 0BB. Used by permission.

681 This is my body

1. This is my body, broken for you,
bringing you wholeness, making you free.
Take it and eat it, and when you do,
do it in love for me.

2. This is my blood, poured out for you,
bringing forgiveness, making you free.
Take it and drink it, and when you do,
do it in love for me.

3. Back to my Father soon I shall go.
Do not forget me; then you will see
I am still with you, and you will know
you're very close to me.

4. Filled with my Spirit, how you will grow!
You are my branches; I am the tree.
If you are faithful, others will know
you are alive in me.

5. Love one another; I have loved you,
and I have shown you how to be free;
serve one another, and when you do,
do it in love for me.

Text: vs. 1 & 2 Jimmy Owens; vs. 3-5 Damian Lundy (1944-1997)
Music: Peter Jacobs
© Copyright 1978 Bud John Songs/EMI Christian Music Publishing. Administered by CopyCare, P.O. Box 77, Hailsham, East Sussex BN27 3EF, UK. Used by permission.

682 This is my will

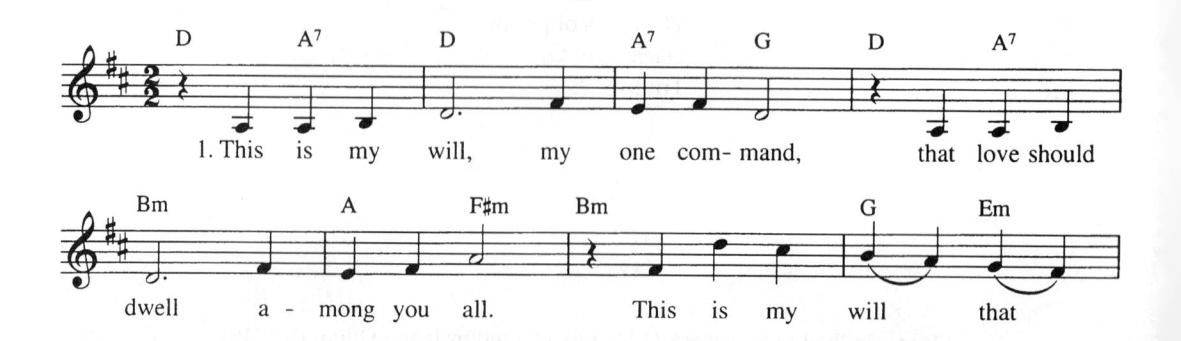

1. This is my will, my one command, that love should dwell among you all. This is my will that

Text © Copyright Geoffrey Chapman, an imprint of Cassell plc, Wellington House, 125 Strand, London WC2R 0BB. Used by permission.

you should love as I have shown that I love you.

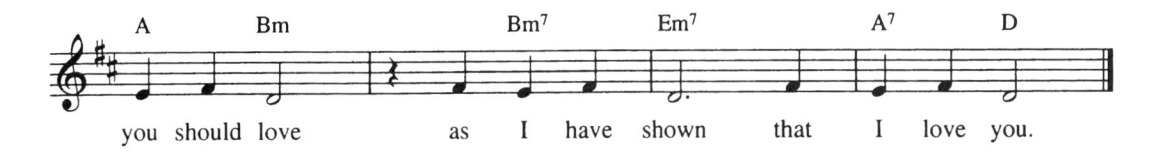

2. No greater love can be than this:
   to choose to die to save one's friends.
   You are my friends if you obey
   all I command that you should do.

3. I call you now no longer slaves;
   no slave knows all his master does.
   I call you friends, for all I hear
   my Father say, you hear from me.

4. You chose not me, but I chose you,
   that you should go and bear much fruit.
   I called you out that you in me
   should bear much fruit that will abide.

5. All that you ask my Father dear
   for my name's sake you shall receive.
   This is my will, my one command,
   that love should dwell in each, in all.

Text: James Quinn (b.1919)
Music: traditional Irish melody

683 This is our faith

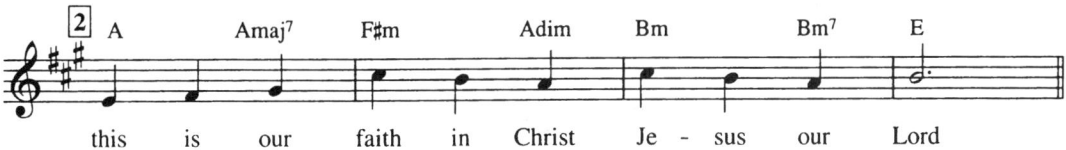

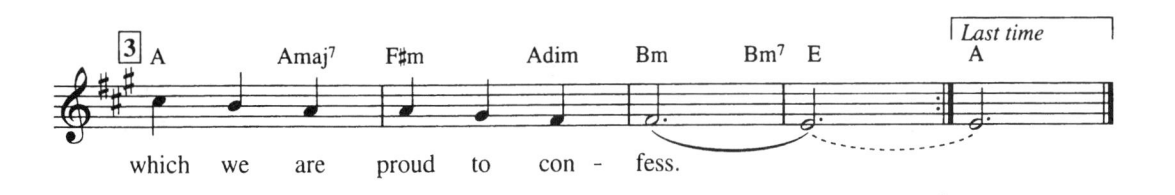

This may be sung as a round, the voices entering as indicated.

1. This is our faith,
2. this is our faith in Christ Je-sus our Lord
3. which we are proud to con-fess.

Text: from the Renewal of Baptismal Promises
Music: Robert B. Kelly (b.1948)
© Copyright 1999 Kevin Mayhew Ltd.

684 This is the day

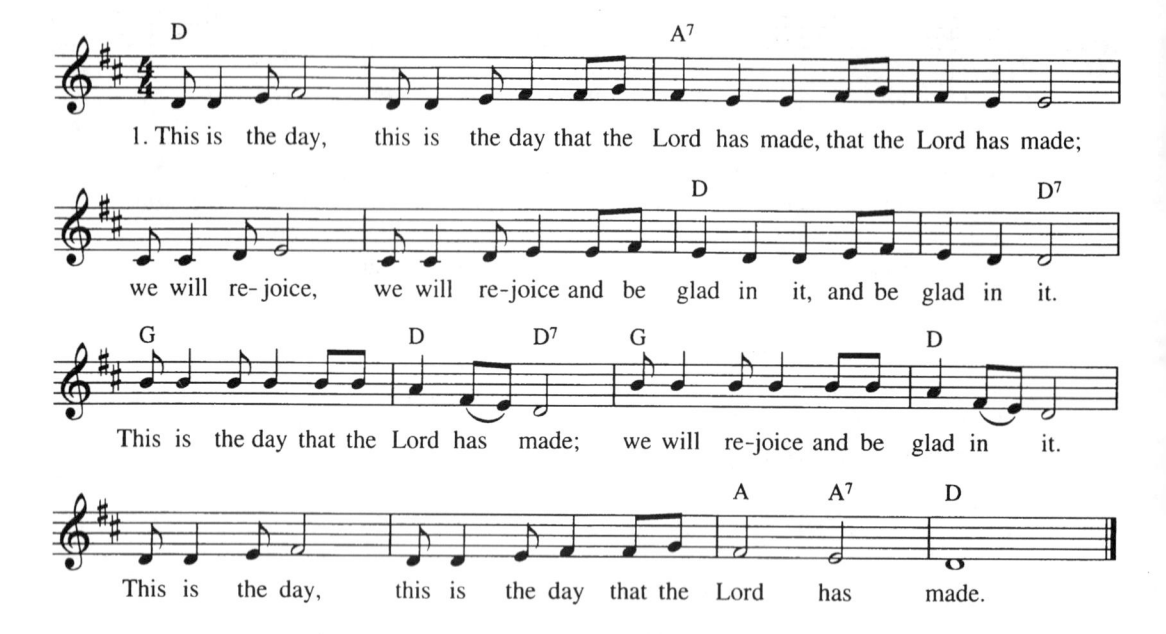

1. This is the day, this is the day that the Lord has made, that the Lord has made;
we will re-joice, we will re-joice and be glad in it, and be glad in it.
This is the day that the Lord has made; we will re-joice and be glad in it.
This is the day, this is the day that the Lord has made.

2. This is the day, this is the day
when he rose again, when he rose again;
we will rejoice, we will rejoice
and be glad in it, and be glad in it.
This is the day when he rose again;
we will rejoice and be glad in it.
This is the day, this is the day
when he rose again.

3. This is the day, this is the day
when the Spirit came, when the Spirit came;
we will rejoice, we will rejoice
and be glad in it, and be glad in it.
This is the day when the Spirit came;
we will rejoice and be glad in it.
This is the day, this is the day
when the Spirit came.

Text and Music: Les Garrett (b.1944)
© Copyright 1967 Scripture in Song, a division of Integrity Music. Administered by Kingsway's Thankyou Music,
P.O. Box 75, Eastbourne, East Sussex BN23 6NW, UK. For the territory of the UK only. Used by permission.

685 This is the image of the queen

IVER 86 86 87 86

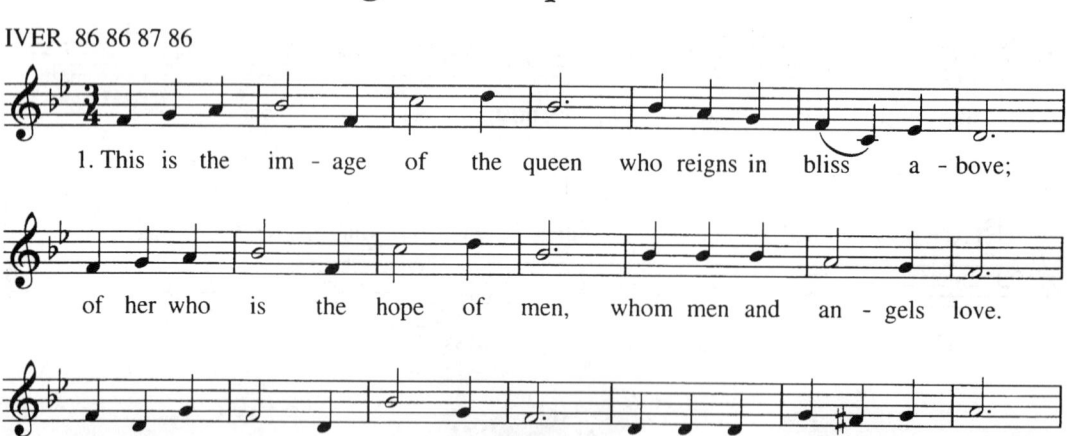

1. This is the im-age of the queen who reigns in bliss a-bove;
of her who is the hope of men, whom men and an-gels love.
Most ho-ly Ma-ry, at thy feet I bend a sup-pli-ant knee;

in this thy own sweet month of May, do thou re-mem-ber me.

    2. The homage offered at the feet
       of Mary's image here
       to Mary's self at once ascends
       above the starry sphere.
       Most holy Mary, at thy feet
       I bend a suppliant knee;
       in all my joy, in all my pain,
       do thou remember me.

    3. How fair soever be the form
       which here your eyes behold,
       its beauty is by Mary's self
       excelled a thousandfold.
       Most holy Mary, at thy feet
       I bend a suppliant knee;
       in my temptations, each and all,
       do thou remember me,

Text: Edward Caswall (1814-1878)
Music: Henri Friedrich Hémy (1818-1888)

686 This joyful Eastertide

THIS JOYFUL EASTERTIDE (VREUCHTEN) 67 67 and Refrain

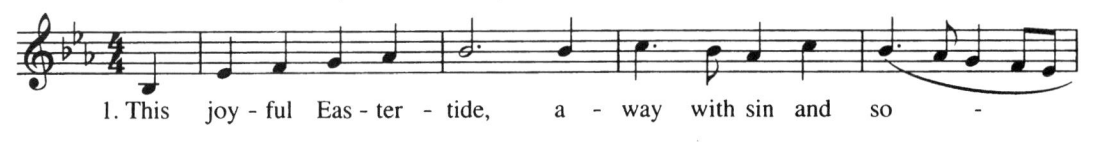

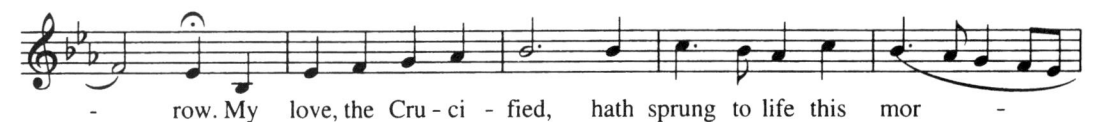

1. This joy-ful Eas-ter-tide, a-way with sin and so-row. My love, the Cru-ci-fied, hath sprung to life this mor-row. Had Christ, that once was slain, ne'er burst his three-day pri-son, our faith had been in vain: but now hath Christ a-ri-sen, a-ri-sen, a-ri-sen, a-ri-sen.

Refrain

    2. My flesh in hope shall rest,
       and for a season slumber;
       till trump from east to west
       shall wake the dead in number.

    3. Death's flood hath lost its chill,
       since Jesus crossed the river:
       lover of souls, from ill
       my passing soul deliver.

Text: George Ratcliffe Woodward (1848-1934)
Music: 17th century Dutch melody
Text © Copyright control

687 This, then, is my prayer

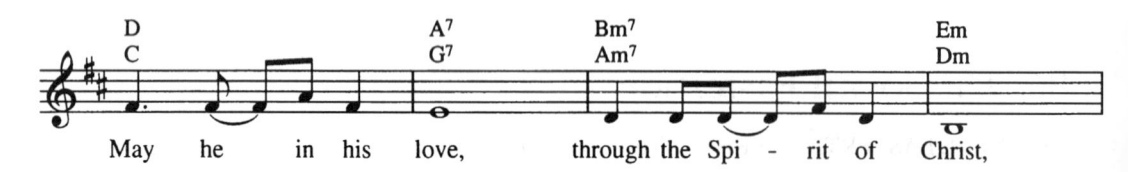

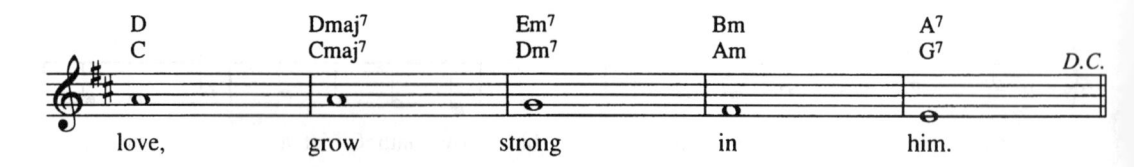

Refrain

This, then, is my prayer, falling on my knees before God who is Father and source of all life. May he in his love, through the Spirit of Christ, give you pow'r to grow strong in your innermost self.

1. May Christ live in your hearts and may your lives, rooted in love, grow strong in him.

2. May you, with all the saints,
   grow in the pow'r to understand
   how he loves you.

3. O how can I explain
   in all its depth and all its scope
   his love, God's love!

4. For his love is so full,
   it is beyond all we can dream:
   his love, in Christ!

5. And so, glory to him
   working in us, who can do more
   than we can pray!

The Refrain is not sung after verse 3.

Text: Damian Lundy (1944-1997) based on Eph. 3:14-21
Music: Gerard Markland (b.1953)
© Copyright 1978 Kevin Mayhew Ltd.

688 Though the mountains may fall

Though the mountains may fall and the hills turn to dust, yet the love of the Lord will stand as a shelter for all who will call on his name. Sing the praise and the glory of God.

1. Could the Lord ever leave you? Could the Lord forget his love? Though the mother forsake her child, he will not abandon you.

2. Should you turn and forsake him,
   he will gently call your name.
   Should you wander away from him,
   he will always take you back.

3. Go to him when you're weary;
   he will give you eagle's wings.
   You will run, you will never tire,
   for your God will be your strength.

4. As he swore to your fathers,
   when the flood destroyed the land,
   he will never forsake you;
   he will swear to you again.

Text: Dan Schutte based on Isaiah
Music: Dan Schutte

© Copyright 1975 Daniel L. Schutte and New Dawn Music, 5536 NE Hassalo, Portland, Oregon 97213, USA. All rights reserved. Used by permission.

689 Thou, whose almighty word

MOSCOW 664 6664

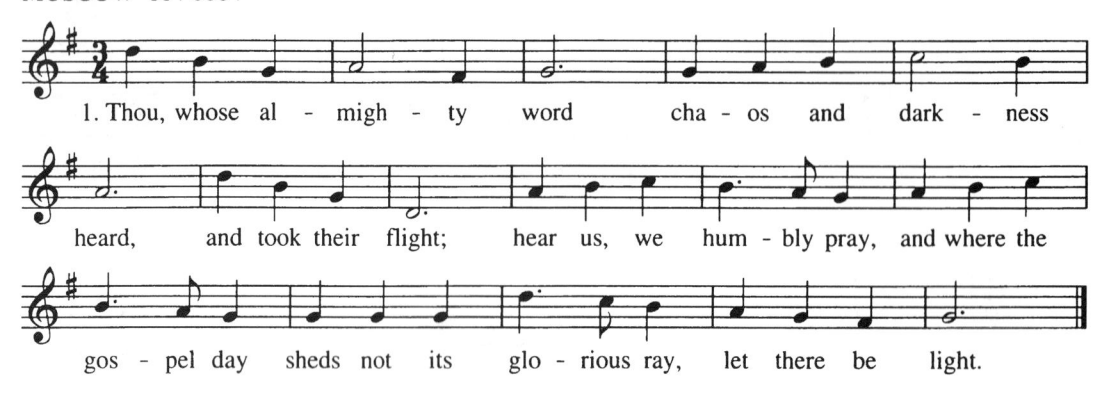

1. Thou, whose almighty word
chaos and darkness heard,
and took their flight;
hear us, we humbly pray,
and where the gospel day
sheds not its glorious ray,
let there be light.

2. Thou, who didst come to bring
on thy redeeming wing,
healing and sight,
health to the sick in mind,
sight to the inly blind,
O now to humankind
let there be light.

3. Spirit of truth and love,
life-giving, holy Dove,
speed forth thy flight;
move on the water's face,
bearing the lamp of grace,
and in earth's darkest place
let there be light.

4. Holy and blessèd Three,
glorious Trinity,
Wisdom, Love, Might;
boundless as ocean's tide
rolling in fullest pride,
through the earth far and wide
let there be light.

Text: John Marriott (1780-1825) alt.
Music: melody from Madan's 'Collection' (1769) adapted by Felice de Giardini (1716-1796)

690 Thy hand, O God, has guided

THORNBURY 76 76 D

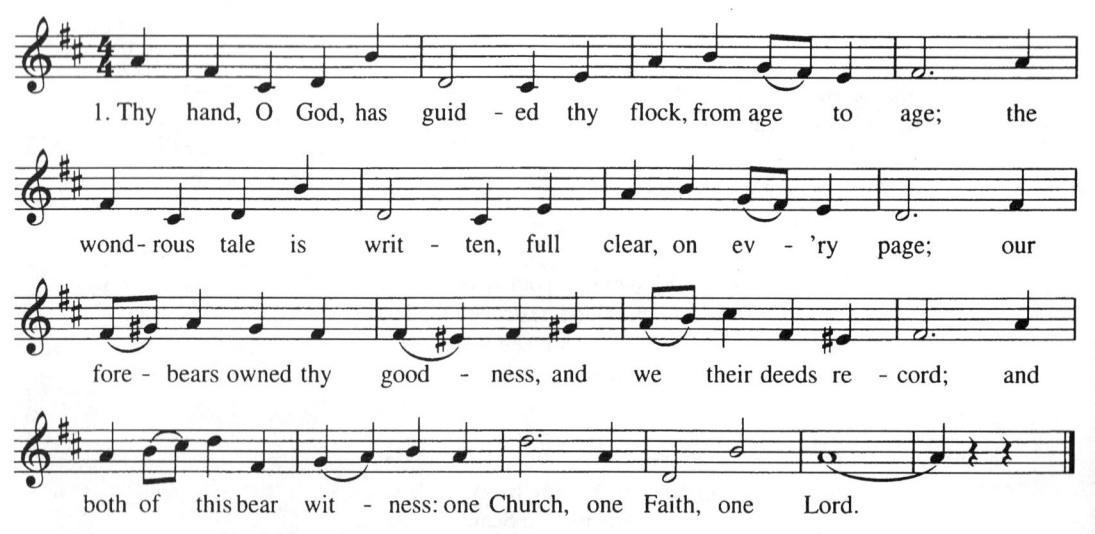

1. Thy hand, O God, has guided thy flock, from age to age;
the wondrous tale is written, full clear, on ev'ry page;
our forebears owned thy goodness, and we their deeds record;
and both of this bear witness: one Church, one Faith, one Lord.

Music © Copyright the Executors of Dr. Basil Harwood. Used by permission of the Trustees
of the late Dr Basil Harwood Settlement Trust, Stewart House, 24 Kingsway, London WC2B 6JX.

2. Thy heralds brought glad tidings
    to greatest, as to least;
    they bade them rise, and hasten
    to share the great King's feast;
    and this was all their teaching,
    in ev'ry deed and word,
    to all alike proclaiming:
    one Church, one Faith, one Lord.

3. Through many a day of darkness,
    through many a scene of strife,
    the faithful few fought bravely
    to guard the nation's life.
    Their gospel of redemption,
    sin pardoned, hope restored,
    was all in this enfolded:
    one Church, one Faith, one Lord.

4. And we, shall we be faithless?
    Shall hearts fail, hands hang down?
    Shall we evade the conflict,
    and cast away our crown?
    Not so: in God's deep counsels
    some better thing is stored:
    we will maintain, unflinching,
    one Church, one Faith, one Lord.

5. Thy mercy will not fail us,
    nor leave thy work undone;
    with thy right hand to help us,
    the vict'ry shall be won;
    and then by all creation,
    thy name shall be adored.
    And this shall be their anthem:
    One Church, one Faith, one Lord.

Text: Edward Hayes Plumptre (1821-1891) alt.
Music: Basil Harwood (1859-1949)

691 To be in your presence
My desire

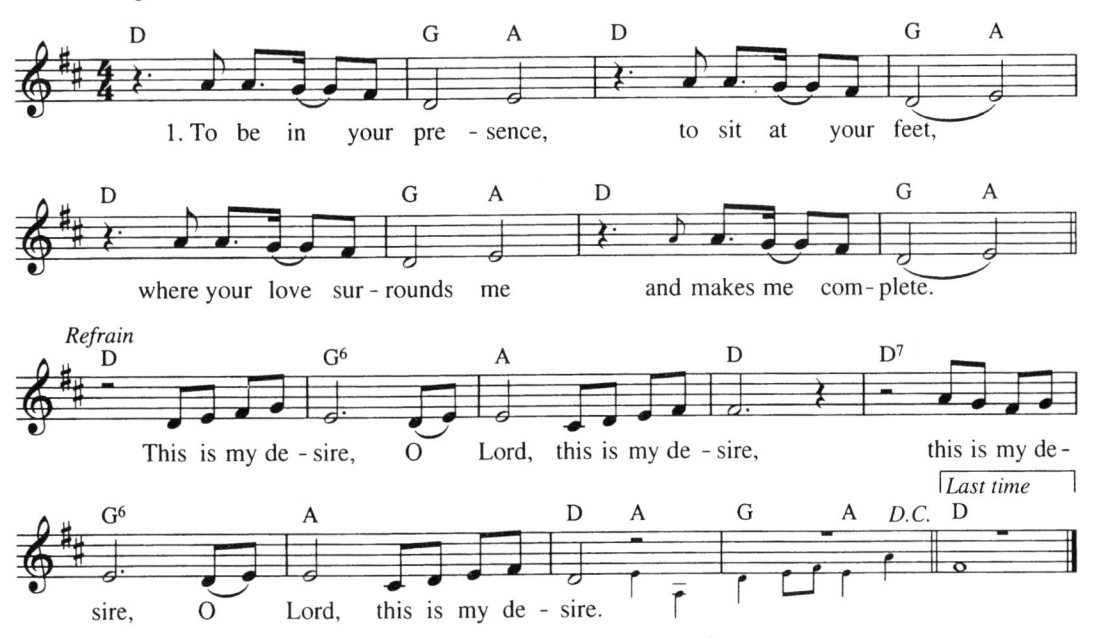

1. To be in your pre - sence, to sit at your feet,
   where your love sur - rounds me and makes me com - plete.

Refrain
This is my de - sire, O Lord, this is my de - sire,
this is my de - sire, O Lord, this is my de - sire.

2. To rest in your presence,
    not rushing away,
    to cherish each moment,
    here I would stay.

Text and Music: Noel Richards
© Copyright 1991 Kingsway's Thankyou Music, P.O. Box 75, Eastbourne, East Sussex BN23 6NW, UK.
Used by permission.

692 To Christ, the Prince of peace

NARENZA SM

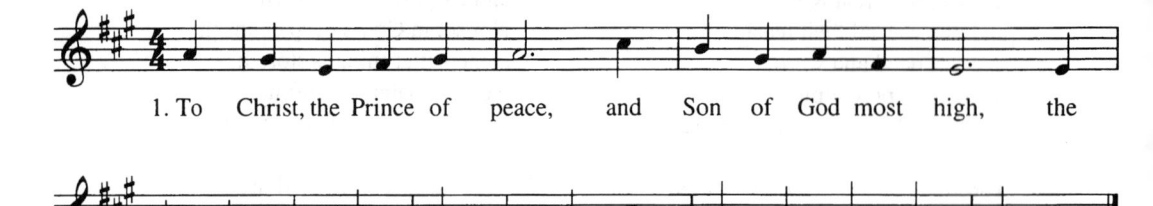

1. To Christ, the Prince of peace, and Son of God most high, the Fa-ther of the world to come, sing we with ho-ly joy.

2. Deep in his heart for us
the wound of love he bore;
that love wherewith he still inflames
the hearts that him adore.

3. O Jesu, victim blest,
what else but love divine
could thee constrain to open thus
that sacred heart of thine?

4. O fount of endless life,
O spring of water clear,
O flame celestial, cleansing all
who unto thee draw near!

5. Hide us in thy dear heart,
for thither we do fly;
where seek thy grace through life, in death
thine immortality.

6. Praise to the Father be,
and sole-begotten Son;
praise, holy Paraclete, to thee,
while endless ages run.

Text: 'Summi parentis filio' from 'Catholicum Hymnologium' (1587) trans. Edward Caswall (1814-1878)
Music: melody from J. Leisentritt's 'Catholicum Hymnologium Germanicum' (1584)
adapted by William Henry Havergal (1793-1870)

693 To Jesus' heart, all burning

COR JESU 76 76 and Refrain

1. To Je-sus' heart, all burn-ing with fer-vent love for men, my heart with fond-est yearn-ing shall raise its joy-ful strain.

Refrain

While a-ges course a-long, blest be with loud-est song the

sa - cred heart of Je - sus by ev - 'ry heart and tongue, the
sa - cred heart of Je - sus by ev - 'ry heart and tongue.

2. O heart, for me on fire
with love that none can speak,
my yet untold desire
God gives me for thy sake.

3. Too true, I have forsaken
thy love for wilful sin;
yet now let me be taken
back by thy grace again.

4. As thou art meek and lowly,
and ever pure of heart,
so may my heart be wholly
of thine the counterpart.

5. When life away is flying,
and earth's false glare is done,
still, Sacred Heart, in dying,
I'll say I'm all thine own.

Text: 'Dem Herzen Jesu singe' by Aloys Schlör (1805-1852) trans. A.J. Christie (1817-1891) alt.
Music: traditional

694 To you, O Lord, I lift up my soul

To you, O Lord, I lift up my soul, I lift up my soul. 1. Teach me, Lord, your ho - ly ways and help me learn your paths. Guide my foot-steps in your truth, my Sa-viour and my God.

2. Good and upright is the Lord
who guides the wand'rer back,
leads the humble in this path
and shows the poor his ways.

3. Faithfulness and love abound
for all who keep his word;
those who love him have a friend
whose promise is made clear.

Text: Susan Sayers (b.1946) based on Psalm 24
Music: Andrew Moore (b.1954)
© Copyright 1996 Kevin Mayhew Ltd.

LITURGICAL
HYMNS OLD & NEW

695 To your altar we bring

Refrain

To your altar we bring you these gifts of bread and wine.
Take, Lord, receive, make them holy and divine. They're our
joys and our hopes, all our failures and our strife.
Take, Lord, and make these gifts our food of life.

1. Take and bless these gifts we offer;
   make them pleasing to you, O Lord.

2. Take these gifts and make them holy
   by the pow'r of your Holy Spirit.

3. They'll become the body and blood
   of your Son, Jesus Christ, our Lord.

Text and Music: Julian Wiener
© Copyright 1999 Kevin Mayhew Ltd.

696 Turn to me

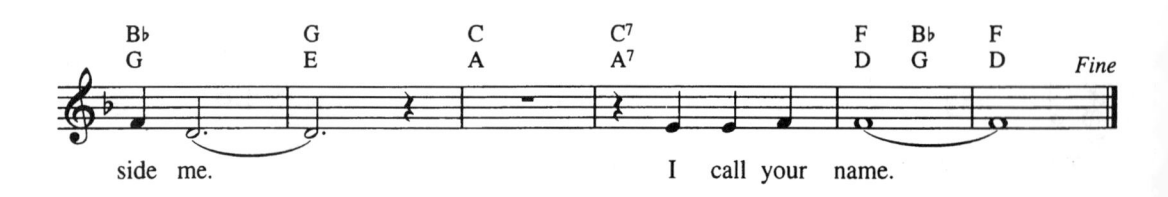

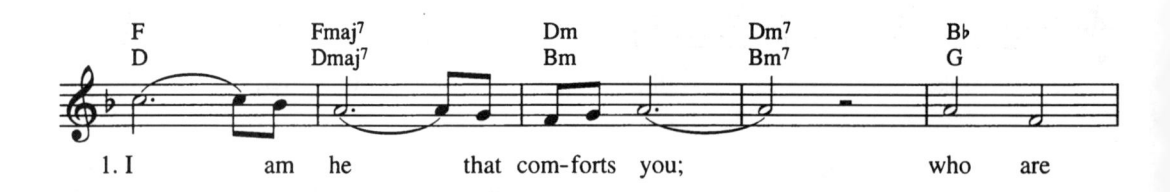

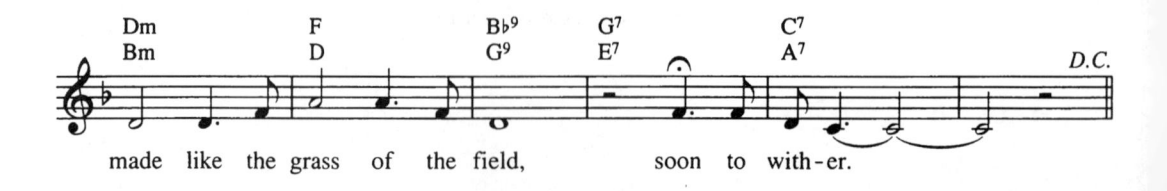

Refrain

Turn to me, O turn and be saved, says the Lord, for I am God; there is no o-ther, none beside me. I call your name.

1. I am he that com-forts you; who are you to be a-fraid of flesh that fades, is made like the grass of the field, soon to with-er.

© Copyright 1975 John B. Foley, SJ and New Dawn Music, 5536 NE Hassalo, Portland, OR 97213, USA.
All rights reserved. Used by permission.

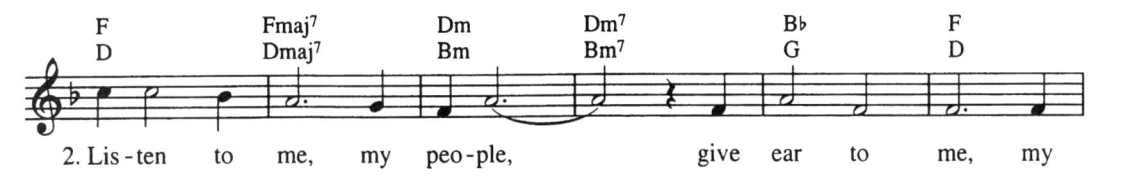

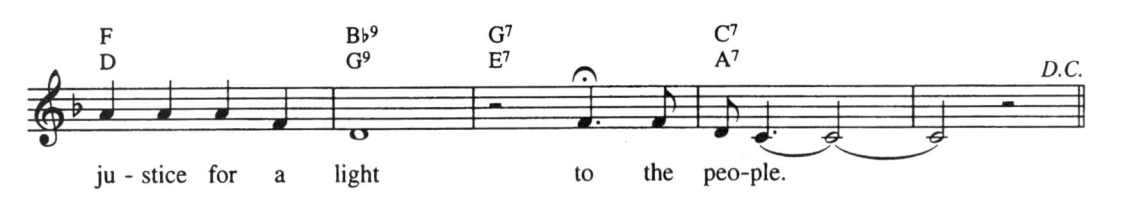

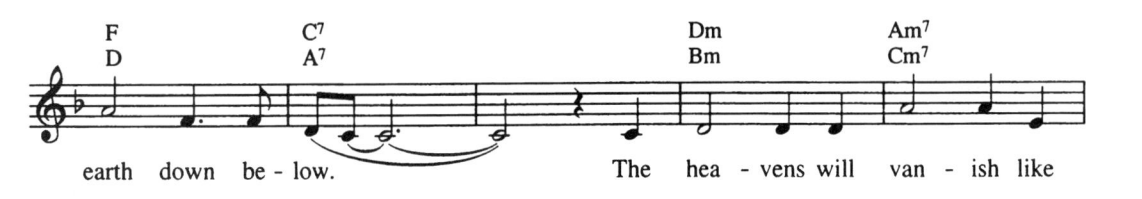

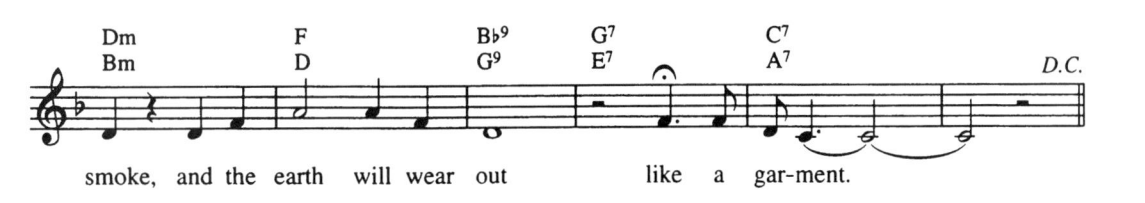

2. Listen to me, my people, give ear to me, my nation: a law will go forth from me, and my justice for a light to the people.

3. Lift up your eyes to the heavens, and look at the earth down below. The heavens will vanish like smoke, and the earth will wear out like a garment.

Text and Music: John B. Foley

697 Unless a grain of wheat

Refrain

Un-less a grain of wheat shall fall up-on the ground and die, it re-mains but a sin-gle grain with no life. (v.2 If)

1. If we have died with him, then we shall live with him; reign with him.
2. an-y-one serves me, then they must fol-low me; ser-vants will be.
3. Make your home in me as I make mine in you; those who re-main in me bear much fruit.
4. If you re-main in me and my word lives in you; then you will be my dis- ci-ples.
5. Those who love me are loved by my Fa-ther; we shall be with them and dwell in them.
6. Peace I leave with you, my peace I give to you; peace which the world can-not give is my gift.

Text: based on Scripture
Music: Bernadette Farrell

© Copyright 1983 Bernadette Farrell. Published by OCP Publications, 5536 NE Hassalo, Portland, OR 97213, USA. All rights reserved. Used by permission.

698 Unto us a boy is born

PUER NOBIS 76 77

1. Unto us a boy is born! King of all creation;
came he to a world forlorn,
the Lord of ev'ry nation,
the Lord of ev'ry nation.

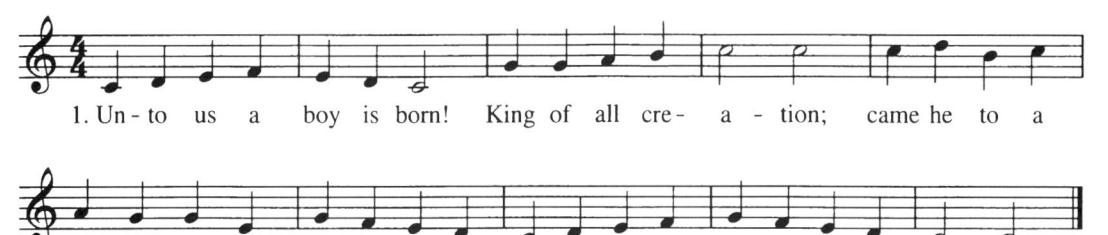

2. Cradled in a stall was he,
watched by cows and asses;
but the very beasts could see
that he the world surpasses,
that he the world surpasses.

3. Then the fearful Herod cried,
'Pow'r is mine in Jewry!'
So the blameless children died
the victims of his fury,
the victims of his fury.

4. Now may Mary's Son, who came
long ago to love us,
lead us all with hearts aflame
unto the joys above us,
unto the joys above us.

5. Omega and Alpha he!
Let the organ thunder,
while the choir with peals of glee
shall rend the air asunder,
shall rend the air asunder.

Text: 'Puer nobis nascitur' (15th century) trans. Percy Dearmer (1867-1936) alt.
Music: from 'Piae Cantiones' (1582)
Text © Copyright Oxford University Press, Great Clarendon Street, Oxford OX2 6DP.
Used by permission from 'The Oxford Book of Carols.'

699 Upon thy table, Lord

DAWBY LM

1. Upon thy table, Lord, we place
these symbols of our work and thine,
life's food won only by thy grace,
who giv'st to all the bread and wine.

2. Within these simple things there lie
the height and depth of human life,
the thought of all, our tears and toil,
our hopes and fears, our joy and strife.

3. Accept them, Lord; from thee they come:
we take them humbly at thy hand.
These gifts of thine for higher use
we offer, as thou dost command.

Text: M.F.C. Wilson (1884-1944) alt.
Music: traditional English melody
Text © Copyright control.

700 Vaster far than any ocean

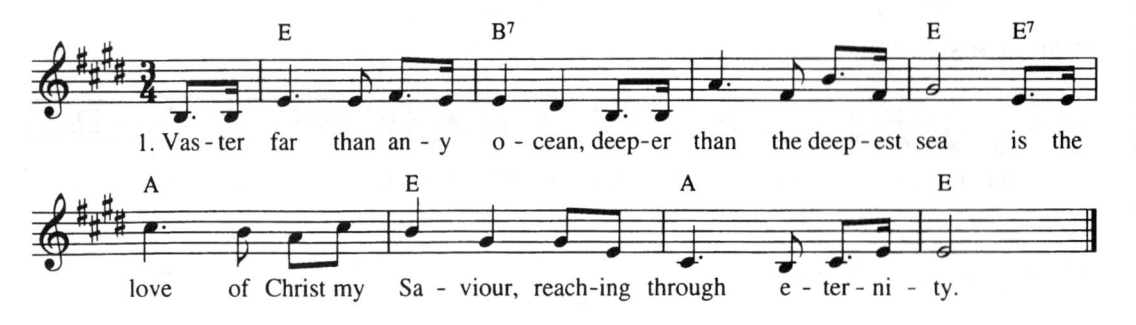

1. Vaster far than any ocean, deeper than the deepest sea
is the love of Christ my Saviour, reaching through eternity.

2. But my sins are truly many,
is God's grace so vast, so deep?
Yes, there's grace o'er sin abounding,
grace to pardon, grace to keep.

3. Can he quench my thirst for ever?
Will his Spirit strength impart?
Yes, he gives me living water,
springing up within my heart.

Text: unknown
Music: Russian folk melody

701 Veni, Creator Spiritus

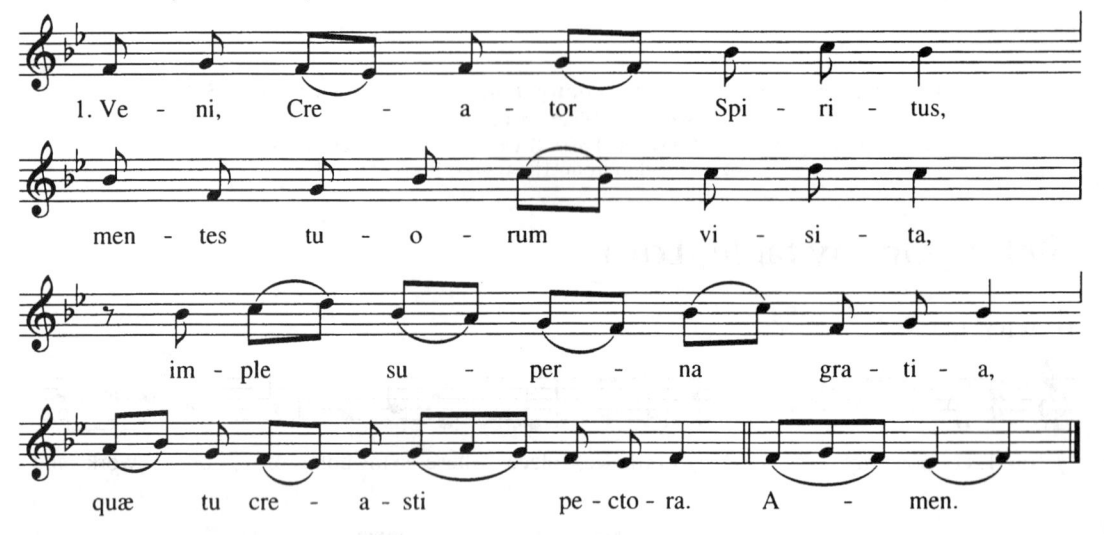

PLAINSONG (MODE VIII)

1. Veni, Creator Spiritus,
mentes tuorum visita,
imple superna gratia,
quæ tu creasti pectora. Amen.

2. Qui diceris Paraclitus,
Altissimi donum Dei,
fons vivus, ignis, caritas,
et spiritalis unctio.

3. Tu septiformis munere,
digitus paternæ dexteræ,
tu rite promissum Patris,
sermone ditans guttura.

4. Accende lumen sensibus,
infunde amorem cordibus,
infirma nostri corporis
virtute firmans perpeti.

5. Hostem repellas longius,
pacemque dones protinus:
ductore sic te prævio,
vitemus omne noxium.

6. Per te sciamus da Patrem,
noscamus atque Filium,
teque utriusque Spiritum
credamus omni tempore.

7. Deo Patri sit gloria,
et Filio, qui a mortuis
surrexit, ac Paraclito,
in sæculorum sæcula. Amen.

Text: ascribed to Rabanus Maurus (776-856)
Music: Plainsong

702 Veni, Sancte Spiritus

PLAINSONG (MODE I)

1. Veni, Sancte Spiritus, et emitte cælitus
2. Veni, pater pauperum, veni, dator munerum,

lucis tuæ radium.
veni, lumen cordium.
3. Consolator optime,
4. In labore requies,

dulcis hospes animæ, dulce refrigerium.
in æstu temperies, in fletu solatium.

5. O lux beatissima reple cordis intima
6. Sine tuo numine, nihil est in homine,

tuorum fidelium. 7. Lava quod est sordidum,
nihil est innoxium. 8. Flecte quod est rigidum,

riga quod est aridum, sana quod est saucium.
fove quod est frigidum, rege quod est devium.

9. Da tuis fidelibus, in te confidentibus,
10. Da virtutis meritum, da salutis exitum,

sacrum septenarium.
da perenne gaudium. Amen. Alleluia.

Text: sequence for Pentecost Sunday ascribed to Stephen Langton (d.1228)
Music: Plainsong (13th century)

LITURGICAL
HYMNS OLD & NEW

703 Victimae Paschali laudes

PLAINSONG (MODE I)

1. Victimae Paschali laudes immolent Christiani.
2. Agnus redemit oves: Christus innocens Patri reconciliavit peccatores.
3. Mors et vita duello conflixere mirando: dux vitae mortuus, regnat vivus.
4. Dic nobis, Maria, quid vidisti in via?
5. Sepulchrum Christi viventis, et gloriam vidi resurgentis:
6. Angelicos testes, sudarium, et vestes.
7. Surrexit Christus spes mea: praecedet suos in Galilaeam.
8. Scimus Christum surrexisse a mortuis vere: tu nobis, victor Rex, miserere. Amen. Alleluia.

Text: attributed to Wipo (c.1030)
Music: Plainsong

704 Waken, O sleeper, wake and rise
BILLING CM

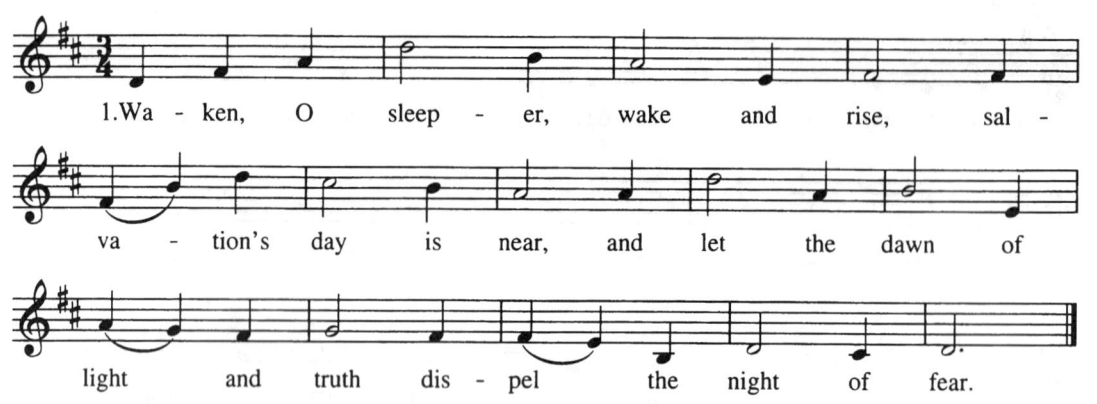

1. Waken, O sleeper, wake and rise,
salvation's day is near,
and let the dawn of light and truth
dispel the night of fear.

A lower setting will be found at No. 582

2. Let us prepare to face the day
of judgement and of grace,
to live as people of the light,
and perfect truth embrace.

3. Watch then and pray, we cannot know
the moment or the hour,
when Christ, unheralded, will come
with life-renewing pow'r.

4. Then shall the nations gather round
to learn his ways of peace,
when spears to pruning-hooks are turned
and all our conflicts cease.

Text: Michael Forster (b.1946)
Music: Richard Runciman Terry (1865-1938)
Text © Copyright 1993 Kevin Mayhew Ltd.
Music © Copyright Burns & Oates Ltd, Wellwood, North Farm Road, Tunbridge Wells, Kent TN2 3QR.
Used by permission.

705 Wake up, O people

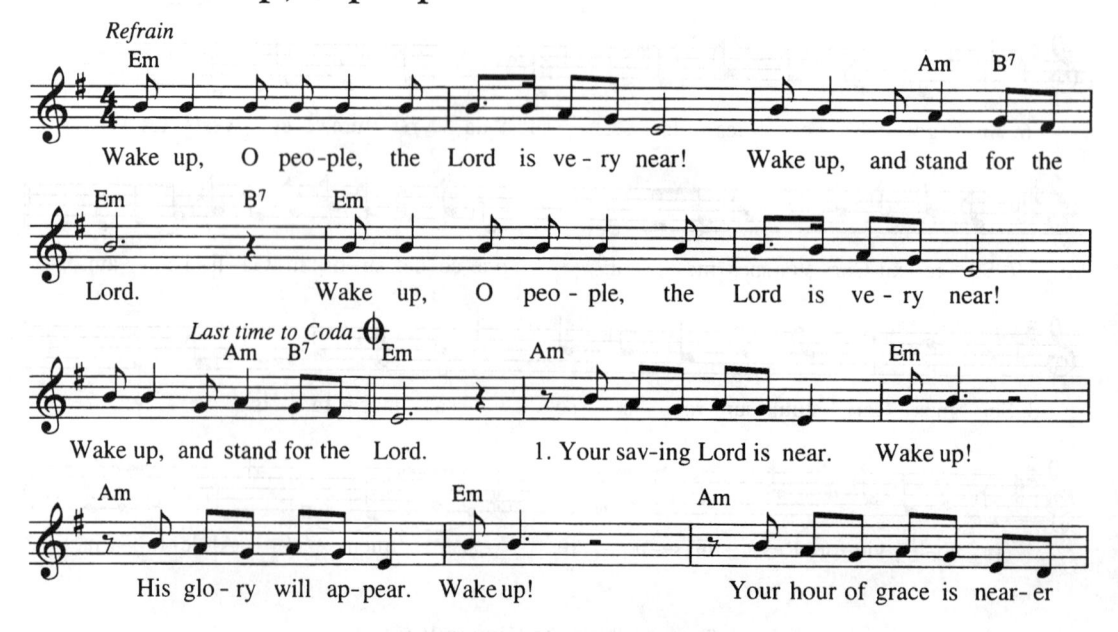

Refrain

Wake up, O people, the Lord is very near! Wake up, and stand for the Lord. Wake up, O people, the Lord is very near! Wake up, and stand for the Lord.

1. Your saving Lord is near. Wake up! His glory will appear. Wake up! Your hour of grace is nearer

© Copyright 1984 Kevin Mayhew Ltd.

than it e-ver was.

2. The night of sin has passed. Wake up!
   The light is near at last. Wake up!
   The day star, Christ, the Son of God,
      will soon appear.

3. To live in love and peace. Wake up!
   To let all quarrels cease. Wake up!
   To live that all you do may stand
      the light of day

4. That Christ may be your shield. Wake up!
   That death to life may yield. Wake up!
   That heaven's gate be opened wide
      again for you.

Text: Marie Lydia Pereira (b.1920) from Romans 13:11-14
Music: Marie Lydia Pereira (b.1920)

706 Walk with me, O my Lord

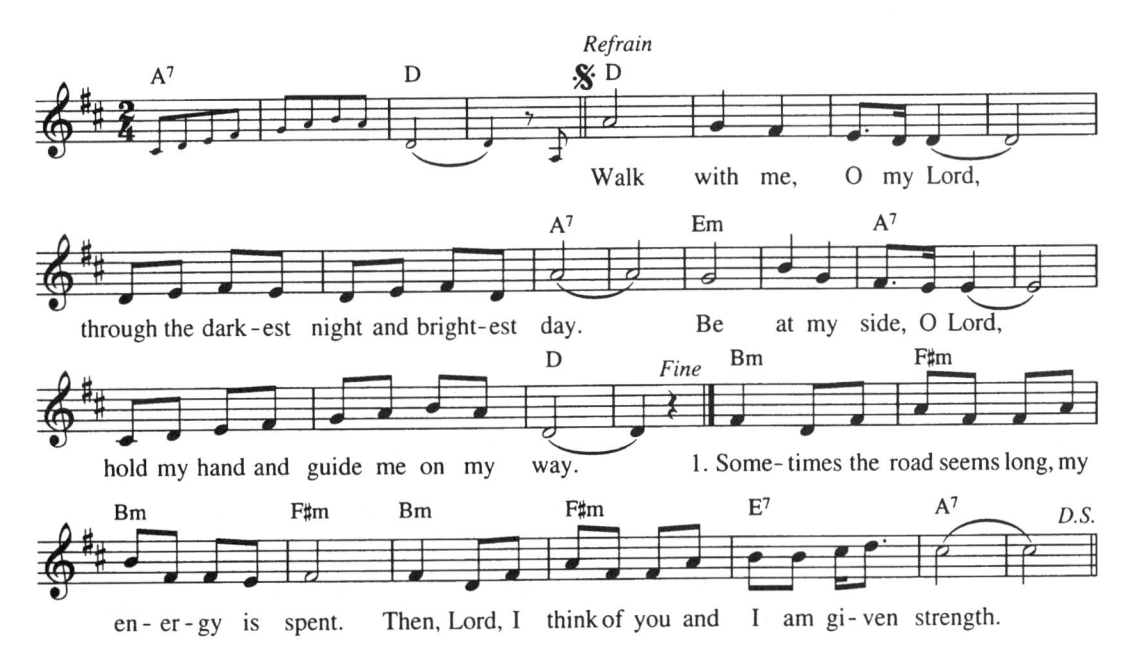

Walk with me, O my Lord, through the dark-est night and bright-est day. Be at my side, O Lord, hold my hand and guide me on my way. 1. Some-times the road seems long, my en-er-gy is spent. Then, Lord, I think of you and I am gi-ven strength.

2. Stones often bar my path
   and there are times I fall,
   but you are always there
   to help me when I call.

3. Just as you calmed the wind
   and walked upon the sea,
   conquer, my living Lord,
   the storms that threaten me.

4. Help me to pierce the mists
   that cloud my heart and mind,
   so that I shall not fear
   the steepest mountain-side.

5. As once you healed the lame
   and gave sight to the blind,
   help me when I'm downcast
   to hold my head up high.

Text and Music: Estelle White (b.1925)
© Copyright 1976 Kevin Mayhew Ltd.

707 We are gathering together

1. We are gathering together unto him.
We are gathering together unto him.
Unto him shall the gath'ring of the people be,
we are gathering together unto him.

2. We are offering together unto him.
We are offering together unto him.
Unto him shall the off'ring of the people be,
we are offering together unto him.

3. We are singing together unto him.
We are singing together unto him.
Unto him shall the singing of the people be,
we are singing together unto him.

4. We are praying together unto him.
We are praying together unto him.
Unto him shall the praying of the people be,
we are praying together unto him.

Text: unknown
Music: traditional melody

708 We are his children
Go forth in his name

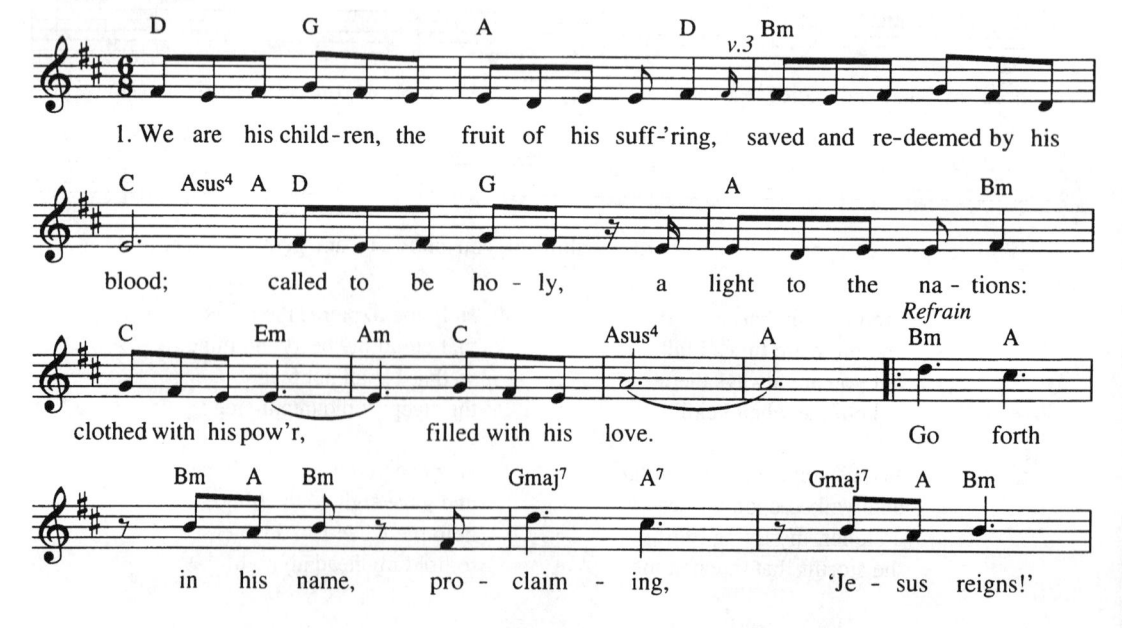

1. We are his children, the fruit of his suff'ring, saved and redeemed by his blood; called to be holy, a light to the nations: clothed with his pow'r, filled with his love.

Refrain
Go forth in his name, proclaiming, 'Jesus reigns!'

© Copyright 1990 Make Way Music, P.O. Box 263, Croydon, Surrey CR9 5AP, UK.
International copyright secured. All rights reserved. Used by permission.

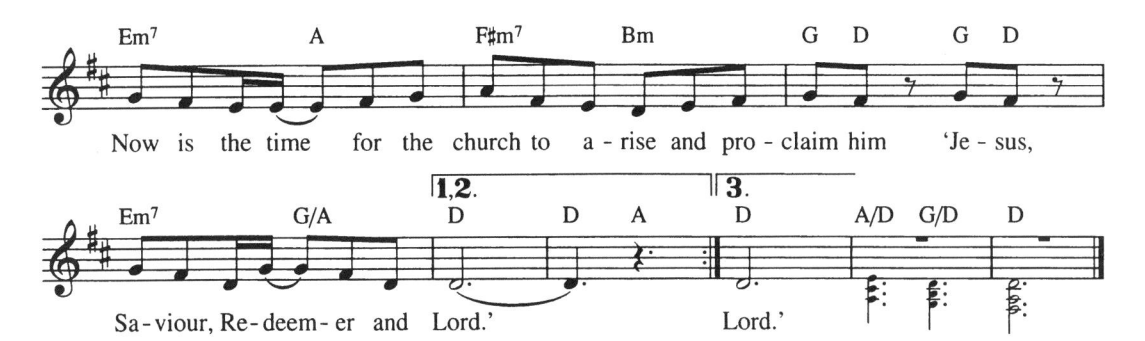

Now is the time for the church to arise and proclaim him 'Jesus, Saviour, Redeemer and Lord.'

2. Countless the souls that are stumbling in darkness,
   why do we sleep in the light?
   Jesus commands us to go make disciples,
   this is our case, this is our fight.

3. Listen, the wind of the Spirit is blowing,
   the end of the age is so near;
   pow'rs in the earth and the heavens are shaking,
   Jesus our Lord soon shall appear!

Text and Music: Graham Kendrick (b.1950)

709 We are his people

We are his people, the sheep of his flock, his people, the sheep of his flock. 1. Shout with gladness to God all the earth, joyfully obey him. Come and gather before him now, singing songs of gladness.

2. Understand that the Lord is our God;
   he it is who made us.
   We his people belong to him,
   he our loving shepherd.

3. O how faithful and good is the Lord,
   loving us for ever;
   rich in mercy and faithfulness,
   true through all the ages.

Text: Susan Sayers (b.1946) based on Psalm 99
Music: Andrew Moore (b.1954)
© Copyright 1995 Kevin Mayhew Ltd.

710 We are marching

We are march-ing in the light of God, we are march-ing in the light of God. We are march-ing in the light of God, We are march-ing in the light of God. God We are march-ing, Oo-ooh! We are march-ing in the light of God. We are march-ing, Oo-ooh! We are march-ing in the light of God.

Text: traditional South African trans. Anders Nyberg
Music: traditional South African
Text © Copyright 1990 Wild Goose Publications, Iona Community,
840 Govan Road, Glasgow G51 3UU. Used by permission.

711 We behold the splendour of God

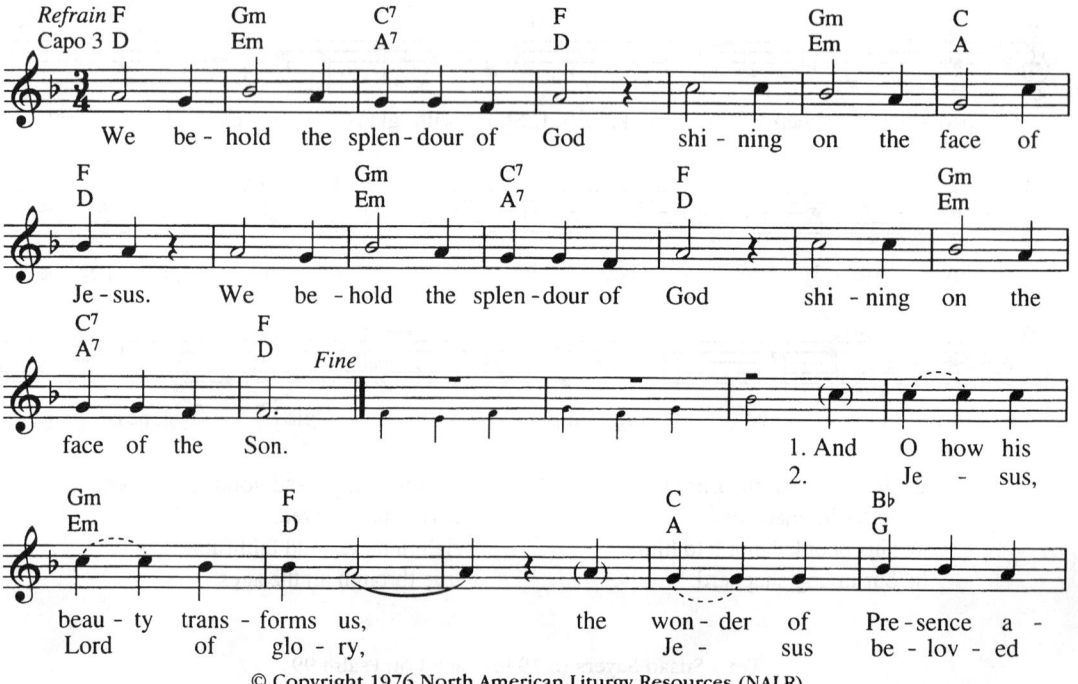

Refrain F Gm C⁷ F Gm C
Capo 3 D Em A⁷ D Em A

We be-hold the splen-dour of God shi-ning on the face of

F Gm C⁷ F Gm
D Em A⁷ D Em

Je-sus. We be-hold the splen-dour of God shi-ning on the

C⁷ F
A⁷ D *Fine*

face of the Son.
1. And O how his
2. Je - sus,

Gm F C B♭
Em D A G

beau-ty trans-forms us, the won-der of Pre-sence a-
Lord of glo - ry, Je - sus be-lov-ed

© Copyright 1976 North American Liturgy Resources (NALR),
5536 NE Hassalo, Portland, Oregon 97213, USA. All rights reserved. Used by permission.

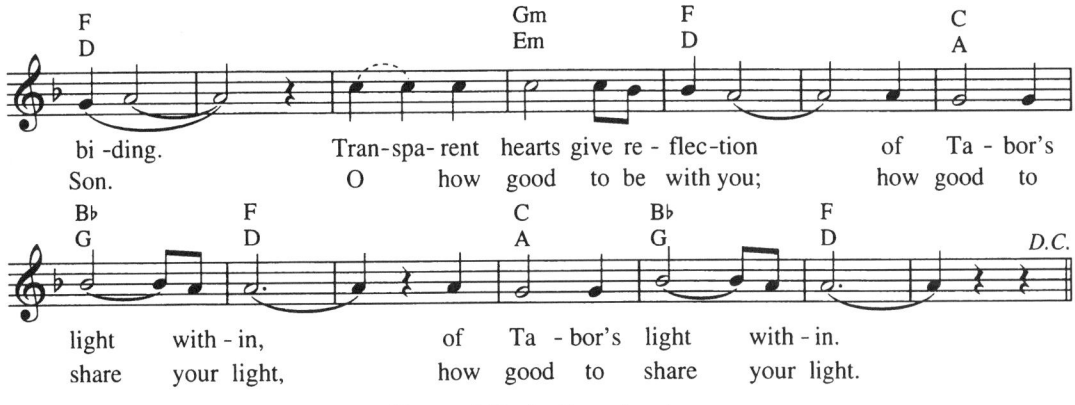

bi-ding. Tran-spa-rent hearts give re-flec-tion of Ta-bor's
Son. O how good to be with you; how good to

light with-in, of Ta-bor's light with-in.
share your light, how good to share your light.

Text and Music: Carey Landry

712 We believe

KENTSTOWN 87 87 87

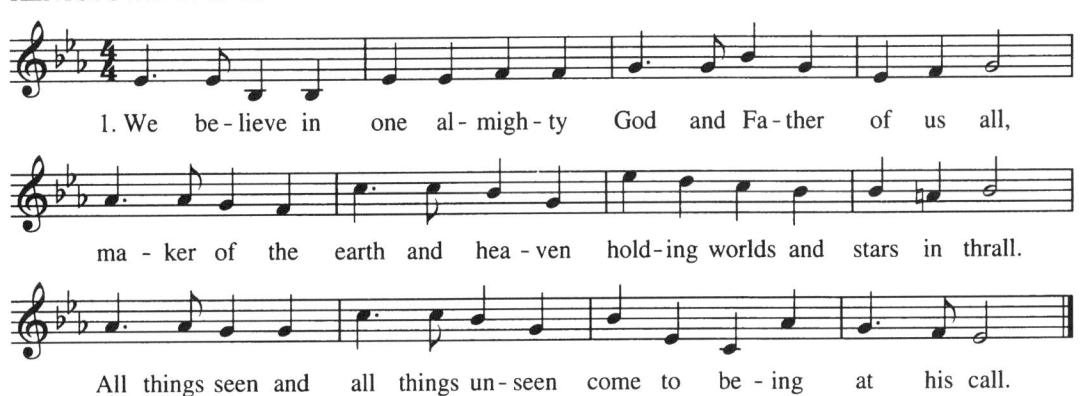

1. We believe in one almighty God and Father of us all,
maker of the earth and heaven holding worlds and stars in thrall.
All things seen and all things unseen come to being at his call.

2. We believe in one Redeemer,
Christ, the Father's only Son.
Timelessly in love begotten,
through him all God's work is done.
Light from Light and God from Godhead,
with the Father's Being, one.

3. All for us and our salvation,
Christ his glory set aside,
by the Holy Spirit's power,
and the womb of virgin bride;
suffered under Pilate's sentence,
for our sake was crucified.

4. He has burst the grave asunder,
rising as the prophets said;
seated in the Father's presence,
he is our exalted head.
He will come again with glory,
judge the living and the dead.

5. We acclaim the Holy Spirit,
of all life the source and Lord;
with the Son and Father worshipped,
ever honoured and adored;
speaking through the holy prophets,
pow'r of sacrament and word.

6. Holy Church, and universal,
apostolic company!
In one sacrament forgiven,
signed by water, his to be.
In the resurrection body
we shall share eternity.

Text: Michael Forster (b.1946) based on the Creed
Music: Colin Mawby (b.1936)
© Copyright 1992 Kevin Mayhew Ltd.

LITURGICAL
HYMNS OLD & NEW

713 We cannot measure

YE BANKS AND BRAES DLM

1. We cannot measure how you heal or answer ev'ry suff'rer's prayer, yet we believe your grace responds where faith and doubt unite to care. Your hands, though bloodied on the cross, survive to hold and heal and warn, to carry all through death to life and cradle children yet unborn.

2. The pain that will not go away,
    the guilt that clings from things long past,
   the fear of what the future holds,
   are present as if meant to last.
   But present too is love which tends
   the hurt we never hoped to find,
   the private agonies inside,
   the memories that haunt the mind.

3. So some have come who need your help
   and some have come to make amends,
   as hands which shaped and saved the world
   are present in the touch of friends.
   Lord, let your Spirit meet us here
   to mend the body, mind and soul,
   to disentangle peace from pain
   and make your broken people whole.

Text: The Iona Community
Music: traditional Scottish melody

Text © Copyright 1989 WGRG/Iona Community, 840 Govan Road, Glasgow G51 3UU.
Used by permission from 'Love from Below' (Wild Goose Publications 1989).

714 We celebrate the new creation

ST CLEMENT 98 98

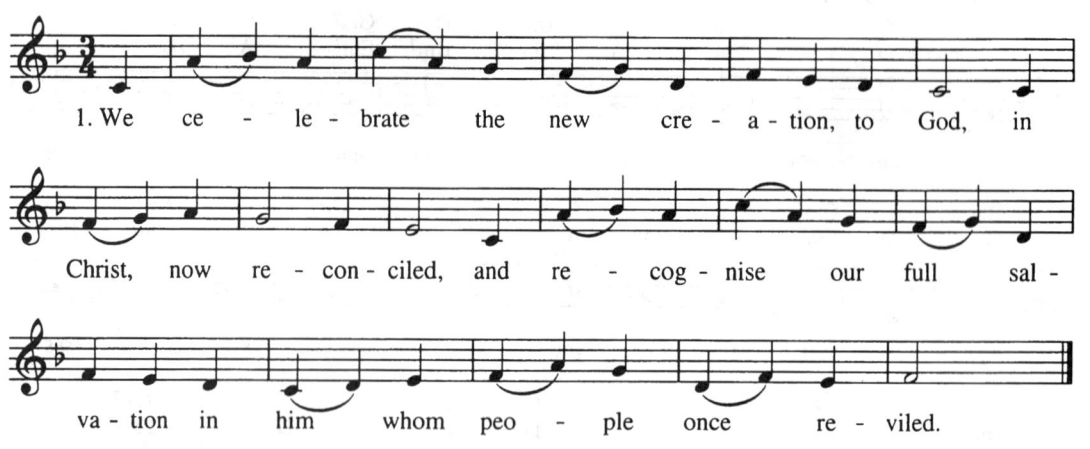

1. We celebrate the new creation, to God, in
Christ, now reconciled, and recognise our full salvation in him whom people once reviled.

A higher setting will be found at No.563

2. In token of our liberation,
   within God's presence now we stand,
   to share the banquet of salvation,
   the harvest of the promised land.

3. The news of reconciliation
   is now entrusted to our care;
   so spread the word throughout creation,
   the feast is here for all to share.

4. Begin the joyful celebration:
   the lost return, the dead arise,
   to see the light of exultation
   which shines from God's forgiving eyes.

Text: Michael Forster (b.1946) based on 2 Corinthians 5:17-21
Music: Clement Cotterill Scholefield (1839-1904)
Text © Copyright 1993 Kevin Mayhew Ltd.

715 We celebrate this festive day

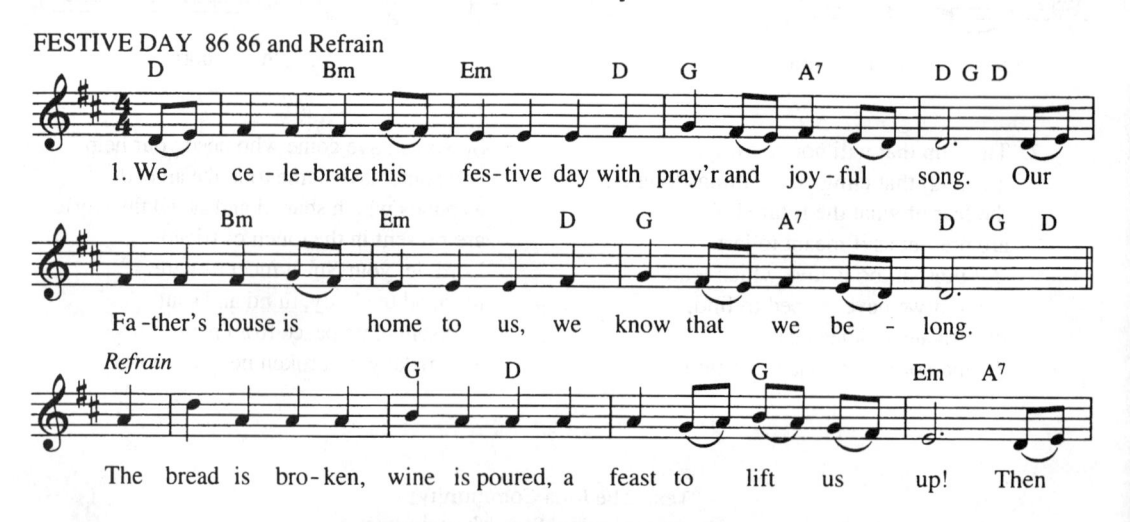

FESTIVE DAY 86 86 and Refrain

1. We celebrate this festive day with pray'r and joyful song. Our Father's house is home to us, we know that we belong.

Refrain

The bread is broken, wine is poured, a feast to lift us up! Then

Text © Copyright 1998 Willard F. Jabusch, 5735 University Avenue,
Chicago, Illinois 60637, USA. Used by permission. All rights reserved.

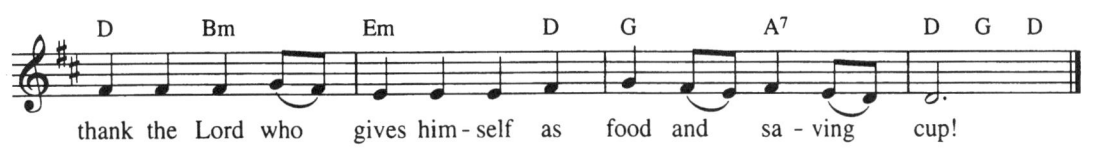

thank the Lord who gives him-self as food and sa-ving cup!

2. The door is open, enter in,
   and take your place by right.
   For you've been chosen as his guest
   to share his love and light.

3. We come together as the twelve
   came to the Upper Room.
   Our host is Jesus Christ the Lord,
   now risen from the tomb.

4. Who travels needs both food and drink
   to help them on their way.
   Refreshed and strong we'll journey on
   and face another day.

5. Who shares this meal receives the Lord
   who lives, though he was dead.
   So death can hold no terrors now
   for those who eat his bread.

Text: Willard F. Jabusch (b.1930)
Music: melody by Johann Sebastian Bach (1685-1750)
adapted by Willard F. Jabusch (b.1950)

716 We have a dream

WOODLANDS 10 10 10 10

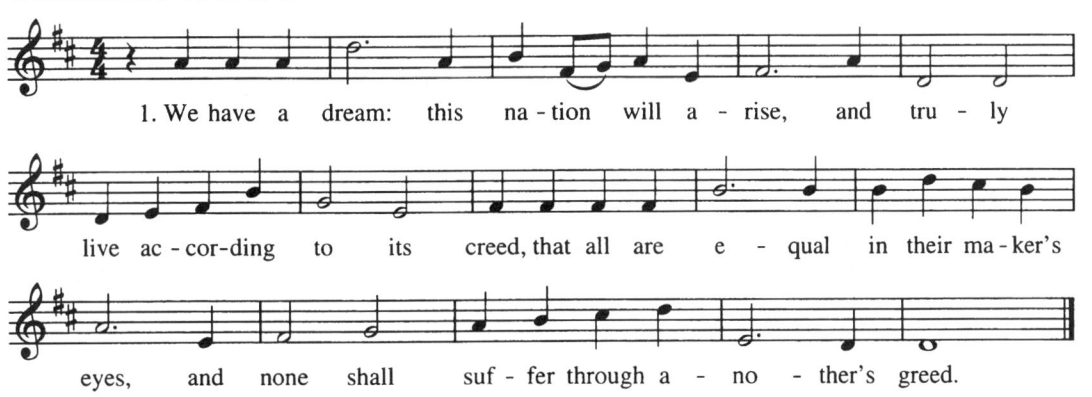

1. We have a dream: this nation will arise, and truly live according to its creed, that all are equal in their maker's eyes, and none shall suffer through another's greed.

2. We have a dream that one day we shall see
   a world of justice, truth and equity,
   where children of the slaves and of the free
   will share the banquet of community.

3. We have a dream of deserts brought to flow'r,
   once made infertile by oppression's heat,
   when love and truth shall end oppressive pow'r,
   and streams of righteousness and justice meet.

4. We have a dream: our children shall be free
   from judgements based on colour or on race;
   free to become whatever they may be,
   of their own choosing in the light of grace.

5. We have a dream that truth will overcome
   the fear and anger of our present day;
   that black and white will share a common home,
   and hand in hand will walk the pilgrim way.

6. We have a dream: each valley will be raised,
   and ev'ry mountain, ev'ry hill brought down;
   then shall creation echo perfect praise,
   and share God's glory under freedom's crown!

Text: Michael Forster (b.1946) based on the speech by Martin Luther King Jr.
Music: Walter Greatorex (1877-1949)
Text © Copyright 1997 Kevin Mayhew Ltd.
Music © Copyright Oxford University Press, Great Clarendon Street, Oxford OX2 6DP.
Used by permission from 'Enlarged Songs of Praise'.

717 We hold a treasure
Earthen vessels

We hold a treasure, not made of gold,
in earthen vessels, wealth untold;
one treasure only: the Lord, the Christ,
in earthen vessels.

1. Light has shone in our darkness;
God has shone in our heart,
with the light of the glory of Jesus, the Lord.

2. He has chosen the lowly,
   who are small in this world;
   in his weakness is glory,
   in Jesus the Lord.

Text: John Foley based on 2 Corinthians 4 and 1 Corinthians 1
Music: John Foley

© Copyright 1975 John B. Foley SJ and New Dawn Music, 5536 NE Hassalo, Portland, Oregon 97213, USA.
All rights reserved. Used by permission.

718 We plough the fields and scatter

WIR PFLÜGEN 76 76 D and Refrain

1. We plough the fields and scatter the good seed on the land, but it is fed and watered by God's almighty hand: he sends the snow in winter, the warmth to swell the grain, the breezes and the sunshine, and soft, refreshing rain.

Refrain
All good gifts around us are sent from heav'n above; then thank the Lord, O thank the Lord, for all his love.

2. He only is the maker
of all things near and far;
he paints the wayside flower,
he lights the evening star;
he fills the earth with beauty,
by him the birds are fed;
much more to us, his children,
he gives our daily bread.

3. We thank thee then, O Father,
for all things bright and good:
the seed-time and the harvest,
our life, our health, our food.
Accept the gifts we offer
for all thy love imparts,
and, what thou most desirest,
our humble, thankful hearts.

Text: Matthias Claudius (1740-1815) trans. Jane Montgomery Campbell (1817-1878) alt.
Music: Johann Abraham Peter Schulz (1747-1800)

719 Were you there when they crucified my Lord?

WERE YOU THERE 10 10 14 10

1. Were you there when they cru-ci-fied my Lord, Were you there when they cru-ci-fied my Lord, O, some-times it caus-es me to trem-ble, trem-ble, trem-ble. Were you there when they cru-ci-fied my Lord?

2. Were you there when they nailed him to a tree? ...

3. Were you there when they pierced him in the side? ...

4. Were you there when they laid him in the tomb? ...

5. Were you there when he rose to glorious life? ...

Text: Spiritual alt.
Music: Spiritual

720 We shall draw water joyfully

Refrain

We shall draw wa-ter joy-ful-ly, sing-ing joy-ful-ly, sing-ing joy-ful-ly; we shall draw wa-ter joy-ful-ly from the well-springs of sal-va-tion.

1. Tru-ly God is our sal-va-tion; we trust, we shall not fear. For the Lord is our strength, the Lord is our song; he be-came our Sa-viour.

© Copyright 1988 Paul Inwood. Administered in England by the St. Thomas More Group.
Published by OCP Publications, 5536 NE Hassalo, Portland, OR 97213, USA. All rights reserved. Used by permission.

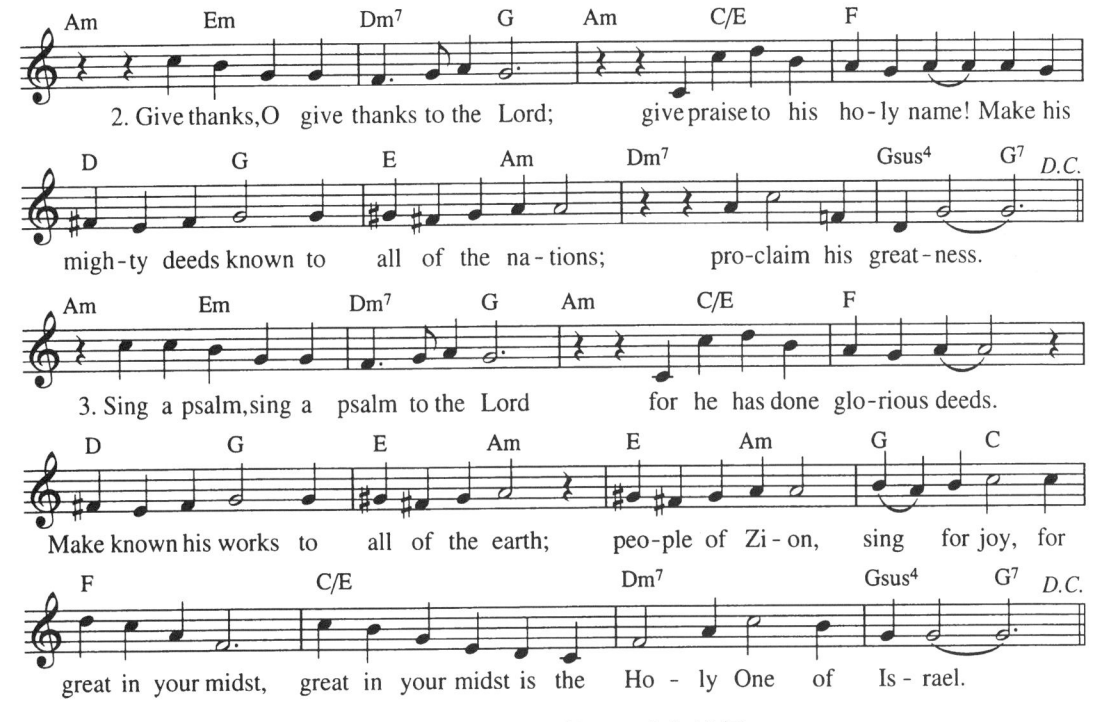

2. Give thanks, O give thanks to the Lord; give praise to his holy name! Make his mighty deeds known to all of the nations; proclaim his greatness.

3. Sing a psalm, sing a psalm to the Lord for he has done glorious deeds. Make known his works to all of the earth; people of Zion, sing for joy, for great in your midst, great in your midst is the Holy One of Israel.

Text and Music: Paul Inwood (b.1947)

721 We shall stay awake
Advent acclamations

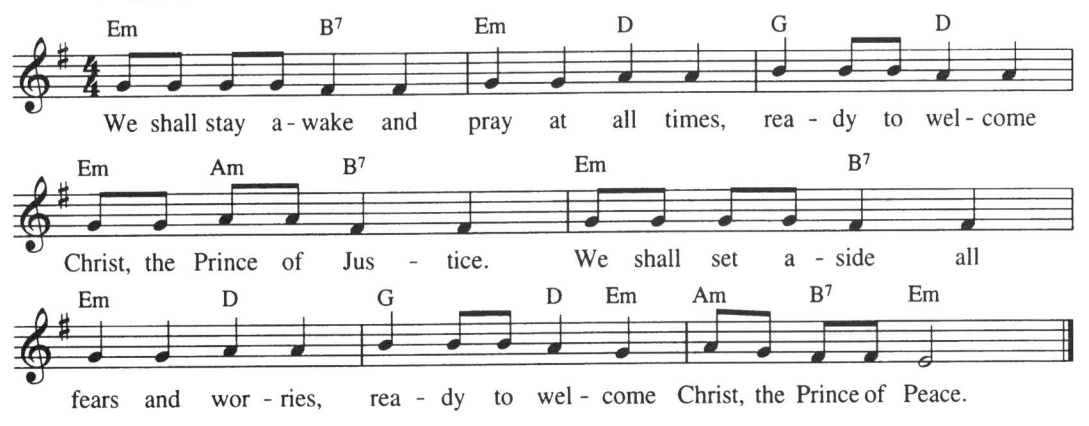

We shall stay awake and pray at all times, ready to welcome Christ, the Prince of Justice. We shall set aside all fears and worries, ready to welcome Christ, the Prince of Peace.

Advent 2

We shall set our sights on what is righteous,
ready to welcome Christ, the Prince of Justice.
We shall smooth the path, prepare the Lord's way,
ready to welcome Christ, the Prince of Peace.

Advent 3

We shall plunge into the saving water,
ready to welcome Christ, the Prince of Justice.
We shall be reborn and rise to new life,
ready to welcome Christ, the Prince of Peace.

Advent 4

We shall hold with faith to what God promised,
ready to welcome Christ, the Prince of Justice.
We shall be attentive to his Spirit,
ready to welcome Christ, the Prince of Peace.

Text: Pierre-Marie Hoog and Robert B. Kelly (b.1948)
Music: Jacques Berthier (1923-1994)
Original text © Copyright Rev. Pierre-Marie Hoog S.J., Eglise St. Ignace, 75006 Paris, France. Used by permission.
English translation and music © Copyright 1999 Kevin Mayhew Ltd.

722 We three kings of Orient are

KINGS OF ORIENT 88 86 and Refrain

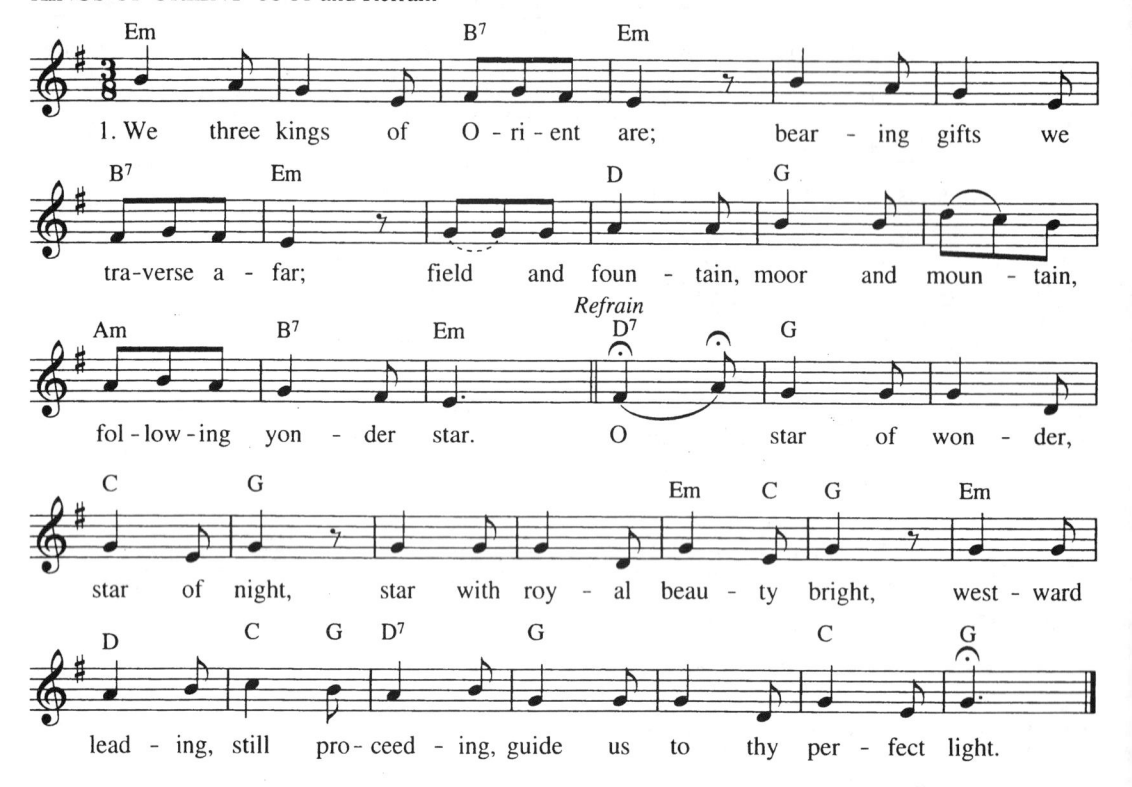

1. We three kings of Orient are;
   bearing gifts we traverse afar;
   field and fountain, moor and mountain,
   following yonder star.

   Refrain
   O star of wonder, star of night,
   star with royal beauty bright,
   westward leading, still proceeding,
   guide us to thy perfect light.

2. Born a King on Bethlehem plain,
   gold I bring, to crown him again,
   King for ever, ceasing never,
   over us all to reign.

3. Frankincense to offer have I,
   incense owns a Deity nigh,
   prayer and praising, gladly raising,
   worship him, God most high.

4. Myrrh is mine, its bitter perfume
   breathes a life of gathering gloom;
   sorrowing, sighing, bleeding, dying,
   sealed in the stone-cold tomb.

5. Glorious now behold him arise,
   King and God and sacrifice;
   alleluia, alleluia,
   earth to heav'n replies.

Text and Music: John Henry Hopkins (1820-1891) alt.

723 What child is this

GREENSLEEVES 87 87 68 67

1. What child is this who, laid to rest,
   on Mary's lap is sleeping?
   Whom angels greet with anthems sweet,
   while shepherds watch are keeping?

This, this is Christ the King, whom shepherds guard and angels sing:
come, greet the infant Lord, the babe, the Son of Mary!

2. Why lies he in such mean estate,
where ox and ass are feeding?
Good Christians, fear: for sinners here
the silent Word is pleading.
Nails, spear, shall pierce him through,
the cross be borne for me, for you;
hail, hail the Word made flesh,
the babe, the Son of Mary!

3. So bring him incense, gold and myrrh,
come rich and poor, to own him.
The King of kings salvation brings,
let loving hearts enthrone him.
Raise, raise the song on high,
the Virgin sings her lullaby:
joy, joy for Christ is born,
the babe, the Son of Mary!

Text: William Chatterton Dix (1837-1898) alt.
Music: traditional English melody

724 What feast of love

GREENSLEEVES 87 87 68 67

1. What feast of love is offered here, what banquet come from heaven? What
food of everlasting life, what gracious gift is given?
This, this is Christ the King, the bread come down from heaven.
O taste and see and sing! How sweet the manna given!

2. What light of truth is offered here,
what covenant from heaven?
What hope of everlasting life,
what wondrous word is given?
This, this is Christ the King,
the Sun come down from heaven.
O see, and list'ning, sing!
The Word of God is given!

3. What wine of love is offered here,
what crimson drink from heaven?
What stream of everlasting life,
what precious blood is given?
This, this is Christ the King,
the sweetest wine of heaven.
O taste and see and sing!
The Son of God is given!

Text: Delores Dufner
Music: Traditional English melody
Text: © Copyright 1993 Delores Dufner. Published by OCP Publications, 5536 NE Hassalo,
Portland, OR 97213, USA. All rights reserved. Used by permission.

725 What kind of greatness

1. What kind of greatness can this be, that chose to be made small?
Exchanging untold majesty for a world so pitiful.
That God should come as one of us, I'll never understand.
The more I hear the story told, the more amazed I am.

Refrain
O what else can I do but kneel and worship you,
and come just as I am,
my whole life an offering.

2. The One in whom we live and move
   in swaddling cloths lies bound.
   The voice that cried, 'Let there be light',
   asleep without a sound.
   The One who strode among the stars,
   and called each one by name,
   lies helpless in a mother's arms
   and must learn to walk again.

3. What greater love could he have shown
   to shamed humanity,
   yet human pride hates to believe
   in such deep humility.
   But nations now may see his grace
   and know that he is near,
   when his meek heart, his words, his works
   are incarnate in us here.

Text and Music: Graham Kendrick (b.1950)

© Copyright 1994 Make Way Music, P.O. Box 263, Croydon, Surrey CR9 5AP, UK.
International copyright secured. All rights reserved. Used by permission.

726 Whatsoever you do

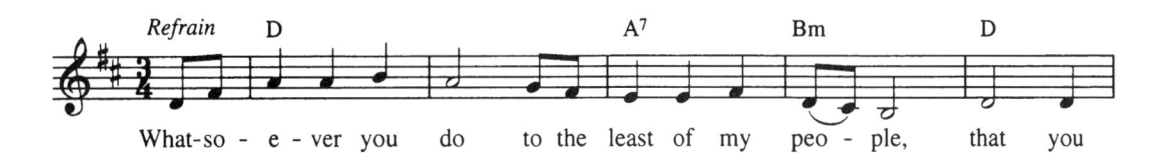

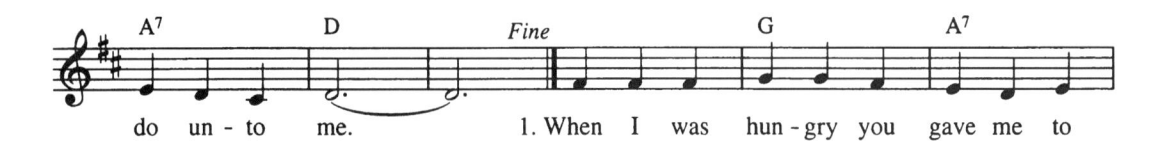

Refrain
What-so-e-ver you do to the least of my peo-ple, that you do un-to me.

1. When I was hun-gry you gave me to eat.
When I was thir-sty you gave me to drink.
Now en-ter in-to the home of my Fa-ther.

2. When I was homeless you opened your door.
When I was naked you gave me your coat.
Now enter into the home of my Father.

3. When I was weary you helped me find rest.
When I was anxious you calmed all my fears.
Now enter into the home of my Father.

4. When in a prison you came to my cell.
When on a sick-bed you cared for my needs.
Now enter into the home of my Father.

5. When I was aged you bothered to smile.
When I was restless you listened and cared.
Now enter into the home of my Father.

6. When I was laughed at you stood by my side.
When I was happy you shared in my joy.
Now enter into the home of my Father.

Text and Music: Willard F. Jabusch (b.1930)
Text and Music © Copyright 1998 Willard F. Jabusch /OCP Publications,
5536 NE Hassalo, Portland, OR 97213, USA. All rights reserved. Used by permission.

727 When Christ our Lord to Andrew cried

ST ANDREW DCM

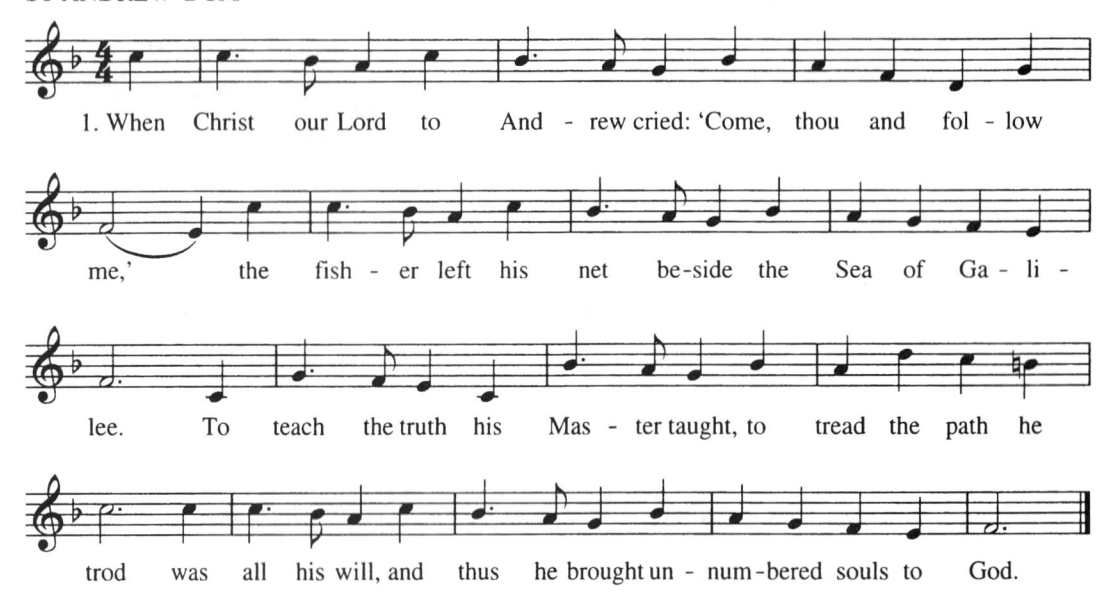

1. When Christ our Lord to Andrew cried: 'Come, thou and follow me,' the fisher left his net beside the Sea of Galilee. To teach the truth his Master taught, to tread the path he trod was all his will, and thus he brought unnumbered souls to God.

2. When Andrew's hour had come, and he
was doomed like Christ to die,
he kissed his cross exultingly,
and this his loving cry:
'O noble cross! O precious wood!
I long have yearned for thee;
uplift me to my only good
who died on thee for me.'

3. Saint Andrew, now in bliss above,
thy fervent prayers renew
that Scotland yet again may love
the faith, entire and true;
that I the cross allotted me
may bear with patient love!
'Twill lift me, as it lifted thee,
to reign with Christ above.

Text: E.M. Barrett
Music: traditional

728 When from bondage we are summoned

FREEDOM 87 87 D

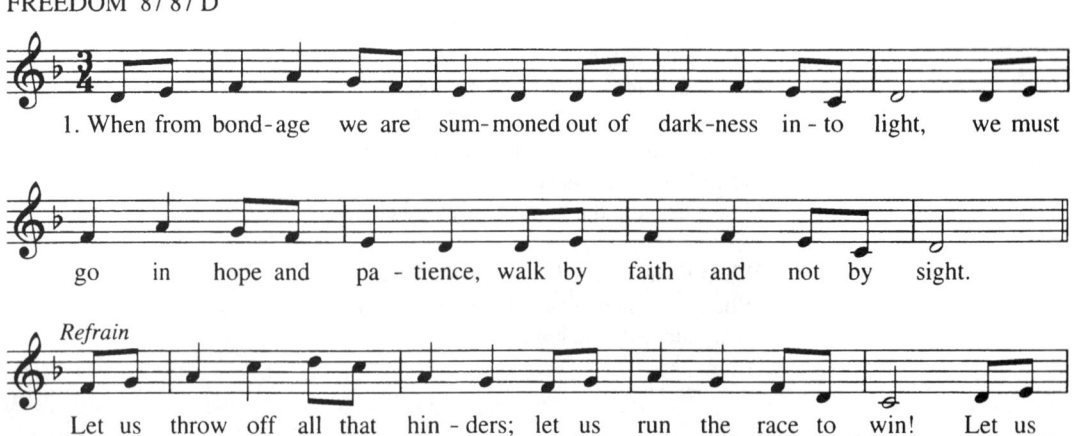

1. When from bondage we are summoned out of darkness into light, we must go in hope and patience, walk by faith and not by sight.

Refrain
Let us throw off all that hinders; let us run the race to win! Let us

Text © Copyright 1984, 1988, 1996 Delores Dufner OSB, Sisters of the Order of St Benedict,
104 Chapel Lane, St Joseph, MN 56374-0220, USA. Used by permission.
Music © Copyright 1984 Jay F Hunstiger, 4545 Wichita Trail,
Hamel, MN 55340, USA. Used by permission.

has-ten to our home-land and, re-joic-ing, en-ter in.

2. When our God names us a people,
   Jesus leads us by the hand
   through a lonely, barren desert,
   to a great and glorious land.

3. Through all stages of the journey
   Christ is with us, night and day,
   with compassion for our weakness
   ev'ry step along the way.

4. We must not lose sight of Jesus
   who accepted pain and loss;
   who, for joy of love unmeasured,
   dared embrace the shameful cross.

5. See the prize our God has promised:
   endless life with with Christ the Lord.
   Now we fix our eyes on Jesus
   walk by faith in Jesus' word.

Text: Delores Dufner
Music: Jay F. Hunstiger

729 When I feel the touch

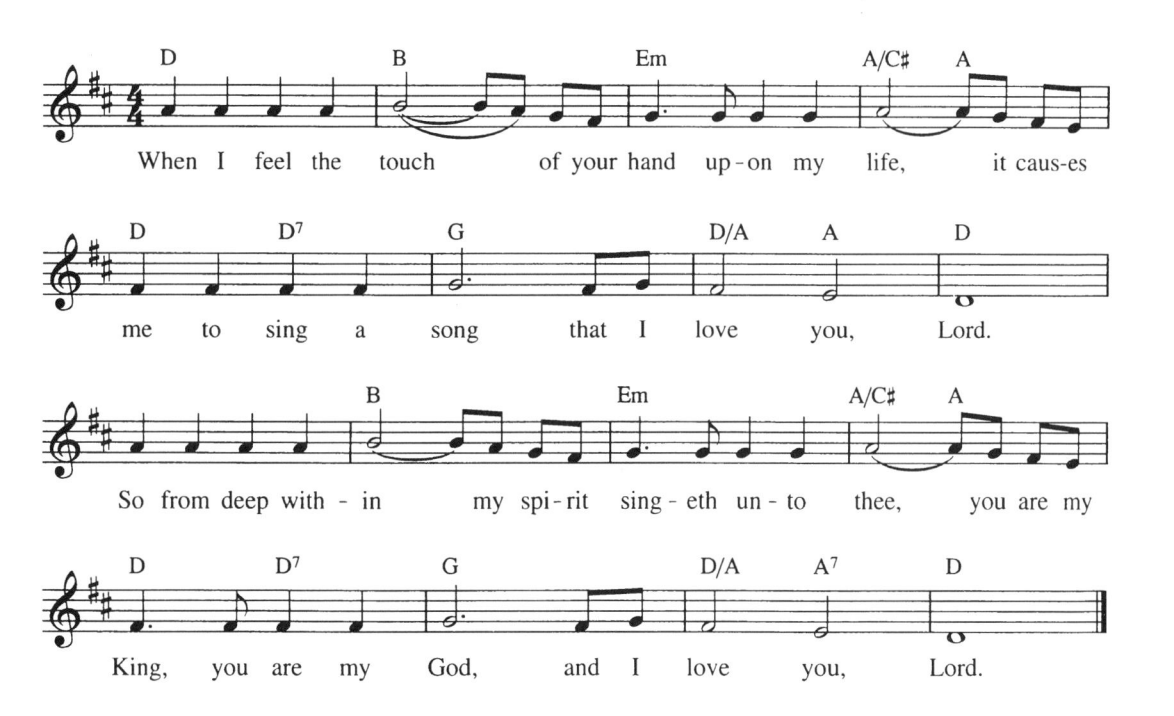

When I feel the touch of your hand up-on my life, it caus-es
me to sing a song that I love you, Lord.
So from deep with-in my spi-rit sing-eth un-to thee, you are my
King, you are my God, and I love you, Lord.

Text and Music: Keri Jones and David Matthew
© Copyright 1978 Word's Spirit of Praise Music. Administered by CopyCare,
P.O. Box 77, Hailsham, East Sussex BN27 3EF, UK. Used by permission.

730 When I needed a neighbour

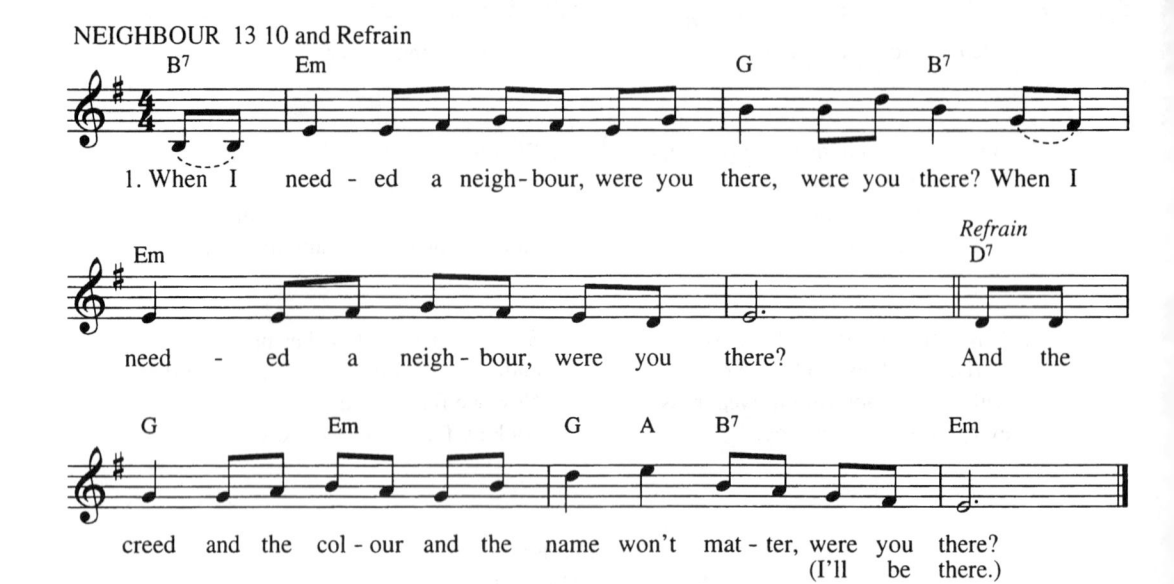

NEIGHBOUR 13 10 and Refrain

1. When I needed a neighbour, were you there, were you there?
When I needed a neighbour, were you there?
And the creed and the colour and the name won't matter, were you there?
(I'll be there.)

2. I was hungry and thirsty,
were you there, were you there?
I was hungry and thirsty,
were you there?

3. I was cold, I was naked,
were you there, were you there?
I was cold, I was naked,
were you there?

4. When I needed a shelter,
were you there, were you there?
When I needed a shelter,
were you there?

5. When I needed a healer,
were you there, were you there?
When I needed a healer,
were you there?

6. Wherever you travel,
I'll be there, I'll be there,
wherever you travel,
I'll be there.

Text and Music: Sydney Carter (b.1915)

© Copyright 1965 Stainer & Bell Ltd, P.O. Box 110, Victoria House,
23 Gruneisen Road, Finchley, London N3 1DZ. Used by permission.

731 When I survey the wondrous cross

TUNE 1: ROCKINGHAM LM

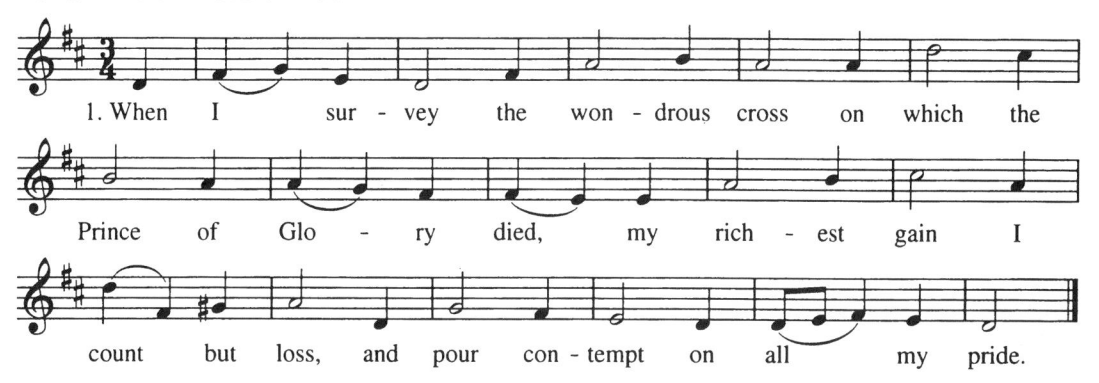

1. When I survey the wondrous cross on which the Prince of Glory died, my richest gain I count but loss, and pour contempt on all my pride.

A lower setting will be found at No. 480

2. Forbid it, Lord, that I should boast,
   save in the death of Christ, my God:
   all the vain things that charm me most,
   I sacrifice them to his blood.

3. See from his head, his hands, his feet,
   sorrow and love flow mingling down:
   did e'er such love and sorrow meet,
   or thorns compose so rich a crown?

4. Were the whole realm of nature mine,
   that were an off'ring far too small;
   love so amazing, so divine,
   demands my soul, my life, my all.

TUNE 2: O WALY WALY LM

Text: Isaac Watts (1674-1748)
Music: Tune 1 – adapted by Edward Miller (1735-1807)
Tune 2 – Somerset folk song collected by Cecil Sharp

732 When the time came

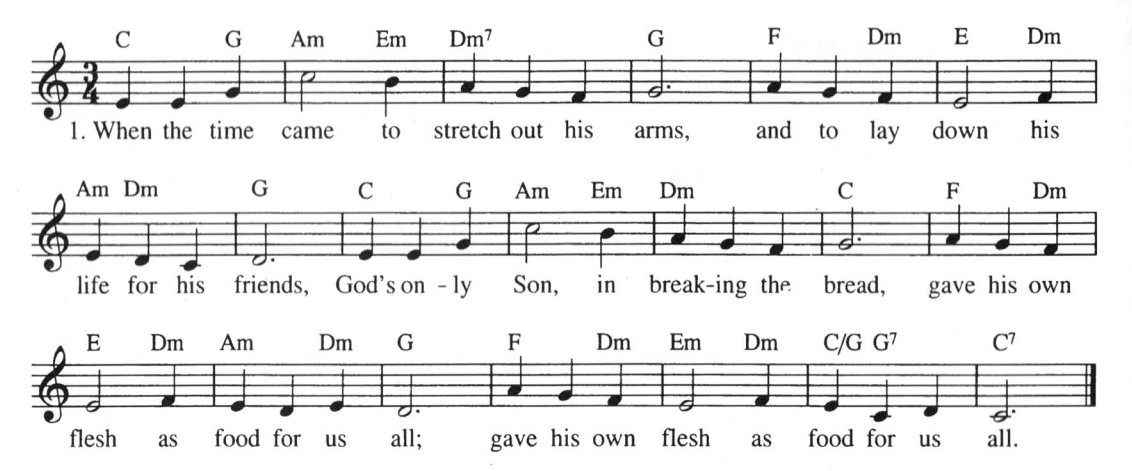

1. When the time came to stretch out his arms, and to lay down his life for his friends, God's on-ly Son, in break-ing the bread, gave his own flesh as food for us all; gave his own flesh as food for us all.

2. This is my flesh, O take it and eat.
   This is my blood, O take it and drink,
   and to proclaim my death for you all,
   this must you do until I return,
   this must you do until I return.

3. Hunger and thirst no longer we fear,
   Christ's holy flesh becomes now our food.
   And when we raise his chalice to drink,
   joy overflows, our hope is renewed,
   joy overflows, our hope is renewed.

4. O bread of life, O banquet divine,
   sign of the love that makes us all one;
   we who now share this gift from above,
   surely have seen the goodness of God,
   surely have seen the goodness of God.

5. Through Jesus Christ, the perfect high Priest,
   and in the Spirit, source of our peace,
   for this great feast which you have prepared,
   Father above, O praised be your name,
   Father above, O praised be your name.

Text: Didier Rimaud trans. Margaret Foley and Robert B. Kelly (b.1949)
Music: Jo Akepsimas
© Copyright Editions Musicales STUDIO SM, 54 Rue Michel Ange 75016, Paris, France. Used by permission.

733 Where are you bound, Mary

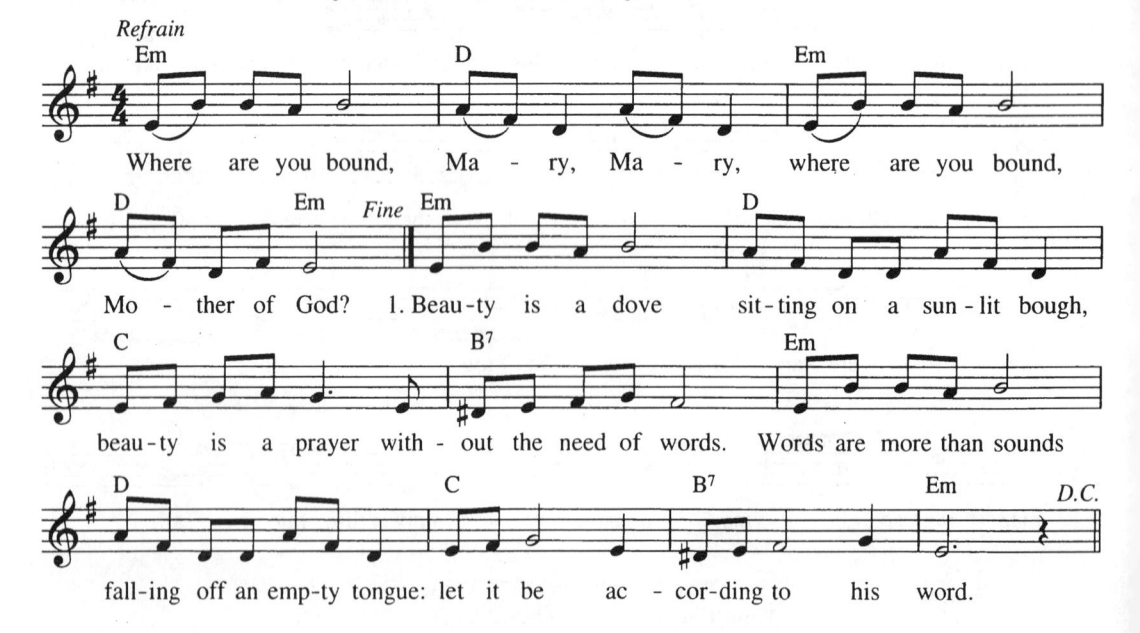

Refrain
Where are you bound, Ma-ry, Ma-ry, where are you bound, Mo-ther of God?

1. Beau-ty is a dove sit-ting on a sun-lit bough, beau-ty is a prayer with-out the need of words. Words are more than sounds fall-ing off an emp-ty tongue: let it be ac-cor-ding to his word.

© Copyright 1976 Kevin Mayhew Ltd.

2. Mary heard the word
spoken in her inmost heart.
Mary bore the Word
and held him in his arms.
Sorrow she has known,
seeing him upon the cross:
greater joy to see him rise again.

3. Where are we all bound,
carrying the Word of God?
Time and place are ours
to make his glory known.
Mary bore him first,
we will tell the whole wide world:
let it be according to his word.

Text and Music: John Glynn (b.1948)

734 Where is love and loving kindness

Refrain

Where is love and lov-ing kind - ness, God is there.

1. The love of Christ has ga-thered us to-ge-ther in one:
let us then re - joice and be glad in him.

2. Let us fear and love the liv-ing God; let us love each o-ther in the depths of our hearts.

3. There-fore when we are to-ge - ther let us take heed not to be di-vid-ed in mind.

4. Let there be an end to bit-ter-ness and quar-rels, an end to strife, and in our midst be Christ our God.

5. And in com-pa-ny with the bles - sed, may we see your face in glo - ry, Christ our God:
pure and un - bound - ed joy for e - ver and e - ver. A - men.

Text: based on 'Ubi Caritas'
Music: Alan Rees (b.1941)
Text © Copyright 1966 Bishop's Conference of England and Wales. Used by permission.
Music © Copyright 1995 Kevin Mayhew Ltd.

735 Where love and charity endure

Refrain

Where love and char-i-ty en-dure, God dwells there-in.

1. The love of Christ has bound us all in-to one fold: let us re-joice and ren-der thanks for his great love.

2. Let us revere and love the ever-living God,
   and by our love for one another prove that love.

3. It is together in one Body that we live:
   make sure that we do not divide it by our deeds.

4. May conflicts, quarrels, bitterness all disappear:
   let Jesus Christ be ever-present in our midst.

5. In heav'n amid the saints may we behold you, Lord,
   and there before the Father's throne your love enjoy.

6. Thus may we have unending happiness and joy
   in heav'n with God through endless ages evermore.

Text: Jean-Paul Lécot (b.1947) based on 'Ubi caritas', trans. W.R. Lawrence (1925-1997)
Music: Paul Décha
© Copyright 1988 Kevin Mayhew Ltd.

736 Where the love of Christ unites us

AR HYD Y NOS 84 84 88 84

1. Where the love of Christ u-nites us, there God is found.
   When we meet as love in-vites us, there God is found.
   Let us come with ju-bi-la-tion to the God of our sal-va-tion;

Text © Copyright 1993 Kevin Mayhew Ltd.

love en-li-vens all cre-a-tion; there God is found.

A higher setting will be found at No. 232

2. Where we meet without division,
   there God is found,
   free from anger and derision,
   there God is found.
   Let all bitter feuds be ended,
   strife resolved and foes befriended,
   pride and fear by love transcended:
   there God is found.

3. Where the blessèd live for ever,
   there God is found;
   bonds of love no pain can sever,
   there God is found.
   Christ in glory, we implore you,
   let us with the saints adore you,
   love resplendent flows before you;
   there God is found.

Text: Michael Forster (b.1946) based on 'Ubi Caritas'
Music: traditional Welsh melody

737 Where true love is found with charity

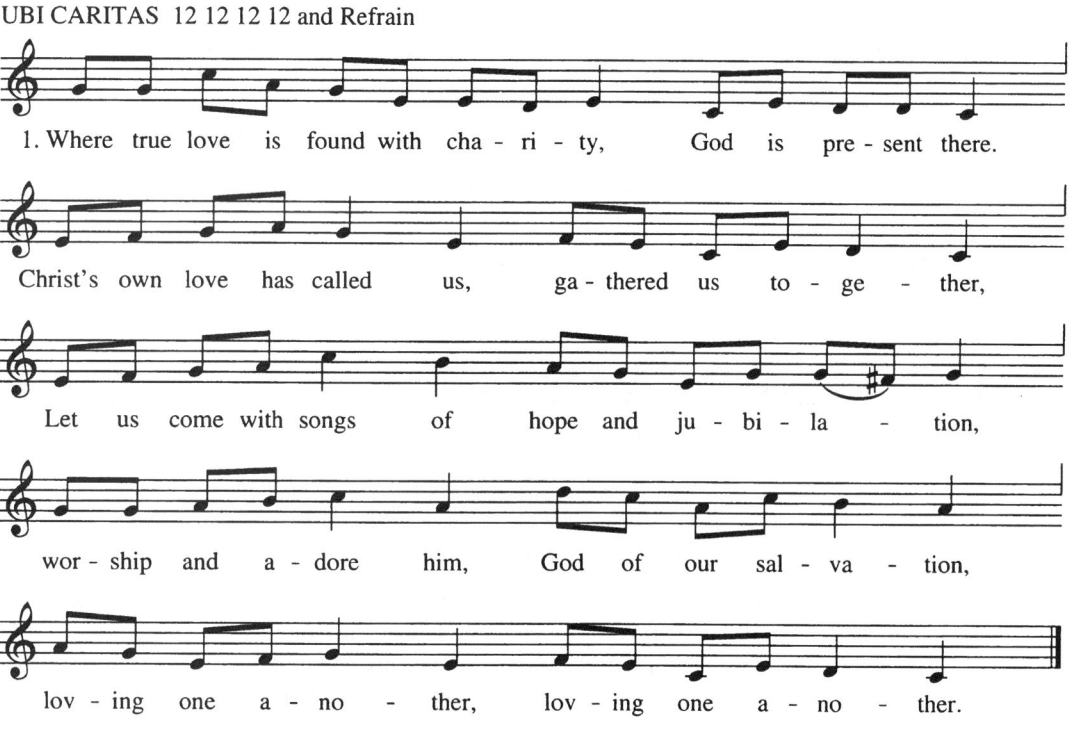

UBI CARITAS 12 12 12 12 and Refrain

1. Where true love is found with cha-ri-ty, God is pre-sent there.
   Christ's own love has called us, ga-thered us to-ge-ther,
   Let us come with songs of hope and ju-bi-la-tion,
   wor-ship and a-dore him, God of our sal-va-tion,
   lov-ing one a-no-ther, lov-ing one a-no-ther.

2. Where true love is found with charity,
   God is present there.
   As his holy people, gathering together,
   let us be united, strife and discord ending.
   Christ, our God, among us, ev'ry fear transcending,
   known in one another, known in one another.

3. Where true love is found with charity,
   God is present there.
   With the saints and martyrs, one in faith together
   let us see your glory, Christ our great salvation,
   sharing in the great eternal celebration,
   there with one another, there with one another.

Text: Michael Forster (b.1946) based on 'Ubi Caritas'
Music: Gregory Murray (1905-1992)
Text: © Copyright 1998 Kevin Mayhew Ltd.
Music: © Copyright The Estate of Gregory Murray. Used by permission of The Trustees of
Downside Abbey, Stratton-on-the-Fosse, Bath BA3 4RH.

738 Where true love is present
Leave your gift

MAKE PEACE 65 65 and Refrain

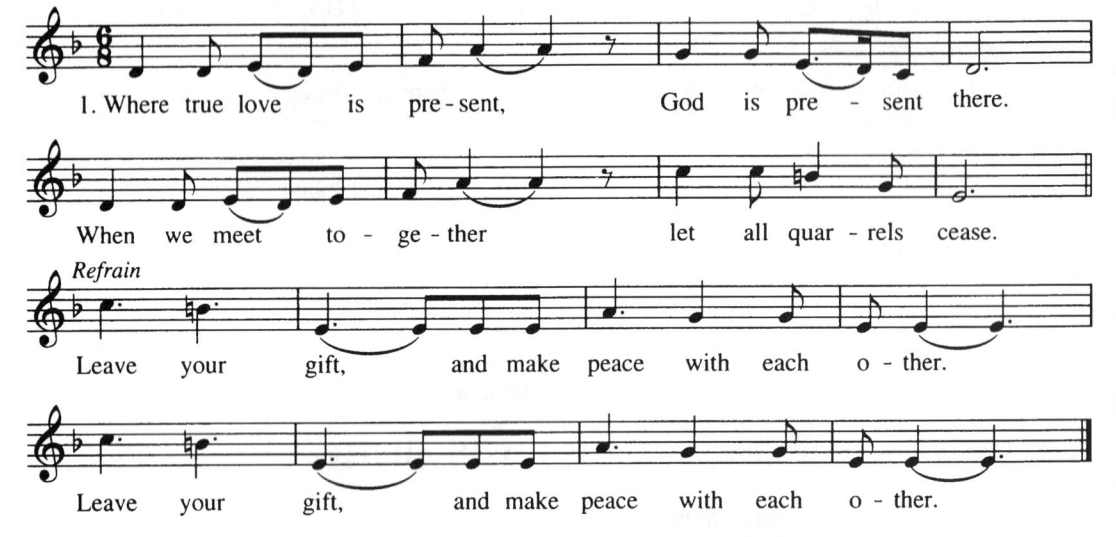

1. Where true love is present,
God is present there.
When we meet together
let all quarrels cease.

Refrain
Leave your gift,
and make peace with each other.
Leave your gift,
and make peace with each other.

2. God is loving kindness; those who love like him
live in God most truly, and he lives in them.

3. Let us put behind us bitterness and strife,
recognising Jesus present in our midst.

Text: H.J. Richards (b.1921) based on Scripture and 'Ubi Caritas'
Music: Christopher Tambling (b.1964)
© Copyright 1997 Kevin Mayhew Ltd.

739 While shepherds watched

WINCHESTER OLD CM

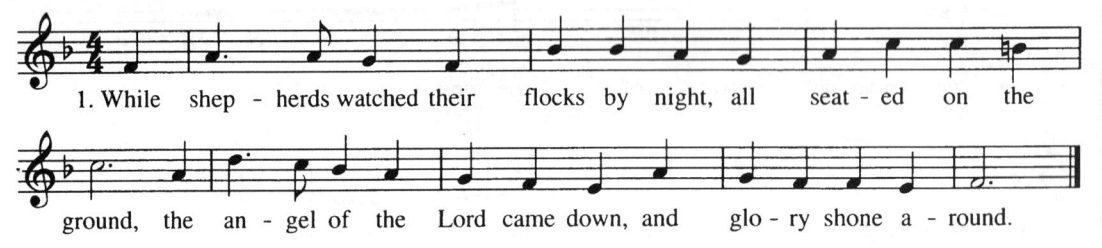

1. While shepherds watched their flocks by night, all seated on the ground, the angel of the Lord came down, and glory shone around.

2. 'Fear not,' said he, (for mighty dread
had seized their troubled mind)
'glad tidings of great joy I bring
to you and all mankind.'

3. 'To you in David's town this day
is born of David's line
a Saviour, who is Christ the Lord;
and this shall be the sign:'

4. 'The heav'nly babe you there shall find
to human view displayed,
all meanly wrapped in swathing bands,
and in a manger laid.'

5. Thus spake the seraph, and forthwith
appeared a shining throng
of angels praising God, who thus
addressed their joyful song:

6. 'All glory be to God on high,
and on the earth be peace,
goodwill henceforth from heav'n to all
begin and never cease.'

Text: Nahum Tate (1652-1715)
Music: from Este's 'Psalter' (1592)

740 Will you come and follow me
The Summons

KELVINGROVE 76 76 77 76

1. Will you come and fol-low me if I but call your name? Will you go where you don't know, and ne-ver be the same? Will you let my love be shown, will you let my name be known, will you let my life be grown in you, and you in me?

    2. Will you leave yourself behind
       if I but call your name?
       Will you care for cruel and kind,
       and never be the same?
       Will you risk the hostile stare
       should your life attract or scare,
       will you let me answer prayer
       in you, and you in me?

    3. Will you let the blinded see
       if I but call your name?
       Will you set the pris'ners free,
       and never be the same?
       Will you kiss the leper clean
       and do such as this unseen,
       and admit to what I mean
       in you, and you in me?

    4. Will you love the 'you' you hide
       if I but call your name?
       Will you quell the fear inside,
       and never be the same?
       Will you use the faith you've found
       to reshape the world around
       through my sight and touch and sound
       in you, and you in me?

    5. Lord, your summons echoes true
       when you but call my name.
       Let me turn and follow you,
       and never be the same.
       In your company I'll go
       where your love and footsteps show.
       Thus I'll move and live and grow
       in you, and you in me.

Text: John L. Bell (b.1949) and Graham Maule (b.1958)
Music: traditional Scottish melody
Text © Copyright 1987 WGRG, Iona Community, 840 Govan Road, Glasgow G51 3UU, Scotland.
Used by permission from the 'Heaven shall not wait' collection.

741 With the Lord there is mercy

Response

With the Lord there is mercy, with the Lord there is mercy and fullness of redemption.

1. From the deep I call to you, hear me, O God. Give attention to my cry and hear my pleading words.

2. If you only saw our guilt, Lord, who would live?
   But forgiveness flows from you, and so we praise your name.

3. How my soul awaits the Lord! In him I trust.
   Longingly I wait for him as watchers for the dawn.

4. Since our great forgiving God comes to redeem,
   all his people will be saved from all their sin and shame.

Text: Susan Sayers (b.1946) based on Psalm 129
Music: Andrew Moore (b.1954)
© Copyright 1995 Kevin Mayhew Ltd.

742 With you, O God

Response

With you, O God, my highest good, with you I am secure.

1. With you, I am always with you, my God, you hold me tight, your hand in mine.

Text © Copyright Burns & Oates Ltd., Wellwood, North Farm Road, Tunbridge Wells, Kent TN2 3QR.
Used by permission.
Music © Copyright 1984 Kevin Mayhew Ltd.

2. All things come to their fulfilment in you;
   you lead me on in your great love.

3. Heaven, what is that if you are not there?
   And here on earth you are my joy.

4. And when life on earth has come to an end,
   then I will be with you, my God.

Text: Huub Oosterhuis based on Psalm 72
Music: Frances M. Kelly (b.1952)

743 Word made flesh

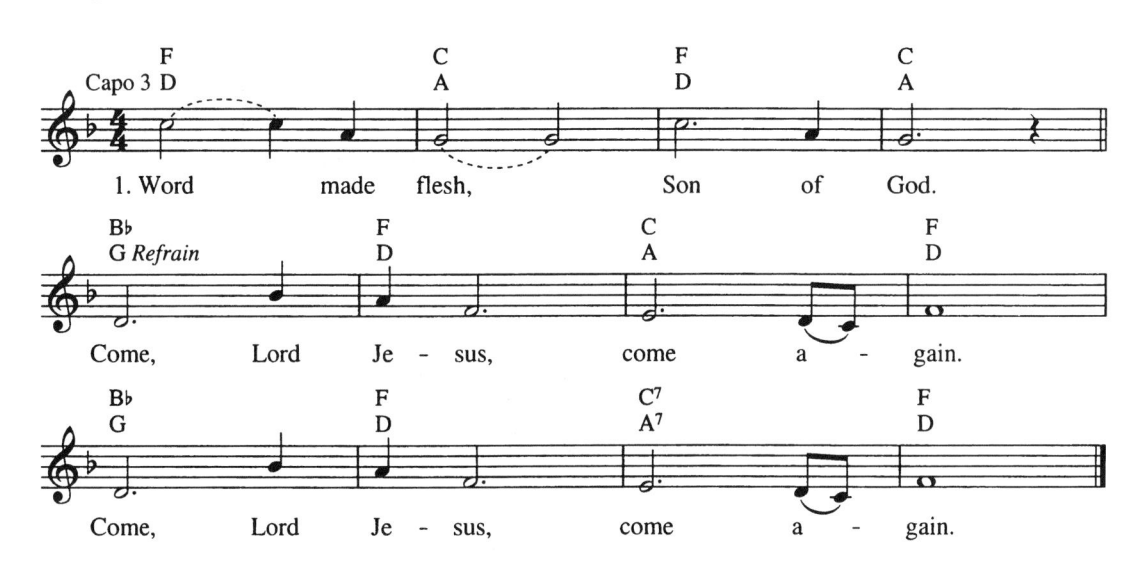

1. Word made flesh, Son of God.

Refrain
Come, Lord Jesus, come again.
Come, Lord Jesus, come again.

2. Lord and Saviour, Son of God.

3. Prince of Peace, Son of God.

4. Alleluia, Son of God.

5. Bread of Life, Son of God.

6. Light of the World, Son of God.

7. Jesus Christ, Son of God.

Text and Music: Virginia Vissing

© Copyright 1974, 1998 Sisters of St Mary of Namur, 909 West Shaw, Ft. Worth, Texas 76110, USA.
All rights reserved. Used by permission.

744 Yahweh, I know you are near

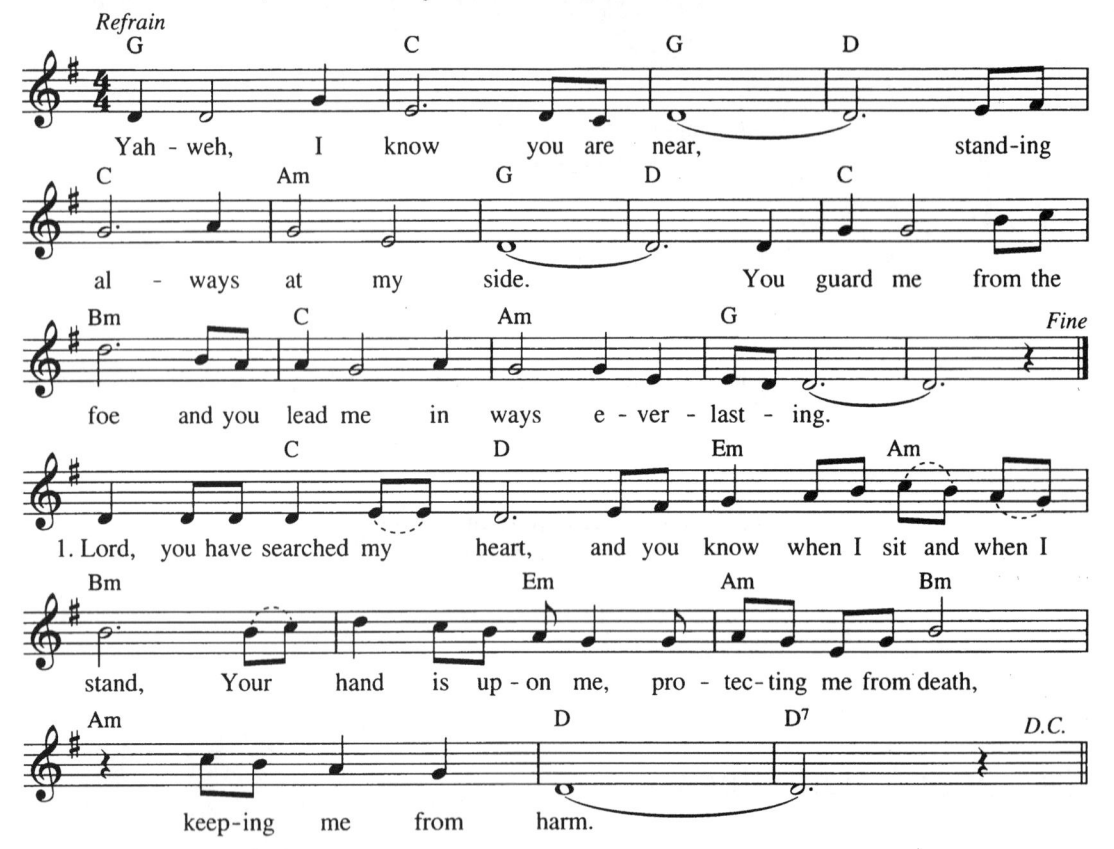

Yah-weh, I know you are near, stand-ing al-ways at my side. You guard me from the foe and you lead me in ways e-ver-last-ing.

1. Lord, you have searched my heart, and you know when I sit and when I stand, Your hand is up-on me, pro-tec-ting me from death, keep-ing me from harm.

2. Where can I run from your love?
If I climb to the heavens you are there.
If I fly to the sunrise or sail beyond the sea,
still I'd find you there.

3. You know my heart and its ways,
you who formed me before I was born,
in the secret of darkness, before I saw the sun
in my mother's womb.

4. Marv'llous to me are your works;
how profound are your thoughts, my Lord!
Even if I could count them, they number as the stars,
you would still be there.

Text: Dan Schutte based on Psalm 138
Music: Dan Schutte
© Copyright 1971, 1974 Daniel L. Schutte.
Administered by New Dawn Music, 5536 NE Hassalo, Portland, OR 97213, USA.
All rights reserved. Used by permission.

745 Yahweh is the God of my salvation

Yah-weh is the God of my sal-va-tion: I trust in

© Copyright 1972 The Benedictine Foundation of the State of Vermont, Inc., Weston Priory,
Weston, Vermont 05161, USA. Used by permission from the recording 'Wherever you go'.

him and have no fear. I sing of the joy which his love gives to me, and I draw deep-ly from the springs of his great kind-ness.

1. O-pen our eyes to the won-der of this mo-ment, the be-gin-ning of a-no-ther day.

2. Be with us, Lord, as we break through with each o-ther to find the truth and beau-ty of each friend.

3. When ev-'ning comes, and our day of toil is o-ver, give us rest, O Lord, in the joy of ma-ny friends.

4. Take us be-yond the vi-sion of this day to the deep and wide ways of your in-fi-nite love and life.

Text: Gregory Norbet based on Isaiah 12
Music: Gregory Norbet

746 Ye choirs of new Jerusalem

ST FULBERT CM

1. Ye choirs of new Jerusalem, your sweetest notes employ, the Paschal victory to hymn in strains of holy joy.

2. For Judah's Lion burst his chains,
   and crushed the serpent's head;
   and brought with him, from death's domain,
   the long-imprisoned dead.

3. From hell's devouring jaws the prey
   alone our leader bore;
   his ransomed hosts pursue their way
   where he hath gone before.

4. Triumphant in his glory now
   his sceptre ruleth all:
   earth, heav'n and hell before him bow
   and at his footstool fall.

5. While joyful thus his praise we sing,
   his mercy we implore,
   into his palace bright to bring,
   and keep us evermore.

6. All glory to the Father be,
   all glory to the Son,
   all glory, Holy Ghost, to thee,
   while endless ages run.

Text: 'Chorus novæ Jerusalem' by St Fulbert of Chartres (c.1028) trans. Robert Campbell (1814-1868)
Music: Henry John Gauntlett (1805-1876)

747 Ye sons and daughters of the Lord

O FILLII ET FILIAE 888 and Alleluias

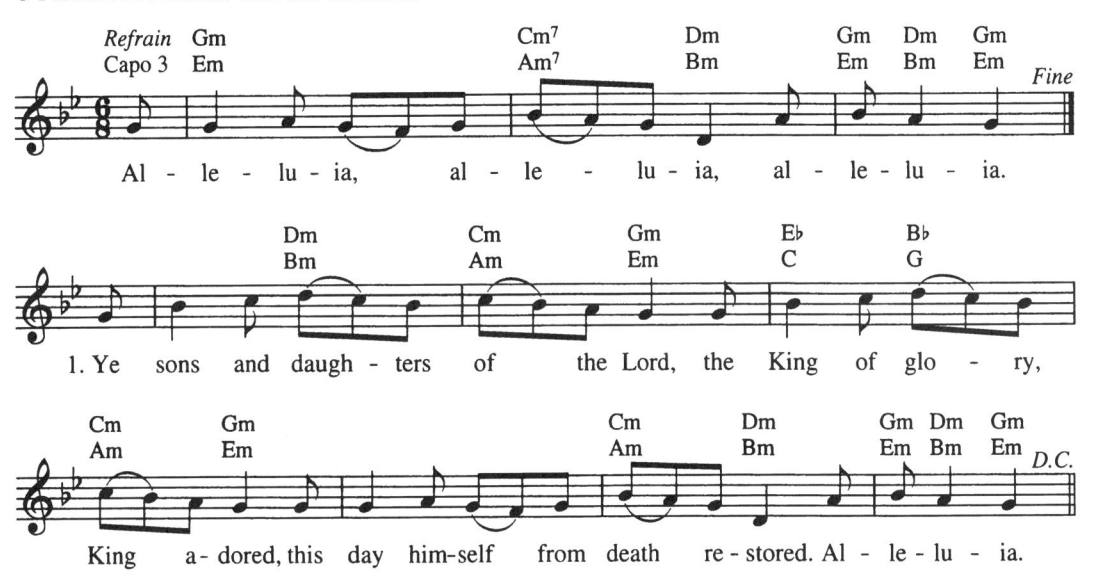

Refrain: Alleluia, alleluia, alleluia.

1. Ye sons and daughters of the Lord, the King of glory,
King adored, this day himself from death restored. Alleluia.

2. All in the early morning grey
went holy women on their way
to see the tomb where Jesus lay.
Alleluia.

3. Then straightway one in white they see,
who saith, 'Ye seek the Lord; but he
is ris'n, and gone to Galilee.'
Alleluia.

4. That self-same night, while out of fear
the doors were shut, their Lord most dear
to his apostles did appear.
Alleluia.

5. But Thomas, when of this he heard,
was doubtful of his brethren's word;
wherefore again there comes the Lord.
Alleluia.

6. 'Thomas, behold my side,' saith he;
'my hands, my feet, my body see,
and doubt not, but believe in me.'
Alleluia.

7. When Thomas saw that wounded side,
the truth no longer he denied:
'Thou art my Lord and God!' he cried.
Alleluia.

8. Now let us praise the Lord most high,
and strive his name to magnify
on this great day, through earth and sky.
Alleluia.

Text: Jean Tisserand (d.1494) trans. Edward Caswall (1814-1878)
Music: Samuel Webbe (1740-1816)

748 You are beautiful
I stand in awe

You are beau-ti-ful be-yond de-scrip-tion, too mar-vel-lous for words, too won-der-ful for com-pre-hen-sion, like no-thing e-ver seen or heard. Who can grasp your in-fi-nite wis-dom? Who can fa-thom the depth of your love? You are beau-ti-ful be-yond des-crip-tion, ma-jes-ty, en-throned a-bove.

Refrain

And I stand, I stand in awe of you. I stand, I stand in awe of you. Ho-ly God, to whom all praise is due, I stand in awe of you.

Words and Music: Mark Altrogge

© Copyright 1987 People of Destiny International. Administered by CopyCare,
P.O. Box 77, Hailsham, East Sussex BN27 3EF, UK. Used by permission.

749 You are salt for the earth
Bring forth the kingdom

Cantor
1. You are salt for the earth, O people: *(All)* salt for the kingdom of God! *(Cantor)* Share the flavour of life, O people: *(All)* life in the kingdom of God! *Refrain* Bring forth the kingdom of mercy, bring forth the kingdom of peace; bring forth the kingdom of justice, bring forth the city of God!

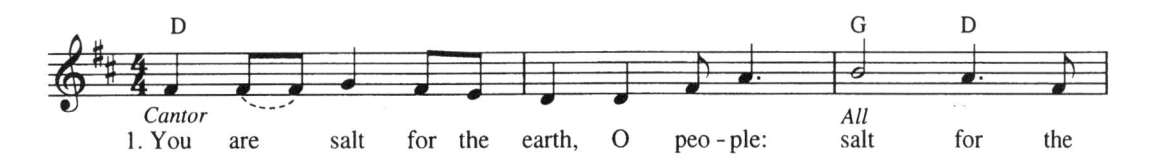

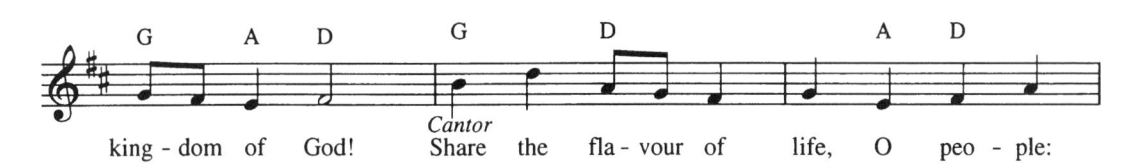

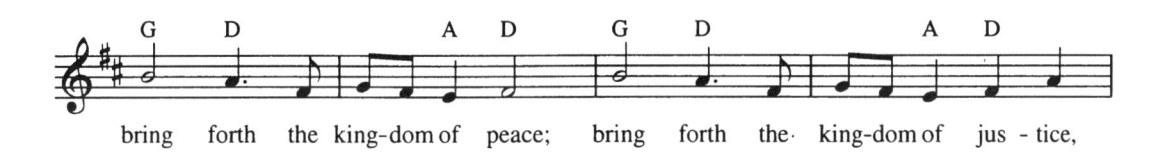

2. You are a light on the hill, O people:
   light for the city of God!
   Shine so holy and bright, O people:
   shine for the kingdom of God!

3. You are a seed of the Word, O people:
   bring forth the kingdom of God!
   Seeds of mercy and seeds of justice,
   grow in the kingdom of God!

4. We are a blest and a pilgrim people:
   bound for the kingdom of God!
   Love our journey and love our homeland:
   love is the kingdom of God!

Text and Music: Marty Haugen (b.1950)

© Copyright 1986 GIA Publications Inc., 7404 S. Mason Avenue, Chicago, Illinois 60638, USA.
All rights reserved. Used by permission.

750 You are the King of Glory
Hosanna to the Son of David

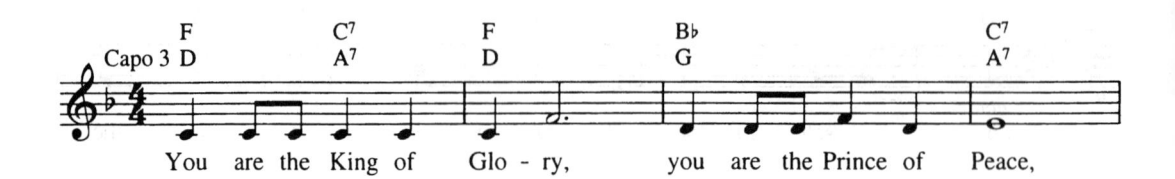

You are the King of Glo-ry, you are the Prince of Peace, you are the Lord of heav'n and earth, you're the Son of right-eous-ness. An-gels bow down be-fore you, wor-ship and a-dore, for you have the words of e-ter-nal life, you are Je-sus Christ the Lord. Ho-san-na to the Son of Da-vid! Ho-san-na to the King of kings! Glo-ry in the high-est hea-ven, for Je-sus the Mes-si-ah reigns.

Text and Music: Mavis Ford

© Copyright 1978 Word's Spirit of Praise Music. Administered by CopyCare, P.O. Box 77, Hailsham, East Sussex BN27 3EF, UK. Used by permission.

751 You are the light
Enfold me in your love

1. You are the light that is e-ver bright,
you fill my heart, giv-ing life;
you give the work I en-dea-vour to do,
mean-ing and pur-pose are bles-sings from you.
Refrain
O hold me, en-fold me in your love.

2. You are the beauty that fills my soul,
you, by your wound, make me whole.
You paid the price to redeem me from death;
yours is the love that sustains my ev'ry breath.

3. You still the storms and the fear of night,
you turn despair to delight.
You feel the anguish, and share in my tears,
you give the hope from the depth of my fears.

4. You are the word full of life and truth,
you guide my feet since my youth;
you are my refuge, my firm cornerstone,
you I will worship and honour alone.

5. You have restored me and pardoned sin,
you give me strength from within.
You called me forth, and my life you made new.
Love is the binding that holds me to you.

6. You are the Way, you are Truth and Life,
you keep me safe in the strife.
You give me love I cannot comprehend,
you guide the way to a life without end.

Text and Music: Margaret Rizza (b.1929)
© Copyright 1998 Kevin Mayhew Ltd.

LITURGICAL
HYMNS OLD & NEW

752 You give, Lord
Nunc Dimittis

1. You give, Lord, the sign to your
servant to go in your peace;
your promise of old has been
honoured, your word is fulfilled.

Refrain
May God give his grace in our
waking and watch as we sleep;
may Christ be our friend in the daylight,
our peace through the night.

2. At last I have seen your salvation,
your gift to the world:
the light of the Gentiles,
the glory in Israel's midst.

3. Give thanks to the Father of mercies,
give thanks to his Son,
give thanks to the joy-giving Spirit,
give thanks to one God.

Text: Gregory Murray (1905-1992) based on Luke 2:29-32
Music: Gregory Murray (1905-1992)
© Copyright 1999 Kevin Mayhew Ltd.

753 You have been baptised in Christ

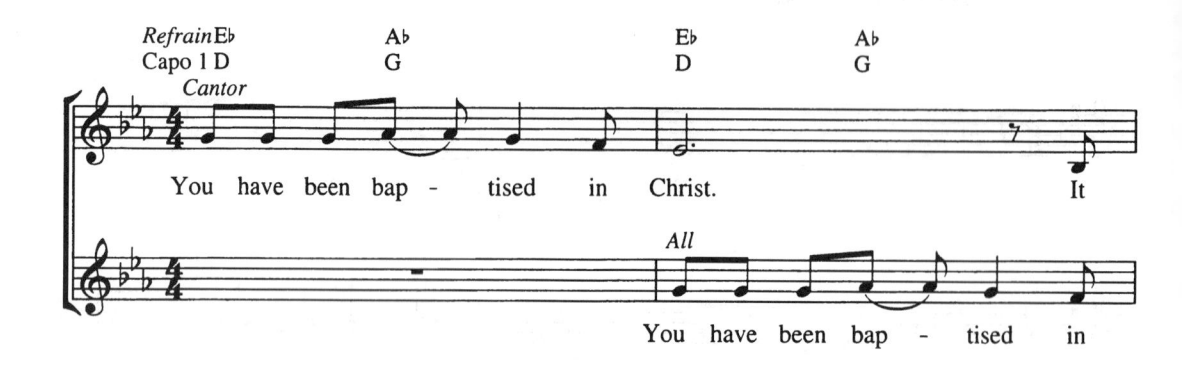

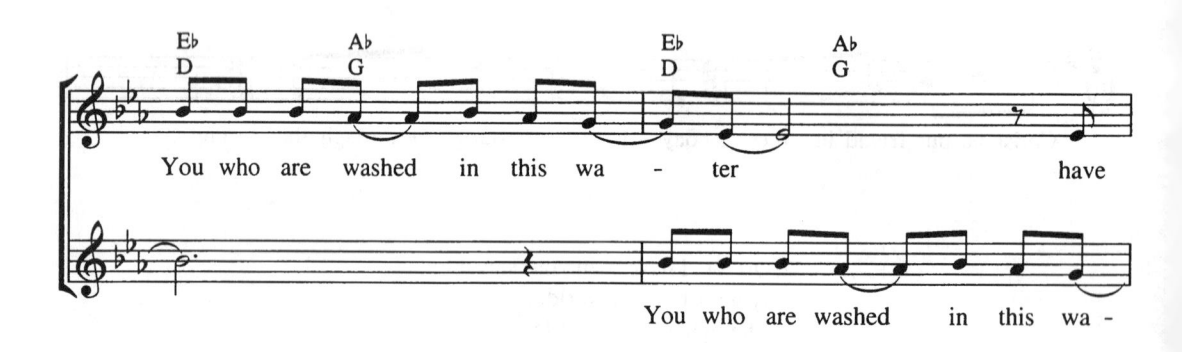

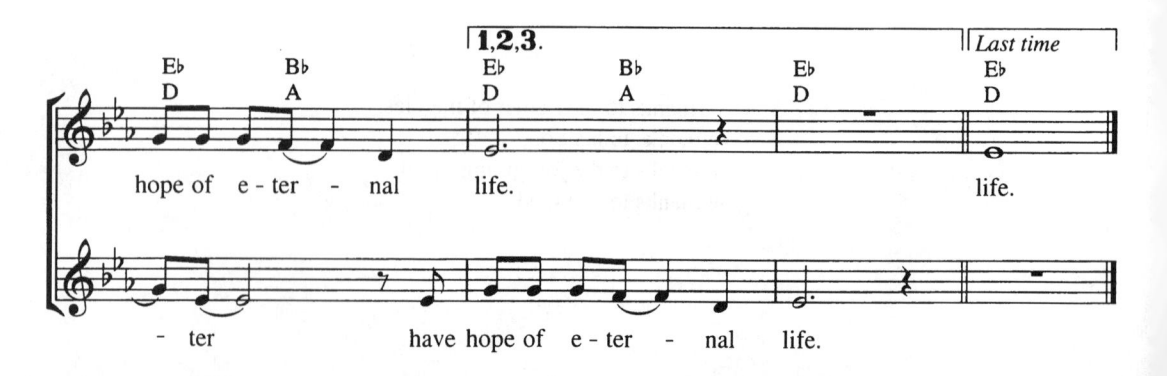

Refrain / Capo 1 D / Cantor

You have been bap-tised in Christ. It

All

You have been bap-tised in

Christ. It is he that you have put on.

is he that you have put on.

You who are washed in this wa-ter have

You who are washed in this wa-

1, 2, 3.

hope of e-ter-nal life.

Last time

life.

-ter have hope of e-ter-nal life.

© Copyright 1976, North American Liturgy Resources (NALR), 5536 NE Hassalo, Portland, OR 97213, USA.
All rights reserved. Used by permission.

1. God the Father has freed you and given you a new birth, and to be a member of his holy people he now anoints you with oil.

2. You are a new creation. In Christ you have been clothed. See in this garment the outward sign of your dignity in him.

3. Receive the light of Christ; keep it burning brightly. Always walk as a child of the light, with his flame alive in your heart.

Text: Carey Landry from the Rite of Baptism
Music: Carey Landry

754 You have called us

Refrain

You have called us out of darkness, out of darkness into your glorious light. You have saved us from the darkness, we rejoice in your power and might. You have called

1. We are a chosen race, a royal priesthood by your grace. We are a holy nation set apart for you. You have called

© Copyright 1990 Integrity's Hosanna! Music. Administered by Kingsway's Thankyou Music, P.O. Box 75, Eastbourne, East Sussex, BN23 6NW, UK. For the UK only. Used by permission.

CODA

We rejoice in your power and might.

2. We are to take your light
to ev'ry nation, tongue and tribe,
so they may see your glory
shining through our lives.

Text and Music: Lynn DeShazo and Martin J. Nystrom

755 You have the message of eternal life

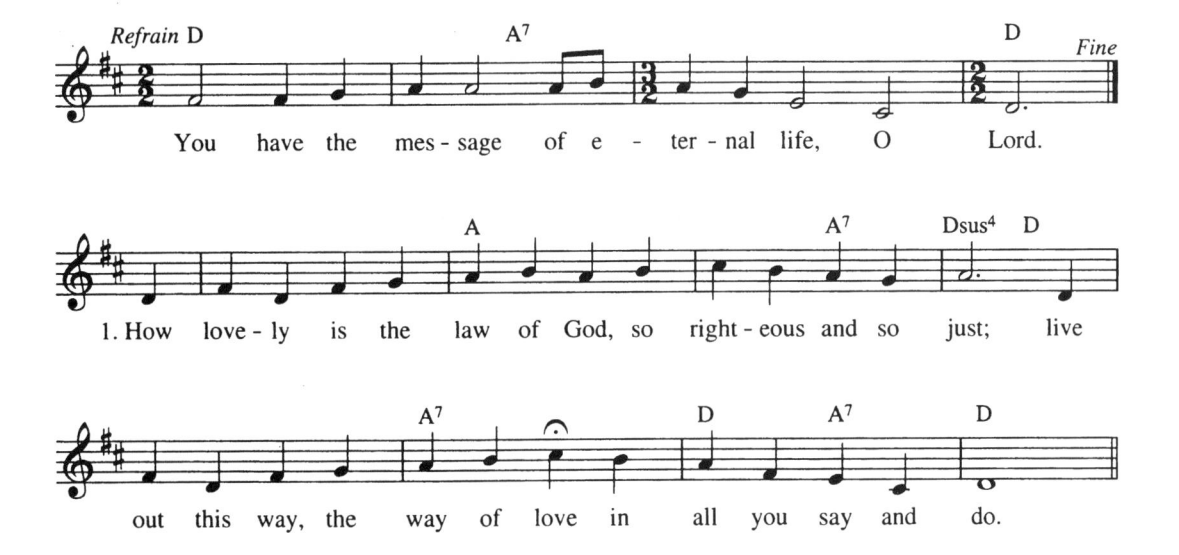

Refrain

You have the message of eternal life, O Lord.

1. How lovely is the law of God, so righteous and so just; live out this way, the way of love in all you say and do.

2. This law alone can soothe the soul,
    give peace and inner joy;
    like solid ground that we may trust,
    and light to travel by.

3. As worldly values shift and slide,
    the love of God holds fast,
    and though our world will pass away
    his faithfulness remains.

Text: Susan Sayers (b.1946) based on Psalm 18
Music: Andrew Moore (b.1954)
© Copyright 1995 Kevin Mayhew Ltd.

LITURGICAL
HYMNS OLD & NEW

756 Your love's greater

Your love's greater (greater), greater than the greatest mountain, your love's deeper (deeper), deeper than the deepest sea; a love that never dies, a love that reaches deep inside, more wondrous than all the universe.

1. You made the heavens, the earth and sea; your pow'r is awesome, and you still love me.

2. Your ways are righteous,
   your laws are just,
   love is your promise,
   and in you I trust.

3. Your love is healing,
   your love endures;
   my life is changed,
   Lord, now I know I'm yours.

Text and Music: Mike Anderson (b.1956)
© Copyright 1999 Kevin Mayhew Ltd.

757 You shall cross the barren desert
Be not afraid

1. You shall cross the barren desert, but you shall not die of thirst. You shall wander far in safety though you do not know the way. You shall speak your words in foreign lands and they will understand. You shall see the face of God and live.

Refrain
Be not afraid. I go before you always. Come, follow me, and I will give you rest.

2. If you pass through raging waters in the sea, you shall not drown. If you walk amid the burning flames, you shall not be harmed. If you stand before the pow'r of hell and death is at your

© Copyright 1975, 1978 Robert J. Dufford S.J., and New Dawn Music, 5536 NE Hassalo, Portland, OR 97213, USA. All rights reserved. Used by permission.

side, know that I am with you through it all.

Refrain
Be not a - fraid. I go be - fore you al - ways.
Come, fol - low me, and I will give you rest.

3. Bles - sed are the poor, for the king-dom shall be theirs.
Blest are you that weep and mourn, for one day you shall laugh. And if wick - ed men in - sult and hate you all be - cause of me, bles - sed, bles - sed are you!

Refrain
Be not a - fraid. I go be - fore you al - ways.
Come, fol-low me, and I will give you rest.

Text: Bob Dufford based on Isaiah 43:2-3, Luke 6:20
Music: Bob Dufford

758 You shall go out with joy
The trees of the field

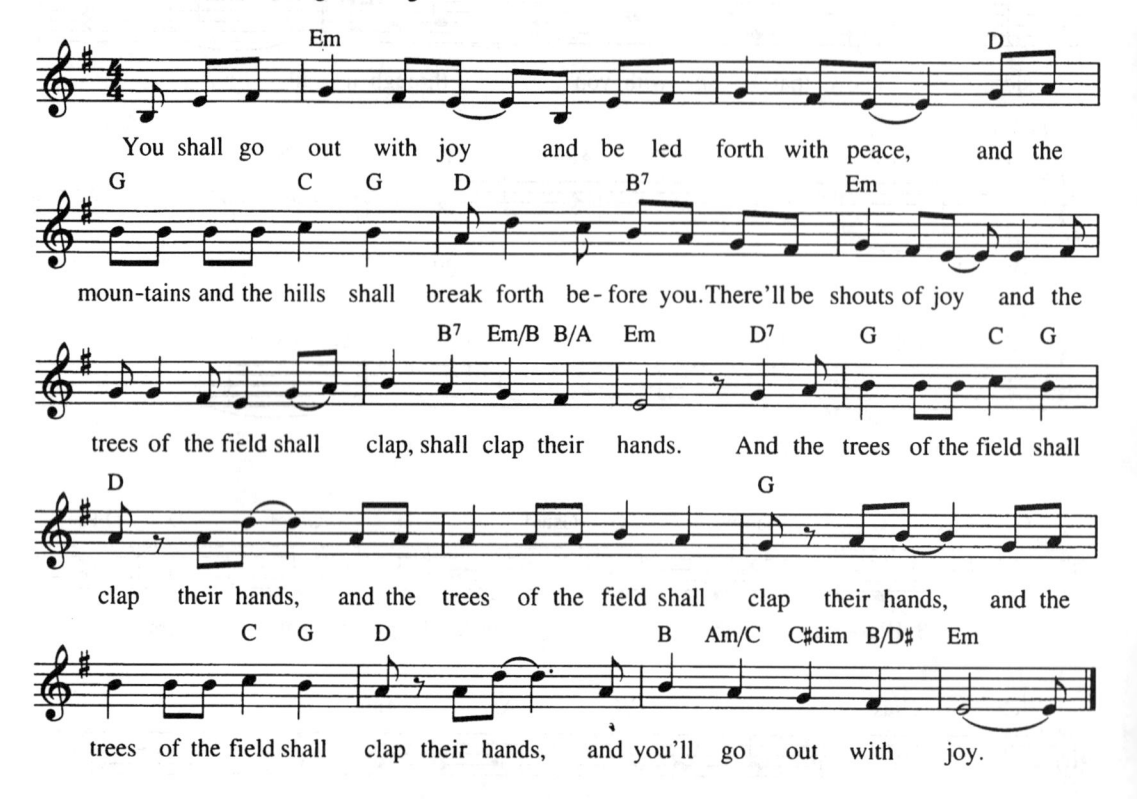

You shall go out with joy and be led forth with peace, and the mountains and the hills shall break forth before you. There'll be shouts of joy and the trees of the field shall clap, shall clap their hands. And the trees of the field shall clap their hands, and the trees of the field shall clap their hands, and the trees of the field shall clap their hands, and you'll go out with joy.

Text and Music: Steffi Geiser Rubin and Stuart Dauermann
© Copyright 1975 Lillenas Publishing Co. Administered by CopyCare,
P.O. Box 77, Hailsham, East Sussex BN27 3EF, UK. Used by permission.

759 You who dwell in the shelter of the Lord
On eagle's wings

1. You who dwell in the shelter of the Lord, who abide in his shadow for life, say to the Lord: 'My refuge, my rock in whom I trust!'

© Copyright 1979, 1991 New Dawn Music, 5536 NE Hassalo, Portland, OR 97213, USA.
All rights reserved. Used by permission.

Refrain

And he will raise you up on ea-gle's wings, bear you on the breath of dawn, make you to shine like the sun, and hold you in the palm of his hand.

To verses / *Last time* Fine

2. The snare of the fow-ler will ne-ver cap-ture you, and fam-ine will bring you no fear. Un-der his wings your ref-uge, his faith-ful-ness your shield. *D.S.*

3. You need not fear the ter-ror of the night, nor the ar-row that flies by day; though thou-sands fall a-bout you, near you it shall not come. *D.S.*

4. For to his an-gels he's giv-en a com-mand to guard you in all of your ways; u-pon their hands they will bear you up, lest you dash your foot a-gainst a stone. *D.S.*

Text: Michael Joncas (b.1951) based on Psalm 90
Music: Michael Joncas (b.1951)

LITURGICAL
HYMNS OLD & NEW

Children's Hymns and Songs

760 A butterfly, an Easter egg
Signs of new life

1. A butterfly, a butterfly, an Easter egg, an Easter egg, a fountain flowing in the park, a fountain flowing in the park.

Refrain
These are signs of new life; the life of Jesus the Lord. And we sing to him, alleluia! We give to him our praise! We sing to him, alleluia! Glory be to him! Glory be to him! Glory be to Jesus the Lord!

2. A helping hand,
a helping hand,
a happy smile,
a happy smile,
a heart so full of hope and joy,
a heart so full of hope and joy.

3. A cup of wine,
a cup of wine,
a loaf of bread,
a loaf of bread,
now blest and broken for us all,
now blest and broken for us all.

Text and Music: Carey Landry
© Copyright 1979 North American Liturgy Resources (NALR), 5536 NE Hassalo, Portland, OR 97213, USA.
All rights reserved. Used by permission.

761 All in an Easter garden

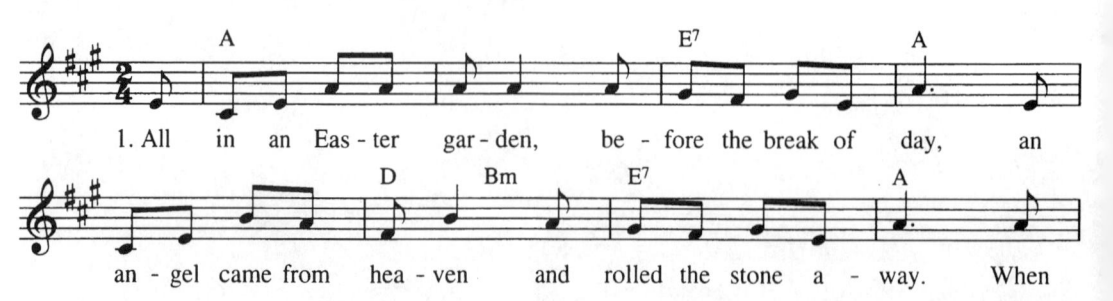

1. All in an Easter garden, before the break of day, an angel came from heaven and rolled the stone away. When

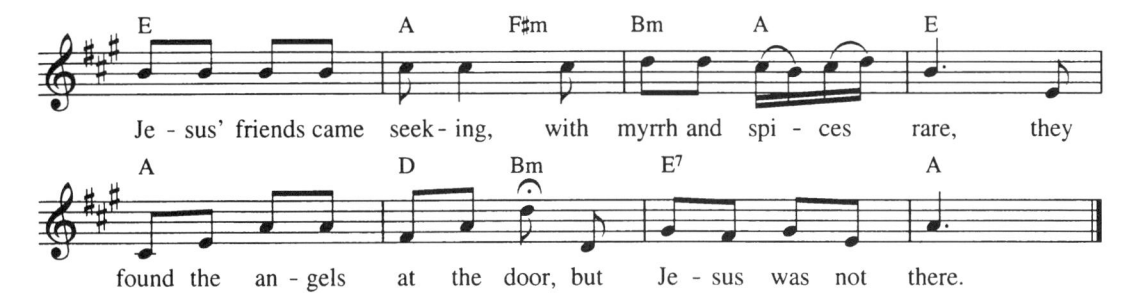

Je-sus' friends came seek-ing, with myrrh and spi-ces rare, they found the an-gels at the door, but Je-sus was not there.

2. All in an Easter garden,
   where water lilies bloom,
   the angels gave their message
   beside an empty tomb:
   'The Lord is here no longer,
   come, see where once he lay;
   the Lord of life is ris'n indeed,
   for this is Easter day.'

Text and Music: traditional

762 All of my heart

All of my heart, all of my soul, all of my mind, all of my strength. With ev'ry-thing with-in me I want to praise you, Lord. I want to love you with all that I am, and bring joy to your heart. Let me bring joy to your heart all of my life.

Text and Music: Doug Marks-Smirchirch
© Copyright Right on the Mark Music. Copyright control.

763 All of the people

Refrain / Capo 5

All of the people on the mountain, all of the people in the valley, all of the people in the villages and the town, say to each other on the way, 'Bring all your friends and don't delay, Jesus of Nazareth is coming here today.'

1. Jesus, Jesus, when we are with you,
   it's strange, and yet it's true,
   we start to feel that there is more to life than living as we do.
   It's richer and more satisfying than we ever knew.

2. Jesus, Jesus, healing as you go,
   your loving seems to flow
   like water from a fountain,
   and as we are touched we want to grow
   in love towards each other –
   just because you love us so!

3. Jesus, Jesus, we have come to see
   that you must really be
   the Son of God our Father.
   We've been with you and we all agree
   that only in your service
   can the world be truly free!

Text and Music: Susan Sayers (b.1946)
© Copyright 1986 Kevin Mayhew Ltd.

764 All the nations of the earth

Refrain

All the nations of the earth, praise the Lord who brings to birth the greatest star, the smallest flow'r. Alleluia.

1. Let the heavens praise the Lord, alleluia.
Moon and stars, praise the Lord, alleluia.

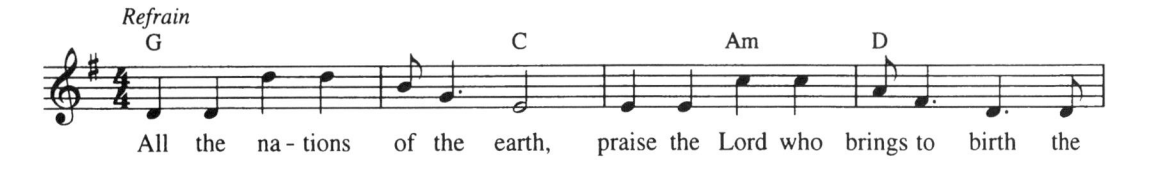

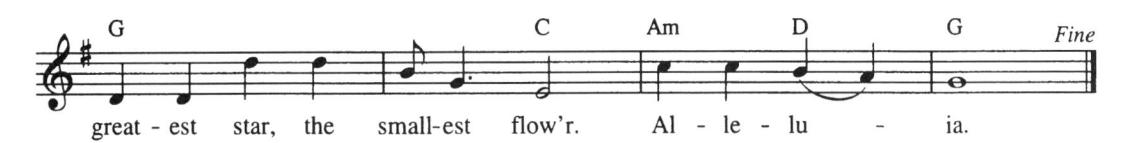

2. Snow-capped mountains, praise the Lord,
   alleluia.
   Rolling hills, praise the Lord,
   alleluia.

3. Deep sea water, praise the Lord,
   alleluia.
   Gentle rain, praise the Lord,
   alleluia.

4. Roaring lion, praise the Lord,
   alleluia.
   Singing birds, praise the Lord,
   alleluia.

5. Earthly monarchs, praise the Lord,
   alleluia.
   Young and old, praise the Lord,
   alleluia.

Text: Michael Cockett (b.1938)
Music: Kevin Mayhew (b.1942)

© Copyright McCrimmon Publishing Co. Ltd., 10-12 High Street, Great Wakering,
Southend-on-Sea, Essex SS3 0EQ. Used by arrangement.

765 And everyone beneath the vine and fig tree

And ev-'ry-one beneath the vine and fig tree shall live in peace and have no fear. And ev-'ry-one beneath the vine and fig tree shall live in peace and have no fear. And in-to plough-shares turn their swords, na-tions shall learn war no more. And in-to plough-shares turn their swords, na-tions shall learn war no more. And ev-'ry- war no more.

This can be sung as a round with the second voices entering at B

Text and Music: unknown

766 As Jacob with travel was weary one day

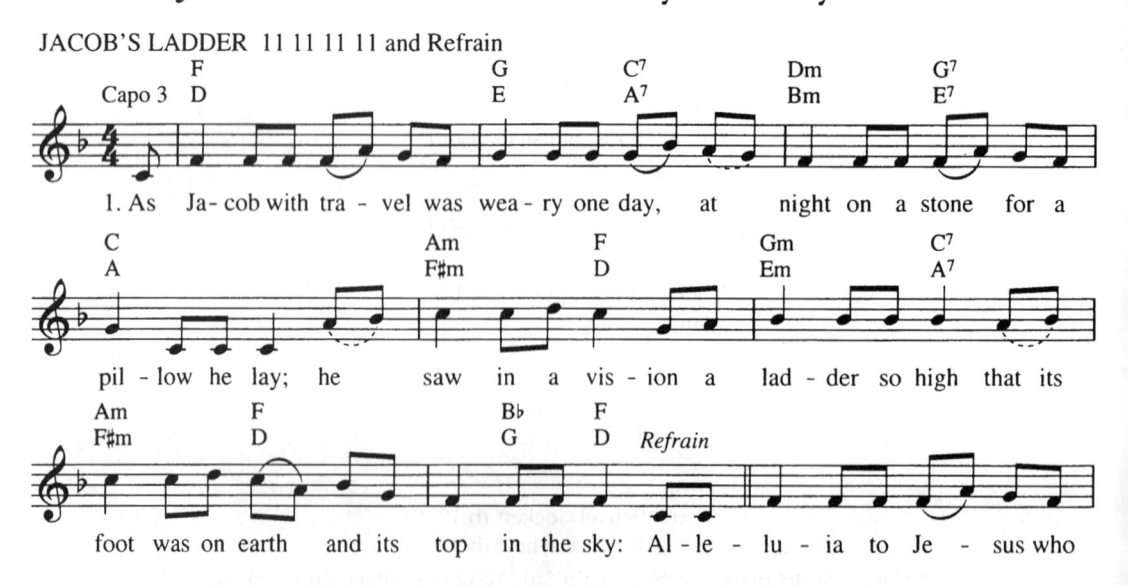

JACOB'S LADDER 11 11 11 11 and Refrain

1. As Ja-cob with tra-vel was wea-ry one day, at night on a stone for a pil-low he lay; he saw in a vis-ion a lad-der so high that its foot was on earth and its top in the sky:

Refrain

Al-le-lu-ia to Je-sus who

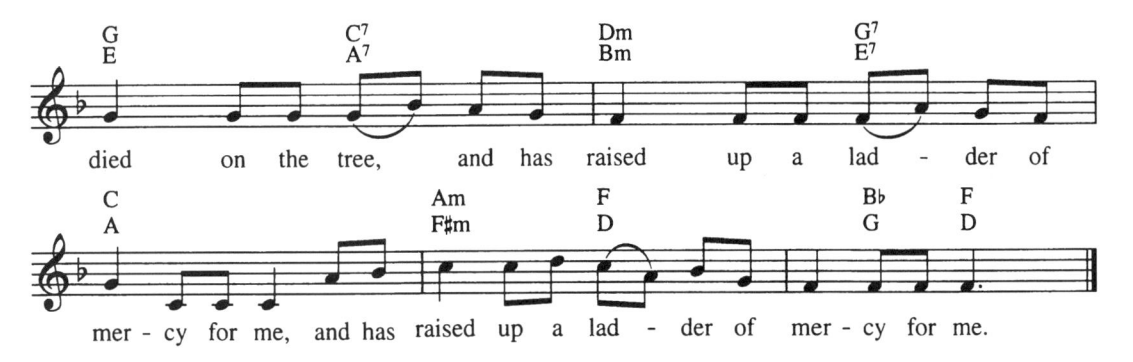

died on the tree, and has raised up a ladder of
mercy for me, and has raised up a ladder of mercy for me.

2. This ladder is long, it is strong and well-made,
has stood hundreds of years and is not yet decayed;
many millions have climbed it and reached Zion's hill,
and thousands by faith are climbing it still:

3. Come let us ascend! all may climb it who will;
for the angels of Jacob are guarding it still:
and remember, each step that by faith we pass o'er,
some prophet or martyr has trod it before:

4. And when we arrive at the haven of rest
we shall hear the glad words, 'Come up hither, ye blest,
here are regions of light, here are mansions of bliss.'
O who would not climb such a ladder as this?

Text: 18th century
Music: 18th century English carol melody

767 Be the centre of my life

1. Be the centre of my life, Lord Jesus, be the
centre of my life, I pray; be my Saviour to forgive me, be my
friend to be with me, be the centre of my life today!

2. Let the power of your presence, Lord Jesus,
from the centre of my life shine through;
oh, let ev'rybody know it,
I really want to show it,
that the centre of my life is you!

Text and Music: Alan J. Price

© Copyright 1990 Daybreak Music Ltd, Silverdale Road, Eastbourne, East Sussex BN20 7AB. Used by permission.

768 Caterpillar, caterpillar

1. Caterpillar, caterpillar, munching, munching, ate through a leaf or two, for caterpillar, caterpillar, munching, munching, didn't have a lot to do. But the leaves were very tasty, and there seemed a lot to spare, so caterpillar, caterpillar went on munching, munching ev'rywhere. me; for he took me as a caterpillar, and he made a butterfly of me.'

2. Caterpillar, caterpillar, feeling sleepy,
   fixed up a silken bed.
   Then caterpillar, caterpillar climbed inside
   and covered up his sleepy head.
   In the dark he slept and rested
   as the days and nights went by,
   till on a sunny morning when the silk bed burst,
   he was a butterfly!

3. Butterfly, oh butterfly, a-flitt'ring, flutt'ring;
   oh what a sight to see.
   And as the lovely butterfly was flutt'ring by,
   I heard him sing a song to me:
   'Oh I never knew God could do
   such a wondrous thing for me;
   for he took me as a caterpillar and he made
   a butterfly of me.'

Text and Music: Susan Sayers (b.1946)
© Copyright 1986 Kevin Mayhew Ltd.

769 Change my heart, O God

Change my heart, O God, make it ever true,
change my heart, O God,
may I be like you.
you.

You are the potter, I am the clay,
mould me and make me, this is what I pray.

Text and Music: Eddie Espinosa
© Copyright 1982 Mercy/Vineyard Publishing/Music Services. Administered by CopyCare, P.O. Box 77, Hailsham, East Sussex BN27 3EF, UK. Used by permission.

770 'Cheep!' said the sparrow
The birds' song

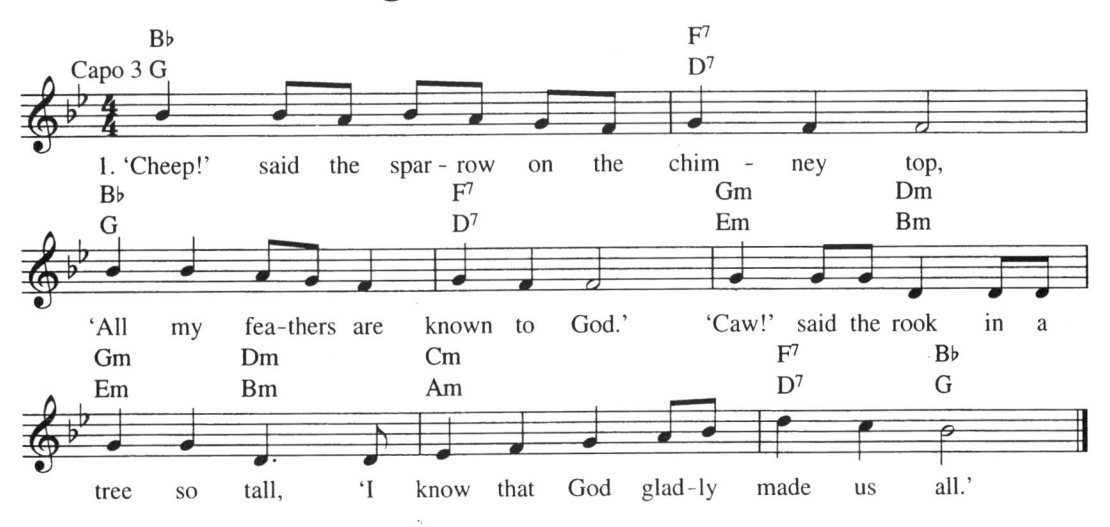

1. 'Cheep!' said the sparrow on the chimney top,
   'All my feathers are known to God.'
   'Caw!' said the rook in a tree so tall,
   'I know that God gladly made us all.'

2. 'Coo!' said the gentle one, the grey-blue dove,
   'I can tell you that God is love.'
   High up above sang the lark in flight,
   'I know the Lord is my heart's delight.'

3. 'Chirp!' said the robin with his breast so red,
   'I don't work at all, yet I'm fed.'
   'Whoo!' called the owl in a leafy wood,
   'Our God is wonderful, wise and good.'

Text and Music: Estelle White (b.1925)
© Copyright 1977 Kevin Mayhew Ltd.

771 Christ is our King

Refrain
Christ is our King, let the whole world rejoice! May all the nations sing out with one voice! Light of the world, you have helped us to see that we are one people and one day we all shall be free!

1. He came to open the eyes of the blind,
letting the sunlight pour into their minds.
Vision is waiting for those who have hope.
He is the light of the world.

2. He came to speak tender words to the poor,
he is the gateway and he is the door.
Riches are waiting for all those who hope.
He is the light of the world.

3. He came to open the doors of the gaol;
he came to help the downtrodden and frail.
Freedom is waiting for all those who hope.
He is the light of the world.

4. He came to open the lips of the mute,
letting them speak out with courage and truth.
His words are uttered by all those who hope.
He is the light of the world.

5. He came to heal all the crippled and lame,
sickness took flight at the sound of his name.
Vigour is waiting for all those who hope.
He is the light of the world.

6. He came to love everyone on this earth
and through his Spirit he promised rebirth.
New life is waiting for all those who hope.
He is the light of the world.

Text and Music: Estelle White (b.1925)
© Copyright 1976 Kevin Mayhew Ltd.

772 Clap your hands, all you people

Clap your hands, all you people. Shout to our God with a voice of triumph.
Clap your hands, all you people. Shout to our God with a voice of praise! Hosanna, hosanna. Shout to our God with a voice of triumph.
Praise him, praise him. Shout to our God with a voice of praise!

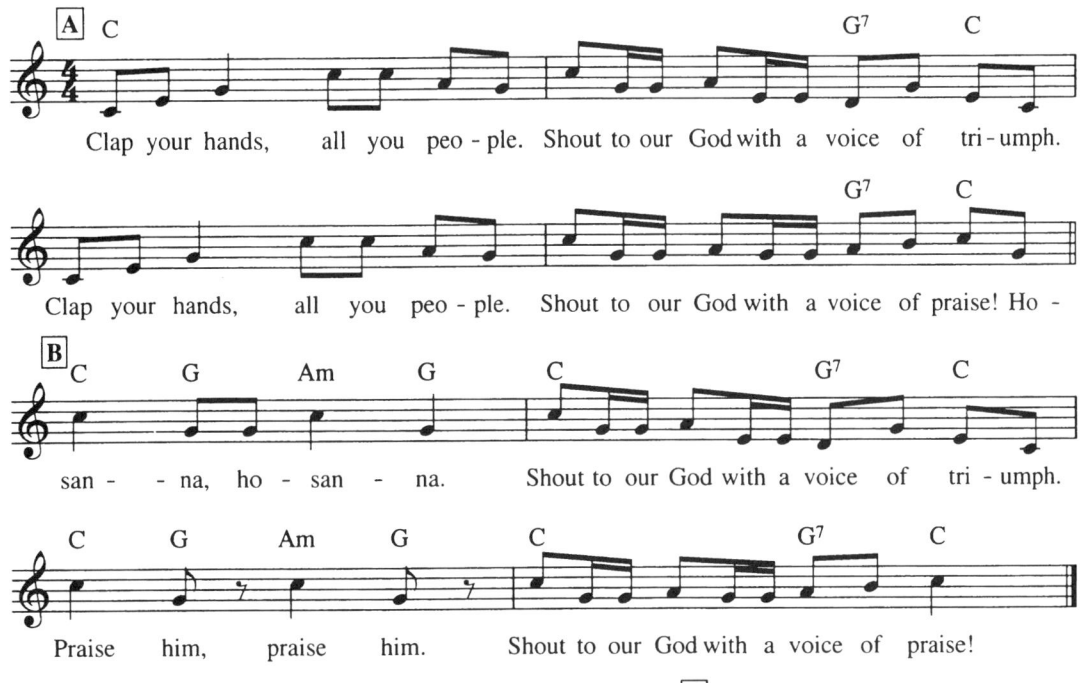

This can be sung as a round with the second voices entering at B

Text and Music: Jimmy Owens
© Copyright 1972 Bud John Songs/EMI Christian Music Publishing. Administered by CopyCare, P.O. Box 77, Hailsham, East Sussex BN27 3EF, UK. Used by permission.

773 Clap your hands and sing this song

MICHAEL ROW THE BOAT 74 74

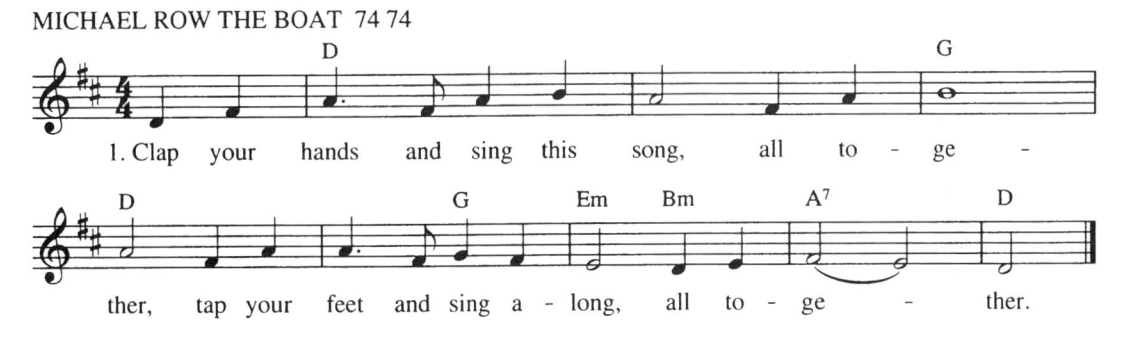

1. Clap your hands and sing this song, all together, tap your feet and sing along, all together.

2. Raise your hands up in the air, all together,
   God can reach you anywhere, all together.

3. Fold your arms across your chest, all together,
   in the arms of God you're blessed, all together.

4. Close your eyes and shut them tight, all together,
   God will keep you in his sight, all together.

5. Now sing softly, whisper low, all together,
   God will hear you even so, all together.

6. Sing out loud and strong and clear, all together,
   so that ev'ryone can hear, all together.

7. Sing with harmony and joy, all together,
   God loves ev'ry girl and boy, all together.

Text: Jean Holloway (b.1939)
Music: traditional
Text © Copyright 1997, 1999 Kevin Mayhew Ltd.

LITURGICAL
HYMNS OLD & NEW

774 Come and praise the Lord our King

MICHAEL ROW THE BOAT 74 74

1. Come and praise the Lord our King, al-le-lu-ia, come and praise the Lord our King, al-le-lu-ia!

2. Christ was born in Bethlehem, alleluia,
   Son of God and Son of Man, alleluia.

3. He grew up an earthly child, alleluia,
   in the world, but undefiled, alleluia.

4. He who died at Calvary, alleluia,
   rose again triumphantly, alleluia.

5. He will cleanse us from our sin, alleluia,
   if we live by faith in him, alleluia.

Text: unknown
Music: traditional melody

775 Come, God's children

MICHAEL ROW THE BOAT 74 74

1. Come, God's children, praise the Lord, al-le-lu-ia. He's our God, and we are his, al-le-lu-ia!

2. Come to him with songs of praise, alleluia,
   songs of praise, rejoice in him, alleluia.

3. For the Lord is a mighty God, alleluia,
   he is King of all the world, alleluia.

4. In his hands are valleys deep, alleluia,
   in his hands are mountain peaks, alleluia.

5. In his hands are all the seas, alleluia,
   and the lands which he has made, alleluia.

6. Praise the Father, praise the Son, alleluia,
   praise the Spirit, the Holy One, alleluia.

Text: unknown
Music: traditional melody

776 Come into his presence

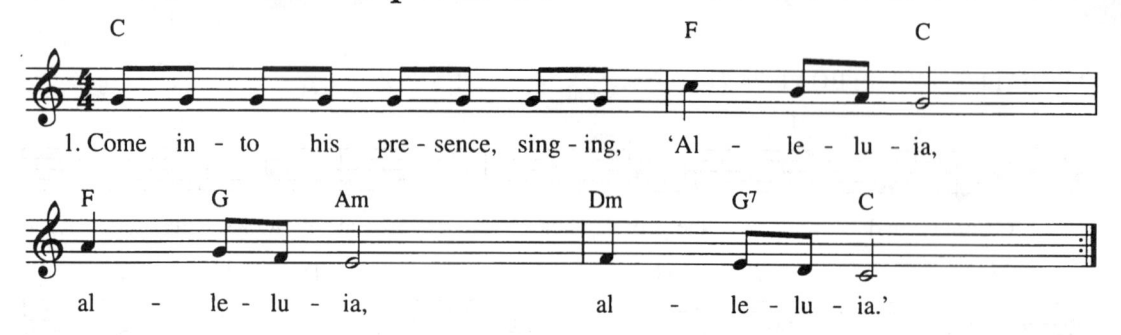

1. Come into his presence, singing, 'Alleluia, alleluia, alleluia.'

2. Come into his presence, singing,
   'Jesus is Lord, Jesus is Lord, Jesus is Lord.'
   Come into his presence, singing,
   'Jesus is Lord, Jesus is Lord, Jesus is Lord.'

3. Come into his presence, singing,
   'Glory to God, glory to God, glory to God.'
   Come into his presence, singing,
   'Glory to God, glory to God, glory to God.'

Text and Music: unknown

777 Come, they told me
The little drummer boy

1. Come, they told me, pah-rum-pum-pum-pum!
our new-born King to see, pah-rum-pum-pum-pum!
Our finest gifts we bring, pah-rum-pum-pum-pum!
to lay before the King, pah-rum-pum-pum-pum! Rum-pum-pum-pum!
Rum-pum-pum-pum! So, to honour him, pah-rum-pum-pum-pum!
when we come.

Last time repeat & fade

© Copyright 1941 EMI Mills Music Inc./Delaware Music Corp, USA.
Worldwide print rights controlled by Warner Bros. Inc., USA/IMP Ltd.
Used by permission of IMP Ltd, Griffin House, 161 Hammersmith Road, London W6 8BS.

2. Baby Jesus, pah-rum-pum-pum-pum!
   I am a poor child too, pah-rum-pum-pum-pum!
   I have no gift to bring, pah-rum-pum-pum-pum!
   that's fit to give a King, pah-rum-pum-pum-pum!
   Rum-pum-pum-pum! Rum-pum-pum-pum!
   Shall I play for you, pah-rum-pum-pum-pum!
   on my drum?

3. Mary nodded, pah-rum-pum-pum-pum!
   The ox and lamb kept time, pah-rum-pum-pum-pum!
   I played my drum for him, pah-rum-pum-pum-pum!
   I played my best for him, pah-rum-pum-pum-pum!
   Rum-pum-pum-pum! Rum-pum-pum-pum!
   Then he smiled at me, pah-rum-pum-pum-pum!
   me and my drum.

Text and Music: Katherine K. Davis, Henry V. Onorati and Harry Simeone

778 Dear child divine

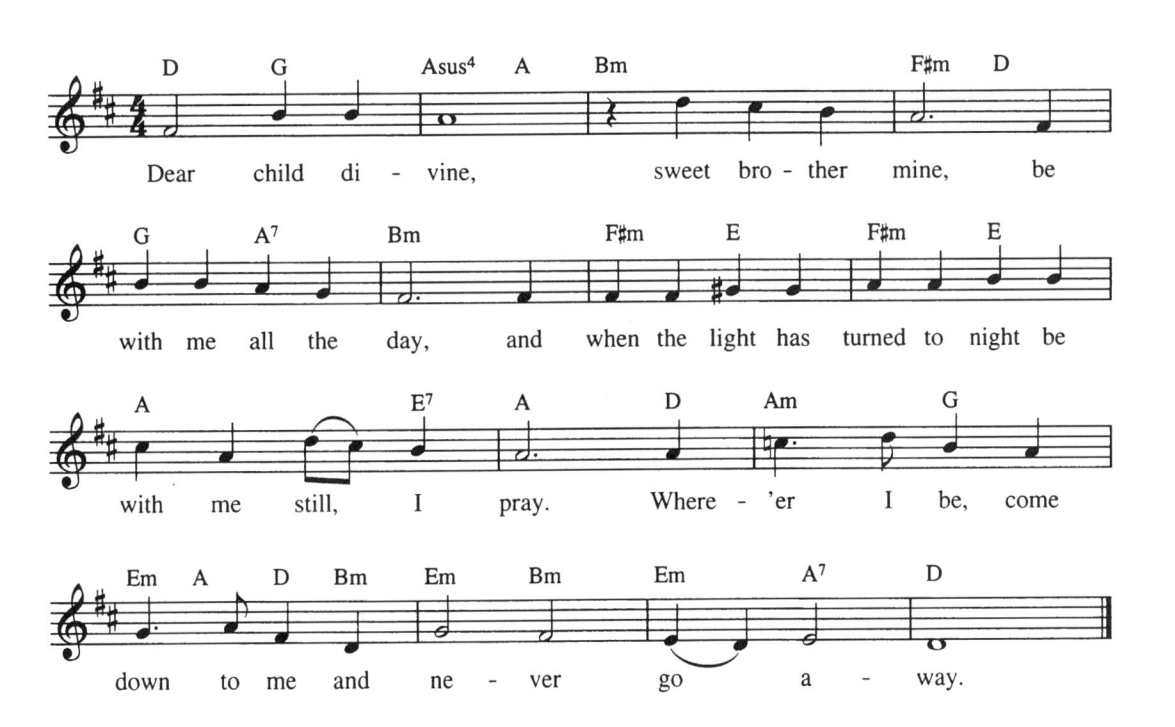

Dear child di-vine, sweet bro-ther mine, be with me all the day, and when the light has turned to night be with me still, I pray. Where-'er I be, come down to me and ne-ver go a-way.

Text: unknown
Music: Alan Rees (b.1941)
Music © Copyright Belmont Abbey Trustees, Belmont Abbey, Hereford HR2 9RZ. Used by permission.

779 Do not worry over what to eat

Do not wor-ry o-ver what to eat, what to wear or put up-on your feet; trust and pray, go do your best to-day, then leave it in the hands of the Lord, leave it in the hands of the Lord.

1. The li-lies of the field, they do not spin or weave, yet Sol-o-mon was not ar-rayed like one of these. The birds of the air, they do not sow or reap, but God tends to them like a shep-herd tends his sheep.

2. The Lord will guide you in his hidden way,
show you what to do and tell you what to say.
When you pray for rain, go build a dam to store
ev'ry drop of water you have asked him for.

3. The Lord knows all your needs before you ask.
Only trust in him for he will do the task
of bringing in your life whatever you must know.
He'll lead you through the darkness wherever you must go.

Text and Music: Sebastian Temple (1928-1998)
© Copyright control.

780 Don't build your house on the sandy land

Don't build your house on the san - dy land, don't build it too near the shore. Well, it might look kind of nice, but you'll have to build it twice, oh, you'll have to build your house once more. You'd bet-ter build your house up - on a rock, make a good foun - da - tion on a sol - id spot. Oh, the storms may come and go but the peace of God you will know.

This song can be sung as a round with the second voice entering at B

Text and Music: Karen Lafferty

© Copyright 1981 Maranatha! Music. Administered by CopyCare, P.O. Box 77, Hailsham, East Sussex BN27 3EF, UK.
Used by permission

781 Do what you know is right

Brightly

Leader Do what you know is right. *All* Do what you know is right. *Leader* Do what you know is good. *All* Do what is good. If no one else does it, don't be a - fraid. Je - sus says, 'I am with you al - ways.'

Text and Music: Bev Gammon

© Copyright 1988 Kingsway's Thankyou Music, P.O. Box 75, Eastbourne, East Sussex BN23 6NW, UK.
Used by permission.

782 Each of us is a living stone
Living stones

Brightly (swinging)

Each of us is a living stone, no one needs to stand a-lone,
joined to o-ther liv-ing stones, we're build-ing the tem-ple of God. *Fine*

1. We're build-ing, we're build-ing the tem-ple of God on earth, but it
needs no walls or stee - ple, for we're ma-king a house of grea-ter worth, we're
build - ing it with peo - ple! *D.C.*

2. The stone that, the stone that the builders once cast aside
has been made the firm foundation,
and the carpenter who was crucified
now offers us salvation.

Text: Michael Forster (b.1946)
Music: James Patten (b.1936)
© Copyright 1997 Kevin Mayhew Ltd.

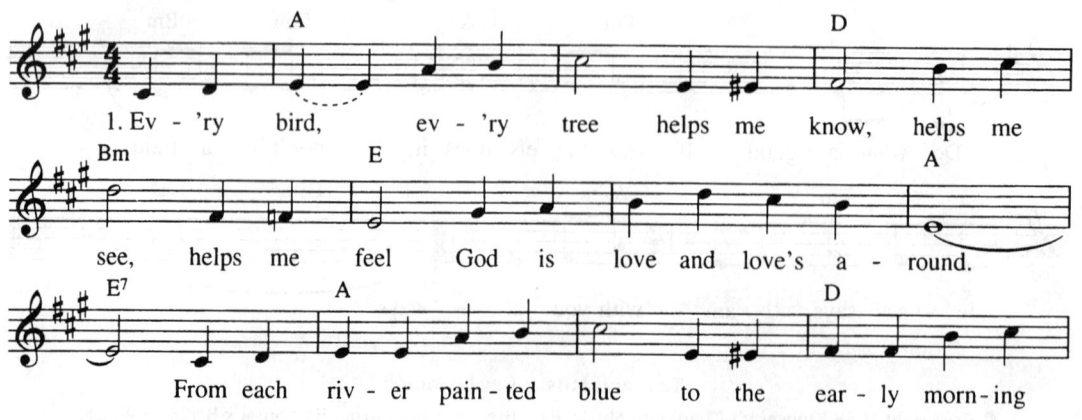

783 Every bird, every tree

1. Ev-'ry bird, ev-'ry tree helps me know, helps me
see, helps me feel God is love and love's a - round.
From each riv-er pain-ted blue to the ear-ly morn-ing

© Copyright 1978 Kevin Mayhew Ltd.

dew this is love, God is love, love's a-round.

2. Ev'ry prayer, ev'ry song
makes me feel I belong
to a world filled
with love that's all around.
From each daybreak to each night,
out of darkness comes the light,
this is love, God is love, love's around.

3. Ev'ry mountain, ev'ry stream,
ev'ry flower, ev'ry dream
comes from God,
God is love and love's around.
From the ever-changing sky
to a new-born baby's cry,
this is love, God is love, love's around.

Text and Music: Peter Watcyn-Jones

784 Father welcomes all his children

Fa-ther wel-comes all his chil-dren to his fam-'ly through his Son. Fa-ther giv-ing his sal-va-tion, life for e-ver has been won. won.

1. Lit-tle chil-dren, come to me, for my king-dom is of these.
Love and new life have I to give, par-don for your sin.

2. In the water, in the word,
in his promise, be assured:
all who believe and are baptised
shall be born again.

3. Let us daily die to sin;
let us daily rise with him –
walk in the love of Christ our Lord,
live in the peace of God.

Text and Music: Robin Mann
© Copyright 1986 Kevin Mayhew Ltd.

785 Fishes of the ocean

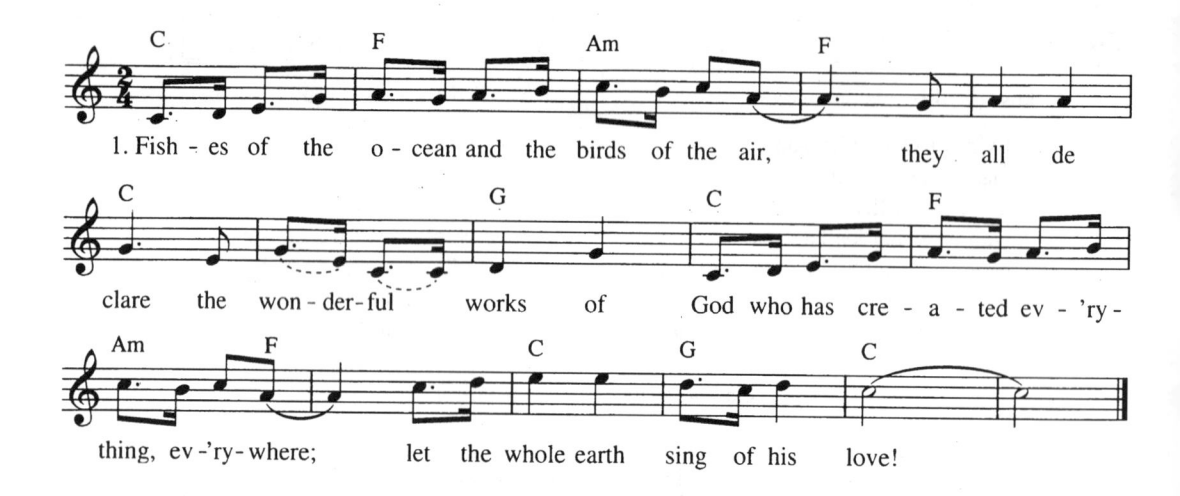

1. Fishes of the ocean and the birds of the air,
they all declare the wonderful works of God
who has created ev-'ry-thing, ev'rywhere;
let the whole earth sing of his love!

2. Apples in the orchard and the corn in the field,
the plants all yield their fruit in due season,
so the generosity of God is revealed;
let the whole earth sing of his love!

3. Energy and colour from the sun with its light,
the moon by night; the patterns of the stars
all winking in the darkness on a frosty cold night;
let the whole earth sing of his love!

4. Muddy hippopotamus and dainty gazelle,
the mice as well, are of his making,
furry ones and hairy ones and some with a shell;
let the whole earth sing of his love!

5. All that we can hear and ev'rything we can see,
including me, we all of us spring from God
who cares for ev'rybody unendingly;
let the whole earth sing of his love!

Text and Music: Susan Sayers (b.1946)
© Copyright 1986 Kevin Mayhew Ltd.

786 Forward in faith

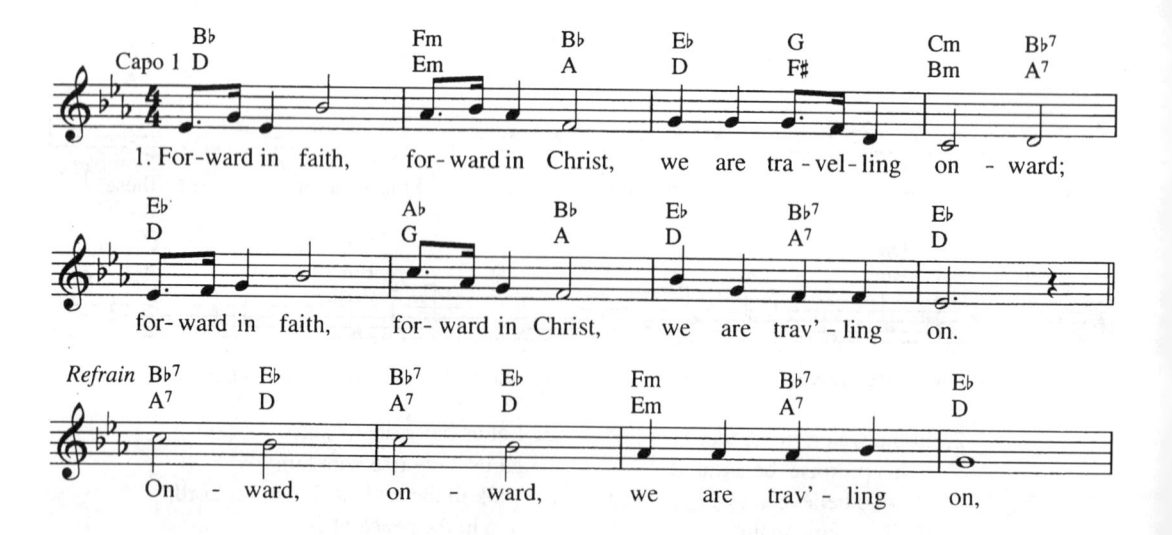

1. Forward in faith, forward in Christ, we are travelling onward;
forward in faith, forward in Christ, we are trav'ling on.

Refrain
Onward, onward, we are trav'ling on,

© Copyright 1983 Palm Tree Press Ltd, assigned 1984 to Kevin Mayhew Ltd.

on - ward, on - ward, we are trav' - ling on. on.

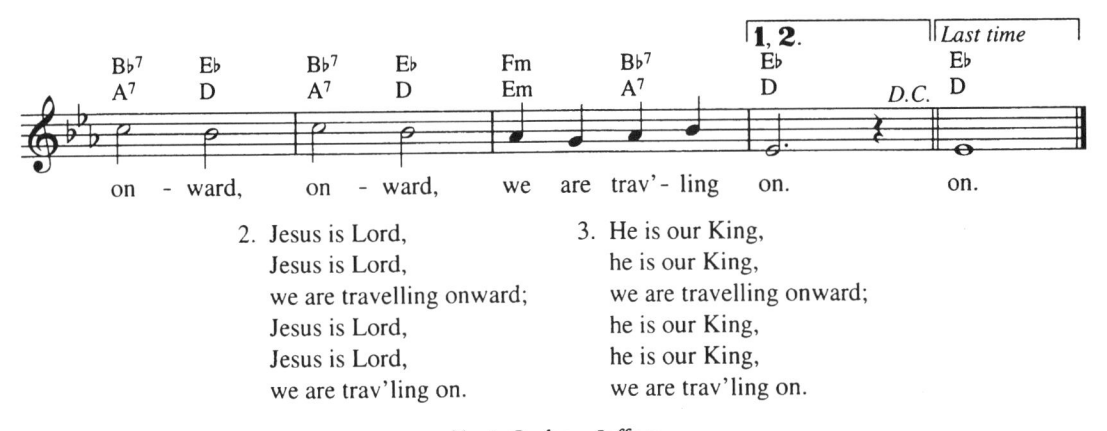

2. Jesus is Lord,
Jesus is Lord,
we are travelling onward;
Jesus is Lord,
Jesus is Lord,
we are trav'ling on.

3. He is our King,
he is our King,
we are travelling onward;
he is our King,
he is our King,
we are trav'ling on.

Text: Graham Jeffery
Music: Kevin Mayhew (b.1942)

787 Friends, all gather here in a circle
Circle of friends

Friends, all ga - ther here in a cir - cle. It has no be - gin - ning and it has no end.
Face to face, we all have a place in God's own cir - cle of friends.
Hey there, *(name)*! How do you do? Who's that friend sit - ting close to you?
Thank the Lord, for *(name)* has a place in the cir - cle too.
Take a look a - round. Find some - one near. Take her/him by the hand, say,
'Glad you're here.' We're to - ge - ther and when we've gone, God's
love like a cir - cle rolls on and on and on.

Text and Music: David Morstad
© Copyright control

788 Give me peace, O Lord

1. Give me peace, O Lord, I pray, in my work and in my play; and inside my heart and mind, Lord, give me peace.

2. Give peace to the world, I pray
let all quarrels cease today.
May we spread your light and love:
Lord, give us peace.

Text and Music: Estelle White (b.1925)
© Copyright 1976 Kevin Mayhew Ltd.

789 God almighty set a rainbow

1. God almighty set a rainbow arching in the sky above, and his people understand it as a signal of his love.

Refrain after each verse:

Thank you, Father, thank you, Father,
thank you, Father, for your care,
for your warm and loving kindness
to your people ev'rywhere.

2. Clouds will gather, storms come streaming
on the darkened earth below –
too much sunshine makes a desert,
without rain no seed can grow.

3. Through the stormcloud shines your rainbow,
through the dark earth springs the wheat.
In the future waits your harvest
and the food for all to eat.

4. God almighty, you have promised
after rain the sun will show;
bless the seeds and bless the harvest.
Give us grace to help us grow.

Text: Caroline Somerville
Music: traditional melody
Text © Copyright 1976 The Central Board of Finance of the Church of England, Church House, Great Smith Street, London SW1P 3NZ. Used by permission from 'Together for Harvest' (CIO, 1976)

790 God gives his people strength

1. God gives his people strength.
   If we believe in his way
   he's swift to repay
   all those who bear the burden of the day.
   God gives his people strength.

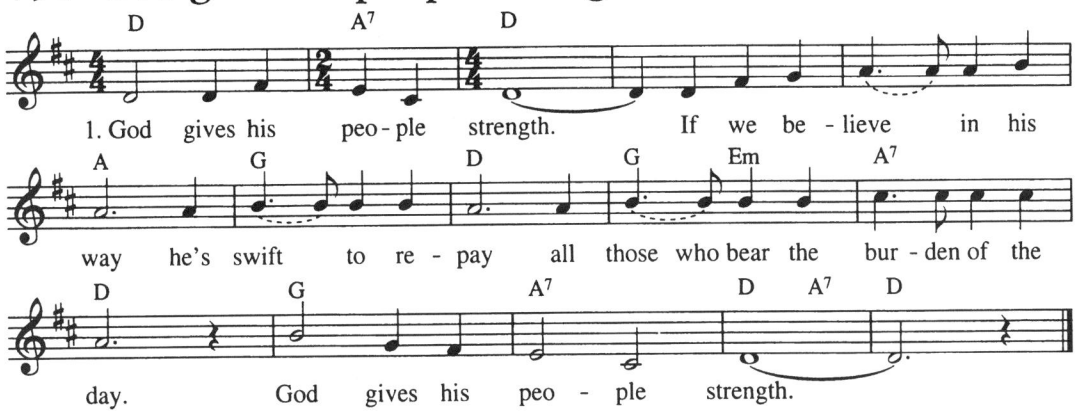

2. God gives his people hope.
   If we but trust in his word
   our prayers are always heard.
   He warmly welcomes anyone who's erred.
   God gives his people hope.

3. God gives his people love.
   If we but open wide our heart
   he's sure to do his part.
   He's always the first to make a start.
   God gives his people love.

4. God gives his people peace.
   When sorrow fills us to the brim
   and courage grows dim
   he lays to rest our restlessness in him.
   God gives his people peace.

Text and Music: Miriam Therèse Winter
© Copyright 1965 Medical Mission Sisters, 92 Sherman Street, Hartford, CT 06105, USA.
Used by permission.

791 God our Father gave us life

1. God our Father gave us life,
   he keeps us in his care;
   help us care for others too:
   Lord, hear our prayer;
   Lord, hear our prayer.

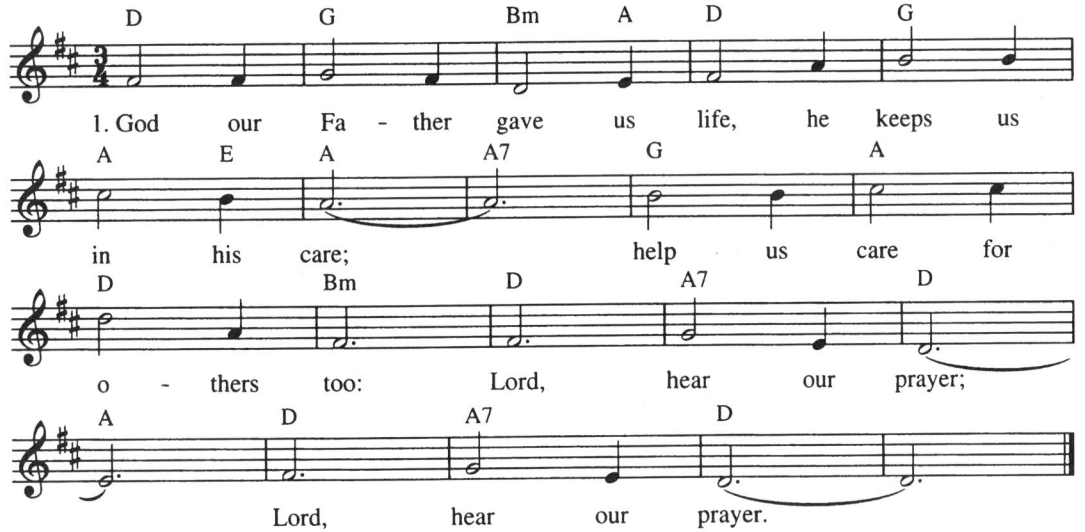

2. When we're frightened, hurt or tired,
   there's always someone there.
   Make us thankful for their love:
   Lord, hear our prayer;
   Lord, hear our prayer.

3. All God's children need his love,
   a love that we can share.
   So, we pray for ev'ryone:
   Lord, hear our prayer;
   Lord, hear our prayer.

Text and Music: Kathleen Middleton
© Copyright 1986 Kevin Mayhew Ltd.

792 God sends a rainbow
Colours of hope

1. God sends a rainbow after the rain,
colours of hope gleaming through pain;
bright arcs of red and indigo light,
making creation hopeful and bright.

Refrain
Colours of hope dance in the sun,
while it yet rains the hope has begun;
colours of hope shine through the rain,
colours of love, nothing is vain.

2. When we are lonely, when we're afraid,
though it seems dark, rainbows are made;
even when life itself has to end,
God is our rainbow, God is our friend.

3. Where people suffer pain or despair,
God can be seen in those who care;
even where war and hatred abound,
rainbows of hope are still to be found.

4. People themselves like rainbows are made,
colours of hope in us displayed;
old ones and young ones, women and men,
all can be part of love's great 'Amen'!

Text: Michael Forster (b.1946)
Music: Christopher Tambling (b.1964)
© Copyright 1997 Kevin Mayhew Ltd.

793 God turned darkness into light

1. God turned darkness into light,
   separated day from night,
   looked upon it with delight,
   and declared that it was good.

Refrain
God was pleased with ev'rything,
God was pleased with ev'rything,
God was pleased with ev'rything,
and declared that it was good.

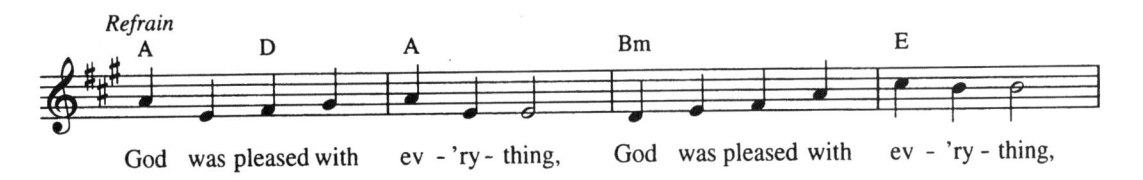

2. God divided land and sea,
   filled the world with plants and trees,
   all so beautiful to see,
   and declared that it was good.

3. God made animals galore,
   fishes, birds and dinosaurs,
   heard the splashes, songs and roars,
   and declared that it was good.

4. God made people last of all,
   black and white, and short and tall,
   male and female, large and small,
   and declared that it was good.

Text: Michael Forster (b.1946)
Music: Christopher Tambling (b.1964)
© Copyright 1997 Kevin Mayhew Ltd.

794 Goliath was big and Goliath was strong
Biggest isn't always best

With vigour

1. Goliath was big and Goliath was strong,
   his sword was sharp and his spear was long;
   he bragged and boasted but he was wrong:
   biggest isn't always best!

   Refrain
   Biggest isn't always best!
   Biggest isn't always best!
   God told David,
   'Don't be afraid, biggest isn't always best!'

2. A shepherd boy had a stone and sling;
   he won the battle and pleased the King!
   Then all the people began to sing:
   'Biggest isn't always best!'

3. So creatures made in a smaller size,
   like tiny sparrows and butterflies,
   are greater than we may realise:
   biggest isn't always best!

Text: Michael Forster (b.1946)
Music: Christopher Tambling (b.1964)
© Copyright 1993 Kevin Mayhew Ltd.

795 Hail, Mary, full of grace

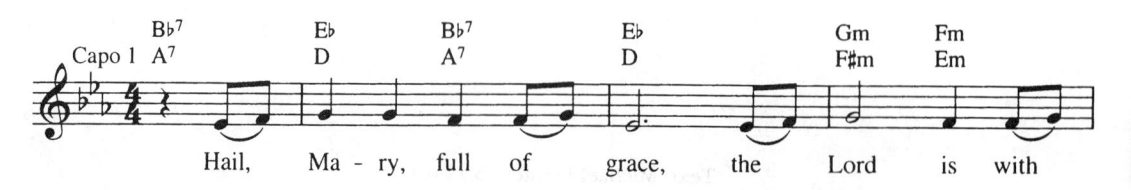

Hail, Mary, full of grace, the Lord is with

Music © Copyright 1986 Kevin Mayhew Ltd.

thee. Blessed art thou among women, and blessed is the fruit of thy womb, Jesus. Holy Mary, mother of God, pray for us sinners, now and at the hour of our death. Amen.

Text: Luke 1:28
Music: Julian Wiener

796 Hallelu, hallelu

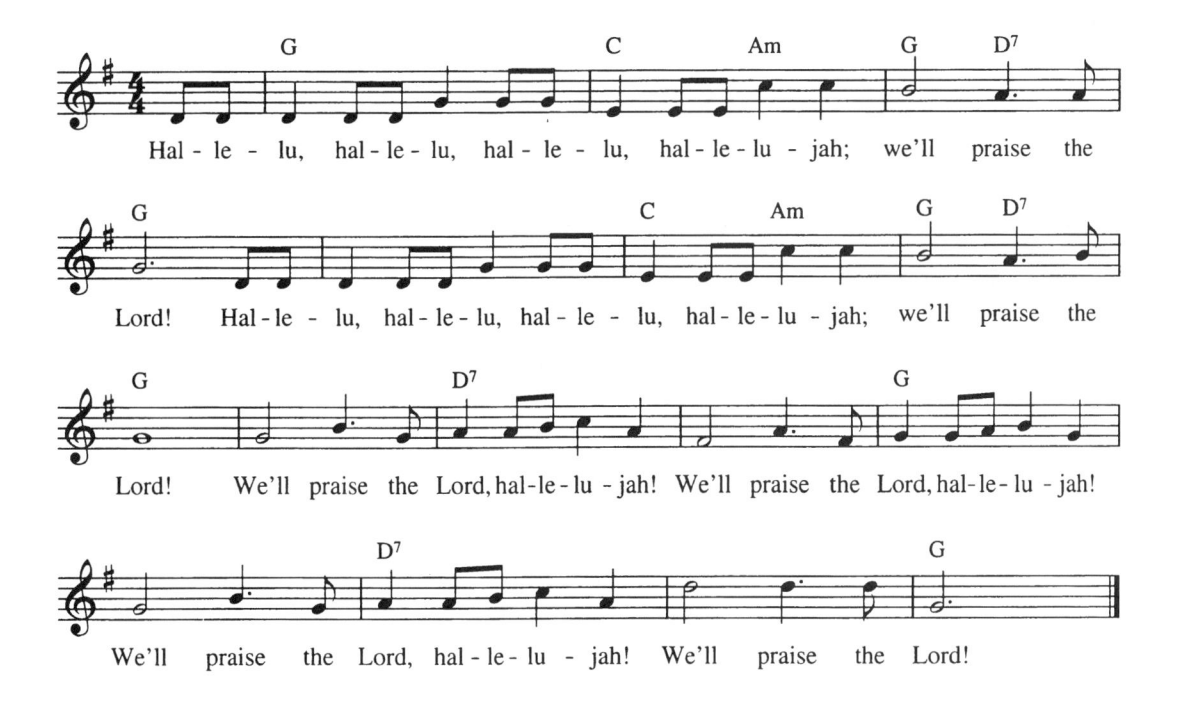

Hallelu, hallelu, hallelu, hallelujah; we'll praise the Lord! Hallelu, hallelu, hallelu, hallelujah; we'll praise the Lord! We'll praise the Lord, hallelujah! We'll praise the Lord, hallelujah! We'll praise the Lord, hallelujah! We'll praise the Lord!

Text and Music: unknown

797 Have you heard the raindrops
Water of life

1. Have you heard the raindrops drumming on the rooftops?
   Have you heard the raindrops dripping on the ground?
   Have you heard the raindrops splashing in the streams and
   running to the rivers all around?

   Refrain:
   There's water, water of life,
   Jesus gives us the water of life;
   there's water, water of life,
   Jesus gives us the water of life.

2. There's a busy worker digging in the desert,
   digging with a spade that flashes in the sun;
   soon there will be water rising in the well-shaft,
   spilling from the bucket as it comes.

3. Nobody can live who hasn't any water,
   when the land is dry, then nothing much grows;
   Jesus gives us life if we drink the living water,
   sing it so that ev'rybody knows.

Text and Music: Christian Strover
© Copyright Christian Strover/Jubilate Hymns, 4 Thorne Park Road, Chelston, Torquay TQ2 6RX, UK.
Used by permission.

798 He is the King

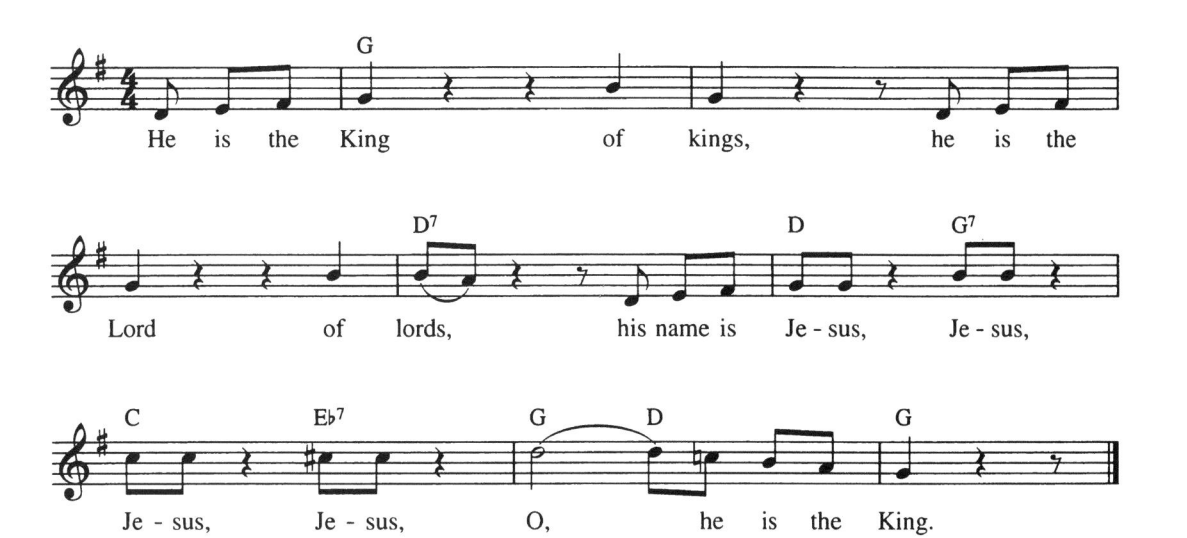

He is the King of kings, he is the Lord of lords, his name is Jesus, Jesus, Jesus, Jesus, O, he is the King.

Text and Music: unknown
This arrangement © Copyright 1999 Kevin Mayhew Ltd.

799 Hey, now, everybody sing

Hey, now, ev-'ry-bo-dy sing, ev-'ry-bo-dy sing to the Lord our God!
Hey, now, ev-'ry-bo-dy sing, ev-'ry-bo-dy sing to the Lord our God!
Ev-'ry-bo-dy join in a song of praise, come and sing a-long with me!
Glo-ry, al-le-lu-ia, glo-ry, al-le-lu-ia, I'm so glad I'm free!
Hey, now, ev-'ry-bo-dy sing, ev-'ry-bo-dy sing to the Lord our God!
Hey, now, ev-'ry-bo-dy sing, ev-'ry-bo-dy sing to the Lord our God!
Ev-'ry-bo-dy sing, ev-'ry-bo-dy sing, ev-'ry-bo-dy sing to the Lord our God!
Ev-'ry-bo-dy sing, ev-'ry-bo-dy sing, ev-'ry-bo-dy sing to the Lord our God!
Ev-'ry-bo-dy sing!

Text and Music: Orien Johnson

© Copyright 1982 Fred Bock Music Company. Administered by Kingsway's Thankyou Music, P.O. Box 75, Eastbourne, East Sussex BN23 6NW, UK. Europe (excl. Germany) & British Commonwealth (excl. Canada). Used by permission.

800 If I were a butterfly

1. If I were a butterfly, I'd thank you, Lord, for giving me wings, and if I were a robin in a tree, I'd thank you, Lord, that I could sing, and if I were a fish in the sea, I'd wiggle my tail and I'd giggle with glee, but I just thank you, Father, for making me 'me'.

Refrain
For you gave me a heart, and you gave me a smile, you gave me Jesus and you made me your child, and I just thank you, Father, for making me 'me'.

2. If I were an elephant,
   I'd thank you, Lord, by raising my trunk,
   and if I were a kangaroo,
   you know I'd hop right up to you,
   and if I were an octopus,
   I'd thank you, Lord, for my fine looks,
   but I just thank you, Father, for making me 'me'.

3. If I were a wiggly worm,
   I'd thank you, Lord, that I could squirm,
   and if I were a billy goat,
   I'd thank you, Lord, for my strong throat,
   and if I were a fuzzy wuzzy bear,
   I'd thank you, Lord, for my fuzzy wuzzy hair,
   but I just thank you, Father, for making me 'me'.

Text and Music: Brian Howard

© Copyright 1975 Mission Hills Music. Administered by CopyCare, P.O. Box 77, Hailsham, East Sussex BN27 3EF, UK. Used by permission.

801 I give my hands

1. I give my hands to do your work and, Jesus Lord, I give them willingly. I give my feet to go your way and ev'ry step I shall take cheerfully,

Refrain
O, the joy of the Lord is my strength, my strength! O, the joy of the Lord is my help, my help! For the pow'r of his Spirit is in my soul and the joy of the Lord is my strength.

2. I give my eyes to see the world
   and ev'ryone, in just the way you do.
   I give my tongue to speak your words,
   to spread your name and freedom-giving truth.

3. I give my mind in ev'ry way
   so that each thought I have will come from you.
   I give my spirit to you, Lord,
   and every day my prayer will spring anew.

4. I give my heart that you may love
   in me your Father and the human race.
   I give myself that you may grow
   in me and make my life a song of praise.

Text and Music: Estelle White (b.1925)
© Copyright 1978 Kevin Mayhew Ltd.

802 I'm black, I'm white, I'm short, I'm tall

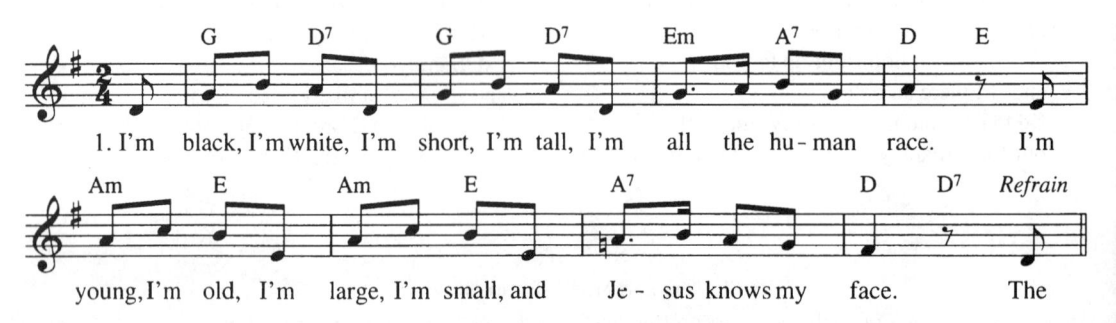

1. I'm black, I'm white, I'm short, I'm tall, I'm all the human race. I'm young, I'm old, I'm large, I'm small, and Jesus knows my face. The

© Copyright 1993 Kevin Mayhew Ltd.

love of God is free to ev-'ry-one, free to ev-'ry-one, free to ev-'ry-one.
The love of God is free, oh yes! That's what the gos-pel says.

2. I'm rich, I'm poor, I'm pleased, I'm sad,
I'm ev'ry-one you see.
I'm quick, I'm slow, I'm good, I'm bad,
I know that God loves me.

3. So tall and thin, and short and wide,
and any shade of face,
I'm one of those for whom Christ died,
part of the human race.

Text: Michael Forster (b.1946)
Music: Christopher Tambling (b.1964)

803 In the upper room
You must do for others

1. In the up-per room, Je-sus and his friends
met to ce-le-brate their fi-nal sup-per.
Je-sus took a bowl, knelt to wash their feet, told them:
'You must do for o-thers as I do for you.'

2. Peter was annoyed: 'This will never do!
You, as Master, should not play the servant!'
Jesus took a towel, knelt to dry their feet, told them:
'You must do for others as I do for you.'

Text and Music: Gerard Fitzpatrick
© Copyright 1986 Kevin Mayhew Ltd.

804 Isn't it good

Isn't it good to be together, being with friends old and new? Isn't it good? The Bible tells us Jesus our Lord is here too! Isn't it good to be together, being with friends old and new? Isn't it good the Bible tells us Jesus our Lord is here too! He's here! By his Spirit he's with us. He's here! His promise is true. He's here! Though we can't see him, he's here for me and you. He's here! By his Spirit he's with us. He's here! His promise is true. He's here! Though we can't see him, he's here for me and you.

Text and Music: Alan J. Price

© Copyright 1992 Daybreak Music Ltd., Silverdale Road, Eastbourne, East Sussex BN20 7AB. Used by permission.

805 It's me, O Lord

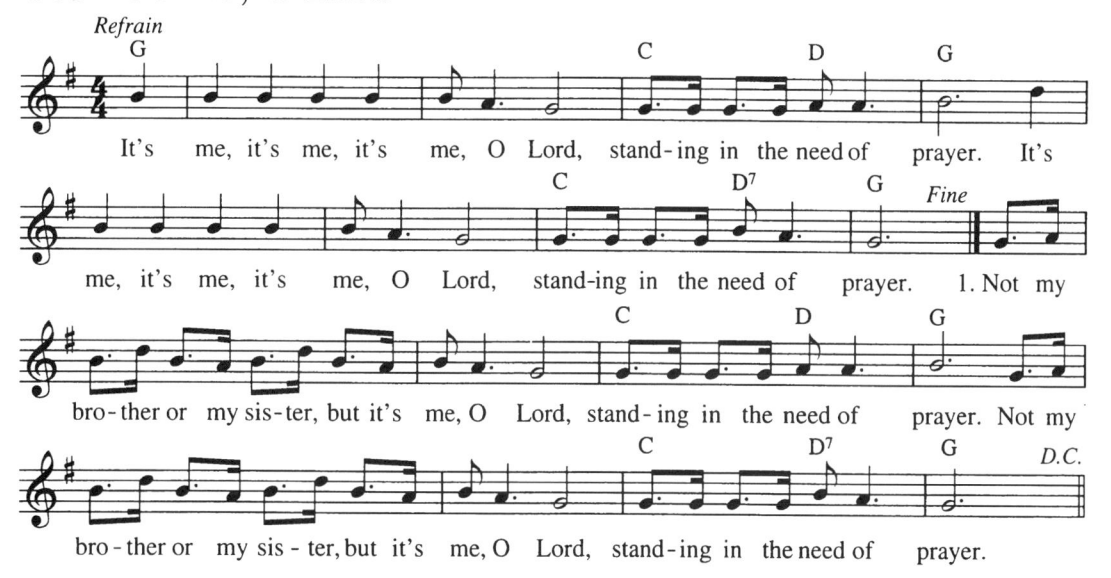

Refrain

It's me, it's me, it's me, O Lord, standing in the need of prayer. It's me, it's me, it's me, O Lord, standing in the need of prayer. *Fine*

1. Not my brother or my sister, but it's me, O Lord, standing in the need of prayer. Not my brother or my sister, but it's me, O Lord, standing in the need of prayer. *D.C.*

    2. Not my mother or my father,
       but it's me, O Lord,
       standing in the need of prayer.
       Not my mother or my father,
       but it's me, O Lord,
       standing in the need of prayer.

    3. Not the stranger or my neighbour,
       but it's me, O Lord,
       standing in the need of prayer.
       Not the stranger or my neighbour,
       but it's me, O Lord,
       standing in the need of prayer.

Text and Music: Spiritual

806 I've got peace like a river

1. I've got peace like a river, I've got peace like a river, I've got peace like a river in my soul.

Last time: I've got ocean in my soul.

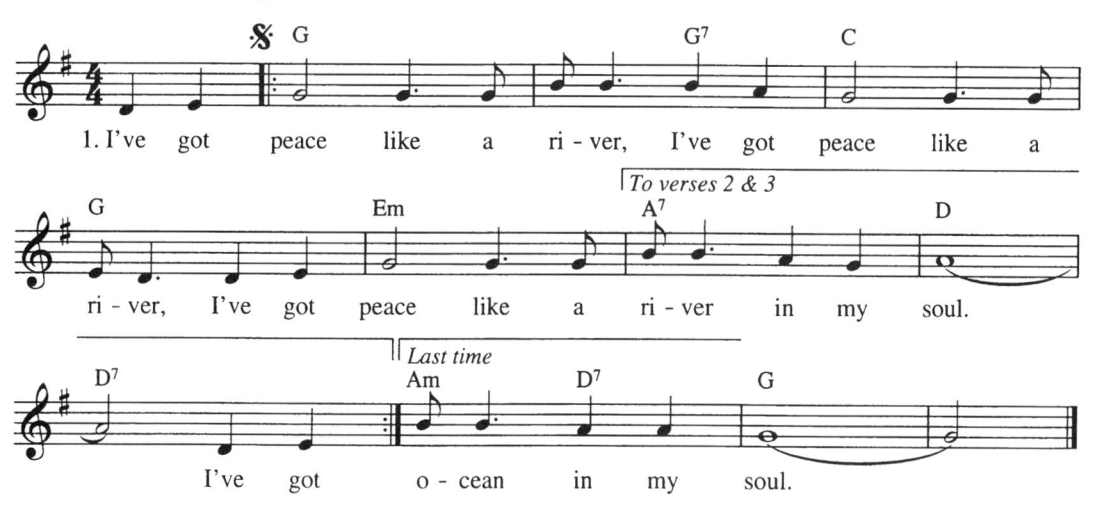

    2. I've got joy like a fountain,
       I've got joy like a fountain,
       I've got joy like a fountain in my soul.

    3. I've got love like an ocean,
       I've got love like an ocean,
       I've got love like an ocean in my soul.

Text and Music: Spiritual

LITURGICAL
HYMNS OLD & NEW

807 I will wave my hands

I will wave my hands in praise and a-dor-a-tion, I will wave my hands in praise and a-dor-a-tion, I will wave my hands in praise and a-dor-a-tion, praise and a-dor-a-tion to the liv-ing God. For he's gi-ven me hands that just love clap-ping: one, two, one, two, three; and he's gi-ven me a voice that just loves shout-ing, 'Hal-le-lu-jah!' He's gi-ven me feet that just love danc-ing: one, two, one, two, three; and he's put me in a be-ing that has no trou-ble see-ing that what-ever I am feel-ing he is wor-thy to be praised. wor-thy to be praised.

Text and Music: Ian Smale

© Copyright 1985 Kingsway's Thankyou Music, P.O. Box 75, Eastbourne, East Sussex BN23 6NW, UK.
Used by permission.

808 Jesus had all kinds of friends

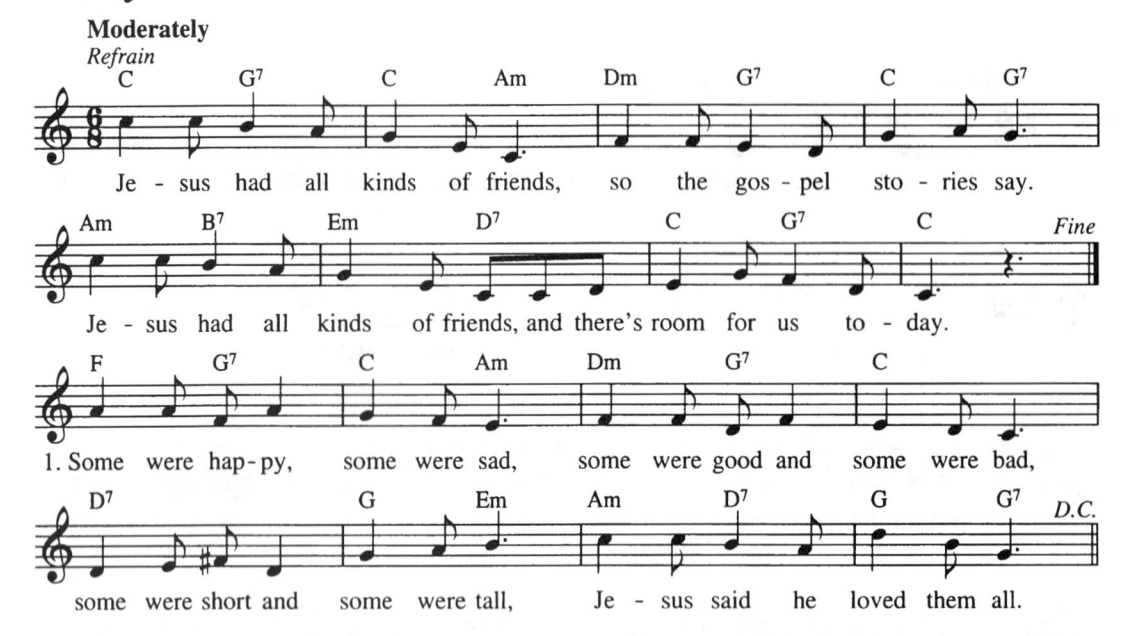

Moderately

Refrain

Je-sus had all kinds of friends, so the gos-pel sto-ries say.

Je-sus had all kinds of friends, and there's room for us to-day.

1. Some were hap-py, some were sad, some were good and some were bad, some were short and some were tall, Je-sus said he loved them all.

2. Some were humble, some were proud,
   some were quiet, some were loud,
   some were fit and some were lame,
   Jesus loved them all the same.

3. Some were healthy, some were sick,
   some were slow and some were quick,
   some were clever, some were not,
   Jesus said he loved the lot!

Text: Michael Forster (b.1946)
Music: Christopher Tambling (b.1964)
© Copyright 1993 Kevin Mayhew Ltd.

809 Jesus is greater

Capo 5 C

Je-sus is great-er than the great-est he-roes, Je-sus is clo-ser than the clo-sest friends. He came from hea-ven and he died to save us, to show us love that ne-ver ends. Son of God, and the Lord of glo-ry, he's the light, fol-low in

© Copyright 1992 Sea Dream Music, P.O. Box 13533, London E7 0SG.
Used by permission.

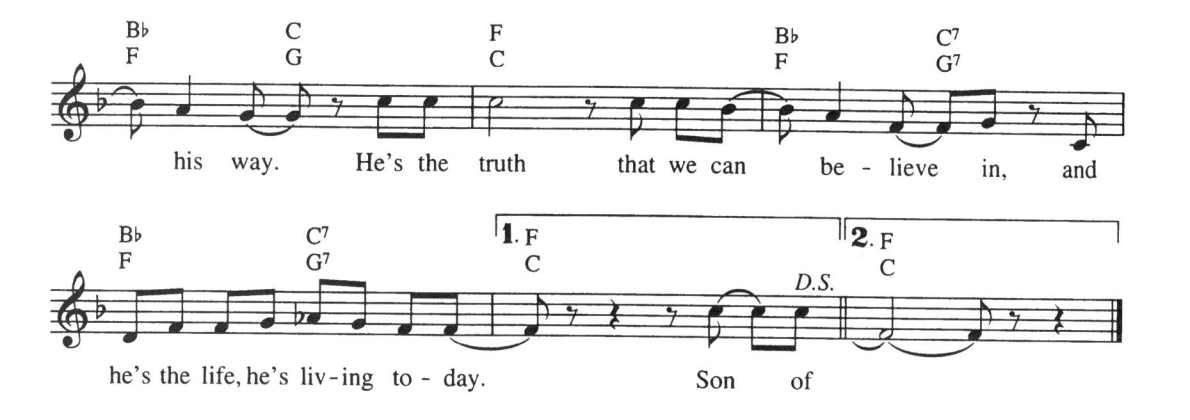

his way. He's the truth that we can be-lieve in, and he's the life, he's liv-ing to-day. Son of

1. F
2. F

D.S.

Text and Music: Gill Hutchinson

810 Jesus put this song

'Hebrew' style, getting faster

1. Je-sus put this song in-to our hearts, Je-sus put this song in-to our hearts; it's a song of joy no one can take a-way. Je-sus put this song in-to our hearts.

3. dance.

Each verse should be sung faster

2. Jesus taught us how to live in harmony,
   Jesus taught us how to live in harmony;
   diff'rent faces, diff'rent races, he made us one.
   Jesus taught us how to live in harmony.

3. Jesus turned our sorrow into dancing,
   Jesus turned our sorrow into dancing;
   changed our tears of sadness into rivers of joy.
   Jesus turned our sorrow into a dance.

Text and Music: Graham Kendrick (b.1950)
© Copyright 1986 Kingsway's Thankyou Music, P.O. Box 75, Eastbourne, East Sussex BN23 6NW, UK.
Used by permission.

811 Jesus went away to the desert

1. Je-sus went a-way to the des-ert, pray-ing,
list-ened for his Fath-er's voice. Then he heard the voice of the
temp-ter say-ing, 'Why not make the ea-sy choice?'

Refrain
Ain't list-'nin' to no temp-ta-tion, ain't fall-in' for
no per-sua-sion, ain't gon-na turn a-way from sal-va-tion, I'm a-
wait-in' on the word of the Lord.

2. 'There's an easy way if you'd only choose it,
you can turn the stones to bread!
What's the good of pow'r if you don't abuse it?
Gotta keep yourself well fed!'

3. 'What about a stunt to attract attention,
showing off your special pow'r?
You'd get more applause than I'd care to mention
jumping from the Temple tow'r!'

4. 'Ev'rything you want will be right there for you,
listen to the words I say!
Nobody who matters will dare ignore you;
my way is the easy way.'

Text: Michael Forster (b.1946)
Music: Christopher Tambling (b.1964)
© Copyright 1997 Kevin Mayhew Ltd.

812 Jesus will never, ever

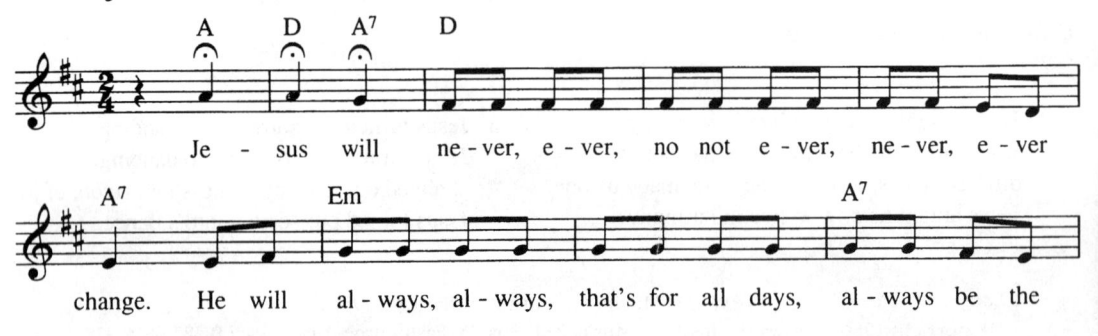

Je-sus will ne-ver, e-ver, no not e-ver, ne-ver, e-ver
change. He will al-ways, al-ways, that's for all days, al-ways be the

© Copyright 1990 Greg Leavers, 1 Haws Hill, Carnforth, Lancs. LA5 9DD. Used by permission.

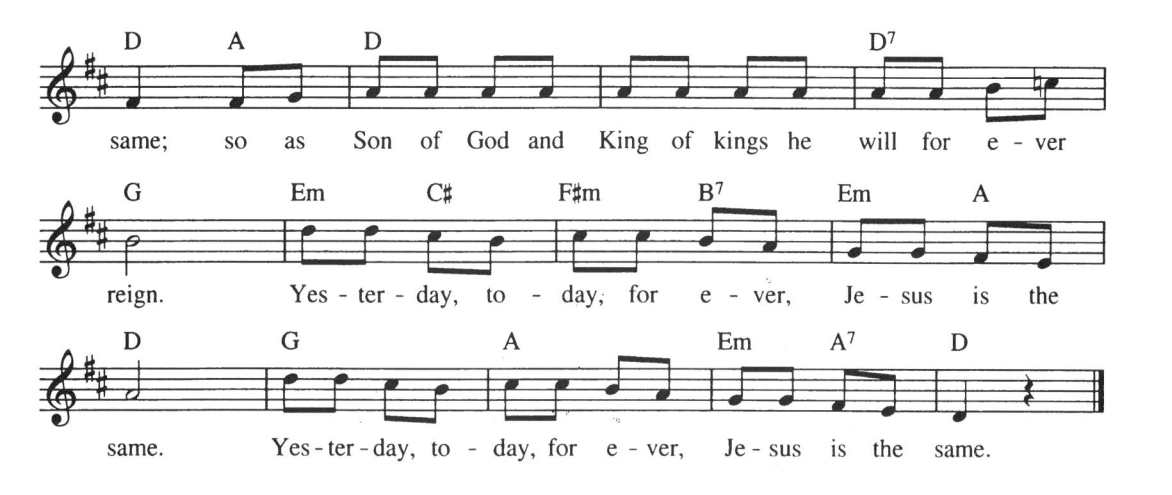

same; so as Son of God and King of kings he will for ever reign. Yes-ter-day, to-day, for e-ver, Jesus is the same. Yes-ter-day, to-day, for e-ver, Jesus is the same.

Text and Music: Greg Leavers

813 Jesus, you love me

Je-sus, you love me more than I can know. Je-sus, you love me more than words can say. I'm spe-cial, I'm planned; I'm born with a fu-ture, I'm in your hands. I'm for-gi-ven, I've been changed; loved by my Fa-ther who knows me by name. I'm loved by my Fa-ther who knows me by name.

Text and Music: David Hind

© Copyright 1992 Kingsway's Thankyou Music, P.O. Box 75, Eastbourne, East Sussex BN23 6NW, UK. Used by permission.

814 Joseph was an honest man

1. Joseph was an honest man, he was an honest man. He pleased the Lord in all his ways because he was an honest man; and God said: 'I am choosing you, because you are an honest man, to care for the one who'll bear my Son, because you are an honest man.'

2. Joseph was a faithful man,
   he was a faithful man.
   He kept the trust the Lord had giv'n
   because he was a faithful man.
   He cared for Mary and her Son,
   because he was a faithful man,
   through days of pain and days of fun,
   because he was a faithful man.

3. Joseph was a working man,
   he was a working man.
   He laboured as a carpenter
   because he was a working man.
   And daily at his work he'd be,
   because he was a working man,
   no idler or a shirker he,
   because he was a working man.

4. Joseph was a praying man,
   he was a praying man.
   He walked with God each single day
   because he was a praying man.
   In joy or pain he'd turn to him,
   because he was a praying man,
   if fear did rage or hope grew dim,
   because he was a praying man.

5. Joseph was an honest man,
   he was an honest man.
   His blameless life won its reward
   because he was an honest man.
   The Lord was pleased and called him home,
   because he was an honest man,
   with him to rest, no more to roam,
   because he was an honest man.

6. Joseph is a helping man,
   he is a helping man.
   He rescues those who turn to him
   because he is a helping man.
   So go to Joseph in your need,
   because he is a helping man,
   you'll see him work with speed and pow'r,
   because he is a helping man.

Text and Music: Marie Lydia Pereira
© Copyright 1976 Kevin Mayhew Ltd.

815 Kum ba yah

1. Kum ba yah, my Lord, kum ba yah, kum ba yah, my Lord, kum ba yah, kum ba yah, my Lord, kum ba yah, O Lord, kum ba yah.

2. Someone's crying, Lord, kum ba yah,
someone's crying, Lord, kum ba yah,
someone's crying, Lord, kum ba yah,
O Lord, kum ba yah.

3. Someone's singing, Lord, kum ba yah,
someone's singing, Lord, kum ba yah,
someone's singing, Lord, kum ba yah,
O Lord, kum ba yah.

4. Someone's praying, Lord, kum ba yah,
someone's praying, Lord, kum ba yah,
someone's praying, Lord, kum ba yah,
O Lord, kum ba yah.

Text and Music: Spiritual

816 Let the mountains dance and sing

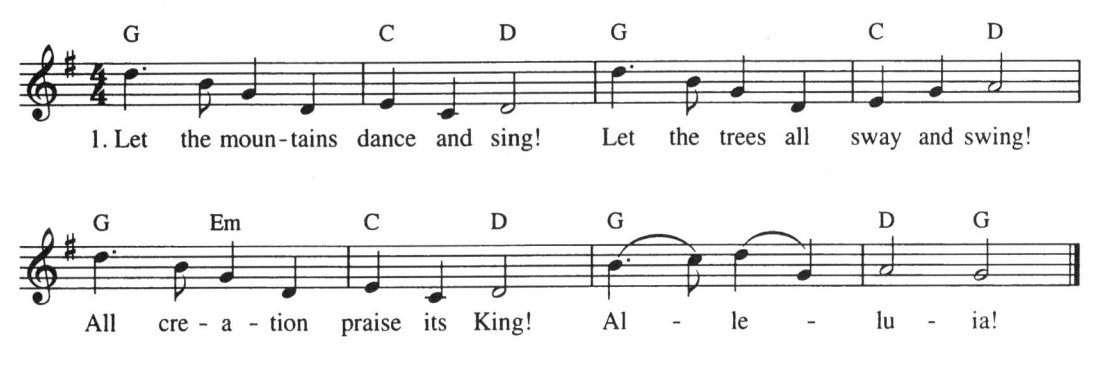

1. Let the mountains dance and sing! Let the trees all sway and swing! All creation praise its King! Alleluia!

2. Let the water sing its song!
And the pow'rful wind so strong
whistle as it blows along!
Alleluia!

3. Let the blossom all break out
in a huge unspoken shout,
just to show that God's about!
Alleluia!

Text and Music: Susan Sayers (b.1946)
© Copyright 1984 Kevin Mayhew Ltd.

817 Life for the poor was hard and tough
Jesus turned the water into wine

Never hurrying

1. Life for the poor was hard and tough, Jesus said, 'That's not good enough; life should be great and here's the sign: I'll turn the water in-to wine.'

Refrain
Jesus turned the water into wine, Jesus turned the water into wine, Jesus turned the water into wine, and the people saw that life was good.

2. Life is a thing to be enjoyed,
　not to be wasted or destroyed.
　Laughter is part of God's design;
　let's turn the water into wine!

3. Go to the lonely and the sad,
　give them the news to make them glad,
　helping the light of hope to shine,
　turning the water into wine!

Text: Michael Forster (b.1946)
Music: Christopher Tambling (b.1964)
© Copyright 1993 Kevin Mayhew Ltd.

818 Little donkey

1. Lit-tle don-key, lit-tle don-key, on the dus-ty road,
got to keep on plod-ding on-wards with your pre-cious load.
Been a long time, lit-tle don-key, through the win-ter's night;
don't give up now, lit-tle don-key, Beth-le-hem's in sight.

Refrain
Ring out those bells to-night, Beth-le-hem, Beth-le-hem,
fol-low that star to-night, Beth-le-hem, Beth-le-hem.
Lit-tle don-key, lit-tle don-key, had a hea-vy day,
lit-tle don-key, car-ry Ma-ry safe-ly on her way.

2. Little donkey, little donkey,
on the dusty road,
there are wise men, waiting for a
sign to bring them here.
Do not falter, little donkey,
there's a star ahead;
it will guide you, little donkey,
to a cattle shed.

Text and Music: Eric Boswell

© Copyright 1959 Warner/Chappell Music Ltd. London W6 8BS.
Used by permission of IMP Ltd., Griffin House, 161 Hammersmith Road, London W6 8BS.

819 Little Jesus, sleep away

1. Little Jesus, sleep away, in the hay,
while we worship, watch and pray.
We will gather at the manger,
worship this amazing stranger:
little Jesus born on earth,
sign of grace and human worth.

2. Little Jesus, sleep away,
   while you may;
   pain is for another day.
   While you sleep, we will not wake you,
   when you cry we'll not forsake you.
   Little Jesus, sleep away,
   we will worship you today.

Text: Christopher Massey (b.1956)
Music: traditional Czech carol
Text © Copyright 1999 Kevin Mayhew Ltd.

820 Lord of the future

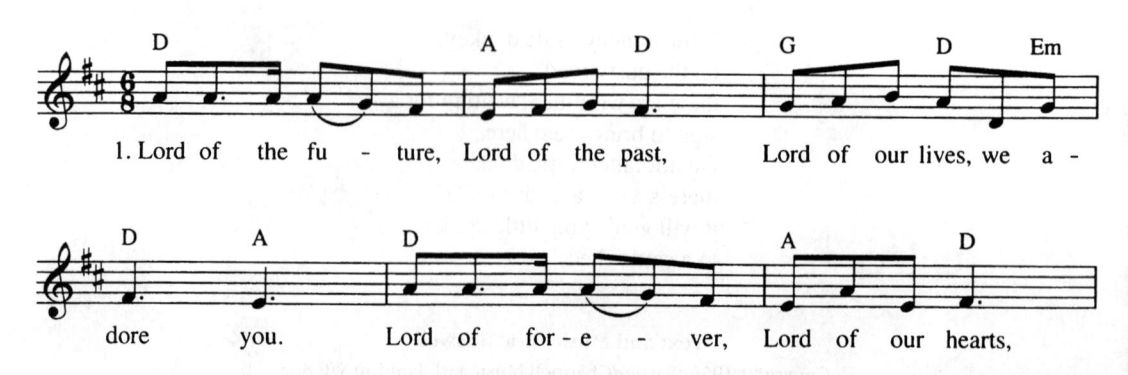

1. Lord of the future, Lord of the past,
Lord of our lives, we adore you.
Lord of forever, Lord of our hearts,

© Copyright 1994 Daybreak Music Ltd., Silverdale Road, Eastbourne, East Sussex BN20 7AB, UK. Used by permission.

we give all praise to you. you.

2. Lord of tomorrow,
Lord of today,
Lord over all, you are worthy.
Lord of creation,
Lord of all truth,
we give all praise to you.

Text and Music: Ian D. Craig

821 Lord, we've come to worship you

With a gentle rhythm

Lord, we've come to wor-ship you, Lord, we've come to praise;
Lord, we've come to wor-ship you in oh so ma-ny ways.
Some of us shout and some of us sing, and some of us whis-per the
praise we bring but, Lord, we all are ga-ther-ing to give to you our praise.

Text and Music: Ian Smale
© Copyright 1989 Kingsway's Thankyou Music, P.O. Box 75, Eastbourne,
East Sussex BN23 6NW, UK. Worldwide (excl. USA and Canada).
Used by permission.

822 Lord, you've promised, through your Son
Lord, forgive us

Lord, you've promised, through your Son, you'll forgive the wrongs we've done; we confess them, ev'ry one, please, dear Lord, forgive us. 1. Things we've done and things we've said, we regret the hurt they spread. Lord, we're sorry. Lord, we're sorry.

3rd time to last refrain

Last refrain:
Lord, you've promised, through your Son, you'll forgive the wrongs we've done; we receive your pardon, Lord, as you forgive us.

2. Sinful and unkind thoughts too,
all of these are known to you.
Lord, we're sorry.
Lord, we're sorry.

3. And the things we've left undone,
words and deeds we should have done.
Lord, we're sorry.
Lord, we're sorry.

Last refrain:
Lord, you've promised, through your Son,
you'll forgive the wrongs we've done;
we receive your pardon,
Lord, as you forgive us.

Text and Music: Alan J. Price
© Copyright 1992 Daybreak Music Ltd., Silverdale Road, Eastbourne, East Sussex BN20 7AB.
Used by permission.

823 My mouth was made for worship

1. My mouth was made for wor-ship, my hands were made to raise, my feet were made for danc-ing, my life is one of praise to Je-sus. And all God's peo-ple said: A-men, hal-le-lu-jah, a-men, praise and glo-ry, a-men, a-men, a-men, a-men.

Wo, wo, wo, wo. 2. My Wo, wo, wo, wo, wo.

2. My heart was made for loving,
   my mind to know God's ways,
   my body was made a temple,
   my life is one of praise to Jesus.
   And all God's people said: Amen,
   hallelujah, amen, praise and glory,
   amen, amen, amen, amen,
   Wo,wo,wo,wo,wo.

Text and Music: Ian Smale

© Copyright 1989 Glorie Music. Administered by Kingsway's Thankyou Music, P.O. Box 75, Eastbourne, East Sussex BN23 6NW, UK. Worldwide. Used by permission.

824 Nobody's a nobody

1. No-bo-dy's a no-bo-dy, be-lieve me 'cause it's true.
No-bo-dy's a no-bo-dy, es-pe-cial-ly not you.
No-bo-dy's a no-bo-dy, and God wants us to see that
ev-'ry-bo-dy's some-bo-dy, and that means e-ven me.

2. I'm no car-toon, I'm hu-man, I have feel-ings, treat me right. I'm
not a su-per he-ro with su-per strength and might. I'm
not a me-ga pop star or su-per ath-e-lete, but
did you know I'm spec-ial, in fact I'm quite u-nique!

Text and Music: John Hardwick
© Copyright 1993 Daybreak Music Ltd., Silverdale Road, Eastbourne, East Sussex BN20 7AB.
Used by permission.

825 Now the Mass is ended

1. Now the Mass is end - ed, Lord, now it's time to go,
but we will not leave a - lone, we will take you too.
In our work, in our play, all through-out our bu - sy day,
we will not be left a - lone, we'll live this day with you.

2. Through this Mass we have received
blessing, grace and pow'r
loving truly as you did,
loving hour by hour,
to be kind, to be true,
just like you in all we do.
Stay with us, we ask you, Lord,
and help us stay with you.

Text and Music: Marie Lydia Pereria
© Copyright 1978 Kevin Mayhew Ltd.

826 O come and join the dance

As a Scottish folk-dance

1. O come and join the dance that all be-gan so long a-go, when Christ the Lord was born in Beth-le-hem. Through all the years of dark-ness still the dance goes on and on, oh, take my hand and come and join the song. Re-joice! Re-joice! Re-joice! Re-joice! O lift your voice and sing, and o-pen up your heart to wel-come him. Re-joice! Re-joice! Re-joice! Re-joice and wel-come now your King, for Christ the Lord was born in Beth-le-hem.

2. Come
3. Let

© Copyright 1998 Make Way Music, P.O. Box 263, Croydon, Surrey CR9 5AP, UK.
International copyright secured. All rights reserved. Used by permission.

3. ... hem. for Christ the Lord was born in Beth-le-hem. For Christ the Lord was born in Beth-le-hem.

2. Come shed your heavy load and dance your worries away,
for Christ the Lord was born in Bethlehem.
He came to break the pow'r of sin and turn your night to day,
oh, take my hand and come and join the song.

3. Let laughter ring and angels sing and joy be all around,
for Christ the Lord was born in Bethlehem.
And if you seek with all your heart he surely can be found,
oh, take my hand and come and join the song.

Text and Music: Graham Kendrick (b.1950)

827 O give thanks

O give thanks to the Lord, all you his people, O give thanks to the Lord, for he is good. Let us praise, let us thank, let us ce-le-brate and dance, O give thanks to the Lord, for he is good.

Text and Music: Joanne Pond
© Copyright 1980 Kingsway's Thankyou Music, P.O. Box 75, Eastbourne, East Sussex BN23 6NW, UK.
Used by permission.

828 O Lord, all the world

1. O Lord, all the world be-longs to you, and you are al-ways mak-ing all things new. What is wrong you for-give, and the new life you give is what's turn-ing the world up-side down.

2. The world's only loving to its friends,
   but you have brought us love that never ends;
   loving enemies too,
   and this loving with you
   is what's turning the world upside down.

3. This world lives divided and apart.
   You draw us all together and we start,
   in your body, to see
   that in a fellowship we
   can be turning the world upside down.

4. The world wants the wealth to live in state,
   but you show us a new way to be great:
   like a servant you came,
   and if we do the same,
   we'll be turning the world upside down.

5. O Lord, all the world belongs to you,
   and you are always making all things new.
   Send your Spirit on all
   in your Church, whom you call
   to be turning the world upside down.

Text and Music: Patrick Appleford
© Copyright 1965 Josef Weinberger Ltd., 12-14 Mortimer Street, London W1N 7RD. Used by permission

829 One hundred and fifty-three!

Refrain

One hun-dred and fif-ty-three! One hun-dred and fif-ty-three! The num-ber of all the fish in the sea: one hun-dred and fif-ty-three!

1. We'd fished all the night for

© Copyright 1993 Kevin Mayhew Ltd.

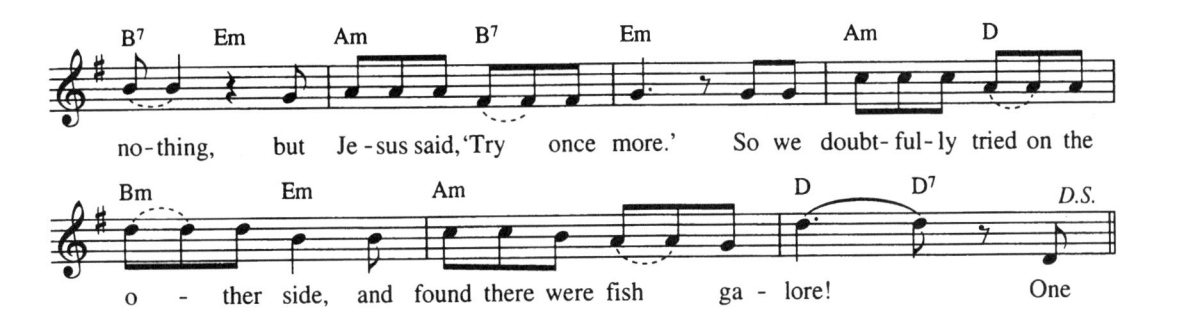

no-thing, but Je-sus said, 'Try once more.' So we doubt-ful-ly tried on the o-ther side, and found there were fish ga-lore! One

2. We got all the fish to the shore,
   we wondered how many there'd be.
   So we started to count,
   and what an amount:
   one hundred and fifty-three!

3. Now here was a wonderful sight
   we'd never expected to see;
   and the net didn't break,
   it was able to take
   the hundred and fifty-three!

4. So whether you're rich or you're poor,
   whatever your race or your sect,
   be you black, white or brown,
   Jesus wants you around,
   there's plenty of room in the net!

Text: Michael Forster (b.1946)
Music: Christopher Tambling (b.1964)
© Copyright 1993 Kevin Mayhew Ltd.

830 Our God is so great

Our God is so great, so strong and so migh-ty, there's no-thing that he can-not do. The ri-vers are his, the moun-tains are his, the stars are his han-di-work too.

Text and Music: unknown

831 Out to the great wide world we go

Joyfully

Refrain

Out to the great wide world we go! Out to the great wide world we go!
Out to the great wide world we go and we sing of the love of Je-sus.

1. Go and tell our neigh-bours, go and tell our friends,
Je-sus gives his peo-ple love that ne-ver ends. So:

2. People sad and lonely,
wond'ring how to cope;
let's find ways of showing
Jesus gives us hope. So:

Text: Michael Forster (b.1946)
Music: Christopher Tambling (b.1964)
© Copyright 1993 Kevin Mayhew Ltd.

832 O when the saints go marching in

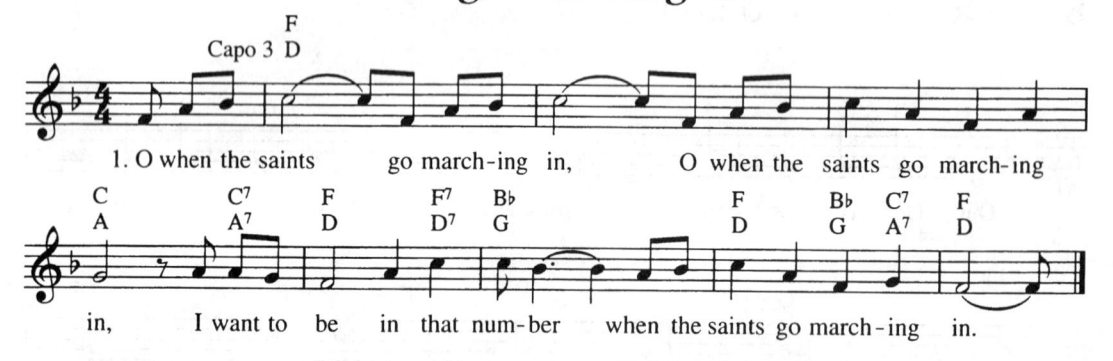

Capo 3 D

1. O when the saints go march-ing in, O when the saints go march-ing in, I want to be in that num-ber when the saints go march-ing in.

2. O when they crown him Lord of all,
O when they crown him Lord of all,
I want to be in that number
when they crown him Lord of all.

3. O when all knees bow at his name,
O when all knees bow at his name,
I want to be in that number
when all knees bow at his name.

4. O when they sing the Saviour's praise,
O when they sing the Saviour's praise,
I want to be in that number
when they sing the Saviour's praise.

5. O when the saints go marching in,
O when the saints go marching in,
I want to be in that number
when the saints go marching in.

Text and Music: traditional

833 Peter and John went to pray
Silver and gold

Peter and John went to pray, they met a lame man on the way. He asked for alms and held out his palms and this is what Peter did say: 'Silver and gold have I none, but such as I have I give thee, in the name of Jesus Christ of Nazareth, rise up and walk!' He went walking and leaping and praising God, walking and leaping and praising God. 'In the name of Jesus Christ of Nazareth, rise up and walk.'

Text: unknown based on Acts 3
Music: unknown

834 Praise and thanksgiving

Praise and thanks-giv-ing let ev-'ry-one bring
un-to our Fa-ther for ev-'ry good thing!
All to-ge-ther joy-ful-ly sing.

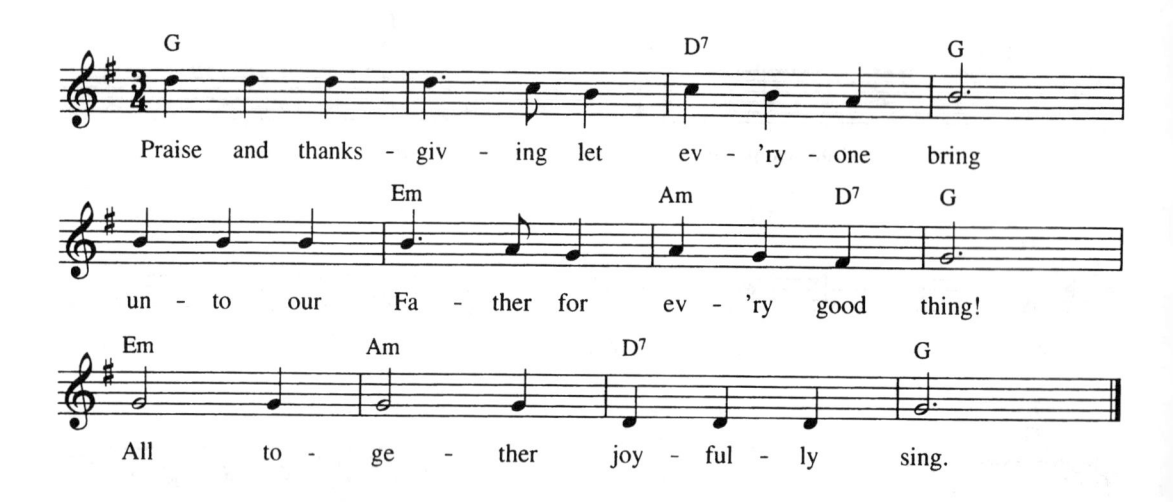

Text and Music: unknown

835 Praise God in his holy place

Lively

1. Praise God in his ho-ly place! He's the God of time and space. Praise him, all the hu-man race! Let ev-'ry-thing praise our God!

To next verse

Last time

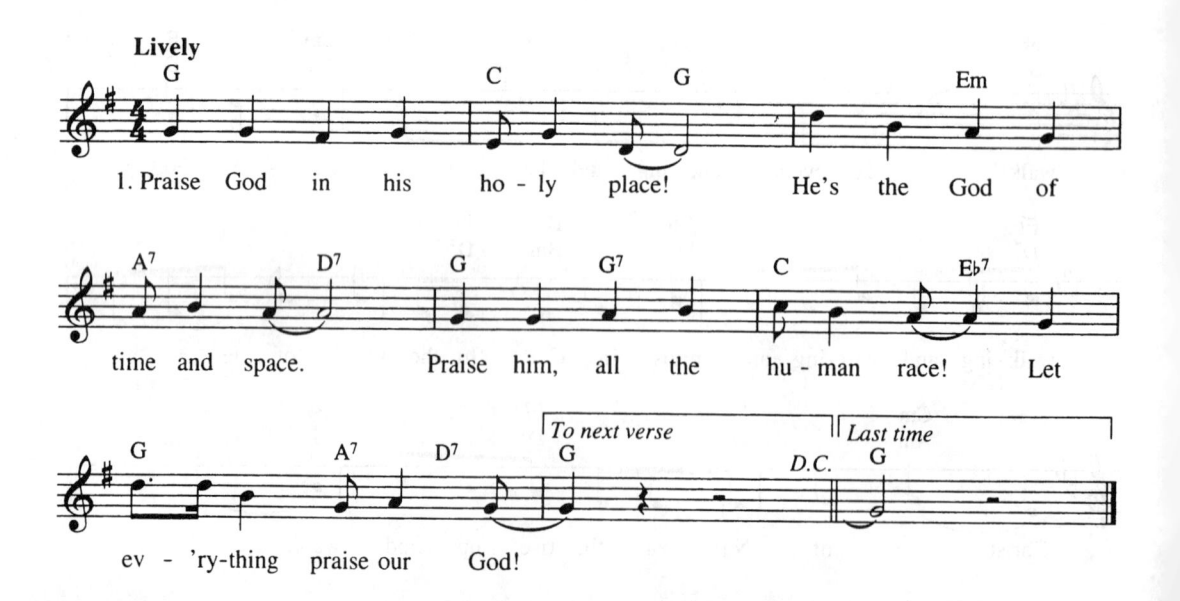

© Copyright 1997 Kevin Mayhew Ltd.

2. Praise him with the ol' wood block!
   Let it swing and let it rock,
   praising God around the clock!
   Let ev'rything praise the Lord!

3. Praise him with the big bass drum,
   if you've got guitars, then strum!
   Now let's make those rafters hum!
   Let ev'rything praise our God!

4. Praise him with the chime bars' chime,
   tell the bells it's party time,
   help those singers find a rhyme!
   Let ev'rything praise our God!

5. Violin or xylophone,
   trumpets with their awesome tone;
   bowed or beaten, bashed or blown,
   let ev'rything praise our God!

6. Cymbals, triangles and things,
   if it crashes, howls or rings,
   ev'rybody shout and sing!
   Let ev'rything praise our God!

Text: Michael Forster (b.1946)
Music: Christopher Tambling (b.1964)

836 Put your trust

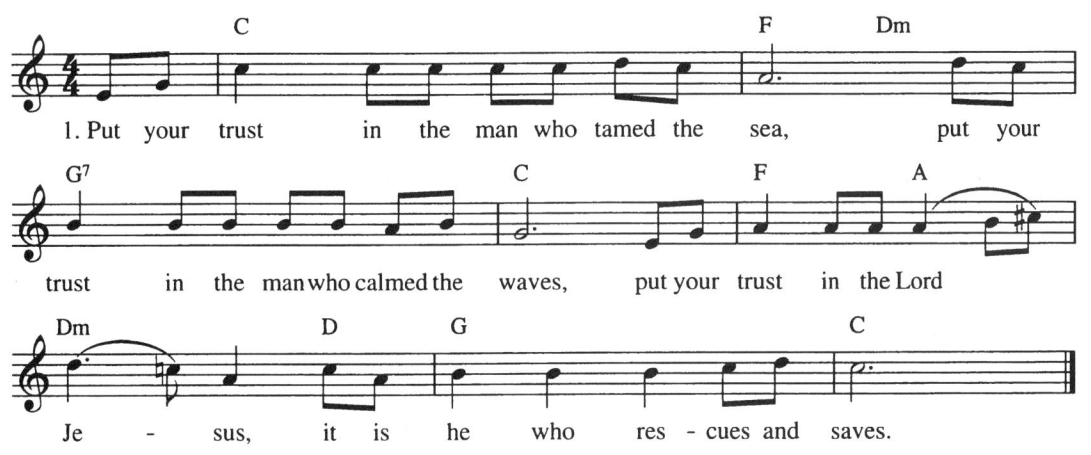

1. Put your trust in the man who tamed the sea, put your trust in the man who calmed the waves, put your trust in the Lord Jesus, it is he who rescues and saves.

2. Put your trust in the man who cured the blind,
   put your trust in the man who helped the lame,
   put your trust in the Lord Jesus,
   there is healing strength in his name.

3. Put your trust in the man who died for you,
   put your trust in the man who conquered fear,
   put your trust in the Lord Jesus,
   for he rose from death and he's near.

4. Put your trust in the man who understands,
   put your trust in the man who is your friend,
   put your trust in the Lord Jesus,
   who will give you life without end.

Text and Music: Estelle White (b.1925)
© Copyright 1983 Kevin Mayhew Ltd.

837 Rise and shine

Rise and shine, and give God his glory, glory. Rise and shine, and give God his glory, glory. Rise and shine, and give God his glory, glory, children of the Lord.

1. The Lord said to Noah, 'There's gonna be a floody, floody.' Lord said to Noah, 'There's gonna be a floody, floody. Get those children out of the muddy, muddy, children of the Lord.'

2. So Noah, he built him,
   he built him an arky, arky,
   Noah, he built him,
   he built him an arky, arky,
   built it out of hickory barky, barky,
   children of the Lord.

3. The animals, they came on,
   they came on, by twosies, twosies,
   animals, they came on,
   they came on by twosies, twosies,
   elephants and kangaroosies, roosies,
   children of the Lord.

4. It rained and poured for
   forty daysies, daysies,
   rained and poured for
   forty daysies, daysies,
   nearly drove those animals crazies, crazies,
   children of the Lord.

5. The sun came out and
   dried up the landy, landy,
   sun came out and
   dried up the landy, landy,
   ev'rything was fine and dandy, dandy,
   children of the Lord.

6. If you get to heaven
   before I do-sies, do-sies,
   you get to heaven
   before I do-sies, do-sies,
   tell those angels I'm comin' too-sies, too-sies,
   children of the Lord.

Text: unknown based on Genesis 6:4
Music: traditional

838 Sing a simple song

1. Sing a simple song unto the Lord, sing a simple song unto the Lord, sing it with your heart, sing it with your soul, sing a simple song unto the Lord. O Lord, I love you, O Lord, I see. O Lord, I love you, I see that you love me.

2. Say a simple prayer unto the Lord,
   say a simple prayer unto the Lord,
   say it with your heart, say it with your soul,
   say a simple prayer unto the Lord.

3. Give a simple gift unto the Lord,
   give a simple gift unto the Lord,
   give it with your heart, give it with your soul,
   give a simple gift unto the Lord.

Text and Music: Carey Landry
© Copyright 1976 North American Liturgy Resources (NALR), 5536 NE Hassalo, Portland, OR 97213, USA.
All rights reserved. Used by permission.

LITURGICAL
HYMNS OLD & NEW

839 Sing praise to God

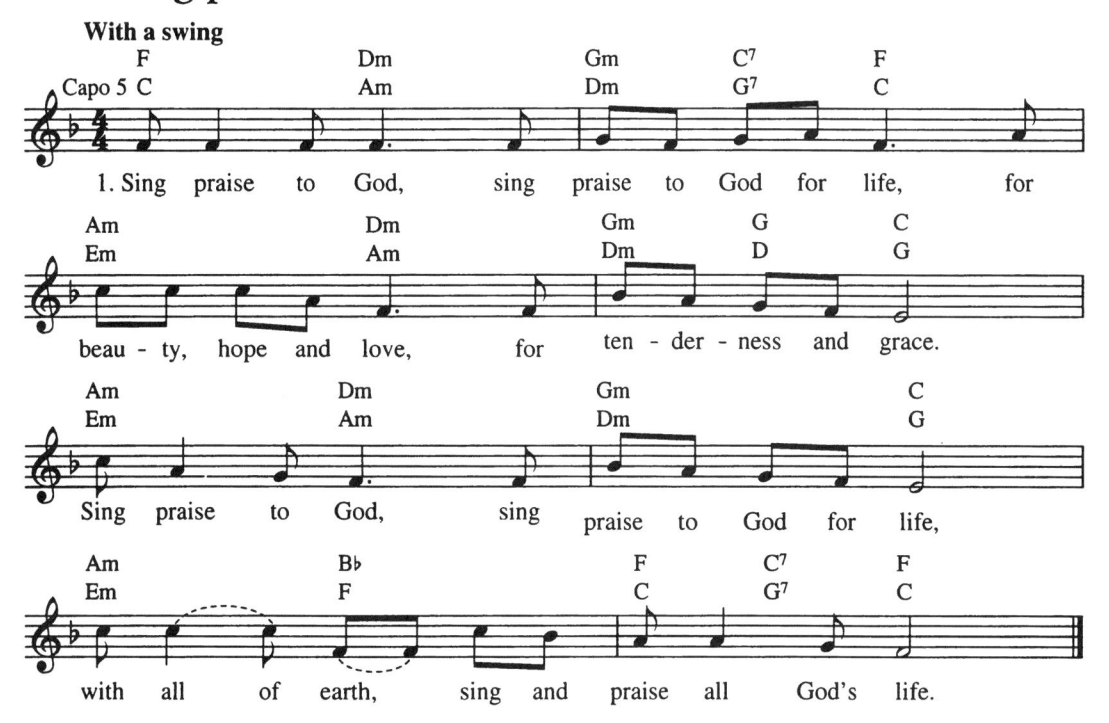

With a swing

1. Sing praise to God, sing praise to God for life, for beauty, hope and love, for tenderness and grace. Sing praise to God, sing praise to God for life, with all of earth, sing and praise all God's life.

2. Lift up your eyes to see the works of God,
   in ev'ry blade of grass, in ev'ry human face.
   Lift up your eyes to see the works of God,
   through all life, in all time and all space.

3. Open your ears to hear the cries of pain
   arising from the poor and all who are oppressed.
   Open your mind and use your wits to find
   who are the causes of this world's unjust ways.

4. Reach out your hands to share the wealth God gave
   with those who are oppressed, and those who feel alone.
   Reach out your hands and gently touch with Christ
   each frozen heart which has said 'No' to love.

5. Open our hearts to love the world with Christ,
   each person in this world, each creature of this earth.
   Open our hearts to love the ones who hate,
   and in their hearts find a part of ourselves.

6. Live life with love, for love encircles all,
   it casts out all our fears, it fills the heart with joy.
   Live life with love, for love transforms our life,
   as we praise God with our eyes, hands and hearts.

Text: W. L. Wallace
Music: Noel Rawsthorne (b.1929)
© Copyright 1997 Kevin Mayhew Ltd.

840 Step by step, on and on
Jesus is the living way

Step by step, on and on, we will walk with Jesus till the journey's done. Step by step, day by day, because Jesus is the living way. 1. He's the one to follow, in his footsteps we will tread. Don't worry about tomorrow, Jesus knows the way ahead. Oh,

2. He will never leave us,
and his love he'll always show,
so wherever Jesus leads us,
that's the way we want to go. Oh,

Text and Music: Gill Hutchinson
© Copyright 1994 Sea Dream Music, P.O. Box 13533, London E7 0SG. Used by permission.

841 Thank you, Lord
Right where we are

1. Thank you, Lord, for this new day, thank you, Lord, for this new day, thank you, Lord, for this new day, right where we are. Alleluia, praise the Lord, alleluia,

© Copyright 1971 Celebration. Administered by Kingsway's Thankyou Music, P.O. Box 75, Eastbourne, East Sussex BN23 6NW, UK. Europe & British Commonwealth (excl. Canada, Australasia & Africa). Used by permission.

praise the Lord, al - le - lu - ia, praise the Lord, right where we are.

2. Thank you, Lord, for food to eat,
thank you, Lord, for food to eat,
thank you, Lord, for food to eat,
right where we are.

3. Thank you, Lord, for clothes to wear,
thank you, Lord, for clothes to wear,
thank you, Lord, for clothes to wear,
right where we are.

4. Thank you, Lord, for all your gifts,
thank you, Lord, for all your gifts,
thank you, Lord, for all your gifts,
right where we are.

Text: Diane Davis Andrew adapted by Geoffrey Marshall-Taylor
Music: Diane Davis Andrew

842 There are hundreds of sparrows
God knows me

1. There are hun - dreds of spar - rows, thou - sands, mil - lions, they're two a pen - ny, far too ma - ny there must be; there are hun - dreds and thou - sands, mil - lions of spar - rows, but God knows ev' - ry one, and God knows me.

2. There are hundreds of flowers, thousands, millions,
and flowers fair the meadows wear for all to see;
there are hundreds and thousands, millions of flowers,
but God knows ev'ry one, and God knows me.

3. There are hundreds of planets, thousands, millions,
way out in space each has a place by God's decree;
there are hundreds and thousands, millions of planets,
but God knows ev'ry one, and God knows me.

4. There are hundreds of children, thousands, millions,
and yet their names are written on God's memory;
there are hundreds and thousands, millions of children,
but God knows ev'ry one, and God knows me.

Text: John Gowans
Music: John Larsson
© Copyright Salvationist Publishing & Supplies. Administered by CopyCare, P.O. Box 77,
Hailsham, East Sussex BN27 3EF, UK. Used by permission.

843 There's a great big world out there

Jaunty, but not fast

There's a great big world out there. Let's go!
There's a great big world out there. Let's go!
There's a great big world out there. Let's go! Celebrate the love of God!

1. We've sung about the love of God,
   now it's time to let it show.
   If we don't act as though it's true,
   how on earth will people know?

2. We've brought to God our prayers and hymns,
   now it's time to live his life,
   to sow a little love and peace
   in the place of selfish strife.

3. We've listened to the word of God,
   now it's time to live it out,
   to show by ev'rything we do
   what the gospel is about.

This can be sung as a round during the third verse, with the second voices entering at the refrain (using the accompaniment to the verse).

Text: Michael Forster (b.1946)
Music: Andrew Gant (b.1963)
© Copyright 1997 Kevin Mayhew Ltd.

844 There's a rainbow in the sky

There's a rainbow in the sky, and it's okay! There's a rainbow in the sky, and it's okay! There's a rainbow in the sky, and it's okay! It's a sign that God is good.

1. Forty days and nights afloat,
all cooped up on Noah's boat!
Now the rain is almost done;
wake up world, here comes the sun!

2. Now we've got another start,
ev'ryone can play a part:
make the world a better place,
put a smile on ev'ry face!

3. Sometimes, still, the world is bad,
people hungry, people sad.
Jesus wants us all to care,
showing people ev'rywhere:

Text: Michael Forster (b.1946)
Music: Christopher Tambling (b.1964)
© Copyright 1993 Kevin Mayhew Ltd.

845 There was one, there were two
The children's band

Refrain

There was one, there were two, there were three friends of Jesus, there were four, there were five, there were six friends of Jesus, there were sev'n, there were eight, there were nine friends of Jesus, ten friends of Jesus in the band. *Fine*

1. Bells are going to ring in praise of Jesus, praise of Jesus, praise of Jesus, bells are going to ring in praise of Jesus, prais-ing Jesus the Lord. *D.C.*

2. Drums are going to boom in praise of Jesus, praise of Jesus, praise of Jesus, drums are going to boom in praise of Jesus, praising Jesus the Lord.

3. Tambourines will shake in praise of Jesus, praise of Jesus, praise of Jesus, tambourines will shake in praise of Jesus, praising Jesus the Lord.

4. Trumpets will resound in praise of Jesus, praise of Jesus, praise of Jesus, trumpets will resound in praise of Jesus, praising Jesus the Lord.

Verses can be added ad lib, for example:

Clarinets will swing in praise of Jesus... Play recorders, too... Triangles will ting...

Fiddles will be scraped... Let guitars be strummed... Chime bars will be chimed...

Glockenspiels will play... Vibraphones will throb... Trombones slide about...

Text: Christina Wilde
Music: traditional American melody
Text © Copyright 1997, 1999 Kevin Mayhew Ltd

846 The voice from the bush
Lead my people to freedom

1. The voice from the bush said: Moses, look snappy,
have I got a job for you! I've looked around and I'm
not very happy. Here is what you have to do:

Refrain
Lead my people to freedom! Lead my people to freedom!
Lead my people to freedom! Got to go to the Promised Land!

2. The people of God were suff'ring and dying,
   sick and tired of slavery.
   All God could hear was the sound of their crying;
   Moses had to set them free:

3. We know that the world is still full of sorrow,
   people need to be set free.
   We've got to give them a better tomorrow,
   so God says to you and me:

Text: Michael Forster (b.1946)
Music: Christopher Tambling (b.1964)
© Copyright 1993 Kevin Mayhew Ltd.

847 The wise man

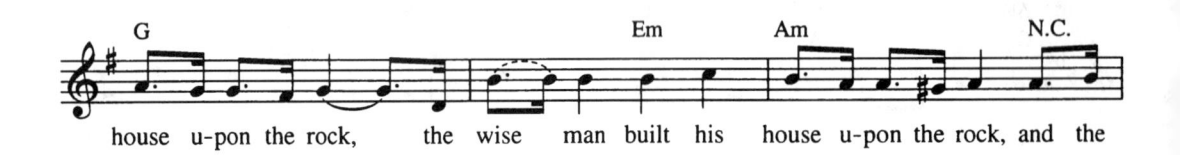

1. The wise man built his house up-on the rock, the wise man built his house up-on the rock, the wise man built his house up-on the rock, and the rain came tum-bling down. And the rain came down and the floods came up, the rain came down and the floods came up, the rain came down and the floods came up, and the house on the rock stood firm.

2. The foolish man built his house upon the sand, *(x3)*
and the rain came tumbling down,
And the rain came down and the floods came up,
the rain came down and the floods came up, *(x2)*
and the house on the sand fell flat.

Text and Music: unknown

848 The world is full of smelly feet

Refrain

The world is full of smel-ly feet, wea-ry from the dus-ty street. The world is full of smel-ly feet, we'll wash them for each oth-er.

1. Je-sus said to his dis-ci-ples, 'Wash those wea-ry toes!
   Do it in a cheer-ful fash-ion, ne-ver hold your nose!'

2. People on a dusty journey
   need a place to rest;
   Jesus says, 'You say you love me,
   this will be the test!'

3. We're his friends, we recognize him
   in the folk we meet;
   smart or scruffy, we'll still love him,
   wash his smelly feet!

Text: Michael Forster (b.1946)
Music: Christopher Tambling (b.1964)
© Copyright 1997 Kevin Mayhew Ltd.

849 This little light of mine

This little light of mine, I'm gonna let it shine.
This little light of mine, I'm gonna let it shine.
This little light of mine I'm gonna let it shine, let it shine, let it shine, let it shine.

1. The light that shines is the light of love, lights the darkness from above, it shines on me and it shines on you, and shows what the power of love can do. I'm gonna shine my light both far and near, I'm gonna shine my light both bright and clear. Where there's a dark corner in this land, I'm gonna let my little light shine.

2. On Monday he gave me the gift of love,
Tuesday peace came from above.
On Wednesday he told me to have more faith,
on Thursday he gave me a little more grace.
On Friday he told me to watch and pray,
on Saturday he told me just what to say,
on Sunday he gave me the pow'r divine
to let my little light shine.

Text and Music: traditional

850 We will praise

We will praise, we will praise, we will praise the Lord, we will praise the Lord be-cause he is good. We will praise, we will praise, we will praise the Lord be-cause his love is e-ver-last-ing.

Bring on the trum-pets and harps, let's hear the cym-bals ring, then in har-mo-ny lift our voi-ces and sing, sing. We will praise, we will praise, we will praise the Lord, we will praise the Lord be-cause he is good. We will praise, we will praise, we will praise the Lord be-cause his love is e-ver-last-ing.

Text and Music: Ian Smale
© Copyright 1984 Kingsway's Thankyou Music, P.O. Box 75, Eastbourne, East Sussex BN23 6NW, UK.
Used by permission.

851 When is he coming

1. When is he com-ing, when, O when is he com-ing, the Re-deem-er? When will we see him, when, O when will we see him, the Re-deem-er?

Refrain
Come, O come, from your king-dom up there, from your king-dom up there a-bove! Come, O come to your peo-ple on earth, to your peo-ple on earth bring love! Em-ma-nu-el! Em-ma-nu-el! Em-ma-nu-el!

2. Long years awaiting,
   many years here awaiting the Redeemer!
   Ready to greet him,
   always ready to meet him, the Redeemer!

3. Spare us from evil,
   from the clutches of evil, O Redeemer!
   Though we are sinners
   we have known your forgiveness, O Redeemer!

Text and Music: David Palmer
© Copyright 1976 Kevin Mayhew Ltd.

852 When the Spirit of the Lord

1. When the Spirit of the Lord is within my heart I will sing as David sang. When the Spirit of the Lord is within my heart I will sing as David sang. I will sing, I will sing, I will sing as David sang. I will sing, I will sing, I will sing as David sang.

2. When the Spirit of the Lord is within my heart
   I will clap as David clapped . . .

3. When the Spirit of the Lord is within my heart
   I will dance as David danced . . .

4. When the Spirit of the Lord is within my heart
   I will praise as David praised . . .

Text and Music: unknown

853 When your Father made the world
Care for your world

1. When your Father made the world, before that world was old, in his eye what he had made was lovely to behold. Help your people to care for your world.

Refrain
The world is a garden you made, and you are the one who planted the seed, the world is a garden you made, a life for our food, life for our joy, life we could kill with our selfish greed.

2. All the world that he had made,
the seas, the rocks, the air,
all the creatures and the plants
he gave into our care.
Help your people to care for your world.

3. When you walked in Galilee,
you said your Father knows
when each tiny sparrow dies,
each fragile lily grows.
Help your people to care for your world.

4. And the children of the earth,
like sheep within your fold,
should have food enough to eat,
and shelter from the cold.
Help your people to care for your world.

Text: Anne Conlon
Music: Peter Rose

© Copyright 1996 Josef Weinberger Ltd, 12-14 Mortimer Street, London W1N 7RD.
Used by permission.

854 Who put the colours in the rainbow?

1. Who put the col-ours in the rain-bow? Who put the salt in-to the sea?
Who put the cold in-to the snow-flake? Who made you and me?
Who put the hump up-on the ca-mel? Who put the neck on the gi-raffe?
Who put the tail up-on the mon-key? Who made hy-e-nas laugh?
Who made whales and snails and quails? Who made hogs and dogs and frogs?
Who made bats and cats and rats? Who made ev-'ry-thing?

2. Who put the gold into the sunshine?
Who put the sparkle in the stars?
Who put the silver in the moonlight?
Who made Earth and Mars?
Who put the scent into the roses?
Who taught the honey-bee to dance?
Who put the tree inside the acorn?
It surely can't be chance!
Who made seas and leaves and trees?
Who made snow and winds that blow?
Who made streams and rivers flow?
God made all of these!

Text and Music: Paul Booth

© Copyright Paul Booth. Administered by CopyCare, P.O. Box 77,
Hailsham, East Sussex BN27 3EF, UK. Used by permission.

855 Yesterday, today, for ever

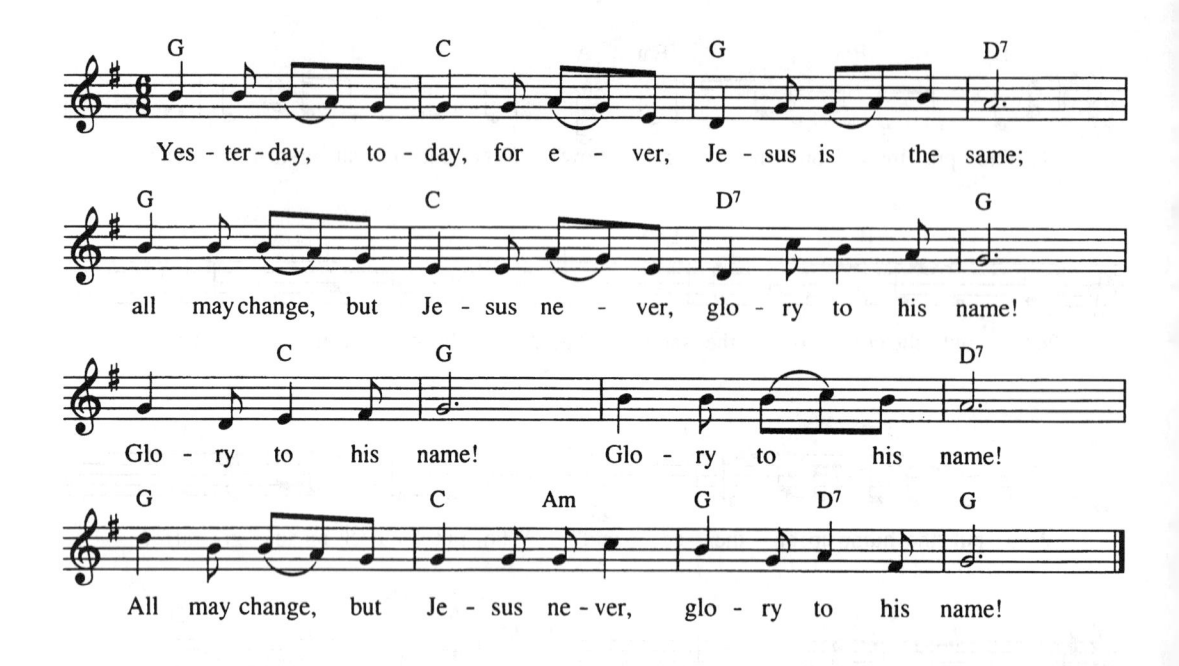

Yes-ter-day, to-day, for e-ver, Jesus is the same;
all may change, but Jesus ne-ver, glory to his name!
Glory to his name! Glory to his name!
All may change, but Jesus ne-ver, glory to his name!

Text and Music: unknown

856 You've got to move

1. You've got to move when the Spirit says move, you've got to move when the Spirit says move, 'cause when the Spirit says move, you've got to move when the Spirit, move when the Spirit says move.

2. You've got to sing ...

3. You've got to clap ...

4. You've got to shout ...

5. You've got to move ...

Text and Music: traditional

857 Zacchaeus was a very little man

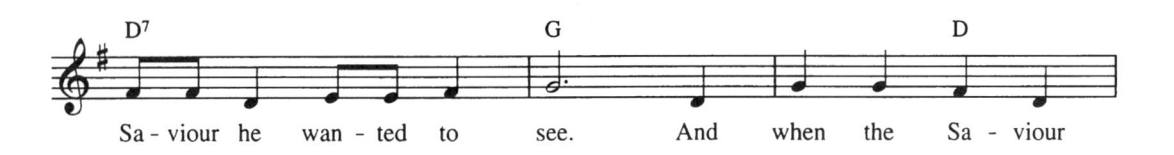

Zacchaeus was a very little man, and a very little man was he. He climbed up into a sycamore tree, for the Saviour he wanted to see. And when the Saviour passed that way, he looked into the tree and said, 'Now Zacchaeus, you come down, for I'm coming to your house for tea.'

Text and Music: unknown

858 Zip bam boo

Brightly

Refrain F / Capo 3 D — B♭ / G

Zip bam boo, za-ma la-ma la boo, there's free-dom in Je-sus Christ.

F / D

Zip bam boo, za-ma la-ma la boo, there's

C⁷ / A⁷ — F / D

free-dom in Je-sus Christ. Though we hung him on a cross till he

F⁷ / D⁷ — B♭⁷ / G⁷

died in pain, three days la-ter he's a-live a-gain.

F / D — B♭ / G — F / D — C⁷ / A⁷

Zip bam boo, za-ma la-ma la boo, there's free-dom in Je-sus Christ.

F / D — B♭ / G — F / D *Fine*

1. This Je-sus was a work-ing man who

B♭⁷ / G⁷ — F / D

shout-ed 'Yes' to life, but did-n't choose to

© Copyright 1972 Kingsway's Thankyou Music, P.O. Box 75, Eastbourne, East Sussex BN23 6NW, UK.
Used by permission.

...set-tle down, or take him-self a wife. To live for God he made his task, 'Who is this man?' the peo-ple ask. Zip bam boo, za-ma la-ma la boo, there's free-dom in Je-sus Christ.

2. He'd come to share good news from God
and show that he is Lord.
He made folk whole who trusted him
and took him at his word.
He fought oppression, loved the poor,
gave the people hope once more.
Zip bam boo, zama lama la boo,
there's freedom in Jesus Christ.

3. 'He's mad! He claims to be God's Son
and give new life to men!
Let's kill this Christ, once and for all,
no trouble from him then!'
'It's death then, Jesus, the cross for you!'
Said, 'Man, that's what I came to do!'
Zip bam boo, zama lama la boo,
there's freedom in Jesus Christ.

Text and Music: Sue McClellan, John Paculabo and Keith Ryecroft

LITURGICAL
HYMNS OLD & NEW

Chants

859 Adoramus te, Domine

Music for All

(Hum) A-do-ra-mus te, Do-mi-ne. ne.

Music for Cantor

1. With the an-gels and arch-an-gels:
2. With the pa-tri-archs and pro-phets:
3. With the Vir-gin Ma-ry, mo-ther of God:
4. With the a-pos-tles and e-van-ge-lists:
5. With all the mar-tyrs of Christ:
6. With all who wit-ness to the Gos-pel of the Lord:
7. With all your peo-ple of the Church through-out the world.

* Choose either part.

The Cantor enters on the upbeat at the end of the first refrain, so that the [A] marked in his/her part falls at the beginning of each repeat of the refrain at the [A] indicated.

Text: Taizé Community
Music: Jacques Berthier (1923-1994)
Text and Music © Copyright Ateliers et Presses de Taizé, Taizé-Communauté, F-71250, France. Used by permission.

860 Adoramus te, Domine Deus

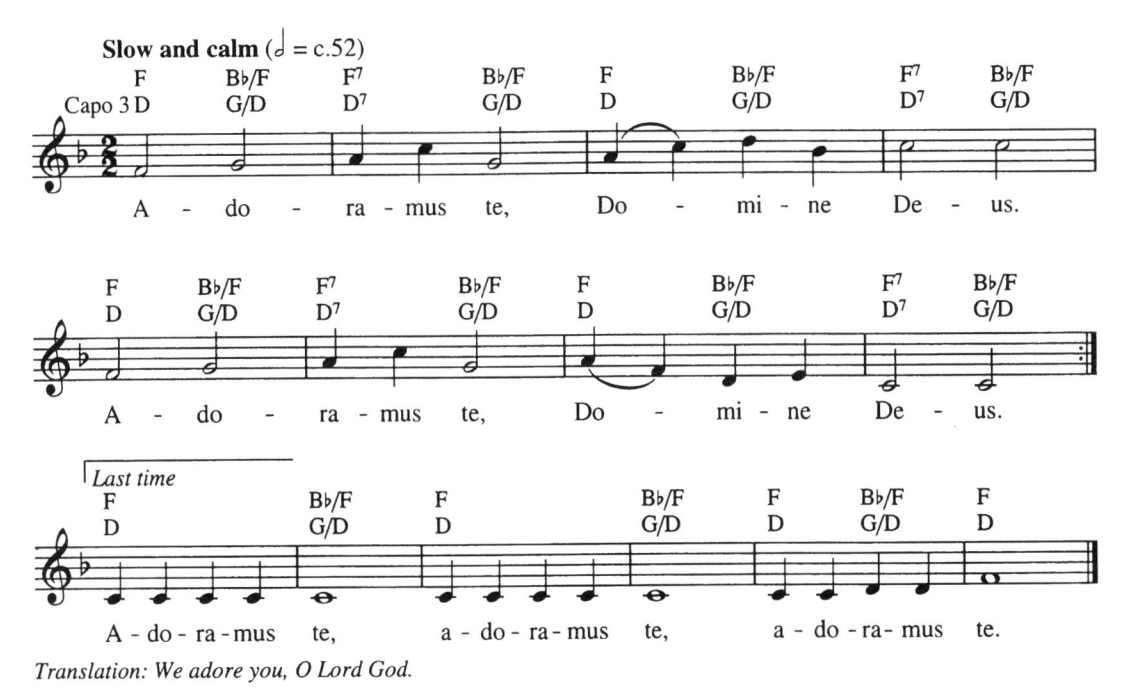

Translation: We adore you, O Lord God.

Text: Traditional
Music: Margaret Rizza (b.1929)
© Copyright 1997 Kevin Mayhew Ltd.

861 Benedictus qui venit

Text: from the Roman Missal
Music: Noel Darros
© Copyright 1988 Kevin Mayhew Ltd.

862 Bless the Lord, my soul

Bless the Lord, my soul, and bless God's ho-ly name.

Bless the Lord, my soul, who leads me in-to life.

Verses: Cantor

1. It is God who for-gives all your guilt, who heals ev-'ry one of your ills, who re-deems your life from the grave, who crowns you with love and com-pas-sion.

2. The Lord is com-pas-sion and love, the Lord is pa-tient and rich in mer-cy. God does not treat us ac-cord-ing to our sins, nor re-pay us ac-cord-ing to our faults.

3. As a fa-ther has com-pas-sion on his chil-dren, the Lord has mer-cy on those who re-vere him; for God knows of what we are made, and re-mem-bers that we are dust.

Text: Taizé Community from Psalm 102
Music: Jacques Berthier (1923-1994)
© Copyright Ateliers et Presses de Taizé, Taizé-Communauté, F71250, France. Used by permission.

863 Calm me, Lord

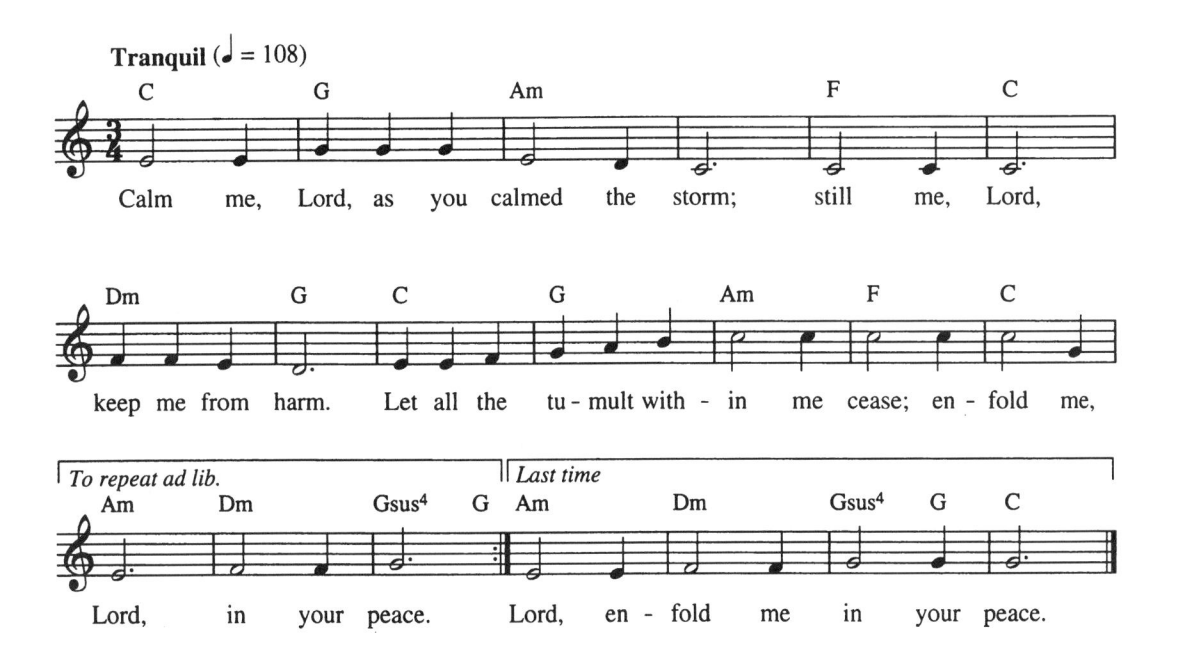

Tranquil (♩ = 108)

Calm me, Lord, as you calmed the storm; still me, Lord, keep me from harm. Let all the tumult within me cease; enfold me, Lord, in your peace. Lord, enfold me in your peace.

To repeat ad lib. | *Last time*

Text: David Adam
Music: Margaret Rizza (b.1929)
Text © Copyright SPCK, Holy Trinity Church, Marylebone Road, London, NW1 4DU.
Used by permission from 'The Edge of Glory'.
Music © Copyright 1998 Kevin Mayhew Ltd.

864 Confitemini Domino

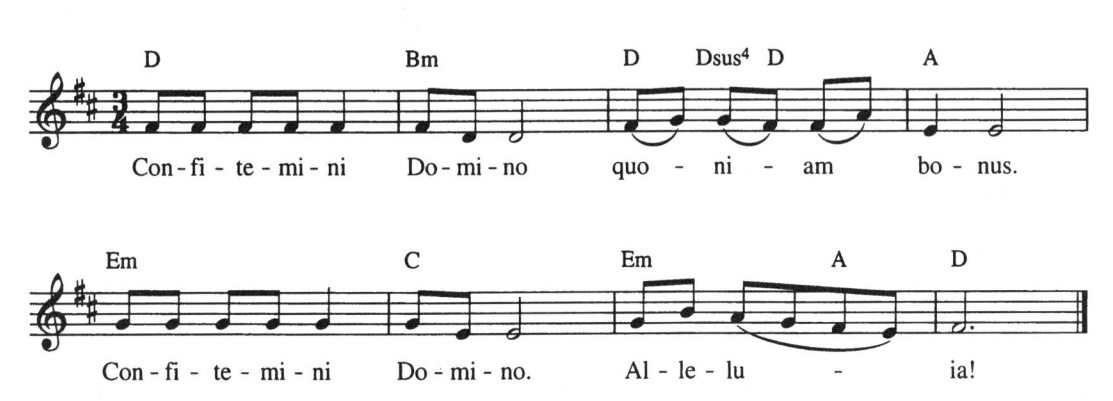

Confitemini Domino quoniam bonus.
Confitemini Domino. Alleluia!

Translation: Give thanks to the Lord for he is good.

Text: Psalm 117
Music: Jacques Berthier (1923-1994)
© Copyright 1981 Ateliers et Presses de Taizé, Taizé-Communauté, F-71250, France.
Used by permission.

865 Eat this bread

Eat this bread, drink this cup, come to him and never be hungry. Eat this bread, drink this cup, trust in him and you will not thirst.

Verses: Cantor

1. Christ is the Bread of Life, the true bread sent from the Father.
2. Your ancestors ate manna in the desert, but this is the bread come down from heaven.
3. Eat his flesh, and drink his blood, and Christ will raise you up on the last day.
4. Anyone who eats this bread will live for ever.
5. If we believe and eat this bread we will have eternal life.

* *Choose either part.*

Text: Taizé Community based on Scripture
Music: Jacques Berthier (1923-1994)

© Copyright Ateliers et Presses de Taizé, Taizé-Communauté, F-71250, France.
Used by permission.

866 Exaudi nos, Domine

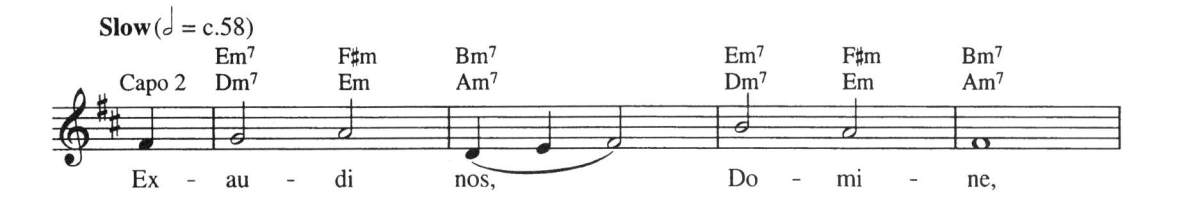

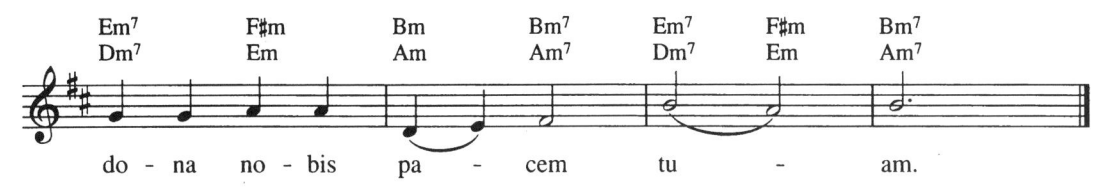

Slow (♩ = c.58)

Ex - au - di nos, Do - mi - ne,

do - na no - bis pa - cem tu - am.

Translation: Hear us, O Lord, give us your peace.

Text: Traditional
Music: Margaret Rizza (b.1929)
Music © Copyright 1998 Kevin Mayhew Ltd.

867 Holy God

Ho-ly God, we place our-selves in-to your hands. Bless us and care for us, be gra-cious and lov-ing to us; look kind-ly up-on us, and give us peace.

Text: Kevin Mayhew based on the Aaronic Blessing (Numbers 6:24-26)
Music: Kevin Mayhew (b.1942)
Music © Copyright 1996 Kevin Mayhew Ltd.

868 In the Lord I'll be ever thankful

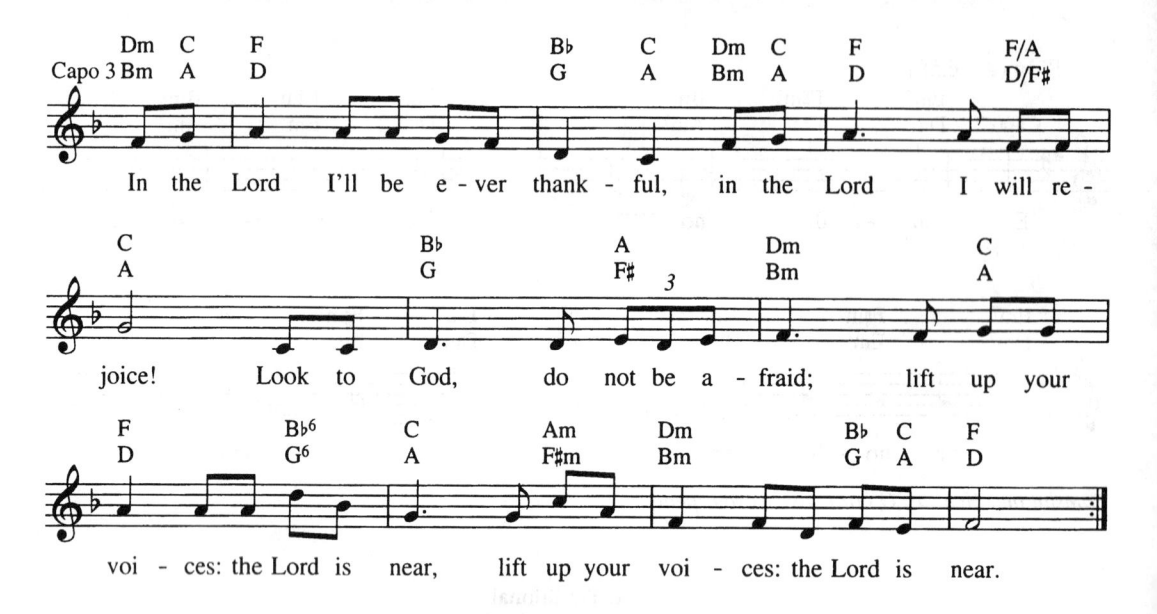

In the Lord I'll be e-ver thank-ful, in the Lord I will re-joice! Look to God, do not be a-fraid; lift up your voi-ces: the Lord is near, lift up your voi-ces: the Lord is near.

Text: Taizé Community
Music: Jacques Berthier (1923-1994)
© Copyright Ateliers et Presses de Taizé, Taizé-Communauté, F-71250, France.
Used by permission.

869 In the Lord is my joy

In the Lord is my joy and sal-va-tion, he gives light to all his cre-a-tion. In the Lord is my joy and sal-va-tion, he gives peace and true con-so-la-tion.

© Copyright 1998 Kevin Mayhew Ltd.

In the Lord is my sal - va - tion.

In the Lord is my sal - va - tion.

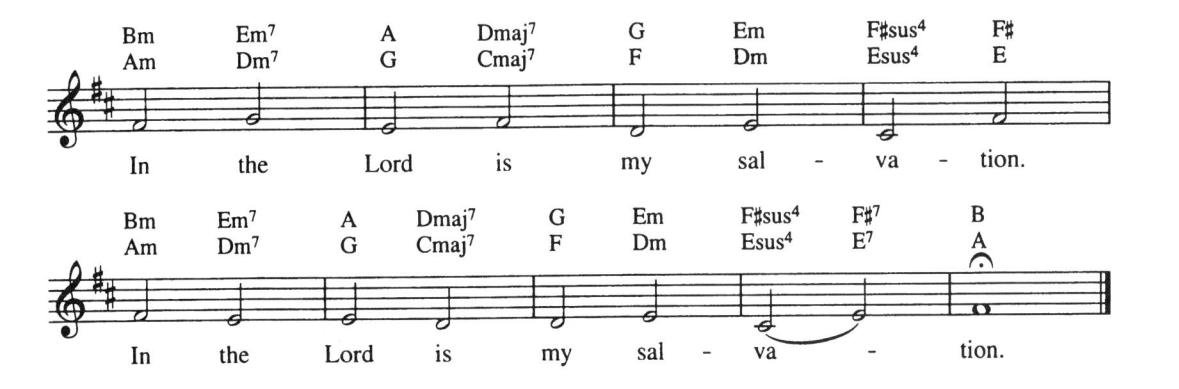

Text and Music: Margaret Rizza (b.1929)

870 Jesus, remember me

Je - sus, re - mem - ber me when you come in - to your king - dom.

Je - sus, re - mem - ber me when you come in - to your king - dom.

Text: Taizé Community based on Scripture
Music: Jacques Berthier (1923-1994)
© Copyright Ateliers et Presses de Taizé, Taizé-Communauté, F-71250, France. Used by permission.

871 Jubilate Deo

This may be sung as a round, the voices entering as indicated.

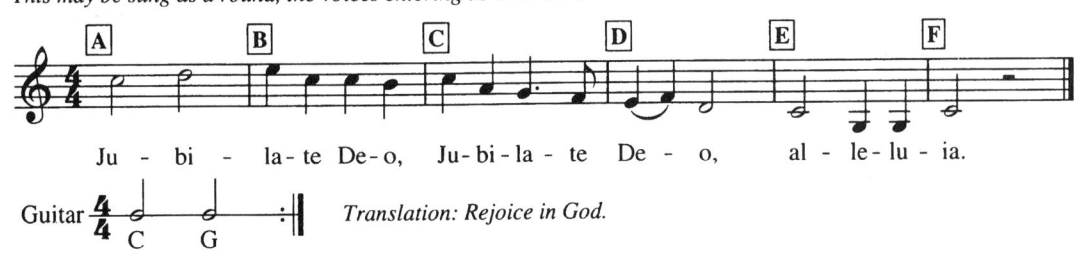

Ju - bi - la - te De - o, Ju - bi - la - te De - o, al - le - lu - ia.

Guitar

Translation: Rejoice in God.

Text: from Psalm 32
Music: Michael Praetorius (1571-1621)
© Copyright Ateliers et Presses de Taizé, Taizé-Communauté, F-71250, France.
Used by permission.

872 Jubilate Deo (Servite)

This may be sung as a 2-part round, the voices entering as indicated.

Joyfully

Ju - bi - la - te De - o om - nis ter - ra.

Ser - vi - te Do - mi - no in læ - ti - ti - a.

Al - le - lu - ia, al - le - lu - ia, in læ - ti - ti - a.

Last time: in læ - ti - ti - a!

Al - le - lu - ia, al - le - lu - ia, in læ - ti - ti - a.

Translation: Rejoice in God, all the earth. Serve the Lord with gladness.

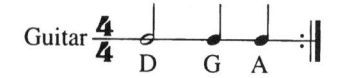

Guitar 4/4 D G A

Text: Traditional
Music: Jacques Berthier (1923-1994)
© Copyright Ateliers et Presses de Taizé, Taizé-Communauté, F-71250, France.
Used by permission.

873 Kindle a flame

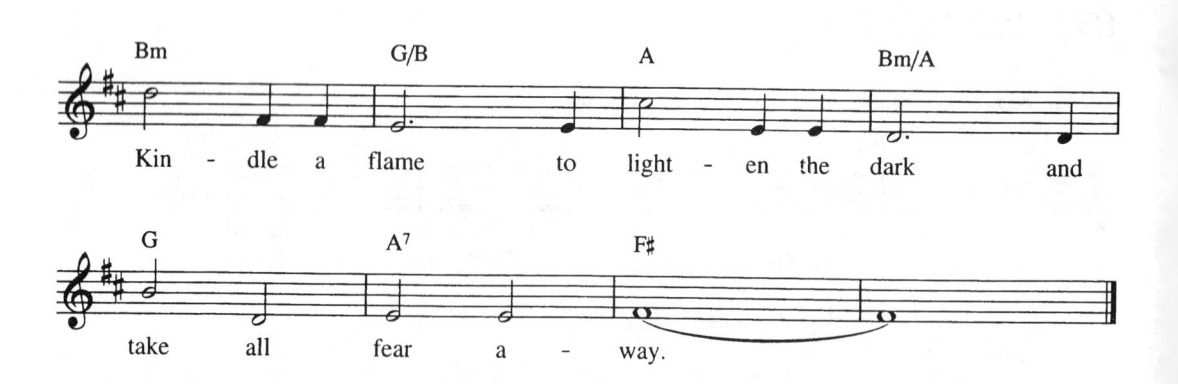

Kin - dle a flame to light - en the dark and take all fear a - way.

Text and Music: John L. Bell (b.1949) and Graham Maule (b.1958)
© Copyright WGRG, Iona Community, 840 Govan Road, Glasgow G51 3UU, Scotland.
Used by permission from 'Heaven Shall Not Wait' (Wild Goose Publications, 1987).

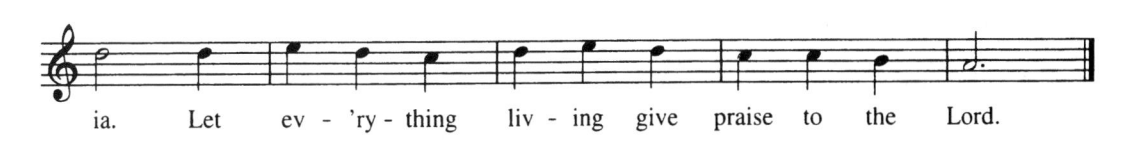

874 Laudate Dominum
Sing praise

Lau - da - te Do - mi - num, lau - da - te Do - mi - num, om - nes
Sing praise and bless the Lord, sing praise and bless the Lord, peo - ples,

gen - tes, al - le - lu - ia. Lau - da - te Do - mi - num,
na - tions, al - le - lu - ia. Sing praise and bless the Lord,

lau - da - te Do - mi - num, om - nes gen - tes, al - le - lu - ia.
sing praise and bless the Lord, peo - ples, na - tions, al - le - lu - ia.

These verses may be sung above the Refrain.

Verses: Cantor

1. Praise the Lord, all you na - tions, praise God all you peo - ples. Al - le - lu - ia. Strong is God's love and mer - cy, al - ways faith - ful for e - ver. Al - le - lu - ia. 2. Al - le - lu - ia, al - le - lu - ia. Let ev - 'ry - thing liv - ing give praise to the Lord. Al - le - lu - ia, al - le - lu - ia. Let ev - 'ry - thing liv - ing give praise to the Lord.

Text: Taizé Community, based on Scripture
Music: Jacques Berthier (1923-1994)
© Copyright Ateliers et Presses de Taizé, Taizé-Communauté, F-71250, France.
Used by permission.

875 Laudate omnes gentes

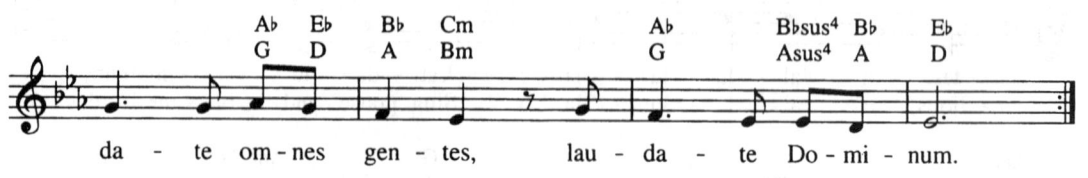

Lau-da-te om-nes gen-tes, lau-da-te Do-mi-num. Lau-da-te om-nes gen-tes, lau-da-te Do-mi-num.

Translation: All peoples, praise the Lord.

Text: from Psalm 116
Music: Jacques Berthier (1923-1994)
© Copyright Ateliers et Presses de Taizé, Taizé-Communauté, F-71250, France.
Used by permission.

876 Lord of creation

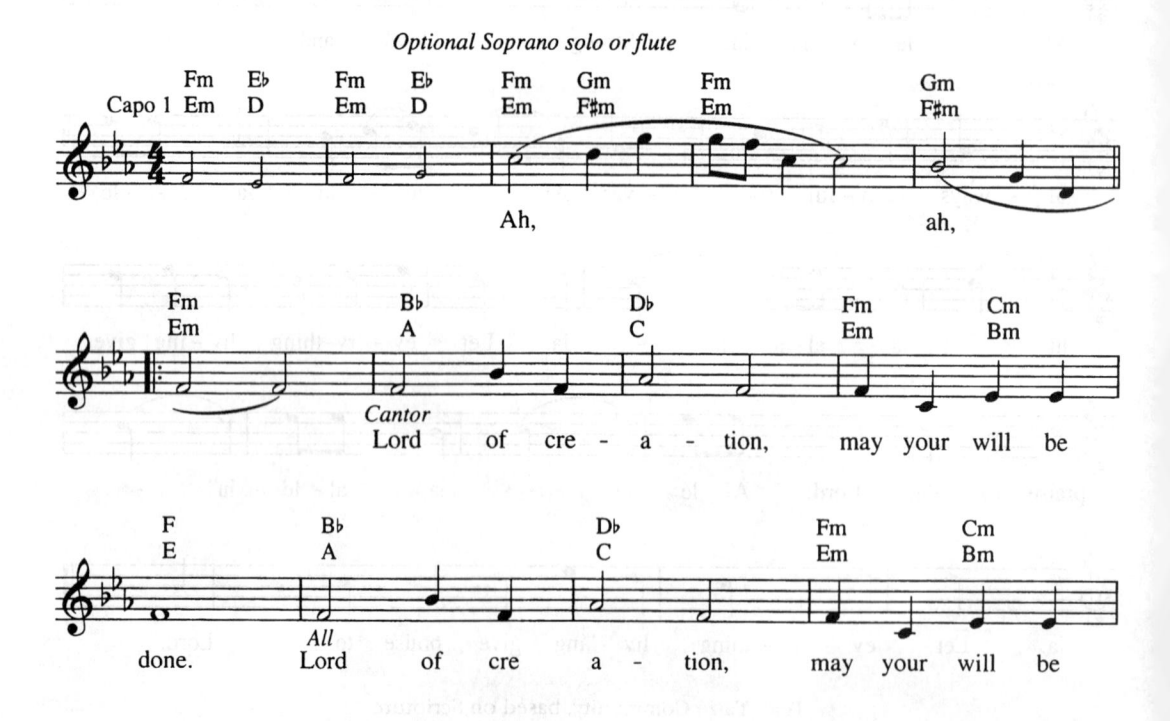

Optional Soprano solo or flute

Ah, ah,

Cantor
Lord of cre-a-tion, may your will be done.
All
Lord of cre-a-tion, may your will be

© Copyright 1991 Kevin Mayhew Ltd.

To repeat
Fm Gm Fm Gm
Em F#m Em F#m

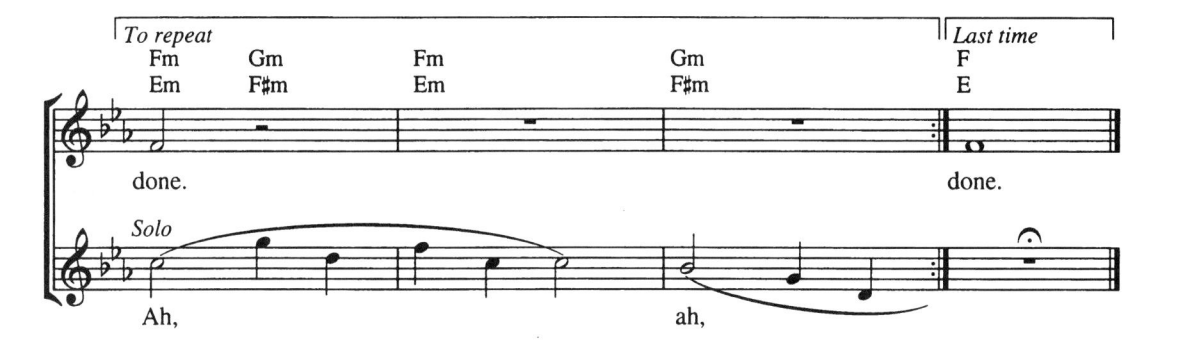

Last time
F
E

done. done.

Solo
Ah, ah,

Text and Music: Colin Mawby (b.1936)

877 Magnificat

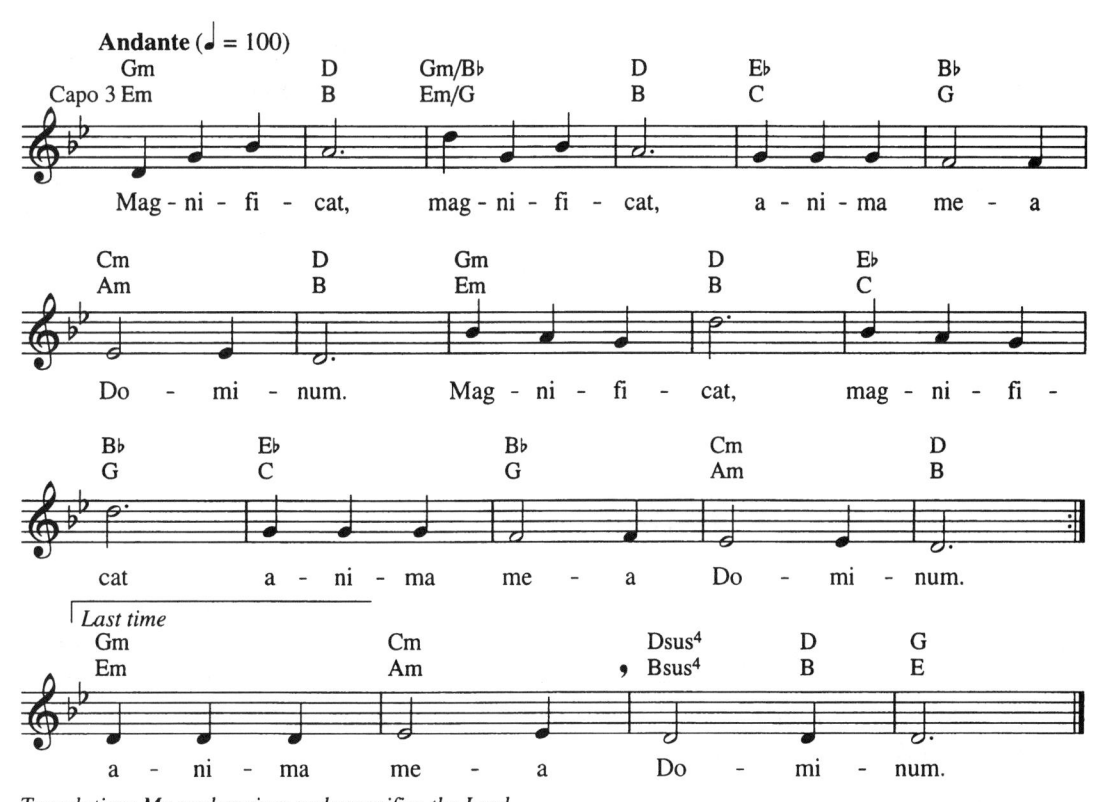

Andante (♩ = 100)

Gm D Gm/B♭ D E♭ B♭
Capo 3 Em B Em/G B C G

Mag - ni - fi - cat, mag - ni - fi - cat, a - ni - ma me - a

Cm D Gm D E♭
Am B Em B C

Do - mi - num. Mag - ni - fi - cat, mag - ni - fi -

B♭ E♭ B♭ Cm D
G C G Am B

cat a - ni - ma me - a Do - mi - num.

Last time
Gm Cm Dsus⁴ D G
Em Am Bsus⁴ B E

a - ni - ma me - a Do - mi - num.

Translation: My soul praises and magnifies the Lord.

Text: Luke 1:46
Music: Margaret Rizza (b.1929)
© Copyright 1997 Kevin Mayhew Ltd.

878 May the Lord bless you
A Blessing

(♩ = c. 63)

May the Lord bless you, may the Lord protect you and guide you, may his strength uphold you, his light shine upon you, his peace surround you, his love enfold you. May the Lord bless you, the Lord bless you, the Lord bless you.

Text: Gaelic Blessing, adapted by Margaret Rizza (b.1929)
Music: Margaret Rizza (b.1929)
© Copyright 1998 Kevin Mayhew Ltd.

879 Misericordias Domini

(♩ =72)

Refrain

Mi-se-ri-cor-di-as Do-mi-ni in æ-ter-num can-ta-bo.

Translation: I will sing for ever of the mercy of the Lord

Verses: Cantor

1. From age to age, through all ge-ne-ra-tions, my mouth shall pro-claim your truth, O Lord.

© Copyright Ateliers et Presses de Taizé, Taizé-Communauté, F071250, France. Used by permission.

2. Who, O God, who in the u-ni-verse can com-pare with you?

3. Blest be the Lord for e-ver through-out e-ter-ni-ty. A-men! A-men!

*Choose either part.

Text: Psalm 88
Music: Jacques Berthier (1923-1994)

880 Nada te turbe
Nothing can trouble

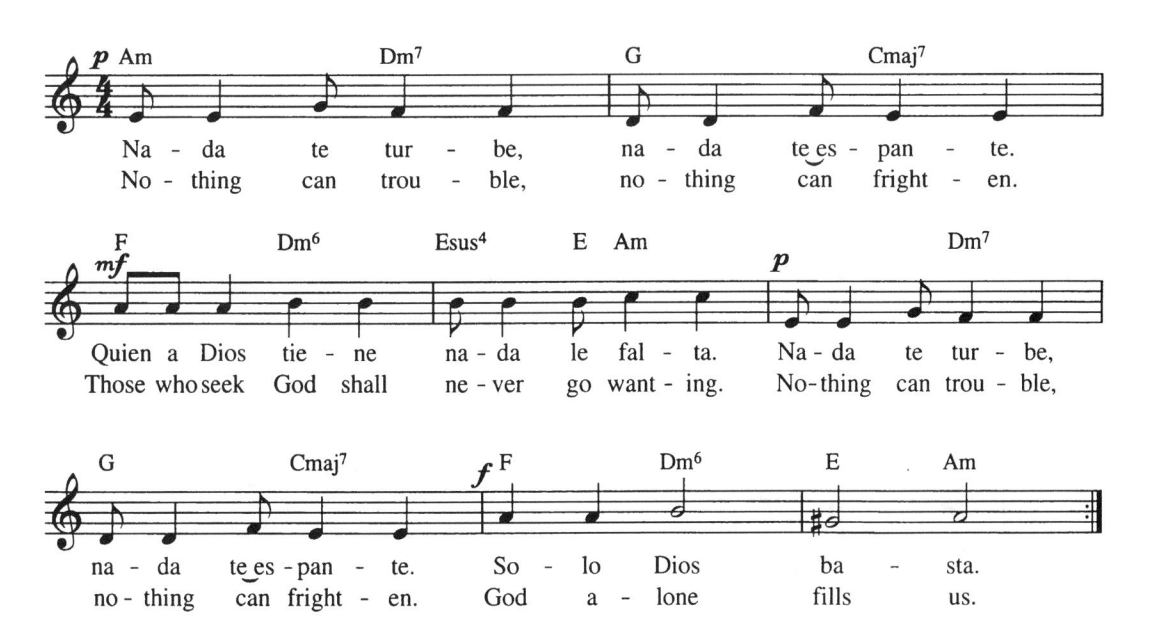

Na - da te tur - be, na - da te_es - pan - te.
No - thing can trou - ble, no - thing can fright - en.

Quien a Dios tie - ne na - da le fal - ta. Na - da te tur - be,
Those who seek God shall ne - ver go want - ing. No-thing can trou - ble,

na - da te_es - pan - te. So - lo Dios ba - sta.
no - thing can fright - en. God a - lone fills us.

Text: St Teresa of Avila
Music: Jacques Berthier (1923-1994)

© Copyright Ateliers et Presses de Taizé, Taizé-Communauté, F-71250, France. Used by permission.

881 O Christe, Domine Jesu

O Chri-ste, Do-mi-ne Je-su, O Chri-ste, Do-mi-ne Je-su! Je-su!

Translation: O Christ, Lord Jesus.

These verses may be sung above the Refrain.

Verses: Cantor

1. The Lord is my shep-herd; there is no-thing I shall want. Fresh and green are the pas-tures where he gives me re-pose. Near rest-ful wa-ters he leads me, to re-vive my drooping spi-rit. He guides me a-long the right path; he is true to his name. If I should walk in the val-ley of dark-ness no e-vil would I fear.

2. You are there with your rod and staff; with these you give me com-fort.

Text © Copyright 1963, 1986, 1993 The Grail, England, taken from 'The Psalms, a New Inclusive Language Version', published by HarperCollins Religious. Used by permission of A. P. Watt, London.
Music © Copyright Ateliers et Presses de Taizé, Taizé-Communauté, F-71250, France. Used by permission.

You have pre-pared a ban-quet for me in the sight of my foes.

My head you have a-noin-ted with oil; my cup is o-ver-flow-ing. Sure-ly

good - ness and kind - ness shall fol - low me all the days of my life.

In the Lord's own house shall I dwell for e - ver and e - ver.

Choose either part.

Text: Psalm 22
Music: Jacques Berthier (1923-1994)

882 O Lord, hear my prayer

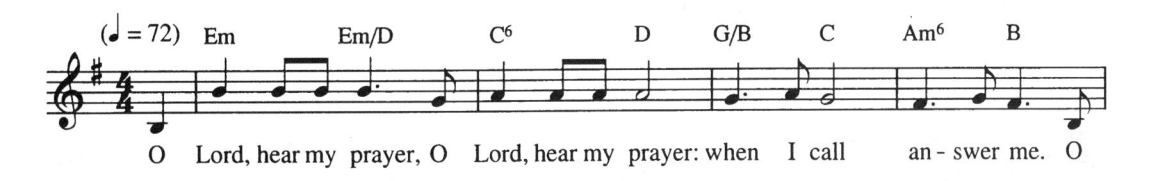

O Lord, hear my prayer, O Lord, hear my prayer: when I call an-swer me. O
Lord, hear my prayer, O Lord, hear my prayer. Come and lis-ten to me.

Text: Taizé Community
Music: Jacques Berthier (1923-1994)

© Copyright Ateliers et Presses de Taizé, Taizé-Communauté, F-71250, France. Used by permission.

883 O Lord, my heart is not proud

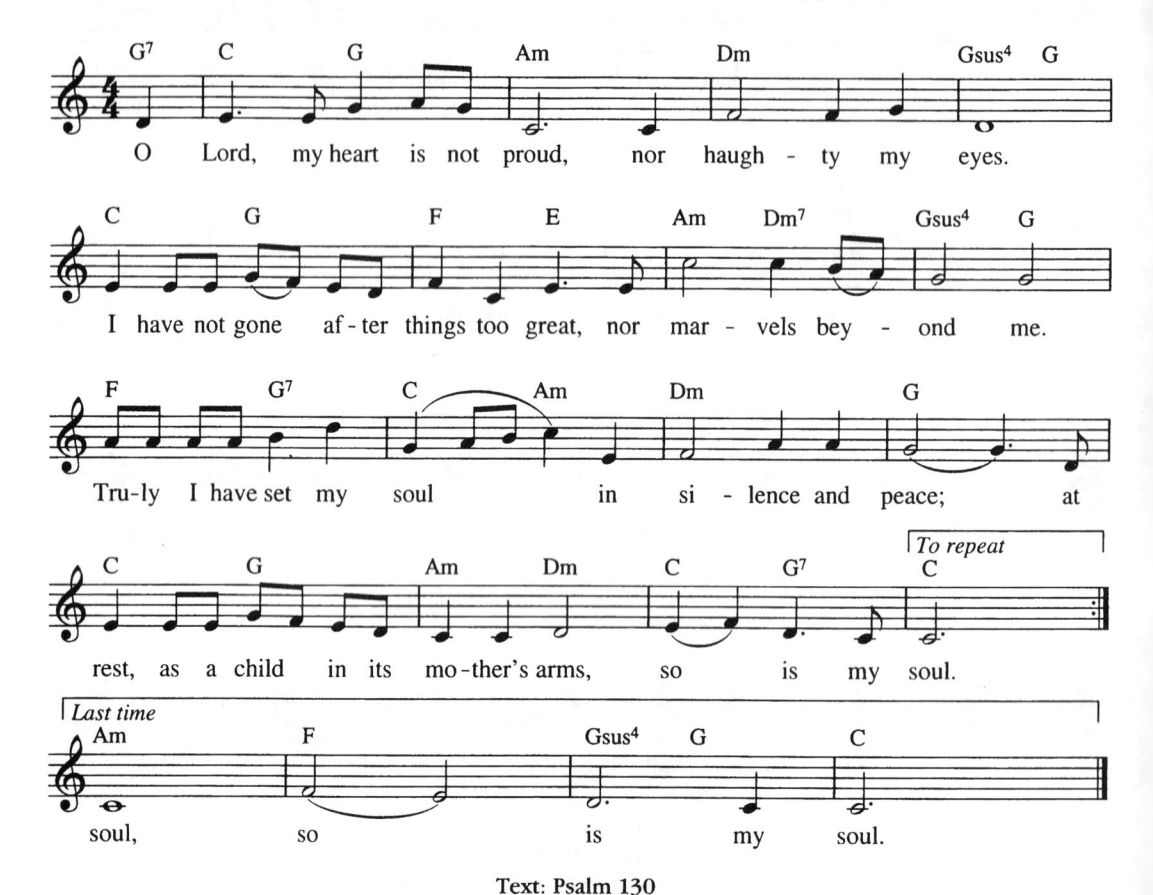

O Lord, my heart is not proud, nor haughty my eyes.
I have not gone after things too great, nor marvels beyond me.
Truly I have set my soul in silence and peace; at rest, as a child in its mother's arms, so is my soul.

Last time: so is my soul.

Text: Psalm 130
Music: Margaret Rizza (b.1929)
Text © Copyright The Grail, England. Used by permission of A.P. Watt Ltd, 20 John Street, London WC1N 2DR.
Music © Copyright 1997 Kevin Mayhew Ltd.

884 O Sacrament most holy

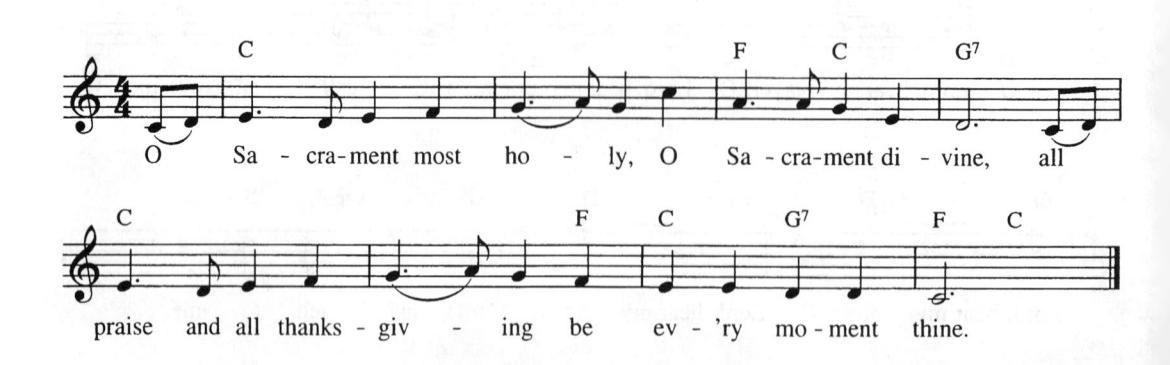

O Sacrament most holy, O Sacrament divine, all praise and all thanksgiving be ev'ry moment thine.

Text and Music: traditional

885 Ostende nobis

This may be sung as a round, the voices entering as indicated.

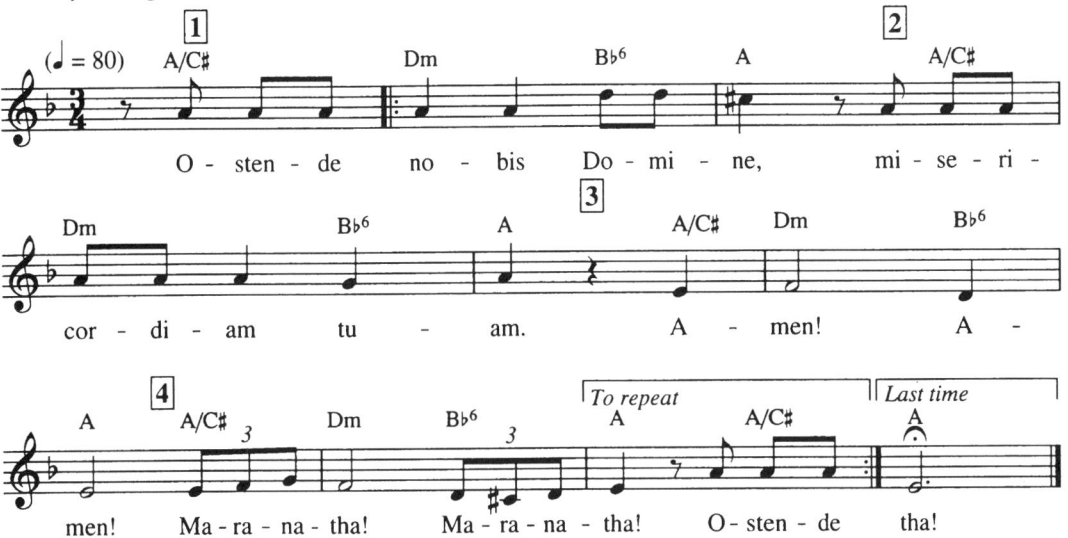

O - sten - de no - bis Do - mi - ne, mi - se - ri - cor - di - am tu - am. A - men! A - men! Ma - ra - na - tha! Ma - ra - na - tha! O - sten - de tha!

Translation: Lord, show us your mercy. Amen! Come soon!

Text: Taizé Community
Music: Jacques Berthier (1923-1994)
© Copyright Ateliers et Presses de Taizé, Taizé-Communauté, F-71250, France. Used by permission.

886 Sanctum nomen Domini

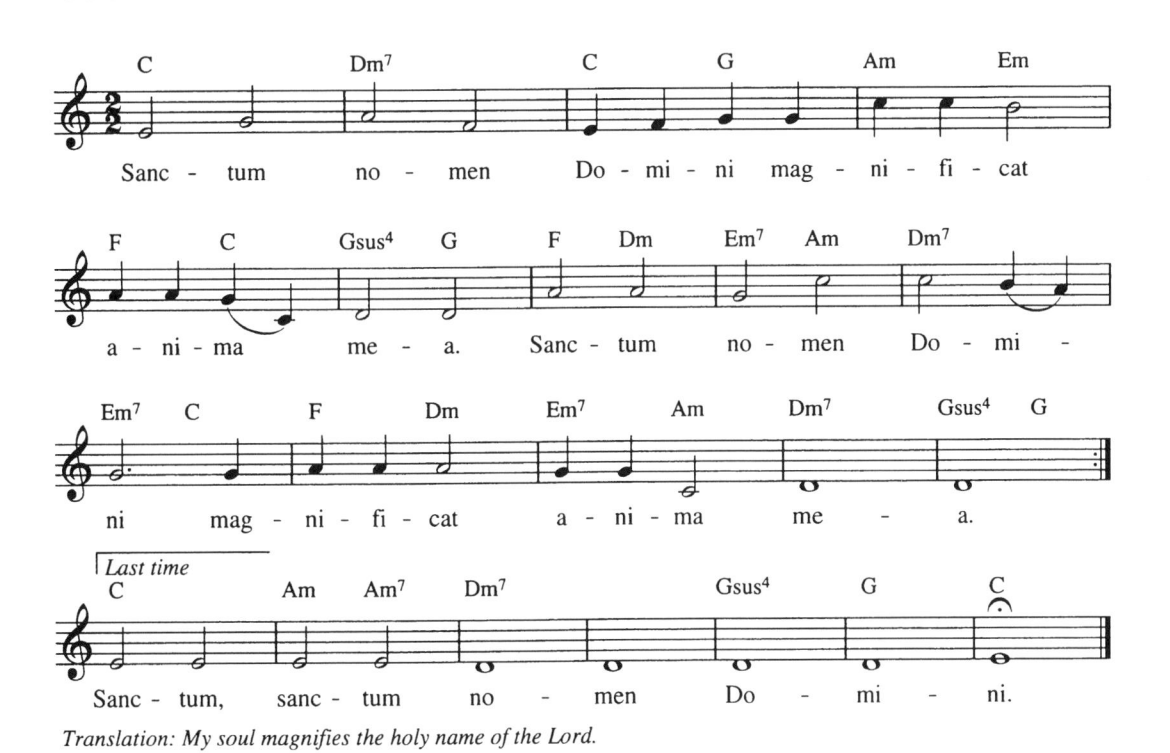

Sanc - tum no - men Do - mi - ni mag - ni - fi - cat a - ni - ma me - a. Sanc - tum no - men Do - mi - ni mag - ni - fi - cat a - ni - ma me - a. Sanc - tum, sanc - tum no - men Do - mi - ni.

Translation: My soul magnifies the holy name of the Lord.

Text: Traditional
Music: Margaret Rizza (b.1929)
© Copyright 1998 Kevin Mayhew Ltd.

887 Silent, surrendered

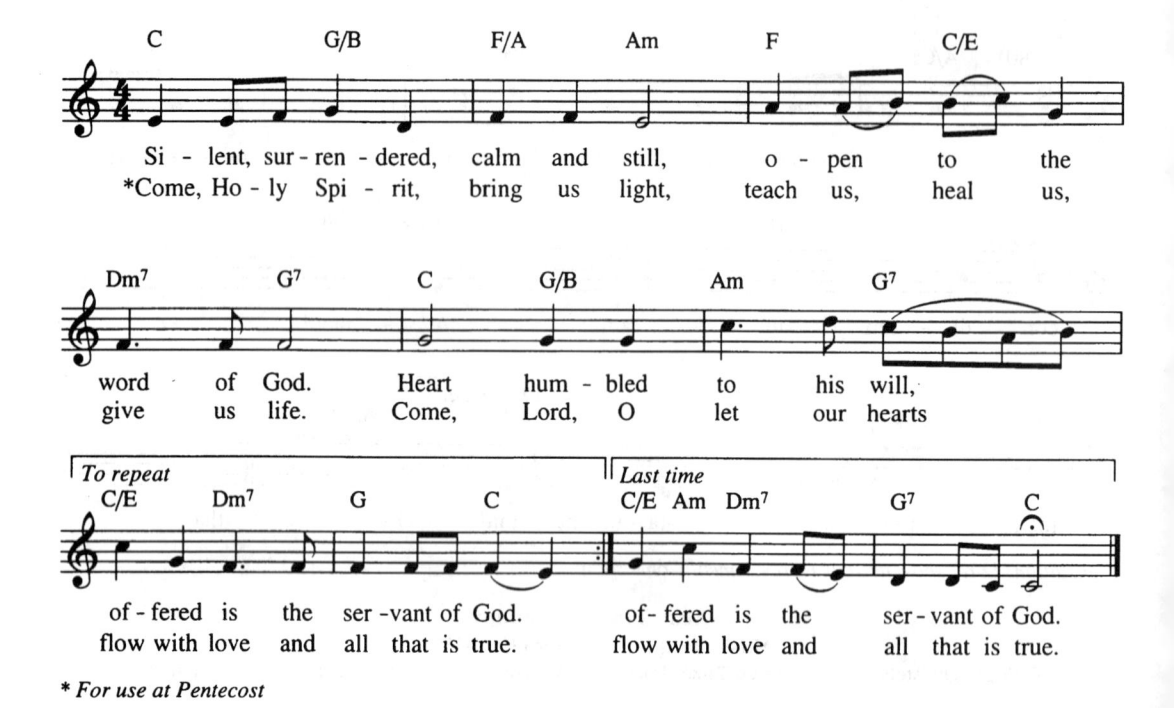

Si - lent, sur - ren - dered, calm and still, o - pen to the word of God. Heart hum - bled to his will, of - fered is the ser - vant of God.

*Come, Ho - ly Spi - rit, bring us light, teach us, heal us, give us life. Come, Lord, O let our hearts flow with love and all that is true.

For use at Pentecost

Text: v. 1: Pamela Hayes; v.2: Margaret Rizza (b.1929)
Music: Margaret Rizza (b.1929)
© Copyright 1998 Kevin Mayhew Ltd.

888 Stay here and keep watch

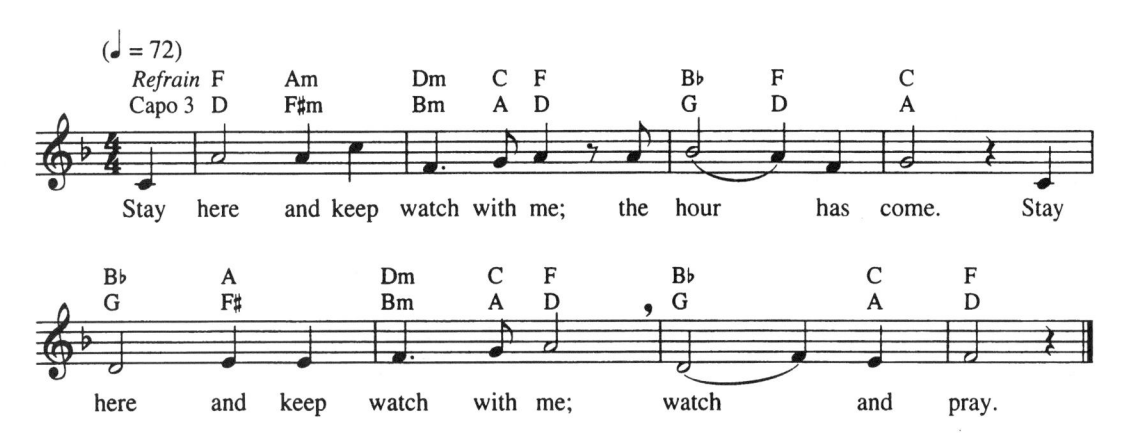

Refrain

Stay here and keep watch with me; the hour has come. Stay here and keep watch with me; watch and pray.

These verses may be sung above the Refrain.

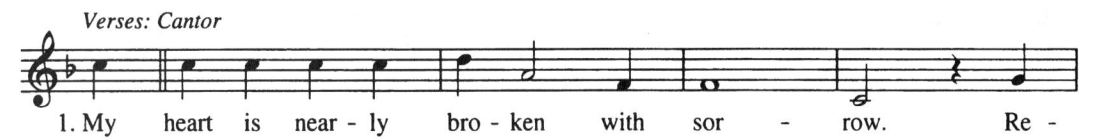

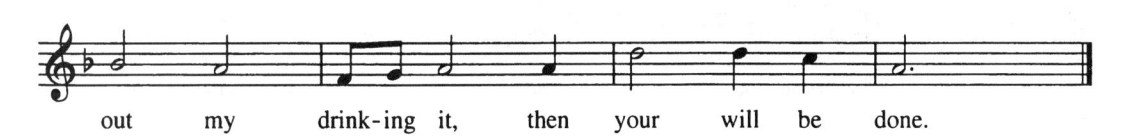

Verses: Cantor

1. My heart is nearly broken with sorrow. Remain here, remain here and stay awake with me.

2. Father, if it is possible, let this cup pass me by.

3. Father, if this cannot pass me by without my drinking it, then your will be done.

Text: Taizé Community from Matthew 26
Music: Jacques Berthier (1923-1994)

© Copyright 1984 Ateliers et Presses de Taizé, Taizé-Communauté, F-71250, France. Used by permission.

889 Stay with me

Refrain

Stay with me, re-main here with me, watch and pray, watch and pray.

Verses: Cantor

1. Stay here and keep watch with me. Watch and pray, watch and pray!

2. Watch and pray not to give way to temp-ta-tion.

3. The Spi-rit is ea-ger, but the flesh is weak.

4. My heart is near-ly bro-ken with sor-row. Re-main here with me, stay a-wake and pray.

5. Fa-ther, if it is pos-si-ble let this cup pass me by.

6. Fa-ther, if this can-not pass me by with-out my drink-ing it, your will be done.

*Choose either part

Text: Matthew 26: 36-42
Music: Jacques Berthier (1923-1994)

© Copyright Ateliers et Presses de Taizé, Taizé-Communauté, F-71250, France. Used by permission.

890 Surrexit Christus

Refrain

(Hum) Sur-re-xit Christus, al-le-lu-ia!

(Hum) Can-ta-te Do-mi-no, al-le-lu-ia!

Translation: Christ is risen. Sing to the Lord.

These verses may be sung above the Refrain.

Verses: Cantor

1. All you heavens, bless the Lord.
Stars of the heavens bless the Lord.

2. Sun and moon, bless the Lord. And you, night and day, bless the Lord.

3. Frost and cold, bless the Lord. Ice and snow, bless the Lord.

4. Fire and heat, bless the Lord. And you, light and darkness, bless the Lord.

5. Spirits and souls of the just, bless the Lord. Saints and the humble-hearted, bless the Lord.

* *Choose either part.*

Text: from Daniel 3
Music: Jacques Berthier (1923-1994)

© Copyright Ateliers et Presses de Taizé, Taizé-Communauté, F-71250, France. Used by permission.

891 The Lord is my light

The Lord is my light, in him I trust. The Lord is my light, in him I trust, in him I trust.

Text: Psalm 26
Music: Margaret Rizza (b.1929)
© Copyright 1998 Kevin Mayhew Ltd.

892 The Lord is my song

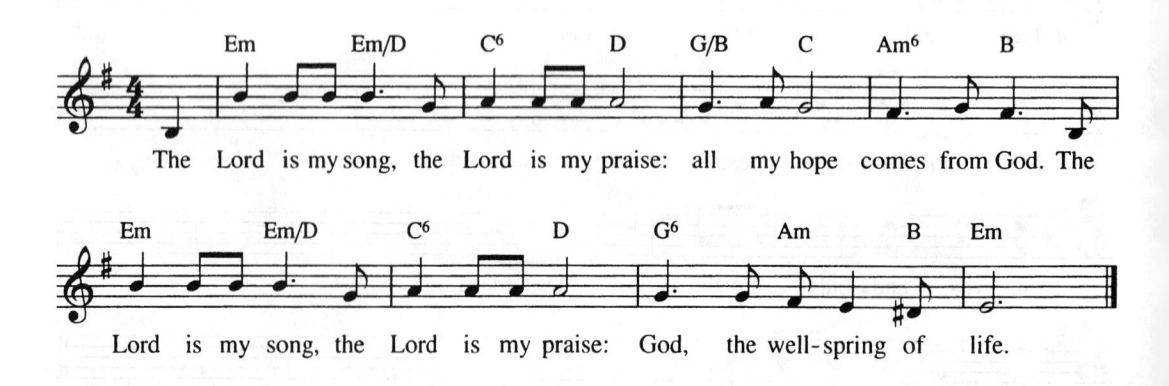

The Lord is my song, the Lord is my praise: all my hope comes from God. The Lord is my song, the Lord is my praise: God, the well-spring of life.

Text: Taizé Community
Music: Jacques Berthier (1923-1994)
© Copyright Ateliers et Presses de Taizé, Taizé-Communauté, F-71250, France. Used by permission.

893 Ubi caritas

Music for All, to be sung 6 times

Ubi caritas et amor.

Ubi caritas Deus ibi est.

Verses for Cantor(s)

1. Your love, O Jesus Christ, has gathered us together.
2. May your love, O Jesus Christ, be foremost in our lives.
3. Let us love one another as God has loved us.
4. Let us be one in love together in the one bread of Christ.
5. The love of God in Jesus Christ bears eternal joy.
6. The love of God in Jesus Christ will never have an end.

* *Choose either part, or divide.*

Text: Taizé Community
Music: Jacques Berthier (1923-1994)

© Copyright Ateliers et Presses de Taizé, Taizé-Communauté, F-71250, France. Used by permission.

LITURGICAL
HYMNS OLD & NEW

894 Veni, lumen cordium
Come, light of our hearts

Veni, lumen cordium. Veni, Sancte Spiritus.
Veni, lumen cordium. Veni, Sancte Spiritus.
Veni, lumen cordium.
Veni, Sancte Spiritus. Amen.

Translation: Come, light of our hearts. Come, Holy Spirit, come.

Text: Stephen Langton (1160-1228)
Music: Margaret Rizza (b.1929)
© Copyright 1998 Kevin Mayhew Ltd.

895 Veni, Sancte Spiritus (Vogler)

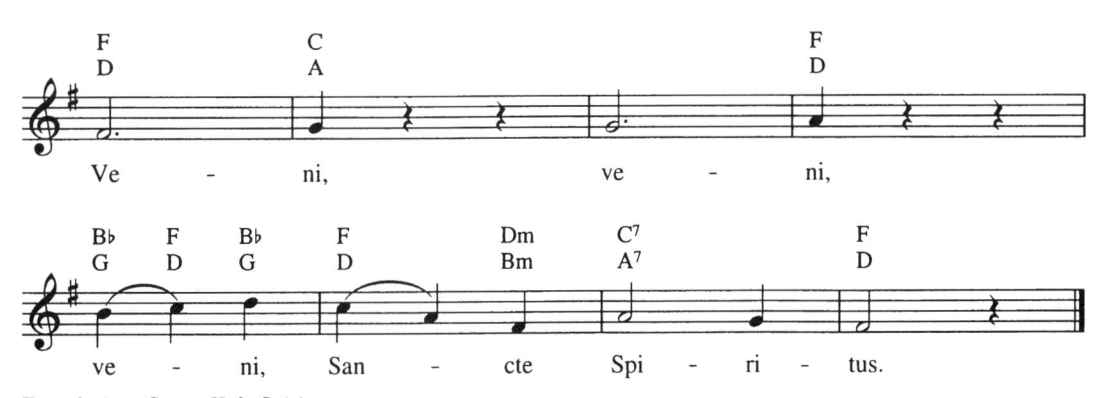

Veni, veni, veni, Sancte Spiritus.

Translation: Come, Holy Spirit.

Music: George Vogler (1749-1814)

896 Veni, Sancte Spiritus (Walker)

Verses: Cantor

1. Holy Spirit, Lord of light, radiance give from celestial height. Come, thou Father of the poor, come now with treasures that endure: Light of all who live.

Congregation to sing 5 times — Capo 1

Veni, Sancte Spiritus; veni, Sancte Spiritus; veni, veni, Sancte Spiritus; veni, Sancte Spiritus.

2. Thou, of all consolers, the best. Thou the soul's delightful guest; refreshing peace bestow. Thou, in toil, my comfort sweet; thou,

© Copyright 1981, 1982, Christopher Walker. Published by OCP Publications, 5536 NE Hassalo, Portland, OR 97213, USA. All rights reserved. Used by permission.

cool-ness in the heat. Thou, my sol - ace in time of woe.

3. Light im - mor - tal, light di - vine; fire of love, our
hearts re - fine, our in - most be - ing fill. Take thy grace a - way and
no - thing pure in us will stay, all our good is turned to ill.

4. Heal our wounds, our strength re - new, on our dry - ness
pour thy dew; wash guilt a - way, bend the stub - born heart, melt the froz - en,
warm the chill and guide the steps that go a - stray.

5. Seven - fold gifts on us be pleased to pour, who thee con - fess and
thee a - dore; bring us thy com - fort when we die; give us life with thee on
high; give us joys, give us joys that ne - ver end.

Text: Stephen Langton (1160-1228), trans. Edward Caswall (1814-1878), alt. Christopher Walker
Music: Christopher Walker (b.1947)

897 Wait for the Lord

Refrain

Wait for the Lord, whose day is near.
Wait for the Lord: keep watch, take heart!

These verses may be sung above the Refrain.

Verses: Cantor

1. Pre-pare the way for the Lord. Make a straight path for God.
Pre-pare the way for the Lord.

2. Re-joice in the Lord al-ways: God is at hand.
Joy and glad-ness for all who seek the Lord.

3. The glo-ry of the Lord shall be re-vealed. All the earth will see the Lord.

4. I wait-ed for the Lord. God heard my cry.

© Copyright Ateliers et Pesses de Taizé, Taizé-Communauté, F-71250, France.
Used by permission.

5. Our eyes are fixed on the Lord our God.

6. Seek first the kingdom of God. Seek and you shall find.

7. O Lord, show us your way. Guide us in your truth.

Text: Taizé Community, based on Scripture
Music: Jacques Berthier (1923-1994)

898 Within our darkest night

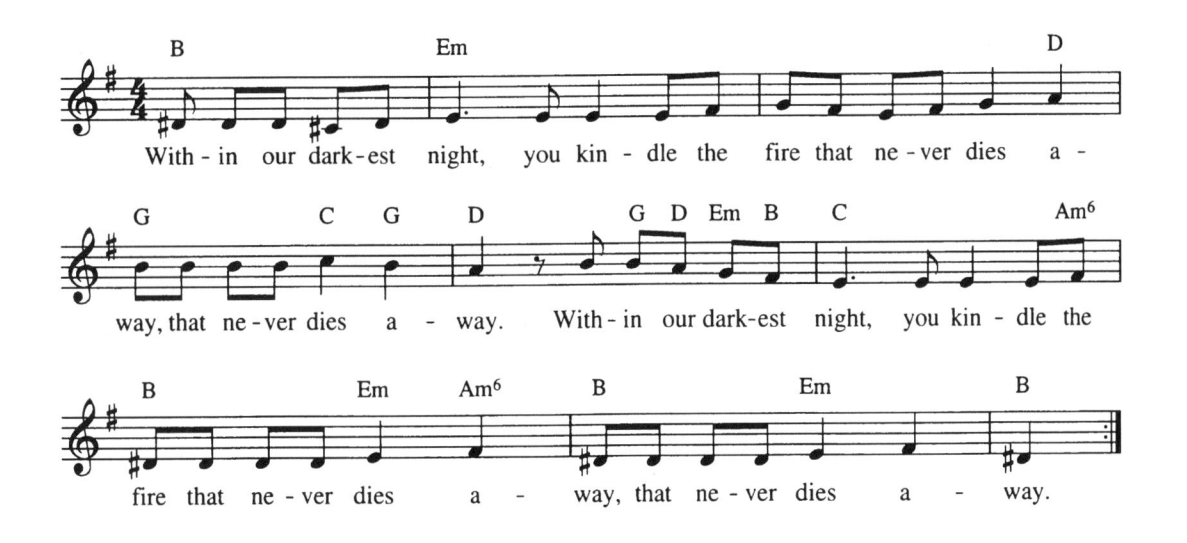

Within our darkest night, you kindle the fire that never dies away, that never dies away. Within our darkest night, you kindle the fire that never dies away, that never dies away.

Text: Taizé Community
Music: Jacques Berthier (1923-1994)
© Copyright Ateliers et Presses de Taizé, Taizé-Communauté, F-71250, France. Used by permission.

899 You are the centre

You are the centre, you are my life, you are the centre, O Lord, of my life. Come, Lord, and heal me, Lord of my life, come, Lord, and teach me, Lord of my life. You are the centre, Lord, of my life. Give me your Spirit and teach me your ways, give me your peace, Lord, and set me free.

1. You are the centre, Lord, of my life. *D.C.*

2. You are the centre, you are my life, you are the centre, O Lord, of my life.

rit. e dim. al fine

Text and Music: Margaret Rizza (b.1929)
© Copyright 1998 Kevin Mayhew Ltd.

Responsorial Psalms

900 1st Advent (A)

Responsorial Psalm Psalm 121:1-2, 4-5, 6-9. ℟ cf. v.1

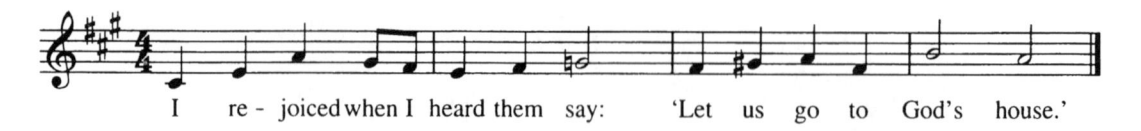

I rejoiced when I heard them say: 'Let us go to God's house.'

1. I rejoiced when I <u>heard</u> them say:
   'Let us go <u>to</u> God's house.'
   And now our <u>feet</u> are standing
   within your gates, <u>O</u> Jerusalem.

2. It is there that the <u>tribes</u> go up,
   the tribes <u>of</u> the Lord.
   For Israel's <u>law</u> it is,
   there to praise <u>the</u> Lord's name.

3. For the peace of Jeru<u>sa</u>lem pray:
   'Peace be <u>to</u> your homes!
   May peace reign <u>in</u> your walls,
   in your pal<u>a</u>ces, peace!'

4. For love of my bre<u>thren</u> and friends
   I say: 'Peace <u>up</u>on you!'
   For love of the house <u>of</u> the Lord
   I will ask <u>for</u> your good.

Gospel Acclamation Psalm 84:8
For musical setting see Nos 36 to 47
   Alleluia.
   Let us see, O <u>Lord</u>, your mercy
   and give us your <u>sa</u>ving help.
   Alleluia.

Response: Andrew Moore Psalm tone: Alan Rees
Text © 1963, 1986, 1993 The Grail, England, taken from 'The Psalms, a New Inclusive Language Version',
published by HarperCollins Religious. Used by permission of A.P. Watt Ltd, London.
Response © Copyright 1998 Kevin Mayhew Ltd.
Psalm tone © Copyright Belmont Abbey, Hereford HR2 9RZ. Used by permission.

901 1st Advent (B)

Responsorial Psalm Psalm 79:2-3, 15-16, 18-19. ℟ v.4

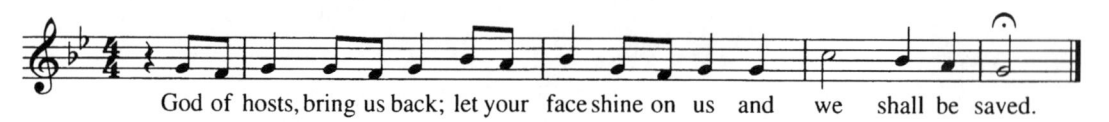

God of hosts, bring us back; let your face shine on us and we shall be saved.

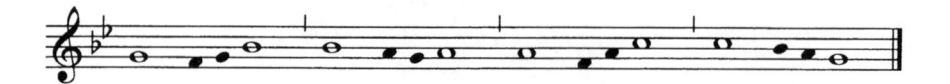

1. O Shepherd of Is<u>ra</u>el, hear us,
   shine forth from your che<u>ru</u>bim throne.
   O Lord, rouse <u>up</u> your might,
   O Lord, come <u>to</u> our help.

2. God of hosts, turn again, <u>we</u> implore,
   look down from hea<u>ven</u> and see.
   Visit this vine <u>and</u> protect it,
   the vine your right <u>hand</u> has planted.

Response: Andrew Moore Psalm tone: Gregory Murray
Text © 1963, 1986, 1993 The Grail, England, taken from 'The Psalms, a New Inclusive Language Version',
published by HarperCollins Religious. Used by permission of A.P. Watt Ltd, London.
Response © Copyright 1998 Kevin Mayhew Ltd.
Psalm tone © Copyright Downside Abbey, Stratton-on-the-Fosse, Bath BA3 4RH. Used by permission.

3. May your hand be on the one <u>you</u> have chosen,
   the one you have gi<u>ven</u> your strength.
   And we shall never forsake <u>you</u> again:
   give us life that we may call up<u>on</u> your name.

Gospel Acclamation Psalm 84:8
For musical setting see Nos 36 to 47
   Alleluia.
   Let us see, O <u>Lord</u>, your mercy
   and give us your <u>sav</u>ing help.
   Alleluia.

902 1st Advent (C)

Responsorial Psalm Psalm 24:4-5, 8-9, 10, 14. ℟ v.1

To you, O Lord, I lift up my soul, I lift up my soul.

1. Lord, make me <u>know</u> your ways.
   Lord, teach <u>me</u> your paths.
   Make me walk in your <u>truth</u>, and teach me:
   for you are <u>God</u> my saviour.

2. The Lord is <u>good</u> and upright.
   He shows the path to <u>those</u> who stray,
   he guides the humble in <u>the</u> right path;
   he teaches his way <u>to</u> the poor.

3. His ways are faithful<u>ness</u> and love
   for those who keep his cove<u>nant</u> and will.
   The Lord's friendship is for those <u>who</u> revere him;
   to them he re<u>veals</u> his covenant.

Gospel Acclamation Psalm 84:8
For musical setting see Nos 36 to 47
   Alleluia.
   Let us see, O <u>Lord</u>, your mercy
   and give us your <u>sav</u>ing help.
   Alleluia.

Response and Psalm tone: Alan Rees
Text © 1963, 1986, 1993 The Grail, England, taken from 'The Psalms, a New Inclusive Language Version',
published by HarperCollins Religious. Used by permission of A.P. Watt Ltd, London.
Response © Copyright 1998 Kevin Mayhew Ltd.
Psalm tone © Copyright Belmont Abbey, Hereford HR2 9RZ. Used by permission.

903 2nd Advent (A)

Responsorial Psalm Psalm 71:1-2, 7-8, 12-13, 17. ℟ cf. v.7

In his days jus-tice shall flou - rish and peace till the moon fails.

1. O God, give your judgement to the king,
to a king's son your justice,
that he may judge your people in justice
and your poor in right judgement.

2. In his days justice shall flourish
and peace till the moon fails.
He shall rule from sea to sea,
from the Great River to earth's bounds.

3. For he shall save the poor when they cry
and the needy who are helpless.
He will have pity on the weak
and save the lives of the poor.

4. May his name be blest for ever
and endure like the sun.
Every tribe shall be blest in him,
all nations bless his name.

Gospel Acclamation Luke 3:4, 6
For musical setting see Nos 36 to 47
Alleluia.
Prepare a way for the Lord and make his paths straight,
and all mankind shall see the salvation of our God.
Alleluia.

Response: Stephen Dean   Psalm tone: Alan Rees
Text © 1963, 1986, 1993 The Grail, England, taken from 'The Psalms, a New Inclusive Language Version', published by HarperCollins Religious. Used by permission of A.P. Watt Ltd, London.
Response © 1989 Stephen Dean. Published by OCP Publications, 5536 NE Hassalo, Portland, OR 97213, USA. Used by permission. Psalm tone © Belmont Abbey, Hereford HR2 9RZ. Used by permission.

904 2nd Advent (B)

Responsorial Psalm Psalm 84:9-14. ℟ v.8

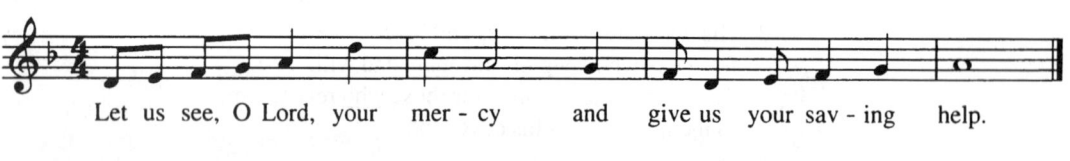

Let us see, O Lord, your mer-cy and give us your sav-ing help.

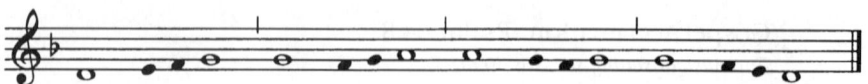

1. I will hear what the Lord God has to say,
a voice that speaks of peace.
His help is near for those who fear him
and his glory will dwell in our land.

2. Mercy and faithfulness have met;
justice and peace have embraced.
Faithfulness shall spring from the earth
and justice look down from heaven.

Response: Stephen Dean   Psalm tone: Laurence Bevenot
Text © 1963, 1986, 1993 The Grail, England, taken from 'The Psalms, a New Inclusive Language Version', published by HarperCollins Religious. Used by permission of A.P. Watt Ltd, London.
Response © 1989 Stephen Dean. Published by OCP Publications, 5536 NE Hassalo, Portland, OR 97213, USA.
All rights reserved. Used by permission.
Psalm tone © Ampleforth Abbey, York YO6 4EN. Used by permission.

3. The Lord will <u>make</u> us prosper
and our earth shall <u>yield</u> its fruit.
Justice shall <u>march</u> before him
and peace shall fo<u>llow</u> his steps.

Gospel Acclamation Luke 3:4, 6
For musical setting see Nos 36 to 47
　　Alleluia.
　　Prepare a way for the Lord and make <u>his</u> paths straight,
　　and all mankind shall see the salvation <u>of</u> our God.
　　Alleluia.

905　2nd Advent (C)

Responsorial Psalm　Psalm 125. ℟ v.3

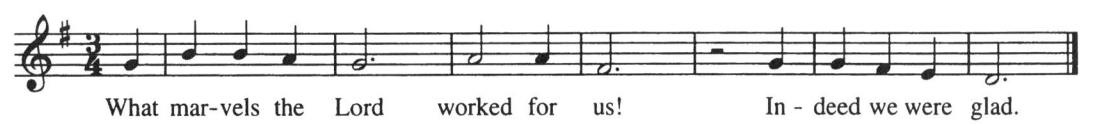

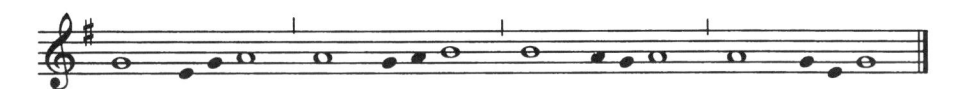

What mar-vels the Lord　worked for us!　In - deed we were glad.

1. When the Lord delivered <u>Zion</u> from bondage,
it seemed <u>like</u> a dream.
Then was our mouth <u>filled</u> with laughter,
on our lips <u>there</u> were songs.

2. The heathens themselves <u>said</u>: 'What marvels
the Lord <u>worked</u> for them!'
What marvels the Lord <u>worked</u> for us!
Indeed <u>we</u> were glad.

3. Deliver us, O Lord, <u>from</u> our bondage
as streams <u>in</u> dry land.
Those who are sow<u>ing</u> in tears
will sing <u>when</u> they reap.

4. They go out, they go out, <u>full</u> of tears
carrying seed <u>for</u> the sowing:
they come back, they come back, <u>full</u> of song,
carry<u>ing</u> their sheaves.

Gospel Acclamation Luke 3:4, 6
For musical setting see Nos 36 to 47
　　Alleluia.
　　Prepare a way for the Lord and make <u>his</u> paths straight,
　　and all mankind shall see the salvation <u>of</u> our God.
　　Alleluia.

Response: Martin Setchell　Psalm tone: Gregory Murray
Text © 1963, 1986, 1993 The Grail, England, taken from 'The Psalms, a New Inclusive Language Version',
published by HarperCollins Religious. Used by permission of A.P. Watt Ltd, London.
Response © Copyright 1998 Kevin Mayhew Ltd.
Psalm tone © Copyright McCrimmon Publishing Co. Ltd, 10-12 High St, Great Wakering,
Essex SS3 0EQ. Used by permission.

906 3rd Advent (A)

Responsorial Psalm Psalm 145:6-10. ℟ cf. Isaiah 35:4

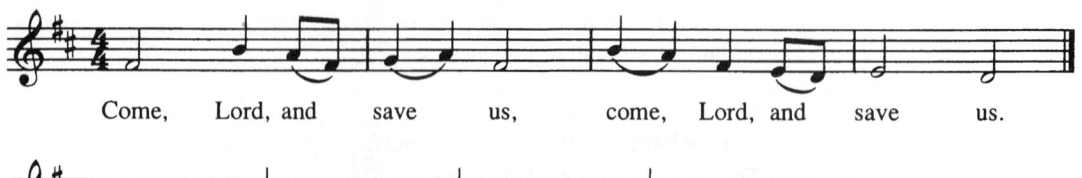

Come, Lord, and save us, come, Lord, and save us.

1. It is the Lord who keeps <u>faith</u> for ever,
   who is just to those who <u>are</u> oppressed.
   It is he who gives bread <u>to</u> the hungry,
   the Lord, who sets pri<u>son</u>ers free.

2. It is the Lord who gives sight <u>to</u> the blind,
   who raises up those who <u>are</u> bowed down,
   the Lord, who pro<u>tects</u> the stranger
   and upholds the wi<u>dow</u> and orphan.

3. It is the Lord who <u>loves</u> the just
   but thwarts the path <u>of</u> the wicked.
   The Lord will <u>reign</u> for ever,
   Zion's God, from <u>age</u> to age.

Gospel Acclamation Isaiah 61:1 (Luke 4:18)
For musical setting see Nos 36 to 47
   Alleluia.
   The spirit of the Lord has been gi<u>ven</u> to me.
   He has sent me to bring good news <u>to</u> the poor.
   Alleluia.

Response: Richard Lloyd   Psalm tone: Andrew Moore
Text © 1963, 1986, 1993 The Grail, England, taken from 'The Psalms, a New Inclusive Language Version',
published by HarperCollins Religious. Used by permission of A.P. Watt Ltd, London.
Response and Psalm tone © Copyright 1998 Kevin Mayhew Ltd.

907 3rd Advent (B)

Responsorial Psalm Luke 1:46-50, 53-54. ℟ Isaiah 61:10

My soul re-joi-ces in my God.

1. My soul glor<u>ifies</u> the Lord,
   my spirit rejoices in <u>God</u>, my Saviour.
   He looks on his servant <u>in</u> her nothingness;
   henceforth all ages will <u>call</u> me blessed.

2. The Almighty works mar<u>vels</u> for me.
   Holy <u>is</u> his name!
   His mercy is from <u>age</u> to age,
   on <u>those</u> who fear him.

Response and Psalm tone: Andrew Moore
Text © 1963, 1986, 1993 The Grail, England, taken from 'The Psalms, a New Inclusive Language Version',
published by HarperCollins Religious. Used by permission of A.P. Watt Ltd, London.
Response and Psalm tone © Copyright 1998 Kevin Mayhew Ltd.

3. He fills the star<u>v</u>ing with good things,
   sends the rich <u>a</u>way empty.
   He protects Isra<u>el</u>, his servant,
   remembe<u>ring</u> his mercy.

Gospel Acclamation Isaiah 61:1 (Luke 4:18)
For musical setting see Nos 36 to 47
  Alleluia.
  The spirit of the Lord has been gi<u>ven</u> to me.
  He has sent me to bring good news <u>to</u> the poor.
  Alleluia.

908 3rd Advent (C)

Responsorial Psalm Isaiah 12:2-6. R̸ v.6

Sing and shout for joy for great in your midst is the Ho-ly One of Is-ra-el.

1. Truly, God is <u>my</u> salvation,
   I trust, I <u>shall</u> not fear.
   For the Lord is my <u>strength</u>, my song,
   he be<u>came</u> my saviour.

2. Give thanks <u>to</u> the Lord,
   give praise <u>to</u> his name!
   Make his mighty deeds known <u>to</u> the peoples!
   Declare the greatness <u>of</u> his name.

3. Sing a psalm to the Lord for he has done glo<u>ri</u>ous deeds,
   make them known to <u>all</u> the earth!
   People of Zion, sing and <u>shout</u> for joy
   for great in your midst is the Holy <u>One</u> of Israel.

Gospel Acclamation Isaiah 61:1 (Luke 4:18)
For musical setting see Nos 36 to 47
  Alleluia.
  The spirit of the Lord has been gi<u>ven</u> to me.
  has sent me to bring good news <u>to</u> the poor.
  Alleluia.

Response: Richard Lloyd   Psalm tone: Laurence Bevenot
Text © 1963, 1986, 1993 The Grail, England, taken from 'The Psalms, a New Inclusive Language Version',
published by HarperCollins Religious. Used by permission of A.P. Watt Ltd, London.
Response © Copyright 1998 Kevin Mayhew Ltd.
Psalm tone © Copyright Ampleforth Abbey, York YO6 4EN. Used by permission.

909 4th Advent (A)

Responsorial Psalm   Psalm 23:1-6. ℟ cf. vv. 7,10

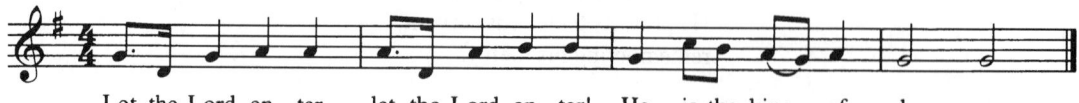

Let the Lord en-ter, let the Lord en-ter! He is the king of glo-ry.

1. The Lord's is the earth <u>and</u> its fullness,
   the world and <u>all</u> its peoples.
   It is he who set it <u>on</u> the seas;
   on the waters he <u>made</u> it firm.

2. Who shall climb the mountain <u>of</u> the Lord?
   Who shall stand in his <u>holy</u> place?
   Those with clean hands <u>and</u> pure heart,
   who desire not <u>worth</u>less things.

3. They shall receive blessings <u>from</u> the Lord
   and reward from the <u>God</u> who saves them.
   Such are the <u>ones</u> who seek him,
   seek the face of the <u>God</u> of Jacob.

Gospel Acclamation   Matthew 1:23
For musical setting see Nos 36 to 47
   Alleluia.
   The virgin will conceive and give birth <u>to</u> a son
   and they will call him Emmanuel, a name which means '<u>God</u>-is-with-us'.
   Alleluia.

Response: Alan Rees   Psalm tone: Laurence Bevenot
Text © 1963, 1986, 1993 The Grail, England, taken from 'The Psalms, a New Inclusive Language Version',
published by HarperCollins Religious. Used by permission of A.P. Watt Ltd, London.
Response © Copyright 1998 Kevin Mayhew Ltd.
Psalm tone © Copyright Ampleforth Abbey, York YO6 4EN. Used by permission.

910 4th Advent (B)

Responsorial Psalm   Psalm 88:2-5, 27, 29. ℟ cf.v.2

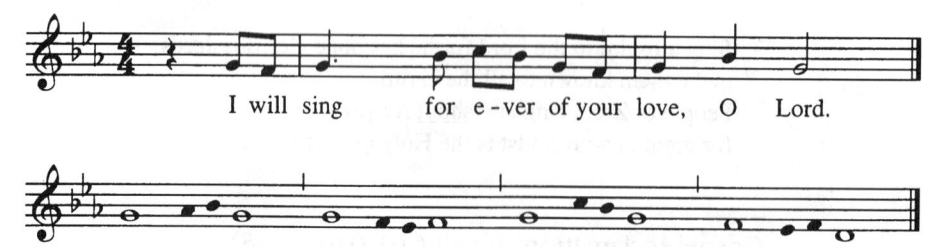

I will sing for e-ver of your love, O Lord.

1. I will sing for ever of your <u>love</u>, O Lord;
   through all ages my mouth will pro<u>claim</u> your truth.
   Of this I am sure, that your love <u>lasts</u> for ever,
   that your truth is firmly established <u>as</u> the heavens.

Response and Psalm tone: Andrew Moore
Text © 1963, 1986, 1993 The Grail, England, taken from 'The Psalms, a New Inclusive Language Version',
published by HarperCollins Religious. Used by permission of A.P. Watt Ltd, London.
Response and Psalm tone © Copyright 1998 Kevin Mayhew Ltd.

2. 'I have made a covenant <u>with</u> my chosen one;
   I have sworn to Da<u>vid</u> my servant:
   I will establish your dynas<u>ty</u> for ever
   and set up your throne <u>through</u> all ages.'

3. He will say to me: 'You <u>are</u> my father,
   my God, the <u>rock</u> who saves me.'
   I will keep my love <u>for</u> him always;
   for him my covenant <u>shall</u> endure.

Gospel Acclamation Luke 1:38
For musical setting see Nos 36 to 47
   Alleluia.
   I am the handmaid <u>of</u> the Lord:
   let what you have <u>said</u> be done to me.
   Alleluia.

911 4th Advent (C)

Responsorial Psalm Psalm 79:2-3, 15-16, 18-19. ℟ v.4

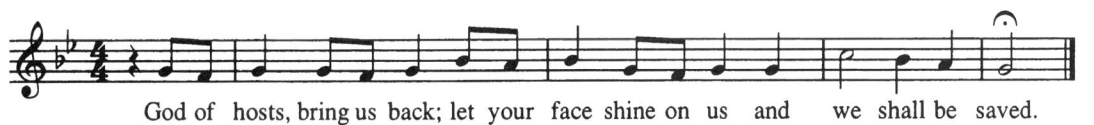

God of hosts, bring us back; let your face shine on us and we shall be saved.

1. O shepherd of Is<u>rael</u>, hear us,
   shine forth from your che<u>ru</u>bim throne.
   O Lord, rouse <u>up</u> your might,
   O Lord, come <u>to</u> our help.

2. God of hosts, turn again, <u>we</u> implore,
   look down from hea<u>ven</u> and see.
   Visit this vine <u>and</u> protect it,
   the vine your right <u>hand</u> has planted.

3. May your hand be on the one <u>you</u> have chosen,
   the one you have gi<u>ven</u> your strength,
   and we shall never forsake <u>you</u> again:
   give us life that we may call u<u>pon</u> your name.

Gospel Acclamation Luke 1:38
For musical setting see Nos 36 to 47
   Alleluia.
   I am the handmaid <u>of</u> the Lord:
   let what you have <u>said</u> be done to me.
   Alleluia.

Response: Andrew Moore Psalm tone: Gregory Murray
Text © 1963, 1986, 1993 The Grail, England, taken from 'The Psalms, a New Inclusive Language Version',
published by HarperCollins Religious. Used by permission of A.P. Watt Ltd, London.
Response © Copyright 1998 Kevin Mayhew Ltd.
Psalm tone © Copyright Downside Abbey, Stratton-on-the-Fosse, Bath BA3 4RH. Used by permission.

912 The Nativity of Our Lord - Midnight Mass (A,B,C)

Responsorial Psalm Psalm 95:1-3, 11-13. ℟ Luke 2:11

To-day a sa-viour has been born to us; he is Christ the Lord.

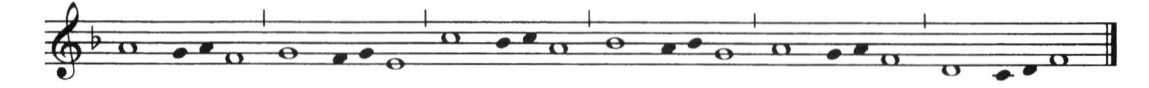

1. O sing a new song <u>to</u> the Lord,
   sing to the Lord <u>all</u> the earth.
   O sing to the Lord, <u>bless</u> his name.
   Proclaim his help <u>day</u> by day,
   tell among the <u>nations</u> his glory
   and his wonders among <u>all</u> the

2. Let the heavens rejoice and <u>earth</u> be glad,
   let the sea and all within it <u>thunder</u> praise,
   let the land and all it <u>bears</u> rejoice,
   all the trees of the wood <u>shout</u> for joy
   at the presence of the Lord <u>for</u> he comes,
   he comes to <u>rule</u> the earth.

Gospel Acclamation Luke 2:10-11
For musical setting see Nos 36 to 47
　　Alleluia.
　　I bring you news <u>of</u> great joy:
　　today a saviour has been born to us, <u>Christ</u> the Lord.
　　Alleluia.

Response: Rosalie Bonighton Psalm tone: Andrew Moore
Text © 1963, 1986, 1993 The Grail, England, taken from 'The Psalms, a New Inclusive Language Version',
published by HarperCollins Religious. Used by permission of A.P. Watt Ltd, London.
Response and Psalm tone © Copyright 1998 Kevin Mayhew Ltd.

913 The Nativity of Our Lord - Mass During the Day (A,B,C)

Responsorial Psalm Psalm 97:1-6. ℟ v.3

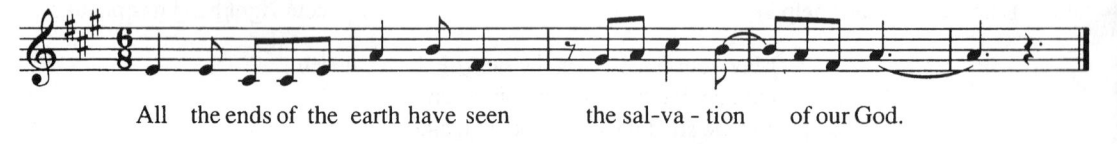

All the ends of the earth have seen the sal-va-tion of our God.

1. Sing a new song <u>to</u> the Lord
   for he <u>has</u> worked wonders.
   His right hand and his <u>ho</u>ly arm
   have <u>brought</u> salvation.

2. The Lord has made known <u>his</u> salvation;
   has shown his justice <u>to</u> the nations.
   He has remembered his <u>truth</u> and love
   for the <u>house</u> of Israel.

Response: Richard Proulx Psalm tone: Alan Rees
Text © 1963, 1986, 1993 The Grail, England, taken from 'The Psalms, a New Inclusive Language Version',
published by HarperCollins Religious. Used by permission of A.P. Watt Ltd, London.
Response © Copyright 1998 Kevin Mayhew Ltd.
Psalm tone © Copyright Belmont Abbey, Hereford HR2 9RZ. Used by permission.

3. All the ends of the <u>earth</u> have seen
   the salvation <u>of</u> our God.
   Shout to the Lord <u>all</u> the earth,
   ring <u>out</u> your joy.

4. Sing psalms to the Lord <u>with</u> the harp,
   with the <u>sound</u> of music.
   With trumpets and the sound <u>of</u> the horn
   accalim the <u>King</u>, the Lord.

Gospel Acclamation
For musical setting see Nos 36 to 47
Alleluia.
Come, you nations, wor<u>ship</u> the Lord,
for today a great light has shone down u<u>pon</u> the earth.
Alleluia.

914 *Sunday in the Octave of Christmas*
The Holy Family (A,B,C)

Responsorial Psalm Psalm 127:1-5. ℟ cf. v.1

O bless-ed are those who fear the Lord, who fear the Lord.

1. O blessed are those who <u>fear</u> the Lord
   and walk <u>in</u> his ways!
   By the labour of your hands <u>you</u> shall eat.
   You will be hap<u>py</u> and prosper.

2. Your wife like a <u>fruit</u>ful vine
   in the heart <u>of</u> your house;
   your children like shoots <u>of</u> the olive,
   ar<u>ound</u> your table.

3. Indeed thus <u>shall</u> the blessed
   the man who <u>fears</u> the Lord.
   May the Lord bless <u>you</u> from Zion
   all the days <u>of</u> your life!

Gospel Acclamation Colossians 3:15, 16
For musical setting see Nos 36 to 47
Alleluia.
May the peace of Christ reign <u>in</u> your hearts;
let the message of Christ find a <u>home</u> within you.
Alleluia.

Response: Andrew Moore Psalm tone: Alan Rees
Text © 1963, 1986, 1993 The Grail, England, taken from 'The Psalms, a New Inclusive Language Version',
published by HarperCollins Religious. Used by permission of A.P. Watt Ltd, London.
Response © Copyright 1998 Kevin Mayhew Ltd.
Psalm tone © Copyright Belmont Abbey, Hereford HR2 9RZ. Used by permission.

915 The Holy Family (B ad lib)

Responsorial Psalm Psalm 104:1-6, 8-9. ℟ vv. 7, 8

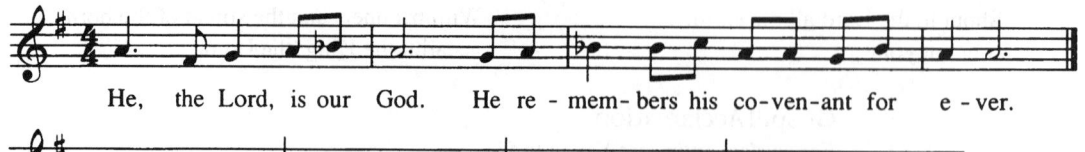

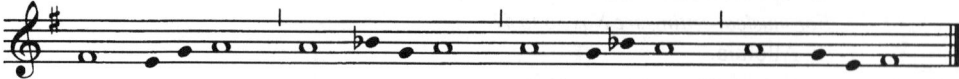

He, the Lord, is our God. He re-mem-bers his co-ven-ant for e-ver.

1. Give thanks to the Lord, <u>tell</u> his name,
   make known his deeds am<u>ong</u> the peoples.
   O sing to him, <u>sing</u> his praise;
   tell all his won<u>der</u>ful works!

2. Be proud of his <u>ho</u>ly name,
   let the hearts that seek the <u>Lord</u> rejoice.
   Consider the Lord <u>and</u> his strength;
   constantly <u>seek</u> his face.

3. Remember the wonders <u>he</u> has done,
   his miracles, the judge<u>ments</u> he spoke.
   O children of Abra<u>ham</u>, his servant,
   O sons of the Ja<u>cob</u> he chose.

4. He remembers his cove<u>nant</u> for ever,
   his promise for a thousand gene<u>rations</u>,
   the covenant he <u>made</u> with Abraham,
   the oath he <u>swore</u> to Isaac.

Gospel Acclamation Hebrews 1:1-2
For musical setting see Nos 36 to 47
   Alleluia.
   At various times <u>in</u> the past
   and in various dif<u>ferent</u> ways,
   God spoke to our ancestors <u>through</u> the prophets;
   but in our own time, the last days, he has spoken to us <u>through</u> his Son.
   Alleluia.
Note: the tone should be sung twice

Response: Stephen Dean Psalm tone: Laurence Bevenot
Text © 1963, 1986, 1993 The Grail, England, taken from 'The Psalms, a New Inclusive Language Version',
published by HarperCollins Religious. Used by permission of A.P. Watt Ltd, London.
Response © 1989 Stephen Dean. Published by OCP Publications, 5536 NE Hassalo, Portland, OR 97213, USA. Used by permission.
Psalm tone © Copyright Ampleforth Abbey, York YO6 4EN. Used by permission.

916 The Holy Family (C ad lib)

Responsorial Psalm Psalm 83:2-3, 5-6, 9-10. ℟ v.5

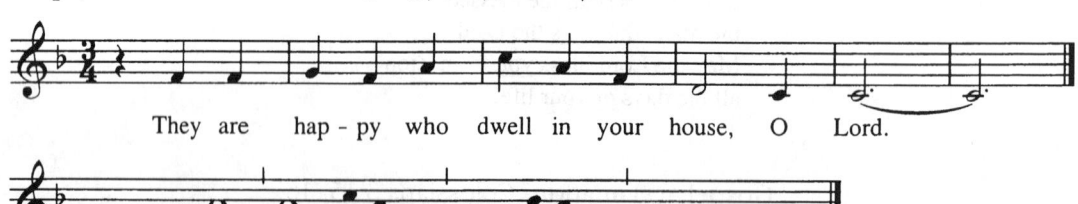

They are hap-py who dwell in your house, O Lord.

1. How lovely <u>is</u> your dwelling place,
   Lord <u>God</u> of hosts.
   My soul is long<u>ing</u> and yearning,
   is yearning for the courts <u>of</u> the Lord.

2. They are happy, who dwell <u>in</u> your house,
   for ever sing<u>ing</u> your praise.
   They are happy, whose strength <u>is</u> in you;
   they walk with ever grow<u>ing</u> strength.

Response: Rosalie Bonighton Psalm tone: Alan Rees
Text © 1963, 1986, 1993 The Grail, England, taken from 'The Psalms, a New Inclusive Language Version',
published by HarperCollins Religious. Used by permission of A.P. Watt Ltd, London.
Response © Copyright 1998 Kevin Mayhew Ltd.
Psalm tone © Copyright Belmont Abbey, Hereford HR2 9RZ. Used by permission.

3. O Lord, God of hosts, <u>hear</u> my prayer,
   give ear, O <u>God</u> of Jacob.
   Turn your eyes, O <u>God</u>, our shield,
   look on the face of <u>your</u> anointed.

Gospel Acclamation cf. Acts 16:14
For musical setting see Nos 36 to 47
   Alleluia.
   Open our <u>heart</u>, O Lord,
   to accept the words <u>of</u> your Son.
   Alleluia.

917 *1 January: Octave of Christmas*
Solemnity of Mary, Mother of God (A,B,C)

Responsorial Psalm Psalm 66:2-3, 5, 6, 8. ℟ v.2

O God, be gra-cious, be gra-cious and bless us.

1. God, be gra<u>cious</u> and bless us
   and let your face shed its <u>light</u> upon us.
   So will your ways be known <u>upon</u> earth
   and all nations learn your <u>saving</u> help.

2. Let the nations be glad <u>and</u> exult
   for you rule the <u>world</u> with justice.
   With fairness you <u>rule</u> the peoples,
   you guide the na<u>tions</u> on earth.

3. Let the peoples praise <u>you</u>, O God;
   let all the <u>peoples</u> praise you.
   May God still give <u>us</u> his blessing
   till the ends of the <u>earth</u> revere him.

Gospel Acclamation Hebrews 1:1-2
For musical setting see Nos 36 to 47
   Alleluia.
   At various times <u>in</u> the past
   and in various dif<u>ferent</u> ways,
   God spoke to our ancestors <u>through</u> the prophets;
   but in our own time, the last days, he has spoken to us <u>through</u> his Son.
   Alleluia.

Note: the tone should be sung twice

Response: Alan Rees **Psalm tone:** Andrew Moore
Text © 1963, 1986, 1993 The Grail, England, taken from 'The Psalms, a New Inclusive Language Version',
published by HarperCollins Religious. Used by permission of A.P. Watt Ltd, London.
Response and Psalm tone © Copyright 1998 Kevin Mayhew Ltd.

918 2nd after Christmas (A,B,C)

Responsorial Psalm Psalm 147:12-15, 19-20. ℟ John 1:14

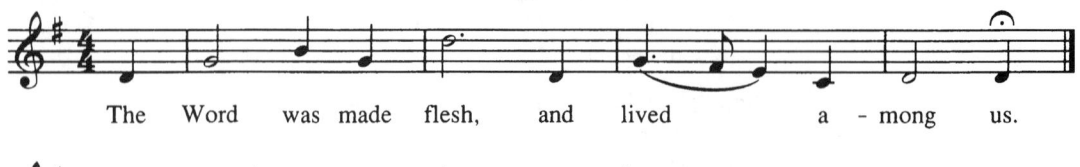

The Word was made flesh, and lived among us.

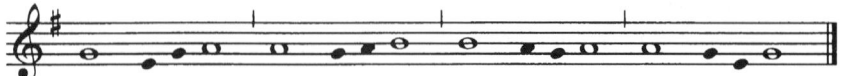

1. O praise the <u>Lord</u>, Jerusalem!
   Zion, <u>praise</u> your God!
   He has strengthened the bars <u>of</u> your gates,
   he has blessed the chil<u>dren</u> within you.

2. He established peace <u>on</u> your borders,
   he feeds you with <u>fin</u>est wheat.
   He sends out his word <u>to</u> the earth
   and swiftly runs <u>his</u> command.

3. He makes his word <u>known</u> to Jacob,
   to Israel his laws <u>and</u> decrees.
   He has not dealt thus with <u>o</u>ther nations;
   he has not taught them <u>his</u> decrees.

Gospel Acclamation cf. 1 Timothy 3:16
For musical setting see Nos 36 to 47
   Alleluia.
   Glory be to you, O Christ, proclaimed <u>to</u> the pagans;
   Glory be to you, O Christ, believed in <u>by</u> the world.
   Alleluia.

Response: Colin Mawby Psalm tone: Gregory Murray
Text © 1963, 1986, 1993 The Grail, England, taken from 'The Psalms, a New Inclusive Language Version',
published by HarperCollins Religious. Used by permission of A.P. Watt Ltd, London.
Response © Copyright 1998 Kevin Mayhew Ltd.
Psalm tone © Copyright McCrimmon Publishing Co. Ltd, 10-12 High St, Great Wakering, Essex SS3 0EQ. Used by permission.

919 *6 January or the Sunday between 2 January and 8 January*
The Epiphany of the Lord (A,B,C)

Responsorial Psalm Psalm 71:1-2, 7-8, 10-13. ℟ cf. v.11

All nations shall fall prostrate before you, O Lord.

1. O God, give your judgement <u>to</u> the king,
   to a king's <u>son</u> your justice,
   that he may judge your peo<u>ple</u> in justice
   and your poor <u>in</u> right judgement.

2. In his days <u>jus</u>tice shall flourish
   and peace till <u>the</u> moon fails.
   He shall rule from <u>sea</u> to sea,
   from the Great River <u>to</u> earth's bounds.

Response: Andrew Moore Psalm tone: Gregory Murray
Text © 1963, 1986, 1993 The Grail, England, taken from 'The Psalms, a New Inclusive Language Version',
published by HarperCollins Religious. Used by permission of A.P. Watt Ltd, London.
Response © Copyright 1998 Kevin Mayhew Ltd.
Psalm tone © Copyright Downside Abbey, Stratton-on-the-Fosse, Bath BA3 4RH. Used by permission.

3. The kings of Tarshish and the sea coasts
      shall <u>pay</u> him tribute.
   The kings of Sheba and Seba shall <u>bring</u> him gifts.
   Before him all kings <u>shall</u> fall prostrate,
   all na<u>tions</u> shall serve him.

4. For he shall save the poor <u>when</u> they cry
   and the needy <u>who</u> are helpless.
   He will have pity <u>on</u> the weak
   and save the lives <u>of</u> the poor.

Gospel Acclamation Matthew 2:2
For musical setting see Nos 36 to 47
   Alleluia.
   We saw his star <u>as</u> it rose
   and have come to pay homage <u>to</u> the Lord.
   Alleluia.

920 The Baptism of the Lord (A)

Responsorial Psalm Psalm 28:1-4, 9-10. ℟ v.11

The Lord will bless his peo-ple, will bless his peo-ple with peace.

1. O give the Lord you chil<u>dren</u> of God,
   give the Lord glo<u>ry</u> and power;
   give the Lord the glory <u>of</u> his name.
   Adore the Lord in his <u>ho</u>ly court.

2. The Lord's voice resounding <u>on</u> the waters,
   the Lord on the immensi<u>ty</u> of waters;
   the voice of the Lord, <u>full</u> of power,
   the voice of the Lord, <u>full</u> of splendour.

3. The God of <u>glo</u>ry thunders.
   In his temple they <u>all</u> cry: 'Glory!'
   The Lord sat enthroned <u>over</u> the flood;
   the Lord sits as <u>king</u> for ever.

Gospel Acclamation cf. Mark 9:8
For musical setting see Nos 36 to 47
   Alleluia.
   The heavens opened and the Father's <u>voice</u> resounded:
   'This is my Son, the Beloved. Lis<u>ten</u> to him.'
   Alleluia.

Response: Richard Lloyd Psalm tone: Alan Rees
Text © 1963, 1986, 1993 The Grail, England, taken from 'The Psalms, a New Inclusive Language Version',
published by HarperCollins Religious. Used by permission of A.P. Watt Ltd, London.
Response © Copyright 1998 Kevin Mayhew Ltd.
Psalm tone © Copyright Belmont Abbey, Hereford HR2 9RZ. Used by permission.

921 The Baptism of the Lord (B ad lib)

Responsorial Psalm Isaiah 12:2-6. ℞ v.6

With joy you will draw water from the wells of salvation.

1. Truly, God is my <u>sal</u>vation
   I trust, I <u>shall</u> not fear.
   For the Lord is my <u>strength</u>, my song,
   he be<u>came</u> my saviour.

2. Give thanks <u>to</u> the Lord,
   give praise <u>to</u> his name!
   Make his mighty deeds known <u>to</u> the peoples!
   Declare the greatness <u>of</u> his name.

3. Sing a psalm to the Lord for he has done glo<u>ri</u>ous deeds,
   make them known to <u>all</u> the earth!
   People of Zion, sing and <u>shout</u> for joy
   for great in your midst is the Holy <u>One</u> of Israel.

Gospel Acclamation cf. John 1:29

For musical setting see Nos 36 to 47

Alleluia.
John saw Jesus coming towards <u>him</u>, and said:
This is the Lamb of God who takes away the sin <u>of</u> the world.
Alleluia.

Response and Psalm tone: Andrew Moore
Text © 1963, 1986, 1993 The Grail, England, taken from 'The Psalms, a New Inclusive Language Version',
published by HarperCollins Religious. Used by permission of A.P. Watt Ltd, London.
Response and Psalm tone © Copyright 1998 Kevin Mayhew Ltd.

922 The Baptism of the Lord (C ad lib)

Responsorial Psalm Psalm 103:1-2, 3-4, 24-25, 27-30. ℞ v.1

Bless the Lord, my soul! Lord God, how great you are.

1. Lord God, how <u>great</u> you are,
   clothed in majes<u>ty</u> and glory,
   wrapped in light as <u>in</u> a robe!
   You stretch out the heavens <u>like</u> a tent.

2. The earth is full <u>of</u> your riches.
   There is the sea, <u>vast</u> and wide,
   with its moving <u>swarms</u> past counting,
   living things <u>great</u> and small.

Response: Andrew Moore Psalm tone: Laurence Bevenot
Text © 1963, 1986, 1993 The Grail, England, taken from 'The Psalms, a New Inclusive Language Version',
published by HarperCollins Religious. Used by permission of A.P. Watt Ltd, London.
Response © Copyright 1998 Kevin Mayhew Ltd.
Psalm tone © Copyright Ampleforth Abbey, York YO6 4EN. Used by permission.

3. All of these <u>look</u> to you
    to give them their food <u>in</u> due season.
    You give it, they gath<u>er</u> it up:
    you open your hand, they <u>have</u> their fill.

4. You take back your sp<u>ir</u>it, they die,
    returning to the dust from <u>which</u> they came.
    You send forth your spirit, they <u>are</u> created;
    and you renew the face <u>of</u> the earth.

Gospel Acclamation cf. Luke 3:16
For musical setting see Nos 36 to 47
Alleluia.
Someone is coming, said John, someone grea<u>ter</u> than I.
He will baptise you with the Holy Spirit <u>and</u> with fire.
Alleluia.

923 Ash Wednesday (A,B,C)

Responsorial Psalm Psalm 50:3-6, 12-14, 17. ℟ v.3

Have mercy on us, Lord, for we have sinned.

1. Have mercy on me, God, <u>in</u> your kindness.
    In your compassion blot out <u>my</u> offence.
    O wash me more and more <u>from</u> my guilt
    and cleanse me <u>from</u> my sin.

2. My offences tru<u>ly</u> I know them;
    my sin is al<u>ways</u> before me.
    Against you, you alone, <u>have</u> I sinned;
    what is evil in your sight <u>I</u> have done.

3. A pure heart create for <u>me</u>, O God,
    put a steadfast sp<u>ir</u>it within me.
    Do not cast me away <u>from</u> your presence,
    nor deprive me of your <u>ho</u>ly spirit.

4. Give me again the joy <u>of</u> your help;
    with a spirit of fer<u>vour</u> sustain me.
    O Lord, o<u>pen</u> my lips
    and my mouth shall de<u>clare</u> your praise.

Gospel Acclamation Psalm 50:12, 14
*One of the responses Nos 53 to 55 should be
sung before and after this text.*

A pure heart create for <u>me</u>, O God,
and give me again the joy <u>of</u> your help.

or cf. Psalm 94:8

Harden not your <u>hearts</u> today,
but listen to the voice <u>of</u> the Lord.

Response and Psalm tone: Andrew Moore
Text © 1963, 1986, 1993 The Grail, England, taken from 'The Psalms, a New Inclusive Language Version',
published by HarperCollins Religious. Used by permission of A.P. Watt Ltd, London.
Response and Psalm tone © Copyright 1998 Kevin Mayhew Ltd.

924 1st Lent (A)

Responsorial Psalm Psalm 50:3-6, 12-14, 17. ℟ v.3

Have mercy on us, Lord, for we have sinned.

1. Have mercy on me, God, in your kindness.
   In your compassion blot out my offence.
   O wash me more and more from my guilt
   and cleanse me from my sin.

2. My offences truly I know them;
   my sin is always before me.
   Against you, you alone, have I sinned;
   what is evil in your sight I have done.

3. A pure heart create for me, O God,
   put a steadfast spirit within me.
   Do not cast me away from your presence,
   nor deprive me of your holy spirit.

4. Give me again the joy of your help;
   with a spirit of fervour sustain me.
   O Lord, open my lips
   and my mouth shall declare your praise.

Gospel Acclamation Matthew 4:4
One of the responses Nos 53 to 55 should be sung before and after this text.

Man does not live on bread alone,
but on every word that comes from the mouth of God.

Response and Psalm tone: Andrew Moore
Text © 1963, 1986, 1993 The Grail, England, taken from 'The Psalms, a New Inclusive Language Version', published by HarperCollins Religious. Used by permission of A.P. Watt Ltd, London.
Response and Psalm tone © Copyright 1998 Kevin Mayhew Ltd.

925 1st Lent (B)

Responsorial Psalm Psalm 24:4-9. ℟ cf. v.10

Your ways, Lord, are faithfulness and love for those who keep your covenant.

1. Lord, make me know your ways.
   Lord, teach me your paths.
   Make me walk in your truth, and teach me:
   for you are God my saviour.

2. Remember your mercy, Lord,
   and the love you have shown from of old.
   In your love remember me,
   because of your goodness, O Lord.

Response: Rosalie Bonighton   Psalm tone: Laurence Bevenot
Text © 1963, 1986, 1993 The Grail, England, taken from 'The Psalms, a New Inclusive Language Version', published by HarperCollins Religious. Used by permission of A.P. Watt Ltd, London.
Response © Copyright 1998 Kevin Mayhew Ltd.
Psalm tone © Copyright Ampleforth Abbey, York YO6 4EN. Used by permission.

3. The Lord is <u>good</u> and upright.
   He shows the path to <u>those</u> who stray,
   he guides the humble in <u>the</u> right path;
   he teaches his way <u>to</u> the poor.

Gospel Acclamation Matthew 4:4
*One of the responses Nos 53 to 55 should
be sung before and after this text.*

Man does not live on <u>bread</u> alone,
but on every word that comes from the <u>mouth</u> of God.

926 1st Lent (C)

Responsorial Psalm   Psalm 90:1-2, 10-15. ℟ v.15

Be with me, Lord, in my dis - tress.

1. He who dwells in the shelter of <u>the</u> Most High
   and abides in the shade of <u>the</u> Almighty,
   says to the <u>Lord</u>: 'My refuge,
   my stronghold, my God in <u>whom</u> I trust!'

2. Upon you no <u>ev</u>il shall fall,
   no plague approach <u>where</u> you dwell.
   For you has he comman<u>ded</u> his angels,
   to keep you in <u>all</u> your ways.

3. They shall bear you up<u>on</u> their hands
   lest you strike your foot a<u>gainst</u> a stone.
   On the lion and the viper <u>you</u> will tread
   and trample the young lion <u>and</u> the dragon.

4. His love he set on me, so <u>I</u> will rescue him;
   protect him for he <u>knows</u> my name.
   When he calls I shall answer: 'I am with you.'
   I will save him in distress and <u>give</u> him glory.

Gospel Acclamation Matthew 4:4
*One of the responses Nos 53 to 55 should
be sung before and after this text.*

Man does not live on <u>bread</u> alone,
but on every word that comes from the <u>mouth</u> of God.

Response and Psalm tone: Andrew Moore
Text © 1963, 1986, 1993 The Grail, England, taken from 'The Psalms, a New Inclusive Language Version',
published by HarperCollins Religious. Used by permission of A.P. Watt Ltd, London.
Response and Psalm tone © Copyright 1998 Kevin Mayhew Ltd.

927 2nd Lent (A)

Responsorial Psalm Psalm 32:4-5, 18-20, 22. ℟ v.22

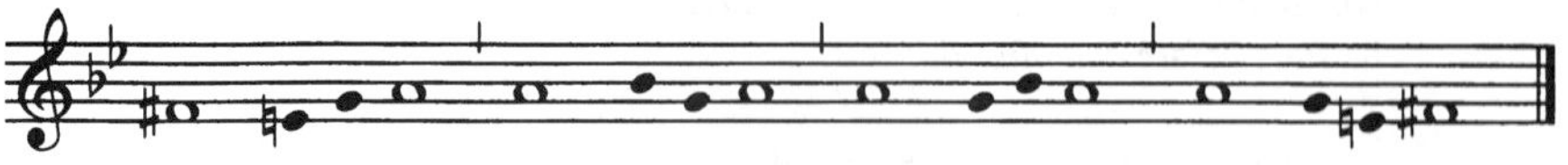

May your love be upon us, O Lord, as we place all our hope in you.

1. The word of the <u>Lord</u> is faithful
   and all his works <u>to</u> be trusted.
   The Lord loves jus<u>tice</u> and right
   and fills the earth <u>with</u> his love.

2. The Lord looks on those <u>who</u> revere him,
   on those who hope <u>in</u> his love,
   to rescue their <u>souls</u> from death,
   to keep them a<u>live</u> in famine.

3. Our soul is waiting <u>for</u> the Lord.
   The Lord is our help <u>and</u> our shield.
   May your love be upon <u>us</u>, O Lord,
   as we place all our <u>hope</u> in you.

Gospel Acclamation Matthew 17:5
*One of the responses Nos 53 to 55 should
be sung before and after this text.*

From the bright cloud the Father's <u>voice</u> was heard:
'This is my Son, the Beloved. Li<u>sten</u> to him.'

Response: Rosalie Bonighton Psalm tone: Laurence Bevenot
Text © 1963, 1986, 1993 The Grail, England, taken from 'The Psalms, a New Inclusive Language Version',
published by HarperCollins Religious. Used by permission of A.P. Watt Ltd, London.
Response © Copyright 1998 Kevin Mayhew Ltd.
Psalm tone © Copyright Ampleforth Abbey, York YO6 4EN. Used by permission.

928 2nd Lent (B)

Responsorial Psalm Psalm 115:10, 15-19. ℟ Psalm 114:9

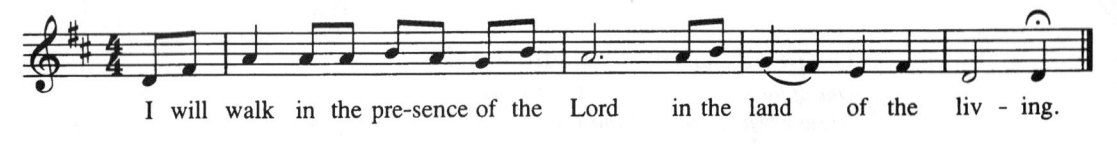

I will walk in the presence of the Lord in the land of the living.

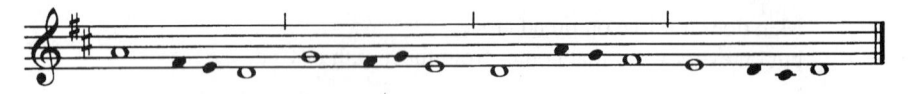

1. I trusted, even <u>when</u> I said:
   'I am sore<u>ly</u> afflicted.'
   O precious in the eyes <u>of</u> the Lord
   is the death <u>of</u> his faithful.

2. Your servant, Lord, your ser<u>vant</u> am I;
   you have loo<u>sened</u> my bonds.
   A thanksgiving sacri<u>fice</u> I make:
   I will call on <u>the</u> Lord's name.

Response and Psalm tone: Andrew Moore
Text © 1963, 1986, 1993 The Grail, England, taken from 'The Psalms, a New Inclusive Language Version',
published by HarperCollins Religious. Used by permission of A.P. Watt Ltd, London.
Response and Psalm tone © Copyright 1998 Kevin Mayhew Ltd.

3. My vows to the Lord I will fulfil
   before all his people,
   in the courts of the house of the Lord,
   in your midst, O Jerusalem.

Gospel Acclamation Matthew 17:5
*One of the responses Nos 53 to 55 should
be sung before and after this text.*

From the bright cloud the Father's voice was heard:
'This is my Son, the Beloved. Listen to him.'

929 2nd Lent (C)

Responsorial Psalm Psalm 26:1, 7-9, 13-14. ℟ v.1

The Lord is my light and my help.

1. The Lord is my light and my help;
   whom shall I fear?
   The Lord is the stronghold of my life;
   before whom shall I shrink?

2. O Lord, hear my voice when I call;
   have mercy and answer.
   Of you my heart has spoken:
   'Seek his face.'

3. It is your face, O Lord, that I seek;
   hide not your face.
   Dismiss not your servant in anger;
   you have been my help.

4. I am sure I shall see the Lord's goodness
   in the land of the living.
   Hope in him, hold firm and take heart.
   Hope in the Lord!

Gospel Acclamation Matthew 17:5
*One of the responses Nos 53 to 55 should
be sung before and after this text.*

From the bright cloud the Father's voice was heard:
'This is my Son, the Beloved. Listen to him.'

Response: Richard Lloyd Psalm tone: Alan Rees
Text © 1963, 1986, 1993 The Grail, England, taken from 'The Psalms, a New Inclusive Language Version',
published by HarperCollins Religious. Used by permission of A.P. Watt Ltd, London.
Response © Copyright 1998 Kevin Mayhew Ltd.
Psalm tone © Copyright Belmont Abbey, Hereford HR2 9RZ. Used by permission.

930 3rd Lent (A)

Responsorial Psalm Psalm 94:1-2, 6-9. ℟ v.8

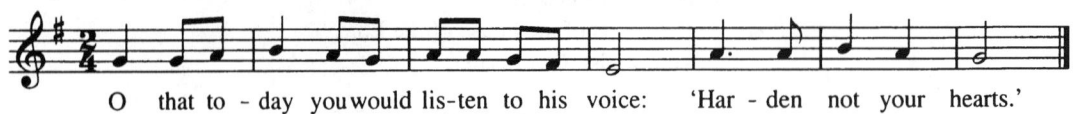

O that to-day you would listen to his voice: 'Harden not your hearts.'

1. Come, ring out our joy <u>to</u> the Lord;
   hail the <u>rock</u> who saves us.
   Let us come before him, <u>gi</u>ving thanks,
   with songs let us <u>hail</u> the Lord.

2. Come in; let us bow <u>and</u> bend low;
   let us kneel before the <u>God</u> who made us
   for he is our God, and we the people who
   belong <u>to</u> his pasture,
   the flock that is led <u>by</u> his hand.

3. O that today you would listen <u>to</u> his voice!
   'Harden not your hearts as <u>at</u> Meribah,
   as on that day as Massah in the desert, when
   your fathers put me <u>to</u> the test;
   when they tried me, though they <u>saw</u> my work.'

Gospel Acclamation cf. John 4:42, 15
*One of the responses Nos 53 to 55 should be
sung before and after this text.*

Lord, you are really the saviour <u>of</u> the world;
give me the living water, so that I may ne<u>ver</u> get thirsty.

Response and Psalm tone: Gregory Murray
Text © 1963, 1986, 1993 The Grail, England, taken from 'The Psalms, a New Inclusive Language Version',
published by HarperCollins Religious. Used by permission of A.P. Watt Ltd, London.
Response and Psalm tone © Copyright McCrimmon Publishing Co. Ltd,
10-12 High St, Great Wakering, Essex SS3 0EQ. Used by permission.

931 3rd Lent (B)

Responsorial Psalm Psalm 18:8-11. ℟ John 6:68

You have the message of eternal life, O Lord.

1. The law of the <u>Lord</u> is perfect,
   it re<u>vives</u> the soul.
   The rule of the Lord is <u>to</u> be trusted,
   it gives wisdom <u>to</u> the simple.

2. The precepts of the <u>Lord</u> are right,
   they <u>gladden</u> the heart.
   The command of the <u>Lord</u> is clear,
   it gives light <u>to</u> the eyes.

Response and Psalm tone: Andrew Moore
Text © 1963, 1986, 1993 The Grail, England, taken from 'The Psalms, a New Inclusive Language Version',
published by HarperCollins Religious. Used by permission of A.P. Watt Ltd, London.
Response and Psalm tone © Copyright 1998 Kevin Mayhew Ltd.

3. The fear of the Lord is holy,
   abiding for ever.
   The decrees of the Lord are truth
   and all of them just.

4. They are more to be desired than gold,
   than the purest of gold
   and sweeter are they than honey,
   than honey from the comb.

Gospel Acclamation John 11:25-26
One of the responses Nos 53 to 55 should be sung before and after this text.

I am the resurrection and the life, says the Lord,
whoever believes in me will never die.

932 3rd Lent (C)

Responsorial Psalm Psalm 102:1-4, 6-8, 11. ℟ v.8

The Lord is com-pas-sion and love, the Lord is com-pas-sion and love.

1. My soul, give thanks to the Lord,
   all my being, bless his holy name.
   My soul give thanks to the Lord
   and never forget all his blessings.

2. It is he who forgives all your guilt,
   who heals every one of your ills,
   who redeems your life from the grave,
   who crowns you with love and compassion.

3. The Lord does deeds of justice,
   gives judgement for all who are oppressed.
   He made known his ways to Moses
   and his deeds to Israel's sons.

4. The Lord is compassion and love,
   slow to anger and rich in mercy,
   for as the heavens are high above the earth
   so strong is his love for those who fear him.

Gospel Acclamation Matthew 4:17
One of the responses Nos 53 to 55 should be sung before and after this text.

Repent, says the Lord,
for the kingdom of heaven is close at hand.

Response: Andrew Moore Psalm tone: Laurence Bevenot
Text © 1963, 1986, 1993 The Grail, England, taken from 'The Psalms, a New Inclusive Language Version',
published by HarperCollins Religious. Used by permission of A.P. Watt Ltd, London.
Response © Copyright 1998 Kevin Mayhew Ltd.
Psalm tone © Copyright Ampleforth Abbey, York YO6 4EN. Used by permission.

933 4th Lent (A)

Responsorial Psalm Psalm 22. ℟ v.1

The Lord is my shep-herd; there is no-thing I shall want, the Lord is my shep-herd; there is no-thing I shall want.

1. The Lord <u>is</u> my shepherd;
   there is nothing <u>I</u> shall want.
   Fresh and green <u>are</u> the pastures
   where he gives <u>me</u> repose.

2. Near restful wa<u>ters</u> he leads me,
   to revive my <u>droop</u>ing spirit.
   He guides me along <u>the</u> right path;
   he is true <u>to</u> his name.

3. If I should walk in the val<u>ley</u> of darkness
   no evil <u>would</u> I fear.
   You are there with your crook <u>and</u> your staff;
   with these you <u>give</u> me comfort.

4. You have prepared a ban<u>quet</u> for me
   in the sight <u>of</u> my foes.
   My head you have anoin<u>ted</u> with oil;
   my cup is <u>o</u>verflowing.

5. Surely goodness and kind<u>ness</u> shall follow me
   all the days <u>of</u> my life.
   In the Lord's own house <u>shall</u> I dwell
   for e<u>ver</u> and ever.

Note: verse 3 may be omitted

Gospel Acclamation John 8:12
*One of the responses Nos 53 to 55 should
be sung before and after this text.*

I am the light of the world, <u>says</u> the Lord;
anyone who follows me will have the <u>light</u> of life.

Response: Andrew Moore Psalm tone: Alan Rees
Text © 1963, 1986, 1993 The Grail, England, taken from 'The Psalms, a New Inclusive Language Version',
published by HarperCollins Religious. Used by permission of A.P. Watt Ltd, London.
Response © Copyright 1998 Kevin Mayhew Ltd.
Psalm tone © Copyright Belmont Abbey, Hereford HR2 9RZ. Used by permission.

934 4th Lent (B)

Responsorial Psalm   Psalm 136. ℟ v.6

O let my tongue cleave to my mouth   if I re-mem-ber you not!

1. By the rivers of Babylon there we <u>sat</u> and wept,
   remem<u>ber</u>ing Zion;
   on the pop<u>lars</u> that grew there
   we hung <u>up</u> our harps.

2. For it was there that they asked us, our cap<u>tors</u>, for songs,
   our oppress<u>ors</u>, for joy.
   'Sing to <u>us</u>,' they said,
   'one of <u>Z</u>ion's songs.'

3. O how could we sing the song <u>of</u> the Lord
   on a<u>lie</u>n soil?
   If I forget <u>you</u>, Jerusalem,
   let my <u>right</u> hand wither!

4. O let my tongue cleave <u>to</u> my mouth
   if I remem<u>ber</u> you not,
   if I prize <u>not</u> Jerusalem
   above <u>all</u> my joys!

Gospel Acclamation   John 3:16
*One of the responses Nos 53 to 55 should
be sung before and after this text.*

God loved the world so much that he gave his <u>only</u> Son;
everyone who believes in him has et<u>er</u>nal life.

Response and Psalm tone: Andrew Moore
Text © 1963, 1986, 1993 The Grail, England, taken from 'The Psalms, a New Inclusive Language Version',
published by HarperCollins Religious. Used by permission of A.P. Watt Ltd, London.
Response and Psalm tone © Copyright 1998 Kevin Mayhew Ltd.

935 4th Lent (C)

Responsorial Psalm Psalm 33:2-7. ℟ v.9

Taste, O taste and see that the Lord is good, that the Lord is good.

1. I will bless the Lord <u>at</u> all times,
   his praise always <u>on</u> my lips;
   in the Lord my soul shall <u>make</u> its boast.
   The humble shall hear <u>and</u> be glad.

2. Glorify the <u>Lord</u> with me.
   Together let us <u>praise</u> his name.
   I sought the Lord <u>and</u> he answered me;
   from all my terrors he <u>set</u> me free.

3. Look towards him <u>and</u> be radiant;
   let your faces not <u>be</u> abashed.
   This poor man called; <u>the</u> Lord heard him
   and rescued him from all <u>his</u> distress.

Gospel Acclamation Luke 15:18
*One of the responses Nos 53 to 55 should
be sung before and after this text.*

I will leave this place and go to my fa<u>ther</u> and say:
'Father, I have sinned against heaven and <u>against</u> you.'

Response and Psalm tone: Alan Rees
Text © 1963, 1986, 1993 The Grail, England, taken from 'The Psalms, a New Inclusive Language Version',
published by HarperCollins Religious. Used by permission of A.P. Watt Ltd, London.
Response © Copyright 1998 Kevin Mayhew Ltd.
Psalm tone © Copyright Belmont Abbey, Hereford HR2 9RZ. Used by permission.

936 5th Lent (A)

Responsorial Psalm Psalm 129. ℟ v.7

With the Lord there is mer-cy and full-ness of re-demp-tion.

1. Out of the depths I cry to <u>you</u>, O Lord,
   Lord, <u>hear</u> my voice!
   O let your ears <u>be</u> attentive
   to the voice <u>of</u> my pleading.

2. If you, O Lord, should <u>mark</u> our guilt,
   Lord, who <u>would</u> survive?
   But with you is <u>found</u> forgiveness:
   for this <u>we</u> revere you.

Response: Alan Rees Psalm tone: Andrew Moore
Text © 1963, 1986, 1993 The Grail, England, taken from 'The Psalms, a New Inclusive Language Version',
published by HarperCollins Religious. Used by permission of A.P. Watt Ltd, London.
Response and Psalm tone © Copyright 1998 Kevin Mayhew Ltd.

3. My soul is waiting <u>for</u> the Lord,
   I count <u>on</u> his word.
   My soul is longing <u>for</u> the Lord
   more than watch<u>man</u> for daybreak.

4. Because with the Lord <u>there</u> is mercy
   and fullness <u>of</u> redemption,
   Israel indeed he <u>will</u> redeem
   from all <u>its</u> iniquity.

Gospel Acclamation John 11:25, 26
*One of the responses Nos 53 to 55 should
be sung before and after this text.*

I am the resurrection and the life, <u>says</u> the Lord;
whoever believes in me will <u>ne</u>ver die.

937 5th Lent (B)

Responsorial Psalm Psalm 50:3-4, 12-15. ℟ v.12

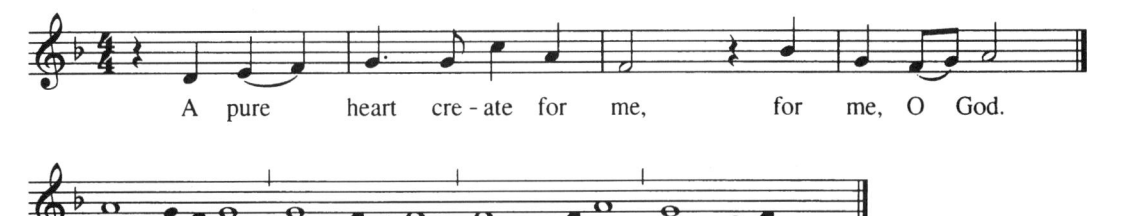

A pure heart cre-ate for me, for me, O God.

1. Have mercy on me, God, <u>in</u> your kindness.
   In your compassion blot out <u>my</u> offence.
   O wash me more and more <u>from</u> my guilt
   and cleanse me <u>from</u> my sin.

2. A pure heart create for <u>me</u>, O God,
   put a steadfast spi<u>rit</u> within me.
   Do not cast me away <u>from</u> your presence,
   nor deprive me of your <u>ho</u>ly spirit.

3. Give me again the joy <u>of</u> your help;
   with a spirit of fer<u>vour</u> sustain me,
   that I may teach transgres<u>sors</u> your ways
   and sinners may re<u>turn</u> to you.

Gospel Acclamation John 12:26
*One of the responses Nos 53 to 55 should
be sung before and after this text.*

If a man serves me, says the Lord, <u>he</u> must follow me,
wherever I am, my servant will <u>be</u> there too.

Response: Richard Lloyd   Psalm tone: Gregory Murray
Text © 1963, 1986, 1993 The Grail, England, taken from 'The Psalms, a New Inclusive Language Version',
published by HarperCollins Religious. Used by permission of A.P. Watt Ltd, London.
Response © Copyright 1998 Kevin Mayhew Ltd.
Psalm tone © Copyright Downside Abbey, Stratton-on-the-Fosse, Bath BA3 4RH. Used by permission.

938 5th Lent (C)

Responsorial Psalm Psalm 125. ℟ v.3

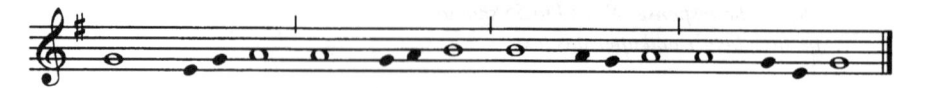

What marvels the Lord worked for us! Indeed we were glad.

1. When the Lord delivered Zion from bondage,
   it seemed like a dream.
   Then was our mouth filled with laughter,
   on our lips there were songs.

2. The heathens themselves said: 'What marvels
   the Lord worked for them!'
   What marvels the Lord worked for us!
   Indeed we were glad.

3. Deliver us, O Lord, from our bondage
   as streams in dry land.
   Those who are sowing in tears
   will sing when they reap.

4. They go out, they go out, full of tears,
   carrying seed for the sowing;
   they come back, they come back, full of song,
   carrying their sheaves.

Gospel Acclamation Amos 5:14
*One of the responses Nos 53 to 55 should
be sung before and after this text.*

Seek good and not evil so that you may live,
and that the Lord God of hosts may really be with you.

Response: Martin Setchell Psalm tone: Gregory Murray
Text © 1963, 1986, 1993 The Grail, England, taken from 'The Psalms, a New Inclusive Language Version',
published by HarperCollins Religious. Used by permission of A.P. Watt Ltd, London.
Response © Copyright 1998 Kevin Mayhew Ltd.
Psalm tone © Copyright McCrimmon Publishing Co. Ltd, 10-12 High St, Great Wakering, Essex SS3 0EQ. Used by permission.

939 Passion Sunday (A,B,C)

Responsorial Psalm Psalm 21:8-9, 17-20, 23-24. ℟ v.2

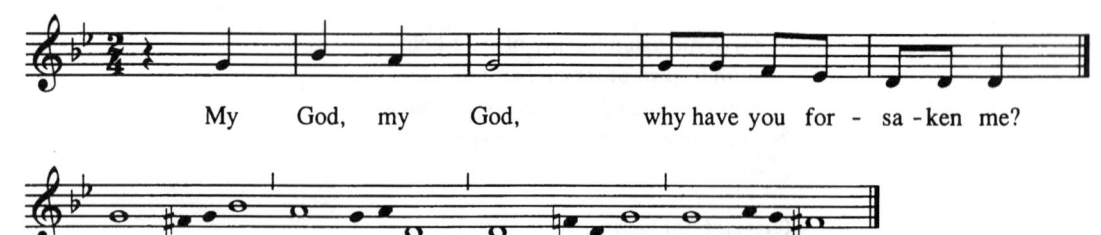

My God, my God, why have you forsaken me?

1. All who see me deride me,
   they curl their lips, they toss their heads.
   'He trusted in the Lord, let him save him;
   let him release him if this is his friend.'

2. Many dogs have surrounded me,
   a band of the wicked beset me.
   They tear holes in my hands and my feet
   I can count every one of my bones.

Response: Gregory Murray Psalm tone: Andrew Moore
Text © 1963, 1986, 1993 The Grail, England, taken from 'The Psalms, a New Inclusive Language Version',
published by HarperCollins Religious. Used by permission of A.P. Watt Ltd, London.
Response © Copyright McCrimmon Publishing Co. Ltd, 10-12 High St, Great Wakering, Essex SS3 0EQ. Used by permission.
Psalm tone © Copyright 1998 Kevin Mayhew Ltd.

3. They divide my clo<u>thing</u> among them.
   They cast lots <u>for</u> my robe.
   O Lord, do not leave <u>me</u> alone,
   my strength, make <u>haste</u> to help me!

4. I will tell of your name <u>to</u> my brethren
   and praise you where they <u>are</u> assembled.
   'You who fear the Lord <u>give</u> him praise;
   all sons of Jacob, <u>give</u> him glory.'

Gospel Acclamation Philippians 2:8-9
*One of the responses Nos 53 to 55 should
be sung before and after this text.*

Christ was humbler yet, even to accepting death, death <u>on</u> a cross.
But God raised him high and gave him the name which is ab<u>ove</u> all names.

940 Holy Thursday -
Evening Mass of the Lord's Supper (A,B,C)

Responsorial Psalm Psalm 115:12-13, 15-18. ℟ cf. 1 Corinthians 10:16

The bless-ing cup that we bless is a com-mu-nion with the blood of Christ.

1. How can I re<u>pay</u> the Lord
   for his good<u>ness</u> to me?
   The cup of salvation <u>I</u> will raise;
   I will call on <u>the</u> Lord's name.

2. O precious in the eyes <u>of</u> the Lord
   is the death <u>of</u> his faithful.
   Your servant, Lord, your ser<u>vant</u> am I;
   you have loo<u>sened</u> my bonds.

3. A thanksgiving sacri<u>fice</u> I make:
   I will call on <u>the</u> Lord's name.
   My vows to the Lord I <u>will</u> fulfil
   before <u>all</u> his people.

Gospel Acclamation John 13:34
*One of the responses Nos 53 to 55 should
be sung before and after this text.*

I give you a <u>new</u> commandment:
love one another just as I have loved you, <u>says</u> the Lord.

Response: Richard Proulx   Psalm tone: Laurence Bevenot
Text © 1963, 1986, 1993 The Grail, England, taken from 'The Psalms, a New Inclusive Language Version',
published by HarperCollins Religious. Used by permission of A.P. Watt Ltd, London.
Response © Copyright 1998 Kevin Mayhew Ltd.
Psalm tone © Copyright Ampleforth Abbey, York YO6 4EN. Used by permission.

941 Good Friday - Celebration of the Lord's Passion (A,B,C)

Responsorial Psalm Psalm 30:2, 6, 12-13, 15-17, 25. ℟ Luke 23:46

Fa - ther, in - to your hands I com-mend my spi - rit.

1. In you, O Lord, <u>I</u> take refuge,
   let me never be <u>put</u> to shame.
   In your justice, <u>set</u> me free.
   It is you who will re<u>deem</u> me, Lord.

2. In the face of <u>all</u> my foes
   I am <u>a</u> reproach,
   an object of scorn <u>to</u> my neighbours
   and of fear <u>to</u> my friends.

3. Those who see me <u>in</u> the street
   run <u>far</u> away from me.
   I am like the dead, forg<u>ott</u>en by all,
   like a thing <u>thrown</u> away.

4. But as for me, I trust <u>in</u> you, Lord,
   I say: 'You <u>are</u> my God.'
   My life is in your <u>hands</u>, deliver me
   from the hands of <u>those</u> who hate me.

5. Let your face shine <u>on</u> your servant.
   Save me <u>in</u> your love.
   Be strong, let your <u>heart</u> take courage,
   all who hope <u>in</u> the Lord.

Gospel Acclamation Philippians 2:8-9
*One of the responses Nos 53 to 55 should be
sung before and after this text.*

Christ was humbler yet, even to accepting death, death <u>on</u> a cross.
But God raised him high and gave him the name which is ab<u>ove</u> all names.

Response and Psalm tone: Gregory Murray
Text © 1963, 1986, 1993 The Grail, England, taken from 'The Psalms, a New Inclusive Language Version',
published by HarperCollins Religious. Used by permission of A.P. Watt Ltd, London.
Response © Copyright McCrimmon Publishing Co. Ltd, 10-12 High St, Great Wakering, Essex SS3 0EQ. Used by permission.
Psalm tone © Copyright Downside Abbey, Stratton-on-the-Fosse, Bath BA3 4RH. Used by permission.

942 Easter Sunday - The Easter Vigil (A,B,C)
After the first Reading

Responsorial Psalm Psalm 103:1-2, 5-6, 10, 12-14, 24, 35. ℟ cf. v.30

Send forth your spi - rit, O Lord, and re - new the face of the earth.

Response and Psalm tone: Andrew Moore
Text © 1963, 1986, 1993 The Grail, England, taken from 'The Psalms, a New Inclusive Language Version',
published by HarperCollins Religious. Used by permission of A.P. Watt Ltd, London.
Response and Psalm tone © Copyright 1998 Kevin Mayhew Ltd.

1. Bless the <u>Lord</u>, my soul!
   Lord God, how <u>great</u> you are,
   clothed in majes<u>ty</u> and glory,
   wrapped in light as <u>in</u> a robe!

2. You founded the earth <u>on</u> its base,
   to stand firm from <u>age</u> to age.
   You wrapped it with the ocean <u>like</u> a cloak:
   the waters stood higher <u>than</u> the mountains.

3. You make springs gush forth <u>in</u> the valleys:
   they flow in be<u>tween</u> the hills.
   On their banks dwell the <u>birds</u> of heaven;
   from the branches they <u>sing</u> their song.

4. From your dwelling you wa<u>ter</u> the hills;
   earth drinks its fill <u>of</u> your gift.
   You make the grass grow <u>for</u> the cattle
   and the plants to <u>serve</u> our needs.

5. How many are your <u>works</u>, O Lord!
   In wisdom you have <u>made</u> them all.
   The earth is full <u>of</u> your riches.
   Bless the <u>Lord</u>, my soul!

After the second Reading

Responsorial Psalm Psalm 15:5, 8-11. ℟ v.1

Pre-serve me, God, I take re-fuge in you.

1. O Lord, it is you who are my por<u>tion</u> and cup;
   it is you yourself who <u>are</u> my prize.
   I keep the Lord ever <u>in</u> my sight:
   since he is at my right hand, I <u>shall</u> stand firm.

2. And so my heart rejoices, my <u>soul</u> is glad;
   even my body shall <u>rest</u> in safety.
   For you will not leave my soul a<u>mong</u> the dead,
   nor let your beloved <u>know</u> decay.

3. O Lord, <u>you</u> will show me
   the <u>path</u> of life,
   the fullness of joy <u>in</u> your presence,
   at your right hand happ<u>iness</u> for ever.

Response: Andrew Moore Psalm tone: Laurence Bevenot
Text © 1963, 1986, 1993 The Grail, England, taken from 'The Psalms, a New Inclusive Language Version',
published by HarperCollins Religious. Used by permission of A.P. Watt Ltd, London.
Response © Copyright 1998 Kevin Mayhew Ltd.
Psalm tone © Copyright Ampleforth Abbey, York YO6 4EN. Used by permission.

After the third Reading

Responsorial Psalm Exodus 15:1-6, 17-18. ℟ v.1

I will sing to the Lord, glorious his triumph!

1. I will sing to the Lord, glori__ous__ his triumph!
   Horse and rider he has thrown in__to__ the sea!
   The Lord is my strength, my song, __my__ salvation.
   This is my God and __I__ extol him,
   my father's God and I __give__ him praise.

2. The Lord __is__ a warrior!
   The Lord __is__ his name.
   The chariots of Pharaoh he hurled in__to__ the sea,
   the flower of his army is drowned __in__ the sea.
   The deeps hide them; they sank __like__ a stone.

3. Your right hand, Lord, glorious __in__ its power,
   your right hand, Lord, has shat__tered__ the enemy.
   In the greatness of your glory you __crushed__ the foe.
   You will lead your people and plant them __on__ your mountain,
   the sanctuary, Lord, which your __hands__ have made.
   The Lord will reign for e__ver__ and ever.

Response: Richard Lloyd   Psalm tone: Andrew Moore
Text © 1963, 1986, 1993 The Grail, England, taken from 'The Psalms, a New Inclusive Language Version',
published by HarperCollins Religious. Used by permission of A.P. Watt Ltd, London.
Response and Psalm tone © Copyright 1998 Kevin Mayhew Ltd.

After the fourth Reading

Responsorial Psalm Psalm 29:2, 4-6, 11-13. ℟ v.2

I will praise you, Lord, you have rescued me.

1. I will praise you, Lord, __you__ have rescued me
   and have not let my enemies rejoice __over__ me.
   O Lord, you have raised my soul __from__ the dead,
   restored me to life from those who sink in__to__ the grave.

Response: Richard Lloyd   Psalm tone: Alan Rees
Text © 1963, 1986, 1993 The Grail, England, taken from 'The Psalms, a New Inclusive Language Version',
published by HarperCollins Religious. Used by permission of A.P. Watt Ltd, London.
Response © Copyright 1998 Kevin Mayhew Ltd.
Psalm tone © Copyright Belmont Abbey, Hereford HR2 9RZ. Used by permission.

2. Sing psalms to the Lord, <u>you</u> who love him,
   give thanks to his <u>ho</u>ly name.
   His anger lasts but a moment; his fa<u>vour</u> through life.
   At night there are tears, but joy <u>comes</u> with dawn.

3. The Lord listened <u>and</u> had pity.
   The Lord came <u>to</u> my help.
   For me you have changed my mourning <u>into</u> dancing,
   O Lord my God, I will thank <u>you</u> for ever.

After the fifth Reading

Responsorial Psalm Isaiah 12:2-6. ℟ v.3

With joy you will draw wa-ter from the wells of sal-va-tion.

1. Truly God is <u>my</u> salvation,
   I trust, I <u>shall</u> not fear.
   For the Lord is my <u>strength</u>, my song,
   he be<u>came</u> my saviour.

2. Give thanks <u>to</u> the Lord,
   give praise <u>to</u> his name!
   Make his mighty deeds known <u>to</u> the peoples,
   declare the greatness <u>of</u> his name.

3. Sing a psalm to the Lord for he has done glo<u>ri</u>ous deeds,
   make them known to <u>all</u> the earth!
   People of Zion, sing and <u>shout</u> for joy
   for great in your midst is the Holy <u>One</u> of Israel.

Response and Psalm tone: Andrew Moore
Text © 1963, 1986, 1993 The Grail, England, taken from 'The Psalms, a New Inclusive Language Version',
published by HarperCollins Religious. Used by permission of A.P. Watt Ltd, London.
Response and Psalm tone © Copyright 1998 Kevin Mayhew Ltd.

After the sixth Reading

Responsorial Psalm Psalm 18:8-11. ℟ John 6:69

You have the message of eternal life, O Lord.

1. The law of the <u>Lord</u> is perfect,
   it re<u>vives</u> the soul.
   The rule of the Lord is <u>to</u> be trusted,
   it gives wisdom <u>to</u> the simple.

2. The precepts of the <u>Lord</u> are right,
   they glad<u>den</u> the heart.
   The command of the <u>Lord</u> is clear,
   it gives light <u>to</u> the eyes.

3. The fear of the <u>Lord</u> is holy,
   a<u>bid</u>ing for ever.
   The decrees of the <u>Lord</u> are truth
   and all <u>of</u> them just.

4. They are more to be de<u>sired</u> than gold,
   than the pur<u>est</u> of gold
   and sweeter are <u>they</u> than honey,
   than honey <u>from</u> the comb.

Response and Psalm tone: Andrew Moore
Text © 1963, 1986, 1993 The Grail, England, taken from 'The Psalms, a New Inclusive Language Version',
published by HarperCollins Religious. Used by permission of A.P. Watt Ltd, London.
Response and Psalm tone © Copyright 1998 Kevin Mayhew Ltd.

After the seventh Reading

Responsorial Psalm Psalm 41:3, 5; 42:3, 4. ℟ 41:2

Like the deer that yearns for running streams, so my soul is yearning for you, my God.

1. My soul is thirs<u>ting</u> for God,
   the God <u>of</u> my life;
   when can I en<u>ter</u> and see
   the <u>face</u> of God?

2. These things will I remember as I pour <u>out</u> my soul;
   how I would lead the rejoicing crowd into the <u>house</u> of God,
   amid cries of gladness <u>and</u> thanksgiving,
   the throng <u>wild</u> with joy.

Response and Psalm tone: Gregory Murray
Text © 1963, 1986, 1993 The Grail, England, taken from 'The Psalms, a New Inclusive Language Version',
published by HarperCollins Religious. Used by permission of A.P. Watt Ltd, London.
Response © Copyright McCrimmon Publishing Co. Ltd, 10-12 High St, Great Wakering, Essex SS3 0EQ. Used by permission.
Psalm tone © Copyright Downside Abbey, Stratton-on-the-Fosse, Bath BA3 4RH. Used by permission.

3. O send forth your light <u>and</u> your truth;
   let these <u>be</u> my guide.
   Let them bring me to your <u>ho</u>ly mountain
   to the place <u>where</u> you dwell.

4. And I will come to the <u>al</u>tar of God,
   the God <u>of</u> my joy.
   My redeemer, I will thank you <u>on</u> the harp,
   O <u>God</u>, my God.

If a Baptism takes place, the Psalm which follows the fifth Reading is used, or the one that follows here.

Responsorial Psalm Psalm 50:12-15, 18, 19. ℟ v.12

A pure heart cre-ate for me, for me, O God.

1. A pure heart create for <u>me</u>, O God,
   put a steadfast sp<u>ir</u>it within me.
   Do not cast me away <u>from</u> your presence,
   nor deprive me of your <u>ho</u>ly spirit.

2. Give me again the joy <u>of</u> your help;
   with a spirit of fer<u>vour</u> sustain me,
   that I may teach transgres<u>sors</u> your ways
   and sinners may re<u>turn</u> to you.

3. For in sacrifice you take <u>no</u> delight,
   burnt offering from me you <u>would</u> refuse,
   my sacrifice, a <u>con</u>trite spirit.
   A humbled, contrite heart you <u>will</u> not spurn.

Response: Richard Lloyd   Psalm tone: Gregory Murray
Text © 1963, 1986, 1993 The Grail, England, taken from 'The Psalms, a New Inclusive Language Version', published by HarperCollins Religious. Used by permission of A.P. Watt Ltd, London.
Response © Copyright 1998 Kevin Mayhew Ltd.
Psalm tone © Copyright Downside Abbey, Stratton-on-the-Fosse, Bath BA3 4RH. Used by permission.

943 Easter Sunday - The Mass of Easter Night (A,B,C)

Responsorial Psalm Psalm 117:1-2, 16-17, 22-23

Al - le - lu - ia, al - le - lu - ia, al - le - lu - ia.

1. Give thanks to the Lord for <u>he</u> is good,
for his love <u>has</u> no end.
Let the family of Is<u>ra</u>el say:
'His love <u>has</u> no end.'

2. The Lord's right <u>hand</u> has triumphed;
his right hand <u>raised</u> me up.
I shall not die, <u>I</u> shall live
and re<u>count</u> his deeds.

3. The stone which the buil<u>ders</u> rejected
has be<u>come</u> the corner stone.
This is the work <u>of</u> the Lord,
a marvel <u>in</u> our eyes.

Response: Martin Setchell   Psalm tone: Alan Rees
Text © 1963, 1986, 1993 The Grail, England, taken from 'The Psalms, a New Inclusive Language Version', published by HarperCollins Religious. Used by permission of A.P. Watt Ltd, London.
Response © Copyright 1998 Kevin Mayhew Ltd.
Psalm tone © Copyright Belmont Abbey, Hereford HR2 9RZ. Used by permission.

944 Easter Sunday - Mass of the Day (A,B,C)

Responsorial Psalm Psalm 117:1-2, 16-17, 22-23. ℟ v.24

This day was made by the Lord; we re-joice and are glad.

1. Give thanks to the Lord for <u>he</u> is good,
for his love <u>has</u> no end.
Let the family of Is<u>ra</u>el say:
'His love <u>has</u> no end.'

2. The Lord's right <u>hand</u> has triumphed;
his right hand <u>raised</u> me up.
I shall not die, <u>I</u> shall live
and re<u>count</u> his deeds.

3. The stone which the buil<u>ders</u> rejected
has be<u>come</u> the corner stone.
This is the work <u>of</u> the Lord,
a marvel <u>in</u> our eyes.

Gospel Acclamation   1 Corinthians 5:7-8
For musical setting see Nos 36 to 47
Alleluia.
Christ, our passover, <u>has</u> been sacrificed;
let us celebrate the feast then, <u>in</u> the Lord.
Alleluia.

Response: Rosalie Bonighton   Psalm tone: Laurence Bevenot
Text © 1963, 1986, 1993 The Grail, England, taken from 'The Psalms, a New Inclusive Language Version', published by HarperCollins Religious. Used by permission of A.P. Watt Ltd, London.
Response © Copyright 1998 Kevin Mayhew Ltd.
Psalm tone © Copyright Ampleforth Abbey, York YO6 4EN. Used by permission.

945 2nd Easter (A)

Responsorial Psalm Psalm 117:2-4, 13-15, 22-24. ℟ v.1

Give thanks to the Lord for he is good, give thanks to the Lord for his love has no end.

1. Let the sons of Is<u>ra</u>el say:
   'His love <u>has</u> no end.'
   Let the sons of <u>A</u>aron say:
   'His love <u>has</u> no end.'
   Let those who fear <u>the</u> Lord say:
   'His love <u>has</u> no end.'

2. I was thrust down, thrust <u>down</u> and falling
   but the Lord <u>was</u> my helper.
   The Lord is my strength <u>and</u> my song:
   he <u>was</u> my saviour.
   There are shouts of <u>joy</u> and victory
   in the tents <u>of</u> the just.

3. The stone which the buil<u>ders</u> rejected
   has be<u>come</u> the corner stone.
   This is the work <u>of</u> the Lord,
   a marvel <u>in</u> our eyes.
   This day was made <u>by</u> the Lord;
   we rejoice <u>and</u> are glad.

Gospel Acclamation John 20:29
For musical setting see Nos 36 to 47

Alleluia.
Jesus said: 'You believe because <u>you</u> can see me.
Happy are those who have not seen and <u>yet</u> believe.'
Alleluia.

Response: Alan Rees Psalm tone: Andrew Moore
Text © 1963, 1986, 1993 The Grail, England, taken from 'The Psalms, a New Inclusive Language Version',
published by HarperCollins Religious. Used by permission of A.P. Watt Ltd, London.
Response and Psalm tone © Copyright 1998 Kevin Mayhew Ltd.

946 2nd Easter (B)

Responsorial Psalm Psalm 117:2-4, 15-18, 22-24. ℞ v.1

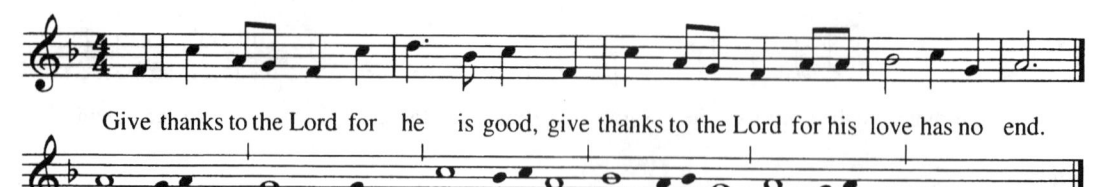

Give thanks to the Lord for he is good, give thanks to the Lord for his love has no end.

1. Let the sons of Is<u>ra</u>el say:
   'His love <u>has</u> no end.'
   Let the sons of <u>Aa</u>ron say:
   'His love <u>has</u> no end.'
   Let those who fear <u>the</u> Lord say:
   'His love <u>has</u> no end.'

2. The Lord's right <u>hand</u> has triumphed;
   his right hand <u>raised</u> me up.
   I shall not die, <u>I</u> shall live
   and re<u>count</u> his deeds.
   I was punished, I was punished <u>by</u> the Lord,
   but not <u>doomed</u> to die.

3. The stone which the buil<u>ders</u> rejected
   has be<u>come</u> the corner stone.
   This is the work <u>of</u> the Lord,
   a marvel <u>in</u> our eyes.
   This day was made <u>by</u> the Lord;
   we rejoice <u>and</u> are glad.

Gospel Acclamation John 20:29
For musical setting see Nos 36 to 47
  Alleluia.
  Jesus said: 'You believe because <u>you</u> can see me.
  Happy are those who have not seen and '<u>yet</u> believe.'
  Alleluia.

Response: Alan Rees Psalm tone: Andrew Moore
Text © 1963, 1986, 1993 The Grail, England, taken from 'The Psalms, a New Inclusive Language Version',
published by HarperCollins Religious. Used by permission of A.P. Watt Ltd, London.
Response and Psalm tone © Copyright 1998 Kevin Mayhew Ltd.

947 2nd Easter (C)

Responsorial Psalm Psalm 117:2-4, 22-27. ℞ v.1

Give thanks to the Lord for he is good, give thanks to the Lord for his love has no end.

1. Let the sons of Is<u>ra</u>el say:
   'His love <u>has</u> no end.'
   Let the sons of <u>Aa</u>ron say:
   'His love <u>has</u> no end.'
   Let those who fear <u>the</u> Lord say:
   'His love <u>has</u> no end.'

2. The stone which the buil<u>ders</u> rejected
   has be<u>come</u> the corner stone.
   This is the work <u>of</u> the Lord,
   a marvel <u>in</u> our eyes.
   This day was made <u>by</u> the Lord;
   we rejoice <u>and</u> are glad.

Response: Alan Rees Psalm tone: Andrew Moore
Text © 1963, 1986, 1993 The Grail, England, taken from 'The Psalms, a New Inclusive Language Version',
published by HarperCollins Religious. Used by permission of A.P. Watt Ltd, London.
Response and Psalm tone © Copyright 1998 Kevin Mayhew Ltd.

3. O Lord, grant us salvation;
O Lord, grant success.
Blessed in the name of the Lord
is he who comes.
We bless you from the house of the Lord;
the Lord God is our light.

Gospel Acclamation John 20:29
For musical setting see Nos 36 to 47
Alleluia.
Jesus said: 'You believe because you can see me.
Happy are those who have not seen and yet believe.'
Alleluia.

948 3rd Easter (A)

Responsorial Psalm Psalm 15:1-2, 5, 7-11. ℟ v.11

Show us, Lord, the path of life.

1. Preserve me, God, I take refuge in you.
   I say to the Lord: 'You are my God.
   O Lord, it is you who are my portion and cup;
   it is you yourself who are my prize.'

2. I will bless the Lord who gives me counsel,
   who even at night directs my heart.
   I keep the Lord ever in my sight:
   since he is at my right hand, I shall stand

3. And so my heart rejoices, my soul is glad;
   even my body shall rest in safety.
   For you will not leave my soul among the dead,
   nor let your beloved know decay.

4. O Lord, you will show me
   the path of life,
   the fullness of joy in your presence,
   at your right hand happiness for ever.

Gospel Acclamation cf. Luke 24:32
For musical setting see Nos 36 to 47
Alleluia.
Lord Jesus, explain the scriptures to us.
Make our hearts burn within us as you talk to us.
Alleluia.

Response: Andrew Moore   Psalm tone: Laurence Bevenot
Text © 1963, 1986, 1993 The Grail, England, taken from 'The Psalms, a New Inclusive Language Version',
published by HarperCollins Religious. Used by permission of A.P. Watt Ltd, London.
Response © Copyright 1998 Kevin Mayhew Ltd.
Psalm tone © Copyright Ampleforth Abbey, York YO6 4EN. Used by permission.

949 3rd Easter (B)

Responsorial Psalm Psalm 4:2, 4, 7, 9. ℟ v.7

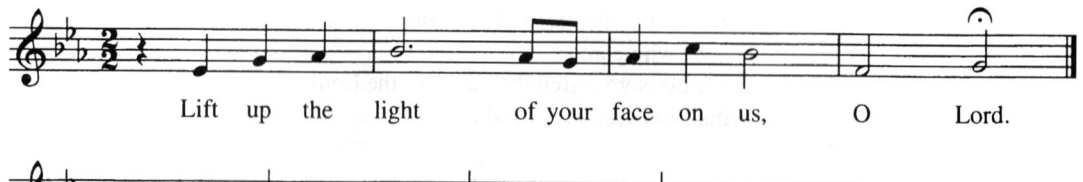

Lift up the light of your face on us, O Lord.

1. When I call, answer me, O <u>God</u> of justice;
   from anguish you release me, have mer<u>cy</u> and hear me!
   It is the Lord who grants favours to those <u>whom</u> he loves;
   the Lord hears me whene<u>ver</u> I call him.

2. 'What can bring us happiness?' <u>many</u> say.
   Lift up the light of your face on <u>us</u>, O Lord.
   I will lie down in peace and sleep <u>comes</u> at once,
   for you alone, Lord, make me <u>dwell</u> in safety.

Gospel Acclamation cf. Luke 24:32
For musical setting see Nos 36 to 47
   Alleluia.
   Lord Jesus, explain the scrip<u>tures</u> to us.
   Make our hearts burn within us <u>as</u> you talk to us.
   Alleluia.

Response and Psalm tone: Andrew Moore
Text © 1963, 1986, 1993 The Grail, England, taken from 'The Psalms, a New Inclusive Language Version',
published by HarperCollins Religious. Used by permission of A.P. Watt Ltd, London.
Response and Psalm tone © Copyright 1998 Kevin Mayhew Ltd.

950 3rd Easter (C)

Responsorial Psalm Psalm 29:2, 4-6, 11-13. ℟ v.2

I will praise you, Lord, you have rescued me.

1. I will praise you, Lord, <u>you</u> have rescued me
   and have not let my enemies rejoice <u>over</u> me.
   O Lord, you have raised my soul <u>from</u> the dead,
   restored me to life from those who sink in<u>to</u> the grave.

Response: Richard Lloyd Psalm tone: Alan Rees
Text © 1963, 1986, 1993 The Grail, England, taken from 'The Psalms, a New Inclusive Language Version',
published by HarperCollins Religious. Used by permission of A.P. Watt Ltd, London.
Response © Copyright 1998 Kevin Mayhew Ltd.
Psalm tone © Copyright Belmont Abbey, Hereford HR2 9RZ. Used by permission.

2. Sing psalms to the Lord, you who love him,
   give thanks to his holy name.
   His anger lasts but a moment; his favour through life.
   At night there are tears, but joy comes with dawn.

3. The Lord listened and had pity.
   The Lord came to my help.
   For me you have changed my mourning into dancing;
   O Lord my God, I will thank you for ever.

Gospel Acclamation cf. Luke 24:32
For musical setting see Nos 36 to 47
   Alleluia.
   Lord Jesus, explain the scriptures to us.
   Make our hearts burn within us as you talk to us.
   Alleluia.

951 4th Easter (A)

Responsorial Psalm Psalm 22:1-6. R︎ v.1

The Lord is my shepherd; there is nothing I shall want, the Lord is my shepherd; there is nothing I shall want.

1. The Lord is my shepherd;
   there is nothing I shall want.
   Fresh and green are the pastures
   where he gives me repose.

2. Near restful waters he leads me
   to revive my drooping spirit.
   He guides me along the right path;
   he is true to his name.

3. If I should walk in the valley of darkness
   no evil would I fear.
   You are there with your crook and your staff;
   with these you give me comfort.

Note: verse 3 may be omitted

4. You have prepared a banquet for me
   in the sight of my foes.
   My head you have anointed with oil;
   my cup is overflowing.

5. Surely goodness and kindness shall follow me
   all the days of my life.
   In the Lord's own house shall I dwell
   for ever and ever.

Gospel Acclamation John 10:14
For musical setting see Nos 36 to 47
   Alleluia.
   I am the good shepherd, says the Lord;
   I know my own sheep and my own know me.
   Alleluia.

Response: Andrew Moore   Psalm tone: Alan Rees
Text © 1963, 1986, 1993 The Grail, England, taken from 'The Psalms, a New Inclusive Language Version',
published by HarperCollins Religious. Used by permission of A.P. Watt Ltd, London.
Response © Copyright 1998 Kevin Mayhew Ltd.
Psalm tone © Copyright Belmont Abbey, Hereford HR2 9RZ. Used by permission.

952 4th Easter (B)

Responsorial Psalm Psalm 117:1, 8-9, 21-23, 26, 28-29. R̷ v.22

The stone which the build-ers re-jec-ted has be-come the cor-ner stone.

1. Give thanks to the Lord for <u>he</u> is good,
   for his love <u>has</u> no end.
   It is better to take refuge <u>in</u> the Lord
   than to <u>trust</u> in mortals;
   it is better to take refuge <u>in</u> the Lord
   than to <u>trust</u> in rulers.

2. I will thank you for you have <u>given</u> answer
   and you <u>are</u> my saviour.
   The stone which the buil<u>ders</u> rejected
   has be<u>come</u> the corner stone.
   This is the work <u>of</u> the Lord,
   a marvel <u>in</u> our eyes.

3. Blessed in the name of the Lord is <u>he</u> who comes.
   We bless you from the house <u>of</u> the Lord;
   I will thank you for you have <u>given</u> answer
   and you <u>are</u> my saviour.
   Give thanks to the Lord for <u>he</u> is good;
   for his love <u>has</u> no end.

Gospel Acclamation John 10:14
For musical setting see Nos 36 to 47
   Alleluia.
   I am the good shepherd, <u>says</u> the Lord;
   I know my own sheep and my <u>own</u> know me.
   Alleluia.

Response: Martin Setchell   Psalm tone: Andrew Moore
Text © 1963, 1986, 1993 The Grail, England, taken from 'The Psalms, a New Inclusive Language Version',
published by HarperCollins Religious. Used by permission of A.P. Watt Ltd, London.
Response and Psalm tone © Copyright 1998 Kevin Mayhew Ltd.

953 4th Easter (C)

Responsorial Psalm Psalm 99:1-3, 5. R̷ v.3

We are his peo-ple, the sheep of his flock.

1. Cry out with joy to the Lord, <u>all</u> the earth.
   Serve the <u>Lord</u> with gladness.
   Come before him, sing<u>ing</u> for joy.

2. Know that he, the <u>Lord</u>, is God.
   He made us, we be<u>long</u> to him,
   we are his people, the sheep <u>of</u> his flock.

Response and Psalm tone: Andrew Moore
Text © 1963, 1986, 1993 The Grail, England, taken from 'The Psalms, a New Inclusive Language Version',
published by HarperCollins Religious. Used by permission of A.P. Watt Ltd, London.
Response and Psalm tone © Copyright 1998 Kevin Mayhew Ltd.

3. Indeed, how good <u>is</u> the Lord,
   eternal his mer<u>ci</u>ful love.
   He is faithful from <u>age</u> to age.

Gospel Acclamation John 10:14
For musical setting see Nos 36 to 47
   Alleluia.
   I am the good shepherd, <u>says</u> the Lord;
   I know my own sheep and my <u>own</u> know me.
   Alleluia.

954 5th Easter (A)

Responsorial Psalm   Psalm 32:1-2, 4-5, 18-19. ℟ v.22

May your love be up-on us, O Lord, as we place all our hope in you.

1. Ring out your joy to the Lord, <u>O</u> you just;
   for praise is fitting for <u>loy</u>al hearts.
   Give thanks to the Lord u<u>pon</u> the harp,
   with a ten-stringed lute <u>sing</u> him songs.

2. For the word of the <u>Lord</u> is faithful
   and all his works <u>to</u> be trusted.
   The Lord loves jus<u>tice</u> and right
   and fills the earth <u>with</u> his love.

3. The Lord looks on those <u>who</u> revere him,
   on those who hope <u>in</u> his love,
   to rescue their <u>souls</u> from death,
   to keep them a<u>live</u> in famine.

Gospel Acclamation John 14:6
For musical setting see Nos 36 to 47
   Alleluia.
   Jesus said: 'I am the Way, the Truth <u>and</u> the Life.
   No one can come to the Father ex<u>cept</u> through me.'
   Alleluia.

Response: Rosalie Bonighton   Psalm tone: Laurence Bevenot
Text © 1963, 1986, 1993 The Grail, England, taken from 'The Psalms, a New Inclusive Language Version',
published by HarperCollins Religious. Used by permission of A.P. Watt Ltd, London.
Response © Copyright 1998 Kevin Mayhew Ltd.
Psalm tone © Copyright Ampleforth Abbey, York YO6 4EN. Used by permission.

955 5th Easter (B)

Responsorial Psalm Psalm 21:26-28, 30-32. ℟ v.26

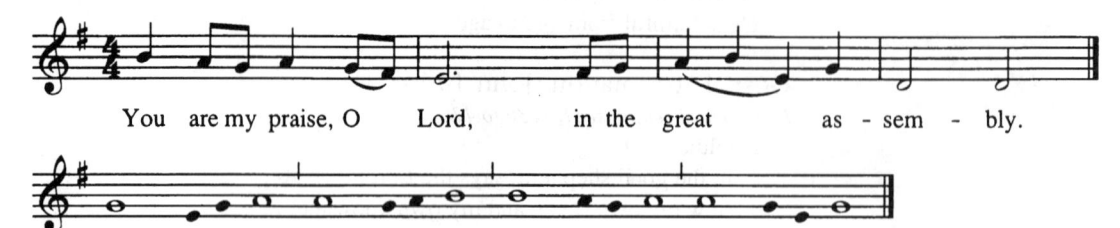

You are my praise, O Lord, in the great assembly.

1. My vows I will pay before <u>those</u> who fear him.
   The poor shall eat and shall <u>have</u> their fill.
   They shall praise the Lord, <u>those</u> who seek him.
   May their hearts live for <u>ev</u>er and ever!

2. All the earth shall remember and return <u>to</u> the Lord,
   all families of the nations wor<u>ship</u> before him.
   They shall worship him, all the mighty <u>of</u> the earth;
   before him shall bow all who go down <u>to</u> the dust.

3. And my soul shall live for him, my <u>chil</u>dren serve him.
   They shall tell of the Lord to generations <u>yet</u> to come,
   declare his faithfulness to peoples <u>yet</u> unborn:
   'These things the <u>Lord</u> has done.'

Gospel Acclamation John 15:4-5
For musical setting see Nos 36 to 47

Alleluia.
Make your home in me, as I make <u>mine</u> in you.
Whoever remains in me bears <u>fruit</u> in plenty.
Alleluia.

Response: Andrew Moore   Psalm tone: Gregory Murray
Text © 1963, 1986, 1993 The Grail, England, taken from 'The Psalms, a New Inclusive Language Version',
published by HarperCollins Religious. Used by permission of A.P. Watt Ltd, London.
Response © Copyright 1998 Kevin Mayhew Ltd.
Psalm tone © Copyright McCrimmon Publishing Co. Ltd, 10-12 High St, Great Wakering, Essex SS3 0EQ. Used by permission.

956 5th Easter (C)

Responsorial Psalm Psalm 144:8-13. ℟ cf. v.1

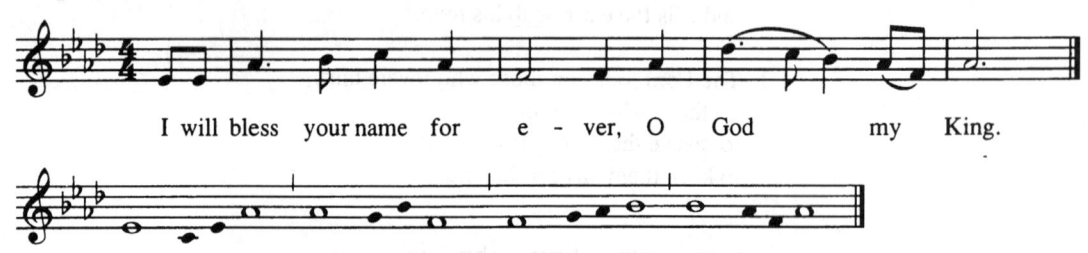

I will bless your name for ever, O God my King.

1. The Lord is kind and full <u>of</u> compassion,
   slow to anger, aboun<u>ding</u> in love.
   How good is the <u>Lord</u> to all,
   compassionate to <u>all</u> his creatures.

2. All your creatures shall thank <u>you</u>, O Lord,
   and your friends shall re<u>peat</u> their blessings.
   They shall speak of the glory <u>of</u> your reign
   and declare your <u>might</u>, O God.

Response: Colin Mawby   Psalm tone: Alan Rees
Text © 1963, 1986, 1993 The Grail, England, taken from 'The Psalms, a New Inclusive Language Version',
published by HarperCollins Religious. Used by permission of A.P. Watt Ltd, London.
Response © Copyright 1998 Kevin Mayhew Ltd.
Psalm tone © Copyright Belmont Abbey, Hereford HR2 9RZ. Used by permission.

3. They will make known to all your <u>migh</u>ty deeds
   and the glorious splendour <u>of</u> your reign.
   Yours is an ever<u>las</u>ting kingdom;
   your rule lasts from <u>age</u> to age.

Gospel Acclamation John 13:34
For musical setting see Nos 36 to 47
   Alleluia.
   Jesus said: 'I give you a <u>new</u> commandment:
   love one another, just as I <u>have</u> loved you.'
   Alleluia.

957 6th Easter (A)

Responsorial Psalm Psalm 65:1-7, 16, 20. ℟ v.1

Cry out with joy to God all the earth.

1. Cry out with joy to God <u>all</u> the earth,
   O sing to the glory <u>of</u> his name.
   O render him glo<u>ri</u>ous praise,
   say to God: 'How tremen<u>dous</u> your deeds!'

2. 'Before you all the <u>earth</u> shall bow;
   shall sing to you, sing <u>to</u> your name!'
   Come and see the <u>works</u> of God,
   tremendous his deeds <u>a</u>mong men.

3. He turned the sea in<u>to</u> dry land,
   they passed through the ri<u>ver</u> dry-shod.
   Let our joy then <u>be</u> in him;
   he rules for ever <u>by</u> his might.

4. Come and hear, all <u>who</u> fear God.
   I will tell what he did <u>for</u> my soul:
   Blessed be God who did not re<u>ject</u> my prayer
   nor with<u>hold</u> his love from me.

Gospel Acclamation John 14:23
For musical setting see Nos 36 to 47
   Alleluia.
   Jesus said: 'If anyone loves me they will <u>keep</u> my word,
   and my Father will love them and <u>we</u> shall come to them.'
   Alleluia.

Response: Rosalie Bonighton Psalm tone: Alan Rees
Text © 1963, 1986, 1993 The Grail, England, taken from 'The Psalms, a New Inclusive Language Version',
published by HarperCollins Religious. Used by permission of A.P. Watt Ltd, London.
Response © Copyright 1998 Kevin Mayhew Ltd.
Psalm tone © Copyright Belmont Abbey, Hereford HR2 9RZ. Used by permission.

958 6th Easter (B)

Responsorial Psalm Psalm 97:1-4. ℟ cf.v.2

The Lord has shown his sal-va-tion to all the na-tions.

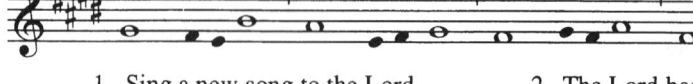

1. Sing a new song <u>to</u> the Lord
   for he <u>has</u> worked wonders.
   His right hand and his <u>ho</u>ly arm
   have <u>brought</u> salvation.

2. The Lord has made known <u>his</u> salvation;
   has shown his justice <u>to</u> the nations.
   He has remembered his <u>truth</u> and love
   for the <u>house</u> of Israel.

3. All the ends of the <u>earth</u> have seen
   the salvation <u>of</u> our God.
   Shout to the Lord <u>all</u> the earth,
   ring <u>out</u> your joy.

Gospel Acclamation John 14:23
For musical setting see Nos 36 to 47
Alleluia.
Jesus said: 'If anyone loves me they will <u>keep</u> my word,
and my Father will love them and <u>we</u> shall come to them.'
Alleluia.

Response: Richard Proulx   Psalm tone: Andrew Moore
Text © 1963, 1986, 1993 The Grail, England, taken from 'The Psalms, a New Inclusive Language Version',
published by HarperCollins Religious. Used by permission of A.P. Watt Ltd, London.
Response and Psalm tone © Copyright 1998 Kevin Mayhew Ltd.

959 6th Easter (C)

Responsorial Psalm Psalm 66:2-3, 5-6, 8. ℟ v.4

Let the peo-ples praise you, O God; let all the peo-ples praise you.

1. O God, be grac<u>ious</u> and bless us
   and let your face shed its <u>light</u> upon us.
   So will your ways be known <u>upon</u> earth,
   and all nations learn your <u>saving</u> help.

2. Let the nations be glad <u>and</u> exult
   for you rule the <u>world</u> with justice.
   With fairness you <u>rule</u> the peoples,
   you guide the <u>nations</u> on earth.

Response: Colin Mawby   Psalm tone: Gregory Murray
Text © 1963, 1986, 1993 The Grail, England, taken from 'The Psalms, a New Inclusive Language Version',
published by HarperCollins Religious. Used by permission of A.P. Watt Ltd, London.
Response © Copyright 1998 Kevin Mayhew Ltd.
Psalm tone © Copyright McCrimmon Publishing Co. Ltd, 10-12 High St, Great Wakering, Essex SS3 0EQ. Used by permission.

3. Let the peoples praise you, O God;
   let all the peoples praise you.
   May God still give us his blessing
   till the ends of the earth revere him.

Gospel Acclamation John 14:23
For musical setting see Nos 36 to 47
   Alleluia.
   Jesus said: 'If anyone loves me they will keep my word,
   and my Father will love them and we shall come to them.'
   Alleluia.

960 The Ascension of the Lord (A,B,C)

Responsorial Psalm Psalm 46:2-3, 6-9. ℟ v.6

God goes up with shouts of joy; the Lord goes up with trum-pet blast.

1. All peoples, clap your hands,
   cry to God with shouts of joy!
   For the Lord, the Most High, we must fear,
   great king over all the earth.

2. God goes up with shouts of joy;
   the Lord goes up with trumpet blast.
   Sing praise for God, sing praise,
   sing praise to our king, sing praise.

3. God is king of all the earth.
   Sing praise with all your skill.
   God is king over the nations;
   God reigns on his holy throne.

Gospel Acclamation Matthew 28:19, 20
For musical setting see Nos 36 to 47
   Alleluia.
   Go, make disciples of all the nations;
   I am with you always; yes, to the end of time.
   Alleluia.

Response: Andrew Moore   Psalm tone: Laurence Bevenot
Text © 1963, 1986, 1993 The Grail, England, taken from 'The Psalms, a New Inclusive Language Version',
published by HarperCollins Religious. Used by permission of A.P. Watt Ltd, London.
Response © Copyright 1998 Kevin Mayhew Ltd.
Psalm tone © Copyright Ampleforth Abbey, York YO6 4EN. Used by permission.

961 7th Easter (A)

Responsorial Psalm Psalm 26:1, 4, 7-8. ℟ v.13

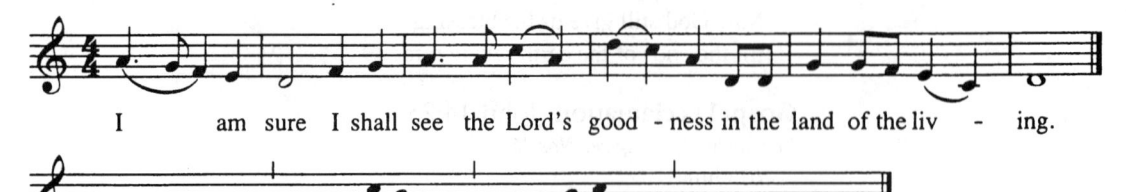

I am sure I shall see the Lord's goodness in the land of the living.

1. The Lord is my light <u>and</u> my help;
   whom <u>shall</u> I fear?
   The Lord is the stronghold <u>of</u> my life;
   before whom <u>shall</u> I shrink?

2. There is one thing I ask <u>of</u> the Lord,
   for <u>this</u> I long,
   to live in the house <u>of</u> the Lord,
   all the days <u>of</u> my life.

3. O Lord, hear my voice <u>when</u> I call;
   have mer<u>cy</u> and answer.
   Of you my <u>heart</u> has spoken;
   '<u>Seek</u> his face.'

Gospel Acclamation cf. John 14:18
For musical setting see Nos 36 to 47
Alleluia.
I will not leave you orphans, <u>says</u> the Lord;
I will come back to you, and your hearts will be <u>full</u> of joy.
Alleluia.

Response: Colin Mawby   Psalm tone: Alan Rees
Text © 1963, 1986, 1993 The Grail, England, taken from 'The Psalms, a New Inclusive Language Version',
published by HarperCollins Religious. Used by permission of A.P. Watt Ltd, London.
Response © Copyright 1998 Kevin Mayhew Ltd.
Psalm tone © Copyright Belmont Abbey, Hereford HR2 9RZ. Used by permission.

962 7th Easter (B)

Responsorial Psalm Psalm 102:1-2, 11-12, 19-20. ℟ v.19

The Lord has set his sway in heaven.

1. My soul, give thanks <u>to</u> the Lord;
   all my being, bless his <u>holy</u> name.
   My soul, give thanks <u>to</u> the Lord
   and never forget <u>all</u> his blessings.

2. For as the heavens are high a<u>bove</u> the earth
   so strong is his love for <u>those</u> who fear him.
   As far as the east is <u>from</u> the west
   so far does he re<u>move</u> our sins.

Response: Andrew Moore   Psalm tone: Gregory Murray
Text © 1963, 1986, 1993 The Grail, England, taken from 'The Psalms, a New Inclusive Language Version',
published by HarperCollins Religious. Used by permission of A.P. Watt Ltd, London.
Response © Copyright 1998 Kevin Mayhew Ltd.
Psalm tone © Copyright Downside Abbey, Stratton-on-the-Fosse, Bath BA3 4RH. Used by permission.

3. The Lord has set his sway in heaven
   and his kingdom is ruling over all.
   Give thanks to the Lord, all his angels,
   mighty in power, fulfilling his word.

Gospel Acclamation cf. John 14:18
For musical setting see Nos 36 to 47
   Alleluia.
   I will not leave you orphans, says the Lord;
   I will come back to you, and your hearts will be full of joy.
   Alleluia.

963 7th Easter (C)

Responsorial Psalm Psalm 96:1-2, 6-7, 9. ℟ vv.1, 9

The Lord is King, the Lord is King, most high a-bove all the earth.

1. The Lord is King, let earth rejoice,
   the many coastlands be glad.
   His throne is justice and right.

2. The skies proclaim his justice;
   all peoples see his glory.
   All you spirits, worship him.

3. For you indeed are the Lord
   most high above all the earth
   exalted far above all spirits.

Gospel Acclamation cf. John 14:18
For musical setting see Nos 36 to 47
   Alleluia.
   I will not leave you orphans, says the Lord;
   I will come back to you, and your hearts will be full of joy.
   Alleluia.

Response and Psalm tone: Andrew Moore
Text © 1963, 1986, 1993 The Grail, England, taken from 'The Psalms, a New Inclusive Language Version',
published by HarperCollins Religious. Used by permission of A.P. Watt Ltd, London.
Response and Psalm tone © Copyright 1998 Kevin Mayhew Ltd.

964 Pentecost Sunday (A,B,C)

Responsorial Psalm Psalm 103:1, 24, 29-31, 34. ℟ cf.v.30

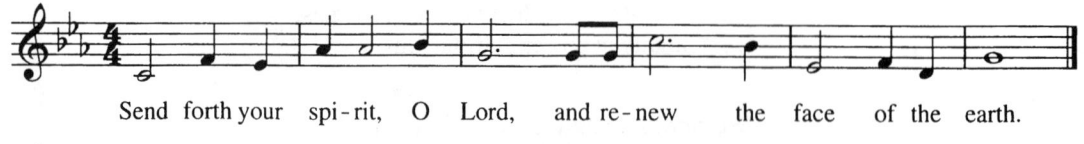

Send forth your spirit, O Lord, and renew the face of the earth.

1. Bless the <u>Lord</u>, my soul!
   Lord God, how <u>great</u> you are.
   How many are your <u>works</u>, O Lord!
   The earth is full <u>of</u> your riches.

2. You take back your sp<u>ir</u>it, they die,
   returning to the dust from <u>which</u> they came.
   You send forth your spirit, they <u>are</u> created;
   and you renew the face <u>of</u> the earth.

3. May the glory of the Lord <u>last</u> for ever!
   May the Lord rejoice <u>in</u> his works!
   May my thoughts be plea<u>sing</u> to him.
   I find my joy <u>in</u> the Lord.

Gospel Acclamation
For musical setting see Nos 36 to 47
   Alleluia.
   Come, Holy Spirit, fill the hearts <u>of</u> your faithful
   and kindle in them the fire <u>of</u> your love.
   Alleluia.

Response and Psalm tone: Andrew Moore
Text © 1963, 1986, 1993 The Grail, England, taken from 'The Psalms, a New Inclusive Language Version', published by HarperCollins Religious. Used by permission of A.P. Watt Ltd, London.
Response and Psalm tone © Copyright 1998 Kevin Mayhew Ltd.

965 *Sunday after Pentecost*
The Most Holy Trinity (A)

Responsorial Psalm Daniel 3:52-56. ℟ v.22

This Psalm is sung as a Litany. The Response is given out and repeated by all and is then repeated at the end of each line.

To you glory and praise for evermore.

1. You are blest, Lord God <u>of</u> our fathers.
   To you glory and praise for evermore.
   Blest your glorious <u>ho</u>ly name.
   To you glory and praise for evermore.

2. You are blest in the temple <u>of</u> your glory.
   To you glory and praise for evermore.
   You are blest on the throne <u>of</u> your kingdom.
   To you glory and praise for evermore.

Response and Psalm tone: Andrew Moore
Text © 1963, 1986, 1993 The Grail, England, taken from 'The Psalms, a New Inclusive Language Version', published by HarperCollins Religious. Used by permission of A.P. Watt Ltd, London.
Response and Psalm tone © Copyright 1998 Kevin Mayhew Ltd.

3. You are blest who gaze in<u>to</u> the depths.
   To you glory and praise for evermore.
   You are blest in the firma<u>ment</u> of heaven.
   To you glory and praise for evermore.

   Gospel Acclamation cf. Revelation 1:8
   For musical setting see Nos 36 to 47
   Alleluia.
   Glory be to the Father, and to the Son, and to the <u>Ho</u>ly Spirit,
   the God who is, who was, and who <u>is</u> to come.
   Alleluia.

966 *Sunday after Pentecost*
The Most Holy Trinity (B)

Responsorial Psalm Psalm 32:4-6, 9, 18-20, 22. R̸ v.12

Hap - py the peo - ple the Lord has cho-sen as his own.

1. The word of the <u>Lord</u> is faithful
   and all his works <u>to</u> be trusted.
   The Lord loves jus<u>tice</u> and right
   and fills the earth <u>with</u> his love.

2. By his word the hea<u>vens</u> were made,
   by the breath of his mouth <u>all</u> the stars.
   He spoke; and they <u>came</u> to be.
   He commanded; they sprang in<u>to</u> being.

3. The Lord looks on those <u>who</u> revere him,
   on those who hope <u>in</u> his love,
   to rescue their <u>souls</u> from death,
   to keep them a<u>live</u> in famine.

4. Our soul is waiting <u>for</u> the Lord.
   The Lord is our help <u>and</u> our shield.
   May your love be upon <u>us</u>, O Lord,
   as we place all our <u>hope</u> in you.

   Gospel Acclamation cf. Revelation 1:8
   For musical setting see Nos 36 to 47
   Alleluia.
   Glory be to the Father, and to the Son, and to the <u>Ho</u>ly Spirit,
   the God who is, who was, and who <u>is</u> to come.
   Alleluia.

Response and Psalm tone: Andrew Moore
Text © 1963, 1986, 1993 The Grail, England, taken from 'The Psalms, a New Inclusive Language Version',
published by HarperCollins Religious. Used by permission of A.P. Watt Ltd, London.
Response and Psalm tone © Copyright 1998 Kevin Mayhew Ltd.

967 *Sunday after Pentecost*
The Most Holy Trinity (C)

Responsorial Psalm Psalm 8:4-9. ℟ v.2

How great is your name, O Lord our God, through all the earth, through all the earth!

1. When I see the heavens, the work <u>of</u> your hands,
   the moon and the stars which <u>you</u> arranged,
   what are we that you should keep <u>us</u> in mind,
   mortals <u>that</u> you care for us?

2. Yet you have made us little <u>less</u> than gods;
   with glory and hon<u>our</u> you crowned us,
   gave us power over the works <u>of</u> your hand,
   put all things un<u>der</u> our feet.

3. All of them, <u>sheep</u> and cattle,
   yes, even the <u>savage</u> beasts,
   birds of the <u>air</u>, and fish
   that make their way <u>through</u> the waters.

Gospel Acclamation cf. Revelation 1:8
For musical setting see Nos 36 to 47
   Alleluia.
   Glory be to the Father, and to the Son, and to the <u>Holy</u> Spirit,
   the God who is, who was, and who <u>is</u> to come.
   Alleluia.

Response: Colin Mawby Psalm tone: Laurence Bevenot
Text © 1963, 1986, 1993 The Grail, England, taken from 'The Psalms, a New Inclusive Language Version',
published by HarperCollins Religious. Used by permission of A.P. Watt Ltd, London.
Response © Copyright 1998 Kevin Mayhew Ltd.
Psalm tone © Copyright Ampleforth Abbey, York YO6 4EN. Used by permission.

968 *Thursday after Trinity Sunday*
The Body and Blood of Christ (A)

Responsorial Psalm Psalm 147:12-15, 19-20. ℟ v.12

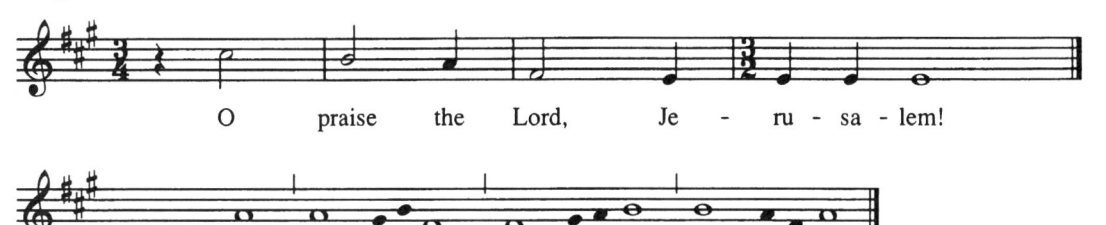

O praise the Lord, Jerusalem!

1. O praise the <u>Lord</u>, Jerusalem!
   Zion, <u>praise</u> your God!
   He has strengthened the bars <u>of</u> your gates,
   he has blessed the chil<u>dren</u> within you.

2. He established peace <u>on</u> your borders,
   he feeds you with <u>fin</u>est wheat.
   He sends out his word <u>to</u> the earth
   and swiftly runs <u>his</u> command.

3. He makes his word <u>known</u> to Jacob,
   to Israel his laws <u>and</u> decrees.
   He has not dealt thus with <u>other</u> nations;
   he has not taught them <u>his</u> decrees.

Gospel Acclamation John 6:51-52
For musical setting see Nos 36 to 47
   Alleluia.
   I am the living bread which has come down from heaven, <u>says</u> the Lord.
   Anyone who eats this bread will <u>live</u> for ever.
   Alleluia.

Response: Rosalie Bonighton   Psalm tone: Alan Rees
Text © 1963, 1986, 1993 The Grail, England, taken from 'The Psalms, a New Inclusive Language Version',
published by HarperCollins Religious. Used by permission of A.P. Watt Ltd, London.
Response © Copyright 1998 Kevin Mayhew Ltd.
Psalm tone © Copyright Belmont Abbey, Hereford HR2 9RZ. Used by permission.

969 *Thursday after Trinity Sunday*
The Body and Blood of Christ (B)

Responsorial Psalm Psalm 115:12-13, 15-18. ℟ v.13

The cup of sal-va-tion I will raise; I will call on the Lord's name.

1. How can I re<u>pay</u> the Lord
 for his good<u>ness</u> to me?
 The cup of salvation <u>I</u> will raise;
 I will call on <u>the</u> Lord's name.

2. O precious in the eyes <u>of</u> the Lord
 is the death <u>of</u> his faithful.
 Your servant, Lord, your ser<u>vant</u> am I;
 you have loos<u>ened</u> my bonds.

3. A thanksgiving sacri<u>fice</u> I make:
 I will call on <u>the</u> Lord's name.
 My vows to the Lord I <u>will</u> fulfil
 before <u>all</u> his people.

Gospel Acclamation John 6:51-52
For musical setting see Nos 36 to 47
 Alleluia.
 I am the living bread which has come down from heaven, <u>says</u> the Lord.
 Anyone who eats this bread will <u>live</u> for ever.
 Alleluia.

Response: Richard Lloyd   Psalm tone: Gregory Murray
Text © 1963, 1986, 1993 The Grail, England, taken from 'The Psalms, a New Inclusive Language Version',
published by HarperCollins Religious. Used by permission of A.P. Watt Ltd, London.
Response © Copyright 1998 Kevin Mayhew Ltd.
Psalm tone © Copyright McCrimmon Publishing Co. Ltd, 10-12 High St, Great Wakering, Essex SS3 0EQ. Used by permission.

970 *Thursday after Trinity Sunday*
The Body and Blood of Christ (C)

Responsorial Psalm Psalm 109:1-4. ℟ v.4

You are a priest for e-ver, a priest like Mel-chi-ze-dek of old.

1. The Lord's revelation <u>to</u> my Master:
 'Sit <u>on</u> my right:
 I will put your foes be<u>neath</u> your feet.'

2. The Lord will <u>send</u> from Zion
 your scep<u>tre</u> of power:
 rule in the midst of <u>all</u> your foes.

Response: Richard Lloyd   Psalm tone: Andrew Moore
Text © 1963, 1986, 1993 The Grail, England, taken from 'The Psalms, a New Inclusive Language Version',
published by HarperCollins Religious. Used by permission of A.P. Watt Ltd, London.
Response and Psalm tone © Copyright 1998 Kevin Mayhew Ltd.

3. A prince from the day of your birth
   on the holy mountains;
   from the womb before the daybreak I begot you.

4. The Lord has sworn an oath he will not change.
   'You are a priest for ever,
   a priest like Melchizedek of old.'

Gospel Acclamation John 6:51-52
For musical setting see Nos 36 to 47
   Alleluia.
   I am the living bread which has come down from heaven, says the Lord.
   Anyone who eats this bread will live for ever.
   Alleluia.

971 2nd in Ordinary Time (A)

Responsorial Psalm Psalm 39:2, 4, 7-10. ℟ vv.8, 9

Here I am, Lord! I come to do your will.

1. I waited, I waited for the Lord and
     he stooped down to me;
   he heard my cry.
   He put a new song into my mouth,
   praise of our God.

2. You do not ask for sacrifice and offerings,
   but an open ear.
   You do not ask for holocaust and victim.
   Instead, here am I.

3. In the scroll of the book it stands written
   that I should do your will.
   My God, I delight in your law
   in the depth of my heart.

4. Your justice I have proclaimed
   in the great assembly.
   My lips I have not sealed;
   you know it, O Lord.

Gospel Acclamation
For musical setting see Nos 36 to 47
   Alleluia.
   Blessings on the King who comes, in the name of the Lord!
   Peace in heaven and glory in the highest heavens!
   Alleluia.

   or John 1:14, 12
   Alleluia.
   The Word was made flesh and lived among us;
   to all who did accept him he gave power to become children of God.
   Alleluia.

Response: Colin Mawby   Psalm tone: Gregory Murray
Text © 1963, 1986, 1993 The Grail, England, taken from 'The Psalms, a New Inclusive Language Version',
published by HarperCollins Religious. Used by permission of A.P. Watt Ltd, London.
Response © Copyright 1998 Kevin Mayhew Ltd.
Psalm tone © Copyright Downside Abbey, Stratton-on-the-Fosse, Bath BA3 4RH. Used by permission.

972 3rd in Ordinary Time (A)

Responsorial Psalm Psalm 26:1, 4, 13-14. ℟ v.1

The Lord is my light and my help.

1. The Lord is my light <u>and</u> my help;
   whom <u>shall</u> I fear?
   The Lord is the stronghold <u>of</u> my life;
   before whom <u>shall</u> I shrink?

2. There is one thing I ask <u>of</u> the Lord,
   for <u>this</u> I long,
   to live in the house <u>of</u> the Lord,
   all the days <u>of</u> my life.

3. I am sure I shall see <u>the</u> Lord's goodness
   in the land <u>of</u> the living.
   Hope in him, hold firm <u>and</u> take heart.
   Hope <u>in</u> the Lord!

Gospel Acclamation Matthew 4:23
For musical setting see Nos 36 to 47
Alleluia.
Jesus proclaimed the Good News <u>of</u> the kingdom,
and cured all kinds of sickness <u>among</u> the people.
Alleluia.

Response: Richard Lloyd   Psalm tone: Alan Rees
Text © 1963, 1986, 1993 The Grail, England, taken from 'The Psalms, a New Inclusive Language Version',
published by HarperCollins Religious. Used by permission of A.P. Watt Ltd, London.
Response © Copyright 1998 Kevin Mayhew Ltd.
Psalm tone © Copyright Belmont Abbey, Hereford HR2 9RZ. Used by permission.

973 4th in Ordinary Time (A)

Responsorial Psalm Psalm 145:7-10. ℟ Matthew 5:3

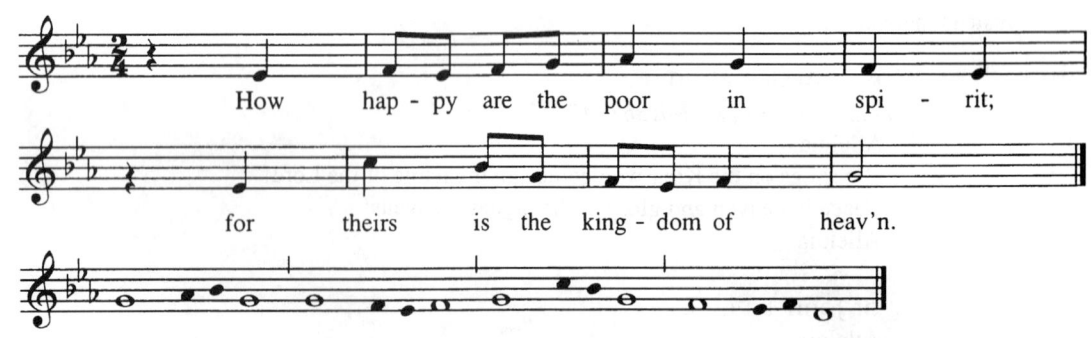

*How happy are the poor in spirit;
for theirs is the kingdom of heav'n.*

1. It is the Lord who keeps <u>faith</u> for ever,
   who is just to those who <u>are</u> oppressed.
   It is he who gives bread <u>to</u> the hungry,
   the Lord, who sets <u>pris</u>oners free.

2. It is the Lord who gives sight <u>to</u> the blind,
   who raises up those who <u>are</u> bowed down,
   the Lord, who pro<u>tects</u> the stranger
   and upholds the wi<u>dow</u> and orphan.

Response: Richard Lloyd   Psalm tone: Andrew Moore
Text © 1963, 1986, 1993 The Grail, England, taken from 'The Psalms, a New Inclusive Language Version',
published by HarperCollins Religious. Used by permission of A.P. Watt Ltd, London.
Response and Psalm tone © Copyright 1998 Kevin Mayhew Ltd.

3. It is the Lord who <u>loves</u> the just
but thwarts the path <u>of</u> the wicked.
The Lord will <u>reign</u> for ever,
Zion's God, from <u>age</u> to age.

Gospel Acclamation Matthew 11:25
For musical setting see Nos 36 to 47
Alleluia.
Blessed are you, Father, Lord of Hea<u>ven</u> and earth,
for revealing the mysteries of the kingdom <u>to</u> mere children.
Alleluia.

or Matthew 5:12
Alleluia.
Rejoice <u>and</u> be glad:
your reward will be <u>great</u> in heaven.
Alleluia.

974 5th in Ordinary Time (A)

Responsorial Psalm Psalm 111:4-9. R℣ v.4

The good will be a light in the dark-ness.

1. They are a light in the darkness <u>for</u> the upright:
they are generous, merci<u>ful</u> and just.
The good take pi<u>ty</u> and lend,
they conduct their af<u>fairs</u> with honour.

2. The just will <u>never</u> waver:
they will be remem<u>bered</u> for ever.
They have no fear of <u>evil</u> news;
with a firm heart they trust <u>in</u> the Lord.

3. With a steadfast heart they <u>will</u> not fear;
open-handed, they give <u>to</u> the poor;
their justice stands <u>firm</u> for ever.
Their heads will be <u>raised</u> in glory.

Gospel Acclamation John 8:12
For musical setting see Nos 36 to 47
Alleluia.
I am the light of the world, <u>says</u> the Lord,
anyone who follows me will have the <u>light</u> of life.
Alleluia.

Response: Martin Setchell Psalm tone: Andrew Moore
Text © 1963, 1986, 1993 The Grail, England, taken from 'The Psalms, a New Inclusive Language Version',
published by HarperCollins Religious. Used by permission of A.P. Watt Ltd, London.
Response and Psalm tone © Copyright 1998 Kevin Mayhew Ltd.

975 6th in Ordinary Time (A)

Responsorial Psalm   Psalm 118:1-2, 4-5, 17-18, 33-34. ℟ v.1

They are hap-py   who   fol-low God's law!

1. They are happy whose <u>life</u> is blameless,
   who fo<u>llow</u> God's law!
   They are happy those who <u>do</u> his will,
   seeking him with <u>all</u> their hearts.

2. You have laid <u>down</u> your precepts
   to be o<u>beyed</u> with care.
   May my foot<u>steps</u> be firm
   to o<u>bey</u> your statutes.

3. Bless your servant and <u>I</u> shall live
   and o<u>bey</u> your word.
   Open my eyes that I <u>may</u> consider
   the wonders <u>of</u> your law.

4. Teach me the demands <u>of</u> your statutes
   and I will keep them <u>to</u> the end.
   Train me to ob<u>serve</u> your law,
   to keep it <u>with</u> my heart.

Gospel Acclamation   1 Samuel 3:9; John 6:68
For musical setting see Nos 36 to 47
   Alleluia.
   Speak, Lord, your ser<u>vant</u> is listening;
   you have the message of e<u>ter</u>nal life.
   Alleluia.

Response: Rosalie Bonighton   Psalm tone: Andrew Moore
Text © 1963, 1986, 1993 The Grail, England, taken from 'The Psalms, a New Inclusive Language Version',
published by HarperCollins Religious. Used by permission of A.P. Watt Ltd, London.
Response and Psalm tone © Copyright 1998 Kevin Mayhew Ltd.

976 7th in Ordinary Time (A)

Responsorial Psalm   Psalm 102:1-4, 8, 10, 12-13. ℟ v.8

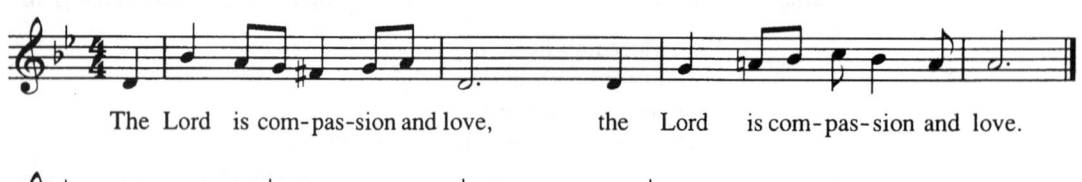

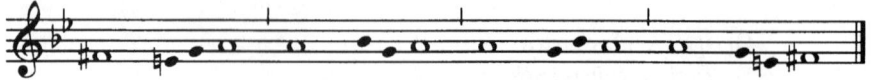

The Lord is com-pas-sion and love,   the   Lord   is com-pas-sion and love.

1. My soul, give thanks <u>to</u> the Lord,
   all my being, bless his <u>holy</u> name.
   My soul, give thanks <u>to</u> the Lord
   and never forget <u>all</u> his blessings.

2. It is he who forgives <u>all</u> your guilt,
   who heals every one <u>of</u> your ills,
   who redeems your life <u>from</u> the grave,
   who crowns you with love <u>and</u> compassion.

Response: Andrew Moore   Psalm tone: Laurence Bevenot
Text © 1963, 1986, 1993 The Grail, England, taken from 'The Psalms, a New Inclusive Language Version',
published by HarperCollins Religious. Used by permission of A.P. Watt Ltd, London.
Response © Copyright 1998 Kevin Mayhew Ltd.
Psalm tone © Copyright Ampleforth Abbey, York YO6 4EN. Used by permission.

3. The Lord is compa<u>ssion</u> and love,
   slow to anger and <u>rich</u> in mercy.
   He does not treat us according <u>to</u> our sins
   nor repay us according <u>to</u> our faults.

4. As far as the east is <u>from</u> the west
   so far does he re<u>move</u> our sins.
   As a father has compassion <u>on</u> his sons,
   the Lord has pity on <u>those</u> who fear him.

Gospel Acclamation John 14:23
For musical setting see Nos 36 to 47
    Alleluia.
    If anyone loves me they will <u>keep</u> my word,
    and my Father will love them and <u>we</u> shall come to them.
    Alleluia.

or 1 John 2:5
    Alleluia.
    When anyone obeys what <u>Christ</u> has said,
    God's love comes to perfec<u>tion</u> in him.
    Alleluia.

977 8th in Ordinary Time (A)

Responsorial Psalm Psalm 61:2-3, 6-9. ℟ v.6

In God a-lone is my soul at rest, at rest.

1. In God alone is my <u>soul</u> at rest;
   my help <u>comes</u> from him.
   He alone is my <u>rock</u>, my stronghold,
   my fortress: <u>I</u> stand firm.

2. In God alone be at <u>rest</u>, my soul;
   for my hope <u>comes</u> from him.
   He alone is my <u>rock</u>, my stronghold,
   my fortress: <u>I</u> stand firm.

3. In God is my safe<u>ty</u> and glory,
   the rock <u>of</u> my strength.
   Take refuge in God <u>all</u> you people.
   Trust him <u>at</u> all times.

Gospel Acclamation John 17:17
For musical setting see Nos 36 to 47
    Alleluia.
    Your word is <u>truth</u>, O Lord,
    consecrate us <u>in</u> the truth.
    Alleluia.

or Hebrews 4:12
    Alleluia.
    The word of God is something a<u>live</u> and active;
    it can judge secret emo<u>tions</u> and thoughts.
    Alleluia.

Response: Rosalie Bonighton   Psalm tone: Alan Rees
Text © 1963, 1986, 1993 The Grail, England, taken from 'The Psalms, a New Inclusive Language Version',
published by HarperCollins Religious. Used by permission of A.P. Watt Ltd, London.
Response © Copyright 1998 Kevin Mayhew Ltd.
Psalm tone © Copyright Belmont Abbey, Hereford HR2 9RZ. Used by permission.

978 9th in Ordinary Time (A)

Responsorial Psalm Psalm 30:2-4, 17, 25. ℟ v.3

Be a rock of refuge for me, O Lord.

1. In you, O Lord, I take refuge.
   Let me never be put to shame.
   In your justice, set me free,
   hear me and speedily rescue me.

2. Be a rock of refuge to me,
   a mighty stronghold to save me,
   for you are my rock, my stronghold.
   For your name's sake, lead me and guide me.

3. Let your face shine on your servant.
   Save me in your love.
   Be strong, let your heart take courage,
   all who hope in the Lord.

Gospel Acclamation John 14:23
For musical setting see Nos 36 to 47
Alleluia.
If anyone loves me they will keep my word,
and my Father will love them and we shall come to them.
Alleluia.

or John 15:5
Alleluia.
I am the vine, you are the branches, says the Lord.
Whoever remains in me, with me in him, bears fruit in plenty.
Alleluia.

Response: Andrew Moore   Psalm tone: Alan Rees
Text © 1963, 1986, 1993 The Grail, England, taken from 'The Psalms, a New Inclusive Language Version',
published by HarperCollins Religious. Used by permission of A.P. Watt Ltd, London.
Response © Copyright 1998 Kevin Mayhew Ltd.
Psalm tone © Copyright Belmont Abbey, Hereford HR2 9RZ. Used by permission.

979 10th in Ordinary Time (A)

Responsorial Psalm Psalm 49:1, 8, 12-15. ℟ v.23

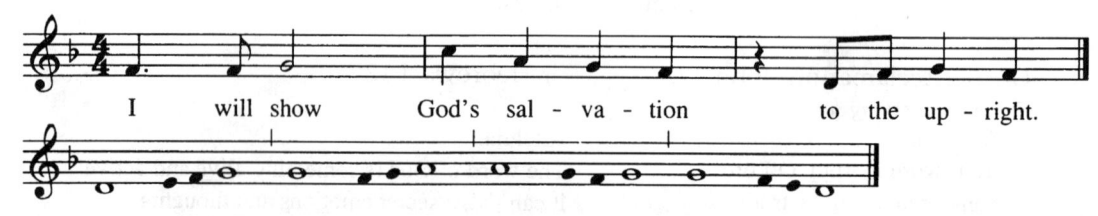

I will show God's salvation to the upright.

1. The God of gods, the Lord, has spoken and summoned the earth,
   from the rising of the sun to its setting.
   'I find no fault with your sacrifices,
   your offerings are always before me.'

Response: Richard Lloyd   Psalm tone: Laurence Bevenot
Text © 1963, 1986, 1993 The Grail, England, taken from 'The Psalms, a New Inclusive Language Version',
published by HarperCollins Religious. Used by permission of A.P. Watt Ltd, London.
Response © Copyright 1998 Kevin Mayhew Ltd.
Psalm tone © Copyright Ampleforth Abbey, York YO6 4EN. Used by permission.

2. 'Were I hungry, I <u>would</u> not tell you,
   for I own the world and <u>all</u> it holds.
   Do you think I eat the <u>flesh</u> of bulls,
   or drink the <u>blood</u> of goats?'

3. 'Pay your sacrifice of thanks<u>giv</u>ing to God
   and render him your <u>vo</u>tive offerings.
   Call on me in the day <u>of</u> distress.
   I will free you and <u>you</u> shall honour me.'

Gospel Acclamation cf. Acts 16:14
For musical setting see Nos 36 to 47
    Alleluia.
    Open our <u>heart</u>, O Lord,
    to accept the words <u>of</u> your Son.
    Alleluia.

or Luke 4:18
    Alleluia.
    The Lord has sent me to bring the good news <u>to</u> the poor,
    to proclaim liber<u>ty</u> to captives.
    Alleluia.

980 11th in Ordinary Time (A)

Responsorial Psalm Psalm 99:2-3, 5. ℟ v.3

We are his peo-ple, the sheep of his flock.

1. Cry out with joy to the Lord, <u>all</u> the earth.
   Serve the <u>Lord</u> with gladness.
   Come before him, sing<u>ing</u> for joy.

2. Know that he, the <u>Lord</u> is God.
   He made us, we be<u>long</u> to him,
   we are his people, the sheep <u>of</u> his flock.

3. Indeed, how good <u>is</u> the Lord,
   eternal his mer<u>ci</u>ful love.
   He is faithful from <u>age</u> to age.

Gospel Acclamation John 10:27
For musical setting see Nos 36 to 47
    Alleluia.
    The sheep that belong to me listen to my voice, <u>says</u> the Lord,
    I know them <u>and</u> they follow me.
    Alleluia.

or Mark 1:15
    Alleluia.
    The kingdom of God is <u>close</u> at hand.
    Repent, and believe <u>the</u> Good News.
    Alleluia.

Response and Psalm tone: Andrew Moore
Text © 1963, 1986, 1993 The Grail, England, taken from 'The Psalms, a New Inclusive Language Version',
published by HarperCollins Religious. Used by permission of A.P. Watt Ltd, London.
Response and Psalm tone © Copyright 1998 Kevin Mayhew Ltd.

981 12th in Ordinary Time (A)

Responsorial Psalm Psalm 68:8-10, 14, 17, 33-35. ℟ v.14

In your great love, in your great love, answer me, O God, answer me, O God, in your love.

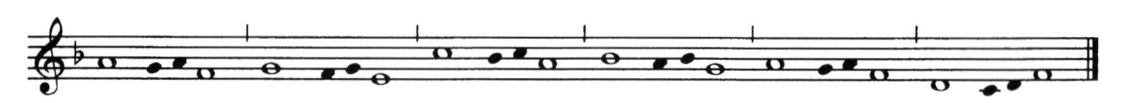

1. It is for you that I <u>suf</u>fer taunts,
   that shame c<u>ov</u>ers my face,
   that I have become a stranger <u>to</u> my brothers,
   an alien to my own <u>moth</u>er's sons.
   I burn with zeal <u>for</u> your house
   and taunts against you <u>fall</u> on me.

2. This is my <u>pray</u>er to you,
   my prayer <u>for</u> your favour.
   In your great love, answer <u>me</u>, O God,
   with your help that <u>nev</u>er fails:
   Lord, answer, for your <u>love</u> is kind;
   in your compassion, <u>turn</u> towards me.

3. The poor when they see it <u>will</u> be glad
   and God-seeking hearts <u>will</u> revive;
   for the Lord listens <u>to</u> the needy
   and does not spurn his servants <u>in</u> their chains.
   Let the heavens and the earth <u>give</u> him praise,
   the sea and all its <u>liv</u>ing creatures.

Gospel Acclamation John 1:14, 12
For musical setting see Nos 36 to 47
   Alleluia.
   The Word was made flesh and <u>lived</u> among us;
   to all who did accept him
   he gave power to become chil<u>dren</u> of God.
   Alleluia

or John 15:26, 27
   Alleluia.
   The Spirit of truth will <u>be</u> my witness;
   and you too will <u>be</u> my witnesses.
   Alleluia.

Response: Richard Proulx   Psalm tone: Andrew Moore
Text © 1963, 1986, 1993 The Grail, England, taken from 'The Psalms, a New Inclusive Language Version',
published by HarperCollins Religious. Used by permission of A.P. Watt Ltd, London.
Response and Psalm tone © Copyright 1998 Kevin Mayhew Ltd.

982 13th in Ordinary Time (A)

Responsorial Psalm Psalm 88:2-3, 16-19. ℟ v.2

I will sing for e-ver of your love, O Lord.

1. I will sing for ever of your <u>love</u>, O Lord;
   through all ages my mouth will pro<u>claim</u> your truth.
   Of this I am sure, that your love <u>lasts</u> for ever,
   that your truth is firmly established <u>as</u> the heavens.

2. Happy the people who acclaim <u>such</u> a king,
   who walk, O Lord, in the light <u>of</u> your face,
   who find their joy every day <u>in</u> your name,
   who make your justice the source <u>of</u> their bliss.

3. For it is you, O Lord, who are the glory <u>of</u> their strength;
   it is by your favour that our might <u>is</u> exalted;
   for our ruler is in the keeping <u>of</u> the Lord;
   our king in the keeping of the Holy <u>One</u> of Israel.

Gospel Acclamation cf. Acts 16:14
For musical setting see Nos 36 to 47
   Alleluia.
   Open our <u>heart</u>, O Lord,
   to accept the words <u>of</u> your Son.
   Alleluia.

   or 1 Peter 2:9
   Alleluia.
   You are a chosen race, a royal priesthood,
      a people set apart to sing the <u>prais</u>es of God
   who called you out of darkness into his won<u>der</u>ful light.
   Alleluia.

Response and Psalm tone: Andrew Moore
Text © 1963, 1986, 1993 The Grail, England, taken from 'The Psalms, A New Inclusive Language Version',
published by HarperCollins Religious. Used by permission of A.P. Watt Ltd, London.
Response and Psalm tone © Copyright 1998 Kevin Mayhew Ltd.

983 14th in Ordinary Time (A)

Responsorial Psalm Psalm 144:1-2, 8-11, 13-14. ℟ v.1

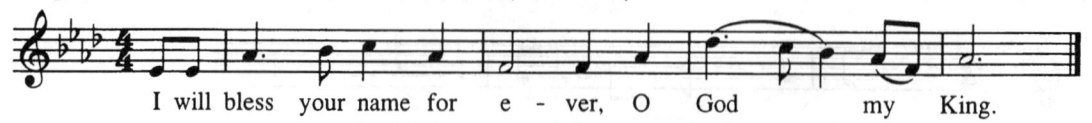

I will bless your name for e-ver, O God my King.

1. I will give you glory, O <u>God</u> my King,
   I will bless your <u>name</u> for ever.
   I will bless you day <u>af</u>ter day
   and praise your <u>name</u> for ever.

2. The Lord is kind and full <u>of</u> compassion,
   slow to anger, aboun<u>ding</u> in love.
   How good is the <u>Lord</u> to all,
   compassionate to <u>all</u> his creatures.

3. All your creatures shall thank <u>you</u>, O Lord,
   and your friends shall re<u>peat</u> their blessing.
   They shall speak of the glory <u>of</u> your reign
   and declare your <u>might</u>, O God.

4. The Lord is faithful in <u>all</u> his words
   and loving in <u>all</u> his deeds.
   The Lord supports <u>all</u> who fall
   and raises all who <u>are</u> bowed down.

Gospel Acclamation cf. Matthew 11:25
For musical setting see Nos 36 to 47
Alleluia.
Blessed are you, Father, Lord of hea<u>ven</u> and earth,
for revealing the mysteries of the kingdom <u>to</u> mere children.
Alleluia.

Response: Colin Mawby Psalm tone: Alan Rees
Text © 1963, 1986, 1993 The Grail, England, taken from 'The Psalms, a New Inclusive Language Version',
published by HarperCollins Religious. Used by permission of A.P. Watt Ltd, London.
Response © Copyright 1998 Kevin Mayhew Ltd.
Psalm tone © Copyright Belmont Abbey, Hereford HR2 9RZ. Used by permission.

984 15th in Ordinary Time (A)

Responsorial Psalm Psalm 64:10-14. ℟ Luke 8:8

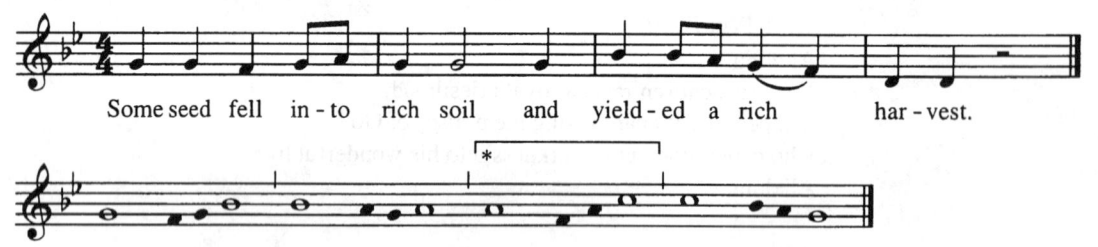

Some seed fell in-to rich soil and yield-ed a rich har-vest.

* Omit in verse 3

1. You care for the earth, <u>give</u> it water,
   you fill <u>it</u> with riches.
   Your river in hea<u>ven</u> brims over
   to pro<u>vide</u> its grain.

2. And thus you provide <u>for</u> the earth;
   you <u>drench</u> its furrows,
   you level it, soften <u>it</u> with showers,
   you <u>bless</u> its growth.

Response: Richard Lloyd Psalm tone: Gregory Murray
Text © 1963, 1986, 1993 The Grail, England, taken from 'The Psalms, a New Inclusive Language Version',
published by HarperCollins Religious. Used by permission of A.P. Watt Ltd, London.
Response © Copyright 1998 Kevin Mayhew Ltd.
Psalm tone © Copyright Downside Abbey, Stratton-on-the-Fosse, Bath BA3 4RH. Used by permission.

3. You crown the year <u>with</u> your goodness.
   Abundance flows <u>in</u> your steps,
   in the pastures of the wilder<u>ness</u> it flows.

4. The hills are gir<u>ded</u> with joy,
   the meadows co<u>vered</u> with flocks,
   the valleys are <u>decked</u> with wheat.
   They shout for joy, <u>yes</u>, they sing.

Gospel Acclamation 1 Samuel 3:9; John 6:68
For musical setting see Nos 36 to 47
   Alleluia.
   Speak, Lord, your ser<u>vant</u> is listening;
   you have the message of e<u>ter</u>nal life.
   Alleluia.

or

   Alleluia.
   The seed is the word of God, <u>Christ</u> the sower;
   whoever finds this seed will re<u>main</u> for ever.
   Alleluia.

985 16th in Ordinary Time (A)

Responsorial Psalm Psalm 85:5-6, 9-10, 15-16. ℟ v.5

O Lord, you are good and for-giv - ing.

1. O Lord, you are good <u>and</u> forgiving,
   full of love to <u>all</u> who call.
   Give heed, O Lord, <u>to</u> my prayer
   and attend to the sound <u>of</u> my voice.

2. All the nations shall come <u>to</u> adore you
   and glorify your <u>name</u>, O Lord:
   for you are great and do mar<u>vell</u>ous deeds,
   you who a<u>lone</u> are God.

3. But you, God of mercy <u>and</u> compassion,
   slow to <u>anger</u>, O Lord,
   abounding in <u>love</u> and truth,
   turn and take <u>pity</u> on me.

Gospel Acclamation cf. Ephesians 1:17, 18
For musical setting see Nos 36 to 47
   Alleluia.
   May the Father of our Lord Jesus Christ enlighten the eyes <u>of</u> our mind,
   so that we can see what hope his call <u>holds</u> for us.
   Alleluia.

or cf. Matthew 11:25
   Alleluia.
   Blessed are you, Father, Lord of hea<u>ven</u> and earth,
   for revealing the mysteries of the kingdom <u>to</u> mere children.
   Alleluia.

Response: Colin Mawby Psalm tone: Gregory Murray
Text © 1963, 1986, 1993 The Grail, England, taken from 'The Psalms, a New Inclusive Language Version',
published by HarperCollins Religious. Used by permission of A.P. Watt Ltd, London.
Response © Copyright 1998 Kevin Mayhew Ltd.
Psalm tone © Copyright Downside Abbey, Stratton-on-the-Fosse, Bath BA3 4RH. Used by permission.

986 17th in Ordinary Time (A)

Responsorial Psalm Psalm 118:57, 72, 76-77, 127-130. ℟ v.97

Lord, how I love your law! Lord, how I love your law!

1. My part, I have re<u>solved</u>, O Lord,
   is to o<u>bey</u> your word.
   The law from your mouth means <u>more</u> to me
   than sil<u>ver</u> and gold.

2. Let your love be ready <u>to</u> console me
   by your promise <u>to</u> your servant.
   Let your love come to me and <u>I</u> shall live
   for your law is <u>my</u> delight.

3. That is why I love <u>your</u> commands
   more than <u>fin</u>est gold.
   That is why I rule my life <u>by</u> your precepts;
   I <u>hate</u> false ways.

4. Your will is wonder<u>ful</u> indeed;
   therefore <u>I</u> obey it.
   The unfolding of your <u>word</u> gives light
   and tea<u>ches</u> the simple.

Gospel Acclamation John 15:15
For musical setting see Nos 36 to 47

Alleluia.
I call you friends, <u>says</u> the Lord,
because I have made known to you everything I have learnt <u>from</u> my Father.
Alleluia.

or cf. Matthew 11:25
Alleluia.
Blessed are you, Father, Lord of hea<u>ven</u> and earth,
for revealing the mysteries of the kingdom <u>to</u> mere children.
Alleluia.

Response: Richard Lloyd   Psalm tone: Alan Rees
Text © 1963, 1986, 1993 The Grail, England, taken from 'The Psalms, a New Inclusive Language Version',
published by HarperCollins Religious. Used by permission of A.P. Watt Ltd, London.
Response © Copyright 1998 Kevin Mayhew Ltd.
Psalm tone © Copyright Belmont Abbey, Hereford HR2 9RZ. Used by permission.

987 18th in Ordinary Time (A)

Responsorial Psalm Psalm 144:8-9, 15-18. ℟ v.16

You open wide your hand, O Lord, you grant our desires.

1. The Lord is kind and full <u>of</u> compassion,
   slow to anger, aboun<u>ding</u> in love.
   How good is the <u>Lord</u> to all,
   compassionate to <u>all</u> his creatures.

2. The eyes of all creatures <u>look</u> to you
   and you give them their food <u>in</u> due time.
   You open <u>wide</u> your hand,
   grant the desires of <u>all</u> who live.

Response: Andrew Moore   Psalm tone: Gregory Murray
Text © 1963, 1986, 1993 The Grail, England, taken from 'The Psalms, a New Inclusive Language Version',
published by HarperCollins Religious. Used by permission of A.P. Watt Ltd, London.
Response © Copyright 1998 Kevin Mayhew Ltd.
Psalm tone © Copyright McCrimmon Publishing Co. Ltd, 10-12 High St, Great Wakering, Essex SS3 0EQ. Used by permission.

3. The Lord is just in <u>all</u> his ways
   and loving in <u>all</u> his deeds.
   He is close to <u>all</u> who call him,
   call on him <u>from</u> their hearts.

Gospel Acclamation Luke 19:38
For musical setting see Nos 36 to 47
Alleluia.
Blessings on the King who comes in the name <u>of</u> the Lord!
Peace in heaven and glory in the <u>high</u>est heavens!
Alleluia.

or Matthew 4:4
Alleluia.
Man does not live on <u>bread</u> alone,
but on every word that comes from the <u>mouth</u> of God.
Alleluia.

988 19th in Ordinary Time (A)

Responsorial Psalm Psalm 84:9-14. ℟ v.8

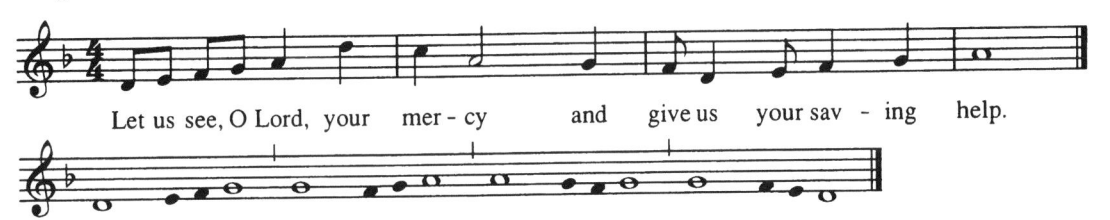

Let us see, O Lord, your mer-cy and give us your sav-ing help.

1. I will hear what the Lord God <u>has</u> to say,
   a voice that <u>speaks</u> of peace.
   His help is near for <u>those</u> who fear him
   and his glory will dwell <u>in</u> our land.

2. Mercy and faithful<u>ness</u> have met;
   justice and peace <u>have</u> embraced.
   Faithfulness shall spring <u>from</u> the earth
   and justice look <u>down</u> from heaven.

3. The Lord will <u>make</u> us prosper
   and our earth shall <u>yield</u> its fruit.
   Justice shall <u>march</u> before him
   and peace shall fo<u>llow</u> his steps.

Gospel Acclamation Luke 19:38
For musical setting see Nos 36 to 47
Alleluia.
Blessings on the King who comes, in the name <u>of</u> the Lord!
Peace in heaven and glory in the <u>high</u>est heavens.
Alleluia.

or Psalm 129:5
Alleluia.
My soul is waiting <u>for</u> the Lord,
I count <u>on</u> his word.
Alleluia.

Response: Stephen Dean   Psalm tone: Laurence Bevenot
Text © 1963, 1986, 1993 The Grail, England, taken from 'The Psalms, a New Inclusive Language Version',
published by HarperCollins Religious. Used by permission of A.P. Watt Ltd, London.
Response © 1984 Stephen Dean. Published by OCP Publications, 5536 NE Hassalo, Portland, OR 97213, USA. Used by permission.
Psalm tone © Copyright Ampleforth Abbey, York YO6 4EN. Used by permission.

989 20th in Ordinary Time (A)

Responsorial Psalm Psalm 66:2-3, 5-6, 8. ℟ v.4

Let the peo-ples praise you, O God; let all the peo-ples praise you.

1. O God, be gra<u>cious</u> and bless us
   and let your face shed its <u>light</u> upon us.
   So will your ways be known <u>up</u>on earth
   and all nations learn your <u>saving</u> help.

2. Let the nations be glad <u>and</u> exult
   for you rule the <u>world</u> with justice.
   With fairness you <u>rule</u> the peoples,
   you guide the na<u>tions</u> on earth.

3. Let the peoples praise <u>you</u>, O God;
   let all the <u>peoples</u> praise you.
   May God still give <u>us</u> his blessing
   till the ends of the <u>earth</u> revere him.

Gospel Acclamation   John 10:27

For musical setting see Nos 36 to 47

Alleluia.
The sheep that belong to me listen to my voice, <u>says</u> the Lord,
I know them <u>and</u> they follow me.
Alleluia.

or cf. Matthew 4:23
Alleluia.
Jesus proclaimed the Good News <u>of</u> the kingdom,
and cured all kinds of sickness a<u>mong</u> the people.
Alleluia.

Response: Colin Mawby   Psalm tone: Gregory Murray
Text © 1963, 1986, 1993 The Grail, England, taken from 'The Psalms, a New Inclusive Language Version',
published by HarperCollins Religious. Used by permission of A.P. Watt Ltd, London.
Response © Copyright 1998 Kevin Mayhew Ltd.
Psalm tone © Copyright McCrimmon Publishing Co. Ltd, 10-12 High St, Great Wakering, Essex SS3 0EQ. Used by permission.

990 21st in Ordinary Time (A)

Responsorial Psalm   Psalm 137:1-3, 6, 8. ℟ v.8

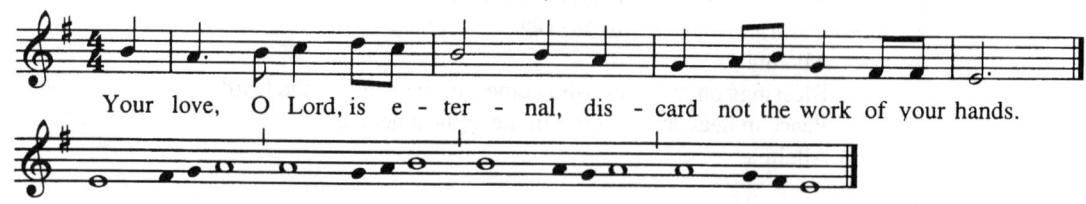

Your love, O Lord, is e-ter-nal, dis-card not the work of your hands.

1. I thank you, Lord, with <u>all</u> my heart,
   you have heard the words <u>of</u> my mouth.
   Before the angels <u>I</u> will bless you.
   I will adore before your <u>holy</u> temple.

2. I thank you for your faithful<u>ness</u> and love
   which excel all we <u>ever</u> knew of you.
   On the day I <u>called</u>, you answered;
   you increased the strength <u>of</u> my soul.

Response: Alan Rees   Psalm tone: Laurence Bevenot
Text © 1963, 1986, 1993 The Grail, England, taken from 'The Psalms, a New Inclusive Language Version',
published by HarperCollins Religious. Used by permission of A.P. Watt Ltd, London.
Response © Copyright 1998 Kevin Mayhew Ltd.
Psalm tone © Copyright Ampleforth Abbey, York YO6 4EN. Used by permission.

3. The Lord is high yet he looks <u>on</u> the lowly
   and the haughty he knows <u>from</u> afar.
   Your love, O Lord, <u>is</u> eternal,
   discard not the work <u>of</u> your hands.

Gospel Acclamation 2 Corinthians 5:19
For musical setting see Nos 36 to 47
   Alleluia.
   God in Christ was reconciling the world <u>to</u> himself,
   and he has entrusted to us the news that <u>they</u> are reconciled.
   Alleluia.

or Matthew 16:18
   Alleluia.
   You are Peter and on this rock I will <u>build</u> my Church.
   And the gates of the underworld can never hold <u>out</u> against it.
   Alleluia.

991 22nd in Ordinary Time (A)

Responsorial Psalm Psalm 62:2-6, 8-9. ℟ v.2

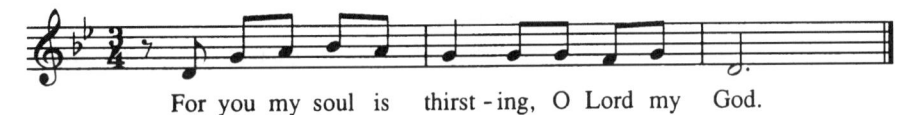

For you my soul is thirst-ing, O Lord my God.

1. O God, you are my God, for <u>you</u> I long:
   for you my <u>soul</u> is thirsting.
   My body <u>pines</u> for you
   like a dry, weary land <u>without</u> water.

2. So I gaze on you <u>in</u> the sanctuary
   to see your strength <u>and</u> your glory.
   For your love is bet<u>ter</u> than life,
   my lips will <u>speak</u> your praise.

3. So I will bless you <u>all</u> my life,
   in your name I will lift <u>up</u> my hands.
   My soul shall be filled as <u>with</u> a banquet,
   my mouth shall praise <u>you</u> with joy.

4. For you have <u>been</u> my help;
   in the shadow of your wings <u>I</u> rejoice.
   My soul <u>clings</u> to you:
   your right hand <u>holds</u> me fast.

Gospel Acclamation cf. Ephesians 1:17, 18
For musical setting see Nos 36 to 47
   Alleluia.
   May the Father of our Lord Jesus Christ enlighten the eyes <u>of</u> our mind,
   so that we can see what hope his call <u>holds</u> for us.
   Alleluia.

Response and Psalm tone: Andrew Moore
Text © 1963, 1986, 1993 The Grail, England, taken from 'The Psalms, a New Inclusive Language Version',
published by HarperCollins Religious. Used by permission of A.P. Watt Ltd, London.
Response and Psalm tone © Copyright 1998 Kevin Mayhew Ltd.

992 23rd in Ordinary Time (A)

Responsorial Psalm Psalm 94:1-2, 6-9. ℟ v.8

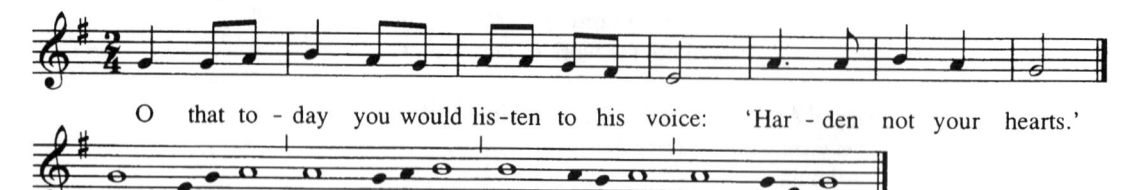

O that to-day you would lis-ten to his voice: 'Har-den not your hearts.'

1. Come, ring out our joy to the Lord;
   hail the rock who saves us.
   Let us come before him, giving thanks,
   with songs let us hail the Lord.

2. Come in; let us bow and bend low;
   let us kneel before the God who made us
   for he is our God, and we the people who
   belong to his pasture,
   the flock that is led by his hand.

3. O that today you would listen to his voice!
   Harden not your hearts as at Meribah,
   as on that day at Massah in the desert, when
   your fathers put me to the test;
   when they tried me, though they saw my work.

Gospel Acclamation John 17:17   or 2 Corinthians 5:19
For musical setting see Nos 36 to 47

Alleluia.
Your word is truth, O Lord,
consecrate us in the truth.
Alleluia.

Alleluia.
God in Christ was reconciling the world to himself,
and he has entrusted to us the news that they are reconciled.
Alleluia.

Response and Psalm tone: Gregory Murray
Text © 1963, 1986, 1993 The Grail, England, taken from 'The Psalms, a New Inclusive Language Version',
published by HarperCollins Religious. Used by permission of A.P. Watt Ltd, London.
Response and Psalm tone © Copyright McCrimmon Publishing Co. Ltd,
10-12 High St, Great Wakering, Essex SS3 0EQ. Used by permission.

993 24th in Ordinary Time (A)

Responsorial Psalm Psalm 102:1-4, 9-12. ℟ v.8

The Lord is com-pas-sion and love, the Lord is com-pas-sion and love.

1. My soul, give thanks to the Lord,
   all my being, bless his holy name.
   My soul, give thanks to the Lord
   and never forget all his blessings.

2. It is he who forgives all your guilt,
   who heals every one of your ills,
   who redeems your life from the grave,
   who crowns you with love and compassion.

Response: Andrew Moore Psalm tone: Laurence Bevenot
Text © 1963, 1986, 1993 The Grail, England, taken from 'The Psalms, a New Inclusive Language Version',
published by HarperCollins Religious. Used by permission of A.P. Watt Ltd, London.
Response © Copyright 1998 Kevin Mayhew Ltd.
Psalm tone © Copyright Ampleforth Abbey, York YO6 4EN. Used by permission.

3. His wrath will come <u>to</u> an end;
   he will not be an<u>gry</u> for ever.
   He does not treat us according <u>to</u> our sins
   nor repay us according <u>to</u> our faults.

4. For as the heavens are high a<u>bove</u> the earth
   so strong is his love for <u>those</u> who fear him.
   As far as the east is <u>from</u> the west
   so far does he re<u>move</u> our sins.

Gospel Acclamation 1 Samuel 3:9; John 6:68
For musical setting see Nos 36 to 47
   Alleluia.
   Speak, Lord, your ser<u>vant</u> is listening:
   you have the message of e<u>ternal</u> life.
   Alleluia.

or John 13:34

   Alleluia.
   I give you a <u>new</u> commandment:
   love one another, just as I have
     loved you, <u>says</u> the Lord.
   Alleluia.

994 25th in Ordinary Time (A)

Responsorial Psalm Psalm 144:2-3, 8-9, 17-18. ℟ v.18

The Lord is close to all who call him.

1. I will bless you day <u>after</u> day
   and praise your <u>name</u> for ever.
   The Lord is great, highly <u>to</u> be praised,
   his greatness can<u>not</u> be measured.

2. The Lord is kind and full <u>of</u> compassion,
   slow to anger, aboun<u>ding</u> in love.
   How good is the <u>Lord</u> to all,
   compassionate to <u>all</u> his creatures.

3. The Lord is just in <u>all</u> his ways
   and loving in <u>all</u> his deeds.
   He is close to <u>all</u> who call him,
   who call on him <u>from</u> their hearts.

Gospel Acclamation Luke 19:38
For musical setting see Nos 36 to 47
   Alleluia.
   Blessings on the King who comes, in the name <u>of</u> the Lord!
   Peace in heaven and glory in the <u>highest</u> heavens!
   Alleluia.

or cf. Acts 16:14
   Alleluia.
   Open our <u>heart</u>, O Lord,
   to accept the words <u>of</u> your Son.
   Alleluia.

Response: Andrew Moore   Psalm tone: Laurence Bevenot
Text © 1963, 1986, 1993 The Grail, England, taken from 'The Psalms, a New Inclusive Language Version',
published by HarperCollins Religious. Used by permission of A.P. Watt Ltd, London.
Response © Copyright 1998 Kevin Mayhew Ltd.
Psalm tone © Copyright Ampleforth Abbey, York YO6 4EN. Used by permission.

995 26th in Ordinary Time (A)

Responsorial Psalm Psalm 24:4-9. ℟ v.6

Re - mem-ber, re - mem-ber your mer-cy, O Lord.

1. Lord, make me <u>know</u> your ways,
   Lord teach <u>me</u> your paths.
   Make me walk in your <u>truth</u>, and teach me;
   for you are <u>God</u> my saviour.

2. Remember your <u>mercy</u>, Lord,
   and the love you have shown <u>from</u> of old.
   Do not remember the sins <u>of</u> my youth.
   In your <u>love</u> remember me.

3. The Lord is <u>good</u> and upright.
   He shows the path to <u>those</u> who stray,
   he guides the humble in <u>the</u> right path;
   he teaches his way <u>to</u> the poor.

Gospel Acclamation John 14:23
For musical setting see Nos 36 to 47
   Alleluia.
   If anyone loves me they will <u>keep</u> my word,
   and my Father will love them and <u>we</u> shall come to them.
   Alleluia.

   or John 10:27
   Alleluia.
   The sheep that belong to me listen to my voice <u>says</u> the Lord,
   I know them and <u>they</u> follow me.
   Alleluia.

Response: Richard Proulx   **Psalm tone:** Alan Rees
Text © 1963, 1986, 1993 The Grail, England, taken from 'The Psalms, a New Inclusive Language Version', published by HarperCollins Religious. Used by permission of A.P. Watt Ltd, London.
Response © Copyright 1998 Kevin Mayhew Ltd.
Psalm tone © Copyright Belmont Abbey, Hereford HR2 9RZ. Used by permission.

996 27th in Ordinary Time (A)

Responsorial Psalm Psalm 79:9, 12-16, 19-20. ℟ Isaiah 5:7

The vine-yard of the Lord is the House of Is-ra-el.

1. You brought a vine <u>out</u> of Egypt;
   to plant it you drove <u>out</u> the nations.
   It stretched out its branches <u>to</u> the sea,
   to the Great River it stretched <u>out</u> its shoots.

2. Then why have you broken <u>down</u> its walls?
   It is plucked by all <u>who</u> pass by.
   It is ravaged by the boar <u>of</u> the forest,
   devoured by the beasts <u>of</u> the field.

Response: Colin Mawby   **Psalm tone:** Laurence Bevenot
Text © 1963, 1986, 1993 The Grail, England, taken from 'The Psalms, a New Inclusive Language Version', published by HarperCollins Religious. Used by permission of A.P. Watt Ltd, London.
Response © Copyright 1998 Kevin Mayhew Ltd.
Psalm tone © Copyright Ampleforth Abbey, York YO6 4EN. Used by permission.

3. God of hosts, turn again, <u>we</u> implore,
   look down from hea<u>ven</u> and see.
   Visit this vine <u>and</u> protect it,
   the vine your right <u>hand</u> has planted.

4. And we shall never forsake <u>you</u> again:
   give us life that we may call u<u>pon</u> your name.
   God of hosts, <u>bring</u> us back;
   let your face shine on us and we <u>shall</u> be saved.

Gospel Acclamation John 15:15
For musical setting see Nos 36 to 47
   Alleluia.
   I call you friends, <u>says</u> the Lord,
   because I have made known to you everything
      I have learnt <u>from</u> my Father.
   Alleluia.

or cf. John 15:16
   Alleluia.
   I chose you from the world to go
      out <u>and</u> bear fruit,
   fruit that will last, <u>says</u> the Lord.
   Alleluia.

997 28th in Ordinary Time (A)

Responsorial Psalm Psalm 22. ℟ v.6

The Lord is my shep-herd; there is no-thing I shall want, the Lord is my shep-herd; there is no-thing I shall want.

1. The Lord <u>is</u> my shepherd;
   there is nothing <u>I</u> shall want.
   Fresh and green <u>are</u> the pastures
   where he gives <u>me</u> repose.

2. Near restful wa<u>ters</u> he leads me,
   to revive my <u>drooping</u> spirit.
   He guides me along <u>the</u> right path;
   he is true <u>to</u> his name.

3. If I should walk in the val<u>ley</u> of darkness
   no evil <u>would</u> I fear.
   You are there with your crook <u>and</u> your staff;
   with these you <u>give</u> me comfort.

4. You have prepared a ban<u>quet</u> for me
   in the sight <u>of</u> my foes.
   My head you have anoin<u>ted</u> with oil;
   my cup is <u>o</u>verflowing.

5. Surely goodness and kind<u>ness</u> shall follow me
   all the days <u>of</u> my life.
   In the Lord's own house <u>shall</u> I dwell
   for <u>ever</u> and ever.

Note: verse 3 may be omitted

Gospel Acclamation John 1:12, 14
For musical setting see Nos 36 to 47
   Alleluia.
   The Word was made flesh and <u>lived</u> among us;
   to all who did accept him he gave power to
      become child<u>ren</u> of God.
   Alleluia.

or cf. Ephesians 1:17, 18
   Alleluia.
   May the Father of our Lord Jesus Christ enlighten
      the eyes <u>of</u> our mind,
   so that we can see what hope his call <u>holds</u> for us.
   Alleluia.

Response: Andrew Moore   Psalm tone: Alan Rees
Text © 1963, 1986, 1993 The Grail, England, taken from 'The Psalms, a New Inclusive Language Version',
published by HarperCollins Religious. Used by permission of A.P. Watt Ltd, London.
Response © Copyright 1998 Kevin Mayhew Ltd.
Psalm tone © Copyright Belmont Abbey, Hereford HR2 9RZ. Used by permission.

998 29th in Ordinary Time (A)

Responsorial Psalm Psalm 95:1, 3-5, 7-10. ℟ v.7

Give the Lord glo-ry and pow-er.

1. O sing a new song <u>to</u> the Lord,
   sing to the Lord <u>all</u> the earth.
   Tell among the na<u>tions</u> his glory
   and his wonders among <u>all</u> the peoples.

2. The Lord is great and wor<u>thy</u> of praise,
   to be feared a<u>bove</u> all gods;
   the gods of the hea<u>thens</u> are naught.
   It was the Lord who <u>made</u> the heavens.

3. Give the Lord, you fam<u>ilies</u> of peoples,
   give the Lord glo<u>ry</u> and power,
   give the Lord the glory <u>of</u> his name.
   Bring an offering and en<u>ter</u> his courts.

4. Worship the Lord <u>in</u> his temple.
   O earth, trem<u>ble</u> before him.
   Proclaim to the nations: '<u>God</u> is king.'
   He will judge the peo<u>ples</u> in fairness.

Gospel Acclamation John 17:17
For musical setting see Nos 36 to 47
   Alleluia.
   Your word is <u>truth</u>, O Lord,
   consecrate us <u>in</u> the truth.
   Alleluia.

or Phillipians 2:15-16

   Alleluia.
   You will shine in the world <u>like</u> bright stars
   because you are offering it the <u>word</u> of life.
   Alleluia.

Response and Psalm tone: Andrew Moore
Text © 1963, 1986, 1993 The Grail, England, taken from 'The Psalms, a New Inclusive Language Version',
published by HarperCollins Religious. Used by permission of A.P. Watt Ltd, London.
Response and Psalm tone © Copyright 1998 Kevin Mayhew Ltd.

999 30th in Ordinary Time (A)

Responsorial Psalm Psalm 17:2-4, 47, 51. ℟ v.2

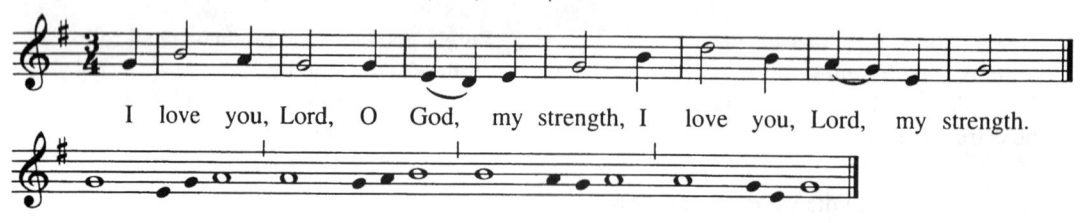

I love you, Lord, O God, my strength, I love you, Lord, my strength.

1. My God is the rock where <u>I</u> take refuge;
   my shield, my mighty <u>help</u>, my stronghold.
   The Lord is worthy <u>of</u> all praise.
   When I call I am saved <u>from</u> my foes.

2. Long life to the <u>Lord</u>, my rock!
   Praised be the <u>God</u> who saves me.
   He has given great victories <u>to</u> his king
   and shown his love for <u>his</u> anointed.

Gospel Acclamation cf. Acts 16:14
For musical setting see Nos 36 to 47
   Alleluia.
   Open our <u>heart</u>, O Lord,
   to accept the words <u>of</u> your Son.
   Alleluia.

Response: Alan Rees   Psalm tone: Gregory Murray
Text © 1963, 1986, 1993 The Grail, England, taken from 'The Psalms, a New Inclusive Language Version',
published by HarperCollins Religious. Used by permission of A.P. Watt Ltd, London.
Response © Copyright 1998 Kevin Mayhew Ltd.
Psalm tone © Copyright McCrimmon Publishing Co. Ltd, 10-12 High St, Great Wakering, Essex SS3 0EQ. Used by permission.

1000 31st in Ordinary Time (A)

Responsorial Psalm Psalm 130

Keep my soul in peace be-fore you, Lord.

1. O Lord, my heart <u>is</u> not proud
   nor haugh<u>ty</u> my eyes.
   I have not gone after <u>things</u> too great
   nor mar<u>vels</u> beyond me.

2. Truly I have set my soul in si<u>lence</u> and peace.
   A weaned child on its mother's breast, even so <u>is</u> my soul.
   O Israel, hope <u>in</u> the Lord
   both now <u>and</u> for ever.

Gospel Acclamation 1 Samuel 3:9; John 6:68
For musical setting see Nos 36 to 47
   Alleluia.
   Speak, Lord, your ser<u>vant</u> is listening;
   you have the message of e<u>ter</u>nal life.
   Alleluia.

Response: Martin Setchell   Psalm tone: Andrew Moore
Text © 1963, 1986, 1993 The Grail, England, taken from 'The Psalms, a New Inclusive Language Version',
published by HarperCollins Religious. Used by permission of A.P. Watt Ltd, London.
Response and Psalm tone © Copyright 1998 Kevin Mayhew Ltd.

1001 32nd in Ordinary Time (A)

Responsorial Psalm Psalm 62:2-8. ℟ v.2

For you my soul is thirsting, O Lord my God.

1. O God, you are my God, for <u>you</u> I long;
for you my <u>soul</u> is thirsting.
My body <u>pines</u> for you
like a dry, weary land with<u>out</u> water.

2. So I gaze on you <u>in</u> the sanctuary
to see your strength <u>and</u> your glory.
For your love is bet<u>ter</u> than life,
my lips will <u>speak</u> your praise.

3. So I will bless you <u>all</u> my life,
in your name I will lift <u>up</u> my hands.
My soul shall be filled as <u>with</u> a banquet,
my mouth shall praise <u>you</u> with joy.

4. On my bed I re<u>mem</u>ber you.
On you I muse <u>through</u> the night
for you have <u>been</u> my help;
in the shadow of your wings <u>I</u> rejoice.

Gospel Acclamation Matthew 24:42, 44
For musical setting see Nos 36 to 47
   Alleluia.
   Stay awake <u>and</u> stand ready,
   because you do not know the hour when the Son of <u>Man</u> is coming.
   Alleluia.

Response and Psalm tone: Andrew Moore
Text © 1963, 1986, 1993 The Grail, England, taken from 'The Psalms, a New Inclusive Language Version',
published by HarperCollins Religious. Used by permission of A.P. Watt Ltd, London.
Response and Psalm tone © Copyright 1998 Kevin Mayhew Ltd.

1002 33rd in Ordinary Time (A)

Responsorial Psalm Psalm 127:1-5. ℟ v.1

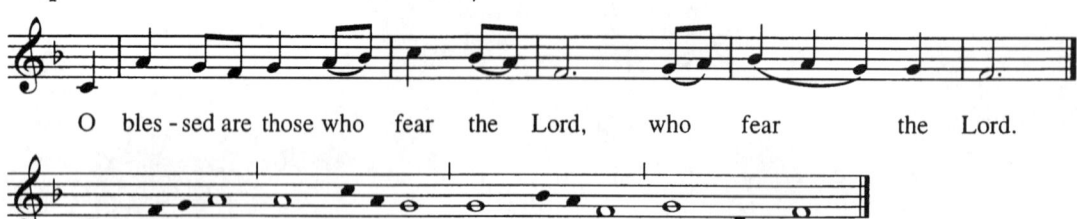

O blessed are those who fear the Lord, who fear the Lord.

1. O blessed are those who <u>fear</u> the Lord
and walk <u>in</u> his ways!
By the labour of your hands <u>you</u> shall eat.
You will be happy and prosper.

2. Your wife like a <u>fruitful</u> vine
in the heart <u>of</u> your house;
your children like shoots <u>of</u> the olive,
a<u>round</u> your table.

Response: Andrew Moore   Psalm tone: Alan Rees
Text © 1963, 1986, 1993 The Grail, England, taken from 'The Psalms, a New Inclusive Language Version',
published by HarperCollins Religious. Used by permission of A.P. Watt Ltd, London.
Response © Copyright 1998 Kevin Mayhew Ltd.
Psalm tone © Copyright Belmont Abbey, Hereford HR2 9RZ. Used by permission.

3. Indeed thus <u>shall</u> be blessed
   those who <u>fear</u> the Lord.
   May the Lord bless <u>you</u> from Zion
   in a hap<u>py</u> Jerusalem.

Gospel Acclamation Revelation 2:10 or John 15:4, 5

For musical setting see Nos 36 to 47

Alleluia.
Even if you have to die, <u>says</u> the Lord,
keep faithful, and I will give you the <u>crown</u> of life.
Alleluia.

Alleluia.
Make your home in me, as I make mine
   in you, <u>says</u> the Lord.
Whoever remains in me bears <u>fruit</u> in plenty.
Alleluia.

1003 *Last Sunday in Ordinary Time*
Our Lord Jesus Christ, Universal King (A)

Responsorial Psalm Psalm 22. ℟ v.1

The Lord is my shep-herd; there is no-thing I shall want, the Lord is my shep-herd; there is no-thing I shall want.

1. The Lord <u>is</u> my shepherd;
   there is nothing <u>I</u> shall want.
   Fresh and green <u>are</u> the pastures
   where he gives <u>me</u> repose.

2. Near restful wa<u>ters</u> he leads me,
   to revive my <u>drooping</u> spirit.
   He guides me along <u>the</u> right path;
   he is true <u>to</u> his name.

3. If I should walk in the val<u>ley</u> of darkness
   no evil <u>would</u> I fear.
   You are there with your crook <u>and</u> your staff;
   with these you <u>give</u> me comfort.

4. You have prepared a ban<u>quet</u> for me
   in the sight <u>of</u> my foes.
   My head you have anoin<u>ted</u> with oil;
   my cup is <u>overflowing</u>.

5. Surely goodness and kind<u>ness</u> shall follow me
   all the days <u>of</u> my life.
   In the Lord's own house <u>shall</u> I dwell
   for e<u>ver</u> and ever.

Note: verse 3 may be omitted

Gospel Acclamation Mark 11:10

For musical setting see Nos 36 to 47

Alleluia.
Blessings on him who comes in the name <u>of</u> the Lord!
Blessings on the coming kingdom of our <u>father</u> David!
Alleluia.

Response: Andrew Moore   Psalm tone: Alan Rees

Text © 1963, 1986, 1993 The Grail, England, taken from 'The Psalms, a New Inclusive Language Version',
published by HarperCollins Religious. Used by permission of A.P. Watt Ltd, London.
Response © Copyright 1998 Kevin Mayhew Ltd.
Psalm tone © Copyright Belmont Abbey, Hereford HR2 9RZ. Used by permission.

1004 2nd in Ordinary Time (B)

Responsorial Psalm Psalm 39:2, 4, 7-10. ℟ vv.8, 9

Here I am, Lord! I come to do your will.

1. I waited, I waited for the Lord
   and <u>he</u> stooped down to me;
   he <u>heard</u> my cry.
   He put a new song in<u>to</u> my mouth,
   praise <u>of</u> our God.

2. You do not ask for sacri<u>fice</u> and offerings,
   but an <u>open</u> ear.
   You do not ask for holo<u>caust</u> and victim.
   Instead, <u>here</u> am I.

3. In the scroll of the book <u>it</u> stands written
   that I should <u>do</u> your will.
   My God, I delight <u>in</u> your law
   in the depth <u>of</u> my heart.

4. Your justice I <u>have</u> proclaimed
   in the <u>great</u> assembly.
   My lips I <u>have</u> not sealed;
   you know <u>it</u>, O Lord.

Gospel Acclamation 1 Samuel 3:9; John 6:68

For musical setting see Nos 36 to 47

Alleluia.
Speak, Lord, your ser<u>vant</u> is listening:
you have the message of e<u>ter</u>nal life.
Alleluia.

or

Alleluia.
We have found the Messiah –
which <u>means</u> the Christ –
grace and truth have <u>come</u> through him.
Alleluia.

Response: Colin Mawby   Psalm tone: Gregory Murray
Text © 1963, 1986, 1993 The Grail, England, taken from 'The Psalms, a New Inclusive Language Version',
published by HarperCollins Religious. Used by permission of A.P. Watt Ltd, London.
Response © Copyright 1998 Kevin Mayhew Ltd.
Psalm tone © Copyright Downside Abbey, Stratton-on-the-Fosse, Bath BA3 4RH. Used by permission.

1005 3rd in Ordinary Time (B)

Responsorial Psalm Psalm 24:4-9. ℟ v.4

Lord, make me know your ways.

1. Lord, make me <u>know</u> your ways.
   Lord, teach <u>me</u> your paths.
   Make me walk in your <u>truth</u>, and teach me:
   for you are <u>God</u> my saviour.

2. Remember your <u>mercy</u> Lord,
   and the love you have shown <u>from</u> of old.
   In your <u>love</u> remember me,
   because of your <u>goodness</u>, O Lord.

Response: Rosalie Bonighton   Psalm tone: Andrew Moore
Text © 1963, 1986, 1993 The Grail, England, taken from 'The Psalms, a New Inclusive Language Version',
published by HarperCollins Religious. Used by permission of A.P. Watt Ltd, London.
Response and Psalm tone © Copyright 1998 Kevin Mayhew Ltd.

3. The Lord is <u>good</u> and upright.
   He shows the path to <u>those</u> who stray,
   he guides the humble in <u>the</u> right path;
   he teaches his way <u>to</u> the poor.

Gospel Acclamation Mark 1:15
For musical setting see Nos 36 to 47
   Alleluia.
   The kingdom of God is <u>close</u> at hand;
   believe <u>the</u> Good News.
   Alleluia.

1006 4th in Ordinary Time (B)

Responsorial Psalm Psalm 94:1-2, 6-9. ℟ v.9

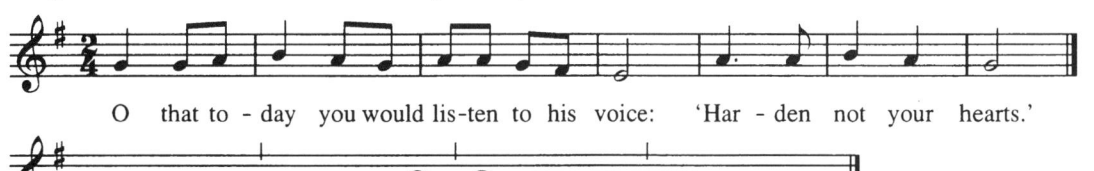

O that to-day you would lis-ten to his voice: 'Har-den not your hearts.'

1. Come ring out our joy <u>to</u> the Lord;
   hail the <u>rock</u> who saves us.
   Let us come before him, <u>giving</u> thanks,
   with songs let us <u>hail</u> the Lord.

2. Come in; let us kneel <u>and</u> bend low;
   let us kneel before the <u>God</u> who made us
   for he is our God, and we the people who
     belong <u>to</u> his pasture,
   the flock that is led <u>by</u> his hand.

3. O that today you would listen <u>to</u> his voice!
     'Harden not your hearts as <u>at</u> Meribah,
     as on that day at Massah in the desert, when
       your fathers put me <u>to</u> the test;
     when they tried me, though they <u>saw</u> my work.'

Gospel Acclamation cf. Matthew 11:25
For musical setting see Nos 36 to 47
   Alleluia.
   Blessed are you, Father, Lord of hea<u>ven</u> and earth,
   for revealing the mysteries of the kingdom <u>to</u> mere children.
   Alleluia.

or Matthew 4:16
   Alleluia.
   The people that lived in darkness have seen <u>a</u> great light;
   on those who dwell in the land and shadow of death a <u>light</u> has dawned.
   Alleluia.

Response and Psalm tone: Gregory Murray
Text © 1963, 1986, 1993 The Grail, England, taken from 'The Psalms, a New Inclusive Language Version',
published by HarperCollins Religious. Used by permission of A.P. Watt Ltd, London.
Response and Psalm tone © Copyright McCrimmon Publishing Co. Ltd,
10-12 High St, Great Wakering, Essex SS3 0EQ. Used by permission.

1007 5th in Ordinary Time (B)

Responsorial Psalm Psalm 146:1-6. ℟ v.3

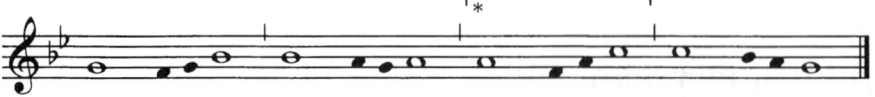

Praise the Lord, praise the Lord who heals the bro-ken-heart-ed.

* Omit in verse 1

1. Praise the Lord for <u>he</u> is good;
   sing to our God for <u>he</u> is loving:
   to him our <u>praise</u> is due.

2. The Lord builds <u>up</u> Jerusalem
   and brings back Is<u>rael</u>'s exiles,
   he heals the <u>bro</u>ken-hearted,
   he binds up <u>all</u> their wounds.

3. Our Lord is great <u>and</u> almighty;
   his wisdom can ne<u>ver</u> be measured.
   The Lord rai<u>ses</u> the lowly;
   he humbles the wicked <u>to</u> the dust.

Gospel Acclamation John 8:12   or Matthew 8:17
For musical setting see Nos 36 to 47

Alleluia.
I am the light of the world, <u>says</u> the Lord,
anyone who follows me will have the <u>light</u> of life.
Alleluia.

Alleluia.
He took our sick<u>nes</u>ses away,
and carried our diseas<u>es</u> for us.
Alleluia.

Response: Richard Lloyd   Psalm tone: Gregory Murray
Text © 1963, 1986, 1993 The Grail, England, taken from 'The Psalms, a New Inclusive Language Version',
published by HarperCollins Religious. Used by permission of A.P. Watt Ltd, London.
Response © Copyright 1998 Kevin Mayhew Ltd.
Psalm tone © Copyright Downside Abbey, Stratton-on-the-Fosse, Bath BA3 4RH. Used by permission.

1008 6th in Ordinary Time (B)

Responsorial Psalm Psalm 31:1-2, 5, 11. ℟ v.7

You are my ref-uge, O Lord; you fill me with the joy of sal-va-tion.

1. Happy are those whose offence <u>is</u> forgiven,
   whose sin <u>is</u> remitted.
   O happy are those to <u>whom</u> the Lord
   im<u>putes</u> no guilt.

2. But now I have acknow<u>ledged</u> my sins;
   my guilt I <u>did</u> not hide,
   and you, Lord, <u>have</u> forgiven
   the guilt <u>of</u> my sin.

Response: Colin Mawby   Psalm tone: Gregory Murray
Text © 1963, 1986, 1993 The Grail, England, taken from 'The Psalms, a New Inclusive Language Version',
published by HarperCollins Religious. Used by permission of A.P. Watt Ltd, London.
Response © Copyright 1998 Kevin Mayhew Ltd.
Psalm tone © Copyright Downside Abbey, Stratton-on-the-Fosse, Bath BA3 4RH. Used by permission.

3. Rejoice, rejoice in the Lord,
   exult, you just!
   O come, ring out your joy,
   all you upright of heart.

Gospel Acclamation cf. Ephesians 1:17, 18   or Luke 7:16
For musical setting see Nos 36 to 47
Alleluia.   Alleluia.
May the Father of our Lord Jesus Christ   A great prophet has appeared among us;
   enlighten the eyes of our mind,   God has visited his people.
so that we can see what hope his call holds for us. Alleluia.
Alleluia.

1009 7th in Ordinary Time (B)

Responsorial Psalm Psalm 40:2-5, 13-14. ℟ v.5

Heal my soul for I have sinned a-gainst you, Lord, heal my soul.

1. Happy are those who consider the poor and the weak.
   The Lord will save them in the day of evil,
      will guard them, give them life, make them happy in the land
   and will not give them up to the will of their foes.

2. The Lord will give them strength in their pain,
   he will bring them back from sickness to health.
   As for me, I said: 'Lord, have mercy on me,
   heal my soul for I have sinned against you.'

3. If you uphold me I shall be unharmed
   and set in your presence for evermore.
   Blessed be the Lord, the God of Israel
   from age to age. Amen. Amen.

Gospel Acclamation John 1:12, 14
For musical setting see Nos 36 to 47
   Alleluia.
   The Word was made flesh and lived among us;
   to all who did accept him he gave power to become children of God.
   Alleluia.

   or Luke 4:18
   Alleluia.
   The Lord has sent me to bring the good news to the poor,
   to proclaim liberty to captives.
   Alleluia.

Response: Alan Rees   Psalm tone: Gregory Murray
Text © 1963, 1986, 1993 The Grail, England, taken from 'The Psalms, a New Inclusive Language Version',
published by HarperCollins Religious. Used by permission of A.P. Watt Ltd, London.
Response © Copyright 1998 Kevin Mayhew Ltd.
Psalm tone © Copyright Downside Abbey, Stratton-on-the-Fosse, Bath BA3 4RH. Used by permission.

1010 8th in Ordinary Time (B)

Responsorial Psalm Psalm 102:1-4, 8, 10, 12-13. ℟ v.8

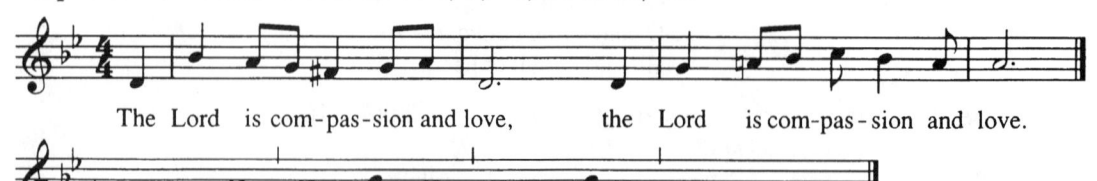

The Lord is com-pas-sion and love, the Lord is com-pas-sion and love.

1. My soul, give thanks <u>to</u> the Lord,
   all my being, bless his <u>ho</u>ly name.
   My soul, give thanks <u>to</u> the Lord
   and never forget <u>all</u> his blessings.

2. It is he who forgives <u>all</u> your guilt,
   who heals every one <u>of</u> your ills,
   who redeems your life <u>from</u> the grave,
   who crowns you with love <u>and</u> compassion.

3. The Lord is compa<u>ssion</u> and love,
   slow to anger and <u>rich</u> in mercy.
   He does not treat us according <u>to</u> our sins
   nor repay us according <u>to</u> our faults.

4. As far as the east is <u>from</u> the west
   so far does he re<u>move</u> our sins.
   As a father has compassion <u>on</u> his sons,
   the Lord has pity on <u>those</u> who fear him.

Gospel Acclamation John 10:27
For musical setting see Nos 36 to 47
Alleluia.
The sheep that belong to me listen to my voice, <u>says</u> the Lord,
I know them <u>and</u> they follow me.
Alleluia.

or James 1:18
Alleluia.
By his own choice the Father made us his children by the message <u>of</u> the truth,
so that we should be a sort of first-fruits of all that <u>he</u> created.
Alleluia.

Response: Andrew Moore Psalm tone: Laurence Bevenot
Text © 1963, 1986, 1993 The Grail, England, taken from 'The Psalms, a New Inclusive Language Version',
published by HarperCollins Religious. Used by permission of A.P. Watt Ltd, London.
Response © Copyright 1998 Kevin Mayhew Ltd.
Psalm tone © Copyright Ampleforth Abbey, York YO6 4EN. Used by permission.

1011 9th in Ordinary Time (B)

Responsorial Psalm Psalm 80:3-8, 10-11. ℟ v.2

Ring out your joy to God our strength.

1. Raise a song and <u>sound</u> the timbrel,
   the sweet-sounding harp <u>and</u> the lute,
   blow the trumpet at <u>the</u> new moon,
   when the moon is full, <u>on</u> our feast.

2. For this is Is<u>rael</u>'s law,
   a command of the <u>God</u> of Jacob.
   He imposed it as a <u>rule</u> on Joseph,
   when he went out against the <u>land</u> of Egypt.

Response and Psalm tone: Andrew Moore
Text © 1963, 1986, 1993 The Grail, England, taken from 'The Psalms, a New Inclusive Language Version',
published by HarperCollins Religious. Used by permission of A.P. Watt Ltd, London.
Response and Psalm tone © Copyright 1998 Kevin Mayhew Ltd.

3. A voice I did not know said to me:
   'I freed your shoulder from the burden;
   your hands were freed from the load.
   You called in distress and I saved you.

4. 'Let there be no foreign god among you,
   no worship of an alien god.
   I am the Lord your God,
   who brought you from the land of Egypt.'

Gospel Acclamation cf. John 6:63, 68
For musical setting see Nos 36 to 47
Alleluia.
Your words are spirit, Lord, and they are life:
you have the message of eternal life.
Alleluia.

or cf. John 17:17
Alleluia.
Your word is truth, O Lord,
consecrate us in the truth.
Alleluia.

1012 10th in Ordinary Time (B)

Responsorial Psalm Psalm 129. ℟ v.7

With the Lord there is mercy and fullness of redemption.

1. Out of the depths I cry to you, O Lord,
   Lord, hear my voice!
   O let your ears be attentive
   to the voice of my pleading.

2. If you, O Lord, should mark our guilt,
   Lord, who would survive?
   But with you is found forgiveness:
   for this we revere you.

3. My soul is waiting for the Lord,
   I count on his word.
   My soul is longing for the Lord
   more than watchman for daybreak.

4. Because with the Lord there is mercy
   and fullness of redemption,
   Israel indeed he will redeem
   from all its iniquity.

Gospel Acclamation John 14:23
For musical setting see Nos 36 to 47
Alleluia.
If anyone loves me they will keep my word,
and my Father will love them and we shall come to them.
Alleluia.

or John 12:31, 32
Alleluia.
Now the prince of this world is to be overthrown, says the Lord.
And when I am lifted up from the earth, I shall draw all men to myself.
Alleluia.

Response: Alan Rees Psalm tone: Andrew Moore
Text © 1963, 1986, 1993 The Grail, England, taken from 'The Psalms, a New Inclusive Language Version',
published by HarperCollins Religious. Used by permission of A.P. Watt Ltd, London.
Response and Psalm tone © Copyright 1998 Kevin Mayhew Ltd.

1013 11th in Ordinary Time (B)

Responsorial Psalm Psalm 91:2-3, 13-16. ℟ v.2

It is good to give you thanks, give you thanks, O Lord.

1. It is good to give thanks <u>to</u> the Lord
to make music to your name, <u>O</u> Most High,
to proclaim your love <u>in</u> the morning
and your truth in the watches <u>of</u> the night.

2. The just will flourish <u>like</u> the palm-tree
and grow like a Le<u>ba</u>non cedar.
Planted in the house <u>of</u> the Lord
they will flourish in the courts <u>of</u> our God.

3. Still bearing fruit when <u>they</u> are old,
still full of <u>sap</u>, still green,
they will proclaim that the <u>Lord</u> is just.
In him, my rock, there <u>is</u> no wrong.

Gospel Acclamation John 15:15
For musical setting see Nos 36 to 47

Alleluia.
I call you friends, <u>says</u> the Lord,
because I have made known to you everything I have learnt <u>from</u> my Father.
Alleluia.

or

Alleluia.
The seed is the word of God, <u>Christ</u> the sower;
whoever finds the seed will re<u>main</u> for ever.
Alleluia.

Response: Colin Mawby   Psalm tone: Alan Rees
Text © 1963, 1986, 1993 The Grail, England, taken from 'The Psalms, a New Inclusive Language Version', published by HarperCollins Religious. Used by permission of A.P. Watt Ltd, London.
Response © Copyright 1998 Kevin Mayhew Ltd.
Psalm tone © Copyright Belmont Abbey, Hereford HR2 9RZ. Used by permission.

1014 12th in Ordinary Time (B)

Responsorial Psalm Psalm 106:23-26, 28-31. ℟ v.1

O give thanks to the Lord, for his love endures for ever.

1. Some sailed to the <u>sea</u> in ships
to trade on the <u>mighty</u> waters.
These have seen <u>the</u> Lord's deeds,
the wonders he does <u>in</u> the deep.

2. For he spoke; he sum<u>moned</u> the gale,
tossing the waves <u>of</u> the sea
up to heaven and back <u>into</u> the deep;
their soul melted away in <u>their</u> distress.

Response and Psalm tone: Andrew Moore
Text © 1963, 1986, 1993 The Grail, England, taken from 'The Psalms, a New Inclusive Language Version', published by HarperCollins Religious. Used by permission of A.P. Watt Ltd, London.
Response and Psalm tone © Copyright 1998 Kevin Mayhew Ltd.

3. Then they cried to the Lord <u>in</u> their need
and he rescued them from <u>their</u> distress.
He stilled the storm <u>to</u> a whisper:
all the waves of the <u>sea</u> were hushed.

4. They rejoiced because <u>of</u> the calm
and he led them to the haven <u>they</u> desired.
Let them thank the Lord <u>for</u> his love,
the wonders he does <u>for</u> his people.

Gospel Acclamation cf. Ephesians 1:17, 18
For musical setting see Nos 36 to 47

Alleluia.
May the Father of our Lord Jesus Christ enlighten the eyes <u>of</u> our mind,
so that we can see what hope his call <u>holds</u> for us.
Alleluia.

or Luke 7:16
Alleluia.
A great prophet has <u>appeared</u> among us;
God has vis<u>it</u>ed his people.
Alleluia.

1015 13th in Ordinary Time (B)

Responsorial Psalm Psalm 29:2, 4-6, 11-13. ℟ v.2

I will praise you, Lord, you have rescued me.

1. I will praise you, Lord, <u>you</u> have rescued me
and have not let my enemies rejoice <u>over</u> me.
O Lord, you have raised my soul <u>from</u> the dead,
restored me to life from those who sink in<u>to</u> the grave.

2. Sing psalms to the Lord, <u>you</u> who love him,
give thanks to his <u>holy</u> name.
His anger lasts but a moment; his fa<u>vour</u> through life.
At night there are tears, but joy <u>comes</u> with dawn.

3. The Lord listened <u>and</u> had pity.
The Lord came <u>to</u> my help.
For me you have changed my mourning <u>into</u> dancing,
O Lord my God, I will thank <u>you</u> for ever.

Gospel Acclamation cf. John 6:63, 68
For musical setting see Nos 36 to 47

Alleluia.
Your words are spirit, Lord, and <u>they</u> are life:
you have the message of et<u>ern</u>al life.
Alleluia.

Response: Richard Lloyd   Psalm tone: Alan Rees
Text © 1963, 1986, 1993 The Grail, England, taken from 'The Psalms, a New Inclusive Language Version',
published by HarperCollins Religious. Used by permission of A.P. Watt Ltd, London.
Response © Copyright 1998 Kevin Mayhew Ltd.
Psalm tone © Copyright Belmont Abbey, Hereford HR2 9RZ. Used by permission.

1016 14th in Ordinary Time (B)

Responsorial Psalm Psalm 122. ℟ v.2

Our eyes are on the Lord till he show us his mercy.

1. To you have I lifted <u>up</u> my eyes,
   you who dwell <u>in</u> the heavens:
   my eyes, like the <u>eyes</u> of slaves
   on the hand <u>of</u> their lords.

2. Like the eyes <u>of</u> a servant
   on the hand <u>of</u> his mistress,
   so our eyes are on the <u>Lord</u> our God
   till he show <u>us</u> his mercy.

3. Have mercy on us, <u>Lord</u>, have mercy.
   We are filled <u>with</u> contempt.
   Indeed all too full <u>is</u> our soul
   with the scorn <u>of</u> the rich.

Gospel Acclamation John 1:12, 14
For musical setting see Nos 36 to 47
   Alleluia.
   The Word was made flesh and <u>lived</u> among us;
   to all who did accept him he gave power to become chil<u>dren</u> of God.
   Alleluia.

   or Luke 4:18
   Alleluia.
   The Lord has sent me to bring the good news <u>to</u> the poor,
   to proclaim liber<u>ty</u> to captives.
   Alleluia.

Response and Psalm tone: Andrew Moore
Text © 1963, 1986, 1993 The Grail, England, taken from 'The Psalms, a New Inclusive Language Version',
published by HarperCollins Religious. Used by permission of A.P. Watt Ltd, London.
Response and Psalm tone © Copyright 1998 Kevin Mayhew Ltd.

1017 15th in Ordinary Time (B)

Responsorial Psalm Psalm 84:9-14. ℟ v.8

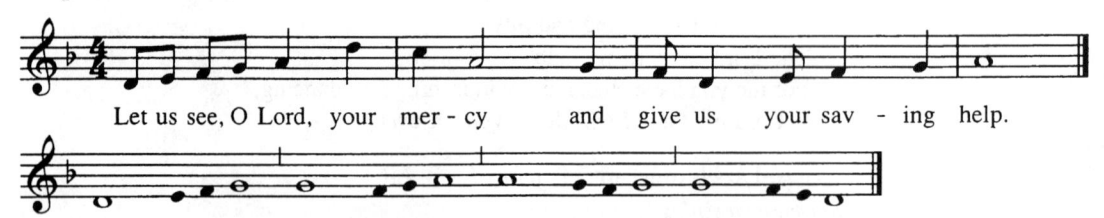

Let us see, O Lord, your mercy and give us your saving help.

1. I will hear what the Lord God <u>has</u> to say,
   a voice that <u>speaks</u> of peace.
   His help is near for <u>those</u> who fear him
   and his glory will dwell <u>in</u> our land.

2. Mercy and faithful<u>ness</u> have met;
   justice and peace <u>have</u> embraced.
   Faithfulness shall spring <u>from</u> the earth
   and justice look <u>down</u> from heaven.

Response: Stephen Dean   Psalm tone: Laurence Bevenot
Text © 1963, 1986, 1993 The Grail, England, taken from 'The Psalms, a New Inclusive Language Version',
published by HarperCollins Religious. Used by permission of A.P. Watt Ltd, London.
Response © 1989 Stephen Dean. Published by OCP Publications, 5536 NE Hassalo, Portland, OR 97213, USA. Used by permission
Psalm tone © Copyright Ampleforth Abbey, York YO6 4EN. Used by permission.

3. The Lord will <u>make</u> us prosper
   and our earth shall <u>yield</u> its fruit.
   Justice shall <u>march</u> before him
   and peace shall fo<u>llow</u> his steps.

Gospel Acclamation cf. John 6:63, 68
For musical setting see Nos 36 to 47
Alleluia.
Your words are spirit, Lord, and <u>they</u> are life:
you have the message of e<u>ter</u>nal life.
Alleluia.

or cf. Ephesians 1:17, 18
Alleluia.
May the Father of our Lord Jesus Christ enlighten
the eyes <u>of</u> our mind,
so that we can see what hope his call <u>holds</u> for us.
Alleluia.

1018 16th in Ordinary Time (B)

Responsorial Psalm Psalm 22. ℟ v.2

The Lord is my shep-herd; there is no-thing I shall want, the Lord is my shep-herd; there is no-thing I shall want.

1. The Lord <u>is</u> my shepherd;
   there is nothing <u>I</u> shall want.
   Fresh and green <u>are</u> the pastures
   where he gives <u>me</u> repose.

2. Near restful wa<u>ters</u> he leads me
   to revive my <u>drooping</u> spirit.
   He guides me along <u>the</u> right path;
   he is true <u>to</u> his name.

3. If I should walk in the va<u>lley</u> of darkness
   no evil <u>would</u> I fear.
   You are there with your crook <u>and</u> your staff;
   with these you <u>give</u> me comfort.

4. You have prepared a ban<u>quet</u> for me
   in the sight <u>of</u> my foes.
   My head you have anoin<u>ted</u> with oil;
   my cup is <u>o</u>verflowing.

5. Surely goodness and kind<u>ness</u> shall follow me
   all the days <u>of</u> my life.
   In the Lord's own house <u>shall</u> I dwell
   for e<u>ver</u> and ever.

Note: verse 3 may be omitted

Gospel Acclamation John 10:27
For musical setting see Nos 36 to 47
Alleluia.
The sheep that belong to me listen to my voice, <u>says</u> the Lord,
I know them <u>and</u> they follow me.
Alleluia.

Response: Andrew Moore Psalm tone: Alan Rees
Text © 1963, 1986, 1993 The Grail, England, taken from 'The Psalms, a New Inclusive Language Version',
published by HarperCollins Religious. Used by permission of A.P. Watt Ltd, London.
Response © Copyright 1998 Kevin Mayhew Ltd.
Psalm tone © Copyright Belmont Abbey, Hereford HR2 9RZ. Used by permission.

1019 17th in Ordinary Time (B)

Responsorial Psalm Psalm 144:10-11, 15-18. ℟ v.16

You open wide your hand, O Lord, you grant our desires.

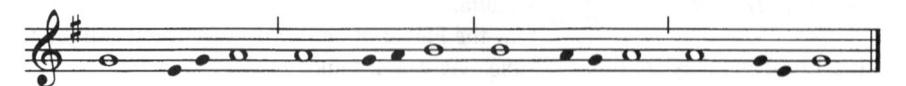

1. All your creatures shall thank <u>you</u>, O Lord,
   and your friends shall re<u>peat</u> their blessing.
   They shall speak of the glory <u>of</u> your reign
   and declare your <u>might</u>, O God.

2. The eyes of all creatures <u>look</u> to you
   and you give them their food <u>in</u> due time.
   You open <u>wide</u> your hand,
   grant the desires of <u>all</u> who live.

3. The Lord is just in <u>all</u> his ways
   and loving in <u>all</u> his deeds.
   He is close to <u>all</u> who call him,
   who call on him <u>from</u> their hearts.

Gospel Acclamation cf. John 6:63, 68   or Luke 7:16
For musical setting see Nos 36 to 47

Alleluia.
Your words are spirit, Lord, and <u>they</u> are life:
you have the message of e<u>ter</u>nal life.
Alleluia.

Alleluia.
A great prophet has ap<u>peared</u> among us;
God has visi<u>ted</u> his people.
Alleluia.

Response: Andrew Moore   Psalm tone: Gregory Murray
Text © 1963, 1986, 1993 The Grail, England, taken from 'The Psalms, a New Inclusive Language Version',
published by HarperCollins Religious. Used by permission of A.P. Watt Ltd, London.
Response © Copyright 1998 Kevin Mayhew Ltd.
Psalm tone © Copyright McCrimmon Publishing Co. Ltd, 10-12 High St, Great Wakering, Essex SS3 0EQ. Used by permission.

1020 18th in Ordinary Time (B)

Responsorial Psalm Psalm 77:3-4, 23-25, 54. ℟ v.24

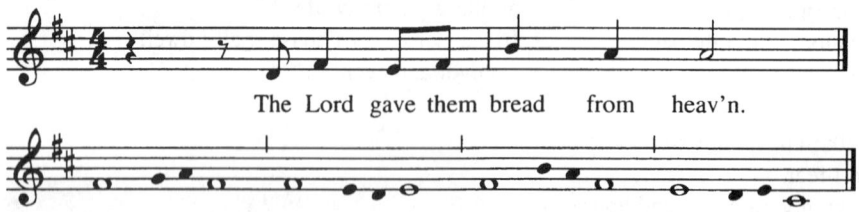

The Lord gave them bread from heav'n.

1. The things we have heard and un<u>der</u>stood,
   the things our fore<u>bears</u> have told us,
   we will tell to the next gene<u>ra</u>tion:
   the glories of the Lord <u>and</u> his might.

2. He commanded the <u>clouds</u> above
   and opened the <u>gates</u> of heaven.
   He rained down manna <u>for</u> their food,
   and gave them <u>bread</u> from heaven.

3. Mere mortals ate the <u>bread</u> of angels.
   He sent them abun<u>dance</u> of food.
   He brought them to his <u>holy</u> land,
   to the mountain which his right <u>hand</u>

Response: Rosalie Bonighton   Psalm tone: Andrew Moore
Text © 1963, 1986, 1993 The Grail, England, taken from 'The Psalms, a New Inclusive Language Version',
published by HarperCollins Religious. Used by permission of A.P. Watt Ltd, London.
Response and Psalm tone © Copyright 1998 Kevin Mayhew Ltd.

Gospel Acclamation John 14:5
For musical setting see Nos 36 to 47
    Alleluia.
    I am the Way, the Truth and the Life, <u>says</u> the Lord;
    no one can come to the Father ex<u>cept</u> through me.
    Alleluia.

or Matthew 4:4
    Alleluia.
    Man does not live on <u>bread</u> alone,
    but on every word that comes from the <u>mouth</u> of God.
    Alleluia.

1021 19th in Ordinary Time (B)

Responsorial Psalm Psalm 33:2-9. ℟ v.9

Taste, O taste and see that the Lord is good, that the Lord is good.

1. I will bless the Lord <u>at</u> all times,
   his praise always <u>on</u> my lips;
   in the Lord my soul shall <u>make</u> its boast.
   The humble shall hear <u>and</u> be glad.

2. Glorify the <u>Lord</u> with me.
   Together let us <u>praise</u> his name.
   I sought the Lord and <u>he</u> answered me;
   from all my terrors he <u>set</u> me free.

3. Look towards him <u>and</u> be radiant;
   let your faces not <u>be</u> abashed.
   When the poor cry out <u>the</u> Lord hears them
   and rescues them from all <u>their</u> distress.

4. The angel of the Lord <u>is</u> encamped
   around those who revere <u>him</u>, to rescue them.
   Taste and see that the <u>Lord</u> is good.
   They are happy who seek ref<u>uge</u> in him.

Gospel Acclamation John 14:23
For musical setting see Nos 36 to 47
    Alleluia.
    If anyone loves me they will <u>keep</u> my word,
    and my Father will love them, and <u>we</u> shall
    come to them.
    Alleluia.

or John 6:51
    Alleluia.
    I am the living bread which has come down
      from heaven, <u>says</u> the Lord.
    Anyone who eats this bread will <u>live</u> for ever.
    Alleluia.

Response and Psalm tone: Alan Rees
Text © 1963, 1986, 1993 The Grail, England, taken from 'The Psalms, a New Inclusive Language Version',
published by HarperCollins Religious. Used by permission of A.P. Watt Ltd, London.
Response © Copyright 1998 Kevin Mayhew Ltd.
Psalm tone © Copyright Belmont Abbey, Hereford HR2 9RZ. Used by permission.

1022 20th in Ordinary Time (B)

Responsorial Psalm Psalm 33:2-3, 10-15. ℟ v.9

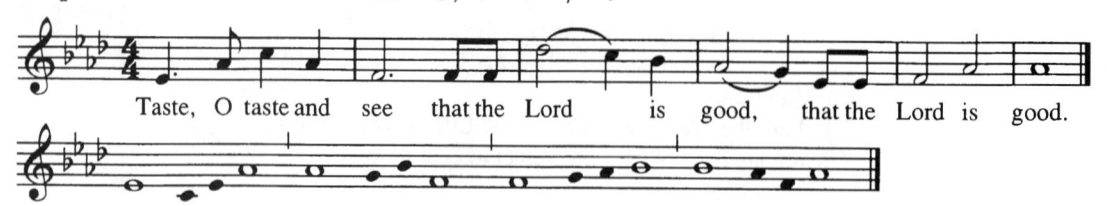

Taste, O taste and see that the Lord is good, that the Lord is good.

1. I will bless the Lord <u>at</u> all times,
   his praise always <u>on</u> my lips;
   in the Lord my soul shall <u>make</u> its boast.
   The humble shall hear <u>and</u> be glad.

2. Revere the Lord, <u>you</u> his saints.
   They lack nothing, those <u>who</u> revere him.
   Strong lions suffer want <u>and</u> go hungry
   but those who seek the Lord <u>lack</u> no blessing.

3. Come, chil<u>dren</u>, and hear me
   that I may teach you the fear <u>of</u> the Lord.
   Who are they who <u>long</u> for life
   and many days, to enjoy <u>their</u> prosperity?

4. Then keep your <u>tongue</u> from evil
   and your lips from spea<u>king</u> deceit.
   Turn aside from evil <u>and</u> do good;
   seek and strive <u>after</u> peace.

Gospel Acclamation John 1:12, 14

For musical setting see Nos 36 to 47

Alleluia.
The Word was made flesh and <u>lived</u> among us;
to all who did accept him he gave power to
   become chil<u>dren</u> of God.
Alleluia.

or John 6:56

Alleluia.
They who eat my flesh and <u>drink</u> my blood
live in me, and I live in them, <u>says</u> the Lord.
Alleluia.

Response and Psalm tone: Alan Rees
Text © 1963, 1986, 1993 The Grail, England, taken from 'The Psalms, a New Inclusive Language Version',
published by HarperCollins Religious. Used by permission of A.P. Watt Ltd, London.
Response © Copyright 1998 Kevin Mayhew Ltd.
Psalm tone © Copyright Belmont Abbey, Hereford HR2 9RZ. Used by permission.

1023 21st in Ordinary Time (B)

Responsorial Psalm Psalm 33:2-3, 16-23. ℟ v.9

Taste, O taste and see that the Lord is good, that the Lord is good.

1. I will bless the Lord <u>at</u> all times,
   his praise always <u>on</u> my lips;
   in the Lord my soul shall <u>make</u> its boast.
   The humble shall hear <u>and</u> be glad.

2. The Lord turns his face a<u>gainst</u> the wicked
   to destroy their remembrance <u>from</u> the earth.
   The Lord turns his eyes <u>to</u> the just
   and his ears to <u>their</u> appeal.

Response and Psalm tone: Alan Rees
Text © 1963, 1986, 1993 The Grail, England, taken from 'The Psalms, a New Inclusive Language Version',
published by HarperCollins Religious. Used by permission of A.P. Watt Ltd, London.
Response © Copyright 1998 Kevin Mayhew Ltd.
Psalm tone © Copyright Belmont Abbey, Hereford HR2 9RZ. Used by permission.

3. They call and <u>the</u> Lord hears
   and rescues them in all <u>their</u> distress.
   The Lord is close to the <u>bro</u>ken-hearted;
   those whose spirit is crushed <u>he</u> will save.

4. Evil brings <u>to</u> the wicked;
   those who hate the <u>good</u> are doomed.
   The Lord ransoms the souls <u>of</u> his servants.
   Those who hide in him shall not <u>be</u> condemned.

Gospel Acclamation cf. John 6:63, 68
For musical setting see Nos 36 to 47
Alleluia.
Your words are spirit, Lord, and <u>they</u> are life:
you have the message of e<u>ter</u>nal life.
Alleluia.

1024 22nd in Ordinary Time (B)

Responsorial Psalm Psalm 14:2-5. ℟ v.1

The just will live in the pre-sence of the Lord.

1. Lord, who shall dwell on your <u>ho</u>ly mountain?
   Those who walk <u>with</u>out fault;
   those who <u>act</u> with justice
   and speak the truth <u>from</u> their hearts.

2. Those who do no wrong <u>to</u> their kindred,
   who cast no slur <u>on</u> their neighbours,
   who hold the godless <u>in</u> disdain,
   but honour those who <u>fear</u> the Lord.

3. Those who keep their pledge, <u>come</u> what may;
   who take no interest <u>on</u> a loan
   and accept no bribes a<u>gainst</u> the innocent.
   Such people will stand <u>firm</u> for ever.

Gospel Acclamation cf. John 6:63, 68
For musical setting see Nos 36 to 47
Alleluia.
Your words are spirit, Lord, and <u>they</u> are life:
you have the message of e<u>ter</u>nal life:
Alleluia.

or James 1:18
Alleluia.
By his own choice the Father made us his children by the
    message <u>of</u> the truth,
so that we should be a sort of first-fruits of all that <u>he</u> created.
Alleluia.

Response: Richard Proulx Psalm tone: Gregory Murray
Text © 1963, 1986, 1993 The Grail, England, taken from 'The Psalms, a New Inclusive Language Version',
published by HarperCollins Religious. Used by permission of A.P. Watt Ltd, London.
Response © Copyright 1998 Kevin Mayhew Ltd.
Psalm tone © Copyright Downside Abbey, Stratton-on-the-Fosse, Bath BA3 4RH. Used by permission.

1025 23rd in Ordinary Time (B)

Responsorial Psalm Psalm 145:7-10. ℟ v.1

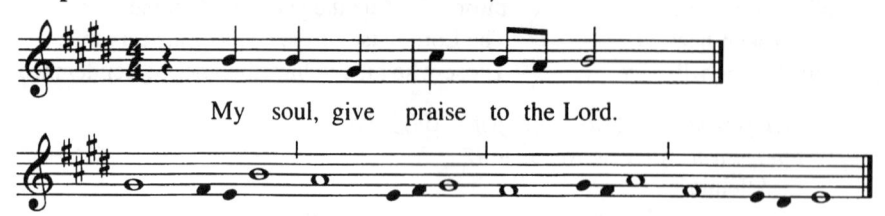

My soul, give praise to the Lord.

1. It is the Lord who keeps <u>faith</u> for ever,
   who is just to those who <u>are</u> oppressed.
   It is he who gives bread <u>to</u> the hungry,
   the Lord, who sets pri<u>son</u>ers free.

2. It is the Lord who gives sight <u>to</u> the blind,
   who raises up those who <u>are</u> bowed down,
   the Lord who <u>loves</u> the just,
   the Lord, who pro<u>tects</u> the stranger.

3. The Lord upholds the wi<u>dow</u> and orphan,
   but thwarts the path <u>of</u> the wicked.
   The Lord will <u>reign</u> for ever,
   Zion's God, from <u>age</u> to age.

Gospel Acclamation 1 Samuel 3:9; John 6:68   or cf. Matthew 4:23
For musical setting see Nos 36 to 47

Alleluia.
Speak, Lord, your ser<u>vant</u> is listening:
you have the message of e<u>ter</u>nal life.
Alleluia.

Alleluia.
Jesus proclaimed the Good News <u>of</u> the kingdom,
and cured all kinds of sickness a<u>mong</u> the people.
Alleluia.

Response: Rosalie Bonighton Psalm tone: Andrew Moore
Text © 1963, 1986, 1993 The Grail, England, taken from 'The Psalms, a New Inclusive Language Version',
published by HarperCollins Religious. Used by permission of A.P. Watt Ltd, London.
Response and Psalm tone © Copyright 1998 Kevin Mayhew Ltd.

1026 24th in Ordinary Time (B)

Responsorial Psalm Psalm 114:1-6, 8-9. ℟ v.9

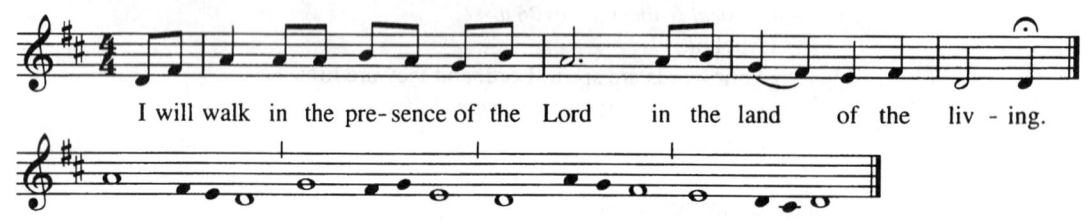

I will walk in the pre-sence of the Lord in the land of the liv-ing.

1. I love the Lord for <u>he</u> has heard
   the cry of <u>my</u> appeal;
   for he <u>turned</u> his ear to me
   in the day <u>when</u> I called him.

2. They surrounded me, the <u>snares</u> of death,
   with the anguish <u>of</u> the tomb;
   they caught me, sorrow <u>and</u> distress.
   O Lord my <u>God</u>, deliver me!

3. How gracious is the <u>Lord</u>, and just;
   our God <u>has</u> compassion.
   The Lord protects the <u>simple</u> hearts;
   I was helpless <u>so</u> he saved me.

4. He has kept my soul from death, my <u>eyes</u> from tears
   and my <u>feet</u> from stumbling.
   I will walk in the presence <u>of</u> the Lord
   in the land <u>of</u> the living.

Response and Psalm tone: Andrew Moore
Text © 1963, 1986, 1993 The Grail, England, taken from 'The Psalms, a New Inclusive Language Version',
published by HarperCollins Religious. Used by permission of A.P. Watt Ltd, London.
Response and Psalm tone © Copyright 1998 Kevin Mayhew Ltd.

Gospel Acclamation John 14:5
For musical setting see Nos 36 to 47
Alleluia.
I am the Way, the Truth and the Life, <u>says</u> the Lord;
no one can come to the Father ex<u>cept</u> through me.
Alleluia.

or Galatians 6:14
Alleluia.
The only thing I can boast about is the cross <u>of</u> our Lord,
through whom the world is crucified to me, and I <u>to</u> the world.
Alleluia.

1027 25th in Ordinary Time (B)

Responsorial Psalm Psalm 53:3-6, 8. ℟ v.6

The Lord up-holds my life, up - holds my life.

* *Omit in verse 2*

1. O God, save me <u>by</u> your name;
   by your power, up<u>hold</u> my cause.
   O God, <u>hear</u> my prayer;
   listen to the words <u>of</u> my mouth.

2. For the proud have <u>risen</u> against me,
   ruthless foes <u>seek</u> my life.
   They have no re<u>gard</u> for God.

3. But I have God <u>for</u> my help.
   The Lord up<u>holds</u> my life.
   I will sacrifice to you with <u>willing</u> heart
   and praise your name for <u>it</u> is good.

Gospel Acclamation John 8:12
For musical setting see Nos 36 to 47
Alleluia.
I am the light of the world, <u>says</u> the Lord,
anyone who follows me will have the <u>light</u> of life.
Alleluia.

or cf. 2 Thessalonians 2:14
Alleluia.
Through the Good News <u>God</u> has called us
to share the glory of our Lord <u>Jesus</u> Christ.
Alleluia.

Response: Colin Mawby Psalm tone: Gregory Murray
Text © 1963, 1986, 1993 The Grail, England, taken from 'The Psalms, a New Inclusive Language Version',
published by HarperCollins Religious. Used by permission of A.P. Watt Ltd, London.
Response © Copyright 1998 Kevin Mayhew Ltd.
Psalm tone © Copyright Downside Abbey, Stratton-on-the-Fosse, Bath BA3 4RH. Used by permission.

1028 26th in Ordinary Time (B)

Responsorial Psalm Psalm 18:8, 10, 12-14. ℟ v.9

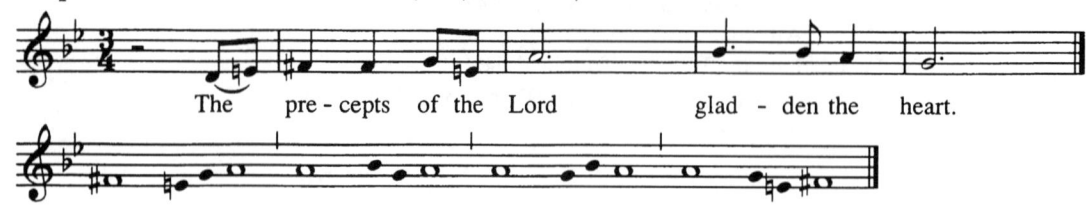

The pre-cepts of the Lord glad-den the heart.

1. The law of the <u>Lord</u> is perfect,
   it re<u>vives</u> the soul.
   The rule of the Lord is <u>to</u> be trusted,
   it gives wisdom <u>to</u> the simple.

2. The fear of the <u>Lord</u> is holy,
   ab<u>id</u>ing for ever.
   The decrees of the <u>Lord</u> are truth
   and all <u>of</u> them just.

3. So in them your servant <u>finds</u> instruction;
   great reward is <u>in</u> their keeping.
   But who can detect <u>all</u> their errors?
   From hidden <u>faults</u> acquit me.

4. From presumption re<u>strain</u> your servant
   and let <u>it</u> not rule me.
   Then shall <u>I</u> be blameless,
   clean <u>from</u> grave sin.

Gospel Acclamation cf. John 17:17
For musical setting see Nos 36 to 47

Alleluia.
Your word is <u>truth</u>, O Lord
consecrate us <u>in</u> the truth.
Alleluia.

Response: Richard Lloyd Psalm tone: Laurence Bevenot
Text © 1963, 1986, 1993 The Grail, England, taken from 'The Psalms, a New Inclusive Language Version', published by HarperCollins Religious. Used by permission of A.P. Watt Ltd, London.
Response © Copyright 1998 Kevin Mayhew Ltd.
Psalm tone © Copyright Ampleforth Abbey, York YO6 4EN. Used by permission.

1029 27th in Ordinary Time (B)

Responsorial Psalm Psalm 127. ℟ v.5

May the Lord bless us all the days of our life.

1. O blessed are those who <u>fear</u> the Lord
   and walk <u>in</u> his ways!
   By the labour of your hands <u>you</u> shall eat.
   You will be happy and prosper.

2. Your wife will be like a <u>fruitful</u> vine
   in the heart <u>of</u> your house;
   your children like shoots <u>of</u> the olive,
   <u>around</u> your table.

3. Indeed thus <u>shall</u> be blessed
   those who <u>fear</u> the Lord.
   May the Lord bless <u>you</u> from Zion
   in a <u>happy</u> Jerusalem.

Response: Rosalie Bonighton Psalm tone: Andrew Moore
Text © 1963, 1986, 1993 The Grail, England, taken from 'The Psalms, a New Inclusive Language Version', published by HarperCollins Religious. Used by permission of A.P. Watt Ltd, London.
Response and Psalm tone © Copyright 1998 Kevin Mayhew Ltd.

Gospel Acclamation cf. John 17:17
For musical setting see Nos 36 to 47
   Alleluia.
   Your word is truth, O Lord,
   consecrate us in the truth.
   Alleluia.

or 1 John 4:12
   Alleluia.
   As long as we love one another
   God will live in us and his love will be complete in us.
   Alleluia.

1030 28th in Ordinary Time (B)

Responsorial Psalm Psalm 89:12-17. ℟ v.14

Fill us with your love, fill us with your love that we may rejoice.

1. Make us know the shortness of our life
that we may gain wisdom of heart.
Lord, relent! Is your anger for ever?
Show pity to your servants.

2. In the morning, fill us with your love;
we shall exult and rejoice all our days.
Give us joy to balance our affliction
for the years when we knew misfortune.

3. Show forth your work to your servants;
let your glory shine on their children.
Let the favour of the Lord be upon us:
give success to the work of our hands.

Gospel Acclamation cf. Matthew 11:25
For musical setting see Nos 36 to 47
   Alleluia.
   Blessed are you, Father, Lord of heaven and earth,
   for revealing the mysteries of the kingdom to mere children.
   Alleluia.

or Matthew 5:3
   Alleluia,
   How happy are the poor in spirit;
   theirs is the kingdom of heaven.
   Alleluia.

Response: Andrew Moore Psalm tone: Alan Rees
Text © 1963, 1986, 1993 The Grail, England, taken from 'The Psalms, a New Inclusive Language Version',
published by HarperCollins Religious. Used by permission of A.P. Watt Ltd, London.
Response © Copyright 1998 Kevin Mayhew Ltd.
Psalm tone © Copyright Belmont Abbey, Hereford HR2 9RZ. Used by permission.

1031 29th in Ordinary Time (B)

Responsorial Psalm Psalm 32:4-5, 18-20, 22. ℟ v.22

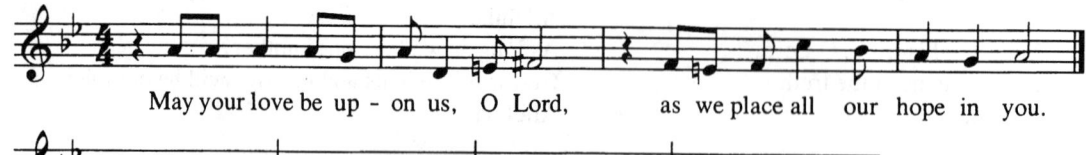

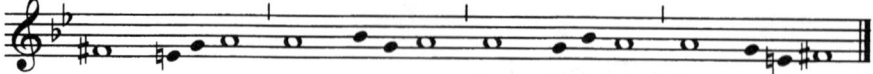

May your love be upon us, O Lord, as we place all our hope in you.

1. The word of the <u>Lord</u> is faithful
   and all his works <u>to</u> be trusted.
   The Lord loves jus<u>tice</u> and right
   and fills the earth <u>with</u> his love.

2. The Lord looks on those <u>who</u> revere him,
   on those who hope <u>in</u> his love,
   to rescue their <u>souls</u> from death,
   to keep them a<u>live</u> in famine.

3. Our soul is waiting <u>for</u> the Lord.
   The Lord is our help <u>and</u> our shield.
   May your love be upon <u>us</u>, O Lord,
   as we place all our <u>hope</u> in you.

Gospel Acclamation John 14:15
For musical setting see Nos 36 to 47
   Alleluia.
   I am the Way, the Truth and the Life, <u>says</u> the Lord;
   no one can come to the Father ex<u>cept</u> through me.
   Alleluia.

   or Mark 10:45
   Alleluia.
   The Son of Man <u>came</u> to serve,
   and to give his life as a ran<u>som</u> for many.
   Alleluia.

Response: Rosalie Bonighton   Psalm tone: Laurence Bevenot
Text © 1963, 1986, 1993 The Grail, England, taken from 'The Psalms, A New Inclusive Language Version',
published by HarperCollins Religious. Used by permission of A.P. Watt Ltd, London.
Response © Copyright 1998 Kevin Mayhew Ltd.
Psalm tone © Copyright Ampleforth Abbey, York YO6 4EN. Used by permission.

1032 30th in Ordinary Time (B)

Responsorial Psalm Psalm 125. ℟ v.3

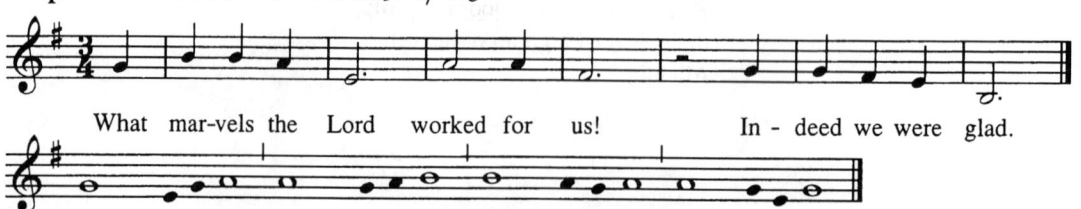

What marvels the Lord worked for us! Indeed we were glad.

1. When the Lord delivered <u>Zion</u> from bondage,
   it seemed <u>like</u> a dream.
   Then was our mouth <u>filled</u> with laughter,
   on our lips <u>there</u> were songs.

2. The heathens themselves <u>said</u>: 'What marvels
   the Lord <u>worked</u> for them!'
   What marvels the Lord <u>worked</u> for us!
   Indeed <u>we</u> were glad.

Response: Martin Setchell   Psalm tone: Gregory Murray
Text © 1963, 1986, 1993 The Grail, England, taken from 'The Psalms, A New Inclusive Language Version',
published by HarperCollins Religious. Used by permission of A.P. Watt Ltd, London.
Response © Copyright 1998 Kevin Mayhew Ltd.
Psalm tone © Copyright McCrimmon Publishing Co. Ltd, 10-12 High St, Great Wakering, Essex SS3 0EQ. Used by permission.

3. Deliver us, O Lord, <u>from</u> our bondage
   as streams <u>in</u> dry land.
   Those who are so<u>wing</u> in tears
   will sing <u>when</u> they reap.

4. They go out, they go out, <u>full</u> of tears,
   carrying seed <u>for</u> the sowing:
   they come back, they come back, <u>full</u> of song,
   carry<u>ing</u> their sheaves.

Gospel Acclamation John 8:12
For musical setting see Nos 36 to 47
Alleluia.
I am the light of the world, <u>says</u> the Lord,
anyone who follows me will have the <u>light</u> of life.
Alleluia.

1033 31st in Ordinary Time (B)

Responsorial Psalm Psalm 17:2-4, 47, 51. ℟ v.2

I love you, Lord, O God, my strength, I love you, Lord, my strength.

1. I love you, <u>Lord</u>, my strength,
   my rock, my for<u>tress</u>, my saviour.
   My God is the rock where <u>I</u> take refuge;
   my shield, my mighty <u>help</u>, my stronghold.

2. The Lord is worthy <u>of</u> all praise:
   when I call I am saved <u>from</u> my foes.
   Long life to the <u>Lord</u>, my rock!
   Praised be the <u>God</u> who saves me.

Gospel Acclamation cf. John 6:63, 68
For musical setting see Nos 36 to 47
Alleluia.
Your words are spirit, Lord, and <u>they</u> are life:
you have the message of e<u>ter</u>nal life.
Alleluia.

or John 14:23
Alleluia.
If anyone loves me they will <u>keep</u> my word,
and my Father will love them and <u>we</u> shall come to them.
Alleluia.

Response: Alan Rees   Psalm tone: Gregory Murray
Text © 1963, 1986, 1993 The Grail, England, taken from 'The Psalms, a New Inclusive Language Version',
published by HarperCollins Religious. Used by permission of A.P. Watt Ltd, London.
Response © Copyright 1998 Kevin Mayhew Ltd.
Psalm tone © Copyright McCrimmon Publishing Co. Ltd, 10-12 High St, Great Wakering, Essex SS3 0EQ. Used by permission.

1034 32nd in Ordinary Time (B)

Responsorial Psalm Psalm 145:7-10. ℟ v.2

My soul, give praise to the Lord.

1. It is the Lord who keeps <u>faith</u> for ever,
who is just to those who <u>are</u> oppressed.
It is he who gives bread <u>to</u> the hungry,
the Lord, who sets pris<u>on</u>ers free.

2. It is the Lord who gives sight <u>to</u> the blind,
who raises up those who <u>are</u> bowed down.
It is the Lord who <u>loves</u> the just,
the Lord, who pro<u>tects</u> the stranger.

3. The Lord upholds the wi<u>dow</u> and orphan
but thwarts the path <u>of</u> the wicked.
The Lord will <u>reign</u> for ever,
Zion's God, from <u>age</u> to age.

Gospel Acclamation Revelation 2:10   or Matthew 5:3
For musical setting see Nos 36 to 47

Alleluia.
Even if you have to die, <u>says</u> the Lord,
keep faithful, and I will give you the <u>crown</u> of life.
Alleluia.

Alleluia.
How happy are the <u>poor</u> in spirit;
theirs is the king<u>dom</u> of heaven.
Alleluia.

Response: Rosalie Bonighton   Psalm tone: Andrew Moore
Text © 1963, 1986, 1993 The Grail, England, taken from 'The Psalms, a New Inclusive Language Version',
published by HarperCollins Religious. Used by permission of A.P. Watt Ltd, London.
Response and Psalm tone © Copyright 1998 Kevin Mayhew Ltd.

1035 33rd in Ordinary Time (B)

Responsorial Psalm Psalm 15:5, 8-11. ℟ v.1

Pre-serve me, God, I take ref-uge in you.

1. O Lord, it is you who are my por<u>tion</u> and cup;
it is you yourself who <u>are</u> my prize.
I keep the Lord ever <u>in</u> my sight:
since he is at my right hand, I <u>shall</u> stand firm.

2. And so my heart rejoices, my <u>soul</u> is glad;
even my body shall <u>rest</u> in safety.
For you will not leave my soul a<u>mong</u> the dead,
nor let your beloved <u>know</u> decay.

3. O Lord, <u>you</u> will show me
the <u>path</u> of life,
the fullness of joy <u>in</u> your presence,
at your right hand happ<u>iness</u> for ever.

Response: Andrew Moore   Psalm tone: Laurence Bevenot
Text © 1963, 1986, 1993 The Grail, England, taken from 'The Psalms, a New Inclusive Language Version',
published by HarperCollins Religious. Used by permission of A.P. Watt Ltd, London.
Response © Copyright 1998 Kevin Mayhew Ltd.
Psalm tone © Copyright Ampleforth Abbey, York YO6 4EN. Used by permission.

Gospel Acclamation Matthew 24:42, 44
For musical setting see Nos 36 to 47
Alleluia.
Stay awake <u>and</u> stand ready,
because you do not know the hour when the Son of <u>Man</u> is coming.
Alleluia.

or Luke 21:36
Alleluia.
Stay awake, praying <u>at</u> all times
for the strength to stand with confidence before the <u>Son</u> of Man.
Alleluia.

1036 *Last Sunday in Ordinary Time*
Our Lord Jesus Christ, Universal King (B)

Responsorial Psalm Psalm 92:1-2, 5. ℟ v.1

The Lord is King, with ma-je-sty en-robed.

1. The Lord is King, with majes<u>ty</u> enrobed;
   the Lord has robed him<u>self</u> with might,
   he has girded him<u>self</u> with power.

2. The world you made firm, not <u>to</u> be moved;
   your throne has stood firm <u>from</u> of old.
   From all eternity, O <u>Lord</u>, you are.

3. Truly your decrees are <u>to</u> be trusted.
   Holiness is fitting <u>to</u> your house,
   O Lord, until the <u>end</u> of time.

Gospel Acclamation Mark 11:9, 10
For musical setting see Nos 36 to 47
Alleluia.
Blessings on him who comes in the name <u>of</u> the Lord!
Blessings on the coming kingdom of our <u>father</u> David!
Alleluia.

Response and Psalm tone: Andrew Moore
Text © 1963, 1986, 1993 The Grail, England, taken from 'The Psalms, a New Inclusive Language Version',
published by HarperCollins Religious. Used by permission of A.P. Watt Ltd, London.
Response and Psalm tone © Copyright 1998 Kevin Mayhew Ltd.

1037 2nd in Ordinary Time (C)

Responsorial Psalm Psalm 95:1-3, 7-10. ℟ v.3

Pro-claim the won-ders of the Lord a-mong all the peo-ples.

1. O sing a new song to the Lord,
   sing to the Lord all the earth.
   O sing to the Lord, bless his name.

2. Proclaim his help day by day,
   tell among the nations his glory
   and his wonders among all the peoples.

3. Give the Lord, you families of peoples,
   give the Lord glory and power,
   give the Lord the glory of his name.

4. Worship the Lord in his temple.
   O earth, tremble before him.
   Proclaim to the nations: 'God is king.'

Gospel Acclamation cf. John 6:63, 68
For musical setting see Nos 36 to 47
Alleluia.
Your words are spirit, Lord, and they are life:
you have the message of eternal life.
Alleluia.

or cf. 2 Thessalonians 2:14
Alleluia.
Through the Good News God has called us
to share the glory of our Lord Jesus Christ.
Alleluia.

Response and Psalm tone: Andrew Moore
Text © 1963, 1986, 1993 The Grail, England, taken from 'The Psalms, a New Inclusive Language Version',
published by HarperCollins Religious. Used by permission of A.P. Watt Ltd, London.
Response and Psalm tone © Copyright 1998 Kevin Mayhew Ltd.

1038 3rd in Ordinary Time (C)

Responsorial Psalm Psalm 18:8-10, 15. ℟ John 6:63

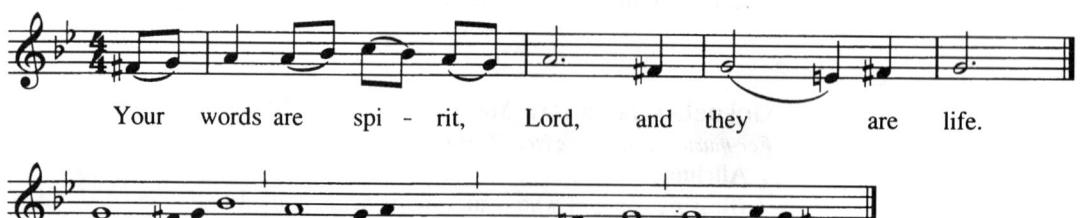

Your words are spi-rit, Lord, and they are life.

1. The law of the Lord is perfect,
   it revives the soul.
   The rule of the Lord is to be trusted,
   it gives wisdom to the simple.

2. The precepts of the Lord are right,
   they gladden the heart.
   The command of the Lord is clear,
   it gives light to the eyes.

Response and Psalm tone: Andrew Moore
Text © 1963, 1986, 1993 The Grail, England, taken from 'The Psalms, a New Inclusive Language Version',
published by HarperCollins Religious. Used by permission of A.P. Watt Ltd, London.
Response and Psalm tone © Copyright 1998 Kevin Mayhew Ltd.

3. The fear of the <u>Lord</u> is holy,
   ab<u>id</u>ing for ever.
   The decrees of the <u>Lord</u> are truth
   and all <u>of</u> them just.

4. May the spoken words <u>of</u> my mouth,
   the thoughts <u>of</u> my heart,
   win favour in your <u>sight</u>, O Lord,
   my rescu<u>er</u>, my rock!

Gospel Acclamation Luke 4:18
For musical setting see Nos 36 to 47
Alleluia.
The Lord has sent me to bring the good news <u>to</u> the poor,
to proclaim liber<u>ty</u> to captives.
Alleluia.

1039 4th in Ordinary Time (C)

Responsorial Psalm Psalm 70:1-6, 15, 17. ℟ v.15

My lips will tell of your help.

1. In you, O Lord, <u>I</u> take refuge;
   let me never be <u>put</u> to shame.
   In your justice res<u>cue</u> me, free me;
   pay heed to <u>me</u> and save me.

2. Be a rock where I <u>can</u> take refuge,
   a mighty strong<u>hold</u> to save me;
   for you are my <u>rock</u>, my stronghold.
   Free me from the hand <u>of</u> the wicked.

3. It is you, O Lord, who <u>are</u> my hope,
   my trust, O Lord, <u>since</u> my youth.
   On you I have leaned <u>from</u> my birth,
   from my mother's womb you have <u>been</u> my help.

4. My lips will tell <u>of</u> your justice
   and day by day <u>of</u> your help.
   O God, you have taught me <u>from</u> my youth
   and I proclaim your <u>won</u>ders still.

Gospel Acclamation John 14:5
For musical setting see Nos 36 to 47
Alleluia.
I am the Way, the Truth and the Life, <u>says</u> the Lord;
no one can come to the Father ex<u>cept</u> through me.
Alleluia.

or Luke 4:18
Alleluia.
The Lord has sent me to bring the good news <u>to</u> the poor,
to proclaim liber<u>ty</u> to captives.
Alleluia.

Response: Colin Mawby Psalm tone: Gregory Murray
Text © 1963, 1986, 1993 The Grail, England, taken from 'The Psalms, a New Inclusive Language Version',
published by HarperCollins Religious. Used by permission of A.P. Watt Ltd, London.
Response © Copyright 1998 Kevin Mayhew Ltd.
Psalm tone © Copyright Downside Abbey, Stratton-on-the-Fosse, Bath BA3 4RH. Used by permission.

1040 5th in Ordinary Time (C)

Responsorial Psalm Psalm 137:1-5, 7-8. ℟ v.1

Before the angels I will bless you, O Lord.

1. I thank you, Lord, with <u>all</u> my heart,
you have heard the words <u>of</u> my mouth.
Before the angels <u>I</u> will bless you
I will adore before your <u>ho</u>ly temple.

2. I thank you for your faithful<u>ness</u> and love
which excel all we <u>ev</u>er knew of you.
On the day I <u>called</u>, you answered;
you increased the strength <u>of</u> my soul.

3. All earth's <u>kings</u> shall thank you
when they hear the words <u>of</u> your mouth.
They shall sing of <u>the</u> Lord's ways:
'How great is the glory <u>of</u> the Lord!'

4. You stretch out your <u>hand</u> and save me,
your hand will do <u>all</u> things for me.
Your love, O Lord, <u>is</u> eternal,
discard not the work <u>of</u> your hand.

Gospel Acclamation John 15:15

For musical setting see Nos 36 to 47

Alleluia.
I call you friends, <u>says</u> the Lord,
because I have made known to you
   everything I have learnt <u>from</u> my Father.
Alleluia.

or Matthew 4:19

Alleluia.
Follow me, <u>says</u> the Lord,
and I will make you fish<u>ers</u> of men.
Alleluia.

Response: Richard Lloyd   Psalm tone: Laurence Bevenot
Text © 1963, 1986, 1993 The Grail, England, taken from 'The Psalms, a New Inclusive Language Version',
published by HarperCollins Religious. Used by permission of A.P. Watt Ltd, London.
Response © Copyright 1998 Kevin Mayhew Ltd.
Psalm tone © Copyright Ampleforth Abbey, York YO6 4EN. Used by permission.

1041 6th in Ordinary Time (C)

Responsorial Psalm Psalm 1:1-4, 6. ℟ Psalm 39:5

Happy are those, happy are those who have placed their trust in the Lord.

* Omit in verses 2 and 3

1. Happy in<u>deed</u> are those
who follow not the counsel <u>of</u> the wicked;
nor linger in the <u>way</u> of sinners
nor sit in the compan<u>y</u> of scorners,
whose delight is the law <u>of</u> the Lord
and who ponder his law <u>day</u> and night.

Response: Alan Rees   Psalm tone: Andrew Moore
Text © 1963, 1986, 1993 The Grail, England, taken from 'The Psalms, a New Inclusive Language Version',
published by HarperCollins Religious. Used by permission of A.P. Watt Ltd, London.
Response and Psalm tone © Copyright 1998 Kevin Mayhew Ltd.

2. They are like a tree that is planted
   beside the flowing waters,
   that yields its fruit in due season
   and whose leaves shall never fade;
   and all that they do shall prosper.

3. Not so are the wicked, not so!
   For they like winnowed chaff
   shall be driven away by the wind.
   For the Lord guards the way of the just
   but the way of the wicked leads to doom.

Gospel Acclamation cf. Matthew 11:25
For musical setting see Nos 36 to 47
   Alleluia.
   Blessed are you, Father, Lord of heaven and earth,
   for revealing the mysteries of the kingdom to mere children.
   Alleluia.

   or Luke 6:23
   Alleluia.
   Rejoice and be glad:
   your reward will be great in heaven.
   Alleluia.

1042 7th in Ordinary Time (C)

Responsorial Psalm Psalm 102:1-4, 8, 10, 12-13. ℟ v.8

The Lord is com-pas-sion and love, the Lord is com-pas-sion and love.

1. My soul, give thanks to the Lord,
   all my being, bless his holy name.
   My soul, give thanks to the Lord
   and never forget all his blessings.

2. It is he who forgives all your guilt,
   who heals every one of your ills,
   who redeems your life from the grave,
   who crowns you with love and compassion.

3. The Lord is compassion and love,
   slow to anger and rich in mercy.
   He does not treat us according to our sins
   nor repay us according to our faults.

4. As far as the east is from the west
   so far does he remove our sins.
   As a father has compassion on his sons,
   the Lord has pity on those who fear him.

Gospel Acclamation cf. Acts 16:14
For musical setting see Nos 36 to 47
   Alleluia.
   Open our heart, O Lord,
   to accept the words of your Son.
   Alleluia.

   or John 13:34
   Alleluia.
   I give you a new commandment: love one another,
   just as I have loved you, says the Lord.
   Alleluia.

Response: Andrew Moore   Psalm tone: Laurence Bevenot
Text © 1963, 1986, 1993 The Grail, England, taken from 'The Psalms, a New Inclusive Language Version',
published by HarperCollins Religious. Used by permission of A.P. Watt Ltd, London.
Response © Copyright 1998 Kevin Mayhew Ltd.
Psalm tone © Copyright Ampleforth Abbey, York YO6 4EN. Used by permission.

1043 8th in Ordinary Time (C)

Responsorial Psalm Psalm 91:2-3, 13-16. ℟ cf. v.2

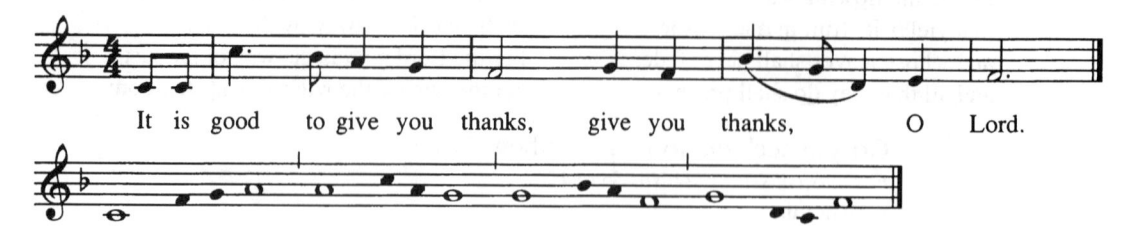

It is good to give you thanks, give you thanks, O Lord.

1. It is good to give thanks to the Lord
   to make music to your name, O Most High,
   to proclaim your love in the morning
   and your truth in the watches of the night.

2. The just will flourish like the palm-tree
   and grow like a Lebanon cedar.
   Planted in the house of the Lord
   they will flourish in the courts of our God.

3. Still bearing fruit when they are old,
   still full of sap, still green,
   they will proclaim that the Lord is just.
   In him, my rock, there is no wrong.

Gospel Acclamation cf. Acts 16:14
For musical setting see Nos 36 to 47
   Alleluia.
   Open our heart, O Lord,
   to accept the words of your Son.
   Alleluia.

or Philippians 2:15-16

   Alleluia.
   You will shine in the world like bright stars
   because you are offering it the word of life.
   Alleluia.

Response: Colin Mawby   Psalm tone: Alan Rees
Text © 1963, 1986, 1993 The Grail, England, taken from 'The Psalms, a New Inclusive Language Version',
published by HarperCollins Religious. Used by permission of A.P. Watt Ltd, London.
Response © Copyright 1998 Kevin Mayhew Ltd.
Psalm tone © Copyright Belmont Abbey, Hereford HR2 9RZ. Used by permission.

1044 9th in Ordinary Time (C)

Responsorial Psalm Psalm 116:1-2. ℟ Mark 16:15

Go out to the whole world and pro-claim the Good News.

1. O praise the Lord, all you nations,
   acclaim him all you peoples!

2. Strong is his love for us;
   he is faithful for ever.

Response and Psalm tone: Andrew Moore
Text © 1963, 1986, 1993 The Grail, England, taken from 'The Psalms, a New Inclusive Language Version',
published by HarperCollins Religious. Used by permission of A.P. Watt Ltd, London.
Response and Psalm tone © Copyright 1998 Kevin Mayhew Ltd.

Gospel Acclamation John 1:14, 12
For musical setting see Nos 36 to 47
  Alleluia.
  The Word was made flesh and <u>lived</u> among us;
  to all who did accept him he gave power to become child<u>ren</u> of God.
  Alleluia.

  or John 3:16
  Alleluia.
  God loved the world so much that he gave his <u>on</u>ly Son
  so that everyone who believes in him may have e<u>ter</u>nal life.
  Alleluia.

1045   10th in Ordinary Time (C)

Responsorial Psalm Psalm 29:2, 4-6, 11-13. ℟ v.2

I will praise you, Lord, you have rescued me.

1. I will praise you, Lord, <u>you</u> have rescued me
   and have not let my enemies rejoice <u>o</u>ver me.
   O Lord, you have raised my soul <u>from</u> the dead,
   restored me to life from those who sink in<u>to</u> the grave.

2. Sing psalms to the Lord, <u>you</u> who love him,
   give thanks to his <u>ho</u>ly name.
   His anger lasts a moment; his fa<u>vour</u> through life.
   At night there are tears, but joy <u>comes</u> with dawn.

3. The Lord listened <u>and</u> had pity.
   The Lord came <u>to</u> my help.
   For me you have changed my mourning <u>into</u> dancing;
   O Lord my God, I will thank <u>you</u> for ever.

Gospel Acclamation cf. Ephesians 1:17, 18
For musical setting see Nos 36 to 47
  Alleluia.
  May the Father of our Lord Jesus Christ enlighten the eyes <u>of</u> our mind,
  so that we can see what hope his call <u>holds</u> for us.
  Alleluia.

  or Luke 7:16
  Alleluia.
  A great prophet has app<u>eared</u> among us;
  God has vis<u>ited</u> his people.
  Alleluia.

Response: Richard Lloyd   Psalm tone: Alan Rees
Text © 1963, 1986, 1993 The Grail, England, taken from 'The Psalms, a New Inclusive Language Version',
published by HarperCollins Religious. Used by permission of A.P. Watt Ltd, London.
Response © Copyright 1998 Kevin Mayhew Ltd.
Psalm tone © Copyright Belmont Abbey, Hereford HR2 9RZ. Used by permission.

1046 11th in Ordinary Time (C)

Responsorial Psalm Psalm 31:1-2, 5, 7, 11. ℟ cf. v.5

For - give, Lord, the guilt of my sin.

1. Happy are those whose offence <u>is</u> forgiven
   whose sin <u>is</u> remitted.
   O happy are those to <u>whom</u> the Lord
   im<u>putes</u> no guilt.

2. But now I have acknow<u>ledged</u> my sins:
   my guilt I <u>did</u> not hide.
   And you, Lord, <u>have</u> forgiven
   the guilt <u>of</u> my sin.

3. Rejoice, rejoice <u>in</u> the Lord,
   ex<u>ult</u>, you just!
   O come, ring <u>out</u> your joy,
   all you up<u>right</u> of heart.

Gospel Acclamation John 14:5
For musical setting see Nos 36 to 47
   Alleluia.
   I am the Way, the Truth and the Life, <u>says</u> the Lord;
   no one can come to the Father ex<u>cept</u> through me.
   Alleluia.

or 1 John 4:10
   Alleluia.
   God so loved us when he <u>sent</u> his Son
   to be the sacrifice that takes our <u>sins</u> away.
   Alleluia.

Response: Martin Setchell Psalm tone: Alan Rees
Text © 1963, 1986, 1993 The Grail, England, taken from 'The Psalms, a New Inclusive Language Version',
published by HarperCollins Religious. Used by permission of A.P. Watt Ltd, London.
Response © Copyright 1998 Kevin Mayhew Ltd.
Psalm tone © Copyright Belmont Abbey, Hereford HR2 9RZ. Used by permission.

1047 12th in Ordinary Time (C)

Responsorial Psalm Psalm 62:2-6, 8-9. ℟ v.2

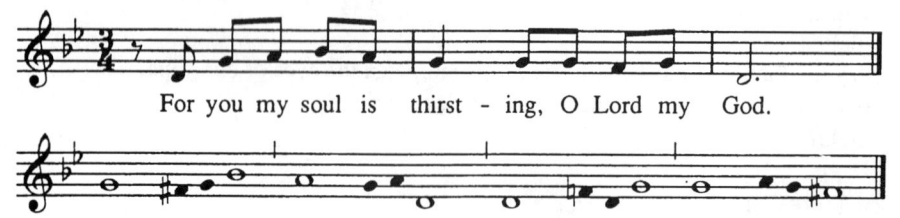

For you my soul is thirst - ing, O Lord my God.

1. O God, you are my God, for <u>you</u> I long;
   for you my <u>soul</u> is thirsting.
   My body <u>pines</u> for you
   like a dry, weary land with<u>out</u> water.

2. So I gaze on you <u>in</u> the sanctuary
   to see your strength <u>and</u> your glory.
   For your love is bet<u>ter</u> than life,
   my lips will <u>speak</u> your praise.

Response and Psalm tone: Andrew Moore
Text © 1963, 1986, 1993 The Grail, England, taken from 'The Psalms, a New Inclusive Language Version',
published by HarperCollins Religious. Used by permission of A.P. Watt Ltd, London.
Response and Psalm tone © Copyright 1998 Kevin Mayhew Ltd.

3. So I will bless you <u>all</u> my life,
   in your name I will lift <u>up</u> my hands.
   My soul shall be filled as <u>with</u> a banquet,
   my mouth shall praise <u>you</u> with joy.

4. For you have <u>been</u> my help;
   in the shadow of your wings <u>I</u> rejoice.
   My soul <u>clings</u> to you;
   your right hand <u>holds</u> me fast.

Gospel Acclamation John 8:12
For musical setting see Nos 35 to 39 and 39 to 47
Alleluia.
I am the light of the world, <u>says</u> the Lord,
anyone who follows me will have the <u>light</u> of life.
Alleluia.

or John 10:27
Alleluia.
The sheep that belong to me listen to my voice, <u>says</u> the Lord,
I know them <u>and</u> they follow me.
Alleluia.

1048 13th in Ordinary Time (C)

Responsorial Psalm Psalm 15:1-2, 5, 7-11. ℟ v.1

Pre-serve me, God, I take ref-uge in you.

1. Preserve me, God, I take re<u>fuge</u> in you.
   I say to the Lord: 'You <u>are</u> my God.'
   O Lord, it is you who are my por<u>tion</u> and cup;
   it is you yourself who <u>are</u> my prize.

2. I will bless the Lord who <u>gives</u> me counsel,
   who even at night di<u>rects</u> my heart.
   I keep the Lord ever <u>in</u> my sight:
   since he is at my right hand, I <u>shall</u> stand firm.

3. And so my heart rejoices, my <u>soul</u> is glad;
   even my body shall <u>rest</u> in safety.
   For you will not leave my soul <u>among</u> the dead,
   nor let your beloved <u>know</u> decay.

4. O Lord, <u>you</u> will show me
   the <u>path</u> of life,
   the fullness of joy <u>in</u> your presence,
   at your right hand happ<u>iness</u> for ever.

Gospel Acclamation 1 Samuel 3:9; John 6:68
For musical setting see Nos 36 to 47
Alleluia.
Speak, Lord, your ser<u>vant</u> is listening:
you have the message of e<u>ternal</u> life.
Alleluia.

Response: Andrew Moore   Psalm tone: Laurence Bevenot
Text © 1963, 1986, 1993 The Grail, England, taken from 'The Psalms, a New Inclusive Language Version',
published by HarperCollins Religious. Used by permission of A.P. Watt Ltd, London.
Response © Copyright 1998 Kevin Mayhew Ltd.
Psalm tone © Copyright Ampleforth Abbey, York YO6 4EN. Used by permission.

1049 14th in Ordinary Time (C)

Responsorial Psalm Psalm 65:1-7, 16, 20. ℟ v.1

Cry out with joy to God all the earth.

1. Cry out with joy to God <u>all</u> the earth,
   O sing to the glory <u>of</u> his name.
   O render him glo<u>ri</u>ous praise.
   Say to God: 'How tremen<u>dous</u> your deeds!'

2. 'Before you all the <u>earth</u> shall bow;
   shall sing to you, sing <u>to</u> your name!'
   Come and see the <u>works</u> of God,
   tremendous his deeds <u>among</u> men.

3. He turned the sea in<u>to</u> dry land,
   they passed through the ri<u>ver</u> dry-shod.
   Let our joy then <u>be</u> in him;
   he rules for ever <u>by</u> his might.

4. Come and hear, all <u>who</u> fear God.
   I will tell what he did <u>for</u> my soul.
   Blessed be God who did not re<u>ject</u> my prayer
   nor with<u>hold</u> his love from me.

Gospel Acclamation John 15:15
For musical setting see Nos 36 to 47

Alleluia.
I call you friends, <u>says</u> the Lord,
because I have made known to you everything I have learnt <u>from</u> my Father.
Alleluia.

or Colossians 3:15, 16

Alleluia.
May the peace of Christ reign <u>in</u> your hearts,
because it is for this that you were called together as parts <u>of</u> one body.
Alleluia.

Response: Rosalie Bonighton Psalm tone: Alan Rees
Text © 1963, 1986, 1993 The Grail, England, taken from 'The Psalms, a New Inclusive Language Version',
published by HarperCollins Religious. Used by permission of A.P. Watt Ltd, London.
Response © Copyright 1998 Kevin Mayhew Ltd.
Psalm tone © Copyright Belmont Abbey, Hereford HR2 9RZ. Used by permission.

1050 15th in Ordinary Time (C)

Responsorial Psalm Psalm 68:14, 17, 30-31, 33-34, 36-37. ℟ cf. v.33

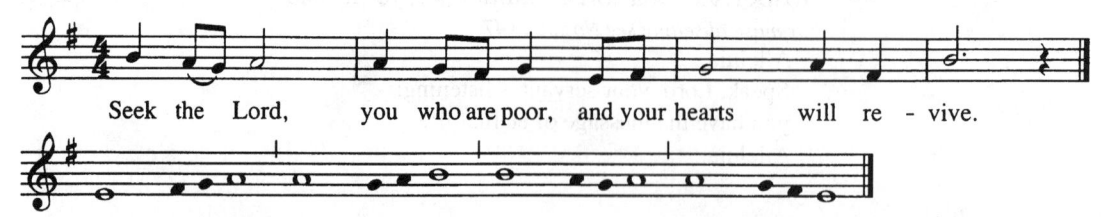

Seek the Lord, you who are poor, and your hearts will revive.

1. This is my prayer to you, my prayer <u>for</u> your favour.
   In your great love, answer <u>me</u>, O God,
   with your help that <u>never</u> fails:
   Lord, answer, for your <u>love</u> is kind.

2. As for me in my pover<u>ty</u> and pain
   let your help, O God, <u>lift</u> me up.
   I will praise God's name <u>with</u> a song;
   I will glorify him <u>with</u> thanksgiving.

Response: Andrew Moore Psalm tone: Laurence Bevenot
Text © 1963, 1986, 1993 The Grail, England, taken from 'The Psalms, a New Inclusive Language Version',
published by HarperCollins Religious. Used by permission of A.P. Watt Ltd, London.
Response © Copyright 1998 Kevin Mayhew Ltd.
Psalm tone © Copyright Ampleforth Abbey, York YO6 4EN. Used by permission.

3. The poor when they see it <u>will</u> be glad
and God-seeking hearts <u>will</u> revive;
for the Lord listens <u>to</u> the needy
and does not spurn his servants <u>in</u> their chains.

4. For God will bring <u>help</u> to Zion
and rebuild the <u>cit</u>ies of Judah.
The sons of his servants <u>shall</u> inherit it;
those who love his <u>name</u> shall dwell there.

The Gospel Acclamation is to be found below.

Alternative Responsorial Psalm   Psalm 18:8-11. R℣ v.9

The pre-cepts of the Lord glad-den the heart.

1. The law of the <u>Lord</u> is perfect,
it re<u>vives</u> the soul.
The rule of the Lord is <u>to</u> be trusted,
it gives wisdom <u>to</u> the simple.

2. The precepts of the <u>Lord</u> are right,
they glad<u>den</u> the heart.
The command of the <u>Lord</u> is clear,
it gives light <u>to</u> the eyes.

3. The fear of the <u>Lord</u> is holy,
abi<u>ding</u> for ever.
The decrees of the <u>Lord</u> are truth
and all <u>of</u> them just.

4. They are more to be de<u>sired</u> than gold,
than the pur<u>est</u> of gold
and sweeter are <u>they</u> than honey,
than honey <u>from</u> the comb.

Gospel Acclamation   John 10:27
For musical setting see Nos 36 to 47
Alleluia.
The sheep that belong to me listen to my voice, <u>says</u> the Lord,
I know them <u>and</u> they follow me.
Alleluia.

or cf. John 6:63, 68
Alleluia.
Your words are spirit, Lord, and <u>they</u> are life:
you have the message of e<u>ter</u>nal life.
Alleluia.

Response: Richard Lloyd   Psalm tone: Laurence Bevenot
Text © 1963, 1986, 1993 The Grail, England, taken from 'The Psalms, a New Inclusive Language Version',
published by HarperCollins Religious. Used by permission of A.P. Watt Ltd, London.
Response © Copyright 1998 Kevin Mayhew Ltd.
Psalm tone © Copyright Ampleforth Abbey, York YO6 4EN. Used by permission.

1051 16th in Ordinary Time (C)

Responsorial Psalm Psalm 14:2-5. ℟ v.1

The just will live in the pre-sence of the Lord.

1. Lord, who shall dwell on your <u>ho</u>ly mountain?
   Those who walk <u>with</u>out fault;
   those who <u>act</u> with justice
   and speak the truth <u>from</u> their hearts.

2. Those who do no wrong <u>to</u> their kindred
   who cast no slur <u>on</u> their neighbour,
   who hold the godless <u>in</u> disdain,
   but honour those who <u>fear</u> the Lord.

3. Those who keep their pledge, <u>come</u> what may;
   who take no interest <u>on</u> a loan
   and accept no bribes <u>against</u> the innocent.
   Such people will stand <u>firm</u> for ever.

Gospel Acclamation cf. Acts 16:14

For musical setting see Nos 36 to 47
Alleluia.
Open our <u>heart</u>, O Lord,
to accept the words <u>of</u> your Son.
Alleluia.

or cf. Luke 8:15
Alleluia.
Blessed are those who, with a noble and <u>gen</u>erous heart,
take the word of God to themselves and yield a harvest
   through their <u>per</u>severance.
Alleluia.

Response: Richard Proulx Psalm tone: Gregory Murray
Text © 1963, 1986, 1993 The Grail, England, taken from 'The Psalms, a New Inclusive Language Version',
published by HarperCollins Religious. Used by permission of A.P. Watt Ltd, London.
Response © Copyright 1998 Kevin Mayhew Ltd.
Psalm tone © Copyright Downside Abbey, Stratton-on-the-Fosse, Bath BA3 4RH. Used by permission.

1052 17th in Ordinary Time (C)

Responsorial Psalm Psalm 137:1-3, 6-8. ℟ v.8

On the day I called, you ans-wered me, O Lord.

1. I thank you, Lord, with <u>all</u> my heart,
   you have heard the words <u>of</u> my mouth.
   Before the angels <u>I</u> will bless you.
   I will adore before your <u>ho</u>ly temple.

2. I thank you for your faithful<u>ness</u> and love
   which excel all we <u>ever</u> knew of you.
   On the day I <u>called</u>, you answered;
   you increased the strength <u>of</u> my soul.

Response: Richard Lloyd Psalm tone: Laurence Bevenot
Text © 1963, 1986, 1993 The Grail, England, taken from 'The Psalms, a New Inclusive Language Version',
published by HarperCollins Religious. Used by permission of A.P. Watt Ltd, London.
Response © Copyright 1998 Kevin Mayhew Ltd.
Psalm tone © Copyright Ampleforth Abbey, York YO6 4EN. Used by permission.

3. The Lord is high yet he looks <u>on</u> the lowly
   and the haughty he knows <u>from</u> afar.
   Though I walk in the midst <u>of</u> affliction
   you give me life and frust<u>rate</u> my foes.

4. You stretch out your <u>hand</u> and save me,
   your hand will do <u>all</u> things for me.
   Your love, O Lord, <u>is</u> eternal,
   discard not the work <u>of</u> your hands.

Gospel Acclamation John 1:12, 14
For musical setting see Nos 36 to 47
Alleluia.
The Word was made flesh and <u>lived</u> among us;
to all who did accept him he gave power to become child<u>ren</u> of God.
Alleluia.

or Romans 8:15
Alleluia.
The spirit you recieved is the spi<u>rit</u> of children,
and it makes us cry out, '<u>Abba</u>, Father!'
Alleluia.

1053 18th in Ordinary Time (C)

Responsorial Psalm Psalm 89:3-6, 12-14, 17. ℟ v.1

O Lord, you have been our ref - uge from one gen-er-a-tion to the next.

1. You turn us back <u>into</u> dust
   and say: 'Go back children <u>of</u> the earth.'
   To your eyes a thousand years are like
   yesterday, <u>come</u> and gone,
   no more than a watch <u>in</u> the night.

2. You sweep us away <u>like</u> a dream,
   like grass which springs up <u>in</u> the morning.
   In the morning it springs <u>up</u> and flowers:
   by evening it wi<u>thers</u> and fades.

3. Make us know the shortness <u>of</u> our life
   that we may gain wis<u>dom</u> of heart.
   Lord, relent! Is your <u>anger</u> for ever?
   Show pity <u>to</u> your servants.

4. In the morning, fill us <u>with</u> your love;
   we shall exult and rejoice <u>all</u> our days.
   Let the favour of the Lord <u>be</u> upon us:
   give success to the work <u>of</u> our hands.

The Gospel Acclamation is to be found on the next page.

Response: Rosalie Bonighton   Psalm tone: Andrew Moore
Text © 1963, 1986, 1993 The Grail, England, taken from 'The Psalms, a New Inclusive Language Version',
published by HarperCollins Religious. Used by permission of A.P. Watt Ltd, London.
Response and Psalm tone © Copyright 1998 Kevin Mayhew Ltd.

Alternative Responsorial Psalm Psalm 94:1-2, 6-9. ℟ vv.7-8

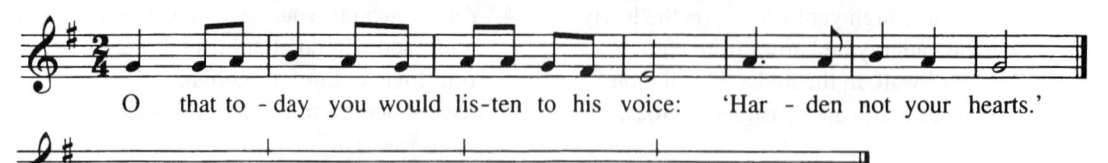

O that to-day you would lis-ten to his voice: 'Har-den not your hearts.'

1. Come, ring out our joy <u>to</u> the Lord;
   hail the <u>rock</u> who saves us.
   Let us come before him, <u>gi</u>ving thanks,
   with songs let us <u>hail</u> the Lord.

2. Come in; let us bow <u>and</u> bend low;
   let us kneel before the <u>God</u> who made us
   for he is our God, and we the people who
      belong <u>to</u> his pasture,
   the flock that is led <u>by</u> his hand.

3. O that today you would listen <u>to</u> his voice!
   'Harden not your hearts as <u>at</u> Meribah,
   as on that day at Massah in the desert, when
      your fathers put me <u>to</u> the test;
   when they tried me, though they <u>saw</u> my work.'

Gospel Acclamation cf. John 17:17   or Matthew 5:3
For musical setting see Nos 36 to 47

Alleluia.   Alleluia.
Your word is <u>truth</u>, O Lord,   How happy are the <u>poor</u> in spirit;
consecrate us <u>in</u> the truth.   theirs is the king<u>dom</u> of heaven.
Alleluia.   Alleluia.

Response and Psalm tone: Gregory Murray
Text © 1963, 1986, 1993 The Grail, England, taken from 'The Psalms, a New Inclusive Language Version',
published by HarperCollins Religious. Used by permission of A.P. Watt Ltd, London.
Response and Psalm tone © Copyright McCrimmon Publishing Co. Ltd,
10-12 High St, Great Wakering, Essex SS3 0EQ. Used by permission.

1054 19th in Ordinary Time (C)

Responsorial Psalm Psalm 32:1, 12, 18-20, 22. ℟ v.12

Hap-py the peo-ple the Lord has cho-sen as his own.

1. Ring out your joy to the Lord, <u>O</u> you just;
   for praise is fitting for <u>loy</u>al hearts.
   They are happy, whose God <u>is</u> the Lord,
   the people he has chosen <u>as</u> his own.

2. The Lord looks on those <u>who</u> revere him,
   on those who hope <u>in</u> his love,
   to rescue their <u>souls</u> from death,
   to keep them a<u>live</u> in famine.

3. Our soul is waiting <u>for</u> the Lord.
   The Lord is our help <u>and</u> our shield.
   May your love be upon <u>us</u>, O Lord,
   as we place all our <u>hope</u> in you.

Response and Psalm tone: Andrew Moore
Text © 1963, 1986, 1993 The Grail, England, taken from 'The Psalms, a New Inclusive Language Version',
published by HarperCollins Religious. Used by permission of A.P. Watt Ltd, London.
Response and Psalm tone © Copyright 1998 Kevin Mayhew Ltd.

Gospel Acclamation cf. Matthew 11:25
For musical setting see Nos 36 to 47
    Alleluia.
    Blessed are you, Father, Lord of hea<u>ven</u> and earth,
    for revealing the mysteries of the kingdom <u>to</u> mere children.
    Alleluia.

or Matthew 24:42, 44
    Alleluia.
    Stay awake <u>and</u> stand ready,
    because you do not know the hour when the Son of <u>Man</u> is coming.
    Alleluia.

1055 20th in Ordinary Time (C)

Responsorial Psalm Psalm 39:2-4, 18. ℟ v.14

Lord, come to my aid, Lord, come to my aid!

* Omit in verse 1

1. I waited, I waited <u>for</u> the Lord
   and <u>he</u> stooped down to me;
   he <u>heard</u> my cry.

2. He drew me from the <u>dead</u>ly pit,
   from the <u>mi</u>ry clay.
   He set my feet u<u>pon</u> a rock
   and made my <u>foot</u>steps firm.

3. He put a new song in<u>to</u> my mouth,
   praise <u>of</u> our God.
   Many shall <u>see</u> and fear
   and shall trust <u>in</u> the Lord.

4. As for me, wretch<u>ed</u> and poor,
   the Lord <u>thinks</u> of me.
   You are my rescu<u>er</u>, my help,
   O God, do <u>not</u> delay.

Gospel Acclamation cf. Acts 16:14
For musical setting see Nos 36 to 47
    Alleluia.
    Open our <u>heart</u>, O Lord,
    to accept the words <u>of</u> your Son.
    Alleluia.

or John 10:27
    Alleluia.
    The sheep that belong to me listen to my voice, <u>says</u> the Lord,
    I know them <u>and</u> they follow me.
    Alleluia.

Response: Colin Mawby   Psalm tone: Gregory Murray
Text © 1963, 1986, 1993 The Grail, England, taken from 'The Psalms, a New Inclusive Language Version',
published by HarperCollins Religious. Used by permission of A.P. Watt Ltd, London.
Response © Copyright 1998 Kevin Mayhew Ltd.
Psalm tone © Copyright Downside Abbey, Stratton-on-the-Fosse, Bath BA3 4RH. Used by permission.

1056 21st in Ordinary Time (C)

Responsorial Psalm Psalm 116. ℟ Mark 16:15

Go out to the whole world and pro-claim the Good News.

1. O praise the Lord, <u>all</u> you nations,
   acclaim him <u>all</u> you peoples!

2. Strong is his <u>love</u> for us;
   he is faith<u>ful</u> for ever.

Gospel Acclamation John 14:23
For musical setting see Nos 36 to 47
   Alleluia.
   If anyone loves me they will <u>keep</u> my word,
   and my Father will love them and <u>we</u> shall come to them.
   Alleluia.

   or John 14:6
   Alleluia.
   I am the Way, the Truth and the Life, <u>says</u> the Lord;
   no one can come to the Father ex<u>cept</u> through me.
   Alleluia.

Response and Psalm tone: Andrew Moore
Text © 1963, 1986, 1993 The Grail, England, taken from 'The Psalms, a New Inclusive Language Version',
published by HarperCollins Religious. Used by permission of A.P. Watt Ltd, London.
Response and Psalm tone © Copyright 1998 Kevin Mayhew Ltd.

1057 22nd in Ordinary Time (C)

Responsorial Psalm Psalm 67:4-7, 10-11. ℟ cf. v.11

In your good-ness, O God, you pre-pared a home for the poor.

1. The just shall rejoice at the <u>presence</u> of God,
   they shall exult and <u>dance</u> for joy.
   O sing to the Lord, make music <u>to</u> his name;
   rejoice in the Lord, exult <u>at</u> his presence.

2. Father of the orphan, defender <u>of</u> the widow,
   such is God in his <u>holy</u> place.
   God gives the lonely a <u>home</u> to live in;
   he leads the prisoners forth <u>into</u> freedom.

Response: Richard Proulx   Psalm tone: Andrew Moore
Text © 1963, 1986, 1993 The Grail, England, taken from 'The Psalms, a New Inclusive Language Version',
published by HarperCollins Religious. Used by permission of A.P. Watt Ltd, London.
Response and Psalm tone © Copyright 1998 Kevin Mayhew Ltd.

3. You poured down, O God, a ge<u>ne</u>rous rain:
   when your people were starved you gave <u>them</u> new life.
   It was there that your people <u>found</u> a home,
   prepared in your goodness, O God, <u>for</u> the poor.

Gospel Acclamation John 14:23
For musical setting see Nos 36 to 47
    Alleluia.
    If anyone loves me they will <u>keep</u> my word,
    and my Father will love them and <u>we</u> shall come to them.
    Alleluia.

or Matthew 11:29
    Alleluia.
    Shoulder my <u>yoke</u> and learn from me,
    for I am gentle and hum<u>ble</u> in heart.
    Alleluia.

1058 23rd in Ordinary Time (C)

Responsorial Psalm Psalm 89:3-6, 12-14, 17. ℟ v.1

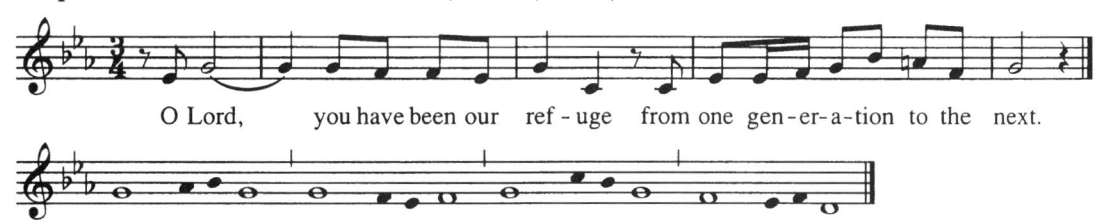

O Lord, you have been our ref-uge from one gen-er-a-tion to the next.

1. You turn us back <u>into</u> dust
   and say: 'Go back, children <u>of</u> the earth!'
   To your eyes a thousand years are like
      yesterday, <u>come</u> and gone,
   no more than a watch <u>in</u> the night.

2. You sweep us away <u>like</u> a dream,
   like grass which springs up <u>in</u> the morning.
   In the morning it springs <u>up</u> and flowers:
   by evening it wi<u>thers</u> and fades.

3. Make us know the shortness <u>of</u> our life
   that we may gain wis<u>dom</u> of heart.
   Lord, relent! Is your <u>anger</u> for ever?
   Show pity <u>to</u> your servants.

4. In the morning, fill us <u>with</u> your love;
   we shall exult and rejoice <u>all</u> our days.
   Let the favour of the Lord <u>be</u> upon us:
   give success to the work <u>of</u> our hands.

    Gospel Acclamation John 15:15
    For musical setting see Nos 36 to 47
        Alleluia.
        I call you friends, <u>says</u> the Lord,
        because I have made known to you everything I have learnt <u>from</u> my Father.
        Alleluia.

    or Psalm 118:135
        Alleluia.
        Let your face shine <u>on</u> your servant,
        and teach me <u>your</u> decrees.
        Alleluia.

Response: Rosalie Bonighton   Psalm tone: Andrew Moore
Text © 1963, 1986, 1993 The Grail, England, taken from 'The Psalms, a New Inclusive Language Version',
published by HarperCollins Religious. Used by permission of A.P. Watt Ltd, London.
Response and Psalm tone © Copyright 1998 Kevin Mayhew Ltd.

1059 24th in Ordinary Time (C)

Responsorial Psalm Psalm 50:3-4, 12-13, 17, 19. ℟ Luke 15:18

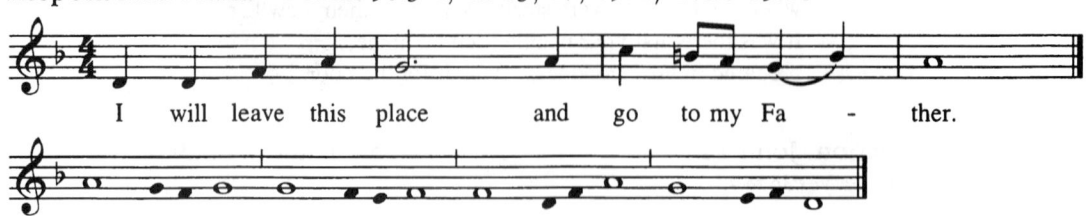

I will leave this place and go to my Father.

1. Have mercy on me, God, <u>in</u> your kindness.
   In your compassion blot out <u>my</u> offence.
   O wash me more and more <u>from</u> my guilt
   and cleanse me <u>from</u> my sin.

2. A pure heart create for <u>me</u>, O God,
   put a steadfast spi<u>rit</u> within me.
   Do not cast me away <u>from</u> your presence,
   nor deprive me of your <u>ho</u>ly spirit.

2. A pure heart create for <u>me</u>, O God,
   put a steadfast spi<u>rit</u> within me.
   Do not cast me away <u>from</u> your presence,
   nor deprive me of your <u>ho</u>ly spirit.

Gospel Acclamation cf. Ephesians 1:17, 18
For musical setting see Nos 36 to 47
   Alleluia.
   May the Father of our Lord Jesus Christ enlighten the eyes <u>of</u> our mind,
   so that we can see what hope his call <u>holds</u> for us.
   Alleluia.

or 2 Corinthians 5:19
   Alleluia.
   God in Christ was reconciling the world <u>to</u> himself,
   and he has entrusted to us the news that <u>they</u> are reconciled.
   Alleluia.

Response: Alan Rees Psalm tone: Gregory Murray
Text © 1963, 1986, 1993 The Grail, England, taken from 'The Psalms, a New Inclusive Language Version',
published by HarperCollins Religious. Used by permission of A.P. Watt Ltd, London.
Response © Copyright 1998 Kevin Mayhew Ltd.
Psalm tone © Copyright Downside Abbey, Stratton-on-the-Fosse, Bath BA3 4RH. Used by permission.

1060 25th in Ordinary Time (C)

Responsorial Psalm Psalm 112:1-2, 4-8. ℟ cf. vv.1, 7

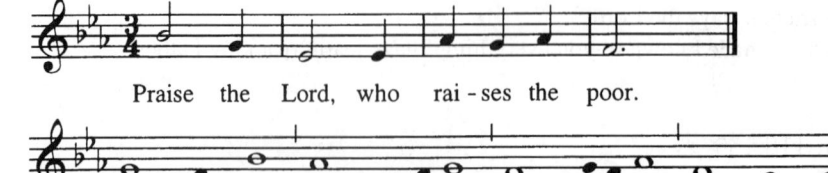

Praise the Lord, who raises the poor.

1. Praise, O servants <u>of</u> the Lord,
   praise the name <u>of</u> the Lord!
   May the name of the <u>Lord</u> be blessed
   both now and for <u>ever</u>more.

2. Who is like the <u>Lord</u>, our God,
   who has risen on high <u>to</u> his throne
   yet stoops from the heights <u>to</u> look down,
   to look down upon hea<u>ven</u> and earth?

Response and Psalm tone: Andrew Moore
Text © 1963, 1986, 1993 The Grail, England, taken from 'The Psalms, a New Inclusive Language Version',
published by HarperCollins Religious. Used by permission of A.P. Watt Ltd, London.
Response and Psalm tone © Copyright 1998 Kevin Mayhew Ltd.

3. From the dust he lifts <u>up</u> the lowly,
   from the dungheap he <u>raises</u> the poor
   to set them in the compa<u>ny</u> of rulers,
   yes, with the rulers <u>of</u> his people.

Gospel Acclamation cf. Acts 16:14
For musical setting see Nos 36 to 47
Alleluia.
Open our <u>heart</u>, O Lord,
to accept the words <u>of</u> your Son.
Alleluia.

or 2 Corinthians 8:9
Alleluia.
Jesus <u>Christ</u> was rich,
but he became poor for your sake, to make you rich <u>out</u> of his poverty.
Alleluia.

1061 26th in Ordinary Time (C)

Responsorial Psalm Psalm 145:6-10. ℟ v.2

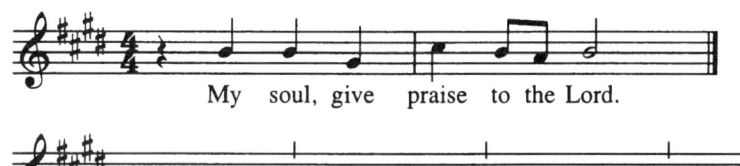

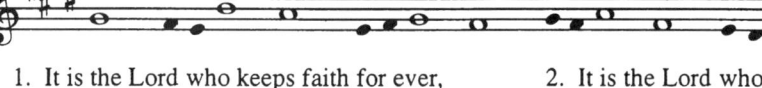

My soul, give praise to the Lord.

1. It is the Lord who keeps <u>faith</u> for ever,
   who is just to those who <u>are</u> oppressed.
   It is he who gives bread <u>to</u> the hungry,
   the Lord, who sets pri<u>son</u>ers free.

2. It is the Lord who gives sight <u>to</u> the blind,
   who raises up those who <u>are</u> bowed down.
   It is the Lord who <u>loves</u> the just,
   the Lord, who pro<u>tects</u> the stranger.

3. He upholds the wi<u>dow</u> and orphan
   but thwarts the path <u>of</u> the wicked.
   The Lord will <u>reign</u> for ever,
   Zion's God, from <u>age</u> to age.

Gospel Acclamation John 10:27
For musical setting see Nos 36 to 47
Alleluia, alleluia!
The sheep that belong to me listen to my voice, <u>says</u> the Lord,
I know them <u>and</u> they follow me.
Alleluia.

or 2 Corinthians 8:9
Alleluia.
Jesus <u>Christ</u> was rich,
but he became poor for your sake, to make you rich out <u>of</u> his poverty.
Alleluia.

Response: Rosalie Bonighton Psalm tone: Andrew Moore
Text © 1963, 1986, 1993 The Grail, England, taken from 'The Psalms, a New Inclusive Language Version',
published by HarperCollins Religious. Used by permission of A.P. Watt Ltd, London.
Response and Psalm tone © Copyright 1998 Kevin Mayhew Ltd.

1062 27th in Ordinary Time (C)

Responsorial Psalm Psalm 94:1-2, 6-9. ℟ v.9

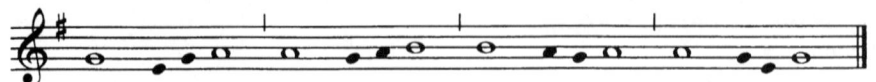

O that to-day you would listen to his voice; 'Harden not your hearts.'

1. Come, ring out our joy to the Lord;
   hail the rock who saves us.
   Let us come before him, giving thanks,
   with songs let us hail the Lord.

2. Come in; let us bow and bend low;
   let us kneel before the God who made us
   for he is our God, and we the people who
      belong to his pasture,
   the flock that is led by his hand.

3. O that today you would listen to his voice!
   'Harden not your hearts as at Meribah,
   as on that day at Massah in the desert, when
      your fathers put me to the test;
   when they tried me, though they saw my work.'

Gospel Acclamation 1 Samuel 3:9; John 6:68 or 1 Peter 1:25
For musical setting see Nos 36 to 47

Alleluia.
Speak, Lord, your servant is listening:
you have the message of eternal life.
Alleluia.

Alleluia.
The word of the Lord remains for ever:
What is this word? It is the Good News
   that has been brought to you.
Alleluia.

Response and Psalm tone: Gregory Murray
Text © 1963, 1986, 1993 The Grail, England, taken from 'The Psalms, a New Inclusive Language Version',
published by HarperCollins Religious. Used by permission of A.P. Watt Ltd, London.
Response and Psalm tone © Copyright McCrimmon Publishing Co. Ltd,
10-12 High St, Great Wakering, Essex SS3 0EQ. Used by permission.

1063 28th in Ordinary Time (C)

Responsorial Psalm Psalm 97:1-4. ℟ cf.v.2

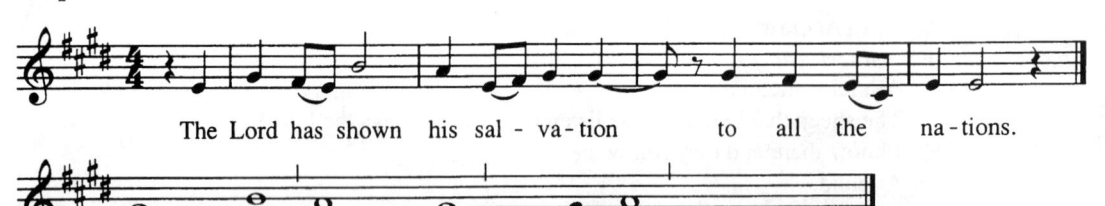

The Lord has shown his salvation to all the nations.

1. Sing a song to the Lord
   for he has worked wonders.
   His right hand and his holy arm
   have brought salvation.

2. The Lord has made known his salvation;
   has shown his justice to the nations.
   He has remembered his truth and love
   for the house of Israel.

Response: Richard Proulx Psalm tone: Andrew Moore
Text © 1963, 1986, 1993 The Grail, England, taken from 'The Psalms, a New Inclusive Language Version',
published by HarperCollins Religious. Used by permission of A.P. Watt Ltd, London.
Response and Psalm tone © Copyright 1998 Kevin Mayhew Ltd.

3. All the ends of the earth have seen
   the salvation of our God.
   Shout to the Lord all the earth,
   ring out your joy.

Gospel Acclamation cf. John 6:63, 68
For musical setting see Nos 36 to 47
   Alleluia.
   Your words are spirit, Lord, and they are life;
   you have the message of eternal life.
   Alleluia.

or cf. 1 Thessalonians 5:18
   Alleluia.
   For all things give thanks,
   because this is what God expects you to do in Christ Jesus.
   Alleluia.

1064 29th in Ordinary Time (C)

Responsorial Psalm Psalm 120. ℟ cf. v.2

Our help is in the name of the Lord who made heav-en and earth.

1. I lift up my eyes to the mountains:
   from where shall come my help?
   My help shall come from the Lord
   who made heaven and earth.

2. May he never allow you to stumble!
   Let him sleep not, your guard.
   No, he sleeps not nor slumbers,
   Israel's guard.

3. The Lord is your guard and your shade;
   at your right side he stands.
   By day the sun shall not smite you
   nor the moon in the night.

4. The Lord will guard you from evil,
   he will guard your soul.
   The Lord will guard your going and coming
   both now and for ever.

Gospel Acclamation cf. Ephesians 1:17, 18
For musical setting see Nos 36 to 47
   Alleluia.
   May the Father of our Lord Jesus Christ enlighten the eyes of our mind,
   so that we can see what hope his call holds for us.
   Alleluia.

or Hebrews 4:12
   Alleluia.
   The word of God is something alive and active;
   it can judge secret emotions and thoughts.

Response: Colin Mawby   Psalm tone: Andrew Moore
Text © 1963, 1986, 1993 The Grail, England, taken from 'The Psalms, a New Inclusive Language Version',
published by HarperCollins Religious. Used by permission of A.P. Watt Ltd, London.
Response and Psalm tone © Copyright 1998 Kevin Mayhew Ltd.

1065 30th in Ordinary Time (C)

Responsorial Psalm Psalm 32:2-3, 17-19, 23. ℟ v.7

The Lord hears the cry of the poor.

1. I will bless the Lord <u>at</u> all times,
   his praise always <u>on</u> my lips;
   in the Lord my soul shall <u>make</u> its boast.
   The humble shall hear <u>and</u> be glad.

2. The Lord turns his face a<u>gainst</u> the wicked
   to destroy their remembrance <u>from</u> the earth.
   The just call and <u>the</u> Lord hears
   and rescues them in all <u>their</u> distress.

3. The Lord is close to the <u>broken</u>-hearted;
   those whose spirit is crushed <u>he</u> will save.
   The Lord ransoms the souls <u>of</u> his servants.
   Those who hide in him shall not <u>be</u> condemned.

Gospel Acclamation cf. Matthew 11:25
For musical setting see Nos 36 to 47

Alleluia.
Blessed are you, Father, Lord of hea<u>ven</u> and earth,
for revealing the mysteries of the kingdom <u>to</u> mere children.
Alleluia.

or 2 Corinthians 5:19

Alleluia.
God in Christ was reconciling the world <u>to</u> himself,
and he has entrusted to us the news that <u>they</u> are reconciled.
Alleluia.

Response: Andrew Moore   **Psalm tone:** Laurence Bevenot
Text © 1963, 1986, 1993 The Grail, England, taken from 'The Psalms, a New Inclusive Language Version',
published by HarperCollins Religious. Used by permission of A.P. Watt Ltd, London.
Response © Copyright 1998 Kevin Mayhew Ltd.
Psalm tone © Copyright Ampleforth Abbey, York YO6 4EN. Used by permission.

1066 31st in Ordinary Time (C)

Responsorial Psalm Psalm 144:1-2, 8-11, 13-14. ℟ cf. v.1

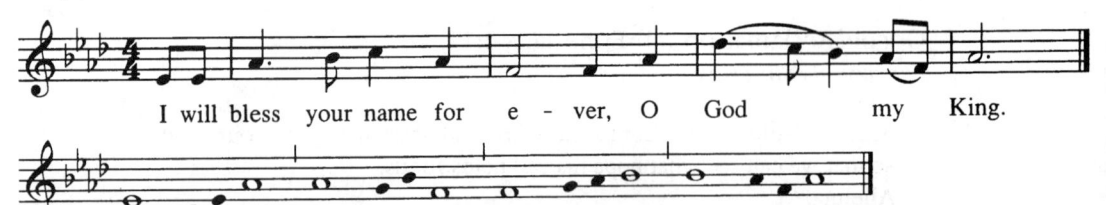

I will bless your name for e-ver, O God my King.

1. I will give you glory, O <u>God</u> my King,
   I will bless your <u>name</u> for ever.
   I will bless you day <u>after</u> day
   and praise your <u>name</u> for ever.

2. The Lord is kind and full <u>of</u> compassion,
   slow to anger, aboun<u>ding</u> in love.
   How good is the <u>Lord</u> to all,
   compassionate to <u>all</u> his creatures.

Response: Colin Mawby   **Psalm tone:** Alan Rees
Text © 1963, 1986, 1993 The Grail, England, taken from 'The Psalms, a New Inclusive Language Version',
published by HarperCollins Religious. Used by permission of A.P. Watt Ltd, London.
Response © Copyright 1998 Kevin Mayhew Ltd.
Psalm tone © Copyright Belmont Abbey, Hereford HR2 9RZ. Used by permission.

3. All your creatures shall thank you, O Lord,
   and your friends shall repeat their blessing.
   They shall speak of the glory of your reign
   and declare your might, O God.

4. The Lord is faithful in all his words
   and loving in all his deeds.
   The Lord supports all who fall
   and raises all who are bowed down.

Gospel Acclamation Luke 19:38
For musical setting see Nos 36 to 47
Alleluia.
Blessings on the King who comes in the name of the Lord!
Peace in heaven and glory in the highest heavens!
Alleluia.

or John 3:16
Alleluia.
God loved the world so much that he gave his only Son,
so that everyone who believes in him may have eternal life.
Alleluia.

1067 32nd in Ordinary Time (C)

Responsorial Psalm Psalm 16:1, 5-6, 8, 15. ℟ v.15

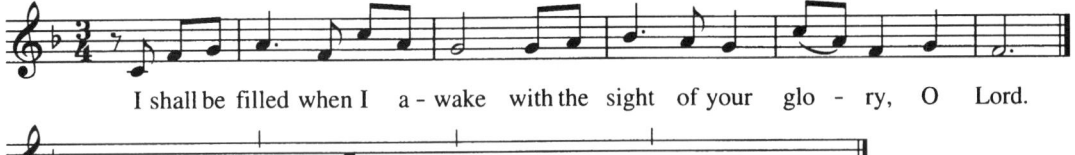

I shall be filled when I a-wake with the sight of your glo-ry, O Lord.

1. Lord, hear a cause that is just,
   pay heed to my cry.
   Turn your ear to my prayer:
   no deceit is on my lips.

2. I kept my feet firmly in your paths;
   there was no faltering in my steps.
   I am here and I call, you will hear me, O God.
   Turn your ear to me; hear my words.

3. Guard me as the apple of your eye.
   Hide me in the shadow of your wings.
   As for me, in my justice I shall see your face
   and be filled, when I awake, with the sight of your glory.

Gospel Acclamation Luke 21:36
For musical setting see Nos 36 to 47
Alleluia.
Stay awake, praying at all times
for the strength to stand with confidence
   before the Son of Man.
Alleluia.

or Revelation 1:5, 6

Alleluia.
Jesus Christ is the First-born from the dead;
to him be glory and power for ever and ever.
Alleluia.

Response: Richard Proulx Psalm tone: Alan Rees
Text © 1963, 1986, 1993 The Grail, England, taken from 'The Psalms, A New Inclusive Language Version',
published by HarperCollins Religious. Used by permission of A.P. Watt Ltd, London.
Response © Copyright 1998 Kevin Mayhew Ltd.
Psalm tone © Copyright Belmont Abbey, Hereford HR2 9RZ. Used by permission.

1068 33rd in Ordinary Time (C)

Responsorial Psalm Psalm 97:5-9. ℟ cf. v.9

The Lord comes to rule the peoples with fairness.

1. Sing psalms to the Lord <u>with</u> the harp
   with the <u>sound</u> of music.
   With trumpets and the sound <u>of</u> the horn
   acclaim the <u>King</u>, the Lord.

2. Let the sea and all with<u>in</u> it, thunder;
   the world, and <u>all</u> its peoples.
   Let the rivers <u>clap</u> their hands
   and the hills ring <u>out</u> their joy.

3. Rejoice at the presence <u>of</u> the Lord,
   for he comes to <u>rule</u> the earth.
   He will rule the <u>world</u> with justice
   and the peo<u>ples</u> with fairness.

Gospel Acclamation Luke 21:36   or Luke 21:28
For musical setting see Nos 36 to 47

Alleluia.
Stay awake, praying <u>at</u> all times
for the strength to stand with confidence
before the <u>Son</u> of Man.
Alleluia.

Alleluia.
Stand erect, hold <u>your</u> heads high,
because your liberation is <u>near</u> at hand.
Alleluia.

Response: Rosalie Bonighton   Psalm tone: Gregory Murray
Text © 1963, 1986, 1993 The Grail, England, taken from 'The Psalms, a New Inclusive Language Version',
published by HarperCollins Religious. Used by permission of A.P. Watt Ltd, London.
Response © Copyright 1998 Kevin Mayhew Ltd.
Psalm tone © Copyright McCrimmon Publishing Co. Ltd, 10-12 High St, Great Wakering, Essex SS3 0EQ. Used by permission.

1069 *Last Sunday in Ordinary Time*
Our Lord Jesus Christ, Universal King (C)

Responsorial Psalm Psalm 121:1-5. ℟ cf. v.2

I rejoiced when I heard them say: 'Let us go to God's house'

1. I rejoiced when I <u>heard</u> them say:
   'Let us go <u>to</u> God's house.'
   And now our <u>feet</u> are standing
   within your gates, <u>O</u> Jerusalem.

2. Jerusalem is built <u>as</u> a city
   strong<u>ly</u> compact.
   It is there that the <u>tribes</u> go up,
   the tribes <u>of</u> the Lord.

Response: Andrew Moore   Psalm tone: Alan Rees
Text © 1963, 1986, 1993 The Grail, England, taken from 'The Psalms, a New Inclusive Language Version',
published by HarperCollins Religious. Used by permission of A.P. Watt Ltd, London.
Response © Copyright 1998 Kevin Mayhew Ltd.
Psalm tone © Copyright Belmont Abbey, Hereford HR2 9RZ. Used by permission.

3. For Israel's <u>law</u> it is,
    there to praise <u>the</u> Lord's name.
    There were set the <u>thrones</u> of judgement
    of the <u>house</u> of David.

Gospel Acclamation Mark 11:9, 10
For musical setting see Nos 36 to 47
    Alleluia.
    Blessings on him who comes in the name <u>of</u> the Lord!
    Blessings on the coming kingdom of our <u>father</u> David!
    Alleluia.

1070 *2 February*
The Presentation of the Lord (A,B,C)

Responsorial Psalm Psalm 23:7-10. ℟ v.8

Who is the King of Glory? It is the Lord.

1. O gates, lift <u>up</u> your heads;
   grow higher, <u>an</u>cient doors.
   Let him enter, the <u>King</u> of Glory!

2. Who is the <u>King</u> of Glory?
   The Lord, the <u>mighty</u>, the valiant,
   the Lord, the vali<u>ant</u> in war.

3. O gates, lift <u>high</u> your heads;
   grow higher, <u>an</u>cient doors.
   Let him enter, the <u>King</u> of Glory!

4. Who is he, the <u>King</u> of Glory?
   He, the <u>Lord</u> of armies,
   he is the <u>King</u> of Glory.

Gospel Acclamation Luke 2:32
For musical setting see Nos 36 to 47
    Alleluia.
    The light to enligh<u>ten</u> the Gentiles
    and give glory to Isra<u>el</u>, your people.
    Alleluia.

Response and Psalm tone: Andrew Moore
Text © 1963, 1986, 1993 The Grail, England, taken from 'The Psalms, a New Inclusive Language Version',
published by HarperCollins Religious. Used by permission of A.P. Watt Ltd, London.
Response and Psalm tone © Copyright 1998 Kevin Mayhew Ltd.

1071 *24 June*
The Birth of St John the Baptist (A,B,C)

Responsorial Psalm Psalm 138:1-3, 13-15. ℟ v.14

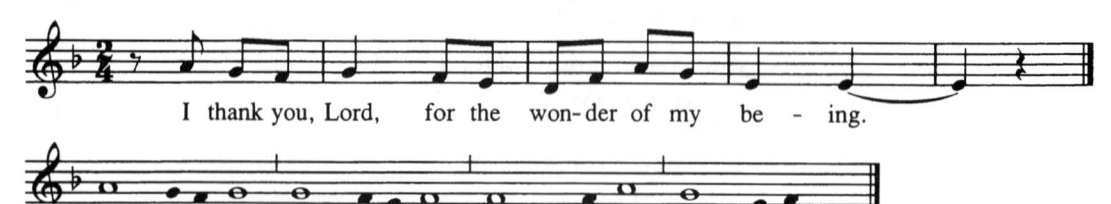

I thank you, Lord, for the wonder of my being.

1. O Lord, you search me and you know me,
   you know my resting <u>and</u> my rising,
   you discern my purpose <u>from</u> afar.
   You mark when I walk <u>or</u> lie down,
   all my ways lie o<u>pen</u> to you.

2. For it was you who cre<u>ated</u> my being,
   knit me together in my <u>mother</u>'s womb.
   I thank you for the wonder <u>of</u> my being,
   for the wonders of all <u>your</u> creation.

3. Already you <u>knew</u> my soul,
   my body held no se<u>cret</u> from you
   when I was being fa<u>shioned</u> in secret
   and moulded in the depths <u>of</u> the earth.

Gospel Acclamation cf. Luke 1:76
For musical setting see Nos 36 to 47

Alleluia.
As for you, little child, you shall be called a prophet
  of God, <u>the</u> Most High.
You shall go ahead of the Lord to prepare his <u>ways</u> before him.
Alleluia.

Response: Richard Proulx Psalm tone: Gregory Murray
Text © 1963, 1986, 1993 The Grail, England, taken from 'The Psalms, a New Inclusive Language Version',
published by HarperCollins Religious. Used by permission of A.P. Watt Ltd, London.
Response © Copyright 1998 Kevin Mayhew Ltd.
Psalm tone © Copyright Downside Abbey, Stratton-on-the-Fosse, Bath BA3 4RH. Used by permission.

1072 *29 June*
SS Peter and Paul, Apostles (A,B,C)

Responsorial Psalm Psalm 33:2-9. ℟ v.5. Alt. ℟ v.8

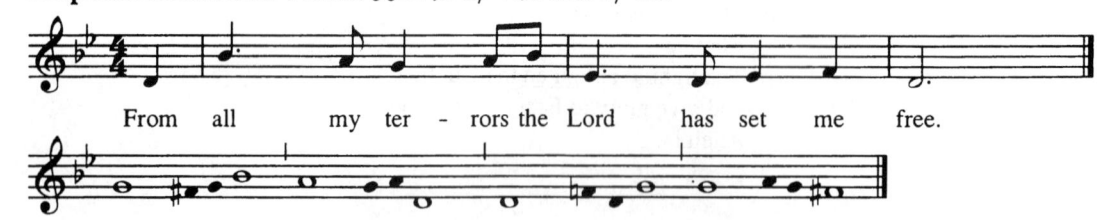

From all my terrors the Lord has set me free.

1. I will bless the Lord <u>at</u> all times,
   his praise always <u>on</u> my lips;
   in the Lord my soul shall <u>make</u> its boast.
   The humble shall hear <u>and</u> be glad.

2. Glorify the <u>Lord</u> with me.
   Together let us <u>praise</u> his name.
   I sought the Lord <u>and</u> he answered me;
   from all my terrors he <u>set</u> me free.

Response and Psalm tone: Andrew Moore
Text © 1963, 1986, 1993 The Grail, England, taken from 'The Psalms, a New Inclusive Language Version',
published by HarperCollins Religious. Used by permission of A.P. Watt Ltd, London.
Response and Psalm tone © Copyright 1998 Kevin Mayhew Ltd.

3. Look towards him <u>and</u> be radiant;
   let your faces not <u>be</u> abashed.
   When the poor cry out <u>the</u> Lord hears them,
   and rescues them from all <u>their</u> distress.

4. The angel of the Lord <u>is</u> encamped
   around those who revere <u>him</u>, to rescue them.
   Taste and see that the <u>Lord</u> is good.
   They are happy who seek re<u>fuge</u> in him.

Gospel Acclamation Matthew 16:18
For musical setting see Nos 36 to 47

Alleluia.
You are Peter and on this rock I will <u>build</u> my church.
And the gates of the underworld can never hold <u>out</u> against it.
Alleluia.

1073 *6 August*
The Transfiguration of the Lord (A,B,C)

Responsorial Psalm Psalm 96:1-2, 5-6, 9. ℟ vv.1, 9

The Lord is King, the Lord is King, most high a-bove all the earth.

1. The Lord is King, let <u>earth</u> rejoice,
   let all the coast<u>lands</u> be glad.
   His throne, jus<u>tice</u> and right.

2. The mountains <u>melt</u> like wax
   before the Lord of <u>all</u> the earth.
   All peoples <u>see</u> his glory.

3. For you indeed <u>are</u> the Lord
   most high above <u>all</u> the earth
   exalted far a<u>bove</u> all spirits.

Gospel Acclamation Matthew 17:5
For musical setting see Nos 36 to 47

Alleluia.
This is my Son, <u>the</u> Beloved,
he enjoys my favour; lis<u>ten</u> to him.
Alleluia.

Response and Psalm tone: Andrew Moore
Text © 1963, 1986, 1993 The Grail, England, taken from 'The Psalms, a New Inclusive Language Version',
published by HarperCollins Religious. Used by permission of A.P. Watt Ltd, London.
Response and Psalm tone © Copyright 1998 Kevin Mayhew Ltd.

1074 *15 August*
The Assumption of the Blessed Virgin Mary (A,B,C)

Responsorial Psalm Psalm 44:10-12, 16. ℞ v.10

On your right hand stands the queen, in gar-ments of gold.

1. The daughters of kings are a<u>mong</u> your loved ones.
   On your right stands the queen in <u>gold</u> of Ophir.
   Listen, O daughter, give ear <u>to</u> my words:
   forget your own people and your <u>father</u>'s house.

2. So will the king de<u>sire</u> your beauty.
   He is your lord, pay ho<u>mage</u> to him.
   They are escorted amid glad<u>ness</u> and joy;
   they pass within the palace <u>of</u> the king.

Gospel Acclamation
For musical setting see Nos 36 to 47
   Alleluia.
   Mary has been taken up <u>into</u> heaven;
   all the choirs of angels <u>are</u> rejoicing.
   Alleluia.

Response: Colin Mawby   Psalm tone: Alan Rees
Text © 1963, 1986, 1993 The Grail, England, taken from 'The Psalms, A New Inclusive Language Version', published by HarperCollins Religious. Used by permission of A.P. Watt Ltd, London.
Response © Copyright 1998 Kevin Mayhew Ltd.
Psalm tone © Copyright Belmont Abbey, Hereford HR2 9RZ. Used by permission.

1075 *14 September*
The Triumph of the Cross (A,B,C)

Responsorial Psalm Psalm 77:1-2, 34-38. ℞ v.7

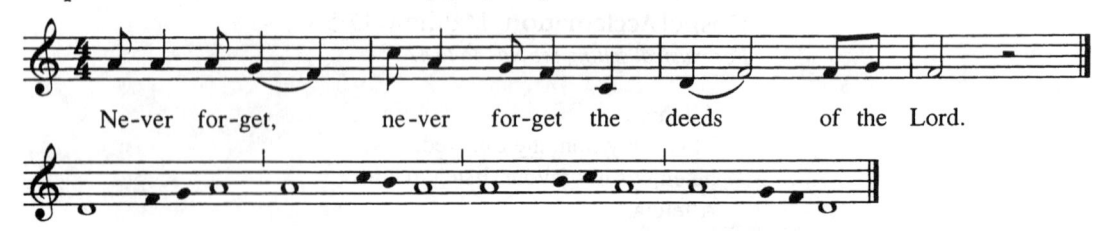

Ne-ver for-get, ne-ver for-get the deeds of the Lord.

1. Give heed, my people, <u>to</u> my teaching;
   turn your ear to the words <u>of</u> my mouth.
   I will open my mouth <u>in</u> a parable
   and reveal hidden lessons <u>of</u> the past.

2. When he slew them then <u>they</u> would seek him,
   return and seek <u>him</u> in earnest.
   They would remember that God <u>was</u> their rock,
   God the Most High <u>their</u> redeemer.

Response: Richard Lloyd   Psalm tone: Alan Rees
Text © 1963, 1986, 1993 The Grail, England, taken from 'The Psalms, A New Inclusive Language Version', published by HarperCollins Religious. Used by permission of A.P. Watt Ltd, London.
Response © Copyright 1998 Kevin Mayhew Ltd.
Psalm tone © Copyright Belmont Abbey, Hereford HR2 9RZ. Used by permission.

3. But the words they spoke <u>were</u> mere flattery;
   they lied to him <u>with</u> their lips.
   For their hearts were not <u>tru</u>ly with him;
   they were not faithful <u>to</u> his covenant.

4. Yet he who is full <u>of</u> compassion
   forgave their <u>sin</u> and spared them.
   So often he held <u>back</u> his anger
   when he might have stirred <u>up</u> his rage.

Gospel Acclamation
For musical setting see Nos 36 to 47
   Alleluia.
   We adore you, O Christ, <u>and</u> we bless you;
   because by your cross you have re<u>deem</u>ed the world.
   Alleluia

1076 *1 November*
All Saints (A,B,C)

Responsorial Psalm Psalm 23:1-6. ℟ cf. v.6

Such are the ones who seek your face, O Lord.

1. The Lord's is the earth <u>and</u> its fullness,
   the world and <u>all</u> its peoples.
   It is he who set it <u>on</u> the seas;
   on the waters he <u>made</u> it firm.

2. Who shall climb the mountain <u>of</u> the Lord?
   Who shall stand in his <u>ho</u>ly place?
   Those with clean hands <u>and</u> pure heart,
   who desire not <u>worth</u>less things.

3. They shall receive blessings <u>from</u> the Lord
   and reward from the <u>God</u> who saves them.
   Such are the <u>ones</u> who seek him,
   seek the face of the <u>God</u> of Jacob.

Gospel Acclamation Matthew 11:28
For musical setting see Nos 36 to 47
   Alleluia.
   Come to me, all you who labour and are <u>o</u>verburdened,
   and I will give you rest, <u>says</u> the Lord.
   Alleluia.

Response: Rosalie Bonighton Psalm tone: Alan Rees
Text © 1963, 1986, 1993 The Grail, England, taken from 'The Psalms, a New Inclusive Language Version',
published by HarperCollins Religious. Used by permission of A.P. Watt Ltd, London.
Response © Copyright 1998 Kevin Mayhew Ltd.
Psalm tone © Copyright Belmont Abbey, Hereford HR2 9RZ. Used by permission.

1077 *2 November*
The Commemoration of all the Faithful Departed (A,B,C)

Responsorial Psalm Psalm 26:1, 4, 7-9, 13-14. ℟ v.1. Alt. ℟ v.13

I am sure I shall see the Lord's goodness in the land of the living.

1. The Lord is my light <u>and</u> my help;
   whom <u>shall</u> I fear?
   The Lord is the stronghold <u>of</u> my life;
   before whom <u>shall</u> I shrink?

2. There is one thing I ask <u>of</u> the Lord,
   for <u>this</u> I long,
   to live in the house <u>of</u> the Lord,
   all the days <u>of</u> my life.

3. O Lord, hear my voice <u>when</u> I call;
   have mer<u>cy</u> and answer.
   It is your face, O Lord, <u>that</u> I seek;
   hide <u>not</u> your face.

4. I am sure I shall see <u>the</u> Lord's goodness
   in the land <u>of</u> the living.
   Hope in him, hold firm <u>and</u> take heart.
   Hope <u>in</u> the Lord!

Gospel Acclamation John 6:39
For musical setting see Nos 36 to 47

Alleluia.
It is my Father's will, says the Lord, that I should lose nothing of all that <u>he</u> has given me,
and that I should raise it up on <u>the</u> last day.
Alleluia.

Response: Colin Mawby   Psalm tone: Alan Rees
Text © 1963, 1986, 1993 The Grail, England, taken from 'The Psalms, a New Inclusive Language Version',
published by HarperCollins Religious. Used by permission of A.P. Watt Ltd, London.
Response © Copyright 1998 Kevin Mayhew Ltd.
Psalm tone © Copyright Belmont Abbey, Hereford HR2 9RZ. Used by permission.

1078 The Dedication of a Church

Responsorial Psalm   Psalm 45:2-3, 5-6, 8-9. ℟ v.5

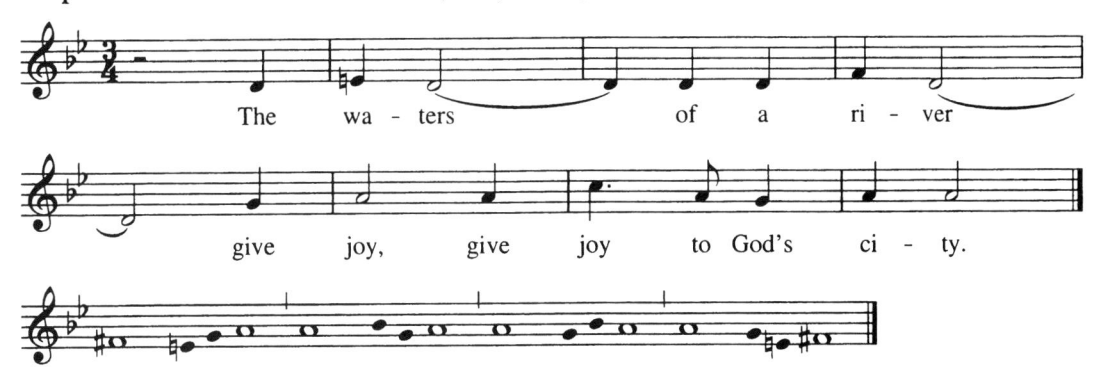

The wa - ters of a ri - ver
give joy, give joy to God's ci - ty.

1. God is for us a <u>ref</u>uge and strength,
   a helper close at hand, in time <u>of</u> distress:
   so we shall not fear though the <u>earth</u> should rock,
   though the mountains fall into the depths <u>of</u> the sea.

2. The waters of a river give joy <u>to</u> God's city,
   the holy place where the <u>Most</u> High dwells.
   God is within, it can<u>not</u> be shaken;
   God will help it at the dawning <u>of</u> the day.

3. The Lord of <u>hosts</u> is with us:
   the God of Jacob <u>is</u> our stronghold.
   Come, consider the works <u>of</u> the Lord
   the redoubtable deeds he has done <u>on</u> the earth.

Gospel Acclamation   2 Chronicles 7:16
For musical setting see Nos 36 to 47
   Alleluia.
   I have chosen and consecrated this house, <u>says</u> the Lord,
   for my name to be <u>there</u> for ever.
   Alleluia.

Response: Rosalie Bonighton   Psalm tone: Laurence Bevenot
Text © 1963, 1986, 1993 The Grail, England, taken from 'The Psalms, a New Inclusive Language Version',
published by HarperCollins Religious. Used by permission of A.P. Watt Ltd, London.
Response © Copyright 1998 Kevin Mayhew Ltd.
Psalm tone © Copyright Ampleforth Abbey, York YO6 4EN. Used by permission.

LITURGICAL
HYMNS OLD & NEW

Eucharistic Adoration with Benediction

1079 O salutaris *O saving victim* (Tune 1)

MELCOMBE LM

1. O salutaris hostia, quae caeli pandis ostium, bella premunt hostilia, da robur, fer auxilium.
2. Uni trinoque Domino sit sempiterna gloria, qui vitam sine termino nobis donet in patria. Amen.

1. O saving victim, op'ning wide
   the gate of heav'n to man below;
   our foes press on from ev'ry side;
   thine aid supply, thy strength bestow.

2. To thy great name be endless praise,
   immortal Godhead, One in Three;
   O grant us endless length of days
   in our true native land with thee. Amen.

1080 O salutaris *O saving victim* (Tune 2)

O SALUTARIS LM

1. O salutaris hostia, quae caeli pandis ostium, bella premunt hostilia, da robur, fer auxilium.
2. Uni trinoque Domino sit sempiterna gloria, qui vitam sine termino nobis donet in patria. Amen.

Text: St. Thomas Aquinas (1227-1274) trans. John Mason Neale (1818-1866)
Music: Tune 1 – Samuel Webbe (1740-1816)
Tune 2 – Abbé Duguet (c.1767)

1081 O salutaris *O saving victim* (Tune 3)

COCKFIELD GREEN LM

1. O sa - lu - ta - ris ho - sti - a, quae cæ - li pan - dis os - ti - um, bel - la pre - munt ho - sti - li - a, da ro - bur, fer au - xi - li - um.
2. U - ni tri - no - que Do - mi - no sit sem - pi - ter - na glo - ri - a, qui vi - tam si - ne ter - mi - no no - bis do - net in pa - tri - a. A - men.

1. O saving victim, op'ning wide
   the gate of heav'n to man below;
   our foes press on from ev'ry side;
   thine aid supply, thy strength bestow.

2. To thy great name be endless praise,
   immortal Godhead, One in Three;
   O grant us endless length of days
   in our true native land with thee. Amen.

1082 O salutaris *O saving victim* (Tune 4)

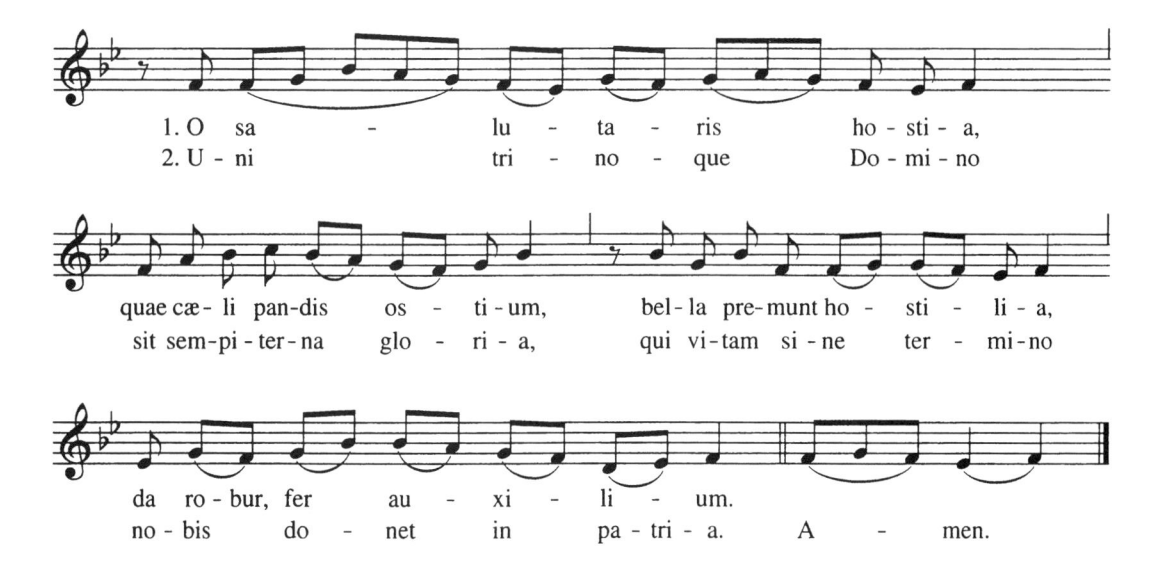

1. O sa - lu - ta - ris ho - sti - a, quae cæ - li pan - dis os - ti - um, bel - la pre - munt ho - sti - li - a, da ro - bur, fer au - xi - li - um.
2. U - ni tri - no - que Do - mi - no sit sem - pi - ter - na glo - ri - a, qui vi - tam si - ne ter - mi - no no - bis do - net in pa - tri - a. A - men.

Text: St. Thomas Aquinas (1227-1274) trans. John Mason Neale (1818-1866)
Music: Tune 3 – unknown
Tune 4 – Plainsong

1083 Tantum ergo *Come adore* (Tune 1)

ST THOMAS 87 87 87

1. Tantum ergo Sacramentum veneremur cernui:
et antiquum documentum novo cedat ritui;
præstet fides supplementum sensuum defectui.

2. Genitori, genitoque laus et jubilatio,
salus, honor, virtus, quoque sit et benedictio;
procedenti ab utroque compar sit laudatio. Amen.

A lower setting will be found at No. 509

1. Come, adore this wondrous presence,
bow to Christ, the source of grace.
Here is kept the ancient promise
of God's earthly dwelling-place.
Sight is blind before God's glory,
faith alone may see his face.

2. Glory be to God the Father,
praise to his co-equal Son,
adoration to the Spirit,
bond of love, in Godhead one.
Blest be God by all creation
joyously while ages run.

Text: St Thomas Aquinas (1227-1274) trans. James Quinn (b.1919)
Music: Samuel Webbe (1740-1816)
Text © Copyright Geoffrey Chapman, an imprint of Cassell plc, 125 Strand, London WC2R 0BB.
Used by permission.

1084 Tantum ergo *Come adore* (Tune 2)

PANGE LINGUA 87 87 87

1. Tantum ergo Sacramentum veneremur cernui:
et antiquum documentum novo cedat ritui;

2. Genitori, genitoque laus et jubilatio,
salus, honor, virtus, quoque sit et benedictio;

Text © Copyright Geoffrey Chapman, an imprint of Cassell plc, 125 Strand, London WC2R 0BB.
Used by permission.

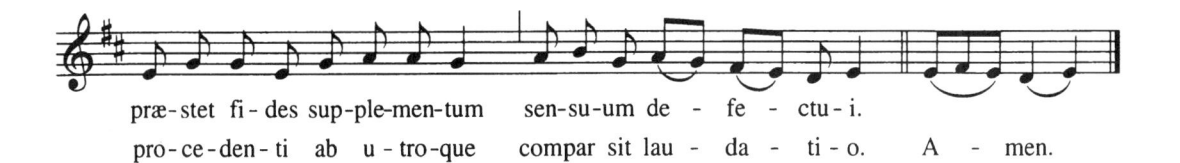

præ-stet fi-des sup-ple-men-tum sen-su-um de - fe - ctu-i.
pro-ce-den-ti ab u-tro-que compar sit lau - da - ti-o. A - men.

1. Come, adore this wondrous presence,
   bow to Christ, the source of grace.
   Here is kept the ancient promise
   of God's earthly dwelling-place.
   Sight is blind before God's glory,
   faith alone may see his face.

2. Glory be to God the Father,
   praise to his co-equal Son,
   adoration to the Spirit,
   bond of love, in Godhead one.
   Blest be God by all creation
   joyously while ages run.

Text: St Thomas Aquinas (1227-1274) trans. James Quinn (b.1919)
Music: Plainsong

1085 Adoremus in æternum

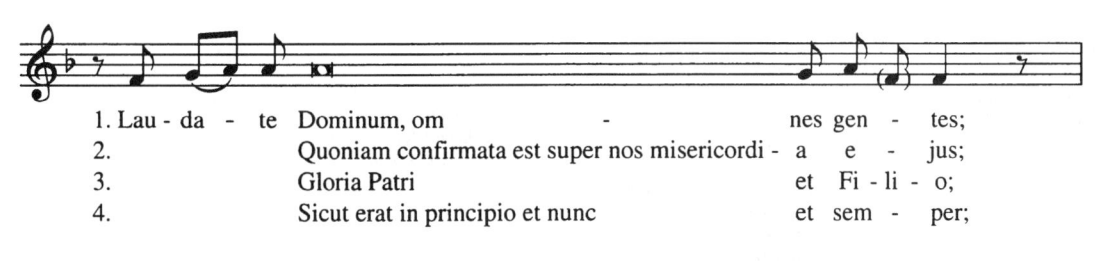

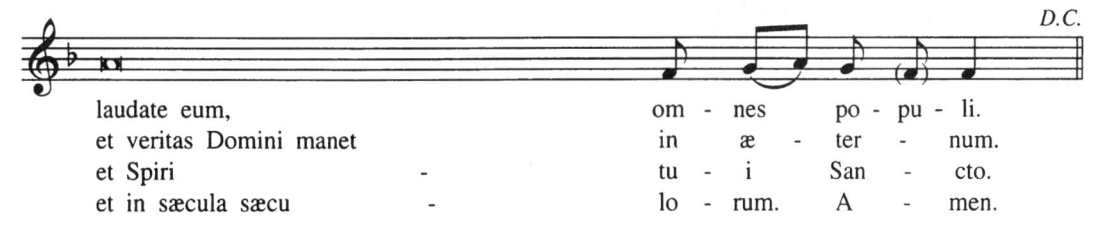

Refrain   *Fine*

A - do - re - mus in æ - ter - num san-ctis-si-mum sa - cra-men - tum.

1. Lau - da - te Dominum, om - nes gen - tes;
2. Quoniam confirmata est super nos misericordi - a e - jus;
3. Gloria Patri et Fi - li - o;
4. Sicut erat in principio et nunc et sem - per;

D.C.

laudate eum, om - nes po - pu - li.
et veritas Domini manet in æ - ter - num.
et Spiri - tu - i San - cto.
et in sæcula sæcu - lo - rum. A - men.

Text: Psalm 116
Music: Plainsong

Index of Composers and Sources of Music

Abbaye de Notre Dame de Tamié 432
Adkins, Donna 254
Ainger, Geoffrey 179
Akepsimas, Jo 732
Altrogge, Mark 748
American traditional 7, 131, 271, 353, 491, 664, 845
Andersen, Frank 250
Anderson, Mike 25, 111, 173, 212, 231, 237, 423, 436, 496, 577, 619, 654, 756,
Andrew, Diane Davis 841
Appleford, Patrick 447, 451, 828
Archer, Malcolm 14, 22, 41, 89, 422, 460

Bach, Johann Sebastian 715
Bain, James Leith Macbeth 661
Bankhead, Dave 219
Baptist traditional 518
Barnard, John 200
Basque traditional 646
Batya, Naomi 409
Beaumont, Geoffrey 522
Beaumont, Richard 374
Beethoven, Ludwig van 177, 257
Bell, John L. 181, 613, 873
Bennard, George 535
Benvenga, Nancy 884
Berthier, Jacques 18, 23, 40, 63, 721, 859, 862, 864, 865, 868, 870, 872, 874, 875, 879, 880, 881, 882, 885, 888, 889, 890, 892, 893, 897, 898
Bevenot, Laurence 47, 159
Bilbrough, Dave 425
Bodley, Se-irse 228
Bohemian Brethren's *Kirchengesang* 519
Bonighton, Rosalie 391
Booth, Paul 854
Boswell, Eric 818
Bourgeois, Louis 121
Bowater, Chris 410
Bower, J. Dykes 315
Brethorst, Leona von 381
Brierley, Michael 147

Caribbean traditional 87
Carter, Andy 206
Carter, Sydney 352, 353, 595, 730
Charu Chose Ngoni 426
Chatfield, Allen William 448
Christian Lyre, The 622
Clark, Jodi Page 440
Clarke, Jeremiah 652
Coelho, Terrye 252
Conty, Sophie 409
Conway, Anne 140, 163
Corbeil, Pierre de 478
Corners Gesangbuch 258
Craig, Ian D. 820
Croatian folk melody 579, 624
Croft, William 514, 568
Crookall, J. 414, 502
Crown of Jesus 397
Crüger, Johann 314, 497, 555, 586
Cull, Robert 545
Cutts, Peter 434
Czech traditional 819

Daniels, Danny 24
Daniels, John 143
Darros, Noel 861
Darwall, John 589
Dauermann, Stuart 758
Davies, Henry Walford 283
Davis, Katherine K. 777
Day's *Psalter* 458
Dean, Stephen 372
Décha, Paul 107, 109, 285, 343, 735
Deiss, Lucien 123, 126, 304, 407, 490, 528
DeShazo, Lynn 754
Donnelly, Noel 61, 70, 222, 377, 386, 596, 629, 631
D'Souza, Anthony 227, 321
Dufford, Bob 600, 626, 757
Duffy, Francis 27
Duffy, Philip 69, 73, 92
Duguet, Abbé 1080
Dunn, Fred 406
Dutch traditional 580, 686
Dvorak's *New World Symphony* 298
Dyer, Max 385
Dykes, John Bacchus 243, 337, 415, 547, 605, 656, 671

Elgar, Edward 395
Elvey, George Job 226, 229, 292, 323
English traditional 31, 125, 296, 331, 375, 512, 526, 537, 627, 651, 653, 699, 723, 724, 766
Espinosa, Eddie 192, 769
Este's *Psalter* 739
Ett, Casper 632
Evans, David J. 165
Ewing, Alexander 387

Farrant, Richard 130
Farrell, Bernadette 439, 585, 697
Filitz, Friedrich 19, 280, 416
Fishel, Donald 105, 657
Fitzpatrick, Gerard 58, 88, 803
Foley, John 354, 449, 525, 538, 625, 658, 696, 717
Ford, Mavis 750
French traditional 134, 135, 216, 238, 262, 293, 360, 390, 401, 418, 468, 498,
Freylinghausen's *Gesangbuch* 466
Fry, Steven 187

Gaelic traditional 193, 194, 388, 476, 680
Gammon, Bev 781
Gant, Andrew 843
Gardiner, William 479
Garrett, Les 684
Gauntlett, Henry John 536, 665, 746
Geistliche Kirchengesang 101, 103, 184
Gelineau, Joseph 137, 221, 384, 486
Genevan Psalter 121, 172
German traditional 136, 167, 196, 230, 300, 340, 399, 606
Gibbons, Orlando 162, 263, 268, 559
Gillard, Richard 169, 186
Glynn, John 342, 573, 733
Gonsalves, Peter 277

Goss, John 312, 576, 601
Greatorex, Walter 614, 644, 716, 614
Grenoble Antiphoner 153

Haas, David 204
Halesworth Setting, The 14
Handel, George Frideric 404, 591, 678
Hardwick, John 824
Harmonischer Lieder-schatz 174
Harwood, Basil 420, 517, 690
Hasidic melody 242
Hassler, Hans Leo 551, 552
Hatton, John 255
Haugen, Marty 13, 152, 217, 319, 327, 749
Havergal, William Henry 174
Haydn, Franz Joseph 579
Hayford, Jack W. 469
Hays, Lee 190
Hearn, Naida 398
Hebrew traditional 612
Heilige Seelenlust 269
Helmore, Thomas 503
Hémy, Henri Friedrich 230, 358, 500, 685
Herbert, George 636
Herrera, J. 659
Hewer, Jenny 251
Hill, David 71, 80
Himmels-Lust 473
Hind, David 813
Hintze, Jacob 146
Holst, Gustav 365, 510
Hopkins, John Henry 722
Hopkirk, James 648
Horsley, William 666
Howard, Brian 800
Howells, Herbert 119
Hughes, John 307, 338
Hunstiger, Jay F. 728
Hutchinson, Gill 809, 840
Hymn Tunes of the United Brethren 428
Hymns and Sacred Poems 516

Ignatius, Sr. Patrick 463
Inwood, Paul 26, 91, 592, 720
Ireland, John 487
Irish traditional 36, 66, 74, 99, 168, 288, 351, 450, 505, 682
Irvine, Jessie Seymour 661
Irwin, Elaine 520
Israeli traditional 9, 305, 441, 546, 655
Italian traditional 441
Iverson, Daniel 630

Jabusch, Willard F. 417, 726
Jackson, Francis 261
Jacobs, Peter 681
Jef, R. 114
Johnson, James G. 191
Johnson, Orien 799
Joncas, Michael 33, 241, 357, 660, 759
Jones, John David 408
Jones, Keri 729
Jones, Peter 20

Katholisches Gesangbuch 333, 499
Kearney, Peter 256
Kelly, Frances M. 35, 515, 578, 742
Kelly, Robert B. 82, 189, 236, 674, 683
Kendrick, Graham 118, 157, 267, 270, 322, 328, 367, 453, 471, 475, 530, 607, 679, 708, 725, 810, 826
Kirkpatrick, William James 155
Knapp, Phoebe Palmer 170
Kocher, Conrad 144

Lafferty, Karen 604, 780
Landry, Carey 94, 382, 413, 662, 711, 753, 760, 838
Larsson, John 842
Leavers, Greg 812
Lécot, Jean Paul 28, 57, 64, 78, 225, 405, 467
Leftley, Francesca 29, 320, 369, 437, 485, 564, 638
Leisentritt, J. 692
Leon, Meyez 291
Lesbordes, Alexandre 158, 373, 411, 554
Lloyd, Richard 34, 108, 171
Lockhart, Charles 182
Lundy, Damian 213, 534, 539, 558, 561
Lyra Davidica 199, 389

McCann, Christine 273, 637
McClean, Don 190
McClellan, Sue 202, 858
MacMillan, James 59, 75
Madan's Collection 689
Madden, Peter 571
Madeleine, Sister 259
Maher, W. J. 628
Mainz Gesangbuch 145
Mann, Robin 784
Mansell, David J. 394
Mark, Robin 484
Markland, Gerard 95, 160, 224, 240, 248, 379, 446, 540, 687
Marks-Smirchirch, Doug 762
Matthew, David 729
Maule, Graham 181, 613, 873
Mawby, Colin 17, 211, 712, 876
Mayhew, Kevin 77, 180, 214, 348, 433, 504, 574, 598, 618, 764, 786, 867
Mendelssohn, Felix 317
Middleton, Kathleen 791
Miller, Edward 731
Milner, Anthony 462, 495
Monk, William Henry 97, 125, 147, 316
Moore, Andrew 2, 35, 39, 43, 44, 46, 55, 104, 124, 139, 150, 265, 347, 370, 380, 402, 452, 464, 482, 556, 643, 694, 709, 741, 755
Morgan, Patricia 219
Morstad, David 787
Murphy, Colin 378
Murray, Gregory 1, 106, 128, 156, 474, 486, 523, 550, 587, 635, 677, 737, 752, 1082
Musikalisches Handbuch 541, 593, 668

Nazareth, Aniceto 175, 203, 245, 299, 306, 350, 359, 435, 562, 594, 599, 609, 642
Nichols, Kevin 362
Nicholson, Sydney Hugo 429
Norbet, Gregory 207, 223, 745
Notre Dame, A Sister of 185
Nurnbergisches Gesangbuch 264
Nystrom, Martin J. 142, 754

O'Carroll, Fintan 37
O'Connor, Roc 430
Osborne, Hayward 102
Owens, Carol 286
Owens, Jimmy 335, 772

Paculabo, John 202, 858
Paderborn Gesangbuch 549
Palestrina, G. P. da 225
Palmer, David 851
Paris Antiphoner 284, 615
Parkinson, Maria 141
Parry, Charles Hubert Hastings 132, 234, 548
Parry, Hubert 93, 138, 669
Patten, James 782
Pearsall, Robert Lucas de 512
Pereira, Marie Lydia 303, 427, 455, 542, 543, 705, 814, 825
Perry, Michael 603
Peruvian traditional 30
Petrie collection 656
Petrus, Theodoricus 508
Piae Cantiones 301, 290, 698
Pitts, William 247, 392
Plainsong 5, 6, 10, 11, 12, 42, 48, 53, 56, 79, 98, 151, 201, 287, 315, 396, 424, 495, 567, 570, 588, 597, 701, 702, 703, 1084, 1085
Polish traditional 326, 364, 492
Pond, Joanne 827
Praetorius, Michael 871
Praxis Pietatis Melica 220, 294, 295, 583, 584
Price, Alan J. 767, 804, 822

Pritchard, Rowland Huw 110
Proulx, Richard 76, 81
Psalmodia Evangelica 668
Psalmody in Miniature, Second supplement 480
Psalms Edinburgh 665
Psalms in English Metre, The 448
Purcell, Henry 197
Purday, Charles Henry 415

Rawsthorne, Noel 839
Rees, Alan 21, 90, 148, 608, 734, 778
Rheinhardt MS 569
Riada, Seán Ó 670
Richards, Hubert J. 297
Richards, Noel 117, 691, 383, 494
Richards, Tricia 383, 494
Richardson, John 188, 313, 442
Ridout, Alan 318
Rigby, Charles 310
Rimsky-Korsakov, Nicolai 85
Rizza, Margaret 4, 16, 465, 507, 610, 640, 751, 860, 863, 866, 869, 877, 878, 883, 886, 887, 891, 894, 899
Rock, Gordon 15
Rose, Peter 853
Rowlands, William Penfro 244, 332, 461
Rubin, Steffi Geiser 758
Russian traditional 700
Ryecroft, Keith 202, 858

Sayers, Susan 763, 768, 785, 816
Scheffler, Johann 269
Schein, Johann Hermann 506, 602
Scholefield, Clement Cotterill 161, 563, 650, 714
Schubert, Franz 62
Schulz, Johann Abraham Peter 718
Schutte, Dan 154, 178, 279, 376, 403, 616, 688, 744
Scottish traditional 198, 272, 489, 645, 713, 740

Select Hymns with Tunes Annext 438
Sharp, Cecil 566
Shaw, Martin 819
Shephard, Richard 176
Shrubsole, William 116
Sibelius, Jean 166, 356
Sicilian traditional 339
Smale, Ian 249, 807, 821, 823, 850
Smart, Henry 197, 444
Smith Jnr., Leonard E. 346
Smith, Henry 276
Somerset folk song 566, 731
South African traditional 82, 266, 355, 611, 710
Spiritual 633, 719, 805, 806, 815
Stainer, John 112, 218, 461
Stanfield, Francis 635
Stassen, Linda 617
Strover, Christian 797
Sullivan, Arthur Seymour 544
Swedish folk melody 529
Swiss folk melody 531

Tallis, Thomas 129, 210, 282, 363
Tambling, Christopher 271, 275, 421, 738, 792, 793, 794, 802, 808, 811, 817, 829, 831, 835, 844, 846, 848
Taylor, Cyril Vincent 459
Temple, Sebastian 122, 278, 470, 623, 639, 663, 779
Terry, Richard Runciman 149, 229, 281, 445, 511, 547, 553, 582, 704
Teschner, Melchior 113
Tochter Sion 127, 130
Toolan, Suzanne 349
Tozer, A. Edmunds 400
Traditional 208, 246, 274, 289, 302, 308, 309, 330, 560, 601, 634, 648, 667, 693, 707, 727, 761, 773, 774, 775, 789, 832, 837, 849, 856
Trotman, Wilfred 517
Turle, James 481

Turner, Roy 120
Tuttle, Carl 344

Vissing, Virginia 96, 527, 743
Vogler, George 895

Wade, John Francis 100, 501
Walker, Christopher 52, 60, 68, 565, 896
Walsh, James 54, 253
Watcyn-Jones, Peter 783
Webbe, Samuel 341, 443, 457, 509, 621, 747, 1079, 1083
Weisse, M. 454
Welch, Eric 368
Welker, Louis 483
Welsh traditional 8, 32, 67, 115, 232, 233, 334, 361, 456, 493, 736
Wesley, Samuel Sebastian 521, 647
West Indian Spiritual 472
West Indian traditional 676
Westlake, F. 532
Westley, Samuel Sebastien 513
White, Estelle 45, 83, 139, 183, 235, 329, 366, 431, 477, 524, 533, 557, 620, 706, 770, 771, 788, 801, 836
Wiener, Julian 84, 695, 795
Williams, A. 480
Williams, Ralph Vaughan 195, 209, 215, 260
Williams, Robert 311
Williams, Thomas 580
Winter, Miriam Therése 790
Wise, Joe 50, 72, 641
Württemberg Gesangbuch 393, 649, 675

Yigdal 291

Zulu traditional 426

Alphabetical Index of Tunes

Some modern tunes have not been given names. They will be found under the first line of text associated with them in the Index of First Lines.

Abbot's Leigh 459
Adeste Fideles 100, 501
Adoro te 287, 396, 424
Ag cr'ost an s'ol 670
All for Jesus 112
All things bright and beautiful 125
Amazing Grace 131, 491
Amor Dei 180
Anima Christi 628
Antioch 404
Aquinas 511
Ar hyd y nos 115, 232, 233, 334, 456, 736
As gentle as silence 557
Aurelia 513, 521, 647
Au sang qu'un Dieu 293
Aus der Tiefe (Heinlein) 264
Austria 579, 624
Ave Maria 149
Ave Maris Stella 632

Battle Hymn 271
Bellwoods 648
Belmont 479
Benedicite 102
Be still and know 164
Billing 582, 704
Birjina gaztettobat zegoen 646
Blackheath 495
Blaenwern 244, 332, 461
Blessed assurance 170
Bransle de L'Official 238
Bridegroom 434
Brixton 433
Bunessan 193, 194, 476, 680

Calypso Carol 603
Cameron's 271
Caritas 368
Carlisle 182
Caswall 19, 280
Christe Sanctorum 284, 615
Christmas morn 601
Cockfield Green 1081
Come to me 391
Come to the manger 208
Comfort 505
Confido 106
Corde Natus (Divinum Mysterium) 508
Cor Jesu 693
Corona 229, 281
Corpus Christi 397
Cradle Song 155
Cranham 365
Creator Alme Siderum 567
Cresswell 462
Crimond 661
Cross of Jesus 218
Crucifer 429
Crüger 314
Culbach 269
Cwm Rhondda 307, 338

Daily, daily 230
Darwall's 148th 589

Dawby 699
Deep calls to deep 235
Deus tuorum militum 153
Diademata 229, 292, 323
Divine Mysteries 635
Dix 144
Dominus regit me 656, 671
Donnybrook 211
Down Ampney 209
Dream Angus 198
Duke Street 255
Dundee 665

East Acklam 261
Easter Hymn 199, 389
Ebenezer (Ton-y-Botel) 580
Edgbaston 627
Eisenach 506, 602
Ellacombe 393, 649, 675
Es ist ein' ros' entsprungen 136
Evelyns 147
Eventide 97
Ewing 387
Ezechiel 446

Farrant 130
Felsham 504
Festive day 715
Finlandia 166, 356
Fons Amoris 634
Forest Green 526
Franconia 174, 648
Freedom 728

Gloria Christi 228
God be in my head 283
God rest you merry 296
Good News 561
Gopsal 591
Grace 524
Grace in Essence 181
Greek 17
Greensleeves 723, 724
Grosser Gott 333, 499
Guiting Power 200
Gwalchmai 408

Hanover 568
Hatherop Castle 522
Helmsley 438
Here I am 376
Herzliebster Jesu 555
Highwood 547
Hillsdown 370
Holy Cross 402
Horsley 666
How great thou art 529
Humility (Oxford) 601
Hyfrydol 110

In Babilone 580
In dulci jubilo 300
Irby 536
Iris 134, 135
Irish 516
Iver 685

Jacob's Ladder 766
Jerusalem 132
Jesus is Lord 394
Jubilate Deo 406

Jucunda Laudatio 587
Kelvingrove 740
Kentstown 712
King Divine 310
King's Lynn 512
Kings of Orient 722

Lambourn 452
Lasst uns erfreuen 101, 103, 184
Laudate Dominum 548, 669
Laudes 313
Laudes Mariae 230
Laurence 553
Laus Deo (Redhead No. 46) 196, 340, 606
Leoni 291
Liebster Immanuel 473
Living God 630
Living Lord 447
Llanfair 311
Lobe den Herren 220, 294, 295, 583, 584
Londonderry Air 351
Lourdes 360
Lord for tomorrow (Providence) 445
Love came down 460
Love Divine 461
Love unknown 487
Luckington 420
Lux Benigna 415
Lux perpetua 474
Lübeck 466

Maccabaeus 678
Make peace 738
Malvern 395
Mannheim 416
Maria Zu Lieben 549
Mary's child 179
Melcombe 457, 1079
Melita 243
Mendelssohn 317
Merton 316
Michael 119
Michael row the boat 773, 774, 775
Miles Lane 116
Mit Freuden Zart 519
Monkland 428
Monks Gate 331
Moscow 689

Narenza 692
Neighbour 730
Nicaea 337, 605
Noel 375
Noel Nouvelet 390, 468, 498
Nun Danket 497, 586

Ode to Joy 177, 257
O King of Might 523
Old Hall Green 502
Old Hundredth 121, 172
Omni die 258
Omni die dic Mariae 230
One cold night 539
Orientis partibus 478
O Salutaris 1080
O Sanctissima 339
O Waly Waly 566, 731

Pange Lingua 570, 1084
Parthenos 618
Passion Chorale 551, 552
Pastor Bonus 677
Personent Hodie (Theodoric) 290
Picardy 262, 418
Pinner 517
Plainsong 315
Plaisir d'amour 560
Pleading Saviour 622
Praise my soul 312, 576
Princethorpe 247, 392
Puer nobis 698

Ravenshaw 454
Regent Square 197, 444
Rejoice, Rejoice 152
Reproaches 534
Repton 93, 138, 234
Resonet in laudibus 399
Rockingham 480, 731
Royal Oak 125

Sacrum Convivium 148
Salve festa dies 195
Salzburg 146
Sanctissimum 635
Sandon 415
Sawston 246
Seek ye first 604
Shine, Jesus, shine 453
Sine Nomine 260
Slane 168, 288, 450
Song 1 268, 559
Song 34 (Angels' Song) 263
Song 46, 162
Southwell (Damon) 448
St Andrew 727
St Anne 514
St Bernard 127, 130
St Catherine (Tynemouth) 500
St Clement 161, 563, 650, 714
St Columba 99
St Denio 361, 493
St Flavian 458
St Fulbert 665, 746
St George's Windsor 226
St Gertrude 544
St Magnus 652
St Patrick 308
St Theodulph 113
St Thomas 443, 509, 621
St Ursula 532
Stabat Mater 145
Standish 315
Stella 309
Stille Nacht 614
Strength and stay 547
Stuttgart 167
Sunset 636
Surrexit 156
Sussex Carol 537
Swavesey 414

Tallis's Canon 129, 282, 363
Tallis's Ordinal 210
Te Lucis 495
Tempus adest floridum 301
Thainake 613
Thaxted 510
The Call 215

The first Nowell 651
The holly and the ivy 653
The old rugged cross 535
This is your God 475
This joyful Eastertide (Vreuchten) 686
Thornbury 517, 690
Tozer 400

Truro 668
Turris Davidica 358

Ubi Caritas 737

Vaughan 442
Venez, Divin Messie 216
Veni Emmanuel 503
Veni Sancte Spiritus 341

Verbum Dei 347

Was Lebet 569
Were you there 719
Westminster 481
Westminster Abbey 197
Westminster Old 188
Whence is that goodly fragrance? 401

Willsbridge 512
Winchester New 541, 593, 668
Winchester Old 739
Wir pflügen 718
Woodlands 644, 716
Wzlobie lezy 326, 364

Ye banks and braes 713

Metrical Index of Tunes

Some modern tunes, because of their free rhythmic patterns, are not listed in this index.

4 6 6 5
Plaisir d'amour 560

4 6 88 4
Laurence 553

4 6 886
Edgbaston 627

4 10 4 10 and Refrain
Deep calls to deep 235

55 53 D
Bunessan 193, 194, 476, 680

65 63
Grace in Essence 181

65 65
Caswall 19, 280
Holy Cross 402

65 65 66 65
Monks Gate 331

65 65 and Refrain
Lourdes 360
Make peace 738

65 65 D
Evelyns 147
Laudes 313
Princethorpe 247, 392

65 65 D and Refrain
St Gertrude 544

664 6664
Moscow 689

666 66 and Refrain
Personent Hodie (Theodoric) 290

66 8 D and Refrain
The old rugged cross 535

66 11 D
Down Ampney 209

66 65 D and Refrain
This is your God 475

66 66
Ave Maris Stella 632
Ravenshaw 454

66 66 44 44
Darwall's 148th 589
Love unknown 487

66 66 88 6
Divine Mysteries 635
Sanctissimum 635

66 66 and Refrain
Gopsal 591

66 84 D
Leoni 291

66 86 SM (Short Metre)
Bellwoods 648
Carlisle 182
Franconia 174, 648
Narenza 692
Southwell (Damon) 448

66 86 66 86 DSM (Double Short Metre)
Corona 229, 281
Diademata 229, 292, 323
Donnybrook 211

67 67
Love came down 460

67 67 66 66
Nun Danket 497, 586

67 67 and Refrain
This joyful Eastertide (Vreuchten) 686

74 74
Michael row the boat 773, 774, 775

74 74 D
Gwalchmai 408

75 75 44 75
Living God 630

76 76
Mary's child 179

76 76 77 76
Kelvingrove 740

76 76 676
Es ist ein' ros' entsprungen 136

76 76 and Refrain
St Theodulph 113

76 76 and Refrain
All things bright and beautiful 125
Cor Jesu 693
Royal Oak 125
Vaughan 442

76 76 D
Aurelia 647, 513, 521
Crüger 314

Ellacombe 393, 649
Ewing 387
Hatherop Castle 522
King's Lynn 512
O King of Might 523
Passion Chorale 551, 552
Pinner 517
Tempus adest floridum 301
Thornbury 517, 690
Turris Davidica 358
Willsbridge 512

76 76 D and Refrain
Wir pflügen 718

76 77
Puer nobis 698

76 86 Irregular and Refrain
The holly and the ivy 653

77 74 D and Refrain
Here I am 376

77 75 D
Benedicite 102

77 77
Aus der Tiefe (Heinlein) 264
Culbach 269
Lübeck 466
Monkland 428
Orientis partibus 478
The Call 215

77 77 77
Dix 144

77 77 and Alleluias
Easter Hymn 389
Llanfair 311

77 77 and Refrain
Bransle de L'Official 238
Christmas morn 601
Humility (Oxford) 601
Iris 135
King Divine 310
Westminster Old 188

77 77 D
Easter Hymn 199
St George's Windsor 226
Salzburg 146

77 77 D and Refrain
Mendelssohn 317

777 11
Resonet in laudibus 399

777 D
Veni Sancte Spiritus 341

77 87 87 6 and Refrain
Battle Hymn 271

78 76 and Refrain
Venez, Divin Messie 216

78 78 77
Grosser Gott 333

7 8 9 8 and Refrain
Reproaches 534

84 84
Lord for tomorrow (Providence) 445

84 84 88 84
Ar hyd y nos 115, 232, 233, 334, 456, 736

84 84 888 4
East Acklam 261

85 85 and Refrain
Guiting Power 200

86 86 CM (Common Metre)
Amazing Grace 131, 491
Antioch 404
Belmont 479
Billing 582, 704
Brixton 433
Crimond 661
Dundee 665
Farrant 130
Horsley 666
Irish 516
Miles Lane 116
St Anne 514
St Bernard 127, 130
St Flavian 458
St Fulbert 665, 746
St Magnus 652
Tallis's Ordinal 210
Tozer 400
Westminster 481
Winchester Old 739

86 86 86 and Refrain
God rest you merry 296

86 86 86 86 DCM (Double Common Metre)
Ellacombe 675
Forest Green 526
Noel 375
St Andrew 727

86 86 87 86
Iver 685

86 86 88
Verbum Dei 347

86 86 and Refrain
Festive day 715
St Ursula 532

86 88 6
Repton 93, 138, 234

86 96 and Refrain
Felsham 504

87 87
All for Jesus 112
Cross of Jesus 218
Dominus regit me 656, 671
Merton 316
Lambourn 452
Laus Deo (Redhead No. 46) 196, 340, 606
Love Divine 461
Omni die 258
St Columba 99
Stuttgart 167

87 87 6
Bridegroom 434

87 87 33 7
Michael 119

87 87 47
Cwm Rhondda 307, 338
Helmsley 438

87 87 68 67
Greensleeves 723, 724

87 87 77
Irby 536

87 87 87
Kentstown 712
Mannheim 416
Pange Lingua 570, 1084
Picardy 262, 418
Praise, my soul 312, 576
Regent Square 197, 444
St Thomas 443, 509, 621, 1083
Sacrum Convivium 148
Westminster Abbey 197

87 87 87 7
Corde Natus (Divinum Mysterium) 508

87 87 88 77
Mit Freuden Zart 519
Wzlobie lezy 326, 364

87 87 and Refrain
Come to me 391
Iris 134
Parthenos 618
Swavesey 414

87 87 D
Abbot's Leigh 459
Au sang qu'un Dieu 293
Austria 579, 624
Blaenwern 244, 332, 461
Daily, daily 230
Ebenezer (Ton-y-Botel) 580
Freedom 728
Hyfrydol 110
In Babilone 580
Laudes Mariae 230
Ode to Joy 177, 257
Omni die dic Mariae 230
Pleading Saviour 622

88 44 88 and Alleluias
Lasst uns erfreuen 101, 103, 184

88 86 and Refrain
Kings of Orient 722

88 87 88 86
Jubilate Deo 406

887
Stabat Mater 145

888
Be still and know 164

888 and Alleluias
O filii et filiae 747
Old Hall Green 502
Surrexit 156

88 88 LM (Long Metre)
Blackheath 495
Cockfield Green 1081
Creator Alme Siderum 567
Dawby 699
Deus tuorum militum 153
Duke Street 255
Grosser Gott 499
Eisenach 506, 602
Melcombe 457, 1079
Old Hundredth 121, 172
O Salutaris 1080
O Waly Waly 566, 731
Rockingham 480, 731
Song 34 (Angels' Song) 263
Tallis's Canon 129, 282, 363
Te Lucis 495
Truro 668
Winchester New 541, 593, 668

88 88 and Refrain LM
(Long Metre) and Refrain
Corpus Christi 397
Sawston 246
Veni Emmanuel 503

88 88 8
Malvern 395

88 88 88
Melita 243
St Catherine (Tynemouth) 500
Sunset 636
Stella 309
Sussex Carol 537

88 88 88 88 DLM
(Double Long Metre)
Grace 524
Jerusalem 132
Ye banks and braes 713

88 88 98 11 7
Ezechiel 446

88 88 and Refrain
Gloria Christi 228

88 97 and Refrain
Cresswell 462

97 87
One cold night 539

98 98
St Clement 161, 563, 650, 714

98 98 87 89
Rejoice, Rejoice 152

98 98 98
Whence is that goodly fragrance? 401

99 10 10 6 and Refrain
Shine, Jesus, shine 453

99 99 10 9
Pastor Bonus 677

9 8 88 83
Living Lord 447

10 4 10 4 10 10
Lux Benigna 415
Sandon 415

10 4 66 66 10 4
Luckington 420

10 7 10 7 and Refrain
Jucunda Laudatio 587

10 9 12 10
As gentle as silence 557

10 10 10 4
Sine Nomine 260

10 10 10 10
Anima Christi 628
Eventide 97
Slane 168, 288
Woodlands 644, 716

10 10 10 10 10 10
Finlandia 166, 356
Song 1 162, 286, 559

10 10 11 11
Hanover 568
Laudate Dominum 548, 669

10 10 12 10
Birjina gaztettobat zegoen 646

10 10 14 10
Were you there 719

10 10 and Refrain
Crucifer 429

10 11 11 11 and Refrain
Maccabaeus 678

10 11 11 12
Slane 450

11 10 11 10
Highwood 547
Liebster Immanuel 473
Strength and stay 547

11 10 11 10 11 10 11 12
Londonderry Air 351

11 10 11 10 88 and Refrain
Fons Amoris 634

11 10 11 10 and Refrain
Ave Maria 149
How great thou art 529

11 11 8 9 and Refrain
Hillsdown 370

11 11 10 11
Noel nouvelet 390, 498

11 11 11 5
Christe Sanctorum 284, 615
Herzliebster Jesu 555

11 11 11 11
Adoro Te 287, 396
Aquinas 511
Comfort 505
Cradle Song 155
Maria Zu Lieben 549
Noel nouvelet 468
St Denio 361, 493
Thainake 613

11 11 11 11 and Refrain
Jacob's Ladder 766
St Patrick 308

11 12 11 12 and Refrain
Jesus is Lord 394

11 12 12 10
Nicaea 337, 605

12 4 11 5
Confido 106

12 12 12 12 and Refrain
Ubi Caritas 737

12 12 and Refrain
Lux perpetua 474

13 8 5 9 8 and Refrain
Caritas 368

13 10 13 10
Was Lebet 569

13 10 and Refrain
Neighbour 730

13 13 13
Amor Dei 180

13 13 13 13 13 13
Thaxted 510

14 14 4 7 8
Lobe den Herren 220, 294, 295, 583, 584

15 15 15 7 and Refrain
Cameron's 271

Irregular
Adeste fideles 100
Ag cr'ost an s'ol 670
Blessed assurance 170
Come to the manger 208
Cranham 365
Dream Angus 198
God be in my head 283
Good News 561
In dulci jubilo 300
O Sanctissima 339
Plainsong 315
Standish 315
Stille Nacht 614
Seek ye first 604
The first Nowell 651

Irregular and Refrain
Adeste Fideles 501
Calypso Carol 603
Salve festa dies 195

Index of Authors and Sources of Text

Aaronic Blessing 867
Adam, David 863
Adkins, Donna 254
Ainger, Geoffrey 179
Alexander, Cecil Frances 125, 536, 666
Alford, Henry 226
Alighieri, Dante 468
Alstyne, Frances Jane van 170
Altrogge, Mark 250, 748
Anderson, Mike 25, 111, 173, 212, 231, 237, 423, 436, 496, 577, 619, 654, 756
Andrew, Diane Davis 841
Anima Christi 628
Appleford, Patrick 447, 451, 828
Aquinas, St Thomas 287, 396, 509, 511, 570, 1079, 1080, 1081, 1082, 1083, 1084
Arnold, J. 389

Baker, Henry Williams 454, 548, 656
Ballantine, John 65
Bankhead, Dave 219
Baring-Gould, Sabine 646
Barrett, E. M. 727
Batya, Naomi 409
Beaumont, Richard 374
Bell, John L. 181, 198, 288, 388, 390, 613, 740, 873
Bell, Maurice F. 519
Bennard, George 535
Benvenga, Nancy 884
Bilbrough, Dave 425
Billington, Sandra Joan 560, 612
Bishop Synesius 448
Bittleston, Henry 230
Blake, William 132
Blount, Walter Kirkham 184
Boberg, Karl 529
Bode, John E. 522
Bonar, Horatius 162
Book of Hours 283
Booth, Paul 854
Borthwick, Jane L. 166
Boswell, Eric 818
Bourne, George Hugh 444
Bowater, Chris 410
Bowers, John E. 195
Brennan, Patrick 310
Brethorst, Leona von 381
Bridges, Matthew 229, 479
Bridges, Robert 119, 552
Brooks, Philip 526
Budry, Edmond Louis 678
Bunyan, John 331
Burgundy, A. 184
Byrne, Mary 168

Campbell, Jane Montgomery 718
Campbell, Robert 146, 648, 746
Caribbean traditional 87
Carter, Andy 206, 491, 352, 353, 595, 730
Caswall, Edward 127, 145, 167, 280, 313, 316, 341, 400, 499, 511, 521, 601, 627, 685, 692, 747, 896
Catholicum Hymnologium 692
Cennick, John 438

Chadwick, James 134, 135
Chandler, John 541
Chartres, St Fulbert of 746
Chesterton, Gilbert Keith 512
Christie, A. J. 693
Christmas Carols, Ancient and Modern 651
Clark, Jodi Page 440
Claudius, Matthias 718
Cluny, St Bernard of 230
Cockett, Michael 106, 259, 368, 620, 764
Coelho, Terrye 252
Coffin, Charles 541, 648
Coles, Vincent Stuckey Stratton 129
Collins, Terence 8
Colvin, Tom 426
Compleat Psalmodist 389
Conlon, Anne 853
Connaughton, Luke 180, 433, 462, 587, 677
Conty, Sophie 409
Conway, Anne 140, 163
Cotterill, Thomas 311
Craig, Ian D. 820
Crossman, Samuel 487
Crum, John Macleod Campbell 498
Crux fidelis 244
Cull, Robert 545

Dale, Alan 297
Damascus, St John of 649
Daniel 3 890
Daniel, Ivor J. E. 196
Daniels, Danny 24
Daniels, John 143
Dauermann, Stuart 758
Davis, Katherine K. 777
Daw Jr, Carl P. 434
De Contemptu Mundi 387
Dean, Stephen 372
Dearmer, Percy 290, 331, 698
Deiss, Lucien 123, 126, 304, 407, 490, 528
DeShazo, Lynn 754
Discendi, amor santo 387
Dix, William Chatterton 110, 144, 723
Doddridge, Philip 480
Donnelly, Noel 222, 377, 386, 629, 631
Draper, William Henry 103
D'Souza, Anthony 227, 321
Dudley-Smith, Timothy 257, 291, 644
Dufford, Bob 600, 626, 757
Duffy, Philip 92
Dufner, Delores 391, 424, 724, 728
Dunn, Fred 406
Dyer, Max 385

Edmeston, James 416
Ellerton, John 650
English carol 18th century 766
English traditional 296, 537
Espinosa, Eddie 192, 769
Evans, David J. 165

Faber, Frederick William 188, 246, 392, 393, 397, 481, 502, 549, 636

Farjeon, Eleanor 476
Farrell, Bernadette 439, 585
Fishel, Donald 105, 657
Fitzpatrick, Gerard 803
Foley, Brian 340, 457, 602,
Foley, John 354, 449, 525, 538, 625, 658, 696, 717
Foley, Margaret 732
Ford, Mavis 750
Forster, Michael 19, 31, 32, 66, 67, 93, 116, 129, 138, 148, 155, 161, 167, 172, 177, 211, 225, 230, 233, 264, 268, 271, 275, 292, 294, 295, 298, 312, 323, 332, 334, 338, 356, 363, 373, 402, 421, 464, 480, 495, 507, 513, 544, 555, 563, 567, 580, 589, 605, 610, 618, 624, 669, 671, 675, 704, 712, 714, 716, 736, 737, 782, 792, 793, 794, 802, 808, 811, 817, 829, 831, 835, 843, 844, 846, 848
Fortunatus, Venantius 621, 668
Foundling Hospital Collection 579
Franz, Ignaz 333
Fry, Steven 187
Fullerton, William Young 351

Gaelic Blessing 878
Gammon, Bev 781
Garrett, Les 684
Gelineau, Joseph 221, 486
Gerhardt, Paul 552
Gillard, Richard 169, 186
Glynn, John 342, 378, 573, 733
Gonsalves, Peter 277
Gowans, John 842
Grail translation 411, 432, 592, 599
Grant, Robert 568
Greally, John 281, 606
Green, Fred Pratt 261
Gurney, Dorothy F. 547

Haas, David 204
Hall's, William John 174
Hamson, Anthony 9
Hardwick, John 824
Hatch, Edwin 182
Haugen, Marty 13, 152, 217, 319, 327, 749
Hayes, Pamela 465, 887
Hayford, Jack W. 469
Hearn, Naida 398
Heber, Reginald 337
Herbert, George 215, 408, 420
Hermann the Lame 128, 597
Hernaman, Claudia Frances 458
Hewer, Jenny 251
Hind, David 813
Hine, Stuart K. 529
Hodgetts, Michael 228, 285
Holloway, Jean 272, 456, 645, 773
Hoog, Pierre-Marie 721
Hopkins, Gerard Manley 287
Hopkins, John Henry 722
How, William Walsham 260
Howard, Brian 800
Hoyle, Richard Birch 678
Hull, Eleanor 168
Hume, Ruth Fox 98

Hurley, Denis E. 99
Hutchinson, Gill 809, 840

Ignatius, Sr. Patrick 463
Inwood, Paul 91, 720
Iona Community, the 713
Irish traditional 35, 36
Irwin, Elaine 520
Iverson, Daniel 630

Jabusch, Willard F. 242, 326, 471, 546, 655, 715, 726
Jeffery, Graham 786
Johnson, James G. 191
Johnson, Orien 799
Joncas, Michael 357, 660, 759
Jones, Keri 729
Josephine, Sister Marie 634

Kaan, Fred 262
Kearney, Peter 256
Keble, John 174
Kelly, Frances M. 515, 578,
Kelly, Robert B. 49, 82, 189, 201, 221, 667, 674, 721, 732
Kelly, Thomas 652
Ken, Thomas 282
Kendrick, Graham 118, 157, 267, 270, 322, 328, 367, 453, 471, 475, 530, 607, 679, 708, 725, 810, 826
Kethe, William 121
Kirkpatrick, William James 155
Kitchin, George William 429
Knox, Ronald Arbuthnott 156, 468, 493, 551
Konstant, David 348

Lafferty, Karen 604, 780
Landry, Carey 94, 382, 413, 662, 711, 753, 760, 838
Langton, Stephen 341, 702, 894, 896
Lawrence, W. R. 64, 158, 343, 405, 554, 659, 735
Lectionary, The 33, 34
Lécot, Jean-Paul 57, 107, 285, 343, 405, 554, 659, 735
Leavers, Greg 812
Leeson, Jane Elizabeth 199, 466
Leftley, Francesca 29, 305, 320, 369, 437, 485, 564, 638
Lingard, John 309
Littledale, Richard F. 209
Liturgy of St James 418
Luke 1:46 877
Lundy, Damian 48, 53, 95, 96, 114, 160, 205, 213, 266, 339, 355, 370, 384, 395, 399, 412, 441, 478, 488, 492, 531, 534, 539, 558, 561, 566, 672, 681, 687
Lutheran Book of Worship 101
Lyte, Henry Francis 97, 576

MacBean, Lachlan 193
McCann, Christine 273, 637
McClellan, Sue 858
MacDonald, Mary 193
MacLeod, Fiona 236
Madan, Martin 317, 438

Madden, Peter 571
Maintzisch Gesangbuch 506
Mann, Robin 784
Mansell, David J. 394
Marchal, Michael 241
Mark, Robin 484
Markland, Gerard 224, 240, 248, 379, 446, 540
Marks-Smirchirch, Doug 762
Marriott, John 689
Marshall-Taylor, Geoffrey 841
Massey, Christopher 819
Matthew, David 729
Maule, Graham 181, 198, 288, 388, 390, 613, 740, 873
Maurus, Rabanus 210, 701
Mawby, Colin 876
Mayhew, Kevin 214, 433, 504, 574
Meine Hoffnung stener feste 119
Memorial Acclamation In paradisum 241
Middleton, Kathleen 791
Milman, Henry Hart 593
Milton, John 428
Mohr, Joseph 614
Monsell, John Samuel Bewley 255, 569
Montgomery, James 314
Morgan, Patricia 219
Morrison, John 665
Morstad, David 787
Moultrie, G. 418
Murray, Gregory 474, 486, 523, 752

Nazareth, Aniceto 133, 175, 203, 245, 299, 306, 350, 359, 435, 562, 594, 609, 642
Neale, John Mason 113, 197, 300, 301, 387, 503, 508, 509, 649, 668, 1079, 1080, 1081, 1082
Neander, Joachim 119, 583, 584
Newbolt, Michael Robert 429
Newman, John Henry 247, 258, 415, 582
Newton, John 131
Nichols, Kevin 244, 362, 452
Noel, Caroline Maria 147
Norbet, Gregory 207, 223, 745
Notre Dame, A sister of 185
Nyberg, Anders 611, 710
Nye, Anthony 516, 517
Nystrom, Martin J. 142, 754

O sola magnarum urbium 167
Oakeley, Frederick 501, 586
O'Connor, Roc 430

Office of Night Prayer, The 598
Omni die dic Mariae 230
Oosterhuis, Huub 742
Osborne, Hayward 102
Osler, Edward 579
Owens, Carol 286
Owens, Jimmy 335, 681, 772
Oxenham, H. N. 315

Paculabo, John 202, 858
Palmer, David 851
Parkinson, Maria 141
Peacey, John Raphael 153
Pearson, Keith D. 401
Pereira, Marie Lydia 303, 427, 455, 542, 543, 705, 814, 825
Perronet, Edward 116
Perry, Michael 347, 510, 603
Peruvian traditional 30
Petti, Anthony G. 136
Philip, Sister Mary of 216
Plumptre, Edward Hayes 690
Pond, Joanne 827
Price, Alan J. 767, 804, 822
Prudentius, Aurelius Clemens 167, 508

Quincunque centum quaeritis 127
Quinn, James 194, 220, 232, 263, 396, 550, 596, 615, 670, 680, 682, 1083, 1084

Reed, Edith Margaret Gellibrand 364
Reeks, Joseph W. 414
Rees, John 131
Renewal of Baptismal Promises 683
Richards, Hubert J. 105, 108, 171, 176, 297, 643, 783
Richards, Noel 383, 494, 691
Richards Tricia 117, 383, 494
Riley, Harold 284
Rimaud, Didier 732
Rinkart, Martin 497
Rite of Confirmation 608
Rizza, Margaret 640, 751, 869, 887, 899
Roman Missal 1, 2, 4, 5, 6, 10, 11, 12, 14, 15, 16, 17, 18, 20, 21, 22, 27, 28, 56, 58, 59, 60, 61, 62, 63, 68, 69, 70, 73, 74, 75, 76, 79, 80, 81, 88, 89, 90, 861
Rossetti, Christina Georgina 365, 460
Rowthorn, Jeffrey 459
Rubin, Steffi Geiser 758

Ryecroft, Keith 202, 858

Salazar, George 26
Sandys, William 651
Saward, Michael 200
Sayers, Susan 124, 265, 318, 380, 482, 556, 694, 709, 741, 755, 763, 768, 785, 816
Schlegal, Katherina von 166
Schlör, Aloys 693
Schutte, Dan 154, 178, 279, 376, 403, 616, 688, 744
Scottish Psalter, The 661
Sears, Edmund Hamilton 375
Shewring, Walter H. 506
Siena, Bianco da 209
Simphonia Sinenum 156
Sister Agnes 308
Sister M 149
Smale, Ian 249, 807, 821, 823, 850
Smith Jr., Leonard E. 346
Smith, Henry 276
Smith, Walter Chalmers 361
Smyttan, George Hunt 264
Somerville, Caroline 789
South African traditional 611
Sparrow-Simpson, William John 112
Spinks, Brian 422
Spiritual 633, 719, 805, 806, 815
St Teresa of Avila 880
St Alphonsus 442, 500, 532
St Bernard of Cluny 387
Stanfield, Francis 553, 635
Stassen, Linda 617
Stone, Samuel John 647
Strover, Christian 797
Struther, Jan 450

Taizé Community 23, 859, 862, 865, 868, 870, 871, 874, 882, 885, 888, 889, 892, 893, 897, 898
Tate, Nahum 739
Taylor, Helen 426
Te Lucis ante terminum 159
Temple, Sebastian 122, 278, 470, 623, 639, 663, 779
Teresine, Sister M. 269, 443
Tisserand, Jean 747
Todi, Jacopone da 145
Toolan, Suzanne 349
Traditional 51, 151, 239, 274, 289, 302, 324, 330, 518, 653, 761, 832, 849, 856, 860, 866, 872, 886
Turner, Roy 120
Turton, William Harry 559
Tuttle, Carl 344

Ubi Caritas 368, 734
Urbs beata Jerasulem 197

Vaughan, Edmund 293, 442, 500, 532
Venerable Bede 493
Veni, Creator Spiritus 210
Victimae Paschali laudes 199
Vissing, Virginia 96, 527, 743
Viva, viva, Gesù 280
Vox clara ecce intonat 316

Waddell, Chrysogonus 505
Wade, John Francis 100, 501
Walker, Christopher 52, 565, 896
Wallace, W. L. 839
Walsh, James 253
Walworth, Clarence 333
Watcyn-Jones, Peter 115, 783
Watts, Isaac 404, 514, 731
Weatherell, F. W. 473
Welker, Louis 483
Wesley, Charles 218, 311, 317, 438, 461, 591
West Indian Spiritual 472
West Indian traditional 676
White, Estelle 45, 139, 183, 235, 329, 366, 431, 477, 524, 533, 557, 706, 770, 771, 788, 801, 836
Whitefield, George 317
Whiting, William 243
Whittier, John Greenleaf 234
Wiener, Julian 695
Wilde, Christina 109, 845
Williams, Peter 307
Williams, William 307
Wilson, M. F. C. 699
Winkworth, Catherine 497, 583, 584
Winter, Miriam Thérése 790
Wipo of Burgundy 199
Wise, Joe 50, 641
Woodward, George Ratcliffe 238, 686
Wright, Ralph 632
Wyse, John 358

Xavier, Sister M. 445

Ylvisaker, John 664
Young, John Freeman 614

Scriptural Index

GENESIS	
1:1	613
1:1-5	228, 508
1:1-31	793, 853, 854
1:2-3	120, 243, 453, 629, 631, 689, 725
1:26	262, 363
1:27	189
2:7	94, 180, 182, 183, 677
2:9	513
2:9-3:7	189
3:14-15	230, 473, 746
4:10	280
6-9	513, 631, 667, 837, 844
9:13	789, 792
12:1-2	417
28:10-22	766

EXODUS	
3:1-6	165, 513, 550
3:7-12	846
3:14-17	372
3-6	477
4:20	513
12:5	184
12:21	146
13-17	356
13:21	307
14	345, 375, 631
14-18	485, 534
15:1-18	942
15:2	892
15:25	513
16	146, 396, 444
16:4	307, 500
17:6-7	334, 444
19-20	503
19:4	159
19:5	206
19:19	292
20:3	471
25:17	481
40:38	728

NUMBERS	
6:24-26	867, 878
11	396
20:11	334

DEUTERONOMY	
6:4	762
8:3	604
32:11	515, 613
33:27	255

JOSHUA	
3	307
3:14-17	678, 686

1 SAMUEL	
3:4	483
3:9	34, 975, 984, 993, 1000, 1025, 1048, 1062
17	794

2 SAMUEL	
6:12-23	852

1 KINGS	
8:27	365
19:12	139, 234, 435
22:17	677

2 KINGS	
2:11	132

2 CHRONICLES	
10:17	1078

1 MACCABEES	
14:12	765

JOB	
19:25	616
38:8-11	243

PSALMS	
1	1041
2:8	351
3:8	686
4	949
4:8	598
5	457
8	967
8:1	345, 529
8:3	257
8:7-8	785
14	1024, 1051
15	942, 948, 1035, 1048
15:5	131, 168
16	1067
16:8	515
17	999, 1033
17:2-3	260, 369
17:28	342
18:1-2	306, 441
18:7-14	755, 931, 942, 1028, 1038, 1050
18:8	756
19:1	117
21	96, 482, 939, 955
22	486, 586, 656, 661, 880, 933, 951, 997, 1003, 1018
22:1-2	223
22:6	383
23	909, 1076
23:1	587
23:2	383
23:6	357, 474
23:7-10	260, 311, 471, 493, 655, 1070
24	694, 902, 995, 1005
24:4-9	592, 925
26	660, 929, 961, 972, 1077
26:1	306, 869
26:8	357, 383, 474
26:11	897
27:1	891
27:7	307
28	920
29	942, 950, 1015, 1045
29:2	164
30	941, 978
30:2-3	260, 369
30:5	251
30:16	662
31	1008, 1046
32	405, 927, 954, 966, 1031, 1054, 1065
32:1	871
32:9	508
33	643, 658, 868, 935, 1021, 1022, 1023, 1072
33:1-9	277, 380
33:8	642, 724
33:18	446. 531
35:9	306
39	971, 1004, 1055
39:1	897
39:5	1041
39:8	483
40	1009
40:1	301
41	433
41:1-2	142, 474
41:7	235
41-42	432, 942
42	359
44	1074
44:6	650
45	1078
45:4	667
45:10	163, 164, 165, 166
46	577, 960
46:1	772, 773
47:3	514
49	979
50	160, 318, 923, 924, 937, 942, 1059
50:7	667
50:10	899
53	1027
54	515
60	321
60:4	515
61	997
62	265, 991, 1001, 1047
62:2	383
62:7	515
64	257, 279, 984
64:7	243
65	126, 279, 430, 957, 1049
67	1057
68	981, 1050
69:4	897
70	245, 1039
70:1	333
70:3	369
70:17	751
71	314, 903, 919
71:6	669
72	742
75:7	383
77	1020, 1075
77:24-25	110, 181, 307, 500, 506, 642
78:9	528
79	600, 901, 911, 996
79:15	677
80	1011
80:16	376
83	916
83:1-2	642
84:8-14	544, 716, 900, 901, 902, 904, 988, 1017
85	985
88	879, 910, 982
88:14-15	154, 716
89	1030, 1053, 1058
89:2-4	514
90	926
90:1-7	178, 759
90:2	260
90:5	499
91	1013, 1043
92	1036
92:1	346
94	556, 775, 930, 992, 1006, 1053, 1062
94:2	307
94:3-5	830
94:8	923
95	171, 625, 912, 998, 1037
95:1	554
96	963, 1073
97	124, 616, 913, 958, 1063, 1068
97:1	554
99	104, 121, 123, 137, 406, 615, 709, 775, 953, 980
99:1-2	180, 776, 872
99:4	195
99:5	756
102	108, 576, 862, 932, 962, 976, 993, 1010, 1042
102:1-2	173, 419, 422, 520
102:3	164
102:10	528
103	568, 609, 610, 922, 942, 964
103:14	257
103:30	96, 182, 103, 608, 629, 899
104	915
104:1-5	426
106	1014
109	970
109:1	591
110:1	107
111	974
112	1060
114	1026
114:9	928
115:10-19	386, 928, 940, 969
116	220, 756, 827, 874, 875, 1044, 1056, 1085
117	275, 626, 943, 944, 945, 946, 947, 952
117:1	107, 119, 850, 864
117:14	195, 801, 869
117:19-24	195, 381, 675, 684, 782
117:25-26	2, 3, 4, 5, 7, 8, 59, 60, 61, 62, 63, 64, 65, 66, 67, 253, 344, 861
118	975, 986
118:35	1068
118:57	131
118:105	306
120	370, 1064
121	900, 1069
122	1016

122:2	897	12:2-6	720, 745, 908, 921, 942	**AMOS**		8:17	1002
125	905, 938, 1032			5:14	938	8:20	259, 350, 477
125:5-6	154, 385, 810	16:1	316, 601	5:24	464, 572	8:23-27	635, 706
127	914, 1002, 1029	24:16	217			8:26	166, 243, 245, 351, 751, 836, 863
129	222, 269, 741, 936, 1012	25:8	367	**MICAH**			
		30:23	669	4:3-4	704, 765	9:9	259, 350, 451, 483, 740, 840
129:5	988	35:1-10	221	6:3-5	356, 534		
130	490, 533, 883, 1000	35:4-7	669			9:36	677
132:1	642, 804	35:5-6	152, 395	**HABAKKUK**		9:38	270
135	428, 827	40:1	154, 218	2:14	120	10:8-9	286, 297
135:1	119, 850	40:1-11	221, 227, 242, 505			10:29-31	842, 853
135:4-6	306	40:4-5	351, 716, 897	**ZEPHANIAH**		10:38	259, 429
136	190, 934	40:8-9	302, 454, 541, 619, 623	1:7	418	11:5	152, 487, 706
137	990, 1040, 1052					11:25	973, 983, 985, 986, 1006, 1030, 1041, 1054, 1065
138	248, 744, 1071	40:31	688	**HAGGAI**			
138:23	453	43:1	813	2:7	218		
140:2	422	43:1-4	240, 757			11:28-30	127, 222, 223, 224, 351, 451, 483, 525, 553, 642, 725, 757, 1057, 1076
144	956, 983, 987, 994, 1019, 1066	43:11	112	**ZECHARIAH**			
		43:20	757	2:13	418		
145	106, 906, 973, 1025, 1034, 1061	45:4	813				
		45:22	696	**MALACHI**		12:8	452
145:9	675	48:18	572	1:11	270	13:1-23	565
146:1-11	384, 1007	49:1-10	757	4:2	317, 395, 750	13:4	350, 509
146:3	351, 437, 446	49:13-16	382, 540, 688, 816			13:8	228
146:4	257, 725	52:7-10	342, 346	**MATTHEW**		13:24-30	670
147:12-20	411, 918, 968	53:1-12	200, 233	1:19	814	13:25	226
147:16	718	53:4-5	193, 564, 751	1:23	33, 208, 317, 398, 526, 550, 646, 655, 671, 851, 909	13:41	147, 226
148	102, 412, 548, 579, 764, 816, 830	54:8-10	662, 688			13:47-50	670
		55:1-2	322, 323, 424, 492, 504, 525, 667			14:13-21	272
148:1-2	508			2:1-12	138, 144, 167, 229, 365, 501, 531, 603, 651, 676, 722, 723, 818	14:22-33	379
149:1	554	55:1-7	602			14:25	243
149:3	231	55:1-13	140			14:29	483
150	173, 548, 578, 835, 845, 850	55:12	758			15:31	706
		58:9	562			16:18	271, 990, 1072
150:3	616	60:1-7	138, 154	2:2	919	16:24	259
150:6	583	61:1	906, 907, 908	2:11	569	16:27	306
		61:1-3	216, 351, 437, 471, 531, 669, 673	2:13-18	698	17:1-8	711
PROVERBS				3:1-3	99, 219, 897	17:5	55, 927, 928, 929, 1073
5:1	96	64:8	94, 192, 638, 769	3:1-12	541, 721		
9:1-6	256	66:1	110	3:11	120	17:20	245
9:5	642			3:13-17	631	18:12-14	99, 131, 310, 350, 677
		JEREMIAH		4:1-11	264, 363, 458, 462, 811	19:14	784
SONG OF SOLOMON		1:4-19	558			20:12	790
2:4	324	31:3	357, 662, 756	4:4	604, 924, 925, 926, 987, 1020	20:28	267, 394, 668
4:11	551	31:31-34	304			21:1-11	113, 487, 593
8:6	147	51:46	255	4:16-17	453, 932, 1006	21:9	3, 4, 5, 7, 8, 59, 60, 61, 62, 63, 64, 65, 66, 67, 253, 274, 344, 750, 772, 861
				4:18-20	234, 259, 350, 451, 483, 727, 740, 1040		
WISDOM OF SOLOMON		**EZEKIEL**					
7:22-8:1	566	1:26	593				
		11:23	461	4:21	353	22:37-40	464, 762
ISAIAH		33:7	302	4:23	972, 989, 1025	24:30-31	13, 316, 438, 521, 529, 686, 708
1:3	723	36:25-26	120, 304, 376, 446, 562, 769	5:3-4	327, 589, 647, 973, 1030, 1034, 1053		
2:4-5	544, 704, 710, 765					24:42-44	704, 721, 1001, 1035, 1054
5:1-4	534	37:5	182, 183	5:3-12	158, 654		
5:7	996	44:1	550	5:8	174	25:4	274
6:2-3	1, 2, 3, 4, 5, 6, 7, 8, 59, 60, 61, 62, 63, 64, 65, 66, 67, 229, 333, 335, 336, 337, 361, 418, 422, 626	47	667	5:12-13	327, 749, 973	25:31	13, 147, 306
		47:1	507	5:14-16	327, 350, 439, 467, 672, 749, 849	25:31-46	228, 595, 726, 730, 766
		47:1-12	372				
		47:12	262	5:23	738	26:6-11	595
6:8	376			5:41	186	26:26-29	225, 273, 295, 459, 509, 523, 539, 570, 642, 681, 715, 732
7:4	255	**DANIEL**		5:44	828		
7:14	33, 152, 317, 398, 503, 566	3:52-90	102, 103, 412, 594, 890, 965	6:9-13	83, 84, 85, 86, 87		
				6:10	559, 876	26:36-42	888, 889
9:1-2	154, 453, 589	7:9	568	6:12-14	470, 851	26:36-27:56	188
9:2-7	665	7:9-22	361	6:25-34	779	26:39	267, 582, 876
9:5-6	91, 229, 242, 310, 317, 320, 409, 444, 559, 692, 698, 721, 743, 750	12:3	467, 759	6:26	477, 770	26:41	544, 849
				6:30	839	27:22	487
		HOSEA		6:33	604, 897	27:29	551, 552
		2:14-25	207	7:7	96, 562, 604	27:32-61	719
11:1-2	136, 210, 340, 341, 503, 513, 566, 608, 701, 702, 986	2:21-25	437	7:9	189	27:46	482
		13:4	112	7:11	718	28:1-10	678, 747, 761
				7:14	144	28:6-7	184, 703
11:1-9	161	**JOEL**		7:24-27	780, 847	28:9	649
11:9	120	2:17	333	8:2	740	28:18	286
		2:28	120				

28:19-20	110, 270, 273, 345, 379, 459, 467, 623, 631, 708, 781, 831, 960	1:38	524, 733	13:10-17	353	3:16	657, 934, 1044, 1066
		1:42	597, 618	14:12-24	376	3:30	663
		1:46	49, 877, 886	14:13	235, 327, 706	4:10	95, 96, 391, 527, 797
		1:46-55	109, 285, 488, 489, 491, 644, 679, 907	15:4-6	99, 131, 241, 310, 350, 656, 677	4:14	507, 700
						4:42	320, 351, 743
MARK		1:52	257	15:11-32	99, 620	5:3	327, 706
1:1-8	541, 721	1:76	1071	15:18	935	5:9	353
1:3	897	1:79	679	15:20	293	6:1-15	272
1:4	99, 220	2:1-7	472, 536	15:32	714	6:16-21	379
1:8	120	2:1-20	229, 296, 601, 603, 723	16:22	241	6:19	243, 706
1:9-11	631			18:15	784	6:31-32	181, 307, 424, 500, 724
1:12-13	264, 363, 458, 462	2:7	208, 725, 819	19:1-10	857		
1:15	980, 1005	2:10-11	912	19:5	483	6:32-58	865
1:16	234	2:8-20	134, 135, 155, 302, 354, 365, 501, 614, 651, 739	19:10	672	6:33	334
1:17	259, 451, 483, 740			19:28-38	113, 487, 593	6:34-40	348, 1077
1:18	350			19:38	2, 3, 4, 7, 9, 59, 60, 61, 62, 63, 64, 65, 66, 67, 253, 750, 861, 971, 987, 988, 994, 1066	6:35	91, 175, 177, 253, 350, 637
1:40	740	2:13-14	1, 3, 7, 20, 21, 22, 23, 24, 25, 26, 27, 28, 29, 30, 31, 32, 100, 130, 152, 238, 317, 375, 399, 526, 676, 776			6:35-68	349
2:14	259, 350, 483, 537, 740, 840					6:48	732, 743
						6:50-52	203, 253, 287, 353, 371, 424, 444, 511, 642, 969, 970, 1021
2:28	452			19:42	607		
4:1-20	565	2:29-32	599, 752, 1070	21:15	779		
4:3	350, 509	2:35	145	21:27-28	13, 306, 521, 524, 1068	6:56-58	203, 424, 1022
4:26-29	180, 226, 261, 351	3:1-18	541, 721			6:63	1038
4:35-41	635, 706	3:3-4	99, 221, 897, 903, 904, 905	21:36	544, 704. 721, 1035, 1067, 1068	6:67-68	34, 379, 750, 755, 931, 975, 984, 993, 1000, 1004, 1011, 1015, 1017, 1019, 1023, 1024, 1025, 1033, 1037, 1048, 1050, 1062, 1063
4:39	166, 243, 245, 351, 751, 836, 863			22:19-20	225, 273, 295, 447, 459, 462, 509, 523, 539, 570, 642, 681, 715, 732		
		3:16	120, 922				
6:31	483	3:21-22	631				
6:32-44	272	4:1-13	264, 363, 458, 462, 811				
6:34	677			22:39-44	888, 889		
6:45-52	379	4:4	604	22:40-23:46	188		
6:48	243	4:18	216, 297, 413, 471, 673, 740, 771, 906, 907, 908, 979, 1009, 1016, 1038, 1039	22:42	267, 582, 876	6:69	160, 165, 410, 942
7:37	125			22:53	539	7:37-39	95, 182, 183, 391, 506, 507, 525, 527, 553, 667, 700, 763, 797
8:34	259, 429			23:21	487		
8.38	306			23:26-55	719		
9:2-8	711	4:34	166	23:34	127, 459, 475, 822	8:12	11, 96, 179, 202, 204, 205, 215, 260, 292, 350, 415, 439, 453, 467, 544, 657, 662, 672, 679, 689, 743, 751, 771, 809, 891, 933, 974, 1007, 1027, 1032, 1047
9:7-8	55, 920	5:11-12	234, 740	23:42-43	241, 287, 396, 511, 870		
10:14	784	5:27	259, 350, 451, 483, 740, 840				
10:21	451			23:46	662, 941		
10:45	267, 394, 668, 1031	6:5	452	24:1-8	678, 747, 761		
11:1-11	113, 487, 593	6:20-23	589, 654, 757, 1041	24:4-7	184		
11:9-10	3, 4, 5, 7, 8, 59, 60, 61, 62, 63, 64, 65, 66, 67, 253, 274, 344, 750, 772, 861, 1003, 1036, 1069	6:27	828	24:13-35	48, 195, 424, 645		
		6:47-49	780, 847	24:15	250		
		7:6	139	24:32	948, 949, 950	8:32	52, 371, 453
		7:16	1008, 1014, 1019, 1045	24:35	272	8:36	385, 544
				24:36-43	143	9:1-41	131, 320
12:28-31	464, 762	7:22	395, 487	24:49-52	165, 493, 708	10:9	771
13:11	297, 779	7:34	110			10:11	96, 241, 350, 474, 624
13:25-26	13, 316, 438, 521, 529, 708	8:4-15	565	**JOHN**			
		8:5	350, 509	1:1-14	401, 508	10:11-18	466, 467, 551, 552
13:33	704, 721	8:8	984	1:3	566, 567	10:14-15	184, 951, 952, 953
14:3-9	595	8:15	1051	1:9-10	415, 487	10:27	513, 980, 989, 995, 1010, 1018, 1047, 1050, 1055, 1061
14:22-25	225, 273, 295, 459, 462, 509, 523, 539, 570, 642, 681, 715, 732	8:22-25	166, 243, 245, 351, 635, 706, 751, 836, 863	1:12-14	34, 971, 981, 997, 1009, 1016, 1022, 1044, 1052		
						11:25-27	96, 115, 182, 349, 353, 467, 931, 936
		9:10-17	272	1:14	48, 91, 100, 147, 168, 200, 247, 317, 444, 478, 501, 509, 567, 585, 622, 723, 743, 751, 918		
14:32-15:41	188	9:23	259, 429			11:43	672
14:34-36	267, 582, 876, 888, 889	9:28-36	711			12:1-8	595
		9:35	55			12:12-15	113, 487, 593, 750
14:38	544, 849	9:58-59	259, 350, 451, 477, 740			12:13	1, 4, 6, 8, 59, 60, 61, 62, 63, 64, 65, 66, 67, 253, 274, 344, 772
15:13	487			1:29	1, 2, 6, 7, 8, 9, 21, 22, 23, 24, 25, 26, 27, 30, 31, 32, 88, 89, 90, 91, 92, 93, 132, 160, 310, 311, 320, 410, 535, 564, 573, 921		
15:17	551, 552	10:2	270				
15:21-47	719	10:6	286				
15:34	482	10:25-29	362, 464, 762			12:21	545
16:1-8	184, 678, 747, 761	10:39	691			12:24	697
16:7	703	11:1	447	1:35-39	234, 483, 727	12:26	522, 697, 937
16:15-18	459, 1044	11:2-4	83, 84, 85, 86, 87, 189, 470, 718	1:43	259, 350, 451, 483, 740, 840	12:28	254, 395
						12:31-32	429, 1012
LUKE		11:9	96, 562			12:35	672
1-2	646	12:6-7	842, 853	1:51	170, 766	12:46	657
1:26-38	343, 508	12:22-32	779	2:1-11	247, 288, 817	13-14	377
1:28	128, 141, 313, 360, 550, 632, 795	12:24	477, 770	3:3	286, 317, 351, 657	13:1-15	475, 803, 848
		12:28	839	3:5	771	13:14	224
1:32	387, 910, 911	12:31	897	3:8	182, 183, 613	13:33	96, 682
1:35	629						

13:34-35	133, 203, 256, 462, 464, 571, 574, 681, 893, 940, 956, 993, 1042	2:4	453	**2 CORINTHIANS**		1:20	324, 423
		2:18	120	1:3	248	1:27	407
		2:23-24	524	3:17-18	94, 231, 354, 453, 461, 527, 763, 858	2:14	423
		2:34	591			3:1	2, 12, 20, 22, 26, 27, 28, 29, 30
13:36	224	3:15	199, 444, 678, 703	4:6	453, 711, 717		
14:6	205, 215, 255, 281, 348, 350, 371, 395, 675, 751, 809, 840, 1020, 1026, 1031, 1039, 1046, 1056	4:12	398, 469	4:7-16	299	3:13	412
		7:49	110	5:7-8	514, 728	3:15-16	263, 914, 1049
		10:38	689	5:14	299		
		13:47	708	5:17	324, 326, 461, 647, 714, 753	**1 THESSALONIANS**	
		16:4	982, 1042			5:5	154
14:16	96, 210, 340, 608, 672, 701, 702	16:14	916, 979, 994, 999, 1043, 1051, 1055, 1060	5:18-19	317, 714, 990, 992, 1059, 1065	5:8	316
						5:18	1063
14:18	110, 163, 259, 345, 382, 623, 804, 840, 961, 962, 963	17:6	828	6:10	352		
		17:28	725	8:9	352, 1060, 1061	**2 THESSALONIANS**	
		20:28	751			1:7	147
14:21	607			**GALATIANS**		2:14	1027, 1037
14:23	957, 958, 959, 976, 978, 995, 1012, 1021, 1033, 1056, 1057	**ROMANS**		2:19-20	105, 203, 219, 267, 500		
		5:5	335			**1 TIMOTHY**	
		5:8	219	3:27-28	189, 538	1:17	361, 475
14:25-27	48, 96, 183, 210, 286, 571, 701, 702, 828	5:10	199, 267, 703, 714	4:5-7	48, 94, 95, 96, 170, 249	3:16	918
		6:3-5	195, 299, 667, 753			4:10	119
14:27	236, 564, 573, 574, 697, 788	6:9	199, 241, 353	5:1	271, 585, 858	6:12	255
		6:18	537, 544	5:22	231		
15:1-9	513, 681	8:1-3	189, 203, 338, 527, 672	5:24	479	**2 TIMOTHY**	
15:1-17	133, 434			6:14-15	461, 731, 1026	1:10	326
15:4-5	97, 697, 955, 978, 1002	8:11	105			2:8-12	407, 697
		8:15	94, 95, 96, 191, 1052	**EPHESIANS**		2:19	324
15:7	697	8:21-22	205, 403, 459, 537	1:3-14	172	4:7	255, 260
15:12	256, 681	8:23-26	527, 540	1:13-14	231, 334, 624		
15:13-17	682, 725	8:29	94	1:17-18	985, 991, 997, 1008, 1014, 1017, 1045, 1059, 1064	**TITUS**	
15:15-16	388, 467, 986, 996, 1013, 1040, 1049, 1058	8:31-39	311, 354, 403, 494			2:13	306
		8:32	529			3:4	672
		8:37	678	1:21-23	469, 508		
15:26-27	981	8:39	700	2:6	324	**HEBREWS**	
16:7	210	10:14-17	347, 561	2:14	407	1:1-2	915, 917
16:13	340	11:33-36	475, 748	2:16	317, 324	1:3	475, 591
16:20-22	154, 163, 616, 810	12:15	186	2:19	478	1:8	650
16:32	259	12:20	642	2:20	197, 324, 540, 751	2:9	832
17	559	13:12	648	3:9	187	2:14	241, 326
17:17	977, 992, 998, 1011, 1028, 1029, 1053			3:14-21	687	2:17	189, 233
		1 CORINTHIANS		3:18-19	464, 700, 748	4-9	110, 146
17:21-22	94, 228, 810	1:25-27	168, 211, 531, 618, 717	4:5	647	4:12	977, 1064
17:24	522			4:15-16	247	4:14-15	233, 728
18:1-19:37	188	3:9	226	4:31-32	368, 412	5:5	233
18:37	290	3:11	197, 647	5:1-2	191, 219, 537, 540	5:10	233
19:2	551, 552	5:7-8	146, 372, 444, 944	5:6-20	153, 154	7:25	311
19:6	487	6:14	187	5:8	672, 704	8-9	732
19:17-42	719	6:20	169	5:14	403, 616, 753	8:1	591
19:25-30	145, 733	7:23	666	6:10-17	168	9:5	481
19:30	233	8:3	481	6:15	342	9:11-14	444
19:34	146, 151, 315, 372, 396, 573, 621, 628, 631, 667, 668, 723	9:24-27	255			10:19-20	294, 453
		10:16-17	424, 538, 559, 674, 893, 940	**PHILIPPIANS**		10:23	728
				2:4	267	11:1	170
20:1-18	326, 678	10:24	267	2:7	338, 648, 828	11:3	508
20:11-18	184, 199, 703	11:23-25	225, 273, 295, 459, 462, 509, 523, 539, 570, 642, 681, 715, 732	2:7-11	53, 55, 147, 189, 475, 563	11:14	728
20:17	271					12:2	2, 12, 20, 21, 22, 26, 27, 28, 29, 728
20:19-31	143, 747			2:8-9	939		
20:21-22	182, 183, 297, 828			2:10-11	105, 196, 204, 325, 336, 346, 385, 394, 395, 400, 447, 469, 776, 786, 832	12:24	280, 294
20:24-29	511, 664	11:27	9, 74, 75, 76			13:8	812, 855
20:27-28	287, 311, 396, 666	12:3-4	105, 538				
20:29	431, 467, 945, 946, 947	12:12	169, 424, 734, 735, 736	2:15-16	998, 1043	**JAMES**	
				3:7-8	295, 731	1:17	97, 255, 361, 718
21:1-11	829	12:27	828	3:8-12	118	1:18	1010, 1024
21:15-17	350, 379	13:1-13	355, 463	3:14	728	1:27	675
21:19	259, 483, 740	13:2	245	3:21	292		
		13:4-8	133	4:4-5	590, 705, 897	**1 PETER**	
ACTS		13:12-13	187, 368, 459, 893	4:7	139	1:3	286
1:4-5	120, 183	15:20	311			1:18-19	170, 184, 647, 666, 751
1:6-11	101, 110, 311, 312, 493	15:26-28	298, 479	**COLOSSIANS**			
		15:45	582	1:12-13	203, 657	1:25	454, 1062
1:8	165, 379, 459, 831	15:52	616, 686	1:13-20	201, 508	2:2	478
1:11	395	15:55-57	97, 169, 385, 399, 431, 678	1:15	363, 475	2:4-8	675, 782
2:1-4	228, 342, 613, 630, 701			1:18	199, 444	2:6	197
		16:22	312, 431, 885				

2:9-10	206, 478, 546, 565, 585, 657, 728, 754, 982	4:12-13	97, 1029	4:12	336	19:6-9	146, 226, 647
		4:16	115, 289, 290, 368, 734, 735, 736, 737, 738	5:5-6	110, 403, 746	19:16	91, 110, 409, 469, 619, 652, 798
				5:6-14	229	20:14	307
		4:19	532	5:9	110, 116, 270, 335, 429, 666, 668	21	387
2 PETER		5:6-8	372			21:1-2	241, 365
1:16-18	55, 711			5:12-13	117, 311, 374, 410, 419, 444, 754	21:3-5	166, 367, 424, 437, 505, 828
		REVELATION		6:10	116	21:9	424
1 JOHN		1:5-6	110, 199, 444, 1067	7:3	429	21:21	260
1:1	388	1:7	316, 438, 521	7:9-12	387, 479, 624, 754, 832	22:1-4	117, 262, 307, 310, 368, 372, 373, 518, 667
1:5	154, 415	1:8	461, 508, 698, 965, 966, 967	7:14-15	143, 146, 170, 187, 387, 641		
1:7	672					22:16-17	91, 323, 566, 589, 663, 705, 797
1:9	7	1:17-18	241, 323, 591	7:17	166, 437, 624		
2:5	976	2:10	1002, 1034	11:15	229	22:17-20	322
2:9-11	162	3:7	503, 566	11:17	374, 593	22:20	213, 214, 312, 431, 566, 743, 885
3:2	368, 481, 536	4:6	110	12:1	550		
3:5	165,	4:8	335, 336, 337, 365, 374, 422	17:14	110, 409, 469		
4:7-20	162			19:1-9	596	22:23	144
4:10	1046	4:10	337, 461				

Index of Uses

THE MASS

ENTRANCE SONGS
(See under general *Entrance Songs* below)

PENITENTIAL RITE

A New People's Mass	1
A Simple Mass	2
Mass of the Spirit	3
Mass of the Bread of Life	4
Missa de Angelis	5
Mass XVIII	6
The American Eucharist	7
The 'Hopwood' Mass	8
The Israeli Mass	9
Lord, have mercy (Orbis Factor)	11
Lord, have mercy (Alme Pater)	12
Kyrie eleison (Haugen)	13
Lord, have mercy (Archer)	14
Lord, have mercy (Rock)	15
Kyrie eleison (Rizza)	16
Kyrie (Mawby)	17
Lord, have mercy on us (Filitz)	19

Also:
Look around you (Kyrie eleison)	440
Lord, have mercy	446

GLORIA

A New People's Mass	1
A Simple Mass	2
Mass of the Spirit	3
Mass of the Bread of Life	4
Missa de Angelis	5
Coventry Gloria	20
Gloria (Rees)	21
Glory to God in the highest (Archer)	22
Gloria (Taizé)	23
Glory, glory in the highest (Daniels)	24
Gloria (Anderson)	25
Gloria (Salazar)	26
Gloria (Duffy)	27
Lourdes Gloria	28
Sing to God a song of glory	29
Peruvian Gloria	30
Glory to God, to God in the height *Country Gardens Gloria*	31
Sing glory to God *Ash Grove Gloria*	32

RESPONSORIAL PSALM
A complete set of Responsorial Psalms will be found at nos. 900-1078. See also *Responsorial Psalm Index*

GOSPEL ACCLAMATION
For specified Sunday and Feast Day Gospel Acclamations see nos. 900-1078.

The 'American' Eucharist	7
Advent Alleluia (Joncas)	33
Alleluia (Lloyd)	34
Scottish Alleluia (Kelly)	35
Irish Alleluia	36
Celtic Alleluia	37
Eightfold Alleluia	38

Alleluia (Easter Season)	39
Alleluia (Berthier)	40
Alleluia (Archer)	41
Alleluia (Plainsong)	42
Alleluia (Moore No 1, No 2, No 3)	43, 44, 46
Alleluia (White)	45
Alleluia (Bevenot)	47
Alleluia (Lundy)	48
Alleluia! Magnificat!	49
Alleluia: We will hear your Word	50
Halle, halle, halle	51
Sing praises to the Lord	52

Also:
Lent and Holy Week Gospel Acclamation (Plainsong)	53, 54, 55
All glory to you, Redeemer and Lord	114
God of the Covenant	294
Lord, thy word abideth	454 (vs 1, 4, 5, 6)
Open your ears, O Christian people	546

CREED

Credo 3	56
Lourdes Credo	57
We believe (Fitzpatrick)	58

Also:
Firmly I believe	258
We believe	712

PRAYER OF THE FAITHFUL

Praise to God in the highest	581
God our Father gave us life	791
O Lord, hear my prayer	882

PREPARATION OF THE GIFTS

All that I am	122
Almighty Father, Lord most high	129
Almighty Father, take this bread	130
At your feet	148
Blessed be God	171
Blest are you, Lord	175
Blest are you, Lord of creation	176
Blest are you, O God	177
Bread from the earth	180
Come on and celebrate	219
God everlasting, wonderful and holy	284
In bread we bring you, Lord	362
Lord, accept the gifts we offer	443
O God, we give ourselves today	516
O holy Lord, by all adored	519
O King of might and splendour	523
Reap me the earth	587
Take and bless our gifts	637
Take our bread	641
To your altar we bring	695
Upon thy table, Lord	699
We are gathering together	707

SANCTUS

A New People's Mass	1
A Simple Mass	2
Mass of the Spirit	3

Mass of the Bread of Life	4
Missa de Angelis	5
Mass XVIII	6
The 'American' Eucharist	7
The 'Hopwood' Mass	8
The 'Israeli' Mass	9
Holy, holy, holy (MacMillan)	59
Celtic Liturgy	60
Sanctus (Donnelly)	61
Holy, holy, holy (Deutsche Messe)	62
Sanctus (Taizé)	63
Lourdes Sanctus	64
Holy, holy, holy is the Lord (Ballantine)	65
Holy, most holy, all holy the Lord *Slane Sanctus*	66
O holy, most holy *Ash Grove Sanctus*	67

Also:
Holy, holy, holy	335
Holy, holy, holy is the Lord	336
Holy, holy, holy! Lord God almighty	337
Hosanna, hosanna	344
Let all that is within me	419
Clap your hands, all you people	772

MEMORIAL ACCLAMATION

The 'American' Eucharist	7
A Simple Mass	2
Let us proclaim (Celtic Liturgy)	68
Christ has died (Duffy)	69
Christ has died (Donnelly)	70
Christ has died (Hill)	71
Christ has died (Wise)	72
Dying you destroyed our death (Duffy)	73
When we eat this bread (Irish melody)	74
When we eat this bread (MacMillan)	75
When we eat this bread (Proulx)	76

Also:
He is Lord	325
Word made flesh	743
Benedictus qui venit	861

GREAT AMEN

Doxology and Great Amen (Mayhew)	77
Doxology and Great Amen (Lourdes)	78
Doxology and Great Amen (Plainsong)	79
Great Amen (Hill)	80
When we eat this bread (Proulx)	81
Great Amen (South African)	82

LORD'S PRAYER

Our Father (White)	83
Our Father (Weiner)	84
Our Father (Rimsky-Korsakov)	85
'Echo' Our Father	86
Our Father (Caribbean)	87

SIGN OF PEACE

Bind us together, Lord	169

Deep peace of the running wave to you	236
Dona nobis pacem	239
Grant us your peace	305
Peace I leave with you	571
Peace is flowing like a river	572
Peace, perfect peace	574
Shalom, my friend	612
Exaudi nos, Domine	866

AGNUS DEI

A New People's Mass	1
A Simple Mass	2
Mass of the Spirit	3
Mass of the Bread of Life	4
Missa de Angelis	5
Mass XVIII	6
The 'American' Eucharist	7
The 'Hopwood' Mass	8
The 'Israeli' Mass	9
Lamb of God (Fitzpatrick)	88
Lamb of God (Archer)	89
Lamb of God (Rees)	90
Jesus, Lamb of God (Inwood)	91
Jesus, Lamb of God (Duffy)	92
O Lamb of God	93

COMMUNION
(See under *Communion* below)

RECESSIONAL SONG
(See under general *Recessional Songs* below)

ADVENT

Abba, Father, send your Spirit	96
Behold, the Saviour of the nations	161
Come, Lord Jesus	213
Come, my Way, my Truth, my Life	215
Come, O divine Messiah!	216
Come, O God of all the earth	217
Come, prepare the way	220
Come, thou long-expected Jesus	221
Comfort, comfort my people	227
Enter in the wilderness	242
For you my soul is thirsting	265
Hark! a herald voice is calling	316
Hear our cry	322
How lovely on the mountains	346
Like a sea without a shore	431
O come, O come, Emmanuel	503
O comfort my people	505
O Jesus Christ, remember	521
On Jordan's bank the Baptist's cry	541
Open your ears, O Christian people	546
O Wisdom, source of harmony	566
Rejoice in the Lord always	590
See, your Saviour comes	607
Sing a new song	616
The coming of our God	648
The Saviour will come, resplendent in joy	669
Waken, O sleeper, wake and rise	704
Wake up, O people	705
We shall stay awake	721
Word made flesh	743

ADVENT: CHILDREN'S SECTION
When is he coming 851

ADVENT: RIZZA, TAIZÉ and OTHER CHANTS
In the Lord I'll be ever thankful 868
Ostende nobis, Domine 885
Wait for the Lord 897

ASCENSION
(See also under *Christ the King*)
A hymn of glory let us sing! 101
Alleluia, sing to Jesus 110
Hail the day that sees him rise 311
Hail the risen Lord, ascending 312
In the tomb so cold 367
New praises be given 493
Praise the Lord 577

BAPTISM
Abba Father, from your hands 95
Abba Father, send your Spirit 96
By the cross of Christ 189
Called to be servants 191
Do not be afraid 240
God forgave my sin 286
Guide me, O thou great Redeemer 307
Here's a child for you, O Lord 329
He's got the whole world in his hand 330
I will never forget you 382
Lord, have mercy 446
My shepherd is the Lord 486
O healing river 518
O let all who thirst 525
O living water 527
O the word of my Lord 558
Springs of water, bless the Lord 631
The King of love my shepherd is 656
The light of Christ 657
The Lord's my shepherd 661
There is a river 667
This is our faith 683
We shall draw water joyfully 720
You have been baptised in Christ 753

BAPTISM: CHILDREN'S SECTION
Father welcomes all his children 784
Have you heard the raindrops 797

BAPTISM: RIZZA, TAIZÉ and OTHER CHANTS
O Christe, Domine Jesu 881

CHRISTMASTIDE
A child is born in Bethlehem 98
Adeste fideles 100
Angels we have heard in heaven 134
Angels we have heard on high 135
A noble flower of Judah 136
Arise to greet the Lord of light 138
As with gladness men of old 144
Awake, awake and greet the new morn 152
Away in a manger 155
Bethlehem, of noblest cities 167
Born in the night, Mary's child 179
Child in the manger 193
Come, come, come to the manger 208
Ding dong, merrily on high 238
God rest you merry, gentlemen 296
Good Christians all, rejoice 300
Good King Wenceslas 301
Go, tell it on the mountain 302
Hail to the Lord's anointed 314
Hark, the herald angels sing 317
Infant holy, infant lowly 364
In the bleak midwinter 365
It came upon the midnight clear 375
Let all mortal flesh keep silence 418
Love came down at Christmas 460
Lovely in your littleness 465
Mary had a baby 472
O come, all ye faithful 501
Of the Father's love begotten 508
O little town of Bethlehem 526
Once in royal David's city 536
On Christmas night all Christians sing 537
O sing a new song 554
See amid the winter's snow 601
See him lying on a bed of straw 603
Silent night 614
Sleep, holy babe 627
The first Nowell 651
The holly and the ivy 653
The race that long in darkness pined 665
The Virgin Mary had a baby boy 676
This Child 679
Unto us a boy is born 698
We three kings of Orient are 722
What child is this 723
What kind of greatness 725
While shepherds watched 739

CHRISTMASTIDE: CHILDREN'S SECTION
Come, they told me 777
Little donkey 818
Little Jesus, sleep away 819
O come and join the dance 826

CHRIST THE KING
All God's people, come together 115
All hail the power of Jesus' name 116
All the ends of the earth 124
And did those feet in ancient time 132
As with gladness men of old 144
At the name of Jesus 147
Be still, for the presence of the Lord 165
Be thou my vision 168
Blest are the pure in heart 174
Christ be beside me 194
Christ is King of earth and heaven 196
Christ triumphant 200
Christus vincit 201
Come and praise him 206
Come on and celebrate 219
Come, praise the Lord 220
Crown him with many crowns 229
Forth in the peace of Christ we go 263
Give me joy in my heart 274
Glorious God, King of creation 278
Hail, Redeemer, King divine 310
He is Lord 325
Hosanna, hosanna 344
How lovely on the mountains 346
I cannot tell 351
Jesus is Lord! Creations voice proclaims it 394
Jesus is Lord! In love he came 395
Joy to the world 404
King of glory, King of peace 408
King of kings and Lord of lords 409
Let the heavens declare 423
Let the world in concert sing 426
Lo, he comes with clouds descending 438
Lord, enthroned in heavenly splendour 444
Majesty, worship his majesty 469
Make way, make way 471
Praise the Lord 577
Rejoice, the Lord is King 591
Sing it in the valleys 619
The head that once was crowned with thorns 652
To Christ, the Prince of peace 692
We are his children 708
What feast of love 724
Ye choirs of new Jerusalem 746
You are the King of Glory 750

CHRIST THE KING: CHILDREN'S SECTION
Christ is our King 771
Come and praise the Lord our King 774
Forward in faith 786
He is the King 798
Jesus will never, ever 812
O when the saints go marching in 832

COMMUNION
Abba, abba, Father 94
Alleluia, sing to Jesus 110
All for Jesus! 112
All I once held dear 118
A new commandment 133
As bread my Lord comes to me 139
As earth that is dry 140
As the deer pants for the water 142
As we are gathered 143
At the Lamb's high feast we sing 146
Ave verum corpus 151
Beloved, let us love 162
Be still and know I am with you 163
Be still and know that I am God 164
Be still, for the presence of the Lord 165
Be thou my vision 168
Bind us together, Lord 169
Blessed be the God of Jesus Christ 172
Blest are the pure in heart 174
Bread is blessed and broken 181
Breathe on me, Breath of God 182
By his grace 187
Christ be beside me 194
Christians, lift up your hearts 195
Come and be filled 203
Come and be light for our eyes 204
Come, Lord Jesus 213
Come, Lord Jesus, come 214
Come, my Way, my Truth, my Life 215
Come to me, all who labour 223
Come to me, come, my people 224
Come to the table of the Lord 225
Deep calls to deep 235
Father and life-giver 247
Father, we come to you 253
Fill my house 256
Freedom for my people 266
From many grains 268
Gather around, for the table is spread 272
Gifts of bread and wine 273
Glorify the Lord 277
God everlasting, wonderful and holy 284
Godhead here in hiding 287
God is my great desire 291
God of the covenant 294
God of the Passover 295
Guide me, O thou great Redeemer 307
Hail, true Body 315
He brings us into his banqueting table 324
He is Lord 325
Here in this place 327
Here is bread 328
Holy God, your pilgrim people 334
Holy, holy, holy is the Lord 336
I am the bread of life (Konstant) 348
I am the bread of life (Toolan) 349
I cannot tell 351
If God is for us 354
I have loved you with an everlasting love 357
In the love of God and neighbour 366
Into one we all are gathered 368
In you, my God 369
In your coming and going 370
I received the living God 371
I will seek your face, O Lord 383
I will walk in the presence of God 386
Jesus calls us 388
Jesus, ever flowing fountain 391
Jesus, gentlest Saviour 392
Jesus, Lord of glory 396
Jesus, my Lord, my God, my all 397
Jesus, the very thought of thee 400
Jesus, the Word, has lived among us 401
Lauda, Jerusalem 411
Let all mortal flesh keep silence 418
Let all that is within me 419
Let the hungry come to me 424
Lord Jesus Christ 447
Lord, we come to ask your healing 456
Love divine, all loves excelling 461
Love is his word 462
Lumen Christi 467
My God, and is thy table spread 480
My shepherd is the Lord 486
My soul is longing for your peace 490
O bread of heaven 500
O food of travellers 506
Of the glorious body telling 509
O Godhead hid 511
O how good is the Lord 520
O King of might and splendour 523
O my Lord, within my heart 533
One bread, one body 538

On this day of joy	542	All I once held dear	118
O Sacred Heart	553	Be still, my soul	166
O, the love of my Lord	557	Be thou my vision	168
O thou, who at thy Eucharist didst pray	559	Day is done, but love unfailing	232
Our God loves us	560	Deep calls to deep	235
Pange lingua gloriosi	570	Do not be afraid	240
Rejoice in the Lord always	590	Dying you destroyed our death	241
See the holy table, spread for our healing	605	Faith in God	245
See us, Lord, about your altar	606	Father God	248
Soul of my Saviour	628	Father, in my life I see	250
Sweet sacrament divine	635	For all the saints	260
Take this and eat	642	For you my soul is thirsting	265
Taste and see the goodness of the Lord	643	Glory to thee, my God, this night	282
Thanks for the fellowship	645	God be in my head	283
The King of love my shepherd is	656	God is my great desire	291
The Lord is my life	660	Going home	298
The Lord's my shepherd	661	Hear my cry	321
The table's set, Lord	674	I am the bread of life (Konstant)	348
This is my body	681	I am the bread of life (Toolan)	349
To be in your presence	691	If God is for us	354
We behold the splendour of God	711	In you, my God	369
We celebrate this festive day	715	In your coming and going	370
We hold a treasure	717	I watch the sunrise	378
What feast of love	724	I will seek your face, O Lord	383
Where is love and loving kindness	734	I will walk in the presence of God	386
Where love and charity endure	735	Jerusalem the golden	387
Where the love of Christ unites us	736	Lead, kindly light	415
Where true love is found with charity	737	Like a sea without a shore	431
Where true love is present	738	Like as the deer	432
Word made flesh	743	Like the deer that yearns	433
		Lord Jesus, think on me	448
COMMUNION: CHILDREN'S SECTION		Lord of life	451
A butterfly, an Easter egg	760	Lord, thy word abideth	454
In the upper room	803	May you see the face of God	474
Isn't it good	804	My God, accept my heart this day	479
		My shepherd is the Lord	486
COMMUNION: RIZZA, TAIZÉ and OTHER CHANTS		My soul is longing for your peace	490
Eat this bread	865	O fountain of life	507
Jesus, remember me	870	O God, our help in ages past	514
May the Lord bless you (A blessing)	878	O Jesus Christ, remember	521
O Christe, Domine Jesu	881	Save us, O Lord (Mayhew)	598
O Sacrament most holy	884	Save us, O Lord (Nazareth)	599
The Lord is my light	891	Steal away	633
Ubi caritas	893	Sweet Saviour, bless us	636
		The King of love my shepherd is	656
EUCHARISTIC ADORATION WITH BENEDICTION		The Lord is my life	660
O salutaris/O saving Victim (1), (2), (3), (4)	1079, 1080, 1081, 1082	The Lord's my shepherd	661
Tantum ergo/Come adore (1), (2)	1083, 1084	The seed is Christ's	670
Adoremus in aeternum	1085	Unless a grain of wheat	697
		With you, O God	742
CONFIRMATION		You give, Lord	752
(See *Discipleship and Dedication* and *Whitsun* below)		You who dwell in the shelter of the Lord	759
CORPUS CHRISTI		**DEATH: CHILDREN'S SECTION**	
(See *Communion* above)		God sends a rainbow	792
DEATH		**DEATH: RIZZA, TAIZÉ and OTHER CHANTS**	
Abide with me	97	Bless the Lord my soul	862
		Jesus, remember me	870
		May the Lord bless you (A blessing)	878
		Nada te turbe (Nothing can trouble)	880
		O Christe, Domine Jesu	881
		O Lord, hear my prayer	882
		The Lord is my light	891
		Within our darkest night	898

DISCIPLESHIP AND DEDICATION		The love I have for you	662
All my hope on God is founded	119	The night was dark	664
All that I am	122	This day God gives me	680
And did those feet in ancient time	132	To be in your presence	691
A new commandment	133	To you, O Lord, I lift up my soul	694
Awake, awake fling off the night	153	Turn to me	696
Come and be filled	203	Unless a grain of wheat	697
Come, Lord Jesus, come	214	Walk with me, O my Lord	706
Come to me, all who labour	223	We are his children	708
Come to me, come, my people	224	We are marching	710
Dear Lord and Father of mankind	234	When I feel the touch	729
Deep calls to deep	235	Will you come and follow me	740
Faith in God	245	With you, O God	742
Faith of our fathers	246	You are the light	751
Father God	248	You have called us	754
Father, in my life I see	250	You have the message of eternal life	755
Father, I place into your hands	251	Your love's greater	756
Fight the good fight	255	You shall cross the barren desert	757
Fill my house	256	You who dwell in the shelter of the Lord	759
Follow me, follow me	259		
From heaven you came	267	**DISCIPLESHIP AND DEDICATION: CHILDREN'S SECTION**	
God be in my head	283	All of my heart	762
God's Spirit is in my heart	297	All of the people	763
He who would valiant be	331	As Jacob with travel was weary one day	766
How shall they hear the word of God	347	Be the centre of my life	767
I am the Light	350	Caterpillar, caterpillar	768
If I am lacking love	355	Change my heart, O God	769
In you, my God	369	Do not worry over what to eat	779
I, the Lord of sea and sky	376	Don't build your house on the sandy land	780
I, the Servant-Lord	377	Do what you know is right	781
I will be with you	379	I give my hands	801
Jesus Christ is waiting	390	Jesus had all kinds of friends	808
Leave your country and your people	417	O Lord, all the world	828
Listen, let your heart keep seeking	435	Put your trust	836
Listen to me, Yahweh	436	Sing a simple song	838
Longing for light	439	Step by step, on and on	840
Lord, for tomorrow and its needs	445	There's a great big world out there	843
Lord of life	451	There's a rainbow in the sky	844
Lord, the light of your love	453	There was one, there were two	845
Lord, you give the great commission	459	The wise man	847
Love is patient	463	The world is full of smelly feet	848
Loving shepherd of thy sheep	466	This little light of mine	849
Lumen Christi	467	Zacchaeus was a very little man	857
Make me a channel of your peace	470	Zip bam boo	858
My God said to me, 'Follow!'	483		
O, come to the water	504	**DISCIPLESHIP AND DEDICATION: RIZZA, TAIZÉ and OTHER CHANTS**	
O fountain of life	507	Calm me, Lord	863
O God, please listen	515	May the Lord bless you (A blessing)	878
O Jesus, I have promised	522	Nada te turbe (Nothing can trouble)	880
O let all who thirst	525	O Lord, my heart is not proud	883
O my Lord, within my heart	533	Silent, surrendered	887
Onward, Christian pilgrims	544		
Open our eyes, Lord	545	**EASTERTIDE**	
O the word of my Lord	558	Alleluia, alleluia, give thanks to the risen Lord	105
Out of darkness	565	All heaven declares	117
Peace I leave with you	571	All I once held dear	118
Remember your mercy, Lord	592	At the Lamb's high feast we sing	146
Seek ye first	604	Battle is o'er, hell's armies flee	156
Send me, Lord	611	Bring all ye dear-bought nations	184
Sing it in the valleys	619	Christ the Lord is risen today	199
Sweet heart of Jesus	634	Come and praise him	206
Take me, Lord	638	Come, Lord Jesus	213
Take my hands	639		
Take my hands, Lord	640		
The kingdom of heaven	654		

Title	No.
From the very depths of darkness	271
He is Lord	325
He is risen, tell the story	326
Holy, holy, holy	335
I danced in the morning	353
In the tomb so cold	367
I saw streams of water flowing	372
Jesus Christ is risen today	389
Jesus is Lord! Creation's voice proclaims it	394
Jesus rose on Easter day	399
Join in the dance	403
Keep in mind	407
New daytime dawning	492
Now the green blade riseth	498
Rejoice, all heavenly powers	589
Sing a new song	616
Sing to the mountains	626
The day of resurrection	649
The head that once was crowned with thorns	652
The King of glory comes	655
The Lord is alive	659
The night was dark	664
Thine be the glory	678
This is our faith	683
This is the day	684
This joyful Eastertide	686
Victimae Paschali laudes	703
Ye choirs of new Jerusalem	746
Ye sons and daughters of the Lord	747

EASTERTIDE: CHILDREN'S SECTION

Title	No.
A butterfly, an Easter egg	760
All in an Easter garden	761

EASTERTIDE: RIZZA, TAIZÉ and OTHER CHANTS

Title	No.
Surrexit Christus	890

ENTRANCE SONGS

(Wherever possible, the Entrance Song should relate to the theme of the day or of the sacrament being celebrated. The songs listed below are general songs of gathering. See also *Praise* below.)

Title	No.
All people that on earth do dwell	121
All the earth proclaim the Lord	123
Arise, come to your God	137
Christians, lift up your hearts	195
Come and go with me	205
God everlasting, wonderful and holy	284
Holy God, of righteous glory	332
I'll turn my steps to the altar of God	359
I will enter his gates	381
Jubilate, everybody	406
Like as the deer	432
Like the deer that yearns	433
Lord our God	452
Lord, the light of your love	453
O God beyond all praising	510
O God, your people gather	517
Open your ears, O Christian people	546
O that today you would listen to his voice	556

Title	No.
Praise to the Lord, the Almighty	583
Sing, all creation	615
We are gathering together	707
We are his people	709

ENTRANCE SONGS: CHILDREN'S SECTION

Title	No.
Come into his presence	776
Lord we've come to worship you	821

EVENING

Title	No.
Abide with me	97
Before the light of evening fades	159
Be thou my vision	168
Day is done, but love unfailing	232
Glory to thee, my God, this night	282
God be in my head	283
Grant us your peace	305
I watch the sunrise	378 (vs. 3, 4)
Lead, kindly light	415
Lord of all hopefulness	450 (vs. 3, 4)
Now as the evening shadows fall	495, 495a
Now with the fast-departing light	499
Save us, O Lord (Mayhew)	598
Save us, O Lord (Nazareth)	599
Sweet Saviour, bless us	636
The day thou gavest, Lord, is ended	650
Yahweh is the God of my salvation	745 (v. 3)
You give, Lord	752

EVENING: CHILDREN'S SECTION

Title	No.
Dear child divine	778

EVENING: RIZZA, TAIZÉ and OTHER CHANTS

Title	No.
Kindle a flame	873

FORGIVENESS

Title	No.
Across the years there echoes still	99
All you who seek a comfort sure	127
Amazing grace	131
As earth that is dry	140
Behold, the Lamb of God	160
Blessed assurance	170
Bread is blessed and broken	181
Change my heart, O God	192
Christians, lift up your hearts	195
Christ's is the world	198
Come back to me	207
Come to me	222
Comfort, comfort my people	227
Deep within my heart	237
From the depths we cry to thee	269
God forgave my sin	286
God of mercy and compassion	293
Grant to us, O Lord	304
Have mercy on us, O Lord	318
Hear our cry	322
Jesus, ever flowing fountain	391
Lead us, heavenly Father, lead us	416
Let the heavens declare	423
Listen to me, Yahweh	436
Listen to my voice	437
Look at the sky	441
Lord, have mercy	446

Title	No.
Lord Jesus Christ	447
Lord, make me a means of your peace	449
Nothing shall separate us	494
O God, your people gather	517, 517a
O Lord, be not mindful	528
O sacred heart	553
O suffering Jesus	555
O, the love of my Lord	557
Praise to you, O Christ, our Saviour	585
Remember your mercy, Lord	592
Sing, my soul	620
To Jesus' heart, all burning	693
Vaster far than any ocean	700
We cannot measure	713
With the Lord there is mercy	741

FORGIVENESS: CHILDREN'S SECTION

Title	No.
Be the centre of my life	767
It's me, O Lord	805
Jesus, you love me	813
Lord, you've promised, through your Son	822

FORGIVENESS: RIZZA, TAIZÉ and OTHER CHANTS

Title	No.
Bless the Lord my soul	862

HARVEST

Title	No.
All things bright and beautiful	125, 125a
Come, ye thankful people come	226
Fill your hearts with joy and gladness	257
For the fruits of his creation	261
Glory and praise to our God	279
Laudato sii, O mi Signore	412
Reap me the earth	587
We plough the fields and scatter	718
God almighty set a rainbow	789

HEALING

Title	No.
Be still and know that I am God	164
Be still, for the presence of the Lord	165
Be still my soul	166
Brother, sister, let me serve you	186
Deep within my heart	237
Do not be afraid	240
For the healing of the nations	262
Healer of our every ill	319
Healer of the sick	320
Hear our cry	322
I will never forget you	382
I will sing a song	384
Jesus Christ is waiting	390
Jesus is Lord! In love he came	395
Lay your hands gently upon us	413
Listen to my voice	437
Lord, make me a means of your peace	449
Lord, we come to ask your healing	456
Lord, you give the great commission	459
Make me a channel of your peace	470
O healing river	518

Title	No.
O, how good is the Lord	520
Ours were the sufferings he bore	564
Sing it in the valleys	619
Spirit of the living God	630
The Spirit of the Lord	673
We cannot measure	713

HEALING: CHILDREN'S SECTION

Title	No.
God sends a rainbow	792
Peter and John went to pray	833

HEALING: RIZZA, TAIZÉ and OTHER CHANTS

Title	No.
Bless the Lord my soul	862
Silent, surrendered	887
You are the centre	899

HOLY SPIRIT

(See *Whitsun* below)

JUSTICE and PEACE

Title	No.
Alleluia, alleluia! I will praise the Father	106
Alleluia, thank you for fathers	111
All God's people, come together	115
Beauty for brokenness	157
Be blest, pure of heart	158
Behold, the Saviour of the nations	161
Be still and know I am with you	163
Christ's is the world	198
Come and be light for our eyes	204
Come O God of all the earth	217
Dona nobis pacem	239
For the healing of the nations	262
Freedom for my people	266
Glorify the Lord	277
God fills me with joy	285
God of eternal light	292
God's Spirit is in my heart	297
Hail to the Lord's anointed	314
How shall they hear the word of God	347
It came upon the midnight clear	375
Jesus Christ is waiting	390
Longing for light	439
Lord, unite all nations	455
Love is the only law	464
Make me a channel of your peace	470
My soul doth magnify the Lord	488
My soul is filled with joy	489
My soul proclaims you, mighty Lord	491
O God of earth and altar	512
O healing river	518
O let all who thirst	525
Onward, Christian pilgrims	544
Peace is flowing like a river	572
Peace is the gift	573
See, your Saviour comes	607
Sing, Holy Mother	618
Sing the gospel of salvation	624
Taste and see the goodness of the Lord	643
Tell out, my soul	644
The kingdom of heaven	654
The Lord hears the cry of the poor	658
The Spirit of the Lord	673
We have a dream	716
Whatsoever you do	726
When I needed a neighbour	730

JUSTICE and PEACE: CHILDREN'S SECTION		Like as the deer	432	Tell out, my soul	644	GOOD FRIDAY	
		Like the deer that yearns	433	The angel Gabriel from heaven came	646	All you who seek a comfort sure	127
And everyone beneath the vine and fig tree	765	Love divine, all loves excelling	461	The sign of hope, creation's joy	671	At the cross her station keeping	145
Give me peace, O Lord	788	Love is his word	462	This is the image of the queen	685	By the blood that flowed from thee	188
God sends a rainbow	792	My heart will sing to you	484	Where are you bound, Mary?	733	By the cross	189
Sing praise to God	839	Now I know what love is	496	MARY: CHILDREN'S SECTION		Day of wrath and day of wonder	233
The voice from the bush	846	O Lord, your tenderness	530	Hail, Mary, full of grace	795	Faithful Cross	244
When your Father made the world	853	O sacred heart	553	MARY: RIZZA, TAIZÉ and OTHER CHANTS		Glory be to Jesus	280
		O, the love of my Lord	557			I give you love	356
LENT		Our God loves us	560	Magnificat	877	Jesus, who condemns you?	402
Across the years there echoes still	99	Our hearts were made for you	562	Sanctum nomen, Domini	886	Lamb of God, Holy One	410
Blest be the Lord	178	The King of love my shepherd is	656	MORNING		Lift high the cross	429
By the blood that flowed from thee	188	The love I have for you	662	Awake, awake: fling off the night	153	My God, my God, why have you forsaken me?	482
By the waters of Babylon	190	To be in your presence	691	Awake from your slumber	154	My people, what have I done to you?	485
Change my heart, O Lord	192	Your love's greater	756	I watch the sunrise	378 (v.1)	My song is love unknown	487
Come back to me	207	LOVE OF GOD: CHILDREN'S SECTION		Lord, for tomorrow and its needs	445	O come and mourn with me awhile	502
Come to me	222			Lord, all hopefulness	450 (v.1)	O God of grace we thank you	513
Dear Lord and Father of mankind	234	God sends a rainbow	792	Lord, when I wake I turn to you	457	O my people, what have I done to you?	534
Fight the good fight	255	MARRIAGE		Morning has broken	476	On a hill far away	535
Follow me, follow me	259	A new commandment	133	My God, accept my heart this day	479	O sacred head ill-used	551
From the depths we cry to thee	269	God in the planning	288	This day God gives me	680	O sacred head sore wounded	552
God forgave my sin	286	God is love	289	Waken, O sleeper, wake and rise	704	O suffering Jesus	555
In company with Christians past	363	Lead us, heavenly Father, lead us	416	Yahweh is the God of my salvation	745 (v.1)	Our Saviour, Christ	563
Leave your country and your people	417	Let love be real	421	MORNING: CHILDREN'S SECTION		Ours were the sufferings he bore	564
Look around you	440	Love divine, all loves excelling	461			See, Christ was wounded	602
Lord, have mercy	446	Love is patient	463	Thank you, Lord	841	Sing, my tongue, the song of triumph	621
Lord Jesus, think on me	448	On this day of joy	542	PASSIONTIDE		There is a green hill far away	666
Lord, who throughout these forty days	458	O perfect love	547	All glory, laud and honour	113	The royal banners forward go	668
Moses, I know you're the man	477	MARRIAGE: CHILDREN'S SECTION		Lauda, Jerusalem	411	Were you there when they crucified my Lord?	719
O, the love of my Lord	557			My song is love unknown	487	When I survey the wondrous cross	731
O the word of my Lord	558	Life for the poor was hard and tough	817	Ride on, ride on in majesty	593		
Save us, O Lord (Dufford)	600			You are the King of Glory	750	PEOPLE OF GOD (CHURCH)	
Seek ye first	604	MARY		PASSIONTIDE: RIZZA, TAIZÉ and OTHER CHANTS		Abba, abba, Father	94
Turn to me	696	Alma redemptoris mater	128			All God's people, come together	115
We behold the splendour of God	711	A noble flower of Judah	136	Benedictus qui venit	861	All over the world	120
You shall cross the barren desert	757	As I kneel before you	141	MAUNDY THURSDAY (See also Communion)		All you nations, sing out your joy	126
You who dwell in the shelter of the Lord	759	At the cross her station keeping	145			And did those feet in ancient time	132, 132a
		Ave Maria, O maiden, O mother	149	Hail, true Body	315	A new commandment	133
LENT: CHILDREN'S SECTION		Ave, Regina caelorum	150	Lauda, Jerusalem	411	As we are gathered	143
Jesus went away to the desert	811	Bring flowers of the rarest	185	Love is his word	462	Awake from your slumber	154
LENT: RIZZA, TAIZÉ and OTHER CHANTS		Daily, daily, sing to Mary	230	Of the glorious body telling	509	Bind us together, Lord	169
		God fills me with joy	285	One bread, one body	538	Brother, sister, let me serve you	186
O Lord, hear my prayer	882	Hail, Queen of heaven	309	One cold night in spring	539	Called to be servants	191
LOVE OF GOD		Hail, thou star of ocean	313	O thou, who at thy Eucharist didst pray	559	Christ is made the sure foundation	197
Abba Father, from your hands	95	Holy Mary, you were chosen	339	Pange lingua gloriosi	570	Christ's is the world	198
Alleluia: all the earth	104	Holy Virgin, by God's decree	343	Said Judas to Mary	595	Christus vincit	201
Alleluia: Praise God	108	I'll sing a hymn to Mary	358	This is my will	682	Colours of day	202
All God's people, come together	115	Immaculate Mary	360	When the time came	732	Come and be light for our eyes	204
All my hope on God is founded	119	Look down, O mother Mary	442	Where is love and loving kindness	734	Come and go with me	205
All you who seek a comfort sure	127	Maiden, yet a mother	468	Where love and charity endure	735	Come and praise him	206
A new commandment	133	Mary immaculate	473	Where the love of Christ unites us	736	Come, Lord Jesus, come	214
As the deer pants for the water	142	Mother of God's living Word	478	Where true love is found with charity	737	Creator of the day	228
Beloved, let us love	162	My soul doth magnify the Lord	488	Where true love is present	738	Faith of our fathers	246
Come down, O love divine	209	My soul is filled with joy	489	MAUNDY THURSDAY: RIZZA, TAIZÉ and OTHER CHANTS		Father, we come to you	253
God is love	289	My soul proclaims you, mighty God	491			Fill my house	256
God is love: his the care	290	O lady, full of God's own grace	524	Stay here and keep watch	888	Firmly I believe	258
God is my great desire	291	O Mary, when our God chose you	531	Stay with me	889	Follow me, follow me	259
If I am lacking love	355	O Mother blest	532	Ubi caritas	893	Forth in the peace of Christ we go	263
I have loved you with an everlasting love	357	O purest of creatures	549			Freedom for my people	266
In the love of God and neighbour	366	O Queen of heaven	550			From heaven you came	267
Let there be love	425	Regina cæli	588				
Like a sea without a shore	431	Salve, Regina	597				
		Sing, Holy Mother	618				
		Sing of Mary, pure and lowly	622				
		Star of sea and ocean	632				

From many grains	268	O when the saints go marching in	832	Glory be to Jesus	280	O, how good is the Lord	520
From the sun's rising	270			Glory to thee, Lord God	281	O Jesus Christ, remember	521
God's Spirit is in my heart	297	**PEOPLE OF GOD (CHURCH): RIZZA, TAIZÉ and OTHER CHANTS**		Glory to thee, my God, this night	282	O Lord, my God	529
Guide me, O thou great Redeemer	307			God everlasting, wonderful and holy	284	O Lord, your tenderness	530
Heaven is open wide	323	Adoramus te, Domine (Taizé)	859	God fills me with joy	285	O praise ye the Lord	548
He brings us into his banqueting table	324	**PRAISE and THANKSGIVING**		Great indeed are your works, O Lord	306	O that today you would listen	556
Here in this place	327	Abba, abba, Father	94	Guide me, O thou great Redeemer	307	Our God loves us	560
Holy God, your pilgrim people	334	Abba, Father, send your Spirit	96	Hear my cry	321	O Word, in uncreated light	567
Holy Jesus, in our likeness born	338	All creation, bless the Lord	102	He's got the whole world in his hand	330	O worship the King	568
Into one we all are gathered	368	All creatures of our God and King	103	Holy God, we praise thy name	333	O worship the Lord in the beauty of holiness	569
I saw the Holy City	373	Alleluia, alleluia! I will praise the Father	106	Holy, holy, holy! Lord God almighty	337	Praise him	575
I, the Servant-Lord	377	Alleluia: all the earth	104	Hosanna, hosanna	344	Praise, my soul, the King of heaven	576
I will never forget you	382	Alleluia, alleluia, give thanks to the risen Lord	105	How great is our God	345	Praise the Lord	577
I will sing a song	384	Alleluia: Let us sing of the Lord	107	How lovely on the mountains	346	Praise the Lord in his holy house	578
Jerusalem the golden	387	Alleluia: Praise God	108	If God is for us	354	Praise the Lord, ye heavens, adore him	579
Jesus calls us	388	Alleluia: Sing my soul	109	Immortal, invisible	361	Praise to God for saints and martyrs	580
Let there be love	425	Alleluia, sing to Jesus	110	I saw the Holy City	373	Praise to the Holiest	582
Like the murmur of the dove's song	434	Alleluia, thank you for fathers	111	I sing a song to you, Lord	374	Praise to the Lord, the Almighty	583, 584
Longing for light	439	All for Jesus!	112	I will bless the Lord	380	Praise to you, O Christ, our Saviour	585
Look at the sky	441	All glory, laud and honour	113	I will enter his gates	381	Praise we our God with joy	586
Love divine, all loves excelling	461	All hail the power of Jesus' name	116	I will sing, I will sing	385	Rejoice, all heavenly powers	589
Love is his word	462	All heaven declares	117	Jesus calls us	388	Ring out your joy	594
Love is the only law	464	All people that on earth do dwell	121	Jesus is God	393	Salvation is God's	596
Lumen Christi	467	All the earth proclaim the Lord	123	Jesus is Lord! Creation's voice proclaims it	394	Sing, all creation	615
Moses, I know you're the man	477	All the ends of the earth	124	Jesus, Name above all names	398	Sing a new song	616
Mother of God's living Word	478	All things bright and beautiful	125	Jesu, the very thought of thee	400	Sing hallelujah to the Lord	617
O, come to the water	504	All you nations, sing out your joy	126	Jesus, the Word, has lived among us	401	Sing, my soul	620
O God of earth and altar	512	Amazing grace	131	Joy to the world	404	Sing praises to the Living God	623
On this house your blessing, Lord	543	Arise, come to your God	137	Jubilate Deo	405	Sing to the Lord, alleluia	625
Open your ears, O Christian people	546	Arise to greet the Lord of light	138	Jubilate Deo	406	Sing to the mountains	626
O thou, who at thy Eucharist didst pray	559	At the Lamb's high feast we sing	146	King of glory, King of peace	408	Taste and see the goodness of the Lord	643
Our God sent his Son long ago	561	Awake, awake: fling off the night	153	King of kings and Lord of lords	409	Tell out, my soul	644
Our hearts were made for you	562	Blessed assurance	170	Lauda, Jerusalem	411	The King of glory comes	655
Out of darkness	565	Blessed be God	171	Laudato sii, O me Signore	412	The Lord is my life	660
Peace is the gift	573	Blessed be the God of Jesus Christ	172	Let all the world in every corner sing	420	Though the mountains may fall	688
Praise to you, O Christ, our Saviour	585	Bless the Lord, my soul	173	Let our praise to you be as incense	422	To Christ, the Prince of peace	692
Salvation is God's	596	Blest be the Lord	178	Let the heavens declare	423	To Jesus' heart, all burning	693
Save us, O Lord (Dufford)	600	Bring all ye dear-bought nations	184	Let the world in concert sing	426	We behold the splendour of God	711
See us, Lord, about your altar	606	By his grace	187	Let us sing your glory	427	We shall draw water joyfully	720
The Church's one foundation	647	Christians, lift up your hearts	195	Let us, with a gladsome mind	428	Yahweh, I know you are near	744
The kingdom of heaven	654	Christ triumphant	200	Lift up your hearts	430	Yahweh is the God of my salvation	745
The temple of the living God	675	Christus vincit	201	Lo, he comes with clouds descending	438	You are beautiful	748
The wandering flock of Israel	677	Come and praise him	206	Lord, enthroned in heavenly splendour	444	Your love's greater	756
This, then, is my prayer	687	Come, let us raise a joyful song	212	Lord, the light of your love	453	**PRAISE and THANKSGIVING: CHILDREN'S SECTION**	
Thy hand, O God, has guided	690	Come on and celebrate	219	Lord, thy word abideth	454		
We are his people	709	Come, praise the Lord	220	Majesty, worship his majesty	469	All of my heart	762
We celebrate the new creation	714	Dear Lord and Father of mankind	234	Meekness and majesty	475	All the nations of the earth	764
When from bondage we are summoned	728	Father God, I wonder	249	Morning has broken	476	As Jacob with travel was weary one day	766
You are salt for the earth	749	Father, I place into your hands	251	My God, how wonderful you are	481	'Cheep!' said the sparrow	770
PEOPLE OF GOD (CHURCH): CHILDREN'S SECTION		Father, we adore you	252	My heart will sing to you	484	Christ is our King	771
		Father, we love you	254	My soul doth magnify the Lord	488	Clap your hands, all you people	772
Each of us is a living stone	782	Fill your hearts with joy and gladness	257	My soul is filled with joy	489	Clap your hands and sing this song	773
Forward in faith	786	Firmly I believe	258	My soul proclaims you, mighty God	491	Come and praise the Lord our King	774
Friends, all gather here in a circle	787	For the fruits of his creation	261	Now I know what love is	496	Come, God's children	775
God gives his people strength	790	For you my soul is thirsting	265	Now thank we all our God	497	Come into his presence	776
Isn't it good	804	From the sun's rising	270	O God beyond all praising	510	Every bird, every tree	783
Jesus put this song into our hearts	810	Give me joy in my heart	274	O God of grace we thank you	513	Fishes of the ocean	785
Lord, we've come to worship you	821	Give thanks to God	275	O God, our help in ages past	514	God almighty set a rainbow	789
O Lord, all the world	828	Give thanks with a grateful heart	276	O holy Lord, by all adored	519	God turned darkness into light	793
One hundred and fifty three!	829	Glorify the Lord	277			Hallelu, hallelu	796
Out to the great wide world we go	831	Glorious God, King of creation	278			Have you heard the raindrops	797
		Glory and praise to our God	279				

Hey, now, everybody sing	799
If I were a butterfly	800
I give my hands	801
I'm black, I'm white, I'm short, I'm tall	802
I've got peace like a river	806
I will wave my hands	807
Jesus is greater	809
Jesus put this song into our hearts	810
Let the mountains dance and sing	816
Life for the poor was hard and tough	817
Lord of the future	820
Lord, we've come to worship you	821
My mouth was made for worship	823
O give thanks	827
Our God is so great	830
Praise and thanksgiving	834
Praise God in his holy place	835
Sing a simple song	838
Sing praise to God	839
Thank you, Lord	841
There are hundreds of sparrows	842
There was one, there were two	845
We will praise	850
When the Spirit of the Lord	852
Who put the colours in the rainbow?	854
Yesterday, today, for ever	855
You've got to move	856

PRAISE and THANKSGIVING: RIZZA, TAIZÉ and OTHER CHANTS

Adoramus te Domine (Rizza)	860
Confitemini Domino	864
In the Lord I'll be ever thankful	868
In the Lord is my joy	869
Jubilate Deo (Servite)	872
Laudate Dominum	874
Laudate Omnes Gentes	875
Lord of creation	876
Magnificat	877
Misericordias Domini	879
O Christe, Domine Jesu	881
O Sacrament most holy	884
Sanctum nomen, Domini	886
The Lord is my song	892

RECESSIONAL SONG

(Sometimes the hymn after Communion is the most apt concluding song. Where the recessional song requires a further song, one of the following could be used. See also *Praise*).

Forth in the peace of Christ we go	263
God's Spirit is in my heart	297
Go in peace	299
Go, the Mass is ended	303
Praise we our God with joy	586
The Mass is ended	663
You shall go out with joy	758

RECESSIONAL SONG: RIZZA, TAIZÉ and OTHER CHANTS

Holy God, we place ourselves	867

SAINTS

For all the saints	260
Hail, glorious St Patrick	308
Heaven is open wide	323
Leader, now on earth no longer	414
Praise to God for saints and martyrs	580
When Christ our Lord to Andrew cried	727

SAINTS: CHILDREN'S SECTION

Joseph was an honest man	814
O when the saints go marching in	832

TRINITY

Eternal Father, strong to save	243
Father, in my life I see	250
Father, we adore you	252
Father, we love you	254
Glorious God, King of creation	278
Heaven is open wide	323
Holy God, we praise thy name	333
Holy, holy, holy! Lord God almighty	337
How great is our God	345
Lead us, heavenly Father, lead us	416
One Father	540

Sing praises to the living God	623
Thou, whose almighty Word	689

UNITY

All for Jesus!	112
As we are gathered	143
Be still and know I am with you	163
Bind us together, Lord	169
Brother, sister, let me serve you	186
Christ is made the sure foundation	197
Christ's is the world	198
Creator of the Day	228
For all the saints	260
Forth in the peace of Christ we go	263
Heaven is open wide	323
Here in this place	327
He's got the whole world in his hand	330
Holy God, your pilgrim people	334
Holy Jesus, in our likeness born	338
Into one we all are gathered	368
I will sing a song	384
I will sing, I will sing	385
Jesus calls us	388
Let there be love	425
Like the murmur of the dove's song	434
Lord, unite all nations	455
Lord, we come to ask your healing	456
O God of earth and altar	512
One Bread, one body	538
O thou, who at thy Eucharist didst pray	559
Praise to you, O Christ, our Saviour	585
See us, Lord, about your altar	606
The Spirit lives to set us free	672
The table's set, Lord	674
This is my will	682
Thy hand, O God, has guided	690
Where is love and loving kindness	734
Where love and charity endure	735
Where the love of Christ unites us	736
Where true love is found with charity	737
Where true love is present	738

WHITSUN

Abba, Father, send your Spirit	96
All over the world	120
Breathe on me, Breath of God	182
Breath of God, O Holy Spirit	183
Colours of day	202
Come down, O love divine	209
Come, Holy Ghost, Creator, come	210
Come, Holy Spirit, come	211
Creator of the Day	228
Dance in your Spirit	231
Grant to us, O Lord	304
Healer of our every ill	319
Holy, holy, holy	335
Holy Spirit, come, confirm us	340
Holy Spirit, Lord of light	341
Holy Spirit of fire	342
Jesus is Lord! Creations voice proclaims it	394
Like the murmur of the dove's song	434
Listen, let your heart keep seeking	435
Lord, the light of your love	453
O, come to the water	504
O living water	527
Send forth your Spirit (Rees)	608
Send forth your Spirit (Nazareth)	609
Send forth your Spirit (Rizza)	610
She sits like a bird	613
Spirit hovering o'er the waters	629
Spirit of the living God	630
The Spirit lives to set us free	672
The Spirit of the Lord	673
This is the day	684
This, then, is my prayer	687
Veni, Creator Spiritus	701
Veni, Sancte Spiritus	702

WHITSUN: CHILDREN'S SECTION

You've got to move	856

WHITSUN: RIZZA, TAIZÉ and OTHER CHANTS

Silent, surrendered	887
Veni, Sancte Spiritus	895
Veni, Sancte Spiritus (Walker)	896
You are the centre	899

Index of Sunday and Feastday Themes

1st SUNDAY OF ADVENT
Year A *Watch for his coming*
216 Come, O divine Messiah
512 O Jesus Christ, remember
544 Onward, Christian pilgrims
704 Waken, O sleeper, wake and rise
721 We shall stay awake

Year B *Wake up*
94 Abba, Abba, Father
152 Awake, awake and greet the new morn
192 Change my heart, O God
307 Guide me, o thou great Redeemer
688 Though the mountains may fall

Year C *Be prepared*
147 At the name of Jesus
316 Hark, a herald voice
705 Wake up, O people
743 Word made flesh
897 Wait for the Lord

2nd SUNDAY OF ADVENT
Year A *The Kingdom is close*
136 A noble flower of Judah
161 Behold the Saviour of the nations
503 O come, O come, Emmanuel
541 On Jordan's bank the Baptist's cry
721 We shall stay awake

Year B *The Lord is coming*
221 Come, prepare the way
227 Comfort, comfort my people
242 Enter in the wilderness
505 O comfort my people
851 When is he coming

Year C *Prepare the way*
431 Like a sea without a shore
541 On Jordan's bank the Baptist's cry
648 The coming of our God
687 This, then, is my prayer
897 Wait for the Lord

3rd SUNDAY OF ADVENT
Year A *The blind will see*
153 Awake, awake: fling off the night
221 Come, prepare the way
395 Jesus is Lord! In love he came
669 The Saviour will come resplendent in joy
706 Walk with me, O my Lord

Year B *Good News for the poor*
285 God fills me with joy
297 God's Spirit is in my heart
541 On Jordan's bank the Baptist's cry
567 O Word, in uncreated light
673 The Spirit of the Lord

Year C *Rejoice*
139 As bread my Lord comes to me
346 How lovely on the mountains
590 Rejoice in the Lord always
868 In the Lord I'll be ever thankful
897 Wait for the Lord

4th SUNDAY OF ADVENT
Year A *God with us*
316 Hark! a herald voice is calling
503 O come, O come, Emmanuel
646 The angel Gabriel from heaven came
671 The sign of hope, creation's joy
851 When is he coming

Year B *Annunciation*
141 As I kneel before you
343 Holy Virgin, by God's decree
508 Of the Father's love begotten
646 The angel Gabriel from heaven came
795 Hail, Mary, full of grace

Year C *Visitation*
167 Bethlehem, of noblest cities
478 Mother of God's living Word
526 O little town of Bethlehem
618 Sing, holy Mother
733 Where are you bound, Mary?

CHRISTMAS (see also *Index of Uses*)
Midnight *Light in the darkness*
134 Angels we have heard on high
418 Let all mortal flesh keep silence
531 O Mary, when our God chose you
614 Silent night
665 The race that long in darkness pined

Dawn *The manger*
208 Come, come, come to the manger
317 Hark, the herald angels sing
365 In the bleak midwinter
651 The first Nowell
739 While shepherds watched

Day *Word made flesh*
100 Adeste fideles
346 How lovely on the mountains
401 Jesus, the Word, has lived among us
508 Of the Father's love begotten
743 Word made flesh

HOLY FAMILY
The Presentation
465 Lovely in your littleness
599 Save us, O Lord (Nazareth)
622 Sing of Mary, pure and lowly
698 Unto us a boy is born
752 You give, Lord

MARY MOTHER OF GOD
Abba Father
94 Abba, Abba, Father
96 Abba Father, send your Spirit
867 Holy God, we place ourselves
877 Magnificat
878 May the Lord bless you

2nd SUNDAY AFTER CHRISTMAS
He dwelt among us
247 Father and life-giver
478 Mother of God's living Word
508 Of the Father's love begotten
622 Sing of Mary, pure and lowly
743 Word made flesh

EPIPHANY
The nations come
144 As with gladness men of old
167 Bethlehem, of noblest cities
651 The first Nowell
722 We three kings of Orient are
723 What child is this

BAPTISM OF THE LORD
The beloved Son
297 God's Spirit is in my heart
525 O let all who thirst
527 O living water
630 Spirit of the living God
631 Springs of water, bless the Lord

ASH WEDNESDAY
Out of the depths
269 From the depths we cry to thee
286 God forgave my sin
333 Holy God, we praise thy name
363 In company with Christians past
446 Lord, have mercy

1st SUNDAY OF LENT (see also *Index of Uses*)
Year A *The second Adam*
94 Abba, Abba, Father
189 By the cross
447 Lord Jesus Christ
582 Praise to the Holiest
811 Jesus went away to the desert

Year B *Repent*
264 Forty days and forty nights
269 From the depths we cry to thee
363 In company with Christians past
558 O the word of my Lord
792 God sends a rainbow

Year C *Trust in God*
99 Across the years there echoes still
222 Come to me
325 He is Lord
458 Lord, who throughout these forty days
759 You who dwell in the shelter of the Lord

2nd SUNDAY OF LENT
Year A *Life beyond death*
178 Blest be the Lord
207 Come back to me
378 I watch the sunrise
417 Leave your country and your people
711 We behold the splendour of God

Year B *The beloved Son*
354 If God is for us
494 Nothing shall separate us
529 O Lord, my God
657 The light of Christ
711 We behold the splendour of God

Year C *Transfigured*
292 God of eternal light
440 Look around you
448 Lord Jesus, think on me
479 My God, accept my heart this day
711 We behold the splendour of God

3rd SUNDAY OF LENT
Year A *Thirst for water*
504 O, come to the water
525 O let all who thirst
527 O living water
667 There is a river
700 Vaster far than any ocean

Year B *Jesus the new Temple*
133 A new commandment
269 From the depths we cry to thee
363 In company with Christians past
600 Save us, O Lord (Dufford)
696 Turn to me

Year C *Jesus the new Moses*
140 As earth that is dry

376	I, the Lord of sea and sky
391	Jesus, ever-flowing fountain
513	O God of grace, we thank you
527	O living water

4th SUNDAY OF LENT
Year A *From darkness into light*
153	Awake, awake: fling off the night
168	Be thou my vision
202	Colours of day
672	The Spirit lives to set us free
689	Thou, whose almighty word

Year B *Saved*
131	Amazing grace
286	God forgave my sin
290	God is love: his the care
324	He brings us into his banqueting table
458	Lord, who throughout these forty days

Year C *The prodigal Father*
293	God of mercy and compassion
461	Love divine, all loves excelling
620	Sing, my soul
714	We celebrate the new creation
753	You have been baptised in Christ

5th SUNDAY OF LENT
Year A *Raised from death*
96	Abba, Father, send your Spirit
182	Breathe on me, Breath of God
183	Breath of God, O Holy Spirit
348	I am the bread of life (Konstant)
672	The Spirit lives to set us free

Year B *Life out of death*
254	Father, we love you
304	Grant to us, O Lord
498	Now the green blade riseth
562	Our hearts were made for you
697	Unless a grain of wheat

Year C *A new start*
118	All I once held dear
133	A new commandment
461	Love divine, all loves excelling
731	When I survey the wondrous cross
757	You shall cross the barren desert

PASSION SUNDAY (PALM)
(See also *Index of Uses*)
He humbled himself
113	All glory, laud and honour
411	Lauda, Jerusalem
593	Ride on, ride on in majesty
861	Benedictus qui venit
870	Jesus, remember me

MAUNDY THURSDAY
When you eat you proclaim his death
509	Of the glorious body telling
538	One bread, one body
736	Where the love of Christ unites us
888	Stay here and keep watch
893	Ubi caritas

GOOD FRIDAY
Burdened with sin
127	All you who seek a comfort sure
552	O sacred head sore wounded
668	The royal banners forward go
719	Were you there when they crucified my Lord?
731	When I survey the wondrous cross

EASTER VIGIL
Entering the Promised Land
105	Alleluia, alleluia, give thanks to the risen Lord
271	From the very depths of darkness
325	He is Lord
326	He is risen, tell the story
399	Jesus rose on Easter day

EASTER DAY (See also *Index of Uses*)
Life out of death
156	Battle is o'er, hell's armies flee
184	Bring, all ye dear-bought nations
199	Christ the Lord is risen today
684	This is the day
686	This joyful Eastertide

2nd SUNDAY OF EASTER
Year A *New birth*
183	Breath of God, O Holy Spirit
297	God's Spirit is in my heart
626	Sing to the mountains
664	The night was dark
747	Ye sons and daughters of the Lord

Year B *Faith*
143	As we are gathered
169	Bind us together, Lord
326	He is risen, tell the story
431	Like a sea without a shore
511	O Godhead hid

Year C *Touch me*
182	Breathe on me, breath of God
508	Of the Father's love begotten
511	O Godhead hid
591	Rejoice, the Lord is King
664	The night was dark

3rd SUNDAY OF EASTER
Year A *Stay with us*
97	Abide with me
184	Bring, all ye dear-bought nations
645	Thanks for the fellowship
686	This joyful Eastertide
751	You are the light

Year B *Prince of life*
143	As we are gathered
199	Christ the Lord is risen today
444	Lord, enthroned in heavenly splendour
678	Thine be the glory
731	When I survey the wondrous cross

Year C *Victory*
229	Crown him with many crowns
350	I am the Light
379	I will be with you
419	Let all that is within me
469	Majesty, worship his majesty

4th SUNDAY OF EASTER
Year A *Healed by his wounds*
156	Battle is o'er, hell's armies flee
310	Hail, Redeemer, King divine
350	I am the Light
466	Loving shepherd of thy sheep
564	Ours were the sufferings he bore

Year B *The Good Shepherd*
114	All glory to you, Redeemer and Lord
147	At the name of Jesus
486	My shepherd is the Lord
661	The Lord's my shepherd
708	We are his children

Year C *The sheep brought to God*
146	At the Lamb's high feast we sing
310	Hail, Redeemer, King divine
373	I saw the Holy City
387	Jerusalem the golden
656	The king of love my shepherd is

5th SUNDAY OF EASTER
Year A *The Way, Truth and Life*
206	Come and praise him
349	I am the bread of life (Toolan)
350	I am the Light
546	Open your ears, O Christian people
675	The temple of the living God

Year B *The Vine*
97	Abide with me
133	A new commandment
434	Like the murmur of the dove's song
681	This is my body
697	Unless a grain of wheat

Year C *God lives among those who love*
132	And did those feet in ancient time
133	A new commandment
373	I saw the Holy City
387	Jerusalem the golden
437	Listen to my voice

6th SUNDAY OF EASTER
Year A *I will not leave you*
110	Alleluia, sing to Jesus
163	Be still and know I am with you
183	Breath of God, O Holy Spirit
209	Come down, O Love divine
345	How great is our God

Year B *Bear fruit by loving*
133	A new commandment
162	Beloved, let us love
289	God is love
681	This is my body
682	This is my will

Year C *Peace*
96	Abba Father, send your Spirit
470	Make me a channel of your peace
571	Peace I leave with you
573	Peace is the gift
697	Unless a grain of wheat

ASCENSION (See also *Index of Uses*)
Raised by God
101	A hymn of glory let us sing
110	Alleluia, sing to Jesus
311	Hail the day that sees him rise
444	Lord, enthroned in heavenly splendour
493	New praises be given

7th SUNDAY OF EASTER
Year A *Eternal life is to know God in Christ*
163	Be still and know I am with you
345	How great is our God
444	Lord, enthroned in heavenly splendour
559	O thou, who at thy Eucharist didst pray
862	Bless the Lord, my soul

Year B *God is love*
289	God is love
290	God is love: his the care
368	Into one we all are gathered
559	O thou, who at thy Eucharist didst pray
735	Where love and charity endure

Year C *May they be one in us*
94	Abba, Abba, Father
169	Bind us together, Lord
214	Come, Lord Jesus, come
297	God's Spirit is in my heart
743	Word made flesh

WHITSUN (See also *Index of Uses*)
Receive the Holy Spirit
182 Breathe on me, Breath of God
210 Come, Holy Ghost, Creator, come
527 O living water
608 Send forth your Spirit (Rees)
630 Spirit of the living God

TRINITY (See also *Index of Uses*)
Year A — *God so loved the world*
94 Abba, Abba, Father
102 All creation, bless the Lord
278 Glorious God, King of creation
630 Spirit of the living God
657 The light of Christ

Year B — *Abba Father*
95 Abba, Father, from your hands
270 From the sun's rising
333 Holy God, we praise thy name
345 How great is our God
379 I will be with you

Year C — *The love of God poured out*
96 Abba, Father, send your Spirit
182 Breathe on me, Breath of God
335 Holy, holy, holy
340 Holy Spirit, come, confirm us
416 Lead us, heavenly Father, lead us

CORPUS CHRISTI
(See also *Index of Uses* under *Communion*)
Year A — *Bread from Heaven*
203 Come and be filled
307 Guide me, O thou great Redeemer
348 I am the bread of life (Konstant)
500 O bread of heaven
511 O Godhead hid

Year B — *Body and Blood*
444 Lord, enthroned in heavenly splendour
462 Love is his word
583 Praise to the Lord, the Almighty
642 Take this and eat
681 This is my body

Year C — *Plenty for all*
273 Gifts of bread and wine
287 Godhead here in hiding
396 Jesus, Lord of glory
538 One bread, one body
738 Where true love is present

SACRED HEART
Year A — *I will give you rest*
127 All you who seek a comfort sure
162 Beloved, let us love
223 Come to me, all who labour
289 God is love
290 God is love: his the care

Year B — *The love of Christ crucified*
95 Abba Father, from your hands
146 At the Lamb's high feast we sing
240 Do not be afraid
628 Soul of my Saviour
687 This, then, is my prayer

Year C — *The loving Shepherd*
350 I am the Light
553 O Sacred Heart
634 Sweet heart of Jesus
692 To Christ, the Prince of peace
693 To Jesus' heart, all burning

SUNDAYS OF THE YEAR
1st SUNDAY (See *Baptism of the Lord*)

2nd SUNDAY
Year A — *Lamb of God*
132 And did those feet in ancient time
160 Behold, the Lamb of God
410 Lamb of God, Holy One
573 Peace is the gift
631 Springs of water, bless the Lord

Year B — *Called*
234 Dear Lord and Father of mankind
259 Follow me, follow me
435 Listen, let your heart keep seeking
483 My God said to me, 'Follow'
727 When Christ our Lord to Andrew cried

Year C — *Bride and Groom*
247 Father and life-giver
288 God in the planning
368 Into one we all are gathered
562 Our hearts were made for you
630 Spirit of the living God

3rd SUNDAY
Year A — *Light has dawned*
154 Awake from your slumber
234 Dear Lord and Father of mankind
350 I am the Light
453 Lord, the light of your love
665 The race that long in darkness pined

Year B — *Follow me*
234 Dear Lord and Father of mankind
259 Follow me, follow me
451 Lord of life
483 My God said to me, 'Follow'
740 Will you come and follow me

Year C — *Good News*
297 God's Spirit is in my heart
471 Make way, make way
673 The Spirit of the Lord
735 Where love and charity endure
736 Where the love of Christ unites us

4th SUNDAY
Year A — *Good News for the poor*
158 Be blessed, pure of heart
174 Blest are the pure in heart
654 The kingdom of heaven
717 We hold a treasure
749 You are salt for the earth

Year B — *The crowds stare*
163 Be still and know I am with you
333 Holy God, we praise thy name
529 O Lord, my God
561 Our God sent his Son long ago
582 Praise to the Holiest

Year C — *Persecuted love*
194 Christ be beside me
355 If I am lacking love
463 Love is patient
557 O, the love of my Lord
644 Tell out, my soul

5th SUNDAY
Year A — *Light*
350 I am the Light
439 Longing for light
467 Lumen Christi
672 The Spirit lives to set us free
749 You are salt for the earth

Year B — *Healing the broken*
164 Be still and know that I am God
202 Colours of day
319 Healer of our every ill
320 Healer of the sick
413 Lay your hands gently upon us

Year C — *Called by the Holy God*
234 Dear Lord and Father of mankind
259 Follow me, follow me
333 Holy God, we praise thy name
376 I, the Lord of sea and sky
740 Will you come and follow me

6th SUNDAY
Year A — *What God demands*
224 Come to me, come, my people
307 Guide me, O thou great Redeemer
390 Jesus Christ is waiting
654 The kingdom of heaven
738 Where true love is present

Year B — *Healing*
283 God be in my head
413 Lay your hands gently upon us
447 Lord Jesus Christ
620 Sing, my soul
740 Will you come and follow me

Year C — *Good News for the poor*
174 Blest are the pure in heart
589 Rejoice, all heavenly powers
654 The kingdom of heaven
757 You shall cross the barren desert
1041 Happy indeed (Psalm 1)

7th SUNDAY
Year A — *Love your enemies*
186 Brother, sister, let me serve you
425 Let there be love
462 Love is his word
464 Love is the only law
828 O Lord, all the world

Year B — *Forgiven and healed*
131 Amazing grace
170 Blessed assurance
195 Christians, lift up your hearts
286 God forgave my sin
304 Grant to us, O Lord

Year C — *Compassion*
94 Abba, Abba, Father
425 Let there be love
464 Love is the only law
470 Make me a channel of your peace
726 Whatsoever you do

8th SUNDAY
Year A — *At rest in God*
382 I will never forget you
445 Lord, for tomorrow and its needs
604 Seek ye first
688 Though the mountains may fall
779 Do not worry over what to eat

Year B — *Wedded to God*
133 A new commandment
169 Bind us together, Lord
207 Come back to me
562 Our hearts were made for you
724 What feast of love

Year C — *Giving yourself away*
194 Christ be beside me
385 I will sing, I will sing
431 Like a sea without a shore
558 O the word of my Lord
678 Thine be the glory

9th SUNDAY
Year A — *Building on rock*
- 119 All my hope on God is founded
- 448 Lord Jesus, think on me
- 514 O God, our help in ages past
- 647 The Church's one foundation
- 847 The wise man

Year B — *Freedom from slavery*
- 266 Freedom for my people
- 299 Go in peace
- 355 If I am lacking love
- 711 We behold the splendour of God
- 717 We hold a treasure

Year C — *Outsiders are welcome*
- 139 As bread my Lord comes to me
- 164 Be still and know that I am God
- 197 Christ is made the sure foundation
- 240 Do not be afraid
- 395 Jesus is Lord! In love he came

10th SUNDAY
Year A — *I want love not ritual*
- 355 If I am lacking love
- 376 I, the Lord of sea and sky
- 462 Love is his word
- 463 Love is patient
- 562 Our hearts were made for you

Year B — *Adam and Satan*
- 168 Be thou my vision
- 186 Brother, sister, let me serve you
- 299 Go in peace
- 582 Praise to the Holiest
- 746 Ye choirs of new Jerusalem

Year C — *The dead raised to life*
- 220 Come, praise the Lord
- 348 I am the bread of life (Konstant)
- 520 O, how good is the Lord
- 561 Our God sent his Son long ago
- 564 Ours were the sufferings he bore

11th SUNDAY
Year A — *Spread the Good News*
- 206 Come and praise him
- 286 God forgave my sin
- 289 God is love
- 303 Go, the Mass is ended
- 546 Open your ears, O Christian people

Year B — *Growth of the Kingdom*
- 120 All over the world
- 123 All the earth proclaim the Lord
- 180 Bread from the earth
- 226 Come, ye thankful people, come
- 351 I cannot tell

Year C — *God forgives*
- 131 Amazing grace
- 237 Deep within my heart
- 258 Firmly I believe
- 620 Sing, my soul
- 862 Bless the Lord, my soul

12th SUNDAY
Year A — *Do not be afraid*
- 240 Do not be afraid
- 370 In your coming and going
- 378 I watch the sunrise
- 582 Praise to the Holiest
- 688 Though the mountains may fall

Year B — *The Conqueror of chaos*
- 166 Be still, my soul
- 416 Lead us, heavenly Father, lead us
- 435 Listen, let your heart keep seeking
- 647 The Church's one foundation
- 706 Walk with me, O my Lord

Year C — *Take up the cross*
- 189 By the cross
- 259 Follow me, follow me
- 429 Lift high the cross
- 483 My God said to me, 'Follow'
- 538 One bread, one body

13th SUNDAY
Year A — *Cups of water are rewarded*
- 259 Follow me, follow me
- 429 Lift high the cross
- 483 My God said to me, 'Follow'
- 667 There is a river
- 753 You have been baptised in Christ

Year B — *Victory over death*
- 325 He is Lord
- 352 I come like a beggar
- 447 Lord Jesus Christ
- 862 Bless the Lord, my soul
- 880 Nada te turbe

Year C — *Follow me*
- 259 Follow me, follow me
- 266 Freedom for my people
- 350 I am the Light
- 585 Praise to you, O Christ, our Saviour
- 754 You have called us

14th SUNDAY
Year A — *Humility*
- 127 All you who seek a comfort sure
- 223 Come to me, all who labour
- 224 Come to me, come, my people
- 377 I, the Servant-Lord
- 725 What kind of greatness

Year B — *Speak out*
- 168 Be thou my vision
- 194 Christ be beside me
- 240 Do not be afraid
- 297 God's Spirit is in my heart
- 331 He who would valiant be

Year C — *Make peace*
- 263 Forth in the peace of Christ we go
- 286 God forgave my sin
- 572 Peace is flowing like a river
- 573 Peace is the gift
- 731 When I survey the wondrous cross

15th SUNDAY
Year A — *The prodigal Sower*
- 140 As earth that is dry
- 350 I am the Light
- 435 Listen, let your heart keep seeking
- 565 Out of darkness
- 639 Take my hands

Year B — *Go and preach*
- 172 Blessed be the God of Jesus Christ
- 270 From the sun's rising
- 286 God forgave my sin
- 297 God's Spirit is in my heart
- 303 Go, the Mass is ended

Year C — *God's Word is near you*
- 214 Come, Lord Jesus, come
- 362 In bread we bring you, Lord
- 444 Lord, enthroned in heavenly splendour
- 464 Love is the only law
- 726 Whatsoever you do

16th SUNDAY
Year A — *The lenient Judge*
- 226 Come, ye thankful people, come
- 261 For the fruits of his creation
- 527 O living water
- 540 One Father
- 670 The seed is Christ's

Year B — *The Shepherd*
- 407 Keep in mind
- 486 My shepherd is the Lord
- 656 The King of love my shepherd is
- 661 The Lord's my shepherd
- 677 The wandering flock of Israel

Year C — *God in the midst*
- 194 Christ be beside me
- 235 Deep calls to deep
- 369 In you, my God
- 557 O, the love of my Lord
- 691 To be in your presence

17th SUNDAY
Year A — *Discernment*
- 94 Abba, Abba, Father
- 369 In you, my God
- 567 O Word, in uncreated light
- 670 The seed is Christ's
- 717 We hold a treasure

Year B — *The hungry are fed*
- 139 As bread my Lord comes to me
- 169 Bind us together, Lord
- 272 Gather around, for the table is spread
- 362 In bread we bring you, Lord
- 690 Thy hand, O God, has guided

Year C — *Never stop asking*
- 83-87 Our Father
- 286 God forgave my sin
- 423 Let the heavens declare
- 604 Seek ye first
- 897 Wait for the Lord

18th SUNDAY
Year A — *God's pity*
- 140 As earth that is dry
- 354 If God is for us
- 504 O, come to the water
- 525 O let all who thirst
- 667 There is a river

Year B — *Bread from Heaven*
- 348 I am the bread of life (Konstant)
- 349 I am the bread of life (Toolan)
- 500 O bread of heaven
- 743 Word made flesh
- 865 Eat this bread

Year C — *Rich before God*
- 194 Christ be beside me
- 262 For the healing of the nations
- 311 Hail the day that sees him rise
- 512 O God of earth and altar
- 779 Do not worry over what to eat

19th SUNDAY
Year A — *Calm after the storm*
- 234 Dear Lord and Father of mankind
- 243 Eternal Father, strong to save
- 379 I will be with you
- 706 Walk with me, O my Lord
- 863 Calm me, Lord

Year B — *The Bread of Life*
- 139 As bread my Lord comes to me

348	I am the bread of life (Konstant)	**23rd SUNDAY**		512	O God of earth and altar
349	I am the bread of life (Toolan)	Year A	*Responsibility for brothers and sisters*	658	The Lord hears the cry of the poor
425	Let there be love	186	Brother, sister, let me serve you	726	Whatsoever you do
642	Take this and eat	289	God is love	730	When I needed a neighbour
Year C	*The virtuous saved*	470	Make me a channel of your peace		
153	Awake, awake: fling off the night	736	Where the love of Christ unites us	Year C	*Riches corrupt you*
240	Do not be afraid	738	Where true love is present	224	Come to me, come, my people
245	Faith in God			255	Fight the good fight
307	Guide me, O thou great Redeemer	Year B	*The deaf hear again*	390	Jesus Christ is waiting
717	We hold a treasure	158	Be blessed, pure of heart	448	Lord Jesus, think on me
		395	Jesus is Lord! In love he came	604	Seek ye first
20th SUNDAY		413	Lay your hands gently upon us		
Year A	*God so loved the whole world*	669	The Saviour will come, resplendent in joy	**27th SUNDAY**	
262	For the healing of the nations			Year A	*Sour grapes*
297	God's Spirit is in my heart	771	Christ is our king	236	Deep peace of the running wave to you
330	He's got the whole world in his hand	Year C	*Counting the cost*	534	O my people, what have I done to you?
658	The Lord hears the cry of the poor	259	Follow me, follow me	571	Peace I leave with you
765	And everyone beneath the vine and fig tree	483	My God said to me, 'Follow'	675	The temple of the living God
		697	Unless a grain of wheat	782	Each of us is a living stone
Year B	*Come and eat*	740	Will you come and follow me		
203	Come and be filled	754	You have called us	Year B	*Man and wife, one body*
256	Fill my house			133	A new commandment
348	I am the bread of life (Konstant)	**24th SUNDAY**		147	At the name of Jesus
371	I received the living God	Year A	*As forgiving as God*	289	God is love
659	The Lord is alive	164	Be still and know that I am God	421	Let love be real
		186	Brother, sister, let me serve you	1029	O blessed are those who fear the Lord
Year C	*Setting the world on fire*	286	God forgave my sin		
168	Be thou my vision	449	Lord, make me a means of your peace	Year C	*Increase our faith*
255	Fight the good fight	862	Bless the Lord, my soul	119	All my hope on God is founded
331	He who would valiant be			245	Faith in God
370	In your coming and going	Year B	*What faith entails*	416	Lead us, heavenly Father, lead us
688	Though the mountains may fall	189	By the cross	417	Leave your country and your people
		259	Follow me, follow me	1062	Come ring out our joy
21st SUNDAY		354	If God is for us		
Year A	*Built on rock*	483	My God said to me, 'Follow!'	**28th SUNDAY**	
197	Christ is made the sure foundation	754	You have called us	Year A	*Everyone is invited*
324	He brings us into his banqueting table			146	At the Lamb's high feast we sing
647	The Church's one foundation	Year C	*The prodigal Father*	256	Fill my house
654	The kingdom of heaven	99	Across the years there echoes still	480	My God, and is thy table spread
690	Thy hand, O God, has guided	131	Amazing grace	661	The Lord's my shepherd
		293	God of mercy and compassion	690	Thy hand, O God, has guided
Year B	*To whom else would we go?*	517	O God, your people gather		
97	Abide with me	700	Vaster far than any ocean	Year B	*The Kingdom is worth every sacrifice*
110	Alleluia, sing to Jesus			259	Follow me, follow me
165	Be still, for the presence of the Lord	**25th SUNDAY**		417	Leave your country and your people
379	I will be with you	Year A	*Generous to a fault*	451	Lord of life
755	You have the message of eternal life	173	Bless the Lord, my soul	558	O the word of my Lord
		178	Blest be the Lord	717	We hold a treasure
Year C	*No east or west*	290	God is love: his the care		
115	All God's people, here together	520	O, how good is the Lord	Year C	*Gratitude*
120	All over the world	620	Sing, my soul	111	Alleluia, thank you for fathers
262	For the healing of the nations			320	Healer of the sick
330	He's got the whole world in his hand	Year B	*Servants of each other*	407	Keep in mind
420	Let all the world in every corner sing	174	Blest are the pure in heart	697	Unless a grain of wheat
		186	Brother, sister, let me serve you	1063	Sing a new song to the Lord
22nd SUNDAY		470	Make me a channel of your peace		
Year A	*A living sacrifice*	533	O my Lord, within my heart	**29th SUNDAY**	
94	Abba, Abba, Father	571	Peace I leave with you	Year A	*God as Supreme King*
259	Follow me, follow me			119	All my hope on God is founded
331	He who would valiant be	Year C	*The right use of money*	120	All over the world
483	My God said to me, 'Follow'	123	All the earth proclaim the Lord	361	Immortal, invisible, God only wise
544	Onward, Christian pilgrims	262	For the healing of the nations	696	Turn to me
		286	God forgave my sin	998	O sing a new song
Year B	*Submit to God's Word*	512	O God of earth and altar		
304	Grant to us, O Lord	658	The Lord hears the cry of the poor	Year B	*Christ tested as we are*
390	Jesus Christ is waiting			114	All glory to you, Redeemer and Lord
558	O the word of my Lord	**26th SUNDAY**		267	From heaven you came
658	The Lord hears the cry of the poor	Year A	*Humble repentance*	444	Lord, enthroned in heavenly splendour
675	The temple of the living God	147	At the name of Jesus	582	Praise to the Holiest
		325	He is Lord	728	When from bondage we are summoned
Year C	*The heavenly Jerusalem for the humble*	338	Holy Jesus, in our likeness born		
224	Come to me, come, my people	385	I will sing, I will sing	Year C	*Unrelenting prayer*
285	God fills me with joy	475	Meekness and majesty	262	For the healing of the nations
327	Here in this place			561	Our God sent his Son long ago
373	I saw the Holy City	Year B	*Whatsoever you do to the least*	644	Tell out, my soul
387	Jerusalem the golden	262	For the healing of the nations	658	The Lord hears the cry of the poor
				1064	I lift up my eyes

30th SUNDAY

Year A	*Loving neighbours is like loving God*
133	A new commandment
464	Love is the only law
658	The Lord hears the cry of the poor
726	Whatsoever you do
762	All of my heart

Year B	*Lord that I may see*
131	Amazing grace
320	Healer of the sick
444	Lord, enthroned in heavenly splendour
658	The Lord hears the cry of the poor
870	Jesus, remember me

Year C	*God prefers sinners*
97	Abide with me
255	Fight the good fight
318	Have mercy on us, O Lord
436	Listen to me, Yahweh
437	Listen to my voice

31st SUNDAY

Year A	*A warning for priests*
174	Blest are the pure in heart
304	Grant to us, O Lord
338	Holy Jesus, in our likeness born
377	I, the Servant-Lord
1000	O Lord, my heart is not proud

Year B	*Loving God and neighbour*
119	All my hope on God is founded
133	A new commandment
362	In bread we bring you, Lord
583	Praise to the Lord, the Almighty
726	Whatsoever you do

Year C	*God saves the lost*
131	Amazing grace
290	God is love: his the care
583	Praise to the Lord, the Almighty
857	Zacchaeus was a very little man
1066	I will give you glory

32nd SUNDAY

Year A	*Keep watch*
153	Awake, awake: fling off the night
154	Awake from your slumber
274	Give me joy in my heart
566	O Wisdom, source of harmony
704	Waken, O sleeper, wake and rise

Year B	*Giving one's all*
213	Come, Lord Jesus
286	God forgave my sin
639	Take my hands
652	The head that once was crowned with thorns
1034	It is the Lord who keeps faith

Year C	*Always alive before God*
220	Come, praise the Lord
348	I am the bread of life (Konstant)
451	Lord of life
649	The day of resurrection
659	The Lord is alive

33rd SUNDAY

Year A	*Using our talents*
122	All that I am
251	Father, I place into your hands
639	Take my hands
705	Wake up, O people
726	Whatsoever you do

Year B	*Saved from disaster*
286	God forgave my sin
438	Lo, he comes with clouds descending
467	Lumen Christi
521	O Jesus Christ, remember
759	You who dwell in the shelter of the Lord

Year C	*Don't give in*
370	In your coming and going
567	O Word, in uncreated light
648	The coming of our God
757	You shall cross the barren desert
1068	Sing psalms to the Lord

34th SUNDAY (CHRIST THE KING)

Year A	*Bandaging the wounded*
228	Creator of the day
311	Hail the day that sees him rise
390	Jesus Christ is waiting
466	Loving shepherd of thy sheep
726	Whatsoever you do

Year B	*Christ Supreme*
124	All the ends of the earth
229	Crown him with many crowns
336	Holy, holy, holy is the Lord
469	Majesty, worship his majesty
652	The head that once was crowned with thorns

Year C	*A place for us in the Kingdom*
201	Christus vincit
314	Hail to the Lord's anointed
423	Let the heavens declare
444	Lord, enthroned in heavenly splendour
870	Jesus, remember me

Responsorial Psalm Index

A complete set of Responsorial Psalms will be found at numbers 900-1078.

Those suggested below are either alternative translations, paraphrases or songs based on the appropriate psalm.

The Lectionary also provides for common psalms for each season which are also noted here.

ADVENT
Common Psalms		Psalm 24	694
		Psalm 84	716

First Sunday
- Year A   Use common psalm
- Year B   Psalm 79   600
- Year C   Psalm 24   694

Second Sunday
- Year A   Psalm 71   314
- Year B   Psalm 84   716
- Year C   Use common psalm

Third Sunday
- Year A   Psalm 145   106
- Year B   Magnificat   109, 285, 488, 489, 491, 644, 679
- Year C   Isaiah 12   720, 745

Fourth Sunday
- Year A   Use common psalm
- Year B   Psalm 88   879
- Year C   Psalm 79   600

THE NATIVITY OF OUR LORD
Common Psalm   Psalm 97   124

Midnight Mass,
- Years A, B, C   Psalm 95   171, 625

Mass during the day,
- Years A, B, C   Psalm 97   124

The Holy Family
- Years A, B, C   Use common psalm
- Year B ad lib   Psalm 104   426
- Year C ad lib   Use common psalm

Solemnity of Mary, Mother of God
- Years A, B, C   Use common psalm

Second Sunday after Christmas
- Years A, B, C   Psalm 147   411

The Epiphany of the Lord
- Years A, B, C   Psalm 71   314

The Baptism of the Lord
- Year A   Use common psalm
- Year B ad lib   Isaiah 12   720, 745
- Year C ad lib   Psalm 103   568, 609, 610

LENT
Common Psalms	Psalm 50	160, 318
	Psalm 90	178, 759
	Psalm 129	222, 269, 741

Ash Wednesday
- Years A, B, C   Psalm 50   160, 318

First Sunday of Lent
- Year A   Psalm 50   160, 31
- Year B   Psalm 24   694
- Year C   Psalm 90   178, 759

Second Sunday of Lent
- Year A   Psalm 32   405
- Year B   Psalm 115   386
- Year C   Psalm 26   660

Third Sunday of Lent
- Year A   Psalm 94   556
- Year B   Psalm 18   755
- Year C   Psalm 102   108, 576, 862

Fourth Sunday of Lent
- Year A   Psalm 22   486, 656, 661
- Year B   Psalm 136   190
- Year C   Psalm 33   643, 658

Fifth Sunday of Lent
- Year A   Psalm 129   222, 269, 741
- Year B   Psalm 50   160, 318
- Year C   Use common psalm

HOLY WEEK
Passion Sunday
- Years A, B, C   Psalm 21   483

Holy Thursday, Evening Mass of the Lord's Supper
- Years A, B, C   Psalm 115   386

Good Friday, Celebration of the Lord's Passion
- Years A, B, C   Psalm 30   369

Easter Sunday, The Easter Vigil
Common Psalm   Psalm 135
- Years A, B, C   Psalm 103   568, 609, 610

After the
- second Reading   Use common psalm
- third Reading   Use common psalm
- fourth Reading   Use common psalm
- fifth Reading   Isaiah 12   720, 745
- sixth Reading   Psalm 18   755
- seventh Reading   Psalm 41-42   142, 432, 433

If Baptism takes place   Use common psalm

Easter Sunday, The Mass of Easter Night
- Years A, B, C   Psalm 117   275

EASTER
Common Psalms	Psalm 117	275
	Psalm 65	126, 430

Easter Sunday, Mass of the Day
- Years A, B, C   Psalm 117   275

Second Sunday of Easter
- Year A   Psalm 117   275
- Year B   Psalm 117   275
- Year C   Psalm 117   275

Third Sunday of Easter
- Year A   Use common psalm
- Year B   Use common psalm
- Year C   Use common psalm

Fourth Sunday of Easter
- Year A   Psalm 22   486, 656, 661
- Year B   Psalm 117   782
- Year C   Psalm 99   104, 121, 123, 137, 406, 615, 709

Fifth Sunday of Easter
- Year A   Psalm 32   405
- Year B   Use common psalm
- Year C   Use common psalm

Sixth Sunday of Easter
- Year A   Psalm 65   126, 430
- Year B   Psalm 97   124
- Year C   Use common psalm

The Ascension of the Lord
- Years A, B, C   Psalm 46   577

Seventh Sunday of Easter
- Year A   Psalm 26   660
- Year B   Psalm 102   108, 576, 862
- Year C   Use common psalm

PENTECOST
Pentecost Sunday
- Years A, B, C   Psalm 103   568, 609, 610

The Most Holy Trinity
- Year A   Daniel 3   594
- Year B   Psalm 32   405
- Year C   Use common psalm

The Body and Blood of Christ
- Year A   Psalm 147   411
- Year B   Psalm 115   386
- Year C   Use common psalm

SUNDAYS OF THE YEAR
Common Psalms	Psalm 18	755
	Psalm 26	660
	Psalm 33	643, 658
	Psalm 62	265
	Psalm 94	556
	Psalm 99	104, 121, 123, 137, 406, 615, 709
	Psalm 102	108, 576, 862
	Psalm 144	
(Last weeks)	Psalm 121	

YEAR A
Second Sunday in Ordinary Time
- Year A   Use common psalm

Third Sunday in Ordinary Time
- Year A   Psalm 26   660

Fourth Sunday in Ordinary Time
- Year A   Psalm 145   106

Fifth Sunday in Ordinary Time
- Year A   Use common psalm

Sixth Sunday in Ordinary Time
- Year A   Use common psalm

Seventh Sunday in Ordinary Time
- Year A   Psalm 102   108, 576, 862

Eighth Sunday in Ordinary Time
- Year A   Use common psalm

Ninth Sunday in Ordinary Time
- Year A   Psalm 30   369

Tenth Sunday in Ordinary Time
- Year A   Use common psalm

Eleventh Sunday in Ordinary Time
- Year A   Psalm 99   104, 121, 123, 137, 406, 615, 709

Twelfth Sunday in Ordinary Time
- Year A   Use common psalm

Thirteenth Sunday in Ordinary Time
- Year A   Psalm 88   879

Fourteenth Sunday in Ordinary Time
- Year A   Use common psalm

Fifteenth Sunday in Ordinary Time
- Year A   Psalm 64   279

Sixteenth Sunday in Ordinary Time
- Year A   Use common psalm

Seventeenth Sunday in Ordinary Time
- Year A   Use common psalm

Eighteenth Sunday in Ordinary Time
- Year A   Use common psalm

Nineteenth Sunday in Ordinary Time
- Year A   Psalm 84   716

Twentieth Sunday in Ordinary Time
- Year A   Use common psalm

Twenty-first Sunday in Ordinary Time, Year A   Use common psalm

Twenty-second Sunday in Ordinary Time, Year A   Psalm 62   265

Twenty-third Sunday in Ordinary Time, Year A   Psalm 94   556

Twenty-fourth Sunday in Ordinary Time, Year A   Psalm 102   108, 576, 862

Twenty-fifth Sunday in Ordinary Time, Year A   Use common psalm

Twenty-sixth Sunday in Ordinary
    Time, Year A   Psalm 24   694
Twenty-seventh Sunday in Ordinary
    Time, Year A   Psalm 79   600
Twenty-eighth Sunday in Ordinary
    Time, Year A   Psalm 22   486, 656, 661
Twenty-ninth Sunday in Ordinary
    Time, Year A   Psalm 95   171, 625
Thirtieth Sunday in Ordinary Time
    Year A   Psalm 17   369
Thirty-first Sunday in Ordinary Time
    Year A   Psalm 130   490, 533, 883
Thirty-second Sunday in Ordinary
    Time, Year A   Psalm 62   265
Thirty-third Sunday in Ordinary Time
    Year A   Use common psalm
Our Lord Jesus Christ, Universal King
    Psalm 22   486, 656, 661

YEAR B
Second Sunday in Ordinary Time
    Year B   Use common psalm
Third Sunday in Ordinary Time
    Year B   Psalm 24   694
Fourth Sunday in Ordinary Time
    Year B   Psalm 94   556
Fifth Sunday in Ordinary Time
    Year B   Psalm 146   384
Sixth Sunday in Ordinary Time
    Year B   Use common psalm
Seventh Sunday in Ordinary Time
    Year B   Use common psalm
Eighth Sunday in Ordinary Time
    Year B   Psalm 102   108, 576, 862
Ninth Sunday in Ordinary Time
    Year B   Use common psalm
Tenth Sunday in Ordinary Time
    Year B   Psalm 129   222, 269, 741
Eleventh Sunday in Ordinary
    Time, Year B   Use common psalm
Twelfth Sunday in Ordinary
    Time, Year B   Use common psalm
Thirteenth Sunday in Ordinary
    Time, Year B   Use common psalm
Fourteenth Sunday in Ordinary Time
    Year B   Use common psalm
Fifteenth Sunday in Ordinary Time
    Year B   Psalm 84   716
Sixteenth Sunday in Ordinary Time
    Year B   Psalm 22   486, 656, 661
Seventeenth Sunday in Ordinary
    Time, Year B   Use common psalm
Eighteenth Sunday in Ordinary Time
    Year B   Use common psalm
Nineteenth Sunday in Ordinary Time
    Year B   Psalm 33   643, 658
Twentieth Sunday in Ordinary Time
    Year B   Psalm 33   643, 658
Twenty-first Sunday in Ordinary
    Time, Year B   Psalm 33   643, 658
Twenty-second Sunday in Ordinary
    Time, Year B   Use common psalm
Twenty-third Sunday in Ordinary
    Time, Year B   Psalm 145   106
Twenty-fourth Sunday in Ordinary
    Time, Year B   Use common psalm
Twenty-fifth Sunday in Ordinary
    Time, Year B   Use common psalm
Twenty-sixth Sunday in Ordinary
    Time, Year B   Psalm 18   755
Twenty-seventh Sunday in Ordinary
    Time, Year B   Use common psalm
Twenty-eighth Sunday in Ordinary
    Time, Year B   Use common psalm
Twenty-ninth Sunday in Ordinary
    Time, Year B   Psalm 32   405
Thirtieth Sunday in Ordinary Time
    Year B   Use common psalm
Thirty-first Sunday in Ordinary Time
    Year B   Psalm 17   369
Thirty-second Sunday in Ordinary
    Time, Year B   Psalm 145   106
Thirty-third Sunday in Ordinary Time
    Year B   Use common psalm
Our Lord Jesus Christ, Universal King
    Use common psalm

YEAR C
Second Sunday in Ordinary Time
    Year C   Psalm 95   171, 625
Third Sunday in Ordinary Time
    Year C   Psalm 18   755
Fourth Sunday in Ordinary Time
    Year C   Psalm 70   245
Fifth Sunday in Ordinary Time
    Year C   Use common psalm
Sixth Sunday in Ordinary Time
    Year C   Use common psalm
Seventh Sunday in Ordinary Time
    Year C   Psalm 102   108, 576, 862
Eighth Sunday in Ordinary Time
    Year C   Use common psalm
Ninth Sunday in Ordinary Time
    Year C   Psalm 116   220, 874
Tenth Sunday in Ordinary Time
    Year C   Use common psalm
Eleventh Sunday in Ordinary Time
    Year C   Use common psalm
Twelfth Sunday in Ordinary Time
    Year C   Psalm 62   265
Thirteenth Sunday in Ordinary Time
    Year C   Use common psalm
Fourteenth Sunday in Ordinary Time
    Year C   Psalm 65   126, 430
Fifteenth Sunday in Ordinary Time
    Year C   Use common psalm
    Alternative   Psalm 18   755
Sixteenth Sunday in Ordinary Time
    Year C   Use common psalm
Seventeenth Sunday in Ordinary
    Time, Year C   Use common psalm
Eighteenth Sunday in Ordinary Time
    Year C   Use common psalm
    Alternative   Psalm 94   556
Nineteenth Sunday in Ordinary Time
    Year C   Psalm 32   405
Twentieth Sunday in Ordinary Time
    Year C   Use common psalm
Twenty-first Sunday in Ordinary
    Time, Year C   Psalm 116   220, 874
Twenty-second Sunday in Ordinary
    Time, Year C   Use common psalm
Twenty-third Sunday in Ordinary
    Time, Year C   Use common psalm
Twenty-fourth Sunday in Ordinary
    Time, Year C   Psalm 50   160, 318
Twenty-fifth Sunday in Ordinary
    Time, Year C   Use common psalm
Twenty-sixth Sunday in Ordinary
    Time, Year C   Psalm 145   106
Twenty-seventh Sunday in Ordinary
    Time, Year C   Psalm 94   556
Twenty-eighth Sunday in Ordinary
    Time, Year C   Psalm 97   124
Twenty-ninth Sunday in Ordinary
    Time, Year C   Psalm 120   370
Thirtieth Sunday in Ordinary Time
    Year C   Psalm 32   405
Thirty-first Sunday in Ordinary Time
    Year C   Use common psalm
Thirty-second Sunday in Ordinary
    Time, Year C   Use common psalm
Thirty-third Sunday in Ordinary Time
    Year C   Psalm 97   124
Our Lord Jesus Christ, Universal King
    Psalm 121

FEAST DAYS
The Presentation of the Lord
    Years A, B, C   Psalm 23   311, 655
The Birth of St John the Baptist
    Years A, B, C   Psalm 138
SS Peter and Paul, Apostles
    Years A, B, C   Psalm 33   643, 658
The Transfiguration of the Lord
    Years A, B, C   Psalm 96
The Assumption of the Blessed
    Virgin Mary
    Years A, B, C   Psalm 44
The Triumph of the Cross
    Years A, B, C   Psalm 77
All Saints
    Years A, B, C   Psalm 23   311, 655
The Commemoration of all the
    Faithful Departed
    Years A, B, C   Psalm 26   660
The Dedication of a Church
    Psalm 45

Index of First Lines

This index is in five parts:
1. Mass Music
2. Hymns and Songs
3. Children's Hymns and Songs
4. Chants
5. Eucharistic Adoration with Benediction

Responsorial Psalms at numbers 900-1078 are not included in this index.

This index gives the first line of each hymn. If a hymn is known also by a title (e.g. As gentle as silence) this is given as well, but indented and in italic.

MASS MUSIC

A New People's Mass (Murray) 1
A Simple Mass (Moore) 2
Mass of the spirit (Mayhew) 3
Mass of the Bread of Life (Rizza) 4
Missa de Angelis (Plainsong) 5
Mass XVIII (Plainsong) 6
American Eucharist 7
Hopwood Mass 8
Israeli Mass 9

Penitential Rite

Lord, have mercy (Missa de Angelis) 10
Lord, have mercy (Orbis Factor) 11
Lord, have mercy (Alme Pater) 12
Kyrie eleison (Haugen) 13
Lord, have mercy (Archer) 14
Lord, have mercy (Rock) 15
Kyrie eleison (Rizza) 16
Kyrie (Mawby) 17
Kyrie (Taizé) 18
Lord, have mercy on us (Filitz) 19

Gloria

Coventry 20
Rees 21
Archer 22
Taizé 23
Daniels 24
Anderson 25
Salazar 26
Duffy 27
Lourdes 28
Leftley 29
Peruvian 30
Country Gardens 31
Ash Grove 32

Gospel Acclamation

Advent (Joncas) 33
Alleluia (Lloyd) 34
Scottish (Kelly) 35
Irish 36
Celtic 37
Eightfold 38
Easter (Moore) 39
Berthier 40
Archer 41
Plainsong 42
Moore No. 1 43
Moore No. 2 44
White 45
Moore No. 3 46
Bevenot 47
Lundy 48
Alleluia! Magnificat! 49
Alleluia: We will hear your Word 50
Halle, halle, halle 51
Sing praises to the Lord 52
Lent and Holy Week (Lundy) 53
Lent and Holy Week (Walsh) 54
Lent and Holy Week (Moore) 55

Creed

Credo 3 56
Lourdes 57
Fitzpatrick 58

Sanctus

MacMillan 59
Celtic Liturgy 60
Donnelly 61
Deutsche Messe 62
Taizé 63
Lourdes 64
Holy, holy, holy is the Lord 65
Slane 66
Ash Grove 67

Memorial Acclamation

Christ has died

Celtic Liturgy 68
Duffy 69
Donnelly 70
Hill 71
Wise 72

Dying you destroyed our death (Duffy) 73

When we eat this bread

Irish 74
MacMillan 75
Proulx 76

Great Amen

Mayhew 77
Lourdes 78
Plainsong 79
Hill 80
Proulx 81
South African 82

Lord's Prayer

White 83
Wiener 84
Rimsky-Korsakov 85
Echo 86
Caribbean 87

Agnus Dei

Fitzpatrick 88
Archer 89
Rees 90
Inwood 91
Duffy 92
Repton 93

HYMNS and SONGS

A

Abba, Abba, Father 94
Abba Father, from your hands 95
Abba, Father, send your Spirit 96
Abide with me 97
A child is born in Bethlehem 98
Across the years there echoes still 99
Adeste fideles 100
  Advent acclamations 721
  Advent song 213
  A healing song 437
A hymn of glory let us sing! 101
All creation, bless the Lord 102
All creatures of our God and King 103
Alleluia: All the earth 104
Alleluia, alleluia, give thanks to the risen Lord 105
Alleluia, I will praise the Father 106
Alleluia: Let us sing of the Lord 107
  Alleluia: My soul praises the glory – see
  Alleluia: Sing, my soul 109
Alleluia: Praise God 108
Alleluia: Sing, my soul 109
Alleluia, sing to Jesus 110
Alleluia, thank you for fathers 111
All for Jesus! 112
All glory, laud and honour 113
All glory to you, Redeemer and Lord 114
All God's people, here together 115
All hail the power of Jesus' name 116
All heaven declares 117
All I once held dear 118
All my hope on God is founded 119
All over the world 120
All people that on earth do dwell 121
All that I am 122
All the earth proclaim the Lord 123
All the ends of the earth 124
All things bright and beautiful 125
All you nations, sing out your joy 126
All you who seek a comfort sure 127
Alma redemptoris mater 128
Almighty Father, Lord most high 129
Almighty Father, take this bread 130
Amazing grace 131
And did those feet in ancient time 132
A new commandment 133
Angels we have heard in heaven 134
Angels we have heard on high 135
A noble flower of Judah 136
Arise, come to your God 137
Arise to greet the Lord of light 138
As bread my Lord comes to me 139
As earth that is dry 140
  As gentle as silence 557
As I kneel before you 141
As the deer pants for the water 142
As we are gathered 143
As with gladness men of old 144
  A touching place 198
At the cross her station keeping 145
At the Lamb's high feast we sing 146
At the name of Jesus 147
At your feet 148
Ave Maria, O maiden, O mother 149
Ave, Regina caelorum 150
Ave verum corpus 151
Awake, awake and greet the new morn 152
Awake, awake: fling off the night 153
Awake from your slumber 154
Away in a manger 155

B

Battle is o'er, hell's armies flee 156
Beauty for brokenness 157
Be blessed, pure of heart 158
Before the light of evening fades 159
Behold, the Lamb of God 160
Behold, the Saviour of the nations 161
  Be humble of heart 224
Beloved, let us love 162
  Be not afraid 757
Be still and know I am with you 163
Be still and know that I am God 164
Be still, for the presence of the Lord 165
Be still, my soul 166
Bethlehem, of noblest cities 167
Be thou my vision 168
Bind us together, Lord 169
Blessed assurance 170
Blessed be God 171
  Blessed be God 175
Blessed be the God of Jesus Christ 172
Bless the Lord, my soul 173
Blest are the pure in heart 174
Blest are you, Lord 175
Blest are you, Lord of creation 176
Blest are you, O God 177
Blest be the Lord 178
Born in the night, Mary's child 179
Bread from the earth 180
Bread is blessed and broken 181
Breathe on me, Breath of God 182
Breath of God, O Holy Spirit 183
  Bridegroom and bride 288
Bring, all ye dear-bought nations 184
Bring flowers of the rarest 185
  Bring forth the kingdom 749
Brother, sister, let me serve you 186
By his grace 187
By the blood that flowed from thee 188
By the cross 189
By the waters of Babylon 190

C

Called to be servants 191
Change my heart, O God 192
Child in the manger 193
Christ be beside me 194
  Christ be our light 439
Christians, lift up your hearts 195
Christ is King of earth and heaven 196
Christ is made the sure foundation 197

Entry	Page
Christ is risen	367
Christ's is the world	198
Christ the Lord is risen today	199
Christ triumphant	200
Christus vincit	201
City of God	154
Close to you	378
Colours of day	202
Come and be filled	203
Come and be light for our eyes	204
Come and go with me	205
Come and praise him	206
Come and see	664
Come back to me	207
Come, come, come to the manger	208
Come down, O Love divine	209
Come, follow me	350
Come, Holy Ghost, Creator, come	210
Come, Holy Spirit, come	211
Come, let us raise a joyful song	212
Come, Lord Jesus	213
Come, Lord Jesus, come	214
Come, my Way, my Truth, my Life	215
Come, O divine Messiah!	216
Come, O God of all the earth	217
Come, O long-expected Jesus	218
Come on and celebrate!	219
Come, praise the Lord	220
Come, prepare the way	221
Come to me	222
Come to me	391
Come to me, all who labour	223
Come to me, come, my people	224
Come to the table of the Lord	225
Come to the water	525
Come, ye thankful people come	226
Comfort, comfort my people	227
Creator of the day	228
Creator of the starry height – see *O Word, in uncreated light*	567
Crown him with many crowns	229

D

Entry	Page
Daily, daily, sing to Mary	230
Dance in your Spirit	231
Day is done, but love unfailing	232
Day of wrath and day of wonder	233
Dear Lord and Father of mankind	234
Dear maker of the stars of night – see *O Word, in uncreated light*	567
Deep calls to deep	235
Deep peace of the running wave to you	236
Deep within my heart	237
Ding dong, merrily on high	238
Dona nobis pacem	239
Do not be afraid	240
Dying you destroyed our death	241

E

Entry	Page
Earthen vessels	717
Enemy of apathy	613
Enfold me in your love	751
Enter in the wilderness	242
Eternal Father, strong to save	243

F

Entry	Page
Faithful Cross	244
Faith in God	245
Faith of our fathers	246
Father and life-giver	247
Father God, gentle Father God	248
Father God, I wonder	249
Father, in my life I see	250
Father, I place into your hands	251
Father, we adore you	252
Father, we come to you	253
Father, we love you	254
Fight the good fight	255
Fill my house	256
Fill your hearts with joy and gladness	257
Firmly I believe	258
Follow me	259
For all the saints	260
For the fruits of his creation	261
For the healing of the nations	262
Forth in the peace of Christ we go	263
Forty days and forty nights	264
For you my soul is thirsting	265
Freedom for my people	266
Freely, freely	286
From heaven you came	267
From many grains	268
From the depths we cry to thee	269
From the sun's rising	270
From the very depths of darkness	271

G

Entry	Page
Gather around, for the table is spread	272
Gather us in	327
Gifts of bread and wine	273
Give me joy in my heart	274
Give thanks to God	275
Give thanks with a grateful heart	276
Glorify the Lord	277
Glorify your name	254
Glorious God, King of creation	278
Glory and praise to our God	279
Glory be to Jesus	280
Glory to thee, Lord God	281
Glory to thee, my God, this night	282
God be in my head	283
God everlasting, wonderful and holy	284
God fills me with joy	285
God forgave my sin	286
Godhead here in hiding	287
(see also *Jesus, Lord of glory* for another translation of this hymn)	
God in the planning	288
God is love	289
God is love: his the care	290
God is my great desire	291
God of eternal light	292
God of mercy and compassion	293
God of the covenant	294
God of the Passover	295
God of the poor	157
God rest you merry, gentlemen	296
God's Spirit is in my heart	297
Go forth in his name	708
Going home	298
Go in peace	299
Good Christians all, rejoice	300
Good King Wenceslas	301
Go tell everyone	297
Go, tell it on the mountain	302

Entry	Page
Go, the Mass is ended	303
Grant to us, O Lord	304
Grant us your peace	305
Great indeed are your works, O Lord	306
Great love	484
Guide me, O thou great Redeemer	307

H

Entry	Page
Hail, glorious St Patrick	308
Hail, Queen of heaven	309
Hail, Redeemer, King divine	310
Hail the day that sees him rise	311
Hail the risen Lord, ascending	312
Hail, thou star of ocean	313
Hail to the Lord's anointed	314
Hail, true Body	315
Hark! a herald voice is calling	316
Hark, the herald angels sing	317
Have mercy on us, O Lord	318
Healer of our every ill	319
Healer of the sick	320
Hear my cry	321
Hear our cry	322
Heaven is open wide	323
He brings us into his banqueting table	324
He has made me glad	381
He is Lord	325
He is risen, tell the story	326
Here I am, Lord	376
Here in this place	327
Here is bread	328
Here's a child for you, O Lord	329
He's got the whole world in his hand	330
He who would valiant be	331
His banner over me is love	324
Holy God, of righteous glory	332
Holy God, we praise thy name	333
Holy God, your pilgrim people	334
Holy, holy, holy	335
Holy, holy, holy is the Lord	336
Holy, holy, holy! Lord God almighty	337
Holy Jesus, in our likeness born	338
Holy Mary, you were chosen	339
Holy Spirit, come, confirm us	340
Holy Spirit, Lord of light	341
Holy Spirit of fire	342
Holy Virgin, by God's decree	343
Hosanna, hosanna	344
Hosanna to the Son of David	750
How great is our God	345
How great thou art	529
How lovely on the mountains	346
How shall they hear the word of God	347

I

Entry	Page
I am the bread of life (Konstant)	348
I am the bread of life (Toolan)	349
I am the Light	350
I cannot tell	351
I come like a beggar	352
I danced in the morning	353
If God is for us	354
If I am lacking love	355
I give you love	356
I have loved you with an everlasting love	357
I'll sing a hymn to Mary	358
I'll turn my steps to the altar of God	359

Entry	Page
Immaculate Mary	360
Immortal, invisible, God only wise	361
In bread we bring you, Lord	362
In company with Christians past	363
Infant holy, infant lowly	364
In the bleak midwinter	365
In the love of God and neighbour	366
In the shadow of your wings	515
In the tomb so cold	367
Into one we all are gathered	368
In you, my God	369
In your coming and going	370
I received the living God	371
I saw streams of water flowing	372
I saw the Holy City	373
I sing a song to you, Lord	374
I stand in awe	748
It came upon the midnight clear	375
I, the Lord of sea and sky	376
I, the Servant-Lord	377
I watch the sunrise	378
I will be with you	379
I will bless the Lord	380
I will enter his gates	381
I will never forget you	382
I will seek your face, O Lord	383
I will sing a song	384
I will sing, I will sing	385
I will sing your praises	249
I will walk in the presence of God	386

J

Entry	Page
Jerusalem	132
Jerusalem the golden	387
Jesus calls us	388
Jesus Christ is risen today	389
Jesus Christ is waiting	390
Jesus, ever flowing fountain	391
Jesus, gentlest Saviour	392
Jesus is God	393
Jesus is Lord! Creations voice proclaims it	394
Jesus is Lord! In love he came	395
Jesus is our joy	465
Jesus, Lord of glory	396
(see also *Godhead here in hiding* for another translation of this hymn)	
Jesus, my Lord, my God, my all	397
Jesus, Name above all names	398
Jesus rose on Easter day	399
Jesu, the very thought of thee	400
Jesus, the Word, has lived among us	401
Jesus, who condemns you	402
Join in the dance	403
Joy to the world	404
Jubilate Deo	405
Jubilate, everybody	406
Judas and Mary	595

K

Entry	Page
Keep in mind	407
Keep we the fast that men of old – see *In company with Christians past*	363
King of glory, King of peace	408
King of kings and Lord of lords	409
Kyrie eleison	440

L

Lamb of God, Holy One	410
Lauda, Jerusalem	411
Laudato sii, O mi Signore	412
Lay your hands gently upon us	413
Leader, now on earth no longer	414
Lead, kindly light	415
Lead us, heavenly Father, lead us	416
Leave your country and your people	417
Leave your gift	738
Let all mortal flesh keep silence	418
Let all that is within me	419
Let all the world in every corner sing	420
Let love be real	421
Let our praise to you be as incense	422
Let the heavens declare	423
Let the hungry come to me	424
Let there be love	425
Let the world in concert sing	426
Let us sing your glory	427
Let us, with a gladsome mind	428
Lift high the cross	429
Lift up your hearts	430
Light up the fire	202
Like a sea without a shore	431
Like as the deer	432
Like the deer that yearns	433
Like the murmur of the dove's song	434
Listen, let your heart keep seeking	435
Listen to me, Yahweh	436
Listen to my voice	437
Living Lord	447
Lo, he comes with clouds descending	438
Longing for light	439
Look around you	440
Look at the sky	441
Look down, O mother Mary	442
Lord, accept the gifts we offer	443
Lord, enthroned in heavenly splendour	444
Lord, for tomorrow and its needs	445
Lord, have mercy	446
Lord Jesus Christ	447
Lord Jesus, think on me	448
Lord, make me a means of your peace	449
Lord of all hopefulness	450
Lord of life	451
Lord of the dance	353
Lord our God	452
Lord, the light of your love	453
Lord, thy word abideth	454
Lord, unite all nations	455
Lord, we come to ask your healing	456
Lord, when I wake I turn to you	457
Lord, who throughout these forty days	458
Lord, you give the great commission	459
Lourdes Hymn	360
Love came down at Christmas	460
Love divine, all loves excelling	461
Love is his word	462
Love is patient	463
Love is the only law	464
Lovely in your littleness	465
Loving shepherd of thy sheep	466
Lumen Christi	467

M

Maiden, yet a mother	468
Majesty, worship his majesty	469
Make me a channel of your peace	470
Make way, make way	471
Maranatha	431
Mary had a baby	472
Mary immaculate	473
May you see the face of God	474
Meekness and majesty	475
Morning has broken	476
Moses, I know you're the man	477
Mother of God's living Word	478
My desire	691
My God, accept my heart this day	479
My God, and is thy table spread	480
My God, how wonderful you are	481
My God loves me – see Our God loves us	560
My God, my God, why have you forsaken me?	482
My God said to me, 'Follow!'	483
My heart will sing to you	484
My people, what have I done to you?	485
My shepherd is the Lord	486
My song is love unknown	487
My soul doth magnify the Lord	488
My soul is filled with joy	489
My soul is longing for your peace	490
My soul proclaims you, mighty God	491

N

New daytime dawning	492
New Lourdes Hymn	343
New praises be given	493
Nothing shall separate us	494
Now as the evening shadows fall	495
Now I know what love is	496
Now thank we all our God	497
Now the green blade riseth	498
Now with the fading light of day – see Now as the evening shadows fall	495
Now with the fast-departing light	499
Nunc Dimittis	752

O

O bread of heaven	500
O come, all ye faithful	501
O come and mourn with me awhile	502
O come, O come, Emmanuel	503
O, come to the water	504
O comfort my people	505
O food of travellers	506
O fountain of life	507
Of the Father's love begotten	508
Of the glorious body telling	509
O God beyond all praising	510
O Godhead hid	511
O God of earth and altar	512
O God of grace, we thank you	513
O God, our help in ages past	514
O God, please listen	515
O God, we give ourselves today	516
O God, your people gather	517
O healing river	518
O holy Lord, by all adored	519
O, how good is the Lord	520
O Jesus Christ, remember	521
O Jesus, I have promised	522
O King of might and splendour	523
O lady, full of God's own grace	524
O let all who thirst	525
O little town of Bethlehem	526
O living water	527
O Lord, be not mindful	528
O Lord, my God	529
O Lord, your tenderness	530
O Mary, when our God chose you	531
O Mother blest	532
O my Lord, within my heart	533
O my people, what have I done to you?	534
On a hill far away	535
Once in royal David's city	536
On Christmas night all Christians sing	537
On eagle's wings	759
One bread, one body	538
One cold night in spring	539
One Father	540
One God	540
On Jordan's bank the Baptist's cry	541
Only a shadow	662
On this day of joy	542
On this house your blessing, Lord	543
Onward, Christian pilgrims	544
Open our eyes, Lord	545
Open your ears, O Christian people	546
O perfect love	547
O praise ye the Lord	548
O purest of creatures	549
O Queen of heaven	550
O sacred head ill-used	551
O sacred head sore wounded	552
O Sacred Heart	553
O sing a new song	554
O suffering Jesus	555
O that today you would listen to his voice	556
O, the love of my Lord	557
O the word of my Lord	558
O thou, who at thy Eucharist didst pray	559
Our God loves us	560
Our God reigns	346
Our God sent his Son long ago	561
Our hearts were made for you	562
Our Saviour, Christ	563
Ours were the sufferings he bore	564
Out of darkness	565
O Wisdom, source of harmony	566
O Word, in uncreated light	567
O worship the King	568
O worship the Lord in the beauty of holiness	569

P

Pange lingua gloriosi	570
Peace I leave with you	571
Peace is flowing like a river	572
Peace is the gift	573
Peace, perfect peace	574
Praise him	575
Praise, my soul, the King of heaven	576
Praise the Lord	577
Praise the Lord in his holy house	578
Praise the Lord, ye heavens, adore him	579
Praise to God for saints and martyrs	580
Praise to God in the highest	581
Praise to the Holiest	582
Praise to the Lord, the Almighty	583
Praise to the Lord, the Almighty (Ecumenical version)	584
Praise to you, O Christ, our Saviour	585
Praise we our God with joy	586

R

Reap me the earth	587
Regina cæli	588
Rejoice, all heavenly powers	589
Rejoice in the Lord always	590
Rejoice, the Lord is King	591
Remember your mercy, Lord	592
Reproaches	356
Ride on, ride on in majesty	593
Ring out your joy	594

S

Said Judas to Mary	595
Salvation is God's	596
Salve, Regina	597
Save us, O Lord (Mayhew)	598
Save us, O Lord (Nazareth)	599
Save us, O Lord (Dufford)	600
See, amid the winter's snow	601
See, Christ was wounded	602
See him lying on a bed of straw	603
Seek ye first	604
See the holy table, spread for our healing	605
See us, Lord, about your altar	606
See, your Saviour comes	607
Send forth your Spirit (Rees)	608
Send forth your Spirit (Nazareth)	609
Send forth your Spirit (Rizza)	610
Send me, Lord	611
Shalom, my friend	612
She sits like a bird	613
Shine, Jesus, shine	453
Silent night	614
Sing, all creation	615
Sing a new song	616
Sing hallelujah to the Lord	617
Sing, holy Mother	618
Sing hosanna	274
Sing it in the valleys	619
Sing, my soul	620
Sing, my tongue, the song of triumph	621
Sing of Mary, pure and lowly	622
Sing out, earth and skies	217
Sing praises to the living God	623
Sing the gospel of salvation	624
Sing to the Lord, alleluia	625
Sing to the mountains	626
Sleep, holy babe	627
Song of farewell	241
Song of the Advent prophets	221

Song of Simeon	599
Soul of my Saviour	628
Spirit hovering o'er the waters	629
Spirit of the living God	630
Springs of water, bless the Lord	631
Star of sea and ocean	632
Steal away	633
Sweet heart of Jesus	634
Sweet sacrament divine	635
Sweet Saviour, bless us	636

T

Take and bless our gifts	637
Take me, Lord	638
Take my hands	639
Take my hands, Lord	640
Take my life	640
Take our bread	641
Take this and eat	642
Taste and see the goodness of the Lord	643
Tell out, my soul	644
Thanks for the fellowship	645
The angel Gabriel from heaven came	646
The Beatitudes	654
The Church's one foundation	647
The coming of our God	648
The day of resurrection	649
The day thou gavest, Lord, is ended	650
The first Nowell	651
The head that once was crowned with thorns	652
The holly and the ivy	653
The kingdom of heaven	654
The King of glory comes	655
The King of love my shepherd is	656
The light of Christ	657
The Lord hears the cry of the poor	658
The Lord is alive	659
The Lord is my life	660
The Lord's my shepherd	661
The love I have for you	662
The Mass is ended	663
The night was dark	664
The Old Rugged Cross	535
The race that long in darkness pined	665
There is a green hill far away	666
There is a river	667
The royal banners forward go	668
The Saviour will come, resplendent in joy	669
The seed is Christ's	670
The Servant King	267
The Servant song	186
The sign of hope, creation's joy	671
The Spirit lives to set us free	672
The Spirit of the Lord	673
The Stations of the Cross	402
The summons	740
The table's set, Lord	674
The temple of the living God	675
The trees of the field	758
The Virgin Mary had a baby boy	676
The wandering flock of Israel	677
Thine be the glory	678
This Child	679
This day God gives me	680
This is my body	681
This is my will	682

This is our faith	683
This is the day	684
This is the image of the queen	685
This is your God	475
This joyful Eastertide	686
This, then, is my prayer	687
Though the mountains may fall	688
Thou, whose almighty word	689
Thuma Mima	611
Thy hand, O God, has guided	690
To be in your presence	691
To Christ, the Prince of peace	692
To Jesus' heart, all burning	693
To you, O Lord, I lift up my soul	694
To your altar we bring	695
Trinity song	250
Turn to me	696

U

Unless a grain of wheat	697
Unto us a boy is born	698
Upon thy table, Lord	699

V

Vaster far than any ocean	700
Veni, Creator Spiritus	701
Veni, Sancte Spiritus	702
Veni, veni, Sancte Spiritus	629
Victimae Paschali laudes	703

W

Waken, O sleeper, wake and rise	704
Wake up, O people	705
Walk in the light	672
Walk with me, O my Lord	706
We are gathering together	707
We are his children	708
We are his people	709
We are marching	710
We behold the splendour of God	711
We believe	712
We cannot measure	713
We celebrate the new creation	714
We celebrate this festive day	715
We have a dream	716
We hold a treasure	717
We plough the fields and scatter	718
Were you there when they crucified my Lord?	719
We shall draw water joyfully	720
We shall stay awake	721
We three kings of Orient are	722
What child is this	723
What feast of love	724
What kind of greatness	725
Whatsoever you do	726
When Christ our Lord to Andrew cried	727
When from bondage we are summoned	728
When I feel the touch	729
When I needed a neighbour	730
When I survey the wondrous cross	731
When the time came	732
Where are you bound, Mary	733
Where is love and loving kindness	734
Where love and charity endure	735
Where the love of Christ unites us	736

Where true love is found with charity	737
Where true love is present	738
While shepherds watched	739
Will you come and follow me	740
With the Lord there is mercy	741
With you, O God	742
Word made flesh	743

Y

Yahweh, I know you are near	744
Yahweh is the God of my salvation	745
Ye choirs of new Jerusalem	746
Ye sons and daughters of the Lord	747
You are beautiful	748
You are salt for the earth	749
You are the King of Glory	750
You are the light	751
You give, Lord	752
You have been baptised in Christ	753
You have called us	754
You have the message of eternal life	755
Your love's greater	756
You shall cross the barren desert	757
You shall go out with joy	758
You who dwell in the shelter of the Lord	759

CHILDREN'S HYMNS and SONGS

A

A butterfly, an Easter egg	760
All in an Easter garden	761
All of my heart	762
All of the people	763
All the nations of the earth	764
And everyone beneath the vine and fig tree	765
As Jacob with travel was weary one day	766

B

Be the centre of my life	767
Biggest isn't always best	794

C

Care for your world	853
Caterpillar, caterpillar	768
Change my heart, O God	769
'Cheep!' said the sparrow	770
Christ is our King	771
Clap your hands, all you people	772
Clap your hands and sing this song	773
Colours of hope	792
Come and praise the Lord our King	774
Come, God's children	775
Come into his presence	776
Come, they told me	777

D

Dear child divine	778
Do not worry over what to eat	779
Don't build your house on the sandy land	780
Do what you know is right	781

E

Each of us is a living stone	782
Every bird, every tree	783

F

Father welcomes all his children	784
Fishes of the ocean	785
Forward in faith	786
Friends, all gather here in a circle	787

G

Give me peace, O Lord	788
God almighty set a rainbow	789
God gives his people strength	790
God knows me	842
God our Father gave us life	791
God sends a rainbow	792
God turned darkness into light	793
Goliath was big and Goliath was strong	794

H

Hail, Mary, full of grace	795
Hallelu, hallelu	796
Have you heard the raindrops	797
He is the King	798
Hey, now, everybody sing	799

I

If I were a butterfly	800
I give my hands	801
I'm black, I'm white, I'm short, I'm tall	802
In the upper room	803
Isn't it good	804
It's me, O Lord	805
I've got peace like a river	806
I will wave my hands	807

J

Jesus had all kinds of friends	808
Jesus is greater	809
Jesus is the living way	840
Jesus put this song into our hearts	810
Jesus turned the water into wine	817
Jesus went away to the desert	811
Jesus will never, ever	812
Jesus, you love me	813
Joseph was an honest man	814

K

Kum ba yah	815

L

Lead my people to freedom	846
Let the mountains dance and sing	816
Life for the poor was hard and tough	817
Little donkey	818
Little Jesus, sleep away	819
Living stones	782
Lord, forgive us	822
Lord of the future	820
Lord, we've come to worship you	821
Lord, you've promised, through your Son	822

M

My mouth was made for worship	823

N
Nobody's a nobody	824
Now the Mass is ended	825

O
O come and join the dance	826
O give thanks	827
O Lord, all the world	828
One hundred and fifty-three!	829
Our God is so great	830
Out to the great wide world we go	831
O when the saints go marching in	832

P
Peter and John went to pray	833
Praise and thanksgiving	834
Praise God in his holy place	835
Put your trust	836

R
Right where we are	841
Rise and shine	837

S
Signs of new life	760
Silver and gold	833
Sing a simple song	838
Sing praise to God	839
Step by step, on and on	840

T
Thank you, Lord	841
The birds' song	770
The children's band	845
The little drummer boy	777
There are hundreds of sparrows	842
There's a great big world out there	843
There's a rainbow in the sky	844
There was one, there were two	845
The voice from the bush	846
The wise man	847
The world is full of smelly feet	848
This little light of mine	849

W
Water of life	797
We will praise	850
When is he coming	851
When the Spirit of the Lord	852
When your Father made the world	853
Who put the colours in the rainbow?	854

Y
Yesterday, today, for ever	855
You must do for others	803
You've got to move	856

Z
Zacchaeus was a very little man	857
Zip bam boo	858

CHANTS

A
A Blessing	878
Adoramus te, Domine (Taizé)	859
Adoramus te, Domine (Rizza)	860

B
Benedictus qui venit	861
Bless the Lord, my soul	862

C
Calm me, Lord	863
Come, light of our hearts	894
Confitemini Domino	864

E
Eat this bread	865
Exaudi nos, Domine	866

H
Holy God, we place ourselves	867

I
In the Lord I'll be ever thankful	868
In the Lord is my joy	869

J
Jesus, remember me	870
Jubilate Deo	871
Jubilate Deo (Servite)	872

K
Kindle a flame	873

L
Laudate Dominum	874
Laudate omnes gentes	875
Lord of creation	876

M
Magnificat	877
May the Lord bless you	878
Misericordias Domini	879

N
Nada te turbe	880
Nothing can trouble	880

O
O Christe, Domine Jesu	881
O Lord, hear my prayer	882
O Lord, my heart is not proud	883
O Sacrament most holy	884
Ostende nobis	885

S
Sanctum nomen Domini	886
Silent, surrendered	887
Sing praise	874
Stay here and keep watch	888
Stay with me	889
Surrexit Christus	890

T
The Lord is my light	891
The Lord is my song	892

U
Ubi caritas	893

V
Veni, lumen cordium	894
Veni, Sancte Spiritus (Vogler)	895
Veni, Sancte Spiritus (Walker)	896

W
Wait for the Lord	897
Within our darkest night	898

Y
You are the centre	899

EUCHARISTIC ADORATION WITH BENEDICTION

Adoremus in aeternum	1085
O salutaris	1079, 1080, 1081, 1082
O saving victim	1079, 1080, 1081, 1082
Tantum ergo	1083, 1084
Come adore	1083, 1084